Property Law

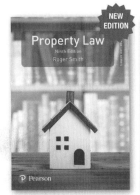

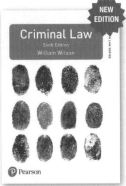

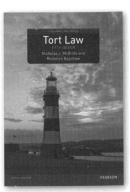

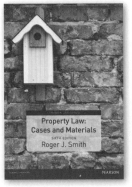

Pearson

Property Law

Ninth Edition

Roger J. Smith

 Pearson

Harlow, England • London • New York • Boston • San Francisco • Toronto • Sydney
Dubai • Singapore • Hong Kong • Tokyo • Seoul • Taipei • New Delhi
Cape Town • São Paulo • Mexico City • Madrid • Amsterdam • Munich • Paris • Milan

PEARSON EDUCATION LIMITED
Edinburgh Gate
Harlow CM20 2JE
United Kingdom
Tel: +44 (0)1279 623623
Web: www.pearson.com/uk

First published 1996 (print)
Second edition published 1998 (print)
Third edition published 2000 (print)
Fourth edition published 2003 (print)
Fifth edition published 2006 (print)
Sixth edition published 2009 (print)
Seventh edition published 2011 (print and electronic)
Eighth edition published 2014 (print and electronic)
Ninth edition published 2017 (print and electronic)

© Addison Wesley Longman Limited 1996, 1998 (print)
© Pearson Education Limited 2000, 2003, 2006, 2009 (print)
© Pearson Education Limited 2011, 2014, 2017 (print and electronic)

Contains public sector information licensed under the Open Government Licence (OGL) v3.0. http://www.nationalarchives.gov.uk/doc/open-government-licence/version/3/.

Contains Parliamentary information licensed under the Open Parliament Licence (OPL) v3.0. http://www.parliament.uk/site-information/copyright/open-parliament-licence/

Pearson Education is not responsible for the content of third-party internet sites.

ISBN: 978-1-292-09559-2 (print)
          978-1-292-09563-9 (PDF)
          978-1-292-16942-2 (ePub)

British Library Cataloguing-in-Publication Data
A catalogue record for the print edition is available from the British Library

Library of Congress Cataloging-in-Publication Data
Names: Smith, Roger J. (Roger John), 1948- author.
Title: Property law/Roger J. Smith.
Description: Ninth edition. | New York : Pearson, 2017.
Identifiers: LCCN 2017006086| ISBN 9781292095592 (print) | ISBN 9781292095639
    PDF | ISBN 9781292169422 (epub)
Subjects: LCSH: Real property—England.
Classification: LCC KD829 .S64 2017 | DDC 346.4104/3—dc23
LC record available at https://lccn.loc.gov/2017006086

10 9 8 7 6 5 4 3 2 1
21 20 19 18 17

Print edition typeset in 10/12.5pt Times LT Pro by iEnergizer Aptara®, Ltd.
Printed in Great Britain by Ashford Colour Press Ltd

NOTE THAT ANY PAGE CROSS REFERENCES REFER TO THE PRINT EDITION

Contents in brief

Contents in detail

Acknowledgement

We are grateful to the following for permission to reproduce copyright material:

Text

Extract on page 19 from *Kay v Lambeth LBC* [2006] 2 AC 465 at 191; Extracts on page 36, page 50 from *National Provincial Bank Ltd v Ainsworth* [1965] AC 1175; Extract on page 65 from *Hibbert v McKiernan* [1948] 2 KB 142; Extract on page 67 from *South Staffordshire Water Company v Sharman* [1896] 2 QB 44; Extract on page 68 from *Parker v British Airways Board* [1982] QB 1004 at 1004; Extracts on page 79, page 82 from *JA Pye (Oxford) Ltd v Graham* [2003] 1 AC 419; Extract on page 94 from *Pole-Carew v Western Counties & General Manure Co. Ltd* [1920] 2 Ch 97; Extract on page 98 from *Hobson v Gorringe* [1897] 1 Ch 182; Extract on page 129 from *T Choithram International SA v Pagarani* [2001] 1 WLR 1 at 11; Extract on page 147 from *Gissing v Gissing* [1971] AC 886 at 905; Extract on page 175 from *Hopgood v Brown* [1955] 1 WLR 213 at 226; Extract on page 181 from *King v Dubrey* [2016] Ch 221 at 55; Extract on page 193 from *Pettitt v Pettitt* [1970] AC 777 at 810; Extracts on page 195, page 217 from *Lloyds Bank plc v Rosset* [1991] 1 AC 107; Extracts on page 199, page 217 from *Grant v Edwards* [1986] Ch 638 at 648; Extract on page 200 from *Stack v Dowden* [2007] 2 AC 432; Extract on page 204 from *Oxley v Hiscock* [2005] Fam 211; Extract on page 204 from *Stack v Dowden* [2005] Fam 211 at 69; Extract on page 233 from *Bailey v Barnes* [1894] 1 Ch 25 at 34; Extract on page 265 from *Bristol & West BS v Henning* [1985] 1 WLR 778; Extract on page 268 from *Williams & Glyn's Bank Ltd v Boland* [1981] AC 487 at 504; Extract on page 308 from *Robertson v Fraser* (1871) LR 6 Ch App 696 at 699; Extract on page 315 from *Burgess v Rawnsley* [1975] Ch 429 at 439; Extract on page 316 from *Nielson-Jones v Fedden* [1975] Ch 222 at 230; Extract on page 323 from *Mortgage Corpn v Shaire* [2001] Ch 743 at 761; Extract on page 344 from *Jones v Jones* [1977] 1 WLR 438 at 442; Extract on page 344 from *Browne v Pritchard* [1975] 1 WLR 1366 at 1371; Extract on page 374 from *Prudential Assurance Co. Ltd v London Residuary Body* [1992] 2 AC 386 at 396; Extracts on page 379, page 380 from *Street v Mountford* [1985] AC 809 at 819 and 825; Extract on page 384 from *Snook v London & West Riding Investments Ltd* [1967] 2 QB 786 at 802; Extract on page 401 from *Hammersmith and Fulham LBC v Monk* [1992] 1 AC 478 at 490–1; Extract on page 403 from *Walsh v Lonsdale* (1882) 21 Ch D 9 at 14–5; Extract on page 405 from *Manchester Brewery Co. v Coombs* [1901] 2 Ch 608 at 617; Extract on page 413 from *Southwark LBC v Mills* [2001] 1 AC 1 at 23; Extract on page 418 from *Mancetter Developments Ltd v Garmanson Ltd* [1986] QB 1212 at 1218; Extract on page 420 from *Quick v Taff Ely BC* [1986] QB 809 at 818; Extract on page 436 from *Horsey Estate Ltd v Steiger* [1899] 2 QB 79 at 91–2; Extract on page 436 from *Rugby School (Governors) v Tannahill* [1935] 1 KB 87 at 91; Extract on page 438 from *Akici v LR Butlin Ltd* [2006] 1 WLR 201 at 71–4; Extract on page 458 from *Grant v Edmondson* [1931] 1 Ch 1 at 28; Extract on page 490 from *Errington v Errington* [1952] 1 KB 290;

Extract on page 491 from *Ashburn Anstalt* v *Arnold* [1989] Ch 1 at 22; Extract on page 515 from *Re Ellenborough Park* [1956] Ch 131 at 174; Extracts on page 522 from *London & Blenheim Estates Ltd* v *Ladbroke Retail Parks Ltd* [1992] 1 WLR 1278 at 1286 and 1288; Extracts on page 526, page 542 from *Union Lighterage Co.* v *London Graving Dock Co.* [1902] 2 Ch 557; Extract on page 527 from *Pwllbach Colliery Co. Ltd* v *Woodman* [1915] AC 634 at 643; Extract on page 528 from *Wheeldon* v *Burrows* (1879) 12 Ch D 31 at 49; Extract on page 528 from *Borman* v *Griffith* [1930] 1 Ch 493 at 499; Extract on page 529 from *Ward* v *Kirkland* [1967] Ch 194; Extract on page 538 from *Hollins* v *Verney* (1884) 13 QBD 304 at 315; Extract on page 539 from *Davies* v *Du Paver* [1953] 1 QB 184 at 207–8; Extract on page 550 from *James* v *Stevenson* [1893] AC 162 at 168; Extract on page 558 from *London & South Western Railway Co.* v *Gomm* (1882) 20 Ch D 562 at 583; Extracts on pages 560–1, page 563 from *Rogers* v *Hosegood*[1900] 2 Ch 388; Extract on page 578 from *Samuel* v *Jarrah Timber & Wood Paving Corporation Ltd* [1904] AC 323 at 326; Extract on page 581 from *Grangeside Properties Ltd* v *Collingwoods Securities Ltd* [1964] 1 WLR 139 at 142; Extracts on page 584, page 587, page 590 from *Royal Bank of Scotland plc* v *Etridge (No. 2)* [2002] 2 AC 773; Extract on page 617 from *Waring* v *London & Manchester Assurance Co. Ltd* [1935] Ch 311 at 318; Extract on page 619 from *Warner* v *Jacob* (1882) 20 Ch D 220 at 224.

Contains public sector information licensed under the Open Government Licence v3.0.

Table of cases

Table of statutes

Table of statutes instruments

Part I
Introducing property law

1

Basic property principles

1. What is property and property law?

This is to start with a deceptively difficult question. Could it be said that property law is that relating to physical objects, such as land and cars? Though understandable, this proposition would be misleading. Not every transaction, or liability, relating to physical objects is regarded as relevant to the law of property. A contract with my garage to service my car is part of the law of contract rather than the law of property. Torts committed in relation to property may be ordinary torts such as negligence. Certain torts have an effect that is more specific to property, nuisance being one example. Even these, however, may be seen as more part of torts than part of property.[1]

A narrower proposition is that property law is concerned with the ownership of objects. This gets closer to property as understood by lawyers. Property is indeed concerned with the ownership of land and of cars. But what is special about property? Why is it different from other legal categories such as contract, restitution or tort? There are, perhaps, two principal elements.[2] The first concerns the attribute of property that it can be bought and sold. Whilst this is a common attribute of property, it is difficult to take it too far. Exceptionally, there are some property rights which cannot be transferred.[3] The converse is also true. Many contracts can be seen as the purchase of something that is not property. I may buy a person's silence concerning information embarrassing to myself, but no property is involved. Similarly, I may sell information to another person, even though the information is neither confidential nor proprietary in nature.[4]

The second element of property concerns the right to exclude others.[5] If I own a car, it is plain that I can stop anybody else from interfering with it.[6] This right to exclude has two principal applications. It may operate against third parties who have no shadow of a right over the property. In addition, it may be applicable against those who do have claims to the property, but whose claims are inferior to that of the owner. Thus, the owner of a car might sell it to A on hire purchase and then purport to sell it outright to B.

---

[1] Nuisance may be committed by a person with no proprietary interest, such as a trespasser.
[2] Harris, *Property and Justice*, Chapter 4.
[3] For example, it is possible to ensure that a right over land terminates on any attempt to transfer it.
[4] A sporting club could sell information regarding progress of, say, a cricket match, to a broadcaster. The information is not confidential, but it may be cheaper to buy it than to send an employee to the event.
[5] Emphasised by Penner, *The Idea of Property in Law*, especially Chapter 4.
[6] A complication in English law is that tort actions are employed to this end; we do not have actions designed specifically as property actions. Contrast the vindicatio in Roman law.

Both A and B claim proprietary rights in the car, but A's rights (A being first in time) will be given priority in any litigation between them. This type of dispute dominates much of property law.

Not limited to ownership

The proposition that property law deals with ownership of objects faces the objection of being too narrow in scope. Property has wider concerns than ownership. The layperson readily equates the physical object with the proprietary right: 'my car', or 'my house'.

Two examples show that this is not always the case. First, many rights to possess land involve a lease: a right to land for a certain period. A person with a short lease (the tenant, or lessee) cannot be said to own the land. At the same time, the lessee's rights are more than contractual. Suppose the owner of the leased land were to sell it to P. Can P evict the lessee? Contractual privity principles quite clearly point in favour of P. Yet, the law does in fact protect the lessee against purchasers; the lease is a proprietary interest. Second, a car may be bought on hire purchase. Although the car does not belong to the purchaser until all the payments are made, we regard the purchaser as having an immediate proprietary right.

It is important to understand that the law recognises a finite number (numerus clausus) of proprietary rights.[7] The parties are never free to create their own, novel, proprietary categories. Thus, a contract to service my car does not create any proprietary interest in the car.[8] Whilst ownership is a concept that the layperson readily understands, other proprietary interests depend upon complex legal rules. Indeed, the great majority of this text will be taken up with the investigation of proprietary interests in land: what they are, what rights they confer and under what circumstances they will bind purchasers.[9]

So far, we have concentrated on physical objects. Yet it would be unduly restrictive to insist that property is so limited. Suppose I own shares in a company; what object do I have? A share certificate, perhaps, but the piece of paper is by itself of little importance. I can buy and sell the shares and assert my rights to them against others: propositions that seem to point towards proprietary status. Yet, as soon as we move away from physical objects, our sense of property becomes much less clear.[10]

Rights of action

Let us consider rights of action held by a person. A good example is provided by a bank account. Unless I am overdrawn, my bank will owe me money. The relationship between myself and my bank is essentially contractual: it would not be regarded as proprietary because it is difficult to say what the property is in. It cannot be the cheques or cash paid into my account, because the bank can use the money for its own purposes. The original property (cheques and cash) has been converted into an obligation to pay the balance of

---

[7] Different rights are recognised for different forms of property.
[8] Although the garage may be a bailee of the car whilst it is in their possession for servicing. Bailment is a proprietary interest based on possession.
[9] See, e.g., Kevin Gray and Susan Francis Gray (Chapter 1) and Bright (Chapter 21) in *Land Law: Themes and Perspectives* (eds Bright and Dewar).
[10] See Penner, *The Idea of Property in Law*, Chapters 5 and 6.

my account on my demand (a debt). However, this debt may itself be seen as the subject matter of property. Thus, I can transfer the debt to another person, and I can stop anybody else from claiming to enforce it.[11]

This is illustrated by the following example. If I am owed a considerable sum from D, I could charge this to M as security for a debt I owe to M. The effect of this would be to allow M to recover the debt owed by D, should I fail to pay M.[12] What happens if I then transfer the debt to a purchaser, P? The law recognises that P may be bound by M's earlier mortgage of the same debt.[13] An example of this principle is that a right of pre-emption can be regarded as 'property' passing on bankruptcy, even though it may not be a proprietary right in the land concerned.[14] In other words, we treat the debt or other right of action in a similar way to land or a car: the subject matter of proprietary claims.

Nevertheless, the status of rights of action continues to cause difficulty. Somebody who takes my car (for example) commits the tort of conversion. However, the House of Lords[15] has held (by a bare majority) that conversion does not apply to choses in action. This means that there is no proprietary remedy as exists for tangible property – the economic torts may apply, but these generally require intentional conduct.

Somewhat similar issues may arise in respect of electronic data. This is neither a chose in possession nor a chose in action, although it may be of vital importance in modern society. Rights to an electronic database were recently considered by the Court of Appeal.[16] The claimant maintained a subscriber database for the defendant. When the contract terminated, the claimant refused to return the database until outstanding fees were paid. In principle, this would have been proper if it had been a physical paper record: the claimant would have had a lien. However, it was held that, like conversion, liens apply only to choses in possession.

The human body and body parts

Not every physical object can be owned. We will mention one example. It has long been clear that there can be no ownership of the human body or of corpses. Other related questions are more difficult. *Yearworth* v *North Bristol NHS Trust*[17] had to consider whether semen was property so that the defendants could be liable for careless storage causing damage. It was held that semen can be owned: it was deliberately produced (by men about to undergo chemotherapy, which might affect fertility) with a view to later use. Furthermore, the men retained control over its use or destruction.

---

[11] Rights of action differ from objects in that the most obvious form of interference – taking possession – is inapplicable.

[12] This is similar to a mortgage of land to secure a bank or building society loan; the security in the example being the debt owed by D rather than land.

[13] There are detailed rules as to precisely when P is bound; generally, M must have given notice to D.

[14] *Dear* v *Reeves* [2002] Ch 1; see p 104 below. A pre-emption is a right of first refusal, should the owner wish to sell.

[15] *OBG Ltd* v *Allan* [2008] AC 1. The issue has caused much debate: e.g. Douglas [2008] LMCLQ 129 and Green (2008) 71 MLR 114.

[16] *Your Response Ltd* v *Datastream Business Media Ltd* [2015] QB 41 (Low (2014) 130 LQR 547). Floyd LJ stressed at [42] that information is not generally regarded as property (a point discussed later in this chapter). The issue was avoided in the case: the defendant had a contractual right to the database's return.

[17] [2010] QB 1; the decision involves complex issues (see, e.g., Wall (2011) 31 OxJLS 783). More generally, cf Moses (2008) 30 Syd LR 639.

Intellectual property

A property analysis is sometimes used in order to recognise novel claims. It is commonly said that the hallmark of property lies in the exclusion of others. An owner of land can prevent others from asserting rights to it. Those with lesser rights (such as leases or rights of way over land) can stop interference with those rights. This exclusionary role of property is pounced upon by those who want to prevent interference with something that is of importance to them. In other words, an extension of property is sought in order to exclude others. As will be seen later in this chapter, most developments in this area have been statutory. Thus statute prohibits the copying of written material (copyright) and the exploitation of others' inventions (patents).

The courts are sometimes asked to develop such analyses themselves. In the well-known American case of *International News Service* v *Associated Press*,[18] the defendant had used news material printed by the claimant on the East coast. Usually, copied news would be stale news and of little significance, but in *INS* the time differences between the East and West coasts meant that the defendant could publish the news on the West coast at the same time as the claimant. As there was no direct copy of the words used, there was no breach of copyright. The claimant argued that they had a novel quasi-proprietary right in their news reports. Such a proprietary right would have the exclusionary effect of preventing anybody else from using it. This analysis was accepted by the Supreme Court but has not found favour with English or Commonwealth courts.[19] This demonstrates the difficulty in persuading courts to recognise new forms of property.

However, even in England, information receives some protection. The courts are prepared to protect *confidential* information against improper use. In many cases, this is based upon the defendant's having received the information on a confidential basis. These cases can be explained without recourse to a proprietary analysis. However, it appears that confidential information may be protected against, for example, telephone tapping. This extension of protection seems to herald a move to a more proprietary basis to justify intervention by the courts,[20] although the area is still being debated. The rights in this section are collectively described as intellectual property.

2. Ownership

Although property is not restricted to ownership, ownership is certainly worthy of investigation. The concept rarely troubles practising lawyers, whose concern is usually as to what property is subject to ownership or else what proprietary rights are recognised. Indeed, the nature of ownership may be seen as more of a jurisprudential question than a legal one.[21] The normal attributes of transmissibility and power to exclude others apply to ownership, but so they do to other proprietary rights.

---

[18] (1918) 248 US 215.
[19] See the instructive Australian High Court decision in *Victoria Park Racing & Recreation Grounds Co Ltd* v *Taylor* (1937) 58 CLR 479 (especially Dixon J at pp 508–510), in which the court denied a claim to prevent the broadcasting, from overlooking premises, of the claimant's racing activities.
[20] Gurry, *Breach of Confidence*, pp 46–56. Note the differing views expressed in *Boardman* v *Phipps* [1967] 2 AC 46.
[21] See the discussion by Honoré in *Oxford Essays in Jurisprudence* (First Series, ed Guest), Chapter 5; also Harris, *Property and Justice*.

What is special about ownership is that it is the ultimate right to use (and abuse) the object or right in question. Difficulties swiftly emerge, however. There is rarely an unlimited right to use property: witness the tort of nuisance and planning permission requirements for land development.[22] In some cases, an owner may have put it out of his or her power to use land by creating a short-term right in another person; a lease, for example. This shows how the law permits the incidents of ownership to be split amongst several people. Perhaps it is best to regard ownership as residing in the person with the ultimate right to the use of the property. If A has leased the land to B for 20 years, we would regard A as the owner, even though B can exercise most[23] of the rights of ownership until that period has elapsed.

In English law, the absence of remedies based upon proof of ownership is remarkable. As will be seen later,[24] our remedies are usually based upon possession and rights to possession. It is generally sufficient simply to prove a better right than the other party and not necessary to prove absolute ownership. This has the consequence that issues relating to ownership are less likely to come before the courts,[25] which are more often concerned with possession. This provides a contrast with some other legal systems.

In particular, few cases involve the nature of ownership,[26] although the extent of the rights of individual owners is frequently litigated. One type of case that has arisen in other jurisdictions is how far group claims to land can fit within property principles. This has caused difficulties with aboriginal land rights.[27] As we have seen, ownership concepts may be employed where it is sought to extend notions of property to novel situations, as in the context of information. There are various statutory references to ownership, but these appear to have caused the courts few problems.[28]

Finally, how crucial is ownership? If a legal system denies ownership, does this preclude a law of property? So long as some rights over objects (or other forms of property) are recognised, and these rights are enforceable against other persons (the exclusionary aspect), it would seem appropriate to see the rules as being proprietary. If the rights were personal and not transmissible, then we might have more doubts, but the point to grasp is that property analyses need not be limited to specific socio-economic structures.[29]

3. Some basic distinctions

The law of property has developed over many centuries. One result of this is that it is encrusted with numerous distinctions, often archaic in their nature and terminology. Many legal systems recognise a distinction between land and other forms of property.

[22] Douglas in *Modern Studies in Property Law*, Vol 7 (ed Hopkins), Chapter 16, discusses the right to use land in the context of freehold estates.
[23] There are limits as to what B can do, particularly as regards damaging the property.
[24] See p 52 below.
[25] The courts may, of course, be called upon to deal with ownership. One example concerns the obligation of a seller to show good title (land: Barnsley, *Conveyancing Law and Practice* (4th edn), pp 266–271) or to show a right to sell (goods: Sale of Goods Act 1979, s 12).
[26] *Melluish v BMI (No 3) Ltd* [1996] AC 454 at pp 474–476 provides an exception, in the context of fixtures.
[27] *Mabo v Queensland* (1992) 107 ALR 1, especially Toohey J at pp 144ff.
[28] Cf *Raymond Lyons & Co Ltd v Metropolitan Police Commissioner* [1975] QB 321.
[29] See Harris (1995) 111 LQR 421 (revised in Harris, *Property and Justice*, Chapter 7).

There are several reasons for this. The permanence of land means that the creation of valuable long-term rights in it is feasible. Furthermore, the effective use of land often demands that permanent arrangements are made with adjoining landowners. One obvious example is that access to the land may require a right of way over a neighbour's land. Another example is that the intended use of land may require limiting the use of adjoining land. Thus, the development of a housing estate may be viable only if an adjoining owner enters into a restrictive covenant, which binds purchasers, preventing the building of a factory.

The result is that a greater variety of rights can be created in land than in other property. For other property, ease of purchase has a higher priority: purchasers of cars, for example, do not expect to undertake investigations to discover whether they are affected by a multitude of other people's rights. There is also a feeling that land is an unusually valuable asset. This is one of the justifications for having formality requirements (writing or, in some cases, deeds) for most land transactions. Of course, some areas of land are small and of little value, whereas other forms of property can have enormous values.

Realty and personalty

In English law, a distinction is made between realty and personalty. In essence, real property is land and personalty covers all other property. The origin of the English distinction lies in the availability of actions to recover land in medieval property law (actions in rem, or real actions). Because leases were not protected by these actions, they counted as personalty despite the eventual development of more effective leasehold remedies. Leases were given the curious categorisation of 'chattels real'. Since the property reforms of 1925, the distinctions between realty and personalty have been greatly reduced, with leases being almost completely assimilated into realty. Nevertheless, it should not be thought that there are no distinctions between realty and personalty today. The range of interests in realty remains far wider than in personalty (see Chapter 5). In addition, most interests in land have to be registered before they can bind purchasers. However, many of the technical rules regulating property now apply identically to realty and personalty.

One important example of this convergence concerns the devolution of property on the death of the owner.[30] Originally, realty would pass directly to the heir or legatee. Personalty would pass to the executor of the deceased's will (or administrator in the case of intestacy), for passing on to legatees or selling for the payment of debts. This led to their being described as personal representatives. Today, all property passes to personal representatives, although the now inaccurate label still survives. The routing of all property through personal representatives is important to ensure that rights to the property can be traced easily. The rights of the personal representatives are established by the grant of probate (of a will) or grant of representation (intestacy).[31] For land, a purchaser, whether direct from the personal representatives or from a beneficiary to whom the property has been transferred, is protected against irregularities in the transfer by the personal representatives.[32]

---

[30] Administration of Estates Act 1925, s 1.
[31] Ibid, s 1.
[32] Ibid, s 36 (especially (6)–(8)).

This ensures that there is no need and, indeed, no right to inspect the will. As wills can be highly complex, this is an important element in ensuring simple and safe property transfer.

Personalty has a wide scope, as it comprises all property other than realty. It is usual to distinguish between choses in possession and choses in action. A chose in possession is a physical object, such as a car. As will be seen later, a car can be transferred by delivery to another person; rights to possession are recognised by creating a bailment of the car. Choses in action are incorporeal in nature: they are legally recognised rights. One obvious example is money in a bank account. I have a right of action against my bank to recover any sum standing to my credit in my account; conversely, my bank can sue me if my account is overdrawn. Choses in action cannot attract all the same rules as choses in possession for the simple reason that physical delivery is not feasible.[33] Instead, we talk about assigning a chose in action: there are special rules for this, which will be considered in Chapter 8.

The line between realty and choses in possession on the one side, and choses in action on the other, is not clear-cut. It would be straightforward if the law were to say that ownership of physical property was to fall on one side of the line and all other rights on the other side. However, that would revert to the error of thinking that property is limited to ownership. Rather, the law recognises numerous rights in land and other objects that are proprietary rights in themselves. One example is the lease: a right to land for a specified period. We regard this as a property right, rather than as a mere chose in action.[34] It does not follow, however, that every transaction relating to land constitutes realty. Suppose I contract with a window cleaning firm that I will employ them for two years to clean my windows. The firm does not have a right that is recognised as being a proprietary right in my land. It is simply a contractual right, regulated as a chose in action.[35]

Intellectual property

It has already been seen that there is a category of intellectual property; it counts as personalty. It is a specialised area, the details of which fall outside the scope of this text. Several rights in intellectual property are recognised, usually as the result of legislation. Examples are copyright in written material, which prevents copying of the material without permission. This inhibits copying of the words; for example, a rival publisher producing copies of a popular novel.[36] It offers less protection against reproducing the ideas in the writing. The primary protection of ideas (or inventions) lies in the law relating to patents. Patents are made public, but the law provides a monopoly in respect of the invention for a period of 20 years. There are other rights, such as registered trade marks and designs. Designs cover items as varied as toys and car exhausts. Registered designs are given a monopoly for 20 years, whilst design right[37] gives protection against copying of unregistered designs for 10 years from their first marketing. Apart from these statutory rules, the

---

[33] Problems may arise where a representative document, such as a building society pass book, is handed over. Although there are some relaxations, the general rule is that this does not transfer the chose in action.
[34] It is also a contract. Leases share many of the characteristics of choses in action and we refer to the assignment both of choses in action and of leases.
[35] Property lawyers describe such a right to enter land as a licence (see Chapter 22).
[36] Protection generally ceases 70 years after death.
[37] Introduced by the Copyright, Designs and Patents Act 1988.

courts have recognised rights based upon the confidentiality of information. This prevents a person from taking advantage of information received in confidence (for example, as an employee) but would not prevent simple copying of an idea or design.[38]

On top of this structure, there are several torts intended to prevent unfair trading practices. These are based upon ideas of not misleading people, though their effect may be to recognise something akin to intellectual property. For example, the tort of passing off prevents the impression being given that goods have been produced by another trader. It is obviously wrong for the seller of cheap trainers to claim that they are Nike trainers. More difficult is the case where, say, a supermarket chain produces cans of a cola drink that resemble Coca-Cola cans. Here, the tort will apply if purchasers are likely to be misled. This produces a result very similar to protecting the design of the can, but it is not subject to the constraints on design protection. It is not a situation in which a property right would normally be said to exist.

Legal and equitable rights

This area is discussed in Chapter 4. Historically, the common law courts recognised a limited range of rights (legal rights), whereas other rights were recognised by the Court of Chancery (equitable rights). Although the courts have been fused for well over a century, the distinction between legal and equitable rights survives. For most equitable interests, the principal importance of the distinction lies in the narrower circumstances in which they may bind purchasers,[39] coupled with a generally more discretionary approach in dealing with them. The most significant equitable development is the trust. This is a device whereby one person (the trustee) has legal ownership and manages the property, whilst another person (the beneficiary) has equitable ownership and enjoys all the benefits of the property. In terms of economic value, the beneficiary is the owner, yet without control over the property. If the property is to be sold in order to be replaced with an alternative asset (as where shares in Shell are sold and replaced with shares in Marks & Spencer), it is the trustee who will sell them.

4. The new property

The language of property has been employed in discussion of claims to advance certain rights of individuals in modern society.[40] These claims include, for example, rights to employment and to benefits such as retirement pensions. The link with property is tenuous. The argument is that the law should recognise these rights in the same way as it recognises property, free from undue governmental control. Secure employment is, for most people, more significant than most of their possessions. The law has not, as yet, protected an individual's right to employment to the extent to which it protects that individual's interest in a car or house. Whether the law should do more to protect such rights is, of course, an arguable question. The property analogy is apt for the purpose of asking whether the law has its priorities correctly ordered. However, there is little serious attempt to argue that

---

[38] Assuming that the idea or design is lawfully in that person's possession.
[39] They are more likely than legal rights to require registration.
[40] Reich (1964) 73 Yale LJ 733; note the discussion by Harris, *Property and Justice*, pp 149–151.

these rights should be proprietary in the sense in which lawyers use that term. The issues arise as regards neither the transmissibility of these rights nor the power to exclude others. In terms of ownership, there is no concern with the extent of use and abuse of the right.

A rather different point is that property may be used as a way of promoting certain state policy objectives. A good example lies in 'commodification' in the context of environmental regulation – creating property rights in fisheries and carbon, for example.[41] This involves the use of property (often to allow the sale of these new property rights) in order that environmental costs are taken fully into account.

Further reading

Honoré, A M (1961) 'Ownership' in *Oxford Essays in Jurisprudence*, First Series (ed A G Guest), Chapter 5.
O'Connor, P (2009) 'The extension of land registration principles to new property rights in environmental goods' in *Modern Studies in Property Law*, Vol 5 (ed M Dixon), Chapter 15.
Reich, C A (1964) 73 Yale LJ 733: The new property.

---

[41] O'Connor in *Modern Studies in Property Law*, Vol 5 (ed Dixon), Chapter 15.

2

The central concerns of property law

Introduction

We saw in the previous chapter that property encompasses not only ownership, but also a wide range of other rights. In this chapter, an attempt will be made to isolate the issues that are of primary concern to property lawyers and to explain the ways in which they are dealt with. Mostly, these issues will be restricted to land and chattels (movable objects, or choses in possession), with the greatest emphasis being placed upon land.

1. What interests bind purchasers?

Although the term property right can be given several different meanings,[1] our central concern is whether a particular right is capable of binding not just the parties who created it, but also third parties.[2] Usually the issue is whether a purchaser from the person who created the right is bound, though the issue may also concern others who interfere with the right.[3] Any system of private ownership necessarily recognises that the owner's rights affect others. However, it does not follow that all rights other than ownership will all have that proprietary effect.

Consider the following examples in relation to land. A agrees with B that B is to clean the windows of A's house monthly for five years for an annual payment of £100. Should A sell the house to C, then B has neither the right to enter C's land to clean the windows nor any right to claim any payment from C. B has a mere contractual right against A; privity of contract principles ensures that C, a stranger to the contract, is not bound. In the second example, D agrees with E, a neighbour, that E can cross D's land in order to gain easy access to a road. D sells the land to F. Here, E has a proprietary interest (a right of way, a form of easement) which will bind F: E can continue to use the access.[4] That the agreement between D and E may also constitute a contract is irrelevant to this result: it is the proprietary nature of the transaction that is crucial.

---

[1] Jackson, *Principles of Property Law*, Chapters 2 and 3, especially pp 39–45 and 67–78.
[2] JW Harris in *Oxford Essays in Jurisprudence* (Third Series, eds Eekelaar and Bell), at pp 180–181, describes the doctrinal cleavage between those interests that bind purchasers and those that do not.
[3] The nature of rights affecting others has been the subject of recent debate: see, e.g., McFarlane in *Landmark Cases in Land Law* (ed Gravells), Chapter 1; Gardner in *Modern Studies in Property Law*, Vol 7 (ed Hopkins), Chapter 15; Jaffey (2015) 131 LQR 377.
[4] Subject to requirements of formality (writing, or a deed) and registration.

Proprietary transactions are thus seen to be special in that they operate outside the normal concepts of privity of contract. Despite recognising a generous range of proprietary interests, the law does not permit the parties to produce novel property rights. In the famous words of Lord Brougham LC,[5] 'it must not therefore be supposed that incidents of a novel kind can be devised and attached to property, at the fancy or caprice of any owner'. This is the numerus clausus principle, mentioned in Chapter 1.[6]

Why does the law take this approach? The answer is based upon two principal factors. First, the courts are wary of imposing unreasonable burdens on the process of buying property. An unlimited range of proprietary interests would make it difficult for purchasers to know what rights to look out for and also to know what the incidents of a novel interest might be. However, some of these problems are less severe now that most rights (but not those held by those in actual occupation) have to be registered before a purchaser will be bound.[7] Second, a wide range of proprietary rights would render ownership less attractive, possibly resulting in economically inefficient use of property.

Land law is a long-established area of law, and most proprietary rights have been recognised for centuries. There is little doubt about their being proprietary, even though their technical rules can still give rise to litigation. There are, however, areas in which the restrictive approach to the range of proprietary interests is controversial. This is most clearly the case as regards licences: permission to enter land not amounting to a lease or easement. According to conventional property thinking, licences are not proprietary interests.[8] This area has been subject to considerable analysis and litigation in recent decades: it is the present front-line in the battle for proprietary status.

It should be noted, however, that the binding of third parties (usually purchasers from the person who created the right) is not a black-and-white issue. There is a substantial armoury of legal weapons available in specific scenarios. These weapons may be used to attack third parties, but this does not mean that any proprietary right is involved. Two examples might be given. A person who induces the breach of a contract may be made liable in tort.[9] It is controversial how far this tort operates in the property context, but its application does not mean that the contract is rendered a proprietary interest. The purchaser is not bound to comply with the contract. Rather, the purchaser's conduct results in tort liability. A second example is where a purchaser persuades the owner to sell by promising that the rights (not previously proprietary) of a third party will be upheld. If the purchaser reneges on the promise, this is viewed as unconscionable behaviour giving rise to a constructive trust binding the purchaser.[10]

For a right to be regarded as proprietary, it is necessary for it to bind purchasers automatically, subject to its being registered (as is required for most interests in land). The crucial emphasis is on the quality of the right to the property, rather than on the purchaser's

---

[5] *Keppell* v *Bailey* (1834) 2 My&K 517 at p 535 (39 ER 1042 at p 1049).

[6] See McFarlane in *Modern Studies in Property Law*, Vol 6 (ed Bright), Chapter 15; also in *Landmark Cases in Land Law* (ed Gravells), Chapter 1.

[7] Edgeworth (2006) 32 Monash ULR 387. See also p 498 below.

[8] See p 50 below for an outline.

[9] See p 500 below.

[10] See pp 143–146 below; JW Harris in *Oxford Essays in Jurisprudence* (Third Series, eds Eekelaar and Bell), at pp 187–191.

conduct. In past centuries (and for a minority of interests today), an equitable interest would bind purchasers with notice: those who know about or should know about the interest. There is a fine line between binding a purchaser because of the purchaser's conduct (not property) and binding the purchaser because there is notice (property).[11] This fine line is crucial to determining what are proprietary interests.

It is commonly said that another aspect of a proprietary right is its assignability. Having a proprietary right is often of limited utility unless its value can be unlocked by sale to a third party. Rights regarded as proprietary can generally be assigned, but closer examination shows that assignability does not always fit perfectly with proprietary status. For a start, some proprietary rights are not assignable. It is possible to provide that an interest shall terminate on assignment,[12] whilst some proprietary rights, such as rights of way, are linked with specific land and cannot be alienated separately from that land.

We have seen that it is exceptional for the burden of non-proprietary rights to bind third parties. However, it is very common for the benefit of such rights to be assigned to third parties who are then able to sue to enforce them. The assignment of the benefit of a contract has long been recognised as an exception to privity rules. Originally, the third party had to join the assignor, but a direct action is now normally available.[13] That the benefit of a right can be assigned does not mean that it is proprietary. Suppose B contracts with A to provide refuse disposal facilities for A's factory for five years. B could assign the benefit of this contract to C,[14] so that C could sue A. This plainly does not give C a proprietary right in the land. What we can say is that the benefit of the contract may be regarded as a proprietary right. This means that C has a right to enforce the contract, good as against other claimants to the contract. If B were to assign the contract a second time to D (inconsistently with C's assignment), then C has a better right than D to the contract.[15] The point to note is that the object of the proprietary right is the contract rather than the land.

Yet another aspect of a proprietary right is sometimes said to be the ability to recover the property.[16] If I cannot get the property back if it is taken by somebody, then how can my right be said to be proprietary? However, this point also is troublesome. Although the taker will normally be liable in damages, it need not follow that the property is recoverable. If my ring is stolen by X, it may be that my remedy is to claim its value from X. Indeed, this was the original state of the law. This 'personal remedy' against X explained why we describe chattels as personal property,[17] but it could scarcely be said that there were no proprietary rights in chattels. Today, specific recovery of chattels can be ordered.[18]

---

[11] The line is illustrated by the rule that an equitable interest will bind a person who is not a purchaser, despite there being no notice: *Re Nisbet and Potts' Contract* [1906] 1 Ch 386 (adverse possession).
[12] A good example is provided by protective trusts: Trustee Act 1925, s 33 (see p 44 below).
[13] Law of Property Act 1925, s 136.
[14] Provided that it is not personal to B.
[15] Subject to the priority rules (considered below, p 126).
[16] 'The traditional dividing line': Jackson, *Principles of Property Law*, p 39.
[17] *Crossley Vaines on Personal Property* (5th edn), p 6.
[18] Currently, Torts (Interference with Goods) Act 1977, s 3. Curwen (2006) 26 LS 570 criticises the narrowness of the application of s 3 and the absence of an adequate proprietary remedy for chattels.

Nor can it be argued that specific enforcement of rights is the same as proprietary status. Over the past century, it has become apparent that the courts will specifically enforce contracts relating to land, even though the limits are as yet unclear.[19] It might be possible in the waste disposal example for B to get an order for specific performance against A, the other contracting party. However, the House of Lords has made it very clear that this does not lead to B's having a proprietary interest in the land that can be enforced against a purchaser from A.[20]

It follows that neither assignability of the benefit nor specific recovery can be used to prove that a right is or is not proprietary. They may be factors that can be brought into an argument over a claim that a particular right should be admitted to the category of proprietary interests binding purchasers, but they are not decisive.

The interests binding purchasers are summarised in Chapter 5. The more important interests in land are considered in detail in Parts III and IV. Except for licences, there is usually little doubt as to whether a particular right constitutes a proprietary interest. However, the qualifying rules for each interest do provide greater scope for disagreements. These form one of the major areas for study.

2. Creation and transfer

Having established that a right is proprietary, the next question concerns methods of creation and transfer. There is much material that is common to all interests, or at least to a range of interests, and this is dealt with in Part II. However, certain interests have rules that are very specific. These rules are addressed in Parts III and IV as the various interests are studied. A good example is provided by easements, such as rights of way. Easements are subject to elaborate rules as to when they will be implied, or arise from long use. Indeed, these rules provide the bulk of the material on easements. For most other interests, it is quite exceptional for them to be created other than expressly.[21]

3. The rights of the parties

Once it has been decided that an interest exists, an obvious question arises as to what rights and duties the parties have. In some areas, there is little to say. Taking covenants (obligations in deeds) as an example, all depends upon what the covenant provides. Nevertheless, many interests have attracted special rules. This is especially true of leases. Because a lease involves one person using another person's land, often for many years, it is vital to sort out their duties and rights. In particular, what obligations are imposed on the landlord to repair the land and on the tenant to take care of it? A related question concerns the enforcement of obligations. Taking leases again, landlords invariably include a right to forfeit the lease if the tenant is in breach of obligations. This right to forfeit is strictly regulated by statute and the courts, giving rise to another large body of law. In leases, these issues are sufficiently important to deserve a chapter to themselves.

---

[19] See below pp 486 et seq.
[20] *National Provincial Bank Ltd v Ainsworth* [1965] AC 1175.
[21] Interests in the family home constitute another exception: see Chapter 11.

4. The effect on purchasers

It has been seen that the essence of proprietary interests is that they are rights capable of affecting third parties. The third party may be a purchaser from the creator of the right, or else a person granted a lease or security interest (mortgage).[22] However, it is not the case that every purchaser is automatically bound by every proprietary interest.

In particular, special rules were applied to equitable interests: a purchaser for value of a legal estate would not be bound if there were no notice. There is notice if the purchaser knows about the equitable interest, or a reasonable purchaser would have discovered it from making the normal inquiries.

In the modern law, the great majority of land is covered by land registration, whereby the ownership is registered. Unless there is a short lease, actual occupation or a non-express easement, nearly every interest, whether legal or equitable, has to be entered on the register. The upshot is that most interests have to be registered before they will bind purchasers; but once registered, it is no longer necessary to prove that the purchaser has notice. Proprietary status remains crucial for deciding whether an interest can be registered and so will bind purchasers. Even where land is not registered, many equitable interests have to be registered under the land charges scheme before a purchaser will be bound. The assumption throughout the text is that land registration applies. Because registration has categories and principles that apply across different interests in land, it will be dealt with in Part II.

A rather different point regarding purchasers is that many interests (especially where there is a trust) are subject to overreaching. This means that, subject to certain safeguards,[23] the land can be sold free from these interests, which will then take effect in respect of the proceeds. This applies to many successive ('to A for life, remainder to B') and concurrent ('to C and D jointly') interests. This concept of overreaching is widely imposed by legislation.[24] Although these successive and concurrent interests will not normally bind purchasers, there are two respects in which they are shown still to be interests in land. First, the rights of the interest holders are the same (at least until sale) as if there were no overreaching. Second, if a sale fails to comply with the overreaching rules, then the interest will bind the purchaser.[25]

Because overreaching applies principally to successive and concurrent interests, detailed treatment is postponed until we reach those topics in Part III. However, it should be remembered that other interests may be affected by overreaching. Indeed, whenever a person has power to sell land free of rights, a form of overreaching will take place. One well-known example arises if there is default by the borrower under a mortgage. The lender, such as a bank or building society, can sell the land and thereby overreach the proprietary interest of the borrower, who becomes entitled to any proceeds of sale left after deducting the loan.

---

[22] The word purchaser is commonly used to include lessees, mortgagees and other successors in title.
[23] Principally, the payment of purchase money to two trustees: this is an attempt to reduce the risk of fraud.
[24] See p 56 below for a summary.
[25] *Williams & Glyn's Bank Ltd* v *Boland* [1981] AC 487 (sale by one trustee, rather than two as required).

Further reading

Gardner, S (2013) '"Persistent Rights" appraised' in *Modern Studies in Property Law*, Vol 7 (ed N Hopkins), Chapter 15.

Harris, J W (1987) 'Legal doctrine and interests in land' in *Oxford Essays in Jurisprudence* (Third Series, eds J Eekelaar and J Bell), Chapter 8.

McFarlane, B (2011) 'The numerus clausus principle and covenants relating to land' in *Modern Studies in Property Law*, Vol 6 (ed S Bright), Chapter 15.

3
Human rights

Introduction

The incorporation of the European Convention for the Protection of Human Rights and Fundamental Freedoms into domestic English law by the Human Rights Act 1998 was a most significant development. This is true for all areas of law, including property law. We will consider the material under three headings: the rights conferred by the Convention (incorporated in Schedule 1 to the Act), how those rights can be enforced and how the courts have been reacting to the 1998 Act in the property context.

The impact of human rights on specific property interests will be undertaken as we study them in later chapters. It is not feasible to include everything in this chapter, as the detailed property rules and their rationale have yet to be explained. Accordingly, this chapter will be restricted to a general review of the impact of human rights. It is also worth observing that we are still in the relatively early stages of a new era when human rights arguments are being worked out by the English courts. We are, perhaps, just reaching the stage when principles are beginning to settle down, so that lawyers can feel confident in asserting when human rights may affect existing property principles.

1. The Convention rights

Three Articles will be mentioned as most likely to surface in property contexts. The first is the protection of property under Article 1 of the First Protocol (A1P1)[1]:

> Every natural or legal person is entitled to the peaceful enjoyment of his possessions. No one shall be deprived of his possessions except in the public interest and subject to the conditions provided for by law and by the general principles of international law.
>
> The preceding provisions shall not, however, in any way impair the right of a State to enforce such laws as it deems necessary to control the use of property in accordance with the general interest or to secure the payment of taxes or other contributions or penalties.

Not surprisingly, *deprivation* of possessions (a word widely interpreted to include, for example, claims to damages) is difficult to justify: normally, compensation will be needed. There are provisions allowing compulsory purchase of land (which are outside the scope of this text), where it is required for purposes such as building a new road; compensation is payable. *Control* over possessions is more readily accepted, subject to issues of proportionality relative to the legitimate end being pursued.

---

[1] This is reviewed in depth in Allen, *Property and the Human Rights Act 1998.*

The application of A1P1 in the adverse possession context was considered by the European Court of Human Rights (Strasbourg) in *JA Pye (Oxford) Ltd* v *United Kingdom*.[2] Adverse possession is the principle whereby ownership can be lost if land is adversely possessed by another person for 12 years; it is studied in Chapter 7. Two general points emerge from *Pye*. The first concerns the UK argument that A1P1 was not engaged because ownership in English law is inherently susceptible to adverse possession: the loss of the land was a natural risk within English property law ownership and not any form of confiscation. This was emphatically rejected. To uphold it would lead to the emasculation of A1P1. However, the second point is that adverse possession was treated as a 'control of use' rather than 'deprivation'. It operates to regulate questions of title rather than deprive owners of their land. A1P1 was still engaged, but this analysis made it easier for the court to justify its conclusion that adverse possession is consistent with human rights, despite the absence of compensation.

Next, Article 8 can be used to protect homes:

1. Everyone has the right to respect for his private and family life, his home and his correspondence.
2. There shall be no interference by a public authority with the exercise of this right except such as is in accordance with the law and is necessary in a democratic society in the interests of national security, public safety or the economic well-being of the country, for the prevention of disorder or crime, for the protection of health or morals, or for the protection of the rights and freedoms of others.

To be a home, it is not necessary for there to be any property right.[3] This raises interesting possibilities for those living with a property owner to rely on Article 8.[4] Many of our legal rules are based on protecting the property owner; the position of others (especially partners and children) is often overlooked. However, human rights arguments cannot be used to create rights to housing (or property interests): they operate in more of a negative fashion to limit interference.[5] In any event, the qualifications in the second paragraph mean that there is nothing approaching an absolute right. Article 8 has been much litigated in the past few years; this is discussed below.

Finally, Article 6 provides that 'In the determination of his civil rights and obligations . . . , everyone is entitled to a fair and public hearing'. This might be relevant to remedies which are exercised out of court: it might be argued that they preclude a hearing to resolve the issue. However, these remedies can be viewed as simply enforcement of existing rights conferred by law, rather than the determination of rights.

2. Enforcement of Convention rights

This is the source of hot debate: are rights conferred simply against the State (so that it cannot, for example, confiscate property) or also against other individuals? On the one

---

[2] (2007) 46 EHHR 1083; Dixon [2007] Conv 552. See also p 27 below.
[3] *Harrow LBC* v *Qazi* [2004] 1 AC 983. The extent to which the recent cases develop the concept of home is considered by Bevan in *Modern Studies in Property Law*, Vol 8 (ed Barr), Chapter 11 (see also p 350, n 209 below).
[4] Nield and Hopkins (2013) 33 LS 431 (directed to the mortgage context, but could be much wider).
[5] Baroness Hale in *Kay* v *Lambeth LBC* [2006] 2 AC 465 at [191].

hand, the origins of the legislation lie in enforcement by the Strasbourg court, which is concerned only with rights against States. In the Act, this is reflected in the provision that public authorities must act consistently with Convention rights.[6] It is sometimes argued that the substantive Convention rights are rights as against States and therefore, by definition, individuals cannot breach them.[7]

On the other hand, two principal arguments are put forward in favour of 'horizontal' effect against individuals. One is that s 3 requires legislation to be read, so far as possible, in a way compatible with Convention rights.[8] This applies regardless of the parties. If a public authority was a party and it was acting in breach of Convention rights, then s 3 would require the legislation to be read so as to avoid a breach. That interpretation, however, has to be the correct interpretation whoever the parties are: we cannot accept that legislation has a different meaning according to the identity of the parties. Perhaps more important is the fact that the State may be in breach of Convention rights by having legislation which conflicts with those rights, even though the beneficiary of that breach may be another individual rather than the State itself. Again, this means that the legislation should be read so that there is no breach; inevitably, this will impact on the individuals involved. Nor is this simply a matter of theory: the cases show that s 3 operates even though both litigants are individuals.[9]

However, legislation will not always be the cause of the problem. This leads to the second argument. This is based upon s 6(3), which includes courts as public authorities. Wade[10] has seized on this to argue that the courts must give effect to Convention rights, so that full horizontal effect is achieved. However, most commentators take a somewhat more cautious stance.[11] It is widely recognised that the State may be liable where Convention rights are denied by individuals: this has been characterised as a positive obligation to ensure that adequate protection is provided. It was early seen in privacy claims under Article 8. It seems probable that the courts will allow horizontal effect in this situation, so that the courts should act so as to ensure that there is no breach.[12]

3. Convention rights in the courts

A. Horizontal effect?

The earlier cases are reflected in the approach of Mummery LJ in *X* v *Y*,[13] when he observed it is unusual for horizontal effect to be crucial: courts are usually able to decide cases on more specific grounds. In particular, the interpretation of legislation under s 3 is

---

[6] Section 6.
[7] Buxton (2000) 116 LQR 48 at p 56.
[8] This enables the courts to go significantly further than normal statutory interpretation principles would permit: *Ghaidan* v *Godin-Mendoza* [2004] 2 AC 557.
[9] *PW & Co* v *Milton Gate Investments Ltd* [2004] Ch 142; *X* v *Y* [2004] ICR 1634 (especially at [49] and [66]); *Ghaidan* v *Godin-Mendoza* [2004] 2 AC 557; *Beaulane Properties Ltd* v *Palmer* [2006] Ch 79 provide examples.
[10] See, e.g., (2000) 116 LQR 217; also Morgan (2002) 22 LS 259.
[11] See Bamforth (2001) 117 LQR 34; Phillipson and Williams (2011) 74 MLR 878.
[12] *Douglas* v *Hello! Ltd* [2001] QB 967 at [128]–[129]; *Venables* v *News Group Newspapers Ltd* [2001] Fam 430 at [24]–[26].
[13] [2004] ICR 1634 at [44]–[46]. Cf Lord Walker in *Doherty* v *Birmingham CC* [2009] AC 367 at [99], who seems to equate challenging the common law and horizontal effect.

likely to cover many property cases, and this explains the use of human rights in cases involving individuals. Property law is sufficiently statutory that most issues can be viewed in terms of interpreting legislation.[14] Similarly, if a challenge is made to a common law rule, then it seems probable that the courts will wish a human rights compliant rule to operate, whether or not the parties include a public authority.

Where horizontal effect could be really important is where Article 8 (respect for home) applies. This may be used both (i) to challenge statutory rules or legal principles and (ii) to challenge decisions to take possession.[15] The former challenge is viable on the basis of what was said earlier in this section, though few challenges have been successful.[16] A useful example concerns applications by trustees in bankruptcy (who realise assets to pay off creditors of the bankrupt) for possession of the bankrupt's family home. *Barca* v *Mears*[17] has suggested that the test for possession fails sufficiently to take into account people's homes and family lives.

However, the more contentious question relates to the second challenge: can it be argued that a decision to order possession in favour of a private landowner is, on the facts of the case, disproportionate? That was the question faced by the Supreme Court in *McDonald* v *McDonald*.[18] Because it follows on cases discussed in the following section, it will be discussed thereafter.

B. Human rights in the exercise of proprietary rights

A highly controversial issue concerns the application of Article 8.[19] Can it be used to challenge the eviction of occupiers from their homes, when the claim against them is based upon an impeccable legal right? This has typically arisen where a local authority has sought possession of a house when either a lease (or licence) has terminated or the occupier's rights are not binding on the local authority. Can occupiers argue that the court, in ordering possession, must take into consideration the effect on their home? There has been a huge amount of litigation in the past decade or so, with very different views being taken in the House of Lords and Strasbourg.

The story starts with *Harrow LBC* v *Qazi*,[20] in which a bare majority of the House of Lords held that the local authority was entitled to exercise its rights as owner, free of any human rights limitations. Then the Strasbourg court held in *Connors* v *UK*[21] that reliance on legal title was insufficient when attempting to evict gypsies. The effect of *Connors* on *Qazi* was controversial, and the issue returned to a seven-judge House of Lords in *Kay* v *Lambeth LBC*.[22] Again by a bare majority, the stance in *Qazi* was maintained.

---

[14] Howell (2007) 123 LQR 618 is more inclined to see these cases as supporting horizontal effect.
[15] These possibilities are recognised in *McDonald* v *McDonald* [2016] 3 WLR 45 at [45].
[16] Examples of unsuccessful challenges are *Sims* v *Dacorum BC* [2015] AC 1336 (joint periodic tenancies; see p 402 below) and *Horsham Properties Group Ltd* v *Clark* [2009] 1 WLR 1255 (mortgagees' powers of sale; see p 27 below).
[17] [2005] 2 FLR 1; see p 349 below.
[18] [2016] 3 WLR 45.
[19] Nield [2013] King's LJ 147.
[20] [2004] 1 AC 983.
[21] [2004] HLR 991.
[22] [2006] 2 AC 465.

This was difficult enough, but subsequent Strasbourg decisions supported the minority in *Qazi* and *Kay*: in particular, *McCann* v *UK*[23] and *Kay* v *UK*.[24] The Strasbourg cases insisted that an independent tribunal should decide upon the proportionality of evicting a person from their home. Proportionality is to be assessed against the background that Article 8 permits interference 'necessary in a democratic society', as detailed above. The scene was then set for a radical review of the area by a nine-judge Supreme Court in 2010 in *Manchester City Council* v *Pinnock*.[25] This overruled both *Qazi* and *Kay*.

Now that the Supreme Court has held that proportionality must be satisfied before evicting an occupier, the intricacies of the earlier cases need not be considered in any detail. It should not be thought that the House of Lords had ignored what was emerging from Strasbourg. It was accepted that the importance of the home had to be recognised, and that this required some adjustment of English law. This adjustment is seen in the *Kay* analysis that the court could reject possession applications by the use of one of two 'gateways'.[26] The first was that the substantive law could be challenged on the basis of inconsistency with Article 8; this would be proved in few cases. The second was that the decision of the local authority to seek possession could be challenged on the basis of judicial review. As the Strasbourg criticisms intensified, the scope of judicial review was widened by the House of Lords in *Doherty v Birmingham CC*.[27]

Fortunately, in *Pinnock,* the Supreme Court took a quite different approach from *Doherty* and recognised that Article 8 requires that proportionality be arguable in all cases. Perhaps surprisingly, the judicial review analysis has not completely disappeared. In *Pinnock* itself, legislation required the court to order possession if certain procedural requirements were satisfied. This appears to preclude the consideration of Article 8, but the Supreme Court reasoned that the decision of the local authority to seek possession could be challenged by judicial review.[28] Importantly, a wide scope for review was accepted. If the local authority failed to accord proper consideration to the loss of a home, then that would be a ground for review – this goes further than traditional review principles. Further, the court should allow the occupier to challenge the local authority's version of the facts, and these questions (unlike normal judicial review challenges) could be decided by the county court judge hearing the possession application. This approach to judicial review built upon and further developed the analyses in *Doherty*.

The quite reasonable question may be asked as to why, prior to *Pinnock,* the English courts were so resistant to the human rights arguments. Part of the answer may lie in too great a deference to the simple enforcement of property rights. This probably explains *Qazi*, though it was early seen to be much too sweeping. The stronger point was a fear that regular reliance on Article 8 would lead to possession proceedings being protracted, clogging the courts.[29] *McCann* was not persuaded that this was a serious risk.

---

[23] [2008] 2 FLR 899. See p 401 below for the landlord and tenant context.

[24] [2011] HLR 13. This followed from the claimant's defeat in *Kay* v *Lambeth LBC*.

[25] [2011] 2 AC 104 (Lord Neuberger delivered the judgment of the court); Thompson [2011] Conv 421, Bright in *Landmark Cases in Land Law* (ed Gravells), Chapter 11.

[26] [2006] 2 AC 465 at [110] (Lord Hope, with all the majority judges' approval).

[27] [2009] AC 367; overruled by *Pinnock* on the role of Article 8.

[28] *Leicester CC* v *Shearer* [2014] HLR 100 (Loveland [2014] Conv 262) provides an example of a public law challenge (based on misrepresentation by the local authority).

[29] *Kay* [2006] 2 AC 465, especially at [54] and [109]. The arguments are strongly expressed in *Doherty* v *Birmingham CC* [2009] AC 367 at [20], though Lord Mance at [163] was unconvinced.

With that in mind, what practical effect is *Pinnock* likely to have? In minority analyses in the earlier House of Lords cases, Lord Bingham thought that a proportionality defence would succeed only in exceptional cases. The Supreme Court thought that this test was 'unsafe and unhelpful': there may be more cases than we presently contemplate. Nevertheless, the courts continue to refer to exceptional and highly exceptional cases.[30] In any event, there is no need for local authorities to plead factors that are obvious, such as the need to regulate a limited housing stock. On the other hand, factors specific to individual cases (such as the need for land for development, where the occupant has one small part of it) do need to be pleaded and proved. Furthermore, Article 8 need only be considered if raised by the occupier; defences should be summarily dismissed unless they stand a reasonable chance of success (for which purpose the facts will need to be assumed to be as alleged by the occupier). So far, the indications are that it is difficult to persuade the court that an arguable case exists – county court decisions in favour of occupiers have generally been overturned on appeal.[31] It seems most likely that human rights defences will succeed when there is some special factor such as vulnerability of the occupier or some attempt by the landlord to bypass the normal protection of tenants.[32]

One of the difficulties in this area is that there are numerous ways in which local authorities allow residential occupation of land, usually under specific statutory schemes. With each of them, there are questions both as to whether the statutory scheme is Article 8 compliant (a major issue in *Pinnock* for what are known as 'demoted tenancies') and whether the way in which they are operated satisfies Article 8. Several of these important questions were dealt with by the Supreme Court in *Hounslow LBC* v *Powell*.[33] However, they are not central to a general review of human rights and (like the tenancies themselves) lie outside the scope of this text.

In the cases immediately before *Pinnock*, a distinction was sometimes drawn[34] as to whether or not the occupier had been given a lease (or licence) by the local authority. If so, then it is easier to argue that the Article 8 considerations are strong. On the other hand, if the occupier is simply a trespasser relative to the local authority, then any defence is unlikely to succeed. Any formal distinction between these categories would be inconsistent with *Pinnock*: there must be scope to raise proportionality issues in every case.[35] Nevertheless, it remains the case that the distinction has some relevance to the way in which questions of proportionality are assessed.[36] On the other hand, questions such as the length of the occupation may be equally important.

[30] See, e.g., *Hounslow LBC* v *Powell* [2011] 2 AC 186 at [92]. *Corby BC* v *Scott* [2012] HLR 366 stresses that it is not enough for the facts to be exceptional: they must show an arguable case based upon proportionality. See Walsh (2015) 131 LQR 585 for an analysis of the operation of *Pinnock*, especially as regards trespassers.
[31] *Corby BC* v *Scott* [2012] HLR 366 (but see Loveland [2012] Conv 512); *Birmingham CC* v *Lloyd* [2012] HLR 681 (trespasser); *Thurrock BC* v *West* [2013] 1 P&CR 175; *Fareham BC* v *Miller* [2013] HLR 282. A decision in favour of the tenant is *Southend-on-Sea BC* v *Armour* [2014] HLR 362 (introductory tenancy).
[32] A high level of vulnerability was insufficient in *R (Plant)* v *Somerset CC* [2016] HLR 416 (trespasser, with offer of other accommodation). The latter situation is illustrated by the *McCann* context, discussed at p 401 below.
[33] [2011] 2 AC 186; Cowan and Hunter (2012) 75 MLR 78. See also *R (N)* v *Lewisham LBC* [2015] AC 1259 (homelessness).
[34] *Central Bedfordshire C* v *Housing Action Zone Ltd* [2010] 1 WLR 446. As in *Kay*, the owner had leased the property with a view to flats being leased to homeless persons (the defendants). This arguably made the defendants more than mere trespassers.
[35] The distinction put *Kay* in the trespasser category; this is inconsistent with the subsequent decision in *Kay* v *UK*.
[36] *Birmingham CC* v *Lloyd* [2012] HLR 681.

C. The exercise of proprietary rights: horizontal effect

The cases discussed in the previous section all concern local authorities. As such, they could be seen as relating more to public authorities than to general property law. But, if they extend to private landowners, then this would make a real difference: rights of private sector landlords and mortgagees (for example) often impact on the family home. In addition, could Article 8 inhibit the recovery of land occupied by trespassers? It would change the balance of the law considerably if Article 8 were to qualify the exercise of rights discussed in this text. On the other hand, there are many contexts in which taking possession depends upon a court order and the court possesses a discretion. This applies to some actions by landlords, mortgagees and trustees. The discretion will almost necessarily take the home into account (sometimes legislation requires this): Article 8 would then be satisfied.[37] Even so, we should not overlook the fact that Article 8 may influence the exercise of the discretion: the home may become a more important factor. The formal impact of Article 8 may be limited, but it may have a marked effect on the way a discretion is exercised.

However, there remain gaps, especially as regards family members. Even if there is a discretion, it may be constrained by the legislation. A good example is found in mortgages, where the discretion applies only if mortgage arrears can be paid off within a reasonable period. Accordingly, we need to know whether proportionality is relevant to the decision to take possession. Take a simple case where a lease has come to an end but the tenant (with no statutory protection, a likely situation today) refuses to leave. A private individual owes no human rights duties. But can it be said that the court – a public authority (s 6(3)) – must comply with Article 8? This was the question faced by the Supreme Court in *McDonald* v *McDonald*.[38] Residential leases are regulated by legislation in several ways: court orders are required before a landlord can recover possession, although the court is required to order possession after the lease ends.

A compelling factor in *McDonald* was that the tenant (the adult daughter of the landlord) had a mental disorder, making it difficult for her to work or to be a satisfactory public sector tenant. The analysis of the Supreme Court was complex. The argument that the court is a public authority was accepted such that 'it may well be that article 8 is engaged' in possession applications. However, the Supreme Court went on to say that this does not justify a different result from that flowing from the contractual relationship between landlord and tenant. It follows that the tenant could not raise issues of proportionality.[39] Several arguments were raised to justify this: the A1P1 protection of property and the oddity of giving a remedy only where possession is taken by court proceedings are both stressed. Overall, the point is made that human rights are designed to prevent state infringement, not to vary parties' contractual agreements.

---

[37] *National Westminster Bank plc* v *Rushmer* [2010] 2 FLR 362 (trusts of land). This is supported by the confidence in *Pinnock* that the termination of secure tenancies, in which the court applies a reasonableness test, satisfies proportionality.

[38] [2016] 3 WLR 45; Lees (2017) 133 LQR 31; Nield [2017] Conv 60 A slightly complicating factor was that the landlord's rights were exercised by a receiver appointed by a mortgagee. This has limited effect on the principles involved. *McDonald* was applied in *Watts* v *Stewart* [2017] HLR 109 (almshouses).

[39] The core of the argument is found at [40]. In any event, possession postponed for six weeks (the maximum allowed under the legislation) would not be disproportionate.

It is not clear how strong the point is, but this analysis is said to apply 'at least' where there are statutory provisions balancing the rights of the parties (as there are for landlord and tenant). It is fair to add that most modern areas of land law have a statutory overlay – so landlord and tenant relationships, mortgages and trusts of land all operate within statutory frameworks. Even if 'at least' is a strong limitation,[40] it is unlikely have a widespread impact in land law cases.

The Supreme Court undertook a fairly detailed review of decisions and dicta of the European Court of Human Rights. It concluded that there was no 'clear and authoritative guidance' that was inconsistent with the conclusions reached. Some of the details of the reasoning of the Supreme Court appear to be based on that guidance.

It has been seen that the Supreme Court places stress on the agreement between the parties: Article 8 cannot be used to argue proportionality contrary to the agreement. That raises the question as to the position if there is no agreement between the parties. Two examples will be considered.

The first concerns cases where one of the occupiers is a person who is not party to any agreement – a child of a tenant or mortgagor is one example. Prior to *McDonald*, it was argued that a child of a mortgagor could argue proportionality.[41] However, it would appear strange if members of a tenant's or mortgagor's family could raise proportionality issues, when the Supreme Court insists that the contractual rights should be given effect to. Although the issue must still be open after *McDonald*, the point that the other occupiers are there only because of the tenant's or mortgagor's possession makes it unlikely that any proportionality argument is viable.

The second example concerns trespassers – an obvious example where there is no agreement. Before *McDonald*, this had arisen in *Malik v Fassenfelt*.[42] The trespassers had lived on the land (restoring it from a polluted and neglected site) for two years. Sir Alan Ward was prepared to hold that the court was bound to take account of Article 8, such that the old rule,[43] whereby virtually immediate possession could be sought from trespassers, was no longer valid (even though such an order was held proportionate on the facts). However, both Lord Toulson and Lloyd LJ held that it was inappropriate to rule on such a controversial point, given that there had been no appeal on it. It might be added that the Court of Appeal in *McDonald*[44] treated the majority as not agreeing with Sir Alan Ward. Nevertheless, at least one High Court case applied the approach of Sir Alan Ward.[45]

How does this stand after the Supreme Court? One perspective is that it would be odd if trespassers were able to raise proportionality arguments when lawful occupiers generally

[40] *Menelaou v Bank of Cyprus UK Ltd* [2016] EWHC 2656 (Ch) at [31] indicates that absence of statutory provisions is unlikely to be crucial.
[41] Nield and Hopkins (2013) 33 LS 431.
[42] [2013] 3 EGLR 99; Lees [2013] Conv 516. See Thompson [2011] Conv 421 for arguments against this application of Article 8. For a broader discussion (including public authority landowners), see Walsh (2015) 131 LQR 585.
[43] *McPhail v Persons Unknown* [1973] Ch 447.
[44] [2015] Ch 357 at [57]. *Malik* is not discussed in the Supreme Court.
[45] *Manchester Ship Canal Developments Ltd v Persons Unknown* [2014] EWHC 645 (Ch). In *Hampson v Orchid Runnymede Ltd* [2015] 11 September, the owner did not contest the application of Article 8. However, immediate possession was ordered in both cases.

cannot do so (absent a public authority landowner, of course). The interference with the A1P1 rights of the landowner is even more pronounced in this setting. In any event, the significance of the point appears to be limited.[46] *Malik* itself shows that it will often be proportionate to order possession immediately. Even if this is not proportionate in an exceptional case, the most that can be expected is postponement for up to six weeks, if there is exceptional hardship. That appears to be the effect of section 89 of the Housing Act 1980.[47] In *McDonald*, it was held that this postponement was the most that could be expected even if proportionality can be argued; Sir Alan Ward had adopted a similar approach in *Malik*. It is theoretically possible that possession might be refused (rather than postponed), but *McDonald* states that 'it is not easy to imagine circumstances' justifying that.

D. The impact of human rights on property principles

In this section, we will consider challenges to property principles, rather than the question (discussed in the previous section) whether a decision to take possession can be challenged as being disproportionate. An initial observation is that, as expressed by Baroness Hale in *Kay*,[48] the Convention began 'as a code of individual civil and political rights, not a code of social and economic rights'. This means that it is not readily used to confer new property rights on individuals, nor to recast the basic principles of property law. Its impact may still be significant, but not so significant as to change the very foundations of property principles.

In which areas of property law might human rights arguments be raised?[49] As regards A1P1, an immediate reaction might be that English law rarely allows the taking of property, leaving aside compulsory purchase. Yet, problems have been encountered as regards confiscation orders following criminal offences – the relevant legislation has had to be read down in order to introduce proportionality.[50] Moving to areas covered by this text, a moment's thought reveals many possible examples. Apart from adverse possession (mentioned earlier in this chapter), what about the effect of registration of title or the forfeiture of leases? In each case, property may be lost and A1P1 engaged; as in *Pye*, however, it may well not amount to deprivation. In other cases, there may be an interference with property rights such as to attract A1P1. One example might be where an easement is acquired by long use (prescription): is this an interference with the owner's rights?

One factor which may come into play in several contexts is that the conduct complained about may be based on the terms of the lease, mortgage, etc, or else implied into such

---

[46] Even for public authority landowners, *Birmingham CC v Lloyd* [2012] HLR 681 at [18] shows that Article 8 will protect the trespasser in only 'the most extraordinarily exceptional circumstances'; cf *R (Plant) v Somerset CC* [2016] HLR 416.

[47] An attack on s 89 in *Hounslow LBC v Powell* [2011] 2 AC 186 failed.

[48] [2006] 2 AC 465 at [192]; the point is stressed by Hughes & Davis [2006] Conv 526 (revisited [2010] Conv 57 in the light of intervening cases). See also Allen, op cit, Chapter 10.

[49] Goymour in *The Impact of the UK Human Rights Act on Private Law* (ed Hoffmann), Chapter 12, contains a useful analysis of the impact so far and likely future developments.

[50] *R v Waya* [2013] 1 AC 294 (Proceeds of Crime Act 2002).

transactions (they would be subject to any contrary provision). Powers to sell land are very common; one example is the powers of trustees of land. In *Horsham Properties Group Ltd v Clark*,[51] Briggs J held that a mortgagee's power of sale (whether express or statutorily implied) did not engage A1P1 – it is not a taking of property where the parties have agreed that a sale may take place on default. This analysis is very similar to that adopted by *McDonald* v *McDonald* in the context of the exercise of rights; it would seem very difficult to challenge it today.

Turning to Article 8, the requirement of respect for family and home might have a very significant impact. Thus, we saw earlier in this chapter that it might be used to challenge the rules on sale of property on bankruptcy. Article 6 could be used to challenge rights which are exercised without a court order. In the property context, this will be unusual. One possible (if unlikely) example is the right of a mortgagee to take possession (in strictly limited situations) without a court order.[52]

However, none of these Convention rights is absolute. Almost always, the question is whether the legal rule in question is a proportionate response to attaining a legitimate aim. This factor is likely to protect the A1P1 examples mentioned above. Indeed, the rights may themselves conflict: protecting an occupier in his home (Article 8) may involve restricting the rights of ownership (A1P1). It is central to the analysis in *Kay* that nearly all legal rules are the result of the careful balancing of the various issues involved. Especially where recent legislation is involved, it is difficult to contemplate a successful human rights challenge to legal rules in other than rare cases.[53]

When we turn to the cases, the impact on the areas of property law considered in this text has so far been very limited.[54] The courts have either found reasons why the Convention rights do not apply at all or else have found that there is no breach. When there has been a successful human rights challenge, it has nearly always been reversed on appeal.[55] Particular examples of human rights arguments will be seen in subsequent chapters.

However, it would be quite wrong to dismiss human rights. For a time, it was thought that one high-profile casualty was the law relating to adverse possession, as it operated in registered land before reforms in 2002. This was found to contravene A1P1 in the first instance decision in *Beaulane Properties Ltd* v *Palmer*[56] and a similar approach was initially taken by Strasbourg in *JA Pye (Oxford) Ltd* v *United Kingdom*.[57] However, the Grand Chamber[58] reversed that decision in 2007 and held that the relevant legislation was human rights compliant. The area is interesting as a challenge to a long-established aspect of property law; it will be studied in Chapter 7.

---

[51] [2009] 1 WLR 1255; any taking would in any event be justified in the public interest. Similar ideas are seen in *Sims* v *Dacorum BC* [2015] AC 1336 (termination of periodic tenancy by single joint tenant).
[52] See p 609 below.
[53] A more alarmist stance is adopted by Howell (2007) 123 LQR 618.
[54] As predicted by Harpum (2000) 4 L&T Rev 4, 29.
[55] Rook [2002] Conv 316 reviews the first year of the legislation; the three principal cases discussed were all subsequently reversed!
[56] [2006] Ch 79 (Strauss QC).
[57] (2006) 43 EHHR 43; the facts arose before the 1998 Act was in force.
[58] (2007) 46 EHHR 1083 (10–7 majority).

Further reading

Bamforth, N C (2001) 117 LQR 34: The true 'horizontal effect' of the Human Rights Act 1998.

Buxton, R (2000) 116 LQR 48: The Human Rights Act and private law.

Goymour, A (2011) Chapter 12 in *The Impact of the UK Human Rights Act on Private Law* (ed Hoffmann).

Phillipson, G and Williams, A (2011) 74 MLR 878: Horizontal effect and the constitutional restraint.

Wade, H W R (2000) 116 LQR 217: Horizons of horizontality.

Walsh, R (2015) 131 LQR 585: Stability and predictability in English property law – the impact of Article 8 of the European Convention on Human Rights reassessed.

4

Trusts and equitable interests

Introduction

Equitable interests form a very significant aspect of English property law, especially regarding land. Indeed, trusts and many other equitable interests in land are vital to the working of the modern law of property. In order to understand how trusts and equitable interests work, it is necessary to understand the court system that gave rise to them.

Today, we think of the courts as administering a unified body of law. There are, it is true, different Divisions of the High Court, but they exist primarily for a convenient distribution of business. Up to the late nineteenth century, things were very different. There were different courts, each exercising its own jurisdiction. The basis of land law was to be found in the common law courts.[1] However, the increasing rigidity of the common law led to the Chancellor's exercising an additional jurisdiction. This jurisdiction, commencing in the fourteenth century, led to the establishment of the Court of Chancery and the development of principles known as equity.

One very important feature of the Chancery jurisdiction is that it builds upon common law principles. Even though the result might be substantially inconsistent with the common law result, the Chancellor never denied that result outright. A good example is found in the jurisdiction to intervene in cases of fraud. The common law might find for a person despite their fraud. The Chancellor would issue an injunction prohibiting that person from enforcing the common law judgment. This procedure does not deny the common law judgment; rather, it seeks to ensure that no benefit shall arise from it. In this instance, it is clear that the practical result is inconsistent with the common law. Any question as to which system would prevail was settled by James I in 1616 in favour of equity. From that time onwards, it has been settled that the common law is subject to such qualifications as equity introduces.

The work of the Chancellor was not confined to property, as shown by the above fraud example. Equitable remedies were of great importance, particularly as regards contracts. Equity would grant specific performance of a contract, whereas the common law remedy was damages. This was to become very important as regards property, as contracts relating to property are those most likely to attract specific performance.

As will be seen later, the common law and Chancery courts were merged by the Judicature Acts 1873–75. Despite occasional doubts, this has not led to a merger of law

---

[1] Common Pleas, Exchequer and King's Bench finally merged in 1880.

(the principles administered by common law courts) and equity (the principles adminis-tered by Chancery).[2] Indeed, it is still possible to talk about the development of new equi-table principles. To talk in these terms sounds distinctly odd today unless the historical background is borne in mind.

1. Trusts[3]

The most significant contribution of equity has been the trust. Looking at it from a func-tional angle, the trust is a mechanism whereby one person (the trustee) manages property for the benefit of another (the beneficiary, or *cestui que trust*). The origins of trusts lie in arrangements whereby A transfers property to B on the understanding that B is to apply it for the benefit of C. So far as the courts of common law were concerned, B was the legal owner of the property and was bound by no obligation towards C. Even if there had been a contract between A and B, privity of contract denied any action by C.

However, it would be unconscionable for B to assert the right to benefit from the prop-erty, as this would be inconsistent with the understanding between A and B. Accordingly, the Chancellor recognised an obligation upon B to apply the property in favour of C, an obligation which C could enforce directly. It should be noted that the Chancellor never denies the ownership of B. Instead, B is forced to yield all benefit from the property to C.

This early form of trust was called a *use* and was recognised from at least the early fifteenth century. The reasons for creating uses varied greatly. Apart from the idea of B's managing the land for C,[4] uses could be used as, in essence, a power to devise property on death[5] and to avoid feudal dues (generally payable to the Crown) which would arise if the beneficiary directly held an estate in the land. Once A could be sure that the Chancellor would force B to give effect to the use, it was used in a wide range of situations.

The effectiveness of the use in reducing liability to feudal dues was a major factor lead-ing to the Statute of Uses 1536. The Statute's effect was to execute uses, so that the ben-eficiary held the legal estate and B held nothing at all. Although this might appear to have put an end to the use, the reality was far more complex. For a start, some uses fell outside the Statute, notably where an active duty was imposed upon B. Much more important, however, were attempts to side-step the Statute by creating a succession of uses. What would be the result if A transferred property to B to the use of C, to the use of D? Could it be argued that the Statute executed the use in favour of C, but that C then held the legal estate to the use of D? Initially, in *Jane Tyrrel's Case*,[6] this argument was rejected. C indeed obtained the legal estate, but the use in favour of D was disregarded: it was repug-nant to the use declared and executed in C's favour.

Subsequently, the virtual elimination of feudal dues by the Tenures Abolition Act 1660 provided an environment more receptive to uses. By the end of that century, the Chancellor had recognised a trust imposed on C for the benefit of D. Despite difficulty in differentiating

[2] Baker (1977) 93 LQR 529.
[3] Simpson, *A History of the Land Law* (2nd edn), Chapter 8.
[4] Perhaps because A was absent.
[5] Wills operating on land were not recognised before the Statute of Wills 1540.
[6] (1557) 2 Dyer 155a (73 ER 336).

this trust from the old use upon a use, the courts came to enforce it. This effectively destroyed the intended effect of the Statute. It should not be thought, however, that the Statute was of no effect. The details lie outside the scope of our investigation, but the Statute was used by conveyancers to produce results that had previously been impossible.[7]

The trust was thus recognised by the early eighteenth century, although the use in favour of C was still executed by the Statute. The Statute of Uses was finally repealed by the Law of Property Act 1925,[8] but this can be viewed as a largely technical reform. The modern trust is used for a variety of purposes. Traditionally, it was used to create successive interests in land. It has also been widely used as a method of avoiding tax. A trust by itself has little or no tax-saving implications, but some beneficial rights created under the trust have enjoyed significant tax savings (although less so today).

However, it is its imposition by statute that has led to the trust being very common in modern society – far more so than in other common law countries such as the United States. It is mandatory today whenever there are successive or concurrent interests in land. This is in order to ensure that there are adequate powers to sell and manage the land.

When a trust is set up, what beneficial rights can be created? Equity permitted the same rights as recognised at common law, so that one can have life interests and remainders, for example. Although most trusts would employ these conventional interests, equity was prepared to recognise some novel rights. One area which opens up considerable flexibility is that of the discretionary trust or power. The settlor can give discretion to the trustees to choose to whom the property (or the income from it) shall go. Thus, there might be a discretionary trust in favour of such of the settlor's children as the trustees select, or a power to select beneficiaries from a wide class of persons.[9] Where there is a specific beneficiary, the trustees may have power to determine how much income shall be paid. This would be relevant if, for example, a trust is set up for the education of the settlor's child, with the balance to go to grandchildren.

Resulting and constructive trusts

Apart from being expressly created or imposed by statute, trusts may also be imposed by the courts. Two important forms of such trusts are the resulting trust and the constructive trust.[10] A resulting trust operates where property is transferred without intending that there should be beneficial ownership in the transferee.[11] Two forms of resulting trust may be identified. If X simply transfers property to Y (or pays for property put in Y's name), then equity presumes that it is to be held on a resulting trust for X unless it can be shown that a gift was intended.

Second, where property is transferred to persons as trustees, the courts infer that the trustees are not intended to have any beneficial interest. Accordingly, a transfer to R on trust

---

[7] Examples are secret conveyances by grant and release and the creation of legal executory interests (Simpson, *A History of the Land Law* (2nd edn), pp 188–190, 196–198).

[8] Schedule 7.

[9] See *McPhail* v *Doulton* [1971] AC 424 and *Re Gulbenkian's Settlements* [1970] AC 508 for certainty requirements.

[10] Swadling [2011] CLP 399 contends that constructive trusts represent equitable obligations rather than true trusts, despite much authority to the contrary.

[11] See p 138 below.

for S for life creates an equitable life interest in S and a resulting trust of the remainder in favour of the transferor. It is controversial as to how far this second form of resulting trust can be rebutted by a contrary intention. It was viewed as 'automatic' by Megarry J,[12] though Lord Browne-Wilkinson regards all resulting trusts as based upon intention.[13] More recent dicta of Lord Millett in *Air Jamaica Ltd* v *Charlton*[14] provide some support for the 'automatic' concept, though they do not use that language and may simply stress that it is not necessary to prove an intention to retain an interest. The true basis for resulting trusts has been the subject of lively debate in recent years, although some form of intention appears central – at least for presumed resulting trusts.[15] Whatever the outcome of this puzzle, it should be remembered that it is possible for a trustee to be given a beneficial interest.[16]

Constructive trusts are imposed by the courts where it would be unconscionable for the holder of the property to take it free from some claim. Most constructive trusts fall within well-defined categories. It is generally said that they arise independently of the parties' intentions. Examples are: when a trustee makes an unauthorised profit out of the position of trustee; or a person intermeddles, in some way, in the administration of the trust. On the other hand, some constructive trusts are imposed to give effect to the intentions of the parties, where some rule would otherwise allow one of them unconscionably to renege on an undertaking. Typically, this is where a trust of land is unenforceable because it fails to comply with a statutory requirement of writing.

Constructive and resulting trusts do not require writing,[17] so they are suitable for giving effect to oral agreements. If land is transferred subject to an oral trust, it would be unconscionable for the transferee (having agreed to the trust) to keep the land beneficially. One specific application of this principle is where two people jointly purchase land, but the legal title is vested in one of them. This is very common on the purchase of family homes. The purchasers' intentions as to beneficial ownership of the land can usually be given effect by way of constructive trust.

2. The trust as a proprietary interest

It has been seen that the trustee owes an obligation in favour of the beneficiary. An unauthorised sale, or other disposition, by the trustee would be a breach of trust. Why should the rights of the beneficiary be regarded as proprietary, binding successors in title to the trustee? The Chancellor considered that a purchaser who was aware of the trust was implicated in the breach; conscience dictated that the purchaser should be bound by the trust.

---

[12] *Re Vandervell's Trusts (No 2)* [1974] Ch 269.
[13] *Westdeutsche Landesbank Girozentrale* v *Islington LBC* [1996] AC 669 at p 708 (expressly doubting the analysis of Megarry J). Chambers, *Resulting Trusts* (1997), also rejects the 'automatic' category.
[14] [1999] 1 WLR 1399 at p 1412 (PC); note the contrasting comments of Rickett and Grantham (2000) 116 LQR 15 and Harpum [2000] Conv 170.
[15] Chambers, *Resulting Trusts* (1997) regards all resulting trusts as being imposed by law because there is no intention to benefit the recipient. He places resulting trusts within the law of restitution. Swadling (2008) 124 LQR 72 is critical of *Westdeutsche* but also of the Chambers analysis. Mee [2014] CLJ 86 is again critical of Chambers, but with a different view of intention than that expressed by Swadling.
[16] Since 1925, most co-owners of land are both trustees and beneficiaries.
[17] Law of Property Act 1925, s 53(2).

This was established by the early sixteenth century. Over the years, ever wider classes of persons were held bound. Notice became crucial to the binding of purchasers.[18] There would be notice if the purchaser was aware of the trust (actual notice), would have been aware if proper investigations had been made (constructive notice) or notice was held by an agent such as a solicitor (imputed notice).

A significant twentieth-century ruling[19] is that everybody will be bound, unless a purchaser of a legal estate without notice. The issue arose in the context of a legal estate based upon adverse possession rather than purchase. The holder of the legal estate had no notice and did not fall within any of the existing categories of persons bound by equitable interests. Nevertheless, there was little difficulty in holding that the equitable interest could be enforced. The original basis of the enforcement, that of unconscionable conduct by the purchaser, has long since given way to the rule that everybody bar the purchaser of a legal estate without notice is bound. We might contrast the constructive trust which may be imposed on a purchaser who promises to be bound by a right. There it is the specific conduct of the purchaser that ensures that the purchaser will be bound.

Whilst fully recognising that purchasers with notice are bound, Maitland argued that equitable interests should be regarded as being personal, stressing that they do not bind purchasers automatically as legal interests do.[20] Though possessing some historical justification, this view is difficult to square with modern analyses.[21] Everybody recognises, of course, that the effect of equitable interests is not identical to that of legal interests. It may be concluded that equitable interests are generally enforceable against successors in title and are properly described as proprietary interests.

A rather different aspect of the alleged personal nature of the beneficiary's interest lies in the nature of the remedies available. The Chancellor would interfere by making an order against a person. The Chancellor did not deny the ownership of the trustee, but ordered the trustee to apply the property for the benefit of the beneficiary. In the modern law, we think of the beneficiary as having an equitable interest in the land, but it is more historically correct to say that the beneficiary has personal remedies against the trustee. The use of the word personal does not signify that purchasers are not affected, but it describes the nature of the remedy. This is enhanced when discretionary trusts are considered: it may be difficult to identify a normal property right possessed by the discretionary beneficiary.

Fortunately, it is rarely necessary to decide the precise nature of the beneficiary's rights. Exceptions, however, do arise, particularly where legislation has to be interpreted. In *Baker* v *Archer-Shee*,[22] a question arose in a taxation setting whether the beneficiary was entitled to income arising from trust assets (as opposed to being entitled to income from the trustees). By a 3:2 majority, the House of Lords decided that the beneficiary was entitled to the income from the trust assets, the trustees being regarded as mere agents for transmitting the income. This decision has remained controversial, but fortunately it has been of little practical significance, even in the taxation setting.

---

[18] This is more fully analysed in Chapter 12.
[19] *Re Nisbet and Potts' Contract* [1906] 1 Ch 386.
[20] *Equity* (2nd ed), Lectures X and XI.
[21] See Pettit, *Equity and the Law of Trusts* (12th edn), pp 84–86; Jaffey (2015) 131 LQR 377.
[22] [1927] AC 844.

Whatever the theoretical position, we normally consider beneficiaries as having equitable rights in the property.[23] If A holds on trust for B, then we say that A has the legal fee simple and B an equitable fee simple. Placed in that stark form, it might appear that there are two rival claimants to the land. It is easier to understand if we remember that B's right is to claim the benefit of the land, to the extent of a fee simple estate, from A. This way of considering the situation is more historically correct and helps to explain the interlocking nature of legal and equitable rights.

3. Other equitable interests

The Chancellor did more than recognise the trust. Many equitable principles have nothing to do with property law and need not be discussed here. However, equitable remedies are important to us.

The Court of Chancery would (where appropriate) order specific performance of contracts, whereas a court of law would simply award damages. This availability of specific performance was particularly significant in contracts for the sale of land.[24] It led to the application of the maxim that equity treats as done that which ought to be done: in other words, equity would treat the purchaser as if he or she already had the interest. By this means, a contract to purchase[25] land was treated as giving the purchaser an equitable interest in the land, subject, of course, to the payment of the purchase price. This interest, which can bind later purchasers, is described as an estate contract.[26]

Other equitable remedies were also significant. Equitable rights to rescind contracts for misrepresentation or undue influence or to rectify contracts on account of mistake can be applied to conveyances of legal estates. These last equitable rights have been categorised as *equities*; they are discussed later in this chapter.

Equity also played a vital role in the development of mortgages. If a person wished to use land as security for a loan, the land could be transferred to the lender (mortgagee) with a right for the borrower (mortgagor) to recover the land if the loan and interest were repaid on a certain date. An obvious problem arose where the borrower failed to repay by the due date: very valuable property could be lost by virtue of a failure to pay what might be a relatively small sum. Equity, therefore, allowed the borrower to recover the property by paying off the loan and interest (*redemption*). This right might last indefinitely, but the lender could cut it short by obtaining a court order for *foreclosure*. The foreclosure proceedings would give time for the sums to be repaid. In the modern law, it is far more likely that the property will be sold, with the proceeds (net of the sums due) going to the borrower.[27]

---

[23] See, e.g., Lord Browne-Wilkinson in *Tinsley* v *Milligan* [1994] 1 AC 340 at p 371. *Shell UK Ltd* v *Total UK Ltd* [2011] QB 86 permits the beneficiary to sue in tort for negligent damage to the trust assets by a third party. However, this is controversial (Hargreaves (2011) 25 *Trust Law International* 163; Edelman (2013) 129 LQR 66); it raises difficult questions relating to the nature of beneficial rights (Gardner in *Modern Studies in Property Law*, Vol 7 (ed Hopkins), Chapter 15).

[24] The uniqueness of land results in specific performance being generally available, whereas contracts relating to other property rarely attract the remedy.

[25] The same reasoning applies to a contract to acquire any legal interest in the land – a lease, for example.

[26] It seems difficult to accept the argument of Hopkins (1998) 61 MLR 486 that there is an equitable right in the land apart from the estate contract: the two are opposite sides of a single coin, the equitable interest being the substance of the right (fee simple, lease, mortgage, etc) which is constituted by the estate contract.

[27] Law of Property Act 1925, ss 91(2), 101, 105.

Estate contracts and the equity of redemption both involve equitable rights to recognised legal interests. Other equitable rights are more unconventional. A good example is provided by the restrictive covenant. In 1848,[28] it was recognised that a right to prevent development on a neighbour's land (or its use for specified purposes) was a proprietary interest which bound purchasers. Recent decades have seen much discussion and litigation on the question whether licences to enter land should join the category of equitable proprietary interests (see Chapter 22).

4. Equities

Equities form a rather dubious group of proprietary interests. Unlike equitable interests, equities are not discussed in detail in later chapters. Like equitable interests, they are a product of the Court of Chancery. Although the category is quite long established, it is unclear how far its existence is justified.[29]

The major distinguishing feature of equities is, for unregistered land, their weaker effect on purchasers, in comparison with equitable interests. There is controversy regarding whether these differing effects require an extra category, or whether the rules on equitable interests are flexible enough to accommodate the differences. The first difference is that a purchaser of an *equitable* interest without notice will defeat an equity, whereas it takes a purchaser of a *legal* estate to defeat an equitable interest. The second difference is that a purchaser is less likely to be held to have notice of an equity. Both these differences will be considered in Chapter 12.

Assuming that equities constitute a discrete category, what are they? It is generally said that there are two broad types of equities. The first is based on certain equitable remedies where, to quote from *Latec Investments Ltd* v *Hotel Terrigal Pty Ltd (in liquidation)*,[30] the claim 'must be made good before an equitable interest can be held to exist' or the claimant 'required the assistance of a court of equity to remove an impediment to his title as a preliminary to asserting his interest'.

Examples are where a conveyance is sought to be set aside for fraud,[31] undue influence or similar reasons and where rectification of a lease is sought. There is ample authority to show that these claims will bind purchasers with notice.[32] It is possible that there are other equities of an analogous character. A problem in assessing some of the cases, especially earlier ones, is that 'equity' and 'equitable interest' are used interchangeably. It is only when contrasts between equities and equitable interests are stressed that the cases begin to develop the discrete category of equities.

These equities operate so as to defeat or modify otherwise valid transactions. The claimant is a party to the transaction, and this is likely to cause a later purchaser to presume that the transaction reflects the true legal situation. These are good reasons why the purchaser should not be bound by such equities as readily as if they were normal equitable

---

[28] *Tulk* v *Moxhay* (1848) 2 Ph 774 (41 ER 1143).

[29] Everton (1976) 40 Conv 209 and, more strongly, Wallace and Grbich (1979) 3 UNSWLJ 175.

[30] (1965) 113 CLR 265 at pp 277 (Kitto J), 286 (Taylor J); but see Chambers, *Resulting Trusts* (1997), Chapter 7.

[31] Aided by Misrepresentation Act 1967, s 1.

[32] *Latec Investments* (fraud); *Bainbrigge* v *Browne* (1881) 18 Ch D 188 (undue influence); *Garrard* v *Frankel* (1862) 30 Beav 445 (54 ER 961); and *Smith* v *Jones* [1954] 1 WLR 1089 (rectification).

interests. The distinction between equities and equitable interests has been said to be based on the discretionary nature of the remedy sought.[33] Yet, this is difficult to comprehend. True, these remedies are discretionary, but so are other remedies such as specific performance of estate contracts: we experience no difficulty in saying that estate contracts are equitable interests.[34]

The limited effect of equities upon purchasers may also extend to equitable interests in certain circumstances. Suppose O transfers property to X on resulting trust, but using the same language as an absolute transfer and not mentioning the trust. There is a good chance that O's interest will be postponed to a later *equitable* mortgage created by X.[35] Similarly, a mortgagor who creates the mortgage by executing a normal conveyance to a mortgagee may find the equity of redemption[36] postponed to a later equitable interest.[37] We reach these results without recourse to the language of equities.

The second broad type of equity consists of rights whose nature is different from conventional equitable interests. At one time, it was thought that a deserted wife's right to occupy the matrimonial home fell into this category.[38] However, the House of Lords, in *National Provincial Bank Ltd* v *Ainsworth*,[39] rejected the deserted wife's right as any sort of equity or equitable interest; it was held to be a personal right against the husband. The fact that it could be enforced by an equitable remedy did not lead to its being capable of binding purchasers. Indeed, Lord Upjohn totally rejected this type of equity: 'a mere "equity" naked and alone is, in my opinion, incapable of binding successors in title even with notice; it is personal to the parties'.[40] Nevertheless, the equity terminology has since been used by the House of Lords in the context of estoppel-based rights.[41] This usage is rather surprising.

It is easy to conclude that this second group of equities is a result of sloppy thinking. They appear to be a lesser form of equitable interest for which the court is not prepared to use the equitable interest terminology. As equities, they might be subject to the different priority rules, although one may doubt whether this requires them to constitute a separate category. There is much to be said for the view of Lord Upjohn that the second group does not exist. If judges want purchasers to be bound, then the right involved should be termed an equitable interest. The equity terminology might be considered as a valuable way for cautious judges to develop what may later become equitable interests,[42] but it is very dubious whether such a halfway house is necessary. It certainly complicates our legal analysis.

---

[33] Wade [1955] CLJ 158; Delany (1957) 21 Conv 195. *Latec Investments* is one of the few cases to consider the nature and extent of the category of equities rather than their effect on purchasers.

[34] See Everton (1976) 40 Conv 209. The point is recognised by Wade [1955] CLJ 158.

[35] *Re King's Settlement* [1931] 2 Ch 294; Chambers, *Resulting Trusts* (1997), p 180. A transfer that does not mention consideration is unlikely to have the same effect: *Shropshire Union Railways & Canal Co* v *R* (1875) 7 HL 496.

[36] An equitable interest, notwithstanding the label.

[37] *Abigail* v *Lapin* [1934] AC 491; *Rice* v *Rice* (1853) 2 Drew 73 (61 ER 646) (unpaid vendor's lien); *Rimmer* v *Webster* [1902] 2 Ch D 163 at p 173.

[38] *Westminster Bank Ltd* v *Lee* [1956] Ch 7.

[39] [1965] AC 1175.

[40] Ibid, at p 1238.

[41] *Shiloh Spinners Ltd* v *Harding* [1973] AC 691 at p 721. The special priority effects of equities have never arisen in the estoppel cases: Neave and Weinberg (1978–1980) 6 UTasLR 24, 115 at p 133.

[42] Neave and Weinberg, above.

Into this already complex situation we now have to fit s 116 of the Land Registration Act 2002. This applies to registered titles – around 95% of all titles. It provides: 'It is hereby declared for the avoidance of doubt that . . . (b) a mere equity, has effect from the time the equity arises as an interest capable of binding successors in title.' It is clear that this was intended to cover the first type of equities described earlier.[43] Its purpose was to clarify their status as being capable of binding purchasers[44] and to bring them within the same priority rules as are applied to equitable interests.

Unfortunately, the use of the term 'mere equity' raises the question of whether the second category is also given proprietary status. Indeed, it might cover any situation where there is an equitable remedy, regardless of whether a conventional property right would result. After all, the House of Lords in *Ainsworth* posed the question for decision as being whether a mere equity bound purchasers, giving a negative answer. To reverse this would amount to a significant change in the law, the ramifications of which could be very wide. Although supported by the literal wording of s 116, it seems a most unlikely result of a provision which is 'enacted for the avoidance of doubt' and which was treated by the Law Commission as 'declaratory of the present law'.

5. Equitable principles today

It has already been noted that the separate courts of law and equity were abolished by the Judicature Acts 1873–75. Insofar as there was any conflict between legal and equitable rules, it was provided that the rules of equity are to prevail.[45] This provision will rarely be significant, as equity set out to modify rather than to contradict the common law. The merger of the courts does, however, require us to consider whether it is either relevant or sensible to maintain a distinction between legal and equitable rights and interests more than a century later.

Despite some suggestions to the contrary and the passing of many decades, it still seems premature to seek to merge legal and equitable principles completely.[46] It is common to observe that the trust depends upon a separation of legal and equitable rights.[47] Furthermore, the trust remains of central importance: the property legislation of 1925 and the Trusts of Land and Appointment of Trustees Act 1996 make very extensive use of trusts for regulating successive and concurrent ownership of land. It is somewhat more difficult to justify the continuing distinction between other legal and equitable interests. Is it meaningful to continue to refer to restrictive covenants, for example, as equitable interests?

As the law stands, there clearly are differences between legal and equitable rights, although these are becoming less significant. The most obvious difference concerns the range of purchasers who may be bound: it has been noted that equitable interests do not bind bona fide purchasers of the legal estate without notice. Yet, the development of

---

[43] Law Com No 271, paras 5.33, 5.36.

[44] Doubts as to this had been expressed from time to time, most recently in *Collings* v *Lee* [2001] 2 All ER 332 at p 338 (fraudulent misrepresentation); cf Nolan [2001] CLJ 477.

[45] Today, see Senior Courts Act 1981, s 49.

[46] Baker (1977) 93 LQR 529.

[47] A proposition challenged by Jaffey (2015) 131 LQR 377 at p 387, arguing for a substantive separation of control and benefit.

registration requirements in the past century has led to a huge erosion of this difference.[48] Although it cannot be said that legal and equitable interests have been equated, many legal and equitable interests have to be entered on the register in order to bind a purchaser. Further developments are likely to be in the direction of treating legal and equitable interests in an identical manner.

There are other differences. Equitable remedies, which lie at the heart of the enforcement of equitable rights, are inherently discretionary.[49] In contrast, legal rights are enforceable as of right. Too much should not be made of the point, however. It is unusual for the courts to refuse a remedy for breach of an equitable proprietary right. At the same time, conduct which denies an equitable remedy may also operate to trigger a defence to a legal right. Examples may be found in estoppel and also in the rules for the priority of mortgages.[50] It may be observed that it is in the area of remedies that the movement towards fusing, or integrating, law and equity is strongest.[51]

In addition, a number of rules apply only to legal rights. These include formality requirements: the creation of a legal right in land generally requires the formality of a deed, whereas most equitable rights in land require only writing. There are also other rules of a more specific nature.[52] Overall, however, the courts are increasingly reluctant to accept differences between legal and equitable interests unless backed by convincing reasons.[53]

Intangible, but possibly important, is the perception of equity as offering greater flexibility than the common law and hence being the natural source of developing legal concepts. This is, of course, based on the traditional idea of Chancery as a court of conscience. Even today, the courts use unconscionability in formulating equitable rules. The result is that many lawyers feel more confident about developing new equitable rules, perhaps in part because they are of a more discretionary nature. Being discretionary, the courts can prevent their use getting out of hand. Nevertheless, it is difficult to argue that judicial innovation would be stifled if legal and equitable principles were fully integrated. Surely, the perceived need for innovation would remain the same and lawyers would simply use different reasoning to justify their conclusions. It is not as if the ideas of unconscionability would disappear; rather, that they would not be linked with equity.

Further reading

Baker, P V (1977) 93 LQR 529: The future of equity.
Everton, A (1976) 40 Conv (NS) 209: 'Equitable interests' and 'equities' – in search of a pattern.
Hargreaves, E (2011) 25 *Trust Law International* 163: The nature of beneficiaries' interests under trusts.
Jaffey, P (2015) 131 LQR 377: Explaining the trust.
Millett, P J (1998) 114 LQR 214: Equity's place in the law of commerce.

---

[48] Discussed at p 295 below.
[49] See pp 403 (equitable leases), 572 (covenants) below.
[50] For estoppel, see *Gafford* v *Graham* (1998) 77 P&CR 73 (acquiescence). For mortgages, see p 225 below.
[51] For arguments in favour of change, see Burrows (2002) 22 OxJLS 1; Worthington (2002) 55 CLP 223.
[52] These include the statutory implication of easements (*Borman* v *Griffith* [1930] 1 Ch 493). This is based upon a contract not being a conveyance, as defined by Law of Property Act 1925, s 205(1)(ii). That definition is likely to be the source of further distinctions.
[53] Lord Browne-Wilkinson in *Tinsley* v *Milligan* [1994] 1 AC 340 at p 371.

5
Property interests

Introduction

In this chapter, we begin to investigate specific property interests in land and in chattels. Many of the issues relating to land will be considered in greater detail in Parts III and IV. Accordingly, the purpose of this chapter is to introduce some of the important categories of interests. It also provides a little detail where the interest does not warrant separate treatment later. It might be added that our concern is with private rights (including those held by public bodies): the law relating to communal rights is relatively ill-developed.[1]

1. Land

A. Tenures[2]

Although the doctrine of tenures has little practical significance today,[3] it is crucial to understanding the development of interests in land. The basic idea is that the Crown owns all land and grants rights to individuals. These individuals do not themselves own land but instead hold of (are tenants of)[4] the Crown. In the past, this was significant because services might be due to the Crown, and the Crown would have valuable rights (incidents), for example, on succession of a new tenant. The nature of both the services and the incidents would vary according to the form of tenure. Tenants could in turn subinfeudate to others, creating a further link in the feudal chain.

Control over tenures has medieval origins. As early as 1290, the statute Quia Emptores stopped the creation of new tenurial relationships (save by the Crown). The most common form of tenure was socage, in which the service was a monetary payment. As inflation reduced the value of these payments, the incidents became the most valuable benefit of the feudal lord, especially the Crown. However, the Tenures Abolition Act 1660 converted nearly all tenures into socage and abolished most of the incidents. Thereafter, tenurial relationships lost virtually all their significance. Inevitably, the identity of mesne lords (those standing between the Crown and the ultimate tenant) became forgotten over the centuries.

---

[1] Clarke (1997) 50 CLP 120.
[2] A much fuller account is found in Megarry and Wade, *The Law of Real Property* (8th edn), Chapter 2.
[3] But note the spirited argument of Nugee (2008) 124 LQR 586 that (especially as regards manorial rights) the feudal system is more important than commonly thought (cf Jessel (2014) 130 LQR 587). For possible reforms, see Bray in *Modern Studies in Property Law*, Vol 5 (ed Dixon), Chapter 4.
[4] The word 'tenants' can be confusing: here, it does not signify a lease.

Does the doctrine of tenures have any modern significance? In exceptional circumstances, the land can still revert to the lord (escheat),[5] although escheat has been drastically limited by legislation. A very different point is that the statute Quia Emptores applied only to freehold land, with the result that new leasehold tenures can still be created. Without this qualification, leases in their present form could not have developed. However, leases are usually fixed-term arrangements involving the payment of rent rather than the provision of services; they never involved the same incidents as in freehold tenures. In other words, the problems afflicting freehold tenurial relationships never applied to leases.

Perhaps the greatest enduring significance of tenures lies in its encouragement of the development of estates in land. That all land is held, ultimately, of the Crown, means that it is strictly incorrect to talk of owning land. Instead, we should refer to holding an estate in land. When a system recognises outright ownership, it may be difficult to split that ownership into parts. Because the common law had to grapple with the concept of the estate rather than physical property, it was easier to develop a far more flexible approach to ownership. For whatever reason, the common law permitted a wide range of estates, often with no one person being regarded as the owner of the land.

B. Freehold estates

The essence of the estate is that it defines the length of time for which the right to the land will last. The two forms today are the life estate and the fee simple. A life estate gives a right to the land for life, whereas a fee simple is a right capable of lasting indefinitely. A fee simple will pass, by will or intestacy, on the death of the holder. The fee simple is by far the most common freehold estate: this is the right which will be held by the average homeowner.

Estates may be held concurrently; that is, two or more persons may own the estate together. Thus, a husband and wife may be concurrent owners of the fee simple of their home. Two forms of concurrent interests are recognised today. In a joint tenancy, the land will vest automatically in the survivors when a joint tenant dies: this is especially appropriate for trustees and is overwhelmingly the choice of persons buying family homes. A tenancy in common differs in that a share in the property will pass under the will (or intestacy) of a deceased co-owner. It is obvious that survivorship will be inappropriate in many cases, whether as between business partners or, for example, on the purchase of a house by a group of friends. It is possible to 'sever' a joint tenancy, at any time before death, so as to create a tenancy in common.

Sometimes, the normal period of enjoyment of an estate may be modified by the settlor. Two possibilities may be identified. First, enjoyment may be postponed in some way. In this case, we would say that it is not in possession.[6] In some such cases, enjoyment is postponed but, sooner or later, will come about. This is true of a gift 'to A for life, remainder

---

[5] Disclaimer by trustee in bankruptcy: *British General Insurance Co Ltd* v *Att-Gen* [1945] LJNCCR 113 at pp 123–128. Death without a will and without heirs results in the property going to the Crown as bona vacantia: Administration of Estates Act 1925 (hereafter AEA), ss 45(1)(d), 46(1)(vi).

[6] A freehold estate remains in possession despite there being a lease of the land: Law of Property Act 1925 (hereafter LPA), s 205(1)(xix). This may be justified by the fact that the freeholder is able to claim rent from the tenant.

in fee simple to B'. Although A's life estate is in possession, B will enjoy the land on A's death. Even if B dies first, the fee simple will pass under B's will. B is said, during A's lifetime, to have a fee simple in remainder; we describe it as an estate vested in interest.[7] By contrast, a gift 'to C in fee simple if she obtains a law degree' provides no certainty that C's fee simple will ever vest in possession. Such a gift is commonly called a contingent gift. Sometimes, there will be no identifiable donee, as where there is a gift 'to the first person to swim the English Channel after my death'. The policy of the law has been to restrict contingent gifts where the contingency may operate far in the future. This is the rule against perpetuities, briefly described in Chapter 17.

Alternatively, the period of enjoyment may be qualified by cutting the estate short after it has vested. An example would be a grant of a life interest to a widow or widower until remarriage. This highly complex area will be considered later in this chapter.

(i) *The fee simple*

A fee simple may be regarded as a perpetual right to the land.[8] It continues notwithstanding the death of the grantee, notwithstanding the absence of heirs and notwithstanding the absence of a will. The intestacy rules apply if there is no will. These are established by legislation[9] and enable the property to pass to the nearest relatives. If there are no relatives within the prescribed classes, then the property will go to the Crown.[10] The rules may be summarised as follows. A spouse[11] will get all the assets if there are no children. If there are children, the spouse will get a fixed sum (at present £250,000)[12] and the 'personal chattels' (furniture, car, etc). The residue goes half to the spouse and half to the children. In the absence of a spouse, the property will go to children, parents, siblings, grandparents or uncles and aunts (in that order). It may be noted that the intestacy rules make no provision for an unmarried partner living with the deceased, regardless of how long they have been living together.[13]

If the fee simple is in possession and is not liable to be cut short, then it is as good as outright ownership.[14] This fee simple absolute in possession is by a huge margin the most common freehold estate today. Colloquially, we often refer to the holder of a fee simple absolute in possession as the owner.

---

[7] Where the holder of the fee simple makes a grant 'to A for life' the fee simple reverts to the grantor, who is said to have a fee simple in reversion.

[8] Strictly, the possibility of escheat means that it is not perpetual: Williams [2015] CLJ 592.

[9] AEA, s 46, as amended by Inheritance and Trustees' Powers Act 2014. The operation of these rules can be challenged, just as wills can be, if they fail to make reasonable financial provision for a spouse, partner (living as husband and wife for the last two years), child or person maintained by the deceased: Inheritance (Provision for Family and Dependants) Act 1975. All these rules apply to every form of property, not just land.

[10] AEA, s 46(1)(vi). The Crown may provide for dependants and those for whom the intestate might have been expected to make provision. This might be a partner with whom the intestate was li ving, where they are not married.

[11] Including those in civil partnerships: see p 331 below.

[12] The fixed sum is specified by SI 2009 No 135.

[13] Law Com No 331 proposed changing this. However, this proposal was not implemented by the Inheritance and Trustees' Powers Act 2014.

[14] J W Harris, 'Ownership of Land in English Law' in *The Legal Mind: Essays in honour of Tony Honoré* (eds MacCormick and Birks), discusses ownership, recognising that several different estates incorporate ownership rights.

The fee simple owner is entitled to the land below the surface and to the air above it. The latter ensures that interferences with airspace constitute trespass.[15] This applies to any intruding structure, but otherwise there is no wrong unless use of the land is affected. Thus flying over the land, at a proper height, and taking photographs is not a trespass.[16] Below surface rights may give entitlement to minerals, subject to statutory controls.[17] The extent of rights below the surface was argued in *Bocardo SA* v *Star Energy UK Onshore Ltd*,[18] in which the defendants had drilled for oil at a great depth under the claimants' land (it was clear that the oil itself did not belong to the claimants). It was held by the Supreme Court that this amounted to a trespass – allowing flying over land did not mean that there could be access below the surface. The significance of this was limited by the majority decision to award only nominal damages.

It is possible to sever land horizontally. The best example of this is found with flats, where different people will have rights to different floors in the building. Unfortunately, the common law has difficulty in coping with the problems that arise between owners of freehold flats,[19] with the result that examples of such 'flying freeholds' have been uncommon.[20] Instead, it is common to use long leases as a substitute for granting the freehold. The entire area raises obvious problems. Suppose the building burns down; how do we treat ownership in a block of air, especially if a lower owner declines to participate in rebuilding? Freehold flats can now be made subject to regulation by the Commonhold and Leasehold Reform Act 2002 (hereafter CLRA).[21] This would make flying freeholds more common, save that the legislation is rarely used.

It has long been possible for grantors to provide that the estate shall terminate in certain circumstances. The result is that the fee simple becomes 'qualified' rather than 'absolute'.[22] In most cases, it is part of an attempt to control the grantees by placing restrictions or obligations upon them. The law on this area is exceptionally technical, and at least some of the rules are impossible to justify. As Porter MR famously observed, it is 'little short of disgraceful to our jurisprudence'.[23] Much of the problem stems from the use of the following two ways of cutting interests short.

(a) Conditional and determinable fees

The conditional fee recognises that there is a fee simple and then provides that it shall terminate on a specified event: a condition subsequent. Conceptually, the grantor gives the entire estate away and then claws it back on breach of the condition. The grantor is said to have a right of entry. With a determinable fee, what is granted is a qualified right from the

---

[15] *Anchor Brewhouse Developments Ltd* v *Berkley House (Docklands Developments) Ltd* (1987) 38 BLR 82 (jib of crane).
[16] *Lord Bernstein of Leigh* v *Skyviews & General Ltd* [1978] QB 479 (a common law rule, though the area is regulated by legislation).
[17] E.g. Petroleum Act 1998, s 2.
[18] [2011] 1 AC 380, adopting views expressed by Howell (2002) 53 NILQ 268.
[19] Duties based on nuisance may cover essential repairs: *Abbahall Ltd* v *Smee* [2003] 1 WLR 1472 (flying freehold resulting from adverse possession).
[20] Lord Keith in *Sovmots Investments Ltd* v *SSE* [1979] AC 144 at pp 183–184.
[21] This is discussed in Chapter 21.
[22] Absolute has no wider meaning, so it can be applied to (for example) the title of an adverse possessor: *Turner* v *Chief Land Registrar* [2013] 2 P&CR 223.
[23] *Re King's Trusts* (1892) 29 LR Ir 401 at p 410.

very beginning. In this case, the entire fee simple is never granted away. Instead, the grantee is to have the land for a limited period (the cases commonly refer to such grants as limitations). The grantor retains a possibility of reverter.

Whichever route is used, the event must be one that is not bound to happen.[24] This may be justified because a fee must be capable of lasting forever and also because the obvious events that are bound to occur are death[25] and the passing of time. These events create a life estate or lease, respectively: a determinable or conditional fee simple would be quite inappropriate.

It is important to note that a grantor can choose which of a conditional fee or a determinable fee to create: all depends upon the words used. 'To Richard until he remarries' creates a determinable fee, whereas 'To Anne on condition that she does not remarry' creates a conditional fee. A determinable fee is created where words such as 'until', 'during', 'as long as' are used; whilst 'on condition that', 'but if a certain event happens' and any phrase indicating forfeiture will create a conditional fee.[26] Although a particular terminating event may more naturally be expressed one way or another, careful drafting can ensure that either a determinable fee or a conditional fee is created.

The effects of determinable and conditional fees are very different, and this forms the basis for criticism of the law. A long-established rule is that a determinable fee terminates automatically when the event occurs, whereas a conditional fee continues until the grantor exercises the right of entry. Terminating events are often held to be invalid. In a determinable fee, this renders the entire grant void,[27] whereas an invalid condition results in the grantee's having a fee simple absolute.[28] This drastic contrast is explained by the two-step analysis of a conditional fee: the grant of the fee simple followed by an attempt to claw it back in certain events. The law strikes down the attempt to claw it back rather than the initial grant.

(b) The validity of determining events

This has given rise to a mountain of authority. An attempt to prevent alienation of a conditional fee is liable to fail as being repugnant[29] to the nature of a fee simple. By contrast, no such rule applies to determinable fees,[30] on the rather dubious analysis that the grantee has never been given the full fee simple.

What happens if, in a conditional fee, there is a limited constraint on alienation? It is universally accepted that a condition permitting an alienation save to one specified person is valid.[31] More difficulty exists where alienation to a limited class is permitted by the grant. In *Re Macleay*,[32] Jessel MR upheld a condition that the land should not be sold out of the family.

---

[24] Challis, *Real Property* (3rd edn, Sweet (ed)), p 251. Unlike other rules, this does not apply to estates other than the fee simple: Challis at p 253.

[25] An attempt to give a person a full beneficial right in property (with power to sell and keep the proceeds) but to provide for its termination on death is likely to be seen as contradictory. It is neither a life interest (because of the right to sell) nor a qualified fee: *Ivin v Blake* (1993) 67 P&CR 263 (treated as a fee simple absolute).

[26] *Mary Portington's Case* (1613) 10 Co Rep 35b at pp 41b, 42a (77 ER 976 at pp 986, 987).

[27] *Re Moore* (1888) 39 Ch D 116; but contrast *Re Brewer's Settlement* [1896] 2 Ch 503 (bankruptcy).

[28] *Re Moore* (1888) 39 Ch D 116; *Re Wilkinson* [1926] Ch 842.

[29] The repugnancy doctrine is criticised by Glanville Williams (1943) 59 LQR 343. See also Jenks (1917) 33 LQR 11 and Sweet (1917) 33 LQR 236, 342.

[30] *Re Leach* [1912] 2 Ch 422, in which the point was substantially assumed.

[31] Co Litt 223a–b.

[32] (1875) LR 20 Eq 186, relying on *Doe d Gill v Pearson* (1805) 6 East 173 (102 ER 1253).

However, this was difficult to justify on the previous authority[33] and has been sharply criticised.[34] The criticism is convincing, even though it is difficult to take the debate seriously
when the identical provision would have been valid if phrased as a determinable fee!

The repugnancy rule also invalidates conditions operating on other forms of alienation,
such as mortgages,[35] or on bankruptcy.[36] Again, a determinable fee (or life estate) is unaffected by these rules.[37] This flexibility of determinable fees is especially important as
regards protective trusts. In a protective trust,[38] an interest is made determinable on bankruptcy or disposition. If it determines, there will then be a discretionary trust for the beneficiary and close family. The settlor's purpose is to ensure that the beneficiary continues
to obtain a flow of income from the property, with no chance of the beneficiary disposing
of the interest and spending the proceeds. Nobody will be willing to buy an interest that
will terminate at the moment of purchase!

Another common terminating event found in the cases is marriage. It has long been held
contrary to public policy to impose a condition preventing marriage.[39] However, conditions restraining *remarriage* are valid, seemingly because it is the status of widow or
widower that provides the reason for the gift[40] and also because it may be entirely appropriate to pay income directly to the grantee's children at the time of the remarriage.[41] A
partial restriction on marriage may be upheld.[42] Accordingly, conditions operating on
marriage to a Scotsman[43] or a domestic servant[44] have been held valid, as would a condition preventing marriage with a specified individual. Once again, all the restrictive rules
can be evaded by the simple expedient of drafting the gift as a determinable fee. This is
remarkable, bearing in mind that the basis of these rules lies in policy.[45]

Public policy may strike down other conditions. Examples are where the provision
encouraged spouses to live apart,[46] where service in the armed forces was inhibited[47] and
where obtaining a dukedom was required.[48] The courts will also strike down provisions
that interfere with parents' upbringing of children.[49] On the other hand, the courts will not

---

[33] *Attwater* v *Attwater* (1853) 18 Beav 330 (52 ER 131); *Re Brown* [1954] Ch 39.
[34] *Re Rosher* (1884) 26 Ch D 801.
[35] *Ware* v *Cann* (1830) 10 B&C 433 (109 ER 511).
[36] *Re Machu* (1882) 21 Ch D 838.
[37] *Brandon* v *Robinson* (1811) 18 Ves 429 (34 ER 379). An attempt to settle one's own property on oneself until
bankruptcy comes too close to defeating the bankruptcy laws and is likely to be struck down on policy
grounds: *Re Brewer's Settlement* [1896] 2 Ch 503.
[38] Trustee Act 1925, s 33. The beneficiary normally has a life interest.
[39] See, e.g., *Harvey* v *Aston* (1738) 1 Atk 361 (26 ER 230).
[40] There are a few examples of conditions being upheld where there is no intention to inhibit a first marriage: *Re
Hewett* [1918] 1 Ch 458.
[41] *Newton* v *Marsden* (1862) 2 J&H 356 (70 ER 1094) (widow); *Allen* v *Jackson* (1875) 1 Ch D 399 (widower).
[42] *Leong* v *Chye* [1955] AC 648 (PC).
[43] *Perrin* v *Lyon* (1807) 9 East 170 (103 ER 538).
[44] *Jenner* v *Turner* (1880) 16 Ch D 188.
[45] *Morley* v *Rennoldson* (1843) 2 Hare 570 at pp 579–580 (67 ER 235 at p 239); *Re Hewett* [1918] 1 Ch 458 at
p 465; *Leong* v *Chye* [1955] AC 648 at p 660. It was this that raised the ire of Porter MR in *Re King's Trusts*
(1892) 29 LR Ir 401.
[46] *Wilkinson* v *Wilkinson* (1871) LR 12 Eq 604; *Re Johnson's Will Trusts* [1967] Ch 387.
[47] *Re Edgar* [1939] 1 All ER 635.
[48] *Egerton* v *Brownlow* (1853) 4 HLC 1 (10 ER 359), distinguished in *Re Wallace* [1920] 2 Ch 274 where a lesser
honour was required.
[49] *Re Boulter* [1922] 1 Ch 75 (limiting residence abroad: German mother); *Re Borwick* [1933] Ch 657 (limiting
religious choice: likely to interfere with parental duty).

use policy to strike down provisions which may be found distasteful, such as restrictions on the religion of those the beneficiary may marry.[50] The applications of public policy in this paragraph (but not the earlier ones) extend to determinable fees.

(c) Certainty requirements

The courts employ a very strict certainty requirement for conditional fees. In the leading case of *Clavering* v *Ellison*,[51] Lord Cranworth required that it must be possible to 'see from the beginning, precisely and distinctly, upon the happening of what event it was that the preceding vested estate was to determine'. This deliberately strict test has been used to strike down conditions relating to residence[52] and conditions relating to Jewish faith and parentage.[53] The cases show a clear tension between the courts' desire to uphold what the settlor has required and a lack of sympathy with many of the conditions imposed.

More recent cases display less inclination to strike down conditions. Thus, a condition against marrying a Roman Catholic was upheld in *Blathwayt* v *Baron Cawley*.[54] Even so, the strictness of the rule for conditions subsequent is well illustrated by a comparison with conditions precedent. Here, there is no need for initial certainty as to the ways in which the condition may apply. It is sufficient if the condition is in fact clearly satisfied.[55] Although the distinction between conditions precedent and subsequent was criticised by Lord Denning MR in *Re Tuck's Settlement Trusts*,[56] he has little support in the cases. Insofar as the rule is based upon a dislike of forfeiture, it should not, logically, apply to determinable fees.[57]

(d) Other aspects of qualified fees

First, it is possible to provide that the fee simple shall terminate on a specific event and go to a third party (to A, but if A remarries, then to B).[58] This is very similar to a conditional fee, although B is said to have a contingent or executory interest rather than a right of entry. Secondly, these rules apply to life estates.[59] Although doubts have on occasion been voiced as to whether all the rules apply in an identical manner,[60] the cases do not support significant distinctions. Finally, the right of entry (on a conditional fee) and possibility of reverter (on a determinable fee) are themselves interests in land capable of being disposed of.[61]

---

[50] *Hodgson* v *Halford* (1879) 11 Ch D 959.
[51] (1859) 7 HLC 707 at p 725 (11 ER 282 at p 289).
[52] *Sifton* v *Sifton* [1938] AC 656, distinguished in *Re Gape* [1952] Ch 743.
[53] *Clayton* v *Ramsden* [1943] AC 320. See Butt (1977) 8 Syd LR 400.
[54] [1976] AC 397, in which the House of Lords expressed reservations about the scope of *Clayton*.
[55] *Re Allen* [1953] Ch 810; the entire gift fails if a condition precedent is void.
[56] [1978] Ch 49.
[57] Yet *Re Wilkinson* [1926] Ch 842 applied the *Clavering* rule (at least, *Re Talbot-Ponsonby's Estate* [1937] 4 All ER 309 presumed that it had done so).
[58] This is sometimes described as a 'shifting use'. There can also be a 'springing use' ('to A if she obtains a law degree').
[59] *Rochford* v *Hackman* (1852) 9 Hare 475 (68 ER 597) (restraint on alienation); *Jones* v *Jones* (1876) 1 QBD 279 (restraint on marriage); *Sifton* v *Sifton* [1938] AC 656 (certainty).
[60] E.g. Sweet (1917) 33 LQR 236.
[61] LPA, s 4(2) specifically includes rights of entry; a possibility of reverter appears included as 'a contingent, executory or future equitable interest'.

A right of entry may be legal if annexed to a legal rentcharge,[62] but is otherwise equitable. It will be seen that the fee simple absolute in possession is the only *legal* freehold estate permitted after 1925.[63] As an exception, conditional fees are deemed to be absolute for this purpose.[64] If the right of entry is legal, then there are two straightforward legal interests: conditional fee followed by right of entry. However, an equitable right of entry (which is most usual) may result in there being a trust of land, governed by the Trusts of Land and Appointment of Trustees Act 1996. Determinable fees and possibilities of reverter exist only in equity.

(e) Conclusions

Stepping back from the detail, it is worth reiterating the oddity of the distinction between conditional and determinable fees. It is not unusual for the law to offer alternative ways of regulating a specific area. Nearly always, however, there are substantial differences between the alternatives, so that it makes sense for the parties to have a choice. An example lies in the two forms of concurrent interests: joint tenancy and tenancy in common. There is a significant difference in that a joint tenancy passes to the survivor of the joint tenants; it will be used where this survivorship is desired. For determinable and conditional estates, the principal differences lie in the range of determining events that the courts will strike down. Any well-advised settlor can avoid most of the restrictions by the simple expedient of creating a determinable fee. There is little attraction in using a conditional fee, save perhaps to avoid the gift failing altogether if the determining event is struck down. It is difficult to think of any reason to retain both forms of qualified fees.

(ii) *The fee tail*

Although very important in past centuries,[65] the fee tail (or entail) became distinctly rare, and the Trusts of Land and Appointment of Trustees Act 1996 prohibits the creation of new entails.[66] Attempts to create entails, whether of land or personalty, take effect as a declaration of trust in favour of the holder of the purported entail. Accordingly, entails will be considered very briefly.

The nature of the entail is that it descends to the lineal descendants of the grantee. Entails ensure that the land remains within the family. Descent is to the eldest male child. This fitted well with ideas of primogeniture, odd as they seem to most people today. It was possible to prescribe different forms of descent, for example, to either male or female children. Somebody else will hold a fee simple in remainder or reversion. If the grantee of the entail and all descendants of the grantee die, then the entail terminates and the land goes to the holder of the remainder or reversion.

However, the operation of entails is inherently unstable. If in possession, the holder of the entail can 'disentail' so as to create a fee simple absolute, destroying the original fee

---

[62] LPA, s 1(2)(e); new rentcharges are restricted by the Rentcharges Act 1977: see p 56 below.
[63] LPA, s 1(1); see p 55 below.
[64] LPA, s 7(1) (as amended by Law of Property (Amendment) Act 1926).
[65] It was the basis of most nineteenth-century settlements of land.
[66] Sched 1, para 5. It is not very happily drafted, but the fears of Histed (2000) 116 LQR 445 and Pascoe [2001] Conv 396 appear exaggerated.

simple in remainder or reversion.[67] If the grantee of the entail is not in possession, disentailing is more difficult. Without the participation of the holder of the prior interest, it is possible to create only a 'base fee'. This is a form of fee simple but terminates if the original grantee's descendants die out.

(iii) *Life estates*

The life estate is fairly straightforward, although it can be qualified (conditional or determinable) in the same way as a fee simple. The operation of life estates is usually simple: the estate ends on death and the land goes to the holder of the next estate. Normally, the life estate will be based on the grantee's lifetime, but it is possible to select the life of a third party (to X as long as Y lives). This is sometimes called a life estate *pur autre vie*.

One area to investigate is the liability of the life tenant for actions or omissions affecting the property. Rules are needed in order to hold a reasonable balance between the life tenant and those with interests in remainder. The rules have traditionally been expressed in terms of *waste*.[68] Acts or omissions may be placed in four categories. At one end of the spectrum is ameliorating waste: conduct which improves the property. Although the tenant for life is supposed not to make permanent changes to the property, ameliorating waste causes no loss and any complaint is most unlikely to find favour with the court,[69] unless, perhaps, the character of the premises is changed. Permissive waste consists of allowing the property to deteriorate. A life tenant is not liable for permissive waste unless an obligation to repair or maintain is expressly imposed.[70]

Voluntary waste consists of doing some unjustified act which diminishes the value of the property; life tenants are liable for such waste. Two different types of situation may be identified. The most obvious is simply damaging the property: perhaps carrying out defective DIY work which requires expensive correction. The second situation concerns taking profits from the land. Obviously, a tenant can take crops, but what about felling mature trees or opening a mine and taking minerals? Without going into details, it should be noted that the law regulates the extent to which a life tenant can derive benefits from the land.

Finally, equitable waste is conduct which is best seen as 'a peculiarly flagrant branch of voluntary waste'.[71] It is significant because liability for voluntary waste is commonly excluded. The courts have been anxious to ensure that this does not give unwarranted protection to life tenants.

These rules were developed against the background that the life tenant would be occupying or managing the land for the duration of the life estate. In the modern law, the legal estate will be held by trustees, though beneficiaries will often be occupying the land and the trustees may delegate management to the life tenant.[72] Whoever manages the land, the voluntary waste rules may still be relevant in influencing decisions and – as regards mining leases, for example – determining the benefits the life tenant should receive.

---

[67] Fines and Recoveries Act 1833. A transfer of the property suffices as, since 1925, does a specific devise of the entailed property by will (LPA, s 176).
[68] See Megarry and Wade, *The Law of Real Property* (8th edn), paras 3-090 et seq.
[69] *Doherty* v *Allman* (1878) 3 App Cas 709 (tenant of lease: injunction refused).
[70] *Re Cartwright* (1889) 41 Ch D 532.
[71] Megarry and Wade, *The Law of Real Property* (8th edn), para 3-095.
[72] Trusts of Land and Appointment of Trustees Act 1996, ss 12, 9.

(iv) *Words of limitation*

What words are necessary in order to create these estates? The rules in the past frequently posed traps. Unless the essential technical words were used ('A and his heirs' for a fee simple; 'B and the heirs of his body' for an entail),[73] a grant would transfer only a life estate.[74] The rules began to be relaxed in the nineteenth century,[75] and the modern law takes a very different stance. Section 60 of the Law of Property Act 1925 enacts that a conveyance passes all the rights of the grantor without words of limitation.[76] In other words, a person who wishes to create a life estate has to ensure that it is made clear that this is intended, although no formal words are required.

Entails can no longer be created, but attempts to create an entail give rise to a trust for the grantee rather than a transfer of the fee simple.[77] Strict words ('to D and the heirs of his body' or 'to E in tail') were essential to create an entail.

C. Leases

A lease is in many respects similar to a freehold estate: a right to enjoy land by reference to the length of enjoyment. The hallmark of a lease is that it is for a certain maximum period, whereas freehold estates are for indefinite (fee simple) or uncertain (entail, life estate) periods. However, the lease has a quite separate history, with the result that leasehold tenure and freehold tenure were subjected to very different rules. In the modern law, the practical consequences of these historical differences are very limited. It may be noted that it has always been possible for life estate holders to create leases (subject to the risk that the life estate might terminate before the intended expiry of the lease) and tenants can create life estates out of leases.

Much more important today is that leases and freehold estates have different roles. Leases may most obviously be compared with life estates, as both are temporary. Leases are used as a means of giving the use of land for a specified period, nearly always in return for rent or a capital payment. On the other hand, life estates are used for a different purpose. They are usually given to members of the settlor's family, not part of a commercial arrangement. More importantly, the purpose is often to provide an income (generally rent from leases) for the holders of the life estates. It is less common, at least in the large nineteenth-century settlements which so influenced the 1925 legislation, for there to be physical enjoyment of the land. This different role of leasehold estates is reflected in the 1925 legislation, considered in Chapter 6.

D. Commonhold

Commonhold (introduced by the Commonhold and Leasehold Reform Act 2002) is a scheme for the ownership and management of interdependent properties, such as flats. The

---

[73] Co Litt, 1a, 7b, 20a.
[74] Co Litt, 1a, 8b.
[75] 'To C in fee simple' was recognised by the Conveyancing Act 1881, s 51.
[76] But if ineffective words of limitation are used, Mee [2008] Conv 129 notes that defective drafting of LPA, s 60 might mean that problems are still caused.
[77] Trusts of Land and Appointment of Trustees Act 1996, Sched 1, para 5.

language of commonhold suggests that it is a new form of estate alongside freehold and leasehold estates. In fact, the estate is one of freehold. The new scheme involves 'commonhold land', and we therefore have freehold estates in commonhold land.[78] It is certainly correct as a matter of substance to view commonhold as a new method of holding land (with new incidents and controls, together with management by the commonhold association), but technically it is not a new estate.

E. Other interests

A wide range of interests, falling short of full enjoyment and possession, can be created in land. Thus easements are rights relating to a neighbour's land. The best-known easement is a right of way, but there are many others. Examples are the right of storage, the right to use a car park, the right to light (so that the neighbour cannot build so as to block light) and the right to advertise one's business. All easements require that land be benefited by the right. Rather similar are profits *à prendre*: rights to take objects (such as minerals or fish) from the servient land. Profits can be held personally ('in gross') or for the benefit of neighbouring land ('appurtenant').

Another very common interest is the mortgage: a security for a loan.[79] Traditionally, the fee simple[80] was conveyed to the lender, the borrower having a right to recover the property on paying off the loan. The viability of mortgages as a widespread form of security was ensured by the equitable rule that the borrower can recover the property at any time, subject to the court's imposing a time limit (by a process called foreclosure). The borrower's rights are termed the equity of redemption. The legal structure of mortgages was changed by the 1925 legislation, and today virtually all mortgages are created by way of 'legal charge'. The legal charge ensures that the fee simple, coupled with an equitable right to redeem, remains in the mortgagor (borrower),[81] whilst the mortgagee obtains a charge.

Equitable interests

These are numerous and quite apart from beneficial interests under trusts. The estate contract is a contractual right to a legal estate. Equity will give specific performance of a contract to create or transfer a legal estate. This, coupled with the maxim that equity treats as done that which ought to be done, results in an equitable interest arising from the contract. The importance of this is that a person who, for example, contracts to buy land has not only a contractual right against the seller but also an equitable proprietary claim enforceable against any person who acquires the land.

The nature of this proprietary claim has been called into question by *Mortgage Business plc* v *O'Shaugnessy*.[82] The Supreme Court held that the purchaser cannot create proprietary

---

[78] CLRA, ss 1(1), 7(2), 9(3). A 'new estate in all but name': Clarke (1995) 58 MLR 486 at p 496.
[79] We commonly talk about a house buyer getting a mortgage, but this is misleading. What the buyer gets is a loan; it is the building society or bank that gets the mortgage, the security interest.
[80] This assumes that the borrower has the fee simple; leases and other interests can be mortgaged in a similar manner.
[81] Every fee simple mortgagor keeps the fee simple today: LPA, s 85.
[82] [2015] AC 385; Hopkins [2015] Conv 245; Sparkes [2015] Conv 301 at pp 307–309.

rights prior to completion. This is difficult to comprehend, as assignments and subleases out of equitable leases (as well as sub-sales) are fully recognised. The result in the case could be justified by saying no right can be created which is greater than the purchaser's right (very small before the price is paid), but the absolute rule laid down is strange. Its weakness is illustrated by Baroness Hale's recognition that it would not apply where a purchaser's rights are equitable because a transfer has not been registered.

Two extensions of the estate contract may be noted. It frequently happens that a transfer or creation of a legal estate is ineffective because of failure to comply with the appropriate formalities, especially the use of a deed. Even without any express prior contract, equity will treat the transaction as a contract whenever there is consideration. The result is that the failed transfer may take effect as an equitable interest, provided that the formality requirements for contracts are satisfied.[83] The second extension is that an option to purchase land (where the purchaser has a choice as to whether to go ahead with the purchase) is also a proprietary interest.[84] This is particularly important because options may be exercisable some considerable time in the future, providing a substantial risk of a change in ownership of the land in the interval.

A quite different equitable interest is the restrictive covenant: an obligation imposed upon a neighbour not to undertake specified activities on the servient land. It is very like an easement, requiring both benefited and burdened land. However, few negative easements (that is, easements which restrict the servient owner rather than confer a right on the dominant owner to do something) are permitted. The restrictive covenant was established in the mid-nineteenth century and is the best 'modern' example of a novel equitable interest.

Recent decades have seen attempts to create other equitable interests. Most of the issues have surrounded licences: rights to use land that fall short of the recognised proprietary interests. Arguments in favour of recognising the so-called 'deserted wife's equity' (a proprietary right to remain in possession of the matrimonial home) were rejected by the House of Lords in *National Provincial Bank Ltd* v *Ainsworth*.[85] Lord Wilberforce[86] provided a useful summary of the requirements for there to be a new proprietary interest: 'Before a right or an interest can be admitted into the category of property, or of a right affecting property, it must be definable, identifiable by third parties, capable in its nature of assumption by third parties, and have some degree of permanence or stability.' This is sometimes criticised as circular,[87] though it probably represents the current approach. Subsequently, the Court of Appeal has denied that contractual licences are proprietary interests binding purchasers.[88]

On the other hand, it seems probable that estoppel licences do bind purchasers, a result confirmed for registered land by s 116 of the Land Registration Act 2002. An estoppel licence may arise where a licensee relies on a representation to their detriment, or the owner acquiesces in the licensee's acting upon a supposition that there are rights to the

---

[83] See p 403 below.
[84] Options are considered further in the formalities setting: p 103 below.
[85] [1965] AC 1175.
[86] Ibid, at pp 1247–1248.
[87] Kevin Gray and Susan Francis Gray in *Land Law: Themes and Perspectives* (eds Bright and Dewar), pp 32–37; Dixon in *Land Law: Issues, Debates, Policy* (ed Tee), pp 16–18.
[88] *Ashburn Anstalt* v *Arnold* [1989] Ch 1.

land. Estoppel licences might be thought to be analogous to estate contracts, with estoppel being substituted for the role of contract. However, the analogy is difficult to maintain both because the remedy given in estoppel may be discretionary[89] and also because estoppels may protect licences as well as estates.

One problem surrounding such novel claims is that s 4(1) of the Law of Property Act 1925 appears to preclude the development of new equitable interests.[90] Though the courts are naturally hesitant to develop new rights, it would be odd if all development were precluded by statute. Perhaps the answer is that the subsection is directed towards the effect of the 1925 legislation, which rendered a number of interests equitable rather than legal. Thus the legislation itself cannot be used to justify a wider range of equitable interests but does not prevent the courts from developing them.

2. Chattels

The position regarding chattels is much less complex. The doctrine of tenures and estates has no operation here: it is entirely accurate to talk of a person's owning a car. Two or more persons can be concurrent owners of chattels. However, the more difficult question concerns the recognition of rights other than ownership.

The one clear example of a legal right is bailment: possession of chattels.[91] Both the bailor and bailee have property rights ('general property' and 'special property', respectively) enforceable against third parties. If the chattel is damaged, then, rather surprisingly, the bailee can recover all the loss to the chattel, not merely his or her loss (there is a duty to account to the bailor).[92] The bailor can sue if there is loss from damage to the reversionary interest (i.e. if there is destruction, or damage lasting beyond the bailment).[93] This does not apply if the bailee has repaired the damage or compensated the bailor.[94]

It is less clear that purchasers from the bailor are bound by the bailment, though this seems probable for chattel leases and pledge.[95] Perhaps the reason why bailment has been so readily accepted is that actions for interference with goods mostly involve interference with possession.[96] The result is that lawyers concentrate far more on possession than property rights as such.[97]

Bailment provides the basis for hire and many more complex transactions. In a hire purchase contract, the hirer (buyer) strictly is a bailee, though it appears that a form of ownership in the goods may be recognised.[98] Bailment also explains security transactions, where the creditor may have possession (pledge, lien) or may have the general property (mortgage).

---

[89] Not only as to whether there should be a remedy, but more crucially as to the extent of the remedy.

[90] See p 492 below.

[91] Permission to leave chattels on a person's land will not suffice: *Ashby v Tolhurst* [1937] 2 KB 242.

[92] *The Winkfield* [1902] P 42.

[93] *Mears v LSW Ry Co* (1862) 11 CBNS 850 (142 ER 1029).

[94] *HSBC Rail (UK) Ltd v Network Rail Infrastructure Ltd* [2006] 1 WLR 643.

[95] See the summary of the present position in RJ Smith, *Plural Ownership*, pp 211–212.

[96] *Crossley Vaines on Personal Property* (5th edn), Chapter 2. Curwen argues that special property represents fragmentation of ownership rather than simply possession: (2000) 20 LS 181, also [2004] Conv 308 as regards actions for conversion.

[97] This has led to underdeveloped principles for actions by owners out of possession: Tettenborn [1994] CLJ 326.

[98] *Wickham Holdings Ltd v Brooke House Motors Ltd* [1967] 1 WLR 295, especially Lord Denning MR at pp 300–301; Hill, *Modern Studies in Property Law*, Vol 1 (ed Cooke), Chapter 2 (not limited to hire purchase).

Although bailment can explain many situations, the result is a fairly limited concept of proprietary interests in chattels.[99] This is welcome in some respects, as the free marketability of chattels is crucial to commerce; it would be compromised if a broad range of proprietary rights were to be recognised. Land is less frequently bought and sold and procedures (such as registration of interests) have been developed to ensure a good balance between the needs of encumbrancers and purchasers. Furthermore, effective use of land often demands the existence of rights over neighbouring land, whilst its permanency ensures its utility as a security. These considerations are much weaker as regards chattels.

It is possible to have equitable interests in chattels, most obviously when a trust has been created.[100] Another good example is an equitable charge, a form of security interest. However, the courts are alert to the risks for commerce and are reluctant to impose the same duty of inquiry on purchasers of chattels as is laid upon purchasers of land.[101] Although equity today plays a central role in commerce,[102] equitable doctrines will not be extended so as to subvert clear and convenient legal rules and 'throw the business world into confusion'.[103]

3. Relative or absolute ownership?

A feature both of estates of land and of ownership of chattels is that it is not necessary for a claimant to prove absolute ownership. All that is generally necessary is to prove a better right than the other party to the dispute.[104] It follows that it is usually insufficient for the defendant to prove that some other person has a better right than the claimant. To a large extent, this stress on relativity of claims may be seen as a result of our not employing special actions to enforce proprietary rights. Instead, we use actions, such as trespass, which are based upon interference with possession. Accordingly, the courts tend to be more interested in possession and rights to possession than in ownership.

For estates, this is best illustrated by the adverse possession rules. If A is in adverse possession of B's land, then A is able to claim the land back should C take it.[105] This remains true for registered land. However, adverse possession against B has a limited role in registered land since reforms in 2002, so that the concept of absolute ownership is more viable.[106] This may have practical effects when considering human rights protection of ownership.[107]

---

[99] See Palmer, *Bailment* (3rd edn), pp 101–108, especially for a comparison with leases. McMeel [2003] LMCLQ 169 is critical of bailment, arguing that its broad scope has stultified the development of personal property principles and that it is redundant.

[100] See, e.g., Bell, *Modern Law of Personal Property in England and Ireland*, Chapters 7–9.

[101] *Manchester Trust* v *Furness* [1895] 2 QB 539 at p 545 ('infinite mischief and paralyzing the trade of the country'), quoted with approval in *Polly Peck International plc* v *Nadir (No 2)* [1992] 4 All ER 769 at p 782.

[102] Millett (1998) 114 LQR 214.

[103] Atkin LJ in *Re Wait* [1927] 1 Ch 606 at pp 636, 640 (passing of property on sale).

[104] The role of relativity in property law is explored by Fox [2006] CLJ 330.

[105] *Asher* v *Whitlock* (1865) LR 1 QB 1; p 89 below.

[106] Land Registration Act 2002, s 58(1) ensures that registration is generally conclusive; for adverse possession, see p 77 below.

[107] See Dixon [2006] Conv 179 at p 184.

An equivalent area for chattels involves finding. Suppose R finds property belonging to S, but T subsequently seizes possession of it. R can recover it from T.[108] It has been a long-standing rule that the defendant (T) cannot raise the defence of *ius tertii* (ownership in a third party). Although this rule was abolished by s 8 of the Torts (Interference with Goods) Act 1977, the impact of this on relativity of title is less than might be imagined. There is still no obligation on the claimant to prove ownership and, although the defendant can request that the third party be joined, failure by that party to appear will lead to the claimant's succeeding.[109] It is only where the third party is known[110] and proves a superior title that the Act makes any difference. In that setting, the claimant can have no legitimate complaint. Despite the legislation, it remains safe to conclude that English law places greater stress on the relativity of the claims of the parties than on absolute ownership.

Further reading

Fox, D [2006] CLJ 330: Relativity of title at law and in equity.
Gray, K and Gray, S F 'The idea of property in land' in *Land Law: Themes and Perspectives* (eds Bright and Dewar), Chapter 1.
Harris, J W 'Ownership of Land in English Law' in *The Legal Mind: Essays in honour of Tony Honoré* (eds MacCormick and Birks), Chapter 9.
Millett, P J (1998) 114 LQR 214: Equity's place in the law of commerce.
Nugee, E (2008) 124 LQR 586: The feudal system and the Land Registration Acts.

[108] *Armory* v *Delamirie* (1722) 1 Stra 505 (93 ER 664); p 64 below. Rostill (2015) 35 OxJLS 31 explores the basis upon which relativity works.
[109] *Civil Procedure 2016 (White Book)*, Vol 1, Rule 19.5A. Failure to join the third party is likely to be fatal to the defendant: *de Franco* v *Metropolitan Police Commissioner* (1987) *The Times*, May 8; Bell, *Modern Law of Personal Property in England and Ireland*, p 84; Battersby [1992] Conv 100 at p 102.
[110] For the unknown owner, see *Costello* v *Derbyshire Chief Constable* [2001] 1 WLR 1437 (p 65 below).

6

The role of legislation and registration for land interests

Introduction

Although most of the central concepts of property law are common law or equity based, there is a vitally important statutory overlay. In particular, the property legislation of 1925[1] made numerous changes to real property and trusts, creating a 'new era'[2] for real property law. Many of the provisions of this legislation will be examined in later chapters, but at this point, an overview will be provided.

Despite the importance of the legislation, it is erroneous to view it as an attempt to codify the law. Rather, it attempted to bring property law up to date and, in particular, to ease the creation and transfer of property interests. Nor should we overestimate what was achieved in 1925 itself, for much of that legislation consolidated important nineteenth-century reforms. With the advantage of hindsight, it may be argued that most of the fundamental reforms were in place by the 1880s. Examples include settled land, implied terms in conveyances and, to a lesser extent, registration.

The 1925 legislation did more, however, than consolidate these earlier reforms. The most pressing problems had already been addressed, but other areas still awaited reform. Equally importantly, the 1925 legislation set out to provide a structure for the law in which the reforms could best operate. Take mortgages as an example. Prior to 1925, the fee simple passed to the mortgagee (lender). Whilst it is easy to comprehend the idea of holding the fee simple as security, this possessed drawbacks. It complicated the title to the fee simple (a mortgage would involve a conveyance of the fee and its reconveyance on paying off the mortgage) and failed to reflect the reality of the situation: the mortgagor is commonly regarded as the owner. The 1925 abolition of this method of creating mortgages had virtually no practical effect on the parties but began to place the legal analysis of mortgages on a more realistic footing.[3]

---

[1] Settled Land Act, Trustee Act, Law of Property Act, Land Registration Act, Land Charges Act, Administration of Estates Act.

[2] Preface to Cheshire, *Modern Law of Real Property* (1st edn, 1925). For criticism of modern assumptions as to the role of the legislation, see Anderson [1984] CLP 63; Bright and Dewar (eds), *Land Law: Themes and Perspectives*, Chapter 4.

[3] Law of Property Act 1925 (hereafter LPA), s 85. One cannot pretend that the substituted 3,000-year lease was an ideal reform (see p 578 below).

The real property reforms contained in the 1925 legislation are many and varied. Apart from improvements to specific areas,[4] three categories of reform may be identified. First, many doctrines of the earlier law were outdated, complex and confusing. Their abolition has caused few problems and may be seen as both overdue and welcome. The nature of these reforms is such that there is no need to investigate them further.

Next, there are numerous sections implying terms into conveyances, leases, mortgages and trusts. These mirror terms previously inserted by lawyers. The effect of the legislation is to shorten documents (beneficial both at the stage of drafting them and when others inspect them in later years) and to reduce the danger of omitting standard clauses. The success of the legislation obviously depends upon whether the draftsmen identified the standard clauses and then drafted implied terms in an appropriate manner. There is always the danger of asking what would be a reasonable provision rather than what is a standard provision. As the implied terms can nearly always be excluded or amended by the parties, a statutory implied term that is unrealistic or out of date will lengthen documents by reason of its exclusion!

Third, and most significant, there are provisions amending the effect of interests on purchasers. A major problem in the past was that it could be difficult for sellers to show an unencumbered right to a fee simple or lease. Legal rights would bind the purchaser automatically. This caused obvious problems for purchasers when so many legal estates could exist in the same property, quite apart from encumbrances such as easements. Equitable rights would bind the purchaser if the purchaser was aware of them (actual notice) or should have been aware of them (constructive notice). This placed a heavy burden on the purchaser to make full inquiries, although even a careful purchaser faced the risk of a court deciding that there was constructive notice. It is this third type of provision upon which, together with reforms of specific areas, we will now concentrate.

1. The 1925 legislation

A. Restricting legal estates and interests

This is undertaken by LPA, s 1. The idea was to limit legal rights to those which really should bind purchasers automatically. For estates, this means those which are essential for the efficient use of land. So far as freehold estates are concerned, only the fee simple absolute in possession[5] is recognised as a legal estate. This is, of course, the interest which most purchasers will wish to acquire. Leases[6] remain legal estates. This is no surprise, as leases provide an ideal way of occupying property, especially on a short-term basis. From the owner's point of view, leasing land provides a good way of obtaining income, with the prospect of increased capital value as well. There is a ready market for fees simple which are subject to leases; in particular, most shops and industrial premises are held under

---

[4] Some are of wide impact: the rules of intestate succession in the Administration of Estates Act 1925, for example.
[5] As defined in Chapter 5. It was seen that a conditional fee is treated as absolute.
[6] Technically, 'terms of years absolute'. Although most leases are liable to be cut short by forfeiture, they remain absolute (LPA, s 205(1)(xxvii)).

leases. The purchaser of the fee simple usually intends to take an income from the land (rent) rather than occupy it personally. From the tenant's point of view, the lease provides an estate that can be sold or otherwise disposed of, quite apart from its principal purpose of giving a right of possession.

So far as other interests are concerned, s 1(2) lists those able to exist as legal interests. They are easements, rentcharges, charges by way of legal mortgage, similar charges not created by an instrument (this covers statutory charges) and certain rights of entry. Some of these require further explanation.

Legal easements are limited to those existing forever or for a term of years: easements for life are excluded. The category covers an 'easement, right or privilege', which will include profits *à prendre* and other incorporeal hereditaments.

A rentcharge is a right to a money payment from land. It is like rent from a lease, save that it is paid by a freeholder. It has become increasingly unusual, and its creation was severely limited by the Rentcharges Act 1977, which prohibits the creation of most new rentcharges. Two exceptions may be noted. It is still possible to create rentcharges where there is a trust of land, provided it lasts no longer than a person's life and there is no consideration.[7] A settlor can thereby require that a sum be paid to, say, her widower, charged on land within a settlement. The second exception occurs where there is an 'estate rentcharge'.[8] This is a rentcharge imposed either to ensure the performance of covenants by the owner of the land or else to recoup the cost of providing services or other benefits to the land.[9] Outside these exceptions, existing rentcharges are phased out over 60 years.[10]

Rights of entry must be one of two types to be legal. The first is a right to enter on breach of covenants in a legal lease. Virtually every landlord has this right. Insofar as the landlord will have a legal estate (whether the freehold or a superior lease), it is good sense for the parallel right of entry to be legal. The second is a right of entry attached to a legal rentcharge. It can be argued that as both legal leases and legal rentcharges bind purchasers, so also should remedies for breach which will be found in the instruments creating them.

All interests outside the statutory list must be equitable.[11] By itself, this does little to aid the position of purchasers, who would still have to take steps to discover them and would be bound by them if there were notice. However, we shall see that the legislation ensures that equitable interests are subject to very different rules than before 1925.

B. Overreaching

We are here mainly concerned with equitable freehold estates, such as life interests and fees simple in remainder. These are often called 'family interests' as they are usually created

---

[7] Trusts of Land and Appointment of Trustees Act 1996, Sched 1, para 3 (family arrangements and marriage consideration are allowed); Rentcharges Act 1977, s 2(3).
[8] Rentcharges Act 1977, s 2(3), defined in s 2(4).
[9] The latter would be most relevant for a block of flats or housing estate, where work such as maintenance of roofs, private roads, paths, etc, is carried out.
[10] Rentcharges Act 1977, s 3.
[11] LPA, s 1(3). A narrow view of the effect of s 1(3) is adopted by Pulleyn [2012] Conv 387 at p 389.

in favour of members of a family. The legislation ensures that the legal fee simple absolute in possession is held by trustees,[12] and it is with these trustees that a purchaser deals. It is provided that the trustees may sell the land and that, on sale, the beneficial interests are transferred to the purchase money. The purchaser of the land is wholly unaffected by the beneficial interests, provided that the purchase money is paid to at least two trustees. This restriction is designed to avoid the relatively high risk that a single trustee might abscond with the purchase money. Following sale, the beneficiary has a right in the purchase money rather than in the land; the process is called 'overreaching'. The practical consequence is that, instead of receiving rent from the land, a life interest holder will obtain interest on the purchase money or, more likely, dividends from shares bought with the money.[13]

This power of sale was originally controversial as it divorced the beneficiaries' rights from the land, which might have been owned by the family for centuries; it introduced the idea of rights in a fund (presently represented by the land).[14] It should not be thought, however, that overreaching is a concept introduced by legislation. It already existed whenever trustees had an express right or duty to sell the land. What was new in the nineteenth century was the conferring of overreaching powers (which the settlor could not exclude) whenever there are successive interests in land. Very important for the modern law was the extension of overreaching in 1925 to persons holding interests in lands concurrently. This is where most of the cases and controversy currently centre. Again, the purpose was to make it easier to buy and sell land;[15] the co-owners will receive their proportionate shares of the purchase price.

Non-family equitable interests, just like legal estates and interests, will rarely be suitable for overreaching. They are generally created for consideration and labelled 'commercial interests'. If a person has a restrictive covenant preventing a neighbour from building, this could never sensibly take effect against money! On the other hand, there is scope for overreaching in limited circumstances. Two instances may be given.

First, a mortgagee has a power to sell the land in order to realise the security constituted by the mortgage, should the borrower default. The interest of the borrower (usually the legal fee simple) is then overreached[16] and takes effect against the proceeds of sale. This means that the lender can recover the money owing, but that any balance has to be paid to the borrower. The second instance is found in the rather detailed ad hoc trust of land provisions; they are rarely encountered. Where the trustees are court approved, or a trust corporation,[17] overreaching is extended in two respects. First, rights prior to the trust can be overreached. Normally, overreaching affects only interests created when the trust is set up (or created later). Secondly, a slightly wider range of rights can be overreached.

---

[12] Where the Settled Land Act 1925 applied, this would usually be the tenant for life.

[13] In some cases, the beneficiaries (if all are adults) may choose to split the capital between them, terminating the trusts. If all the beneficiaries act together, they are entitled to terminate a trust: *Saunders* v *Vautier* (1841) 4 Beav 115 (49 ER 282), affirmed Cr&Ph 240 (41 ER 482).

[14] Note the distinction which Rudden draws between things as thing and things as wealth: (1994) 14 OxJLS 81. Rudden would not seek to put each right into a specific category (as does the family/commercial dichotomy), but successive family interests provide a good example of things as wealth.

[15] See p 302 below.

[16] See LPA, s 2(1)(iii), which also recognises overreaching where a personal representative sells land.

[17] See p 354 below.

C. Registration of land charges

Most equitable rights are prized because they affect purchasers. The challenge is to find ways in which to ensure that purchasers are bound, but without the expense and uncertainty of nineteenth-century conveyancing and the doctrine of notice. The solution was found in registration. Under the land charges scheme, many equitable rights (now listed in the Land Charges Act 1972) must be entered on a register if they are to bind a purchaser. It is then relatively easy for the purchaser to discover them.

It may be seen in summary that legal estates and interests are those that purchasers must still take steps to discover. Most equitable interests will either not bind a purchaser because they are overreachable family interests or, if commercial interests, require registration before a purchaser can be bound. A few equitable interests, nevertheless, remain subject to the doctrine of notice.

D. Assessing the 1925 legislation

Looking back at the legislation more than 90 years later, it is remarkable how long much of it survived and how few amendments there have been to its fundamental principles. This is a tribute to its drafting, though significant parts of the legislation have for many years been in need of overhaul. The need for reform is reflected in reports of the Law Commission covering such central areas as trusts of land,[18] mortgages, land registration[19] and easements and covenants.

More generally, the focus of property law has changed significantly over the past century. At least up to and including the 1925 legislation, a large part of the subject was devoted to interests that would be created in family settlements. This was of enormous significance when land constituted the principal class of assets and a relatively small number of wealthy families owned much of the land in the country. The economic and political significance of land settlements was incalculable. Things have now changed dramatically. Land is no longer the most important form of capital (a role overtaken by shares in companies), and settlements are relatively uncommon. The stress on making sale and other dispositions of land more straightforward remains a prime consideration, but it is balanced by a much greater concern with the use of land. The idea of an interest in a fund was vital to the nineteenth-century reform of settlements, but it is at odds with how most people now view interests in the family home. Overall, the 1925 legislation bears the appearance of a successful attempt to deal with the problems of the past rather than addressing the concerns of the present.

2. Land registration

A registration scheme far more comprehensive than land charges is found today in the Land Registration Act 2002. Its origins pre-date 1925, though the major expansion of the system took effect under the Land Registration Act 1925. Whilst land charges are limited

---

[18] Implemented by the Trusts of Land and Appointment of Trustees Act 1996.
[19] Implemented by the Land Registration Act 2002.

to the protection of mainly equitable and statutory rights, land registration is based upon the registration of legal estates. The principal significance of this is that the register tells the purchaser who owns the legal estate (whether fee simple or lease). The old title deeds are redundant: because the law guarantees the title of the purchaser (once registered), there is no need to make inquiries off the register about title.

The system, moreover, is not limited to legal estates. Subject to some exceptions (the notorious category of overriding interests), all legal and equitable interests must be entered on the register if they are to bind a purchaser. There is no role for land charges; that scheme ceases to apply once title is registered. It follows that land charges are rapidly diminishing in importance.

It may be noted that the traditional differences in the effect of legal and equitable interests on purchasers are swept aside by land registration: the doctrine of notice has no application. Nevertheless, only legal estates and interests can be registered (in the sense of being guaranteed by the State): equitable interests can merely be protected on the register. Furthermore, several legal interests (especially short leases and some non-express easements) are overriding interests, and as such, they bind purchasers without any entry on the register. Equitable interests are overriding interests only if accompanied by actual occupation. Overriding interests mean that purchasers are not able to rely on the register alone: they form the most controversial aspect of registration.

Registration of title (the alternative description of land registration) has been extended rather slowly over the years. By 1980, about half of all titles were registered; but today, the figure is around 95%. Within the next decade (probably sooner), virtually every dealing with land will involve registered land. Accordingly, this book places stress on the registered land rules, with those for unregistered land being summarised more quickly. Despite the enormous significance of registered land, however, the unregistered land rules remain of importance in shaping the structure of our thinking about property principles. Although the Land Registration Act 2002 makes a determined attempt to move away from the older principles (such as the doctrine of notice and the rules relating to the priority of two competing equitable interests),[20] it would be rash to assume that the old principles will not influence the thinking of the courts.

The Land Registration Act 2002 considerably amends property law as it applies to registered land. The earlier legislation could be seen as changing the procedures for protecting interests and for buying land, together with making significant changes to priority rules. Today, this narrow approach is no longer tenable. The new legislation will make revolutionary changes to our rules relating to the creation and transfer of interests in land: for most interests, electronic creation will, some time in the future, become both sufficient and necessary. This will largely replace our present formality rules. A second vitally important change is that adverse possession (claiming ownership of land by possession adverse to the owner) is changed almost beyond recognition – contested claims to adverse possession will rarely succeed in the future. Indeed, throughout the text, we need to bear in mind that principles may be changed by the 2002 legislation.[21]

---

[20] This appears clearly from Law Com No 271: see paras 2.17, 5.16, 5.21.

[21] One example is that it is declared that estoppel claims to registered land can bind purchasers, removing uncertainty which was the source of many an examination question.

3. Other modern legislation and overview

Unsurprisingly, there are dozens of statutes impacting on property law. However, mention will be made of three statutes which are especially important; all will be discussed in later chapters.

It has been observed that the treatment of an interest under a trust as an interest in a fund has been thought to be out of date for modern property law. The problems were greatest for concurrent interests, especially where a couple own the family home. The area was reformed by the Trusts of Land and Appointment of Trustees Act 1996.[22] Although the practical changes introduced by that Act are limited, it provides a fuller and more modern structure for regulating the holding and management of successive and concurrent interests in land. In particular, the rather odd (if workable) trust for sale previously imposed on co-owners is replaced by the more modern trust of land.

The running of covenants in leases was restructured by the Landlord and Tenant (Covenants) Act 1995. This forms the basis for most of Chapter 20. Finally, a long-needed system for holding and managing flats was introduced in 2002: commonhold.[23]

Conclusion

To a much greater extent than other forms of property, land is subject to often elaborate statutory provision. In part, this reflects the age of the rules applying to land: many became out of date and required statutory reform. It also reflects the need to provide clarity and certainty for land transactions, especially as a broad range of interests in land has long been recognised. Yet, many of our most basic principles remain rooted in common law and equity: it would be a serious error to believe that legislation provides all the solutions for issues arising in land law.

Further reading

Rudden, B (1994) 14 OxJLS 81: Things as things and things as wealth.

---

[22] See Chapter 16.

[23] Commonhold and Leasehold Reform Act 2002: see Chapter 21. It is rarely encountered in practice.

Part II

General principles: creation and transfer of property interests

7
Original acquisition of property interests

Introduction

The huge majority of interests in property are created by the current owner, or by the courts' imposing an obligation, such as a trust, on the current owner.[1] However, some interests do not derive from another person's ownership. The first of three such examples dealt with in this chapter is finding, where the finder is often given a better right to the thing than anyone except the owner who had lost it. The second is adverse possession, whereby rights to ownership can be acquired by a long period of possession adverse to the owner.[2] These two areas are interesting because they have required the development of principles relating to possession, principles which are rarely to the fore in other contexts.[3] The third example is that of fixtures, whereby objects fixed to land, or to a more important object, become by law part of the land or other object.

1. Finding

The rights of finders have long interested lawyers, more than one might suppose from the relatively small number of cases. One reason is that they illustrate what counts as possession in English law and the extent to which legal rights are grounded on possession rather than ownership. The fascination of commentators is enhanced by the inconsistent analyses employed in the cases. Many of the cases could have been decided on any of several grounds; frequently, the ground upon which a case was decided has subsequently been doubted. This has led to the explanation of earlier cases on grounds that are barely recognisable from reading them.

One crucial point is that disputes frequently involve multiple parties. Take this example. Land is leased by L to T. T employs contractors (C) to undertake work on the premises. One of C's employees (F) finds a gold bracelet on the premises. A jealous colleague, E, takes it from F. An inscription on the bracelet indicates that it belongs to O, who at present cannot be traced. E has physical possession of the bracelet but could face claims by O, L, T, C and F.[4] The fact that one of these parties may have a better right than another

---

[1] Others with proprietary interests, such as lessees, can create interests out of their own interests.
[2] In a similar manner, easements can be acquired by long user. This is called prescription and will be dealt with in Chapter 23 on easements.
[3] Possession is also important in the gift of chattels, addressed in Chapter 8.
[4] Based on *City of London Corporation* v *Appleyard* [1963] 1 WLR 982, save that there was no E. T was held to have a better right than C or F on the facts, but L won by virtue of a term in the lease; O was never discovered.

does not necessarily mean that they can keep it. For example, C will have a better right than F (and thereby E) by virtue of being the employer. Whether L as owner and T as occupier have better rights than C involves difficult points of law, but it is clear that O, if traced, can claim the property from whoever has it.

This example tells us that it is simplistic to talk about finders owning what they have found.[5] They may have better rights than those who take the property from them (such as E), but this does not mean that their claims will prevail against other claimants. Because of this, our analysis will be based upon investigating specific relationships; these provide the building blocks for the resolution of complex problems like that described earlier.

A. Things found on, in or under land

(i) *Finder – true owner disputes*

Where the owner of a lost article is known, that person can reclaim it from whoever has it. This simple rule was applied in *Moffatt* v *Kazana*.[6] It was proved that the owner of a bungalow had hidden a tin containing nearly £2,000 in the loft. Some 10 years later, the bungalow was sold to the defendant and, oddly enough, the owner forgot about the tin. In the course of building work, the tin was discovered three years later. The original owner had since died. Wrangham J held that his personal representatives could claim it from the defendant. Furthermore, it had not been sold together with the bungalow; we will return to this aspect of the decision later.

The one qualification on the owner's claim is that it must be brought within the limitation period of six years.[7] However, time begins to run only from the time the object is demanded from the finder, not from the date of the finding.[8] The consequence is that the finder may have to return the object many years after the initial finding, although any sale of the goods may well constitute a conversion causing time to begin to run.[9]

(ii) *Finder – dispossessor disputes*

The classic case is *Armory* v *Delamirie*[10] in 1722. A chimney sweep's boy found a ring, in which a stone was set. He took it to a jeweller, who removed the stone and refused to return it. Pratt CJ was emphatic that the finder 'has such property as to keep it against all save the rightful owner'. Indeed, the jeweller was held liable for the most valuable stone that would fit the ring, unless he returned the original stone. Therefore, the finder has a better right than anybody who interferes with their possession.[11] This applies even

---

[5]   Rostill (2015) 35 OxJLS 31 argues that the courts treat the finder (or other possessor) as if they have a property right, rather deciding that that person actually acquires a property right.
[6]   [1969] 2 QB 152.
[7]   Limitation Act 1980, s 2.
[8]   *Spackman* v *Foster* (1883) 11 QBD 99.
[9]   Marshall (1949) 2 CLP 68 at p 70.
[10]   1 Stra 505 (93 ER 664); Hickey in *Landmark Cases in Property Law* (ed Douglas, Hickey and Waring), Chapter 6.
[11]   Whether the finder can claim against subsequent claimants is less clear: Fox [2006] CLJ 330 at pp 345–348.

where the finder is a wrongdoer or a thief and the property has been seized by the police.[12] Although some courts have been reluctant to enunciate such a rule, any other principle would allow a free-for-all fight for possession, especially where the true owner is not known.

If the finder hands the property to another person in order to find the owner, it is clear that the finder is not relinquishing any rights to the property and can reclaim it if the owner is not found. Commonly, the property is handed to the occupier of the premises where it has been found. Should the occupier have any rights, it will be as a result of occupation rather than because of the handing over of the object.[13]

(iii) *Finder – occupier disputes*

This is where the real problems have arisen. The difficult question is whether occupation of land carries rights to chattels whose existence the occupier is ignorant of. The question can quite often be side-stepped by applying one of three rules.

(a) Wrongdoers

The idea that a finder could unlawfully enter another person's land and claim property found on that land has been found repulsive by many judges. This is especially the case where there is an intention to steal the property (that is, not to return it to its true owner even if that person can be identified). The courts are insistent that such finders cannot claim the property; assuming there is no stronger claimant, the occupier is to be treated as being entitled to possession. As Donaldson LJ pointed out in *Parker* v *British Airways Board*,[14] examples of this rule are virtually non-existent. However, it can be observed in several cases based on theft.[15]

The best known of these cases is probably *Hibbert* v *McKiernan*,[16] in which the accused had taken golf balls, lost by players, from a golf course. The case raised the issue whether the golf club, as occupiers, could be treated as possessing the lost golf balls. Lord Goddard CJ[17] thought it unnecessary to resolve the general rights of occupiers: 'Every householder or occupier of land means or intends to exclude thieves and wrongdoers from the property occupied by him, and this confers on him a special property in goods found on his land sufficient to support an indictment.' Inevitably, this special property would also allow the occupier to claim a better right to possession, relative to the thief.[18]

This rule seems pretty well established for trespassers who possess the mens rea for theft. It is not so clear how the rule will apply to those who enter as lawful visitors but who

---

[12] *Costello* v *Derbyshire Chief Constable* [2001] 1 WLR 1437; *Webb* v *Merseyside Chief Constable* [2000] QB 427. Hickey in *Modern Studies in Property Law*, Vol 7 (ed Hopkins), Chapter 18, is critical of this protection of thieves.

[13] *Parker* v *British Airways Board* [1982] QB 1004.

[14] [1982] QB 1004. See also *Bird* v *Fort Frances* [1949] OR 292.

[15] *Cartwright* v *Green* (1803) 8 Ves 405 (32 ER 412) (carpenter finding money in bureau being repaired); *R* v *Rowe* (1859) Bell 93 (169 ER 1180) (taking iron from bottom of canal).

[16] [1948] 2 KB 142; Hickey (2006) 26 LS 584.

[17] Ibid, at pp 149–150.

[18] Harris in Guest (ed), *Oxford Essays in Jurisprudence* (First Series), at p 96.

stray slightly beyond their permission in finding the object. An example would be a person who finds a lost object on grass adjacent to a path which is being lawfully used as access to a front door of a house.[19] One can but guess as to the outcome.

(b) Agreement

A finder who is not a trespasser will nearly always have permission to be on the premises. The terms of this permission may expressly or implicitly limit the rights of the finder, especially where the object is an integral part of the realty and it is found in the course of work being done on the premises.[20] Express provision for finding may be made in some formal agreements,[21] but it is unclear how readily terms will be implied to cut down finders' rights.

(c) Employees and agents

There is extensive authority that employees and agents must account to their employers and principals for property received by reason of the employment.[22] A good example is the Irish case of *M'Dowell* v *Ulster Bank*,[23] in which Palles CB held that a bank porter could not keep bank notes found whilst sweeping out the bank floor. This most obviously applies where property is found on the employer's premises. Especially where there is public access to the premises, it can readily be taken to be one of an employee's responsibilities to hand in lost property.[24]

Where property is found elsewhere, it may be more difficult to prove that the finding is in the course of the employment, rather than the employment being merely the occasion of the finding.[25] There is little English authority, but dicta support the employer.[26] Indeed, Donaldson LJ in *Parker* appeared to suggest that the same applies to independent contractors who find property,[27] but the cases offer no support.

(d) Other situations[28]

Outside the three situations described, there has been considerable dispute as to the occupier's claim. It is possible to reconcile the decisions in the cases only by qualifying what the judges have held.

---

[19] Marshall (1949) 2 CLP 68 at pp 83–84, also raising the question whether it must be an intentional trespass.

[20] *Parker* v *British Airways Board* [1982] QB 1004 at p 1010.

[21] As in the lease in *City of London Corporation* v *Appleyard* [1963] 1 WLR 982 and in some building contracts (Hoath [1990] Conv 348 at p 357).

[22] Most cases are unrelated to finding. Well-known examples include *Parker* v *McKenna* (1874) LR 10 Ch App 96; *Att-Gen* v *Goddard* (1929) 98 LJKB 743; *Reading* v *Att-Gen* [1951] AC 507.

[23] (1899) 33 ILT 225. See also *Willey* v *Synan* (1937) 57 CLR 200 (boatswain finding coins aboard ship).

[24] In this context, the handing in is likely to be seen as a surrender of any rights as finder: *Willey* v *Synan* (1937) 57 CLR 200; *Grafstein* v *Holme & Freeman* (1958) 12 DLR 2d 727 (see Sommerfeld (1958) 36 Can BR 558).

[25] *Byrne* v *Hoare* [1965] Qd 135 (majority held police officer entitled to property found on private premises); contrast *Crinion* v *Minister for Justice* [1959] Ir Jur Rep 15.

[26] *City of London Corporation* v *Appleyard* [1963] 1 WLR 982 at p 988; *Hannah* v *Peel* [1945] KB 509 at p 519; *Parker* v *British Airways Board* [1982] QB 1004 at pp 1014, 1017.

[27] [1982] QB 1004 at p 1014. Any reliance upon *City of London Corporation* v *Appleyard* [1963] 1 WLR 982 appears unjustified.

[28] The cases and writings in this area are fully reviewed by Hickey, *Property and the Law of Finders*, Chapter 2 (see also Chapters 5 and 6).

Things attached to or under the land

Pollock and Wright[29] support the occupier regarding such things, based upon the occupier's power and intent to exclude unauthorised interference. Examples are rings found in mud at the bottom of a pool in *South Staffordshire Water Company* v *Sharman*,[30] a prehistoric boat found six feet below the surface in *Elwes* v *Brigg Gas Company*[31] and bank notes found in a wall safe in *City of London Corporation* v *Appleyard*.[32] In *Parker*,[33] Donaldson LJ accepted the superior rights of the occupier in such cases, partly on the theory that what is found in these cases constitutes part of the land.[34]

This theory was adopted by the Court of Appeal in *Waverley BC* v *Fletcher*.[35] The finder had used a metal detector to find a gold brooch some nine inches below the surface of a public park.[36] The court held that the local authority owning the park had a superior right to the brooch. To support the part of the land theory, reliance was placed upon the likelihood of damaging the land and the fact that the true owner is less likely to be discovered than when property is found on land. Even if this last point is correct as a matter of fact, it is questionable why the law should favour the landowner. Nevertheless, the case shows that the finder will rarely have rights to things found in or attached to land.

Things found on land

Greater uncertainty surrounds things found on the land. The first major case in this area, *Bridges* v *Hawkesworth*[37] in 1851, involved bank notes dropped on the floor of a shop. The court held that the finder had a better title than the occupier. The decision was sharply distinguished in *Sharman* because the notes had been found in a public area of the shop in *Bridges*, not a factor emphasised in *Bridges* itself. Academic response to *Bridges* was hostile,[38] although it was followed in *Hannah* v *Peel*.[39] Lord Russell CJ in *Sharman*[40] had stated the principle as follows: 'where a person has possession of house or land, with a manifest intention to exercise control over it and the things which may be upon it or in it, then, if something is found on that land, whether by an employee of the owner or by a stranger, the presumption is that the possession of that thing is in the owner of the locus in quo'. Subsequent dicta have both denied[41] and accepted[42] that the reference to 'on the land' constituted an extension of the 'attached to or under' test.[43] In any event, the scene

---

[29] *Possession in the Common Law* (1888), p 41.
[30] [1896] 2 QB 44. See also *R* v *Rowe* (1859) Bell 93 (169 ER 1180) (iron on bed of canal).
[31] (1886) 33 Ch D 562.
[32] [1963] 1 WLR 982.
[33] [1982] QB 1004 at p 1017.
[34] But *Elwes* v *Brigg Gas Company* (1886) 33 Ch D 562, in the context of the rights of a tenant, does not accept this theory (pp 569–570). Nor would the theory seem to deny the rights of the true owner of the object.
[35] [1996] QB 334.
[36] For public parks, see MacMillan (1995) 58 MLR 101.
[37] (1851) 15 Jur 1079; 21 LJQB 75.
[38] Especially Goodhart (1929) 3 CLJ 195, reprinted in *Essays in Jurisprudence and the Common Law* (1931).
[39] [1945] KB 509.
[40] [1896] 2 QB 44 at p 47. The case could have been decided on the basis that the finder was an employee.
[41] *City of London Corporation* v *Appleyard* [1963] 1 WLR 982 at p 987.
[42] *Hannah* v *Peel* [1945] KB 509 at p 518.
[43] *Waverley BC* v *Fletcher* [1996] QB 334 rejects any need to prove a manifest intention to exercise control when the thing is attached to or under the land.

was set for dispute as to whether the occupier's rights were grounded on the exclusion of others, de facto control or an intention to possess.[44]

The issue subsequently resurfaced in the Court of Appeal in *Parker* v *British Airways Board*,[45] in which a passenger found a gold bracelet in an airport lounge. In finding in favour of the passenger, the court displayed an approach more favourable to finders than many commentators had expected. Donaldson LJ accepted the test in *Sharman*, stressing the requirement that, for the occupier to succeed, 'the occupier's intention to exercise control over anything which might be on the premises was manifest'.[46]

This requirement is destructive of the argument that occupiers always have better rights to things found on their land, but it does leave the boundaries unclear. The intention to exercise control may be implied where it is obvious, as in the case of property found in a bank vault. Eveleigh LJ added that owners of private houses restrict access and that this would invariably be enough to make the intention manifest. It seems probable that we have returned in substance to the public/private distinction drawn in *Sharman*. This distinction is not strictly the legal test (so we need not bother with what technically counts as public), but it is likely to be a major factor in deciding whether the intention to exercise control has been made manifest.

Donaldson LJ buttressed his analysis by arguing that an occupier in possession of lost objects is under a duty to inform the rightful owners and to care for the objects. Where such obligations seem inappropriate, the occupier should not be treated as possessing the lost objects.[47] However, this analysis seems difficult to apply. Similar problems could apply as regards objects attached to or under the land and yet they have caused no difficulty. Nor did they deter Eveleigh LJ from asserting possession in the occupier of a house. Although the duty of care of a finder is clear,[48] any duty prior to discovery of the object is unlikely to be onerous.

Finally, it is occupation rather than ownership of the land which gives rise to possession of objects on the land. In *Hannah* v *Peel*,[49] an owner who had never been in possession failed as against an honest finder. Although Birkett J had not stressed the absence of possession, *Appleyard* treated it as the crucial feature. It is unclear whether a non-possessing owner would have rights to things attached to or under the land, at least where they do not amount to fixtures.

(iv) *Finder – predecessor in title disputes*

Who has the better right as between a finder (assumed to be also the occupier) and that person's predecessor? The problem is as follows. The predecessor may be treated as having been in possession of the lost object by virtue of possession of the land. Unless that

---

[44] See the summary in Goodhart (1929) 3 CLJ 195; also *Hannah* v *Peel* [1945] KB 509 at pp 516–517.
[45] [1982] QB 1004. See Roberts (1982) 45 MLR 683; Kohler [1993] CLP Part 1 69, p 90.
[46] [1982] QB 1004 at p 1014.
[47] The same point had been relied upon in *Bridges* v *Hawkesworth* (1851) 15 Jur 1079; 21 LJQB 75.
[48] *Newman* v *Bourne & Hollingsworth* (1915) 31 TLR 209. The basis of the duty is discussed by Hickey in *Modern Studies in Property Law*, Vol 4 (ed Cooke), Chapter 5, doubting the bailment analysis employed by Donaldson LJ.
[49] [1945] KB 509. See also MacMillan (1995) 58 MLR 101 as regards public parks.

possession of the object is given up on selling the land, it remains superior (as prior in time) to that of the purchaser of the land who finds the object. This raises the question whether a conveyance passes lost objects in or on the land.

Perhaps surprisingly, there is no clear answer. In *Moffatt* v *Kazana*,[50] the conveyance was held not to include bank notes hidden in the loft, but there the seller was also the true owner of the bank notes. Although the reasoning is unhelpful to purchasers, the case does not resolve rights to property belonging to a third party.[51] It has been suggested[52] that rights based on occupation alone should pass as a common law incident of ownership. This is a sensible idea, given that prior occupiers have no better moral claim than the finder. Unfortunately, it is not supported by authority.

Where the finder is a tenant under a lease and the thing was attached to or under the land at the time of the grant, the freeholder has the better right.[53] The lawful possession enjoyed by the tenant is second in time to the freeholder's possession, and the lease is unlikely to be interpreted as conferring rights upon the tenant. The same applies if an object is lawfully removed by the tenant – the normal implication is that it belongs to the landlord, though the tenant may have a right to remove and dispose of it (applicable to rubble, for example). Thus, a valuable Banksy mural, cut from a wall, was held to belong to the landlord in *Creative Foundation* v *Dreamland Leisure Ltd*.[54] However, it may be argued that, for things found on the land, the ultimate question should turn on the control exercised by the landlord and the tenant.[55] On this basis, the tenant may be able to claim as finder under the rules in *Parker*.

B. Things found in chattels

There are not many cases in this area, although one would expect the principles to be similar to those applying to land. The facts of *Merry* v *Green*[56] provide an excellent example of the problems that can arise. After buying a bureau at auction, the purchaser found a secret drawer containing a purse. It was held that delivery of the bureau was insufficient to pass possession of the contents, there being no intention that contents should pass to the purchaser. This reasoning is satisfactory if the seller was the owner of the purse (it accords with *Moffatt*), but it is highly inconvenient if it had been owned by a third party (as appears to have been the case). Indeed, if sale does not pass rights to the contents, it is not clear that the seller of the bureau (not being the owner of the contents) can claim possession. *Appleyard* accepted the proposition that possession of an object generally includes possession of its contents. Although that case did not involve buyer and seller, it embodies a more satisfactory principle.[57]

---

[50] [1969] 2 QB 152. It would be much easier to argue in favour of the purchaser if the property had amounted to a fixture.

[51] Outside the land context, *Merry* v *Green* (1841) 7 M&W 623 (151 ER 916), discussed in the next section, supports the seller.

[52] Hoath [1990] Conv 348.

[53] *Elwes* v *Brigg Gas Company* (1886) 33 Ch D 562. This appears to give rise to a most unfortunate distinction between a lessee for 999 years and a purchaser.

[54] [2016] Ch 253.

[55] Kohler [1993] CLP Part 1 69, p 90.

[56] (1841) 7 M&W 623 (151 ER 916). The case concerned a fraudulent taking and issues of theft; it might be distinguished on this basis.

[57] See (1964) 80 LQR 151.

C. Treasure

Special rules apply where the object is treasure. It then belongs to the Crown, although compensation is normally paid. In the modern law, the rules are designed to ensure that hidden treasure is available to museums, which in effect have the opportunity to buy it from the finder. The property is returned if it is disclaimed by the Crown.[58] A finder who fails to disclose treasure is liable to prosecution.[59]

Until the Treasure Act 1996, the area was governed by ancient common law principles. These contained numerous flaws, notably that they applied only to gold and silver objects and then only where they had been hidden: loss or abandonment would not suffice.[60] With increasing numbers of archaeological finds with metal detectors, these deficiencies became glaring, and the Treasure Act 1996[61] now regulates the area.

The Act applies to gold and silver objects with a 10% precious metal content and to finds of more than 10 coins, provided that they are at least 300 years old.[62] Although this extends to objects which are part of the same find (such as a pot containing coins), it is important to note that objects of historical or archaeological importance are not automatically included. However, there is power to extend the provisions by statutory instrument to objects over 200 years old; this power has been exercised for certain prehistoric objects.

There is a Code of Practice which sets out the principles upon which compensation is to be calculated and to whom it is to be paid.[63] A finder who has permission to search will receive the compensation, though illegality, other inappropriate conduct or trespassing will result in some or all of the payment being made to the occupier. Accidental finds will result in sharing between the finder and occupier. Where the occupier has no right to give permission to search or has a weaker right to the object than the landowner, then the payment will normally be to the landowner.

The cost of compensation is to be borne by the museum to which the object has been transferred. Rather oddly, there is no provision for compensation unless the object is transferred to a museum, though compensation is, of course, unnecessary if the object is disclaimed. Apparently, the Secretary of State could decide that the object be transferred to a body other than a museum[64] or, for example, that it be displayed in 10 Downing Street, without triggering compensation. It is possible that *ex gratia* compensation might be paid.

---

[58] Treasure Act 1996, s 6.

[59] Ibid, s 8. There may also be a prosecution for theft: *R v Hancock* [1990] 2 QB 242.

[60] *Att-Gen of the Duchy of Lancaster* v *GE Overton (Farms) Ltd* [1982] Ch 277; *Att-Gen* v *Trustees of the British Museum* [1903] 2 Ch 598. Hickey [2016] Conv 28 argues that abandonment is not (and should not) be recognised as a way of divesting title; cf Waring in *Landmark Cases in Property Law* (ed Douglas, Hickey and Waring), Chapter 11.

[61] Marston and Ross [1997] Conv 273, [1998] Conv 252; Bray [2013] Conv 265.

[62] Treasure Act 1996, s 1; single coins are excluded, even if gold or silver. Occasionally, the pre-Act rules as to what constitutes treasure may be wider. If so, the Treasure Act 1996 still applies.

[63] Ibid, ss 10, 11 (Code, paras 71–84); the Code also deals with the return of disclaimed objects (para 50). Prior to the Act, compensation was paid to the finder.

[64] Ibid, s 6, confers apparently unlimited power on the Secretary of State to direct transfer or disposal of the object.

2. Adverse possession

Within nearly every area of law, court actions must be brought within a certain time. For example, actions for breach of contract must be brought within six years. In the property setting, a special effect of these limitation rules may be to extinguish property rights after the relevant period has elapsed: 12 years[65] for unregistered land and six years for chattels. This section concentrates upon adverse possession of land. If S enters O's land without permission and stays there for 12 years, O's rights may be extinguished; S will be the new owner. This is much stronger than simply saying that O cannot sue S for the benefits obtained by S in the past, as O loses all future rights as well.

It is, however, most important to note that completely new procedures have been introduced for registered land by the Land Registration Act 2002 (hereafter LRA, or 2002 Act). Their effect is to restrict adverse possession (unless uncontested) to boundary disputes. Indeed, adverse possession never operates automatically against registered estates: an application for registration is a minimum requirement.

Adverse possession raises a number of challenging issues. It is, in the words of Professor Wade,[66] a 'remarkably efficient catalyst for revealing the fundamental notions of title to land and of the system of estates'. In particular, it provides interesting analyses of possession. An obvious question is why the law is so favourable to squatters. We shall see that most of the reasons are no longer thought to be compelling, resulting in the changes in the 2002 Act.

One important factor, even though not featured in all legal analyses, is whether S believes that he or she owns the disputed land. Frequently, the disputed land is next to S's plot and is believed by S to be part of it. Alternatively, there may be some technical defect in S's title, of which S is unaware. In both of these cases, S believes it to be his or her land, and the courts generally welcome the result that S succeeds. Adverse possession here serves to clarify S's title. Contrast the case where S enters land knowing that it belongs to somebody else. Here, the courts are much less inclined to lean in S's favour: S can be treated as a land thief, not deserving to benefit by adverse possession.[67]

With chattels, a thief cannot take advantage of limitation rules, although a subsequent bona fide purchaser can do so.[68] Generally, it is not a crime to take possession of another's land. However, trespassing in a residential building was criminalised in 2012. It was argued in *R (Best)* v *Chief Land Registrar*[69] that this precluded adverse possession. The Court of Appeal disagreed: the 2012 legislation was not intended to limit adverse possession, for which there were strong policy justifications.[70]

---

[65] Thirty years for Crown land (60 years if foreshore): Limitation Act 1980, Sched 1, Part II.

[66] (1962) 78 LQR 541.

[67] Note the description of the claim in *Lambeth LBC* v *Bigden* (2000) 33 HLR 478 at p 482: 'millions of pounds worth of public housing stock in one of the poorest boroughs in the country has passed gratis into private ownership'.

[68] Limitation Act 1980, s 4.

[69] [2016] QB 23; the relevant legislation was the Legal Aid, Sentencing and Punishment of Offenders Act 2012, s 144.

[70] Sales and McCombe LJJ employed an illegality analysis, whereas Arden LJ preferred to base her approach on construction of the legislation. The majority placed stress on the analogous position in prescription of easements: *Bakewell Management Co Ltd* v *Brandwood* [2004] 2 AC 519 (p 541 below).

Nevertheless, adverse possession reflects dislike of deliberate wrongdoers in two ways. First, the courts, especially in the past,[71] tended to operate the rules in such a way as to diminish the intentional squatter's chances of success. That is not to say that such claims always failed, simply that they faced a series of hurdles that would often deny success. Much more importantly, the intentional squatter will nearly always be debarred from adverse possession under the new rules introduced by the 2002 Act.

Discussion of adverse possession will focus on four issues. The first will be the justification for having adverse possession rules. Next, we will consider the rules for registered land: these will govern the great majority of future cases. Then will come the question of what suffices as adverse possession, a much litigated issue. Finally, we will consider the effect of adverse possession. This has caused huge problems where leases are involved.

A. Justifications for adverse possession

One justification for any limitation rule is the elimination of stale claims. Where the events complained of took place in the distant past, it can be difficult to prove the claim and, just as important, to prove defences: litigation can become too much of a lottery. This argument is less significant as regards title to land, because titles are normally document-based and this evidence of title can still be reliable even after many years have passed.

Another justification is that those who sleep on their rights should not be able to enforce them years later. In a similar vein, the law seeks to encourage effective land use, and this is stultified if an owner cannot be bothered to use the land.[72] Persons with future interests have no concern with current possession and cannot be said to sleep on their rights. Accordingly, limitation rules do not operate to extinguish future interests, including the landlord's reversion to a lease.[73] Time begins to run when these interests come into possession, the time when their holders have the right to object. On the other hand, it is a mistake to think that fault on the part of O must be shown.[74] This is particularly clear in the case of chattels. A purchaser in good faith from a thief will obtain a good title after six years, regardless of O's inability to trace the thief or the purchaser.[75]

Why is sleeping on rights objectionable? From S's point of view, it may be unjust to allow very old claims to be asserted.[76] S may have treated the land as his or her own for many years and may well have built upon it or made other improvements.[77] In some

---

[71] More recent cases readily support S: *Red House Farms (Thorndon) Ltd v Catchpole* [1977] 2 EGLR 125; *Buckinghamshire CC v Moran* [1990] Ch 623; *Colchester BC v Smith* [1991] Ch 448 (upheld [1992] Ch 421); *JA Pye (Oxford) Ltd v Graham* [2003] 1 AC 419.

[72] An argument raised by the UK in *JA Pye (Oxford) Ltd v United Kingdom* (2007) 46 EHHR 1083.

[73] See p 87 below.

[74] *Rains v Buxton* (1880) 14 Ch D 537. Adverse possession of underground strata (or a cellar, as in *Rains*) may well not be obvious; nor is it necessary for O to be aware of his title (*Palfrey v Palfrey* (1973) 229 EG 1593). (But see p 80 below as to what is required for adverse possession.)

[75] Limitation Act 1980, ss 2, 4; *RB Policies at Lloyds v Butler* [1950] 1 KB 76 (on the law before 1980) and *Kurtha v Marks* [2008] EWHC 336 (QB) at [8].

[76] Or even cruelty: Best CJ in *A'Court v Cross* (1825) 3 Bing 329 at p 333 (130 ER 540 at p 541).

[77] *Cholmondeley v Clinton* (1820) 2 Jac&W 1 at p 140 (37 ER 527 at p 577).

respects, adverse possession may be seen as a form of estoppel: S has been encouraged to spend money on the land because of O's acquiescence.[78] Yet, there are considerable differences. Crucially, adverse possession depends upon the passing of time rather than upon proof of detrimental reliance.

The argument in favour of S is based upon two principal factors. The first is that a person who has occupied land over an extensive period is likely to treat it as if that person owns it. This is especially significant where S is unaware that the land is owned by another person. The law is likely to lead to criticism and even violence if old claims are pursued. The second factor is that, where S is aware that another person is the true owner, the most efficient use of the land will be stultified if O can at any time reclaim the land and take advantage of any improvements S may make. These are convincing reasons, but they do not tell the full story. It has been seen that future interests are not subject to limitation rules until they fall into possession. This is difficult to square with analyses, as just discussed, that put the major emphasis on the position of S.

Conveyancing justifications

A rather different justification for adverse possession is that it renders conveyancing workable.[79] In the nature of things, it is usually impossible to prove conclusive ownership of the fee simple: to do that, it would be necessary to trace title back through vast numbers of documents to a Crown grant many centuries ago. Adverse possession, however, means that proof of exercise of rights to the land over a reasonable period can generally be relied upon as defeating any earlier ownership claim. However, there are limits to this: possession as if owner for 12 years does not necessarily guarantee a good title to the land. The most notorious problem concerns long leases, where the freeholder can still assert title to the land when the leasehold term eventually expires.

Nevertheless, long possession is generally treated as a good indicator that a vendor of land has a good title. This is reflected in the modern rule[80] that the vendor must produce title deeds dating back at least 15 years. In practice, it is most unusual for land to be sold by a person who has no entitlement to it at all. Where there is an ownership problem, it is more likely to be based upon inaccuracy concerning boundaries or the incorrect execution of deeds; these problems are highly likely to be cured by adverse possession.

These factors provide a cogent justification for adverse possession. Without it, the purchase of land could not avoid being considerably more complex, unsafe and expensive. However, this justification overlooks the significance of registration of titles to land. Once a title is registered, this removes any uncertainty as to the state of the title.[81] Indeed, to allow adverse possession can be argued to be inconsistent with the principle that the register should be exclusive evidence of ownership of land. Now that all but relatively few titles are registered, the conveyancing justification for adverse possession is undermined.

---

[78] Singer (1988) 40 Stanford LR 611, especially pp 665–670; Nield [2004] Conv 123.
[79] Goodman (1970) 33 MLR 281; Dockray [1985] Conv 272.
[80] Law of Property Act 1969, s 23, subject to express contractual provision.
[81] Even though only general boundaries are guaranteed: see p 238 below.

Reform of adverse possession

The disappearance of the conveyancing justification is so significant that the Law Commission[82] concluded that adverse possession is no longer justified in registered land, save in a very few cases. The reasons in its favour were thought to be outweighed by an appreciation that it fails to draw an appropriate balance between O and S and conflicts with the 'fundamental concept of indefeasibility of title' in registered land. Neuberger J stated in *JA Pye (Oxford) Ltd* v *Graham*[83] that the law is 'illogical and disproportionate': illogical because the owner cannot be seen to have done anything wrong, and disproportionate because the squatter can obtain an undeserved windfall at the expense of the owner. However, some writers have stressed that the position is not so one-sided: there remain legitimate reasons for supporting adverse possession of registered land.[84]

The Land Registration Act 2002 now limits adverse possession to three types of case. The first is where O fails to assert rights to the land when given an opportunity to do so. This meets the policy objective of ensuring that the land can be efficiently used when there is clear sleeping on rights. The second is where S reasonably believes that the land is part of S's adjoining plot. This covers the problem that boundaries in the documents (and the register) commonly fail to reflect the position on the ground, coupled with the fact that registration guarantees only the general boundary, not its precise line.[85] These two possibilities are well justified: it is important that the register should accord with reality.[86]

Finally, where S can lay claim to the land on grounds other than adverse possession, then adverse possession can be relied upon. This is intended to apply, for example, where O has acquiesced in S's use of the land, giving rise to an estoppel claim. This third case is not really an example of adverse possession at all.

Human rights consideration

Following the comments of Neuberger J (echoed by Lords Bingham and Hope in the House of Lords),[87] there was extensive discussion of the compatibility of adverse possession with human rights. This debate was conducted almost entirely in the context of registered land before the 2002 reforms. It is generally accepted that adverse possession plays a useful role in settling titles in unregistered land. As for registered land today, the 2002 Act both limits adverse possession and protects O against inadvertently losing ownership. Now that we have an authoritative ruling of the European Court of Human Rights in *JA Pye (Oxford) Ltd* v *United Kingdom*,[88] the earlier cases can be dealt with quickly.

Strauss QC held in *Beaulane Properties Ltd* v *Palmer*[89] that adverse possession, as it operated in registered land prior to the 2002 Act, was inconsistent with Article 1 of the

---

[82] Law Com No 271, paras 14.1–14.4; see also Law Com No 254, paras 10.5–10.19. Scots Law Com No 222, Part 35 appears to take a different view, although the effect of registration is different in Scotland.
[83] [2000] Ch 676 at p 710.
[84] Clarke (2004) 57 CLP 239, at pp 245–263 (though her views as to the impact of the new legislation may be too alarmist); Cobb and Fox (2007) 27 LS 236.
[85] Although the disputed area may be far greater than might be uncertain under the general boundaries principle.
[86] Cf the reintroduction of adverse possession in New South Wales: Part VIA of the Real Property Act, 1900 (inserted in 1979); Woodman and Butt (1980) 54 ALJ 79.
[87] *JA Pye (Oxford) Ltd* v *Graham* [2003] 1 AC 419 at [2], [73].
[88] (2007) 46 EHRR 1083 (Grand Chamber).
[89] [2006] Ch 79; Cloherty and Fox [2005] CLJ 558.

First Protocol (peaceful enjoyment of possessions). Despite the judge's lengthy review of the material, the result was surprising: the Court of Appeal in *Pye* had been unpersuaded of the human rights argument. Whilst it can certainly be argued that the pre-2002 law failed to strike an appropriate balance between O and S, it is less clear that it falls outside the range of proportionate responses: much depends upon an assessment of the arguments (summarised earlier) in favour of adverse possession.

The question then went to the European Court of Human Rights in *JA Pye (Oxford) Ltd v United Kingdom*. It may be observed that the facts in *Pye* arose before the Human Rights Act 1998 was in force, so there was no opportunity for the House of Lords to deal with the question. Adverse possession engages A1P1, as seen in Chapter 3.[90] The principal point of difficulty was as to how far the adverse possession rules constitute a proportionate response to the issues. By the barest of majorities, the court initially held the rules to be disproportionate and upheld the application.[91] However, the Grand Chamber reversed that finding by a 10:7 majority: the legislation was within the wide margin of appreciation allowed to national legislatures, especially in areas of complex law involving rights between individuals.

The decision in *Pye* is conclusive that human rights considerations do not strike down the adverse possession rules; this has been confirmed by the English courts.[92] A fortiori, there can be no successful human rights challenge as regards either unregistered land or the 2002 Act rules for registered land. The arguments raised in *Pye* were only ever powerful for the obsolescent operation of LRA 1925.

The human rights outcome does not, of course, mean that the judges thought that the 2002 Act changes were not desirable. The differences between the judges reflect some difference in perception as to the benefits of adverse possession,[93] but owe more to contrasting approaches to the margin of appreciation allowed to legislatures. Whatever the human rights outcome, the 2002 reforms have widespread (if not universal) support.

B. Adverse possession against registered estates

The first point to note is that we are dealing with claims to registered estates. If adverse possession is sought against an unregistered interest, then the new scheme will not apply even if the fee simple is registered. This is relevant, for example, to adverse possession as against another (unregistered) adverse possessor.[94]

When there is a claim to a registered estate, the old rules as to the effect of adverse possession are disapplied[95] and S must rely on the far more demanding provisions of LRA, Sched 6. It may be added that adverse possession completed before the 2002 Act continues to be governed by the old law,[96] so some claims under the old law will continue to be litigated.

---

[90] See p 19 above.
[91] (2006) 43 EHHR 43; 4:3 majority.
[92] *Ofulue* v *Bossert* [2009] Ch 1 (welcomed by Dixon [2008] Conv 160); this was not challenged on appeal to the House of Lords: [2009] AC 990 at [72].
[93] This is seen most clearly in the dissent of Judges Loucaides and Kovler.
[94] Law Com No 271, para 14.10, Explanatory Notes, para 436(iv).
[95] LRA, s 96.
[96] Ibid, Sched 12, para 18.

There are three possible stages: application by S, resolution of an objection by O and further application by S.

(i) *Applying for registration*

After 10 years of adverse possession of a registered estate, S may apply under para 1 to be registered as proprietor. The use of 10 years for adverse possession is designed to match more general proposed reforms of limitation rules.[97] Paragraph 1 involves points which are foreign to older concepts of adverse possession. Thus, a new requirement is that adverse possession must be for the *last* 10 years, no matter how long adverse possession may have lasted in the past.

There is an essential relaxation for cases where S has been in adverse possession for 10 years but has been evicted (without a court order) within the past six months. This ensures that O cannot negate S's rights to registration, very limited as such rights are, by evicting S. Specific rules apply to court proceedings by O. O cannot avoid S's limited rights to registration by a pre-emptive application for a court order, as no order can be made if adverse possession entitles S to be registered as proprietor.[98] On the other hand, S cannot apply under para 1 if there are pending proceedings against him or her asserting O's right to possession,[99] or if there has been a judgment for possession within the past two years.

The application by itself confers no right to be registered. It triggers notification by the registrar to the proprietor of the estate in question.[100] If there is objection to registration, then the rules detailed in the following section will apply. If there is no objection, then registration of S as proprietor will automatically follow.[101] Here, we see one of the policy objectives coming into play: if O is unwilling to assert any claim to the land, then S should be registered so that best use of the land may be made.

One point to observe is that notification will be given to O at the address held by the land registry. If this is the disputed land (or is out of date), then it will not reach O, and registration of S is almost inevitable.[102] Many examples of adverse possession have involved owners who control large areas of land (making it difficult for them to exercise practical control). These owners will almost always have addresses at which they can be notified, and they are likely to object. This factor is likely to dissuade many adverse possessors from making applications.[103]

(ii) *Resolution of objections*

If O objects, registration will be refused unless one of three conditions is satisfied.[104] The first is where it would be unconscionable by reason of an equity by estoppel for O to

---

[97] Law Com No 270, para 4.130; Law Com No 271, para 14.19.
[98] LRA, s 98, referring to Sched 6, para 5(4) (contested boundaries).
[99] Paragraph 1(3). This did not apply where O sought an antisocial behaviour injunction (based on S's trespass): *Swan Housing Association Ltd* v *Gill* [2013] 1 WLR 1253.
[100] Schedule 6, para 2: other persons (such as chargees) also have to be notified.
[101] Ibid, paras 3, 4: objection has to be made within 65 business days: Land Registration Rules 2003, r 65.
[102] Law Com No 271, paras 14.18, 14.34.
[103] Cobb and Fox (2007) 27 LS 236 at p 257.
[104] Schedule 6, para 5.

dispossess S.[105] Because estoppel remedies are discretionary in extent, provision is made for cases where a less extensive remedy than registration is appropriate.[106] The second condition is that S has some other entitlement to be registered. An example is where the money for a purchase has been paid but no transfer has been executed.[107] The Law Commission recognises that it is not strictly necessary to make provision for these two conditions, as S has a good claim regardless of 10 years' adverse possession. However, their intention is to provide a simple procedure to resolve such disputes.[108] It might be added that disputes will be resolved by the adjudicator, a post instituted by the 2002 Act.[109]

The third condition (para 5(4)) is much more interesting. It requires that S already owns adjoining land and reasonably believes that the disputed land belongs to him or her.[110] The timing of the belief has raised some difficulty. Paragraph 5(4) requires that it must last for at least 10 years of adverse possession, but the courts seem to assume that it must be the *last* 10 years.[111] However, these decisions favour the squatter in that the assertion of O's claim is not readily treated as rendering S's longstanding belief immediately unreasonable. Paragraph 5(4) does not apply to the rare case where the boundaries have been fixed, although it is not limited to cases where the boundary line is initially uncertain.[112] It is intended to cover cases where the boundary on the register fails to match that on the ground. This is a common problem. It may result from an encroachment by S's predecessor in title on to O's land, but it is more likely to be the result of inaccurate placing of fences on the initial development of the land.[113]

Several factors combine to ensure the failure of many claims that would have succeeded in the past. The requirement that there be adjoining land is one obvious limiting factor. Furthermore, if S has knowingly encroached on O's land, then it is unlikely that the test of reasonable belief that it belongs to S will be satisfied.[114] A successful claim by S will likely lead to the boundaries being fixed on the register.[115]

(iii) *Further application for registration*

If S's application is unsuccessful under the provisions discussed so far, one further possibility remains. If O fails to take steps to evict S, then para 6 permits S to make a further

---

[105] The links between estoppel and adverse possession are considered by Nield [2004] Conv 123.

[106] Ibid, para 5(2)(b), also s 110(4): Law Com No 271, paras 14.39–14.42. For estoppel remedies, see p 164 below.

[107] *Bridges* v *Mees* [1957] Ch 475 (p 83 below).

[108] Law Com No 271, para 14.36. Law Com CP 227, para 17.32 leaves open whether these two conditions should be retained. Dixon considers that these conditions could be used to reintroduce much of the old law ([2003] Conv 136 at pp 152–153), although this seems improbable.

[109] LRA, s 73 and Part 11; Dixon [2011] Conv 335. But see p 25, n 93 below.

[110] Unreasonable belief on the part of O's solicitor is not fatal: *IAM Group plc* v *Chowdery* [2012] 2 P&CR 282 stresses that it is O whose belief must be reasonable.

[111] *Zarb* v *Parry* [2012] 1 WLR 1240 at [17]; *IAM Group plc* v *Chowdery* [2012] 2 P&CR 282. These cases are persuasively criticised by Milne [2012] Conv 342. Law Com CP 227, para 17.47, proposes that it should be the last 10 years but with six months to apply after the reasonable belief has ended.

[112] O'Connor in *Modern Studies in Property Law*, Vol 4 (ed Cooke), p 208. She puts the case for specific legislation, as found in Commonwealth jurisdictions, to deal with encroachment disputes.

[113] Law Com No 271, para 14.46.

[114] Note that S's successor is likely to satisfy the test but will require a further 10 years' adverse possession. The Law Commission does not regard the reasonable belief test as overly demanding: Law Com No 271, paras 14.50–14.52.

[115] LRA, s 60(3); Law Com No 271, para 9.13.

application after two years. Paragraph 7 provides that such an application automatically gives an entitlement to registration: this time, there is no provision for notification or objection by O. O's objection at the first stage is not enough to provide permanent protection. If O is not prepared to take the land back by evicting S, then effective land management, coupled with the need for a decisive result, supports S's being entitled to the land thereafter.

What requirements are there for a further application to be made? Unsurprisingly, adverse possession must continue for the two years after the rejection of the para 1 application. For example, accepting a licence from O would be fatal. However, there is no need for adverse possession to continue to the date of the para 6 application and no apparent time limit for that application. It follows that, once the two years are completed, it is irrelevant if O evicts S (unless under a court order, as we shall see) or S leaves the land for other reasons. Furthermore, O is debarred from taking court proceedings once S is entitled to make a para 6 application.

However, any one of three factors relating to court proceedings will prevent a para 6 application; they all mirror rules for para 1 applications. The first is that proceedings for possession are being pursued: the law requires that O take steps within two years, not that the process of evicting S be completed. On the other hand, simply telling S to leave is plainly insufficient. The second is that a judgment for possession has been given within the last two years.[116] The time limit shows that O cannot obtain judgment and then do nothing: that would leave future rights to the land too uncertain. Finally (and unsurprisingly), S must not have been evicted from the land pursuant to a court judgment.

(iv) *The relevance of the unregistered land rules*

How relevant is the mountain of case law on what constitutes adverse possession? In theory, the answer is that it all remains relevant, as adverse possession is determined by reference to the old law.[117] However, it may be predicted that many of the problems will in practice disappear. In most cases, S's claim will succeed only if O fails to act. The single example where adverse possession will operate, despite objection by O, concerns boundary disputes between neighbours.[118]

Few of the difficult cases under the pre-2002 law arose in disputes between neighbours. This is especially true as regards issues relating to S's intention. When S reasonably believes the land belongs to him or her, problems regarding intention are unlikely to surface. S must show adverse possession for a para 1 or 6 application, but disputes are improbable if O chooses not to oppose S's application. However, the older difficult cases can become relevant if O either omits to oppose the application or never received notification of it (perhaps because of an outdated address being used). If S has been registered, O can seek to rectify S's new title (under statutory powers to alter the register) on the basis that there was insufficient adverse possession.[119]

---

[116] Where applications can be made under para 1 or para 6 of Schedule 6, s 98(2), (4) provides for judgments to be unenforceable after two years.
[117] Schedule 6, para 11(1).
[118] The other conditions for registration in para 5 are likely to turn on issues other than adverse possession.
[119] *Baxter* v *Mannion* [2011] 1 WLR 1594: omission to oppose.

(v) *Other issues; successive adverse possessors*

Other points arising from the 2002 Act (including the effect of registration of S) will be considered later, when they can usefully be compared with the position for unregistered land. One point which will be dealt with at this stage concerns the effect of there being successive adverse possessors.

If an adverse possessor transfers the land (including the disputed area), then the successor can count both periods together for the purposes of Sched 6.[120] This reflects the present law, but the position is different (and has changed) if S^2 evicts S.[121] S^2 has to start a fresh period of adverse possession, not only as regards S but also as against O. The reason is that, otherwise, S^2 might be able to be registered when S would have a superior claim. An example would be if S had possessed for eight years and then S^2 for five years. Such a result is incompatible with registering S^2 as proprietor.

A minor exception operates if S in turn evicts S^2: S can include the period S^2 was there. In this case, of course, there is little danger of S^2 being able to evict S.[122] It might be added that, because S's interest is not a registered estate, S^2 can employ the old rules of adverse possession against S. It follows that if S^2 is in adverse possession for 12 years, then S's rights are extinguished. The rights of S^2 against O will, of course, be determined by the normal rules applying to registered estates.

C. Requirements for adverse possession

(i) *Possession*

Traditionally, it was said that either O must have discontinued possession (whereupon S has taken possession), or that O must have been dispossessed by S.[123] Although this categorisation is still used, it is rare for O to have discontinued possession[124]: the real question is whether O has been dispossessed (though without any requirement of physical ouster). The categorisation is of little practical use today.[125] In the words of Lord Browne-Wilkinson in *JA Pye (Oxford) Ltd* v *Graham*[126]: 'The question is simply whether the defendant has dispossessed the paper owner by going into ordinary possession of the land for the requisite period without the consent of the owner.'

Possession will be clear in some cases. Examples are if S builds on land, occupies and uses a building[127] or incorporates land into his or her farm, using it just as other land already owned.[128] On the other hand, a mere trespass is not enough: occasional walking

---

[120] Paragraph 11(2)(a).

[121] Paragraph 11(2)(b). For the unregistered land position, see p 87 below.

[122] But might there be a problem if S^2 had enjoyed adverse possession for 12 years and therefore had established a better title than S? There is nothing in Sched 6 to defeat the claim of S^2.

[123] *Rains* v *Buxton* (1880) 14 Ch D 537 at pp 539–540 (or S receives rent from a tenant or licensee who has so acted: *Roberts* v *Swangrove Estates Ltd* [2007] 2 P&CR 326, not challenged on appeal [2008] Ch 439).

[124] Simple non-use is clearly insufficient: *Buckinghamshire CC* v *Moran* [1990] Ch 623.

[125] *Treloar* v *Nute* [1976] 1 WLR 1295 at p 1300; *Buckinghamshire CC* v *Moran* [1990] Ch 623 (Nourse LJ); but see *Hounslow LB* v *Minchinton* (1997) 74 P&CR 221.

[126] [2003] 1 AC 419 at [36]–[38].

[127] *Mount Carmel Investments Ltd* v *Peter Thurlow Ltd* [1988] 1 WLR 1078.

[128] *Seddon* v *Smith* (1877) 36 LT 168; *Bligh* v *Martin* [1968] 1 WLR 804.

over another person's land certainly does not count as adverse possession. It is worth remembering that S's possession must be exclusive possession[129] and that any significant use by O or others will be inconsistent with S's claim.[130]

Most litigated cases involve equivocal conduct, often when O has been content to leave land vacant for the time being. Everything depends upon the circumstances; in particular, the nature of the land can be vitally important. Where land is suitable for very limited uses, it will be relatively easy to show adverse possession. A good example is found in *Red House Farms (Thorndon) Ltd* v *Catchpole*,[131] where a small island had been formed by a river's changing its course. Since the island was unsuitable for any significant agricultural purpose, S's shooting on the land sufficed as adverse possession. Many cases arise from other jurisdictions, where it is common for land to be used less intensively than in the United Kingdom.[132] If the nature of the land is such that it is suitable for use only at certain times of the year, it suffices if it has been used only at those times.[133]

Perhaps the most useful starting point is that fencing the land is a good indicator of possession. It was described as the 'strongest possible evidence' in *Seddon* v *Smith*.[134] Nevertheless, *Seddon* itself held that fencing is not necessary and several cases have held that it is not conclusive. In *Powell* v *McFarlane*,[135] grazing a cow coupled with making hay and limited repairs to the fencing did not suffice; the fact that S was aged 14 at the start made the proof of intention more difficult. Later use of the land by S's business, including erecting a notice board on it, did constitute adverse possession but had not lasted for 12 years. Once one gets to marginal cases of possession, other factors analysed later in this chapter will likely come into play. In particular, it may be disputed whether there is sufficient intention to possess and possibly whether the possession is adverse.

It has already been observed that use of the land by others, in particular by O, will be inconsistent with S's claim. The more ephemeral S's acts of possession, the easier it will be to show that O has acted so as to maintain possession. The presumption that possession lies with the true owner[136] helps to explain why relatively minor acts by O will suffice to keep possession and render S a mere trespasser[137] rather than an adverse possessor. On the other hand, minimal and very occasional activities on O's part will not deny S's claim.[138]

---

[129] Pollock and Wright, *Possession in the Common Law* (1888), p 20. Emphasised in *Powell* v *McFarlane* (1977) 38 P&CR 452 at p 470; *Buckinghamshire CC* v *Moran* [1990] Ch 623 at p 643; *Marsden* v *Miller* (1992) 64 P&CR 239 at p 243.

[130] *Leigh* v *Jack* (1879) 5 Ex D 264 (O repairing fence); *Maguire* v *Browne* (1913) 17 CLR 365; *Bligh* v *Martin* [1968] 1 WLR 804.

[131] [1977] 2 EGLR 125. The principle is generally based on *Lord Advocate* v *Lord Lovat* (1880) 5 App Cas 273 at p 288. A less sympathetic approach was taken in *Wilson* v *Martin's Executors* [1993] 1 EGLR 178.

[132] *Kirby* v *Cowderoy* [1912] AC 599 (British Columbia); *West Bank Estates Ltd* v *Arthur* [1967] 1 AC 665 (West Indies).

[133] *Bligh* v *Martin* [1968] 1 WLR 804; *Hamson* v *Jones* (1988) 52 DLR 4th 143.

[134] (1877) 36 LT 168 at p 169, more fully explained in *Littledale* v *Liverpool College* [1900] 1 Ch 19 at p 25; *Hounslow LB* v *Minchinton* (1997) 74 P&CR 221. Contrast *Boosey* v *Davis* (1987) 55 P&CR 83 (incomplete fencing).

[135] (1977) 38 P&CR 452; this 'remarkable judgment' was approved by the House of Lords in *JA Pye (Oxford) Ltd* v *Graham* [2003] 1 AC 419 at [31].

[136] *Powell* v *McFarlane* (1977) 38 P&CR 452 at p 470.

[137] As in *Leigh* v *Jack* (1879) 5 Ex D 264.

[138] *Red House Farms (Thorndon) Ltd* v *Catchpole* [1977] 2 EGLR 125; *J Alston and Sons Ltd* v *BOCM Pauls Ltd* [2008] EWHC 3310 at [77], [2009] 1 EGLR 93; *Zarb* v *Parry* [2012] 1 WLR 1240. See also Mee [2015] Conv 455.

Nor will O's acts on a small area of the disputed land affect adverse possession of the remainder.[139] Quite clearly, there may be adverse possession where O's acts are permitted by S[140] or are in assertion of a right less than possession.[141]

(ii) *Animus possidendi*

In addition to enjoying physical possession, S must intend to possess. It is commonly said that intention to possess is especially significant where the acts of possession are equivocal.[142] Slade J in *Powell v McFarlane*[143] required 'clear and affirmative evidence that the trespasser . . . not only had the requisite intention to possess, but made such intention clear to the world'. The element of making the intention clear has led to some difficulty. Peter Gibson LJ has stressed that otherwise, it would be unjust to destroy O's rights.[144] On the other hand, S is not prejudiced by choosing to adopt a low profile.[145] More recently, David Richards J has held that, following *Pye*, there is no separate test of whether the possession is obvious to an observer, though factual possession will almost always be apparent to O.[146]

There should be no problems with animus possidendi where S believes that he or she owns the land, as there will naturally be an intention to treat the land as owned.[147] It might be more problematic if S is a tenant of adjoining land and wrongly believes that the landlord is the true owner of the disputed land.[148]

Problems are most likely where S knows that O is the owner. It will be an unusual and outrageous case where S proclaims ownership to the land after evicting O, although doing so will satisfy adverse possession requirements. The more usual case is where O has no current use for the land, but S enters and starts using it. Commonly, the land is vacant and awaiting future development. This type of situation, typical of very many adverse possession disputes, poses genuinely difficult problems. It can be said that S has taken possession wrongfully and that this is enough to trigger the Limitation Act 1980. On the other hand, it seems harsh to penalise O for not evicting S when O has no real objection to S's using the property for the time being. This sort of claim is almost certain to fail under the new rules applicable to registered land, at least where O opposes an application by S.

This situation has manifested itself in various legal issues. It can sometimes be said that S's acts do not amount to possession.[149] More relevant to our present discussion is whether S has the necessary intention.

---

[139] *Topplan Estates Ltd v Townley* [2005] 1 EGLR 89.
[140] *Bligh v Martin* [1968] 1 WLR 804 (acting as S's contractor and, later, lessee).
[141] *Williams v Usherwood* (1981) 45 P&CR 235 (O entered thinking there was a right to enter to maintain the side of his house, but not realising that he was the owner).
[142] *Littledale v Liverpool College* [1900] 1 Ch 19; *Powell v McFarlane* (1977) 38 P&CR 452 (burden of proof is on S when the acts are equivocal).
[143] (1977) 38 P&CR 452 at p 472.
[144] *Prudential Assurance Co Ltd v Waterloo Real Estate Inc* [1999] 2 EGLR 85 at p 87.
[145] *Purbrick v Hackney LB* [2004] 1 P&CR 553 (derelict building used for storing; doorway secured).
[146] *Wretham v Ross* [2005] EWHC 1259 (Ch) at [31]–[32].
[147] Confirmed by *Williams v Usherwood* (1981) 45 P&CR 235 at p 251; *Pulleyn v Hall Aggregates (Thames Valley) Ltd* (1992) 65 P&CR 276; *Roberts v Swangrove Estates Ltd* [2008] Ch 439.
[148] *Batt v Adams* (2001) 82 P&CR 406 held no adverse possession, but contrast *J Alston and Sons Ltd v BOCM Pauls Ltd* [2008] EWHC 3310 at [95], [2009] 1 EGLR 93.
[149] See p 84 below.

The meaning of intention

The Act makes no reference to intention at all and the animus possidendi rules are spelt out of the requirement that the possession be adverse.[150] To require S to intend to possess as owner would be to ask the impossible in most of these cases and would scarcely be consistent with the legislation. The Court of Appeal in *Buckinghamshire CC v Moran*[151] rejected any such strict requirement, and this has been approved by the House of Lords.[152] However, the court did accept that it is necessary to intend to possess to the exclusion of O. It is not fatal that S is aware that a claim persisted in by O must succeed and is prepared, if necessary, to pay rent: the rule does not require S to be prepared to break the law in physically repelling O.[153] Nor does it matter that S believes that rent is being paid; the intention to possess (albeit as tenant) suffices.[154]

The application of intention in the cases

So when will there be the necessary intention if S is aware that O has no present use for the land? In earlier cases, the courts sometimes found in O's favour because there was 'an intent merely to derive some enjoyment from the land wholly consistent with such use as the true owner might wish to make of it'.[155] This was considered by the House of Lords, in *JA Pye (Oxford) Ltd v Graham*,[156] as part of an important review of adverse possession. It was held that too much had been read into the 'adverse' element of adverse possession. There was criticism of earlier cases restricting adverse possession in cases of this type: 'there will be few occasions in which such inference [to occupy until the land is needed by O] could properly be drawn in cases where the true owner has been physically excluded'. However, treating O as having continuing responsibilities for the land will be fatal.[157]

Another type of case in which intention is significant is where S's actions can be seen as being in the exercise of some other right. In *George Wimpey & Co Ltd v Sohn*,[158] S had an easement to use the disputed area as a garden. Although S fenced it so as to prevent entry by strangers, this act of possession could be seen as enhancing the easement. Even though not justified by the easement, S's actions were referable to an intention to enjoy the easement rather than to possession in the *Moran* sense. However, the motive for fencing

---

[150] *Lambeth LBC v Blackburn* (2001) 82 P&CR 494 at [18]; the role of animus is seen as limited at [36]. See also Lord Browne-Wilkinson in *JA Pye (Oxford) Ltd v Graham* [2003] 1 AC 419 at [40].

[151] [1990] Ch 623, criticised by Tee [2000] Conv 113 and [2002] Conv 50 but contrast Radley-Gardner and Harpum [2001] Conv 155. Earlier contrary suggestions in *Littledale v Liverpool College* [1900] 1 Ch 19, *George Wimpey & Co Ltd v Sohn* [1967] Ch 487 and, possibly, *Powell v McFarlane* (1977) 38 P&CR 452 were not clearly expressed and must now be read in the particular contexts of those cases.

[152] *JA Pye (Oxford) Ltd v Graham* [2003] 1 AC 419 at [43].

[153] *Ocean Estates Ltd v Pinder* [1969] 2 AC 19 (PC); *JA Pye (Oxford) Ltd v Graham* [2003] 1 AC 419 at [43], [46]. Slade J in *Powell v McFarlane* (1977) 38 P&CR 452 at pp 471–472 qualifies the intention as follows: 'so far as is reasonably practicable and so far as the processes of the law will allow' (approved in *Moran*).

[154] *Lodge v Wakefield MCC* [1995] 2 EGLR 124.

[155] *Tecbild Ltd v Chamberlain* (1969) 20 P&CR 633 at p 643.

[156] [2003] 1 AC 419; see especially [36]–[38], [45] (Lord Browne-Wilkinson); Thompson [2002] Conv 480. *Pye* was applied by the Privy Council in *Wills v Wills* [2004] 1 P&CR 612.

[157] *Pavledes v Ryesbridge Properties Ltd* (1989) 58 P&CR 459.

[158] [1967] Ch 487. See also *Littledale v Liverpool College* [1900] 1 Ch 19.

is by no means conclusive. Fencing to keep animals in may well constitute intention as developed in *Moran* and *Pye*.[159]

Although we may feel comfortable with the outcome of the modern cases, it may be thought that the concept of possession in English law requires further analysis. It should be added that the role of animus in possession is notoriously controversial.[160]

(iii) *The possession must be adverse*

As has just been seen, *Pye* rejects any special meaning for 'adverse'. However, it remains correct that there is no possession (or dispossession) if there is actual consent by O,[161] and the same is true if the possession is pursuant to a legal right (a lease would be the best example).[162] Where permission is given for a specific period, possession may well become adverse at the termination of that period.[163] In the case of leases, it is presumed for adverse possession purposes that an oral periodic tenancy ends when rent ceases to be paid,[164] although possession will not be adverse if O cannot claim possession.[165]

What is the position if the permission terminates without S being aware? It appears that S does have the necessary intention to possess, despite a belief that possession is by permission of O.[166]

An interesting question concerns what happens if S takes possession under an agreement which is never formally completed by a transfer. It might be thought that O gives consent, so that adverse possession cannot operate. However, that would prevent the use of adverse possession to cure bad titles in this type of case. Fortunately, *Bridges* v *Mees*[167] treated such possession as being adverse.

Nevertheless, some similar cases still cause difficulty. In *ER Ives Investment Ltd* v *High*,[168] the Court of Appeal rejected adverse possession where there was an informal agreement that the foundations of S's building could remain on O's land. Perhaps more difficult is *Hyde* v *Pearce*,[169] in which S took possession under a contract of sale but never

---

[159] *Chambers* v *Havering LBC* [2012] 1 P&CR 373. Differing views were expressed (Etherton LJ at [40]; Lewison LJ at [65]) on the rejection of intention on similar facts in *Inglewood Investment Co Ltd* v *Baker* [2003] 2 P&CR 319.

[160] Dias, *Jurisprudence* (5th edn), Chapter 13, especially pp 275–277 and 289–290. Its origins and role in adverse possession are explored by Radley-Gardner (2005) 25 OxJLS 727.

[161] *Pye* at [37]. In statutory terms, no action will have accrued to O (Limitation Act 1980, s 15) and the possession is not adverse (Limitation Act 1980, Sched 1, para 8).

[162] *Thomas* v *Thomas* (1855) 2 K&J 79 at p 83 (69 ER 701 at p 703); *Hughes* v *Griffin* [1969] 1 WLR 23. The same applies if S is the registered proprietor: *Parshall* v *Hackney* [2013] Ch 568 (criticised by Lees [2013] Conv 222 and Xu (2013) 129 LQR 477) in the context of O and S having competing registered titles.

[163] *Colchester BC* v *Smith* [1991] Ch 448 at p 489; *Sandhu* v *Farooqui* [2004] 1 P&CR 19 at [20].

[164] Limitation Act 1980, Sched 1, para 5; *Hayward* v *Chaloner* [1968] 1 QB 107. This applies even if there is a written agreement for a lease: *Long* v *Tower Hamlets LBC* [1998] Ch 197; Perkins (1997) 113 LQR 394.

[165] *Smith* v *Lawson* (1997) 75 P&CR 466 (estoppel), relying on Limitation Act 1980, Sched 1, para 8.

[166] *J Alston and Sons Ltd* v *BOCM Pauls Ltd* [2008] EWHC 3310 at [100], [2009] 1 EGLR 93, not following the contrary opinion in *Clowes Developments (UK) Ltd* v *Walters* [2006] 1 P&CR 1.

[167] [1957] Ch 475. The reasoning – somewhat questionable – was that consent ended when the unpaid vendor's lien terminated on payment of the purchase price. See also *Palfrey* v *Palfrey* (1973) 229 EG 1593.

[168] [1967] 2 QB 379.

[169] [1982] 1 WLR 560; Dockray (1983) 46 MLR 89.

paid the purchase money. The Court of Appeal held that the original consent under which S entered governed the entire 14 years' possession, with the result that there was no adverse possession. Similarly, in *Sandhu v Farooqui*,[170] consent was said to operate until completion (which never took place) or until there was communication of its withdrawal. One can see that S's claim to the land is far less meritorious than if the money has been paid (as in *Bridges*), but is not the possession more clearly adverse in *Hyde* and *Sandhu*?

Implied permission

A more controversial question has been whether there is an implied licence for S to possess, particularly where O has no current use for the land. Especially in the past, the courts were inclined to favour O in these circumstances. The Court of Appeal in *Wallis's Cayton Bay Holiday Camp Ltd v Shell-Mex & BP Ltd*[171] went so far as to imply a licence automatically in such cases. This controversial analysis was seen as having the effect of defeating the statutory provisions.[172] It has been overturned by the Limitation Act 1980[173] and need not be explored further. However, the 1980 Act still permits the implication of a licence on the facts of the particular case. This is likely to require some form of dealing between S and O, with acts probative of (not merely consistent with) a licence.[174] Simply taking possession of O's land will not justify implying a licence.

A related analysis, found in cases such as *Wallis*,[175] was that there would be no dispossession where O's intended future use of the land was not affected by S's actions. This idea was based upon dicta of Bramwell LJ in *Leigh v Jack*.[176] It was rejected by the Court of Appeal in *Buckinghamshire CC v Moran*[177]; the House of Lords in *Pye* regarded as a 'heresy' the idea that the intention of O may determine whether S is in possession.[178] Whilst it is acceptable to say that S's acts in a particular case are not enough to amount to possession (many of the earlier cases can be so explained), there is no rule that dispossession requires S to act inconsistently with O's intended future user. Factual possession, coupled with an intention to exclude all others, suffices.

Defences

Before leaving this area, it might be added that, at least for unregistered land,[179] the legislation prevents the running of time where the claim is based on S's fraud, deliberate concealment of relevant facts or a mistake.[180] Few adverse possession cases will fall within

---

[170] [2004] 1 P&CR 19 (mortgage fraud, of which the purchaser was unaware).
[171] [1975] QB 94.
[172] *Powell v McFarlane* (1977) 38 P&CR 452 at p 484.
[173] Schedule 1, para 8(4). It is also rejected as a common law concept by *Smith v Molyneaux* [2017] 1 P&CR 80.
[174] Cases include *Batsford Estates (1983) Co Ltd v Taylor* [2006] 2 P&CR 64 (licence found); *Hicks Developments Ltd v Chaplin* [2007] 1 EGLR 1 and *J Alston and Sons Ltd v BOCM Pauls Ltd* [2008] EWHC 3310, [2009] 1 EGLR 93 (no licence); see also n 190 in this chapter.
[175] [1975] QB 94 at pp 115–116 (Ormrod LJ).
[176] (1879) 5 Ex D 264. See also *Williams Brothers Direct Supply Ltd v Raftery* [1958] 1 QB 159 and *Tecbild Ltd v Chamberlain* (1969) 20 P&CR 633, possibly supported by *West Bank Estates Ltd v Arthur* [1967] 1 AC 665.
[177] [1990] Ch 623.
[178] [2003] 1 AC 419 at [45].
[179] See p 86 below for registered land.
[180] Limitation Act 1980, s 32. Innocent purchasers from S are unaffected by this rule.

this rule; it is certainly not enough that it is difficult to discover the adverse possession[181] or that there is a false assertion of title.[182] In any event, time will start to run when O is (or ought to be) aware of the problem.[183] Somewhat differently, if O is under a disability, then there is protection for O in both the unregistered and registered land regimes.[184]

(iv) *Stopping time running*

A question of obvious importance to O is how to stop the time running. The one clear answer is that bringing a claim is effective.[185] However, the stopping of time running depends on the claim's being pursued. If it is not and O brings a further claim after 12 years in total, then S wins.[186] It is certainly not enough merely to demand that S should leave.[187]

If O is unwilling to bring a claim (perhaps because eviction of an elderly possessor would result), can time be stopped by expressly giving permission for the possession to continue? This question was raised in *BP Properties Ltd* v *Buckler*,[188] in which O had told S that she could stay there for life. The Court of Appeal held that, thereafter, O could not have evicted S[189] and the possession could no longer be seen as adverse. It was open to S to reject the licence, but her silence when the permission was given did not amount to rejection.[190] This offers a valuable escape route for O.[191] Remember, however, that S can reject the licence; further, an offer of a *non-gratuitous* licence will not be treated as accepted by silence.[192]

Acknowledging O's title

Turning to conduct of S, a written acknowledgment of O's title will stop time running.[193] This applies if S requests to O not to sell the property[194] or offers to buy from O (or claims a right to do so).[195] Indeed, any acknowledgment (written or not) of O's claim may be

---

[181] *Rains* v *Buxton* (1880) 14 Ch D 537.

[182] *Willis* v *Earl Howe* [1893] 2 Ch 545.

[183] Limitation Act 1980, s 32(1); *Willis* v *Earl Howe* [1893] 2 Ch 545.

[184] Limitation Act 1980, s 28; LRA, Sched 6, para 8. If this is overlooked (perhaps because O does not respond to a notification), then rectification of the register could be sought.

[185] *BP Properties Ltd* v *Buckler* (1987) 55 P&CR 337 (if an order is obtained but not enforced, a fresh period of adverse possession will start running).

[186] *Markfield Investments Ltd* v *Evans* [2001] 1 WLR 1321 (initial claim dismissed for want of prosecution).

[187] *Mount Carmel Investments Ltd* v *Peter Thurlow Ltd* [1988] 1 WLR 1078 at p 1083 (the contrary suggestion was 'novel, and indeed startling').

[188] (1987) 55 P&CR 337. Though criticised by Law Com No 271, para 14.56, n 187 (see also Wallace [1994] Conv 196 and Thompson [2001] Conv at p 347), it was applied by the Privy Council in *Smith* v *Molyneaux* [2017] 1 P&CR 80.

[189] The basis for this was not explained.

[190] It was held in *Colin Dawson Windows Ltd* v *King's Lynn BC* [2005] 2 P&CR 333 that 'it is natural to draw an inference of permission where a person is in possession pending negotiations for the grant of an interest in that land'.

[191] It does not merely suspend the running of the period: any future adverse possession has to start afresh (Limitation Act 1980, Sched 1, para 8(2)).

[192] *Pavledes* v *Ryesbridge Properties Ltd* (1989) 58 P&CR 459 at p 476.

[193] Limitation Act 1980, ss 29–30. This extends to documents in which S forges O's signature, at least if they are received by O: *Rehman* v *Benfield* [2007] 2 P&CR 317.

[194] *Lambeth LBC* v *Bigden* (2000) 33 HLR 478.

[195] *Ofulue* v *Bossert* [2009] AC 990. The acknowledgment is not normally continuing; a new period may commence thereafter.

evidence showing that there is no animus possidendi,[196] although the acknowledgment by itself would not be conclusive. Once the adverse possession period is completed, even written acknowledgment is ineffective as O's title has already been extinguished.[197]

The simplicity of this last point is undermined by *Colchester BC v Smith*.[198] S's claim to adverse possession was disputed by O. As a compromise, the position was regularised by the grant of a lease to S, with S acknowledging that O was owner and that no right had been acquired by adverse possession. Although finding that S had acquired a good title by adverse possession, the Court of Appeal held that the compromise was effective to deny S's rights. The court accepted that a simple acknowledgment would be ineffective, but a compromise agreement acted upon by O will estop S from relying upon adverse possession. Provided that there is a genuine and freely negotiated compromise,[199] there is everything to be said for enforcing a clear agreement of the parties rather than requiring the uncertainty and expense of litigation.[200]

Registered land

Not all these rules apply to registered land. Possession must, of course, be adverse, so licensed possession will no more be effective under the statutory scheme than for unregistered land. However, there is no need to recognise other ways of stopping time running, given that the passage of time does not by itself destroy O's title. Accordingly, the bringing of a claim does not stop time running,[201] though we have seen that a para 1 or 6 application cannot be brought if possession proceedings are current or if there has been a judgment for possession within the past two years.

The Law Commission states that ss 29–32 of the Limitation Act will not apply[202]: these include acknowledgment of claims. However, it is not easy to see how the 2002 Act gives effect to this. Even if they are inapplicable, one might argue that acknowledgment of a claim could result in possession ceasing to be adverse. This would be fatal to a para 1 application (and to a para 6 application if the further two years' adverse possession had not been completed). In any event, the analysis in *Colchester* would still appear to be available.

(v) *Twelve years*

The adverse possession must not be interrupted: it is fatal if it either ceases or becomes permissive during the period. Any future adverse possession, then, has to start from scratch.[203] However, it is not necessary that the same person is the adverse possessor for

---

[196] *Pavledes v Ryesbridge Properties Ltd* (1989) 58 P&CR 459 at p 481; *Blakeney v MacDonald* (1980) 116 DLR 3d 402.

[197] *Sanders v Sanders* (1881) 19 Ch D 373; *Nicholson v England* [1926] 2 KB 93.

[198] [1992] Ch 421.

[199] Ibid, at p 435 (Butler-Sloss LJ). It would be wrong if O could trick S out of the statutory rights.

[200] The contrary is argued by Dixon [1991] CLJ 234; [1992] CLJ 420, who considers that the parties cannot thus contract out of the legislation. However, the legislation was not designed to protect persons with inadequate bargaining power: Law Reform Committee 21st Report (1977) Cmnd 6923, para 2.55.

[201] Schedule 6, para 11(3)(a).

[202] Law Com No 271, para 14.11.

[203] Limitation Act 1980, Sched 1, para 8(2). See also Law Com No 270, paras 4.54 et seq.

the entire period. The legislation concentrates upon the accrual of a right of action to recover the land.[204] It follows that S can sell an uncompleted adverse possession. What happens if S^2 dispossesses S? The common law rule is that S^2 can count the possession of both of them, so long as there is no gap in the adverse possession of S and S^2.[205] We have seen that this does not apply in registered land.

The normal period of 12 years applies where O has an interest in possession. Adverse possession against a future interest is effective six years after that future interest comes into possession (subject to the normal minimum of 12 years from the start of adverse possession).[206] This includes future interests under trusts of land: the law is generous to beneficiaries in not allowing adverse possession as against the trustees.[207] The landlord's reversion on a lease is counted as a future interest.[208] This means that a squatter of leased land can be evicted by the freehold owner for at least six years after the end of the lease. On the other hand, where S receives the rent, then this is adverse possession against the freehold owner.[209] This rule, which does not apply to registered land,[210] never affected the tenant.

There are somewhat different rules for registered estates, quite apart from the point that a para 1 application requires only 10 years' adverse possession. The provisions of Sched 6 apply only to the estate over which there is adverse possession. It follows that adverse possession over leased land is adverse possession against the tenant but not against the landlord, and any registration of S is in respect of the leasehold title.[211] There are no special periods relating to adverse possession against future interests: when a lease terminates, there will need to be 10 years' adverse possession against the landlord before a para 1 application may be made as regards the landlord's registered estate. The position as regards trusts is slightly remodelled in order to emphasise adverse possession of the registered estate rather than as against beneficial interests. Adverse possession operates only if each of the beneficiaries has an interest in possession.[212]

D. The effect of adverse possession

(i) *General principles: unregistered land*

The completion of adverse possession confers no right on S: we will see later that S's rights are based on the initial adverse possession. Rather, the effect is to extinguish the title of O.[213] Any ancillary rights of O are also extinguished at the end of the period, so O cannot

---

[204] Limitation Act 1980, s 15(1); *Sze* v *Kung* [1997] 1 WLR 1232.

[205] *Willis* v *Earl Howe* [1893] 2 Ch 545 at pp 553–554; *Mount Carmel Investments Ltd* v *Peter Thurlow Ltd* [1988] 1 WLR 1078; *Site Developments (Ferndown) Ltd* v *Cuthbury Ltd* [2011] Ch 226. The rights of S and S^2 against each other are considered later in this chapter.

[206] Limitation Act 1980, s 15(2), Sched 1, para 4. Under the reforms proposed in Law Com No 270, the 12-year period would be reduced to 10, and the special six-year period would be deleted (so that 10 years from the time the future interest comes into possession would be required); see especially paras 4.130 and 4.134.

[207] Limitation Act 1980, s 18.

[208] *St Marylebone Property Co Ltd* v *Fairweather* [1963] AC 510 at pp 536, 544.

[209] Limitation Act 1980, Sched 1, para 6 (minimum £10 p.a. rent).

[210] LRA, Sched 6, para 11(3)(b).

[211] LRA, Sched 6, paras 1, 4, 7, 11(1).

[212] Presumably, future beneficiaries could seek rectification if there were a successful para 1 or para 6 application in ignorance of their rights.

[213] Limitation Act 1980, s 17.

claim for S's use of the land[214] or for rent.[215] At one time, it was thought that there was a statutory transfer of O's title to S. This was rejected in the leading case of *Tichborne* v *Weir*.[216] In most cases it makes little difference, but it becomes especially significant where there is adverse possession against tenants, a topic discussed later in this chapter.

It should be noted that S is bound by all proprietary interests held by persons other than O. These include equitable interests, regardless of whether S has notice: there is no purchase to take advantage of the rules in favour of bona fide purchasers[217] or of failure to register. On a similar basis, there is no conveyance into which implied rights, such as easements, can be inserted.[218]

(ii) *General principles: registered land*

As we have seen, adverse possession (in the few cases in which it operates against registered estates) applies only as a result of applications under paras 1 and 6. Paras 4 and 7 make it clear that S is registered as the new proprietor of the estate in question. This is equivalent to the statutory transfer that was rejected in *Tichborne* v *Weir*. The Law Commission states that O's ancillary rights (for trespass or rent) will disappear. However, this is not explicit in the 2002 Act. One point to note is that under the Land Registration Act 1925, a trust in favour of S arose after adverse possession was complete and before it was entered on the register. This was rather controversial[219] and no longer applies under the 2002 Act.

Registration of S does not affect the priority of any interest. It follows that any interest binding O (whether or not entered on the register) will remain binding on S: the same result as in unregistered land. Two points need to be mentioned. The first is an exception: a registered charge affecting the estate is discharged by the registration of S. The purpose behind this is to produce a clean break, against the background that notification of a para 1 application will be given to the chargee, who will normally object and then evict S. This discharge does not apply[220] in the situations in para 5 when S can override any objection.[221]

The second point concerns the effect on O. How far does the removal of O as proprietor terminate all O's rights to the land? It must be implicit in the scheme that the rights are terminated. If there is some irregularity in the procedure, then the most appropriate response is to seek rectification of the register.[222] This might apply where no notification of S's application had reached O, who now disputes whether the facts justify adverse possession. A slightly different example concerns a beneficiary with an interest in possession, in circumstances where the trustee (O) has failed to object.

---

[214] *Mount Carmel Investments Ltd* v *Peter Thurlow Ltd* [1988] 1 WLR 1078.
[215] *Re Jolly* [1900] 2 Ch 616.
[216] (1892) 67 LT 735.
[217] *Re Nisbet & Potts' Contract* [1906] 1 Ch 386.
[218] *Wilkes* v *Greenway* (1890) 6 TLR 449.
[219] Cooke (1994) 14 LS 1, supported by *Central London Commercial Estates Ltd* v *Kato Kagaku Co Ltd* [1998] 4 All ER 948 at p 953; Law Com No 254, paras 10.28 et seq, 10.70–10.72; Law Com No 271, para 14.70.
[220] LRA, Sched 6, para 9(3), (4). There is provision for apportioning the charge as between the areas of land charged: para 10.
[221] Estoppel, other rights to be registered, disputes between neighbours.
[222] *Baxter* v *Mannion* [2011] 1 WLR 1594, see p 78 above.

(iii) *Before the adverse possession is completed*

It has been observed earlier that the Limitation Act 1980 itself confers no right on S. So what rights does S enjoy? The answer is that adverse possession confers a fee simple on S from the beginning.[223] This might seem odd, in that both O (until adverse possession is completed) and S have a fee simple.[224] However, it ties in with the relativity of title that underlies English property law. Actions to enforce property rights do not depend upon showing an absolute right to the land.[225] Rather, it is sufficient to show a better right than the other party.[226]

This is best demonstrated by the situation where S takes adverse possession for, say, eight years and then is dispossessed by S². It has been seen that, for unregistered land, adverse possession will be completed after a further four years, when the required total of 12 years has elapsed. But who is then entitled, S or S²? *Asher* v *Whitlock*[227] established that S has a good claim against S², always presuming that S² is sued within 12 years of dispossessing S. This is subject to S's not having abandoned any right to the property.[228] Abandonment by O would virtually never be inferred but is more credible as regards S when S has been in adverse possession for a relatively short period. There may be other contexts (other than claims against S²) in which S's rights prior to the completion of adverse possession may be important. For example, *Perry* v *Clissold*[229] held that S had a right which qualified for compensation on compulsory purchase.

These principles apply in a broadly similar fashion to registered land.[230] In particular, it is worth noting that, even in registered land, there can be two (or more) competing legal fees simple. This exemplifies the continued role of ideas of relativity of title, even though the circumstances where S's claim will be stronger than O's are very limited. Two points may be added. The first is that S's rights[231] constitute a proprietary interest capable of binding O's successors in title, at least where S is in actual occupation so as to have an overriding interest. Thus if S has been in adverse possession for, say, five years and then O sells to P, then a para 1 application may be made after a further five years' adverse possession against P. The second is that if S is registered as proprietor following a para 1 or para 6 application, then the original title of S as squatter is extinguished. As we will see, this is most relevant for adverse possession against tenants.

---

[223] Co Litt 2a, 297a; *Rosenberg* v *Cook* (1881) 8 QBD 162 at p 165; *Mabo* v *Queensland* (1992) 107 ALR 1 at pp 161–164 (Toohey J). *Turner* v *Chief Land Registrar* [2013] 2 P&CR 223 provides a more recent example in registered land.

[224] Curwen [2000] Conv 528 argues that it is historically correct to see O as losing the fee simple, but this does not accord with most modern thinking (let alone registration principles).

[225] Hargreaves (1940) 56 LQR 376. Holdsworth's arguments to the contrary (*History of English Law*, Vol 7, pp 62–68; (1940) 56 LQR 479) have not been generally accepted. See also *Allen* v *Roughley* (1955) 94 CLR 98; Wade [1956] CLJ 177.

[226] *Doe d Hughes* v *Dyeball* (1829) M&M 346 (173 ER 1184); *Doe d Humphrey* v *Martin* (1841) Car&M 32 (174 ER 395).

[227] (1865) LR 1 QB 1.

[228] *Mount Carmel Investments Ltd* v *Peter Thurlow Ltd* [1988] 1 WLR 1078.

[229] [1907] AC 73 (PC). Horrendous problems could arise in valuing the right (in *Perry*, the rightful owner was unknown at all relevant times).

[230] Except if S² evicts S, when S² cannot count the period when S was in adverse possession against O: p 79 above.

[231] Including a statutory right to be registered: Law Com No 271, para 14.64.

(iv) *Adverse possession against tenants: unregistered land*

It has already been seen that adverse possession against a tenant (T) does not affect the right of the landlord (O) to recover the property at the end of the lease.[232] Indeed, T can recover the property if O grants a new lease to T at that time, although not if T is exercising an option to renew the lease.[233] In these circumstances, the nature of the rights acquired by S has caused very severe difficulties. Any idea that S acquires the lease previously enjoyed by T is inconsistent with the 'no statutory transfer' doctrine.

The leading case is *Tichborne* v *Weir*,[234] in which S was held not liable on the covenants in the lease. Rejection of the statutory transfer doctrine meant that S could not be regarded as a transferee of the lease and, therefore, was not to be treated as tenant to O, such as would have permitted the covenants to run. Nevertheless, S will be well advised to comply with the covenants. Any breach will normally entitle O to forfeit the lease; O will thereby gain a right to immediate possession which can be enforced against S. Furthermore, S cannot assert T's rights to relief against forfeiture.[235]

The most controversial issues arise when T purports to surrender the lease to O after the completion of adverse possession. Is the surrender effective so as to confer upon O an immediate right to possession against S? By a majority, the House of Lords in *St Marylebone Property Co Ltd* v *Fairweather*[236] held in O's favour. Two significant hurdles must be overcome before this result can be justified.

The first hurdle is that s 17 of the 1980 Act extinguishes T's title. Yet, the section can scarcely extinguish the lease, for that would leave O with an immediate right of possession, a result wholly inimical to S. Nor is the lease vested in S, for that would be inconsistent with *Tichborne* v *Weir*. Indeed, S appears[237] to have a fee simple, 'arcane and counter-intuitive'[238] as that may be. It may well be that the statutory transfer concept would have provided the best explanation of S's position,[239] but it was much too late to argue that point in *Fairweather*. It seems inescapable that the lease remains vested in T and that it is only as between T and S that T's interest is treated as extinguished. Despite one's initial scepticism of *Fairweather* because of the uncompromising drafting of s 17, it really does seem that, as between O and T, the lease survives adverse possession.

The second hurdle lies in explaining how O and T can, by surrender, create rights against S that neither enjoyed previously. It is on this ground that the decision is convincingly criticised by Professor Wade.[240] The Privy Council[241] has recognised the force of the

---

[232] E.g. *Taylor* v *Twinberrow* [1930] 2 KB 16 (periodic tenancy).
[233] *Chung Ping Kwan* v *Lam Island Development Co Ltd* [1997] AC 38 (PC).
[234] (1892) 67 LT 735.
[235] *Tickner* v *Buzzacott* [1965] Ch 426.
[236] [1963] AC 510 (Lord Morris dissented).
[237] Lord Radcliffe in *Fairweather* at p 535.
[238] Harpum (1999) 115 LQR 187 at p 191.
[239] Wallace (1981) 32 NILQ 254. It would face the objection that O, as landlord, might be landed with an assignee without his consent: Law Reform Committee, 21st Report (1977) Cmnd 6923, para 3.45.
[240] (1962) 78 LQR 541. Sub-tenants are protected against surrender by T. The majority distinguished this principle as resting upon non-derogation from grant. Non-derogation cannot benefit S because there is, as all agree, no grant to a squatter. Hopkins [1996] Conv 284 would protect S by analysing surrenders as assignments. *Fairweather* had rejected this.
[241] *Chung Ping Kwan* v *Lam Island Development Co Ltd* [1997] AC 38 at p 47.

criticism, whilst choosing not to pronounce on the correctness of *Fairweather*. As things stand, however, the effect of *Fairweather* is to reduce S's protection in these cases to close to vanishing point.

(v) *Adverse possession against tenants: registered land*

It is clear under the 2002 Act that S is registered as proprietor of the lease.[242] Although the common law views S as having a fee simple, this result is qualified for registered land. S may initially have a fee simple (one that T could have defeated prior to S's being entitled to be registered), but registration of S terminates that fee simple.[243] Because we now have a statutory transfer of the lease, it is easy to conclude that the analysis in *Fairweather* no longer applies. It might be added that a welcome result of the registration of S as proprietor of the lease (rather than a fee simple) is that there will be liability on the covenants on the normal principles under the Landlord and Tenant (Covenants) Act 1995.[244]

What about the position before S is registered? Prior to the 2002 Act, S was protected in registered land on the basis of the statutory trust.[245] Now that there is no longer a statutory trust, there seems no reason for departing from the unregistered land analysis that T can surrender the lease to O. Although many of the reforms of adverse possession are very welcome, this return to technicality is less so. It may mean that T can surrender even after a para 1 application has been made. Of course, the much reduced scope for adverse possession renders the entire area of limited significance.

(vi) *Adverse possession by tenants*

Tower Hamlets LBC v *Barrett*[246] confirms the presumption that a tenant who adversely possesses land close to that leased does so on behalf of the landlord. However, the tenant is protected in that the lease is treated as extending to the land acquired.[247] Further, a purchase of the leased land by the tenant is taken to include the adversely possessed land.

3. Fixtures

Ownership may be affected when one object is fixed to another. Take this simple example. Suppose I build a house and, by mistake, use bricks belonging to X. It is clear that X loses ownership of the bricks, which are now incorporated into the house. X will almost certainly have a remedy for my misuse of the bricks, but that is a different matter. This principle can

---

[242] Similar results had previously been reached by Browne-Wilkinson J in *Spectrum Investment Co* v *Holmes* [1981] 1 WLR 221.

[243] LRA, Sched 6, para 9(1); a result previously supported by *Holmes* and *Kato Kagaku* (see n 245 in this chapter).

[244] Section 28 includes assignments by operation of law, which appears applicable to LRA, Sched 6. However, such assignments leave T liable on the covenants, contrary to the normal position; s 11 of the 1995 Act.

[245] *Central London Commercial Estates Ltd* v *Kato Kagaku Co Ltd* [1998] 4 All ER 948; Cooke [1999] Conv 136; Harpum (1999) 115 LQR 187; Pascoe [1999] Conv 329.

[246] [2006] 1 P&CR 132; Fox [2007] CLJ 16. Lees [2015] Conv 110 at pp 120–122 considers the problems in applying this to registered land.

[247] This applies also to land owned by the landlord. Lees [2015] Conv 110 argues persuasively that this is encroachment rather than adverse possession and should not be governed by the 2002 Act.

apply when one chattel is incorporated in another,[248] but most problems arise when chattels are fixed to land. That is the focus of the following analysis.

Most cases involve chattels belonging to the person fixing them.[249] There may be said to be two categories. The first is where the person affixing the chattel is the owner of the land. Its status as a fixture becomes important on any dealing with the land. If the owner contracts to sell the land, the purchaser will be entitled to fixtures unless the contract provides otherwise. Similarly, a mortgagee of the land will have a better right to fixtures than the owner (or other creditors)[250] and a devise of a house in a will includes fixtures.[251]

The second category is where the person fixing the chattel has a limited right to the land. This may be a life interest, but most cases involve tenants under leases. The consequences discussed in the previous paragraph again apply.[252] Further, the courts have long recognised that it would be grossly unfair if fixtures added by tenants always belonged to landlords. It would also discourage tenants from improving the property.[253] For centuries, the courts have allowed trade and ornamental fixtures to be removed during or at the end of the tenancy.[254]

This is part of a growing tendency to diminish the severity of the traditional fixture rules.[255] Does this development affect the question whether there has been a fixture in the first place? The conventional view certainly is that trade and ornamental fixtures are part of the land, but that there is a right to remove them. However, it will be seen that intention plays a significant role in deciding whether or not there is a fixture. This was used to argue that many trade and ornamental fixtures are not true fixtures because they are attached to the land without the intention that they should become part of the land but merely for use or enjoyment. This role for intention would be especially important outside the landlord and tenant setting, when there is no right to remove fixtures. However, the House of Lords in *Elitestone Ltd* v *Morris*[256] endorses the conventional view that they are fixtures; we will return to the issue later.

A. General principles

The early cases placed great emphasis upon the extent of physical annexation, but a more sophisticated approach was taken by Blackburn J in the leading case of *Holland* v *Hodgson*[257]:

> Perhaps the true rule is, that articles not otherwise attached to the land than by their own weight are not to be considered as part of the land, unless the circumstances are such as to shew that they

---

[248] The issues were well discussed by Roman lawyers: Justinian, *Institutes*, 2.1.20–2.1.34.

[249] The most common exception is where the chattel is held under a contract of hire or hire purchase.

[250] *Mather* v *Fraser* (1856) 2 K&J 536 (69 ER 895), regarded as settled law in *Reynolds* v *Ashby & Son* [1904] AC 466. Chattels do not pass to a mortgagee: *Hulme* v *Brigham* [1943] KB 152.

[251] *Fisher* v *Dixon* (1845) 12 Cl&F 312 (8 ER 1426); *Re Whaley* [1908] 1 Ch 615.

[252] *Meux* v *Jacobs* (1875) LR 7 HL 481 (mortgage by tenant); *Bain* v *Brand* (1876) 1 App Cas 762 (destination under will of tenant).

[253] Lord Kenyon CJ in *Penton* v *Robart* (1801) 2 East 88 at p 90 (102 ER 302 at p 303).

[254] *Poole's Case* (1703) 1 Salk 368 (91 ER 320).

[255] *Leigh* v *Taylor* [1902] AC 157.

[256] [1997] 1 WLR 687 at pp 690–691, 694–696; it is said to be preferable not to use the word fixture to describe chattels which become part of the land (a house being a prime example). This 'part and parcel' analysis is criticised by Luther (2008) 28 LS 574.

[257] (1872) LR 7 CP 328 at p 335 (Exchequer Chamber). For the earlier law, see Luther (2004) 24 OxJLS 597.

were intended to be part of the land . . . on the contrary, an article which is affixed to the land even slightly is to be considered as part of the land, unless the circumstances are such as to shew that it was intended all along to continue a chattel. . . .

Blackburn J gave useful examples where fixing is not conclusive one way or the other. A dry stone wall will be a fixture even though it is not fixed to the land. By contrast, an anchor does not become part of the soil in which it is embedded.[258] Here, the fixing serves a temporary purpose and is readily removed; similar reasoning applies to a carpet that is tacked to the floor. Nevertheless, the court held that machinery nailed to the floor did constitute a fixture so as to pass under a mortgage. Although it was fixed in order to be used effectively and it could be easily removed, this was insufficient to counter the physical annexation. There are countless cases reaching similar conclusions on trade machinery.[259]

Subsequent cases have sought to give greater stress to intention than to the degree of fixing,[260] although this has been principally in the context of ornamental fixtures. Items such as tapestries hung on walls have been litigated on several occasions. If it is possible to show that they were fixed so as to be a permanent part of the house, then they will be fixtures.[261] This will be much easier to prove where they were fixed by a previous occupier. The courts have been inclined to hold that ornamental fixtures fixed by the current occupier are fixed simply so that they can be enjoyed, rather than as a permanent addition to the land.[262]

Many of these cases involved tenants for life, but *Berkley* v *Poulett*[263] raised the question whether the vendor of the fee simple could remove pictures firmly screwed into recesses in the panelling of Hinton House. A majority of the Court of Appeal held that the pictures were fixed in order to enjoy them rather than to be a part of the house. Although the result fits the ornamental fixture cases well, a problem with this type of analysis is that it applies equally well where machinery has to be bolted, nailed or screwed to the floor to ensure its stability. *Holland* v *Hodgson* was emphatic that this did not render it a chattel. The argument in favour of there being no fixture will be enhanced if the objects were moved frequently, as this demonstrates the temporary nature of the fixing.

Third-party owners and intention

Is it relevant that the object belongs to a third party? A typical case is where it has been hired or has been bought on hire purchase.[264] Where there is hire purchase, the cases have been content to hold that the object is a fixture.[265] In cases of hire, it may be easier to

---

[258] Applied in *Bradshaw* v *Davey* [1952] 1 All ER 350 (yacht mooring) and *Chelsea Yacht and Boat Co Ltd* v *Pope* [2001] 1 WLR 1941 (moored houseboat).

[259] Leading cases include *Mather* v *Fraser* (1856) 2 K&J 536 (69 ER 895) and *Reynolds* v *Ashby & Son* [1904] AC 466. The criminal law case of *Billing* v *Pill* [1954] 1 QB 70 (sectional hut bolted to base: chattel) appears difficult to justify.

[260] *Leigh* v *Taylor* [1902] AC 157; *Berkley* v *Poulett* [1977] 1 EGLR 86.

[261] *Norton* v *Dashwood* [1896] 2 Ch 497; *Re Whaley* [1908] 1 Ch 615. See also *D'Eyncourt* v *Gregory* (1866) LR 3 Eq 382 (a dubious decision: *Re De Falbe* [1901] 1 Ch 523) and *Re Lord Chesterfield's Settled Estates* [1911] 1 Ch 237.

[262] *Hill* v *Bullock* [1897] 2 Ch 482 (collection of stuffed birds, lightly fixed to cases themselves fixed to the wall); *Leigh* v *Taylor* [1902] AC 157 (tapestries).

[263] [1977] 1 EGLR 86.

[264] Ownership does not pass until all payments have been made.

[265] *Hobson* v *Gorringe* [1897] 1 Ch 182; *Reynolds* v *Ashby & Son* [1904] AC 466; *Crossley Brothers Ltd* v *Lee* [1908] 1 KB 86.

convince the court that there was an intention that it should remain a chattel, at any rate where there is a low level of fixing.[266] However, the House of Lords has more recently stressed that the result is not determined by the intention of the parties that the object should, or should not, be a fixture.[267] Insofar as intention is relevant, it is only as regards the object of the annexation.

Fixture without fixing?

Where the object rests on its own weight on land without any fixing, the courts have usually applied the prima facie rule that it remains a chattel.[268] Exceptions have been allowed where a house rests on piles,[269] where fixed grates have been replaced by heavy dog grates[270] and, more generally, where the objects form part of the 'architectural design' of the property. This last category is controversial, although it may well be helpful where there is some fixing. It was applied in *D'Eyncourt* v *Gregory*[271] to carved figures, marble vases, stone lions and garden seats. Although the principle seems valid, subsequent cases have been quick to distinguish *D'Eyncourt*.[272]

Damage; connected objects

In all cases, one significant factor is whether the object can be removed without substantial damage. If it cannot, then this is a strong pointer to its being a fixture.[273] A rather different sort of problem arises where one object, not itself fixed, is an integral part of other objects (usually machinery) that are fixed. This arose in *Pole-Carew* v *Western Counties & General Manure Co Ltd*,[274] in which some of the structures rested on their own weight. Because they formed 'a necessary and integral part of a sulphuric acid plant', the Court of Appeal held them to be fixtures. Although this led to a sensible result in *Pole-Carew*, it certainly cannot be concluded that everything in a factory will be a fixture. Free-standing machines connected to fixed motors have been held not to be fixtures[275] and nor were batteries connected to a fixed engine and dynamo.[276]

---

[266] *Lyon & Co* v *London City & Midland Bank* [1903] 2 KB 135 (chairs in hippodrome; contrast *Vaudeville Electric Cinema Ltd* v *Muriset* [1923] 2 Ch 74, where there was no hire); *NH Dunn Pty Ltd* v *LM Ericsson Pty Ltd* [1979] 2 BPR 9241 (New South Wales: telephone switchboard).

[267] *Melluish* v *BMI (No 3) Ltd* [1996] AC 454 at p 473; *Elitestone Ltd* v *Morris* [1997] 1 WLR 687; see also *Hobson* v *Gorringe* [1897] 1 Ch 182 at p 195.

[268] *Wiltshear* v *Cottrell* (1853) 1 El&Bl 674 (118 ER 589) (granary); *Hulme* v *Brigham* [1943] KB 152 (heavy printing machines); *HE Dibble Ltd* v *Moore* [1970] 2 QB 181 (greenhouses); *Deen* v *Andrews* [1986] 1 EGLR 262 (large greenhouse).

[269] *Elitestone Ltd* v *Morris* [1997] 1 WLR 687 (removal not feasible short of demolition), followed in *Spielplatz Ltd* v *Pearson* [2015] 2 P&CR 365; *Reid* v *Smith* (1905) 3 CLR 656 (then a common building method in Queensland). Contrast the houseboat placed on a platform in *Tristmire Ltd* v *Mew* [2012] 1 WLR 852, as that could have been removed and the houseboat floated.

[270] *Monti* v *Barnes* [1901] 1 KB 205.

[271] (1866) LR 3 Eq 382.

[272] *Hill* v *Bullock* [1897] 2 Ch 482; *Re De Falbe* [1901] 1 Ch 523; *Tower Hamlets LB* v *Bromley LB* [2015] EWHC 1954 (Ch) (Henry Moore sculpture).

[273] *Elitestone Ltd* v *Morris* [1997] 1 WLR 687.

[274] [1920] 2 Ch 97.

[275] *Hulme* v *Brigham* [1943] KB 152; *National Australia Bank Ltd* v *Blacker* (2000) 179 ALR 97 (irrigation equipment).

[276] *Jordan* v *May* [1947] KB 427.

Modern application of the rules

The Court of Appeal in *Botham* v *TSB Bank plc*[277] has more recently given a useful ruling on household objects, applying the test whether they are, objectively, intended to be a permanent and a lasting improvement to the house. Baths and their taps, as well as fitted kitchen units, are usually fixtures. However, 'white goods' (cooker, refrigerator, washing machine, etc) in fitted units are not fixtures, as they can readily be removed without significant damage.[278] Carpets, curtains, most light fittings and gas fires simply connected to the gas supply also failed to count as fixtures.

Standing back from these details, how conclusive is physical annexation today? It is plain that it is far too simplistic to rely on that factor alone. Nevertheless, it remains the basis for deciding most cases. As soon as one places stress on intention, one encounters a very slippery concept. For a start, it has been seen that the parties' intentions as to whether there is a fixture are, as such, irrelevant.

What may be relevant is whether the fixing is for the temporary enjoyment of the object as a chattel, or for the use or enjoyment of the land. Yet, as has been noted, objects are nearly always fixed for their enjoyment or use as chattels. To ask whether a machine is fixed to a factory floor to make it a better factory or for the use of the machine is virtually meaningless: it would be rare that the two could be distinguished. Nearly always in the machine cases, the result is that there is a fixture. Stress on the degree of annexation may be a crude method of resolving disputes, but extensive reliance on intention is likely to lead to a sophistication of analysis which cannot be justified by the facts or intentions of the parties.

B. Removable fixtures

Tenants and life interest holders have long been allowed to remove trade and ornamental fixtures. It is sometimes said that the law is most generous to tenants,[279] but the decisions reveal little, if any, difference between the two groups. Both are described as tenants in this section.

There are three categories: (1) landlord's fixtures: cannot be removed; (2) tenant's fixtures: part of the land but can be removed; and (3) chattels.

(i) *Landlord's fixtures*

This category applies where, first, the fixture is neither trade nor ornamental or, second, the nature of the fixture is that it represents a permanent part of the land. Although entire buildings can be tenant's fixtures,[280] buildings with solid foundations will be landlord's fixtures as a permanent part of the land.[281] Additions to existing buildings that form an integral part of them, such as central heating and lifts[282] or windows and doors,[283] will similarly be landlord's fixtures.

---

[277] (1996) 73 P&CR D1.

[278] Contrast *Hawkins* v *Farley* [1997] 2 Qd R 361, where stress was placed upon the degree of fixing where pipes are involved and the unsightly hole left by removal. The result, however, seems less consistent with public expectations.

[279] *Elwes* v *Maw* (1802) 3 East 38 (102 ER 510); *Norton* v *Dashwood* [1896] 2 Ch 497.

[280] *Webb* v *Frank Bevis Ltd* [1940] 1 All ER 247.

[281] *Pole-Carew* v *Western Counties & General Manure Co Ltd* [1920] 2 Ch 97.

[282] *Stokes* v *Costain Property Investments Ltd* [1983] 1 WLR 907.

[283] *Climie* v *Wood* (1869) LR 4 Ex 328; *Bishop* v *Elliott* (1855) 11 Exch 113 (156 ER 766) (noting that they may not be in the trade or ornamental categories anyway); *Boswell* v *Crucible Steel Company* [1925] 1 KB 119.

(ii) *Tenant's fixtures*

These must be either trade or ornamental fixtures. Early suggestions that tenants can remove all their fixtures have long been rejected.[284] Trade fixtures plainly constitute a very wide category. Ornamental fixtures include tapestries,[285] panelling and ornamental chimney pieces.[286] It is no objection that minor damage will be caused on removal, although damage to the land must be paid for.[287] Agricultural fixtures are not trade fixtures,[288] although the Agricultural Tenancies Act 1995 re-enacts a broad statutory right to remove.[289] There is, generally, no obligation to remove trade fixtures.[290] It should be remembered that all these rules are subject to contractual variation, although the courts require plain language to exclude the right to remove.[291]

A lessee must normally exercise the right to remove before the end of the lease.[292] However, the courts are willing to allow a tenant who remains in possession to exercise the right, especially where there is an expectation that the lease will be extended.[293] It is sometimes said that the tenant has a reasonable time after the termination of the lease to remove tenant's fixtures,[294] but this may not apply where the lease expires at the end of the term.[295] Rather harshly, the right is lost following peaceable re-entry on forfeiture, even if no notice has been given to the tenant.[296]

A tenant who surrenders a lease and leaves the premises will be treated as giving up the right to remove.[297] However, a surrender on the grant of a new lease will not affect the right.[298]

(iii) *Chattels*

The application of the *Holland v Hodgson*[299] test may, of course, mean that there is no fixture at all. It should be noted that the right to remove is quite different from saying that the object remains a chattel. Although many cases would be decided in the same way whether the object is removable or remains a chattel, differences do exist. There appears to be no right to exercise commercial rent arrears recovery (seizing goods for unpaid

---

[284] *Elwes v Maw* (1802) 3 East 38 (102 ER 510); *Buckland v Butterfield* (1820) 2 Br&B 54 (129 ER 878); *Bishop v Elliott* (1855) 11 Exch 113 (156 ER 766).

[285] *Re De Falbe* [1901] 1 Ch 523 (upheld [1902] AC 157).

[286] *Spyer v Phillipson* [1931] 2 Ch 183.

[287] *Spyer v Phillipson* [1931] 2 Ch 183; *Mancetter Developments Ltd v Garmanson Ltd* [1986] QB 1212.

[288] *Elwes v Maw* (1802) 3 East 38 (102 ER 510); market gardening fixtures can be removed (*Mears v Callender* [1901] 2 Ch 388).

[289] Section 8 (exclusive of any other right to remove). Unusually, the fixtures remain the property of the tenant before removal.

[290] *Never-Stop Railway (Wembley) Ltd v British Empire Exhibition (1924) Incorporated* [1926] Ch 877.

[291] *Re British Red Ash Collieries Ltd* [1920] 1 Ch 326.

[292] *Minshall v Lloyd* (1837) 2 M&W 450 (150 ER 834); *Ex parte Stephens* (1877) 7 Ch D 127; *Smith v City Petroleum Co Ltd* [1940] 1 All ER 260.

[294] *Smith v City Petroleum Co Ltd* [1940] 1 All ER 260.

[293] *Penton v Robart* (1801) 2 East 88 (102 ER 302); *Pugh v Arton* (1869) LR 8 Eq 626.

[295] *Ex p Brook* (1878) 10 Ch D 100; *Leschallas v Woolf* [1908] 1 Ch 641.

[296] *Pugh v Arton* (1869) LR 8 Eq 626; *Re Palmiero* [1999] 3 EGLR 27.

[297] *Ex p Brook* (1878) 10 Ch D 100.

[298] *New Zealand Government Property Corporation v HM & S Ltd* [1982] QB 1145. Lord Denning MR and Dunn LJ were happy to apply this to express surrender, although Fox LJ appeared more willing to construe express surrender as giving up the right, as in *Leschallas v Woolf* [1908] 1 Ch 641.

[299] (1872) LR 7 CP 328.

rent)[300] against removable fixtures.[301] In addition, fixtures pass to a mortgagee[302] or other transferee[303] of the lease. Their status as fixtures also helps to explain the requirement of removal of tenant's fixtures before the end of the lease.

Although the conventional view is that a trade or ornamental fixture is not a chattel,[304] there have been suggestions that the tenant's intention that they should be removed results in their remaining chattels. This approach was taken by the Earl of Halsbury LC in *Leigh* v *Taylor*.[305] Whilst the temporary nature of a tenant's fixing may be a factor in assessing the object of annexation, it is contrary to a long line of authority to treat tenants' fixtures as chattels. Any idea that *Leigh* v *Taylor* had significantly expanded the chattel category was soon rejected in *Re Whaley*,[306] and the House of Lords in *Elitestone Ltd* v *Morris*[307] stresses the need to separate the issues of whether it is a fixture and whether it can be removed.

C. Is a right to remove fixtures a property interest?

The question here is whether a right to remove fixtures can bind purchasers of the land. One thing is clear: the right to remove tenant's fixtures binds any person bound by the lease.[308]

Greater problems arise where the original owner of the fixture reserves a contractual right to enter and remove it.[309] Most commonly, this has been where the fixture owner has let it on hire purchase, but it applies equally where a supplier has not been paid. No one doubts that there is a valid contractual right against the occupier of the land who fixed it, but can it be exercised against, for example, the occupier's mortgagee?[310] Without such a right to remove, the general rule is that fixtures pass to the mortgagee: the original owners lose their property.[311]

If the object is fixed after the mortgage, any right to remove must be subsequent to the mortgage and prima facie unenforceable.[312] However, it has been held in *Gough* v *Wood & Co*[313] that a mortgagee who allows the mortgagor to remain in possession, carrying on business, impliedly permits fixtures to be removed under such hire purchase contracts.

---

[300] See p 445 below.
[301] On the old law on distraint, see *Crossley Brothers Ltd* v *Lee* [1908] 1 KB 86. Contrast execution in respect of a debt: *Poole's Case* (1703) 1 Salk 368 (91 ER 320).
[302] *Meux* v *Jacobs* (1875) LR 7 HL 481; *Gough* v *Wood & Co* [1894] 1 QB 713.
[303] *Bain* v *Brand* (1876) 1 App Cas 762 (legatee).
[304] E.g. *Holland* v *Hodgson* (1872) LR 7 CP 328 at p 333; *Mancetter Developments Ltd* v *Garmanson Ltd* [1986] QB 1212 at pp 1218–1219. The contrary suggestion in *Re Hulse* [1905] 1 Ch 406 is difficult to support.
[305] [1902] AC 157 at p 159. Lord Shand was more guarded in his analysis.
[306] [1908] 1 Ch 615. See also *Never-Stop Railway (Wembley) Ltd* v *British Empire Exhibition (1924) Incorporated* [1926] Ch 877; *Spyer* v *Phillipson* [1931] 2 Ch 183; *Smith* v *City Petroleum Co Ltd* [1940] 1 All ER 260.
[307] [1997] 1 WLR 687.
[308] *Sanders* v *Davis* (1885) 15 QBD 218 (landlord's mortgagee).
[309] Guest and Lever (1963) 27 Conv 30. See also McCormack [1990] Conv 275; Bennett and Davis (1994) 110 LQR 448.
[310] Where the occupier is a tenant, the fixture owner can normally exercise the tenant's right to remove trade fixtures: *Becker* v *Riebold* (1913) 30 TLR 142 at p 143; *Crossley Brothers Ltd* v *Lee* [1908] 1 KB 86.
[311] *Reynolds* v *Ashby & Son* [1904] AC 466.
[312] Ibid.
[313] [1894] 1 QB 713.

This permission terminates when the mortgagee takes possession[314] and can be contractually excluded.[315] Although the mortgagee's claim to subsequent fixtures is unmeritorious (they provide an unexpected increase to the security),[316] it is unlikely that *Gough* will be widely applied. It was distinguished almost out of existence by the Court of Appeal in *Hobson* v *Gorringe*,[317] and Farwell LJ observed that 'I do not think it has ever been cited except to be distinguished.'[318]

If the object is fixed before the mortgage, any right to remove must be proprietary in nature if it is to bind the mortgagee. Parker J held in *Re Samuel Allen & Sons Ltd*[319] that it was an equitable interest.[320] Although this had slender support from the earlier cases, it was approved by the Court of Appeal a few years later.[321] Although the right has been held not registrable as a land charge in unregistered land,[322] the better view is that it must be entered on the register to bind a registered transferee of registered land.[323]

Further reading

Finding

Goodhart, A L (1929) 3 CLJ 195: Three cases on possession.

Marshall, O R (1949) 2 CLP 68: The problem of finding.

Rostill, L (2015) 35 OxJLS 31: Relative title and deemed ownership in English personal property law.

Adverse possession

Cobb, N and Fox, L (2007) 27 LS 236: Living outside the system? The (im)morality of urban squatting after the Land Registration Act 2002.

Dockray, M [1985] Conv 272: Why do we need adverse possession?

Radley-Gardner, O (2005) 25 OxJLS 727: Civilized squatting.

Wade, H W R (1962) 78 LQR 541: Landlord, tenant and squatter.

Fixtures

Guest, A and Lever, J (1963) 27 Conv 30: Hire-purchase, equipment leases and fixtures.

Luther, P (2004) 24 OxJLS 597: Fixtures and chattels: a question of more or less. . . .

---

[314] *Hobson* v *Gorringe* [1897] 1 Ch 182; *Reynolds* v *Ashby & Son* [1904] AC 466.

[315] *Ellis* v *Glover & Hobson Ltd* [1908] 1 KB 388.

[316] Goode, *Hire Purchase Law and Practice* (2nd edn), pp 740–741. Bennett and Davis (1994) 110 LQR 448 argue that the supplier's right to remove should have priority by analogy to *Abbey National BS* v *Cann* [1991] 1 AC 56. Without the right to remove, the object would not have been sold and would not have been acquired by the mortgagee.

[317] [1897] 1 Ch 182. On one interpretation, it does not apply when the removal is intended to defeat the mortgagee's rights, as opposed to being a normal incident of the hiring contract.

[318] *Ellis* v *Glover & Hobson Ltd* [1908] 1 KB 388 at p 401.

[319] [1907] 1 Ch 575.

[320] *Hobson* v *Gorringe* [1897] 1 Ch 182 confirmed that purchasers of the legal estate without notice are not bound.

[321] *Re Morrison, Jones & Taylor Ltd* [1914] 1 Ch 50.

[322] *Poster* v *Slough Estates Ltd* [1968] 1 WLR 1515.

[323] Guest and Lever (1963) 27 Conv 30 at pp 42–43. The suggestion of Cross J in *Poster* v *Slough Estates Ltd* [1968] 1 WLR 1515 at p 1521 that it might not bind purchasers of registered land seems unfounded.

8

The transfer and creation of property interests

Introduction

We have seen that the law recognises a wide range of property interests. No less complex are the rules relating to how those interests are created and transferred. This chapter is concerned with what is often described as derivative acquisition of interests: where the right is acquired from another person. Original modes of acquisition – for example, finding an abandoned article – were dealt with in Chapter 7.

There are two basic ways in which a person transfers (or creates) a property interest. The first is that the interest may be passed by transferring possession to the acquirer. This method is available for transferring ownership of personal property. Most obviously, I make a gift of a box of chocolates by handing it over. The second method is for the holder to express (orally or in writing) the intention to create a property right.

It is unusual for an oral expression of intention by itself to create a property right. As will be seen later, consideration is often required. Thus, an agreement to sell a car can be effective to transfer ownership, whereas no amount of intention can, without delivery, effect a gift of a car. However, there are occasional exceptions where unilateral oral intention suffices. An example is declaring oneself a trustee of property for another person as beneficiary.

It is common for the law to require that the transfer or creation of an interest be in writing. Writing is generally required for interests in land and for transfers of equitable interests. The major reason for this is to promote certainty. This is a good thing, but writing requirements may frustrate people's intentions and, in some cases, be a source of injustice. This has led to the development of several exceptions to the need for writing. Formality requirements are studied in this chapter. The rationale for them, together with the exceptions, will be considered in Chapters 9, 10, and 11.

1. Deeds

One particular form of writing is the document under seal, or deed. Deeds are powerful: more or less any interest may be created or transferred by deed, whether or not there is consideration or delivery. Even where writing would not suffice (an example is a gift of a chattel), a deed will be effective. Deeds are also effective in creating obligations. It is a basic common law proposition that gratuitous promises are not enforceable: contracts require consideration. Yet, even gratuitous deeds are enforceable.

A deed is essential for the transfer or creation of most legal interests in land.[1] Although the early law allowed transfer of land by giving possession (technically called feoffment with livery of seisin), this has long been obsolete.[2]

What is a deed? The traditional answer was that it is a document that is signed, sealed and delivered. The rules were amended by the Law of Property (Miscellaneous Provisions) Act 1989 (hereafter 1989 Act),[3] although the changes as to sealing and witnesses apply only to deeds entered into by individuals. Section 1 swept aside the need for sealing, which had survived only in the vestigial form of a wafer or a printed circle. The next requirement, delivery, is thoroughly misleading: it means no more than an intention to be bound by the deed.[4] Such an intention is readily found because it is possible to execute a deed conditional upon some event (the condition is rarely expressed in the deed). The deed is valid and cannot be revoked, although it will never come into effect if the condition is not fulfilled. It is called an *escrow*.

A common example is the everyday purchase of a house. The seller normally signs the transfer before completion of the purchase, entrusting his or her solicitor with the deed until the buyer pays the purchase money.[5] This enables the seller to be busy moving house at the time of completion, whilst ensuring that the buyer does not become the owner of the house until he or she pays. On the other hand, where negotiations are still continuing, it is likely there will be no intention to be bound at the time of signing and therefore no delivery.[6]

The 1989 Act requires that the deed be witnessed, the witness being present at the time of signature.[7] Although this is a new rule, it had long been common for deeds to be witnessed. To sum up, a deed entered into by an individual today merely needs to be signed, witnessed and delivered. This leaves the question: what is a deed? In the past, a seal was the major distinguishing factor. Today, a seal is neither essential nor a guarantee that there is a deed. Section 1(2) of the 1989 Act states: 'An instrument shall not be a deed unless . . . it makes it clear on its face that it is intended to be a deed . . . (whether by describing itself as a deed or expressing itself to be executed or signed as a deed or otherwise).' Clearly, a document calling itself a deed satisfies this. However, having a sealed document is not itself enough.[8] Will the courts be prepared to say that because a person goes to the trouble of having a document witnessed, he or she intends for it to be a deed? *HSBC Trust Company (UK) Ltd* v *Quinn*[9] held that simply having witnesses is not enough. Although the word 'deed' is not essential, there must be something more than an intention of a

---

[1] Law of Property Act 1925 (hereafter LPA), s 52. As will be seen, registration is normally required.
[2] LPA, s 51. The earlier history is recounted in Simpson, *A History of the Land Law* (2nd edn), p 280.
[3] Giving effect to Law Com No 163.
[4] *Alan Estates Ltd* v *WG Stores Ltd* [1982] Ch 511 at p 526.
[5] Even if handed to the purchaser's solicitor, it may be an escrow if (in particular) the purchase money has not been paid: *Bank of Scotland plc* v *King* [2008] 1 EGLR 65 (not an escrow on the facts).
[6] *Bolton MBC* v *Torkington* [2004] Ch 66, also confirming that delivery is required for deeds sealed by corporations.
[7] Section 1(3). Two witnesses are required if the deed is signed not by the individual but by a person on his behalf (all must be present). See Dray [2013] Conv 298 for exactly what is required.
[8] 1989 Act, s 1(2A), inserted in 2005.
[9] [2007] EWHC 1543 (Ch).

formal binding document. This is a strict test, especially as regards people who are unfamiliar with legal technicalities.[10]

It might be added that it is possible for estoppel to be used where the requirements for a deed have not been complied with.[11] However, there are distinct limits on how far this goes – Newey J has held that it does not apply where the defect is apparent on the face of the supposed deed.[12]

2. Contracts for sales and dispositions of interests in land

Before looking at the rules for transferring and creating interests, it should be observed that the transfer or creation will often be preceded by a contract. Such a contract is almost invariably entered into when land is sold. What requirements are there for such prior contracts? At first sight, this is simply the province of the law of contract, and we should just look at normal contract rules such as those on consideration. It is indeed correct that these rules must be complied with. However, contracts for interests in land have two special characteristics. First, we have seen that they take effect as estate contracts[13] and are thereby equitable interests in the land. The second characteristic is that there are writing requirements. It is with these requirements that we are now concerned.

There has been legislation in this area since the Statute of Frauds 1677, re-enacted as s 40 of the Law of Property Act 1925. These contracts were unenforceable unless evidenced in writing. This seemingly innocuous provision gave rise to a huge amount of litigation over the centuries. Fortunately, much of this can be discarded following the reformulation of the law in s 2 of the 1989 Act. Less fortunately, the 1989 Act has come under attack for introducing new uncertainties and traps for the unwary: the flow of cases continues.

Today, the contract must be in writing (not merely evidenced by writing), contain all the terms expressly agreed and be signed by both parties. If the rules are not complied with, then there is simply no contract. This is to be contrasted with the old principle that there was a contract, but it was unenforceable.[14]

After the buyer and seller agree on a price, a delay of several weeks is likely before there is a binding contract. The interval is required for lawyers to make extensive inquiries about the land, to ensure that the purchaser can safely bind himself or herself to buy. It is not unusual for the contract to be virtually contemporaneous with the completion of the sale. In the past, it was necessary to guard against correspondence rendering the initial oral agreement enforceable. This was achieved by making all correspondence 'subject to

---

[10] Compare the creation of trusts over property, where it is no objection that the settlor is unaware of the language of trusts but (without trying to make an outright gift) makes it clear that he or she wishes the beneficiary to enjoy it: *Paul v Constance* [1977] 1 WLR 527.

[11] *Shah v Shah* [2002] QB 35 (unknown by the covenantee, witnesses of the covenantor's signature added after deed signed).

[12] *Briggs v Gleeds* [2015] Ch 212 (no witnesses), applied in *Bank of Scotland plc v Waugh* [2014] EWHC 2117 (Ch).

[13] Based upon the availability of the equitable remedy of specific performance. Unless relating to land, sale contracts are not generally specifically enforceable.

[14] Several differences follow. For example, the new formulation implicitly abrogates the principle that one who is allowed to partly perform an oral contract may thereafter enforce it.

contract'.[15] Today, the need for the contract to be in writing and signed by both parties considerably reduces the risk of an 'accidental' enforceable contract.

The delay between initial agreement and formal contract provides an opportunity for either party to withdraw: most notoriously, a seller who has received a higher offer. This is the practice called gazumping, which is particularly prevalent in a rising market. A purchaser who wishes to avoid the danger of being gazumped can contract so that the seller agrees not to consider other offers for a specified period. Such a lockout agreement has been held to be effective and outside the s 2 requirement of writing.[16]

A. Complying with the 1989 Act

(i) *What transactions are included?*

Section 2 applies not only to sales of land,[17] but also to any contract for an interest in land, such as a lease or mortgage[18] and contracts disposing of such interests.[19] It is important to remember that it does not apply to the actual disposal (sale, lease, charge) – different requirements (discussed later in this chapter) then operate.[20] The interest contracted for may be either legal or equitable. There are some statutory exclusions.[21] We shall see that some short leases do not need to be in writing; contracts for such leases are explicitly excluded. Another exclusion is for sales at public auction. It is generally very clear that the parties have agreed to sell and to buy, and the terms are invariably specified in a draft contract available at the auction.[22] A contract simply relating to land is not caught: contracts to clean windows do not require writing!

Problems have arisen where the contract does not take the normal form of V contracting to sell to P. In *Nweze v Nwoko*,[23] the parties agreed that property should be sold and the proceeds be paid to one of them. It was held that this was not caught by s 2: it was more a contract to market the land than one under which an interest is sold. It seems likely that a contract whereby the land is to be sold to a specific third party is within the section,[24] although doubts were expressed in *Nweze*. If such contracts are covered, who must sign? The statutory requirement is that the parties to the contract must each sign. Neuberger J has held that there is no need for the third party to sign the contract.[25]

---

[15] Reaffirmed in *Tiverton Estates Ltd* v *Wearwell Ltd* [1975] Ch 146. The formula is still useful to help avoid an estoppel claim: Adams [2001] Conv 449.

[16] *Pitt* v *PHH Asset Management Ltd* [1994] 1 WLR 327.

[17] Land includes fixtures such as buildings (*Lavery* v *Pursell* (1888) 39 Ch D 508), although crops that are to be harvested may be excluded (*Marshall* v *Green* (1875) 1 CPD 35).

[18] See LPA, s 205(1)(ii), applied by s 2(6) of the 1989 Act.

[19] *Jarvis* v *Jarvis* (1893) 63 LJ Ch 10 (mortgage of a mortgagee's interest: a sub-mortgage).

[20] *Helden* v *Strathmore Ltd* [2011] HLR 635 at [27]; *Rollerteam Ltd* v *Riley* [2017] 2 WLR 870 (nor does it apply to a unilateral contract whereby money is to be paid in consideration of the disposal).

[21] 1989 Act, s 2(5).

[22] The contract would normally be signed straightaway.

[23] [2004] 2 P&CR 667, criticised by Thompson [2004] Conv 323 but welcomed by Heller (2005) 147 PLJ 91.

[24] *Jelson Ltd* v *Derby CC* [1999] 3 EGLR 91.

[25] *RG Kensington Management Co Ltd* v *Hutchinson IDH Ltd* [2003] 2 P&CR 195 at [57], not following *Jelson Ltd* v *Derby CC* [1999] 3 EGLR 91. The third party will have no liability and will not be able to sue unless either the benefit is assigned or the Contracts (Rights of Third Parties) Act 1999 applies.

Similar issues arise if there are two joint purchasers and the contract is signed by only one (not authorised by the other). *Rabiu* v *Marlbray* Ltd holds that there is a good contract binding the person who signed – as the Court of Appeal observed, it would be odd if that person could use his lack of authority to avoid liability.

The application of s 2 also raises problems where neighbours agree on the line of the boundary between their plots. It has been held[27] that clarifying an unclear boundary is outside the section. An agreement settling ownership (which may be wider than boundary disputes) is not a contract *for* sale, etc.[28] The purpose of the parties is to resolve an uncertainty rather than to transfer land. Even though the boundary line is in fact changed, this need not be limited to a trivial amount of land.[29] The intention of the court is to avoid the intrusion of legal complexity into issues that are likely to be solved informally.[30] On the other hand, a simple agreement that a trivial area should belong to one of two neighbours does fall within s 2 – there has to be a purpose of defining an uncertain boundary.[31]

Before the 1989 Act, a question had arisen as to whether writing was needed for a contract by a beneficiary to sell a beneficial interest under a trust for sale.[32] Today, s 2(6) of the 1989 Act confirms that such contracts require writing.[33] Unfortunately, s 2(6) appears to apply to all contracts relating to proceeds of sale of land. Suppose that an owner is contemplating selling land, or has indeed entered into a binding contract. If the owner contracts to assign his or her right to the proceeds of sale, or charge them in favour of an agent,[34] do these transactions have to be in writing? This would be surprising, although it is unclear how the language of the 1989 Act can be limited.

Options and pre-emptions

Spiro v *Glencrown Properties Ltd*[35] deals with the application of the 1989 Act to options to buy or lease land. One standard analysis of an option is that it constitutes an irrevocable offer by the owner to sell.[36] The offer is accepted by the exercise of the option, this acceptance of the offer constituting a normal contract of sale. When the purchaser seeks specific performance, this is enforcing the new contract of sale rather than the option.[37] This two-stage analysis involves two contracts: the entry into the option and the subsequent contract of sale. The original option clearly has to be in writing, but does the exercise of the option require compliance with the Act?

---

[26] [2016] 1 WLR 5147.

[27] *Joyce* v *Rigolli* [2004] EWCA Civ 79; [2004] 1 P&CR D55 (Thompson [2004] Conv 224).

[28] *Rollerteam Ltd* v *Riley* [2017] 2 WLR 870 reminds us that s 2 will not apply if the there is a purported actual transfer (such that LPA, s 52 applies): s 2 requires a promise to transfer. Presumably, the relaxation considered in this paragraph may extend to s 52.

[29] *Yeates* v *Line* [2013] Ch 363.

[30] Estoppel will often justify the same outcome: *Joyce* v *Rigolli* at [35]–[36]. Harwood (2004) 154 NLJ 406 observes that the intensity of boundary disputes may justify a writing requirement.

[31] *Nata Lee Ltd* v *Abid* [2015] 2 P&CR 48.

[32] Since the Trusts of Land and Appointment of Trustees Act 1996, trusts for sale have been less common.

[33] Confirming *Cooper* v *Critchley* [1955] Ch 431.

[34] A well-known example is *Thomas* v *Rose* [1968] 1 WLR 1797.

[35] [1991] Ch 537, supported by *Trustees of Chippenham Golf Club* v *North Wiltshire DC* (1991) 64 P&CR 527 at pp 530–531.

[36] *Beesly* v *Hallwood Estates Ltd* [1960] 1 WLR 549 (affirmed on other grounds: [1961] Ch 105).

[37] *Mountford* v *Scott* [1975] Ch 258.

The principal problem is that the Act requires the contract to be signed by both parties, whereas the exercise of an option is invariably a unilateral act by the option holder. It would be very inconvenient to introduce the Act at this stage, and Hoffmann J declined to do so.[38] His argument was that an option may also be regarded as a conditional contract and, given that both this analysis and the irrevocable offer analysis are merely ways of looking at options rather than strict legal analyses, there is no compelling reason to apply the 1989 Act.

Options are clearly established as interests in land. More uncertain is the status of a pre-emption: a right to buy the land if the owner chooses to sell. Although *Pritchard* v *Briggs*[39] held that a pre-emption is not an interest in land, this has been reversed for registered land by s 115 of the Land Registration Act 2002. In unregistered land, the 1989 Act is thought not to apply to the pre-emption contract,[40] but it may be difficult for it to be satisfied thereafter.[41]

(ii) *The requirement of writing; terms of the contract*

The contract itself must be in writing and not merely evidenced in writing. This is intended to be a stricter approach than under the earlier law.[42] What happens if the parties reach an oral agreement and then sign a document merely recording their oral agreement – is the written document the contract? It is likely that the courts will hold that it is.[43] In any event, all expressly agreed terms must be included.[44]

So far as identifying the land is concerned, it has been held that extrinsic evidence can be employed to complete an identification which is otherwise unclear.[45] In the past, this went as far as permitting the land to be described as 'Property purchased at £420 at the Sun Inn, Pinxton, on the above date'[46] or 'my house'.[47] It remains to be seen whether as much generosity will still be shown now that all the terms have to be in writing.

Questions of identification of the parties could arise today if the contract is signed by an agent. An initial point is that the agent must be authorised to enter into the contract; this cannot be taken for granted, as a solicitor has no general authority to enter into a contract.[48]

---

[38] Similarly, there is only one contract for the purposes of protection on the register: *Armstrong & Holmes Ltd* v *Holmes* [1993] 1 WLR 1482.

[39] [1980] Ch 338; it has been heavily criticised (see *Dear* v *Reeves* [2002] Ch 1 at [32], [43]). As recognised by the majority in *Pritchard*, an option may arise when the pre-emption is activated (*Tiffany Investments Ltd* v *Bircham & Co Nominees (No 2) Ltd* [2004] 2 P&CR 144), though this depends upon the owner's being unable to withdraw at that stage (*Speciality Shops* v *Yorkshire and Metropolitan Estates Ltd* [2003] 2 P&CR 410).

[40] Pettit [1989] Conv 431 at p 433.

[41] *Bircham & Co, Nominees (2) Ltd* v *Worrell Holdings Ltd* (2001) 82 P&CR 427.

[42] *Firstpost Homes Ltd* v *Johnson* [1995] 1 WLR 1567; Thompson [1995] Conv 488.

[43] *Sir Hari Sankar Paul* v *Kedar Nath Saha* [1939] 2 All ER 737.

[44] This may include express terms that would in any event have been implied: Pettit [1989] Conv 431 at p 436.

[45] *Freeguard* v *Rogers* [1999] 1 WLR 375 ('9, Graffham Close' included an adjoining garage, registered under a separate title), though the issue was more one of construction of the contract than the application of the 1989 Act.

[46] *Shardlow* v *Cotterell* (1881) 20 Ch D 90, followed in *Harewood* v *Retese* [1990] 1 WLR 333 (PC).

[47] Recognised in *Sheers* v *Thimbleby* (1897) 76 LT 709.

[48] *H Clark (Doncaster) Ltd* v *Wilkinson* [1965] Ch 694 at p 702. The authority may be oral: *McLaughlin* v *Duffill* [2010] Ch 1.

Once authorised, the older cases held it sufficient for the agent to refer to the seller as proprietor,[49] but not 'the vendor'.[50] Although extrinsic evidence is not available today to identify a vendor who is not referred to in the contract,[51] it remains unclear what latitude (if any) will be permitted.

A rather different point concerns agents who contract without disclosing that they are agents. Pre-1989, this did not prevent the undisclosed principal from suing or being sued on the contract,[52] in accordance with normal agency rules. Presumably, this rule would still apply today. So long as an agent signs so as to make it his contract, this satisfies the statutory requirement that the parties be identified. It does not matter that there is an undisclosed principal, simply because that does not depend upon any of the terms of the contract. Clear as this result appears to be, it may cause some surprise that a person may be liable on the contract even though his name does not appear in it.

Omitted terms

What happens if a term is omitted from the signed document?[53] Prima facie, the contract is void. However, the Law Commission envisaged that the omission of a term might sometimes be corrected by rectification of the signed contract.[54] Rectification has been ordered where the written contract omitted a reference to contents being included in the price.[55] However, the omission must represent a mistake in the drafting of the contract: rectification does not apply simply because the omission renders the contract void.[56] In particular, a deliberate omission of a term – for example, where an extra term is agreed upon after the written contract has been settled in draft – will not trigger rectification.[57]

Where rectification is not available, an omitted term may still take effect under a collateral contract. Consider this example. V agrees to sell his house to P, and contracts are on the point of being exchanged. P receives a survey indicating that a chimney needs to be rebuilt. Very concerned about the likely cost, P telephones V. V, who is eager to sell the house, assures P that he will rebuild the chimney if P exchanges contracts. Can V argue that the obligation to build the chimney is not binding upon him, or that the entire contract is invalid as not being wholly in writing? The long-established answer is that the obligation to build the chimney is not part of the sale contract. Instead, it is part of a collateral contract under which V is to rebuild the chimney in return for P's entering into the contract.[58]

The real question is how far this principle can be taken. It is quite clear that it was intended to survive the 1989 Act.[59] There is a conflict between two laudable objectives. On

---

[49] *Rossiter* v *Miller* (1878) 3 App Cas 1124.
[50] *Potter* v *Duffield* (1874) LR 18 Eq 4.
[51] *Rudra* v *Abbey National plc* (1998) 76 P&CR 537.
[52] *Davies* v *Sweet* [1962] 2 QB 300.
[53] For implications of the parol evidence rule, see McLauchlan, *The Parol Evidence Rule*, especially pp 37–38.
[54] Law Com No 164, para 5.6.
[55] *Wright* v *Robert Leonard Developments Ltd* [1994] EGCS 69.
[56] Treitel, *The Law of Contract* (14th edn), para 6-029; *Francis* v *F Berndes Ltd* [2012] 1 EGLR 117 (failure to identify obligation to buy).
[57] *Oun* v *Ahmad* [2008] EWHC 545 (Ch), especially at [51].
[58] *De Lassalle* v *Guildford* [1901] 2 KB 215.
[59] Law Com No 164, para 5.7.

the one side, it is desired that the written contract should record all the agreed terms. On the other hand, it is seen as unreasonable to deny all effect to a written agreement when a non-core clause has been omitted.

The decision of Judge Paul Baker QC in *Record* v *Bell*[60] shows a clear preference for giving effect to the contract. The vendor had been unable to obtain a copy of the land certificate proving his title. The purchaser agreed to enter into a contract on the basis that the vendor warranted the state of the registered title. This was agreed to by correspondence, but there was no reference to it in the contract. Counsel argued that the statute was not satisfied, bearing in mind the rule that the contract must be in a single signed document. However, the judge held that the vendor's warranty was in a collateral contract and that, therefore, all the terms of the contract of sale were in the signed agreement.[61] *Record* v *Bell* is more than a case of simply omitting a term. There really was an arguable collateral contract: an agreement to sign the contract if the warranty was given. What is more difficult is that the warranty looks as if it was intended to vary the terms of the contract[62] rather than operating outside it (contrast the example about the chimney).

Apart from a collateral contract as described earlier, the parties may decide to embody part of their agreement in a separate contract. The cases in this area were reviewed by the Court of Appeal in *North Eastern Properties Ltd* v *Coleman*.[63] It is quite possible for the parties to use separate contracts, provided that the land contract is not conditional on performance of the separate contract. It does not matter that the two agreements form a single commercial deal. What is especially useful for the parties is that they may indicate that the land contract is not conditional, which might be by the inclusion of an 'entire agreement' clause.

A final issue on the omission of terms is that, before 1989, a person with the benefit of an omitted term could waive it and then enforce the rest of the contract.[64] Although the legislation is not explicit, *Record* v *Bell*[65] supports the view that such waiver is no longer possible.

(iii) *The one document rule*

Not only must the contract record all the agreed terms, but it must also take the form of a single document. It follows that, if a term is left out by mistake and the parties sign a separate document to cover it, then the statute is not satisfied. It is not enough that the second document refers to the main contract, unless the second document can be construed as the contract of sale.

---

[60] [1991] 1 WLR 853. See [1991] CLJ 399; [1991] Conv 471; (1992) 108 LQR 217.
[61] The warranty had been complied with; the question was whether the signed contract could be enforced.
[62] This may explain why a collateral contract argument failed in *Sukhlall* v *Bansoodeb* [2013] EWHC 952 (Ch) (attempt to put part of purchase price in collateral contract).
[63] [2010] 1 WLR 2715; see also *Keay* v *Morris Homes (West Midlands) Ltd* [2012] 1 WLR 2855. Earlier cases include *Tootal Clothing Ltd* v *Guinea Properties Ltd* (1992) 64 P&CR 452 and *Grossman* v *Hooper* [2001] 3 FCR 662.
[64] Likewise if the person bound by a term agreed to comply with it. *Martin* v *Pycroft* (1852) 22 LJ Ch 94; *Scott* v *Bradley* [1971] Ch 850.
[65] [1991] 1 WLR 853. The claimant had in fact performed the omitted term; under the old law, this would have rendered its omission irrelevant. See also *Emmet on Title* (19th edn), para 2.030, although Pettit [1989] Conv 431 at p 438 is less certain.

When land is sold, it is common for the contract to be in two identical parts. Each of the parties signs one part and hands it to the other. It is from this procedure that we talk about exchange of contracts. Section 2(3) allows this to continue 'where contracts are exchanged'. The Court of Appeal in *Commission for the New Towns* v *Cooper (Great Britain) Ltd*[66] has held that this applies only to a conventional exchange of contracts and not to a contract by correspondence (written offer and written acceptance).

The essence of exchange is that there has been a prior agreement as to the terms; the two parts each include all the terms and are intended to effect the formal contract. The strictness of the approach in *Cooper* can be justified as it avoids disputes as to the timing of the contract and its terms. It also reduces the risk of important land contracts being entered into without full thought and the opportunity of seeking professional advice.

Although the basic rule is that the contract must contain all the terms agreed, it is possible for terms in another document to be incorporated by reference.[67] This adopts the earlier law in *Timmins* v *Moreland Street Property Co Ltd*.[68] *Timmins* stressed that the signed memorandum must expressly or by necessary implication refer to another document[69]: it is not sufficient that the documents fit together when put side by side. Presumably, a similar rule will apply under the 1989 Act. A related question is whether, without express reference, a document is incorporated by physically attaching it to the signed document, by a clip or staple, for example. This question was raised, but not settled, in *Record* v *Bell*.[70]

(iv) *Signature*

There is no requirement that the document be signed in any particular place. It may be noted that the document can be signed before there is any contract. A common example is where separate parts of a contract are signed before exchange. If there is then an amendment before the contract comes into being, there appears to be no effective signature.[71]

A very generous approach in the older cases allowed merely writing a name in a document to count as a signature. Thus, issuing a document containing your name would suffice once it was signed by the other party.[72] Under the 1989 Act, however, it is not enough for the name to be printed or typed, at least in the form of an addressee of a letter.[73] On the other hand, the use of a signature writing machine does suffice.[74] It has already been seen that signature may be by an agent.

---

[66] [1995] Ch 259 at pp 283–289 and 292–295; Thompson [1995] Conv 319.
[67] 1989 Act, s 2(2); cf *Firstpost Homes Ltd* v *Johnson* [1995] 1 WLR 1567.
[68] [1958] Ch 110 (cheque for deposit held not to refer to receipt).
[69] *Elias* v *George Sahely & Co (Barbados) Ltd* [1983] 1 AC 646 (PC) allowed incorporation of an oral transaction, of which there was a written record. It would seem unsafe to rely upon this after the 1989 Act, which requires a reference 'to some other document'.
[70] [1991] 1 WLR 853 at p 860.
[71] *New Hart Builders Ltd* v *Brindley* [1975] Ch 342, criticised by Emery (1975) 39 Conv 336.
[72] *Leeman* v *Stocks* [1951] Ch 941.
[73] *Firstpost Homes Ltd* v *Johnson* [1995] 1 WLR 1567; Balcombe LJ is more dismissive of the old law. Compare the rule for wills: p 133 below.
[74] *Ramsay* v *Love* [2015] EWHC 65 (Ch) at [7]; the point was not contested.

(v) *Subsequent variation and rescission*

McCausland v *Duncan Lawrie Ltd*[75] holds that the strict requirements of the 1989 Act
are applicable to variations of the contract. The original contract remains enforceable if
the variation is ineffective. As for oral rescission, this was effective under the old law.
There seems to be no reason why a rescission should be treated any more as a contract for
the sale of land than before 1989. As was pointed out in *Morris* v *Baron & Co*,[76] rescission
of a contract may be seen as the compromise of an action upon it. It would be odd if such
a compromise had to be in writing signed by both parties.

B. Enforcing contracts that do not comply with the 1989 Act

The normal position, of course, is that there is no contract unless the 1989 Act is complied
with. As we have seen, collateral contracts and rectification may come to the rescue when
terms have been omitted, but they apply only in a very limited range of circumstances.
What happens if a party acts to his detriment on a contract that has fallen foul of the Act?

In the past, the requirement of writing was overlooked by equity when there had been
part performance of the contract: the person who partly performed, to the knowledge of
the other, could thereafter enforce the contract. For example, entering into possession (or
permitting entry into possession) was treated as part performance. The Law Commission
was critical of the part performance rule because of the uncertainties concerning its application.[77] Although nothing in the 1989 Act specifically abolishes part performance, *United
Bank of Kuwait plc* v *Sahib*[78] confirms that the doctrine can no longer apply: the doctrine
depended upon the old theory that an oral contract was unenforceable rather than void.[79]

This has particular significance for mortgages. It had long been the law that the
deposit of title deeds with the lender was part performance of an agreement to mortgage
land. *United Bank of Kuwait*[80] confirms both that such mortgages are created by way of
a contract and that they can no longer be created orally. Although lenders nearly always
required borrowers to sign documents confirming the transaction, these would not normally be signed by the lender and therefore would not satisfy the 1989 Act, which
requires signature by both parties. This is a distinct trap for mortgagees; it was not
clearly intended.[81]

It is desirable that some remedy be available where a person has been allowed to act to
his detriment upon the assumption that there is a valid and enforceable contract.
Constructive, resulting and implied trusts are exempted by s 2(5) of the 1989 Act from the
effect of that Act.[82] Before the Act, a constructive trust had been recognised in exceptional
cases where it would be a fraud on a statute for the promisor to deny liability on the

[75] [1997] 1 WLR 38, confirming the old law in *Morris* v *Baron & Co* [1918] AC 1.
[76] [1918] AC 1, relied upon in *McCausland* v *Duncan Lawrie Ltd* [1997] 1 WLR 38.
[77] *Steadman* v *Steadman* [1976] AC 536 had widened its scope.
[78] [1997] Ch 107, especially at pp 139–140. See also *Yaxley* v *Gotts* [2000] Ch 162 at p 172.
[79] Law Com No 164, para 4.13.
[80] [1997] Ch 107 at pp 135–141.
[81] Hill (1990) 106 LQR 396.
[82] Section 2(5).

contract.[83] However, the Law Commission saw estoppel as being the appropriate remedy to deal with cases of unconscionable conduct,[84] despite the legislation containing no reference to estoppel.

Unfortunately, the lack of any statutory exemption for estoppel led to its role being queried in *Yaxley* v *Gotts*.[85] There are, indeed, problems in ensuring that the policy of the legislation is not undermined by devices such as estoppel. As Neuberger LJ later stated,[86] the law must 'avoid regarding [s 2(5)] as an automatically available escape route from the rigours of section 2(1)'.

The Court of Appeal in *Yaxley* held in favour of the purchaser, but mainly on the basis of a constructive trust analysis. It was recognised that estoppels and constructive trusts overlap considerably. Whether estoppel is itself an exception was not made entirely clear, although there are dicta of Beldam and Clarke LJJ which support this. Although most subsequent cases treated the 1989 Act as not precluding estoppel claims,[87] *Kinane* v *Mackie-Conteh*[88] stated that estoppel was likely to apply only where the circumstances also give rise to a constructive trust.

In *Cobbe* v *Yeoman's Row Management Ltd*,[89] Lord Scott expressed the opinion that s 2 cannot be avoided by the application of estoppel. Though there is a fair amount of support for the continued operation of estoppel,[90] the Court of Appeal has recently doubted whether this is possible.[91] If estoppel can apply, but only where a constructive trust is available,[92] *Dudley Muslim Association* v *Dudley MBC*[93] illustrates its limits. Estoppel was argued as a defence to a contractual obligation to re-transfer property (there had been a representation that the obligation would not be enforced). As the Court of Appeal stressed, the claimant (against whom the estoppel was argued) did not hold any property which could be held on a constructive trust. Any estoppel would have to be freestanding, and that is not permissible in the s 2 context.

---

[83] *Lyus* v *Prowsa Developments Ltd* [1982] 1 WLR 1044.

[84] Davis (1993) 13 OxJLS 99.

[85] [2000] Ch 162; RJ Smith (2000) 116 LQR 11; Thompson [2000] Conv 245.

[86] *Kinane* v *Mackie-Conteh* [2005] WTLR 345 at [40]. Contrast the willingness of McFarlane [2005] Conv 501 to apply estoppel as a separate cause of action. Dixon (2010) 30 LS 408 would require an assurance that the obligation will be complied with, notwithstanding the failure to fulfil formality requirements. See also n 90 in this chapter.

[87] *James* v *Evans* [2000] 3 EGLR 1 at p 4; *Shah* v *Shah* [2002] QB 35 (on s 1 of the 1989 Act, limited by *Briggs* v *Gleeds* [2015] Ch 212); *Joyce* v *Rigolli* [2004] EWCA Civ 79 at [35]–[36]; [2004] 1 P&CR D55; *McGuane* v *Welch* [2008] 2 P&CR 530.

[88] [2005] WTLR 345 at [25]–[26] (Arden LJ) and at [41]–[51] (Neuberger LJ); Dixon [2005] Conv 247. *Kinane* was applied in *S* v *S and M* [2007] 1 FLR 1123.

[89] [2008] 1 WLR 1752 at [29]; Lord Walker chose not to consider the point.

[90] *Herbert* v *Doyle* [2009] WTLR 589 at [15] (upheld (2010) [2015] WTLR 1573 without explicit comment on this); *Whittaker* v *Kinnear* [2011] EWHC 1479 (QB); *Muhammad* v *ARY Properties Ltd* [2013] EWHC 1698 (Ch) (not citing *Dudley Muslim Association*). Extra-judicially, Lord Neuberger has suggested that estoppel should operate where there is a belief (encouraged by O) that there is a binding obligation: [2009] CLJ 537 at p 546.

[91] *Dudley Muslim Association* v *Dudley MBC* [2016] 1 P&CR 176; earlier, see *Hutchison* v *B&DF Ltd* [2009] L&TR 206 at [68].

[92] *Brightlingsea Haven Ltd* v *Morris* [2009] 2 P&CR 169. Though criticised by McFarlane and Robertson [2008] LMCLQ 449 at pp 456–457 (see also Dixon (2010) 30 LS 408 at p 416), the constructive trust analysis was readily applied in *Dowding* v *Matchmove Ltd* [2017] 1 WLR 749.

[93] [2016] 1 P&CR 176.

Estoppel, together with its links with constructive trusts, will be considered in later chapters.[94] *Cobbe* is important in restricting the application of estoppel, especially in commercial transactions.[95] Even if not excluded by s 2, this may well make it more difficult to argue estoppel in the sale of land context, especially where the claimant is a businessman. If estoppel can be relied upon, an important aspect of it (but not necessarily of constructive trusts) is that the courts possess a wide range of remedies. Part performance led to the enforcement of the contract, no matter how trivial the act of part performance. As Arden LJ has observed,[96] s 2(5) 'plays a similar role to part performance, although it operates more flexibly'. This flexibility of remedy in estoppel may be seen as an advantage, although it leads to difficulty in predicting the outcome of litigation. Whether there is such a discretion in constructive trusts is less clear. This will become important if, after *Yaxley* and *Cobbe*, it is necessary to rely on a constructive trust.[97] Overall, it may well be concluded that the abolition of part performance is not easily justified.[98]

Finally, it was at one stage thought that a contract rendered void by the 1989 Act could be enforced, once the provisions relating to the transfer of property had been executed.[99] In other words, a clause omitted from the written contract could be enforced after completion. This is very surprising, as it appears to follow that a void contract becomes enforceable after completion, insofar as it contains provisions intended to have effect after completion. Fortunately, the Court of Appeal in *Keay* v *Morris Homes (West Midlands) Ltd*[100] has denied that the cases have any such effect.

C. Conclusions as to the 1989 Act

The 1989 Act enables much of the old law to be forgotten; that is to be welcomed. Nevertheless, there are still plenty of doubts and uncertainties surrounding the need for writing. The flood of cases in the last few years has demonstrated that it has not put paid to litigation. Perhaps most worrying is the uncertainty caused by the reliance upon estoppel in cases previously covered by part performance. Overall, one cannot help thinking that the Act is a disappointment.

D. Electronic conveyancing

Some of the above rules will become of increasingly marginal significance when electronic conveyancing is introduced. This is considered in the following section on land.

---

[94] Chapter 10 and p 215 below. The views of Lord Scott on estoppel generally have been heavily qualified, although this may not impact on his dicta on s 2.

[95] Previously, *Kinane* had supported the need for a representation that there is a binding contract. Bently and Coughlan (1990) 10 LS 325 prefer a restitutionary approach; this gains some support from *Cobbe*.

[96] *Kinane* v *Mackie-Conteh* [2005] WTLR 345 at [32].

[97] See p 220 below.

[98] Note the damning criticism of s 2 by Neuberger [2009] CLJ 537 at p 545. See also Davis (1993) 13 OxJLS 99; Thompson [1994] Conv 465; Griffiths [2002] Conv 216.

[99] *Tootal Clothing Ltd* v *Guinea Properties Ltd* (1992) 64 P&CR 452, followed by Lewison J in *Kilcarne Holdings Ltd* v *Targetfollow (Birmingham) Ltd* [2005] 1 P&CR 105 at [197]–[198] (despite expressing considerable doubts) and *Mirza* v *Mirza* [2009] 2 FLR 115, and with support from *North Eastern Properties Ltd* v *Coleman* [2010] 1 WLR 2715 at [49].

[100] [2012] 1 WLR 2855.

3. Land

We can now look at the various rules for the transfer and creation of interests. The possibilities will be considered by looking at different categories of property: land provides our first category. For all categories, it is assumed that the transferor (or disponor) is the owner of whatever is being transferred, with power to transfer (or otherwise deal with) it.

A. Transfer

The position regarding land transfers is straightforward: it is necessary to use a deed to transfer a legal interest in land.[101] Originally, estates were transferred by a process that was, in essence, delivery: feoffment with livery of seisin. This has long since disappeared.[102]

A few qualifications should be mentioned. First, the transfer of most interests is incomplete without registration. The use of a deed by itself will not then transfer a legal estate, though it is an essential prerequisite to registration. Next, there are a few statutory exceptions to the necessity of a deed. One worth mentioning in the context of transfers is that the personal representatives of a deceased person may transfer land to the persons entitled by an assent: a document in writing.[103] Somewhat surprisingly, it has been held that a deed can be varied by an oral contract.[104] Although this is plainly correct for deeds generally, it is far from clear that it is good policy where land is involved: absent a fresh deed, the rules for land contracts should be complied with.

What happens if a deed is required but not used? Prima facie, the transfer is ineffective. However, a qualification is illustrated by the treatment of informal leases. Leases quite commonly fall foul of the requirement of a deed, but the courts treat such an ineffective lease as an agreement for a lease and enforce it as such.[105] Since the Law of Property (Miscellaneous Provisions) Act 1989, there must be writing signed by both parties for there to be a valid agreement for a lease.[106] It will be recalled that any estate contract (including a written agreement for a lease) confers an equitable interest upon its holder. Indeed, equity will, so far as possible, place the equitable lessee in the same position as if there were a legal lease: equity treats as done what ought to be done.

The same reasoning would apply to a transfer of any legal interest where there is no deed. It follows that the transferee would have an equitable fee simple (or whatever is being attempted to be transferred), provided that there is consideration and writing. Gifts, however, do require a deed to be effective: the donee cannot rely on the earlier analysis, as specific performance is unavailable without consideration.[107]

---

[101] LPA, s 52.

[102] Writing was required by the Statute of Frauds 1677, and the requirement of a deed was introduced by the Real Property Act 1845, s 3. See now LPA, ss 51, 52.

[103] LPA, ss 52(2)(a), 53.

[104] *Target Holdings Ltd* v *Priestley* (1999) 79 P&CR 305; criticised by Thompson [1999] Conv 414.

[105] E.g. *Parker* v *Taswell* (1858) 2 De G&J 559 (44 ER 1106). A recent example is provided by *Bank of Scotland plc* v *Waugh* [2014] EWHC 2117 (Ch) (equitable charge, when requirements for a legal charge not satisfied)

[106] *United Bank of Kuwait plc* v *Sahib* [1997] Ch 107 at p 140.

[107] But the gift may be valid in equity on other grounds: see p 177 below.

So far we have been dealing with transfers of legal interests. There is a specific provision requiring all transfers of interests in land to be in writing. This adds little: we shall see that a substantially identical requirement operates for transfers of all equitable interests.[108] The transfer of equitable interests (in land and other property) will be dealt with later as a separate topic.

B. Creation of interests

The creation of interests in land is regulated by the Law of Property Act 1925. The general rules are that all interests must be created by writing signed by the person creating the interest (s 53(1)(a)) and that legal interests must be created by deed (s 52).[109] In addition, s 53(1)(b) requires trusts of land to be evidenced in writing.

There are two principal exceptions to the need for a deed for legal interests. An assent by a personal representative requires only writing, as has been seen already in the context of transfers.[110] More interesting is the exception for short leases.

It is common for short leases to be entered into without great formality. This is recognised by s 54(2), which allows oral leases to be effective if 'taking effect in possession for a term not exceeding three years . . . at the best rent which can be reasonably obtained without taking a fine'.[111] A fine is a capital sum (sometimes called a premium) paid by the tenant; it is usually found in longer tenancies. The best rent means the market rent, not simply what the parties have agreed.[112] Doubtless, it will remain easy to show that the agreed rent is the market rent unless there are factors in the negotiations showing that the parties were not bargaining for the best rent reasonably obtainable.[113] Arguing that the rent could have been, say, 5% higher is unlikely to be successful. Taking effect in possession means that the lease must not be postponed. It follows that a lease for a period of a year, but which is to commence in six months' time, falls outside s 54(2) and requires a deed.[114]

This may lead to some very fine distinctions. An agreement that a lease for a year will be granted in six months' time is an agreement for a lease which, when granted, will take effect in possession. Both agreement[115] and lease may be oral. It is only if there is an immediate lease, taking effect in the future, that a deed is required. It does not take much

---

[108] LPA, s 53(1)(a), (c).

[109] As with transfers, registration will often be necessary before there can be a legal estate or interest. A deed, however, is a prerequisite for registration. Pulleyn [2012] Conv 387 considers the scope of s 53(1)(a).

[110] See p 111 above.

[111] For details see Sparkes [1992] Conv 252, 337. A lease exceeding three years, but which may be cut short according to its terms, falls outside s 54(2): *Kushner* v *Law Society* [1952] 1 KB 264. The subsection expressly applies even though there is provision for extending the term to a total over three years; cf *Gerraty* v *McGavin* (1914) 18 CLR 152.

[112] *Fitzkriston LLP* v *Panayi* [2008] EWCA Civ 283; [2008] L&TR 412 (evidence that it was a third of market rent); criticised by Brown [2009] Conv 54.

[113] The rent may be higher than the market rent: a 'remarkably good bargain' in *Looe Fuels Ltd* v *Looe Harbour Commissioners* [2009] L&TR 40 at [30].

[114] James Munby QC in an extensive and analytically convincing judgment in *Long* v *Tower Hamlets LBC* [1998] Ch 197. The law before 1925 had been different and Bright [1998] Conv 229 observes that the case 'flies in the face of accepted understanding and practice'.

[115] 1989 Act, s 2(5).

imagination to understand that parties to informal arrangements will not think in these terms and that oral arrangements may be susceptible to either analysis. It is also worrying that many informal agreements take effect a few days in the future and thus fall foul of the legislation.

Section 54(2) includes what are called periodic tenancies. It is possible to create weekly, monthly or yearly leases. Unless terminated by either party, periodic tenancies will continue indefinitely. Because at no time is there a lease for a term exceeding three years, they do not require a deed or writing, provided they take effect in possession.[116] It is interesting that these leases not exceeding three years do not even need to be in writing. Although it may be thought generous (and inviting disputes) to allow oral arrangements to be effective in the land context,[117] the law has long implied periodic tenancies from the payment of rent, and this would be impossible if writing were required. Although contracts for these short leases need not be in writing, transfers of short leases do require a deed.[118] This may constitute something of a trap, although transfer of short leases is unusual.

As noted earlier, the general rule is that the creation of all interests in land (legal and equitable) must be in writing.[119] Three exceptions are worth noting,[120] applicable to each of the provisions in s 53(1). The first, just discussed, is the short lease. Next, s 53(2) excludes resulting, implied and constructive trusts; these will be studied in the context of assignment of equitable interests. This exception is of enormous importance, as it underpins the huge mass of case law dealing with informal joint purchase of land, considered in Chapter 11. The third exception is for part performance. It is deeply unclear when this applies. For contracts, part performance has not been available since 1989.[121] It may well be that part performance applies only to declarations of trust of land within s 53(1)(b)[122] and has no application to s 53(1)(a) or (c).[123]

C. Electronic conveyancing

The Law Commission gave the title 'A Conveyancing Revolution' to its 2001 report on land registration, regarding these changes as more far-reaching than the 1925 reforms.[124] When fully implemented, e-conveyancing will render most of the present formality rules for land obsolete or of minimal importance. As will be seen, the Land Registration Act

---

[116] *Ex p Voisey* (1882) 21 Ch D 442.
[117] But lessees enjoy statutory protection, and landlords ought not to be able to avoid this by the simple expedient of not signing the lease.
[118] *Crago* v *Julian* [1992] 1 WLR 372.
[119] Section 53 does not apply to contracts (the 1989 Act applies instead): *McLaughlin* v *Duffill* [2010] Ch 1 and *Helden* v *Strathmore Ltd* [2011] HLR 635 at [26]–[29].
[120] LPA, ss 53(2), 54(2), 55. Also excluded are dispositions by will and adverse possession.
[121] See p 108 above.
[122] See p 130 below. It seems odd that part performance can apply where there is no contract, although this has been suggested: Picarda, *Law and Practice Relating to Charities* (4th edn), p 312.
[123] Ford and Lee, *Principles of the Law of Trusts* (3rd edn), para 6090; contra the American authorities: Scott, *Trusts* (5th edn), para 14.7.
[124] Law Com No 271, para 1.1. See Harpum in *Modern Studies in Property Law*, Vol 1 (ed Cooke), Ch 1; Capps [2002] Conv 443. Howell [2006] Conv 553 adds a more sceptical view.

2002 (hereafter LRA), makes provision for e-conveyancing. However, after a decade of work, the project was halted in 2011.[125] The future of the area is discussed in a recent Law Commission Consultation Paper.[126] The halting of the original project does *not* mean that electronic developments are shunned. One good example is that electronic delivery of applications for registration is encouraged by a halving of fees, resulting in 83% of such applications being made this way.[127] The structure discussed below (initial optional use of electronic transfers, followed by their becoming compulsory) will be maintained.

(i) *Electronic Communications Act 2000*

This legislation provides for the use of electronic means of entering into transactions and disapplies existing formality requirements. The 2000 Act was partly overtaken by the LRA, but only the 2000 Act applies to contracts for the sale of land. A draft order relating to contracts was published by the Land Registry early in 2007. A significant consequence would be that the writing requirements of the 1989 Act would cease to be required, although all the terms would have to be incorporated into the electronic instrument.

(ii) *Land Registration Act 2002, s 91*

When implemented, Section 91 will 'switch on' optional e-conveyancing. It applies to any disposition (obviously including a transfer) of a registered interest or an interest protected by notice on the register.[128] Its exact application will be settled by rules, so we do not yet know the types of dispositions to be covered. The electronic disposition is treated as a deed for statutory purposes and therefore satisfies all formality requirements.

As originally intended, the significance of e-conveyancing was not limited to the simple replacement of conventional documentation. Entries would be placed on the register electronically, by action of the parties. The present three stages of creating an interest, application to the registry and entry on the register would be collapsed into one: simultaneous completion and registration. It is this aspect of the scheme that has been postponed indefinitely. Interests will be created electronically and applications will be made to the Registry electronically. However, the third stage will remain separate: entries on the register will be made by the Land Registry.[129]

One aspect of e-conveyancing is that it would be operated by conveyancers. The obvious question arises as to what happens if the electronic disposition is not authorised by the parties involved. In order to avoid the necessity for non-electronic checks as to

---

[125] Land Registry Annual Report and Accounts 2010–2011, p 26.

[126] Law Com CP 227, Chapter 20.

[127] Land Registration Fee Order 2013 (SI 2013 No 3174), art 3(5); Land Registry Annual Report and Accounts 2015–2016.

[128] Also dispositions triggering the requirement of registration. Contracts are not included: these are covered by the draft order under the Electronic Communications Act 2000.

[129] An unfortunate consequence is that there will remain a 'registration gap' between completion and registration; this causes a number of problems in the operation of land registration.

authority,[130] the conveyancer is deemed to have the necessary authority.[131] This is a far-reaching provision and may be thought significantly to undermine the security of registered titles.[132] Naturally, any fraudulent electronic entry would spell the end of the conveyancer's career and, most likely, their liberty.

(iii) *Land Registration Act 2002, s 93*

The next stage of e-conveyancing will involve the compulsory use of electronic conveyancing ('switching off' the use of deeds), a step which will lie some years after s 91 is implemented. By contrast, the 2000 Act and LRA, s 91 provide merely an alternative to the use of conventional documents.

Once electronic conveyancing becomes standard, s 93 is likely to be activated. It would also be applied to estate contracts. The importance of s 93 should not be underestimated. Without electronic creation, there will be no proprietary interest. This means that there would be no question of the interest's being protected as an actual occupation overriding interest, affecting a trustee in bankruptcy or having priority over subsequent minor interests.[133] Less obviously, there would not even be a contractual or other personal right.[134] This means that the electronic creation requirement is similar to the requirement of writing under s 2 of the 1989 Act: if it is not complied with, then there is no form of obligation.

It should be noted, however, that not all dispositions will trigger electronic entry requirements. Many interests are created informally or by operation of law and it would be unrealistic (and unjust) to expect these to be the subject of an electronic entry on the register. The Law Commission expects the following exceptions to apply[135]:

(1) rights arising without any express grant or reservation;
(2) dispositions taking effect by operation of law;
(3) interests under trusts; and
(4) leases which are overriding interests (those not exceeding seven years).

The first and third categories merit further discussion. The first includes rights by proprietary estoppel, adverse possession, implied and prescriptive easements and mere equities (such as the right to set aside a transfer for fraud). Turning to interests under trusts, these are important if only because trusts are involved in so many of the cases on the overriding interest of persons in actual occupation. As with the first category, entry on the register cannot be expected for constructive and resulting trusts. It would be truly surprising if statute were to deny effect to these trusts as imposed by the courts. It is less clear that express trusts deserve such protection,[136] although these have caused relatively little difficulty in practice.

---

[130] Law Com No 271, paras 13.60–13.62.
[131] Schedule 5, para 8. The conveyancer would require a 'network access agreement' with the Land Registry.
[132] There is provision for requiring those with network access to have adequate insurance: Sched 5, para 11(3)(c).
[133] For the priority rules, see p 253 below.
[134] Under s 93(2), the disposition or contract 'only has effect' if the requirements are satisfied.
[135] Law Com No 254, para 11.12; they do not appear in the legislation, as they will feature in rules implementing s 93.
[136] The Law Commission defends the proposal by invoking the principle that references to trusts should be excluded from the register (cf LRA, s 78).

(iv) *Implementing and assessing the changes*

There will be no 'big bang' approach applying to all types of interests and disposition. E-conveyancing will be phased in as experience and training develop.

The operation of electronic conveyancing will impact most substantially on the practice of conveyancers. However, the changes will, at least when s 93 is in force, radically alter our perception of formality requirements. Much of the old structure of formality requirements would disappear. During the first stages (before s 93 is implemented), they would cease to be essential: electronic dispositions and contracts would provide alternatives. Once s 93 is implemented, they will cease to be sufficient for registered land (which by then will cover all but a tiny proportion of titles). The old formality rules will apply only to the exceptions to compulsory electronic dispositions; many of these exceptions already lie outside writing requirements.

The present rules on contracts for the sale of land illustrate the use of estoppels and constructive trusts as means of enforcing arrangements which fail the statutory formality requirements. It may be anticipated that the new rules on electronic dispositions would trigger a similar response. This looks like a potent area of growth for estoppel-based arguments,[137] although this lies many years in the future when s 93 is implemented.

4. Chattels

A. Transfer

For chattels, there are three methods of transfer of ownership: delivery, deed and sale.[138]

(i) *Sale*

Most chattels change ownership following a sale. The contract of sale accomplishes the transfer: there is no need for a separate delivery or formal transfer of ownership. Sale of goods constitutes a large area of law, and the details lie outside the scope of this text. A brief overview follows.

For property to pass at all, the rule originally was that the goods must be ascertained.[139] It is fairly obvious that the law will not allow the transfer of property in 1,000 tons of oil from a cargo of 10,000 tons, for how are we to tell which part of the oil belongs to the buyer?[140] However, the Sale of Goods (Amendment) Act 1995[141] permits ownership in common where there is an identified bulk. For ascertained goods, s 17 of the Sale of Goods Act 1979[142] provides for property to pass when intended by the parties. Section 18 lays

---

[137] Dixon in *Modern Studies in Property Law*, Vol 2 (ed Cooke), Ch 9, especially pp 169–172.
[138] For discussion of the civil law concepts of abstract and causal transfers, see van Vliet, *Transfer of Movables*, pp 111 et seq.
[139] Sale of Goods Act 1979, s 16.
[140] *Re Goldcorp Exchange Ltd* [1995] 1 AC 74 (PC).
[141] Authority to deal with the bulk is regulated, something which a common law analysis could not readily achieve.
[142] The 1979 Act consolidated earlier legislation based on the Sale of Goods Act 1893.

down five rules which apply in the absence of a contrary intention. The most important of these is Rule 1: property passes immediately, even though delivery and payment are postponed. It may come as some surprise that title passes at this early stage,[143] although the results are less dramatic than might be thought. In particular, the purchaser cannot claim the goods without paying for them.[144] As regards unascertained goods, property will pass under Rule 5 immediately upon goods being appropriated to the contract or, under Rule 5(3),[145] the bulk being reduced to the quantity contracted for. Similar rules probably apply to other contracts whereby property is to pass. An obvious example is found in contracts of barter or exchange, where the consideration is another chattel or services rather than money as in sale.[146]

(ii) *Gift: intention*

We can now turn to gifts of chattels. For any gift to be effective, it is necessary that both donor and donee should intend a gift. So far as the donor is concerned, it is important that an immediate gift should be intended; the burden lies on the donee to prove this.[147] Words indicating an intention to give in the future will be insufficient, and this applies even where the donee is given (or already has) possession.[148] However, if the donor gives chattels to the donee and says that the donee will own them as from a year's time, it might be possible to give effect to this (after a year) as a delayed gift rather than a promise of a gift.

It is generally thought that the donee must agree to the gift. In the majority of cases, of course, this will not be a problem: gifts are generally welcome. However, in some cases, the donee will not want to accept the gift.[149] In *Dewar* v *Dewar*,[150] Goff J held that the donee's intention to accept the money as a loan did not preclude a gift: after accepting the money, 'He could not force the donor to take it back.' Even if this is correct because the money had been accepted (albeit as a loan), it does not mean that a donee can be forced to accept a gift. Where the gift is by deed, it seems clear that the gift is immediately effective even if the donee is wholly ignorant of it. The donee is allowed a reasonable time to repudiate the deed after becoming aware of it, but the donor has no right to cancel the gift in the meantime.[151]

---

[143] *RV Ward Ltd* v *Bignall* [1967] 1 QB 534 and *Michael Gerson (Leasing) Ltd* v *Wilkinson* [2001] QB 514 suggest that a contrary intention will readily be found.

[144] Section 39.

[145] Provided that there is no other buyer from the bulk.

[146] Bell, *Modern Law of Personal Property in England and Ireland*, pp 323–327.

[147] *Seldon* v *Davidson* [1968] 1 WLR 1083 (gift or loan of money).

[148] *Shower* v *Pilck* (1849) 4 Exch 478 (154 ER 1301) (Alderson B). Contrast a licence to the donee to take the property in the future, where the gift will be complete on the future taking.

[149] In the leading case of *Hill* v *Wilson* (1873) 8 Ch App 888, there would have been a corresponding reduction in a future legacy to the donee's wife.

[150] [1975] 1 WLR 1532, followed in *Day* v *Harris* [2014] Ch 211 (delivery of manuscripts: donor's intention crucial). It is criticised by Roberts (1975) 38 MLR 700 and Thornely [1976] CLJ 47, but see the more balanced analysis by Hill (2001) 117 LQR 127 as part of a study of the role of the donee's consent.

[151] *Standing* v *Bowring* (1885) 31 Ch D 282.

(iii) *Gift: deeds*

It is always possible to use a deed to transfer chattels, although few gifts will have the formality of a deed unless a lawyer has been involved. Unless possession has been transferred, a deed can cause a further complication. A transfer based upon a document, without delivery, may require registration under the Bills of Sale Acts 1878 and 1882.[152] The purpose of this legislation is to ensure that people are not able to give the impression of wealth by the continued possession of chattels that have in fact been transferred (absolutely or by way of mortgage) to another. An unregistered transfer is invalid as regards creditors.[153] Although the legislation also applies to sales, the normal purchaser is rarely content to pay the purchase money and leave the seller in possession.

(iv) *Gift: delivery*

Generally, of course, gifts will be made by delivery. For lawyers, the real interest of gifts lies in the stress on delivery. Gift is one of the relatively few areas of English law in which possession plays a leading role and gift helps us understand how possession is transferred.

Delivery is straightforward in many cases, such as giving a book to a friend as a Christmas present. A moment's thought will show that other cases are more difficult. Suppose I buy a piano and have it delivered secretly to my house. When my wife returns home, I tell her that I am giving it to her as a birthday present. How do I deliver it to her? I will scarcely pick it up and hand it over! Similar problems arise when a large number of chattels are being given: most obviously, when the contents of a house are being given. Although the donor could pick up many of the objects and hand them over to the donee, it would take hours to do so and is plainly unrealistic. These problems are most acute when gifts are made within a common household,[154] as physical handing over is unlikely. Occasionally, the donor seeks to resile from the gift, but more frequently the donor has become bankrupt and the trustee in bankruptcy (or a creditor) is claiming the property in question.

The result has been the growth of a considerable body of law as to what is required for delivery. There was a lively nineteenth-century debate as to whether delivery was indeed required, but in 1890 *Cochrane* v *Moore*[155] settled once and for all that delivery is essential: words of gift are by themselves insufficient. Since that time, the requirement of delivery has not been seriously questioned, although there have been many cases elaborating the concept of delivery.

(a) Actions less than handing over

Three instances will be considered: handing over a representative object or symbol, handing over a key and touching the object being given. The first of these applies where what is being given is a collection of chattels: furniture or collections of silver or china provide

---

[152] Law Com No 369, Chapter 10, proposes that absolute transfers should no longer require registration.
[153] For more detail, see Thornely [1953] CLJ 355.
[154] See Thornely [1953] CLJ 355 for a full analysis.
[155] (1890) 25 QBD 57, accepting *Irons* v *Smallpiece* (1819) 2 B&Ald 551 (106 ER 467).

good examples. It is plainly silly to expect every plate and cup in a dinner service to be handed over in a gift within a household. There is authority that a representative object will suffice in this type of case; for example, handing over a chair as representative of furniture.[156] One objection to allowing delivery in cases such as these is that it is likely to be entirely fortuitous whether such representative delivery in fact takes place. Whilst the donor may well hand an item over, this is more likely to be to show the donee what is being given rather than as a formal completion of the gift. However, it seems that there is a good delivery. What about handing over a symbol, perhaps a receipt for the object? Although there have been dicta supporting this,[157] it seems right to agree with Diamond that 'only a fool would rely on it'.[158]

The handing over of a key is important because it gives access to whatever is locked up: the key may be to a deposit box, trunk, room or warehouse. The law has recognised delivery of possession following the delivery of a key, although none of the cases involves an inter vivos gift. They involve transfers for consideration or else donationes mortis causa (gifts in contemplation of death),[159] for which the rules as to delivery are generally more relaxed. Nevertheless, the cases do suggest that delivery of a key will suffice for inter vivos transfers, although probably only for bulky goods where actual delivery would be difficult.[160]

There appear to be two conditions. The first is that the key must give the donee access. This may be thought to be an obvious result of having a key, but what if the locked object or place is within the donor's control? The donor may be unable to gain access to the object, but nor can the donee if the donor excludes him from his house. This has been said to be fatal to delivery.[161] If the donee is living with the donor, then this is unlikely to be a problem.[162] What happens if the locked object or place is within the control of a third party? It is difficult to say that the donee has access in this case, although the donor has excluded his own control. On principle, it seems that there should be no delivery, although such dicta as we have are inconsistent.[163] Recognition by the third party of the donee's rights will complete the gift, but this is on the different principle of attornment, to be considered later. The second condition is that the donor must relinquish access to what is given. Thus, there will be no delivery if the donor keeps a duplicate key.[164]

Rawlinson v *Mort*[165] held that an organ belonging to the donor and situated in a church could be delivered by the donor's placing his hand on the organ and telling the donee that

[156] *Lock* v *Heath* (1892) 8 TLR 295 (where the point appears to have been conceded), approved in *Re Cole* [1964] Ch 175. See also *Re Harcourt* (1883) 31 WR 578 (representative dish), although Pollock B thought delivery unnecessary.
[157] The only decision favouring it is *Rawlinson* v *Mort* (1905) 93 LT 555, regarded with great suspicion.
[158] (1964) 27 MLR 357 at p 360. Symbolic delivery was rejected in *Ward* v *Turner* (1752) 2 Ves Sen 431 (28 ER 275) in the donationes mortis causa context, even though the rules as to delivery are there more relaxed.
[159] See p 181 below.
[160] *Re Wasserberg* [1915] 1 Ch 195.
[161] *Wrightson* v *McArthur & Hutchisons (1919) Ltd* [1921] 2 KB 807 (good delivery if the transferee gives consideration, because there will then be an irrevocable licence to enter).
[162] *Re Mustapha, Mustapha* v *Wedlake* (1891) 8 TLR 160.
[163] *Wrightson* v *McArthur & Hutchisons (1919) Ltd* [1921] 2 KB 807 supports delivery; *Re Wasserberg* [1915] 1 Ch 195 denies delivery.
[164] *Re Craven's Estate* [1937] Ch 423 at p 428. Retention of a key is not fatal if the donee, independently of keys, has possession: *Woodard* v *Woodard* [1995] 3 All ER 980.
[165] (1905) 93 LT 555.

it was to be his. This is a surprising result, and the authority of the case is weakened by dicta supporting an impossibly generous view of delivery, yet it was cited with approval in *Re Cole*[166] in 1964.

Would *Rawlinson* apply if the donee were to lay hands on it? This is what happened in *Re Cole*, where there was a purported gift of the contents of a house to the donor's wife. She was taken to their new house and told that the contents were hers. As she went around the house, she placed her hands upon some of the contents.[167] It was held that there was no sufficient delivery. It has been suggested that the case means that handling by the donee cannot amount to delivery,[168] but the reasoning in the case appears to be that the wife handled the goods not so as to take delivery but simply in order to inspect or (later) use them. There is certainly no rule that the donor must actively deliver.[169]

Whatever the explanation, the law is shown to be exceptionally technical. Perhaps the most that one can say is that, whilst delivery is insisted upon even for bulky objects, the courts have accepted the necessity of relaxing the rules. This relaxation is, nevertheless, largely unprincipled and subject to somewhat arbitrary limits.

(b) Constructive delivery

The cases considered so far involve some sort of delivery at the date of the gift. In other cases, constructive delivery has been accepted. By this is meant that no physical change in possession has taken place, but the nature of the possession has changed. Four examples will be considered.

Possession before the gift

It has long been accepted that there is a good delivery where the donee already has possession at the time of the gift. Whilst *Cochrane* v *Moore*[170] requires delivery in all cases, this is not taken as extending to requiring a second delivery in such cases.[171] As has been stressed, it would be very strange to insist upon delivery back to the donor followed by redelivery to the donee (not that this area of law lacks strange requirements). This principle seems fairly well settled, as shown in its application in *Pascoe* v *Turner*[172] to a gift by a former lover of the contents of the house in which the donee was living. Although the nature of the possession after the gift must be as donee,[173] this causes little difficulty.

Taking possession after the gift

In this scenario, there is a gap between the words of gift and taking possession. In *Thomas* v *Times Book Co Ltd*,[174] Dylan Thomas had left the manuscript of *Under Milk Wood* in a

---

[166] [1964] Ch 175.
[167] If there were a good gift of these objects, they could be treated as representative of the contents as a whole.
[168] Thornely [1964] CLJ 27.
[169] Thus, there can be delivery of goods held by a third party, or a licence to the donee to take possession: *Thomas* v *Times Book Co Ltd* [1966] 1 WLR 911.
[170] (1890) 25 QBD 57.
[171] *Re Stoneham* [1919] 1 Ch 149.
[172] [1979] 1 WLR 431. See also *Woodard* v *Woodard* [1995] 3 All ER 980.
[173] Wills J in *Kilpin* v *Ratley* [1892] 1 QB 582 at p 585.
[174] [1966] 1 WLR 911.

public house or taxi. As he was about to fly to the United States, he told the donee (a BBC producer) that he could keep the manuscript if he found it. Plowman J held that there was a completed gift when the donee subsequently found the manuscript.

Possession held by a third party

Take the example of a third party storing the property as bailee. How is a gift made if it is desired that the bailment should not be disturbed? The answer is that the bailee may recognise that he or she holds for the donee: this is called attornment. Thereafter, the bailee holds for the donee, and this is a sufficient change of possession in the eyes of the law.[175] It is not sufficient for the donor to give authority (even if irrevocable) to the bailee to deliver or to hand to the donee a receipt, upon production of which the goods will be released. In all cases, the bailee must acknowledge the right of the donee.

A rather different point is that certain documents of title form a special category. These documents[176] actually represent the goods, so that delivery of the documents counts as delivery of the goods. The most important example is a bill of lading provided by shippers.

Donor remaining in possession

At first sight, it seems remarkable that a gift should be possible, given the insistence upon delivery. Yet it has been argued that, if a third party can recognise that he or she holds for the transferee (attornment), then a transferor should be able to do likewise. Such a change of possession is more likely to be recognised where the donor has a business of storing goods, although the cases involve sale rather than gift.[177] The transferor's status changes from that of owner to that of (say) warehouseman. In other cases, it will be more difficult to explain the retention of possession by the donor. If it is made clear that the donor holds as bailee for the donee, then this will suffice,[178] but otherwise the continued possession will need to be explained. The gift will, of course, be complete if the goods are delivered to the donee and returned to the donor.

(c) Making gifts in a common household

This is the source of many cases, especially where the gift is of contents of a house which are used both before and after a purported gift. There is a principle that, where possession is unclear, the owner is to be treated as being in possession.[179] It has been argued that this may be used in the typical case of a husband making a gift of household contents to a wife. Unfortunately, the argument is flawed.[180] Until there is a transfer of possession, the donee is not the owner: it follows that the donee cannot argue that possession follows title simply

[175] *Official Assignee of Madras v Mercantile Bank of India Ltd* [1935] AC 53.
[176] For their scope, see Benjamin's *Sale of Goods* (9th edn), para 18-007.
[177] *Elmore v Stone* (1809) 1 Taunt 458 (127 ER 912) (livery stable keeper); *Castle v Sworder* (1861) 6 H&N 828 (158 ER 341) (warehouse).
[178] *Marvin v Wallis* (1856) 6 El&Bl 726 (119 ER 1035) (sale: loan of horse back to the vendor, at his request); *Michael Gerson (Leasing) Ltd v Wilkinson* [2001] QB 514 (sale and leaseback).
[179] *Ramsay v Margrett* [1894] 2 QB 18 and *French v Gething* [1922] 1 KB 236 are the leading cases. For situations when possession is unclear, see *Youngs v Youngs* [1940] 1 KB 760 and *Koppel v Koppel* [1966] 1 WLR 802.
[180] *Re Cole* [1964] Ch 175.

because title has not been proved. However, the principle is useful in the case of sale[181] or gift by deed,[182] where the deemed possession of the transferee takes the case outside the Bills of Sale legislation.

Re Cole[183] is an example of the attitude of the courts. As we have seen, the husband attempted to make a gift of the contents of a house to his wife. They subsequently lived in the house and assumed that the wife owned the contents for some 16 years until the husband's bankruptcy. The court refused to accept that there had been a delivery. It was not enough that it could be said that possession was in doubt on the facts: the husband was the owner, and he would be treated as in possession. Taken literally, *Re Cole* makes it very difficult for gifts of contents to be made in a common household. Yet, such gifts are an everyday occurrence. Is it really the case that, without physically handing over each item, there is no valid gift? After all, few normal people will consult a lawyer and be told that a deed should be used. It may well be that the court was concerned by the potential for creditors of the donor to be defeated by gifts subsequently concocted by family members.

Given the need for delivery, however, it does seem that *Re Cole* was correctly decided. It follows other cases taking an equally harsh approach over an extended period.[184] There has, nevertheless, been pressure for centuries to allow gifts where it is impracticable to transfer possession and there is a case for considering the matter again 50 years after *Re Cole*.

B. Creation of interests

The range of interests in chattels is much narrower than in land. One consequence is that there is less concern with how they are created. There appear to be three possibilities: contract, deed and delivery.

Charges over chattels are permitted. In a commercial setting, the creation of charges will almost invariably be by contract. The other type of interest worth considering is bailment. This will be created by delivery of the chattel. The nature of bailment is possession of the chattel, and it is difficult to see how it can exist without delivery,[185] even if there is a deed or contract.

Another form of interest in chattels is co-ownership. In *Cochrane* v *Moore*,[186] there was an attempted gift of a quarter share in a horse. The case was actually decided on the ground that there was a declaration of trust; it was left open whether such a share could be given by delivery. The problem, of course, is that a chattel is a physical object capable of delivery, whilst a quarter share is a legal right rather than a physical object.

---

[181] *Ramsay* v *Margrett* [1894] 2 QB 18.
[182] *French* v *Gething* [1922] 1 KB 236.
[183] [1964] Ch 175.
[184] *Bashall* v *Bashall* (1894) 11 TLR 152; *Valier* v *Wright & Bull Ltd* (1917) 33 TLR 366; *Hislop* v *Hislop* [1950] WN 124.
[185] In the extended sense in which delivery is understood for gifts. Thus, the intended bailee may already have physical possession.
[186] (1890) 25 QBD 57.

5. Choses in action

It has long been possible for the holder of a chose in action (such as a creditor who is owed £1,000) to transfer it to another: we refer to this as an assignment. Originally, the common law courts did not recognise assignments, but equity did. One thing to stress is that we are dealing with the benefit of the chose in action. It is not possible to transfer the burden of a chose in action unless it also forms a proprietary interest binding property. For example, suppose O, the owner of land, contracts to sell land to P but subsequently transfers the land in breach of contract to Q. Q is bound by the obligation to sell to P[187]: P has an estate contract, an equitable interest in land. Non-proprietary contracts entered into by O would not bind Q.

A. Assignable rights

One overriding requirement is that the chose in action must be susceptible to assignment. If the obligation is personal in nature or the contract specifically precludes assignment,[188] then no assignment is allowed.[189] On the other hand, the creditor can still declare a trust of the benefit of such a contract,[190] even though the beneficiary can (by joining the trustee/creditor) sue the debtor.[191]

Public policy may also inhibit assignment, most notably in respect of a bare right to litigate.[192] This means that most tort claims and claims for unliquidated contract damages cannot be assigned unless the assignee has a sufficient interest as to justify recognising an assignment.[193] The fear in this context is of trafficking in rights to litigate, though this factor has progressively diminished in importance over the years. However, the great majority of contractual rights may be assigned.[194] Some choses in action have special methods of transfer. Shares in companies provide the best example. Shares are transferred by entry in the share register, and no assignment is recognised which would defeat this rule.[195]

---

[187] Subject to registration requirements.

[188] Precluding assignment will soon be invalid for book debts: Small Business, Enterprise and Employment Act 2015, s 1). If the contract gives rise to a proprietary interest, then that interest may be assigned even if the contract stipulates otherwise. Thus, a lease is assignable even if in breach of covenant, though the assignee is likely to face forfeiture of the lease: *Old Grovebury Manor Farm Ltd* v *Seymour Plant Sales & Hire Ltd (No 2)* [1979] 1 WLR 1397.

[189] *Linden Gardens Trust Ltd* v *Lenesta Sludge Disposals Ltd* [1994] 1 AC 85. For recent discussion, see Turner [2008] LMCLQ 306; Goode [2009] LMCLQ 300. More recently, Tolhurst and Carter [2014] CLJ 405 and Bridge (2016) 132 LQR 47 investigate how far contract or property principles are applicable.

[190] *Don King Productions Inc* v *Warren* [2000] Ch 291; criticised by Tettenborn [1999] LMCLQ 353.

[191] *Barbados Trust Co Ltd* v *Bank of Zambia* (2007) 9 ITELR 689 (Hooper LJ disagreeing); Tolhurst [2007] LMCLQ 278; Trukhtanov (2007) 70 MLR 848; M Smith (2008) 124 LQR 517.

[192] Statute precludes the assignment of some rights (especially pensions and social security payments).

[193] *Trendtex Trading Corporation* v *Crédit Suisse* [1982] AC 679; *Simpson* v *Norfolk NHS Trust* [2012] 1 All ER 1423. Assignment of the proceeds from litigation (even future litigation) is permitted.

[194] Extended by the High Court of Australia to restitutionary claims: *Equuscorp Pty Ltd* v *Bassat* (2012) 246 CLR 498 at [53], [79], [156] and [159].

[195] Gower and Davies, *Principles of Modern Company Law* (10th edn), paras 27–8. This does not prevent equity from recognising a trust over the shares, which may put the beneficiary in a situation little different from an assignee.

B. Statutory assignments

Until the Judicature Act 1873, assignment of the benefit of a chose in action was allowed only by equity. It had the slight disadvantage that the assignor had to be joined as a party to any litigation, being the person to whom the legal obligation was owed. Equitable assignment is still possible today, but normally assignments take effect under statute. The current legislation, s 136(1) of the Law of Property Act 1925, provides that:

> Any absolute assignment by writing under the hand of the assignor (not purporting to be by way of charge only) of any debt or other legal thing in action, of which express notice in writing has been given to the debtor, trustee or other person from whom the assignor would have been entitled to claim such debt or thing in action, is effectual in law (subject to equities having priority over the right of the assignee) to pass . . . the legal right to such debt or thing in action . . .

The law relating to assignment is voluminous and can only be summarised in this chapter. The statute establishes three basic requirements: the assignment must be in writing, it must be absolute and express written notice must have been given to the person who owes the obligation (debtor, for short).

Although the assignment must be in writing, there is no need to use technical language so long as it is clear that the chose in action is intended to be transferred. Dangers lie if the language can be construed as a promise to assign in the future[196] or if the purported assignment takes the form of instructions to the debtor. In the latter case, there may be difficulty in distinguishing between an authority (or revocable instruction) to pay the 'assignee' and a true assignment.[197] If the debtor accepts an obligation to the third party, then a direct obligation to that person will result,[198] at least where notice has been given to him or her. An assignment is apparently not complete unless notice is given to the assignee.[199]

The requirement that the assignment be absolute means that assignments of part of an obligation (for example, assignment of £500 of a £1,000 debt)[200] or for a limited time or purpose (such as an assignment by way of charge) fall outside the statute. Its justification is that the debtor must know whom to pay and should not be open to multiple actions.

The third requirement is that written notice of the assignment must be given to the debtor. This is important for several reasons. It ensures that the debtor does not pay to the assignor. A debtor who pays the assignor after notice has to pay for a second time, to the assignee.[201] The giving of notice also reduces the chances of the assignor's fraudulently assigning the same chose in action twice over. A further factor (discussed in the following section) is that notice is relevant as regards certain obligations owed by the assignor to the debtor.

---

[196] *Re McArdle* [1951] 1 Ch 669.
[197] *Morrell v Wootten* (1852) 16 Beav 197 (51 ER 753); *Curran v Newpark Cinemas Ltd* [1951] 1 All ER 295.
[198] *Shamia v Joory* [1958] 1 QB 448 (no emphasis on notice to the assignee).
[199] *Morrell v Wootten* (1852) 16 Beav 197 (51 ER 753); *Curran v Newpark Cinemas Ltd* [1951] 1 All ER 295; *Alexander v Steinhardt, Walker & Co* [1903] 2 KB 208. The requirement is questioned by Hill (2001) 117 LQR 127 at p 137. *Alexander* holds that notice is complete on posting, but contrast *Timpson's Executors v Yerbury* [1936] 1 KB 645 at p 657. Posting is insufficient for notice to the debtor: *Holt v Heatherfield Trust Ltd* [1942] 2 KB 1.
[200] Examples are *Re Steel Wing Co Ltd* [1921] 1 Ch 349 and *Williams v Atlantic Assurance Co Ltd* [1933] 1 KB 81.
[201] *Brice v Bannister* (1878) 3 QBD 569.

C. Claims by the debtor

Assignment is said to take effect subject to 'equities': defences available to the debtor in a claim by the assignor. This area is complex, but there are two basic rules. The first is that obligations owed by the assignor will affect the assignee if 'flowing out of and inseparably connected with' the debtor's obligation.[202] This means that most claims for breach of the same contract and claims that go to the validity of the contract[203] will affect the assignee. One cannot simply accept an assignment of those parts of a contract that happen to be valuable and expect the debtor to look to the assignor (who might be bankrupt) for the rest. These equities extend to unliquidated damages, and it does not matter whether they arise before or after notice to the debtor.

The second rule is that liquidated claims[204] may be set off against the assignee if they arise before notice to the debtor. There is some obvious sense in this notice requirement: if the debtor lends money to the assignor after notice, then there is no reason at all why the assignee should be affected. The debtor has taken upon himself the risk of default by the assignor. Yet, it is by no means clear that the debtor's protection is adequate. The debtor has no protection for accrued claims to *unliquidated* damages[205] and no protection for future liabilities of the assignor under an existing contract. Suppose the debtor leases property to the assignor. The debtor receives no protection in respect of rent becoming due (and unpaid) after notice of the assignment of a separate debt.[206] It might be argued that assignees could not be sure of their position if such later claims could be set off, but the existing rules already ensure that they need to look out for equities. There is certainly an argument that, provided an obligation is undertaken before assignment, the assignee should take the risk of the assignor's default.[207]

D. Equitable assignments[208]

These have fewer requirements than statutory assignments. Apart from the chose in action having to be capable of assignment, the one clear rule is that the assignee must have notice. There is no need for the assignment to be absolute: there can be a valid equitable assignment by way of charge or of part of a debt. Any problems for the debtor as a result of this are avoided because the assignor normally must be a party to the action[209]: the entire liability of the debtor should be settled in a single court action.

---

[202] *Government of Newfoundland* v *Newfoundland Railway Co* (1888) 13 App Cas 199 at p 213. Contra if payment has already been made to the assignee: *Pan Ocean Shipping Co Ltd* v *Credit Corporation Ltd* [1994] 1 WLR 161; Tolhurst [1999] CLJ 546.

[203] Surprisingly, this does not extend to claims for damages for being fraudulently induced to enter the contract: *Stoddart* v *Union Trust Ltd* [1912] 1 KB 181 (doubted by Tettenborn [1987] Conv 358, who justifiably criticises many of the rules in this area).

[204] I.e. sums fixed by the parties, thus excluding tort claims and most contractual claims other than debt.

[205] *Stoddart* v *Union Trust Ltd* [1912] 1 KB 181.

[206] *Watson* v *Mid-Wales Railway Co* (1867) LR 2 CP 593.

[207] If the debtor owes money to X in a year's time, she will be happy to sell goods (up to the amount of the debt) to X with payment to be made after three months. Why should all her calculations be thrown out by a notice of assignment of the original debt within those three months?

[208] Edelman and Elliott (2015) 131 LQR 228 ask whether equitable assignments work by way of transfer (the dominant view today) or, as they support, trust.

[209] For relaxation of this practice, see Tolhurst (2002) 118 LQR 98.

Notice to the debtor is not essential, but the effect of the assignment is limited unless there is notice (written or oral). For example, if there is no notice, the assignee will lose out if the debtor pays the assignor; there is also the risk of further equities arising. What is the significance of an assignment without notice to the debtor, if it is subject to such restricted consequences? Apart from the fact that the assignor cannot resile from the assignment, the assignor may become bankrupt. Even though notice has not been given to the debtor, the assignee and not the trustee in bankruptcy will be entitled to the chose in action.[210]

A further reason for giving notice is that it protects the assignee against subsequent assignments. If there are successive assignments, it is the first to give notice who has priority.[211] This is known as the rule in *Dearle* v *Hall*.[212] Originally applied to dealings with interests under trusts, it is generally taken to extend to all choses in action.[213] The notice must be in writing, at least where the assignment is of an interest under a trust.[214]

Almost certainly, the most difficult and controversial question relating to equitable assignments is whether consideration is required[215]; it is not required for legal assignments. It may be argued that there is insufficient reason for equity to recognise an assignment if the assignee has not given consideration. On the other hand, there is much to be said for the view that, once the assignor has done everything in his power to make an effective assignment, an equitable assignment will be recognised. There have been cases supporting this latter analysis from early in the nineteenth century,[216] although other cases have stated that consideration is essential.[217] This is especially important for assignments of parts of debts, which cannot be statutory. If equitable assignments do require consideration, past consideration (a pre-existing obligation) suffices.[218] Indeed, one common reason for making an assignment is to pay off an existing debt owed to the assignee.

Whatever the position is generally, it is clear that consideration is necessary when the assignment is of a future chose in action. There cannot be an immediate assignment (there is nothing to assign), and an obligation to assign in the future requires consideration. What is a future chose in action? There is a present chose even if the debt or other obligation will not fall due until the future or depends upon work to be done by the assignor in the future.[219] What is vital is that there is an existing contract or other obligation under which

[210] *Gorringe* v *Irwell India Rubber & Gutta Percha Works* (1886) 34 Ch D 128.
[211] Priority over earlier assignments requires consideration for the later assignment: *United Bank of Kuwait plc* v *Sahib* [1997] 1 Ch 107 at pp 118–120 (Chadwick J, not considered on appeal: p 142).
[212] (1828) 3 Russ 1 (38 ER 475).
[213] *Marchant* v *Morton, Down & Co* [1901] 2 KB 829. Oditah (1989) 9 OxJLS 513 argues that the bona fide purchaser without notice rule should be employed rather than the rule in *Dearle* v *Hall*, but contrast de Lacy [1999] Conv 311.
[214] LPA, s 137(3), (10). For links with registration provisions, see Howell [1993] Conv 22.
[215] Treitel, *The Law of Contract* (14th edn), pp 809–817; Hall [1959] CLJ 99; Megarry (1943) 59 LQR 58; Sheridan (1955) 33 Can BR 284. Consideration is not required if the assignment is by way of declaration of trust, nor if the debtor agrees to hold for the assignee (*Shamia* v *Joory* [1958] 1 QB 448).
[216] *Fortescue* v *Barnett* (1834) 3 My&K 36 (40 ER 14). The most recent authority directly on the point is *Holt* v *Heatherfield Trust Ltd* [1942] 2 KB 1. See also Bridge (2016) 132 LQR 47 at pp 55-56.
[217] *Re Westerton* [1919] 2 Ch 104 (for the law before the Judicature Act 1873).
[218] This was left open in *Holt* v *Heatherfield Trust Ltd* [1942] 2 KB 1, but quickly reaffirmed by commentators: Hollond (1943) 59 LQR 129; Megarry (1943) 59 LQR 208.
[219] *Brice* v *Bannister* (1878) 3 QBD 569; *Earle (G & T) (1925) Ltd* v *Hemsworth RDC* (1928) 140 LT 69.

the obligation will arise.[220] Thus, present assignment of a business's future book debts is impossible.[221] Expectancies, such as 'rights' under the will of a living person or under a trust, should one become the next of kin of a living person, are similarly incapable of assignment.[222]

E. Creation of interests

It is possible to create a charge over a chose in action. Charges take effect only by equitable assignment, as they are not absolute.

6. Declarations of trust and equitable interests

A. Declaration of trust

The owner of any form of property may declare a trust in respect of it. Declarations of trust do not need generally to be in any special form, though writing is required in some instances considered below.[223] All that is necessary is that the person declaring the trust intends another person immediately to obtain a beneficial interest. It will be seen at once that a declaration of trust is unusually powerful. It is unusual in English law in that it requires no delivery of the underlying property (contrast a gift of chattels), no notice to or participation by the beneficiary[224] (contrast sale and assignments of choses in action), no consideration (contrast sale) and no formal document or even writing (contrast wills and deeds). Other methods of transfer or creation frequently dispense with some of these elements, but it is exceptional for transactions to be effective where all are absent.

The courts recognise the remarkable strength of declarations of trust and are correspondingly reluctant to find that there was in fact an irrevocable declaration, sometimes expressing unease as to the state of the law.[225] Suppose that, whilst having a bath and thinking aloud, I say 'I really should make provision for my nieces. I know what I will do. I declare myself a trustee of my Tesco shares[226] for them.' In theory, that is a binding trust which I cannot resile from after stepping back into the real world from the beguiling comfort of a warm bath. Obviously, it may be difficult to prove what has been said, but this can be overcome if there is sufficient evidence. In *Re Cozens*,[227] it was alleged that a

---

[220] *Roxburghe* v *Cox* (1881) 17 Ch D 520.
[221] If there is consideration, they take effect in equity (cf estate contracts) when the book debts arise: *Tailby* v *Official Receiver* (1888) 13 App Cas 523.
[222] *Meek* v *Kettlewell* (1843) 1 Ph 342 (41 ER 662). By analogy, they cannot be disclaimed (even by deed): *Smith* v *Smith* [2001] 1 WLR 1937.
[223] See p 130.
[224] The beneficiary can disclaim the beneficial interest on discovering it: *Re Stratton's Disclaimer* [1958] Ch 42 (rights under a will); *Smith* v *Smith* [2001] 1 WLR 1937.
[225] Described by Lord Cranworth LC as 'unfortunate': *Jones* v *Lock* (1865) LR 1 Ch App 25 at p 28.
[226] The subject matter of the trust must be certain, but (controversially) '50 of my ICI shares' suffices: *Hunter* v *Moss* [1994] 1 WLR 452; Hayton (1994) 110 LQR 335; Martin [1996] Conv 223. For the contrast with trusts of chattels, see *Re Harvard Securities Ltd* [1997] 2 BCLC 369, in which Neuberger J was 'not particularly convinced' by the distinction but was bound by *Hunter*.
[227] [1913] 2 Ch 478.

deceased person had declared a trust by pencil entries in his personal accounts. Neville J had little difficulty in holding that there was no irrevocable declaration of trust. The absence of communication was taken as a strong indicator that any declaration was intended to be revocable.[228]

Pretty obviously, the main problem in this area lies in discovering what will count as an effective declaration of trust, particularly where the word 'trust' is not used. It is not necessary for the settlor to have any comprehension as to what trusts are. What is necessary is that the settlor should intend (1) to retain formal control over the property but (2) that another person (or persons) should have the benefit of that property.

A commonly cited example is *Paul v Constance*.[229] Mr Constance obtained damages in a personal injuries action. The money was placed in a bank deposit account in his name, and Mr Constance told the claimant (with whom he had been living for some six years) that 'The money is as much yours as mine.' This was later repeated, despite the fact that he had taken a conscious decision to have the account in his name, possibly to avoid publicising that he was not married to the claimant. Problems arose when Mr Constance died and his executors denied that the claimant had any rights. The Court of Appeal held that these facts justified a finding of a declaration of trust. The decision seems correct, as Mr Constance intended to retain ownership but at the same time intended that the claimant should share the beneficial rights to the money.

There is one type of situation in which it is almost impossible to prove a declaration of trust. Gifts are sometimes ineffective because the proper means of transfer have not been complied with. The intended transferee may then argue that the court should find a declaration of trust in order to give effect to the transferor's intention to part with the property. This argument is regarded as hopeless. The transferor is intending to retain no right to the property. This factor is treated as inconsistent, with continued legal ownership of the property subject to a trust. If a trust is intended, the owner is not intending to part with all proprietary rights.

Two cases may be cited as examples. In *Jones v Lock*,[230] a father gave a cheque to his nine-month-old son and said, 'I give this to baby for himself.' Lord Cranworth LC held that there was no declaration of trust, displaying an overt reluctance to impress onerous legal consequences on 'loose conversations of this sort'. Similarly, there was an ineffective gift of a lease to a child in *Richards v Delbridge*.[231] Jessel MR stressed the contrast between a trust and 'words of present gift [which] shew an intention to give over property to another, and not retain it in the donor's own hands for any purpose, fiduciary or otherwise'.

As Maitland has observed,[232] it is far more common to intend to give property away than to intend to declare oneself a trustee. The two are quite distinct, and the court will not allow

---

[228] Examples of trusts being recognised where there has been communication but without a formal declaration of trust are *Gray v Gray* (1852) 2 Sim (NS) 273 (61 ER 345) and *Gee v Liddell (No 1)* (1866) 35 Beav 621 (55 ER 1038).

[229] [1977] 1 WLR 527, followed by *Rowe v Prance* [1999] 2 FLR 787 (trust of valuable boat).

[230] (1865) LR 1 Ch App 25.

[231] (1874) LR 18 Eq 11. Other well-known cases are *Antrobus v Smith* (1805) 12 Ves 39 (33 ER 16) (chose in action) and *Heartley v Nicholson* (1875) LR 19 Eq 233 (shares).

[232] *Equity* (2nd edn), p 72.

one to be used merely because the other was intended but has failed. Yet, there does not seem to be a logical imperative whereby the courts could not find a declaration of trust. As will be seen later, a donor who has done all in his power to make a gift is treated as a trustee.[233]

One particular type of case where declarations of trust are more readily found is where a transferee has agreed to benefit somebody. An old example is *Cochrane* v *Moore*,[234] in which a chargee said that a donee of a quarter share would be 'all right'. More recent cases of this type have used constructive rather than express trusts. They will be dealt with in Chapter 9.

Transfers to trustees

Declarations of trust over one's own property are not the normal way of setting up a trust. It is far more common for property to be transferred to trustees and the trusts binding the trustees to be stipulated. In this situation, a trust will be properly constituted if there is an effective transfer of the property to the trustees in accordance with the rules relating to transfers.[235] What happens if the transfer is ineffective? Unlike the cases on failed gifts considered earlier, there is no difficulty in asserting that a trust is intended.

In the leading case of *Milroy* v *Lord*,[236] the settlor purported to assign shares to trustees but failed to do so because there was no entry of the transfer in the share register; he subsequently died. The Court of Appeal in Chancery was emphatic that there was no properly constituted trust. Although the settlor had intended a trust, he had not intended that he should be a trustee. Just as in the failed gift cases already considered, the settlor intended an outright transfer and not to impose a trust upon himself.

The law in *Milroy* is clear, although it might be thought that the settlor's wishes are being trampled upon. Arguably, his primary intention was that there should be a trust and that the character of the intended transferees as trustees was incidental to that primary intention. In other contexts, it is said that equity will not allow a trust to fail for want of a trustee.[237] A good example is found in the context of wills. A legacy lapses if the legatee dies before the testator.[238] Nevertheless, if the legatee is a trustee, then a new trustee will be appointed and the legacy does not lapse.[239]

It is frequently observed that equity will not assist a volunteer. This means that there will not be a trust unless the proper procedures have been followed. However, some modern developments show a more generous approach. In *T Choithram International SA* v *Pagarani*,[240] Lord Browne-Wilkinson observed that 'Although equity will not aid a volunteer, it will not strive officiously to defeat a gift.' This is quite harmless, but Clarke LJ[241] came close to overturning *Milroy* v *Lord* when he applied this dictum soon afterwards.

---

[233] *Re Rose* [1949] Ch 78, p 177 below.
[234] (1890) 25 QBD 57. The validity of the gift to the donee was contested.
[235] There are also certainty rules, but these are within the province of books on trusts.
[236] (1862) 4 De GF&J 264 (45 ER 1185); distinguished in *T Choithram International SA* v *Pagarani* [2001] 1 WLR 1 (PC), where the donor was also one of the trustees.
[237] Snell's *Equity* (33rd edn), para 27-007. A trust will not fail if the trustee disclaims the trust; *Mallott* v *Wilson* [1903] 2 Ch 494, criticised by Matthews [1981] Conv 141.
[238] *Elliot* v *Davenport* (1705) 1 P Wms 83 (24 ER 304).
[239] E.g. *Re Smirthwaite's Trusts* (1871) LR 11 Eq 251.
[240] [2001] 1 WLR 1 at p 11.
[241] *Pennington* v *Waine* [2002] 1 WLR 2075 (see p 178 below).

Actions following a failed transfer

If a transfer (whether on trust or not) fails, then there is nothing to stop a living transferor from later declaring himself a trustee. However, the courts will not infer such a declaration merely because the transferor has acted on the assumption that the gift is valid, at least where he or she is unaware of its invalidity. It is, for example, insufficient to pay the income from the asset to an intended donee.[242]

However, a subsequent transfer to the intended trustees will complete the trust, and this is so even if it is a transfer from a third party. An excellent example is provided by *Re Bowden*.[243] The claimant executed a voluntary transfer to trustees of property which she would become entitled to under the will of her father (then living). Such a transfer was ineffective because there was no proprietary right until the father died. Following the father's death, his personal representatives transferred the daughter's interest to the trustees in accordance with the incomplete trust. Bennett J held that the trustees had authority to receive the property and, as the authority had not been revoked, the trust was complete. The claimant was unable to recover the property.

Formalities

Presuming that the court finds an irrevocable declaration of trust, are any formalities required? Generally, the answer is no. Trusts of land (or of an interest in land) provide an exception: s 53(1)(b) of the Law of Property Act 1925 requires them to be 'manifested and proved' by writing signed by the person declaring the trust.[244] This seems similar[245] to the old provisions relating to contracts for the sale of land which were replaced by the Law of Property (Miscellaneous Provisions) Act 1989. Declarations of trust over an equitable interest (in property other than land) are considered in the following section.

B. Transfer of equitable interests

Equitable interests are choses in action and fall within s 136 of the Law of Property Act 1925 (statutory assignments),[246] although this has little, if any, consequence. They have attracted some special rules. Equity never required the assignor of an equitable interest to be joined as a party where the assignment was absolute, for in absolute assignments there is no prejudice to the debtor. Consideration is not necessary for an immediate assignment of an equitable chose to be effective. This was settled in the nineteenth century in *Kekewich* v *Manning*[247] and has never since been seriously doubted. It can be concluded that the advantages of statutory assignments were already enjoyed by equitable choses in action.

The most important point regarding equitable choses is that s 53(1)(c) of the Law of Property Act 1925 requires any 'disposition' of them to be in writing.[248] It is clear beyond

---

[242] *Heartley* v *Nicholson* (1875) LR 19 Eq 233 (dividends on shares).
[243] [1936] Ch 71.
[244] See Youdan [1984] CLJ 306.
[245] Wilde in *Contemporary Property Law* (eds Jackson and Wilde), Chapter 10, takes the contrary view.
[246] *Re Pain* [1919] 1 Ch 38.
[247] (1851) 1 De GM&G 176 (42 ER 519).
[248] Battersby [1979] Conv 17; Green (1984) 47 MLR 385.

doubt that this covers assignments. There are two central problems. The first is exactly what dealings, other than assignments, with equitable interests are covered. The second concerns the scope of the s 53(2) exception for 'the creation or operation of resulting, implied or constructive trusts'. These issues take us deep into difficult equity theory – rather too difficult for a general book on property!

Section 9 of the Statute of Frauds 1677 had required that 'grants and assignments' of equitable interests be in writing. In *Grey* v *IRC*,[249] it was argued that s 53 should be interpreted as consolidating legislation, not changing the previous law. The beneficiary in *Grey* had instructed the trustee to hold on trust for another. There was no doubt that this effected a transfer of the beneficial interest, but it was not a 'grant or assignment'. The House of Lords held that the Law of Property Act 1925[250] was, in this context, more than consolidating and that the word 'disposition' should be given its natural interpretation. Once this was decided, it was easy to conclude that the instructions to the trustees effected a disposition and must be in writing.

The significance of requiring writing in *Grey* was that stamp duty was payable on a document confirming the instruction. Stamp duty is chargeable on certain transfers, but only if there is writing. It illustrates the point that taxation lies behind many of the cases on formalities.

Other forms of dispositions

Declarations of trust do not normally require writing (unless over land).[251] Is writing required if a beneficiary declares a trust over an equitable interest? There is an argument that the first beneficiary drops out of the picture so that the original trustee holds on trust for the new beneficiary.[252] However, *Nelson* v *Greening & Sykes (Builders) Ltd*[253] rejected the analysis that the original trustee drops out of the picture. How does this impact on s 53(1)(c)? Before *Nelson*, it might have been thought that there was in effect a transfer to the new beneficiary. This would be similar to a direct assignment to the new beneficiary or an instruction to trustees, both of which constitute dispositions within s 53(1)(c). Following *Nelson*, it is much less likely that there is a disposition within the section. The absence of writing may mean that it is unclear what route (assignment, instruction to trustees, declaration of trust) was intended by the holder of the equitable interest. The court may then feel free to adopt a route (especially declaration of trust) that does not require writing.[254]

Even if there were to be a disposition, this does not end the matter. Any principle that the first beneficiary drops out of the picture operates only where there is a simple declaration of trust in favour of the new beneficiary, not where the initial beneficiary either does not dispose of the entire interest or has an active role to play under the new trust.[255]

---

[249] [1960] AC 1.
[250] Technically, the Law of Property (Amendment) Act 1924, which itself was consolidated by the 1925 Act.
[251] *Kinane* v *Mackie-Conteh* [2005] WTLR 345 at [17] confirms that s 53(1)(c) applies only if there is a subsisting equitable interest.
[252] *Grainge* v *Wilberforce* (1889) 5 TLR 436; criticised by Green (1984) 47 MLR 385, who argues that all declarations of trust over equitable interests require writing.
[253] [2008] 1 EGLR 59, especially at [57]. It might be regarded as obiter: see [58]. See also Pawlowski and Brown (2015) 170 T&ELJ 4, suggesting that policy reasons point towards writing being required.
[254] *Drakeford* v *Cotton* [2012] WTLR 1135 at [80].
[255] *Onslow* v *Wallis* (1849) 1 Mac&G 506 (41 ER 1361); *Re Lashmar* [1891] 1 Ch 258.

Suppose the beneficiary declares a discretionary trust in favour of X and Y, under which he is to decide what shares X and Y are to take. In this case, the initial beneficiary does not drop out of the picture, and it is much more difficult to argue a disposition of the equitable interest.

A surrender of a beneficial interest (having the effect that the interest terminates and the next interest under the trust is accelerated) is clearly a disposition.[256] Thus if shares are held on trust for A for life, remainder to B for life, remainder to C absolutely, a written surrender of A's life interest will result in B's life interest coming into possession so that B is entitled to the income. By contrast, disclaiming an interest before it has been accepted does not require writing.[257]

Another way of affecting the beneficial interest is by giving instructions to the trustees. We have seen that *Grey* held that instructions to hold on trust for another person constitute a disposition. What if the beneficiary issues instructions to the trustee to transfer the legal estate? This may be done where the beneficiary holds the entire beneficial interest, or by all the beneficiaries acting together.[258] If the trustee is told to transfer to the beneficiaries themselves, then it is quite clear that there is no transfer of an equitable interest. More difficult is the case where the beneficiaries authorise (or direct) the trustees to transfer the legal title directly to a third party. Such a transfer will have the effect of terminating their equitable interests, although the third party enjoys the legal title rather than an equitable title. The House of Lords held in *Vandervell v IRC*[259] that such transactions fall outside s 53(1)(c), although the ratio is difficult to discern.[260] Perhaps the best analysis is that the interest is defeated rather than disposed of. Once the trustees have disposed of the legal title with the permission of the beneficiary, equity would not allow the beneficiary to assert the equitable title, just as it cannot be asserted against a bona fide purchaser without notice.[261]

Resulting, implied and constructive trusts

The exclusion of these trusts is natural. They are imposed by courts, and there is no desire to curb the powers of the court. The difficulty is that many of these trusts are ultimately based upon the intention of the parties. Two examples of constructive trusts are where specific performance of a contract is available or it would be unconscionable (on the facts of the case) to refuse to fulfil a promise. Can a party argue that an oral contract[262] gives rise to such a constructive trust, where that trust will effect a disposition of an equitable interest?

[256] *IRC v Buchanan* [1958] Ch 289 (interpreting 'disposition' in tax legislation).
[257] *Re Paradise Motor Co Ltd* [1968] 1 WLR 1125.
[258] *Saunders v Vautier* (1841) 4 Beav 115 (49 ER 282), affirmed Cr&Ph 240 (41 ER 482).
[259] [1967] 2 AC 291. Subsequent litigation (*Re Vandervell's Trusts (No 2)* [1974] Ch 269) also involved formality problems: Battersby [1979] Conv 17 at pp 31–37; Green (1984) 47 MLR 385 at pp 413–421.
[260] Lord Upjohn, with whom Lord Pearce agreed, held the section inapplicable where the person instructing the trustees controls both the legal and equitable estate ([1967] 2 AC 291 at p 311); there is no problem for the trustees in knowing that the instruction is genuine. This would be compelling but for the fact that it appears to be equally true in *Grey v IRC*. It is of interest that Lord Upjohn decided *Grey* at first instance, being reversed on appeal.
[261] Hackney, *Understanding Equity and Trusts*, p 90. Nolan [2002] CLJ 169 employs a somewhat analogous overreaching analysis.
[262] Contracts generally require writing only if relating to interests in land.

Such an argument was attempted in *Oughtred* v *IRC*.[263] A beneficiary had a reversionary interest in shares held on trust. His mother had the life interest. They decided to terminate the trust by the mother's buying the reversionary interest. A simple transfer of this beneficial interest would, of course, require writing. However, it was argued that the mother's agreement to purchase the reversion was specifically enforceable in equity and that this gave rise to a constructive trust. Lord Radcliffe, who dissented, approved this argument. The majority did not need to decide the point as they decided that writing was required for different reasons, but Lord Denning rejected the argument. Lord Cohen (dissenting) appears to accept the argument that there is a constructive trust, but not such as to transfer the beneficial interest.

Subsequently, the Court of Appeal has held in *Neville* v *Wilson*[264] that the constructive trust argument is sound: a specifically enforceable oral contract is effective to transfer a beneficial interest. Given the doubts expressed in *Oughtred* this is a bold decision, but one may welcome the settlement of this controversial issue.

Conclusions

It is plain that s 53(1)(c) gives rise to a great deal of difficulty. It raises in acute form how far it is justifiable to insist upon writing in some cases but not in others. It is, of course, true that secret transfers of equitable interests are difficult to spot: there is, after all, no tangible asset that is handed over. In particular, one can sympathise with trustees who are faced with a person claiming the benefit of an oral transfer. Yet, a legal chose in action can be assigned in equity without writing, and the debtor faces similar difficulties. It may well be thought that it is impossible to produce rational results from a statutory structure which depends upon 'disposition' and 'equitable interest'. Even so, it appears that the courts are more concerned with interpreting the legislation than producing a coherent structure to the requirement of writing.

7. Wills

So far we have been looking at inter vivos transfers, those taking effect during the transferor's lifetime. Property may, of course, be left by will, effective on death. The will determines who is entitled to the deceased's property: it does not itself transfer the property. On death, property vests in the personal representatives (called executors when appointed by will, otherwise administrators).[265] In due course, the personal representatives will transfer the assets to those entitled under the will.

To be valid, wills must satisfy special formality requirements. Section 9 of the Wills Act 1837[266] requires that the will be signed by the testator in the presence of two witnesses,[267] each of whom must sign as a witness.[268] Until 1982, it was necessary that the testator sign at the end, but the repeal of this requirement has not solved all difficulties. In

---

[263] [1960] AC 206.
[264] [1997] Ch 144; see also *Re Holt's Settlement* [1969] 1 Ch 100 at p 116. For the Australian position, see Turner [2006] Conv 390.
[265] Administration of Estates Act 1925, s 1.
[266] As amended by the Administration of Justice Act 1982, s 17.
[267] Alternatively, a prior signature may be acknowledged.
[268] Or acknowledge his or her signature in the presence of the testator.

Wood v *Smith*,[269] the testator commenced his will by writing 'my will by Percy Winterborne'. Although writing one's name in this way can amount to a signature, it is required by s 9 that the signature must intend to give effect to the will. It was held that the writing of the will was a single operation on the facts of the case and that the signature was effective. The Court of Appeal left open the question whether the signature would have been valid if the will had been written on two separate occasions, so that it could not be regarded as a single operation.[270]

The witnessing rules provide traps. In particular, a will is invalid if both witnesses are not present together when the testator signs the will (or acknowledges his signature). Another trap is that a witness (or their spouse)[271] cannot take any benefit under a will. It is, however, possible to avoid this if (most unusually) there are two other witnesses, neither of whom is also a beneficiary.

Wills are revoked by the subsequent marriage of the testator, save where it appears from the terms of the will that it is made in contemplation of marriage to a particular person and it is not intended that the will should be revoked.[272] Somewhat similarly, divorce (or annulment of marriage) has the effect of invalidating provisions in favour of the former spouse. However, in the case of divorce, other provisions in the will remain valid.[273] A will may also be revoked by another will or by 'burning, tearing or otherwise destroying' it with the intention of revoking it.[274]

Merely losing the will does not necessarily invalidate it. In many cases, there will be no record of the contents and the will must necessarily fail. However, it suffices if the terms are known. An obvious circumstance would be where a copy is retained by the testator's solicitors, although a more colourful example is provided by *Sugden* v *Lord St Leonards*.[275] Lord St Leonards, a former Lord Chancellor, lavished such care on his will that he constantly talked about it with his daughter. When he died and the will could not be found, the daughter's recollection of the will was sufficient to render it effective. Her recollection was not perfect, but that was no more significant than if part of a will has been rendered illegible or a codicil (a later supplement to a will) has been lost. In all these cases, the courts will give effect to what does exist.

8. Restrictions upon transfers

This area will be considered very briefly. There are several rules, not of a formality nature,[276] that restrict the effectiveness of transfers, especially gifts. The only area

---

[269] [1993] Ch 90; the will was in fact held invalid as the testator lacked testamentary capacity. See also *Weatherhill* v *Pearce* [1995] 1 WLR 592.

[270] An amendment of an existing will clearly cannot rely on a signature in that will: *Re White* [1991] 1 Ch 1.

[271] Civil partnerships have the same status as marriage for the purpose of the rules for wills: see p 331 below.

[272] Wills Act 1837, s 18.

[273] Ibid, s 18A (as substituted by Law Reform (Succession) Act 1995, s 3).

[274] Wills Act 1837, s 20. Destroying part of a will may revoke that part: *Re Everest* [1975] Fam 44; *In the Goods of Woodward* (1871) LR 2 P&D 206.

[275] (1876) 1 PD 154. The controversial questions were whether conversations after the execution of the will were admissible as evidence of its contents and whether it should be inferred that the testator had revoked the will by destroying it.

[276] The Bills of Sale provisions (see p 118 above) combine some formality elements together with registration requirements. For registration requirements in respect of land transactions, see Chapters 12 and 13.

considered in this section is that of bankruptcy.[277] One obvious risk is that a person about to become bankrupt might give all his property to, for example, his wife. If valid, this would defeat the creditors, whilst keeping the property in the family. Several statutory restrictions have been developed to cope with such problems.

Section 423 of the Insolvency Act 1986[278] enables the court to reopen gifts and transactions at a significant undervalue if the purpose was to defeat or prejudice creditors. That provision has no time limit, being based upon the purpose of the transferor.[279] Rather different is s 339 of the 1986 Act. This enables the court to reopen gifts and transactions at a significant undervalue[280] if they have been made within two years of bankruptcy (five years if the transferor was insolvent at the time of the gift). There is no requirement of any purpose regarding creditors. It may be added that preferences shown to creditors are regulated by s 340, without any gift requirement.

Further reading

Bridge, M (2016) 132 LQR 47: The nature of assignment and non-assignment clauses.

Edelman, J and Elliott, S (2015) 131 LQR 228: Two conceptions of equitable assignment.

Hall, J C [1959] CLJ 99: Gift of part of a debt.

Harpum, C (2001) 'Property in an electronic age', in *Modern Studies in Property Law*, Vol 1 (ed E. Cooke), Chapter 1.

Tettenborn, A [1987] Conv 358: Fraud, cross-claims and the assignment of choses in action.

Thornely, J W A [1953] CLJ 355: Transfer of choses in possession between members of a common household.

---

[277] Another well-known example is that transfers intended to defeat a spouse's rights on marriage breakdown may be defeated: Matrimonial Causes Act 1973, s 37 (purchasers in good faith are protected); similar rules apply to civil partnership.

[278] Replacing earlier legislation. For details, see Miller [1998] Conv 362.

[279] It may therefore apply to a 'precautionary' transfer, despite solvency at the time and no contemplation of an early hazardous transaction. *Midland Bank plc* v *Wyatt* [1995] 1 FLR 696.

[280] For an example in a matrimonial breakdown scenario, see *Re Kumar* [1993] 1 WLR 224. Court orders on matrimonial breakdown will not normally be caught. *Hill* v *Haines* [2008] Ch 412.

9

Formalities: rationale and trusts

Introduction

In the previous chapter, it was seen that legislation often requires writing (sometimes a deed) before a disposition can be effective, especially where land is involved. It is not surprising that there are frequent problems arising from failure to comply with these requirements. The first section of this chapter will consider the reasons for having formality rules. This will help us assess the arguments for and against the development of exceptions by the courts. Resulting and constructive trusts provide major exceptions; these will be considered in the second part of this chapter. The most significant modern use of these trusts (mainly the constructive trust) has been in the context of the family home, where there is a mass of controversial case law. This is the subject matter of Chapter 11. Estoppels provide another particularly significant exception, and they will be considered in Chapter 10. Estoppels and constructive trusts overlap to a considerable extent, and it is debated how far they should be assimilated. This is also considered in Chapter 11, after both areas have been studied.

It should be added that resulting and constructive trusts perform a dual role (as is also true for estoppel). The first is that they may be used to impose obligations where none would otherwise exist. This is not a formality function, but for convenience, aspects of it will be dealt with in this chapter. The most significant aspect of this role is that it governs the holding of interests in the family home, whenever the transfer fails to stipulate the interests of the family members. The second role, of course, is that these trusts enable formality rules to be avoided. Not surprisingly, these roles shade into one another. A good example is the resulting trust. If A contributes to the purchase of property by B, then B will hold the property on resulting trust for A in proportion to the contribution. The resulting trust both confers an interest on A and enables it to be enforced notwithstanding a lack of writing.

1. Reasons for formality requirements

An obvious effect of any formality requirement is that it may defeat the intentions of the parties. This effect must be justified.[1]

---

[1] The discussion will concentrate upon writing requirements. Other requirements, such as delivery for gifts, play a similar role. They are described by Gulliver and Tilson (1941) 51 Yale LJ 1 at p 4 as performing a 'ritual function'. For a more recent discussion, see Howard and Hill (1995) 15 LS 356.

Most of our present rules date back to the Statute of Frauds 1677. As its name indicates, the statute was designed to avoid the fraudulent assertion of contracts, trusts and assignments that in truth did not exist. This purpose is still relevant today, although most commentators believe that the circumstances of the seventeenth century made such fraud infinitely more likely than it is today. It is paradoxical that, when fraud is discussed in the cases today, it is almost invariably the fraud of the person who relies on the lack of writing as a technical justification for denying an obligation.

It is common to explain the purposes of formality requirements as threefold: evidential, cautionary and channelling.[2]

The evidential function may be said to be twofold. First, it makes it clear that an obligation has been undertaken. It is obvious that fraudulent or mistaken assertions of obligations are reduced by a requirement of writing. Next, writing clarifies the terms of the agreement or trust. The problems are not limited to fraud. The parties may have genuinely different impressions of what has been orally promised or whether matters have progressed from negotiation to contract.

The cautionary function is intended to be protective of the promisor. The problem is that people frequently make oral promises that they have not thought through. Indeed, it is a common (and erroneous) public perception that there can never be legal liability without writing. When we require writing, we give the promisor an opportunity to reflect upon what obligations are really intended. This is further enhanced as regards the witnessing requirements for wills[3] and deeds: in these cases, even a hastily prepared written promise is likely to fall foul of the rules.

The channelling function is to persuade people to use standard forms (often utilising professional advice), which will make it clear what sort of obligation is being undertaken and what the detailed terms are. This makes it easier to draft the promise and reduces problems of interpretation and the need to imply terms. Two examples may be given. A will is generally recognised as requiring a special form. It follows that it is rare for scraps of paper to be argued to be parts of a will. Similarly, contracts for the sale of land are normally in a detailed form used by lawyers, dealing with most of the problems that might arise. The use of this form not only makes it clear that a contract really is intended but also renders litigation concerning its performance less likely. Nobody can pretend that writing requirements will always result in the appropriate forms being used, but they do encourage their use.

Whilst the benefits of writing are widely recognised, it is equally widely accepted that injustice would result from too rigid an insistence upon them.[4] Within a few decades of the Statute of Frauds, exceptions had been developed, generally based upon the idea that statutory writing requirements cannot be insisted upon where it would be fraudulent to do so. Otherwise, a statute designed to inhibit fraud on the part of a claimant could be used as a cloak to hide fraud practised on the claimant. A clear example would be if B persuades A to transfer land

---

[2] Fuller (1941) 41 Col LR 799. See also Youdan [1984] CLJ 306; Moriarty (1984) 100 LQR 376 at pp 398–404. The Law Commission considered that the purposes justified strengthening the formality requirements for contracts to sell land: Law Com No 164, paras 2.6–2.13.

[3] Protection of the testator from undue deathbed influence was an original purpose of the Wills Act 1837, although of little significance today. Gulliver and Tilson (1941) 51 Yale LJ 1 (especially p 10).

[4] Critchley in *Land Law: Themes and Perspectives* (eds Bright and Dewar), Chapter 20, whilst also identifying benefits extending beyond the interests of the parties.

to him on the oral understanding that B will hold on trust for A. It would be fraudulent for B to deny the trust obligation. There have been suggestions for more broadly based relaxations of the operation of the rules,[5] but these do not at present form part of English law.

Much of the early case law on these exceptions is based upon what became the law of part performance of contracts, though this will have little, if any, effect after the Law of Property (Miscellaneous Provisions) Act 1989. The two general principles operating today are those of resulting or constructive trusts and estoppel.

2. Resulting and constructive trusts

The principles of resulting and constructive trusts are of general application within the law; they are not limited to the formalities context. In this section, we will consider only those constructive trusts relating to formalities; there are many other examples of them. The exclusion of resulting and constructive trusts from formality requirements[6] was, it seems, intended to allow them to continue to function. Consider two examples. If A transfers property to trustees without declaring beneficial interests, then there will be a resulting trust in favour of A. In the second example, a trustee obtains, for himself, property that ought to belong to the trust. A constructive trust will be imposed upon him. It was no part of the legislative policy to prevent either trust from being enforced. In neither of them is the trust being employed by the courts as a device to get around the need for writing.

A. Presumption of resulting trust

The presumption of resulting trust[7] (that is, that the beneficial interest results back to the person providing the property or money) provides one way of dealing with the question of who owns land or other property. If A provides £120,000 and B £60,000, but the legal title is conveyed to A alone, then A will hold the legal title on resulting trust for them in proportion to their contributions. Equity has long presumed that an unexplained transfer of property is not a gift but gives rise to a resulting trust.[8] Similarly, the provision of money for a purchase from a third party is seen as giving rise to a trust which attaches to the property bought with the money.[9]

The proposition that a transfer of property to another gives rise to a trust for the transferor does, at first sight, look distinctly odd. Indeed, Hope JA described it as 'completely anachronistic'.[10] One might suppose that a gift is intended when property is transferred to another. Yet some cases do not look like gifts. A transfer of assets to one's solicitor would not normally be intended to benefit the solicitor personally, though this example does involve a fiduciary. Further, the presumption comes into its own when considering substantial transfers

---

[5] Perillo (1974) 43 Fordham LR 39 argues for enforcement if there is 'clear and convincing' evidence of the promise.
[6] Going back to Statute of Frauds 1677, s 8.
[7] See p 31 above.
[8] Chambers (2001) 15 *Trust Law International* 26 observes the lack of authority for direct transfers of land before *Lohia v Lohia* [2001] WTLR 101.
[9] *Dyer v Dyer* (1788) 2 Cox 92 (30 ER 42).
[10] *Dullow v Dullow* (1985) 3 NSWLR 531 at p 535.

of property. People do not normally make such transfers without making it plain why they are doing so. Take the facts of *Sekhon* v *Alissa*.[11] A mother gave her daughter £22,500 to enable a house to be bought. The daughter argued that this was a gift and that any obligation owed to her mother was merely a moral one. However, Hoffmann J stressed that the money represented virtually all the mother's savings and found that the true intention was to take part in a commercial venture, her name being omitted on the basis of tax advice. Looking at these factors and bearing in mind that there were two other children, one can see that it would be odd to conclude that there was a gift.

Where family homes are involved, today we employ a constructive trust analysis rather than a resulting trust.[12] However, it remains true to assert that we do not regard contributions to the purchase of a house as a gift. In any event, the presumption of resulting trust is generally of small importance. This is because there will be evidence showing that a gift was or, as the case may be, was not intended. Thus, the facts of *Sekhon* v *Alissa* showed clearly that no gift was intended. Nevertheless, the presumption can be a useful starting point.

Transfers of land

One special problem concerns the transfer of land, where it is argued that there is a resulting trust for the transferor. Section 60(3) of the Law of Property Act 1925 provides that 'In a voluntary conveyance a resulting trust for the grantor shall not be implied merely by reason that the property is not expressed to be conveyed for the use or benefit of the grantee.' The reason for this provision is tied in with conveyancing changes introduced in 1925.[13] For many years, its effect was not entirely clear,[14] but in a full review of the area, Nicholas Strauss QC at first instance in *Lohia* v *Lohia*[15] held that s 60(3) ousts the presumption. Perhaps unfortunately, the Court of Appeal did not find it necessary to decide the point and clearly regarded it as open for argument.[16] The effect of s 60(3) remains unclear! Given the weakness of the presumptions today, it is important only in those rare cases where there is no other evidence as to intentions. In any event, the provision is inapplicable in the more common case where money is provided towards the cost of purchase. In this situation nobody is arguing that the seller of the land (the grantor) has a resulting trust in his favour: it is the contributor who argues that there is a trust.

Presumption of advancement

To counter the presumption of resulting trust, the contrary presumption of advancement operated in certain cases. Thus, husbands were presumed to make gifts to wives (but not vice versa) and fathers to children. The origin of advancement lay in the obligation to maintain the transferee, though increasing stress was placed upon the greater likelihood of gifts being intended where the presumption applies.

---

[11] [1989] 2 FLR 94.
[12] See p 187 below.
[13] The repeal of the Statute of Uses, coupled with an intention that such words should no longer be necessary.
[14] See *Hodgson* v *Marks* [1971] Ch 892 at p 933; *Tinsley* v *Milligan* [1994] 1 AC 340 at p 371.
[15] [2001] WTLR 101. Mee [2012] Conv 307 reaches a similar result but by reference to the operation of resulting trusts.
[16] [2001] EWCA Civ 1691 at [24], [25]; (2002) 16 *Trust Law International* 231; see also *M* v *M* [2014] 1 FLR 439 at [171]–[174]. The analysis of Strauss QC was cited with approval in *Ali* v *Khan* (2002) 5 ITELR 232 at [24], but apparently in ignorance of the Court of Appeal dicta.

It is easy to conclude that advancement seems to belong to a much earlier and very different family and social structure. The House of Lords in *Pettitt* v *Pettitt*[17] considered that, as between husbands and wives, the presumption was outdated and of little effect. More radically, s 199 of the Equality Act 2010[18] abolishes advancement (although it had not been brought into effect by the end of 2016). It should not be thought that this will render it difficult to make a gift: especially with transfers from wealthy parents to children, the courts are likely to find an intention of gift.[19]

Bank accounts

One particular asset merits attention: joint bank accounts. The ownership of joint accounts is important for two reasons. First (and obviously), there may be a dispute as to ownership of the balance in the account. More significant may be the ownership of assets bought out of the account, most especially when the account funds the payment of mortgage instalments. Where both parties are earning and their salaries go into the account, it is almost inevitable that the money will be jointly owned. No court will wish to quantify their contributions to the account.[20] If one party provides virtually all the money, then the outcome is less clear. The money is likely to be jointly owned[21] unless either it was a joint account for reasons of convenience only[22] or money is placed in the account in such a way as to show that it is not jointly owned. Suppose A and B are living together and have a joint account. B has significant assets given to him by his parents. B decides to realise some of these assets and buy shares with the proceeds. The proceeds are paid into the joint account, out of which the shares are to be bought. Can A claim a beneficial interest in this money in the account? The answer appears to be no: it seems merely incidental that the money is passing through the account.[23]

Turning to the issue of ownership of assets bought from a jointly owned account, the normal rule is that they belong to the parties equally.[24] The parties may, of course, intend that either can draw on the account for investments in their own names which will not be jointly owned,[25] but this would seem to be exceptional.[26] It is easy to conclude that if a joint account is funded from the income of both parties and assets are purchased (or mortgage instalments funded) from the account, then both parties have beneficial interests in those assets, even if they are placed in the name of one of them.[27] It is revealing that few of the many cases on ownership of homes have involved joint accounts.

[17] [1970] AC 777. See Lord Reid at p 793, Lord Hodson at p 811, Lord Upjohn at pp 813–815 and Lord Diplock at pp 823–824.
[18] Glister (2010) 73 MLR 807.
[19] Contrast *Fowkes* v *Pascoe* (1875) LR 10 Ch App 343 (wealthy mother-in-law: gift) and *Sekhon* v *Alissa* [1989] 2 FLR 94 (transfer by mother of entire savings: no gift).
[20] *Jones* v *Maynard* [1951] Ch 572.
[21] *Re Figgis* [1969] 1 Ch 123, although some reliance was placed on the presumption of advancement (since abolished) in reaching this result.
[22] *Marshal* v *Crutwell* (1875) LR 20 Eq 328.
[23] *Jansen* v *Jansen* [1965] P 478 (money borrowed by wife placed in account for a building project that never came to fruition); *Drake* v *Whipp* [1996] 1 FLR 826.
[24] *Jones* v *Maynard* [1951] Ch 572. This does not apply to assets purchased on another person's credit card, there being no joint account out of which payment is made: *Ebner* v *Official Trustee* (2003) 196 ALR 533.
[25] *Re Bishop* [1965] Ch 450.
[26] Samuels (1965) 28 MLR 480, but contrast *Daly* v *Gilbert* [1993] 3 NZLR 731.
[27] Lord Neuberger in *Stack* v *Dowden* [2007] 2 AC 432 at [133]; *Abbott* v *Abbott* [2008] 1 FLR 1451 (PC).

B. Transfers for fraudulent purposes

When A transfers property to B or property is purchased in B's name, one possible motive is to avoid unwanted consequences which might follow if A is the owner. The most likely unwanted consequences are the loss of the property if A becomes bankrupt, a taxation liability or inability to claim social security benefits. The problem is that A's plan can succeed only if A really does have no ownership: retention of even an equitable interest will be fatal to it. Almost invariably, the cases involve transfers within a family, where there is obviously scope for supposing that a gift was intended.[28]

The transferor's thinking is that, as between the family members, it will not matter much who owns the property. In the great majority of cases, this will be justified. Unfortunately, marriages and other relationships break down, quite apart from other changes of mind or misunderstandings on the part of transferees. If A wishes to recover the property, then he has to prove a trust in his favour. Yet, such a trust is inconsistent with A's objectives in transferring the property. Not only is there an inconsistency, but A is planning to act fraudulently. He is saying that, should he become bankrupt (to take one example), then he will assert that B is the owner with the result that A's creditors lose out, whilst the understanding between A and B is that B is not the beneficial owner. This is to intend a fraud on the creditors. B may have a moral obligation to return the property to A if there is no bankruptcy, and there is certainly no reason why he should not do so, but these propositions do not bear on the question of ownership.

The modern basis for illegality

The illegality test applied in recent decades has been whether the claimant (A) needs to rely on the illegality in order to make out the case for a trust in their favour. If so, then *Tinsley* v *Milligan*[29] held that the claim must fail. This led to a resulting trust analysis being crucial. If the claimant could rely on a resulting trust, then there would be no need to rely on the illegality and the claim could succeed. However, this would also apply to a common intention constructive trust, where the intention could be proved without recourse to the illegality.[30]

Very recently, however, the *Tinsley* reliance test has been rejected by the Supreme Court in *Patel* v *Mirza*.[31] The new test is based upon policy and proportionality. This appears to render much of the older material in this area redundant. It does not mean, of course, that illegality may never be relevant in such cases.

However, one strand of reasoning may survive. Suppose that it is unclear whether A intended to be able to recover the property should the need for the transfer evaporate. Such were the facts in *Tinker* v *Tinker*.[32] Fearing the collapse of his business, a husband purchased a house in his wife's name. The business prospered whilst the marriage soon collapsed.

---

[28] In other situations, there is likely to be a resulting trust for A. *Rowan* v *Dann* (1992) 64 P&CR 202.
[29] [1994] 1 AC 340.
[30] *Davies* v *O'Kelly* [2015] 1 WLR 2725, applied in *Hniazdzilau* v *Vajgel* [2016] EWHC 15 (Ch). The claim would fail where reliance on the unlawful purpose was essential: *Barrett* v *Barrett* [2008] 2 P&CR 345.
[31] [2016] 3 WLR 399 (6:3 majority): see especially Lord Toulson at [101]. Reform had earlier been proposed by Law Com No 320; Davies [2010] Conv 282.
[32] [1970] P 136.

The husband sought to reclaim the house. The Court of Appeal was not prepared to hold that the husband was planning a fraud on his creditors (by hiding his assets) and accordingly held that he had never intended a trust.

C. Constructive trusts: an oral promise by a transferee to hold on trust for the transferor

Suppose A transfers property to B, A and B orally agreeing that B should hold on trust for A during A's lifetime. This is an express oral trust of land in favour of A, which s 53(1)(b) of the Law of Property Act 1925 requires to be evidenced in writing. These were the facts of *Bannister* v *Bannister*,[33] in which the Court of Appeal imposed a constructive trust upon B. It is apparent that failure to enforce a trust would have enabled B to make a windfall profit on the transfer. B had bought the property for a price discounted by some 40%, and it would be most unjust if B could ignore his promise. The court rested its decision on the fraudulent conduct of the purchaser. Although it was held that fraud at the time of the transfer was not necessary (the purchaser then intended to perform his promise), it was fraudulent for the purchaser thereafter to assert the legal title and deny the promise.

The enforcement of the trust in *Bannister* is widely supported. It is based on a long line of cases insisting that the Statute of Frauds cannot be used as an instrument of fraud.[34] It is, however, debated whether the trust is an express one, recognised because a statute cannot be used as an instrument of fraud, or a constructive trust imposed to prevent fraud. *Bannister* treated the trust as constructive. This fits within the s 53(2) exception and appears to be the dominant view today, despite the fact that most earlier cases, including the previous leading authority *Rochefoucauld* v *Boustead*,[35] had taken the former view. Ultimately, it seems to make little difference whatever view is taken.[36]

Could these cases be analysed as giving rise to a resulting trust? If A transfers property to B, then there will be a resulting trust in favour of A unless a gift to B is intended. Why, then, have the courts not simply held that no gift was intended and that there is a resulting trust? There may be two answers. First, the resulting trust is most appropriate where A is to retain ownership in equity. It would be difficult to apply in *Bannister*, where the transferor was claiming a life interest. The second answer is that the conveyances in these cases invariably contain wording which would preclude a resulting trust. It follows that a separate oral agreement has to be relied upon to show that there is a trust. Accordingly, it has been thought impossible to rely upon a resulting trust.[37] This makes it surprising that Russell LJ used a resulting trust analysis in *Hodgson* v *Marks*.[38]

---

[33] [1948] 2 All ER 133.
[34] Allan (2014) 34 LS 419 argues that fraud continues to be at the heart of the trusts here being discussed.
[35] [1897] 1 Ch 196 (at least for the purposes of the limitation legislation); Swadling [2011] CLP 399 at p 416; Allan (2014) 34 LS 419 at pp 425, 431–434 (noting that the case may require somewhat different classification).
[36] Possibly, the fraud analysis might not bind a subsequent purchaser. This seems unlikely on the authorities but was left open in *Hodgson* v *Marks* [1971] Ch 892. A separate point is that the express trust analysis might more readily support third-party enforcement (discussed below), but see Ford and Lee, *Principles of the Law of Trusts* (3rd edn), para 6090. See also McFarlane (2004) 120 LQR 667 at pp 675–676.
[37] *Young* v *Peachy* (1741) 2 Atk 254 (26 ER 557).
[38] [1971] Ch 892. The use of a resulting trust is criticised by Birks, *An Introduction to the Law of Restitution*, pp 60–62.

One point already noted is that the trust does not depend upon fraud at the time of transfer to the trustee. The fraud may exist in the subsequent assertion of the lack of writing, even though the trustee had originally intended to perform the trust. In these circumstances, does a trust exist before the assertion of lack of writing? Before that stage, of course, there is no fraud. Even so, it seems extremely likely that the trust arises at the time of transfer.[39] We can say that it *would be* fraudulent to raise the defence in the future and on that basis, the transferor can be said to have an immediate interest. This is of great importance for taxation purposes.[40] It would establish (as is surely right) that the income and the capital belong to the transferor, even in cases where the transferee at all times complies with the trust and therefore cannot be accused of fraud.

D. Constructive trusts: an oral promise by a transferee to recognise the rights of a third party[41]

Refusal to recognise agreed third-party rights can be just as fraudulent as the conduct in cases such as *Bannister* v *Bannister*. However, the third-party cases illustrate a range of problems. These may be summarised as follows:

(1) Has the transferee agreed to hold for the third party such that it would be fraudulent to deny the trust?
(2) Who can enforce the trust?
(3) What is the nature of the trust?

A fourth question is how far these constructive trusts are proprietary interests binding subsequent purchasers. This is particularly problematic where the rights under the trust are not of a proprietary nature; it will be considered in Chapter 22 in the licences context.[42]

(i) *Agreement to hold for the third party*

Proof of this has caused considerable difficulty. At heart, it is a simple factual inquiry as to whether a trust has been declared. If a trust is expressly declared,[43] then on normal principles there will be a completely constituted trust and, unless land is involved, writing will generally be unnecessary. An example of a trust's being found where the parties have not used the word 'trust' is *Cochrane* v *Moore*,[44] in which a chargee said that a third party would be 'all right'. The recurring question in the cases is whether the words used give rise to a trust.

---

[39] *Ottaway v Norman* [1972] Ch 698 at p 713 (secret trust, similarly imposed to avoid fraud). This also applies to the equivalent Australian constructive trust (p 213 below): *Parsons v McBain* (2001) 192 ALR 772.
[40] It also ensures that a successor to the transferee is bound by the trust: *Re Duke of Marlborough* [1894] 2 Ch 133 (creditors of deceased transferee).
[41] See McFarlane (2004) 120 LQR 667, describing the principle behind this (and some other examples of constructive trusts) as a being of a 'novel kind' (p 686).
[42] See p 493 below.
[43] The trust is generally declared jointly by both parties. In cases where no consideration is given, it would seem to be the seller who declares the trust (Feltham (1982) 98 LQR 17). See also Youdan [1984] CLJ 306 at pp 315–320.
[44] (1890) 25 QBD 57 (p 129 above).

As might be expected, almost invariably, it is the seller who wishes there to be a trust. The purchaser buys on these terms only because they are insisted upon by the seller. The third party's beneficial interest in these cases is rarely a full right to the property, but rather some lesser right to it. The purchaser usually pays a reduced price and is accordingly content to agree to the third-party right.[45] Simply because the purchaser will have paid less by virtue of the agreement, the courts are relatively keen to find a declaration of trust.

Such a case is *Binions* v *Evans*.[46] Lord Denning MR employed a constructive trust where the contract of sale contained a special clause whereby the property was sold 'subject to' the claimant's rights. Indeed, Lord Denning was willing to impose a constructive trust whenever a purchaser impliedly takes subject to the claimant's rights and thought that such an implication could be made whenever the claimant was in actual occupation. This would result in the contractual rights of virtually every occupier binding purchasers.

A constructive trust was also recognised in *Lyus* v *Prowsa Developments Ltd*.[47] A developer had contracted to sell to the claimant a house on an estate being developed. The developer became insolvent, and his mortgagees sold the estate. It is important to note that the starting point was that the mortgagees (and purchasers from them) were not bound by the claimant's contract, as the contract was subsequent to the mortgage. Nevertheless, the mortgagees wished the contract to be honoured. They sold the land subject to the contract and obtained the purchaser's assurance that the claimant's rights would be quickly dealt with. Dillon J held that this gave rise to a trust. His approach is narrower than that of Lord Denning in that Dillon J requires that the promise be taken in order to benefit the third party. Lord Denning had appeared to lump together all cases in which a purchaser agrees to take subject to another person's rights.[48]

The meaning of 'subject to' promises
Binions and *Lyus* are illustrations of purchasers buying 'subject to' the rights of the third party. These simple and common words are ambiguous: they can bear very different interpretations. The first and most likely is that the purchaser is promising not to raise any objections if it transpires that the rights exist and he is bound by them. The promise is not intended to benefit the third party at all but to relieve the seller from potential legal liability to the purchaser and to remove the risk that the purchaser may rescind the contract. This interpretation obviously fails Dillon J's test: there is no intention to benefit the third party.

The second interpretation is that the purchaser promises to give effect to the third party's rights, for the benefit of the third party. This was readily proved in *Lyus*: the seller was plainly not bound by the claimant's estate contract and had no need for protection as described in the first interpretation. The only reason for extracting the promise from the purchaser could be to benefit the claimant. This interpretation clearly satisfies Dillon J's test.

---

[45] Just as in *Bannister* v *Bannister* [1948] 2 All ER 133, where the purchaser bought at a 40% discount and subject to a life interest in the transferor.

[46] [1972] Ch 359. Megaw and Stephenson LJJ held that the claimant had a life interest before the sale.

[47] [1982] 1 WLR 1044. A similar approach was taken by the High Court of Australia in *Bahr* v *Nicolay (No 2)* (1988) 62 ALJR 268.

[48] Quite apart from cases in which Lord Denning would imply a 'subject to' promise. There is little or no scope for this in Dillon J's analysis.

A third and middle interpretation is where the purchaser promises to benefit the third party, but the reason for the promise is to avoid the seller's being liable to the third party. In this case, the only reason the seller extracts the promise is to protect himself: the third party's benefit is merely the means to this end.

The cases were reviewed by the Court of Appeal in *Ashburn Anstalt* v *Arnold*.[49] A purchaser had bought land subject to the rights of the claimant, but the court refused to recognise a constructive trust. The conclusion on the facts in *Binions* was supported because it was a fair inference that the parties' intention was for the purchaser to give effect to the claimant's rights, especially as the purchaser had paid less for the land. More significantly, however, the generous approach of Lord Denning was rejected. In accordance with Dillon J's analysis, it was held necessary for the purchaser to accept an obligation to give effect to the claimant's rights: this will be a new obligation accepted by the purchaser.[50] Such an obligation will not be inferred from the simple fact that the purchaser has agreed to buy 'subject to' those rights. It was significant that in *Ashburn Anstalt*, there was no evidence that the purchaser had paid a lower price. The approach of *Ashburn Anstalt* was followed by the Court of Appeal in *Chaudhary* v *Yavuz*.[51] It was stressed that a promise to buy subject to claims, without identifying the specific claim, will almost never support a constructive trust.

A large body of authority establishes this as the current state of the law.[52] The basis for the constructive trust is unconscionable or inequitable conduct on the part of the purchaser[53]: this will be found if the purchaser obtains the transfer by promising to respect the claim and then goes back on the promise.[54] How readily a trust will be found may well depend upon reactions to the third interpretation of promises to hold 'subject to': namely that the purchaser promises to respect the claim but primarily for the benefit of the seller. It may not be too difficult to convince the court that the seller is worried not just about the purchaser's suing him in respect of the claim[55] but also about the possibility of an action being brought by the claimant. If the claimant will have no viable claim against the seller after sale, then *Lyus* shows that a trust will readily be found. However, the result appears to be that, if there is a viable claim, then the 'subject to' promise may still oblige the purchaser to respect the claim, leading to a constructive trust. This view of the trust may be somewhat wider than appears from reading *Ashburn Anstalt*, and there is no clear authority regarding the third situation. It is certainly arguable that the obligation to the seller is an insufficient reason for finding a trust which the claimant can enforce.

---

[49] [1989] Ch 1. See also *Markfaith Investment Ltd* v *Chiap Hua Flashlights Ltd* [1991] 2 AC 43.
[50] *Lloyd* v *Dugdale* [2002] 2 P&CR 167 at [52].
[51] [2013] Ch 249 (term in *Standard Conditions of Sale*); McFarlane [2013] Conv 74.
[52] See *IDC Group Ltd* v *Clark* [1992] 1 EGLR 187, upheld 65 P&CR 179; *Kewal Investments Ltd* v *Arthur Maiden Ltd* [1990] 1 EGLR 193; *Lloyd* v *Dugdale* [2002] 2 P&CR 167; *Groveholt Ltd* v *Hughes* [2013] 1 P&CR 342. Hayton (1993) 109 LQR 485 at p 488 argued for a more broadly based constructive trust, but this is difficult to square with the cases.
[53] Hopkins (2006) 26 LS 475 analyses and supports the role of conscionability.
[54] *Clowes Developments (UK) Ltd* v *Walters* [2006] 1 P&CR 1 imposed a constructive trust in the special context of a transfer within a group of companies, when both transferor and transferee expected the claim to be unaffected. Unusually, the unconscionable conduct lay in the impact on the claimant.
[55] I.e. should there be no 'subject to' promise.

The effect of the sale price

It has been seen that the payment of a lower price by the purchaser is a significant pointer towards there being a constructive trust. Even this, however, requires some qualification. In *Lyus* itself, there was no reduction in price, proof that it is not essential. In New Zealand, Mahon J has stated that 'The key to this type of inquiry in my opinion lies in the question whether the transferor would have parted with his property but for the oral undertaking of the transferee.'[56] On the other hand, the presence of a reduced price is not enough to prove a trust. Even where it is clear that neither seller nor purchaser wants the purchaser to respect the interest, they may recognise a significant risk that he may be bound by it. In this type of situation, no sane purchaser would pay the full normal market price (especially where the purchaser does not obtain vacant possession): some reduction will be necessary to take account of the risk.

Consider the facts of *Binions*. The purchaser agreed to buy 'subject to the tenancy' of the claimant, who was living in the property. Suppose that the intention had been merely to protect the seller against objection by the purchaser, although the parties thought that the claimant had no rights. The reality is that money would be spent gaining occupation and a reduced purchase price would be inevitable. As is commonly said, few people are interested in purchasing a law suit. It is only where the reduction in price goes beyond a reflection of the risk that a promise to respect the interest can be inferred. That said, there is an understandable reluctance to allow a purchaser to reap a windfall profit where there has been a significant reduction in price. The facts of *Binions* justified the imposition of a constructive trust. The claimant's husband had worked for the sellers and lived in their cottage throughout his life, and there is every reason to suppose that the sellers wanted the occupation of his widow, aged 78, to be protected.

(ii) *Who can enforce the trust?*

One aspect of the promise in cases such as *Binions* is that an agreement between seller and purchaser confers rights on a third party. Although this looks surprising in terms of traditional contract rules, the operation of the constructive trust appears to reach virtually identical results to the Contracts (Rights of Third Parties) Act 1999.[57] In any event, it has always been possible to create trusts in favour of third parties so long as they are completely constituted: *Cochrane v Moore*[58] provides a good example. It should be noted that the trust is not of the promise (when the promisee seller would be the trustee) but of the property itself (so that the promisor purchaser is the trustee). This avoids the traditional reluctance to recognise trusts of promises.[59]

When formality requirements are not satisfied, a constructive trust (or similar analysis) is employed to prevent the transferee from keeping the property free from his undertaking. However, does the avoidance of fraud require that the third party be permitted to enforce

---

[56] *Avondale Printers & Stationers Ltd* v *Haggie* [1979] 2 NZLR 124 at p 163; cf McFarlane (2004) 120 LQR 667 at pp 686–687.

[57] Bright [2000] Conv 398 prefers the contractual claim to the use of the constructive trust. However, contract may not always provide an answer, especially where formalities are absent: Hopkins (2006) 26 LS 475 at pp 485–486.

[58] (1890) 25 QBD 57.

[59] *Re Schebsman* [1944] Ch 83 at p 89, cited in *Lyus*.

the trust?[60] Allowing a resulting trust for the seller would ensure that the transferee obtains no benefit.[61] The seller could thereafter (if so desired) declare a trust for the third party. On the other hand, the cases (*Binions, Lyus, Ashburn Anstalt*) do support the possibility of enforcement by the third party.[62] One argument in favour of this is that the right is often a specific and limited one. In *Lyus*, it was a right to buy a house, and in *Ashburn Anstalt*, an option to take a lease. Whilst there could be a trust to this effect in favour of the seller, it is unlikely that the seller would be interested in exercising this type of right. Even more difficult would be a case where the right is a right of way for a third party. It would be impossible for the seller (who does not own the land to be benefited) to enjoy such a right. The argument in favour of a trust enforceable by the third party (or a contract claim under the 1999 Act) appears to be much the stronger.

(iii) *The nature of the trust*

It is easy to understand that the trust is described as constructive when there is failure to satisfy formality requirements, as it justifies side-stepping these requirements. In many of the cases, however, the issue has turned on the interpretation of the purchaser's promise rather than the lack of writing. In each of *Binions, Lyus* and *Ashburn Anstalt*, the promise was in writing. This did not stop the courts from describing the trust as constructive, although *Cochrane* v *Moore* was apparently based on an express trust.[63] In nearly all the cases, this is merely a matter of a label. The same interpretation of the promise as would lead to a trust (express trust) also makes it fraudulent for the promisor to deny a trust (constructive trust). It may be significant that the use of the constructive trust in the modern cases derives from *Bannister* v *Bannister*. Whilst it is clear that the trust in *Bannister* was a constructive trust, it is equally clear that the only reason for this was to get around the requirement of writing. It follows that *Bannister* is no authority for written promises giving rise to constructive trusts. So, does the use of the constructive trust have any significance apart from formalities? Two possibilities may be considered.

First, it is commonly said that the test for a constructive trust in this sort of case 'is whether the owner of the property has so conducted himself that it would be inequitable to allow him to deny the claimant an interest in the property'.[64] It might be possible to have a case where the purchaser pays the full purchase price and *at his own suggestion* (and in order to benefit the third party) he agrees in writing to buy subject to the third party's rights. In such a case, it could be argued that it is not inequitable for him to change his mind,[65] but an express trust could be enforced because of the writing.

---

[60] Feltham [1987] Conv 246. See also Ford and Lee, *Principles of the Law of Trusts* (3rd edn), paras 6090–6100 and Thompson, *Landmark Cases in Land Law* (ed Gravells), p 169.
[61] Note that a resulting trust (in favour of the seller) was found by Russell LJ in the two-party case of *Hodgson* v *Marks* [1971] Ch 892 (p 142 above).
[62] Also *Neale* v *Willis* (1968) 19 P&CR 836; *Staden* v *Jones* [2008] 2 FLR 1931; Youdan [1988] Conv 267.
[63] The High Court of Australia split as to the nature of the trust in *Bahr* v *Nicolay (No 2)* (1988) 62 ALJR 268, although this was partly because of differing views as to the interpretation of a written undertaking. Mason CJ and Dawson J suggested that the constructive trust was employed because of the difficulty in using a contract between vendor and purchaser to give rise to an express trust in favour of a third party.
[64] *Gissing* v *Gissing* [1971] AC 886 at p 905.
[65] Just as it is not inequitable to fail to honour an unenforceable oral declaration of trust over one's own land.

The second possibility is that words that are too vague to declare a trust may yet justify a constructive trust. This is an interesting idea in the present area, for we have seen that the words used are frequently ambiguous: there is no explicit declaration of trust. There is much to be said for the argument that the unconscionable behaviour of the purchaser should be a sufficient basis for a remedy. However, it is not universally agreed that the normal requirements for trusts can be avoided in this way.[66] Further discussion of the role of constructive trusts is best postponed until they are considered in the context of the joint acquisition of family homes.

Looking at this material as a whole, it appears that formality requirements are unlikely to hinder effective declarations of trust where property is transferred to another. It is far more difficult to surmount formality problems where the owner of property declares himself a trustee.[67] Unless the beneficiary should subsequently act to his detriment on the assumption that he has a beneficial interest,[68] it cannot be said that it is inequitable to deny the trust.

Further reading

Bright, S [2000] Conv 398: The third party's conscience in land law.

Gulliver, A G and Tilson, C J (1941) 51 Yale LJ 1: Classification of gratuitous transfers.

Hopkins, N (2006) 26 LS 475: Conscience, discretion and the creation of property rights.

McFarlane, B (2004) 120 LQR 667: Constructive trusts arising on a receipt of property *sub conditione*.

Mee, J [2012] Conv 307: Resulting trusts and voluntary conveyances of land.

Swadling, W J (2008) 124 LQR 72: Explaining resulting trusts.

Youdan, T G [1984] CLJ 306: Formalities for trusts of land, and the doctrine in *Rochefoucauld* v *Boustead*.

---

[66]   Thus, Nourse J in the somewhat analogous area of mutual wills has stressed the need for the certainties normally required for trusts: *Re Cleaver* [1981] 1 WLR 939; see also *Thwaites* v *Ryan* [1984] VR 65.

[67]   *Bannister* v *Bannister* [1948] 2 All ER 133 at p 135, explaining *Buck* v *Howarth* [1947] 1 All ER 342.

[68]   These circumstances might give rise to an estoppel.

10
Formalities: estoppel

Introduction

This chapter will consider the use of proprietary estoppel to establish rights to property and how it can be used to avoid formality requirements. Its relationship with the constructive trust of the family home will be considered in Chapter 11. A few quite different methods of avoiding formality requirements will also be looked at towards the end of this chapter.

Estoppel[1] has at its heart the proposition that a person who has made a representation or allowed another to labour under a misapprehension should not be allowed, after the other person has acted upon it to his detriment, to deny that which has been represented or misapprehended. It is a principle of law that has many applications. A common example is found in the law of agency.[2] If I tell B that A is my agent and has my authority to sell my car, then I cannot deny A's authority. Suppose that B, relying upon what I have said, contracts with A to buy my car for £5,500. I may have told A that he is not to sell the car for less than £6,000, but I am still bound if A disregards this instruction.

1. The nature and use of estoppel

The classic form of estoppel is a representation of fact. It was extended relatively early to cases of acquiescence in the mistake of another, and the acquiescence cases have been most influential in the development of the law. Estoppel originally required a representation of fact: a promise would not suffice. As most readers will be aware, this limitation was significantly restricted by the *High Trees* case[3] and the development of promissory estoppel. However, this form of estoppel was soon limited to being a defence: it could not be the basis of a cause of action.[4] In the property context, the stress in earlier decades was on acquiescence rather than promises. However, the line between the two is not easy to draw and, despite some recent hesitation, it is clear that effect is routinely given to promises. Most significantly, the courts have been prepared to go well beyond allowing estoppel to act as a mere defence. It is common for the courts to decide that the claimant is entitled to a lease, easement or even the fee simple. In many modern cases, a monetary remedy has been awarded.

---

[1] The traditional text is Spencer Bower and Turner, *Estoppel by Representation* (4th edn, 2004). See also *McFarlane, The Law of Proprietary Estoppel*; Finn, *Essays in Equity*, Chapter 4; Cooke, *The Modern Law of Estoppel*.

[2] *Freeman & Lockyer* v *Buckhurst Park Properties (Mangal) Ltd* [1964] 2 QB 480 at p 503; *Armagas Ltd* v *Mundogas SA* [1986] AC 717 at pp 731 (CA), 777 (HL).

[3] *Central London Property Trust Ltd* v *High Trees House Ltd* [1947] KB 130.

[4] *Combe* v *Combe* [1951] 2 KB 215.

Estoppel cases from the beginning of the nineteenth century are still frequently cited.[5] However, the speech of Lord Kingsdown in *Ramsden* v *Dyson*[6] is commonly referred to as the basis of the modern law, despite the fact that he was dissenting on the facts. His dicta relate to the leasehold context of the litigation:

> If a man, under a verbal agreement with a landlord for a certain interest in land, or, what amounts to the same thing, under an expectation, created or encouraged by the landlord, that he shall have a certain interest, takes possession of such land, with the consent of the landlord, and upon the faith of such promise or expectation, with the knowledge of the landlord, and without objection by him, lays out money upon the land, a Court of equity will compel the landlord to give effect to such promise or expectation.

The past half century has seen a distinct revival of interest in estoppel. Alongside constructive trusts, it has provided remedies where parties have acted on an informal basis. This lack of formality may lie in not identifying the precise interest to be acquired or not using the appropriate formalities (deeds or writing) for land transactions. The movement has been towards using a general formula, much less specific than that employed by Lord Kingsdown. Typical of modern approaches is the following dictum of Oliver LJ[7]:

> If A under an expectation created or encouraged by B that A shall have a certain interest in B's land, thereafter, on the faith of such expectation and with the knowledge of B and without objection by him, acts to his detriment in connection with such land, a court of equity will compel B to give effect to such expectation.

Before proceeding to the estoppel rules, it is worth identifying two special contexts within which estoppel is important. First, the presence of estoppel will overcome lack of formalities.[8] This is, of course, especially important in land transactions, where writing is nearly always essential and quite often a deed is required. Secondly, estoppel may operate where the expectation is not of a conventional property right but non-proprietary in nature. Thus it seems that a licence (generally a purely personal right to reside on land or do some other act on land) may be capable of binding purchasers if protected by an estoppel. This third area in particular displays the flexibility of estoppel in overcoming the normal constraints of property law; it will be considered in Chapter 22 on licences.

2. When will an estoppel arise?

The requirements for estoppel will be considered under three heads: (a) representation or assurance to the claimant (C) by the land owner (O); (b) reliance; and (c) detriment. These

---

[5] *Dann* v *Spurrier* (1802) 7 Ves 231 (32 ER 94); *Taylor* v *Needham* (1810) 2 Taunt 278 (127 ER 1084); *Gregory* v *Mighell* (1811) 18 Ves 328 (34 ER 341). Somewhat later cases include *Duke of Beaufort* v *Patrick* (1853) 17 Beav 60 (51 ER 954); *Unity Joint-Stock Mutual Banking Association* v *King* (1858) 25 Beav 72 (53 ER 563) and *Dillwyn* v *Llewelyn* (1862) 4 De GF&J 517 (45 ER 1285). Development of the principles is well charted by Cooke, *The Modern Law of Estoppel*, pp 42–53.

[6] (1866) LR 1 HL 129 at p 170.

[7] *Midland Bank Ltd* v *Farmpride Hatcheries Ltd* [1981] 2 EGLR 147 at p 151; see also *Taylors Fashions Ltd* v *Liverpool Victoria Trustees Co Ltd* [1982] QB 133 at p 144.

[8] This may involve some difficult policy questions: Dixon (2010) 30 LS 408; Cartwright in *Rationalizing Property, Equity and Trusts* (ed Getzler), Chapter 3; also p 109 above. It is less likely that registration requirements can be so readily avoided: *Lloyds Bank plc* v *Carrick* [1996] 4 All ER 630 (unless the expectation is that the interest will be enforceable without registration).

heads were adopted by the House of Lords in *Thorner* v *Major*.[9] It is worth mentioning that there have been two quite recent House of Lords decisions on estoppel; this is remarkable, as there had been no House of Lords decision for some 150 years. The first decision, *Cobbe* v *Yeoman's Row Management Ltd*,[10] threatened to restrict the application of proprietary estoppel (especially as regards promises). However, *Thorner*, just a year later, re-established estoppel as it had been thought to operate. Elements of these decisions permeate all the modern law in this area, but a detailed consideration of them will be left until the earlier cases have been considered.

Estoppel will be considered as relevant to property transactions: no attempt will be made to provide a comprehensive analysis of estoppel. Such an analysis no more belongs to a book on property than an analysis of contract. A point on terminology should be added. The estoppel that is being discussed is frequently described as proprietary estoppel, and this terminology will be adopted (often shortened to estoppel). The cases contain references to equitable estoppel and estoppel by acquiescence. These descriptions relate to the root of the estoppel, but in the property context, they are unlikely to have characteristics differing from proprietary estoppel.

One general point needs to be addressed at the outset. In the past, courts laid down fairly strict requirements before an estoppel could be proved. The origin of much of this lay in the judgment of Fry J in *Willmott* v *Barber*.[11] The case concerned acquiescence, but Fry J identified five requirements (generally known as *probanda*) which have received support in estoppel generally.[12] They may be summarised as follows:

(1) C must have made a mistake as to his rights.
(2) C must have expended money or done some act (not necessarily on O's land) because of the mistake.
(3) O must be aware of his right (relevant to its being unconscionable to assert his title).
(4) O must be aware of C's mistake.
(5) O must have encouraged C's expenditure, either directly or by not asserting his rights.

It has been clear for a long time that not all the probanda have to be satisfied where there is a representation. In particular, it is not necessary for O to know of his own right.[13] More generally, Oliver J declared in *Taylors Fashions Ltd* v *Liverpool Victoria Trustees Co Ltd*[14] that the probanda should not be seen as strict rules. He stresses that the modern formulation of estoppel is much broader than in the nineteenth century and asks[15] 'whether, in all the circumstances of this case, it was unconscionable for the defendant to seek to take advantage of the mistake which, at the material time, everybody shared'. Oliver J admitted, however, that the probanda might have to be more strictly observed in a case

---

[9] [2009] 1 WLR 776; see, e.g., Lord Walker at [29].
[10] [2008] 1 WLR 1752.
[11] (1880) 15 Ch D 96.
[12] See, e.g., Scarman LJ in *Crabb* v *Arun DC* [1976] Ch 179 at p 194.
[13] *Plimmer* v *Mayor of Wellington* (1884) 9 App Cas 699; *Hopgood* v *Brown* [1955] 1 WLR 213.
[14] [1982] QB 133 (decided 1979); Dixon in *Landmark Cases in Land Law* (ed Gravells), Chapter 4.
[15] [1982] QB 133 at p 155. Unconscionability in equity is explored by Delany and Ryan [2008] Conv 401; contrast Handley [2008] Conv 382 (also (2010) 84 ALJ 239).

where O has merely acquiesced in the expenditure.[16] Most cases go beyond acquiescence. Typically, there are negotiations or discussions between the parties, often with positive encouragement of the expenditure.

Cobbe[17] adopts Oliver J's more general approach, and the general liberalisation of estoppel rules he espouses is seen throughout the analyses in *Thorner*.[18] Indeed, he had been repeatedly supported by the Court of Appeal.[19] Unconscionability permeates estoppel and, in the words of Lord Walker, plays a 'unifying and confirming' role.[20] Two warnings should be added. The first is that the cases have taken differing approaches: it is easy to find dicta which could be used to support a stricter approach. Indeed, this may be seen as the basis of Lord Scott's approach in *Cobbe* (subsequently disowned by *Thorner*). The second warning is that it is inappropriate to rely directly on unconscionability: the courts are hostile to suggestions that estoppel provides a justification for judges to come conclusions they think to be appropriate. It was made clear in *Cobbe*[21] that the requirements of estoppel have to be proved; this was repeated in *Thorner*.[22]

A. Representation or assurance

For convenience, this will be considered in two parts: the nature of the representation or assurance and the encouragement or acquiescence by O. Especially as regards promises, these issues shade into each other.

(i) *The nature of the representation or assurance*

The first of the probanda requires a mistake, whereby C believes that there was a right or interest. Clearly, no such mistake is essential today. It may be true that some mistake will be present, but this may be as whether the stated intentions of the other party will be carried out.

The leading twentieth-century case of *Crabb v Arun District Council*[23] provides an example in a contractual setting. C was negotiating with O for an easement of access. An outline agreement was reached, although apparently insufficient for a claim in contract.[24]

---

[16] However, *Lester* v *Woodgate* [2010] 2 P&CR 359 applies a flexible approach to acquiescence; see especially [39]. McFarlane [2013] CLP 267 at pp 302–304 is critical of Oliver J's assimilation of estoppel by acquiescence and proprietary estoppel based upon promises. See also Samet (2015) 78 MLR 85, examining the basis for imposing liability for acquiescence.

[17] Especially Lord Walker [2008] 1 WLR 1752 at [58].

[18] See also *Commonwealth* v *Verwayen* (1990) 170 CLR 394 (High Court of Australia) and, more recently, *Hoyl Group Ltd* v *Cromer TC* [2016] 1 P&CR 45.

[19] Examples are *Habib Bank Ltd* v *Habib Bank AG Zurich* [1981] 1 WLR 1265; *Nationwide Anglia BS* v *Ahmed & Balakrishnan* (1995) 70 P&CR 381; *Lloyds Bank plc* v *Carrick* [1996] 4 All ER 630; *Gillett* v *Holt* [2001] Ch 210. See also *Blue Haven Enterprises Limited* v *Dulcie Ermine Tully* [2006] UKPC 17 at [23].

[20] *Cobbe* [2008] 1 WLR 1752 at [92]. Dixon (2010) 30 LS 408 promotes the role of unconscionability, although seeking to define it so as to confine the operation of estoppel. Balen and Knowles [2011] Conv 176 are critical of the unconscionability analysis, preferring one based on failure of basis (rooted in unjust enrichment ideas).

[21] Ibid at [16] (Lord Scott); [46] and [59] (Lord Walker).

[22] [2009] 1 WLR 776 at [92] (Lord Neuberger). Contrast Gardner's far wider vision of how estoppel operates: [2014] Conv 202.

[23] [1976] Ch 179.

[24] Atiyah (1976) 92 LQR 174.

O erected substantial gates to allow access by C, who was permitted to start using the access. Believing that this indicated that all was well, C proceeded to dispose of a part of the land which had provided the only alternative access. This rendered the retained part landlocked, unless the new access could be used. O now denied use of this access, at least without a very substantial payment by C. It was held that these facts gave rise to an estoppel, even though C could not be said to have made a mistake as to his rights. It was, nevertheless, reasonable for him to believe that he would be given an easement after O had gone to the expense of erecting gates.

Cases in a family setting are unlikely to involve contracts but frequently contain promises that are detrimentally relied upon. In *Griffiths* v *Williams*,[25] C was assured by O (her mother, now dead) that their home would be hers for life. The Court of Appeal had no difficulty in rejecting the argument that there was no mistake as to rights. It was enough that it would be unconscionable for O to go back on this representation. In a family setting, a distinction between O's saying that C has a right and that C will be given a right would be extraordinarily difficult to draw.

It is essential that C should believe that there is an interest or that O is committed to creating it, although this will be easier to prove if there is very substantial detriment.[26] If C has no such belief, he may still act to his detriment in the hope that all will turn out well. If his hopes are dashed, then estoppel is unlikely to provide a remedy.[27] C has taken a gamble and lost. One application of this is where C assumes that a longstanding practice will continue: this is not by itself enough to give rise to an estoppel.[28]

Estoppel where negotiations are incomplete

The courts have been particularly concerned that estoppel should not give legal effect to negotiations or explicitly non-binding agreements, most especially where there is 'subject to contract' correspondence.[29] An example is *Att-Gen of Hong Kong* v *Humphreys Estate (Queen's Gardens) Ltd*.[30] Whilst a contract was being negotiated, C was allowed into occupation. C's licence made it clear that it might be revoked. Despite significant detriment incurred by C, the Privy Council had little hesitation in rejecting C's claim. Reliance on incomplete or non-binding negotiations is therefore unlikely by itself to give rise to an estoppel.[31] It would be wrong for one party, by undergoing a detriment, to foist an obligation upon the other.[32]

---

[25] [1978] 2 EGLR 121.
[26] *Bibby* v *Stirling* (1998) 76 P&CR D36 ('major construction': substantial and costly greenhouse).
[27] Several cases have involved tenants believing (without encouragement from O) that various irregularities will be sorted out or overlooked. Their claims have not been viewed sympathetically: *Boxbusher Properties Ltd* v *Graham* [1976] 2 EGLR 58; *Brinnand* v *Ewens* [1987] 2 EGLR 67. See also *Swallow Securities Ltd* v *Isenberg* [1985] 1 EGLR 132.
[28] *Keelwalk* v *Waller* [2002] 3 EGLR 79 (renewal of leases at a ground rent only).
[29] Subject to contract clauses were discussed at p 101 above.
[30] [1987] AC 114. See also *Akiens* v *Salomon* (1992) 65 P&CR 364; *Pridean Ltd* v *Forest Taverns Ltd* (1996) 75 P&CR 447; *James* v *Evans* [2000] 3 EGLR 1 (criticised by McMurtry [2001] Conv 86); *Taylor* v *Inntrepreneur Estates (CPC) Ltd* (2001) 82 P&CR D9; *Edwin Shirley Productions Ltd* v *Workspace Management Ltd* [2001] 2 EGLR 16; *Haq* v *Island Homes Housing Association* [2011] 2 P&CR 277.
[31] Stressed (after *Cobbe*) in *Herbert* v *Doyle* (2010) [2015] WTLR 1573.
[32] Whether or not the detriment was incurred for this purpose. The claim is clearly hopeless if it was.

However, there have been some indications of a more flexible approach. It has always been possible to point to something outside the negotiations as justifying an expectation. Thus in *Crabb*, O had encouraged the expectation by constructing the gate and allowing access. In *Salvation Army Trustee Co Ltd* v *West Yorkshire MCC*,[33] O acquiesced in a letter from C warning that detriment was going to be incurred. C incurred the detriment and the claim succeeded. More controversial is the majority Court of Appeal decision in *JT Developments Ltd* v *Quinn*.[34] O had made an offer to C. C acted to their detriment, but subsequently, O purported to withdraw the offer. It was held that an estoppel had arisen, such that the offer could not be withdrawn. The case is a reminder that the reason for there not being a contract may not be so important for estoppel. In *Quinn*, it appears that O was happy to accept an obligation so long as C agreed to the terms offered; this is different from other cases in which terms were still being negotiated.

Negotiations form the basis of *Cobbe*; this will be discussed below. Suffice to say at present that the House of Lords adopted the *Att-Gen of Hong Kong* approach.

Promises to leave property by will

A number of cases have involved promises that C will inherit property on O's death. This is particularly difficult because there is often an extended period over which O's intentions may change, coupled with the inherent freedom of testators to decide to whom to give their property and to amend existing wills. In *Re Basham*,[35] Nugee QC was prepared to find an estoppel in such a case. This approach was adopted by the Court of Appeal in *Gillett* v *Holt*.[36] In this important case, a wide view of estoppel was adopted. Whilst it would go too far to say that a simple statement of intention to leave property in a will constitutes a sufficient assurance, the fact that there were repeated assurances, before witnesses, over a substantial period was compelling. The revocability of wills was seen as irrelevant to the assurances given: the assurances were not expressed in terms consistent with their being revocable. Additionally, the assurance that property would belong to C, rather than being linked to making a will, made the case stronger. A type of case that has been relatively common recently is where C is caring for O in O's old age and O responds by promising to leave property to C.[37]

Cobbe and *Thorner*

As stated earlier, *Cobbe* was a case involving negotiations. C undertook considerable expenditure in obtaining planning permission for O's land, which he was to buy under an agreement being negotiated with O. The essence of the arrangement was that they would

---

[33] (1980) 41 P&CR 179 (Woolf J). *Att-Gen of Hong Kong* treated *Salvation Army* as an exceptional case, based in part on its compulsory purchase background.

[34] (1990) 62 P&CR 33.

[35] [1986] 1 WLR 1498 (no will made); see also *Wayling* v *Jones* (1993) 69 P&CR 170. For estoppel claims to future interests, see Davis [1996] Conv 193.

[36] [2001] Ch 210 (will made and revoked), Thompson [2001] Conv 78; see also *Jennings* v *Rice* [2003] 1 P&CR 100, *Jiggins* v *Brisley* [2003] WTLR 1141 (a strong case as C had paid 30% of the cost of the flat), *Evans* v *HSBC Trust Co (UK) Ltd* [2005] WTLR 1289. In Canada, such facts may justify a constructive trust based on unjust enrichment: *Ogle* v *Ogle* (2005) 248 DLR 4th 626.

[37] *Campbell* v *Griffin* [2001] WTLR 981; *Jennings* v *Rice* [2003] 1 P&CR 100; *Powell* v *Benney* [2007] EWCA Civ 1283.

share the uplift in value attributable to planning permission. The House of Lords had no hesitation in holding that both parties were well aware that there was no contract – C had proceeded in the hope that their outline agreement would come to fruition. This was a wholly inadequate ground for estoppel: C was claiming a contractual right when he had been well aware that there was no contract.

The lower courts had found in favour of C. This was largely attributable to C's substantial expenditure (coupled with significant gains in the value of O's property). The House of Lords was able to deal with this by allowing a claim based upon unjust enrichment, whereby C could recover his expenditure.

Few would challenge the correctness of the result in the House of Lords.[38] However, the expressed reasons provide real difficulty. Lord Scott seems to treat proprietary estoppel as a form of promissory estoppel, requiring a representation of fact (or mixed fact and law). This would make it highly problematic for the huge numbers of cases which have enforced promises. Lord Walker takes a markedly different line, in that he distinguishes between commercial and family (or domestic) cases. He notes that commercial cases are usually about contracts, when the parties are well aware of the significance as to whether there is a contract and the relevant legal rules. By contrast, in the family setting, the parties are more likely to be dealing with expectations of property interests and to have little understanding of the legal principles. Even so, he seems to require that C believes that the assurance is 'binding and irrevocable'.[39] It is far from clear that most of the cases satisfy this test. Both judgments appeared to leave estoppel with a sharply reduced role.[40]

Thorner,[41] by contrast, has facts rather similar to *Gillett*. It is made very clear that *Cobbe* is not as highly restrictive as had been feared: it has no 'apocalyptic' effect.[42] One of the problems in considering the two cases together is that relatively little was said about *Cobbe* – there is, for example, no explanation of what Lord Walker says about the nature of C's belief. The extent of the departure from *Cobbe* is well illustrated by Lord Scott's preference in *Thorner* to treat the case as an example of constructive trust rather than estoppel. He was not prepared to adopt the flexibility propounded for estoppel by the other judges; significantly, none supported his constructive trust analysis.

The facts of *Thorner* were weaker than those in *Gillett* in that there was no overt representation. O was a taciturn individual who rarely made things clear: he was not a man to announce his intentions. Rather, they had to be understood from inferences and conduct. The House of Lords (adopting the decision of the trial judge) was prepared to find an assurance. There was discussion as to how far there is a requirement for the assurance to be 'clear and unequivocal'. Lord Walker[43] adopted a test that the assurance be 'clear

---

[38] It was followed on somewhat similar facts (no final agreement on significant issues) in *Crossco No 4 Unlimited* v *Jolan Ltd* [2012] 2 All ER 754.

[39] [2008] 1 WLR 1752 at [66].

[40] McFarlane and Robertson [2008] LMCLQ 449. Cf Mee in *Modern Studies in Property Law*, Vol 6 (ed Bright), Chapter 8.

[41] It has attracted several useful analyses: McFarlane and Robertson (2009) 125 LQR 535; Uguccioni [2009] LMCLQ 436; Piska (2009) 72 MLR 998; Dixon [2009] Conv 260.

[42] [2009] 1 WLR 776 at [31] (Lord Walker). But see n 48 in this chapter for commercial cases.

[43] Ibid, at [56] supported by Lord Rodger at [26].

enough', not wishing to be tied to technicalities. Though Lord Neuberger adopted the clear and unequivocal test, he sought to apply it in a manner that produces the same results.[44]

It seems, therefore, to be accepted that promises can readily form the basis for estoppel. A test adopted in *Thorner* is that there must be reasonable reliance on the assurance (linked with its being reasonably foreseeable that C may act on it). Knowledge that O frequently changes his mind might well be relevant to issues of reasonableness of reliance.[45] It is not necessary (as the Court of Appeal had thought) that O should have intended reliance – we are dealing with an objective test. It seems to be here that the difference between commercial and familial situations will come into play, as such reliance will rarely be justified in a commercial setting if the parties are aware that there is no contract.[46] What are commercial transactions? It appears that those acting at arms' length and with legal advice available will fall on the commercial side of the line. However, the courts have shown a willingness still to apply estoppel.[47]

What, then, is the significance of the two cases? Much remains as before, though some of the tests and issues have been clarified. It is probably the case that proof of estoppel in commercial cases (at least those based on promises) has been made significantly more difficult.[48]

The role of certainty

It has frequently been argued that estoppel recognises expectations even though the parties have not specified any interest. Despite the requirement by Oliver LJ[49] of a 'certain interest', numerous cases have made it clear that it is unnecessary for the parties to specify the interest. Though Lord Scott in *Cobbe* placed much emphasis on certainty, Lord Walker adopted a far more flexible approach.

We shall see later that the court has a discretion as to what remedy to give. This flexibility as to remedy helps explain why uncertainty as to expectation is tolerated. The uncertainty may take several forms. In a commercial setting, it may be that some terms have not been agreed with sufficient precision[50] or the interest not specified,[51] although *Cobbe* shows that failure to establish agreement will often be fatal. Flexibility is much more important in a family setting; owners and claimants tend not to think in categories of

---

[44] Ibid, at [84]–[86]. Only Lord Scott appears to adopt a strict clear and unequivocal test. Though *Shirt* v *Shirt* [2013] 1 FLR 232 illustrates how, on broadly similar facts, it may be found that no assurance was made, Mee [2013] Conv 280 fears that some courts are unduly generous to claimants.

[45] *Stallion* v *Albert Stallion Holdings (GB) Ltd* [2010] 2 FLR 78 at [129].

[46] *Thorner* [2009] 1 WLR 776 at [96]–[97] (Lord Neuberger). Mee is critical of the commercial/family distinction in *Modern Studies in Property Law*, Vol 6 (ed Bright), pp 192–197; Hopkins (2011) 31 LS 175 supports it as an 'explanatory tool' but not as a basis for different rules.

[47] *Herbert* v *Doyle* (2010) [2015] WTLR 1573; also *Whittaker* v *Kinnear* [2011] EWHC 1479 (QB) and *Dowding* v *Matchmove Ltd* [2017] 1 WLR 749 (constructive trust). An agreement between a separating couple in *Ely* v *Robson* [2016] WTLR 1383 was not commercial, even though they were represented by lawyers.

[48] Extra-judicially, Lord Neuberger has supported the idea that *Cobbe* may represent (and rightly so) the death of proprietary estoppel in most commercial cases: [2009] CLJ 537 at p 543. Nevertheless, examples still exist. *Hoyl Group Ltd* v *Cromer TC* [2016] 1 P&CR 45 provides one recent example, based more on encouraging a belief in a right of way being available than a promise.

[49] *Midland Bank Ltd* v *Farmpride Hatcheries Ltd* [1981] 2 EGLR 147 at p 151, quoted at p 150 above.

[50] *Lim* v *Ang* [1992] 1 WLR 113.

[51] *Plimmer* v *Mayor of Wellington* (1884) 9 App Cas 699.

interests in land. The courts accept such uncertainty.[52] The major issue has concerned the recognition of claims to licences which lie outside conventional categories of proprietary interests. This will be discussed in Chapter 22.

There may be greater difficulty where the uncertainty relates to the property over which the expectation exists. This was discussed at length in *Thorner*, where the assurance concerned a farm. It was recognised that the farm might increase or decrease in size over the years, as in fact happened. This was thought not to be a problem, so long as the court could identify the farm at the date the assurance came to be enforced.[53] Lord Walker indicated that some element of certainty is required: a reference to 'financial security' would be very different. He was undecided whether the application of estoppel in *Re Basham*[54] to the residue of a deceased person's estate was justified. Subsequently, it has been said that *Re Basham* should be treated 'with the utmost caution'.[55]

(ii) *Encouragement or acquiescence by the owner*

It is essential that O has some responsibility for what C has done. If O is ignorant of C's claim and of the detriment, then it will not be unconscionable to deny C's claim. However, it must be remembered that *Thorner* establishes an objective test – we are not concerned with what O actually thought or intended.[56]

So far as awareness of C's claim is concerned, this is likely to cause difficulty in only two cases. The first is where O and C are genuinely mistaken: C expecting one thing and O another. An example might be where C thinks that there is (or will be) an interest, but O believes the detriment is undertaken in the mere hope of an interest. Here, the objective test is important. The second case is where O merely acquiesces in C's expectation. In practice, most expectations arise from representations by O or joint misapprehensions[57] in the course of dealings between O and C: O can scarcely plead ignorance in these cases. Cases of pure acquiescence are rare, but the requirement of knowledge will then become important. As Nourse LJ observed, 'You cannot encourage a belief of which you do not have any knowledge.'[58]

It is also thought necessary for O to be aware of the detriment incurred by C, for the detriment lies at the heart of the claim that O's conduct is unconscionable.[59] Again, most cases raise no difficulty. The expectation and detriment generally occur at the same time,

---

[52] E.g. *Inwards v Baker* [1965] 2 QB 29; *Flinn v Flinn* [1999] 3 VR 712 at pp 739–744 (a full discussion). See Pawlowski (2008) 93 Trusts and Estates & Tax J 4.

[53] This was a major problem for Lord Scott and the principle reason for his preferring a constructive trust.

[54] [1986] 1 WLR 1498.

[55] *Macdonald v Frost* [2009] WTLR 1815 at [19] (where a house is the sole significant asset, then probably a reference to residue can be construed as meaning the house).

[56] This is also supported by Lord Walker in *Cobbe*: [2008] 1 WLR 1752 at [92].

[57] It is not necessary for O to have created or encouraged the expectation: *John v George* (1995) 71 P&CR 375 (joint assumption).

[58] *Brinnand v Ewens* [1987] 2 EGLR 67; *Barclays Bank plc v Zaroovabli* [1997] Ch 321 at pp 330–331. *Hoyl Group Ltd v Cromer TC* [2016] 1 P&CR 45 stresses that the dictum has to be read in its context: encouraging a person to act does not carry any such limitation.

[59] *Gillett v Holt* [1998] 3 All ER 917 at p 929 (Carnwath J, but not affected by the appeal; any need for the detriment to be agreed is clearly rejected).

so that the acquiescence or encouragement will apply to both together. Especially in the family setting, O will nearly always be aware of C's actions.

How precise must O's knowledge be? *Crabb* v *Arun District Council*[60] considered this issue. It may be recalled that C, thinking that a right of access would be allowed, sold off part of the plot, thereby rendering the retained part landlocked. This sale constituted the detriment. O denied awareness of the specific sale, although there was knowledge of the general intentions of C as to the land. Whilst accepting that the problem was not covered by authority, the Court of Appeal had no difficulty in holding that O's general awareness was sufficient.

So far, it has been assumed that awareness of the detriment is necessary. Is this assumption justified? It may readily be accepted that awareness is essential in cases of pure acquiescence.[61] Knowledge of C's assumption or expectation is not of itself enough to describe O's assertion of his legal title as unconscionable. However, the position is less clear where O has made a representation to C or has participated in a dealing involving a joint assumption as to the interest. If C thereafter acts to his detriment, it is arguable that O should not be free to resile from his representation or assumption, at least where it is reasonably foreseeable that C might act to his detriment. Suppose O tells C that a plot of land between their houses belongs to C. When C builds on the land some years later, O is out of the country and so is unaware of the detriment. Should not O's denial of C's claim be regarded as unconscionable? The argument in favour of C is supported by the broad estoppel analyses of Oliver J in *Taylors Fashions* and of the House of Lords in *Thorner*.[62]

A final point to consider in relation to O is whether O must be aware of his own rights or, to put it another way, his right to object to C's claim. This point lies at the heart of *Taylors Fashions*: O was unaware that C's claim (a right to renew a lease) had become unenforceable. Oliver J was reluctant to allow O to escape by virtue of this, although it was a factor taken into consideration in his conclusion that it was not unconscionable for O to resist the exercise of the option. Although Oliver J would deny a sharp distinction between representation and acquiescence, O's lack of awareness is less likely to be a defence in cases where O has encouraged the assumption or expectation.[63] In *Taylors Fashions* itself, O had dealt with a second tenant on the basis that a similar claim was valid. It was held that an estoppel had arisen to protect the second tenant. The transaction with the second tenant involved a greater responsibility on O's part for that tenant's assumption.

B. Reliance

C must act in reliance on the representation or assurance. We have seen that *Thorner* establishes that reliance must be reasonable. This will usually be relevant where there is a promise: if there has been a representation (or understanding) that C is the owner, then it is difficult to imagine any reliance being unreasonable.

---

[60] [1976] Ch 179. Followed in *JT Developments Ltd* v *Quinn* (1990) 62 P&CR 33 on less convincing facts, also *Joyce* v *Epsom & Ewell BC* [2013] 1 EGLR 21 at [39] (knowledge of intention to act sufficient).
[61] *Matharu* v *Matharu* (1994) 68 P&CR 93 (especially Dillon LJ at p 98, although he dissented on the facts).
[62] See also McFarlane and Robertson (2009) 125 LQR 535 at p 540.
[63] See p 152 above.

The main problem is that motives for most acts are mixed: it is then difficult to identify specific reasons for acting. Fortunately, the law has not taken an overly strict approach. In *Greasley* v *Cooke*,[64] Lord Denning MR held that the burden was on O to prove that C did not rely upon the assumption or expectation; this has been accepted in later cases.[65] C had been assured by O (a family) that she could stay in the house for her life. She had originally arrived as a maid but lived with a member of the family for nearly 30 years. She looked after the house and a mentally ill family member.[66] O argued that C's conduct was explicable by her living with a member of the family, but the court held that the burden was on O to prove this. So long as the assumption or expectation is one of the reasons for the detriment, that will suffice.[67]

On the other hand, O can seek to prove that C either did not rely upon the assumption or expectation at all or, possibly, that the detriment would have been incurred in any event.[68] At least two subsequent cases have rebutted the presumption of reliance.[69]

More recently, the idea of reversing the burden of proof has come under greater scrutiny. As a matter of principle, it was doubted by Neuberger LJ in *Steria Ltd* v *Hutchison*,[70] and it has been rejected by the High Court of Australia.[71] As those cases stress, this may make little difference in practice. The circumstances of cases such as *Greasley* are such that it is easy to infer that there was reliance – the result is reached by inference rather than presumption.

One specific point is whether O can argue that C's conduct would have been exactly the same if the expectation had never existed. This is plausible in the moderately common scenario where C's conduct commences before the promise giving rise to the expectation (the conduct may induce a generous promise). The courts have been able to find reliance by asking whether C would have acted differently if the promise had been repudiated (i.e. reliance on non-repudiation rather than on the promise itself).[72]

Before leaving reliance, it should be noted that it is not necessary for C to rely on O's conduct.[73] Examples would be found in many cases of acquiescence, where C believes the land belongs to him. There, C relies on his own mistake and is likely to be quite unaware of O's rights or to place any specific reliance on O's conduct. So far as C is concerned, O may be one of dozens of people who are aware of what he is doing.

---

[64] [1980] 1 WLR 1306. See, generally, Nield in *Modern Studies in Property Law*, Vol 1 (ed Cooke), Chapter 5.
[65] *Grant* v *Edwards* [1986] Ch 638; *Coombes* v *Smith* [1986] 1 WLR 808; *Re Basham* [1986] 1 WLR 1498; *Wayling* v *Jones* (1993) 69 P&CR 170.
[66] This last point may be the significant detriment: *Bostock* v *Bryant* (1990) 61 P&CR 23.
[67] *Amalgamated Investment & Property Co Ltd* v *Texas Commerce International Bank Ltd* [1982] QB 84 (Robert Goff J); *Steria Ltd* v *Hutchison* [2007] ICR 445 at [117] (a 'significant factor'; but for causation not required).
[68] *Western Fish Products Ltd* v *Penwith DC* [1981] 2 All ER 204 (decided in 1978, before *Greasley* v *Cooke*); Treitel, *The Law of Contract* (14th edn), pp 414–420 (on misrepresentation, seemingly the source of the *Greasley* v *Cooke* analysis). Contra Lord Denning MR in *Brikom Investments Ltd* v *Carr* [1979] QB 467.
[69] *Coombes* v *Smith* [1986] 1 WLR 808; *Layton* v *Martin* [1986] 2 FLR 227; see also *Walsh* v *Singh* [2010] 1 FLR 1658 at [58].
[70] [2007] ICR 445 at [128]–[129] (not a proprietary estoppel case).
[71] *Sidhu* v *van Dyke* (2014) 251 CLR 505.
[72] *Wayling* v *Jones* (1993) 69 P&CR 170 (Cooke (1995) 111 LQR 389; Davis [1995] Conv 409); *Campbell* v *Griffin* [2001] WTLR 981 at pp 991–993; *Grundy* v *Ottey* [2003] WTLR 1253 (Thompson [2004] Conv 137). This analysis seems to be overlooked in *Macdonald* v *Frost* [2009] WTLR 1815 at [128].
[73] It is not required by Fry J's probanda in *Willmott* v *Barber* (1880) 15 Ch D 96: see p 151 above.

C. Detriment

It is not enough for C to rely on the representation or assurance; detriment to C must be proved. These are not completely separate tests: several cases have explained how they are intertwined.[74]

The origins of proprietary estoppel lie in expenditure on the land. Although this remains the most obvious example of detriment, it may take quite different forms and certainly need not benefit O. Numerous examples are found in the cases: building a garage on one's land on the basis of a right of access[75]; selling part of one's land leaving the remainder landlocked[76]; leaving one's existing home where there is a right to remain and also an existing job[77]; failure to adopt other opportunities for self-advancement[78]; looking after O or members of O's family[79]; buying and building on replacement land in reliance upon a sale of land originally owned.[80] Somewhat generously, it has been held that expenditure by C's husband may constitute detriment because of the reduced amount left for family expenditure.[81]

The language of detriment is sometimes criticised: it has been said to be sufficient for C to act on the assumption or expectation in such a way as to render it unconscionable for O to assert his legal title.[82] However, the modern approach is that detriment is necessary, although it is not to be viewed as a 'narrow or technical concept'.[83] It seems unlikely that simply acting upon a representation would ever be sufficient. Thus, if O tells C that he will provide C with a home and C moves into the house, the act of moving will not by itself ground a claim.[84] In this example, the provision of a free home is a benefit rather than a detriment. On the other hand, it is vital not to consider the question too narrowly. In moving to O's house, C may give up security of tenure in a previous home and thereby incur detriment.[85]

Frequently, O and C are living together, O providing the home. If C decides not to work as a result, can this failure to maintain alternative sources of support be a detriment? It is a commonplace observation that it is difficult to re-enter the labour market after not having worked for some years; pension rights may also be lost. This form of detriment was rejected in *Coombes v Smith*[86] on the basis that a free home should be regarded as a benefit.

---

[74] *Coombes v Smith* [1986] 1 WLR 808; *Gillett v Holt* [2001] Ch 210 at p 225; *Henry v Henry* [2010] 1 All ER 988 at [55].

[75] *ER Ives Investment Ltd v High* [1967] 2 QB 379.

[76] *Crabb v Arun DC* [1976] Ch 179.

[77] *Jones v Jones* [1977] 1 WLR 438; *Evans v HSBC Trust Co (UK) Ltd* [2005] WTLR 1289.

[78] *Henry v Henry* [2010] 1 All ER 988 provides a recent example.

[79] *Greasley v Cooke* [1980] 1 WLR 1306.

[80] *Salvation Army Trustee Co Ltd v West Yorkshire MCC* (1980) 41 P&CR 179. The decision appears remarkable for enforcing an obligation to buy (rather than to sell), but it was explained as being part of an equity whereby C could have enforced an obligation to sell the replacement land.

[81] *Matharu v Matharu* (1994) 68 P&CR 93 (O was the husband's father).

[82] Lord Denning MR in *Greasley v Cooke* [1980] 1 WLR 1306; contrast Dunn LJ's more conventional analysis. See Cooke, *The Modern Law of Estoppel*, pp 106–108.

[83] *Gillett v Holt* [2001] Ch 210 at p 232.

[84] *Coombes v Smith* [1986] 1 WLR 808.

[85] *Maharaj v Chand* [1986] AC 898 (PC); cf *Tanner v Tanner* [1975] 1 WLR 1346 (consideration) and *Henry v Henry* [2010] 1 All ER 988. A recent example is provided by *Southwell v Blackburn* [2015] 2 FLR 1240.

[86] [1986] 1 WLR 808 (Parker QC). See *Horrocks v Forray* [1976] 1 WLR 230 for a similar analysis as regards contractual consideration.

Much will depend upon the facts of the particular case. Acceptance of detriment in cases such as *Coombes* v *Smith* would mean that detriment would almost invariably be found in the family setting. This might be thought to give estoppel too wide an effect. On the other hand, the loss of a more specific opportunity may be treated more generously. In the Australian case of *Cameron* v *Murdoch*,[87] C worked O's farm in the expectation that he would be able to acquire it on advantageous terms. If he had not been there, C would have built up a farming business elsewhere. Although C benefited from occupation of the farm, the transaction as a whole was rightly viewed as a detriment, and the court allowed C to purchase O's farm at a discount.

Detriment will not be found where C's actions can be viewed as contributions to the costs of running the home or a substitute for rent. This was the approach in *Lee-Parker* v *Izzet (No 2)*,[88] whilst in *Bostock* v *Bryant*[89] the installation of new windows and other improvements were explained as referable to the free occupation enjoyed by C. A variation on this theme is that C may already have a limited right to the land and the detriment may be related to that right. Thus, in *Taylors Fashions*,[90] it was highly relevant that C's expenditure benefited the lease held by C (as distinct from the claimed renewal of the lease); and in *Stilwell* v *Simpson*,[91] it was said that work done by a tenant was for his own benefit as tenant.

Detriment in family relationships

Perhaps the most difficult issues arise where O and C are living together.[92] In any normal family setting, the parties go out of their way to assist one another. How far can their activities within the home count as a detriment? *Coombes* v *Smith*[93] involved such a claim. The parties became lovers. When C became pregnant, she moved to a house provided by O. C claimed detriment in leaving her husband, becoming pregnant and raising a daughter, failing to look for a job and doing work on the house. Each of these argued detriments was rejected. So far as leaving her husband was concerned, this was explicable by the break-up of an unhappy marriage. She became pregnant because she wanted a child: not in reliance on any representation. In any event, the judge was dubious as to whether pregnancy could be viewed as a detriment. Failing to look for a job is, as has been discussed, difficult to rely upon. Finally, the work on the house, such as decorating, was undertaken because she was living there, rather than because of any assumption or expectation of a right to the house; in any event, it could not be regarded as a detriment when it enhanced her own occupation.

The decision appears harsh, although two points need to be remembered. First, O had accepted that C and her daughter could live in the house until the daughter reached 17: it was not a case where C faced immediate eviction. The second point is that the case is

---

[87] [1983] WAR 321, upheld (1986) 63 ALR 575 (PC). *Gillett* v *Holt* [2001] Ch 210, *Suggitt* v *Suggitt* [2012] WTLR 1607 and *Moore* v *Moore* [2016] EWHC 2202 (Ch) are somewhat similar.
[88] [1972] 1 WLR 775 (expenditure of £500 much less than the value of five years' occupation).
[89] (1990) 61 P&CR 23.
[90] [1982] QB 133. O is likely to believe that the expenditure is undertaken because of the existing right.
[91] (1983) 133 NLJ 894. The claim was hopeless as no assumption or expectation could be proved.
[92] Lawson (1996) 16 LS 218.
[93] [1986] 1 WLR 808. The court also found that no assumption or expectation had been proved. See also *Lissimore* v *Downing* [2003] 2 FLR 308 at [21], where the question was asked whether the conduct 'goes beyond what might normally be expected of the relationship'. The facts were less compelling than in *Coombes*.

similar to thousands of others. It raises in an acute form the question whether normal family activity should be regarded as sufficient to make representations binding. If it is so regarded, then the law runs the risk of placing much weight on pretty random evidence as to what has been discussed regarding future occupation.[94] It is obvious that a more generous approach would allow many more claims to succeed. *Coombes* v *Smith* will be regarded as a missed opportunity by those who regard the plight of those in failed relationships outside marriage as deserving of court intervention whenever possible.[95]

A more relaxed approach is supported by other cases. In *Grant* v *Edwards*,[96] Sir Nicolas Browne-Wilkinson V-C thought that 'Setting up house together, having a baby, making payments to general housekeeping expenses . . .' would suffice. More recently, the Court of Appeal in *Gillett* v *Holt*[97] stressed the need to look at all the circumstances (not limited to financial disadvantages) and accepted that giving up other opportunities may at least count towards detriment. It remains to be seen where this leaves *Coombes* v *Smith*.

Finally, we need to consider some consequences of the modern test emphasising unconscionability.[98] One point is that if C has obtained significant benefits already (most obviously in the form of free occupation), it may be argued that the detriment does not justify any remedy: there is no equity to satisfy.[99] More generally, even substantial detriment may not, viewing the facts 'in the round', be sufficient to make O's conduct unconscionable.[100]

3. The effect of the estoppel

A. Use as a sword

Outside property law, it is generally thought that an estoppel cannot give rise to a cause of action: it is said to act as a shield rather than a sword. Thus, it seems difficult to bring an action upon a promissory estoppel.[101] This may be based upon the origins of estoppel as a procedural rule: the person estopped is debarred from denying his representation. It is fiendishly difficult to work out when a claim is really founded upon an estoppel: it is patently facile to rely upon who happens to be the claimant.[102] Just because land is involved does not mean that proprietary estoppel can be argued. Thus, it appears that a right to planning permission[103] and a right to force another to buy land[104] cannot exist under proprietary estoppel.

---

[94] Compare the criticism made of the common intention constructive trust on joint purchase of land: pp 197, 212 below.

[95] Cf Zuckerman (1980) 96 LQR 248.

[96] [1986] Ch 638 at p 657.

[97] [2001] Ch 210, criticised by Wells [2001] Conv 13.

[98] Discussed by Dixon in *Modern Studies in Property Law*, Vol 2 (ed Cooke), Chapter 9; cf (2010) 30 LS 408.

[99] Hobhouse LJ in *Sledmore* v *Dalby* (1996) 72 P&CR 196 (Roch and Butler-Sloss LJJ used this factor in deciding upon the remedy); Milne [1997] CLJ 34. The point was recognised (but was not applicable on the facts) in *Henry* v *Henry* [2010] 1 All ER 988.

[100] *Murphy* v *Burrows* (2004) 7 ITELR 116 (the vagueness of O's assurances was also relevant).

[101] *Combe* v *Combe* [1951] 2 KB 215.

[102] See, e.g., Brandon LJ in *Amalgamated Investment & Property Co Ltd* v *Texas Commerce International Bank Ltd* [1982] QB 84 at pp 131–132.

[103] *Western Fish Products Ltd* v *Penwith DC* [1981] 2 All ER 204 (in addition to problems relating to statutory discretion); cf *Newport City C* v *Charles* [2009] 1 WLR 1884.

[104] *Salvation Army Trustee Co Ltd* v *West Yorkshire MCC* (1980) 41 P&CR 179: see p 160 above.

Whatever the general role of estoppel, it is clear that it can have a positive effect in the property context. As a defence, it would be limited to denying O the right to recover possession from C. Yet estoppel has been used to enable C to claim a right in the land. At one extreme, the claimant may be able to force a transfer of the fee simple[105] and, in other cases, has received a lease[106] or easement.[107] The courts have accepted this quite openly. As has been seen, the origins of proprietary estoppel lie in mistakes or assumptions as to rights. In this context, it is not surprising that the courts are prepared to enforce the rights C thought he had, given the encouragement or acquiescence of O. An early example is *Stiles* v *Cowper*[108] in 1748, in which O was forced to recognise the validity of a lease.

The issue becomes much more difficult where the essence of the expectation is that O will fulfil a representation or promise. It looks here as if the law of estoppel is encroaching upon the law of contract: giving effect to promises that are (in many cases) unenforceable for lack of consideration.[109] Yet the House of Lords enforced an obligation to transfer land in *Dillwyn* v *Llewelyn*[110] without perceiving any such difficulty. More recently, *Thorner* accepted that proprietary estoppel has frequently been applied to promises. This seems correct. Whilst the lawyer can distinguish between an assurance that property belongs to C and an assurance that property will be transferred to C, it is unlikely that C will distinguish between the two assurances once he has been given possession. C will simply treat the property as his. It would be unfortunate to draw fine distinctions as to the precise nature of the representation.

How can we justify this use of estoppel as a sword? Consider two cases. In the first, O tells C that C can have (for ever) a house owned by O. In reliance upon this, C leaves the house in which he has security of tenure. O subsequently denies C any right to the house. In the second case, O promises to give C £100,000 in order that C can buy a house near O. Again, C gives up secure accommodation and again O refuses to fulfil his promise. Is there any reason to allow C's claim in the first example but not in the second? The question has not been squarely faced in the cases. The answer may lie in the approach to the remedy.[111] In proprietary estoppel, as will be seen below, the remedy is sometimes more closely related to C's detriment than to O's promise. Thus estoppel is doing something quite different from enforcing promises: it is remedying the inequity resulting from O's encouragement or acquiescence in C's detriment.[112] Unless promissory estoppel (applicable to the second case)[113] can employ a similar discretionary remedy, this may justify a distinction between the two cases.

---

[105] *Dillwyn* v *Llewelyn* (1862) 4 De GF&J 517 (45 ER 1285); *Pascoe* v *Turner* [1979] 1 WLR 431; *Lim* v *Ang* [1992] 1 WLR 113.

[106] *Siew Soon Wah* v *Yong Tong Hong* [1973] AC 836 (PC); *JT Developments Ltd* v *Quinn* (1990) 62 P&CR 33.

[107] *Crabb* v *Arun DC* [1976] Ch 179.

[108] (1748) 3 Atk 692 (26 ER 1198).

[109] Briggs [1981] Conv 212, convincingly criticised by Thompson [1983] Conv 50 and Moriarty (1984) 100 LQR 376; [1983] Conv 285. See also Finn, *Essays in Equity*, Chapter 4.

[110] (1862) 4 De GF&J 517 (45 ER 1285).

[111] The approach in Australia (p 166 below): *Waltons Stores (Interstate) Ltd* v *Maher* (1988) 164 CLR 387; *Commonwealth* v *Verwayen* (1990) 170 CLR 394; Spence (1991) 107 LQR 221.

[112] This need not be restitutionary in nature, as the detriment may not have conferred a benefit on O: Birks, *An Introduction to the Law of Restitution*, pp 290–293. For links with restitution, see Hopkins in *Modern Studies in Property Law*, Vol 2 (ed Cooke), Chapter 8.

[113] McFarlane and Sales (2015) 131 LQR 610 argue for a promise-detriment analysis, separate from the label of proprietary estoppel. This, they argue, could lead to the developing of estoppel claims outside the proprietary setting.

B. The remedy

It has already been observed that some estoppel rules may be coloured by the nature of the remedy, especially its discretionary character. The extent of this discretion is a major issue. It is commonly said that the court recognises the equity arising from C's expenditure or other detriment.[114] Relating the equity to the expenditure or detriment makes it look as if the court is doing something quite different from enforcing the assumption or expectation. Nevertheless, this point needs to be treated cautiously. The old law on part performance of oral contracts for the sale of land was based upon a similar approach,[115] and yet the courts invariably enforced the contract whenever there was part performance. In truth, stress on the equity arising from the expenditure explains why equity intervenes rather than determines the remedy.

Moriarty has argued that proprietary estoppel is to be seen as a device to avoid formality requirements.[116] This appears not to allow any scope for discretion and it has been attacked on this ground.[117] It runs counter to most lawyers' understanding of the law.[118] However, the fact that similar promises of a home seem to have led to very different results in the cases (sometimes to a fee simple,[119] sometimes to a right to reside for life[120]) is no proof of the operation of a discretion. Moriarty correctly observes that in each of these cases, the remedy is what had been promised to the claimant. It may be a valid criticism of the cases that the courts could have done more to explain why they interpreted each promise as they did, but the result in each case did coincide with the court's interpretation.

Whatever the law as to the scope of the discretion, one rule does stand out. The Court of Appeal in *Baker* v *Baker & Baker* establishes that no remedy can be given which exceeds the assumption or expectation.[121] At least for this purpose, it is necessary to know what was promised. It follows that where the expectation is of a right to land, no remedy can exceed the value of the land.[122]

A narrow discretion?

Initially, it might have been feasible to adopt a very narrow view of the discretion – discretion merely as to how to give effect to the promise.[123] It may be inappropriate to enforce the

---

[114] See *Dillwyn* v *Llewelyn* (1862) 4 De GF&J 517 (45 ER 1285); *Pascoe* v *Turner* [1979] 1 WLR 431. Finn, *Essays in Equity*, Chapter 4, notes the movement towards a broad formulation of estoppel in these terms and deprecates a development of a generalised approach based upon unconscionable conduct.

[115] *Maddison* v *Alderson* (1883) 8 App Cas 467.

[116] (1984) 100 LQR 376.

[117] Thompson [1986] Conv 406. It also fails to take into account the recognition of uncertain expectations and the enforcement of non-proprietary rights.

[118] JD Davies (1979) 8 Syd LR 578; (1980) 7 Adelaide LR 200.

[119] *Dillwyn* v *Llewelyn* (1862) 4 De GF&J 517 (45 ER 1285); *Pascoe* v *Turner* [1979] 1 WLR 431; *Voyce* v *Voyce* (1991) 62 P&CR 290.

[120] *Inwards* v *Baker* [1965] 2 QB 29; *Griffiths* v *Williams* [1978] 2 EGLR 121; *Williams* v *Staite* [1979] Ch 291; *Greasley* v *Cooke* [1980] 1 WLR 1306.

[121] (1993) 25 HLR 408 (C had intended that the detriment should benefit O); see also *Watson* v *Goldsbrough* [1986] 1 EGLR 265 and *Burrows & Burrows* v *Sharp* (1989) 23 HLR 82.

[122] *Jules* v *Robertson* [2012] BPIR 126 (land with no value because of charges).

[123] Gardner (1999) 115 LQR 438 identified four hypotheses. The narrow discretion in the text is closest to hypothesis 2. The wider discretion in the text below is closest to hypothesis 3 but somewhat wider. Hypothesis 4 involves an unfettered discretion.

promise directly, perhaps because C has died[124] or because literal enforcement of the promise will lead to a result not contemplated or desired by the parties. In each case, a monetary award may be more appropriate. Another example is where enforcing the representation would involve two persons, who now hate each other, sharing a house. The court may be very reluctant to order that they both live in the same house, or to order O to leave in order that C may live there.[125] Again, a monetary remedy in favour of C is the best way of fulfilling C's expectations. Such a monetary remedy is especially useful where there is uncertainty in what was promised: the court has to work out the appropriate remedy.[126] Indeed, some have argued that a monetary award should be the standard outcome.[127]

Movement to a wider discretion

It has become clear in recent years that the discretion is much more extensive than described above. Even so, a totally unfettered discretion seems unacceptable.[128] This wider discretion seems to be based upon Scarman LJ's dictum in *Crabb* v *Arun DC*[129] that the courts should confer upon C 'the minimum equity to do justice'. This formulation appears to move the stress away from the expectations of the parties (not that they become irrelevant) and towards the reliance.

The most extensive discussion of the principles is found in *Jennings* v *Rice*.[130] First, we will consider four earlier cases.[131] In *Dodsworth* v *Dodsworth*,[132] there was an expectation of a right to reside for life. The Court of Appeal decided that it was not appropriate to give effect to this expectation, as it would give rise to unintended and undesired legal consequences.[133] However, the court calculated the monetary award by reference to C's expenditure rather than the value of the expectation. It was said that this was not unfair because C had enjoyed rent-free accommodation. Whilst this is true, it applies to most family cases.

The second case is the well-known and controversial decision in *Pascoe* v *Turner*.[134] O and C had been living together for some nine years. O then left C, telling her that the house and its contents were hers and that he would put the matter in the hands of his solicitors.

---

[124] *Raffaele* v *F & G Raffaele* [1962] WAR 29.
[125] *Burrows & Burrows* v *Sharp* (1989) 23 HLR 82 explicitly ruled out a remedy that would result in the quarrelling parties sharing a small house. See also *Dodsworth* v *Dodsworth* (1973) 228 EG 1115; *Baker* v *Baker & Baker* (1993) 25 HLR 408; *Stallion* v *Albert Stallion Holdings (GB) Ltd* [2010] 2 FLR 78 at [138].
[126] *Cameron* v *Murdoch* (1986) 63 ALR 575 (PC) provides a good example. C had an expectation of inheriting property but did not expect to get it for free. The court decided that C could purchase for two-thirds of the value of the property. See also *Gillett* v *Holt* [2001] Ch 210 and pp 167–169 below.
[127] Bright and McFarlane [2005] CLJ 449. Although the Privy Council stated in *Clarke* v *Swaby* [2007] 2 P&CR 12 at [18] that estoppels will often be best satisfied by monetary remedies, Robertson [2008] Conv 295 shows the continuing vitality of expectation relief.
[128] *Jennings* v *Rice* [2003] 1 P&CR 100 at [43] (discussed below), rejecting Gardner's hypothesis 4. See also Bright and McFarlane [2005] CLJ 449 and Gardner (2006) 122 LQR 492.
[129] [1976] Ch 179 at p 198.
[130] [2003] 1 P&CR 100.
[131] See other cases cited in *Jennings* v *Rice* [2003] 1 P&CR 100; also dicta in *Watson* v *Goldsbrough* [1986] 1 EGLR 265; *Burrows & Burrows* v *Sharp* (1989) 23 HLR 82 and *Roebuck* v *Mungovin* [1994] 2 AC 224 at p 235.
[132] (1973) 228 EG 1115.
[133] Prior to the Trusts of Land and Appointment of Trustees Act 1996, such a right could result in the licensee's being entitled to the legal fee simple under the Settled Land Act 1925.
[134] [1979] 1 WLR 431.

Although O was moderately well off, he failed to transfer legal title to C. Following later quarrels, O sought to evict C. In the meantime, C had spent £230 of her £1,000 capital in improving the house with O's encouragement; by the time of the litigation, she had only £300 left. The court held that O should transfer the fee simple to C.

The Court of Appeal emphasised that the expenditure was quite small and was more compatible with C's being awarded a right to reside for life. She was eventually given the fee simple for two reasons: the expenditure of £230 represented a substantial part of her capital, and the court thought that O would do everything possible to deny her full enjoyment of a lesser right, such as a right to reside. The first of these reasons is most unconvincing: it may explain why some remedy should be given, but it could be reflected in a monetary award and scarcely justifies giving the fee simple. The second reason is more convincing, although one cannot help thinking that the dangers were exaggerated out of sympathy for C. Whatever the result should have been, the important point is that the court considered that it had a choice: it was not a matter of automatically giving effect to the promise.

Thirdly, *Sledmore v Dalby*[135] involved work being undertaken on property in reliance upon a representation that C could live there.[136] The Court of Appeal held that no remedy should be given, bearing in mind that C had enjoyed 18 years' free occupation, C had little need for the property and O was in desperate need of money. This clearly shows a wide use of discretion, although it is surprising to see the stress on the respective needs of C and O.[137] Such factors seem more appropriate to the exercise of family law discretions than the determination of rights to property.[138] It is interesting that Hobhouse LJ saw the remedy as restitutionary,[139] adopting the analysis of the High Court of Australia in *Commonwealth v Verwayen*,[140] linking the remedy to the reliance rather than the expectation and stressing the need for proportionality between the reliance and the remedy.[141] However, this has been held not to inhibit Australian courts from giving a remedy going beyond reliance,[142] and their modern approach seems more inclined to enforce expectations than has sometimes been the case in England.[143]

Fourthly, *Gillett v Holt*[144] saw the Court of Appeal identifying the assurance as representing the maximum extent of the equity and then considering what minimum remedy

---

[135] (1996) 72 P&CR 196; the free occupation point was approved in *Clarke v Swaby* [2007] 2 P&CR 12 (PC).

[136] The case was complicated by the fact that the representation was primarily in favour of C's wife (the daughter of O), who had since died.

[137] Pawlowski (1997) 113 LQR 232; Adams [1997] Conv 458; Gardner (2006) 122 LQR 492.

[138] Note Hobhouse LJ's alternative and rather simpler analysis that it was not inequitable to deny the expectation.

[139] At p 208. The use of restitutionary analyses in relation to reliance may be doubted: see n 112 in this chapter.

[140] (1990) 170 CLR 394. Such justification is more necessary in Australia because cases such as *Verwayen* promote a wide role for estoppel in founding causes of action. It is more based on reliance and discretion than restitution; the stress of Hobhouse LJ on restitution may be unintended. The useful analysis by Robertson (1996) 20 MULR 805 demonstrates that this approach has its own problems and has yet to be fully accepted by Australian courts.

[141] *Pascoe v Turner* is difficult to justify on this basis. In *Sledmore*, neither Roch nor Butler-Sloss LJJ chose to agree with Hobhouse LJ.

[142] *Giumelli v Giumelli* (1999) 196 CLR 101, stressing the role of discretion; see the useful discussion by Burns (2001) 22 Adelaide LR 123.

[143] *Donis v Donis* (2007) 19 VR 577 at [32].

[144] [2001] Ch 210 at p 237; also p 227 ('modest restitutionary relief' sometimes appropriate).

was required. Although the facts were complex and literal implementation of the assurance not practicable, the court certainly did not set out to give effect to O's assurance.

At this stage, it can be seen that expectation and reliance are relevant factors in deciding what remedy should be awarded. However, the cases are unhelpful in working out how they operate. Thus, Dyson LJ has observed that 'the two approaches [expectation and detriment] are fundamentally different. The cases are replete with examples, but short on analysis of the reason why one approach is adopted rather than another.'[145]

The approach in *Jennings* v *Rice*

An attempt to work out some of the issues was made in *Jennings* v *Rice*.[146] The facts were similar to *Gillett* in that there was a promise of property on O's death; C had provided household and personal service to the elderly O. In contrast to the earlier cases, the Court of Appeal conducted a thorough analysis of the principles applicable to the granting of a remedy, with full citation of cases and academic writing. Although C had been promised a house (valued at over £400,000), the court awarded £200,000, which was the same as the cost if a live-in carer had been employed.[147] It emerges very clearly that there is no right to fulfilment of the expectation. As Aldous LJ stated,[148] 'The most essential requirement is that there must be proportionality between the expectation and the detriment.'

However, it is the judgment of Robert Walker LJ (with whom Aldous and Mantell LJJ agreed) which is most interesting. He draws a distinction between cases where there is a 'mutual understanding in reasonably clear terms' as to what C is to receive (so that there is something like an agreement between them)[149] and those where the expectations are uncertain, which is likely to be the case with many claims. Where there is certainty, Robert Walker LJ recognises that the risk of disproportionality is reduced and the natural response is to fulfil the expectations.[150] Indeed, this can possess real advantages, as detriment can frequently be difficult to evaluate.[151] This goes a long way towards explaining the fact that in many cases, the courts have given effect to expectations without considering issues of discretion,[152] especially where the detriment is far less than the value of the expectation.[153] Indeed, frequently the courts consider the 'minimum equity' in terms of

---

[145] *Cobbe* v *Yeoman's Row Management Ltd* [2006] 1 WLR 2964 at [121] (Court of Appeal).

[146] [2003] 1 P&CR 100; Thompson [2003] Conv 225. Robertson [2008] Conv 295 provides a useful analysis of the more recent cases.

[147] Cf *Campbell* v *Griffin* [2001] WTLR 981 (cited in *Jennings*). The facts were not dissimilar; the court awarded £35,000 in lieu of the promised life interest in a £160,000 house, which was thought to be disproportionate.

[148] [2003] 1 P&CR 100 at [36].

[149] [2003] 1 P&CR 100 at [50], see also [45]; *Yaxley* v *Gotts* [2000] Ch 162 is seen as a good example, where there would have been a contract but for lack of formalities. There must also be certainty as to what C is to do: *Powell* v *Benney* [2007] EWCA Civ 1283.

[150] This can be seen to be analogous to the Australian approach: Robertson (1998) 18 LS 360, noting that the reliance-based approach 'operates at the margins' (p 366) and [2008] Conv 295.

[151] A factor stressed in *Thorner* v *Curtis* [2008] WTLR 155: expectation worth over £3 million allowed, when very extensive detriment over several decades (upheld in the House of Lords [2009] 1 WLR 776).

[152] In addition to the cases cited in the following footnotes, see *Hopgood* v *Brown* [1955] 1 WLR 213; *Wayling* v *Jones* (1993) 69 P&CR 170.

[153] Examples are *Griffiths* v *Williams* [1978] 2 EGLR 121; *Jones* v *Jones* [1977] 1 WLR 438; *Voyce* v *Voyce* (1991) 62 P&CR 290 (it is not clear whether the Court of Appeal perceived itself as exercising a broad discretion).

the expectation rather than the reliance.[154] It also fits very well the general absence of discussion of remedy in cases in the commercial setting, where an intention of gratuitous benefit is improbable.[155]

In the second group of cases, however, the uncertain expectation is merely the starting point, and the court is likely to look at the detriment to assess what remedy is appropriate. As Robert Walker LJ stressed, the overall objective is to avoid unconscionable conduct: justice to O must be done. A more limited remedy is appropriate if the expectations are 'uncertain, or extravagant, or out of all proportion to the detriment'.[156] Yet, even here, the expectation is not disregarded. The court can look at a wide range of considerations to decide what remedy should be given and does not simply look to detriment.[157] One such consideration may be that mere acquiescence in C's mistaken assumption can justify a lesser remedy.[158]

The application of *Jennings* v *Rice*

The distinction between the two classes of cases is by no means clear – many cases could be analysed either way. Although the existence of a clear bargain may be relevant in deciding what the most appropriate remedy should be, it is less clear that a distinction as firm as that proposed by Robert Walker LJ is justified.[159] Some later cases have quoted his dicta with apparent approval,[160] though the Court of Appeal has recognised that they are open to criticism.[161]

To illustrate the problems, how does the law react to an expectation which is certain but does not arise from a mutual understanding? *Pascoe* may provide a good example. Probably Robert Walker LJ would recognise the expectation as providing a starting point, but it would not be too difficult to prove it to be extravagant or disproportionate. This would also seem to apply to some mutual understandings.[162] Suppose O explicitly agrees that C should have a home for life in return for caring for him. If O unexpectedly dies very soon after C commences caring for him, it might readily be said to be a case where a home for life is disproportionate to a few months' assistance. Similarly, the expectation may be based on a contemplation that a relationship will continue. Should the relationship break down, this would be a relevant factor in limiting the award to C.[163]

---

[154] RJ Smith in Rose (ed), *Consensus ad Idem* at pp 240–243; Cooke (1997) 17 LS 258.

[155] *Ramsden* v *Dyson* (1866) LR 1 HL 129 (Lord Kingsdown); *Chalmers* v *Pardoe* [1963] 1 WLR 677 (PC); *Midland Bank Ltd* v *Farmpride Hatcheries Ltd* [1981] 2 EGLR 147 (Oliver LJ: 'a court of equity will compel B to give effect to such expectation'); *Liverpool CC* v *Walton Group plc* [2002] 1 EGLR 149 at [82]. Similar family cases involving a mutual understanding include *Griffiths* v *Williams* [1978] 2 EGLR 121; *Re Sharpe* [1980] 1 WLR 219; *Re Basham* [1986] 1 WLR 1498.

[156] At [50]. The role of unconscionability is discussed by Delany and Ryan [2008] Conv 401 at pp 407–414.

[157] See [51]–[52], [56].

[158] Finn, *Essays in Equity*, Chapter 4. It might be going too far to deprive O of his land merely because C incurs expenditure thinking the land to be his and O is aware of this.

[159] Gardner (2006) 122 LQR 492.

[160] *Bexley LBC* v *Maison Maurice Ltd* [2007] 1 EGLR 19 at [52].

[161] *Powell* v *Benney* [2007] EWCA Civ 1283 at [20]–[21].

[162] In *Grundy* v *Ottey* [2003] WTLR 1253 at [58], Arden LJ regards proportionality as an overarching requirement.

[163] *Grundy* v *Ottey* [2003] WTLR 1253. Arden LJ suggests at [49] that an expectation itself might be conditional on the continuance of the relationship (criticised by Thompson [2004] Conv 137).

At heart, the remedy is designed to avoid an unconscionable result; this represents the very essence of proprietary estoppel. Thus, *Grundy* v *Ottey*[164] employs a test of 'appropriate remedy in respect of the unconscionable conduct'. In doing this, the courts consider the factors central to proof of estoppel: most obviously, expectation and detrimental reliance. Yet this singularly fails to tell us how the courts are to choose a remedy on the facts of any given case. If the value of detriment and expectation is roughly the same, we have no difficulty, but what otherwise? In many cases, the detriment will be unquantifiable: this makes it easier to justify giving effect to the expectation,[165] and it may be urged that it is inappropriate to try to calculate a mathematical equivalent of the detriment.[166] Perhaps this explains the approach seen in some more recent cases to award the expectation.[167] Thus, in *Suggitt* v *Suggitt*,[168] the Court of Appeal approved a remedy worth over £3 million when the claimant (a son of O) had 'positioned his whole life' on the expectation, albeit that he had done rather little and received numerous benefits. Arden LJ denied that the relied has to be proportionate to the detriment: she preferred the 'out of all proportion' test. This does appear to be much more generous than *Jennings* v *Rice* might lead one to expect.[169]

Most recently, the Court of Appeal returned to the question in *Davies* v *Davies*,[170] another case involving promises relating to a farm. The fundamental inconsistency between the expectation and detriment measures, as identified by Dyson LJ, was recognised. A preference for the detriment measure was expressed, although the court did not need to reach a conclusion. The circumstances that the promises varied over the years, coupled with C's not varying out all her side of the bargain, justified an award reflecting her detriment. Overall, the approach is less favourable towards the expectation measure than *Suggitt*, though the facts were much less compelling.

Disproportionate advantage

A different aspect or proportionality was discussed by the Court of Appeal in *Cobbe* v *Yeoman's Row Management Ltd*.[171] Despite a very large difference between the detriment and the expectation, the court upheld a remedy based upon the expectation. The main reason seems to have been that O would make substantial gains if the expenditure basis were taken (O would be 'disproportionately advantaged'). The facts of *Cobbe* are exceptional: O's making substantial gains in excess of the detriment is absent from virtually all the other cases.[172] One element of the analysis is that it is assumed that the remedy has to

---

[164] [2003] WTLR 1253 at [61]. In *Murphy* v *Burrows* (2004) 7 ITELR 116, the judge would have awarded double the detriment, when the expectation was 10 times higher. Is this the sort of response Robert Walker LJ was seeking?

[165] As in *Q* v *Q* [2009] 1 FLR 935 at [146] (expenditure a quarter of expectation, but there were other factors).

[166] Robertson [2008] Conv 295, noting that Robert Walker LJ doubted the adoption of an hourly rates calculation: *Jennings* v *Rice* [2003] 1 P&CR 100 at [54].

[167] Contrast Mee's argument that the only role of expectation should be to provide a cap for the remedy: *Modern Studies in Property Law*, Vol 5 (ed Cooke), Chapter 16.

[168] [2012] WTLR 1607; also *Bradbury* v *Taylor* [2013] WTLR 29 and *Lothian* v *Dixon* [2014] 28 November. Note the criticism of McFarlane and Sales (2015) 131 LQR 610 at pp 619–620.

[169] Mee [2013] Conv 280.

[170] [2016] 2 P&CR 241.

[171] [2006] 1 WLR 2964; see p 154 above.

[172] One exception may be *Strover* v *Strover* [2005] WTLR 1245 (gain under life insurance policy).

adopt either an expectation or a reliance basis. The possibility of finding some middle-ground solution[173] is disregarded.

The issue was not relevant, of course, in the House of Lords as there was held to be no estoppel. However, it appears very unlikely that the same result would have been reached. As regards the unjust enrichment claim, C's detriment in obtaining planning permission was seen as unlocking the value inherent in the land, rather than increasing its value.[174] This more sceptical approach means that there will be very few cases where O is 'dispro-portionately advantaged'.

Purchasers

The Privy Council[175] has established that there need be no separate investigation of the discretion (or unconscionability) when purchasers are bound by an estoppel. Generally, the purchaser steps into the shoes of O as being bound by the appropriate remedy. However, it is possible that there might be circumstances which are special to a purchaser (or which were special to O alone) which should be taken into account.

C. Misconduct by the claimant[176]

We have already seen that O's conduct was taken into account in *Pascoe v Turner*, espe-cially the way it might affect future enjoyment of the house by C. Similarly, C's conduct may also be taken into account. Misconduct towards O may influence the extent of the remedy or prevent its being unconscionable to deny C's expectation.[177] Anticipated future misconduct may also be important. If C is likely to damage the house during occupation, then this could be a proper reason for denying an occupation remedy. Perhaps more diffi-cult is *J Willis & Son v Willis*,[178] in which the Court of Appeal took into account C's fla-grant lies and fabrications in the litigation and decided that it was proper not to grant any remedy. This ties in with the equitable maxim that he who comes to equity must come with clean hands.[179]

Is misconduct after the court has declared the remedy relevant? If O has been ordered to transfer a property interest to C (most obviously in the case of the fee simple), then it seems too late to complain about misconduct. However, it is not quite so clear where C is given merely an equitable interest or a mere right to reside. It is arguable that C is depend-ent upon a continuing exercise of equitable rights, and this requires continuing 'clean hands'.[180] The courts are reluctant to accede to this argument. In *Williams v Staite*,[181] the

---

[173] Gardner (2006) 122 LQR 492 at p 500. It is not easy to see how a figure is reached (see Mee, n 167 in this chapter), though difficulty in calculating the detriment dictates a broad-brush approach.

[174] [2008] 1 WLR 1752 at [41].

[175] *Henry v Henry* [2010] 1 All ER 988 at [56].

[176] See Thompson [1986] Conv 406.

[177] *McGuane v Welch* [2008] 2 P&CR 530, especially at [51]; *Bye v Colvin-Scott* [2010] WTLR 1 (County Court: no remedy).

[178] [1986] 1 EGLR 62. See also *Gonthier v Orange Contract Scaffolding Ltd* [2003] EWCA Civ 873.

[179] Snell's *Equity* (33rd edn), para 5-010.

[180] Just as an equitable lessee may lose an equitable interest if he breaches the terms of the lease: *Coatsworth v Johnson* (1886) 55 LJQB 220 (see p 404 below).

[181] [1979] Ch 291.

county court had earlier conferred a licence to reside on C. The Court of Appeal refused to accept that C's misconduct (he had gone out of his way to frustrate O's enjoyment of his adjoining land) could terminate the licence. Lord Denning MR thought that exceptional facts might achieve such a result, but this appears to be a minority opinion.

4. The proprietary status of the estoppel

Does an estoppel give rise to a proprietary interest: a right that may bind a purchaser? An immediate distinction needs to be drawn between the position before and after the court has declared the remedy. The position after a remedy is quite straightforward. Once C has had the fee simple, lease or other interest conferred upon him, then that interest will bind purchasers in the normal way. Just two points of detail require attention. First, the court order is unlikely to confer a legal interest directly: there will be an order that O transfer or create the interest. Until O does this, C can have no more than an equitable interest. The second point is that the court may order that C can have a right not generally recognised as a proprietary interest: a licence is the best example. This will be discussed in Chapter 22.

A. The status of the estoppel before a remedy is given

This becomes important if, for example, the land subject to the estoppel is sold before the court is called upon to give a remedy.[182] Many cases involve successors in title, as it is common for changes in ownership to trigger disputes. Most cases will today be decided by s 116 of the Land Registration Act 2002 (hereafter LRA), by which it is 'declared for the avoidance of doubt' that an 'equity by estoppel . . . has effect from the time the equity arises as an interest capable of binding successors in title'. This applies only to registered land, but that includes around 95% of all titles. The previous position was much debated, with many commentators believing that proprietary status is inappropriate: the proposals for change[183] received a very mixed response. The question of how far estoppels deserve proprietary status is still a question worth asking, as it assists our understanding of the attributes we expect of interests which bind successors in title. However, given their lack of significance today, the earlier cases will be considered relatively briefly.

We should first consider s 116 itself. Its purpose is clearly to confer proprietary status on estoppel claims, or 'inchoate equities' as they are sometimes described.[184] It seems tolerably clear that it achieves that objective, though two points might be noted. The first is that it operates 'from the time that the equity arises'. This appears to be the time at which there is detrimental reliance: there is no need for O to have repudiated the expectation.[185] A second point concerns the role of the crucial words 'as an interest capable of binding successors'. One reading would link them with the immediately preceding words 'from the time the equity arises'. This might mean that estoppels have effect from the time they are (by the general law) proprietary in nature: an interpretation which would allow no role at

---

[182] O's bankruptcy provides another example.
[183] Law Com No 271, para 5.30.
[184] Ibid, paras 5.29–5.31. The impact of s 116 after a remedy is given is considered below, p 495.
[185] *Walden* v *Atkins* [2013] WTLR 1465 at [48].

all for s 116! Such an interpretation cannot be likely. The correct analysis is to link those words ('as an interest . . .') with the earlier words 'has effect'[186]: this gives practical effect to the section and is clearly what is intended by the Law Commission.

Why is it controversial as to whether estoppels should bind purchasers? The most obvious problem is that nobody knows exactly what C is entitled to. This may be because the nature of the assumption or expectation is unclear or because the remedy lies in the court's discretion. One might reply that the court's decision as to remedy is retrospective, but this fails to recognise the need of purchasers to know what is binding upon them. More difficulties arise if a monetary remedy is thought proper: how could that be treated as something that could bind a purchaser? A right to money is not by itself an interest in land.[187] Section 116 is more understandable if we view the estoppel itself as binding the purchaser, rather than the interest eventually given.[188] What binds the purchaser is C's right to the exercise of the court's discretion. An order that money be paid would then be a direct order that the *purchaser* should pay. By way of contrast, McFarlane[189] has argued that we should not distinguish between the position before and after the court order – a purchaser is bound by the remedy C is entitled to, provided that it is proprietary in nature. However, this underplays the role of discretion as regards the remedy and is difficult to reconcile with s 116.

What is the position for unregistered land? Most of the pre-s 116 cases seem clear that estoppels do bind successors in title, even before the court has given a remedy.[190] There are cases binding O's devisees after death,[191] O's trustee in bankruptcy,[192] donees[193] and purchasers with notice.[194] It is true that this aspect is not stressed in some of the cases, but quite a few go out of their way to stress that successors in title are in no better position than O,[195] subject to the normal priority rules for equitable interests. On the other hand,

---

[186] This is assumed in *Halifax plc* v *Curry Popeck* [2008] EWHC 1692 (Ch) at [26]; it would be the obvious interpretation if there had been commas around the words 'from the time the equity arises'. See also McFarlane [2003] CLJ 661 at p 693.

[187] Unless there is a lien or charge (*Unity Joint-Stock Mutual Banking Association* v *King* (1858) 25 Beav 72 (53 ER 563)) or a right to reside on the land until the money is paid (cf *Re Sharpe* [1980] 1 WLR 219).

[188] Though *Birmingham Midshires Mortgage Services Ltd* v *Sabherwal* (1999) 80 P&CR 256 (in the overreaching context) looks to the remedy to be given: Dixon [2000] Conv 267 at p 273.

[189] [2003] CLJ 661; see p 496 below.

[190] Law Com No 254, para 3.35; No 271, para 5.30. See also Moriarty (1984) 100 LQR 376 at p 377 (rejecting doubts expressed by Todd [1981] Conv 347); Baughen (1994) 14 LS 147; RJ Smith in Rose (ed), *Consensus ad Idem*, pp 237–238; Thompson [1996] Conv 295; Battersby in *Land Law: Themes and Perspectives* (eds Bright and Dewar), Chapter 19.

[191] *Dillwyn* v *Llewelyn* (1862) 4 De GF&J 517 (45 ER 1285); *Jones* v *Jones* [1977] 1 WLR 438.

[192] *Re Sharpe* [1980] 1 WLR 219 (if it was a proprietary estoppel that was in issue). A proprietary claim is essential if the claim is to rank ahead of unsecured creditors.

[193] *Voyce* v *Voyce* (1991) 62 P&CR 290.

[194] *Taylor* v *Needham* (1810) 2 Taunt 278 (127 ER 1084); *Duke of Beaufort* v *Patrick* (1853) 17 Beav 60 (51 ER 954) (constructive notice); *Mold* v *Wheatcroft* (1859) 27 Beav 510 (54 ER 202) (constructive notice); *Birmingham & District Land Co* v *London & North Western Railway Co* (1888) 40 Ch D 268; *Gresham Life Assurance Society* v *Crowther* [1914] 2 Ch 219; *Hopgood* v *Brown* [1955] 1 WLR 213; *ER Ives Investment Ltd* v *High* [1967] 2 QB 379; *Siew Soon Wah* v *Yong Tong Hong* [1973] AC 836; *JT Developments Ltd* v *Quinn* (1990) 62 P&CR 33 (conceded by counsel); *Locabail (UK) Ltd* v *Bayfield Properties Ltd* [1999] *The Times*, 31 March.

[195] See especially *Taylor* v *Needham*; *Duke of Beaufort* v *Patrick*; *Mold* v *Wheatcroft*; *Hopgood* v *Brown*; *Inwards* v *Baker* [1965] 2 QB 29 at p 37; *ER Ives Investment Ltd* v *High*; *Shiloh Spinners Ltd* v *Harding* [1973] AC 691 at p 721; *Voyce* v *Voyce*; *Locabail (UK) Ltd* v *Bayfield Properties Ltd*; *Vehicles and Supplies Ltd* v *Financial Institutions Services Ltd* [2005] UKPC 24.

there have been influential contrary suggestions from Professor Hayton and Lord Browne-Wilkinson.[196] Though the Court of Appeal in *United Bank of Kuwait plc* v *Sahib*[197] held in 1996 that an estoppel did not bind a purchaser, other recent cases support proprietary status.[198]

One important reason for the surfacing of doubts in recent years may be that the wide discretion as to remedy has been recognised only in the past few decades. This may require us to regard the earlier cases with some suspicion:[199] it would be easier to accept proprietary status if estoppels were simply exceptions to formality requirements. Even so, we have seen that recent cases continue to recognise the binding of purchasers. Another factor counting against the estoppel's proprietary status may be its use to protect non-proprietary interests. Again, much of this development has been in recent years. It is natural to have doubts about binding purchasers outside normal proprietary categories.[200] Yet, the courts do not appear to share these qualms.[201] It has also been suggested that only purchasers with actual notice should be bound,[202] but this solution would add complexity to the law and appears to have little or no support from the cases.

Underlying this debate are the problems caused to purchasers. But how great are they? Of course, any relaxation of formality requirements is liable to cause problems for purchasers: discovering rights is always going to be difficult when they are not in writing. In this respect, estoppels are in no different a position than, for example, common intention constructive trusts. What does mark out the estoppel is the uncertainty as to the remedy. How far this is a matter of great concern may be open to doubt. The response of the purchaser to discovering a claim such as an estoppel will nearly always be to pull out of the transaction, at least until the claim is sorted out. In other words, it is sufficient that the purchaser should be able to discover the claim. If the purchaser wishes to proceed and take the risk, then he can safely assume that the court will not give a remedy in excess of the assumption or expectation.[203]

It is, therefore, of the greatest importance that the purchaser should be able to discover that there is a claim. In the great majority of cases, the claimant will be in actual occupation and thereby able to assert an overriding interest (assuming title is registered). It is common practice for purchasers to make inquiries of occupiers. Purchasers will be protected if the occupier fails to respond to an inquiry.[204] If the claimant is not in actual occupation, then it seems clear that the purchaser will not be bound unless the estoppel is

---

[196] Hayton [1990] Conv 370; Sir Nicolas Browne-Wilkinson, Presidential Address to the Holdsworth Club, 1990–91, reprinted (1996) 10 *Trust Law International* 98. See also Ferguson (1993) 109 LQR 114 at zpp 121–123. Battersby (1995) 58 MLR 637 at p 642 supports proprietary status.

[197] [1997] Ch 107 at pp 141–142; Critchley [1998] Conv 502. The issue was treated in a very cursory manner.

[198] *Lloyds Bank plc* v *Carrick* [1996] 4 All ER 630 at p 642; *Locabail (UK) Ltd* v *Bayfield Properties Ltd* [1999] *The Times*, 31 March; *Bhullar* v *McArdle* (2001) 82 P&CR 481 at [50]; *Vehicles and Supplies Ltd* v *Financial Institutions Services Ltd* [2005] UKPC 24 at [24]–[25]; *Sweet* v *Sommer* [2005] EWCA Civ 227.

[199] Stressed by Hayton [1990] Conv 370. However, his argument at p 382 that the courts fulfil the assumption or expectation only in 'the exceptionally rare case' seems wrong.

[200] JD Davies (1980) 7 Adelaide LR 200 (in the constructive trust context); Baughen (1994) 14 LS 147; McFarlane [2003] CLJ 661. The question is considered in the licences context: p 495 below.

[201] *Ashburn Anstalt* v *Arnold* [1989] Ch 1 (as regards both trusts and estoppels).

[202] Thompson [1983] Conv 50. It was left open, not having been argued, in *Re Sharpe* [1980] 1 WLR 219.

[203] *Baker* v *Baker & Baker* (1993) 25 HLR 408.

[204] LRA, Sched 3, para 2(b).

protected on the register. Finally, it should be remembered that formality does not mean that a right is easily discovered. Even if C has writing to prove the claim, this may have a minimal effect on a purchaser's ability to discover that there is a claim in the first place. What writing does achieve is the eradication of most uncertainty as to the validity and extent of the claim, once it has been discovered.

A different sort of point, relevant to both registered and unregistered land, is whether estoppels can be overreached on a sale by two trustees. This will be considered in Chapter 11, as part of the comparison with constructive trusts.

B. Can the claimant transfer the benefit of an estoppel?

An attribute of most proprietary rights is that their benefit can be transferred. Is this true of an estoppel claim, especially before the court has declared the remedy? The issue has never been squarely addressed or settled in the cases. Insofar as the burden of the claim can be imposed on third parties, it would be odd if the claimant could not transfer the benefit. It is, of course, true that estoppel claims are highly discretionary, but this is scarcely sufficient to insist that C alone can claim the remedy. At most, one might argue that the discretion as to remedy might be exercised differently when C is not bringing the claim. Thus, in the Australian case of *Raffaele* v *F&G Raffaele*,[205] C had died; it was held that C's estate was entitled to a monetary remedy, equal to the value of the claim.

Nevertheless, the point can be made that several cases involve a right to reside in a house. The nature of this expectation is such that it is personal to C and is not susceptible of transfer to anyone else. Such a right is indeed not assignable, but this has little to do with the status of estoppel and everything to do with the nature of the particular promise. It has been suggested that licences are not assignable in the family context,[206] but this would appear to generalise to an unnecessary extent. Take the facts of *Dillwyn* v *Llewelyn*.[207] C built a house after his father had made an informal gift of the land. It would be extraordinary if C were to be unable to sell or mortgage the land,[208] or if the benefit could not be asserted by his personal representatives or trustee in bankruptcy.[209]

Turning to the cases, what little authority there is supports the assignability of the benefit.[210] Winn LJ appears to have left the issue open in *ER Ives Investment Ltd* v *High*,[211] but the general tenor of the judgments favours assignability.[212] There are many examples of courts saying that rights are personal to C, but these are explicable by the nature of the

---

[205] [1962] WAR 29.
[206] Dewar (1986) 49 MLR 741 at p 749.
[207] (1862) 4 De GF&J 517 (45 ER 1285).
[208] Naturally, nobody would be likely to buy or lend on mortgage if they were aware of the informal nature of the gift. Nevertheless, third-party rights are possible, for example, where a charge is drafted so as to apply to all land owned by C.
[209] The benefit of an estoppel passed to the trustee in bankruptcy in *Webster* v *Ashcroft* [2012] 1 WLR 1309 and *Walden* v *Atkins* [2013] WTLR 1465.
[210] *Unity Joint-Stock Mutual Banking Association* v *King* (1858) 25 Beav 72 (53 ER 563); *Brikom Investments Ltd* v *Carr* [1979] QB 467 (Lord Denning MR).
[211] [1967] 2 QB 379.
[212] Crane (1967) 31 Conv 332; *Joyce* v *Epsom & Ewell BC* [2013] 1 EGLR 21 (the contrary was not argued).

rights in the particular cases.[213] Whilst it is true that proprietary interests are generally assignable, there is little justification for its being an essential characteristic in every case. More difficult may be the question whether the benefit should pass automatically on the sale of land benefited by an estoppel, at least where a non-proprietary remedy is awarded.[214]

5. Other means of getting around formality requirements

Resulting and constructive trusts, together with estoppel, represent the most significant ways of limiting the effects of formalities requirements. Brief consideration will be given here to other approaches developed by the courts.

A. Mutual benefit and burden[215]

This shares some common elements with estoppel, though its most interesting effects lie outside the formalities context. It is common for an agreement between two persons to confer rights that are dependent upon performance of corresponding duties under the agreement. Unless there are formality problems, those duties can be contractually enforced between the original parties. However, it may be that a later purchaser is not bound by his seller's duties.

A good example is provided by *Halsall* v *Brizell*.[216] A developer sold off 174 plots, agreeing with the purchasers to provide and maintain central facilities such as roads and sewers. The purchasers promised to contribute to their upkeep. A dispute arose as to the payment of contributions by successors in title to the purchasers. It was common ground that, although the obligation to pay was not a claim that could bind successors in title, they could not insist on the right to use the central facilities without accepting the obligation to make contributions. In other words, they could not take the benefit of the agreement without accepting the burden. In the earlier words of Evershed MR[217]: 'as a matter of plain justice and of law, . . . a person who is enjoying one part of such reciprocal licences cannot at the same time purport to revoke the other part which imposes a burden on him'.

The House of Lords in *Rhone* v *Stephens*[218] has made it clear that the doctrine is restricted to situations where the benefit is made conditional upon the performance of the burden. Unless explicitly conditional, this will require reciprocity and relevance of the burden to the exercise of the benefit. If V sells to P, imposing a number of obligations on P in the conveyance, this does not create the necessary reciprocity to enable V to enforce those obligations on purchasers from P. Although those purchasers take their title under the conveyance to P (and so can be said to take the benefit of an arrangement), any liability would virtually destroy the law's insistence that only recognised interests in land bind purchasers. Further, it appears from *Rhone* that the benefit must be one that could, in theory, be repudiated: simply applying a condition (burden) to the fee simple (benefit) would not qualify.

---

[213] The best example is *Maharaj* v *Chand* [1986] AC 898.
[214] Mee [2013] Conv 156 at pp 160–161.
[215] Davis [1998] CLJ 522, especially pp 537–553.
[216] [1957] Ch 169.
[217] *Hopgood* v *Brown* [1955] 1 WLR 213 at p 226.
[218] [1994] 2 AC 310 at p 322, rejecting the 'pure principle of benefit and burden' asserted in *Tito* v *Waddell (No 2)* [1977] Ch 106; applied in *Thamesmead Town Ltd* v *Allotey* (1998) 79 P&CR 557.

The origins of the rule lie in denying being a party to a deed whilst taking the benefit of it, but the modern law contains no such limitation to deeds.[219] However, even apart from *Rhone*, there are limits to *Halsall*. It will not apply to benefits which are not actively asserted: payment for upkeep of communal areas and landscaping is likely to be excluded. This applies even if payment has to be made in respect of rights which are exercised (such as to roads and sewers), with the rather messy result that costs have to be apportioned.[220] However, apportionment may not be possible (especially where a fixed sum has to be paid), and then the full payment is due.[221]

The benefit and burden doctrine was applied by the Court of Appeal in *ER Ives Investment Ltd* v *High*.[222] There had been agreement that the defendant would allow the foundations of a block of flats to remain on his land, provided that he was given a right of access to the garage to his house across the back of the flats. The defendant's access right was in the nature of an easement, but no legal easement was ever executed and no equitable easement was protected by registration. The flats were sold to the claimants, who denied the defendant's right of access. The court had no hesitation in holding that, at least whilst the flats remained with their foundations on the defendant's land, the defendant had a right to cross the back of the flats. As in *Halsall*, the practical result was that the purchaser was bound. On the facts of *Ives*, the defendant had also acted to his detriment (principally by building a garage for his car, accessible from across the back of the flats) and this gave rise to an estoppel. The two grounds for the decision are intertwined in the judgments: each operates to avoid unconscionable conduct.

Although the benefit and burden doctrine and estoppel have similar origins, they operate in somewhat different ways. So far as the benefit and burden doctrine is concerned, the purchaser is made liable because of his continuing to take the benefit rather than because the other party has any interest in land. In other words, it is what he does after buying the land that affects him. Accordingly, the doctrine operates outside the normal rules relating to interests in land and, in particular, the registration rules.[223] It may be that the conscience of a purchaser would not be affected if unaware of the burden at the time of purchase – although this is unlikely in most cases. Another important difference is that the burden is imposed only so long as the benefit is being asserted.[224] What happens if the benefit is not of a continuing nature? It seems possible that the benefit and burden doctrine will still apply, so that a person who has taken the benefit in the past cannot deny the continuing and corresponding burden.[225] However, a purchaser from the person benefiting will not be bound in these circumstances as the purchaser has done nothing to justify an equitable claim.[226]

[219] Described by Megarry V-C in *Tito* v *Waddell (No 2)* [1977] Ch 106 at p 294 as 'a substantial expansion of the principle'.
[220] *Thamesmead Town Ltd* v *Allotey* (1998) 79 P&CR 557.
[221] *Wilkinson* v *Kerdene Ltd* [2013] EWCA Civ 44; [2013] 2 EGLR 163.
[222] [1967] 2 QB 379. The attempt by Battersby (1995) 58 MLR 637 at p 649 to link *Ives* with the estoppel in *Taylors Fashions Ltd* v *Liverpool Victoria Trustees Co Ltd* [1982] QB 133 appears somewhat tenuous.
[223] *Bhullar* v *McArdle* (2001) 82 P&CR 481 at [52]; *Elwood* v *Goodman* [2014] Ch 442 at [36]. One problem with *Elwood* is that it stressed that the burden (paying towards the upkeep of a right of way) is not registrable. That reasoning would not apply to a case such as *Ives* v *High* (unregistered right of way).
[224] *Parkinson* v *Reid* (1966) 56 DLR 2d 315.
[225] *Tito* v *Waddell (No 2)* [1977] Ch 106 at p 308 (benefit and burden is discussed at pp 289–311). See Aughterson [1985] Conv 12.
[226] *Bhullar* v *McArdle* (2001) 82 P&CR 481 at [50].

There are many problems yet to be resolved. Suppose, for example, that in *Ives*, the owner of the flats had sold just the access land (excluding the flats) to the claimants. Could the claimants bar access when the benefit of the foundations is being enjoyed not by them, but by the owners of the flats?[227] Would their success (if they can succeed) terminate the right of the owners of the flats to keep the foundations on the defendant's land? We do not know the answers.

B. Donor doing all in his power

Some forms of property cannot be transferred by the actions of the parties alone. The best examples are found in transfers of shares and of land. Shares cannot be transferred until the transfer is registered by the company (which may have a discretion not to accept the transfer), and land transfers require registration under the title registration scheme. Does the transferee have any right prior to full transfer? If there is a contract, then an equitable right may be obtained by virtue of the right to specific performance of the contract. In the case of a gift, this analysis is plainly inapplicable. Nor, at first sight, can the donee rely on a trust: we saw in Chapter 8 that equity will not spell out a declaration of trust from a failed gift.

The leading case taking this hard approach towards incomplete gifts is *Milroy v Lord*.[228] Turner LJ required that the settlor (the case involved a gift into a trust) 'must have done everything which, according to the nature of the property comprised in the settlement, was necessary to be done in order to transfer the property and render the settlement binding upon him'. It is important to note that the donor is required to do all that is necessary. If the wrong form is used, then that is fatal and equity will not step in to provide a remedy. Yet, what if the element required to complete the gift lies outside the donor's control? The donor cannot, for example, control the time of registration of the transfer of land or of shares.

In the context of voluntary assignment of choses in action, the courts of equity had long accepted the principle that a gift is effective if the donor has done all in his power.[229] The context was somewhat different, as it was impossible for legal assignment to take place at that time. It was not until the 1948 decision of Jenkins J in *Re Rose*[230] that English courts recognised that a gift might be complete in equity when a legal gift is possible and the donor has done all in his power to make such a gift. This was soon confirmed by the Court of Appeal in a different case, confusingly also called *Re Rose*.[231] The principle has been readily accepted in subsequent cases and is often referred to as the *Re Rose* principle.[232] It should be remembered, however, that its origin lies in dicta in *Milroy v Lord* and that the High Court of Australia had articulated it some 40 years earlier.[233]

---

[227] *Bhullar v McArdle* (2001) 82 P&CR 481 recognised that the doctrine might apply where the benefit was received from a third party, under an 'integral and interdependent' tripartite agreement, although the action would require joinder of the third party.

[228] (1862) 4 De GF&J 264 at p 274 (45 ER 1185 at p 1189).

[229] *Fortescue v Barnett* (1834) 3 My&K 36 (40 ER 14); cf *Re Patrick* [1891] 1 Ch 82.

[230] [1949] Ch 78.

[231] [1952] Ch 499.

[232] See, for example, Lord Wilberforce in *Vandervell v IRC* [1967] 2 AC 291 at p 330. For problems in explaining the theoretical basis of the principle, see Garton [2003] Conv 364.

[233] *Anning v Anning* (1907) 4 CLR 1049. See Meagher, Gummow and Lehane, *Equity: Doctrines and Remedies* (5th edn), paras 6.075–6.155.

The operation of the principle has given rise to a number of issues. First, it seems irrelevant that more might be required of the donor in the future. An excellent example is that a transfer of shares in a private company may require the consent of the directors. When a donor executes a transfer and hands it to the donee together with the share certificate, the gift is complete.[234] It is not material that the directors might seek extra information or assurances from the donor later and, one presumes, immaterial that they actually do so.[235] By contrast, Romer J had earlier held in *Re Fry*[236] that, where Treasury consent was required, it had to be obtained and not just applied for.

The second issue concerns what the donor must do. One possible test is that he has to do all that he could possibly do (including acts that could be undertaken by others). Such a strict approach is rejected in *Mascall v Mascall*.[237] The donor handed over a transfer of registered land together with the land certificate. Problems arose when the donor managed to recover possession of the documents before an application for registration had been submitted to the land registry. The donor could have made such an application, although the donee would normally be the applicant. The Court of Appeal held the gift to be complete in equity. Indeed, further flexibility was exhibited by the Court of Appeal in *Pennington v Waine*.[238] A good equitable gift of shares was found even though the share transfer had not been handed to the transferee. Very generously, it was enough that the donor regarded the gift as complete and had informed the donee.[239] This seems justified only if there is detrimental reliance by the donee.[240]

Finally, what happens if the transfer is never in fact completed? In most of the reported cases,[241] the transfer has been completed and the trust can be seen as avoiding the effects of the necessary hiatus between transfer and formal legal effect.[242] If the transfer is never completed (perhaps because directors refuse consent to a share transfer), it would appear that the gift is still complete in equity: the donor holds on trust for the donee. It is here that one sees something of a conflict with the insistence in *Milroy v Lord* that the trust cannot be used as an alternative to a failed legal gift.[243] More significantly, it is arguable that the donor, once the gift has failed at law, might wish to do something different with the shares.

---

[234] The actual result in *Re Rose*.

[235] Criticised by McKay (1976) 40 Conv 139.

[236] [1946] Ch 312.

[237] (1984) 50 P&CR 119. Lawton LJ stressed that it was the transferee who would normally seek registration.

[238] [2002] 1 WLR 2075, especially Arden LJ at [65]–[67] (principally on unconscionability grounds). The analysis of Clarke LJ is based on transfer of an equitable interest, but how can such an interest exist without a declaration of trust? Commentators have been critical: Tijo and Yeo [2002] LMCLQ 296; Ladds (2003) 17 *Trust Law International* 35; Doggett [2003] CLJ 263; Halliwell [2003] Conv 192 ('completely irreconcilable with all the earlier authorities'). Tham [2006] Conv 411 suggests other ways of justifying the outcome.

[239] Less generosity was shown in *Zeital v Kaye* [2010] WTLR 913. A trust was found in *Shah v Shah* [2011] WTLR 519, but was justified by the wording of the transfer.

[240] *Curtis v Pulbrook* (2011) 15 ITELR 342 (welcomed by Luxton [2012] Conv 70). Briggs J expressed doubts whether the rules serve any rational policy objective.

[241] An exception is *Mascall*, but there the donee would become legal owner following success in the action. The situation discussed in the text is where the donee never becomes the legal owner.

[242] See Evershed MR in *Re Rose* [1952] Ch 499.

[243] The problems might be diminished if one were to accept the suggestion of Lowrie and Todd [1998] CLJ 46 that (following dicta of Lord Browne-Wilkinson in *Westdeutsche Landesbank Girozentrale v Islington LBC* [1996] AC 669 at p 706) the equitable interest of the donee might exist without there being a trust. But might this not also suggest that *Milroy v Lord* requires reconsideration?

Imposing a trust in these circumstances is very different from the purely supplemental role of the trust where formal legal transfer is merely delayed. Yet it appears futile to make these points given that the *Re Rose* decisions are treated as having settled the law.

C. Rules relating to death

There are several ways in which trusts are imposed or gifts recognised on death, thereby avoiding the impact of the Wills Act 1837. Details are found in books on equity and trusts.

(i) *Secret trusts*

If T leaves property to L in his will, but on the oral understanding that L shall hold on trust for B, then a trust (a secret trust) will be enforced by the court if L denies liability. At first sight, this trust is ineffective because it is not in the will and fails to comply with the formality requirements of the Wills Act. However, it is plain that it would be fraudulent for L to keep the property, when he has agreed to accept the trust and, in all probability, the property was left to him only because he had agreed to hold on trust. The case is similar to the inter vivos transfer in *Bannister* v *Bannister*[244] where the trust was not in writing. It may be noted that the intended trust is given effect to: there is no question in this context of there being a mere resulting trust to T. It is, of course, too late for T (now in his grave) to correct the lack of formality.

Perhaps surprisingly, as there is no risk of fraud, the same rule applies where the will states that L is to hold on trust but without specifying the beneficial interests. If the beneficial interests are never communicated to L, the property will be held on trust for the residuary legatees. However, communication of the trust before the execution of the will gives rise to what is called a half-secret trust. It may be noted that communication must be before the will, whereas for fully secret trusts it can be any time before death.[245]

Secret trusts are most likely constructive. Apart from the obvious point that the Wills Act is being avoided, there is also the problem that the declaration of trust is over future property (rights under a will of a living person) and such declarations are not generally effective.

(ii) *Mutual wills*

Two people sometimes make wills leaving property to each other and, should the other predecease the testator, to the same third party. The obvious joint intention is that the survivor will enjoy the other's property, but that all the property should end up with the agreed third party. If the survivor should change his or her mind, the courts may impose a trust to give effect to their agreed intentions. It would be fraudulent to take the first person's property and then to dispose of it elsewhere (though there can still be fraud without taking property).[246]

---

[244] [1948] 2 All ER 133; see p 142 above.
[245] *Re Keen* [1937] Ch 236 at p 246. Perhaps the reason is that there is greater temptation to delay communication in half-secret trusts. In fully secret trusts, L really will get the property if T dies without communicating, and T may be reluctant to take this risk. T will generally be less worried about the property going to residuary legatees in the equivalent half-secret trust.
[246] *Re Dale* [1994] Ch 31.

However, it is essential that the parties intend that the survivor should be under such an obligation; the mere fact that they make identical wills does not by itself prove it.[247] Indeed, *Re Goodchild Deceased*[248] restricted mutual wills to cases where there is a contract whereby the survivor will not revoke: understandings and moral obligations do not suffice. *Healey v Brown*[249] takes the contract analysis so seriously that formality requirements for contracts have to be satisfied where land is involved.

Mutual wills take effect as constructive trusts (avoiding the Wills Act), binding the property on the first death.[250] The authorities on the operation of the trust are few in number, but it gives rise to some very awkward questions. In particular, the survivor can generally dispose of the property inter vivos: it is what is left on death that is caught by the trust. This seems a very strange trust; there is uncertainty as to the extent of the survivor's power to make inter vivos dispositions. *Goodchild* rightly described mutual wills as 'anomalous', and there is much to be said against their use.[251]

(iii) *Strong v Bird*

A very generous principle has been recognised favouring gifts to a personal representative or administrator[252] of a deceased person. An ineffective but immediate gift becomes complete on the donor's death if the donee is appointed personal representative or administrator, provided that there is a continuing intention to give. The rule does not depend upon any theory that appointing the donee as personal representative is intended to complete the gift or that an imperfect gift is being completed. Instead, the analysis is that the legal title is in the donee and, accordingly, the beneficiaries under the will must rely on equity to assert their claim in priority to the ineffective gift. However, equity sees no reason to assist them.

Strong v Bird[253] itself provides a good example of the rule. The deceased purported to release a debt owed by her stepson. The release was ineffective as not being by deed. Jessel MR stressed that appointing the stepson as executor released the debt at law: death achieved what she had failed to do. Whilst equity would normally force an executor to pay debts he owed to the deceased, it would not do so where the deceased had intended to release the debt. A similar analysis has been applied to gifts of other forms of property, where appointment as executor or administrator vests legal title in the donee.[254]

The intention to make a gift must be an immediate intention. A future gift is ineffective,[255] justified by the fact that it appears testamentary in character and therefore subject

---

[247] *Re Cleaver* [1981] 1 WLR 939, reviewing the law on mutual wills.
[248] [1997] 1 WLR 1216.
[249] [2002] WTLR 849; Davis [2003] Conv 238; Pawlowski and Brown [2012] Conv 467. Contrast *Olins* v *Walters* [2009] Ch 212; Luxton [2009] Conv 498.
[250] *Olins* v *Walters* [2009] Ch 212.
[251] Liew (2016) 132 LQR 664 supports the retention of mutual wills (noting their overlap with other equitable principles), whilst urging development of their rules.
[252] See *Re James* [1935] Ch 449 for the extension to administrators, questioned in *Re Gonin* [1979] Ch 16 (but see Kodilinye [1982] Conv 14).
[253] (1874) LR 18 Eq 315; Jaconelli [2006] Conv 432.
[254] *Re Stewart* [1908] 2 Ch 251.
[255] *Re Innes* [1910] 1 Ch 188.

to the requirements of the Wills Act. Any change of mind by the deceased renders the rule inapplicable.[256]

It is difficult to resist the conclusion that the rule is unduly generous. Whilst rigid insistence on formality requirements is to be decried, it is not at all clear that appointment as executor or administrator provides a defensible basis for an exception. Indeed, it might be argued that persons in this position should be the last to be able to rely on informal gifts in order to diminish their fiduciary duties. It is significant that the doctrine has never been based upon the deceased's intention regarding the choice of executor. It might have been more acceptable (and narrower in scope) if it had been so based.

Finally, it is possible that the doctrine might have some impact outside the context of personal representatives. There is probably a general principle that a gift is complete however the property reaches the donee.[257] Normally this will not be a problem, as there will be a continuing intention of a gift which can be given effect to.[258] The problem is more acute in *Strong* v *Bird* because a gift on death needs to satisfy the Wills Act.

(iv) *Donationes mortis causa*

These gifts have some similarity with the rule in *Strong* v *Bird* in that they take effect half inter vivos and half on death. If a person contemplating death makes a gift conditional upon death, then the gift will be effective even though it satisfies neither the requirements for inter vivos gifts nor those specified in the Wills Act. An example would be if a traveller gives somebody a bank deposit book before embarking on a hazardous journey, telling them that the money is to be theirs should the traveller be killed. Its conditional nature distinguishes it from inter vivos gifts. On the other hand, it has an immediate element and therefore is distinguishable from testamentary dispositions. It is important to note that delivery is essential before this form of gift is effective. This, however, is not as onerous as might be thought. Delivery of indicia of title[259] will suffice despite the fact that it would be inadequate for an inter vivos gift.

There is quite a lot of authority on the scope of donationes mortis causa, the history of which goes back as far as Roman law.[260] Although the concept involves an odd mixture of inter vivos and testamentary ideas, in 1991, *Sen* v *Headley*[261] extended it to gifts of unregistered land by handing over the title deeds. More recently, the Court of Appeal in *King* v *Dubrey*[262] expressed doubts about the need for the principle, at least outside the context of deathbed gifts (when making a will may be impractical). It was stressed that there has to be a 'good reason to anticipate death in the near future from an identified cause'. It is not enough that an elderly donor is aware that they do not have long to live. Donationes mortis causa are encountered relatively infrequently.

---

[256] *Re Freeland* [1952] Ch 110; *Re Wale* [1956] 1 WLR 1346.
[257] *Re Ralli's Will Trusts* [1964] Ch 288.
[258] *Re Bowden* [1936] Ch 71.
[259] *Birch* v *Treasury Solicitor* [1951] Ch 298. The crucial requirement is that the document must be necessary before the money can be obtained. The application of this in the modern context of dematerialised investments (and landholding) is considered by Roberts [2013] Conv 113.
[260] *Tate* v *Hilbert* (1793) 2 Ves Jun 111 (30 ER 548).
[261] [1991] Ch 425.
[262] [2016] Ch 221 at [55].

Further reading

Bright, S and McFarlane, B [2005] CLJ 449: Proprietary estoppel and property rights.

Davis, C J [1998] CLJ 522: The principle of benefit and burden.

Dixon, M (2010) 30 LS 408: Confining and defining proprietary estoppel: the role of unconscionability.

Gardner, S (2006) 122 LQR 492: The remedial discretion in proprietary estoppel – again.

Handley, K R [2008] Conv 382: Unconscionability in estoppel by conduct: a triable issue or underlying principle?

McFarlane, B [2013] CLP 267: Understanding equitable estoppel: from metaphors to better laws.

Mee, J [2013] Conv 280: Proprietary estoppel and inheritance: enough is enough?

Neuberger, Lord [2009] CLJ 537: The stuffing of Minerva's owl? Taxonomy and taxidermy in equity.

Robertson, A [2008] Conv 295: The reliance basis of proprietary estoppel remedies.

11
The family home

Introduction

This chapter deals with issues relating to ownership of the family home. Ideally, couples should expressly state what rights they have. As will be seen, this is normally conclusive. Unfortunately, many couples fail to consider and express their intended rights. Either the question is overlooked at the time of purchase (who wants to tell their partner that he or she is not trusted?) or a person moves in with an existing owner. The principles applied in this area are derived from resulting and constructive trusts, although modern analyses employ the common intention constructive trust. This chapter also considers the links between the common intention constructive trust and estoppel.

Although it forms the basis of this chapter, the family home is not a technical category. The same basic principles have often been applied when, for example, parents and children buy a house, whether or not they are all living there. Comparable principles have been applied as between friends and, much more controversially, in commercial settings.[1] They can also apply to assets other than homes.[2] That said, the greatest concern has been felt for the rights of couples to their family home, and this has been the setting for most of the cases and academic analysis. Recent developments have been more specifically based on the special circumstances and needs of a couple regarding their home. Although the general principles continue to be applied to other family relationships, the inferences drawn may well differ. In particular, it may be unsafe to apply the modern law to a commercial setting.[3]

Most cases, at least up to the past few years, have arisen where legal ownership is vested in the name of one of a couple. They may well have purchased the house by their joint efforts. This may be shown by the non-owner putting money towards the purchase, helping to pay the mortgage instalments or paying other expenses so that the legal owner can undertake the purchase. These examples involve monetary contribution, but in other situations, it may still be expected that some right in the land will be recognised. Most obviously, a spouse or partner who looks after young children may not be at work earning money but is still contributing significantly to the welfare of the family and may reasonably expect a share in the family home. As soon as the relationship breaks down, questions of ownership have to be faced.

---

[1] Cf *Banner Homes Group plc* v *Luff Developments Ltd* [2000] Ch 372; Thompson [2001] Conv 265.
[2] *Rowe* v *Prance* [1999] 2 FLR 787 involved a valuable boat.
[3] See the differing views expressed in *Crossco No 4 Unlimited* v *Jolan Ltd* [2012] 2 All ER 754.

This problem has bedevilled the courts of many countries for decades. Most of the earlier cases involved husband and wife, but for over 40 years most disputes between husband and wife have been decided on the basis of a statutory discretion on the breakdown of the marriage.[4] It is significant that this statutory discretion applies only if the parties are married or in a civil partnership. As a result, most of the recent cases involve those living with unmarried partners. Of course, the nature of the relationship may affect the inferences drawn by the courts as to the parties' intentions regarding ownership. In any event, even for relationships attracting the statutory discretion, some disputes do not trigger the discretion. These include actions by mortgagees, the bankruptcy of the legal owner (when assets have to be sold to meet debts) and rights on the death of the legal owner.[5]

It is possible to settle some, though not all, of these problems by having a statutory scheme of joint ownership of family homes. In England there is no such scheme,[6] although the operation of the statutory discretion may be regarded as recognising deferred community property.[7] Problems would arise less frequently if there were discretion to adjust property rights of unmarried cohabitants,[8] although no such discretion would cover all possible disputes. Reform proposals to allow such a discretion are considered later in this chapter.

1. Declaring the beneficial interests

If the conveyance of the legal title declares the beneficial interests in the land, then the courts treat this as conclusive. This is a powerful tool for the parties and their lawyers. In the absence of mistake or fraud, it will preclude investigation of intentions or contributions (at least at the time of purchase). It is very common for conveyances to spouses or partners to declare that they are to share the beneficial interest equally. This is likely to reflect the true intentions of the parties[9] and prevents one of them from subsequently arguing that he (or she) contributed more than the other.

This rule has long been the law, but dicta in *Bedson* v *Bedson* caused doubts to surface.[10] The conventional view was reasserted in both the House of Lords and Court of Appeal, but *Goodman* v *Gallant*[11] may be treated as finally settling the law. A wife

---

[4] Matrimonial Causes Act 1973, s 24 (criteria for the exercise of the discretion are specified by ss 25, 25A). An order for the transfer of property gives an immediate equitable interest in it from the time of the order: *Mountney* v *Treharne* [2003] Ch 135.

[5] Although there is discretion in the court to reallocate assets if a will fails to make reasonable provision for family members (Inheritance (Provision for Family and Dependants) Act 1975), it is necessary to sort out property rights as a first step. See Miller (1986) 102 LQR 445.

[6] Despite the recommendations in Law Com No 86 (1978), never implemented. Such schemes are principally found in parts of the United States: Powell, *Real Property*, Chapter 53.

[7] Cretney (2003) 119 LQR 349.

[8] Family Law Act 1996, s 36 provides a limited discretion to allow unmarried partners, without property rights, to possess for up to a year.

[9] Yet Douglas, Pearce and Woodward [2008] Conv 365 argue that equal shares are often not understood as being a consequence of a joint tenancy. See also Pawlowski and Brown (2013) 27 *Trust Law International* 3.

[10] [1965] 2 QB 666 at pp 682, 685 (contrast Russell LJ at p 689).

[11] [1986] Fam 106. In *Mortgage Corpn* v *Shaire* [2001] Ch 743, on similar facts but without an express declaration, the wife had a three-quarters share.

and her new partner purchased her husband's share in the former matrimonial home. The conveyance declared the wife and partner to be beneficial joint tenants. When the wife and partner separated, the wife claimed a three-quarters share: her original half share prior to the marriage breakdown and half of the husband's share purchased by herself and the partner. Her claim may well have represented a reasonable solution,[12] but the Court of Appeal held that the conveyance was conclusive. On the authorities, the result seems inevitable. It has the advantage of avoiding uncertainty as to the effect of conveyances.[13]

The rule operates only if the claimant is a party to the conveyance. Thus, if A, B and C contribute to the purchase and the conveyance is to A and B beneficially, this cannot shut out C's claim.[14] On the other hand, it is not essential that the conveyance be signed by the transferees.[15] So long as the transferees have agreed the terms of the conveyance, they will be bound.[16]

As has been observed, mistake or fraud can still justify the conveyance's being set aside or rectified. A simple example is provided by *Wilson* v *Wilson*.[17] Because the purchaser's income was not large enough for a mortgage, his brother was brought in as a party to the conveyance and mortgage so that his income could be counted for the purpose of obtaining mortgage finance. The brother intended to take no role other than to facilitate the mortgage. The purchaser's solicitor misunderstood what was going on and inserted a term that they were beneficial joint tenants. Rectification of the conveyance was ordered: it was plain that the term was included by mistake.

Pankhania v *Chandegra*[18] confirms that the declaration remains conclusive despite the analysis in recent cases (discussed below) as to how shares are to be determined in joint names transfers. Those cases, with their stress on common intention, are relevant only if there is no express declaration. That must be correct, as we want to avoid uncertainty and litigation as far as possible. The question whether the shares can be varied by a subsequent common intention raises difficult issues. It would be surprising if contributions to the mortgage repayments (unless radically different from what was intended) or moderate improvements could suffice, as these would seem insufficient to oust the intention as evinced in the declaration. However, an agreement on breakdown of a relationship[19] might well be seen in a different light – there is some support for a constructive trust or estoppel varying the shares.[20]

---

[12] It might well be upheld under the Law Commission's proposals discussed at p 214 below.
[13] In a transfer into joint names, the commonly inserted term enabling the survivor to give a valid receipt on a disposition of the land is not conclusive in favour of a joint tenancy: *Stack* v *Dowden* [2007] 2 AC 432 at [51] (confirming earlier cases), criticised by Sparkes [2012] Conv 207.
[14] *City of London BS* v *Flegg* [1988] AC 54.
[15] Conveyances are valid if signed by the transferor alone.
[16] *Re Gorman* [1990] 1 WLR 616; *Roy* v *Roy* [1996] 1 FLR 541.
[17] [1969] 1 WLR 1470. See Chandler [2008] Fam Law 1210.
[18] [2013] 1 P&CR 238 (nephew and aunt).
[19] As in *Jones* v *Kernott* [2012] 1 AC 776, p 191 below (no express declaration).
[20] Warren J in *Clarke* v *Meadus* [2013] WTLR 199 at [42], [56], [83], doubted by Pawlowski [2011] Conv 245 but welcomed by Gardner [2015] Conv 199. Where there is a variation in favour of a third party, *Arif* v *Anwar* [2016] 1 FLR 359 holds that a constructive trust is inappropriate, but assignment and estoppel principles can apply.

2. An overview of the leading cases

The law has been dominated by two pairs of leading cases. Over 40 years ago, the basic structure of the law was established by the House of Lords in *Pettitt* v *Pettitt*[21] and, 15 months later, *Gissing* v *Gissing*.[22] Both involved married couples – they pre-dated the statutory discretion enabling courts to allocate property on divorce. What is important about these cases is that they established that ownership of family homes is to be determined on trusts principles – there is no general discretion, as is often encountered in legislation in the family setting. In particular, a trust will be found where there is a common intention as to how the property is to be owned. Most of the problems over the intervening years have been based on working out when there is a common intention.

Within the past decade, we have had a further pair of cases: *Stack* v *Dowden*[23] in the House of Lords and *Jones* v *Kernott*[24] in the Supreme Court. These cases (both involving unmarried couples) have attempted to develop common intention so that it fits modern social conditions and can respond to the many criticisms of the application of trusts principles. One significant factor is they stress that the starting point for beneficial ownership reflects legal ownership. If there is a transfer into the name of one of a couple (single name transfer), then the other party has the burden of proving a common intention that beneficial ownership should be shared. But if there is a transfer into both their names (joint names transfer), then they hold equal shares unless one can prove a common intention that they should have a greater share.

One element that has become apparent since the influential Court of Appeal decision in *Oxley* v *Hiscock*[25] is that there are two questions to investigate. The first (Stage 1) is whether there is a common intention that one partner (not otherwise entitled) should have an interest in the property (or a greater than 50% share in a joint names transfer). The second (Stage 2) concerns the size of the shares. We shall see that both *Oxley* and *Jones* v *Kernott* adopt different tests for Stage 1 and Stage 2. Stage 2 will be addressed under the heading of 'Quantification of shares', although some of the issues will be looked at earlier when we investigate the imputing of intentions. The great majority of cases have arisen at Stage 1.

In between these two pairs of cases there is another House of Lords decision: *Lloyds Bank plc* v *Rosset*.[26] *Rosset* dealt with the question as to how to establish common intention at Stage 1. It showed that common intention can be established in two ways. The first is from discussions between the parties. Even if they did not explicitly state that they wanted to establish shares in the property, the court could read that into what they said and agreed. Alternatively, common intention could be inferred. It is the inference of common intention that has proved most controversial. *Rosset* said that such inference could be made

---

[21] [1970] AC 777.
[22] [1971] AC 886.
[23] [2007] 2 AC 432.
[24] [2012] 1 AC 776. See Hayward in *Landmark Cases in Land Law* (ed Gravells), Chapter 10, on these two cases.
[25] [2005] Fam 211, discussed at p 204 below.
[26] [1991] 1 AC 107. Fox Mahoney in *Landmark Cases in Property Law* (ed Douglas, Hickey and Waring), Chapter 8, discusses *Rosset* (and subsequent developments) in the political culture of property law.

only if there were a direct financial contribution (by deposit or mortgage instalments) to the purchase of the property. It may be observed that this inference of common intention frequently feels far removed from what the parties actually thought, although it possesses the merit of being based on objective facts and being slightly easier to establish whether it exists.

Many considered that *Rosset* concentrated far too much on financial considerations, such that homemaking activities (most obviously caring for children) were undervalued. It seems clear that *Stack* sought to relax the *Rosset* requirements by introducing a very wide range of factors (often described as a holistic view of the situation) that the court should take into account. A still controversial question is to what extent *Stack* is a complete break with the past – do the earlier cases still provide guidance as to when a common intention is to be found, even if some modification is required? This will be investigated later in this chapter.

3. Resulting or constructive trust?

In *Gissing*, Lord Diplock left the question open as to whether a resulting trust or a constructive trust analysis operates. Although some subsequent cases used the resulting trust,[27] there was a movement towards the constructive trust.[28] We need to distinguish between express common intention and common intention arising from contributions.

Cases based upon express (but not written) common intentions[29] are clearly constructive trusts. The fact that we are not basing the trust on contributions means that a resulting trust analysis is quite inappropriate: the entire question is whether it is unconscionable to deny the claimant a promised share in beneficial ownership.[30]

Turning to contributions, a resulting trust is readily established by contributions at the time of purchase. However, it had long been clear that a common intention is established by making contributions to mortgage instalments – any other outcome would be quite unacceptable when it is realised that cash contributions to purchases frequently represent a minute proportion of the cost. This provides real difficulties for a resulting trust analysis. It is sometimes argued that English courts accept that contributions to mortgage instalments give rise to a resulting trust,[31] but this is questionable. In any event, the modern basis[32] for both express intention and contribution categories is that of common intention, and it would be rational to recognise a constructive trust across the board.

---

[27] *Cowcher* v *Cowcher* [1972] 1 WLR 425; *Burns* v *Burns* [1984] Ch 317; *Walker* v *Hall* (1984) 5 FLR 126 (especially Lawton LJ); *Sekhon* v *Alissa* [1989] 2 FLR 94; *Springette* v *Defoe* (1992) 65 P&CR 1. This approach is taken in Ireland: Mee [1993] Conv 359. See also Thompson [1990] Conv 314 (also [2004] Conv 496); Gardner (1991) 54 MLR 126; Glover and Todd (1996) 16 LS 325.

[28] *Re Sharpe* [1980] 1 WLR 219; *Lloyds Bank plc* v *Rosset* [1991] 1 AC 107; *Hammond* v *Mitchell* [1991] 1 WLR 1127; *Midland Bank plc* v *Cooke* [1995] 4 All ER 562; *Drake* v *Whipp* [1996] 1 FLR 826. See also Hayton [1990] Conv 370; Sparkes (1991) 11 OxJLS 39.

[29] See p 197 below.

[30] *Grant* v *Edwards* [1986] Ch 638; *Oxley* v *Hiscock* [2005] Fam 211 at [30].

[31] Hayton [1990] Conv 370 at p 383, (1993) 109 LQR 485 at p 486; see also Gardner (1991) 54 MLR 126.

[32] *Lloyds Bank plc* v *Rosset* [1991] 1 AC 107.

Why is the debate as to constructive or resulting trust important? The answer must be that constructive trusts provide much greater flexibility. In particular, they more readily allow recognition of non-financial or indirect contributions and – an important factor in several cases – permit greater flexibility in considering the quantification of the beneficial interest. This fits the modern analysis, seen in *Stack*, that less stress should be placed on financial contributions.

The Court of Appeal in *Oxley* v *Hiscock*[33] reviewed the cases and concluded that the trust is constructive. This was based on two principal factors. The first was the flexibility shown in the cases in quantifying the shares, not being limited to factors present at the time of purchase. The second was the emphasis, in recent decades, on express common intention.

Stack[34] approves the *Oxley* preference for the constructive trust. As we will see below, the House of Lords rejected a resulting trust analysis for joint names purchasers of family homes. This rejection of the resulting trust is resoundingly approved in *Jones* v *Kernott*.[35] It would seem most unlikely that the resulting trust will feature in future family home cases.[36] The only possible exception is where the house is bought without a mortgage, but even that looks unlikely.

4. Inferring and imputing intentions

This area lies at the heart of *Jones* v *Kernott*, so much of the earlier material can be summarised. We have seen that the courts may infer common intentions from conduct and this will be studied in detail below. However, *Gissing* treated it as vitally important to distinguish imputed intention from inferred intention. It is impermissible to impute an intention to parties that they never in fact possessed. On the other hand, it is legitimate to infer from conduct that the parties did form a common intention, even though there may be no direct evidence of it from conversations.

The line between this form of inferring intentions and imputing intentions is often thought to be very narrow. In *Stack* v *Dowden*,[37] Lord Walker indicated his belief that, when the courts have been inferring intentions, they have in fact been imputing them. Confusion increases because a number of judges have used the word 'impute' when it seems clear that an inferred intention (in the sense intended by Lord Diplock in *Gissing*) is under discussion.[38] Lord Walker receives some support from Baroness Hale's reference to imputed intentions,[39] although she does not stress the point. Lord Neuberger strongly disagreed,[40] regarding the distinction as important. Although in a minority judgment, he is well supported by the cases.

---

[33] [2005] Fam 211, discussed at p 204 below.
[34] [2007] 2 AC 432, especially at [31] (Lord Walker), [60] Baroness Hale. See also *Abbott* v *Abbott* [2008] 1 FLR 1451 at [4] (PC).
[35] [2012] 1 AC 776 at [23]–[25], [60].
[36] It was recognised in a parent/child dispute in *Chaudhary* v *Chaudhary* [2013] 2 FLR 1526, although the common intention constructive trust is commonly used in such cases.
[37] [2007] 2 AC 432 at [20]–[23].
[38] Lord Pearson in *Gissing*; Waller LJ in *Burns* v *Burns* [1984] Ch 317; Waite J in *Hammond* v *Mitchell* [1991] 1 WLR 1127 at p 1137; Ward LJ in *Carlton* v *Goodman* [2002] 2 FLR 259 at [42]. More recently, this might be true of *Webster* v *Webster* [2009] 1 FLR 1240 at [32].
[39] [2007] 2 AC 432 at [60], repeated in *Abbott* v *Abbott* [2008] 1 FLR 1451 at [6] (PC).
[40] Ibid, at [125]–[127], supported by Swadling (2007) 123 LQR 511.

This is not just a question of terminology. An approach based on inferred intentions is asking what the parties intended. One based on imputed intentions enables the court to produce a fair result – a version, if you like, of the discretion the courts possess on marriage breakdown.[41] One of the problems of relying on real (inferred) intentions is that many couples give no thought to ownership of the family home. This can cause great difficulty when the relationship breaks down and it is sought to find a common intention.

In *Jones* v *Kernott*, Lord Neuberger's distinction between the two types of intention is approved.[42] However, his rejection of imputing intentions was heavily qualified by the Supreme Court. All the justices considered that intentions could be imputed at the quantification stage – we will return to this when dealing with quantification. However, it seems clear that at Stage 1, intentions can only be inferred,[43] and that has been accepted by the Court of Appeal.[44] Why the difference between Stage 1 and Stage 2, one might ask. Perhaps the best answer is that the parties may well be found to have agreed that shares shall be different from the starting point (Stage 1), but may well not have specified what they should be – particularly likely if one person's share changes over the years in response to their contributions. The law cannot simply state that they have not specified shares and so the Stage 1 common intention must fail – there has to be some way of establishing what the shares are.

Where does this take us as regards Stage 1? The simple proposition that imputing intentions does not apply is no more than a starting point. To begin with, one may doubt whether such a distinction between Stage 1 and Stage 2 can survive in the long term – it looks too artificial. In *Jones* v *Kernott*,[45] Lord Wilson was very welcoming of imputing intentions and gave some encouragement to the idea of an extension to Stage 1.

More important in the short term may be the relationship between imputing and inferring intentions. Lady Hale, Lord Walker and Lord Collins regard the two as overlapping in virtually all cases, so that it matters little which we apply. That suggests that the very wide discretion available in imputed intentions can be replicated in a flexible application of inferred intentions. On the other hand, Lords Kerr and Wilson quite strongly disagree. They see a narrower role for inferred intention and would have decided *Jones* v *Kernott* on the basis of an imputed intention (whereas the other justices found an inferred intention). The choice of analysis has little consequence for quantification (the issue in question in *Jones*), but is crucial for Stage 1. Commentators have generally expressed preference for the approach of Lords Kerr and Wilson.[46] Although a fairly wide scope for inferring

---

[41] The proper role of discretion in land law is considered by Hayward in *Landmark Cases in Land Law* (ed Gravells), Chapter 10. See also Lower [2016] Conv 453.

[42] [2012] 1 AC 776, especially [31], [73].

[43] Ibid, at [31], [51(3)], [64].

[44] Most clearly in *Barnes* v *Phillips* [2016] HLR 24; see also *Geary* v *Rankine* [2012] 2 FLR 1409 at [19] and *Capehorn* v *Harris* [2016] 2 FLR 1026 at [17]. Contrary dicta in *Bhura* v *Bhura* [2015] 1 FLR 153 must be regarded as misguided.

[45] [2012] 1 AC 776 at [84]: 'will merit careful thought'. This may gain some support from Lord Kerr at [76]. See also Pawlowski (2015) 29 *Trust Law International* 3.

[46] Gardner and Davidson (2012) 128 LQR 178; Mee [2012] Conv 167; Doyle and Brown (2012) 26 *Trust Law International* 96 (although commentators hold differing views as to the most appropriate approach at Stage 1). This also gains support from *Aspden* v *Elvy* [2012] 2 FLR 807: Lee [2012] Conv 421 at p 426.

intentions remains apparent,[47] *Capehorn* v *Harris*[48] provides a recent example where a finding of an imputed intention at Stage 1 was rejected by the Court of Appeal and there was no inferred intention.

5. Transfer into joint names

As has been seen, a declaration as to the beneficial interests is conclusive. Yet a simple transfer into joint names, perhaps surprisingly, was traditionally not conclusive. The surprise is because the parties have given thought to issues of ownership (unlike a transfer into a single name). If the transfer expresses the beneficial interests, then this is conclusive on the basis discussed above. However, quite a few cases have involved joint transfers which made no mention of beneficial interests. Since 1998, the land transfer form has required the form of the trust to be declared.[49] Although this does not guarantee compliance,[50] the problem should diminish as fewer pre-1998 transfers feature in the cases.

The issue arose in *Stack* v *Dowden*.[51] There was a transfer into the joint names of an unmarried couple: the woman contributed significantly more to the cost than the man. The House of Lords faced a choice between saying that the starting point was joint beneficial ownership or a resulting trust in proportion to their contributions. The resulting trust analysis has support from older co-ownership cases[52] and had been adopted by several lower courts. However, the majority of the House of Lords held that, as regards the family home, it was appropriate to treat joint beneficial title as the intended outcome.[53] As was stressed, only a lawyer would regard a transfer into joint names as giving rise to a trust in unequal shares. The result was seen as best fitting the intention of the purchasers and also in providing clarity. The transfer can be taken at face value: a transfer into joint names is just that.

However, there is no more than a presumption of joint beneficial ownership.[54] To rebut it, there must be proof of a common intention to that effect, something that will be found only in 'very unusual' cases. It is perhaps unfortunate that the clarity of the presumption was clouded by the finding that there were exceptional circumstances in *Stack*. It seems clear that simple inequality of contributions is not sufficient: the court should consider a

---

[47] *Barnes* v *Phillips* [2016] HLR 24.

[48] [2016] 2 FLR 1026 (a case with business overtones).

[49] Land Registration Rules 2003, Form TR1. Concern has long been expressed over solicitors' failure to clarify the beneficial interests: e.g. Dillon LJ in *Walker* v *Hall* (1984) 5 FLR 126; Ward LJ in *Carlton* v *Goodman* [2002] 2 FLR 259 at [44].

[50] *Stack* v *Dowden* [2007] 2 AC 432 at [52]; Moran [2007] Conv 364. See Cooke [2011] Fam L 1142 for problems in improving the form.

[51] [2007] 2 AC 432 (Pawlowski [2007] Conv 354; Piska (2008) 71 MLR 120; Harding [2009] Conv 308). In Australia, cf *Trustees of Cummins* v *Cummins* (2006) 126 CLR 278 (Sarmas (2012) 36 Melb ULR 216).

[52] See p 310 below.

[53] Baroness Hale delivered the leading speech, with which Lords Hoffmann, Hope and Walker agreed. Lord Neuberger disagreed. Note the criticism of Swadling (2007) 123 LQR 511. Hopkins (2011) 31 LS 175 is critical of having separate rules for family and commercial settings, but Hayward [2012] CFLQ 284 welcomes rules designed to meet the familial aspects of modern cases.

[54] The view has been expressed that the starting point will rarely make a difference (*Montalto* v *Popat* [2016] EWHC 810 (Ch) at [109]), but that underplays the significance of *Stack*.

wide range of financial and other factors in assessing the parties' intentions.[55] On the facts in *Stack*, the parties kept their finances 'rigidly separate' over a relationship lasting well over 20 years (there were four children). This was regarded as an exceptional factor, although one may doubt how far this is factually justified.[56]

Although a significant number of cases have found a common intention to vary the shares, *Fowler* v *Barron*[57] allays suspicions that exceptional circumstances will routinely be found. The fact that one party paid all the costs of the purchase, mortgage and ongoing property costs was not enough. *Stack* was distinguished because the parties in *Fowler* (although without a joint bank account) pooled their income; they had no other assets. There is a suspicion that a party paying part of the costs is in a weaker position (relative to one who pays none), because there is then a percentage which can be pointed to as an intended share – almost nobody argues that paying none of the costs should lead to a zero share. This was appreciated in *Fowler*, where the reply is that one has to find a shared intention for the shares to be other than equal; that simply was not present on the facts.

Pre-*Stack* cases provide illustrations of when the equal shares presumption might be challenged: if the names are joint only because the mortgagee funding the purchase insists upon both their names being on the deeds[58] or the extra name is included solely so that the borrowers have sufficient income for the required loan.[59] These are situations in which exceptional circumstances may rebut the joint ownership presumption. Even here, however, the joint names may be more than a mere technicality.[60]

The question of shares in a joint names transfer was raised in *Jones* v *Kernott* in the Supreme Court.[61] Even though *Stack* was not challenged, the court went out of its way to confirm the *Stack* analysis – this means that any attempt to argue a resulting trust is likely to be doomed to failure. The woman argued in *Jones* that, although the shares were equal on the purchase, the circumstances of the breakdown of the relationship justified finding that they were changed for the future. To a large extent, this involved a decision on the facts – it seems to have been agreed that the man would buy his own house and make no more contributions to the mortgage or other expenses of the jointly owned property. The court accepted a finding of the trial judge that there was a common intention that his share should crystallise when the couple split up. An extraordinary feature of the case is that the man resurfaced to claim a half share in the property after an absence of over 14 years, even though the common intention was found to exist soon after they split. The major issue concerned the quantification of the shares: the man was awarded just 10%. This will be considered when we look at quantification.

---

[55] Baroness Hale at [69]. These factors will be studied in more detail below in the context of single name transfers.
[56] Probert [2007] Fam Law 924, also doubting whether joint beneficial ownership reflects true intentions; George [2008] JSWL 49.
[57] [2008] 2 FLR 831; Piska [2008] Conv 451.
[58] Lord Diplock in *Pettitt* v *Pettitt* [1970] AC 777 at p 824; *Abbey National Bank plc* v *Stringer* [2006] EWCA Civ 338; [2006] 2 P&CR D38 (mother and son), criticised by Dixon [2006] Conv 577; see also the discussion at p 194 below.
[59] *Carlton* v *Goodman* [2002] 2 FLR 259 (not the parties' family home).
[60] *Crisp* v *Mullings* [1976] 2 EGLR 103.
[61] [2012] 1 AC 776. See the somewhat similar case of *Barnes* v *Phillips* [2016] HLR 24.

It must be remembered that *Stack* relates to a couple's home. Other joint transfers are encountered in a family context, often between parents and children. *Stack* has been held to apply to a home purchased by mother and son, though it will not be difficult to rebut the joint ownership presumption outside the cohabitation context[62]; in particular, rigid separation of finances is likely. Sometimes, of course, joint ownership is clearly intended.[63] In the business context, it seems that a resulting trust analysis is still applicable. *Laskar* v *Laskar*[64] is something of a middle situation: a house was purchased by mother and daughter as an investment. The Court of Appeal held that a resulting trust analysis was appropriate (rather than the *Stack* equality principle). The cases show that, even in a business setting, a common intention constructive trust can be relied upon to vary the prima facie shares.[65]

6. Transfer into a single name

A. Early developments: *Pettitt* and *Gissing*

It has already been seen that resulting trusts provide an inadequate basis for establishing rights to family homes. Often, more than 90% of the purchase cost is funded from a mortgage loan. In reality, the purchase is funded by paying off the mortgage. Even when resulting trust ideas were dominant, the courts rejected any suggestion that contributing to mortgage payments was no more than payment of another person's debts.[66]

In the 1960s, the courts began to develop a number of ideas to provide greater flexibility. Two approaches, both resonating with much modern thinking, were to impute intentions and to develop a theory of family property. Under the latter, family assets acquired from family income were treated as belonging to both parties, regardless as to who is named as the legal owner.

It was against this background that *Pettitt*[67] and *Gissing* were decided. It was established in *Pettitt* that common intention was the basis for this area – all the judges agreed that this was the only route whereby an interest could be claimed by the partner without legal title. The House of Lords split three to two in rejecting imputed intentions. The family assets approach gained support only from the minority judgment of Lord Diplock, who would have used it as a basis for imputing intentions. It might be added that the family asset argument was in one respect easier to assert at the time of *Pettitt*. Prior to the

---

[62] See *Adekunle* v *Ritchie* [2007] WTLR 1505 (County Court, but approved in *Laskar* v *Laskar* [2008] 1 WLR 2695 at [16]).
[63] As in *Crossley* v *Crossley* [2006] 2 FLR 813.
[64] [2008] 1 WLR 2695; if *Stack* had been applicable, then (as in *Adekunle*) the presumption would have been rebutted. *Laskar* was followed in *Erlam* v *Rahman* [2016] EWHC 111 (Ch): purchase of buy-to-let property by spouses.
[65] This frequently operates in single names transfers. The cases include *Morris* v *Morris* [2008] EWCA Civ 257; *Aspden* v *Elvy* [2012] 2 FLR 807, *Geary* v *Rankine* [2012] 2 FLR 1409; *Agarwala* v *Agarwala* [2014] 2 FLR 1069; *Capehorn* v *Harris* [2016] 2 FLR 1026.
[66] *Rimmer* v *Rimmer* [1953] 1 QB 63. Australian courts felt greater difficulty in applying resulting trusts, leading to an earlier move to constructive trusts: *Calverley* v *Green* (1984) 155 CLR 242, *Baumgartner* v *Baumgartner* (1987) 76 ALR 75.
[67] [1970] AC 777.

jurisdiction to reallocate property on divorce, the great majority of cases involved married couples: the concept of the family was readily applied. Today, unmarried couples dominate the cases. The nature of these relationships is that they are far more variable. Quite a lot closely resemble marriage, whereas others involve much less settled relationships, sometimes with a deliberate intention of avoiding the commitment and sharing involved in marriage.

The cases immediately following *Pettitt* demonstrated that its effect was far from clear. In *Gissing* v *Gissing*,[68] the House of Lords clarified the effect of their earlier decision. What is most significant in *Gissing* is that Lord Diplock recognises that he was in a minority in *Pettitt* in his willingness to impute non-existent intentions; he proceeds to formulate the law in such a way as to reflect the majority approach. His judgment has been the most influential. It is settled that the common intention of the parties, inferred rather than imputed, provides the basis of any trust in the family purchase area. In the words of Lord Morris, 'The court does not decide how the parties might have ordered their affairs: it only finds how they did.'

It is made clear that the trust does not need to be in writing. Nor is it necessary for the parties explicitly to agree that there should be joint beneficial interests under a trust. As Lord Hodson had observed in *Pettitt*,[69] 'The conception of a normal married couple spending the long winter evenings hammering out agreements about their possessions appears grotesque . . .'.

B. The development of common intention prior to *Stack*: inferring intentions

The stress in most of the cases following *Gissing* was upon the type of conduct from which a common intention may be inferred. Perhaps surprisingly, the courts were willing to infer a common intention almost automatically whenever there was a significant financial contribution to the purchase or mortgage instalments. The common intention test is frequently criticised as being based upon a substantially fictitious intention,[70] but at least it enabled the English courts to confer beneficial interests in cases of financial contribution.

The facts in *Gissing* provide a good example of the problems faced by the courts. The husband and wife were both working. When their matrimonial home was bought, the legal title was placed in the husband's name. Both parties maintained separate bank accounts and treated their finances as separate. The wife paid for clothing and other expenses and both of them saved part of their earnings. The earlier cases had indicated that contributions to a purchase need not be direct payments of the deposit or mortgage instalments. If the claimant undertook expenditure that allowed the legal owner to meet the mortgage instalments, then the courts would infer that there was the requisite common intention. This acceptance of such indirect contributions (an issue which later became controversial)

---

[68] [1971] AC 886. Note the criticism of Mee, *The Property Rights of Cohabitees*, especially Chapter 5.
[69] [1970] AC 777 at p 810.
[70] This criticism goes back many years: Steyn LJ expressed doubts in *Huntingford* v *Hobbs* (1992) 24 HLR 652 at pp 663–664. See also *Allen* v *Snyder* [1977] 2 NSWLR 685 (Mahoney JA); *Pettkus* v *Becker* (1980) 117 DLR 3d 257.

proclaims that it is immaterial how the parties decide to split their expenditure. Nevertheless, the claim in *Gissing* was doomed to failure. It could not be said to be a case where the wife's contributions enabled the husband to pay the mortgage instalments and, as Lord Diplock observed, the way in which they kept their finances separate, rather than pooling their resources, militated against finding a common intention.

Non-financial contributions

Gissing demonstrates that it is not enough for a party to be contributing to the welfare of the family, even financially. It is this sort of situation which has proved most troublesome. The rejection of non-financial contributions is best illustrated by *Burns v Burns*.[71] The case involved an unmarried couple whose relationship lasted some 19 years. The family home was bought by the man when the woman was pregnant with their second child. She made no financial contribution to the purchase, although she started work five years before their separation. Her wages were spent, in part, on household bills and she undertook redecoration of the house. Although Waller LJ was sympathetic to her claim, Fox and May LJJ were emphatic that the facts disclosed no common intention that she should have a share. General contributions to the family are insufficient to infer such an intention, for this would be to return to the concept of family assets rejected in *Pettitt* and *Gissing*. As for her earnings, these had to refer to the purchase of the home in order for any inference to be possible. On the facts, her earnings represented extra income that the claimant chose to earn and could not be related to the initial purchase. The case marks a preference for a relatively certain and easily applied test: financial contribution is essential and it must be referable to the purchase.

Direct financial contributions

Returning to financial contributions, these readily lead to an inferred common intention where there is direct payment of part of the purchase price[72] or regular payment of mortgage instalments[73] by the claimant, or where the parties pool their income which is then used for such expenditure.[74] A common feature in several cases is that an occupier of a council house has been in receipt of a discount (often as much as half the value) when purchasing it. When a partner or children assist in the purchase, the occupier is treated as having contributed the amount of the discount.[75] Indeed, even though the partner or children join in the mortgage and pay some mortgage instalments, this may be consistent with the occupier being intended to be the sole beneficial owner.[76]

---

[71] [1984] Ch 317.

[72] *Cowcher* v *Cowcher* [1972] 1 WLR 425 and *Passee* v *Passee* [1988] 1 FLR 263 are examples.

[73] *Bernard* v *Josephs* [1982] Ch 391 is one of many cases. The payment of a few instalments, especially some time after purchase, may well not suffice: *McKenzie* v *McKenzie* [2003] EWHC 601 (Ch) at [82]; [2003] 2 P&CR D15 (cf *Buggs* v *Buggs* [2004] WTLR 799).

[74] *Walker* v *Hall* (1984) 5 FLR 126.

[75] *Laskar* v *Laskar* [2008] 1 WLR 2695; earlier, see *Springette* v *Defoe* (1992) 65 P&CR 1 and *Evans* v *Hayward* [1995] 2 FLR 511. Where a child (not living in the house) funds the balance of the cost, the intention may be that the occupier is to have a life interest rather than a proportionate share: *Buggs* v *Buggs* [2004] WTLR 799.

[76] *McKenzie* v *McKenzie* [2003] EWHC 601 (Ch); [2003] 2 P&CR D15; *Driver* v *Yorke* (2003) 6 ITELR 80; *Kyriakides* v *Pippas* [2004] 2 FCR 434.

Indirect financial contributions

It has been seen that *Gissing* involved alleged indirect contributions: where the household expenditure is split between the parties so that the legal owner of the home pays the mortgage instalments and the claimant pays other expenses. The contribution is indirect because the claimant does not directly pay off the mortgage but makes it feasible, or at least easier, for the legal owner to do so. One can readily see the attraction of the argument that the parties between them pay the various household bills and it is a matter of convenience as to who actually pays which bill. It appears that *Gissing* supports the sufficiency of indirect contributions.

Although cases after *Gissing* asserted that such indirect contributions would suffice,[77] a more cautious approach became evident in the 1980s. In the influential case of *Grant* v *Edwards*,[78] Nourse LJ left the matter open, whilst Mustill LJ expressed the opinion that indirect contributions would not by themselves suffice. More importantly, however, the House of Lords reconsidered the area in *Lloyds Bank plc* v *Rosset*.[79] Lord Bridge, delivering the only speech, concluded[80] that 'it is at least extremely doubtful whether anything less [than direct contributions] will do'. Many lawyers considered that this was too restrictive, especially given that there was little discussion of the relevant cases. Indeed, *Le Foe* v *Le Foe*[81] subsequently recognised a common intention arising from relatively small indirect contributions, and this was supported by the Law Commission Discussion Paper on Sharing Homes.[82]

Although this section is concentrating on the law before *Stack*, it is worth observing that dicta in the House of Lords support the recognition of indirect contributions.[83] It now seems to be assumed that they can be taken into account.[84]

One possible problem lies in establishing what constitutes an indirect contribution. Cases such as *Gissing* and *Burns* indicate that they are contributions to family expenditure without which the legal owner would have been unable to pay the mortgage instalments. They will be difficult to prove if the legal owner pays all the family expenses until the claimant later obtains a job and contributes to family expenditure – usually when children no longer require full-time attention. However, the courts since *Stack* place more stress on pooling expenditure than on enabling the mortgage to be paid,[85] and this may well justify a more generous approach to what counts as an indirect contribution.

---

[77] *Falconer* v *Falconer* [1970] 1 WLR 1333; *Hargrave* v *Newton* [1971] 1 WLR 1611; *Burns* v *Burns* [1984] Ch 317.
[78] [1986] Ch 638.
[79] [1991] 1 AC 107.
[80] Ibid, at p 133.
[81] [2001] 2 FLR 970 (Nicholas Mostyn QC). There had been significant direct contributions later. The more generous approach is welcomed by Pawlowski [2002] Fam Law 190 and Thompson [2002] Conv 273; Mee (2004) 24 LS 414 at pp 431–432 is more cautious.
[82] Law Com No 278, para 4.26.
[83] [2007] 2 AC 432 at [26] (Lord Walker); also Lord Hope at [12] (unless limited to quantification), Baroness Hale at [63]. This is confirmed by *Abbott* v *Abbott* [2008] 1 FLR 1451 at [5] (PC).
[84] *Webster* v *Webster* [2009] 1 FLR 1240 at [33].
[85] *Fowler* v *Barron* [2008] 2 FLR 831 (joint names); *Webster* v *Webster* [2009] 1 FLR 1240.

Other forms of contribution

A very different form of contribution is working in a business owned by the legal owner of the family home. Frequently, the claimant partner is not paid. Where the work would otherwise have required the employment of somebody, it is more than casual help.[86] The cases have taken the approach that this is in effect a business partnership, entitling the claimant to a share in the profits and assets of the business.[87] If the business owner has used these funds to finance the purchase of the family home, some courts have treated this as a joint contribution to the purchase.[88] However, there is some reluctance to take that last step unless a common intention to share beneficial ownership really can be inferred.[89] It may be observed that work in a business is more readily recognised than work within the family home,[90] although the sort of work in the cases goes far beyond casual assistance.[91]

Next, some forms of financial contribution will be disregarded. If the payment can be seen as being a form of rent paid to the legal owner in return for possession, then a common intention will not be inferred from it. This approach is most readily applied where the parties are not spouses or partners.[92] As between spouses and partners living in a long-term relationship, it is generally inappropriate to regard the pooling of expenditure as a form of rent: this is not the way in which the parties view the contribution.[93]

Another form of payment that will not count is a loan. If the contributor intends to be able to get the money back on demand, then the transaction is a loan, and this is inconsistent with having a share in the land purchased.[94] Where the parties are living together, it would not normally be appropriate (without clear evidence) to find that they intended a loan. Other relationships may call for different responses.[95] A loan will, of course, be preferred for ease of return of the money and to guard against reductions in property values.[96]

A third form of payment is where the legal owner is a lessee paying rent and the claimant contributes towards the rent. This will not generally be treated as giving rise to a trust. It is more for current use rather than acquiring an asset.[97] The conclusion is convenient, avoiding complex trust issues arising when people move into (and out of) flat-sharing arrangements.

---

[86] *Hammond* v *Mitchell* [1991] 1 WLR 1127.

[87] *Re Cummins* [1972] Ch 62.

[88] *Nixon* v *Nixon* [1969] 1 WLR 1676; *Muetzel* v *Muetzel* [1970] 1 WLR 188 (where there was also a small financial contribution).

[89] *James* v *Thomas* [2008] 1 FLR 1598.

[90] In *Lloyd* v *Pickering* [2004] EWHC 1513 (Ch) at [48], Blackburne J stressed that such work establishes much of the value of a business, in contrast to the family home.

[91] *Green* v *Green* (2003) 5 ITELR 888 at [22] (PC: 'regular and substantial' work); *Lloyd* v *Pickering* [2004] EWHC 1513 (Ch) at [49]; (2004) 154 NLJ 1014 (joint venture in running a gym).

[92] *Annen* v *Rattee* [1985] 1 EGLR 136 (student sharing flat: payment not 'an exorbitant payment for what could be called a licence fee and household expenses, or a kind of rent . . .').

[93] *Baumgartner* v *Baumgartner* (1987) 76 ALR 75 at p 84. Cf (1982) 98 LQR 517.

[94] *Re Sharpe* [1980] 1 WLR 219, although there was a licence to remain until the loan was repaid. Cf *Dibble* v *Pfluger* [2011] 1 FLR 659.

[95] *Vajpeyi* v *Yusaf* [2004] WTLR 989 (investment property).

[96] The parties may agree that what starts as a loan becomes a share in the property, generously applied in *Risch* v *McFee* (1990) 61 P&CR 42; see also *CPS* v *Piper* [2011] EWHC 3570 (Admin). Contrast the horror greeting a suggestion that a contribution may have become a loan: *Stokes* v *Anderson* [1991] 1 FLR 391.

[97] *Savage* v *Dunningham* [1974] Ch 181. The result may be otherwise if the parties are regarded as entering into the lease together: *Malayan Credit Ltd* v *Jack Chia-MPH Ltd* [1986] AC 549 (PC).

C. The development of common intention prior to *Stack*: express common intentions

So far, we have concentrated on inferring a common intention from the conduct and contributions of the parties. Express or actual (but not written) common intentions first came to the fore in *Grant* v *Edwards*[98] in 1986. At the time of her partner's purchasing a family home, the claimant was in the process of divorcing her husband. The reason for not including her as a party to the conveyance was that this might cause problems in the divorce proceedings. It was not difficult to construe conversations about this as an agreement that she should have an interest in the land, albeit that it would be better for her name not to appear on the deeds. The Court of Appeal treated *Eves* v *Eves*[99] as being decided on the same basis. There, the legal owner had told the claimant that her name could not appear on the title deeds as she was under 21 years old. Again, this indicated an agreement that she should have an interest, but that it could not be on the deeds.

Lloyds Bank plc v *Rosset*[100] recognised these cases as examples of express common intention. In *Rosset*, it was argued that conversations showed that the restoration of the home was undertaken by the parties as a joint venture and that the property should be their home. However, as Lord Bridge observed, such intentions do not specifically relate to ownership and shed no light on the parties' intentions as to ownership.[101] Strictly speaking, this is quite correct, although one might reply that a layperson will not always couch his or her conversation in terms of ownership. Discussions as in *Rosset* need not necessarily indicate that ownership is joint,[102] but it seems harsh to reject them completely.

An obvious problem with express common intentions is that it is difficult to prove discussions many years ago. As Waite LJ has observed, 'the barrenness of the terrain in which judges . . . are required to search for the small evidential nuggets . . .'[103] requires pleading and proof of 'the tenderest exchanges of a common law courtship'.[104] The difficulty faced by the law is obvious. If the parties have reached an agreement, then the courts will wish to give effect to it.[105] Yet, the nature of the relationship is such that proof of the agreement is agonisingly difficult. There is much to be said for the view that it is better to infer intentions from conduct than to strain to find express intentions. The latter approach is too prone to produce hit-and-miss results.

---

[98] [1986] Ch 638; see also *Rowe* v *Prance* [1999] 2 FLR 787 (valuable boat), criticised by Baughen [2000] Conv 58.

[99] [1975] 1 WLR 1338.

[100] [1991] 1 AC 107.

[101] Regarding the house as the family home is insufficient: *Ivin* v *Blake* (1993) 67 P&CR 263 and *Thomson* v *Humphrey* [2010] 2 FLR 107. This was extended to the purchase of property as an investment in *Buggs* v *Buggs* [2004] WTLR 799 (criticised by Thompson [2003] Conv 411): intending practical family benefit from the investment is not the same as intending joint ownership.

[102] They could indicate a right to live in the property: *Ungurian* v *Lesnoff* [1990] Ch 206.

[103] *Midland Bank plc* v *Cooke* [1995] 4 All ER 562 at p 567.

[104] *Hammond* v *Mitchell* [1991] 1 WLR 1127 at p 1139 (Waite J).

[105] This is equally true where the courts operate more broadly based constructive trusts: *Gillies* v *Keogh* [1989] 2 NZLR 327.

Objective intentions and excuses

One objection to the use of the actual intention approach in the leading cases of *Eves* v *Eves* and *Grant* v *Edwards* is that the legal owner did not intend to share ownership. The reason why the claimant's name was not put on the deeds was in each case an excuse, the legal owner having no intention of giving up sole ownership. It is often argued that this is yet another factor showing how fictitious the common intention is.[106] Yet, this objection is not overwhelming. As far back as *Gissing*,[107] Lord Diplock stressed that the common intention is to be tested objectively.[108] If one party leads the other to believe that a common intention exists, then private reservations will not refute the common intention.[109]

A more convincing criticism is that an excuse standing by itself is weak proof of the intention.[110] This was recognised by Lewison LJ in *Curran* v *Collins*,[111] observing that a specious excuse does not necessarily or even usually justify finding a common intention. At first sight, it does appear odd that *Eves* and *Grant* centre upon agreements that the claimant's name should not be on the deeds.[112] What was special about each of those cases is that there was an assurance that there would be joint ownership – just not legal ownership. Suppose the claimant asks whether they are to co-own. It may be suggested that the outcome depends on whether the answer is 'yes, but not legal ownership' (good claim) or 'no, because . . .' (bad claim). In *Curran*, the excuse that it was too expensive was no basis for finding a common intention.

Acting on the common intention

Finding a common intention, whether inferred or express, is not enough. It could give rise to an express trust, but that would fall foul of the need for writing.[113] It is necessary for the claimant to act on the intention in such a way as to render it inequitable for the legal owner to deny the claimant's interest, although there is no principle that the common intention should itself identify the detriment.[114] Equity will then impose a constructive trust. In *Rosset*, Lord Bridge observed that, in each of *Eves* v *Eves* and *Grant* v *Edwards*, the conduct would not have led to any inferred intention but did suffice as detriment.

---

[106] Eekelaar [1987] Conv 93 at p 96; JD Davies (1990) 106 LQR 539.

[107] [1971] AC 886 at p 906.

[108] Identical intentions held by each party, but not communicated, will not suffice: *Springette* v *Defoe* (1992) 65 P&CR 1, Steyn LJ observing at p 8 that 'Our trust law does not allow property rights to be affected by telepathy.' See also *Lightfoot* v *Lightfoot-Brown* [2005] 2 P&CR 377.

[109] This is made very clear by *Vinaver* v *Milton Ashbury Ltd* [2006] WTLR 1675 at [30].

[110] Gardner (1993) 109 LQR 263 at p 265. In *van Laethem* v *Brooker* [2006] 2 FLR 495, Lawrence Collins J recognised the criticisms and preferred an estoppel analysis.

[111] [2016] 1 FLR 505 at [69]–[74]. Arden LJ, delivering the other substantive judgment, more simply declined to interfere with the trial judge's finding of no common intention. In *Mo Ying* v *Brillex Development Ltd* (2015) 17 ITELR 950 at [7.7] (Hong Kong Court of Appeal), a similar point is made that to 'brush off' the claimant does not give rise to a common intention.

[112] See also *Hyett* v *Stanley* [2004] 1 FLR 394, although there was an express statement that the claimant had a right to the property.

[113] *Midland Bank plc* v *Dobson* [1986] 1 FLR 171.

[114] *Parris* v *Williams* [2009] 1 P&CR 169.

What, then, is required? Conduct which is normal within a relationship is unlikely to suffice.[115] *Midland Bank plc v Dobson*[116] held that payments of money for household expenses and redecorating were no more than one would expect from members of a family. In *Lloyds Bank plc v Rosset*, the claimant had spent a lot of time supervising restoration work on the house as well as doing some work herself. Lord Bridge was very dubious whether this would have been sufficient to count as detriment, even if there had been an actual common intention. However, other cases have been less demanding.[117] A rather unusual form of detriment was recognised in *Cox v Jones*.[118] The claimant wanted to purchase a flat above hers, but was finding it difficult to raise money. When her partner agreed to buy as a nominee for her, she took no further steps to find funding. This standing aside was sufficient to count as detriment.

In *Grant v Edwards*,[119] Nourse LJ required 'conduct on which the woman could not reasonably have been expected to embark unless she was to have an interest in the house'. The court regarded it as significant that her conduct (contributing to expenses such that the legal owner could pay mortgage instalments) was referable to the purchase. On the other hand, Sir Nicolas Browne-Wilkinson V-C argued that the law relating to estoppel provides a useful analogy and may justify a more relaxed view as to detriment.[120] This is considered further in the final section of this chapter.

It has been suggested[121] that the requirement of acting on the intention does not survive *Stack*, given that no mention of it is made in the analyses in the House of Lords. The fact that express intentions were not discussed in *Stack* renders the failure to discuss acting on the detriment unsurprising; a distinct change in the law seems unlikely. It was therefore to be expected that Lewison LJ stated in *Curran v Collins*[122] that *Stack* and *Jones* have made no change in this respect.

D. *Stack v Dowden* and *Jones v Kernott*

A prefatory point is that, even before *Stack*, there was some pressure to adopt an approach significantly more flexible than that recognised by *Rosset*. A good example of this is *Midland Bank plc v Cooke*,[123] with its stress on 'general equitable principles' and a fierce attack by Waite LJ on the operation of the present law.

---

[115] Lawson stresses the anomalies that this sort of rule is likely to cause, especially the gender stereotyping involved: (1996) 16 LS 218, especially pp 224–231.

[116] [1986] 1 FLR 171.

[117] See *Cox v Jones* [2004] 2 FLR 1010 (supervising extensive building work) and *Parris v Williams* [2009] 1 P&CR 169 (sufficient if more than trivial). In *Hammond v Mitchell* [1991] 1 WLR 1127, Waite J rather generously found detriment in supporting ventures which, if they failed, would have resulted in the loss of their home, even though the claimant had no prior interest in it.

[118] [2004] 2 FLR 1010, relying on *Banner Homes Group plc v Luff Developments Ltd* [2000] Ch 372. Probert [2005] Conv 168 notes the potential significance of this approach in expanding the forms of recognised detriment.

[119] [1986] Ch 638 at p 648.

[120] See also *Stokes v Anderson* [1991] 1 FLR 391.

[121] Gardner (2008) 124 LQR 422; Etherton [2008] CLJ 265 at p 277 (repeated more cautiously [2009] Conv 104 at pp 109–110). It is fair to add that the imputed intention analysis provided one of the reasons for the suggestion; this is less powerful following the *Jones v Kernott* [2012] 1 AC 776 analysis that imputed intentions operate only at the quantification stage (p 189 above).

[122] [2016] 1 FLR 505 at [78]. At least five earlier Court of Appeal decisions had assumed that that detrimental reliance remains essential.

[123] [1995] 4 All ER 562; Wylie [1995] Fam Law 633.

Stack v *Dowden*[124] is important as the first House of Lords decision on the family home for over 15 years. It is clear that the House of Lords is aware of the practical issues regarding the importance of the family home and the way cohabitants look at property issues. Further, the artificiality of much of the previous law is well understood. The question to be considered is the extent to which it introduces radical changes in inferring common intentions.

One clear point is that there is no break with the *Gissing* common intention test: this is clearly at the core of the approaches of all the judges in *Stack*. Many argue that this is an inadequate basis for development of a rational legal structure for ownership of family homes,[125] but the rejection in *Jones* v *Kernott* of imputed intentions at Stage 1 indicates that such a change is not yet on the judicial agenda.

As will be seen, the Court of Appeal in *Oxley* v *Hiscock*[126] introduced flexibility into the quantification of shares. This was explained in *Stack* as being based upon common intention. Baroness Hale in *Stack* counsels against a purely arithmetical approach in finding a common intention. The courts are to take a 'holistic' approach, taking account of the whole course of dealing between the parties and their conduct which illuminates their intentions. It might be added that *Jones* v *Kernott* says less about the factors to be taken into account, although it is apparent that the courts are to look at all available evidence. Indeed, Lady Hale stressed that the factors she mentioned in *Stack* are not exhaustive.

It may be helpful to quote some of her relevant dicta in *Stack*[127]:

> In law, 'context is everything' and the domestic context is very different from the commercial world. Each case will turn on its own facts. Many more factors than financial contributions may be relevant to divining the parties' true intentions. These include: any advice or discussions at the time of the transfer which cast light upon their intentions then . . . ; the nature of the parties' relationship; whether they had children for whom they both had responsibility to provide a home; how the purchase was financed, both initially and subsequently; how the parties arranged their finances, whether separately or together or a bit of both; how they discharged the outgoings on the property and their other household expenses. When a couple are joint owners of the home and jointly liable for the mortgage, the inferences to be drawn from who pays for what may be very different from the inferences to be drawn when only one is owner of the home. The arithmetical calculation of how much was paid by each is also likely to be less important. . . . The parties' individual characters and personalities may also be a factor in deciding where their true intentions lay. In the cohabitation context, mercenary considerations may be more to the fore than they would be in marriage, but it should not be assumed that they always take pride of place over natural love and affection.

How far do these dicta apply to Stage 1 in single name cases, given that they relate more to quantification of shares in a joint names transfer?[128] The fact that they are directed towards inferring a common intention indicates that they should apply at any stage

---

[124] [2007] 2 AC 432, especially at [26] and [63] for comments on *Rosset*.
[125] Gardner (2008) 124 LQR 422; Etherton [2008] CLJ 265.
[126] [2005] Fam 211.
[127] [2007] 2 AC 432 at [69].
[128] Following *Jones* v *Kernott* [2012] 1 AC 776, we can see that *Stack* involved Stage 1 in a joint names transfer. The operation of the two stages in joint names transfers was not fully appreciated at the time of *Stack*.

of the investigation into common intention – including Stage 1 in single name transfers. It therefore comes as no surprise that the dicta are routinely referred to in the single name cases.[129]

Nevertheless, Baroness Hale recognised that the inferences to be drawn in single name cases may be different from those in joint names cases. In joint names cases, we have seen that the starting point is equality of shares. The factors the court considers often have the effect of confirming that starting point – against any inference that might be drawn from differing financial contributions. In single name transfers, our starting point is very different – the claimant has no share. Here, more has to be shown before the claimant has a share, let alone a half share.

E. The application of *Stack* and *Jones*

It would be idle to suppose that *Stack* makes no difference. Even though stress is placed upon the significance of the legal title establishing the outcome, Baroness Hale recognises the argument that *Rosset* 'set [the] hurdle rather too high'. This proposition was repeated rather more forcefully in *Abbott* v *Abbott*.[130] Lord Walker also criticises the strictness of the old *Rosset* requirements, most specifically as regards indirect financial contributions. But does this mean that *Rosset* is simply relaxed or, as many argue,[131] should be completely forgotten? This question is not directly addressed by any of the subsequent cases, whether before or after *Jones* v *Kernott*.

Under the old *Rosset* approach, there were two routes to proving a common intention. Either the claimant could point to conversations which indicated that he or she should have a share, or else a common intention could be inferred from certain conduct. Inferred intention seems to have worked very much like a limited form of imputed intention: the courts would infer an intention from specified contributions without further ado.[132] It appears that these routes to finding a common intention still apply. There is no reason not to recognise express common intentions where they exist – even if a broader approach resulting from *Stack* means that they may be less frequently called upon.

The cases following *Stack* seem to fall into two categories.[133] In the first, cases cite the dicta of Baroness Hale in *Stack* and ask whether a common intention can be found.[134]

---

[129] *Abbott* v *Abbott* [2008] 1 FLR 1451 (Gardner (2008) 124 LQR 422; Lee (2008) 124 LQR 209; Pawlowski (2010) 247 PLJ 22); Etherton J in *Bindra* v *Chopra* [2008] 3 FCR 341 at [86] (the issue was not raised on appeal [2009] 2 FLR 786); *Geary* v *Rankine* [2012] 2 FLR 1409 at [19]; *CPS* v *Piper* [2011] EWHC 3570 (Admin) at [7]; *Barnes* v *Phillips* [2016] HLR 24; see also *Q* v *Q* [2009] 1 FLR 935 at [114] and *De Bruyne* v *De Bruyne* [2010] 2 FLR 1240 at [42].

[130] [2008] 1 FLR 1451 (PC); see Dixon [2007] Conv 456 and Lee (2008) 124 LQR 209. Note the prominence of a broad approach to common intention in *Fowler* v *Barron* [2008] 2 FLR 831 (joint names transfer).

[131] See, for example, Gardner (2008) 124 LQR 422, Dixon [2012] Conv 83, Lees [2012] Conv 412, Newnham [2013] Fam L 718; contra Roche [2011] Conv 123, Yip [2012] Conv 159.

[132] This is not so surprising when Lady Hale and Lord Walker characterise the resulting trust as an example of imputed intention: *Jones* v *Kernott* [2012] 1 AC 776 at [29].

[133] Sloan (2015) 35 LS 226 undertakes an extensive survey of the cases, concluding that *Stack* and *Jones* have had very limited effects on the *Rosset* requirements and, in particular, the outcome of cases.

[134] See the cases in n 129 above. *Re Ali* [2013] 1 FLR 1061 at [142] appears to stand alone in explicitly holding that the holistic survey does not apply at Stage 1.

However, it is difficult to find cases in which a common intention has been found in circumstances falling outside the *Rosset* principles plus indirect financial contributions. In the second category, other cases take an approach that seems to replicate *Rosset*.[135] A possible explanation for this is that the factors identified by Baroness Hale are so broad that judges sometimes feel at a loss in deciding what to make of them. Indeed, some cases have continued to apply *Rosset* (albeit modified by *Stack*).[136] Perhaps most striking is *Thomson* v *Humphrey*,[137] citing with approval *Burns* v *Burns*[138] on the insufficiency of non-financial contributions.

How do we make sense of this bewildering variety of positions? One observation is that there will be few relationships in which the claimant has made no financial contribution to family expenditure.[139] On the assumptions that indirect financial contributions are recognised after *Le Foe* and *Stack* and that a broad view will be taken as to what counts as a financial contribution,[140] there will be few cases in which a revised *Rosset* test will not provide a basis for finding a common intention.

However, this fails to do justice to the straightforward reliance on *Stack* in many of the recent cases. It has been seen that the inferring of common intention in financial contribution cases is a pretty automatic exercise. It may remain the case that non-financial contributions will not have this effect. The continuing importance of financial contributions in inferring common intentions is seen in *Dibble* v *Pfluger*,[141] in which the Court of Appeal expressed surprise that the judge had not found a common intention as a result of significant contributions. However, it does appear that courts are more directly asking the question as to what the parties intended – without requiring express discussions as ownership (the old express intention category).[142] This seems faithful to the common intention as articulated in *Gissing* and developed by *Stack*. The twofold division in *Rosset* between inferences from conduct (fairly automatic) and express intentions can now be seen as unduly restrictive. The analysis here proposed leaves some role for *Rosset*, whilst enabling the courts to find a common intention in appropriate cases.

At this point, it is worth reverting to the analysis of inferred and imputed intention in *Jones* v *Kernott*.[143] It was seen that Lady Hale, Lord Walker and Lord Collins see inferred intention as being so wide that it is similar to imputing intentions on grounds of fairness.

---

[135] Examples are to be found in *Tackaberry* v *Hollis* [2008] WTLR 279; *Morris* v *Morris* [2008] EWCA Civ 257; *James* v *Thomas* [2008] 1 FLR 1598 (Ralton [2008] Fam Law 424; Probert [2009] CLP 316 at pp 332–336); *Thomson* v *Humphrey* [2010] 2 FLR 107; *Re Ali* [2013] 1 FLR 1061. Indeed, Piska, *Modern Studies in Property Law*, Vol 5 (ed Dixon), Chapter 9, argues that they may be more restrictive than the pre-*Stack* law, although this seems improbable.

[136] *Webster* v *Webster* [2009] 1 FLR 1240; *Thomson* v *Humphrey* [2010] 2 FLR 107; *Re Ali* [2013] 1 FLR 1061.

[137] [2010] 2 FLR 107; the facts were less compelling than those in *Burns*. See also *Mo Ying* v *Brillex Development Ltd* (2015) 17 ITELR 950 at [7.22] (Hong Kong Court of Appeal)

[138] [1984] Ch 317; p 194 above. Gardner [2013] CLJ 301 argues that a common intention probably would be found today in a case like *Burns*.

[139] Probert [2000] Fam Law 925.

[140] See p 195 above.

[141] [2011] 1 FLR 659. See also *Amin* v *Amin* [2009] EWHC 3356 (Ch) at [274].

[142] For examples, see *CPS* v *Piper* [2011] EWHC 3570 (Admin) and also the unsuccessful claim in *Cattle* v *Evans* [2011] WTLR 947. *Ullah* v *Ullah* [2013] BPIR 928 might indicate a stricter approach, although it did not involve a family home.

[143] [2012] 1 AC 776, p 189 above.

The narrower approach of Lords Kerr and Wilson would allow for inferred intention in far fewer cases. This highlights the problem that looking at the totality of the relationship may prove little about what the parties actually intended. This is scarcely surprising as regards the many couples who never think about ownership of the home. The danger with the approach of the majority is that cases may be decided on the views of the judge deciding the case, with lack of predictability and consistency between judges.[144]

Although the relationship may by itself be an inconclusive factor, specific developments relating to the property may be more compelling. Thus, in *Barnes v Phillips*,[145] the fact that one of the parties extracted a quarter of the value of the property for his own purposes (at a stage close to relationship breakdown) was sufficient to infer an intention that the shares should be varied. This is in a joint names setting, but remains a useful example of inference in operation.

7. Quantification of shares

Now that we have the authoritative decision of the Supreme Court in *Jones v Kernott*, the earlier material deserves no more than a brief summary. A general observation is that earlier cases reveal debate between resulting trust ideas (shares depending on contributions) and constructive trust ideas (greater discretion, with stress on the nature of the relationship). As has been seen, the constructive trust has prevailed.

Midland Bank plc v Cooke[146] is worth mentioning as an earlier case adopting a broad fair proportion approach. The Court of Appeal explicitly accepted that factors falling outside the *Rosset* requirements could be considered in assessing shares: 'the duty of the judge is to undertake a survey of the whole course of dealing between the parties relevant to their ownership and occupation of the property and their sharing of its burdens and advantages'.[147] This is particularly important because it allowed factors other than financial contributions (direct or indirect) to be brought into play.[148]

In *Cooke*, the parties had been married for 24 years (seven at the date of the relevant mortgage) and shared everything in life equally[149]: all pointed to a presumed intention to share ownership equally, although there was no evidence of conversations which could justify an express common intention. Whilst some flexibility in assessing shares is highly desirable, the result in *Cooke* was startling at a time when Stage 1 was dominated by financial contributions. The financial contribution was under 7%, yet the court felt free to find a 50% share.

---

[144] Cf Garland [2012] JSWFL 479.
[145] [2016] HLR 24 (Hayward [2016] Conv 233); this was coupled with non-payment of mortgage instalments for five years afterwards. The facts bear a distinct resemblance to those in *Jones v Kernott*.
[146] [1995] 4 All ER 562 (Dixon [1997] Conv 66; Gardner (1996) 112 LQR 378; O'Hagan (1997) 60 MLR 420); followed in *Le Foe v Le Foe* [2001] 2 FLR 970.
[147] *Midland Bank plc v Cooke* [1995] 4 All ER 562 at p 574.
[148] Supported by *Grant v Edwards* [1986] Ch 638 at pp 657–658; *Stokes v Anderson* [1991] 1 FLR 391 and *Hammond v Mitchell* [1991] 1 WLR 1127.
[149] It was distinguished in *Trowbridge v Trowbridge* [2003] 2 FLR 231, where the couple kept their finances separate.

Drake v *Whipp*,[150] decided soon afterwards, provides something of a contrast. The claimant provided 19% of the overall cost of purchase and conversion of a barn and undertook a 30% share of the labour involved in the conversion. Given these factors, that they had a joint bank account, that the claimant contributed to family expenses and that it was intended to be their home, the Court of Appeal awarded the claimant a one-third share. The court avowedly took a 'broad brush' approach, but its conclusion looks more justifiable in the light of the 1990s authorities than that in *Cooke*.

It was against this background that *Oxley* v *Hiscock*[151] was decided. This influential Court of Appeal decision rejected any need for the common intention to establish the size of the shares. In actual common intention cases, the courts have awarded shares (for example, the quarter share in *Eves* v *Eves*)[152] which cannot be explained on the basis of any common intention that the parties might be supposed to have possessed. The test of fairness, as articulated in several earlier cases, was therefore adopted[153]: 'that share which the court considers fair having regard to the whole course of dealing between them in relation to the property'.[154] The test was justified by a comparison with estoppel; this comparison is discussed in the final section of this chapter.

However, Baroness Hale in *Stack* v *Dowden*[155] criticised the fairness test. It is not the role of the court to invent a fair outcome (such an approach is redolent of the pre-*Pettitt* law), but rather the courts should establish the intention of the parties. On the other hand, she fully approved the approach to resolving the case: having regard to 'the arrangements which they make from time to time in order to meet the outgoings (for example, mortgage contributions, council tax and utilities, repairs, insurance and housekeeping) which have to be met if they are to live in the property as their home'.[156] Yet, it is remarkable that the test is applied in *Oxley* to produce, arguably, the identical result (a 40% share for the claimant) as would have been reached had a resulting trust approach been utilised, taking a generous interpretation of contributions! *Oxley* is not a case where, because the parties pool their expenditure, equal shares result.[157]

What was really significant on the facts in *Oxley* is that both parties contributed capital towards the purchase of the house, as well as taking a mortgage loan for a quarter of the cost. These capital contributions were very material to the outcome. This is different from a young couple purchasing their first home. If it can be shown that the young couple pool their resources, then (regardless of whoever actually pays the mortgage) the courts are likely to give them equal shares.

---

[150] [1996] 1 FLR 826; Dunn [1997] Conv 467. See also *Mollo* v *Mollo* [1999] EGCS 117, [2000] WTLR 227.
[151] [2005] Fam 211 (Chadwick LJ delivered the only judgment); Gardner (2004) 120 LQR 541; Thompson [2004] Conv 496.
[152] [1975] 1 WLR 1338. A quarter share was also awarded, applying *Oxley*, in *Cox* v *Jones* [2004] 2 FLR 1010 (overseeing building work).
[153] [2005] Fam 211 at [69], echoing words used in previous cases.
[154] The analysis was limited to cases where 'the property is bought as a home for a couple who, although not married, intend to live together as man and wife': [68]. However, it was extended in *Ledger-Beadell* v *Peach* [2007] 2 FLR 210 to quantifying the share of parents who contributed to their son's home with the defendant.
[155] [2007] 2 AC 432 at [61]; see also Lord Neuberger at [144].
[156] [2005] Fam 211 at [69] (approved in *Stack* at [36] and [61]).
[157] Gardner (2004) 120 LQR 541 at pp 544–545 suggests that *Oxley* stresses financial aspects more than earlier cases such as *Cooke* and *Drake*, but this may be to read *Oxley* too narrowly.

That approach is also illustrated by the Privy Council decision in *Abbott* v *Abbott*.[158] The purchase was funded by a gift and mortgage payments from a joint bank account into which the claimant's earnings were paid. The claimant was awarded a half share. This effect of pooling of resources may be seen as something of an advance on financial contributions. Further, Baroness Hale in *Stack* counsels against a purely arithmetical approach. The courts are to take a 'holistic' approach, taking account of the whole course of dealing between the parties and their conduct which illuminates their intentions.

The scene was set for the review of quantification by the Supreme Court in *Jones* v *Kernott*,[159] which has been previewed in discussing inferred and imputed intentions. Although an actual or inferred intention will be given effect to, it was recognised that it will sometimes be impossible to infer any intention as to shares. This is quite likely unless it is intended either that the shares should be equal or that they should represent financial contributions. In such a case, shares can be imputed.

Not a lot is said about how imputing intentions is to work. Lady Hale and Lord Walker state that it accords with what Chadwick LJ had said about fair shares in *Oxley*, even though the court should take into account the range of factors identified in *Stack*. This may reduce the stress on financial considerations in *Oxley*. One suggestion[160] is that *Jones* v *Kernott*, in finding 90%/10% shares, was seeking to replicate the outcome where parties are married and the statutory discretion applies. This idea has some merit, but it courts considerable political controversy[161] and is certainly not what Lady Hale and Lord Walker professed to be doing.

We have already observed that, in *Jones*, the justices differed as to whether it was possible to infer intentions as to quantification on the facts of the case. Of interest also is Lord Kerr's analysis that imputed intentions have nothing to do with intention. He much prefers the direct approach of Chadwick LJ to apply directly a test based upon fairness. There is a lot to be said for this view, although Lord Kerr recognised that imputed intentions are too firmly entrenched in legal terminology to be excised at this stage.

Before looking at subsequent cases, two comments will be made. The first is a reminder that these principles apply both to single name and joint names transfers. *Oxley* was a single name case, whereas both *Stack* and *Jones* v *Kernott* involved joint names transfers. *Jones* is explicit that its dicta on inferred and imputed intention also apply to single name transfers.[162] On the other hand, there is no starting point or presumption of equal shares in single names cases,[163] as already seen in *Oxley*. The second is that, as between parents and

---

158 [2008] 1 FLR 1451. It was also material that the claimant was liable on the mortgage loan.
159 [2012] 1 AC 776, p 189 above.
160 Gardner and Davidson (2012) 128 LQR 178. The approach in *Graham-York* v *York* [2016] 1 FLR 407 (p 206 below) appears inconsistent with their argument.
161 It goes far beyond what Law Com 307 was prepared to recommend, and even their weaker proposals have been sidelined for the time being.
162 Ibid, at [52]; applied in *Aspden* v *Elvy* [2012] 2 FLR 807 at [127]. Little was said in *Aspden* as to how the 25% share was justified.
163 *Graham-York* v *York* [2016] 1 FLR 407 at [25] (25% awarded). Although the relationship spanned four decades, it was dysfunctional: 'not much natural love and affection'. As observed by Greer and Pawlowski [2015] Conv 512, both *Oxley* and *Graham-York* lean towards an emphasis on financial contributions.

children (perhaps other family relationships), it may be appropriate to find a common intention that one is to have a life interest, rather than a share in fee simple.[164] It would be exceptional for this to be the outcome for couples.

Two cases after *Jones* demonstrate contrasting outcomes in assessing shares. *Thompson* v *Hurst*[165] is a case in which the couple intended to put title in their joint names. Because of the man's bad employment record, they were advised that the best way of obtaining a mortgage was to put the property in the woman's name alone, which they did. She in fact was the principal breadwinner for the family, even though the man contributed (when in work) to housekeeping and council tax. Etherton LJ upheld an award to the man of 10%. This looks to be a distinctly financially driven outcome, given a 20-year relationship in which the man had contributed when able to do so. The court rejected an argument based upon an intention of joint legal ownership, in which case *Stack* would have given him 50%. Whilst 50% might well have been overly generous given that they kept their finances separate, 10% has the appearance of a nominal award.

CPS v *Piper*[166] involved a more sharing relationship, although the relevant events took place early in it. Holman J had little hesitation in awarding the wife a 50% share, based upon an inferred intention. The outcome in these two cases is plainly very different. This may be explained by the extent to which finances were shared in each relationship: an important factor in *Stack*. However, this may not be a safe ground upon which to rest such radically different outcomes – especially as separating finances is by no means uncommon.[167]

A question of some importance is the extent to which the factors to be taken into account must relate to the property. This surfaced in *Barnes* v *Phillips*[168] in the context of the role taken in supporting (or not supporting) children. This factor was listed as one of those relevant by Lady Hale in *Stack*. *Barnes* holds that it is important not only for inferring intentions but also for determining the quantification of shares under an imputed intention. On the other hand, a distinctly narrower approach had been adopted eight months earlier by a differently constituted Court of Appeal in *Graham-York* v *York*.[169] The court expressly rejected any jurisdiction to exercise 'redistributive justice' and relied upon the statement in *Oxley* that what is relevant is the whole course of dealing 'in relation to the property' (dicta quoted in *Stack* and *Jones*). To reconcile these dicta, we might say the position of children is special, as being based on the dicta of Lady Hale. Alternatively (perhaps preferably), we could say that the parties' conduct in relation to the children must be related in some way to the property – most obviously that a parent caring for children is less able to contribute financially.

---

[164] *Amin* v *Amin* [2009] EWHC 3356 (Ch) at [276]. Where shares are appropriate, *Sandhu* v *Sandhu* [2016] EWCA Civ 1050 illustrates the significance of financial contributions (father and son).
[165] [2014] 1 FLR 238.
[166] [2011] EWHC 3570 (Admin).
[167] See p 191 above.
[168] [2016] HLR 24.
[169] [2016] 1 FLR 407 at [22]; Gardner (2016) 132 LQR 373.

8. Common intention after purchase: improvements

The archetypal case for a common intention constructive trust is where a couple buy a house, often towards the beginning of a relationship. If it is put into the name of just one of them, there will often be evidence from which an intention can be inferred that they should both be beneficial owners. However, there is no rule that the common intention must exist at the time of purchase: several leading cases have recognised that a subsequent intention will be effective.[170] This common intention may either give the claimant a share for the first time or vary the shares which had originally been held. The latter is, of course, the outcome in *Jones* v *Kernott*. It has been seen[171] that it is unclear how far shares established by an express declaration of trust can be varied in this way.

There have been suggestions that subsequent common intentions are more difficult to prove.[172] Somewhat surprisingly, this reluctance to find a common intention has operated even if there is payment of mortgage instalments.[173] It may be hoped that the liberalisation seen in *Stack* and *Jones* will spill over into this context.

A rather different way of changing the shares is illustrated by *Gallarotti* v *Sebastianelli*.[174] Two friends purchased a house to share, paying around 60% from savings. S paid a lot more than G, but G was expected to pay more towards the mortgage. Although the property was put in S's name, they agreed to own it equally. In fact, S paid nearly all the mortgage instalments in the period until their friendship terminated. Although there was a clear common intention for equal shares, the Court of Appeal held that this was on the basis that they would contribute comparable sums overall. Once that expectation was falsified, the court should give effect to an intention that their shares should reflect their contributions. This stress on financial contributions is probably explained by the fact that they were friends rather than a couple. However, the idea of the initial intention being frustrated might have a role in quite different circumstances. Could it be argued that when a couple agree to equal shares, this is on the basis that their relationship will survive for a considerable period? This might mean that different shares are appropriate if they break up after a relatively short time. Acts of apparent generosity between couples may well be explained on this basis, although there is little in the cases to support such an analysis.[175]

An increasingly common scenario is that one of the parties owns the future family home at the time the marriage or relationship commences. What happens if the parties thereafter pool their resources in order to pay the mortgage instalments? Although the early decision

---

[170] *Gissing* v *Gissing* [1971] AC 886 (Lord Diplock at p 906); *Austin* v *Keele* (1987) 61 ALJR 605 (PC). More recently, see *Mirza* v *Mirza* [2009] 2 FLR 115 at [122].

[171] See p 185 above.

[172] *Austin* v *Keele* (1987) 61 ALJR 605 (PC); Griffiths LJ in *Bernard* v *Josephs* [1982] Ch 391, especially at p 404; *James* v *Thomas* [2008] 1 FLR 1598 at [24]; *Williams* v *Lawrence* [2012] WTLR 1455.

[173] In *McKenzie* v *McKenzie* [2003] EWHC 601 (Ch); [2003] 2 P&CR D15, the court asked whether mortgage contributions showed an intention to share the property at the time of purchase; see also *Buggs* v *Buggs* [2004] WTLR 799.

[174] [2012] 2 FLR 1231; no cases were cited.

[175] It replicates the thinking in Law Com No 307 (see p 214 below); *Quaintance* v *Tandan* [2014] WTLR 1609. Similar ideas have been articulated in the estoppel context: p 168, n 163 above.

in *Kowalczuk* v *Kowalczuk*[176] showed reluctance to recognise any beneficial interest in these circumstances, more recent cases demonstrate greater flexibility.[177] It might be added that there are less likely to be discussions justifying an express common intention in such cases – such discussions are far more likely to occur when a property is bought. A conversation along the lines of 'I will agree to move in with you, but only if I have a half share in your house' seems distinctly improbable.

Quantification of shares is likely to be particularly difficult in these cases. As *Abbott* v *Abbott*[178] shows, it is easy to conclude that equal shares are intended where the parties pool expenditure, especially through a joint bank account. This fits what Gardner has described as a materially communal relationship, in which it is appropriate that the parties have equal shares.[179] Even if this analysis is accurate (we have seen that courts do not routinely award equal shares in single name cases), it does not seem appropriate when the property is owned outright by one of the couple before the relationship commences. In such cases, it seems preferable to limit the equal sharing to the proportion of the value of the house that is attributable to the period of the relationship.

Improvements

Improvements to the home may also be difficult to link with a common intention. Not that this is impossible: it may be argued that time and, especially, money would not have been spent unless there had been an agreement for a beneficial interest. But in many cases the parties are likely to base their actions on the fact that they are improving the family home, as opposed to a jointly owned home. *Pettitt* v *Pettitt*[180] is a leading authority. This makes it clear that improving property by itself is not enough; there must be a common intention that the improver should gain a beneficial interest. The claim in *Pettitt* was remarkably weak: the husband had done no more than minor jobs in the home which any spouse or partner would undertake.[181] The failure of the claim in *Pettitt* gives little guidance as to when a common intention will be inferred. The future battleground may centre on cases such as *Jansen* v *Jansen*,[182] in which a partner who worked full time on converting the premises into flats succeeded. The four judges in *Pettitt* who dealt with *Jansen* were equally divided as to whether it was correctly decided.[183]

Subsequent cases have indicated a fairly strict approach. In many, however, the improvement is just one of a number of factors relied upon by the claimant – this fits well

---

[176] [1973] 1 WLR 930. The court would have inferred a common intention if the parties had been married at the time of the acquisition.
[177] *Webster* v *Webster* [2009] 1 FLR 1240. See also *James* v *Thomas* [2008] 1 FLR 1598 at [27], although indicating that the court will still be slow to infer intentions from conduct.
[178] [2008] 1 FLR 1451, p 205 above.
[179] (2008) 124 LQR 422, developing earlier views (1993) 109 LQR 263 and (2004) 120 LQR 541 at pp 547–548; cf the doubts of Bottomley in *Land Law: Themes and Perspectives* (eds Bright and Dewar), Chapter 8.
[180] [1970] AC 777. See, generally, Pawlowski [2009] Fam Law 680.
[181] The facts in *Lloyds Bank plc* v *Rosset* [1991] 1 AC 107 were viewed in the same way; cf also *Walsh* v *Singh* [2010] 1 FLR 1658. *Williams* v *Lawrence* [2012] WTLR 1455 seems best explained on this basis.
[182] [1965] P 478. The weaker case of *Appleton* v *Appleton* [1965] 1 WLR 25 was overruled in *Pettitt*. Lord Denning MR considered that his decision in *Jansen* survived: *Davis* v *Vale* [1971] 1 WLR 1022.
[183] Correct: Lords Reid and Diplock. Incorrect: Lords Hodson and Upjohn.

with the *Stack* adoption of broader considerations when inferring common intentions. It is likely[184] to be taken into account in deciding what share the claimant is to have, even if the improvement by itself would not lead to the inference of a common intention.[185] Where the work is substantial, then it may be possible to persuade the court to find a common intention from the improvements alone.[186] The threshold for this will be high: the work must be of the type that a contractor would normally be brought in to undertake.[187] Even quite heavy work renovating run-down property has been said to fall far short of what is required.[188] Although there is not much authority on the point, it is more likely that a common intention will be inferred from a substantial financial contribution to improvements.[189] However, where the parties have earlier agreed to have equal shares (perhaps by express declaration of trust or transfer into joint names), it would seem that more would be required before a common intention could properly be inferred to vary those shares – the parties have shown that they are more interested in sharing than in rewarding financial contributions.

Statutory intervention

In one context, statute has intervened. Within marriage or civil partnership, substantial improvements give a share (or enlarged share) in the home.[190] This response to *Pettitt* will normally be eclipsed by the statutory discretion to adjust rights on divorce.[191] Whilst it may be generally welcomed, it can produce some very odd results. If a wife purchases land out of her own money and has the legal title placed in the names of her husband and herself beneficially, it means that any subsequent improvement by the husband will give him a share in excess of half.[192] Although the statutory alteration of property rights is subject to a contrary intention, an initial intention to purchase on an equal basis may not suffice as a contrary intention. What is a 'substantial' contribution? The statute provides that it may be in money or money's worth; this includes doing the work oneself.[193] In one case, the expenditure of what looked like 5% of the value of the house was rejected,[194] although expenditure of half that percentage was accepted by Pennycuick V-C in a later case.[195] He held that a series of improvements can be linked together to find a substantial improvement.

[184] *Smith v Baker* [1970] 1 WLR 1160; *Cooke v Head* [1972] 1 WLR 518; *Passee v Passee* [1988] 1 FLR 263; *Drake v Whipp* [1996] 1 FLR 826; *Oxley v Hiscock* [2005] Fam 211.
[185] *Grant v Edwards* [1986] Ch 638 (Mustill LJ); *Thomas v Fuller-Brown* [1988] 1 FLR 237 (despite the improvement's being substantial).
[186] *Stack v Dowden* [2007] 2 AC 432 at [34] (Lord Walker), [70] (Baroness Hale), [139] (Lord Neuberger).
[187] *Button v Button* [1968] 1 WLR 457; *Windeler v Whitehall* [1990] 2 FLR 505.
[188] *Lloyds Bank plc v Rosset* [1991] 1 AC 107, commenting on *Eves v Eves* [1975] 1 WLR 1338.
[189] *Hussey v Palmer* [1972] 1 WLR 1286; *Aspden v Elvy* [2012] 2 FLR 807 (after separation). However, some recent cases have been less generous: *Williams v Lawrence* [2012] WTLR 1455, *Re Ali* [2013] 1 FLR 1061 at [100].
[190] Matrimonial Proceedings and Property Act 1970, s 37.
[191] *Griffiths v Griffiths* [1974] 1 WLR 1350.
[192] *Re Nicholson* [1974] 1 WLR 476, where the original equal shares were based upon a common intention. It may also sever an existing joint tenancy.
[193] *Davis v Vale* [1971] 1 WLR 1022.
[194] *Harnett v Harnett* [1973] Fam 156.
[195] *Re Nicholson* [1974] 1 WLR 476.

9. Accounting

Discovering the existence and size of shares is not always the only issue. An initial point is that the shares are valued at the date of litigation. The suggestion that the claimant's share should be valued at the time of separation has been rejected.[196] There is no justification for refusing claimants a share in the post-separation increase in value in what is, after all, their property.

Accounting is the basis upon which benefits or expenditure may be taken into account, without altering the underlying shares of the parties. Thus one person may be credited with expenditure on the property or debited with the value of sole occupation.[197] In the context of the family home, accounting is likely to apply only after the relationship has broken down and one of the couple has left the home.

(i) The *Stack* v *Dowden* approach

It is common for one of the parties to move out when their relationship breaks down. The other will stay in the house, often paying all the mortgage instalments. It may take several years before litigation sorts out the ownership issues. At that stage, the occupier may claim to have been paying all the mortgage instalments, whilst the other will assert that they have had no enjoyment of their valuable share for that period.

As will be explained below,[198] *Stack* v *Dowden* held that claims for rent should today be considered under the trusts of land legislation. The relevant statutory criteria include the intention of the purchase and the needs of children. These criteria are rather different than those employed in earlier cases (discussed immediately below), although it seems probable that the broad approaches will remain much the same.

The pre-*Stack* approach was to say that, in principle, the payer is entitled to credit for the instalments but then must also account for having sole use of the house.[199] The court would usually treat these two calculations as cancelling each other out.[200]

The courts adopted two further principles. The first is that the payer is still entitled to credit for the capital element of the instalments. In most cases, this will be small. Next, more precise accounting may be employed on bankruptcy of one of the parties.[201] This would also seem appropriate if mortgage instalments are small (or if there is no mortgage).

---

[196] *Turton* v *Turton* [1988] Ch 542. The court was particularly critical of any suggestion that the trust ended on separation. This was, however, the practical result (although not the analysis) in *Jones* v *Kernott* [2012] 1 AC 776.

[197] Where they have equal shares, the net benefit or charge will be half the expenditure or benefit – the other half is attributable to their beneficial interest.

[198] See p 333 below.

[199] *Re Byford* [2004] 1 P&CR 159, especially [31], [41]; Conway [2003] Conv 533. There is unlikely to be liability to account if there is an understanding that the occupier can live there with the parties' children: *Wright* v *Johnson* [2002] 2 P&CR 210, especially at [32]–[33].

[200] *Suttill* v *Graham* [1977] 1 WLR 819 (unless the non-occupier pays the instalments: *Young* v *Lauretani* [2007] 2 FLR 1211). The occupying payer will have a right to credit if the other party has broken an undertaking (on separation) to pay the mortgage instalments: *Re Gorman* [1990] 1 WLR 616.

[201] *Re Pavlou* [1993] 1 WLR 1046.

(ii) *Initial capital contributions*

Accounting has also been used to take account of initial capital contributions. Normally, these will be reflected (if at all) in the size of the parties' shares. However, occasionally cases have allowed such contributions to be offset against the half (or other) share.[202] Generally, the courts have come to this result without discussion and it seems inappropriate save in exceptional circumstances. It certainly seems inapplicable if the conveyance declares the beneficial interests.[203]

However, there will be circumstances when such accounting can be justified. An illustration is provided by the Australian case of *Muschinski* v *Dodds*.[204] Two people living together agreed to buy a plot and erect a house and crafts centre upon it. Muschinski provided $20,000 for the purchase of the plot, the idea being that Dodds's contribution would be the building. The plot was conveyed to them as tenants in common. In fact, they separated before building was commenced. All the members of the High Court agreed that the property was owned in equal shares, but subject to Muschinski's right to the return of the $20,000. It seems entirely proper that Muschinski's contribution should not be overlooked. In England, the Court of Appeal has been willing to adjust shares when one party has failed to carry out his or her part of an arrangement.[205] This is not quite the same as accounting, although dealing with the same problem.

(iii) *Improvements*

Accounting can also be important as regards improvements. It has sometimes been held that an improvement that does not give a share in the property can give rise to a credit in accounting. The difference between giving a share and accounting is that in accounting, no profit will be made from inflation in house prices. An example of accounting for improvements is *Bernard* v *Josephs*,[206] in which credit was given for £2,000 spent on repairs. It is interesting that in the early case of *Jansen* v *Jansen*[207] Russell LJ refused to agree with Lord Denning MR and Davies LJ that the improver had a share in the property, but reached the same result by saying that he should get £1,000 for his work.

Wilcox v *Tait*[208] held that, in cohabitation cases, such accounting is available only as regards expenditure after separation. This makes particular sense in the context of an earlier agreement to have equal beneficial interests, as it is unlikely that the parties intended this to be affected by the expenditure. However, there is no absolute rule, and *Wilcox* recognises an exception if the other party has failed to comply with the basis on which the property was acquired.

[202] *Hine* v *Hine* [1962] 1 WLR 1124; *Bernard* v *Josephs* [1982] Ch 391.
[203] It would be inconsistent with *Goodman* v *Gallant* [1986] Fam 106.
[204] (1984) 62 ALR 429; see also *Young* v *Lauretani* [2007] 2 FLR 1211.
[205] *Bothe* v *Amos* [1976] Fam 46. See also *Gallarotti* v *Sebastianelli* [2012] 2 FLR 1231 (p 207 above) and Mustill LJ in *Grant* v *Edwards* [1986] Ch 638.
[206] [1982] Ch 391. Improvements are discussed in the trusts of land context: p 335 below.
[207] [1965] P 478. See also *Huntingford* v *Hobbs* (1992) 24 HLR 652 (£2,000 conservatory); *Mortgage Express Ltd* v *Robson* [2002] 1 FCR 162 at [29] (granny flat).
[208] [2007] 2 FLR 871, approving *Clarke* v *Harlowe* [2007] 1 FLR 1.

(iv) *Accounting or adjusting the shares?*

Prior to *Jones* v *Kernott*, adjusting shares was unusual, although an example is *Passee* v *Passee*.[209] One of three people jointly purchasing a house died. Her share was assessed at 10%, bearing in mind that the others had made significant contributions after her death. It appears that her share would have been 15% at the date of her death. The normal principle is that the shares of the parties are assessed (but not valued) at the time of separation;[210] the equivalent time in *Passee* was the time of death. It is unclear on what basis her share was reduced, although it does provide a simpler solution than accounting.

A rather different point is that it might be argued that the parties intended a change in the size of their shares after separation. This was the point in issue in *Jones* v *Kernott*,[211] in which one party had occupied the house (paying all expenses) for over 15 years: she claimed a larger share than her 50% as joint owner. As we have seen, the Supreme Court accepted the finding of a common intention that her share should be 90%. This provides an alternative to accounting, one which Lady Hale and Lord Walker[212] much preferred as it avoids the complexity involved in accounting over such a long period. Accounting might not have been as favourable to the man who had left the home as it might be thought. It was likely that no rent would be charged for the period during which the woman was looking after children in the house, whereas she would be credited with her mortgage payments.

This gives rise to the question as to when such an adjustment of shares will be applied, rather than accounting. The period between separation and sale was unusually long in *Stack*. In addition, the parties' conduct in realising a related insurance policy (putting the man in funds to assist in purchasing a replacement house) provided a basis upon which a common intention to vary the shares could be found. It remains to be seen how far the *Jones* approach is exceptional or mainstream.

10. Looking to the future

Few would argue that the common intention analysis is ideal or that it reflects real intentions; it has been described in Canada as a 'phantom intent'.[213] As we have seen, the 'express' common intention is very difficult to operate in practice. The inferred common intention may well have been rejuvenated by *Stack* v *Dowden*, although it remains to be seen how it will be applied in practice, especially where there have been no financial contributions.[214]

For married couples, the problems are usually bypassed by the statutory discretions. Now that these discretions have been extended to civil partnerships,[215] the failure of the

---

[209] [1988] 1 FLR 263.
[210] *Bernard* v *Josephs* [1982] Ch 391.
[211] [2012] 1 AC 776; pp 189 and 205 above.
[212] Ibid, at [50]; criticised by Mee [2012] Conv 167.
[213] Dickson J in *Pettkus* v *Becker* (1980) 117 DLR 3d 257 at p 270.
[214] Gardner [2013] CLJ 301 regards the law as developed by *Stack* and *Jones* as defensible (and preferable to the Law Commission's proposals).
[215] See p 331 below.

law to deal with other relationships has become even more obvious.[216] Virtually every commentator on this area is critical of the law's reliance on common intention as the essential requirement for dealing with the issues flowing from cohabitation; this is seen in comments on the Law Commission's 2002 review of the area, discussed below.

Commonwealth developments

We have been concentrating upon English cases, but Commonwealth courts[217] have been experimenting with more broadly based constructive trusts. This has been most interesting in Australia, as the Australian courts had previously been the most outspoken critics of Lord Denning's attempts to establish a broadly based constructive trust.[218]

The Australian High Court in *Baumgartner* v *Baumgartner*[219] has developed a constructive trust which is independent of common intention, but is instead based upon unconscionability. It seems that the High Court intends that particular situations should justify the imposition of a constructive trust, rather than adopting a totally open judicial discretion. When assessing *Baumgartner*, it should be borne in mind that earlier Australian cases had taken a distinctly narrow view as to when a common intention might be inferred. It is arguable that the *Baumgartner* constructive trust operates in much the same way as the English common intention developed in *Stack*.[220]

Alongside the constructive trust, two further approaches have been developed. In Canada, the constructive trust seems substantially based upon the unjust enrichment of the legal owner, where the work or contributions of the claimant enable the property to be bought or enhance its value.[221] The Supreme Court of Canada has recently given prominence to a more specifically unjust enrichment approach,[222] but this does not preclude a proprietary claim through a remedial constructive trust.[223] Although in joint family ventures, an award should represent a share of wealth proportionate to the claimant's contributions, there is no need for 'duelling quantum meruits'. Unjust enrichment recognises a significantly wider range of contributions and activities than the English courts do, but a discussion of it lies outside the scope of this text. Another approach is that of estoppel, which at one time had particular support in New Zealand.[224] New Zealand developments

---

[216] Douglas, Pearce and Woodward [2007] Fam Law 36 survey the operation of the law in practice. For arguments that the law might fall foul of human rights (improbable), see Wong [2005] JSWL 265.

[217] Gardner (1993) 109 LQR 263 at pp 269–282; Mee, *The Property Rights of Cohabitees*, Chapters 7–9; Rotherham [2004] Conv 268 at pp 281–286.

[218] See especially Glass JA and Samuels JA in *Allen* v *Snyder* [1977] 2 NSWLR 685 and Brennan J in *Muschinski* v *Dodds* (1984) 62 ALR 429.

[219] (1987) 76 ALR 75. The High Court developed ideas of Mahoney JA in *Allen* v *Snyder* [1977] 2 NSWLR 685 and Deane J in *Muschinski* v *Dodds* (1984) 62 ALR 429.

[220] *Gillies* v *Keogh* [1989] 2 NZLR 327 (Cooke P); *Lankow* v *Rose* [1995] 1 NZLR 277; Hayton [1988] Conv 259; Riley (1994) 16 Syd LR 412. For non-direct contributions, see Bryan (1990) 106 LQR 25; Bailey-Harris (1997) 113 LQR 227; *Parij* v *Parij* (1997) 72 SASR 153; *Lloyd* v *Tedesco* (2002) 25 WAR 360.

[221] *Pettkus* v *Becker* (1980) 117 DLR 3d 257; *Sorochan* v *Sorochan* (1986) 29 DLR 4th 1. See also Toohey J in *Baumgartner* and Hammond J in *Daly* v *Gilbert* [1993] 3 NZLR 731. The development of unjust enrichment to cover homemaking activities can lead to astonishing results: *Peter* v *Beblow* (1993) 14 DLR 4th 621 (Supreme Court of Canada).

[222] *Kerr* v *Baranow* (2011) 328 DLR 4th 577.

[223] *Frame* v *Rai* (2013) 361 DLR 4th 42 at [26]–[30], [88] (British Columbia Court of Appeal).

[224] *Gillies* v *Keogh* [1989] 2 NZLR 327.

now utilise constructive trusts and reasonable expectations, based upon direct or indirect contributions to the property.[225]

In England, of course, *Stack* v *Dowden* and *Jones* v *Kernott* have retained the common intention constructive trust. However, its application has been liberalised, such that the contrasts with these Commonwealth approaches are less marked than in the past. One idea that has been mooted is the introduction of a remedial constructive trust to develop restitutionary remedies.[226] However, it clearly is not yet part of English law.[227]

Law Commission proposals

The Law Commission issued a Discussion Paper on Sharing Homes in July 2002.[228] An attempt was made to draft a scheme of property ownership,[229] not tied to specific relationships or financial contribution.[230] Unfortunately, it proved impossible to produce a sufficiently broad scheme whilst avoiding inappropriate results in specific examples where the scheme applied. In short, the attempt to get away from the intentions of the parties did not succeed, although it might have been easier if specific relationships had been concentrated upon. The use of common intention is generally approved,[231] although it is thought that a wider range of contributions (including indirect contributions, as recognised in *Le Foe* and, now, *Stack*) should suffice.

More encouraging, but still controversial,[232] is a 2007 Law Commission report on cohabitants.[233] This report does not address property rights directly, but rather the obligations of the parties on relationship breakdown. As such, it can be seen as having a similar function to the Matrimonial Causes Act jurisdiction on marriage breakdown. However, the Law Commission is keen to stress that its scheme will work on a quite different basis than the matrimonial jurisdiction. The area is becoming more family law than property law and lies on the margins of property law.

The proposed scheme would apply to cohabitants (a 'couple who share a household') if they have children or have been cohabiting for a period (suggested to be between two and five years), although the couple could opt out. It may be noted that it would not apply to relatives or friends who share a home: the 2002 Paper demonstrated the problems in seeking a single solution for diverse circumstances. The court would have power to order

---

[225] *Lankow* v *Rose* [1995] 1 NZLR 277 (the rules are most clearly expressed by Tipping J at p 294).
[226] Lord Browne-Wilkinson in *Westdeutsche Landesbank Girozentrale* v *Islington LBC* [1996] AC 669 at p 716. Etherton [2008] CLJ 265 has argued that *Stack* should be seen as a remedial constructive trust based upon unjust enrichment; cf Douglas, Pearce and Woodward (2009) 72 MLR 24.
[227] Most recently, see Etherton LJ in *Crossco No 4 Unlimited* v *Jolan Ltd* [2012] 2 All ER 754 at [84].
[228] Law Com No 278; Bridge in *Modern Studies in Property Law*, Vol 2 (ed Cooke), Chapter 19.
[229] See Dewar in *Land Law: Themes and Perspectives* (eds Bright and Dewar), Chapter 13, for criticism of too much stress on ownership. See also Wong in *Feminist Perspectives on Equity and Trusts* (eds Scott-Hunt and Lim), Chapter 7.
[230] Cf the proposals of Barlow and Lind (1999) 19 LS 468.
[231] An approach which surprised many commentators. Rotherham [2004] Conv 268 is especially critical of this complacency.
[232] Hughes, Davis and Jacklin [2008] Conv 197; Deech [2010] Fam Law 39 criticises it as (in particular) an expensive and unnecessary inroad on the parties' autonomy.
[233] Law Com No 307; Bridge [2007] Fam Law 911, 998. See Douglas, Pearce and Woodward [2008] Conv 365 (also (2009) 72 MLR 24) for the demographic and conveyancing background; also Probert [2009] CLP 316. Compare Australian reforms, discussed by Leigh and Barry [2011] Fam L 404.

money or property transfers, although not normally periodic payments. In deciding how much to award and the most appropriate form of relief, wide discretionary factors (including the needs and resources of the parties and the welfare of children) would operate.

For the court to be able to make an order, two factors would need to be present. First, the claimant must have made 'qualifying contributions'. These are widely defined and cover, for example, looking after children. Next, there must be either 'retained benefit' or 'economic disadvantage'.[234] Retained benefit means that the claimant's contribution has provided the defendant with an enduring benefit after separation. This applies to contributions which enable property to be required; it appears little wider than direct and indirect contributions. Economic disadvantage is more interesting.[235] It will include loss of earning power or pension rights caused by being out of the labour market whilst undertaking the contribution (but not lost earnings during the relationship, unless lost savings can be proved). In some cases, the weaker financial party might lose out relative to the present law.[236] Suppose a couple purchase a house, which is put in joint names but financed entirely by one of them. The party who financed the purchase may be able to recover the benefit reaped by the other.

The likely impact of these reforms on the present law needs to be considered. It is proposed that it should operate to the exclusion of resulting and constructive trusts (and estoppel) in claims between the cohabitants. However, the old law will remain relevant for other relationships (parents and children feature quite frequently in the cases) and for disputes arising in other ways. Examples of the latter are where one of the parties mortgages the property or becomes bankrupt. The matrimonial jurisdiction similarly leaves these areas to the equitable principles. Overall, however, the significance of the equitable principles and their perceived injustice will be greatly diminished. It is difficult to predict whether this would lead the courts to restrict their operation.

Early implementation of these proposals, already a decade old, appears unlikely. A rather similar reform was introduced in Scotland in 2006. In the course of an appeal to the Supreme Court in *Gow* v *Grant*,[237] Baroness Hale explained in some detail how the reform had proved practical and fair. She urged that such a reform, based on the proposals just discussed, should be introduced in England and Wales. She usefully identified differences between the two systems, with guidance as to where each seems preferable.

11. Constructive trusts and estoppels: the links

In this section, we will compare the operation of common intention constructive trusts and estoppel. It should be remembered that there are different forms of constructive trusts: we are looking only at those based on common intention.

---

[234] This is to avoid drawing up a balance sheet of benefits (and detriment) during the relationship. This objective is also seen in the estoppel case of *Southwell* v *Blackburn* [2015] 2 FLR 1240 at [18].

[235] But it may be difficult to apply: Probert [2006] Fam Law 1060. More generally, see Douglas, Pearce and Woodward [2008] Fam Law 351.

[236] Gardner [2013] CLJ 301 argues that this might contravene human rights principles (Article 1 protection of possessions).

[237] 2012 SLT 828; Lords Wilson and Carnwath agreed with Baroness Hale. See Bray [2012] Fam L 1505.

A. Protection of the estoppel by constructive trust

Quite apart from suggestions that the two doctrines are similar, it is sometimes asserted that estoppels take effect by virtue of a constructive trust. The analysis seems to be that a constructive trust is necessary in order to justify the avoidance of formality rules. Constructive trusts are, of course, exempted from formality requirements,[238] whereas there is no specific exemption for estoppels. The constructive trust is thus, according to this assertion, being imposed simply as a way of giving effect to the remedy, with little apparent significance for either estoppels or constructive trusts. Although support for it was pretty meagre,[239] it has been brought into significance because of the recent doubts as to the use of estoppel to avoid writing requirements for contracts for the sale of land.[240]

B. Similarities between constructive trusts and estoppel[241]

It is apparent that broadly similar principles underpin both equitable doctrines: both exist to prevent unconscionable use of the legal title. Too much should not be made of this: it is rather like saying that two legal rules are similar because they are based on preventing injustice. Much more significant is that the common intention constructive trust and proprietary estoppel both look at the intentions of the parties and the way the claimant has acted upon those intentions, although acquiescence has been developed solely within the estoppel framework. Until the 1980s, the similarities had gone largely unnoticed, at least by the cases. There was a line of cases on constructive trusts and a separate line of cases on estoppel. Even when both issues were raised in cases, they were generally dealt with separately.

Perhaps the most contentious issue in the constructive trust cases has been whether a common intention can be inferred from the circumstances. This has been the principal focus of the law since *Gissing* v *Gissing*.[242] It has little to do with the concerns of proprietary estoppel, where there is generally direct evidence of the assumption or expectation. Much of the stress in estoppel cases has been on questions of detriment and reliance. These in turn have played a lesser role in constructive trusts: financial and non-financial contributions are pretty obvious detrimental reliance. The catalyst for bringing the two doctrines together has been the development of the actual common intention constructive trust, exemplified by the analyses in *Grant* v *Edwards*[243] and *Lloyds Bank plc* v *Rosset*.[244] Once there is an actual common intention, then attention turns to the way in which that intention has been acted upon. That is, of course, very similar to the way estoppel operates. This link has also been seen in the context of informal contracts for the sale of land.

---

[238] Law of Property Act 1925, s 53(2).
[239] *Timber Top Realty Pty Ltd* v *Mullens* [1974] VR 312; *Re Sharpe* [1980] 1 WLR 219; *Re Basham* [1986] 1 WLR 1498 at p 1504 ('a species of constructive trust'); Sir Christopher Slade, 'The Informal Creation of Interests in Land' (Child & Co Oxford Lecture 1984).
[240] See p 109 above. In *Joyce* v *Rigolli* [2004] EWCA Civ 79 at [35], Arden LJ opined that *Yaxley* v *Gotts* [2000] Ch 162 'held that proprietary estoppel involved a constructive trust'. See also Lord Neuberger (2010) 84 ALJ 225 at p 235.
[241] Hayton [1990] Conv 370 and (1993) 109 LQR 485; Ferguson (1993) 109 LQR 114; Gardner (1993) 109 LQR 263; Nield (2003) 23 LS 311; Etherton [2009] Conv 104.
[242] [1971] AC 886.
[243] [1986] Ch 638.
[244] [1991] 1 AC 107.

What is the significance of this convergence? If the two really are the same, then would it be simpler to merge them and avoid the inconsistencies that are inevitable if two similar doctrines operate side by side? Before attempting to answer these very difficult questions, it is necessary to see what the courts have said and how (if at all) the two areas presently differ. The following analysis places little emphasis upon the inferred common intention constructive trust or on estoppel by acquiescence, as these are areas in which each doctrine has developed its own special rules.

C. Court comparisons

The first considered English comparisons come in 1986. Sir Nicolas Browne-Wilkinson V-C observed in *Grant* v *Edwards*[245] that 'The two principles have been developed separately without cross-fertilisation between them: but they rest on the same foundation and have on all other matters reached the same conclusions.' The reference to 'other matters' appears to relate to the elements of detriment and reliance, which are separately discussed below. At much the same time, Nugee QC in *Re Basham*[246] was drawing on general constructive trust principles to support a conclusion that estoppel could operate on unspecified property. It is interesting that *Grant* approaches these issues from the constructive trust perspective, whereas *Basham* does so from that of estoppel.

This linking has received support from numerous cases, including the Privy Council in *Austin* v *Keele*[247] and the House of Lords in *Lloyds Bank plc* v *Rosset*.[248] Although neither case contains a full discussion, Lord Bridge stated in *Rosset* that, were there to have been agreement and detrimental reliance, 'this could have given rise to an enforceable interest in her favour by way either of a constructive trust or of a proprietary estoppel'. It seems obvious that he sees little difference between them. Subsequently, *Yaxley* v *Gotts*[249] recognised that, although there are areas in which the doctrines do not overlap (acquiescence, for example), in the actual common intention context, the constructive trust is 'closely akin to, if not indistinguishable from', proprietary estoppel. It followed that an exclusion of constructive trusts from writing requirements enabled the court to give a remedy to a purchaser under an oral contract for the purchase of land, in circumstances where estoppel might have been expected to apply. However, the opinions do not all go one way. Lord Walker stated in *Stack* v *Dowden*[250] that his dicta in *Yaxley* may have been too enthusiastic as regards complete assimilation of the doctrines.

Some of the most thoughtful (if ultimately inconclusive) comments come from Nourse LJ in *Stokes* v *Anderson*.[251] He observed that the earlier cases had linked the doctrines and

---

[245] [1986] Ch 638 at p 656.
[246] [1986] 1 WLR 1498 (reliance on mutual wills and secret trusts, rather than common intention trusts). His conclusion has been doubted in the House of Lords (see Chapter 10, above p 157).
[247] (1987) 61 ALJR 605 at p 609.
[248] [1991] 1 AC 107 at pp 129, 132–133. See also *Ungurian* v *Lesnoff* [1990] Ch 206 and, more recently, *Ely* v *Robson* [2016] WTLR 1383 at [42].
[249] [2000] Ch 162; see also *Banner Homes Group plc* v *Luff Developments Ltd* [2000] Ch 372 at pp 384–385.
[250] [2007] 2 AC 432 at [37], discussed below.
[251] [1991] 1 FLR 391 at pp 398–399 (views repeated in *Hyett* v *Stanley* [2004] 1 FLR 394 at [27]). See also Neuberger LJ in *Kinane* v *Mackie-Conteh* [2005] WTLR 345 at [51], drawing the line where there is an element of agreement or common understanding.

thought that they might be assimilated in the future, despite 'their separate development out of basically different factual situations'. However, he was unwilling to treat the two doctrines as one. For the present, the courts should apply *Gissing* principles in the context of joint acquisition of property. It is plain, nevertheless, that he sees the future of the law as involving closer integration. This leads us to an investigation of the present differences.

D. Is common intention the same as assumption or expectation?

The doctrines might appear to operate in somewhat different circumstances. The common intention operates rather like a contract: the parties agree to purchase property (or otherwise to deal with it) so as to lead to their both acquiring interests in it. There may not be a contract, but there is a mutuality of purpose. The typical estoppel claim is very different: either C operates under a mistaken assumption or else O makes a representation that C relies upon.[252] It is less usual for the detriment to arise out of a joint enterprise by the parties.[253]

The above distinction is not applicable to every case, but it helps to identify the paradigm constructive trust and estoppel situations. It is more difficult to say whether it can be used to justify differences in the operation of the principles. There is an attraction to the argument that a court faced with a bilateral agreement should give effect to it. In estoppel, by contrast, there is not so much an agreement as a representation or promise. Greater stress on the detriment in deciding upon a remedy may then be justified. In short, enforcing agreements is not the same as enforcing gratuitous promises, representations or understandings.[254]

The problem with this analysis is that the line between agreements and representations is not a sharp one, although it may help to explain how the present rules have evolved in their present form. Now that there is greater overlap of estoppels and constructive trusts in the cases, it seems unlikely that the courts will feel happy in having to decide whether there is an agreement or representation on the facts before them. Trying to force the understandings of members of a family into these categories is likely to lead to yet more artificial analysis. It might also be observed that both constructive trusts and estoppels draw distinctions as to whether familial or commercial situations are involved.[255]

Common intention may also differ from the estoppel rules in that it may require a somewhat greater certainty as to the interest being claimed,[256] although this is not to argue for great precision in constructive trusts. It is possible to see estoppel as being less precise in its operation, reflecting its somewhat weaker discretionary remedy.

---

[252] *Gillett* v *Holt* [2001] Ch 210 at p 230; cf *Jennings* v *Rice* [2003] 1 P&CR 100. JD Davies has observed the contrasting emphasis on undertakings (constructive trusts) and inducements (estoppels), although he denies that a real line can be drawn between them: (1980) 7 Adelaide LR 200.

[253] This is so even where, as in some commercial cases, the claim is to be entitled to a contractual right of some description.

[254] Not every estoppel involves a gratuitous promise, but the discretion in choice of remedy is most likely to be important where there is no consideration: Robert Walker LJ in *Jennings* v *Rice* [2003] 1 P&CR 100.

[255] This is seen in *Stack* in constructive trusts. For estoppel, see *Cobbe* v *Yeoman's Row Management Ltd* [2008] 1 WLR 1752 (Lord Walker) and *Thorner* v *Major* [2009] 1 WLR 776.

[256] The opposite was argued by Lord Scott in *Thorner* v *Major* [2009] 1 WLR 776, but this was a minority view.

It may be argued that the artificiality involved in finding the common intention will be reduced if the law looks to estoppel rather than the common intention constructive trust.[257] Because unconscionability is more to the fore in estoppel, there is no need for the parties to have specified their intentions in any particular fashion. It is interesting that Lord Browne-Wilkinson now supports this approach, although his analysis in *Grant v Edwards* is most often cited as support for linking estoppel and constructive trusts together. The approach has much to commend it.

Finally, a less controversial point may be made. The constructive trust has generally been applied where there is a common intention to share ownership, but not where there is a common intention as to non-freehold interests in property. There seems to be no reason why it should not apply regardless of the form of proprietary interest intended.[258]

E. Detrimental reliance[259]

The principal issue in the earlier cases concerned the necessary link between the detriment and the common intention (constructive trust) or expectation (estoppel). There are two elements to this. The first is whether it can be proved that the common intention or expectation was the cause of the detriment. In estoppel, there is a presumption that the detriment was incurred as a result of the expectation.[260] In *Grant v Edwards*,[261] Sir Nicolas Browne-Wilkinson V-C drew attention to the similarities between the doctrines and expressed the opinion that estoppel could assist in developing the law as to detrimental reliance in constructive trusts: an area in which earlier courts had given little guidance. He would apply the presumption of causation in estoppel to constructive trusts; this appears to be accepted,[262] at least in the family context.[263]

The second element is whether the detriment must be referable to the common intention or expectation. What referability appears to mean is that a person looking at the detriment would conclude that there was a common intention or expectation, such as that relied upon. An alternative meaning is that the detriment must be contemplated as part of (or at the same time as) the common intention.

In the constructive trust cases, it is commonly said that the detriment must be referable to the intention. This is based on dicta in *Gissing v Gissing*[264] and *Eves v Eves*,[265] where stress is placed on there being an initial intention that the claimant contribute in some way.

[257] Sir Nicolas Browne-Wilkinson (1996) 10 *Trust Law International* 98; *Mollo v Mollo* [1999] EGCS 117, [2000] WTLR 227.
[258] This is illustrated by the recent cases, such as *Yaxley v Gotts*, on informal contracts for the sale of land. However, McFarlane has expressed doubts: [2005] Conv 501 at pp 518–520.
[259] Lawson (1996) 16 LS 218.
[260] *Greasley v Cooke* [1980] 1 WLR 1306.
[261] [1986] Ch 638.
[262] It is supported by dicta of Lord Bridge in *Lloyds Bank plc v Rosset* [1991] 1 AC 107; see also *Stokes v Anderson* [1991] 1 FLR 391 and *Risch v McFee* (1990) 61 P&CR 42. Contrast Peter Smith J in *Pritchard Englefield v Steinberg* [2004] EWHC 1908 (Ch) at [54].
[263] Lord Oliver adopts a more restrictive approach in *Austin v Keele* (1987) 61 ALJR 605 at p 610 (PC).
[264] [1971] AC 886.
[265] [1975] 1 WLR 1338.

The requirement of referability also has an analogy in the old law as to part performance of oral contracts for the sale of land. There appears to be little reason or justification for the requirement of referability in constructive trusts.[266] There is no trace of any such rule in estoppel: in particular, there is no requirement that the detriment should take the form of expenditure on the land.

The issue was discussed by Sir Nicolas Browne-Wilkinson V-C in *Grant* v *Edwards*. Whilst estoppel was seen as providing the way forward, he was reluctant to take an emphatic line on a point that had not been fully argued. Nourse LJ was less generous in requiring 'conduct on which the woman could not reasonably have been expected to embark unless she was to have an interest in the house' for the constructive trust, although in *Stokes* v *Anderson*[267] he too contemplated a link with estoppel principles. In neither case was it necessary to come to a decision on the matter, and it must be regarded as undecided.[268]

It may be concluded that, if the two doctrines are similar in other respects, differences in detrimental reliance rules are very difficult to support.

F. The form of the remedy

Differences are apparent when remedies are examined. The common intention constructive trust leads to joint ownership in the huge majority of cases, sole ownership in a few. By way of contrast, although estoppels have very rarely resulted in shared ownership, extremely varied remedies are given. This contrast in remedy is largely explained by the circumstances in which they are employed. The constructive trust is most commonly argued when the parties have, in some sense, jointly purchased a home or other property. Estoppel is used in a wider range of factual situations. Now that the overlap between the doctrines has been recognised, it may be expected that each will deploy the same range of remedies.

More important is the question of court discretion in determining what remedy to give. It has been seen that there is a distinct discretion as regards the remedy in estoppel, most fully discussed in *Jennings* v *Rice*.[269] In the common intention constructive trust, the conventional view was that the court would give effect to the common intention. However, in *Oxley* v *Hiscock*,[270] the Court of Appeal used estoppel principles as a way of developing discretionary constructive trust remedies, based on fairness.

However, there are two flaws in the *Oxley* analysis. The first is that it is by no means clear that the approach in the constructive trust cases in fact mirrors the approach in estoppel.[271] No case, including *Oxley*, begins to explain how the estoppel principles as to

---

[266] *Parris* v *Williams* [2009] 1 P&CR 169 holds that detriment need not be identified as part of the common intention.

[267] [1991] 1 FLR 391 at pp 398–399.

[268] *Austin* v *Keele* (1987) 61 ALJR 605 (PC) is hostile in the commercial context, but the estoppel approach gains support from other cases, including *Risch* v *McFee* (1990) 61 P&CR 42.

[269] [2003] 1 P&CR 100.

[270] [2005] Fam 211 (p 204 above); see also *van Laethem* v *Brooker* [2006] 2 FLR 495 at [78]–[80], [263].

[271] Gardner (2004) 120 LQR 541 at pp 545–546 (perhaps exaggerating the differences).

remedies operate in the family home constructive trust. The second problem is that the *Oxley* fair shares analysis is applied only where the parties have not stipulated what the shares should be in their actual common intention. Yet, estoppel principles of fairness (more often expressed in terms of unconscionability and proportionality) still apply where there is a clear representation as to rights. It is not explained why estoppel principles lie behind some, but not all, constructive trust remedies.

Though *Stack v Dowden*[272] rejected the fairness analysis in *Oxley*, we have seen that it was reinstated by the Supreme Court in *Jones v Kernott*[273] under the guise of an imputed intention. However, it remains significant that it is used only in default of an inferred intention – generally, quantification is not discretionary. It may be concluded that, although estoppel and constructive trusts are not applying identical principles, it cannot be said that they are wildly different.

G. The remedy and purchasers

The discretion as to remedy in estoppel led to suggestions that purchasers should not be bound in advance of the court's giving a remedy. In the light of LRA, s 116, this is no longer a significant issue: purchasers, at least of registered land, are clearly bound. There are, of course, many cases of the highest authority showing that purchasers are bound by constructive trusts. Although Deane J stated in *Muschinski v Dodds*[274] that the wide form of constructive trust favoured by Australian courts will not affect purchasers prior to the court order, later Australian cases support prior proprietary effect for common intention constructive trusts.[275]

A different point concerns overreaching. Constructive and resulting trusts can be over-reached on a sale by two trustees, whereas we might expect estoppels to be subject to normal priority requirements (entry on the register or overriding interest). In *Birmingham Midshires Mortgage Services Ltd v Sabherwal*,[276] the claimant could clearly claim a resulting trust, but chose to argue estoppel in an attempt to avoid overreaching. The Court of Appeal, unsurprisingly, rejected this. Just as estoppel cannot be used to avoid the effect of failure to register,[277] so also it cannot be used to avoid the effects of overreaching.

However, the analysis in *Sabherwal* goes further than this. Whenever the claim is to a family interest (perhaps better regarded as an interest under a trust), then overreaching will operate. This has the consequence that most estoppel claims in the family context will be capable of being overreached, whereas the claim to, for example, the easement in *Crabb v Arun District Council*[278] could not be. One might surmise that the claim in *Pascoe v Turner*[279] to the fee simple would not be overreachable as it was a claim to a legal estate,

---

[272] [2007] 2 AC 432, p 204 above.
[273] [2012] 1 AC 776; p 205 above.
[274] (1984) 62 ALR 429 at p 458.
[275] *Parsons v McBain* (2001) 192 ALR 772.
[276] (1999) 80 P&CR 256; Harpum (2000) 116 LQR 341. See also Thompson [2003] Conv 157 at pp 166–167.
[277] *Lloyds Bank plc v Carrick* [1996] 4 All ER 630: p 499 below.
[278] [1976] Ch 179.
[279] [1979] 1 WLR 431, raising in an acute form whether the expectation or probable remedy is relevant.

even though in some such cases the court might choose to award a life interest. Although *Sabherwal* treats different estoppel claims in different ways, it avoids an unfortunate contrast with overreaching under trusts. In practice, many estoppel claims will be against a single proprietor, so that overreaching (which requires two trustees) would not in any event be feasible.

H. Tentative conclusions

It may be suggested that the law has three basic choices. It could simply go on as at present, developing two separate lines of authority. This would be unfortunate. The cases in the two areas have so much similarity that it cannot be right to ignore points of contact. A slightly more positive approach would be to recognise the doctrines as separate but to allow them to overlap to a greater extent than at present. It would be necessary to consider how they are separated (would a common intention require some form of quid pro quo?) and whether rules from one could profitably be adopted by the other. The third approach is to recognise their great similarities and assimilate them completely. This approach, which at one stage reflected the way things were going,[280] has the merit of simplifying our legal structure. That simplification might, however, be bought at a cost.[281] Although the position as to remedies may be evolving, it is still broadly accurate to say that the law at present recognises one route to identifying beneficial owners (constructive trust) and another route, rather more easily travelled, to a discretionary remedy when an equitable claim is made against the conscience of the owner (estoppel). This was made clear by Lord Walker in *Stack* v *Dowden*.[282] If it is the case that the core situations underpinning the two doctrines are different, the law should not give up lightly the possibility of continuing a separate constructive trust with greater certainty both as to when it operates and the results when it does.[283]

Further reading

Douglas, G, Pearce, J and Woodward, H (2009) 72 MLR 24: Cohabitants, property and the law: a study of injustice.

Fox Mahoney, L (2015) 'The politics of *Lloyd's Bank* v *Rosset*' in *Landmark Cases in Property Law* (ed S Douglas, R Hickey and E Waring), Chapter 8.

Gardner, S (2008) 124 LQR 422: Family property today.

Gardner, S [2013] CLJ 301: Problems in family property.

Hopkins, N (2011) 31 LS 175: The relevance of context in property law: a case for judicial restraint?

Hughes, D, Davis, M and Jacklin, L [2008] Conv 197: 'Come live with me and be my love': a consideration of the 2007 Law Commission proposals on cohabitation breakdown.

Rotherham, C [2004] Conv 268: The property rights of unmarried cohabitees: the case for reform.

---

[280] See *Stokes* v *Anderson* [1991] 1 FLR 391; *Oxley* v *Hiscock* [2005] Fam 211 (however, note the critical comments of Gardner (2004) 120 LQR 541 and Thompson [2004] Conv 496 at pp 505–506).
[281] Welstead [1995] Conv 61.
[282] [2007] 2 AC 432 at [37].
[283] Ferguson (1993) 109 LQR 114; cf McFarlane [2005] Conv 501 and Owen and Rees [2011] Conv 495 (placing stress on differences in remedies).

12

Purchasers: general principles and the need for registration

Introduction

The position of the purchaser is crucial in any property system. When considering what interests should be proprietary, we take into account whether it is reasonable for purchasers to be bound by them. However, it is simplistic to think that purchasers are always bound by proprietary rights. There is a large and difficult mass of legal rules dictating under what precise circumstances a purchaser will be bound. When we refer to purchasers in this context, this means anybody taking a proprietary right, including lessees and mortgagees.

It is, nevertheless, fair to observe that the law's traditional starting point has been that a proprietary interest will bind any subsequent purchaser. It is articulated in the Latin maxim often employed in the context of personal property: *nemo dat quod non habet*. Nobody can pass on a title that he does not have. It follows that if an owner, O, has sold and delivered a car to a purchaser, P, then O is later unable to pass on any rights to any later purchaser. O's sale to P means that P is now the owner and O no longer has anything left to transfer to anyone else. A slightly more sophisticated analysis may be required in many examples involving land. When a person creates a proprietary right, it is as if that person disposes of part of the land. If I create a right of way (an easement) over my land in favour of R, then R obtains a proprietary interest. I cannot sell or otherwise deal with my land so as to defeat R's easement because I no longer have unencumbered ownership of the land.[1]

This is, nevertheless, only a starting point. For personal property, there are many exceptions whereby a purchaser from a non-owner can obtain a good title.[2] For example, a seller who retains possession of the property sold is able to transfer ownership to a subsequent purchaser who is given possession.[3] This is because the first purchaser has enabled the seller to appear as if he still has power to sell the property. The rules applying to land are particularly complex, and the remainder of this chapter concentrates upon them. It should be noted that most priority disputes will today be resolved by land registration principles,

---

[1] Although R may agree that his right will not have priority: *Owen v Blathwayt* [2003] 1 P&CR 444.
[2] Bell, *Modern Law of Personal Property in England and Ireland*, Chapter 21.
[3] Sale of Goods Act 1979, s 24(1). This does not mean that the first sale is without effect. The first purchaser may run the risk of accidental damage to the property and (subject to s 24(1)) is able to transfer ownership.

which are dealt with in the following chapter. Under land registration, most rights will not bind registered purchasers unless they are entered on the register.

Nevertheless, the old rules are important for a number of reasons, quite apart from those few titles remaining unregistered. They form the basis of lawyers' thinking about priority issues and have been influential in the development of registered land principles, for example as regards the overriding interest of those in actual occupation. Further, they remain relevant for priority issues relating to property other than land: particularly important for trusts. Some of the ideas (especially regarding time order) remain of great significance for registered land. However, it is not necessary to study all the old rules at the level of detail which would have been appropriate in the past.

1. Rules for legal interests

Legal interests affect purchasers automatically, just as in the case of personal property. From the purchaser's point of view, this presents two huge problems. First, if the seller does not own the land, then the purchaser will obtain no ownership of it at all. The true owner will have legal ownership which binds all who come into contact with the land. The purchaser's second problem is that there may be legal interests short of full ownership which may affect him. Thus, he may be bound by a legal lease or right of way.

How could the purchaser avoid these problems? Prior to land registration, the answer was that he would inspect the land and the title deeds. If all appeared in order, then the purchaser would go ahead, pay his money and accept a conveyance of the land. It must be remembered that this procedure does not guarantee that he will obtain a good title; all he can do is take the maximum amount of care.

The most crucial and time-consuming part of this process lies in inspecting the title deeds. The title deeds are documents transferring the land from one owner to another, together with other documents relevant to the land (an example would be a lease affecting the land being sold). In the nineteenth century, the seller would have to produce these documents stretching back over at least 60 years, but the period was gradually reduced and, since 1969, has been just 15 years.[4] The reduction in the length of titles can be attributed to a number of causes: titles are simpler today, there is demand for cheap and speedy conveyancing and there is little evidence of problems for purchasers materialising as the period has been progressively reduced. The chances of ownership being in somebody other than the seller are fairly remote. Even then, that person's claim is likely to fail: the modern period of 15 years comfortably exceeds the 12 years that suffices to establish adverse possession in unregistered land.

Nevertheless, problems can still arise. There will be some cases where adverse possession will not operate to defeat others' claims to the land,[5] and there is always the danger that the title deeds might contain a forgery or be based on a mistake. A relatively common

---

[4] Law of Property Act 1969, s 23 (reducing the 30-year period in the Law of Property Act 1925 (hereafter LPA), s 44(1)).

[5] A good example is *St Marylebone Property Co Ltd v Fairweather* [1963] AC 510 (see p 90 above).

problem is that the seller might earlier have sold off part of the land. If no note of this has been placed on the title deeds, it is all too easy to overlook the earlier sale. The purchaser may believe he is getting all the land in the title deeds, and he is likely to be sorely disappointed. Even so, such examples are rare.

A more likely source of difficulty is that legal rights such as leases and easements may have been created by documents which are not shown to a purchaser or not created in writing at all. We shall see[6] that easements are often implied into conveyances, binding land retained by the seller. If this retained land is later sold, how can a purchaser be aware of implied easements? Some might be obvious from an inspection of the land, but inspection cannot be guaranteed to identify all unknown legal interests.

Before leaving legal rights, it may be worth observing that in a very few cases, a legal right might not bind the purchaser. The best example is found in the law of mortgages. In virtually every mortgage, the mortgagee (the lender) has a right to the title deeds.[7] This is vitally important as the absence of title deeds warns any later purchaser that there is a mortgage. It has been held that failure to obtain the title deeds causes the mortgagee to lose priority as against any later purchaser.[8] If the law were otherwise, the lender's failure to comply with the universal practice of mortgagees would have enabled the later purchaser to be defrauded.

2. The development of equitable rules

We have already seen that equity played a vital role in the development of English property law. The origins of equity lie in enforcing obligations where the conscience of the defendant is affected. When land affected by a trust was wrongly sold, the purchaser's conscience was considered as being vitally important. This is an application of the maxim that equity acts in personam. Traditionally, equity does not talk about proprietary rights so much as obligations imposed on individuals. It follows that it is more accurate from a historical perspective to say that equitable rights are proprietary because purchasers can be bound by them than to say that purchasers are bound because the rights are proprietary.

The rule that eventually emerged was that a purchaser's conscience would be bound unless he was a bona fide purchaser of a legal estate for valuable consideration and without notice, actual, imputed or constructive, of the equitable right. Over time, these rules became more settled and it became natural to view the beneficiary's rights as if they were property interests binding purchasers, albeit not in exactly the same way as legal interests.[9] By 1925, this approach had prevailed, and the 1925 legislation treats equitable interests as a species of proprietary interest.

---

[6] See p 524 below.
[7] In practice, only the first mortgagee has this right: the deeds cannot be split or duplicated.
[8] *Jones* v *Rhind* (1869) 17 WR 1091. See also *Walker* v *Linom* [1907] 2 Ch 104 (purchaser rather than mortgagee not obtaining all the title deeds).
[9] The older view is powerfully expressed by Professor Maitland, *Equity* (2nd edn), Lectures X and XI.

3. The doctrine of notice

There will be actual notice if the purchaser is aware of the interest, constructive notice if a reasonable purchaser's inquiries and inspections would have disclosed the interest and imputed notice where his solicitor or agent has actual or constructive notice.

Before looking at these requirements in detail, why should we depart from the first in time rule which applies to legal interests? An historical explanation is based on the application of ideas of conscionability by the Court of Chancery. Equity was reluctant to interfere with the legal titles of transferees from the original trustee unless the conscience of the transferee could be said to be affected. In time, this produced the bona fide purchaser rule. Today, it is pretty far removed from ideas of conscience, but it has given beneficiaries under trusts a protection against purchasers that has enabled their interests to be classed as proprietary.

Why, if at all, should the doctrine of notice continue to operate today? One answer is that beneficiaries who rely upon a trustee (and whose settlor has selected the trustee) have a claim inferior to that of a person who later deals in good faith with the trustee and without notice of the trust. Indeed, that argument has been used in Ireland to give protection to a purchaser of an equitable interest without notice.[10] However, it has been firmly established for more than a century in England that the purchaser is required to have a legal estate.[11] In any event, this explanation of the rule is inapplicable to equitable interests such as restrictive covenants. The holder of a restrictive covenant no more relies on the legal owner than the grantee of a legal easement.

We may then be forced into arguing that legal interests are the oldest, most necessary, most formal and most obvious interests. Equitable interests tend to be less obvious (partly because they are more likely to be created informally) and less crucial to the efficient use of land. They should, therefore, be subject to more onerous rules before a purchaser is bound. This can be further justified because the sale and development of land might be impeded if a purchaser could find himself or herself bound by a vast range of legal and equitable interests which he or she could not discover. In truth, however, it is difficult to give completely convincing modern justifications for the differing rules.

We can now turn to the requirements for the bona fide purchaser defence.

A. Bona fide

This has been little discussed. If the purchaser is not in good faith, then this will nearly always be because there is actual notice of the equitable interest. In such cases, of course, the notice will defeat the purchaser anyway. Lord Wilberforce has emphasised that bona fides remains an independent requirement,[12] although it seems that deception practised on the vendor is irrelevant.[13]

---

[10] *Re Ffrench's Estate* (1887) LR 21 Ir 283, per Fitzgibbon J.
[11] *Phillips v Phillips* (1861) 4 De GF&J 208 (45 ER 1164).
[12] *Midland Bank Trust Co Ltd v Green* [1981] AC 513 at p 528.
[13] *Corbett v Halifax BS* [2003] 1 WLR 964.

B. Purchaser for value

Purchasers include disponees such as mortgagees and lessees. Value will be satisfied by marriage consideration.[14] Satisfaction of a debt is treated as consideration for the purposes of the bona fide purchaser defence.[15]

C. Legal estate

It has already been seen that a legal estate is required; an equitable interest does not suffice. This apparently simple rule has caused considerable difficulty. A fairly obvious consequence is that there must be no notice at the time the legal estate is acquired, even though money may have been paid before notice was acquired.[16] A rather odd exception developed when the legal estate was acquired without conduct amounting to a breach of trust.[17] Far stricter is the suggestion that consideration must be given at the time the legal estate is acquired: earlier consideration will not suffice.[18] There seems to be little reason (or authority) for such a rule. A perplexing relaxation of the need for a legal estate is that a better right to the legal estate will suffice. It seems to operate where the legal owner acknowledges that he holds for the purchaser, without (at least knowingly) committing a breach of trust.[19]

D. Notice

(i) *Actual notice*

This gives rise to little difficulty, although hearing rumours will not suffice.[20] Once there is notice of an interest, it is no defence that the purchaser believes that it is safe to purchase. An example is a belief that an equitable mortgage has been repaid.[21] This may be thought harsh if the belief is reasonable.

(ii) *Constructive notice*

The scope of constructive notice is crucial in evaluating the protection of equitable interests. Although the language of earlier cases indicates that purchasers would not lightly be bound,[22] by the end of the nineteenth century the burden on purchasers was regarded as

---

[14] This will cover the old form of settlement executed on a marriage. For its limits, see *Att-Gen* v *Jacobs Smith* [1895] 2 QB 341.
[15] *Thorndike* v *Hunt* (1859) 3 De G&J 563 (44 ER 1386).
[16] *Wigg* v *Wigg* (1739) 1 Atk 382, 384 (26 ER 244, 245). The consideration must be paid before notice is acquired: *Tourville* v *Naish* (1734) 3 P Williams 307 (24 ER 1077).
[17] Discussed in *Macmillan Inc* v *Bishopsgate Investment Trust plc (No 3)* [1995] 1 WLR 978 at pp 1002–5.
[18] *Mumford* v *Stohwasser* (1874) LR 18 Eq 556.
[19] *Assaf* v *Fuwa* [1955] AC 215; Wade [1955] CLJ 32.
[20] *Barnhart* v *Greenshields* (1853) 9 Moo PC 18 (14 ER 204). See also *Smith* v *Morrison* [1974] 1 WLR 659 (good faith in land charges context).
[21] *Jared* v *Clements* [1903] 1 Ch 428.
[22] *Jones* v *Smith* (1841) 1 Hare 43 at p 56 (66 ER 943 at p 949); *Ware* v *Lord Egmont* (1854) 4 De GM&G 460 (43 ER 586) ('gross negligence').

intolerable. Today, s 199 of the Law of Property Act 1925 provides that a purchaser will be affected only if the equitable interest 'would have come to his knowledge if such inquiries and inspections had been made as ought reasonably to have been made by him'. Although this originated in a consensus that constructive notice should be restricted, it is difficult to point to specific changes.[23]

(a) Inspecting deeds

We have seen that purchasers are entitled to inspect title deeds going back at least 15 years, although the vendor and purchaser are free to provide for a different period.[24] If an equitable interest is mentioned in these title deeds, or in a document referred to by these deeds, then a purchaser has notice of it.[25] Similarly, unusual documents may oblige a purchaser to make further inquiries.[26] If a purchaser contracts for a shorter title, it is clear that he is bound if the normal title inquiries would have disclosed the equitable interest.[27] A purchaser from a person who has acquired title by adverse possession will not obtain title deeds, and it follows that no use can be made of the bona fide purchaser defence.[28] Until the Land Registration Act 2002 (hereafter LRA), a tenant was not entitled to inspect any title deeds relating to the fee simple;[29] and, rather generously, it was enacted that there is no notice of what is in the deeds.[30] Today, the title deeds can be inspected if the lease will be subject to compulsory registration, generally meaning that it is for more than seven years.[31]

A rather different issue relating to title deeds concerns the equitable mortgagee who holds them as security. The first mortgagee (legal or equitable) almost invariably takes possession of the title deeds in order to prevent fraudulent transactions by the mortgagor. A purchaser who ignores the absence of deeds will have notice of the equitable mortgage.[32]

(b) Inspecting the land

To be safe, a purchaser of unregistered land needs to discover the identity of all possessors and to make inquiries of them. Once a person is in possession, there is notice of all that person's rights, regardless of how unusual or unlikely they are.[33] It has long been established that a purchaser must make inquiries of any tenant in possession[34] and is bound by all the tenant's interests, even if not contained in the lease.[35] The purchaser need not,

---

[23] Maitland, *Equity* (2nd edn), pp 119–121: perhaps 'an excuse for rejecting some of the more extreme applications of the doctrine'. *Woolwich plc* v *Gomm* (1999) 79 P&CR 61 at p 74 confirms that there is no need to act as a suspicious purchaser would.
[24] LPA, s 44(1), (11); Law of Property Act 1969, s 23.
[25] *Bisco* v *Earl of Banbury* (1676) 1 Ch Cas 287 (22 ER 804).
[26] *Kennedy* v *Green* (1834) 3 My&K 699 (40 ER 266).
[27] *Peto* v *Hammond* (1861) 30 Beav 495 (54 ER 981).
[28] *Re Nisbet and Potts' Contract* [1906] 1 Ch 386. The adverse possessor is not a purchaser at all.
[29] LPA, s 44(2)–(4), although a sub-tenant is entitled to see the head lease.
[30] LPA, s 44(5), applied in *Shears* v *Wells* [1936] 1 All ER 832.
[31] LPA, s 44(4A) (inserted by LRA 2002).
[32] *Peto* v *Hammond* (1861) 30 Beav 495 (54 ER 981). The contents of the deeds would not, of course, reveal the equitable mortgage.
[33] *Midland Bank Ltd* v *Farmpride Hatcheries Ltd* [1981] 2 EGLR 147.
[34] *Taylor* v *Stibbert* (1794) 2 Ves Jun 437 (30 ER 713); *Barnhart* v *Greenshields* (1853) 9 Moo PC 18 (14 ER 204).
[35] *Daniels* v *Davison* (1809) 16 Ves 249 (33 ER 978); *Allen* v *Anthony* (1816) 1 Mer 282 (35 ER 679).

however, go further and make inquiries as to whom rent is paid. If the landlord (not being the vendor) holds an equitable interest, the purchaser has no notice of that interest.[36] More generally, there is no requirement that the vendor be in possession.[37]

The twentieth-century cases usually involved occupiers who were beneficiaries under trusts. The courts have accepted that a contribution to the purchase price or an agreement to own the property jointly may (by virtue of the infamous common intention) give rise to a trust. Most commonly, this arises between spouses or persons living together, where the legal title is vested in one of them. The title deeds will not disclose the trust, and the question is whether notice results from the possession of the beneficiary. There is clearly notice if the beneficiary is the sole possessor.

The problem arises where the vendor (the trustee) is living in the house with the beneficiary. Can the purchaser rely on the occupation of the vendor, or must he go further and make inquiries of all those in possession? In *Caunce* v *Caunce*,[38] Stamp J took the approach that the wife's occupation was entirely consistent with the husband's beneficial ownership: it did not act as a warning that the wife had a beneficial interest. The same argument could be used for relatives and, probably, friends living with or visiting the vendor. The identical problem has arisen in the registered land system, which does protect the beneficiary. The issue is fully discussed in that context[39]; the status of *Caunce* today is unclear.

(iii) *Imputed notice*

The great majority of purchasers employ a solicitor or other agent. It will come as little surprise that the agent's actual or constructive notice is imputed to the purchaser. If the law were otherwise, few purchasers would be bound by notice. Two particular problems have arisen. The courts have long been reluctant to impute notice where there is fraud by the solicitor,[40] although notice will still be imputed if an honest solicitor would have discovered the equitable interest.[41] The second problem concerns the position if the solicitor has received notice of the equitable interest when acting in a different transaction. The liability of purchasers in such situations was seen as a 'grievous injustice'[42] and was removed in 1882.[43]

E. Other considerations

A purchaser who cannot prove the bona fide purchaser defence may have other arguments. Three possibilities may be mentioned. The first relates to the conduct of the equitable interest holder. If that person enables the legal owner to appear to be free of the equitable

---

[36] *Hunt* v *Luck* [1902] 1 Ch 428.
[37] *Jones* v *Smith* (1841) 1 Hare 43 (66 ER 943); *Hunt* v *Luck* [1902] 1 Ch 428.
[38] [1969] 1 WLR 286.
[39] See p 268.
[40] See, e.g., *Cave* v *Cave* (1880) 15 Ch D 639.
[41] *Kennedy* v *Green* (1834) 3 My&K 699 (40 ER 266).
[42] *Re Cousins* (1886) 31 Ch D 671 at p 676 (Chitty J).
[43] See now LPA, s 199(1)(ii)(b).

interest, then the equitable interest may well be postponed.[44] A representation by the beneficiary to the purchaser that there is no equitable interest will clearly defeat the beneficiary[45]: this can readily be explained as an example of estoppel. A similar case is where the beneficiary has implicitly authorised the transaction. This is dealt with later in the context of registered land.[46]

The second possibility is best explained by an example. Suppose V contracts to sell to P1 and then (inconsistently) to sell to P2. P1's estate contract will have priority over P2 as being the first in time. Suppose that the legal estate is then conveyed to P1 who, by then, is aware of P2's contract. P1 can still rely upon the priority accorded by his contract and is not adversely affected by his later notice.[47] The same principle has been applied to registered land, where P2's contract is protected on the register.[48]

Finally, suppose that A, a purchaser without notice of an equitable interest, later sells the land to B. B has notice of the interest. A will have taken clear of the equitable interest, but is it relevant that B has notice? For centuries, it has been held that B enjoys the same protection as A.[49] Not only does B derive his title from A's unencumbered title, but if B were to be bound, this would make it virtually impossible for A to sell. Such a result would be quite inconsistent with A's initially being free of the equitable interest. The sole (and unsurprising) exception is where B is the original trustee (who had wrongfully sold to A).[50]

4. Two competing equitable interests

The basic principle is that the first in time wins.[51] Although this applies only where the equities are equal,[52] it is unusual for the principle to be upset, and we shall see that it has been adopted without qualification for registered land.[53] Earlier cases were inclined to see the time order as being the fall-back rule, to be applied if there was no other way to distinguish the interests.[54] Today, something akin to conduct leading to the holder of the prior interest being estopped from asserting priority will be required to upset the time order. Thus, a 'thoroughly artificial transaction', designed to give the impression of unencumbered ownership, was postponed to a later interest.[55] Overall, the rules are not dissimilar to those applying to two legal interests,[56] although it may be slightly easier to postpone a first equitable interest.

---

[44] *Kettlewell* v *Watson* (1884) 26 Ch D 501.
[45] Any controversy is likely to be as to whether such a representation can be inferred: *Midland Bank Ltd* v *Farmpride Hatcheries Ltd* [1981] 2 EGLR 147.
[46] *Bristol & West BS* v *Henning* [1985] 1 WLR 778; p 265 below.
[47] *Barclays Bank Ltd* v *Bird* [1954] Ch 274, although the issue was not discussed.
[48] See p 251, n 88 below.
[49] *Harrison* v *Forth* (1695) Prec Ch 51 (24 ER 26); *Wilkes* v *Spooner* [1911] 2 KB 473.
[50] *Gordon* v *Holland* (1913) 82 LJPC 81.
[51] *Barclays Bank Ltd* v *Taylor* [1974] Ch 137 provides a relatively recent example.
[52] Snell's *Equity* (33rd edn), para 4-047. Notice on the part of the second interest may provide a separate ground for the first to win: *Moffett* v *Dillon* [1999] 2 VR 480.
[53] LRA, s 28.
[54] *Rice* v *Rice* (1853) 2 Drew 73 (61 ER 646).
[55] *Freeguard* v *The Royal Bank of Scotland plc* (1998) 79 P&CR 81.
[56] In the context of mortgages (where most priority disputes arise), see Megarry (1940) 7 CLJ 243 at p 247.

The above principles operate where a legal owner creates two or more competing equitable interests. Special rules apply where there are successive transfers of the same equitable interest, as where an equitable life interest holder purports to sell his interest first to A and later to B. These rules form a specialised aspect of the law of assignment.[57]

5. Priority rules for equities

There is a recognised category of 'equities' (as seen in Chapter 4)[58] – generally discretionary claims to defeat or amend property interests. Examples are a right to rectify a lease so as to correct the rent payable and a right to set a conveyance aside for fraud. Somewhat different priority rules are applied in respect of equities. It has been accepted since *Phillips* v *Phillips*[59] in 1861 that purchasers of equitable interests will defeat equities, presuming that there is no notice.

It is interesting that *Latec Investments Ltd* v *Hotel Terrigal Pty Ltd (in liquidation)*,[60] the fullest twentieth-century discussion of equities, contains two contrasting analyses. Kitto J accepted the *Phillips* analysis that the equitable mortgagee without notice would defeat an earlier equity (it was based upon a fraudulently obtained conveyance). Taylor J came to the same result but by virtue of the discretionary remedy sought by the person defrauded. This remedy would not lie when the mortgagee had relied upon the conveyance. A variation on the approach of Taylor J is to stress that the equities are not equal as between the 'equity' and the equitable interest. The conduct of the party claiming the equity, in executing the conveyance, has encouraged the equitable interest holder to believe that all is well.

Another special effect upon purchasers concerns constructive notice. The problem is that a purchaser normally has notice of all the rights of occupiers, such as tenants. This was not automatically extended to equities.[61] This makes good sense where the occupation is consistent with the documentary rights of the occupier (the occupation does not call for explanation in such cases).

In registered land, equities and equitable interests are equated for priority purposes, within the statutory priority rules laid down.[62]

6. The time order

Nearly all priority rules depend in some way upon the order of the competing interests. This can apply almost as much to registered land as to unregistered land. Normally, their order will be obvious, but this is not always the case. If it appears that two interests are created at the same time (usually one of them is a mortgage), then we need some rule to

---

[57] See p 126 above. The first transferee to give notice to the trustee will generally have priority.
[58] Page 35 above.
[59] 4 De GF&J 208 (45 ER 1164); see *Allied Irish Banks Ltd* v *Glynn* [1973] IR 188. O'Sullivan argues that the courts were wrong to interpret *Phillips* this way: (2002) 118 LQR 296.
[60] (1965) 113 CLR 265.
[61] *Smith* v *Jones* [1954] 1 WLR 1089 (rectification); *Westminster Bank Ltd* v *Lee* [1956] Ch 7 (deserted wife's equity).
[62] LRA, ss 28–9, 116(b).

separate them. The notoriously difficult scintilla temporis (moment in time) doctrine was developed in order to produce a time order for their creation.

An example found in some of the earlier cases is when a purchaser purports to grant a lease before the conveyance (or transfer of registered land) to that purchaser is executed. The law confers a lease on the lessee when the legal estate is later transferred to the purchaser. In many cases, however, this purchase of the freehold will be possible only because of a loan secured by a mortgage, which will be executed contemporaneously with the conveyance or transfer. Which comes first, the lease or the mortgage? The original approach of the courts[63] was that the purchaser could not, logically, mortgage the land until it had been conveyed to him. There might be only a notional split second between the conveyance and the mortgage, but this scintilla temporis was long enough for the lease to attach itself to the property before the mortgage.

The obvious objection to this analysis is that the land could not have been bought without the mortgage and yet the mortgagee finds that the land, the purchase of which it has financed, has already been encumbered by the purchaser. One possible way out would be to say that the mortgagee has an equitable mortgage arising by operation of law prior to the conveyance, but this fails to answer all the problems: the agreement with the lessee may have pre-dated any agreement to mortgage.

The issue arose in the House of Lords in *Abbey National BS* v *Cann*.[64] Mrs Cann argued that, by virtue of her contribution to the purchase of a house by her son, she obtained an equitable interest in the land at the moment of transfer. Her son raised the balance of the purchase money by a mortgage. Mrs Cann argued that, applying the scintilla temporis doctrine, her interest arose before the mortgage. Stressing the economic reality underpinning purchases funded by mortgages, the House of Lords rejected the scintilla temporis doctrine and overruled the earlier authorities.

At first sight, it seems only reasonable to reject scintilla temporis as a complex theory which lacks 'a very powerful grasp on reality'.[65] But the decision in favour of the mortgagee leaves other questions unanswered. If the mortgagee funds substantially all the purchase price, then the decision seems fully justified: it would indeed be odd if a person promised a half share could assert that right as against the mortgagee.[66] Yet, in *Cann* itself, Mrs Cann provided £15,000 (out of the proceeds of another house being sold). Her son, so far as Mrs Cann was concerned, needed to raise just £4,000 to fund the balance of the cost of the house being purchased. In fact, he raised £25,000 on mortgage. It was held that the mortgagee had priority to the full extent of the loan. Yet, why should the mortgagee win completely? After all, Mrs Cann contributed £15,000 and the mortgagee £25,000. The scintilla temporis doctrine may have erred in saying that Mrs Cann should win completely, but that is no reason for jumping to the opposite

---

[63] The leading case was *Church of England BS* v *Piskor* [1954] Ch 553.
[64] [1991] 1 AC 56.
[65] Lord Hoffmann in *Ingram* v *IRC* [2000] 1 AC 293 at p 303.
[66] The mortgagee might have other arguments, depending on the facts. In particular, the beneficiary is unlikely to be in actual occupation at the time of completion (for registered land) and may well have authorised the mortgage (see p 265 below); both these arguments were successfully advanced in *Cann*.

extreme. At present, we seem to have a rule designed solely to benefit mortgagees.[67] Certainly, its effect is that a mortgagee funding the purchase of property seems to have nothing to fear.[68]

Two points on the application of *Cann* have arisen in recent cases. Although *Cann* treats the purchase and mortgage as a single transaction, it remains the case that the mortgagee deals with the purchaser, not the seller. This is important if there is a trust of land and the mortgagee wishes to rely on overreaching by dealing with the seller (two trustees).[69]

Next, *Cann* concerns funding sources for the purchase (Mrs Cann and the building society). What if the rival claimant is the seller? The problem has arisen in equity release schemes, whereby an owner sells land but retains occupation rights in it (usually a lease). In *Mortgage Business plc* v *O'Shaughnessy*,[70] there were thought to be two questions. The first was whether purchasers could create proprietary rights prior to completion. If so, the second question was whether *Cann* protected the mortgagee. Despite holding that no proprietary rights could be created,[71] the Supreme Court proceeded to split on the irrelevant second question. By a three-to-two majority, it was held that the *Cann* indivisibility of transfer and mortgage should not be extended so as to render contract, transfer and mortgage indivisible. It was stressed that the lenders are not parties to the contract and may not emerge until a later stage. It follows that any rights created by the purchaser prior to completion (probably none) may bind the mortgagee.

7. Assessing the legal and equitable rules

It will be clear that equitable interests (and equities) cause uncertainty both for holders of these interests and for purchasers. The interest holders cannot be sure that their interests will not be defeated and the purchaser may be held to have notice of an equitable interest and so get a bad title. Prior to the 1925 reforms, the strictness and unfairness of the constructive notice rule was notorious: 'the doctrine must not be carried to such an extent as to defeat honest purchasers . . . this limitation has sometimes been lost sight of . . .'.[72] Professor Maitland described the standard as 'the care of the most prudent solicitor of a family aided by the skill of the most expert conveyancer'.[73] The purchaser's problem was exacerbated by the fact that equitable interests were many and various and, most crucially, the fact that they might not appear on the title deeds.

[67] See (1990) 106 LQR 545 for further development of this argument.
[68] According to Lord Jauncey (*Abbey National BS* v *Cann* [1991] 1 AC 56 at pp 101–102), this might not be the case if the mortgage is not necessary to enable the purchase to go ahead (where the purchaser has enough money from other sources). This would be unusual, but the facts in *Cann* came close to it.
[69] *HSBC Bank plc* v *Dyche* [2010] 2 P&CR 58: Gravells [2010] Conv 169. Normally the purchaser can rely on overreaching and pass a good title to the mortgagee, but this did not apply in *Dyche* as the purchaser was not in good faith.
[70] [2015] AC 385; contrast *Perpetual Trustee Co Ltd* v *Smith* (2010) 273 ALR 469 at [51] (*Cann* was not cited).
[71] See p 49 above.
[72] *Bailey* v *Barnes* [1894] 1 Ch 25 at p 34 (Lindley LJ).
[73] *Equity* (2nd edn), p 119.

The impact of these defects might be put into two categories. The first concerns the time and therefore money spent in the conveyancing process. Going back over past documents is inherently repetitive. Successive purchasers each have to look at the earlier documents and convince themselves that a good title is proved and that nothing untoward is disclosed. It is wasteful that essentially the same work has to be repeated by successive purchasers, but the underpinning reality is that only an extremely foolhardy purchaser (or lawyer) would skip reading all the documents. Even if the purchaser were foolhardy, it is inconceivable that a mortgagee funding the purchase would do anything other than check the deeds carefully. The longer the period over which deeds must be produced, and the more complex the deeds, the greater this waste of effort.

The second category of defects concerns the lack of certainty involved. Purchasers may be bound by legal or equitable rights that they are unaware of. We have seen that a wide range of circumstances may produce this result. Sometimes the seller may have fraudulently suppressed the earlier interest,[74] but more frequently a genuine mistake has been made.[75] The outcome is that the purchase of land is rendered hazardous, bringing the law into disrepute.

8. Registration as a solution

Most legal systems seek to solve these problems by the registration of interests in land. If an interest is registered, then a purchaser can readily discover it. Accordingly, registration systems assure interest holders that their interests, once registered, cannot be defeated by purchasers. Greater problems arise where the interest is not registered. Certainty demands that the purchaser be protected. However, it may be unduly harsh to insist that the interest holder must always lose if, for example, the purchaser is aware of the interest.

Registration systems may be split into three types. Historically, the first was that of *registration of deeds*. This type of registration looks to the method of creating property rights. It will not assist where, for example, interests are created informally, without writing. It does, of course, guard against suppressed or forgotten deeds. Although it is the basis of the modern conveyancing system in most of the United States, it never gained success in England. It was employed only in Middlesex and Yorkshire and was finally abolished by the Law of Property Act 1969.

The second type of registration system requires registration of specified interests. In England, *land charges registration* requires certain equitable and statutory interests to be registered. Despite its name, it is not limited to financial charges. This system looks to the substance of the interest rather than the form of creation. Its role is best seen as replacing the doctrine of notice. It leaves in place virtually all the existing law relating to legal interests and has little impact on the conveyancing process. A purchaser has to inspect the title deeds and the land in order to discover legal interests that might affect him. What the land charges registration does achieve is a greater degree of certainty (for interest holders and purchasers alike) in respect of a wide range of equitable interests.

---

[74] Many examples arise when the seller is close to bankruptcy and is desperately attempting to raise money to pay off his debts.

[75] The purchaser may sometimes have a remedy against the seller based on the 'covenants for title' implied into conveyances: Law of Property (Miscellaneous Provisions) Act 1994.

The third form of registration is that of *registration of title*. It is the most modern of the three, dating from the late nineteenth century. It is radically different from the others in that it replaces the old system of conveyancing based on the production of title deeds. As its name indicates, registration of title shows who is owner of the land. Most importantly, ownership is guaranteed. If a mistake has been made on the register, the purchaser will still end up owning the land he has bought and registered. Rights adverse to the seller will be entered on the register. Unlike the land charges scheme, registration of legal interests is required. Indeed, most interests can be legal only when entered on the register.[76] As one might expect, there are important exceptions to this protection of the purchaser. Most of the difficult and interesting questions in land registration concern the extent of these exceptions.

Registration of title has been compulsory in certain parts of England and Wales since the Land Transfer Act 1897. Over time, these compulsory areas were extended from London and the more densely populated areas of the country until complete coverage was achieved in December 1990. However, this does not mean that all land now has registered title. Compulsory registration bites only when land is transferred,[77] and until then, all the old rules apply. This means that there are still many titles that are not registered. There are about 24.5 million registered titles (approximately 95% of all titles); around 110,000 unregistered titles become registered in a typical year.[78] Given that relatively little unregistered land remains and that every sale of land involves registration, this book concentrates on the registered land position.

9. The land charges scheme

First, however, the land charges scheme requires brief attention. Our investigation is designed to enable the differences between the land charges and land registration schemes to be pointed out, not to provide a comprehensive analysis of land charges. The principal difference is, of course, that the land charges scheme does not do away with the inspection of title deeds. Its provenance is significant but relatively limited in scope. It should be noted that land charges and land registration are mutually exclusive systems: they cannot both apply to a single title.[79]

The land charges scheme was introduced in its present form by the Land Charges Act 1925, re-enacted in the Land Charges Act 1972. It applies mainly to statutory financial charges and equitable interests, but this still means that it has the vitally important effect of emasculating the doctrine of notice. At the heart of the scheme lie two crucial rules. A registered land charge will bind a purchaser automatically: notice is irrelevant.[80] The second is that an unregistered land charge will not affect a purchaser, regardless as to whether the

---

[76] LRA, s 27(1).
[77] LRA, s 4; this includes an assent by personal representatives.
[78] Land Registry Annual Report and Accounts 2015–16, pp 16, 97.
[79] Except that after title is registered, the land charges scheme is still used to provide notice of a person's bankruptcy. As bankruptcy is inherently personal, land charges as a name-based system is ideal as the first step in getting an entry on to registers of title: Ruoff and Roper, *Registered Conveyancing*, para 34.003.
[80] LPA, s 198.

purchaser has notice.[81] It can be seen that registration or absence of registration is conclusive. Where the system applies, the uncertainties of notice are banished and replaced by the simple question: is the interest registered? An important limitation, however, is that interests protected on the register are not guaranteed to exist. Any flaw in an interest, such as a contract being voidable for misrepresentation, is quite unaffected by its entry on the register.

Not every equitable interest is covered by the scheme. There is a list in the legislation of those covered: the most interesting categories are second mortgages, estate contracts (including equitable leases), restrictive covenants, equitable easements[82] and statutory rights to occupy the family home.[83] The list has given rise to much litigation, though we will not go into this. Anything not falling within the list is not covered. Thus unusual rights such as rights of re-entry[84] and newer rights such as those based on estoppel[85] are unlikely to be covered by the land charges scheme.

A large gap in the list is formed by the absence of interests under trusts of land. This is deliberate as such interests will be overreached on a sale by two trustees[86] and thus will not affect a purchaser; there would be no point in requiring registration. However, a purchaser faces real problems if the trust is not apparent from the title deeds, as with the common intention constructive trust affecting many family homes. The purchaser is likely to be unaware that payment to two trustees is required. If the proceeds of sale are paid to the vendor as a single trustee, the only way to defeat the beneficial interest will be reliance on the purchaser without notice rules.[87]

The real weakness of the system, however, lies in the practicalities of its operation. Registration is against the name of the owner of the land at that time. This is far simpler than attempting to identify plots of land affected by charges. It enables registrations and searches to be carried out quickly and cheaply. However, this simplicity is bought at a significant cost. Far too frequently, errors are made in spelling names. Thus, Brian commonly emerges as Brain.[88] The simplicity enabled a commendably early use of computers, but the use of computerised records means that the slightest error will mean that an entry is missed on a search. It is a source of criticism that the computer will not link a search against Erskine Owen Alleyne with a registration against Erskine Alleyne.[89] It is even more odd where the fuller version of the name is correct according to the birth certificate, as the land charges cases adopt the name as found on the title deeds.[90]

[81] Land Charges Act 1972, s 4; LPA, s 199(1)(i); *Midland Bank Trust Co Ltd v Green* [1981] AC 513. Unlike registered land, actual occupiers receive no special protection, a contrast highlighted in *Lloyds Bank plc v Carrick* [1996] 4 All ER 630 at p 642.
[82] For equitable easements generally, see Barnsley (1999) 115 LQR 89; also Pulleyn [2012] Conv 387.
[83] Family Law Act 1996, ss 30–31.
[84] *Shiloh Spinners Ltd v Harding* [1973] AC 691.
[85] *ER Ives Investment Ltd v High* [1967] 2 QB 379.
[86] The beneficial interests are transferred to the proceeds of sale held by the trustees.
[87] *Caunce v Caunce* [1969] 1 WLR 286.
[88] Ruoff, *Searching without Tears*, p 45.
[89] *Diligent Finance Ltd v Alleyne* (1972) 23 P&CR 346; Adams [1987] Conv 135.
[90] *Standard Property Investments plc v British Plastics Federation* (1985) 53 P&CR 25. The use of the name on the title deeds is the only practical approach for conveyancers.

A potentially disastrous problem has been widely discussed since the 1950s. A purchaser must search against the names of every owner of the land since 1925 when the system started; there is no procedure to update entries to the name of the current owner. The purchaser discovers these names by looking at the title deeds. The problem is not difficult to see. A purchaser in 2017 can only look at deeds as far back as the first conveyance older than 15 years. Thus, if the seller bought the land from George in 1990, the purchaser may see only the conveyance from George to the seller. The purchaser can search against the seller's name and that of George. Yet, George himself may only have purchased the land in 1980. This means that any entry between 1925 and 1980 is undiscoverable, although the scheme still operates to give notice to the purchaser.[91]

Predictions of doom and gloom abounded and resulted in the setting up of a statutory compensation scheme for purchasers in 1969.[92] Yet, for the next 20 years, there was not a single claim for compensation.[93] Why were the sceptics confounded? The answer lies in the fact that most land charges have a short life and that those with long-term effects (especially restrictive covenants) are likely to be repeated in successive conveyances and so be brought to the purchaser's attention. At the same time, it is general practice to retain past search certificates with the title deeds. This provides another route for purchasers to discover older charges. We may conclude that the system is flawed, but it is nowhere close to breaking down.

Further reading

Megarry, R E (1940) 7 CLJ 243: Priority after 1925 of mortgages of a legal estate in land.

---

[91] Similarly, a lessee may not be entitled to inspect any title deeds but is still bound by registered charges: *White v Bijou Mansions Ltd* [1937] Ch 610, affirmed [1938] Ch 351 (contrast the rules relating to notice: see p 228 above).

[92] Law of Property Act 1969, s 25.

[93] There was one claim in 1989–1990: Land Registry Annual Report 1989–1990, p 11.

13

Purchasers: registration of title

1. Introduction: the scheme and its objectives

The essence of land registration is that the title to each building or plot of land is registered with its own file. The registered title provides information as to ownership of the land (this is guaranteed) and interests in the land. It is split into three parts.[1] The proprietorship register identifies the owner (the registered proprietor) and any limits on powers to dispose of the land. The property register identifies the land and specifies any benefits such as easements operating in its favour. Finally, the charges register lists interests adverse to the land. The proprietorship register, property register and charges register are simply subdivisions of the registered title: they are not independent documents or files. There will also be a map identifying the land. Whilst only the general boundaries are usually guaranteed,[2] the quality of mapping is a great improvement on maps found in old-style conveyances. The system is decentralised and based on district registries. Although there can be personal searches of the register, it is far more common for applications for entries on the register and searches to be made by post or, increasingly, electronically.

Several major Law Commission reviews[3] of land registration culminated in the Land Registration Act 2002.[4] It made very significant changes to many of the fundamental principles of land registration; the detail is almost completely redrafted. It follows that the pre-2002 material is of limited value when looking at the new system. Many of the issues debated in the older cases are explicitly resolved by the legislation. Those cases may, however, remain of use in illustrating the policy questions involved and (where they are confirmed by the 2002 Act) how the legislation is likely to be applied. In 2016, the Law Commission issued a Consultation Paper[5] reviewing the operation of the 2002 Act. This paper deals with many detailed points (some of which will be mentioned in the relevant sections in

---

[1] Land Registration Rules 2003 (hereafter LRR), rr 5, 8, 9.

[2] Land Registration Act 2002 (hereafter LRA, or 2002 Act), s 60; for the application of this, contrast *Drake* v *Fripp* [2012] 1 P&CR 69 and *Parshall* v *Hackney* [2013] Ch 568. Law Com CP 227, para 15.35 proposes clearer guidance as to the limits of the general boundary rule. The rule reduces the cost of producing maps and, just as important, reduces the scope for bitter disputes between neighbours over small areas of land at the time of first registration. However, fixed boundaries are possible and might become more common: Law Com No 271, paras 9.10–9.13.

[3] Law Com No 158 (1987) was not implemented, though some of its thinking has found its way into the reforms. Law Com No 254 (1998) contains a full analysis of the reasons for change. Law Com No 271 (2001) contains the draft Bill and explains how it is intended to operate.

[4] Cooke [2002] Conv 11 provides a useful commentary on the new provisions; see also Dixon [2003] Conv 136. For changes to adverse possession and e-conveyancing, see pp 74 and 113 above.

[5] Law Com CP 227 (March 2016).

this chapter) but does not challenge the basic structure and policies established in 2002. However, there is a particularly full analysis of rectification and indemnity (areas that have received considerable academic and judicial attention) and more will be said in those areas.

For many years, the register was closed to the public. This secrecy was largely based on the inherent privacy of unregistered conveyancing. Over the years, secrecy became more out of tune with the times and more obviously different from the practice of other countries. The position was changed by the Land Registration Act 1988,[6] which opened the registers to the public. Today, LRA, s 66, provides for access to the register and to documents referred to in the register. However, access to documents can be limited, especially if they contain commercially sensitive information.[7]

An open register has several advantages. Obviously, it enables owners of land to be identified. This may be important simply in order to know to whom to make an offer to buy the land or whom to contact about a nuisance. In addition, knowing the nature of another person's title may be very important because it might disclose rights over one's own land. Tenants form a significant group of persons benefited by the public register. For example, a tenant may not know whether the landlord is the freeholder or is the holder of a head lease; the landlord's title can now be inspected. This may be of vital importance both in deciding whether to take a lease and also if subsequent difficulties arise.[8]

It is sometimes said[9] that three principles underpin registration systems: the mirror principle, curtain principle and insurance principle. The mirror principle is that all facts material to the title are to be found on the register. The curtain principle means that purchasers need not look behind the register and, in particular, are not concerned with the operation of trusts.[10] Finally, the insurance principle provides that where any flaw occurs so that the register fails to reflect the title properly, the person who loses should receive compensation. However, these are very much ideals. It would be wrong to think either that registration was intended to put these principles into effect or that it would always be good policy to do so. There may be competing considerations which justify different approaches. Overriding interests provide the most obvious exception, as a purchaser is bound by these interests (which include trust beneficiaries in actual occupation) despite their not being on the register; no compensation is payable.

2. Types of interests

Land registration may be said to recognise four types of interest: registrable interests, interests created by registrable dispositions, minor interests and overriding interests. Taking registrable interests first, these are principally legal fees simple and leases.[11] Registrable dispositions are those dispositions by a registered proprietor which the legislation

---

[6] See Law Com No 148.

[7] LRR, rr 136–137 ('prejudicial information', defined by r 131). In 2007, identity fraud concerns forced the Land Registry to limit online access to documents.

[8] If title is not registered, an intending tenant has limited rights to inspect the landlord's title deeds: Law of Property Act 1925 (hereafter LPA), s 44(2), (4)–(4A).

[9] Ruoff, *An Englishman Looks at the Torrens System*, Chapter 2.

[10] This is greatly aided by overreaching, which is applicable to both registered and unregistered land. Owen and Cahill [2017] Conv 26 suggest that the curtain principle could be modified.

[11] LRA, s 3. Also included are rentcharges, franchises and profits in gross, though we will not consider these in detail.

requires to be completed by registration.[12] They include transfers, leases, charges and mortgages. Minor interests form a residual category of interests that must be protected on the register before a purchaser can be bound. Overriding interests are quite different: they affect purchasers despite not being entered on the register.

The first three categories all must be entered on the register: we generally refer to *registering* registrable interests and dispositions and *protecting* minor interests. Why do we distinguish between them? The first category (registrable interests) is special in that these are the only interests which can have their own files. Thus a charge (not a registrable interest) is not registrable by itself, but only as a disposition by a registered proprietor: it forms part of the proprietor's title. On the other hand, a lease for, say, 10 years can be registered (indeed, has to be registered) whether or not the landlord is registered. There are then separate registered titles for the freehold (if registered) and lease.

Registrable dispositions are limited to specified grants (transfers, leases, etc) by an existing registered proprietor. They are special, relative to other dispositions constituting minor interests, because they are guaranteed to exist and have priority protection over earlier but unprotected interests.[13] This protection of registered dispositions is illustrated by the following examples. Suppose Andrew confers on Brenda (by contract) an option to purchase Redacre; this is not protected on the register. Andrew then sells and transfers Redacre to Caroline, whose transfer is registered. Caroline's registration gives priority over Brenda's unprotected option. By way of contrast, suppose that, instead of selling to Caroline, Andrew contracts to sell Redacre to Dawn, who protects the contract on the register. Dawn has merely a minor interest and therefore loses out to Brenda, despite the fact that Brenda's interest was never protected and Dawn's was.

Why should we give this greater effect to registered interests and dispositions?[14] As regards registrable interests, perhaps the best explanation is that registration concentrates upon those interests which are most likely to be bought and sold. It enables the purchaser to discover all the details of the interest involved and to rely upon their being correct. This readily explains why fees simple and leases are registrable: they are the interests most likely to be sold. It is more difficult to justify giving less protection to minor interests than to other registered dispositions. It may be observed that registrable interests and registered dispositions (once registered) involve legal estates and interests, whilst minor interests are nearly always equitable. Although this by itself fails to justify making the distinction, it might be asserted that those taking registrable dispositions are most likely to be paying large sums of money, most interested in the disponor's title and willing to pay higher registration fees to obtain greater protection.

A. Registrable interests: first registration

In this section, we will look at the initial registration of fees simple and leases, when the grantor's title is not already registered. Once the grantor's title is registered, then we are

---

[12] Ibid, s 27.

[13] LRA, s 29. They also attract very significantly higher registration fees than the entry of minor interests.

[14] E-conveyancing will reduce the differences: only those unprotected interests which are exempt from electronic disposition requirements would be valid and thus capable of affecting a subsequent interest.

in the realm of registrable dispositions, to be considered in the following section. As around 95% of titles are registered, this means that this section covers the small number still unregistered.

(i) *The fee simple*

For most practical purposes, the legal fee simple absolute in possession may be regarded as equivalent to ownership. It therefore comes as no surprise that registration of the legal fee simple lies at the heart of the registration system. Any holder of the legal fee simple can apply for registration.[15]

What happens if a person believes that he or she might be prejudiced by a future first registration? Entry of a land charge (where available) will ensure that the interest so protected is discovered on first registration and then entered on the register. For other rights, it is possible to enter a *caution against first registration*. Such cautions are uncommon, but they ensure that the person entering the caution has the opportunity to object to the registration and, where appropriate, to have a notice entered on the register.[16] However, it is not possible for a person claiming the fee simple (or lease) to enter such a caution. If it is desired to advance a claim to the fee simple, then the appropriate action is to apply for voluntary registration of it.[17]

(a) **Compulsory registration**

Initial registration usually takes place as a result of the provisions for compulsory registration. LRA, ss 4–8 provide for registration of the fee simple within two months of a conveyance (either on sale or gift), a first legal mortgage or an assent by personal representatives. Thus, compulsory registration operates only after there has been a transfer of the legal title or mortgage. There are several justifications for this. The fact that lawyers are likely to be involved means that the need to register is unlikely to be overlooked. Further, the title to the land will usually have been approved on an unregistered land purchase. This latter factor enables the registry more quickly to approve the fee simple for registration.

It has taken over 150 years for registration to cover 95% of all titles. Partly, the explanation is that it is only since 1990 that compulsory registration has operated throughout England and Wales. Until then, registration was limited to designated areas; their expansion determined the growth of registration. Now that relatively little land remains unregistered, getting the remainder on to the register requires expansion of the 'triggers' for first registration (summarised in the previous paragraph). Extra triggers have already been introduced under powers contained in LRA, s 5.[18]

It has been observed that around 95% of titles are registered. However, the proportion of the land mass is smaller – around 88% in 2016. This is partly because large estates tend to change hands infrequently and partly because registration was initially concentrated on

---

[15] LRA, s 3.
[16] LRA, s 16. Sections 15–22 regulate cautions against first registration.
[17] Ibid, s 15(3); Law Com No 271, para 3.58.
[18] SI 2008 No 2872 (partition; appointment of new trustees).

urban areas. Plot sizes are smaller in those areas, making them quicker to map and register. Complete registration is still some years away, but we can look forward to the time when unregistered land principles will cease to have much practical impact. The Land Registry has targeted large landowners (seeking voluntary registration)[19] and has enjoyed considerable success in increasing the proportion of the registered land mass in recent years. It is currently increasing by around 2% a year.

Failure to register within two months results in the loss of the legal estate.[20] However, the transferee retains the equitable interest in the land.[21] In cases of oversight, the Chief Land Registrar is generally willing to allow registration outside the normal period.[22]

(b) Forms of registered titles

Perhaps surprisingly, there are three forms of freehold title with which a person can be registered. In virtually every case, a fee simple *absolute* is registered; this indicates that there is nothing wrong or dubious about the title as submitted for registration. It need not, however, be perfect. Some registration systems look for perfection in titles presented for registration, but our scheme uses more of a cost-benefit approach: do the merits of allowing registration without stringent inquiries outweigh the remote chance of having to pay compensation if an error is later discovered?[23] Technical and remotely relevant flaws in a title will not generally act as a bar to registration: it is sufficient if the registrar believes that any defect 'will not cause the holding under the title to be disturbed'.[24]

If there is a specific problem with the title (perhaps a deed has been lost), then there may be registration with *qualified* title.[25] This means that there is no guarantee in respect of the specified defect. Otherwise, it is the same as an absolute title. Qualified titles are very rare: those that do exist may be upgraded to absolute titles if the registrar is satisfied as to the title.[26]

Possessory titles provide our third category.[27] They are designed for cases where a documentary title cannot be proved and the title depends upon adverse possession. Possessory title confers no guarantee of title at the time of registration. However, subsequent problems, such as forgery of the newly registered proprietor's signature on a transfer, will be covered by the guarantee. Possessory titles may be upgraded into absolute titles, and there is normally entitlement to conversion after being in possession as proprietor for 12 years.[28]

---

[19] Voluntary registration is encouraged by a 25% reduction in fees: Land Registration Fee Order 2013 (SI 2013 No 3174), art 2(5).
[20] LRA, s 7. This extends to cancelled applications: *Sainsbury's Supermarkets Ltd* v *Olympia Homes Ltd* [2006] 1 P&CR 289 at [70].
[22] LRA, s 6(4), (5); Ruoff and Roper, *Registered Conveyancing*, para 8.011.
[21] But dealing with the land may be difficult: *Pinekerry Ltd* v *Needs (Kenneth) (Contractors) Ltd* (1992) 64 P&CR 245. The cost of replacement conveyances is imposed on the transferee: LRA, s 8.
[23] Ruoff, *An Englishman Looks at the Torrens System*, pp 35–36.
[24] LRA, s 9(3); the general test is that the title must be such as a professional adviser would approve (s 9(2)).
[25] Ibid, s 9(4), (6).
[26] Ibid, s 62.
[27] Ibid, s 9(5), (7).
[28] Ibid, s 62(1), (4).

(c) The effect of first registration

In every case, the legal fee simple is vested in the proprietor, regardless of whether that person previously held such a title.[29] That, however, is only the beginning. Where there is first registration with absolute title, the effect of LRA, s 11(4) is that the estate is vested in the proprietor subject only to interests protected on the register and overriding interests. We will investigate overriding interests later, but it might be noted that the relevant over-riding interests are found in Sched 1. It will be remembered that qualified and possessory titles enjoy more limited protection.

There are two further exceptions to the protection of absolute titles. Where the proprie-tor is a trustee, the beneficiaries' interests bind the proprietor if he has notice of them.[30] Second, adverse possession claims will bind a first proprietor who has notice of them.[31] Normally, the adverse possessor will have an overriding interest by virtue of being in actual occupation. This second exception is needed for the less common context where adverse possession has been completed but there is no actual occupation – one example would be if the adverse possessor had leased the land to a tenant.

An important task of the registrar on inspecting the title is to discover adverse rights such as restrictive covenants and to protect them on the register, usually by way of entry of a notice. It may be recalled that the entry of a notice on the register does not guarantee the interest so protected. This is important if the interest either has never existed or has become unenforceable. Goff LJ confirmed this in *Kitney v MEPC Ltd*.[32] As he observed, the object of registration is intended to be curative of the proprietor's title, whereas to guarantee a minor interest would be destructive of the proprietor's title.

What happens if the first registered proprietor did not own the land prior to registration? On the face of it, registration confers a good title upon the proprietor, but the previous owner has a number of arguments available. Most obviously, a claim for alteration of the register may be available.[33] Controversially, Palk has questioned whether the previous leg-islation did indeed transfer an *equitable* title to the proprietor.[34] This analysis appears to be inconsistent with the wording of s 11[35] and is unlikely to survive the analysis in *Swift 1st Ltd v Chief Land Registrar*.[36] There, the Court of Appeal held that a good equitable title is conferred by registration of a forged disposition. Even if the previous owner is in actual occupation, it seems most unlikely after *Swift 1st* that there could be an overriding interest.[37]

(ii) *Leases*

A legal lease for a period exceeding seven years may be registered in exactly the same way as a fee simple. One remarkable aspect of this is that there may be two titles (more, if there

[29] Ibid, s 58.
[30] Ibid, s 11(5).
[31] Ibid, s 11(4)(c). Under the previous law, all interests by adverse possession were binding as overriding interests.
[32] [1977] 1 WLR 981 (option earlier made void by the land charges legislation); see also p 251 below.
[33] See p 280 below.
[34] (1974) 38 Conv 236.
[35] Wilde [1999] Conv 382 at p 385; Harpum in *Rationalizing Property, Equity and Trusts* (ed Getzler), pp 191–195.
[36] [2015] Ch 602, discussed at pp 250, 264 below.
[37] This is discussed at p 264 below.

are subleases) in respect of the same plot of land: one for the fee simple and the other for the lease. This does no harm because they will cross-refer to each other. There are two justifications for having separate registered titles for leases. The first is that there are many long leases where the freehold is unregistered. It would impede dealings with such leases to say that they cannot be registered. The second reason is that leases may be bought and sold, be mortgaged and have other subordinate interests created out of them. All of this could in theory be reflected in a single register based on the fee simple. In practice, such a register might become unduly cumbersome because rights affecting the lease would have to be distinguished from those affecting the fee simple (and vice versa). The justification of the seven-year period will be considered when we consider leases as registrable dispositions.[38]

(a) Compulsory registration

Whether the landlord's title is registered or not, every grant of a lease for more than seven years must be registered. In this section, we are interested only in those cases where the landlord is not registered (otherwise, there is a registered disposition). There are the same two months for registration as in the case of freeholds and, again, the result of failure to register is the loss of the legal estate. Some pre-2002 leases are not registered because registration was not compulsory at the time they were granted. If such leases are assigned today, then they must be registered within two months, provided that more than seven years are left at the time of assignment.[39]

(b) Special categories of leases

So far, we have been dealing with what may be described as 'normal' leases. Two special categories, however, will be considered,[40] the rules varying as to whether we are considering grants out of unregistered land or registrable dispositions. For convenience, the rules for registered dispositions are included in this section.

Perhaps most important is the future lease: a lease (not merely a contract for a lease)[41] under which possession will be taken in the future. Before the 2002 Act, a short future lease could be an overriding interest; this formed a trap for purchasers as future leases are not discoverable from inspecting the land. To avoid this, they are no longer overriding interests and must be registered when granted, regardless of their length.[42] There is a relaxation for grants taking effect in possession within three months: this provides for the common case where the grant (or renewal) is shortly before commencement. However, it may be noted that some leases (for example, to students in respect of the following academic year) commonly exceed this three-month period.[43]

---

[38] See p 247 below.
[39] LRA, s 4(1)(a), (2).
[40] Other special categories are of less general interest.
[41] The distinction has been considered in the context of formality rules: p 112 above. Leases may commence in up to 21 years' time: LPA, s 149(3).
[42] LRA, ss 4(1)(d) (grants out of unregistered land), 27(2)(b)(ii) (registrable dispositions).
[43] In any event, all future leases have to be by deed to be legal: *Long* v *Tower Hamlets LBC* [1998] Ch 197. This is important for overriding interest status: Brown and Pawlowski [2010] Conv 146.

The second special category is that of the discontinuous lease. An example is a lease for the first week in August for the next four years. For similar reasons as with future leases, it is thought desirable that short discontinuous leases should be registered. As well as voluntary registration being possible, they constitute registrable dispositions: they are not overriding interests binding transferees of registered land. However, they are not subject to compulsory registration on grant out of unregistered land[44]; such leases constitute overriding interests binding the proprietor once the fee simple is later registered.

(c) Forms of leasehold titles and their effect

The various forms of freehold title (absolute, qualified and possessory) and their effects apply to leases. Leases pose one special problem. If the freehold is not registered, then how is the registrar to know whether the landlord owns the fee simple (essential if the lease is to be effective) and whether the land is free from encumbrances such as restrictive covenants?[45] To cover this situation, the legislation utilises *good leasehold* title. Its effect is to guarantee the lease, but not against any defects in the landlord's title.[46] If the freehold is later registered, then the earlier uncertainty is cleared away and the lease can be upgraded to absolute title.[47] As unregistered land becomes progressively rarer, so will good leasehold titles.

(iii) *Other registrable interests*

These are rentcharges, franchises and profits *à prendre* in gross (i.e. where there is no land benefited by the profit). Voluntary registration is possible, although there is no provision for compulsory registration. If the grantor is registered, however, then the rules below on registrable dispositions will operate.

B. Registrable dispositions

Unsurprisingly, a registered proprietor, whether of a fee simple or a lease, has wide powers. LRA, s 23 provides that these are, in essence, the same as the powers permitted by the general law for unregistered titles.[48] This means that the proprietor can, for example, sell, lease or mortgage the title. The registered chargee can both deal with the charge and exercise a chargee's rights (including sale) over the charged estate.[49]

Section 26 is a very important provision. This deems the powers of the proprietor to be 'free of any limitation', though the proprietor remains liable for any breach of duty if a limitation is disregarded. This is particularly important for trusts of land, as such limitations are most likely to be found in the trust of land context. An example would

---

[44] Law Com CP 227 para 3.76 proposes making registration compulsory.
[45] Until the 2002 Act, a lessee had no right to inspect the title to the fee simple (see now LPA, s 44(4A)).
[46] LRA, ss 10(3), 12(6).
[47] Ibid, s 62(2).
[48] A disposition can be registered even though it pre-dates the registered proprietor's obtaining a transfer (and being registered): *First National Bank plc* v *Thompson* [1996] Ch 231 (estoppel based).
[49] *Skelwith (Leisure) Ltd* v *Armstrong* [2015] Ch 345, doubted by Law Com CP 227, paras 5.41, 19.09.

be an exclusion of the power of the trustees to sell. Section 26 will be considered in detail as part of trusts of land,[50] but two points are worth noting now. The first is that, as one might expect, limitations protected by entry on the register are exempted from the effect of s 26. The second point is that there is (quite deliberately) no exemption for overriding interests. It follows that a beneficiary who wishes to enforce a limitation on trustees' powers cannot rely on being in actual occupation: it is essential to enter a restriction on the register.

Section 27 details those dispositions which are registrable. Registration requirements must be satisfied before they can be legal. We will now consider how these rules operate and then the effect of registration. We will assume that the grantor's estate is a fee simple, though the rules also apply to dispositions of registered leases.

(i) *Dispositions within s 27*

(a) Transfers

The most obvious disposition is an outright transfer. As observed above, no legal title will pass until the purchaser is registered as proprietor[51]; there is no two-month period as allowed for first registration. This is more than a technicality: delay in registration may prejudice the purchaser if other interests are protected or (for some interests) become overriding prior to registration.[52]

Before registration of the transfer, the purchaser will have an equitable interest by virtue of giving consideration, provided that there is writing to satisfy formality requirements.[53] What if there is a transfer by way of gift, when there is no consideration? The answer is that the donee may utilise the principle that, if a donor does everything in his power to complete a gift, then equity will treat the gift as complete: the donor will hold on trust for the donee.

Until the 2002 Act, registration of a transfer required the production of the land certificate. This certificate was, essentially, a copy of the register and was possessed by the proprietor. It told the proprietor that he or she was the proprietor. Today, there is no longer a land certificate,[54] although proprietors are given a 'title information document'. This document looks the same as the old land certificate, but it is not mentioned in the legislation and has no legal role. The reason why the land certificate used to be required on transfer was to prevent fraud. An obvious danger to a proprietor is that anybody could forge a signature on a transfer, and this might well not be spotted by the Land Registry. Requiring the certificate to be produced minimised this risk as long as the proprietor safeguarded the certificate. It was dropped in order to enable e-conveyancing to operate in a

---

[50] See p 360 below. Section 26 is not limited to registrable dispositions.

[51] LRA, s 27(1); Ferris in *Contemporary Property Law* (ed Jackson and Wilde), Chapter 7.

[52] See pp 260 and 273 below. Although LRA, s 24 enables owner's powers to be exercised, delay in registering may have serious consequences – for example, difficulty in enforcing rights as an assignee of a leasehold reversion: (*Rother District Investments Ltd v Corke* [2004] 2 P&CR 311) and giving notice to quit (*Stodday Land Ltd v Pye* [2017] 1 P&CR 56).

[53] By analogy with the case of informal leases: *Walsh v Lonsdale* (1882) 21 Ch D 9. For a registration example, see *Barclays Bank Ltd v Taylor* [1974] Ch 137.

[54] LRA, Sched 10, para 4 authorises the issue of land certificates, but has not been activated.

paper-free environment.[55] However, it may be no coincidence that there have been many more instances of fraud in recent years; the reform may be regretted, especially given the delays in introducing e-conveyancing.

(b) Leases

Leases granted for more than seven years are registrable dispositions. Registration will take the form of a new leasehold title, with a notice on the grantor's title.[56] It should be noted that there is no two-month period as for leases granted by an unregistered landlord. A registrable disposition, just like a transfer, simply has no effect at law until registered. The period of seven years represents a significant reduction from the pre-2002 period of 21 years. Shorter leases may be overriding interests, not requiring entry on the register.

Why are short leases not registrable, and why do we have a period of seven years today? The answer lies in the attempt to identify those short leases which are relatively unlikely to be sold and mortgaged. A registration requirement for these short leases would bring little benefit and, indeed, be both unrealistic and unduly burdensome (as well as clogging up the register). The reduction in the period was justified partly because the length of many commercial leases has declined over recent decades, partly because it enables the true state of the title to be discovered from the register and partly because the cost and complexity of registration is less than it used to be.[57]

There is provision for the seven-year period to be reduced.[58] This was intended to link in with e-conveyancing; the Law Commission does not now envisage it to be acted on in the near future.[59] In any event, reduction below three years would not seem feasible. Given that leases under three years can be created orally or in writing, it is less likely that legal advisers will be involved and any requirement of registration would be unrealistic.

Finally, we have seen[60] that future and discontinuous leases constitute registrable dispositions regardless of their length.

(c) Registered charges

Unlike fees simple and leases, charges (mortgages) do not have their own titles. They can be entered only on an existing registered title. A fresh provision in the 2002 Act is that the only form of legal mortgage that can be created and registered is a legal charge: mortgages by long lease are not permitted.[61]

(d) Easements and profits

Like charges, easements do not have their own separate titles. If legal, they may be registered on the title of the land benefited by the easement and a notice is entered on the title of the servient land.[62]

---

[55] Law Com No 271, para 9.88.
[56] LRA, Sched 2, para 3; also s 38.
[57] Law Com No 271, paras 3.14–3.16.
[58] Ibid, para 3.17; LRA, s 118 authorises this.
[59] Law Com CP 227, para 3.94
[60] See pp 244–245 above.
[61] LRA, ss 23(1)(a), 27(2)(f). For mortgages by long lease, see p 578 below.
[62] Ibid, ss 59(1) (registration), 38 (notice); Sched 2, para 7; LRR, rr 73–74 (servient title unregistered).

Compulsory registration operates only where there is an express grant.[63] This means that the many implied easements, including those passing under the 'general words' implied into transfers,[64] and those arising by prescription do not have to be registered: they will usually be overriding interests. A notice may be placed on the register to protect these non-express easements.[65]

Failure to comply with compulsory registration means that the easement can be only equitable, so that an entry on the register will be essential for a purchaser to be bound.[66] One peculiarity is that easements contained in short leases have to be registered, even though the lease itself may be an overriding interest.[67] This constitutes a significant trap, given that such easements are quite common. Where compulsory registration does not apply, voluntary registration is permitted.[68]

Profits appurtenant to land are treated in a generally identical manner. However, profits in gross (those not for the benefit of land) have their own titles, rather than being registered on the title to the dominant land.[69]

(ii) *The effect of registration*

LRA, s 29 provides for the effect of registered dispositions. So long as the transfer is for valuable consideration,[70] it defeats any earlier unprotected interest, unless that interest is overriding (as listed in Sched 3). This protection for registered dispositions is vitally important, as it establishes that the transferee (or other disponee) can safely rely upon the register.[71] Several contrasts with first registration may be noted: the need for valuable consideration is introduced and there is no special protection for trust interests or adverse possession.[72]

Several difficult problems emerge. Under the previous law, there was much debate as to whether the transferee must be in good faith. This is such a large issue that it will be considered separately later,[73] together with the related question as to whether a purchaser can be bound by unprotected claims that are personal in nature. The principal problem to

---

[63] LRA, s 27(2)(d). Law Com CP 227, para 16.32 would exclude easements in short leases not requiring registration.
[64] LPA, s 62 (p 531 below): see LRA, s 27(7).
[65] LRA, ss 32, 34.
[66] Reversing the previous law: *Celsteel Ltd* v *Alton House Holdings Ltd* [1985] 1 WLR 204 (see p 276 below).
[67] Note that the easement will affect adjoining land, whereas the lease as an overriding interest affects only the landlord's title to the leased land.
[68] LRA, s 13(a); LRR, rr 73–74. There is also provision (LRA, ss 37, 71) for discovering and protecting unregistered easements when later transfers are registered.
[69] Ibid, s 3 (voluntary registration) and Sched 2, paras 6, 7 (registrable dispositions).
[70] *Midland Bank Trust Co Ltd* v *Green* [1981] AC 513 at p 532 (land charges context) shows that this is not a demanding requirement. However, nominal consideration does not suffice (LRA, s 132(1)); Law Com CP 227, para 7.66 suggests that this should change. A case can be made for protecting volunteers: O'Connor in *Modern Studies in Property Law*, Vol 2 (ed Cooke), pp 90–91.
[71] Although the need to protect purchasers is often taken for granted, Cooper in *Modern Studies in Property Law*, Vol 8 (ed Barr), Chapter 17 argues that it is often taken too far (an analysis not limited to s 29).
[72] Adverse possession claims may constitute actual occupation overriding interests, though the modern scope for adverse possession in registered land is very limited (see p 74 above).
[73] See p 254 below.

be considered now concerns the effect of forged transfers.[74] Three situations need to be distinguished, in each of which P is the original registered proprietor.

If A forges P's signature on a transfer to himself and is then registered, it seems obvious that A cannot be protected as a result of his fraudulent and criminal conduct, even though this is not explicitly stated in the legislation. The second situation is where A forges P's signature on a transfer to himself and, having obtained registration, later sells the land to B. Presuming that B is unaware of the forgery, he will obtain a good title to the land on being registered.[75] This is because s 29(1) provides that unprotected interests (here, the claim of P, whose signature was forged) are defeated by a registered transfer.

The third and most difficult situation is where A forges P's signature on a transfer direct to C, where C is registered and believes in good faith that she is buying from P. On the one hand, C has not been misled by the register. Instead, she has been duped by A into believing that she is dealing with P. Protecting C will reduce the incentive for purchasers to ensure that documents are genuine. On the other hand, C has been registered as the new proprietor, and it may be argued that, having paid for registration, she should obtain the same guarantee as any other purchaser. Discussion of this problem in Torrens registration systems in Australia and New Zealand[76] contrasts immediate indefeasibility (favouring a purchaser such as C) and deferred indefeasibility (protecting a subsequent purchaser such as B). Currently, immediate indefeasibility generally applies.[77] In assessing the question in our registration system, it should be remembered that rectification may in any event defeat C's protection.

Under the pre-2002 law, *Malory Enterprises Ltd* v *Cheshire Homes (UK) Ltd*[78] held that there was no disposition where there was a forgery – s 29 did not therefore apply. This was applied to the 2002 Act by Newey J in *Fitzwilliam* v *Richall Holding Services Ltd.*[79] This approach was widely criticised by commentators. Leaving aside more technical arguments, the situation provides a good test of the extent to which registration merely reflects existing rights to land, as contrasted with establishing conclusively what those rights are – in unregistered land, C clearly loses. Two specific criticisms emerged. The first was that s 58 vests title in C,[80] though this section refers explicitly to the *legal estate*. Nobody doubts

---

[74] Fox in *Modern Studies in Property Law*, Vol 3 (ed Cooke), Chapter 2. Other void transfers raise similar issues: Harpum in *Rationalizing Property, Equity and Trusts* (ed Getzler), p 189. Scottish Law Commission Discussion Paper No 125, para 7.16. (with Discussion Paper No 128) contains the fullest analysis of the issues regarding void transfers: Cooke [2004] Conv 482.

[75] *Pinto* v *Lim* [2005] EWHC 630 (Ch) provides an example under the old law.

[76] Torrens registration was first introduced in South Australia by Sir Robert Torrens in 1858 and has been enacted by many Commonwealth countries. It developed far more quickly than land registration in England.

[77] *Frazer* v *Walker* [1967] 1 AC 569. Modern arguments tend to question immediate indefeasibility (O'Connor in *Modern Studies in Property Law*, Vol 3 (ed Cooke), Chapter 3 and (2009) 13 Edin LR 194) and it has been rejected in Scotland in favour of a form of deferred indefeasibility (Land Registration etc (Scotland) Act 2012, ss 50, 86).

[78] [2002] Ch 216 at [65]; for an earlier contrary suggestion, see RJ Smith (1985) 101 LQR 79. See also the useful comparative survey by Harding and Bryan in *Modern Studies in Property Law*, Vol 5 (ed Dixon), Chapter 1.

[79] [2013] 1 P&CR 318, criticised by Dixon (2013) 129 LQR 320, Cooke [2013] Conv 344, Lees (2013) 76 MLR 924. Gardner [2013] Conv 530 supports *Fitzwilliam*.

[80] Harpum in *Rationalizing Property, Equity and Trusts* (ed Getzler), pp 197–202. Harpum's analysis is supported by Cooke [2004] Conv 482 at pp 485–486, but Hill-Smith's narrower explanation of s 58 ([2009] Conv 127 at pp 133–135) is persuasive.

that C has the legal estate; the question is whether A has a proprietary right that can be asserted against that legal estate. Secondly, even a forged transfer should count as a 'disposition' so as to receive the protection of s 29.[81]

The issue was reviewed by the Court of Appeal in *Swift 1st Ltd* v *Chief Land Registrar*.[82] Noting the above criticisms, the court held that *Malory* had been decided per incuriam: in particular, s 114 of the 1925 Act had not been dealt with and that section assumes that s 29 (technically, its predecessor in the 1925 Act) applies to void transfers. This reasoning is somewhat curious, given that s 114 was not re-enacted in the 2002 Act and had not been relied upon by any of the critics. However, it seems likely that *Swift 1st* will settle the controversy and be generally approved. It must be remembered that it may well not represent the final answer.[83] A will often be able to claim rectification; indeed, C had not opposed rectification in *Swift 1st*. The issue in the case (discussed later in this chapter) was whether C had a right to payment of indemnity from the Land Registry. It is worth noting that the reasoning in *Swift 1st* does not distinguish clearly between the s 29 and s 58 arguments. This can be important, as s 29 (unlike s 58) requires valuable consideration and is subject to overriding interests. However, the s 114 point appears to relate to s 29 and that the court assumes that overriding interests can affect C.

A few points on specific dispositions should be added. An interesting rule for leases is that even short leases (ones which do not need to be registered) enjoy the benefits of registration.[84] A separate point is that a transfer of a lease carries with it liability on covenants affecting the land. This means that, for example, a restrictive covenant binding a tenant in a lease need not be entered on the register.[85] As regards easements, the benefits of registration apply even if the benefited land is not registered, so that the only entry is a notice on the grantor's title.

C. Minor interests

Minor interests constitute a residuary category, covering all interests in land. Although the 2002 Act ceases to employ the term 'minor interest', it remains a useful descriptive label. Two points should be noted in this respect. The first is that, although we will be dealing with methods of protection of minor interests, the restriction can be used where there is no interest in land. Second, minor interests can overlap other registered land categories. Thus, most overriding interests can be protected by way of notice, as can a registrable interest.

We are dealing with an enormous range of interests, from restrictive covenants to a fee simple that lacks legal status only because it is not registered. Perhaps the most

---

[81] Cogently argued by Hill-Smith [2009] Conv 127.

[82] [2015] Ch 602 (Lees (2015) 131 LQR 515; Smith [2015] CLJ 401; Milne [2015] Conv 356).

[83] The question whether A, if in actual occupation, can assert an overriding interest is considered at p 264 below.

[84] LRA, s 29(4): treated as registered at the time of grant. An example under the similar previous law is *Barclays Bank plc* v *Zaroovabli* [1997] Ch 321 at p 327. The operation of s 29(4) is considered in Law Com CP 227, paras 8.51 *et seq.*

[85] Ibid, s 29(2)(b). This, by virtue of s 29(4), appears also to apply to overriding interest leases.

important characteristic of a minor interest is that it will not bind a registered disposition unless it is entered on the register. Most minor interests will be equitable, but this is not an invariable rule.[86]

(i) *Methods of protection*

The wide range of minor interests is one reason for having two different ways of protecting them: notice and restriction. Protection by notice[87] has the simple effect that a purchaser is bound, although the interest is not guaranteed.[88] The general position is that any interest can be protected by notice. We might note three exceptions.[89]

The first is straightforward: interests under trusts of land (and old Settled Land Act settlements) must be protected by restriction rather than notice. The reason, as we will see shortly, is that the restriction is ideally suited to this type of overreachable interest. Next, leases not exceeding three years cannot be protected. We have observed the reasons why leases not exceeding seven years should be overriding interests rather than registrable dispositions. The upshot is an option to protect leases between three and seven years, although it is difficult to comprehend why that option was not extended to all short leases.

The final exception covers restrictive covenants between landlord and tenant (nearly all leases contain such covenants). Despite the lack of any entry on the register, covenants binding the tenant are enforceable against the assignee following a transfer of the lease.[90] This is justified as those dealing with the lease will read it and discover the covenants. Furthermore, any other rule would require entries in respect of virtually every lease. However, a covenant which binds land other than the leased land must be protected by notice.[91] These last covenants will often be landlord covenants. As those dealing with the landlord's adjoining land will rarely consult the lease, it makes sense to insist on entry in the register.

The proprietor may wish to challenge the existence of the interest. To meet this possibility, the legislation distinguishes between 'agreed' and 'unilateral' notices.[92] Unsurprisingly, a notice is agreed if the proprietor applied for it or consented to it. Less obviously, it also applies if the registrar is satisfied as to its validity. Any other notice is unilateral, in which case the proprietor has to be told about it by the registrar and may apply for it to be cancelled, whereupon it must be justified by the person who entered it.[93]

---

[86] Thus an implied easement which fails the requirements for overriding interest status (p 277 below) is still legal.

[87] LRA, s 32. There is no requirement to identify the interest protected: *Bank of Scotland plc* v *Joseph* [2014] 1 P&CR 302.

[88] Thus, a purchaser who has a contract predating (and having priority to) the interest protected on the register may rely on the priority of that contract: *A2 Dominion Homes Ltd* v *Prince Evans Solicitors* [2015] EWHC 2490 (Ch); see also p 230 above.

[89] Ibid, s 33.

[90] Ibid, s 29(2)(b).

[91] This changes the pre-2002 Act position: *Oceanic Village Ltd* v *United Attractions Ltd* [2000] Ch 234.

[92] LRA, s 34. Law Com CP 227, para 9.116 would change the terminology to 'full' and 'summary' notices.

[93] Ibid, ss 35–36. Disputes will be resolved by the First-tier Tribunal (the successor to the adjudicator), with an appeal to the Upper Tribunal: s 73 and Part 11. The details of justifying notices are considered in Chapter 9, Law Com CP 227.

The entry of a unilateral notice could still damage the proprietor, especially if it causes a sale to fall through. To cover this, compensation is payable if it is entered without reasonable cause; the same applies to restrictions and more generally when a person objects to applications to the registrar.[94] In addition, the court may order an entry to be removed, even if there is reasonable cause – for example, where loss would be caused to the proprietor and compensation could not be afforded.[95]

Restrictions

The principal feature of a restriction is that it may prevent a future entry on the register: registration will be refused if the terms of the restriction are not complied with.[96] The trust of land provides an excellent example. The trustees can sell the land, overreaching the beneficial interests, so long as the purchase money is paid to two trustees. The two-trustee requirement can be reflected in a restriction that a transfer by fewer than two trustees cannot be registered. A restriction is helpful to purchasers because they know what to do in order to be registered and take clear of the beneficial interests. It is also more effective for the beneficiary than a notice. Instead of having to argue a case against a registered transferee, the beneficiary knows that no wrongful registration can take place. Indeed, so appropriate is the restriction that interests under trusts of land cannot be protected by notice. On the other hand, a restriction only prevents a registration: it does not confer any priority on the interest.[97]

It is significant that the circumstances in which a restriction can be entered are unlimited; in particular, it is not limited to the protection of interests in land. An interesting example of this is provided by positive covenants, which do not constitute interests in land binding purchasers.[98] A purchaser entering into such a covenant (in favour of the seller) may agree to a restriction that any subsequent transfer will require the consent of the original seller, that consent to be given if that transferee agrees with the original seller to comply with the covenant. In this way, the seller can ensure that no subsequent transfer takes place without there being a fresh contract with the transferee: the practical effect is that the covenant can be made enforceable against the transferee.[99]

Largely because of this flexibility, there are elaborate provisions governing the entry of restrictions. They can be entered by the registrar (which may be obligatory where joint proprietors are registered)[100] or by application[101] and may be ordered by the

---

[94] LRA, s 77.

[95] *Nugent v Nugent* [2015] Ch 121, applied in *Williams v Seals* [2015] WTLR 339. This jurisdiction arises outside the 2002 Act.

[96] Ibid, ss 40–41.

[97] Law Com No 271, para 6.44, observing that in some cases entry of both notice and restriction may be made (but not for trusts, where notices are prohibited). An interest protected by restriction may, for example, be at risk from a short overriding interest lease: LRA, s 29(4).

[98] See p 552 below. This use of the restriction is considered in Law Com No 254, para 6.36 and Law Com No 271, para 6.40.

[99] The result will be perpetuated by a similar restriction on the transferee's title.

[100] LRA, ss 42 (power), 44 (obligation). Ruoff and Roper, *Registered Conveyancing*, para 44.004 exclude beneficial joint tenants from s 44. This is sensible (the survivor is solely entitled), although not apparent from the wording.

[101] Ibid, s 43; this is obligatory where a beneficial tenancy in common results (other than from a registrable disposition): LRR, r 94.

court.[102] On application, the registrar may reject the restriction if it falls outside standard forms which are specified by rules[103]: this helps to ensure that restrictions are reasonable and workable.

Just as there are unilateral notices, there are 'notifiable' restrictions where applications are made without the consent of the proprietor.[104] A person claiming a beneficial interest under a resulting or constructive trust, for example, may wish to enter a restriction even though the beneficial interest is hotly denied by the registered proprietor (the obligatory restriction is limited to joint proprietors). A notifiable restriction is not entered until the proprietor has been given a chance to object.[105]

(ii) Priorities

The general priority rule is found in LRA, s 28. This establishes, for the first time in legislation,[106] that the priority of an interest is not affected by a later disposition even if that disposition is entered on the register (subject to the s 29 priority enjoyed by registered dispositions). Suppose A declares a trust in favour of B, which is not entered on the register. Subsequently, A sells an option to C to purchase the land. C searches the register and finds that A has, apparently, an unencumbered title. C enters a notice to protect the option. Despite having done everything possible, C's option will be subject to B's beneficial interest and is likely to be worthless.

It is disappointing that the system provides no protection for persons such as C. The Law Commission originally justified this on the basis that the risk would be minimised by compulsory e-conveyancing.[107] Now that e-conveyancing is much delayed, it is welcome that the Law Commission suggests that an interest protected by notice should defeat earlier unprotected interests.[108] In any event, the original justification was not a complete response, as several interests (including the trust in our example) would be likely to lie outside the electronic entry rules.

The priority rule in s 28 is stated to be 'absolute', the Law Commission noting its superiority over the uncertainties of the old equitable rule that the first in time has priority only if the 'equities are equal'.[109] Doubtless we can forget the old equitable rule and be thankful for that. Nevertheless, some of the old law was based on concepts close to estoppel.[110] This would include cases where the first interest is an artificial transaction designed to mislead those later dealing with the proprietor; in such circumstances, it would be surprising if s 28 were to be treated as conclusive.

---

[102] Ibid, s 46.
[103] Ibid, s 43(3); LRR, r 91 (and Sched 4).
[104] Ibid, s 45.
[105] Contrast the procedure for unilateral notices, where the entry is made but then can be objected to.
[106] It confirms the earlier cases of *Barclays Bank Ltd* v *Taylor* [1974] Ch 137 and *Mortgage Corporation Ltd* v *Nationwide Credit Corporation Ltd* [1994] Ch 49.
[107] Law Com No 271, para 5.3. Most interests would have to be entered on the register before they can exist.
[108] Law Com CP 227, para 6.30. Less welcome is the apparent consequence that prior interests protected by restriction will also be defeated (para 6.42).
[109] Law Com No 271 para 5.4.
[110] *Freeguard* v *The Royal Bank of Scotland plc* (1998) 79 P&CR 81.

One additional general point deserves mention. In unregistered land, the category of 'equities' attracts special rules, reflecting the fact that they are marginal interests and often difficult to discover. Section 116 enacts that, for registered land, they are interests capable of binding purchasers. As well as settling any doubts concerning their proprietary status,[111] this has the consequence that their priority is governed by ss 28 and (for registered dispositions) 29. Accordingly, the principle that an equity can be defeated by a bona fide purchaser of an *equitable* interest is overthrown.

(a) Registered dispositions: general principles

The result if the minor interest is protected is clear. An interest protected by notice affects the purchaser, insofar as the interest is valid. Where there is a restriction, an inconsistent registration is most unlikely. However, the restriction would not cause the purchaser, once registered, to be bound.[112]

Subject to the following discussion, it seems clear that an unprotected interest is defeated by a registered disposition: this is the clear effect of s 29 and is an explicit exception to the normal first in time priority rule in s 28.[113]

(b) Registered dispositions: bad faith and actual notice

One of the most difficult questions faced by any registration system is what to do with an unprotected interest, when the purchaser is (or should be) aware of it.[114] Some systems give no special protection to the purchaser, who must rely on the normal priority rules. Other systems give protection to the purchaser in every case, save only cases of fraud.[115]

The English system protects the holder of a minor interest who is in actual occupation, for then there will be an overriding interest. This is a useful safety valve, saving many of those who are unaware that their rights to their home (or other land) technically require protection on the register. The question to be considered here is whether purchasers can be bound in any other circumstances.

Until the 2002 Act, it was highly controversial as to whether purchasers had to be in good faith to defeat unprotected interests. There were few cases on the question, but in 1976, Graham J came to the surprising conclusion in *Peffer* v *Rigg*[116] that good faith was essential. Given the changes in the legislation, the reasoning employed need not be investigated. However, the facts indicate the way in which the problem may arise. The case involved a registered transfer of a house from Mr Rigg to Mrs Rigg on the breakdown of their marriage. As Mrs Rigg was aware, the house had been purchased by Mr Peffer (her brother-in-law) and Mr Rigg as a home for her mother. Mr Rigg held the legal title on a

---

[111] The wording might possibly extend the range of proprietary equities: see p 37 above and p 492 below.

[112] It is not 'protected' for the purposes of s 29; Law Com No 271, para 6.44. This is similar to the previous law regarding cautions: *Clark* v *Chief Land Registrar* [1994] Ch 370.

[113] Dixon (2009) 125 LQR 401 discusses whether the protection extends to a person deriving title from the purchaser, suggesting a surprisingly narrow restriction to those acquiring the identical interest (see p 230 above for unregistered land). The problem is considered in Chapter 8, Law Com CP 227.

[114] See Thompson [1985] CLJ 280.

[115] See the useful international survey in Garro, *The Louisiana Public Records Doctrine and the Civil Law Tradition*, pp 163 et seq.

[116] [1977] 1 WLR 285. See Jackson (1978) 94 LQR 239.

constructive or resulting trust for himself and Mr Peffer. The problem arose because the register contained no mention of Mr Peffer's rights. It is easy to see that Mrs Rigg's claim lacked any merit: whatever the strict legal position, one can understand the judge's desire to hold her bound.

It is instructive that the House of Lords in *Midland Bank Trust Co Ltd v Green*[117] reached a very different conclusion for land charges: good faith is not required. Clearly, it may be distinguished as the legislation is different. What is important, however, is the open hostility shown by the House of Lords to the suggested requirement of good faith. Lord Wilberforce stresses that it would involve an investigation of purchasers' motives; the propensity for motives to be mixed renders such an investigation very complex.

The question is not explicitly addressed by the 2002 Act. However, it is made abundantly clear by the Law Commission[118] that neither actual notice of the unprotected interest nor bad faith will have any effect upon the statutory protection of the purchaser. No sympathy is shown to those who, by ignorance or oversight, fail to protect their interests.[119]

Turning back to the 2002 Act, although there is no explicit statutory rejection of bad faith or actual notice, there is simply no basis for importing those ideas into the current scheme.[120] Accordingly, there is no longer scope for debate on this question; the law for land charges and that for land registration has been established to be the same. However, some fraudulent transactions may persuade the court that there is no consideration, as required by s 29.[121] We will now undertake two types of investigation. The first is whether there are ways (in addition to overriding interests) whereby the purchaser can be attacked, and the second is whether the 2002 Act represents sound legal policy.

(c) Registered dispositions: fraud and constructive trusts

Bad faith may be irrelevant, but it seems more possible that fraud on the part of the purchaser will defeat the s 29 protection: the courts commonly state that statutes cannot be used as instruments of fraud. The best example in registered land is *Lyus v Prowsa Developments Ltd*,[122] in which a purchaser obtained a transfer by promising to respect an unprotected interest. Dillon J held that it would be fraudulent for the purchaser to plead that the interest was not on the register and that a statute cannot be used as an instrument of fraud. However, some argue that fraud does not exclude the statutory protection, which makes no reference to fraud.[123]

---

[117] [1981] AC 513; Thompson in *Landmark Cases in Land Law* (ed Gravells), Chapter 7.
[118] Law Com No 271, para 5.16.
[119] The arguments are more fully expounded in Law Com No 254, paras 3.45–3.46. It is observed that the problem will be less common if compulsory e-conveyancing is introduced: most interests simply will not exist without an entry on the register.
[120] *Peffer* relied upon LRA 1925, s 59(6); this is not replicated in the 2002 Act.
[121] *Halifax plc v Curry Popeck* [2008] EWHC 1692 (Ch).
[122] [1982] 1 WLR 1044. For critical comment, see Clarke [1982] All ER Rev 165.
[123] Cooke and O'Connor (2004) 120 LQR 640 at pp 658–659, implicitly supported by *Halifax plc v Curry Popeck* [2008] EWHC 1692 (Ch). Personal liability (discussed below) may render the point of limited significance.

The next question is whether a constructive trust can be imposed on a purchaser. Graham J used this as an alternative ground for deciding against the purchaser in *Peffer* v *Rigg*, although without any explanation. *Lyus* v *Prowsa* also employed a constructive trust, but this is more readily justified by the purchaser's promise in that case. The limits of the constructive trust in property transfers were clarified by the Court of Appeal in *Ashburn Anstalt* v *Arnold*, approving *Lyus*.[124] *Ashburn Anstalt* turned on the effect of a promise to buy land 'subject to' an interest. It was stressed that a purchaser who buys 'subject to' an interest is likely to intend no more than that he will not complain to the seller if the interest turns out to exist. This will not suffice to prove a constructive trust. That requires the purchaser to promise that he will respect the interest. More recently, the Court of Appeal in *Chaudhary* v *Yavuz*[125] confirmed the *Ashburn Anstalt* approach, stressing that *Lyus* (whilst correct on its facts) is an exceptional case and has never been successfully applied so as to avoid the effects of failure to protect an interest on the register.

Where there is no promise by the purchaser, actual knowledge may suffice for a different form of constructive trust – that based on 'knowing receipt' of trust property. Alternatively, there may be liability under the economic torts. These possibilities are best regarded as branches of a head of liability known as personal liability, to which we will now turn.

(d) Registered dispositions: personal claims

Personal claims are best explained by an example. Suppose S contracts to sell to P. P immediately contracts to resell the land to P2. S executes a transfer in favour of P, who is registered as proprietor. Can P argue that he is not subject to P2's estate contract because it has not been protected on the register? Common sense dictates that P2 should be able to assert that P had contracted to sell to him and that he can enforce that contract regardless of registration issues. Similarly, take the common case where spouses or partners buy property together and a constructive trust is imposed. Could it be argued that (assuming no actual occupation) the trust fails because it has not been entered on the register?[126] Again, the argument is totally unmeritorious.

Most registration systems recognise the principle that personal claims survive the destructive effect of registration.[127] In the words of Brennan J in the High Court of Australia,[128] the protection of purchasers is 'designed to protect a transferee from defects in the title of the transferor, not to free him from interests with which he has burdened his own title'. Despite some early indications that personal obligations would not be recognised in the English registration system,[129] it seems likely that personal claims will be

---

[124] [1989] Ch 1 at pp 24–25; see p 145 above.
[125] [2013] Ch 249.
[126] Wilde [1999] Conv 382 so argues.
[127] See, e.g., *Frazer* v *Walker* [1967] 1 AC 569 at p 585 (Privy Council appeal from New Zealand), applied in *Gardener* v *Lewis* [1998] 1 WLR 1535 (PC).
[128] *Bahr* v *Nicolay (No 2)* (1988) 62 ALJR 268 at p 288.
[129] *Orakpo* v *Manson Investments Ltd* [1977] 1 WLR 347 at p 360 (affirmed on other grounds: [1978] AC 95). Contrast *Lyus* v *Prowsa Developments Ltd* [1982] 1 WLR 1044; *First National Bank plc* v *Thompson* [1996] Ch 231 (estoppel); *Eagle Trust plc* v *SBC Securities Ltd* [1993] 1 WLR 484 at pp 503–504.

recognised under the 2002 Act. The priority accorded to purchasers defeats an unprotected 'interest affecting the estate immediately before the disposition'.[130] Quite apart from the wording being more appropriate to cover claims against the *transferor* than claims directly against the *transferee*, many (possibly all) personal claims will not involve the necessary interest in land.[131] The Law Commission stresses that personal claims should be recognised and enforced against the registered purchaser.[132]

What, then, are personal claims? They may be said to include claims based on a contractual, equitable or tort duty arising between the claimant and transferee. Where an obligation has been accepted by the purchaser, it seems only sensible for the court to give effect to it, whether it be based upon contract or trust. Thus, it is defensible to recognise a constructive trust when a purchaser promises to give effect to an interest in a case such as *Lyus* v *Prowsa*.[133] Assuming that the personal obligation relates to a proprietary interest (such as an estate contract), does it create a proprietary interest affecting later purchasers? *Halifax plc* v *Curry Popeck*[134] concluded that it does not; this fits the Law Commission analysis discussed immediately below.

More problematic are cases where an obligation is imposed upon, rather than accepted by, a purchaser. Examples provided by the Law Commission are a constructive trust imposed on a purchaser for knowing receipt of trust property[135] (probably the best explanation for *Peffer* v *Rigg*) or tort liability for inducing breach of contract. These examples show that the protection of the purchaser with actual notice may prove to be illusory. Although the Law Commission makes much of the point that the liability is personal rather than proprietary,[136] this masks the reality that the purchaser will barely spot the difference: liability feels the same by whatever route it arrives.[137] The extent of these heads of personal liability has yet to be clarified in England, but it would be a foolhardy purchaser who ignores them. At least at present, liability probably requires actual notice on the part of the purchaser,[138] but the potential for these heads of liability to spill over into constructive

[130] LRA, s 29(2).
[131] *Lictor Anstalt* v *Mir Steel UK Ltd* [2014] EWHC 3316 (Ch), especially at [293]–[294].
[132] Law Com 254, paras 3.48–3.49; also recognised in Law Com No 271, paras 4.11 (knowing receipt) and 7.7, n 31 (interference with contract, now better described as inducing breach).
[133] McFarlane (2004) 120 LQR 667, especially pp 667–668; he observes at p 672 that it is then unnecessary to rely on fraud.
[134] [2008] EWHC 1692 (Ch). The contrary appears to operate in Torrens jurisdictions: Harding and Bryan in *Modern Studies in Property Law*, Vol 5 (ed Dixon), Chapter 1.
[135] Note the doubts expressed by Ferris and Battersby [2001] Conv 221 at pp 224–225; also Thompson, *Landmark Cases in Land Law* (ed Gravells), p 177.
[136] See Smith, *Landmark Cases in Land Law* (ed Gravells), pp 144–148 for an argument that the liability can have proprietary consequences. Harding (2008) 31 Melb ULR 343 adopts an approach similar to that of the Law Commission, but contrast Wu (2008) 32 Melb ULR 672 (a useful Australian survey) and Low (2009) 33 Melb ULR 205 at pp 228–232. See also Moses and Edgeworth (2013) 35 Syd LR 107.
[137] See Conaglen and Goymour in *Constructive and Resulting Trusts* (ed Mitchell), Chapter 5 and Smith, *Landmark Cases in Land Law* (ed Gravells), p 148, but contrast Dixon [2012] Conv 439. See also p 500 below (tort in the licences context).
[138] For knowing receipt, see *BCCI (Overseas) Ltd* v *Akindele* [2001] Ch 437 at p 455: knowledge such that it is unconscionable to retain the benefit of the receipt. Calls for a more restitutionary basis for liability (e.g. Lord Millett in *Twinsectra Ltd* v *Yardley* [2002] 2 AC 164 at [105]) were rejected by the High Court of Australia in *Farah Constructions Pty Ltd* v *Say-Dee Pty Ltd* (2007) 230 CLR 89.

notice should set alarm bells ringing.[139] Although the recognition of personal claims has much to commend it,[140] we must appreciate that it also carries dangers. Without great care, such claims could be used to undercut the statutory protection of purchasers.

Personal obligations have long been recognised and discussed in Torrens registration systems, especially in Australia. Australian cases have contained extensive discussions of constructive trust liability, recognising the fear that the protection of purchasers might be unduly prejudiced. This culminated in the High Court of Australia decision in *Farah Constructions Pty Ltd v Say-Dee Pty Ltd*[141] that the receipt-based constructive trust cannot be employed against a proprietor who is not the primary wrongdoer. To apply it in such cases would fly in the face of the statutory protection of purchasers. If the proprietor is the primary wrongdoer, then of course personal liability can be enforced. By way of contrast, New Zealand cases appear to recognise personal liability so wide that one may fear that purchasers receive inadequate protection.[142]

These analyses indicate that the Law Commission's approach is unduly and dangerously simplistic. It is impossible to predict whether English courts will adopt the same arguments: personal liability represents virtually virgin territory so far as the courts are concerned. Of course, we must remember that the correct construction of s 29 (rather than policy considerations) may be held to determine the outcome.

(e) Registered dispositions: policy factors and definitions

That purchasers with actual notice or in bad faith are protected by s 29 seems fairly clear today (if somewhat contradicted by personal liability), but what should the law provide? The general principle that purchasers should be protected against unprotected interests is a good starting point. But is it necessary to extend this to purchasers who have actual notice, or to those in bad faith? To a certain extent, this represents a dispute as to how far compromising the registration system outweighs the ethical arguments in favour of some requirement of good faith. The Law Commission plainly believes that there is little justification for failing to place an entry upon the register.

Nevertheless, the suggestion that purchasers should be protected only in respect of constructive notice, not actual notice, is at first sight attractive; it gained support in the years before the 2002 Act.[143] After all, a major concern of the registration system is to do

---

[139] See Hughson, Neave and O'Connor (1997) 21 MULR 460. Contrast the approach of Stevens and O'Donnell in *Torrens in the Twenty-first Century* (ed Grinlinton), pp 141–156.

[140] Bright [2000] Conv 398 prefers it to very broadly based constructive trust liability. She would limit liability to cases where a transfer is a direct breach of duty, rather than disabling performance.

[141] (2007) 230 CLR 89 (Butt (2007) 81 ALJ 713), applying *Macquarie Bank Ltd v Sixty-Fourth Throne Pty Ltd* [1998] 3 VR 133 and *LHK Nominees Pty Ltd v Kenworthy* (2002) 26 WAR 517 (especially Pullin J at p 571). *Tara Shire Council v Garner* [2003] 1 Qd R 556 supported a wider application of constructive trusts. The use of personal claims for constructive trusts and unjust enrichment is considered by Conaglen and Goymour in *Constructive and Resulting Trusts* (ed Mitchell), Chapter 5; Bant [2011] Conv 309 and Owen [2013] Conv 377.

[142] *Smith v Hugh Watt Society Inc* [2004] 1 NZLR 537 at [79]–[88], relying on *CN & NA Davies Ltd v Laughton* [1997] 3 NZLR 705 (the facts of which more readily justify a personal claim).

[143] Note the instinctive reaction of Staughton LJ in *Overseas Investment Services Ltd v Simcobuild Construction Ltd* (1995) 70 P&CR 322 at p 330; see also Battersby (1995) 58 MLR 637 at p 655 and Howell [1996] Conv 34 at pp 40–43.

away with the uncertainties of constructive notice; it is arguable that actual notice involves little uncertainty. The difficulty, however, lies in defining the scope of actual notice. The line between the two forms of notice is unclear. Typically, the purchaser may have discovered the interest but have been convinced by the seller that the interest no longer exists.[144] Alternatively, the purchaser may have heard a rumour that some adverse claim exists. More tenuously, the purchaser may be aware of facts which a reasonable man would treat as highly suspicious. Perhaps if we were to limit liability to purchasers who are unambiguously aware that there is an unprotected right, then this would be well justified. For other purchasers, one can foresee extensive litigation. Paradoxically, however, the 2002 Act does introduce actual knowledge in some overriding interest contexts.[145]

What about a requirement of bad faith? A very substantial problem is the lack of clarity in our terminology. Even fraud is a word that is difficult to interpret.[146] Useful indicators may be found in Commonwealth countries that identify fraud as the primary exception to a purchaser's protection under Torrens registration systems. It has been much litigated[147] and appears to include dishonouring promises to respect unprotected interests (similar to *Lyus*)[148] and sales aimed at defeating an unprotected interest. The second of these categories appears to be excluded by *Green* in England, counting merely as bad faith.[149]

The meaning of bad faith is even less clear, although a prime motive to defeat the unprotected interest would seem to be caught. Presumably, it encompasses more than fraud. Notwithstanding this uncertainty, the Law Commission recommended in the 1980s that protection should require good faith, whilst making it clear that actual notice will not defeat purchasers.[150] A major problem with this (it was never implemented and was subsequently rejected by the Law Commission) is that the good faith test is so uncertain in application. On the other hand, it might be workable if actual notice could be considered as an indicator of bad faith.[151] This would avoid the problems of determining exactly what is actual notice, whilst ensuring that purchasers do not win on entirely technical and unmeritorious arguments relating to failure to register.

A separate question is whether it is sensible for the law to distinguish between proprietary and personal liability, as approved by the Law Commission. It has already been argued that, welcome as personal liability is, the principles need to be dovetailed with proprietary liability in order to produce a coherent and comprehensible legal structure. This is not to argue that the two should always be the same, but that apparent contradictions should be avoided.

---

[144] Such a purchaser has been held to be in good faith for the purposes of the Land Registration (Official Searches) Rules: *Smith v Morrison* [1974] 1 WLR 659.

[145] It defeats an argument that actual occupation is not obvious (Sched 3, para 2(c)(ii); see also para 3(1)(a) for easements). These rules are defended by Law Com No 271, para 5.21.

[146] Sheridan, *Fraud in Equity*, especially at p 209.

[147] See the useful summary by Cooke and O'Connor (2004) 120 LQR 640 at pp 646–648.

[148] *Loke Yew v Port Swettenham Rubber Co Ltd* [1913] AC 491; *Bahr v Nicolay (No 2)* (1988) 62 ALJR 268 (especially Mason CJ and Dawson J); Lane (1988) 62 ALJ 1036.

[149] Cooke and O'Connor (2004) 120 LQR 640 at p 655.

[150] Law Com No 158, para 4.15.

[151] RJ Smith in *The Reform of Property Law* (eds Jackson and Wilde), at pp 135–137.

(iii) *Search certificates and priority protection*

As part of the sale process, the seller will obtain an up-to-date official copy of the register and give this to the purchaser. For the purposes of showing good title, this takes the place of the title deeds in unregistered land. The purchaser will rely on this, together with an inspection of the land, to establish the state of the seller's title.

Some time will elapse between the date of the official copy and the date of the actual transfer, leading to the risk of there being new entries on the register. To cover this possibility, the purchaser checks with the registry, shortly before the transfer, that there have been no new entries. In the great majority of sales, the search certificate from the registry will confirm that there is no new entry; the purchaser will accept a transfer.

One problem remains. A transfer is effective only when it is registered. Technically, the registration dates back to the date of application, and so this is the really crucial date.[152] There is a risk that the purchaser will be bound by a minor interest entered on the register in the gap between the date of the search certificate and the subsequent application to register the transfer. Such a risk is unacceptable to purchasers because some delay is inevitable before registration; the purchaser has done all that can be expected. The solution is found in the priority protection afforded by LRA, s 72.[153] This protects the purchaser if an entry is made within 30 working days from the date of the search.[154]

A final problem concerns mistakes in searches. Suppose an official search certificate omits a protected minor interest. Can the purchaser who has taken a transfer claim that the minor interest will not bind him? Under the previous legislation it was held that, prior to registration, the purchaser remains bound: there was simply nothing in the legislation protecting the purchaser in such a case.[155] The same appears to be correct under the 2002 Act, although compensation will be paid.[156]

D. Overriding interests

Overriding interests constitute the most important exception to normal registration principles. They are not found on the register, and yet they bind a purchaser. Not only that, but they can also lead to alteration of the register with no compensation being payable to the purchaser. Little wonder, then, that a former Chief Land Registrar has referred to them as 'a stumbling block on registration of title. They may, perhaps, be described as *the* stumbling block.'[157]

Why do we have them? At one time, it was argued that the register replaces the title deeds and that the registration system should not protect purchasers in respect of interests

---

[152] LRA, s 74.

[153] See also LRR, r 131.

[154] Failure to register within that period may postpone the purchaser to an intervening entry on the register: *Baker v Craggs* [2016] EWHC 3250 (Ch). But if the minor interest was created after the contract to purchase, the purchaser would have priority by virtue of having the first of two competing equitable interests.

[155] *Parkash* v *Irani Finance Ltd* [1970] Ch 101. Oddly, the land charges scheme expressly protects a purchaser in similar circumstances: Land Charges Act 1972, s 10(4).

[156] LRA, Sched 8, para 1(1)(c).

[157] Stewart-Wallace, *Principles of Land Registration*, p 32.

not generally found in title deeds. Although this seems correct as a historical explanation,[158] the Law Commission has rejected it as an approach fit for the modern law. Their view is that[159]:

> in the interests of certainty and of simplifying conveyancing, the class of right which may bind a purchaser otherwise than as the result of an entry in the register should be as narrow as possible but . . . interests should be overriding where protection against purchasers is needed, yet it is either not reasonable to expect or not sensible to require any entry on the register.

Another important factor, permeating the changes introduced by the 2002 Act, is the extent to which a purchaser may be expected to discover overriding interests without making extensive inquiries. In assessing overriding interests, we must consider a combination of the unreasonableness of requiring protection by the interest holder and the extent to which it is fair to bind the purchaser.

Overriding interests are listed in Scheds 1 (first registration) and 3 (registered dispositions). The differences between the schedules are based upon the recognition that first registration need not be linked to the purchase of land: issues such as discoverability or inquiry of the occupier are relevant only for registered dispositions. Although the same categories are found in each schedule, each of short leases, actual occupation and easements has a more limited application in Sched 3. Because registered dispositions vastly out-number first registrations, we will study the Sched 3 overriding interests. The contrasts with Sched 1 will be noted as the relevant categories are considered. The objective of the Law Commission was to limit overriding interests as much as possible: their success in this endeavour will be considered once the various categories have been studied.

(i) *Paragraph 1: legal leases*[160]

Legal leases not exceeding seven years constitute overriding interests.[161] As one would expect, short leases requiring registration under s 4 (compulsory first registration) or s 27 (registrable dispositions) are excluded. Although not explicit in the legislation, legal status was required by the Court of Appeal in *City Permanent BS* v *Miller*.[162] This was based partly on the wording ('granted' indicating a deed and thus legal status) and partly on the fact that legal leases, but not equitable leases, bind purchasers of unregistered land automatically. *Miller* was decided on LRA 1925, but the same reasoning and result are supported by the wording of para 1.

The reasons for not requiring registration of short leases have already been considered[163]: much the same reasons lie behind their being overriding interests (rather than requiring protection by notice). We might also note that many short leases are executed

---

[158] Ibid, pp 33–35.
[159] Law Com No 158, para 2.6; a similar approach is taken in No 254, para 4.4 and No 271, para 8.6. The term 'overriding interests' was dropped in the 2002 Act: the Schedules refer to 'interests which override'.
[160] For their priority as regards *earlier* interests, see p 250 above.
[161] See *Barclays Bank plc* v *Zaroovabli* [1997] Ch 321 for leases protected by the Rent Acts: statutory tenants are not protected.
[162] [1952] Ch 840.
[163] See p 247 above. It was seen that there is power to reduce the seven-year period.

without legal advice; to require entry on the register would in practice be unrealistic. It is also true that these short leases are likely to be at a full rent, so that a purchaser who cannot obtain vacant possession will at least receive income instead.[164]

The 2002 Act removes overriding interest status from future and discontinuous leases: we have already seen that they must be registered.[165] This change removes what in many cases would be undiscoverable risks for purchasers. However, it would be dangerous for purchasers to assume that para 1 lessees will always be in occupation. It is quite possible that a lessee may have granted a sublease or licence. Thus, it is essential to check of an occupier whether rent is being paid: the recipient may well be a tenant with a para 1 overriding interest. Although actual occupation (para 2) no longer includes receipt of rent, purchasers still need to inquire about payment of rent.

A short final point is that issues concerning the running of covenants are considered in the context of leasehold covenants.[166]

(ii) Paragraph 2: actual occupation

This is one of the most controversial areas of land registration. Paragraph 2 (formerly LRA 1925, s 70(1)(g)) covers the 'interests belonging at the time of the disposition to a person in actual occupation of the land, so far as relating to land of which he is in actual occupation'. There follow some qualifications and exclusions, which we will consider later. It might be noted that, unlike the other paragraphs, para 2 does not identify specific interests which bind purchasers. Instead, it identifies a basis – actual occupation – upon which virtually any interest will bind purchasers.

(a) Application to equitable interests

In the early decades after the 1925 Act, it seemed to be assumed that the paragraph was of limited scope. The first big issue was how far it covered equitable interests, which can be protected by notice or restriction. With the advantage of hindsight, one can see that the paragraph really must include equitable interests: it is difficult to think of convincing examples of legal interests which did not already (as registered interests or overriding interests in other categories) bind purchasers. Doubts[167] about the overlap of minor and overriding interests were removed by *Bridges* v *Mees*[168] (equitable right to the fee simple) in 1957 and *Webb* v *Pollmount*[169] (option to purchase) in 1965.

The most controversial application of this overlap came in the House of Lords' landmark decision in *Williams & Glyn's Bank Ltd* v *Boland*.[170] Mr Boland held land on trust for sale for himself and his wife as beneficiaries. He mortgaged the land to the bank

---

[164] Law Com No 254, paras 3.7–3.12.
[165] See pp 244–245, 247 above. This applies to discontinuous leases only if granted by registrable disposition.
[166] See p 456 below.
[167] See Potter, *Registered Land Conveyancing*, pp 268–269.
[168] [1957] Ch 475.
[169] [1966] Ch 584.
[170] [1981] AC 487. The result is even clearer following drafting changes in the 2002 Act.

without his wife's knowledge. There could be no overreaching because the mortgage money was not paid to two trustees.[171] The House of Lords had little hesitation in holding that the wife's beneficial interest could be an actual occupation overriding interest. The facts in *Boland* are very common, so this protection of the occupier has a significant impact on purchasers and, especially, upon mortgagees.

(b) The range of rights protected

It is essential to remember that the rights of occupiers bind purchasers and not the occupation itself. The claimant must always prove two elements: actual occupation and an interest in land. Paragraph 2 overriding interests are restricted to normal proprietary interests in land: 'rights in reference to land which have the quality of being capable of enduring through different ownerships of the land, according to normal conceptions of title to real property'.[172] Thus, *National Provincial Bank Ltd* v *Ainsworth*[173] held the deserted wife's equity (right to occupation) to be a mere personal right against her husband; her occupation made no difference.

A significant issue in *Boland* was whether the existence of a trust for sale precluded an overriding interest: it did not. Fortunately, any remaining doubt has been settled by the Trusts of Land and Appointment of Trustees Act 1996.[174] This makes it perfectly clear that beneficial interests under trusts of land are capable of being overriding interests.[175]

Which rights are proprietary?

Although the question as to whether a right is a proprietary one or not involves issues relevant to land law generally rather than land registration,[176] the 2002 Act establishes that three types of claim are proprietary for registered land. Equities – claims to equitable remedies – provoked litigation under the older law. Rights to rectification were recognised in *Blacklocks* v *JB Developments (Godalming) Ltd*[177] and *DB Ramsden & Co Ltd* v *Nurdin & Peacock plc*,[178] though doubts as to mere equities were later raised in *Collings* v *Lee*.[179] Today, s 116 makes it clear that equities can bind purchasers of registered land and, accordingly, can be overriding interests. Whilst this is to be welcomed, they may provide a trap for purchasers. Take a tenant who asserts a right to rectify the lease so as to have the rent reduced. A purchaser cannot assume that the tenant's rights are as stated in the lease and must make enquiries of the tenant.[180]

---

[171] LPA, ss 2(1)(ii), 27.
[172] Russell LJ in *National Provincial Bank Ltd* v *Hastings Car Mart Ltd* [1964] Ch 665 at p 696 (approved in the House of Lords sub nom *National Provincial Bank Ltd* v *Ainsworth*). See also *Mortgage Business plc* v *O'Shaugnessy* [2015] AC 385 at [59].
[173] [1965] AC 1175.
[174] Section 3; see p 362 below.
[175] Jackson (2006) 69 MLR 214 has argued – somewhat heretically – that this is wrong and that beneficial interests under trusts were never intended to bind purchasers of registered land (criticised by Owen [2015] Conv 226).
[176] An example is the rejection of the contractual licence as an interest in land in *Ashburn Anstalt* v *Arnold* [1989] Ch 1.
[177] [1982] Ch 183.
[178] [1999] 1 EGLR 119; Pascoe [1999] Conv 421.
[179] [2001] 2 All ER 332 at p 338 (CA: fraudulent misrepresentation); cf Nolan [2001] CLJ 477.
[180] Cf *DB Ramsden & Co Ltd* v *Nurdin & Peacock plc* [1999] 1 EGLR 119; Pascoe [1999] Conv 421.

Other rights whose proprietary status is clarified by the 2002 Act are estoppel claims (s 116) and rights of pre-emption (s 115). There may indeed be a question as to how far these statutory categories extend,[181] but the general principles are now settled. Most of the earlier cases can be put aside.

One further point deserves mention. It has been argued by the successful counsel in *Blacklocks* that the case was based upon the right to rectify the register (now described as a right to alter).[182] Discussion of this will be postponed until the right to rectify is studied later in this chapter.[183]

Owners' rights

Suppose the owner of land loses the legal title as the result of registration. This might be because the wrong person is registered as first proprietor or because a transfer is forged. Does the losing owner have a right that can be protected by actual occupation? It is quite clear from LRA, s 58 that the new registered proprietor has the legal estate and *Swift 1st* tells us that a beneficial title is also received. In *Malory*,[184] the owner was thought to have rights sufficient to support an overriding interest, but this seems not to survive *Swift 1st*. Newey J in *Fitzwilliam v Richall Holding Services Ltd*[185] had noted the problem that the owner does not have any separate equitable interest prior to the registration of the purchaser; the legal estate is, of course, now held by the purchaser. He did not need to resolve the question, but he regarded as unattractive the proposition that the owner is the one person with a property interest who cannot claim an overriding interest. The original owner was in actual occupation in *Swift 1st*. Although the right to rectify was treated as an overriding interest, there was no explicit consideration of ownership rights as an overriding interest – one must assume that the court implicitly rejected such an analysis.[186] Accordingly, it appears most unlikely that the courts will recognise such an overriding interest.[187]

The effect of being overriding

Once there is an overriding interest, it is important to note that this status does not improve the nature of the right at all: it merely protects it against the effect of registration of (typically) a transfer or charge. We have seen that *Boland* recognised that a beneficiary under a trust could have an overriding interest when mortgage monies were paid to a single trustee. What happens when there are two trustees? In this situation, the trustees have power to overreach the beneficial interests, so that the beneficiaries can normally look only to the proceeds of sale to satisfy their interests.[188]

---

[181] See p 37 above and p 495 below.
[182] [1983] Conv 169, 257, 361. Beyond doubt, the claimant did seek rectification of the register as a result of the overriding interest. However, such rectification would be a consequence of an overriding interest and does not appear to be the reason why the judge found an overriding interest.
[183] See p 287 below.
[184] [2002] Ch 216 at [65].
[185] [2013] 1 P&CR 318 (criticised by Cooke [2013] Conv 344 and Goymour [2013] CLJ 617, though Gardner [2013] Conv 530 takes a contrary approach).
[186] A rather different, if unconventional, argument is that there may be more than one legal title in registered land (as recognised by Law Com No 254, para 10.27 in the adverse possession context), such that the original owner retains a legal title as an overriding interest.
[187] Law Com CP 227, paras 13.44–13.50, criticising *Malory*.
[188] LPA, ss 2(1)(ii), 27.

This issue arose in *City of London BS* v *Flegg*.[189] The House of Lords held that the overriding interest gave no protection against overreaching. The case was quite different from *Boland*, in which there was a single trustee. The presence of two trustees means that the mortgage may be treated as authorised by the trust, so that the mortgagee is not open to attack.[190] Although it may be questioned whether it is good legal policy for two trustees to be able to overreach occupiers' rights,[191] there is no reason at all why occupiers' interests should receive extra protection only in registered land.

The occupier who approves the disposition

Similar reasoning is employed where the occupier approves the registered transaction. Our first case, *Bristol & West BS* v *Henning*,[192] involved two people buying a house together. As both were aware, a mortgage was required in order to fund the purchase, but the conveyance and mortgage were taken in the name of the man. Could his partner claim an interest binding the mortgagee? The Court of Appeal held that she could not: 'it is . . . impossible to impute to them any common intention other than that she authorised Mr Henning to raise the money by mortgage'.[193] Whilst the use of the language of *imputed* intentions may be unfortunate,[194] the only correct analysis seems to be that she did want there to be a mortgage: she was well aware that otherwise, the house could not have been purchased. By no stretch of the imagination could it be argued that Mr Henning was in breach of trust in raising the purchase money on mortgage. If he was acting properly in creating the mortgage, how could she claim that her interest bound the mortgagee? We may regard the case as one of express authorisation: an application of agency principles.

Henning involved unregistered land, but it was almost immediately applied to registered land by *Paddington BS* v *Mendelsohn*.[195] As Browne-Wilkinson LJ observed: 'If the rights of the person in actual occupation are not under the general law such as to give any priority over the holder of the registered estate, there is nothing in s 70 [now Sched 3] which changes such rights into different and bigger rights.' Other cases have used an estoppel analysis: the equitable owner acquiesces in the mortgagee's belief that the legal owner can create an effective mortgage.[196] It has also been said that estoppel is an appropriate analysis when the facts do not fit an agency analysis.[197]

---

[189] [1988] AC 54. See Harpum [1987] CLJ 392; Gardner (1988) 51 MLR 365; RJ Smith (1987) 103 LQR 520; Thompson [1988] Conv 108. Conaglen (2006) 69 MLR 583 notes that this and other qualifications on *Boland* are inherent in the law: they do not reflect changes in judicial attitudes.

[190] Mortgagees are protected against improper purposes in the creation of mortgages: Trustee Act 1925, s 17.

[191] Law Com No 188 proposed reforming the law on this point; see p 356 below.

[192] [1985] 1 WLR 778.

[193] Browne-Wilkinson LJ [1985] 1 WLR 778 at p 782.

[194] Thompson (1986) 49 MLR 245; *Bank of Scotland* v *Hussain* [2010] EWHC 2812 (Ch) at [101].

[195] (1985) 50 P&CR 244. *Henning* and *Mendelsohn* are approved in *Mortgage Business plc* v *O'Shaugnessy* [2015] AC 385 at [88].

[196] *Skipton BS* v *Clayton* (1993) 66 P&CR 223 at p 229; Crabb [1993] Conv 478. Ignorance as to the effect of the mortgage protected the occupier on the facts of the case. See also *Woolwich BS* v *Dickman* [1996] 3 All ER 204.

[197] Newey J in *Bank of Scotland* v *Hussain* [2010] EWHC 2812 (Ch) at [102] (occupier with limited capacity).

The upshot of this is that a mortgage approved by the occupier, especially one to fund the purchase, will generally be immune from attack. Other developments have shown that the mortgagee is in any event likely to win: the mortgage is treated as first in time and there is usually no actual occupation at the time of completion of the purchase.[198] As a result, *Henning* issues are most likely to be important for mortgages entered into after the purchase of the property.

For example, a mortgage to enable an extension to be built, if the occupier is aware of it and approves it, would seem to be within *Henning*. However, a later mortgage may well be for the proprietor's sole benefit – a common example is where it supports the proprietor's business (as in *Boland*). Whenever the occupier clearly approves such a mortgage, it would seem that the mortgagee can rely on *Henning*: the legal owner has committed no breach of trust in entering into the mortgage. What is likely to be very problematic is the situation where the occupier is aware of the mortgage, but approval is neither sought nor given.[199] Here, it may well be going too far to say that the mortgage is authorised.

A related point is that *Henning* has been applied to a subsequent mortgage which replaces an initial authorised mortgage. In *Equity & Law Home Loans Ltd* v *Prestidge*,[200] the Court of Appeal held that the initial authorisation must be taken as extending to the subsequent mortgage. Although the result seems pretty reasonable, the imputation of consent on these facts does seem to go beyond what the parties put their minds to: it looks as if the court is attempting to reach a sensible conclusion for the parties.

It should be noted, however, that the consent is restricted to the amount of the first mortgage. If the subsequent mortgage is for a greater sum (as in *Prestidge*), then it will defeat the occupier only up to the amount of the initial mortgage. It may well be that subrogation provides an alternative and preferable route to the result in *Prestidge*.[201] As the subsequent mortgagee steps into the shoes of the earlier mortgagee by paying off the loan, most of the problems disappear.

Finally, *Henning* may have an effect that is significantly broader than that discussed above. One small aspect of this was seen in *Abbey National BS* v *Cann*.[202] Mrs Cann was aware that some money had to be raised by her son on their joint purchase, but the son raised far more than was necessary for the purchase. The House of Lords held that the mortgagee had priority to the full extent of the mortgage loan. This was supported by earlier cases, although it may be seen as overly generous to the mortgagee who was unaware of Mrs Cann's existence (let alone the limited authority).

---

[198] *Abbey National BS* v *Cann* [1991] 1 AC 56; see p 232 above and p 273 below.
[199] It was held in *Ulster Bank Ltd* v *Shanks* [1982] NI 143 that, in unregistered land, the mortgagee had no notice where the occupier was present when the mortgagee was discussing the mortgage with the legal owner at their home and was fully aware of the intention to mortgage. This may point to the result in registered land.
[200] [1992] 1 WLR 137; RJ Smith (1992) 108 LQR 371.
[201] *Castle Phillips Finance* v *Piddington* [1995] 1 FLR 783 (but not always available: *Locabail (UK) Ltd* v *Bayfield Properties Ltd* [1999] *The Times*, March 31). Dixon in *Modern Studies in Property Law*, Vol 1 (ed Cooke), Chapter 11, observes that a subrogation approach is more easily found where the occupier is a party to the first mortgage (not the position in *Prestidge*).
[202] [1991] 1 AC 56; the relevant figures are detailed at p 232 above.

However, the principle underpinning this extension might go much further. It seems to be held by the Court of Appeal in *Wishart* v *Credit and Mercantile plc*[203] that a person who allows the title to be held by another person takes the risk of that person's entering into unauthorised transactions. If applied literally, this could provide a defence to most claims based on *Boland*. Remarkably, there is no element of consent as seen in the *Henning* line of cases, nor any benefit to the occupier. *Wishart* arose in a commercial setting and may not apply to family home cases (such as *Boland*) where the mortgage is quite separate from the purchase of the home.[204]

Reviewing the scope of para 2

Turning to a policy viewpoint, what rights should fall within para 2? Although one might not accept the argument that all rights, whether or not personal, should be covered,[205] it is possible that a wider range of interests should be recognised as proprietary now that registered land is the norm. Risks to purchasers are limited when they are bound only if the right is protected on the register or the claimant is in actual occupation. This lends support to the 2002 Act clarification of the status of estoppels, equities and rights of pre-emption.

(c) Actual occupation

This may be subdivided into two issues: the approach to be taken by the courts and its application to particular cases. Initially, however, it should be noted that the previous law also protected the receipt of rent. This extension of actual occupation has been dropped from para 2: today, the person receiving rent must protect their interest on the register.[206] However, this does little to ease the burden on purchasers. We have seen that a purchaser who does not inquire as to the payment of rent is taking the risk that the recipient could be the holder of a lease within para 1.

The meaning of actual occupation

There was a long-running battle between those who took actual occupation to be what the words signify (a dictionary definition) and those who saw the term as embodying the doctrine of notice. Whilst most lawyers accept that actual occupation is the registration equivalent of the doctrine of notice, there was acute disagreement as to how far the paragraph is governed by those old rules. The arguments in favour of departing from the old notice rules are that the section does not refer to notice and that the legislation seeks to get away from the old uncertainties involved in the doctrine of notice. It is asserted that actual

---

[203] [2015] 2 P&CR 322; criticised by Dixon [2015] Conv 285 as rendering *Boland* a dead letter. See also the analysis of Televantos [2016] Conv 181 that it is a misconception that ostensible authority can arise simply from the setting up of a trust.

[204] As suggested by Sampson [2016] CLJ 21. However, the court did refer to the family cases, making no such distinction.

[205] Such is argued by Tee [1998] CLJ 328, but this would be a fundamental change and might introduce too much uncertainty. It would be difficult not to allow personal rights to be protected as minor interests. It is, furthermore, difficult to reconcile with electronic entry requirements.

[206] The impact of failure of the landlord's interest on the tenant (who may be protected by para 1 or para 3) is unclear.

occupation is easier to assess than questions based upon notice. One point is clear – without actual occupation, there can be no overriding interest simply because the state of the land makes it obvious that there is an interest.[207]

Fortunately, these old debates relating to notice seem redundant in the light of the 2002 Act. Whilst the Law Commission goes out of its way to stress that the doctrine of notice is not being applied,[208] para 2(c) explicitly provides that a purchaser is not bound by an interest, absent actual knowledge, if the 'occupation would not have been obvious on a reasonably careful inspection of the land at the time of the disposition'. This new provision seems well justified. Although one may readily accept that actual occupation provides much more certainty than the old doctrine of notice, rights that are difficult to discover surely do not deserve overriding interest status.[209] Earlier attempts to import the doctrine of notice frequently resulted from problems caused by occupation that was not obvious.[210]

A vitally important aspect of the statutory formulation is that it is the occupation that must be obvious, not the fact that an occupier has a beneficial interest.[211] When we look at the older cases, the problem has most frequently been that the occupier (usually a wife with a beneficial interest in the family home) has been living with the registered proprietor in circumstances which are not indicative of any hostile claim. In unregistered land, Stamp J in *Caunce* v *Caunce*[212] held that there would not be constructive notice of such a wife's interests. In *Boland*, the House of Lords was faced with a similar claim in registered land. Lord Wilberforce was unambiguous in rejecting the relevance of the doctrine of notice[213]:

> In my opinion . . . the law as to notice as it may affect purchasers of unregistered land . . . has no application even by analogy to registered land. . . . In the case of registered land, it is the fact of occupation that matters. If there is actual occupation, and the occupier has rights, the purchaser takes subject to them. If not, he does not. No further element is material.

He was disdainful of any suggestion that spouses might be subject to a special rule and rejected the submission that actual occupation excludes occupation that is consistent with the mortgagor's title. Quite apart from the difficulty in applying such a test in modern conditions (wives and other occupiers are likely to have proprietary interests), it is simply not what the paragraph says.

What does the future hold? We need to distinguish two questions. The first concerns a person who is living on the land in the circumstances exemplified by *Caunce* and *Boland*.

---

[207] *Chaudhary* v *Yavuz* [2013] Ch 249 (access by iron staircase obvious); see p 272 below.

[208] Law Com No 271, para 8.62; generally, see paras 5.16–5.21. As with the doctrine of notice, there is no necessity for an inspection actually to take place: *Thompson* v *Foy* [2010] 1 P&CR 308 at [132].

[209] Sparkes [1989] Conv 342.

[210] Notably in the Court of Appeal decisions in *Lloyds Bank plc* v *Rosset* [1989] Ch 350 (see RJ Smith (1988) 104 LQR 506; Thompson [1988] Conv 453) and *Abbey National BS* v *Cann* [1989] 2 FLR 265. Both cases went to the House of Lords on other issues: *Rosset* [1991] 1 AC 107; *Cann* [1991] 1 AC 56.

[211] This was very deliberate: Law Com No 271, para 8.62. The Law Commission explains that it is 'less demanding' than constructive notice: para 5.21. It might be added that the protection does not apply if there is actual knowledge *of the interest*.

[212] [1969] 1 WLR 286; see p 229 above.

[213] [1981] AC 487 at p 504. Earlier, see *Hodgson* v *Marks* [1971] Ch 892; more recently, *Mortgage Express* v *Lambert* [2017] Ch 93 at [21], [41]–[42]. For the impact of *Boland*, see Smith in *Landmark Cases in Land Law* (ed Gravells), Chapter 6.

That person cannot be denied to be in actual occupation on any tenable interpretation of those words; equally clearly, the occupation will be obvious to the purchaser. Any argument that a purchaser should not be bound unless that actual occupation provides notice of the person's rights seems doomed to failure under the 2002 Act. Both the analysis by the Law Commission and the introduction of the 'obvious on a reasonably careful inspection' test point to there being no further qualification upon para 2.

The second question is whether there is actual occupation in the first place. Difficulties are unlikely to arise when the claimed occupation is normal living in a house or the use of business or manufacturing premises. In other contexts, the express provisions of para 2 produce the appropriate answer: there is no need at all to resort to the doctrine of notice. In practical terms, it is unlikely that results of many cases will be different (the leading cases are considered below). This is because, where there was any doubt as to actual occupation, the courts already looked to the question whether the occupation would be obvious to a purchaser.[214] Accordingly, it is difficult to think of cases where para 2 will provide a different result.

Nevertheless, the facts of *Kingsnorth Finance Co Ltd* v *Tizard*[215] provide one possibility. A wife who had separated from her husband claimed to be in actual occupation. She no longer lived in the house, but visited it every day to look after the children. Occasionally, she would stay overnight if the husband was away, and she kept clothes there. Judge Finlay QC was clear that there was actual occupation.[216] Although she was not living there, her daily activities might be regarded as just sufficient to justify that result. The facts are all-important in such a case, although an instinctive response is that it is a very borderline decision. Even if the finding of actual occupation is justified, it might well be regarded today as not obvious on a reasonably careful inspection.

One specific problem relates to the position of minor children of the registered proprietor. In the pre-2002 law, *Hypo-Mortgage Services Ltd* v *Robinson*[217] held that they were not in actual occupation. This convenient ruling was partly based upon their having no independent right to occupy, but that provides some difficulty: the source of the occupation is generally irrelevant. More credible, at least for young children, is the argument that it is not feasible to make inquiries.[218] We must presume that the same result will apply under para 2.

The application of actual occupation

Not surprisingly, actual occupation of houses has come up most frequently. Following *Boland*, it is clear that living in a house counts as actual occupation, regardless of whether the proprietor is living there as well.

---

[214] This can be seen in the analysis of Mustill LJ in *Lloyds Bank plc* v *Rosset* [1989] Ch 350 at p 397; also Ralph Gibson LJ in *Abbey National BS* v *Cann* [1989] 2 FLR 265 at p 278 and Arden LJ in *Malory Enterprises Ltd* v *Cheshire Homes (UK) Ltd* [2002] Ch 216 at [81].

[215] [1986] 1 WLR 783. See also *Kling* v *Keston Properties Ltd* (1984) 49 P&CR 212 (p 272 below).

[216] The *Boland* test was applied despite title being unregistered.

[217] [1997] 2 FLR 71; [1997] Conv 84.

[218] Compare the protection as regards children's consents in Trusts of Land and Appointment of Trustees Act 1996, s 10 and the proposals of the Law Commission as regards overreaching in Law Com No 188, paras 4.8–4.10.

One question has concerned actual occupation prior to completion of the purchase. Two cases may be contrasted. In *Lloyds Bank plc* v *Rosset*,[219] a husband held on trust for himself and his wife as beneficiaries.[220] The house being purchased was semi-derelict, and work was done (both before and after completion) by builders to put it in a habitable state. Because Mr Rosset was frequently away, much of the day-to-day control of the builders was undertaken by Mrs Rosset. Could Mrs Rosset be said to be in actual occupation at the time of completion, in order for her interest to bind the mortgagee bank? The question was nicely balanced. A majority of the Court of Appeal held that Mrs Rosset was, on the facts, in actual occupation. This was based partly on her activities on the land and partly on the actual occupation of the builders as agents for Mr and Mrs Rosset. It is clear that occupation through an agent or employee suffices for any type of property: the easiest example is that of a caretaker.[221]

The second, and rather different, case is *Abbey National BS* v *Cann*.[222] The claimant, Mrs Cann, was the mother of the legal owner. When the property was bought, her furniture was moved into the house 35 minutes before the relevant time for actual occupation. Mrs Cann had very sensibly gone on holiday to the Netherlands at the time of the move into the house. The House of Lords held that acts preparatory to completion do not count as actual occupation; in the words of Lord Oliver,[223] there must be 'some degree of permanence and continuity which would rule out mere fleeting presence'. Although the facts in *Cann* are very different from the examples given by Lord Oliver of measuring up for curtains and planning decorations, it may be viewed as a convenient result. It avoids asking whether the purchaser moved in a few minutes before or after completion. Whatever one's view of actual occupation, it is difficult to justify drawing such very fine distinctions.

The facts in *Rosset* were significantly different from those in *Cann* and justify a finding of actual occupation when building work had been carried out over a period exceeding five weeks. In both these cases, the 2002 requirement that the occupation must be 'obvious on a reasonably careful inspection' might be argued today. However, it seems likely that the results in each would remain the same, albeit that the analysis today might well be couched in the terms of the statutory language.[224]

Let us return to the point made as regards *Rosset* that the builders were agents for Mr and Mrs Rosset. There are limits to this analysis. The mere fact that a person allows a licensee into occupation does not mean that the licensee is treated as occupying on the licensor's behalf. In *Strand Securities Ltd* v *Caswell*,[225] a licensor had allowed his stepdaughter to occupy a flat rent-free. It was held that the stepdaughter was occupying on her own behalf and not as an agent for the licensor, who accordingly was not in actual occupation.

---

[219] [1989] Ch 350.
[220] The House of Lords held that the wife had no beneficial interest and therefore did not discuss the issues raised in the Court of Appeal: [1991] 1 AC 107.
[221] *Strand Securities Ltd* v *Caswell* [1965] Ch 958 at pp 981, 984–985.
[222] [1991] 1 AC 56.
[223] Ibid, at p 93.
[224] See the analysis of the cases by Jackson (2003) 119 LQR 660, who argues that the Law Commission misunderstood the nature of the problem.
[225] [1965] Ch 958.

Several recent cases deal with occupiers who leave their homes. It will come as no surprise that an occupier who goes out to shop or to work during the day retains actual occupation. In *Chhokar* v *Chhokar*,[226] the occupier had gone to hospital to give birth to her second child. Whilst she was away, her husband transferred the house to a purchaser, and the purchaser changed the locks to stop her from returning. Going into hospital for a few days no more changes occupation than going on holiday, and Ewbank J felt no hesitation in deciding that she retained actual occupation. We have already considered *Kingsnorth Finance Co Ltd* v *Tizard*,[227] in which a separated wife who visited the house every day to look after the children was regarded as being in actual occupation.

The problem with cases such as *Chhokar* and *Tizard* is to know how to draw the line. If I take leave of absence and visit America for a year, do I remain in actual occupation? Does it make any difference if my wife continues to live in the house? Or if I allow somebody else to occupy the house whilst I am away? *Strand Securities* indicates that allowing somebody else to occupy is inconsistent with actual occupation. The presence of the licensor's furniture made no difference. This fits quite well with the modern requirement that the occupation should be obvious on a reasonable inspection.

How far do we consider the specific circumstances of the individual purchaser in this type of case? The result in *Chhokar* seems clear, but what if the seller had removed all evidence of the wife (clothes, possessions) before the sale? Living in a house is usually obvious to a purchaser, but it is difficult to say that the occupation was obvious to the specific purchaser who inspects after the evidence has been removed. The stress in para 2(c) on the 'time of the disposition' lends strong support to the purchaser. Alternatively, the seller might bring along his girlfriend and assert that the wife's clothes and possessions belong to the girlfriend. The wife's claim might be stronger in those circumstances.

Thompson v *Foy*[228] raises a slightly different question as to when occupation ends. The occupier had removed her personal belongings but had left furniture and bedding there (unlike *Strand Securities*, nobody else had taken possession). It was held that her intention to leave the property permanently was fatal to actual occupation. The analysis in *Thompson* was soon approved by the Court of Appeal in *Link Lending Ltd* v *Bustard*.[229] The facts in *Bustard* took a more extreme form of *Chhokar*: the occupier had been in a residential care institution for over a year, although she was intending to return home when her mental health improved. It was stressed that there is no single test, but the involuntary nature of her absence and her intention to return to what was her only home were crucial factors in deciding that she was in actual occupation. More generally, the permanence and continuity of occupation and the length of the absence were relevant factors. The facts in each of these cases are fairly close to the borderline. One interesting element is the relevance of the occupier's subjective intention in both cases. This is not seen in the earlier cases and

---

[226] [1984] FLR 313 (Ewbank J). The issue did not arise in the Court of Appeal.
[227] [1986] 1 WLR 783; see p 269 above.
[228] [2010] 1 P&CR 308; Dixon [2009] Conv 285. Any occupation would have been obvious on a reasonably careful inspection.
[229] [2010] 2 EGLR 55. The recent cases are considered by Bogusz [2011] Conv 268 and criticised (not wholly persuasively) by Bevan [2016] Conv 104.

will almost never be obvious to a purchaser. It would be especially worrying if it operates to extend actual occupation,[230] rather than to limit it where the physical evidence is sufficient for actual occupation. However, it can be defended because para (c) protects the purchaser if the occupation is not obvious and this does not allow issues of intention to operate.[231]

Occupation of premises other than houses has come up less frequently. If the land is derelict, then it appears that fencing it and undertaking minor ownership activities such as storage may suffice.[232] Alongside *Rosset*, this demonstrates that the nature of the premises is a highly relevant factor in working out what actual occupation requires. Two cases involve the parking of cars. In *Epps* v *Esso Petroleum Co Ltd*,[233] Templeman J held that parking on a vacant lot of land would not suffice. Such conduct seems insufficiently substantial to count as actual occupation. What really impressed the judge was that the position of a boundary wall made it look as if the land belonged to the registered proprietor, rather than to the person parking his car. This element indicates that the occupation (if there was actual occupation in the first place, which was rejected) was not obvious.

An interesting contrast is found in *Kling* v *Keston Properties Ltd*,[234] which involved parking a car in a garage. Without citing *Epps*, it was held that this did amount to actual occupation. This also seems to be correct. The sort of occupation that one expects with a garage is the parking of cars, and it is appropriate to assess actual occupation according to the nature of the premises. Today, one must ask whether the nature of parking in a garage is such that it is obvious to a purchaser.[235]

Can the exercise of an easement ever constitute actual occupation?[236] *Chaudhary* v *Yavuz*[237] held that exercise of a right of access by an external metal staircase did not suffice: it was an example of use rather than occupation. The court left open the exercise of an easement of storage or car parking, which looks closer to occupation.

Occupation of part of premises

Is it necessary to occupy the entirety of the premises over which the overriding interest is claimed? This question is now settled by the wording of para 2: the overriding interest relates only to land over which there is actual occupation.[238] This avoids a risk for a purchaser that an apparently innocuous occupation of a small area might protect an interest affecting the entire plot being transferred. It fits well with the Law Commission's determination to limit overriding interests as far as is reasonably possible.

---

[230] This would mean that it operates well outside the context of leaving the property: see Bogusz [2014] Conv 27.
[231] *Thomas* v *Clydesdale Bank Plc* [2010] EWHC 2755 (Ch) at [38]–[40].
[232] *Malory Enterprises Ltd* v *Cheshire Homes (UK) Ltd* [2002] Ch 216 at [82].
[233] [1973] 1 WLR 1071.
[234] (1984) 49 P&CR 212.
[235] Dicta of Vinelott J at pp 221–222 indicate doubts as to this: cars are normally garaged for only part of the day.
[236] Gray and Gray, *Elements of Land Law* (5th edn), para 8.2.89 suggest not, citing Thompson [1986] Conv 31.
[237] [2013] Ch 249 at [31]; McFarlane [2013] Conv 74, especially at p 81.
[238] This reverses the previous law as enunciated in *Ferrishurst Ltd* v *Wallcite Ltd* [1999] Ch 355 (*Ferrishurst* is supported by Hill (2000) 63 MLR 113 but criticised by Harpum, *Modern Studies in Property Law*, Vol 1 (ed Cooke), pp 17–19). The new rule was applied in *Thompson* v *Foy* [2010] 1 P&CR 308 at [128]–[129].

Nevertheless, it remains probable that actual occupation of an entire plot does not require physical occupation of every inch of it: the question is whether the conduct of the occupier suffices as actual occupation of the entire area claimed.[239] Thus, it should not matter if an occupier of a house has never ventured into parts of the large garden at the rear. It would be different where the disputed part of the premises appears distinct: a person occupying one of two adjoining houses comprised in a single title would provide an example. Nor would there be actual occupation if another person is in occupation of the other part of the premises.

(d) The time of actual occupation

The general rule, found in s 74, is that registration takes effect from the date of registration (technically the date of application), rather than the date of completion of the purchase. Thus, an interest protected by notice or restriction may be valid even if protected after the date of completion.[240] Although there was little supporting authority, the House of Lords in *Cann*[241] held that the date of registration also applies to overriding interests; this now finds statutory recognition in s 29.

However, this general rule does not apply to every overriding interest. *Cann* itself held that the appropriate date for actual occupation (para 2) is the date of completion. One major reason for this was that protection is given to those who make inquiries; this makes sense only in relation to the date of completion. From a practical angle, it would be very odd if an overriding interest was to arise after completion, as the new proprietor may not be able to prevent the occupation[242] and yet has finally committed himself or herself by paying for the land. The presence of this 'registration gap' was thought to be a severe problem – militating against use of the date of registration. It is unnecessary to consider *Cann* further, as para 2 now makes it clear that actual occupation must exist at the date of the disposition (completion). It is less clear whether it must continue to the time of registration. Although most commentators reject such a requirement, Lewison J has supported it on a close reading of s 29 and para 2.[243]

A rather different point is that there is no requirement for actual occupation to continue to the time the dispute comes to court. The issue of priority between purchaser and occupier is decided once and for all at the time of purchase.[244]

(e) Protection for the purchaser who makes inquiries

The purchaser has a statutory defence to an overriding interest if inquiry is made of the occupier, but the rights are not disclosed.[245] This is a clear hint to a purchaser as to what

---

[239] An analogy can be drawn with adverse possession: *Higgs* v *Nassauvian Ltd* [1975] AC 464 (PC).

[240] As in *Elias* v *Mitchell* [1972] Ch 652 (caution). Normally, however, the purchaser will be protected by a clear official search certificate: see p 260 above.

[241] [1991] 1 AC 56 (Lord Bridge dissented on this point); *Barclays Bank plc* v *Zaroovabli* [1997] Ch 321 (short lease). Dangers for mortgagees are highlighted by Robinson (1997) 113 LQR 390.

[242] Examples are most likely if the new proprietor is not entitled to occupation.

[243] *Thompson* v *Foy* [2010] 1 P&CR 308 at [122]–[126], expressing no final view. *Cann* appeared to support the opposite view on the old legislation: [1991] 1 AC 56 at pp 83, 104, 106.

[244] *London & Cheshire Insurance Co Ltd* v *Laplagrene Property Co Ltd* [1971] Ch 499.

[245] Schedule 3, para 2(b).

should be done. Those in actual occupation must be discovered and then asked what their interests are. In practice, purchasers tend to rely on the seller to tell them who is in actual occupation. This may be convenient, but gives purchasers no protection.[246] Once an occupier has been identified, the purchaser must be careful to ask the occupier what interests he or she has, rather than why they are present. This is because there is no necessity for the overriding interest to be the source of the actual occupation.[247]

One change introduced by para 2 is that failure to disclose the right is relevant only if the occupier could reasonably have been expected to disclose it. How does this apply to occupiers who do not appreciate that they have any interest? Although one cannot expect occupiers to identify specific interests in land, it is reasonable to expect them to say whether or not they are making any claim to the land.[248] Nevertheless, there have been indications that it may sometimes be reasonable not to disclose even rights the occupier is aware of.[249]

A danger faced by mortgagees in particular is that any disclaimer or waiver by the occupier may be held to have been secured by undue influence exercised by the proprietor. The mortgagee should ensure that the occupier has received independent legal advice.[250] This is more fully dealt with as part of mortgages.[251]

(f) Statutory exclusions

Four types of interest are expressly excluded from para 2. Statutory possession rights of spouses and those in civil partnerships are not capable of being overriding interests.[252] The onus is on claimants to register their statutory rights if they wish to prevent a sale or mortgage. The reason for this appears to be that, otherwise, purchasers would need to make awkward inquiries in huge numbers of cases, when few such occupiers will in fact oppose dispositions. Much of this reasoning has lost its force after *Boland*. A purchaser who fails to make inquiry of any occupier, spouse or not, is today taking a great risk of being bound by a beneficial interest.[253] The second (obsolescent) exclusion is that beneficial interests under old Settled Land Act settlements cannot be overriding interests.[254] There has never been any equivalent exclusion of beneficial interests under trusts of land.

Third, a new exclusion is that of future leases (those postponed for more than three months) which have not yet taken effect in possession. Such future leases are registrable

---

[246] *Hodgson* v *Marks* [1971] Ch 892.
[247] *Webb* v *Pollmount Ltd* [1966] Ch 584 (actual occupation by virtue of a lease; option to purchase freehold was an overriding interest).
[248] *Mortgage Express* v *Lambert* [2017] Ch 93 at [41].
[249] Judge Behrens in *Begum* v *Issa* [2014] 5 November at [100] (see Dixon [2015] Conv 97 at p 100). This may be explained by there being no direct inquiry on the facts.
[250] *Barclays Bank plc* v *O'Brien* [1994] 1 AC 180 and *Royal Bank of Scotland plc* v *Etridge (No 2)* [2002] 2 AC 773 are the leading cases. There is an argument for this extending to the implied consent in *Henning*: Kenny [2002] Conv 94.
[251] See p 583 below.
[252] Family Law Act 1996, s 31(10); it is unfortunate that this exception (like the fourth) is not found in para 2 itself.
[253] The risk is minimal if there are two trustees (*Flegg*), but it is rare for there to be two trustees where there is a statutory right of occupation.
[254] Paragraph 2(a).

dispositions and fall outside para 1. They also fall outside para 2, even if the future tenant occupies by virtue of some other right (an earlier lease is the most likely example). Once the future lease comes into possession, then it will fall within para 2. However, it remains an unregistered registrable disposition and accordingly cannot be legal or fall within para 1. Finally, rights to 'overriding leases' (a confusing label) under the Landlord and Tenant (Covenants) Act 1995[255] are excluded by s 20(6) of that Act.

(g) An assessment of para 2

Given that the actual occupation overriding interest is a controversial and much-litigated part of registered land, is it justified as an exception to the protection of purchasers? It is, ultimately, a question of balancing the need for purchasers to be able to buy land quickly, cheaply and with confidence in the register with the desirability of protecting those who are occupying land and are ignorant of the need to register. One of the problems is that many overriding interests are created informally and without legal advice. Given that we are frequently dealing with family homes, para 2 plays a role in ensuring that the registration system fits human rights principles – in particular the Article 8 right to respect for homes. We have to accept that the occupier may never heard of registered land, let alone be aware of the need to register. To require registration is the practical equivalent to denying all proprietary force to such interests. Yet, para 2 applies to interests that have been created expressly and with legal advice: it cannot be seen as directed solely at informally created interests. The Law Commission has considered this and concluded that the scope of para 2 should not be restricted[256]; in part, this is because it is reasonable for purchasers to be protected by way of overriding interest in the registration gap between disposition and registration.

Looking at the steps which purchasers have to take, it might be said that the register should provide conclusive proof as to the documentary title to the land. Investigation of the land itself is quite different: a purchaser who fails to investigate the rights of occupiers has only himself or herself to blame. Indeed, it may be regarded as more efficient to bring potential problems into the open at the time of purchase or mortgage. The alternative is to deprive significant numbers of occupiers of their homes. The disruption that this involves, admittedly in a relatively small number of cases, may well be worse than a limited duty of inquiry on purchasers.

In any event, it appears that problems arise far more frequently for second mortgagees than for purchasers of land.[257] The reasons are plain: the occupation will be an obvious stumbling block to a purchaser who is seeking vacant possession. In addition, it would be rare for the occupier to be ignorant of a sale or not to object to it. On the other hand, a mortgage involves no change in occupation and is relatively likely to be executed without the occupier being aware. We may not wish to waste many tears on second mortgagees who fail to make inquiries of occupiers.

---

[255] See p 464 below.
[256] Law Com CP 227, para 11.30 (and preceding analysis).
[257] See Harpum [1990] CLJ 277 at pp 312–315, 324.

Even if the actual occupation overriding interest were to be abolished (almost unthinkable today), it cannot be assumed that the problem would simply go away. Although actual occupation overriding interests are not generally found in registration systems in other countries, those systems tend to have much more litigation on fraud as an exception to the effect of registration. The lesson may be that some sort of safety valve must be found within a registration system. Yet too many or too extensive safety valves may cause purchasers to be denied adequate protection. Whilst willing to defend para 2, we must be alert not to extend it too far – especially where the occupier may be expected to have legal advice. The requirement for the occupation to be obvious on reasonable inspection is especially valuable in establishing a balance between occupier and purchaser.

(h) First registration and Sched 1

Because first registration does not necessarily involve any purchase, it is inappropriate to refer either to inquiries of an occupier or to the rights being obvious on inspection of the land. Whilst the sense of this is plain, very many first registrations will follow upon purchase of the land. It seems odd to deny protection to these proprietors if they have made inquiry of the occupier or the occupation is not obvious.[258] The future lease exception is also omitted: the lease cannot have been a registrable disposition if the landlord's title was not registered.

(iii) *Paragraph 3: easements and profits*[259]

No distinction is drawn by para 3 between easements and profits, and we will, for simplicity, refer to easements. The reforms introduced by para 3 are as great as with any overriding interest.[260] One major change[261] is that equitable easements are no longer included. The principal significance of this concerns express easements which have not been registered as registrable dispositions.[262] They can be only equitable interests, but pre-2002 nevertheless bound purchasers as overriding interests. Because para 3 explicitly requires a legal interest, this unregistered equitable easement is no longer overriding.

The change fits in well with the Law Commission's desire to limit the number of unprotected rights that will bind purchasers. However, an interesting contrary policy argument is that easements are likely to be more beneficial to the dominant land than harmful to the servient land.[263] According to this argument, it would be most efficient for purchasers to

---

[258] Although we should recall that (1) the interest may have been defeated on the initial unregistered purchase of the legal estate and (2) failure to respond to inquiries may well estop the occupier from asserting the interest.

[259] For the operation of easements under the legislation, see Kenny [2003] Conv 304 and Battersby [2005] Conv 195. A comparative survey (linked with current reform proposals for easements) is found in Burns, *Modern Studies in Property Law*, Vol 5 (ed Dixon), Chapter 3.

[260] Law Com No 271, para 8.65.

[261] Recognised in *Chaudhary* v *Yavuz* [2013] Ch 249 at [27]. The previous law was established by the surprising decision in *Celsteel Ltd* v *Alton House Holdings Ltd* [1985] 1 WLR 204. Law Com CP 227, para 16.40 proposes a limited exception for easements in leases not exceeding three years (those easements may be equitable because of the absence of a deed).

[262] Even if the dominant land is not registered, it is necessary to enter notice of the easement on the servient land's title.

[263] Prichard [1987] Conv 328.

be bound but then be compensated. Nevertheless, a wider range of overriding interests reduces the reliability of the register, encourages a purchaser to make potentially expensive inquiries and reduces the incentive to register easements.

We should recall that only express easements constitute registrable dispositions and are thereby outside para 3.[264] It follows that para 3 encompasses implied and prescriptive easements, together with those created prior to the first registration of the land.

The Law Commission was concerned that many of these easements are not obvious to purchasers, especially because easements can survive many years (indeed, centuries) of nonuse. Accordingly, para 3 limits overriding interest status where a right has not been exercised for a year before the disposition. This means that any holder of an easement which has not been so exercised should consider placing an entry on the register, although very often the holder will be ignorant of the easement's existence. Circumstances may mean that even regularly exercised easements suffer an extended interruption, perhaps because the benefited land is vacant for a time. However, the purchaser remains bound by an unexercised easement if there is either knowledge of it or it would have been obvious on a reasonably careful inspection of the land (the same test as applied to occupation in para 2). By their nature, many easements will be obvious on inspection,[265] although the ease of proving this is unclear.[266]

Whilst the Law Commission rightly regards this protection of purchasers as important, one may feel that protecting rights exercised within a year fails to solve the problem of undiscoverable easements. Further, its significance is hugely reduced by an additional factor. The new provisions do not apply to easements that were already overriding at the time Sched 3 came into effect.[267] Pre-2002 easements will be of importance for many decades: non-exercised easements are far more likely to be old easements rather than twenty-firstcentury easements. The result is to limit sharply the practical benefit of this protection.

Two final points may be added. First, it is planned that procedures on transfer and registration will encourage the identification and registration of easements that would otherwise be overriding. This is a laudable attempt to reduce the practical likelihood of being bound by a para 3 easement, without prejudicing anybody in the process. Second, Sched 1 omits the protection against non-exercised easements. This is because the 'obvious on reasonable inspection' test is inappropriate for cases where registration is not immediately linked to sale.[268]

(iv) *Other overriding interests*

There remains a list of less interesting overriding interests.[269] They comprise: customary rights, public rights, local land charges (these have their own local registers), interests in

---

[264] See p 248 above.

[265] At least if inspection includes making inferences from the presence of adjoining buildings: Kenny [2003] Conv 304 at p 309.

[266] Might it include all 'continuous and apparent' easements, implied under *Wheeldon* v *Burrows* (1879) 12 Ch D 31? Law Com No 271, para 8.70 refers to drains and pipes, perhaps indicating a narrower construction.

[267] LRA, Sched 12, para 9. Old easements over *unregistered* land will not enjoy this protection as regards dispositions after first registration of that land.

[268] It would also be difficult to protect the easement, a caution against first registration being the only possibility.

[269] As well as those listed in Sched 3, see also LRA, s 90(5) (PPP leases).

coal, certain mines and minerals (created and title registered before 1898). These categories represent a more streamlined version of the previous law. The list was originally longer, but the following rights ceased to be overriding interests in 2013: franchises, manorial rights, Crown rents, liability in respect of embankments and sea and river walls, payments in lieu of tithe and chancel repair liability. The delay to 2013 was to avoid human rights issues in removing overriding interest status: it provided a decade in which these rights could be entered on the register.[270]

(v) *Reducing overriding interests*

We have observed that the Law Commission set out to reduce the number and significance of overriding interests so far as possible. How successful was that endeavour?

(a) Categories abolished

Two categories disappeared immediately. The first – interests exempted from the effect of registration of qualified, possessory and good leasehold titles – is purely cosmetic. The exempted rights still bind purchasers.[271] The second is a genuine reduction: adverse possession claims. We have already seen that the role of adverse possession is hugely reduced by the 2002 Act. Those claims that survive will not automatically affect purchasers as overriding interests,[272] although the adverse possessor will normally be protected by para 2 as being in actual occupation. Absent actual occupation, the risk of a purchaser being bound without the interest being discoverable is too great to be acceptable. We have seen that, on first registration, the proprietor is bound if he knows of the adverse possession claim or has notice of it.[273]

In addition, we have seen that several 'relics from past times', as the Law Commission described them, were abolished in 2013.

(b) Other forms of reduction

Three forms of reduction will be mentioned. The first consists of changes to individual categories so as to limit them as far as possible. We have considered these when looking at leases, actual occupation and easements and profits. Views may vary as to how far-reaching the changes are. Whilst keeping virtually all the leading categories, there has been some pruning (significant in part) of their operation. The result is extensive tinkering rather than root-and-branch reform. More radical change would, for example, have required removal of actual occupation as an overriding interest.

The second and very valuable reform is to encourage the entry of overriding interests (other than leases not exceeding three years) on the register. Thus, the new proprietor, both as regards first registration and registrable dispositions, must provide details as to

---

[270] LRA, s 117 and SI 2003 No 2431; see Law Com No 271, paras 8.81–8.89 (Nugee (2008) 124 LQR 586).
[271] LRA, s 29(2)(a)(iii).
[272] It should be remembered that adverse possession will never operate automatically (LRA, s 96): there is a right to apply to the registrar.
[273] LRA, s 11(4)(c).

overriding interests, which the registrar may then enter on the register.[274] Without prejudicing anybody, this may have quite a significant effect in reducing the danger of purchasers being faced with unpleasant surprises.

Third, once an interest has been protected by notice (but not restriction), it can never thereafter constitute an overriding interest.[275] The operation of this regarding unilateral notices is problematic when the proprietor successfully objects to the notice and it is accordingly cancelled. If the interest is subsequently proved to exist, it seems that it cannot take effect as an overriding interest. Accordingly, if there is a risk that there will be difficulty in proving the interest, there may be good reason not to apply for a notice where there is an overriding interest.[276]

3. Alteration

It is inevitable that the register will not always be perfect: mistakes are inevitable. The wrong person may be registered as proprietor, the extent of the land registered may be wrong or some adverse right, such as an option, may be omitted from the register. Alteration of the register may be available in these cases to put the error right. It should be noted that the provisions in the 2002 Act represent a radical departure from the previous law, as regards both terminology and substantive rights to alteration. This is an area in which one must be very careful in relying on earlier authorities.

An initial distinction – new in 2002 – is between rectification and other alterations. Rectification (the term previously used for all alterations) applies only to an alteration which corrects a mistake and which adversely affects the title of the registered proprietor.[277] A distinction is thereby drawn between what may be called administrative alterations and those which change the legal position as it stood immediately before alteration: only the latter constitute rectification.

There are many circumstances when administrative alteration is required to make the register accord with existing legal rights: to give effect to an overriding interest claim, for example. This form of alteration does not qualify the reliability of the register and need not be of concern to proprietors. The narrower category of rectification is more interesting: it may significantly reduce the reliability of the register. Even though compensation may be paid, it means that the register ceases to be conclusive. The separating out of this narrower category not only has some specific legal consequences (to be discussed in this chapter), but also concentrates our minds on when it operates and when it should be permitted. As with overriding interests, rectification provides a test of our resolve to move away from traditional conveyancing concepts; there has been much recent discussion of this in the literature.

---

[274] LRR, rr 28, 57. LRA, s 37 provides more generally for the registrar to enter notice of overriding interests.
[275] LRA, s 29(3).
[276] This argument persuaded the Law Commission that it is 'evenly balanced' as to whether s 29(3) should remain: Law Com CP 227, para 11.53.
[277] LRA, Sched 4, para 1. Correction of a general boundary (see p 238 above) is not rectification as the boundary is not guaranteed (*Drake* v *Fripp* [2012] 1 P&CR 69), with the consequence that no indemnity is payable (see p 289 below).

Alteration may be ordered by the court or the registrar, although alteration by the registrar is likely to be most common. However, any dispute is to be referred to the First-tier Tribunal, with an appeal to the Upper Tribunal.

A. Grounds for alteration and rectification

Alteration is regulated by LRA, Sched 4. Paragraphs 2 and 5 provide four grounds. The first, mistake, will be fully considered in this section. Bringing the register up to date is the second ground: the Law Commission gives the examples of entering an easement which has arisen by prescription and deleting a lease terminated by forfeiture proceedings. The third ground is giving effect to interests excepted from the effect of registration: this relates to possessory, qualified and good leasehold titles.[278] Finally, applicable to alterations by the registrar, we have the removal of superfluous entries. This is designed to prevent redundant or spent entries clogging up the register. These last three grounds seem fairly straightforward, and no more need be said about them.

Rectification requires the correction of a mistake, where the title of the proprietor will be adversely affected. Deciding whether the alteration 'prejudicially affects' the proprietor is straightforward: is the proprietor affected by the interest prior to alteration? If not, it is rectification. An obvious example of there being no rectification is where the proprietor is bound by an overriding interest. But what is meant by mistake? The real core of our investigation must concern the standard by which mistake is gauged and also whose mistake is required (a person who forgets to protect an interest, the registered proprietor, or the registry?). These questions are made more difficult because the Law Commission provides examples of administrative alteration, but not of rectification.[279]

Probably, the best test for mistake is whether the Land Registry would have made the entry if it had been aware of the true facts.[280] We will now consider a few situations when rectification has been applied and then return to the nature of the test.

Registering the wrong person

A common situation in which rectification was sought pre-2002 was where the wrong person had been registered as first proprietor. The almost invariable cause for this is that the physical extent of the registered land is erroneous – it includes land previously owned by somebody else.[281] It may be confidently assumed that this will be an example of a mistake under the 2002 Act – this was the approach in *Sainsbury's Supermarkets Ltd* v *Olympia Homes Ltd*.[282]

---

[278] See LRA, ss 11, 12, 29(2)(a)(iii).
[279] See the useful analysis of 'mistake' by Cooper [2013] CLJ 341.
[280] See Ruoff and Roper, *Registered Conveyancing*, para 46.009; Megarry and Wade, *The Law of Real Property* (8th ed), para 7-133.
[281] LRA 1925, s 82(1)(g) provided explicit authority to rectify where the wrong person was registered. Mistakes as to the extent of the land may also be made when part of the registered title is transferred.
[282] [2006] 1 P&CR 289 at [84]; Dixon [2005] Conv 447. See also *Derbyshire CC* v *Fallon* [2007] 3 EGLR 44 at [26]; Dixon [2008] Conv 238 and *Walker* v *Burton* [2014] 1 P&CR 116 at [91].

There are statements by the Law Commission[283] that giving effect to rights conferred by the Act is not a mistake. However, that was in the adverse possession context, and it comes perilously close to saying that there can never be rectification, for the situation where the register does not accord with registered land rules is one of administrative alteration. It seems safe to assume that rectification is available where the wrong person is registered. Similarly, a failure to enter a claim to the land (a restrictive covenant, for example) on the register on first registration, so that the claim is defeated by the registration, is likely to be a mistake.[284]

Rather more straightforward is the rare case where the same area is registered in two different titles (most likely a strip of land between registered plots). Both cannot have the same land (whatever guarantee is given by registration), so rectification of one is inevitable.[285]

Forgery and other challenges to transfers

We have seen that *Swift 1st Ltd* v *Chief Land Registrar*[286] holds that registration of a forged transfer confers a good title on the transferee. It seems uncontroversial that this constitutes a mistake enabling rectification – there had in fact been rectification (by consent) in *Swift 1st*.

An analogous type of case is where a transfer is challenged on grounds such as misrepresentation or undue influence.[287] The Law Commission denies rectification.[288] They argue that the register was originally accurate and it is only the subsequent order setting aside the transfer which is in issue. Here, we need to consider the true meaning of mistake. The approach by the Law Commission looks to some sort of mistake *by the Land Registry*. However, it is not clear that this is required by the legislation. Even if their approach is correct, the conduct in question may in any event give rise to a claim against the transferee. This will be sufficient to justify administrative alteration, based upon bringing the register up to date once the transfer has been set aside.

Adverse possession and other mistakes

It seems likely that mistakes will be encountered in a broad variety of circumstances. In *Baxter* v *Mannion*,[289] an adverse possession claim was accepted by the Land Registry and the adverse possessor was registered as proprietor. However, there had not in fact been sufficient acts of adverse possession. The registration of the adverse possessor was held to constitute a mistake. *Baxter* is important in demonstrating that there is no need for the Land Registry to have done anything wrong: on the facts, it had applied the adverse

---

[283] Law Com No 271, para 3.47.
[284] A pre-2002 example is provided by *Freer* v *Unwins Ltd* [1976] Ch 288 (see p 286 below).
[285] Law Com No 271, para 10.13; *Parshall* v *Hackney* [2013] Ch 568 (criticised by Xu (2013) 129 LQR 477), discussed in Law Com CP 227, paras 13.132–13.151.
[286] [2015] Ch 602.
[287] As in the old leading case of *Norwich & Peterborough BS* v *Steed* [1993] Ch 116.
[288] Law Com No 271, para 10.7, n 23; see also Ruoff and Roper, *Registered Conveyancing,* para 46.009. However, Jacob LJ in *Baxter* v *Mannion* [2011] 1 WLR 1594 at [31] expressed distinct doubts about this.
[289] [2011] 1 WLR 1594; see also pp 78, 88 above.

possession procedures properly.[290] However, the decision fits well the proposition that there is a mistake when the Land Registry would have acted differently if it had been aware of the full circumstances.

A quite different example of mistake is encountered in *MacLeod* v *Gold Harp Properties Ltd*,[291] studied in more detail later in this chapter. A registered freeholder persuaded the Land Registry that a registered lease had been terminated; the lease was removed from the register. In fact, the lease had not terminated. It was uncontroversial that the removal of the lease was a mistake; rectification restored it to the register.

Subsequent registrations

Suppose that a forged transfer results in the registration of F. F subsequently leases the land for 10 years to an innocent lessee, P. Is it possible to rectify P's title? Similar problems could apply whenever there is a mistake in F's registration. This gives rise to two questions. The first is whether the registration of P constitutes a mistake. The second is whether the rectification of F's title can affect P. In this section, we will consider the first of these questions.

The traditional response was that, given that F is a registered proprietor, he has the powers of an owner (see LRA, ss 58 and 23) and there is no mistake in the registration of P – it is central to the system that purchasers should be able to rely on the register as being accurate. This was the approach taken, under the 1925 Act, in *Norwich & Peterborough BS* v *Steed*.[292] Under the 2002 Act, a similar analysis was seen in *Barclays Bank plc* v *Guy*.[293] We will see later that rectification has been allowed against P in recent cases. Though the main analysis has been based on the mistake in the registration of F (such a mistake is plain), there have been some suggestions that registration of P was a further mistake.[294] At least at first sight, this seems difficult to support on principle. However, a broad approach to the meaning of mistake might produce a very different picture.

The width of the power rectify

What do these examples tell us about the meaning of mistake? One of the problems is that none of the cases attempts an analysis of the meaning of mistake. *Baxter* v *Mannion* is clear that a procedural error by the Land Registry is not required. Otherwise we get little further than saying that the cases are generally consistent with the view, mentioned earlier, that there is a mistake if the Land Registry would have acted differently if it had been aware of the true facts. Yet the problem with this is that it is not what the legislation actually says. This opens the door to the possibility – one which the Law Commission would

---

[290] The problem arose because the original proprietor had not responded to a notice from the Land Registry, explicable by family tragedies at the time.
[291] [2015] 1 WLR 1249.
[292] [1993] Ch 116.
[293] [2008] 2 EGLR 74.
[294] See the influential decision of the Deputy Adjudicator in *Knights Construction (March) Ltd* v *Roberto Mac Ltd* [2011] 2 EGLR 123 at [131].

oppose[295] – that the test is whether the position in registered land is different from that if title were not registered.[296] Some commentators have indeed suggested this as the outcome.[297] This would, for example, point to there being a mistake as regards subsequent registrations following a forgery, an issue mentioned above. Unease may be expressed at any wholesale reintroduction of unregistered land rules in the rectification context (it clearly does not fit the approach of the Law Commission), but the failure to define mistake opens up this possibility.

B. The proprietor in possession

As under the pre-2002 law, the proprietor in possession is given extensive protection against rectification. This is very important. A wide scope for rectification is much easier to defend when the proprietor in possession is protected. It is easy to comprehend why it is sensible to protect those in possession. If one of two innocent parties must lose a right to the land and instead be compensated, is it not better for that to be the person out of possession? Greater disruption will be caused if we require the person in possession to leave the land.

Where there is possession at the time of the rectification application, para 3[298] restricts rectification (but not administrative alteration) to two instances considered below. It may be noted that a human rights argument that possession results in denial of the claimant's title is unlikely to succeed: there is a legitimate public interest in enhancing registration and the losing party will be indemnified.[299]

The meaning of possession

The 2002 Act employs a test of physical possession. The Court of Appeal in *Kingsalton Ltd v Thames Water Developments Ltd*[300] considered that a proprietor will normally be in possession unless dispossessed. This means that, where possession is disputed, the proprietor is normally in possession.

Certain relationships give rise to possession without physical possession on the part of the proprietor.[301] Those protected are landlords (tenants possessing), mortgagors (mortgagees possessing), licensors (licensees possessing) and trustees (beneficiaries possessing). This means that the great majority of proprietors (except chargees) will be protected. It limits the frequency of rectification and, more specifically, protects those physically possessing against the possibility of landlords', etc, titles being rectified.[302]

---

[295] See Law Com No 254, para 8.11; contrast the views of the present author in (1993) 109 LQR 187.

[296] Deliberately adopted in Scotland: Scot Law Com No 222, especially para 17.40.

[297] See, recently, Gardner (2014) 77 MLR 763 at pp 771–773.

[298] Replicated in para 6 for rectification by the registrar. The protection is limited to registered estates: this excludes registered chargees in possession (LRA, s 132(1)).

[299] *Kingsalton Ltd* v *Thames Water Developments Ltd* [2002] 1 P&CR 184 at [45].

[300] [2002] 1 P&CR 184 at [21].

[301] LRA, s 131. It appears that double use of s 131 is possible. An example is a landlord's possession if a tenant allows a licensee into possession.

[302] A mischievous thought is as to what happens if (most unusually) the person in physical possession is the person seeking rectification.

When can there be rectification against the proprietor in possession?

Assuming the proprietor does not consent, para 3 allows just two situations.[303] The first is where the proprietor 'has by fraud or lack of proper care caused or substantially contributed to the mistake'.[304] There had been more limited protection of the proprietor (especially the first registered proprietor) until 1977. However, there is still some evidence of an inclination to exercise discretion in favour of the previous owner, as against the first registered proprietor.[305]

It is uncertain what will amount to lack of proper care. At one extreme, this could reintroduce much of the law of constructive notice into the registered land system. Fortunately, it appears that the courts will not be overly zealous in finding lack of proper care.[306]

The second instance where rectification may be ordered is where 'it would for any other reason be unjust for the alteration not to be made'.[307] The use of the double negative ('unjust . . . not to be made') shows that the person seeking rectification must prove a strong case. *Epps* v *Esso Petroleum Co Ltd*[308] provides a rare example of the very similar provision in the 1925 Act being considered judicially. Part of the claimant's land had been mistakenly registered in a title now held by Esso. The claimant was largely to blame for the mistake: his failure to build a new wall along the true boundary had contributed substantially to the mistake being made. Thus far, the justice of the case, far from making it unjust not to rectify, pointed in the direction of refusing rectification. However, the claimant stressed that the indemnity rules at the time of *Epps* had the effect that he would not be compensated should his rectification claim fail.[309] On the other hand, Esso would be compensated if their title was rectified. Therefore, the claimant argued that, for nobody to lose financially, rectification should be ordered. Although Templeman J was prepared to take this argument into account, he did not consider it strong enough to oust the protection of the proprietor in possession.

Similar issues were argued in *Hounslow LB* v *Hare*,[310] in which rectification was sought to delete the defendant's registered lease. Knox J took into account the facts that the defendant would be compensated if there were rectification and that the defendant's title would have been bad but for registration. Nevertheless, he concluded that the defendant had been wholly blameless, and it would not be 'unjust not to rectify' (the statutory wording pre-2002) her title when she faced the loss of the lease of her home. The few cases in

---

[303] Two further instances in the previous law are dropped. That relating to overriding interests is cosmetic – they do not require listing because giving effect to them will be administrative alteration rather than rectification. The old 'order of the court' situation was puzzling and regarded as unnecessary: Law Com No 271, para 10.16.

[304] Schedule 4, para 3(2)(a).

[305] *Johnson* v *Shaw* [2004] 1 P&CR 123 (on LRA 1925), although a range of more specific factors also favoured rectification; contrast *Pinto* v *Lim* [2005] EWHC 630 (Ch).

[306] *Walker* v *Burton* [2014] 1 P&CR 116.

[307] Schedule 4, para 3(2)(b).

[308] [1973] 1 WLR 1071.

[309] Indemnity is discussed below; see especially n 351 in this chapter.

[310] (1990) 24 HLR 9 (rectification was sought because the lease was void under charities legislation); also *Pinto* v *Lim* [2005] EWHC 630 (Ch) at [102] (quantum of indemnity).

which this exception to the proprietor in possession's protection has been the sole ground for allowing rectification have involved distinctly unusual circumstances.[311]

C. Deciding whether to order alteration

Is there any discretion whether or not to order alteration, once a ground for alteration has been established? Absent 'exceptional circumstances', administrative alteration must be allowed.[312] This seems correct: as the interest already binds the proprietor, there will rarely be justification for an entry not being put on the register. However, it might be otherwise if the proprietor has some other (as yet unlitigated) claim to the land.[313]

Paragraphs 3(3) and 6(3) apply the same test to rectification. Although the Law Commission views this as codifying cases indicating that rectification normally results,[314] it does look as though the 2002 Act changes the balance in favour of rectification. Under the previous law, the Court of Appeal[315] referred to the 'balance of the rival considerations', which sounds rather different from the new test of 'exceptional circumstances'.

D. The effect of rectification

If A is registered as proprietor when B is the true owner, then rectification may place B on the register as proprietor. B becomes the owner and A loses his title. But what happens to interests created by A, in favour of C, before rectification? If they are themselves registered, then B will need to obtain rectification against C as well as in respect of A's fee simple. This has been the basis of much debate in the past few years. It can readily be understood that C has relied on A's being registered as proprietor. If C's title can be rectified, then the reliability of registered titles may be seen as seriously diminished.[316] On the other hand, it will frequently be the case that C would lose in unregistered land – this would be the case if the transfer to B had been forged (whether or not B was complicit in the forgery).

It has already been seen that it is doubtful whether C's registration is itself a mistake. However, other approaches might enable an attack on C to be mounted.[317] A very important consideration is that B (the original proprietor) might not receive an indemnity if rectification against C is unavailable. This has caused the courts to want rectification to be available in order to preclude possible human rights objections (in respect

---

[311] In *Sainsbury's Supermarkets Ltd* v *Olympia Homes Ltd* [2006] 1 P&CR 289 at [95], rectification was allowed where the proprietor had expected to be bound by an option omitted from the register by mistake; *Baxter* v *Mannion* [2011] 1 WLR 1594 involved the proprietor's 'unjustified attempt to get himself title'.

[312] LRR, r 126. Although this applies only to court alterations, the same is thought to apply to alteration by the registrar: *Derbyshire CC* v *Fallon* [2007] 3 EGLR 44 at [28].

[313] *Derbyshire CC* v *Fallon* [2007] 3 EGLR 44 (estoppel).

[314] Law Com No 271, para 10.18. See *Paton* v *Todd* [2012] 2 EGLR 19 for the operation of the new test in unusual circumstances.

[315] *Kingsalton Ltd* v *Thames Water Developments Ltd* [2002] 1 P&CR 184 at [26]–[28], [34]; see also *Pinto* v *Lim* [2005] EWHC 630 (Ch).

[316] An argument made by Lees (2015) 78 MLR 361, criticising the lack of certainty in the overall system.

[317] See Goymour [2013] CLJ 617 at pp 633–638.

of B's being deprived of ownership without compensation).[318] It might be noted that B can claim indemnity even if rectification is not in fact ordered, as where C is protected as being in possession. There have been suggestions that the registration of C is part of the mistake in the registration of A and (perhaps the same idea) that rectification of C's title is required to remedy the initial mistake in A's registration.[319] Alongside this, there has been discussion of the question whether rectification can be retrospective.[320]

Differing approaches were taken by Land Registry Adjudicators, but today we can turn to the decision of the Court of Appeal in *MacLeod* v *Gold Harp Properties Ltd*.[321] After a full analysis of the cases and the recommendation of the Law Commission, the court relied on para 8 of Schedule 4 in allowing rectification against C. Paragraph 8 provides that the powers to rectify 'extend to changing for the future the priority of any interest affecting the registered estate'.

There appears a strong argument that the natural reading of these words permits rectification against C. The words 'for the future' mean only that C cannot be made liable for an act prior to the rectification. Any feeling that C is being harshly treated are countered by the fact that C will receive the normal protection of the proprietor in possession (as recognised in *Gold Harp*) and that indemnity may be paid if rectification is in fact ordered.[322]

In *Gold Harp*, the subsequent interest was registered, but para 8 applies to 'any interest'. Thus, it can apply to an overriding interest, or one protected by notice. Prior to the 2002 Act, *Freer* v *Unwins Ltd*[323] had rejected the idea that rectification was retrospective so as to defeat intervening minor and overriding interests. Whilst this is doubtless correct if the rectification does not purport to affect those interests, it seems clear that para 8 now permits the court to order that the rectification shall affect those interests.

It has been seen that a variety of ideas were employed before *Gold Harp* in order to permit rectification to affect dispositions subsequent to the initial mistaken registration. Now that *Gold Harp* relies on para 8 to produce this result, can these other ideas be forgotten? It would be advantageous for the law to have a single basis, one firmly based on the 2002 Act. However, two doubts may be expressed.[324]

The first problem is that para 8 contemplates the rectification of A's title having an effect on C. This was readily applied in *Gold Harp*, where C held a registered lease granted by A. It is more difficult to apply if A has sold the freehold to C and C is registered as proprietor. A no longer has a title that can be rectified. The only rectification that can be sought is of

---

[318] See *Knights Construction (March) Ltd* v *Roberto Mac Ltd* [2011] 2 EGLR 123 (Deputy Adjudicator); Lees (2013) 76 MLR 62 argues that indemnity might still be available.

[319] Lord Neuberger MR in *Barclays Bank plc* v *Guy* [2011] 1 WLR 681.

[320] Differing views were expressed in *Malory Enterprises Ltd* v *Cheshire Homes (UK) Ltd* [2002] Ch 216 at [79], [87], [89].

[321] [2015] 1 WLR 1249. Commentators have been generally supportive: Dixon (2015) 131 LQR 207, Goymour [2015] Conv 253, Lees (2015) 78 MLR 361, Smith [2015] CLJ 10. A wide power to rectify is advocated by Law Com CP 227, paras 13.189–13.196 (and also 13.64–13.74).

[322] In *Gold Harp*, C was acting in concert with A (who had persuaded the registrar that B's registered lease had terminated and should be removed from the register) such that the merits of the case were entirely on B's side. Cooper (2015) 131 LQR 108 argues, taking into account economic aspects, that it is preferable that disputes involving C should be resolved by rectification.

[323] [1976] Ch 288 (rectification to enter a restrictive covenant omitted on the first registration of the servient land; it did affect an overriding interest lease created prior to rectification).

[324] See RJ Smith [2015] CLJ 10.

C's title – this appears to fall outside the wording 'any interest affecting the registered estate'. Yet, this would be a huge and unprincipled limitation on the effect of rectification: to allow rectification against the holder of a very long lease (or a charge for more than the value of the property) but not against a purchaser of the fee simple seems indefensible.

The second problem (probably less serious) arises if the alteration of A's title does not amount to rectification, where A was already bound by B's claim. Paragraph 8 explicitly refers to rectification. Again, any such limit appears to be anomalous (and probably unintended). In *Gold Harp* it appears that A was affected by B's claims prior to alteration, yet the court had no hesitation in applying para 8. This robust approach to the provision is to be welcomed.

If one or both of these doubts is proved to be justified, then one can predict that the other ideas mentioned above (including treating the registration of C as a mistake) will return to prominence. It is less easy to predict which of them would be seen as the strongest.

E. Rights to rectify as overriding interests

As observed in the actual occupation overriding interest section, it has been argued that the overriding interest in *Blacklocks* v *JB Developments (Godalming) Ltd*[325] was the statutory right to rectify the register. This is questionable, but two later cases directly cover the point.

Malory Enterprises Ltd v *Cheshire Homes (UK) Ltd*[326] is the leading case. The Court of Appeal ruled that a statutory right to rectify under LRA 1925 could constitute an overriding interest. There is little justification for this conclusion: the court appears to treat it as following from the recognition of the equitable right to rectify as an overriding interest. Yet these two rights are quite different, having different origins (equity; statute) and applying in different situations – even if they may overlap. Noting that *Malory* on this point had been generally accepted,[327] the Court of Appeal in *Swift 1st Ltd* v *Chief Land Registrar*[328] applied it.

If this is right, what is the effect of the overriding interest? Most obviously, one would expect that a later purchaser would be affected by the right. Yet this is the effect of para 8, as recently held in *Gold Harp*. Unless there are limits on the applications of para 8, it appears unnecessary to rely on any overriding interest.

In each of *Malory* and *Swift 1st*, the overriding interest bound the person taking under a forged disposition. This is curious, as there is clearly a right to rectify when there is a forgery – it is a clear example of a mistake. Might it mean that rectification will be automatic, such that the normal proprietor in possession defence does not apply?[329] It is not clear that this is a correct reading of the legislation, let alone a defensible outcome.

---

[325] [1982] Ch 183; see [1983] Conv 169, 257, 361.
[326] [2002] Ch 216 at [66]–[70]; Sheehan (2003) 119 LQR 31.
[327] Harpum in *Rationalizing Property, Equity and Trusts* (ed Getzler), pp 197–198; Fox in *Modern Studies in Property Law*, Vol 3 (ed Cooke), Chapter 2, p 30. But Cooke [2004] Conv 482 at p 486 and Goymour [2013] CLJ 617 at p 640 have been less impressed; most recently, see the criticism of Milne [2015] Conv 356.
[328] [2015] Ch 602.
[329] It would anyway be unusual for the disponee to be in possession when the original owner was in actual occupation at the time of the disposition.

We might conclude that this overriding interest is unprincipled and plays no useful role. All it achieved on the facts of *Swift 1st* was to complicate the payment of indemnity, as will be seen in the following section. It is welcome that the Law Commission proposes that it should cease to be an overriding interest.[330]

F. Assessment of alteration; reform

Administrative alteration is not problematic: it is essentially a book-keeping exercise. Rectification, by way of contrast, represents an important limitation upon the protection accorded to registered proprietors. Much recent interest in the scope of rectification is based upon this factor, coupled with its being a way of recognising principles of unregistered land that determine the priority of rival proprietary claims.[331] However, two factors demonstrate that it is less destructive of the protection of purchasers than are overriding interests. These are the protection of the proprietor in possession and the availability of indemnity for the proprietor whose title is rectified. These factors permit us to be more relaxed about a wide scope for rectification, although it is unsatisfactory that there remains so much uncertainty surrounding the meaning of 'mistake'.

Rectification is considered in some detail by the Law Commission in its review of the 2002 Act.[332] It is apparent that the Law Commission sees rectification as the most appropriate way to resolve many priority disputes – it permits a more fact-sensitive analysis than a simple rule favouring the registered proprietor (or another person). It is also apparent that rectification is seen as having a much wider role than contemplated in the Reports leading to the 2002 Act. The Law Commission proposes one significant change to the existing rules: there will be a long-stop period of 10 years.[333] In order to introduce further finality, after 10 years, there will be no rectification unless the claimant is in possession or the proprietor is guilty of fraud or lack of proper care. This would be a useful provision, albeit one with limited effect.

4. Indemnity

One of the perennial difficulties in property law is that there are so often two innocent parties, one of whom must lose. Priority principles provide all-or-nothing resolutions of disputes: there is no equivalent to contributory negligence. The losing party may well have done nothing wrong and be exceptionally unfortunate, but that is little consolation for losing. In the United States, this problem is tackled by title insurance. However, this can be expensive and tends to be structured in favour of mortgagees (who insist on such insurance) rather than purchasers.[334]

---

[330] Law Com CP 227, paras 13.60–13.63, 13.83–13.87.
[331] See, e.g., Cooper [2013] CLJ 341 at pp 341–343, Goymour [2013] CLJ 67 at pp 627–641, Gardner (2014) 77 MLR 763 at pp 771–773.
[332] Law Com CP 227, especially paras 13.98–13.126. It is not thought feasible to define 'mistake': para 13.81.
[333] Ibid, para 13.101.
[334] Payne [1976] Conv 11. For its potential alongside title registration, see Morgan in *Contemporary Property Law* (eds Jackson and Wilde), Chapter 8.

One of the merits of a registration system is that it can offer compensation ('indemnity') out of Land Registry funds to those who lose out in priority disputes. Perhaps the most natural use of compensation is for cases where the registration system has caused loss. Thus, if the wrong person is registered as proprietor and the register is not rectified, it is easy to see a case for the original owner being compensated. In fact, most claims arise from minor (often administrative) errors within the Land Registry, usually causing little, if any, loss.

However, limiting indemnity to such cases would be insufficiently imaginative. Indemnity can be used to compensate for losses where the registration system itself has not caused the loss. This is feasible because the incidence of loss is very low relative to the huge numbers of purchasers. The laudable approach of the Law Commission in 1987 was to regard indemnity as a form of insurance: 'insuring all titles against interests not on the register and all interests against the adverse effect of registration'.[335] It will be necessary to consider the extent to which the present law[336] matches that description.

A. Rights to indemnity

Indemnity is dealt with by LRA, Sched 8. Paragraph 1 lists the grounds. Many of them cover essentially administrative errors, such as mistakes in searches or official copies of the register, or the loss of documents. However, two more general and interesting grounds are: (a) rectification and (b) a mistake whose correction would require rectification of the register. In the latter type of claim, the decision is postponed until after it has been decided whether or not to rectify: this is necessary so that we know whether it is the claimant or the proprietor who loses the land.

One initial point to note is that administrative alteration of the register is not here relevant: there must be rectification in the narrow sense of correction of a mistake which prejudicially affects the proprietor.[337] Thus an alteration giving effect to an overriding interest cannot be a ground for indemnity, for this is not rectification. This seems correct, as the loss is caused to the proprietor by the overriding interest, not by the alteration of the register.[338]

The complementary nature of rectification and indemnity is seen in these provisions. Suppose that, by mistake, A is registered as proprietor of B's land. B will seek rectification. If that fails (A might be in possession), then B can claim indemnity. If rectification succeeds, then the loss is shifted to A, who accordingly can claim indemnity. However, in some instances, there may be rectification which does not entirely correct the problem.[339] In such a case, indemnity for B's remaining loss is payable under para 1.

[335] Law Com No 158, paras 3.25–3.26. The merits of indemnity are considered by Cooper in *Modern Studies in Property Law*, Vol 5 (ed Dixon), Chapter 2, stressing its potential to affect behaviour of the Land Registry and lawyers.
[336] The present law was established by the Land Registration Act 1997 (implementing Law Com No 235); the 2002 Act made few changes.
[337] LRA, Sched 8, para 11(2).
[338] This was the analysis employed under LRA 1925 to reach the identical result: *Re Chowood's Registered Land* [1933] Ch 574.
[339] This is most likely if a subsequent disposition (by A) is not affected by the rectification.

One somewhat paradoxical point may be considered. When investigating rectification, we saw that there is a case for mistake being given a relatively limited meaning; this renders the title of the proprietor less vulnerable. Unfortunately, one side effect of a narrow interpretation of mistake (and, therefore, rectification) is to limit the scope of indemnity. Overall, this is welcome to the present proprietor, of course. However, the person who loses out as a result will have no claim to indemnity: his or her claim depends upon there being a mistake which would require rectification to correct it. It would be unacceptable (and quite possibly breach human rights) for the registration scheme not to compensate the innocent person who has lost his or her land. This itself is a strong reason for adopting a wider meaning of mistake.[340]

The most acute problems were thought likely to be encountered when B creates rights in other persons. However, now that *Gold Harp* allows rectification to affect such persons, this issue seems to have been resolved. We saw that there might be limits to the application of *Gold Harp*, which was based on para 8 of Sched 4. The indemnity problems will arise only if those limits are shown to apply and no other route to affecting such persons by the rectification (of A's title) can be found. That seems unlikely.

B. Overriding interests and indemnity

It has been seen that alteration of the register to give effect to overriding interests does not result in indemnity being payable. The reason is simple and convincing: no loss has been caused by the alteration and there is no rectification. But should proprietors bound by overriding interests be indemnified, regardless of whether there is alteration? In 1987, the Law Commission[341] recommended that purchasers bound by overriding interests should be entitled to compensation. This was an excellent suggestion, reflecting the insurance basis for indemnity in the modern law. Unfortunately, it was opposed by the Land Registry and never implemented. In order to facilitate the 2002 reforms, the Law Commission dropped indemnity for overriding interests.[342]

Why is the point so controversial? Admittedly, it extends indemnity to risks off the register, but indemnity has long protected against risks which are not the fault of the registry but would operate in unregistered land. The real problem was that liability to pay indemnity would be open-ended and possibly too expensive. Yet, in practice, purchasers discover nearly all overriding interests, in which case indemnity could not be claimed. In most other cases, the purchaser ought to have discovered the overriding interest, and (as discussed later in this chapter) this will either exclude or reduce the claim for indemnity. Indeed, it is probable that the reform would have led to few successful claims. Even so, it is difficult to quantify the likely number. It should be borne in mind that the current level of indemnity claims runs at around £8–10 million per annum, compared to total annual fee income around £300 million (with an annual surplus).[343] These figures show that even a moderately significant rise in indemnity payments would have a limited effect on fee levels.

---

[340] *Baxter* v *Mannion* [2011] 1 WLR 1594 at [34]; for mistake, see p 280 above.
[341] Law Com No 158, paras 2.10–2.14.
[342] Law Com No 254, paras 4.17–4.20.
[343] Figures taken from Land Registry Annual Reports and Accounts.

C. Forgeries

Paragraph 1(2)(b) allows indemnity where a proprietor's title is rectified on account of a forgery. Obviously, if it is the forger's own title that is rectified, there is no question of indemnity being paid. The more likely case is where a rogue forges a transfer to an innocent purchaser. Prior to 1925, it had been held that the purchaser obtained a bad title, even before rectification, and therefore suffered no loss from rectification.[344] The purpose of para 1(2)(b), repeating provisions in the LRA 1925, is to ensure that compensation would be paid in such circumstances.

Is para 1(2)(b) needed today? The Court of Appeal held in *Swift 1st Ltd v Chief Land Registrar*[345] that registration of a forged transfer does confer good title. This appears to mean that the purpose of the provision (which was fully recognised by the Court of Appeal) is today redundant: alteration really will prejudicially affect the proprietor.

However, a further point posed problems in *Swift 1st*. The original proprietor was in actual occupation, and it was held that this gave rise to an overriding interest, in the form of a right to rectify. It was held that the wording of para 1(2)(b) was strong enough to apply even though there was an overriding interest. In other words, a provision designed to apply where no loss is caused because registration of a forgery gave a bad title (the position prior to *Swift 1st*) applied also where that title was also bad by virtue of an overriding interest.[346] Although this appears to be fortuitous – outside forgery, no indemnity is payable if there is an overriding interest – it can be defended. Forgery has the unique characteristic that the purchaser believes that he or she is dealing with the person in actual occupation. Making enquiries of the occupier appears totally superfluous in such cases.

This relates to a question discussed earlier in this chapter:[347] is the overriding interest status of the right to rectify justified? It was there argued that it is both unprincipled and superfluous. *Swift 1st* shows that it also might be positively harmful in the indemnity context. It is only because of para 1(2)(b) that its effect was negated. Rights to rectify outside the forgery context will continue to cause indemnity problems. Removing the right to rectify as an overriding interest would, it seems, leave absolutely no role for para 1(2)(b), which might then be usefully repealed. Some might think that a purchaser who ignores actual occupation does not deserve indemnity, but that can be dealt with by the restrictions on indemnity now discussed.

D. Restrictions on indemnity

As might be expected, the operation of indemnity is subject to further rules and statutory limits.

---

[344] *Att-Gen v Odell* [1906] 2 Ch 47.

[345] [2015] Ch 602. Dixon [2016] Conv 382 cogently argues that overriding interests based upon rights to rectify should not preclude indemnity, regardless of para 1(2)(b).

[346] A point unsuccessfully raised at first instance ([2014] EWHC 4866 (Ch); see especially [35]) was that para 1(2)(b) could not apply anyway because there was alteration rather than rectification. This would rob para 1(2)(b) of any effect and the Court of Appeal decision implicitly rejects it.

[347] See p 287 above.

(i) *Fraud or lack of proper care*[348]

Not surprisingly, loss caused by the claimant's fraud is excluded. Where there is lack of proper care, this will debar indemnity if it is the sole cause of the loss.[349] If it is a contributory cause, then it will merely reduce indemnity,[350] in a similar fashion to contributory negligence in tort. In the context of compensating for losses caused by the registration system, this makes sense, but it is less clear that fault has a role to play in an insurance-based approach.

(ii) *Quantum and time limits*

There are important and sometimes arbitrary limits on the amount of compensation and the time limits within which it may be claimed. Looking first at time limits, the claim must be brought within six years of knowledge of it, or the time there should have been knowledge.[351]

The amount of compensation is more problematic. Where there is rectification, the rules work well enough. The claimant affected by rectification is limited to the value of the estate or interest at that time.[352] However, the rules are more controversial where there is a mistake (not corrected by rectification). The claimant is limited to the value of the estate or interest at the time of the mistake.[353]

An example will illustrate the problem. A is the registered proprietor of land that is left vacant. In 2011, B forges a transfer in favour of himself and is registered as proprietor but does not go into possession. In 2017, B transfers the land to C, who is duly registered and enters possession. Very shortly afterwards, A realises that C is possessing 'his' land. A immediately takes steps to evict C, but then discovers that C is the registered proprietor. Worse still, rectification is refused because C is in possession. When A turns to the registry to seek indemnity, he will be told that the error was in 2011 and that his claim is limited to the 2011 value of the land,[354] which is much lower than its present value. The obvious reason why this is unfair is that there was no way in which A could have been expected to know that B had fraudulently obtained registration in 2011. Nevertheless, the Law Commission[355] originally supported this result, arguing that interest is added to the indemnity award from the time of the error.[356] It is said that this makes it unnecessary to use current land values. Yet, inflation of land values has frequently been very different from

---

[348] Schedule 8, para 5. Donees are affected by their predecessors' conduct: para 5(3).

[349] This applies if its 'significance and causative effect' is such that the loss should be regarded as wholly resulting from it: *Prestige Properties Ltd v Scottish Provident Institution* [2003] Ch 1 at [36]. It is not necessarily enough that the lack of proper care was a 'but for' cause of the loss: *Dean v Dean* (2000) 80 P&CR 457.

[350] Schedule 8, para 5(2).

[351] Ibid, para 8. Law Com CP 227, paras 14.127–14.136 would base the running of time on the date of the rectification decision.

[352] Ibid, para 6(a).

[353] Ibid, para 6(b).

[354] Confirmed by *Hounslow LB v Hare* (1990) 24 HLR 9 at p 25.

[355] Law Com No 235, para 4.7. Contrast earlier proposals: Law Com No 158, para 3.30.

[356] LRR, r 195.

interest rates; the interests of claimants seem to have been damaged by this approach.[357] It is pleasing that the Law Commission has now changed its position on this question and recommends that current land values be used.[358]

E. The significance of indemnity

This requires an investigation into the frequency and size of compensation payments. The figures show that about £8–10 million is paid in a typical year, representing about £30 for each £1,000 of registry income, or about £2.50 for every dealing.[359] These figures can be variously used to argue that the rules are unduly strict in allowing indemnity or that the figures are a credit to the Land Registry in that there are few errors causing compensation to be paid. The latter is a dangerous argument, because it encourages the idea that indemnity is linked with failures within the Land Registry, or the system of registration. This can encourage a too restrictive approach to indemnity. As we have seen, such arguments have no place in a true insurance approach.

There are around 1,000 successful claims each year. The majority are on account of minor administrative errors within the Land Registry, such as losing documents. The sums involved for these are small; in any event, the number of claims is tiny in comparison with around four and a half million registrations each year (leaving aside other entries on the register and searches). More serious problems (best illustrated in the cases on rectification) are rare but can be expensive when they occur. Thus, claims based upon fraud or forgery amount to around 5% of the numbers of indemnity claims, but cost around 60% of what is paid.

5. Assessing land registration

Today, the land registration system works well in providing a quick and efficient service to those buying and selling land – greatly aided by the increasing use of computerised systems. One of the main reasons for introducing land registration was the waste of time involved in checking title deeds every time land is sold. Registration is a significant improvement upon the old system. It is clearly easier to discover the current state of the title from the register, rather than to have to investigate successive title deeds.[360] Ultimately, the best test of the efficiency of the registered system is whether it is less expensive for buyers and sellers, relative to unregistered land. To the surprise of many, lawyers' fees are generally the same whether title is registered or not. It may be slightly simpler to deal with registered land, yet the difference does not seem large enough to justify a different fee structure.[361]

---

[357] Tee [1996] CLJ 241 at p 247. The Law Commission also argues that there might be changes to the land after the time of the error, which it would not be appropriate to take into account. This may be correct, but reform could surely have accommodated it.

[358] Law Com CP 227, paras 14.147–14.176.

[359] RJ Smith [1986] CLP 111 (figures updated). The ratio of indemnity to income has more than quadrupled since 1986. This may be explained by the presence of large claims based on fraud, coupled with reductions in fees.

[360] Some title registration systems (Australian systems provide examples) record a series of transfers of the registered estate. This is less helpful than the English practice of recording the identity of the current owner.

[361] *Property & Reversionary Investment Corporation Ltd* v *Secretary of State for the Environment* [1975] 1 WLR 1504 at p 1507.

Does this cast doubt upon the improvements brought by registration? The answer seems to be that registration has been successful, but that at the same time, it has become much easier to investigate title to unregistered land. There are many reasons for this. Since 1969, it has been necessary to go back only to a 15-year root of title. Conveyances are drafted more simply and concisely than in the past. Many of the horrors that might be found in earlier decades, such as complex settlements, are now rare. Cases in which the title deeds involve extensive investigation have become unusual. Where there are complications, it is likely to be because of complex covenants (especially in leases). Registration cannot solve this: it is still necessary to read and interpret the relevant documents relating to leases and covenants. Much of the work of lawyers today will not be related to investigating title, but rather dealing with issues such as local authority searches[362] and drafting the contract and conveyance or transfer. It is the dominance of this work that ensures that the time taken is much the same whether title is registered or not.

If title is registered, then the Land Registry will charge a fee for registration. At present, the average house value is around £214,000, or £319,000 for detached houses.[363] The fee is £270 (halved for electronic applications) for sales above £200,000.[364] This cost represents an added expense in purchasing registered land. It would surprise the nineteenth-century proponents of registration to learn that, far from cutting costs, registration of title makes it more expensive to buy land. On a more optimistic note, the level of fees has been significantly reduced over the past two decades. Even without e-conveyancing, the efficiency of computerised systems is having a welcome effect.

A rather different argument in favour of registration is that it offers better protection to encumbrancers and purchasers. The purchaser knows that he or she can rely on getting a good title if the seller is the registered proprietor. The extent of the land will be as described on the filed plan. Any adverse claim, such as a mortgage or restrictive covenant, must be on the register as a registered or protected minor interest. It seems that all the doubts of unregistered conveyancing have disappeared. Yet, this is but a dream. In reality, overriding interests and rectification mean that a purchaser cannot rely on the register alone. That is not to attack the use of overriding interests and rectification, but it has to be recognised that they are incompatible with any complete conclusiveness of the register.

We must be able to demonstrate that the modern law of registration provides more certain and reliable titles, if we are not to be left with the unpalatable conclusion that the registered system makes conveyancing more expensive without any useful improvement in the quality of titles. One could reply that registration offers compensation if things go wrong. This is a huge potential advantage for the registered system. However, we have seen that the actual number of payments, other than for minor administrative mistakes, is quite small.

---

[362] These searches are not designed to discover title-related matters, but rather to establish if there are plans for the property or the area which would affect its value.
[363] Land Registry House Price Index, June 2016.
[364] Land Registration Fee Order 2013 (SI 2013 No 3174).

6. The role of the rules of law and equity: do we have a system of title by registration?

Chapter 12 commenced with a discussion of the ways in which purchasers are bound by existing interests in land, according to the rules of law and equity. Do these rules have any relevance within the modern registered land system? There have been suggestions, encouraged by the Law Commission,[365] that we now have a system of title by registration, such that it is simply what is on the register that counts. But to the contrary, Baroness Hale has opined that land registration is 'purely conveyancing machinery'.[366] This whole area raises very complex issues: this discussion can do little more than scratch the surface.[367]

We will start by asking whether it makes sense to continue to distinguish legal and equitable interests. Though registration rules may have blurred the differences (both may require registration, whilst both may be overriding interests), we cannot simply ignore the old distinctions. It is widely recognised that registration systems involve 'bijural ambiguity':[368] a sometimes uncomfortable mix of registration rules and common law rules. At the most obvious level, the concept of the trust demands a division into legal and equitable interests. We need to be able to say that the beneficiary has equitable proprietary rights, whilst the trustee has the legal title. That an interest is equitable may also be important in terms of remedies. Equitable remedies are not available as of right but depend upon the discretion of the court.[369]

Closer within the registration system, legal or equitable status is still important. It is interesting that only legal estates can be registered[370] and that some overriding interests are specifically limited to legal interests.[371] This might be seen as the legislation's clinging to old terminology, but it probably represents a more substantial policy. The requirement that legal estates be created by deed[372] ensures that registrable rights will be formally created and, accordingly, easily identified.

Where registration may be expected to provide its own set of rules is in the context of priority disputes: disputes between different interests. If, say, X is registered as proprietor of a lease,[373] is this conclusive that X has a lease and that there are no interests (other than

---

[365] Law Com No 271, para 1.10.

[366] *Mortgage Business plc* v *O'Shaugnessy* [2015] AC 385 at [96], although the context (the ability to create proprietary interests) indicates that this should not be taken literally. The dicta are criticised by Hopkins [2015] Conv 245.

[367] The language of title by registration was used by Cooke [2002] Conv 11 at p 16; this, like the Law Commission's analysis, was linked to e-conveyancing. See also Harpum in *Rationalizing Property, Equity and Trusts* (ed Getzler), p 188 and Dixon (2013) 129 LQR 320. Doubts about this approach are seen in the recent contributions by Goymour [2013] CLJ 617 and Gardner (2014) 77 MLR 763.

[368] Scot Law Com No 222, paras 3.1, 13.7; their solution is to remove protection from registration of invalid transfers so that (generally) the unregistered land outcome prevails. See also O'Connor (2009) 13 Edin LR 194; Harding and Hickey in *Modern Studies in Property Law*, Vol 6 (ed Bright), Chapter 14.

[369] Thus a remedy for breach of a restrictive covenant will be denied if there is acquiescence in the breach: see, e.g., *Shaw* v *Applegate* [1977] 1 WLR 970.

[370] LRA, ss 2, 3(1), 4 (first registration), 27(2) (registrable dispositions).

[371] Ibid, Sched 3, paras 1 (leases), 3 (easements).

[372] LPA, s 52.

[373] For protected interests, LRA s 28 provides priority rules based upon date of creation: very different, but still stipulated by the Act.

those protected on the register) affecting it? We will identify three particular areas[374] in which X's position may be challenged: overriding interests, forgeries and rectification. It should be stressed that those advocating title by registration fully recognise these three areas, though their approach will tend to be to narrow their scope.

Overriding interests provide what is, perhaps, the most obvious area. They form a very deliberate qualification upon the protection of the proprietor and clearly require a purchaser (or lessee or chargee) to look beyond the register. We have seen that actual occupation operates in a manner similar to the doctrine of notice, whilst not replicating it. More recently, the effect of registration of forgeries has attracted much attention. The decision in *Swift 1st* that a good title is given seems a strong argument in favour of title by registration. On the other hand, the wider approach to rectification in *Gold Harp* points in the opposite direction.

All this might be seen as good evidence of confusion as to what the proper role of registration should be. It is suggested that the English approach is practical rather than dogmatic. Neither the idea of title by registration nor the idea that the old principles should be given prominence is, it is suggested, correct. Instead, we are feeling our way forward to results that make good practical sense. Thus, one good reason for welcoming *Swift 1st* is that it enables rectification to be used to produce an end result sensitive to the facts of the case: 'responsive to the reality on the ground'.[375] In turn, possession is a crucial element in assessing rectification. We can accept a relatively wide scope for rectification because of the protection of the proprietor in possession (as well as the availability of indemnity). Of particular interest is the protection accorded to possession: whether in the form of the actual occupation overriding interest or the protection of the proprietor in possession against rectification. This may reveal what the system is truly seeking to achieve. That possession is much wider in its application than actual occupation does not alter the big picture.

Further reading

Bogusz, B [2014] Conv 27: The relevance of 'intentions and wishes' to determine actual occupation: a sea change in judicial thinking?

Cooke, E J and O'Connor, P A (2004) 120 LQR 640: Purchaser liability to third parties in the English registration system: a comparative perspective.

Cooper, S (2015) 131 LQR 108: Resolving title conflicts in registered land.

Goymour, A [2013] CLJ 617: Mistaken registration of land: exploding the myth of 'title by registration'.

Harpum, C (2003) 'Registered land: a law unto itself?' in *Rationalizing Property, Equity and Trusts*, (ed J Getzler), Chapter 9.

Jackson, N (2003) 119 LQR 660: Title by registration and concealed overriding interests: the cause and effect of antipathy to documentary proof.

Pottage, A (1995) 15 OxJLS 371: The originality of registration.

Thompson, M P [1985] CLJ 280: Registration, fraud and notice.

---

[374] The position of the proprietor who is aware of an unprotected interest might be added. Since 2002, it has been clear that there is protection, but it is becoming increasingly clear that this may be qualified by personal liability.
[375] Cooke [2014] Conv 444 at p 446.

Part III

Rights to enjoy land: estates and commonhold

14

Successive and concurrent interests: introduction

Introduction

The law relating to successive and concurrent interests is marked by extensive amendment and regulation by the 1925 legislation and, more recently, the Trusts of Land and Appointment of Trustees Act 1996 (hereafter TLATA). We shall begin by considering the material under two major headings: the interests recognised by the law and the legal regulation of those interests.

1. The recognised interests

The most important successive interests were considered in Part I. A very simple form of settlement is where Andrew holds property for life and Brian has a fee simple in remainder. The settlor's intention is that Andrew should, during his lifetime, have the income (rent) or else occupy the land and that Brian should become the absolute owner on Andrew's death. There will also be successive interests if there is a qualified form of fee simple (to Charles, but if he fails his university exams, then to Diana). It should be added that successive interests are not concerned with the creation of leases.[1] If Rachel leases land to Simon for five years, it might look as if Rachel and Simon have successive interests in the land. Nevertheless, we do not regard this as a settlement.

There are several explanations for this. In a formal sense, Rachel has the fee simple absolute in possession[2] in the land: her interest is not postponed until Simon's interest ends. It is true that she cannot exercise any right to physical occupation during the lease, but the law is far more interested in her estate in the land. Rachel is entitled to rent during the lease, and this shows that enjoyment of her interest is not postponed. However, the most important factor is that, as we shall see, successive interests are subject to a detailed statutory regime. This regime is designed to enable the land to be sold free of the successive interests, which are nearly always created by a trust in favour of members of a family. Leases are created in order that the lessee can use the land for a specified period. There is

---

[1] Life interests and remainders may be created out of leases in the same way as out of a fee simple, though short leases are unlikely to be settled in this way.
[2] Law of Property Act 1925 (hereafter LPA), s 205(1)(xix).

no need for it to be possible to sell the land free from leases,[3] and such a power would destroy the commercial utility of leases as a method of possessing land.

Concurrent interests (co-ownership) exist where two or more people enjoy property (or an interest in it) at the same time. Most people living together choose to have their home placed in their joint names; it follows that the law on concurrent interests is of vital importance in regulating the legal relationships of millions of people today. The growth of co-ownership of the family home is a feature of the past half century and, as will be seen, placed such great pressures on the 1925 legal structure that the 1996 reforms became essential. It is possible to have co-ownership of virtually all property rights, including leases and life interests. This last point shows how successive and concurrent interests can co-exist. A very simple example is a gift 'to my widow for life, remainder to my children Rose and Tony'. Rose and Tony are co-owners of a fee simple in remainder. We shall concentrate, however, on co-ownership of the fee simple absolute in possession.

Forms of co-ownership

English law recognises more than one form of co-ownership. The two which have survived to the present day are the joint tenancy and tenancy in common, the latter sometimes called undivided shares (the use of the word 'tenancy' has nothing to do with leases). The principal distinguishing feature of the joint tenancy is the right of survivorship: when one of the joint tenants dies, that person's share does not pass under a will or intestacy. Instead, the surviving joint tenants are entitled to the property. It follows that the joint tenant who outlives all the others will become the sole owner.

Obviously, survivorship does not suit all co-owners. Two people in business as partners would regard it as very odd if the survivor were to be entitled to all the property. Joint tenancy has several inflexible requirements, notably that the shares must be the same in nature and size: it is impossible for the shares to reflect the contributions of the co-owners. This is a result of the unity of interest: one of the *four unities* which are essential for a joint tenancy to be created. Tenancies in common provide a more flexible form of co-ownership. There is no right of survivorship (so the share can be devised by will or pass on intestacy), and the shares can be of whatever size the parties desire.

The joint tenancy possesses two advantages. First, the right of survivorship suits many people. By far the most common example of co-ownership today is of the family home. Nearly always, the parties will wish the surviving spouse or partner to have the home and will utilise the joint tenancy. The second advantage is quite different and is based upon conveyancing considerations. A purchaser will find it far easier to purchase from joint tenants because it avoids any proliferation of co-owners on the death of one joint tenant. Indeed, on death there is one fewer to deal with. By contrast, a tenancy in common can cause greater problems. When a tenant in common dies, the share passes under the will or intestacy. Not only must the purchaser trace the share to those currently entitled (rather

---

[3] It is common to sell land subject to leases. The purchaser will see the land as a source of income (rent). By contrast, the purchase of land subject to a life interest is less appealing. Not only is it uncertain how long the life interest will last, but no income will be received whilst it subsists.

than rely on the death certificate as in the joint tenancy), but then it may be found that the share belongs to several people. Instead of death reducing the number of co-owners to be bargained with, it may well increase the number.

The upshot of these factors[4] was that the common law presumed a joint tenancy whenever the four unities were satisfied, subject to the expression of a contrary intention. Equity, more mindful of the wishes of the parties,[5] was more ready to recognise a tenancy in common. Rather than outright rejection of the common law presumption, equity recognised an equitable tenancy in common in certain specific cases (considered in Chapter 15).

Finally, it should be noted that a joint tenancy can be converted into a tenancy in common: a process termed 'severance'. There are complex rules in this area and the law is somewhat confused. The possibility of severance of a joint tenancy had the important consequence that purchasers could not assume that surviving joint tenants could sell the land: this would only be the case if there had been no severance.

2. Legal regulation

The question as to how the law should regulate successive and concurrent interests has been highly controversial over the past 150 years. In the nineteenth century, wealthy families owned much of the land in the country. It was usual for the land to be subject to complex settlements, often with the senior male member of the family having a life interest, his descendants having interests in remainder and others (brothers, sisters, wife) having specified income rights. It could be difficult and time-consuming to sell the land. The purchaser would have to deal with all those with interests in the land, which would be impossible if interests were held by infants or persons as yet unborn. The problem could be cured if the land was held by trustees with power to sell the land, but otherwise recourse to a private Act of Parliament was necessary and, indeed, quite common.[6]

The solution to the problem lay in the concept of overreaching. The essence of overreaching is that, on the sale of the land, the successive interests are taken away from the land and become interests in the proceeds of sale. Overreaching is no new concept in the reforming legislation, as any trust with a power of sale permits overreaching of the beneficial interests. Suppose that Martin and Nicola hold on trust for Wanda for life, remainder to Charles and Clare; the trust gives Martin and Nicola a power of sale. Wanda, Charles and Clare have equitable interests in the land under the trust. Even without statutory overreaching provisions, once the trustees exercise their power, the beneficial interests are transferred to the proceeds of sale. Wanda will then be entitled to the income from the proceeds of sale (this may mean dividends on shares bought with the proceeds) rather than rent from the land or occupation of it. There is no question of the rights of the beneficiaries binding the purchaser. That the purchaser has notice of them is irrelevant: the power of sale ensures that they are overreached on to the proceeds of sale.

---

[4] Historically, feudal services were also relevant: Megarry and Wade, *The Law of Real Property* (8th edn), para 13-015.

[5] See, e.g., *R v Williams* (1735) Bunb 342 (145 ER 694): 'survivorship is looked upon as odious in equity'.

[6] The problems may have been exaggerated as regards small house sales: Anderson, *Lawyers and the Making of English Land Law 1832–1940*, pp 78, 128.

What was significant in the nineteenth-century reforms was that statute extended over-reaching to all situations where there were successive interests. There would always be somebody with either a power or a duty to sell the land. Of course, it was not intended that land should always be sold; rather, that if it was desirable to sell, there should be a small number of vendors to deal with and no complex trust interests to be bound by. From today's perspective, it is difficult to comprehend how significant and controversial these reforms were. It is no longer the case that so much land is held under complex trusts as to justify imposing overreaching. But in the nineteenth century, land was still seen as the basis of power and wealth, with some families having owned large landed estates for centuries. Not surprisingly, the reforms were viewed with suspicion. Overreaching treats successive interests as being interests in a fund, currently represented by land, rather than as interests in the land itself for all time.

It has been seen that the reforms did not apply to leases. Quite apart from the fact that it is both easy and common to sell land subject to a lease, the viability of leases depends upon occupation of the land. In contrast, successive interests may be viewed more as a source of income; income may be derived from assets, whether in the form of land or of (for example) shares.

Turning to concurrent interests, we have seen that tenancies in common can cause problems for purchasers. The legislative response in 1925 was to introduce overreaching in this area as well.[7] The essence of the scheme is that the legal title must be held by joint tenants. This ensures that a small and, indeed, reducing number of persons are involved in selling the legal title. These joint tenants hold the land on trust for the co-owners, who are equitable joint tenants or tenants in common as the case may be. In most cases, this means that the legal tenants hold on trust for themselves. Simply creating a trust would not of itself confer overreaching powers, but this is achieved by conferring a power to sell; it was a trust for sale before TLATA. From the point of view of overreaching, this change in 1996 made no difference. Both forms of trust enable the land to be retained (and occupied) or sold.

The trust for sale, as employed by the 1925 legislation, came under considerable criticism. The doctrine of conversion, operating as a consequence of the obligation to sell, meant that the beneficial interests should be treated as being in money (the proceeds of the future sale) rather than in land. This treatment of rights to the family home as rights in money appeared to subvert the wishes of millions of home owners. It might be replied that, in the majority of situations, it mattered little. The co-owners normally held the legal estate as joint tenants and would not sell until they wanted to. Nevertheless, problems could arise when family relationships broke down, most especially when not all the co-owners were trustees.

Fortunately, TLATA replaced the trust for sale with the trust of land as the modern form of landholding for both concurrent and successive interests. It is discussed in Chapter 16, together with the surviving aspects of trusts for sale. Many of the problems encountered

---

[7] Underhill thought that tenancies in common caused greater problems than successive interests: (1920) 36 LQR 107 at p 116. See also Grant [1987] CLP 159 at pp 166–167; Anderson, *Lawyers and the Making of English Land Law 1832–1940*, pp 286 et seq.

in the past are now covered by statutory provisions. Although relatively few cases will be differently decided as a result of TLATA, the legal structure is both more clearly laid out and more defensible.

It will also be seen that overreaching has come under attack. Overreaching is part of the 1925 approach which views beneficial interests as being in a fund rather than specific property. It has been argued that protecting the financial interests of the beneficiaries is not enough: their rights to their homes also demand recognition. Although overreaching is largely unaffected by TLATA, the doctrine of conversion has been abolished.

15

Joint tenancy and tenancy in common

Introduction

The previous chapter distinguished the two forms of co-ownership – joint tenancy and tenancy in common. These are the subject matter of this chapter. We will now concentrate on the nature and creation of joint tenancy and tenancy in common and on the severance of a joint tenancy so as to convert it into a tenancy in common.

The essence of joint tenancy is very much that each owns the whole, rather than any form of share in it. The principles discussed in this chapter are ancient in origin and, perhaps more than in any other area of law, are still very much as described by Coke[1] and Blackstone.[2] Coke describes the joint tenants as holding *per my et per tout*: holding nothing (that is, as a separate interest) and everything.[3] In the words of Dixon J, they 'are jointly seised for the whole estate they take in land and no one of them has a distinct or separate title'.[4]

When survivorship operates on the death of a joint tenant (so that the surviving joint tenants are entitled), it is inaccurate to talk about the share passing to the survivors. In the view of the law, each of the survivors already owns the whole: the crucial change is that there are now fewer of them. Yet one cannot take this too far.[5] Statute has provided for exceptions as regards financial provision for dependants of a deceased joint tenant, liability for inheritance tax and liability to creditors.[6] The courts recognised that each is entitled to a share of the income (usually rent). Each co-owner can dispose of his or her share, thereby creating a tenancy in common by severance. On a termination of the joint tenancy, each will again be entitled to a proportionate share.[7] Although each is treated as owning the whole, no individual joint tenant can enter into transactions binding the whole.[8] By

---

[1] Co Litt 181a et seq.

[2] *Commentaries on the Laws of England*, Vol ii, Chapter 12.

[3] Co Litt 186a. See *Daniel v Camplin* (1845) 7 Man&G 167 at p 172 (135 ER 73 at p 75) and *Murray, Ash & Kennedy v Hall* (1849) 7 CB 441 at p 455, n (a) (137 ER 175 at p 180).

[4] *Wright v Gibbons* (1949) 78 CLR 313 at p 329.

[5] Lord Nicholls has recently described it as an 'esoteric concept . . . remote from the realities of life': *Burton v Camden LBC* [2000] 2 AC 399 at p 404.

[6] Inheritance (Provision for Family and Dependants) Act 1975, s 9(1) (see p 41 above); Inheritance Tax Act 1984, s 171; Insolvency Act 1986, s 421A. Goulding [2016] Conv 90 is critical of the breadth of these provisions and asks whether they might infringe human rights principles.

[7] Whether part of the land on partition or part of the proceeds of sale.

[8] *Hammersmith and Fulham LBC v Monk* [1992] 1 AC 478 at pp 490–491; *Hounslow LBC v Pilling* [1993] 1 WLR 1242 (discussed below, p 339).

way of contrast, a tenancy in common, often described as undivided shares in the 1925 legislation,[9] involves the idea of having a share in the land. It is, of course, an undivided share at present (otherwise, there would be separate ownership of different parts of the land), but there is no notion of owning the whole.[10]

Survivorship is the most significant characteristic of the joint tenancy. The reason why we need to know whether a joint tenancy has been created or severed is nearly always that one of the parties wishes to rely on survivorship. Survivorship prevails over provisions in a will of a deceased joint tenant, even if the will refers expressly to the joint tenancy. A will operates only on death and by that time the interest has terminated.[11] In the past, companies could not be joint tenants because they do not die, but the Bodies Corporate (Joint Tenancy) Act 1899 reversed that rule. This is useful because trustees hold property as joint tenants; the law needs to allow for natural persons and companies to be trustees together.

The main difficulty that arises in the operation of survivorship concerns the order of death when a single accident kills two or more joint tenants. A common problem in the cases involves wartime bombs, but problems could just as well arise where death is caused in a road accident and the order of death is not clear. This problem of ascertaining the first to die arises in a variety of circumstances, not just joint tenancy. The response is a statutory presumption[12] that the oldest died first. Albeit an arbitrary solution, it at least has the merit of providing an answer. The presumption applies where 'it is uncertain which of them survived'. The courts have applied the section quite widely. It operates even if the parties may have died instantaneously[13] and, most likely, despite the fact that the courts could, if necessary, make a finding on the balance of probabilities that one of them died first.[14]

However, survivorship is not the only difference between joint tenancies and tenancies in common. One that can be significant is that obligations are joint in a joint tenancy, but may be separate in a tenancy in common. A prominent example of this is found in the law relating to leases. Joint tenants of a lease are each bound to fulfil the covenants: in particular, each is liable to the landlord for the entire rent.[15] Another difference concerns gifts in wills, where one of the donees predeceases the testator. A gift to two joint tenants operates as a gift to the survivor, whereas a gift to tenants in common fails as to the share of the predeceasing devisee.[16] This is analogous to survivorship, though it may present something of a trap for testators.

A final point to note is that other forms of co-ownership have at times been recognised. Until 1925, there could also be a tenancy by entireties and coparcenary, but it is not necessary to consider them today. Apart from these two obsolete concepts, other legal analyses can be used to achieve results similar to co-ownership.[17] One example is timesharing,

---

[9] The terminology puzzled some lawyers: (1944) 9 Conv NS 37.

[10] Though each tenant in common had a common law entitlement to occupy the whole: *Jacobs v Seward* (1872) LR 5 HL 464.

[11] Co Litt 185a, b; *Swift d Neale v Roberts* (1764) 3 Burr 1488 at p 1496 (97 ER 941 at p 946); *Gould v Kemp* (1834) 2 My&K 304 at pp 309–310 (39 ER 959 at p 962).

[12] Law of Property Act 1925 (hereafter LPA), s 184.

[13] *Hickman v Peacey* [1945] AC 304 (3:2 majority).

[14] *Re Pechar* [1969] NZLR 574, following *Re Bate* [1947] 2 All ER 418. The statutory presumption is excluded only if the order of death is a 'defined and warranted conclusion'.

[15] *Mikeover Ltd v Brady* [1989] 3 All ER 618, basing this on the unity of title (discussed below, p 393).

[16] *Robertson v Fraser* (1871) LR 6 Ch App 696. A gift to a class (e.g. my children) goes to the survivors.

[17] Grant [1987] CLP 159 at pp 159–164.

whereby different persons have the use of property (usually a holiday home) at different times of the year. We may not categorise timesharing as co-ownership (it is certainly not subject to the same legal regulation), but it fulfils a similar function.

1. Joint tenancy or tenancy in common?

The basic proposition is that, where the *four unities* are present, any disposition in favour of two or more co-owners is presumed to create a joint tenancy. This was the presumption at law, and it was also adopted by equity.[18] A tenancy in common will exist in three situations. The first, obviously, is where one of the four unities is absent, the second is where parties expressly provide for a tenancy in common or use language pointing towards it ('words of severance') and the third is where equity presumes a tenancy in common from special circumstances.

Is it then true to say that the parties' intentions as to type of co-ownership will be given effect to? The second situation sets out to give effect to an intention to have a tenancy in common and the third rests on a presumption that a tenancy in common is intended. Their combined effect is that the courts will never impose a joint tenancy where it is made clear by the parties or the circumstances that a tenancy in common is intended, but the danger remains that a joint tenancy will be presumed when the parties have not made their intentions clear. On the other hand, a tenancy in common will be imposed even in defiance of the parties' wishes if the four unities are not present.

A. The four unities

Every joint tenancy must have unity of possession, unity of interest, unity of title and unity of time. They form ancient requirements of the joint tenancy.[19] Their analytical basis lies in a working out of the concept of each owning the whole. Nevertheless, in the modern law, they appear very much as a hurdle to be jumped over. In the words of Challis,[20] the requirement is more justified by its 'captivating appearance of symmetry and exactness, than by reason of its practical utility'.

(i) *Unity of possession*

This requires that each co-owner be entitled to possession of the whole. It is what distinguishes co-ownership from separate ownership of the various parts of the land and is the only unity required for a tenancy in common. It is not necessary for each co-owner actually to occupy the whole: the law concentrates on their rights. Unity of possession continues despite a lease or licence by the co-owners,[21] or a lease or licence of a co-owner's share.[22] There is a large body of cases relating to rights to possession. These will be dealt with in Chapter 16.

---

[18] *Cray v Willis* (1729) 2 P Wms 529 (24 ER 847); *Campbell v Campbell* (1792) 4 Bro CC 15 (29 ER 755).
[19] Blackstone, *Commentaries on the Laws of England*, Vol ii, p 180.
[20] *Real Property* (3rd edn), p 367.
[21] *Doe d Aslin v Summersett* (1830) 1 B&Ad 135 (109 ER 738).
[22] See the cases on severance (based on shattering the unity of title) where there is a lease: p 313 below.

(ii) *Unity of interest*

Joint tenants must have interests of the same type and quantum. It is quite impossible for one to have, say, two-thirds and the other one-third. Consequently, on severance the shares as tenants in common will automatically be of the same size.[23] A rather different application of unity of interest is that the nature of the interests must be the same. A gift 'to A and B for life and concurrently to C in fee simple' makes A, B and C tenants in common. Although C has the right to enjoy the land with A and B, this is by virtue of a different estate: a fee simple as opposed to a life interest. However, a gift 'to A and B for life, remainder to B' creates a joint tenancy: the law separates out B's life interest from the fee simple remainder.[24] Unity of interest is also said to explain the requirement that joint tenants act together in order to bind the land,[25] although the same rules apply to tenants in common.[26]

(iii) *Unity of title*

This demands that the interests derive immediately from the same title (generally a deed or a will). This unity is significant when a joint tenant transfers his or her share. The purchaser's title is different from that of the other joint tenants. The title of the other joint tenants is the document creating the joint tenancy, whereas the purchaser's title is the conveyance of the share. A transfer by one joint tenant forms a standard example of severance. In the nature of things, unity of title will rarely cause problems on the initial creation of concurrent interests.

(iv) *Unity of time*

This final unity is the weakest. Its essence is that each of the joint interests must vest at the same time. There will be problems if there is a gift 'to the children of D at 21', as D's children will reach 21 and attain vested interests at different times.

However, the weakness of the requirement is that it does not apply to gifts by will or conveyances to uses. The modern equivalent of conveyances to uses is the trust.[27] As has been observed in Chapter 14, concurrent interests always take effect today under a trust. It is therefore arguable that the unity of time has no role to play in the modern law and can be discarded altogether.

It may be concluded that the unity of interest is the most likely unity to cause problems when creating joint tenancies. In particular, the requirement that the shares be of the same size restricts the utility of the joint tenancy. It can make sense to want shares of differing sizes, whilst at the same time desiring survivorship on death. For one thing, the parties may contemplate a possible severance and desire that their shares on severance should reflect the size of their contributions. More immediately practical may be taxation implications consequent upon the size of each person's interest.

---

[23] *Goodman v Gallant* [1986] Fam 106, subject to an express agreement for different shares on severance.

[24] *Wiscot's Case* (1599) 2 Co Rep 60b (76 ER 555). Contrast subsequent purchase of the reversion: p 314 below.

[25] Megarry and Wade, *The Law of Real Property* (8th edn), para 13-006. A joint tenant is free to lease or otherwise deal with his or her own share: Co Litt 186a, *Doe d Aslin v Summersett* (1830) 1 B&Ad 135 (109 ER 738).

[26] *Jacobs v Seward* (1872) LR 5 HL 464.

[27] Williams, *Real Property* (24th edn), p 199; *Kenworthy v Ward* (1853) 11 Hare 196 (68 ER 1245).

The single justification for keeping the beneficial joint tenancy (i.e. in addition to the tenancy in common) is that it provides the right of survivorship.[28] It is not obvious that we should require all four unities in their present form. Yet, it is easy to see why theory requires unity of interest: it really does reflect the concept that each owns the whole rather than a notional part. Further, survivorship would make little sense if the co-owners have different types of interest (lease and fee simple, for example). It may be concluded that it would be difficult to ditch the four unities completely, but that there should be scope for relaxation of some of the rules.

B. Words of severance

There has never been any doubt that an express desire to create a tenancy in common will be effective.[29] So long as there is unity of possession, there will be a tenancy in common: the other unities are not required.

The courts have been quick to interpret the wording of documents so as to show an intention to create a tenancy in common. As has been discussed, the nature of a joint tenancy is that each owns the whole. Any suggestion that the parties have shares in the land (as opposed to owning the entire land) is inconsistent with a joint tenancy. As Lord Hatherley LC said,[30] anything 'which in the slightest degree indicates an intention to divide the property must be held to abrogate the idea of a joint tenancy'. It might be added that such 'words of severance' are recognised by both common law and chancery. In practice, as a matter of convenience, many judges refer to joint tenants having shares. Although, strictly speaking, this is inappropriate, that terminology is adopted in this chapter.

Common examples of words of severance occur in references to parties holding 'equally'[31] or 'in equal shares'.[32] Others are 'amongst',[33] 'divided'[34] and 'participate'.[35] One may doubt whether, in using these terms, the parties always intended a tenancy in common, but it is clear that the courts have been anxious, whenever possible, to reverse the long-standing preference for joint tenancy.[36] However, it is a question of interpretation of the document as a whole.[37]

C. Equitable presumption of tenancy in common

For all its distaste of survivorship, equity normally follows the common law's preference for joint tenancy. However, there are three situations in which equity considers that survivorship

---

[28] Joint tenancies have effects other than survivorship, but these are relatively insignificant.

[29] Blackstone, *Commentaries on the Laws of England*, Vol ii, p 193.

[30] *Robertson v Fraser* (1871) LR 6 Ch App 696 at p 699.

[31] *Lewen v Cox* (1599) Cro Eliz 695 (78 ER 931); *Right d Compton v Compton* (1808) 9 East 267 (103 ER 575).

[32] *Brown v Oakshot* (1857) 24 Beav 254 (53 ER 355); *Re Davies* [1950] 1 All ER 120.

[33] *Campbell v Campbell* (1792) 4 Bro CC 15 (29 ER 755); *Richardson v Richardson* (1845) 14 Sim 526 (60 ER 462).

[34] *Peat v Chapman* (1750) 1 Ves Sen 542 (27 ER 1193).

[35] *Robertson v Fraser* (1871) LR 6 Ch App 696.

[36] See Joyce J in *Re Woolley* [1903] 2 Ch 206 at p 211.

[37] *Clerk v Clerk* (1694) 2 Vern 323 (23 ER 809): joint tenancy despite the use of 'equally to be divided'.

is so odd that there must be a tenancy in common.[38] The technique employed by equity was never a direct rejection of the common law joint tenancy, but an insistence that the legal joint tenants hold on trust for themselves as tenants in common in equity.[39] Since 1925, every co-ownership involves a trust, and this fits in well with the operation of the equitable presumptions: the trust in concurrent interests has become universal rather than exceptional. It should be remembered that equity is giving effect to the parties' presumed intentions: a joint tenancy will still exist in these three situations if it is really intended.[40]

(i) *Partners in a business*

Not surprisingly, survivorship is seen as inconsistent with a business relationship. This has been recognised for several centuries[41] and ensures that survivorship is avoided in many cases inappropriate for it. The presumption operates in a broad and reasonable fashion. The fact that the parties are merchants does not of itself bring it into play: the property must be acquired in their business as merchants.[42] Even when part of partnership assets, the courts accept proof that survivorship was intended. Thus, *Barton* v *Morris*[43] regarded partnership of a guest house as not being conclusive when it was also the home of the co-owning couple.

Modern attitudes are shown by *Malayan Credit Ltd* v *Jack Chia-MPH Ltd*.[44] The parties took a lease of business premises as joint tenants. They had agreed that each would occupy a specific part of the premises[45] and contribute towards the rent and other expenses in proportion to the area occupied. Strictly speaking, they were not partners, as they had separate businesses. The Privy Council was emphatic that the equitable presumptions should not be rigidly treated as closed categories. Holding premises for separate business purposes was adequate to ensure that they held on trust for themselves as tenants in common in equity.

(ii) *Mortgagees*

Similar to a business relationship is that of two persons who lend money on mortgage. Although the land may be mortgaged to them as joint tenants, equity presumes a tenancy in common.[46] Even though they may not strictly be partners, their relationship is seen as

---

[38] In addition, a tenancy in common will often be preferred if the court is called upon to determine the detailed terms to be inserted in a trust: *Mayn* v *Mayn* (1867) LR 5 Eq 150.

[39] *Morley* v *Bird* (1798) 3 Ves Jun 628 (30 ER 1192).

[40] *Winsper* v *Perrett* [2002] WTLR 927 (unequal contribution); it was said that detrimental reliance was necessary, but this seems dubious where the intention simply rebuts the presumption of a resulting trust.

[41] *Lake* v *Craddock* (1732) 3 P Wms 158 (24 ER 1011) (Varny MR, more fully reported 1 Eq Cas Abr 290 (21 ER 1052), sub nom *Lake* v *Gibson* (1729)).

[42] *Tan Chew Hoe Neo* v *Chee Swee Cheng* (1928) LR 56 Ind App 112.

[43] [1985] 1 WLR 1257 (in the severance context). In *Bathurst* v *Scarborow* [2005] 1 P&CR 58 the partners were merely friends, but they had expressed a desire for survivorship.

[44] [1986] AC 549.

[45] This did not preclude unity of possession: the law does not stop the co-owners from agreeing how they are to occupy.

[46] *Morley* v *Bird* (1798) 3 Ves Jun 628 (30 ER 1192).

being of a business nature: survivorship is out of place. What is remarkable is that a stand-ard mortgage term provides that the money is lent on a joint account,[47] with the purpose of ensuring that the loan can be safely repaid to the surviving lenders. *Re Jackson*[48] held that such a term, despite its reference to a joint account in law and in equity, did not oust the presumption of tenancy in common. It is plain that the courts have recognised the clause's purpose of facilitating repayment by the borrower: it does not affect the rights of the lenders as between themselves.

(iii) *Unequal contribution*

The third situation is where the co-owners have contributed to the purchase price in une-qual shares. The problem here is not so much to do with survivorship, but rather that joint tenancy requires identical sizes of shares. The shares are determined by a resulting trust analysis and this produces the unequal shares. In several cases, unequal contribution has been linked with a business or partnership relationship,[49] but this is not essential.

Outside the business setting, this area of law can be linked with the resulting or con-structive trust imposed when there is contribution to the purchase of property, especially the family home. However, it was seen in Chapter 11 that a transfer of the parties' home into joint names is presumed to operate as a joint tenancy in equity: the resulting trust analysis is not applied, despite the contributions being unequal.[50] The family home pro-vides a context where survivorship works well: a joint tenancy is nearly always chosen whenever the conveyance specifies the beneficial interests.

This leads to an issue in transfers of the family home into a single name. When there is a common intention constructive trust, are the beneficial interests held as joint tenants or tenants in common? If the courts award unequal shares, then a tenancy in common is the only feasible outcome. However, in many cases, the shares in the home are equal. The existence of a joint tenancy will be most important when one of the couple dies after they have separated. In principle, there should be a joint tenancy, as none of the reasons for a tenancy in common seems applicable. However, Baroness Hale has observed that the cases reveal no example of a joint tenancy.[51]

Three cases have involved the death of one of the co-owners, raising the question of survivorship. Two of these three cases presumed that there is no survivorship, meaning that there was a tenancy in common.[52] This may be justified by the recognition[53] that the

[47] Implied by LPA, s 111.
[48] (1887) 34 Ch D 732.
[49] *Lake v Gibson* (1729) 1 Eq Cas Abr 290 (21 ER 1052); *Malayan Credit Ltd v Jack Chia-MPH Ltd* [1986] AC 549.
[50] *Stack v Dowden* [2007] 2 AC 432, especially at [66]; p 190 above.
[51] *Stack v Dowden* [2007] 2 AC 432 at [66], though *Eves v Eves* [1975] 1 WLR 1338 at p 1345 (Brightman J) and *Supperstone v Hurst* [2006] 1 FLR 1245 at [11]–[12] lend some support to joint tenancy. A tenancy in common is supported by *Waller v Waller* [1967] 1 WLR 451 (although it is unclear that the shares were equal; Crane (1967) 31 Conv 141) and *Ulrich v Ulrich* [1968] 1 WLR 180 at p 186 (Lord Denning MR).
[52] *Smith v Baker* [1970] 1 WLR 1160; *Re Cummins* [1972] Ch 62. *Burgess v Rawnsley* [1975] Ch 429 is similar, but involved a resulting trust on the failure of a purpose. The exception is *Chandler v Clark* [2003] 1 P&CR 239, in which the Court of Appeal inclined towards a joint tenancy.
[53] Cf *Stack v Dowden* [2007] 2 AC 432, especially at [61]–[62].

shares may vary during the relationship, something that is inconsistent with a joint tenancy. That factor should be enough to justify a tenancy in common, even in cases where the shares turn out to be of equal size.

2. Severance of the joint tenancy[54]

One or all of the parties may decide that they do not wish survivorship to continue. In the great majority of the modern cases, this is because the relationship (most often marriage) between the parties has broken down. Alternatively, the joint tenancy may have been created by a settlor or testator and not reflect the donees' wishes. Although most joint tenants are happy for survivorship to operate, it has never been the policy of the law to stop the severance of the joint tenancy into a tenancy in common.[55] It should be stressed that severance has to be undertaken during the joint tenant's lifetime: trying to sever by will is too late.[56]

The difficulty is that there are specified ways in which a joint tenancy may be severed. A joint tenant with good legal advice has never had any difficulty in severing. Very often, however, the parties and their advisers have not put their minds to severance. Problems are especially likely to arise where a joint tenant dies unexpectedly, before the co-owners regard survivorship as significant.

At the outset, two statutory points must be considered. First, because a tenancy in common cannot exist at law since 1925, only the equitable joint tenancy can be severed.[57] In the past, lawyers would distinguish between severance in law and the more generous severance principles recognised in equity. That distinction is of little importance today. The second point is that s 36(2) of the Law of Property Act 1925 both recognises the old forms of severance[58] and adds a new method of severance: written notice.

A. The old forms of severance

The judgment of Page-Wood V-C in *Williams* v *Hensman*[59] is universally taken as the starting point:

> A joint tenancy may be severed in three ways: in the first place, an act of any one of the persons interested operating upon his own share may create a severance as to that share. The right of each joint tenant is a right by survivorship only in the event of no severance having taken place of the share which is claimed under the *ius accrescendi*.[60] Each one is at liberty to dispose of his own interest in such manner as to sever it from the joint fund – losing, of course, at the same time, his own right of survivorship. Secondly, a joint tenancy may be severed by mutual agreement. And,

---

[54] McClean (1979) 57 Can BR 1; Butt (1982) 9 Syd LR 568.

[55] Unless there is an agreement not to sever, recognised in *White* v *White* [2001] EWCA Civ 955 at [38].

[56] Although making mutual wills may amount to a lifetime agreement to sever: *Re Wilford's Estate* (1870) 11 Ch D 267. Indeed, such an agreement may be found even if the strict requirements for mutual wills are not satisfied: *Re Woolnough* [2002] WTLR 595, distinguished in *Carr* v *Isard* [2007] WTLR 409.

[57] LPA, s 36(2).

[58] Technically, the old forms of severance applicable to personalty. These are taken to be identical to those applicable to land (*Nielson-Jones* v *Fedden* [1975] Ch 222), but it is odd that the reference to personalty survives the abolition of conversion by the Trusts of Land and Appointment of Trustees Act 1996.

[59] (1861) 1 J&H 546 at pp 557–558 (70 ER 862 at p 867). See Luther (1995) 15 LS 219.

[60] Right of survivorship.

in the third place, there may be a severance by any course of dealing sufficient to intimate that the interests of all were mutually treated as constituting a tenancy in common. When the severance depends on an inference of this kind without any express act of severance, it will not suffice to rely on an intention, with respect to the particular share, declared only behind the backs of the other persons interested. You must find, in this class of cases, a course of dealing by which the shares of all the parties to the contest have been affected . . .

(i) *Acts operating on the joint tenant's share*

This form of severance is based upon common law severance: should any of the four unities cease to exist, then the joint tenancy must terminate. Conveyance of a share means that the title of the purchaser is different from that of the other joint tenants: this shatters the unity of title. This form of severance is straightforward in the case of outright transfers of a joint tenant's share.

It should be noted that there is no need for all the joint tenants to be involved or even to know about the conveyance. Furthermore, it can be used by a joint tenant who wishes to keep an interest as tenant in common. The conveyance could be to a trustee on trust for the former joint tenant. This was the standard method of unilaterally severing joint tenancies before the introduction of severance by written notice in 1925.[61] Indeed, it is today possible to convey property to oneself, and this would seem to effect severance should a written notice be impossible.[62] The lack of involvement of the other joint tenants, though well established, fits badly with much of the thinking and policy relating to severance.[63]

The effect of severance

The effect of severance where there are three or more joint tenants requires discussion. Suppose Andrew, Brenda and Carla are joint tenants. Carla transfers her interest to David. Beyond doubt, this severs Carla's share by shattering the unity of title. However, Andrew and Brenda continue as joint tenants as to their combined two-thirds share. Survivorship continues to operate as between the two of them, but not as regards David. If all three were to die, the result would be that David's estate would have one-third and the estate of the last to die of Andrew and Brenda would have two-thirds.

What happens if Carla transfers her interest to Andrew? A potential problem here is that Andrew has Carla's one-third share as well as his original share in the joint tenancy. Does this affect the unity of interest, as clearly Andrew is entitled to more than Brenda? The courts' answer is that the severance of Carla's share leaves Andrew and Brenda as joint tenants of a two-thirds share.[64] As regards this two-thirds share, there is unity of interest (and of title). It is irrelevant that, outside the joint tenancy, one of the parties has a further interest in the underlying property.

---

[61] *Cray* v *Willis* (1729) 2 P Wms 529 (24 ER 847).
[62] LPA, s 72 (assuming applicable to transfers of equitable interests); *Re Sammon* (1979) 94 DLR 3d 594; *Samuel* v *District Land Registrar* [1984] 2 NZLR 697. See Tooher (1998) 24 Mon ULR 422.
[63] In Australia, Deane J has made the interesting suggestion that this severance may not operate against a joint tenant who is kept in ignorance of it: *Corin* v *Patton* (1990) 92 ALR 1 at p 33. Crown (2001) 117 LQR 477 seeks to reduce the scope of severance by partial alienation (discussed below) for this reason.
[64] *Re Hewett* [1894] 1 Ch 362; *Wright* v *Gibbons* (1949) 78 CLR 313 at pp 324, 332.

Acts other than transfers

Equity recognises severance where there is an enforceable contract to convey the joint tenant's share.[65] Bankruptcy vests the bankrupt's property in the trustee in bankruptcy and this clearly effects a severance.[66] Rather more difficult is the question of whether transactions other than outright transfer will sever. Although *Williams* v *Hensman* refers to 'an act . . . operating upon his own share', the courts have been slow to extend it beyond transfers.[67]

There is authority that a mortgage effects a severance.[68] This must be correct in the classic form of mortgage, where the mortgagee obtains title to the property (subject to the equity of redemption). However, in Victoria, it has been strongly argued that charges do not sever because the chargee does not receive the property charged.[69] Although this has much to commend it in terms of severance principles,[70] the resultant distinction between mortgages and charges is difficult to justify in either practical terms or authority.[71] Although charges over a beneficial interest are likely to arise by chance[72] rather than be created deliberately, the absence of severance would pose a huge trap for the chargee if the chargor should be first joint tenant to die.

What is the effect of a lease of a joint tenant's interest? The problem is that the lessee takes an interest carved out of the joint tenant's interest: there is no claim to the jointly held interest itself. It seems fairly clear that the lessee is not affected by the death of the lessor, so to that extent there is severance.[73] Whether there is a full severance so that there can be no survivorship after the expiry of the lease is less clear. Although the early position was hostile to full severance,[74] the question has rarely been addressed by more modern English cases.

The Australian view is against full severance.[75] This may be justified because the lessee can claim shared entitlement with the other joint tenants for the duration of the lease; to that extent, there is a title (and an interest) which is different from that of the other joint tenants. The lessor joint tenant, however, still possesses the four unities with the others as regards the fee simple.[76]

---

[65] *Brown* v *Raindle* (1796) 3 Ves Jun 256 (30 ER 998); *Re Hewett* [1894] 1 Ch 362.

[66] *Re Rushton* [1972] Ch 197 at p 203. There is controversy as to when severance operates; if the bankruptcy order is after the bankrupt's death, there is no severance: *Re Palmer* [1994] Ch 316. However, the survivor may have to compensate the creditors: Insolvency Act 1986, s 421A.

[67] Co Litt 184b–185a; Nield [2001] Conv 462 at p 470.

[68] *York* v *Stone* (1709) 1 Salk 158 (91 ER 146); more recently, see *Cedar Holdings Ltd* v *Green* [1981] Ch 129; *First National Securities Ltd* v *Hegerty* [1985] QB 850 at pp 854, 862 and *First National Bank plc* v *Achampong* [2004] 1 FCR 18 at [54].

[69] *Lyons* v *Lyons* [1967] VR 169.

[70] Nield [2001] Conv 462.

[71] See the modern cases cited in n 68 above. None of this is affected by the 1925 reforms of mortgages of legal estates: we are dealing with a mortgage of the joint tenant's equitable interest.

[72] As a result either of a failed attempt to charge the legal estate or of a charging order.

[73] See, e.g., *Harbin* v *Barton* (1595) Moo KB 395 (72 ER 650) and *Clerk* v *Clerk* (1694) 2 Vern 323 (23 ER 809).

[74] Co Litt 185a.

[75] *Frieze* v *Unger* [1960] VR 230; *Wright* v *Gibbons* (1949) 78 CLR 313 at p 330 (Dixon J); da Costa (1962) 3 MULR 433 at p 454; contra McClean (1979) 57 Can BR 1 at pp 8–10.

[76] But there may be awkward questions as to who is entitled to income from the land and liable on the covenants after the death of the lessor joint tenant. See the full study of the area by Fox [2000] Conv 208, who supports temporary severance.

Shattering other unities?

It will be recalled that the shattering of any of the four unities terminates a joint tenancy. So far, we have concentrated upon the unity of title, by far the most significant for severance. Unity of time cannot be shattered: once the interests have vested at the same time, that cannot be undone.[77] The unity of possession may be shattered by vesting parts of the land in the co-owners: a process called partition. This creates separate ownership of the parts of the land. It cannot create a tenancy in common as that also requires unity of possession. The final unity is that of interest. If one of the joint tenants acquires an interest that is different from that of the others, then there will be severance if the two interests merge,[78] although in most cases unity of title will also be shattered. A more modern application would arise from a common intention after purchase that the shares in a family home should be unequal.[79]

(ii) *Mutual agreement*

Occasionally, judges object to severance because none of the unities has been shattered,[80] but the better view is that this is relevant only at common law; equity permits severance on its own terms.[81]

One such equitable method is mutual agreement to sever. It should be noted that there must be mutual agreement: it does not suffice if, say, two out of three joint tenants agree to sever.[82] Nor can there be severance just as between the two who wish to sever: with whom would the third person be a joint tenant?

It has been held that agreements to sever do not require writing. In *Burgess* v *Rawnsley*,[83] the two joint tenants orally agreed that one should buy out the other. One of them pulled out of the agreement, whereupon the other died. If the agreement had been in writing, then it would have fallen within Page-Wood V-C's first head as an equitable transfer. However, the lack of writing rendered it unenforceable and thereby precluded any equitable transfer. This did not prevent the Court of Appeal from saying that the parties had agreed not only to buy and sell the share, but also that there should be severance. This agreement to sever did not require writing. As Browne LJ observed, the third head, course of dealing, will of its nature often be oral. Further, one may accept that an agreement to sever is not a contract for the 'sale or other disposition of an interest in land'[84] and that it is quite irrelevant that it is spelt out of such a contract. Perhaps less clearly, it does not seem that an interest in land is 'created'[85]; instead, the nature of the interest is changed.

---

[77] Blackstone, *Commentaries on the Laws of England*, Vol ii, p 185.
[78] *Wiscot's Case* (1599) 2 Co Rep 60b (76 ER 555) (purchase of reversion by one life tenant); cf p 307 above. For merger, see Megarry and Wade, *Law of Real Property* (8th edn), para 13-048.
[79] Pawlowski and Brown (2013) 27 Trust Law International 59, 172, arguing that formalities are not required when shares are varied on severance.
[80] *Nielson-Jones* v *Fedden* [1975] Ch 222 at p 228; see also *Corin* v *Patton* (1990) 92 ALR 1 at p 6 (Mason CJ and McHugh J).
[81] *Burgess* v *Rawnsley* [1975] Ch 429 at p 438; *Corin* v *Patton* (1990) 92 ALR 1 at p 24 (Deane J).
[82] *Wright* v *Gibbons* (1949) 78 CLR 313.
[83] [1975] Ch 429, followed in *Hunter* v *Babbage* [1994] 2 FLR 806.
[84] Law of Property (Miscellaneous Provisions) Act 1989, s 2.
[85] LPA, s 53(1)(a).

Burgess must be taken as representing the law at present,[86] but it may not be impregnable. The interpretation of the legislation is not beyond question, and *Burgess* seems to violate the policy that transactions relating to land should be in writing or evidenced in writing. It is significant that Australian analyses seem to favour the need for writing.[87]

The major question in practice is as to whether the parties have agreed to sever, and in particular whether an agreement should be implied from their conduct and discussions. This shades into the next method of severance.

(iii) *Course of dealing*

This head of severance has given rise to the greatest controversies, both as to what is required and its application to relationship breakdown. The first point to consider is its relationship to mutual agreement. In *Nielson-Jones* v *Fedden*,[88] Walton J viewed course of dealing as being based upon an implied agreement to sever. Within a year, this had been rejected by the Court of Appeal in *Burgess* v *Rawnsley*.[89] Perhaps the most useful comments are made by Sir John Pennycuick,[90] who stresses that a common intention, rather than a binding agreement, is what is required. This has been accepted in England,[91] notwithstanding that earlier cases provide considerable support for Walton J.[92]

The differences between common intention and binding agreement may not be great, but a far more radical view was taken by Lord Denning MR in *Burgess*.[93] His analysis was that 'It is sufficient if there is a course of dealing in which one party makes clear to the other that he desires that their shares should no longer be held jointly but be held in common.' This introduces unilateral declaration as a method of severance, provided that it is communicated to the other party.

There was some authority for unilateral declaration: it had been accepted by Havers J in *Hawkesley* v *May*[94] and Plowman J in *Re Draper's Conveyance*.[95] However, these cases had been comprehensively demolished by Walton J in *Nielson-Jones* v *Fedden*. Havers J had said that unilateral declarations 'obviously' fall within Page-Wood V-C's first head. This is indefensible nonsense, as the first head is limited to actual transfers and other dispositions. Plowman J did no more than blindly follow Havers J. Furthermore, the old method of severance by a transfer to a trustee (overtaken by the statutory written notice) would have been senseless if a unilateral declaration sufficed. It seems impossible to refute Walton J's conclusion that unilateral declarations are not permitted. Sir John Pennycuick

---

[86] Its correctness was taken for granted in *Greenfield* v *Greenfield* (1979) 38 P&CR 570.

[87] *Lyons* v *Lyons* [1967] VR 169 at p 171; Butt (1976) 50 ALJ 246.

[88] [1975] Ch 222 at p 231.

[89] [1975] Ch 429.

[90] Ibid, at p 447.

[91] *Greenfield* v *Greenfield* (1979) 38 P&CR 570; *Carr* v *Isard* [2007] WTLR 409. Australian views are discussed in *Saleeba* v *Wilke* [2007] QSC 298 at [31]–[37] (Conway [2009] Conv 67).

[92] McClean (1979) 57 Can BR 1 at p 16. The question was left open by Deane J in *Corin* v *Patton* (1990) 92 ALR 1 at p 25.

[93] [1975] Ch 429 at p 439. Commentators have been critical: Hayton [1976] CLJ 20; Butt (1976) 50 ALJ 246.

[94] [1956] 1 QB 304.

[95] [1969] 1 Ch 486.

seems to reject Lord Denning's analysis, for he requires that the intention be a common one and expressly excludes oral declarations.

Subsequent cases have provided limited clarification. Whilst it is true that *Harris* v *Goddard*[96] approved *Re Draper's Conveyance*, this was clearly on the basis of statutory written notice (discussed later in this chapter). *Gore & Snell* v *Carpenter*[97] is implicitly inconsistent with Lord Denning's analysis. Overseas, judges have lined up to offer criticism of Lord Denning and support for Walton J.[98] It seems fairly safe to assume that they are right.

Our next question is as to when a course of dealing will show a common intention to sever. For a start, neither an agreement to sell the property nor, indeed, the actual sale of it will always suffice. These are perfectly consistent with an intention that the joint tenancy should continue in the proceeds of sale and assets purchased with the proceeds.[99] Such agreements were considered by the Court of Appeal in *Davis* v *Smith*.[100] It was thought that an agreement to divide the proceeds would suffice, although simply agreeing to sell in the knowledge that equal division was inevitable might be a 'step too far'. What happens if there is sale of part of the land and division of the proceeds amongst the joint tenants? This does not necessarily sever as regards the remaining land, although the extent of sales may well point to an intention of a tenancy in common.[101] The test has been said to be satisfied where 'over the years the parties have dealt with their interests in the property on the footing that they are interests in common'.[102] It may be added that it does not suffice that each in fact intends to sever: the courts look for a shared intention or understanding.[103]

Most modern cases have arisen on the breakdown of the relationship (often marriage) between the parties. It would be exceptional for survivorship to be appropriate in these circumstances: rarely would it be desired by the parties. *Nielson-Jones* v *Fedden* involved a marriage breakdown, with the parties negotiating their financial position at the time the husband died. They had agreed that the jointly owned house should be sold and a smaller house purchased for the husband out of the proceeds. Walton J held that the parties had not agreed what was to happen to the beneficial interests, thus precluding severance under Page-Wood V-C's first head. As to the second and third heads, the problem was that the parties had not reached agreement, even though both looked forward to a termination of the joint tenancy. Walton J held that there was no agreement to sever: 'when parties are negotiating to reach an agreement, and never do reach any final agreement, it is quite impossible to say that they have reached any agreement at all.'[104]

[96] [1983] 1 WLR 1203; Dillon LJ is most explicit.
[97] (1990) 60 P&CR 456 (Judge Blackett-Ord).
[98] See especially *Corin* v *Patton* (1990) 92 ALR 1; *Re Sorensen and Sorensen* (1977) 90 DLR 3d 26; Butt (1982) 9 Syd LR 568 at pp 586–587.
[99] *Hayes' Estate* [1920] 1 IR 207; *Re Allingham* [1932] VLR 469.
[100] [2012] 1 FLR 1177; the case was decided on the basis of the actual division of proceeds of an associated insurance policy and its effect on the future sale proceeds. See also *Saleeba* v *Wilke* [2007] QSC 298; Butt (2008) 82 ALJ 75.
[101] *Crooke* v *De Vandes* (1805) 11 Ves 330 (32 ER 1115); *Re Denny* [1947] LJR 1029.
[102] *Gore & Snell* v *Carpenter* (1990) 60 P&CR 456 at p 462.
[103] *Carr* v *Isard* [2007] WTLR 409 (making wills inconsistent with survivorship).
[104] [1975] Ch 222 at p 230.

It is difficult to see how this approach can survive the criticisms made by the Court of Appeal in *Burgess*. If we use the common intention test, it seems plain that there was a common intention that they should be tenants in common. Even on the agreement analysis, why cannot it be said that the parties had agreed to sever, regardless of whether they reached final agreement on sharing out the proceeds? It is not as if refusal to agree to a severance could be used as a bargaining ploy: either could sever unilaterally by a written notice.

The later decision in *Gore & Snell* v *Carpenter*[105] comes as a surprise. On facts very similar to those in *Nielson-Jones* v *Fedden*, Judge Blackett-Ord concluded that, because negotiations were still continuing when the husband committed suicide, there was no common intention to sever. It is true that Sir John Pennycuick had said in *Burgess* that an offer and counter-offer would not by themselves suffice, but he had earlier stressed that a common intention can be inferred even though negotiations break down: all depends upon the particular facts. Commonwealth courts[106] have been prepared to find a common intention in this type of case, and this seems far more consistent with *Burgess*.

B. Section 36(2): notice in writing

Section 36(2) provides that 'where a legal estate . . . is vested in joint tenants beneficially, and any tenant desires to sever the joint tenancy in equity, he shall give to the other joint tenants a notice in writing of such desire . . .'. This is an extremely useful provision: it provides a simple way for a joint tenant to sever a joint tenancy unilaterally without going through the charade of a conveyance to trustees. It is advantageous in that the other joint tenants are made aware of the severance and the requirement of writing tends to reduce subsequent disputes. Presumably, when one of three or more joint tenants gives notice, it severs only that person's interest (but not the joint tenancy as between the others) – the same effect as a transfer of his or her interest.

It does, however, have its limits. In particular, the joint tenants must hold the legal estate beneficially. Although there is no authority, this would appear to require that the same persons hold the legal estate and beneficial interests. In many cases, one person will hold the legal title on trust for those contributing to the purchase. Should they be joint tenants in equity, a strict reading of the section would not allow severance by written notice. The section would more clearly be inapplicable if a trust is created whereby different persons are trustees and beneficiaries. One can see good reasons for notice to be given to both trustees and beneficiaries, but little reason for them to have to be the same persons.

It should also be noted that the section applies only to land: witness the reference to 'legal estate'. If the land is sold, the proceeds may be held on a joint tenancy. It is then too late to use written notice to sever. It seems to be this gap that persuaded Lord Denning MR in *Burgess* to attempt to recognise unilateral declarations as effective in equity. Apart from

---

[105] (1990) 60 P&CR 456; *McDowell* v *Hirschfield Lipson & Rumsey* [1992] 2 FLR 126 (Judge Stockdale) is similar.
[106] *Re Walters and Walters* (1977) 79 DLR 3d 122, upheld (1978) 84 DLR 3d 416n; *Robichaud* v *Watson* (1983) 147 DLR 3d 626; *Abela* v *Public Trustee* [1983] 1 NSWLR 308; *Hansen Estate* v *Hansen* (2012) 347 DLR 4th 491.

relying on *Williams* v *Hensman*, Lord Denning MR also inferred from the wording of s 36(2)[107] that written notices had always sufficed for severance of interests in personalty. This forced reading of the section has little or no support in the earlier cases: it would have been out of character for the common law or equity to have developed rules based on *written* notice. Sir John Pennycuick expressed doubts as to Lord Denning's argument, whilst Browne LJ blew hot and cold.

A quite different question is as to what suffices as a written notice. If a joint tenant writes that he or she wishes to sever a joint tenancy, then that is conclusive. In many of the cases, however, it has been argued that a desire to sever should be read into documents that, on their face, are not directed towards severance. *Re Draper's Conveyance*[108] held that a court summons requesting sale and division of the proceeds constituted a good notice; it was a process that would inevitably lead to severance. This was criticised by Walton J in *Nielson-Jones* v *Fedden* on the basis that the summons and hence the notice were revocable. That criticism was rejected by the Court of Appeal in *Burgess*: it is difficult to comprehend what an irrevocable notice might be. *Re Draper's Conveyance* was later confirmed by the Court of Appeal in *Harris* v *Goddard*.[109]

Rather surprisingly, subsequent cases have been slow to apply the section. In *Harris* itself,[110] severance was denied because the claim sought a variety of remedies. In part, the problem was that the claim looked to a future severance on the making of the court order, whilst the notice must be a notice of immediate severance. In addition, there could be a remedy that did not involve severance. These points do make sense, but their effect is markedly to narrow the effect of *Re Draper's Conveyance*. One suspects that severance by the bringing of a claim may be virtually random, according to the words used by lawyers who have not addressed the severance question. To be safe, a specific notice of severance is essential.

Gore & Snell v *Carpenter*[111] deals with a slightly different point. On marriage breakdown, the spouses entered into negotiations concerning the future of two houses they owned as joint tenants. The negotiations included a proposed severance. The husband chose not to serve a notice of severance because he did not wish to be seen to be acting in a hostile manner. Following the husband's death, Judge Blackett-Ord held that there was no notice of severance: the proposal put forward in negotiations was not intended as an independent notice of severance. This highlights the problem faced by the courts. Whilst it is clear from *Re Draper's Conveyance* that a notice does not need to state that it is a s 36(2) notice, how far will the courts go in discovering notices from correspondence? Does every letter need to be read in case an inference of a desire to sever can be extracted from it? If so, there will frequently be considerable uncertainty as to whether severance has taken place. Most of the cases have dealt with court applications, a context in which the cases do at least give some guidance as to what will suffice.

---

[107] It reads 'give . . . a notice in writing . . . or do such other acts or things as would, in the case of personal estate, have been effectual to sever the tenancy in equity . . .'. The argument is that the word 'other' equates written notice and the pre-1925 modes of severance, thereby assuming that both were effective before 1925. For criticism, see Hayton [1976] CLJ 20.

[108] [1969] 1 Ch 486.

[109] [1983] 1 WLR 1203.

[110] Reluctantly followed in *Hunter* v *Babbage* [1994] 2 FLR 806. Henderson J took a more generous view to find severance in *Quigley* v *Masterson* [2012] 1 All ER 1224 (application to Court of Protection).

[111] (1990) 60 P&CR 456.

At what time is a notice effective? In *Kinch v Bullard*,[112] W posted a notice to H. Before H received it, he suffered a heart attack. W (still living in the matrimonial home) destroyed the notice on its arrival, as severance was no longer likely to benefit her; H then died. Applying provisions in the Law of Property Act 1925, it was held that the severance was good when the letter was delivered so that H's estate could rely upon it.[113] It was irrelevant that W then no longer desired severance, that she destroyed the notice and that H was never aware of it. Exceptions would have existed if W had told H of her change of mind before delivery, or if it were W who had been relying on the notice. In the latter case, W (W's estate in practice) could not assert severance by a notice which she had hidden from H. The case provides a clear and relatively simple set of rules.

C. Public policy

In exceptional circumstances, severance may result from the application of public policy. The criteria applied here are quite independent of the ideas already discussed. A clear example is the murder of one joint tenant by the other: any suggestion that the murderer should benefit by survivorship is repulsive. This public policy, based on ideas of forfeiture, is applied similarly if the murderer claims under the victim's will or in any similar fashion[114]: it is not specific to joint tenancies. Accordingly, we will not deal with the details of when forfeiture operates: suffice to say that it extends to manslaughter where there is an intention to harm or alarm the victim.[115]

How exactly does this public policy operate in a joint tenancy? Commonwealth cases[116] have held that there was no severance of the joint tenancy, but impose a constructive trust so that the murderer holds the victim's share on trust for the victim's estate.[117] The question arose for the first time in England in *Re K*.[118] Vinelott J noted that in England, there is no question today of severing the legal title, so that he could more simply hold that there was severance of the equitable joint tenancy.

The choice between a simple severance and constructive trust was not material on the facts of *Re K*, but it would become vitally important if there were three joint tenants. A severance analysis would give the victim's estate one-third, with the murderer and third co-owner (T) as joint tenants of the remaining two-thirds. A constructive trust analysis would concentrate upon ensuring that the murderer obtains no benefit, but it would not stop T from benefiting from the victim's death.[119] This, indeed, is the approach taken in

---

[112] [1999] 1 WLR 423.

[113] Section 196(3): notices valid if 'left at the last-known place of abode or business'. Letters sent by special delivery or recorded delivery are presumed to arrive at the normal time of delivery: s 196(4).

[114] The leading case is *Cleaver v Mutual Reserve Fund Life Association* [1892] 1 QB 147; see Youdan (1973) 89 LQR 235.

[115] *Re Hall's Estate* [1914] P 1; *Gray v Barr* [1971] 2 QB 554; *Re K* [1985] Ch 85 (upheld [1986] Ch 180).

[116] See especially *Schobelt v Barber* (1966) 60 DLR 2d 519; *Re Pechar* [1969] NZLR 574; *Rasmanis v Jurewitsch* (1970) 70 SR NSW 407. See also *Cawley v Lillis* [2013] WTLR 559 (Ireland).

[117] One American approach is to restrict the murderer to a half-share for life, in recognition of the fact that the victim has lost a possible full ownership by survivorship: Scott, *Trusts* (4th edn, 1989), para 493.2 (constructive trusts are excluded from the 5th edn). This has not gained approval in Commonwealth jurisdictions: see the cases in the previous note.

[118] [1985] Ch 85 at p 100 (not considered on appeal: [1986] Ch 180).

[119] As happens where the victim has been murdered by a person other than a joint tenant.

Australia.[120] The Law Commission has expressed a preference for the simple severance analysis.[121]

Finally, it should be noted that the court has a discretion under the Forfeiture Act 1982 to amend this operation of public policy, at least where there is no conviction for murder. This was the principal issue in *Re K*,[122] in which a wife had been convicted of manslaughter of her husband who had been assaulting her. It was held that, on the facts, it would be unfair to deprive her of any of the rights she had acquired on the husband's death.

D. Conclusions

It is inappropriate to assess the severance rules individually: they have to be looked at as a whole. There is no justification for the law to place unnecessary hurdles in the way of a joint tenant who wishes to sever, as severance is always possible with good legal advice. Once the relationship between the joint tenants has broken down, then survivorship frequently seems so strange that anything which might lead to severance should be seized upon. Many will therefore sympathise with Lord Denning's approach that a unilateral declaration should sever, whether or not it is supported by the authorities.[123] Nevertheless, the written notice is the statutory response to the need for a simple and effective mode of severance. It may be argued that the courts should not develop other means of severance that introduce greater uncertainty because they do not require writing. The problem, of course, is that analyses that encourage uncertainty and litigation may be as harmful as the operation of survivorship itself.

The present restrictions on when written notice can be given certainly need to be relaxed: they seem both arbitrary and unnecessary. More difficult is the question as to how explicit a notice of severance must be. It seems clear that the notice need not explicitly say 'I hereby sever', but any substantial expansion beyond *Re Draper's Conveyance* would reintroduce uncertainty and largely nullify the benefits of the writing requirement.

3. Do we need both the joint tenancy and the tenancy in common?

It is plain that problems arise in determining whether a joint tenancy or tenancy in common has been created and also whether there has been severance. Criticism can also be levied that the preference for joint tenancy introduces survivorship into cases in which it is not intended and that this is compounded by the operation of survivorship after the relationship between the joint tenants has broken down. We need to consider whether there are benefits which justify retaining both joint tenancy and tenancy in common.

Two propositions are pretty straightforward. First, the tenancy in common has to be retained. No legal system could justify insisting upon survivorship and unity of interest in every case of co-ownership. The second proposition is that joint tenancy is an extremely

---

[120] *Rasmanis v Jurewitsch* (1970) 70 SR NSW 407. The court gave T a tenancy in common as to one-third and T and the murderer a joint tenancy as to two-thirds. Arguably, this is too generous to T.

[121] Law Com No 295, paras 2.27, 3.21–3.24.

[122] [1985] Ch 85; on appeal [1986] Ch 180.

[123] Tooher (1998) 24 Mon ULR 422 at pp 446–449.

valuable method for holding the legal estate. Indeed, it is crucial to the 1925 scheme for clarifying title and rendering the sale of land relatively easy and inexpensive. However, it is far from clear that we should continue to recognise the equitable joint tenancy. Strong arguments have been raised that it is both unnecessary and harmful.[124]

The equitable joint tenancy is strictly unnecessary. There is no reason why a share under a tenancy in common should not be left by will to the survivor. Furthermore, it has to be conceded that there are cases in which survivorship is harmful because the parties have failed to sever after their relationship has broken up. Nor should we forget the costs of legal complexity. Complexity is apt to cause expense in litigation and the inevitable making of mistakes from time to time, quite apart from making books longer and the study of law more difficult. Indeed, if one could be confident that co-owners would always make wills reflecting their intentions (and change them, as necessary), then the case for abolishing the equitable joint tenancy would be very strong.

On the other hand, purchasers of family homes nearly always opt for a joint tenancy when equitable interests are specified.[125] This may owe a lot to the suggestions of their lawyers, but it also shows that survivorship really is intended in the great majority of cases.[126] Odd as the preference for the joint tenancy might seem in many settings, it is very often realistic as regards the family home. In settings other than the family home, the equitable presumptions in favour of a tenancy in common normally ensure that a joint tenancy exists only where survivorship is intended. However, there will be gaps: purchase by friends who contribute equally does not look like an appropriate context for survivorship. Another example may be where a couple have children from previous relationships: they may well not intend that their new partners should benefit at the expense of their own children. These sorts of situations encourage the idea that the starting presumption should favour a tenancy in common, with joint tenancy operating only where it is shown to be intended.

Survivorship problems generally occur when one of the joint tenants has died unexpectedly, often at an early age. If we were to recognise only the tenancy in common, it is most unlikely that all co-owners would have made wills before dying. The intestacy rules might operate satisfactorily for most surviving spouses (and those in civil partnerships), but others may find to their horror that members of the deceased's family are claiming a share in the home.[127]

This problem for the tenancy in common has to be offset against unwanted survivorship when the relationship between joint tenants breaks down. Such unwanted survivorship seems impossible to eradicate,[128] even if amendment of the severance rules would reduce it. Yet, equivalent problems exist for the tenancy in common. A will leaving the share to the survivor (which would be common if there were no survivorship) may itself operate in an unwanted fashion if not amended following relationship breakdown.[129] This seems to

---

[124] Thompson [1987] Conv 29, 275; note the reply by Prichard [1987] Conv 273.

[125] Todd and Jones, *Matrimonial Property*, p 78; estimated at 90% of married co-owners in 2005 (*Administration of Estates – Review of the Statutory Legacy*, pp 31–32 (DCA CP 11/05)). For exceptions, see Pawlowski and Brown (2013) 27 *Trust Law International* 3 at p 9.

[126] Survivorship is better understood than the equality of shares central to a joint tenancy: Douglas, Pearce and Woodward [2008] Conv 365.

[127] This problem would largely disappear if the proposals in Law Com No 331 were implemented.

[128] Absent the unlikely possibility of a court discretion to sever retrospectively.

[129] Provisions for a spouse terminate on divorce: Wills Act 1837, s 18A.

be just as likely as failing to sever a joint tenancy. Indeed, the courts' willingness to accept severance from negotiations may mean that such failure to amend a will could be a more serious problem!

One may conclude that the dangers of not making a will or failing to amend it pose as many problems for the tenancy in common as survivorship does for the joint tenancy. Although one might think twice about introducing the joint tenancy if it did not already exist, the fact that it is used by so many owners of family homes does militate against radical reform.

Further reading

Butt, P (1982) 9 Syd LR 568: Severance of joint tenancies in matrimonial property.
Luther, P (1995) 15 LS 219: *Williams* v *Hensman* and the uses of history.
McClean, A J (1979) 57 Can BR 1: Severance of joint tenancies.
Thompson, M P [1987] Conv 29: Beneficial joint tenancies – a case for abolition? (see also the reply by Prichard, AM [1987] Conv 273 and the response at p 275).

16

Trusts of land

Introduction

The Trusts of Land and Appointment of Trustees Act 1996[1] (hereafter TLATA) ensures that nearly all concurrent and successive interests take effect under the trust of land regime which it establishes. In this chapter, we shall first consider when there is a trust of land and then turn to its operation. The most important topics will be beneficiaries' rights to occupy, the management of the land (with particular emphasis upon sale) and the protection of purchasers by overreaching. Although TLATA does not distinguish between concurrent and successive interests, there may be some practical differences in the way the provisions operate. In this chapter, the main emphasis will be upon concurrent interests: successive interests form the focus of Chapter 17.

The use of a trust for concurrent interests is not new. A trust for sale had been imposed since 1925, with the aim of simplifying purchase of the land.[2] One important point to grasp is that trusts for sale, whether created before or after TLATA, are trusts of land and regulated by that Act.[3] Although all future trusts will be 'simple' trusts of land (save for the rare cases where a trust for sale is expressly created), there are many millions of pre-TLATA trusts for sale. Those imposed by statute became simple trusts of land,[4] but a large proportion will have been created expressly, and these remain trusts for sale.[5] In any event, the consequences of there being a trust for sale are today minimal (they will be considered later in this chapter), as the regulatory regime is the same for all trusts of land.

When considering the modern trust of land, do the pre-1996 authorities remain relevant? It will be seen that few areas are radically changed by TLATA. It follows that, especially where a discretion is conferred on the court, the earlier cases may provide a guide as to the most likely outcome. The question was considered by Neuberger J in *Mortgage Corpn* v *Shaire*.[6] He expressed the view that 'they have to be treated with caution, in the light of the change in the law, and in many cases they are unlikely to be of

---

[1] Hopkins [1996] Conv 411. It gives effect to Law Com No 181; Pottage (1989) 52 MLR 683; RJ Smith [1990] Conv 12.

[2] The pre-1996 problems (primarily for tenancies in common) are described on pp 300–302.

[3] Section 1(2).

[4] TLATA, s 5(1), Sched 2.

[5] Pettit (1997) 113 LQR 207 (rejecting some unguarded comments to the contrary).

[6] [2001] Ch 743 at p 761 (see p 351 below); criticised by Pascoe [2000] Conv 315.

great, let alone decisive, assistance'. However, that dictum was in a context in which the legislation really did point to a new approach, and it may underestimate the utility of the earlier cases in other areas.[7] If we look further back at pre-1925 authority, it must be remembered that concurrent interests frequently formed a source of income rather than providing a home to be lived in. These old cases certainly cannot be presumed to apply without modification to modern circumstances.

1. When is there a trust of land?

A. Successive interests

TLATA contains no provisions specifically relating to successive interests. Instead, trusts of land are defined by s 1(1)(a) to mean 'any trust of property which consists of or includes land'.[8] Since 1925, successive interests always involve equitable interests, as only the fee simple absolute in possession can be a legal freehold estate.[9] It follows that successive interests take effect under a trust and are within TLATA.

Prior to TLATA, settlements (unless by express trust for sale) would take effect under the Settled Land Act 1925.[10] No new settlements can be created under that Act, but existing settlements within the Act continue to be governed by it rather than TLATA.[11]

B. Joint tenancy

Most modern conveyances to co-owners expressly create a trust, the beneficial interests being a joint tenancy or tenancy in common according to the parties' expressed wishes. What happens if there is no express trust? First, we will consider joint tenancies.

Under s 36 of the Law of Property Act 1925 (hereafter LPA), a trust is imposed whenever joint tenants are the beneficial holders of the legal estate. This means that a conveyance to A and B as joint tenants ensures that they hold on trust for themselves as joint tenants in equity. Why is a trust of land imposed? The normal reason for a statutory trust is to aid the sale of land, but it might be objected that a trust is not required either for A and B together to sell their land or for the survivor to sell.

There are two answers. First, the trust of land is regulated by statute. One very important example is that, under TLATA, s 14, the courts have a wide controlling discretion over the functions of the trustees, especially important as regards sale. It is clearly necessary that this regulation should apply to all forms of co-ownership. The second answer is that the joint tenancy may subsequently be severed, creating a tenancy in common. Insofar as a trust is essential at that stage for the protection of purchasers, it is easiest to have a trust from the beginning.

---

[7] A more guarded view of the effect of TLATA is found in *Notting Hill Housing Trust v Brackley* [2002] HLR 212 at [24].
[8] Section 1(2)(a) provides that any form of trust, whether express, implied, resulting or constructive, is included.
[9] See p 55 above.
[10] See p 365 below.
[11] TLATA, ss 1(3), 2.

C. Tenancy in common

LPA, s 1(6) enacts that a tenancy in common cannot be a legal estate: this ensures that tenancies in common can take effect only behind a trust. Section 34(1) states that an undivided share in land cannot be created save as provided by that section.[12] This is singularly inept drafting. It apparently prohibits express trusts in favour of tenants in common, as the rest of the section makes no mention of them. Common sense dictates that it has no such effect.

When we consider s 34(2), things get no better. Where 'land is expressed to be conveyed to any persons in undivided shares', the legal title is vested in them (if adults) as joint tenants on trust for themselves as tenants in common in equity. If there are more than four tenants in common, the legal title is vested in the first four. This last point has no effect on the beneficial interests but ensures that a reasonably small number of persons control dealings with the land.

Section 34(2) readily applies in the straightforward case of a conveyance to tenants in common. However, it was quickly apparent that it is full of gaps.[13] There are several examples where there would have been a tenancy in common before 1925 but which fall outside the wording of the section.[14] If s 34(1) is to be taken seriously, the result is that no tenancy in common is allowed. We have seen that if two people contribute to the purchase of land, but the legal title is vested in one of them, then that person will hold the legal title on trust for both of them. Where the contributions are unequal, they will often be tenants in common. Here, it is impossible to say that there is a conveyance to them in undivided shares: the tenancy in common arises from a resulting or (in a family setting) constructive trust.

The first case[15] to grapple with the problem was *Bull* v *Bull*,[16] in which Denning LJ relied upon s 36(4) of the Settled Land Act 1925. The result was that the owner of the legal estate held it on trust for the contributors as equitable tenants in common. The problem is that s 36(4) says little more than LPA, s 34(1): how it avoids the gaps in the legislation remains a puzzle.[17] Whatever the lack of statutory justification for Lord Denning's analysis, it is the only sensible result. Subsequent cases have assumed that the result is correct[18] and it would seem hopeless to challenge it today.

What happens if a tenancy in common is created by a will? Simplifying somewhat, s 34(3) states that a devise to tenants in common operates as a devise to the testator's personal representatives on trust for the persons interested (the tenants in common). There is no reason why the personal representatives should not retire as trustees, appointing the

---

[12] Or, for old settlements, under the Settled Land Act 1925.

[13] (1944) 9 Conv NS 37.

[14] Apart from the cases discussed below, there are problems if one of the tenants in common is an infant and if the tenancy in common is created by declaration of trust.

[15] Earlier, *Re Buchanan-Wollaston's Conveyance* [1939] Ch 738 placed reliance on LPA, s 36, but did the court appreciate that there was a tenancy in common? See also Ormrod LJ in *Williams & Glyn's Bank Ltd* v *Boland* [1979] Ch 312 at p 333 and Lord Denning MR in *Jackson* v *Jackson* [1971] 1 WLR 1539 at p 1542.

[16] [1955] 1 QB 234.

[17] See Rudden (1963) 27 Conv 51, noting that earlier decisions had assumed the same result.

[18] See especially *Williams & Glyn's Bank Ltd* v *Boland* [1981] AC 487 and *City of London BS* v *Flegg* [1988] AC 54 at pp 77–78.

co-owners in their place. It appears that the section also operates if there is a devise to trustees on trust for tenants in common, the legal estate initially being held by the personal representatives.[19]

It may be concluded that every beneficial joint tenancy or tenancy in common exists behind a trust, despite the inadequacies of the legislation. It is unfortunate that TLATA,[20] which amends the sections so as to create a simple trust rather than a trust for sale, did not address the problems discussed above.

D. Bare trusts and special cases

Trusts of land are not limited to successive and concurrent interests. Bare trusts (as where Rachel holds on trust for Sally) were previously unregulated, but they now fall within the trust of land regime.[21] It follows that a sale by two trustees may overreach the beneficial interest. There is no need for any explicit provision: they are obviously trusts of land.

The Settled Land Act 1925 extended overreaching to a number of special cases. TLATA continues this where there is a conveyance to a minor[22] or land is subjected to family charges (non-contractual payments like annuities). In each case, a trust of land is imposed,[23] ensuring that the land can be sold and the relevant rights overreached. The trust may have very unfortunate consequences where the conveyance takes the form of a lease to a minor: because the landlord is also a trustee, the normal powers of the landlord cannot be exercised when they would prejudice the tenant.[24]

E. Other cases?

The situations dealt with above are the obvious and intended examples of a trust of land. However, the question must be asked whether the definition of trusts of land is such as to drag other situations within the net. Before TLATA, the question whether the particular equitable interest takes effect under a trust was not normally relevant. The danger is that the courts may recognise a trust where it is quite inappropriate for the trusts of land regime to apply. One example would be some constructive trusts giving effect to contractual or estoppel licences,[25] although it is difficult to assess the extent of any problem.[26]

---

[19] *Re House* [1929] 2 Ch 166; s 34(3A) includes trustees within the 'persons interested'.
[20] Schedule 2, paras 3 (s 34), 4 (s 36).
[21] As recommended by Law Com No 188, paras 2.17, 3.10, 4.27; other proposals relating to overreaching are not implemented.
[22] A legal estate cannot be held by a minor: LPA, s 1(6).
[23] TLATA, Sched 1, paras 1–3.
[24] *Hammersmith & Fulham LBC* v *Alexander-David* [2010] Ch 272; Turano-Taylor *Modern Studies in Property Law*, Vol 7 (ed Hopkins), Chapter 6.
[25] *Ashburn Anstalt* v *Arnold* [1989] Ch 1 at pp 22–26; RJ Smith [1990] Conv 12 at pp 14–15. Also estate contracts: Hopkins (1998) 61 MLR 486 at p 490.
[26] It would be appropriate for TLATA to apply if the constructive trust gives effect to a right to reside for life, tantamount to a life interest: *Pritchard Englefield* v *Steinberg* [2004] EWHC 1908 (Ch).

2. Occupation

A. Background

Three issues are frequently mixed up together in the cases: sale of the property, occupation of it and rent or other compensation. In this section we shall consider occupation and financial considerations; sale will be dealt with in the following section (management of the land).

Starting with the position before 1925, unity of possession involved the proposition that each co-owner is entitled to occupy the entire property. It could not be objected that one person was occupying and taking profits from the entire land. This applied as much to agricultural land as to houses.[27] In reality, there was little difficulty, for any co-owner could insist on partition or sale.[28] The threat of this would often produce agreement between them as to the future of the land. The many cases on occupation do not question this basic right to occupy; rather, they deal with conduct amounting to eviction of one co-owner and with claims for improvements.

Since 1925, there has been no automatic right to sale or partition.[29] This means that rights to future occupation have become more significant. Today, rights to occupy are regulated by TLATA and it is unlikely that the earlier cases retain any significance. It has been argued[30] that equitable co-owners had full rights of occupation before TLATA and that there is nothing in the Act to exclude their continuing application. However, there is little authority[31] to support the first proposition, and the true position appears to be that the courts recognised a right to occupy where this was the purpose of the purchase or the trust.[32] In any event, although one may concede that the Act nowhere excludes the previous law, it would be amazing if a court were to stultify the modern statutory code relating to occupation (especially the statutory powers given to trustees to regulate possession).[33]

B. Trusts of Land and Appointment of Trustees Act 1996

Section 12 confers a right to occupy, and s 13 provides for its regulation where, as will be very common in concurrent interests, two or more persons have such a right.[34] These provisions need to be considered in some detail. As stated above, this right to occupy appears

---

[27] *Jacobs v Seward* (1872) LR 5 HL 464 (three fields); *M'Mahon v Burchell* (1846) 2 Ph 127 (41 ER 889) (house).

[28] See Lindley LJ in *Leigh v Dickeson* (1884) 15 QBD 60 at p 69: '. . . unfit for persons who cannot agree amongst themselves; but the evils attaching to it can be dealt with only in a suit for partition or sale . . .'.

[29] Cocks [1984] Conv 198.

[30] Barnsley [1998] CLJ 123, relying in part upon the unity of possession. However, it may well be that possession, as applied to equitable interests, refers to enjoyment of the interest rather than physical possession of the land (just as we can describe an equitable interest as vested in possession regardless of physical occupation).

[31] But see *Bull v Bull* [1955] 1 QB 234.

[32] *Williams & Glyn's Bank Ltd v Boland* [1981] AC 487; *City of London BS v Flegg* [1988] AC 54 (especially Lord Oliver).

[33] Supported by Lightman J in *IRC v Eversden* [2002] STC 1109 at [24] (upheld on other grounds (2003) 75 TC 340). However, in *French v Barcham* [2009] 1 WLR 1124 Blackburne J appears to accept that there can be a right to occupy (in a bankruptcy setting) outside the statute: compare [18] and [35].

[34] Ross Martyn [1997] Conv 254 at pp 258–261; Pascoe [2006] Conv 54.

to be exclusive of any other right of beneficial occupation. It would follow that the holder of the legal estate could not claim to occupy personally, unless entitled by s 12 as a beneficiary.[35] It should be noted that occupation is not limited to the obvious case of the family home. It may apply to any form of property and therefore to occupation of a farm or a factory.

When is there a right to occupy?

Only beneficiaries with interests in possession can have a right to occupy. This excludes, for example, remainder interests in successive interest trusts. It may require the beneficiaries to be ascertained, excluding members of a class of discretionary beneficiaries.[36] Section 12 confers the right provided that one of two conditions is satisfied. The first condition is that the purposes of the trust include occupation, and the second is that the land is held by the trustees to be available for occupation.

An important question is whether these conditions have to be satisfied only at the commencement of occupation (so that we are referring to a right to go into occupation) or whether they must continue to be satisfied for the beneficiary to be entitled to remain in occupation.[37] There is much to be said in favour of the first, 'snapshot', interpretation, as it would mean that beneficiaries are safe in their homes once occupation has commenced. However, two factors point towards the second view.[38] As will be seen later,[39] the court may have no jurisdiction to limit occupation rights; this renders it less likely that a permanent right to occupy is conferred by the legislation. The second factor is that s 12(1) appears to contemplate that the purpose must be continuing[40]; the fact that it might have existed earlier does not suffice.

The first condition for the s 12 right (purposes) substantially mirrors the previous law. It will apply in the great majority of concurrent interest trusts,[41] excepting the few where land is purchased as an investment or for other non-occupation purposes.[42] It will also apply to successive interests where, for example, a widow or widower has a life interest in the family home and is intended to continue to reside there. If s 12 requires the condition to continue to be satisfied, difficult problems may be predicted. Suppose a widowed mother and daughter purchase a house for their joint occupation. To everyone's surprise, the mother remarries and goes to live with her new husband. Can it[43] be argued that the purpose was for joint occupation and that this terminates when one of the parties no longer

---

[35] Contrary to a pre-TLATA suggestion of Lord Denning MR in *Bedson v Bedson* [1965] 2 QB 666 at p 678. See also *Wight v CIR* [1982] 2 EGLR 236.

[36] In the context of inheritance tax, see *Pearson v IRC* [1981] AC 753. Interests in possession are also significant for ss 9(1) (delegation of powers) and 11(1) (consultation of beneficiaries).

[37] They need not be satisfied when the trust first arises: Barnsley [1998] CLJ 123 at pp 132–133.

[38] Supported by Hopkins [1996] Conv 411 at p 420 and Megarry and Wade, *The Law of Real Property* (8th edn), para 12-028.

[39] See p 340 below.

[40] '[E]ntitled . . . to occupy the land at any time if *at that time* . . .' (emphasis added). Further, s 13(1) contemplates continuing control by trustees, as witnessed by the limits in s 13(7).

[41] It appears safe to assume that the purpose need not be articulated in the disposition creating the trust.

[42] E.g. *Re Buchanan-Wollaston's Conveyance* [1939] Ch 738, in which land was purchased in order to prevent its being built upon and thereby to enhance the amenity of other land.

[43] Unsurprisingly, s 12 does not apply merely because the settlement gives power to the trustees to allow occupation: *Smith v Herbert* [2016] WTLR 897.

wishes to share the house? This analysis was usually accepted in the pre-1996 law regarding sale.[44] Given that disputes are most likely to arise when facts change and, especially, relationships break down, the operation of s 12 may well be anything but straightforward.

The second condition ('held by the trustees so as to be so available') appears intended to allow the trustees to treat land as available for occupation or to purchase land for occupation.[45] That trustees can do this seems acceptable, whether or not other beneficiaries believe that it is the best use of the trust's assets. What is more difficult is that the section purports to confer a right to occupy. Unless the snapshot view of the conditions is adopted, to describe this as a right seems meaningless insofar as it depends upon a continuing intention upon the part of the trustees.

It might be argued that the second condition has a much more radical effect: it applies whenever land is held by the trustees and is free for occupation by beneficiaries. For example, trustees may hold a farm leased to a tenant. The land is not available for occupation by beneficiaries. Should the tenant give up the lease, the land becomes available for occupation by beneficiaries, and they have a right to occupy. This interpretation would give a much wider right to occupy and would render the purpose condition superfluous. It seems most unlikely.

In all cases, s 12(2) excludes the right to occupy if the land is either 'unavailable or unsuitable for occupation by him'. Unavailable presumably means that it is in the occupation of another person such as a tenant (but not another beneficiary).[46] Unsuitability is more interesting. It was said in *Chan v Leung*[47] to 'involve a consideration not only of the general nature and physical characteristics of the particular property but also a consideration of the personal characteristics, circumstances and requirements of the particular beneficiary'. That a house was large and expensive to maintain was not sufficient to deny a claim, although it was significant that the occupation was intended to last only a short period.

Do we take a snapshot or continuing view of the exclusion, a similar question to that for the conditions? Suppose that a widow has a life interest in the family home. After several decades, her age is such that she is unable to look after the house: the result is that both she and the house are at risk. It may be clear that it is no longer suitable for occupation by her, but can the trustees use this to insist that she moves to more suitable accommodation to be offered by the trust? It seems to have been assumed in *Chan v Leung*[48] that the land must continue to be suitable.

Trustee control

Section 12 confers an entitlement upon the beneficiary but subject to s 13 discretions of trustees. Two principal elements may be identified. First, the trustees have power

---

[44] *Jones v Challenger* [1961] 1 QB 176; *Rawlings v Rawlings* [1964] p 398 (both cases involving married couples); see p 342 below. In the exceptional case of *Chan v Leung* [2003] 1 FLR 23, the purpose was found to be for occupation by one of a couple, despite their splitting up.

[45] Law Com No 181, para 13.3 emphasises future purchase of land.

[46] *Smith v Herbert* [2016] WTLR 897. It is not sufficient that a tenancy could be terminated by the trustees.

[47] [2003] 1 FLR 23 at [101].

[48] [2003] 1 FLR 23 at [100]–[102]. See also Hopkins [1996] Conv 411 at p 420 and Megarry and Wade, *Law of Real Property* (8th edn), para 12-028; contra Barnsley [1998] CLJ 123 at p 135 and Pascoe [2006] Conv 54 at p 62.

to determine the exercise of entitlements where two or more beneficiaries have a right to occupy.[49] However, beneficiaries' entitlements cannot be excluded or restricted unreasonably, and the trustees cannot deny occupation to all entitled beneficiaries.[50] *Rodway* v *Landy*[51] holds it possible for occupation of different areas to be split between the beneficiaries, even though this means that, in part, the rights of every beneficiary are restricted. Section 13 confers a useful power, but few disputes will be resolved by the trustees. As we have seen, virtually every co-ownership involves the beneficiaries being also the trustees. The section offers no help in such cases: there are no independent trustees who can exercise the statutory discretion. However, the court can (as in *Rodway*) make an order under its general s 14 discretion (discussed later in this chapter).

The second element is that the trustees can impose reasonable conditions upon the beneficiary in occupation.[52] Whether or not there is more than one entitled beneficiary, the occupier may thereby be required to pay outgoings and expenses and assume obligations in relation to the land. This could obviously cover keeping the property in good repair but also the cost of putting the property in an appropriate condition for possession.[53] Equally important is the power to require compensation payments to be made to beneficiaries whose rights of occupation have been limited by the trustees.[54] This, of course, enables justice to be done as between the beneficiaries. It may be observed that different types of trust may attract different responses. In a trust in favour of siblings, it will often be appropriate for one occupying sibling to compensate the others. However, if one of a couple leaves the other with a child in the home, then the response may be quite different.[55]

In all cases, the trustees must take into account the views of the settlor, the purposes for which the land is held and the circumstances and wishes of entitled beneficiaries.[56] An important protection for beneficiaries is that, without court approval, the trustees cannot exercise these powers so as to force out those already in occupation (whether or not by virtue of s 12).[57]

Finally, it should be noted that any questions relating to the functions of the trustees regarding occupation may be resolved by the courts under s 14. The normal criteria[58] for consideration by the court will be applied, save that the circumstances and wishes of those entitled to occupy under s 12 (rather than those with interests in possession) are relevant.[59]

---

[49] TLATA, s 13(1).

[50] Ibid, s 13(2), (1). For the use of s 13 in sale applications, see n 142 in this chapter.

[51] [2001] Ch 703 (medical practice: surgery split between two doctors).

[52] TLATA, s 13(3)–(5). The effect of non-compliance is not stipulated.

[53] *Rodway* v *Landy* [2001] Ch 703 at [41] (cost of dividing the property into two units).

[54] TLATA, s 13(6) (alternatively, other payments or benefits under the trust may have to be forgone). It is to be hoped that this jurisdiction cannot be side-stepped by arguing that the other beneficiary is not entitled to occupy because the land is not available, so that the trustees have not limited occupation: Ross Martyn [1997] Conv 254 at p 261.

[55] *Stack* v *Dowden* [2007] 2 AC 432 at [94].

[56] TLATA, s 13(4).

[57] Ibid, s 13(7). Quaere the result if the occupier cannot afford to make compensation payments: Ross Martyn [1997] Conv 254 at p 261.

[58] See p 341 below.

[59] TLATA, s 15(2).

C. Civil partnerships, spouses, cohabitants and associated persons

First, we should note that the Civil Partnership Act 2004 introduced the concept of civil partnership. This applies only as between persons of the same sex; the partnership has to be registered before any special status is given. From that point on, civil partnership is treated in the same way as marriage. It follows that references (including those in other chapters) to married couples and spouses should today be taken as applying also to those in civil partnerships. More recent legislation allows marriage between same-sex couples.[60]

The Family Law Act 1996[61] contains a number of provisions conferring rights and discretions on the court in cases involving spouses and those in civil partnerships, cohabitants or other 'associated persons'.[62] This area shades into family law, and only a brief summary of the main provisions will be given. It may be noted that the discretions extend to cases where only one party has an interest in the land: the focus is on occupation of family homes rather than concurrent ownership. Property which has not been, or intended to be, used as the family home is not covered.[63]

Taking spouses and those in civil partnerships first, the party with no property interest (or merely an equitable interest) is given a statutory right to retain occupation or, with the leave of the court, to go into occupation.[64] No directly equivalent right is given outside these relationships. However, for all categories the court has power to vary rights to occupation where both parties possess a right to occupy, whether based on property rights (including TLATA, s 12) or the special right to occupy described above.[65] In essence, when the relationship breaks down, the court can order that either party should occupy the land and that the other should leave, or otherwise regulate occupation.[66] Relevant criteria include the housing needs of the parties and any children, their financial resources, the effect of any order on them and their conduct. Particularly important is the likelihood of significant harm to a party or the children, whether an order is made or not. The court may make an order for a specific or an indefinite period.

In the case of cohabitants[67] where only one has a right to occupy, the court again has discretion to allow the other party to enter and restrict the respondent's right to occupy.[68] The court is to consider, amongst other things, the nature and length of the relationship and the level of commitment involved.[69] One important element is that the order cannot last

---

[60] Marriage (Same Sex Couples) Act 2013.

[61] Murphy (1996) 59 MLR 845.

[62] Defined by s 62(3) to include those living in the same household (excluding those such as lodgers but including same-sex couples), relatives, parents and children, parties to family proceedings; it was extended by Domestic Violence, Crime and Victims Act 2004 (hereafter DVCVA), s 4 to include any 'intimate personal relationship . . . of significant duration'.

[63] Family Law Act 1996, ss 30(7), 33(1)(b), 35(1)(c), 36(1)(c).

[64] Ibid, s 30.

[65] Ibid, s 33. For former spouses with no right to occupy (rights normally end on divorce), slightly different provision is made by s 35.

[66] Eviction is treated as draconian and only to be used as a last resort: *Re Y* [2000] 2 FCR 470.

[67] Defined by Family Law Act 1996, s 62(1): 'living together as husband and wife or as if they were civil partners'.

[68] Family Law Act 1996, s 36.

[69] Ibid. The old provision (s 41) making relevant their failure to accept the commitment involved in marriage has been repealed by DVCVA, s 2.

more than six months and can be extended once only. This short-term protection is in part a legacy of its origin in domestic violence, an origin which may be difficult to shake off.[70]

In all cases, the court may impose obligations on the parties as to repairs and discharge of outgoings on the property or to compensate for loss of occupation.[71] This is similar to trustees' powers in trusts of land, although the court is required to take financial needs and resources into account.

It is difficult to assess the relationship of these provisions with those relating to trusts of land. It is unfortunate that two statutes enacted at the same time fail to clarify this. Of course, the trusts of land discretions are conferred on the trustees rather than the court, but the court may be asked to rule on occupation disputes under TLATA, s 14. It is to be noted that the criteria to be taken into account (both as regards occupation and compensation) differ under the two statutes, and this opens the spectre of different results according to which route is taken. Perhaps the best guide comes from a similar issue relating to applications for the sale of property, when the matrimonial jurisdiction is also available. It was held by the Court of Appeal in *Miller Smith* v *Miller Smith*[72] that applications should normally be made under the matrimonial legislation. This is a possible pointer to the use of the Family Law Act 1996 in preference to the trust of land powers. On the other hand, it may be that orders under the Family Law Act 1996 are likely to be for shorter periods, so that longer-term disputes are properly dealt with under the trust of land provisions.

D Rent and other financial adjustments[73]

This may be divided into three areas: payment of rent (or other compensation) as a condition of future occupation; payment of rent (or other compensation) for past occupation; and compensation for improvements made to the land. The first and second areas raise the question whether the beneficiary in occupation is bound to pay others who are not. Payment for future occupation is today covered by TLATA, s 13(6) and has already been discussed. The trustees and, under s 14, the court have powers to order payments, at least in favour of beneficiaries entitled to occupy under s 12.

(i) *Payment for past occupation*

If the trustees or the court have decided under TLATA, s 13(6) what compensation, if any, should be paid, then this would appear to be conclusive.[74] However, it will frequently be the case that the trustees have taken no decision. One of the beneficiaries may simply have gone into occupation or, more commonly, the trustees and beneficiaries will be the same persons and be unable to reach decisions. There are two ways in which this question might be approached. The first is that the court may possess a discretion under TLATA, s 14 to

---

[70] Though *Chalmers* v *Johns* [1999] 1 FLR 392 requires 'exceptional circumstances' to exclude a property owner, verbal abuse of a psychiatrically vulnerable partner sufficed in *Dolan* v *Corby* [2012] 2 FLR 1031.

[71] Family Law Act 1996, s 40.

[72] [2010] 1 FLR 1402 at [18]; see p 346 below.

[73] Cooke [1995] Conv 391; Conway in *Modern Studies in Property Law*, Vol 3 (ed Cooke), Chapter 6; Bright [2009] Conv 378 (assessing the modern impact of TLATA).

[74] Subject to any application under s 14 to challenge the decision of the trustees.

order the occupier to make payments. The second is that, in the absence of such an order, the older cases (on equitable accounting) may indicate when compensation is payable.

The argument in favour of the statutory discretion is that the trustees could, under s 13, have made a decision that the occupier pay compensation. Section 14 confers a power for the court to make 'such order . . . relating to the exercise by the trustees of any of their functions . . . as the court thinks fit'. Although this is principally directed towards the future management of the land, the courts may review trustees' past decisions (or failure to make decisions) and decide what, if any, compensation should be paid.

Until recently, the courts applied the older equitable accounting rules. The most typical context was one of the parties having sole occupation of their former family home following breakdown of a relationship. However, *Stack* v *Dowden*[75] established that the s 14 jurisdiction should be employed. Although *Stack* itself seemed to relate to future occupation, it was soon applied to past occupation by the Court of Appeal in *Murphy* v *Gooch*.[76] However, the House of Lords indicated that the results under the old law and under TLATA would often be the same. The real difference is that the court must consider additional criteria in s 15. These are considered later in this chapter, but the intention behind the purchase and the interests of children are most likely to be significant.

One point to note is that s 13 operates only when the excluded party has a right to occupy under s 12. This will apply to virtually all disputes between those who purchase family homes, but not necessarily to other examples of co-ownership.[77] In particular, *French* v *Barcham*[78] demonstrates that s 13 does not apply when one of the parties is bankrupt – the trustee in bankruptcy does not have a statutory right to occupy. An argument that s 13(6) provides the only basis for payments was rejected. The outcome is that the non-bankrupt occupier will normally have to pay rent.

The older principles

We should start with the position before the 1925 legislation. Because every co-owner was entitled to occupation, there was generally no question of one of them paying rent to the others, even if enjoying exclusive occupation of the entire property. This was equally true as regards houses[79] and as regards agricultural property which one co-owner had profitably farmed.[80]

There were, however, several situations in which payment was required. An agreement between the parties might provide for payment.[81] Further, a statute of 1705[82] provided that a co-owner was liable 'for receiving more than comes to his just share or proportion', but this applied only to direct receipts. It had no operation where a co-owner

---

[75] [2007] 2 AC 432 at [93]–[94], [150].
[76] [2007] 2 FLR 934.
[77] As in *Rahnema* v *Rahbari* [2008] 2 P&CR D11 at [28] (property intended to be rented).
[78] [2009] 1 WLR 1124, applying *Re Pavlou* [1993] 1 WLR 1046 and *Re Byford* [2004] 1 P&CR 459. This disproves the analysis that equitable accounting is dead after *Stack*: Cooke [2007] Fam Law 1024.
[79] *M'Mahon* v *Burchell* (1846) 2 Ph 127 (41 ER 889).
[80] *Jacobs* v *Seward* (1872) LR 5 HL 464.
[81] Whether as rent (*Leigh* v *Dickeson* (1884) 15 QBD 60) or as part of a management agreement (not readily implied: *Kennedy* v *De Trafford* [1897] AC 180).
[82] 4 Anne c 16, s 27. There was no common law duty to account: *Wheeler* v *Horne* (1740) Willes 208 (125 ER 1135).

occupied the land for his or her own benefit as a farmer and thereby made profits.[83] The profits are seen as resulting as much from the farmer's work and money as from the land itself. Although the 1705 provision was repealed by the 1925 legislation, it is thought that there is a similar duty to account today. The receipts will normally accrue to the holder of the legal title, who is a trustee with a duty to ensure that the beneficiaries get their fair shares.[84]

Ouster of the claimant provides another and flexible route to payment. Although a co-owner is perfectly entitled to occupy the entire land, there is no right to exclude the others. If they are excluded, then compensation must be paid.[85] One of the best-known cases is *Jacobs* v *Seward*,[86] in which one party entered upon the property (three fields, close to London), put a lock on the gate, cut the grass and took it away. No objection could be taken to this activity. So far as the lock on the gate was concerned, this was intended to keep the public out, and there was no proof that the claimant was prevented from obtaining access. Whilst cutting hay was held to be consistent with the claimant's rights of occupation, removal of significant quantities of soil would be seen as partial destruction of the subject matter and a form of ouster.[87]

Application to the family home

Most of the modern English cases involve the family home, when the relationship has broken down and one party remains living there. A particular feature of these cases is that the occupier almost invariably pays the mortgage. In these circumstances, the courts usually allow the mortgage interest payments and the value of occupation to cancel each other out,[88] at least where there are no children.[89] Subject to that, the tenor of the cases suggests that there is a duty to account from the date of the breakdown of the relationship.[90] It should be remembered that the courts may sometimes find it preferable to vary the parties' shares (by finding a common intention to that end) rather than operate complex accounting rules; this is especially significant where there is a substantial delay before the property is sold.[91]

The ouster principle was originally used to justify payment. One such case is *Dennis* v *McDonald*,[92] in which a woman left the home because of her partner's violence. This was treated by both Purchas J and the Court of Appeal as a clear case of ouster. However, a broader approach was developed by Millett J in *Re Pavlou*.[93] He held that equity would

---

[83] *Henderson* v *Eason* (1851) 17 QB 701 (117 ER 1451). See also *M'Mahon* v *Burchell* (1846) 2 Ph 127 (41 ER 889).

[84] *Re Landi* [1939] Ch 828.

[85] *Pascoe* v *Swan* (1859) 27 Beav 508 (54 ER 201).

[86] (1872) LR 5 HL 464. It might be unsafe to assume the same conclusion would be reached under TLATA.

[87] *Wilkinson* v *Haygarth* (1847) 12 QB 837 (116 ER 1085).

[88] *Leake* v *Bruzzi* [1974] 1 WLR 1528; *Suttill* v *Graham* [1977] 1 WLR 819: see p 210 above. This is not generally applied on bankruptcy.

[89] *Jones* v *Kernott* [2012] 1 AC 776 at [50].

[90] *Suttill* v *Graham* [1977] 1 WLR 819; *Young* v *Lauretani* [2007] 2 FLR 1211 (decided after *Stack*).

[91] *Jones* v *Kernott* [2012] 1 AC 776; see p 212 above.

[92] [1982] Fam 63; Martin [1982] Conv 305. Applied in *Biviano* v *Natoli* (1998) 43 NSWLR 695 to reach the unsurprising result that exclusion by court order does not constitute ouster; see Conway [2000] Conv 49.

[93] [1993] 1 WLR 1046; applied in *Re Byford* [2004] 1 P&CR 159. There is no reason to limit this to the family home.

order payment whenever necessary in order to do equity between the parties. Once a relationship has broken down, then the person who leaves is to be treated as excluded from the home regardless of ouster: it is not reasonable to expect them to occupy. However, if one party leaves voluntarily and the occupier would be happy to have that person back, then it would not normally be fair to order payment. In any event, no payment will be due if the non-occupier is happy for the other to have sole occupation, especially where their children are living there.[94]

Where ss 12 and 13 of TLATA apply, the *Re Pavlou* approach has been modified by adding the TLATA criteria. The idea of doing equity fits the general TLATA discretion well, although we have seen that the s 15 criteria may provide additional factors.

(ii) *Payments for improvements*

Quite different problems arise where one co-owner has undertaken expenditure in improving the land. There appears to be no TLATA jurisdiction to take account of improvements. Indeed, improvements may well occur when only the improver has a right to occupy.

The basic position is that the improver (usually the occupier) cannot recoup the expenditure: it is a voluntary act that benefits another person and, as such, falls outside restitutionary principles.[95] On the other hand, recovery will be allowed if the improvement has been authorised by the other co-owners[96] or if the expenditure satisfies a legal duty on them.[97]

The improver benefits from a more generous approach where there is sale (or partition, in the older cases). This unlocks the value of the improvement and the courts have long permitted it to be brought into account.[98] It does not matter whether or not it is the improver who seeks sale[99] and there is no distinction between joint tenancies and tenancies in common.[100]

As one would expect, the amount that can be claimed is limited to the amount by which the value of the property has been increased, taken as at the date of the action, and cannot exceed the amount expended.[101] One aspect of a claim for improvements is that it opens the improver up to a claim for rent for the improver's use of the property. However, in most cases today, this will be overtaken by the TLATA jurisdiction.

Turning to the modern law, improvement claims are relatively uncommon in the family home context. Where the improvement is made during the continuance of the relationship, the courts may be inclined to say that it is not intended to give rise to accounting on future

---

[94] *Wright* v *Johnson* [2002] 2 P&CR 210, especially at [32]–[33].
[95] *Leigh* v *Dickeson* (1884) 15 QBD 60.
[96] *Squire* v *Rogers* (1979) 27 ALR 330.
[97] *Leigh* v *Dickeson* (1884) 15 QBD 60 (Cotton LJ at p 66). Payment of mortgage interest may justify a claim on the basis that it relieves the property from a charge for its payment: *Re Gorman* [1990] 1 WLR 616 at p 626; *Re Byford* [2004] 1 P&CR 159 at [23].
[98] *Swan* v *Swan* (1819) 8 Price 518 (146 ER 1281); *Leigh* v *Dickeson* (1884) 15 QBD 60; *Re Jones* [1893] 2 Ch 461; *Re Cook's Mortgage* [1896] 1 Ch 923.
[99] *Brickwood* v *Young* (1905) 2 CLR 387 at p 395. Mortgagees' sales also trigger recoupment: *Re Cook's Mortgage* [1896] 1 Ch 923.
[100] The equality inherent in joint tenancies is not an overriding consideration: *Re Pavlou* [1993] 1 WLR 1046.
[101] *Re Jones* [1893] 2 Ch 461.

sale.[102] Otherwise, improvement will affect the payment on sale.[103] Capital repayments of a mortgage loan are treated as analogous to improvements.[104]

3. Management of the land

The core proposition is that the trustees manage the land. TLATA, s 6 confers unlimited powers upon them, which means, for example, that they can sell, lease or mortgage as they think fit. They also have power to buy land, under TLATA, s 6(3).[105] Having unlimited powers does not mean that the trustees can do as they please. Section 6 itself stresses that the trustees must have regard to the rights of beneficiaries, comply with legal requirements and exercise care.[106] Under equitable principles, trustees cannot act capriciously[107]: they must exercise their powers in a proper manner and, of course, act in the best interests of the beneficiaries. *Preedy* v *Dunne*[108] recently held that the statutory powers are administrative rather than dispositive. More surprisingly, it was also held that estoppel claims do not fall within s 6, which is limited to 'formally and substantively complete transactions'.[109]

Since TLATA, it has been possible for the settlor to exclude any of the powers save, curiously, the power to postpone sale.[110] This little-heralded freedom to exclude powers[111] runs counter to the pro-sale and pro-overreaching developments of the nineteenth and early twentieth centuries. In the past, the major emphasis of property reform was to ensure that land could always be sold. Today, tying land up for generations is no longer the objective of more than a handful of settlors: few seem likely to avail themselves of their new freedom. In any event, exclusion of the power of sale might not be conclusive in all circumstances.[112]

When considering management, however, it is not simply a matter of looking at the powers of the trustees. Two other elements are of crucial importance. The first is that the beneficiaries are given sometimes important roles in the decision-making process. The second is that the court, under TLATA, s 14, has power to make orders in respect of the exercise of the trustees' functions.

---

[102] *Noack* v *Noack* [1959] VR 137; *Wilcox* v *Tait* [2007] 2 FLR 871 (p 211 above).

[103] *Mayes* v *Mayes* (1969) 210 EG 935; as between husband and wife and those in civil partnerships, see Matrimonial Proceedings and Property Act 1970, s 37 (discussed at p 209 above).

[104] *Leake* v *Bruzzi* [1974] 1 WLR 1528. For mortgage interest, see n 97 above.

[105] Since Trustee Act 2000, s 8, all trustees possess this power.

[106] TLATA, s 6(5), (6), (9). As regards rights of beneficiaries, surely trustees must give effect to them rather than merely 'have regard to' them. Ferris and Battersby (2003) 119 LQR 94 at pp 100–102 suggest that future and non-financial rights are here involved; a wider construction of rights is proposed at [2009] Conv 39.

[107] See, e.g., *Klug* v *Klug* [1918] 2 Ch 67; Pettit, *Equity and the Law of Trusts* (12th edn), pp 487–490.

[108] [2015] WTLR 1795 (upheld [2016] EWCA Civ 805, not discussing this point). But an estoppel might arise in respect of other powers held by trustees: *Fielden* v *Christie-Miller* [2015] WTLR 1165 (power of appointment).

[109] Ibid, at [47]–[48].

[110] TLATA, ss 8(1), 4. The power to postpone operates where there is a trust for sale; s 4 invalidates any exclusion of the power, even for pre-1996 trusts for sale. It may also be that powers conferred other than by ss 6 and 7 (such as the power to delegate) cannot be excluded.

[111] It might be argued that exclusion of sale is void as contravening the policy that land should be alienable (see p 43 above): Sydenham [1997] Conv 242. However, this policy never applied to powers of trustees: otherwise, the nineteenth-century reforms would have been largely unnecessary!

[112] Watt [1997] Conv 263. The most promising possibility is a court order under Trustee Act 1925, s 57, where sale is 'expedient'. For court orders under TLATA, s 14, see p 339 below.

The way in which these elements fit together will be considered in relation to decisions as to sale of the land: the most commonly litigated issue. Similar principles are likely to apply to other decisions by the trustees, such as leasing or mortgaging the land. After sale, we shall look at a few less significant aspects of management.

A. Sale

The trustees' power to sell the land does not mean that they can proceed without constraint. We will start with two specific statutory protections for beneficiaries.

(i) *Consent requirements*

The first protection is that the disposition creating the trust may require the consent of a person (usually, though not necessarily, a beneficiary) before trustees' powers are exercised.[113] It might, for example, be the settlor's wish that her children, who hold a fee simple in remainder, should have the opportunity to live in the family house when the life interest holder (her widower) dies. It would make sense to require their consent to any sale or lease of the land. If a consent cannot be obtained, then the court has jurisdiction under s 14 (considered below) to authorise sale.[114]

Cases before 1996 demonstrate that courts were prepared to imply the need for consent.[115] It might be argued that only express consents are allowed, given the wording of s 8(2): 'If the disposition . . . makes provision . . .'. However, similar wording was found in the old legislation[116] and it would be unsafe to presume that implied consents will never be recognised.

The cases in which such implications were made may be split into two categories. The first is where consent was implied to protect the occupation of a beneficiary.[117] Now that there is a statutory right to occupy, there should be less need for such implication.

The second category is where the nature of the trusts makes it necessary to imply consent for their proper working. Where a person is given rights over property which would be defeated if there were to be a sale, the courts are likely to reason that it is appropriate to imply a requirement of consent to sale in order to make those rights effectual. Thus, in *Re Herklots' Will Trusts*,[118] Ungoed-Thomas J implied the need for consent of a remainderman who had a right to take the property in part satisfaction of his share. It may be noted that the result may be to make the land almost completely unsaleable. Suppose a beneficiary enjoys an interest only if the land is not sold. That person is not going to consent to sale, and it is hard to see that the court would defeat the interest by ordering sale

[113] TLATA, s 8(2). Consent of a parent or guardian suffices where the person is not of full age (18): s 10(3).
[114] *Page* v *West* [2010] EWHC 504 (Ch); [2010] WTLR 1811 provides an example, despite there being no specific sale in view and the consent requirement having been bargained for. However, *Finch* v *Hall* [2013] EWHC 4360 (Ch) indicates that the courts will be slow to override refusal of consent, at least where the need for consent has been agreed by the co-owners and there has been no material change of circumstances.
[115] Problems for purchasers who are unaware of the need for consent have been redressed: pp 357–361 below.
[116] LPA, s 26(1), (2).
[117] *Bull* v *Bull* [1955] 1 QB 234; *Irani Finance Ltd* v *Singh* [1971] Ch 59.
[118] [1964] 2 All ER 66.

under s 14.[119] This second form of implied consent seems just as likely to arise after TLATA, though it will remain relatively uncommon.

(ii) *Consultation requirements*

TLATA, s 11 requires trustees, before exercising any of their functions, to consult those beneficiaries who are adults with interests in possession. The trustees are to give effect to the wishes of the majority 'so far as consistent with the general interest of the trust'.[120] The old law contained a similar requirement, although it did not apply to express trusts. Section 11 applies to all post-TLATA trusts, though it can be excluded.[121]

Past experience has shown that the consultation rules are of little effect.[122] In a successive interest trust, the trustees will have to weigh the interests of life tenants against those of remaindermen. It is only the wishes of life interest holders that fall within s 11, and it is by no means obvious that they should prevail. In most concurrent interest cases, there will be two beneficiaries each holding a 50% share. Insofar as they disagree, s 11 provides no solution. Furthermore, the same people are likely to be both trustees and beneficiaries, in which case the dispute can be resolved only by an application to the court under s 14.

It is interesting that the court is to have regard to the views of the majority,[123] although it remains unclear how this will relate to the other criteria introduced by s 15.[124] Whatever their significance, the status accorded to the views of the beneficiaries is interesting. There is no obligation on trustees of other property to consult beneficiaries, still less to comply with their wishes. Indeed, all the beneficiaries together cannot tell the trustees what to do.[125]

(iii) *The decision to sell*

Once trustees have obtained any necessary consents and consulted beneficiaries, how, then, is the decision taken? It is easy if all the trustees agree, as they will decide to sell or to retain the land as the case may be, remembering that they must take the decision for proper reasons and take (under s 11) the wishes of beneficiaries into account. Rather surprisingly, the factors to be considered by the court (s 15, discussed below) are not extended to trustee decisions.[126]

Where trustees are divided, two different analyses produce the result that the land cannot be sold. For a start, a contract or conveyance will require the participation of all the trustees. If one refuses to participate (whether or not justifiably), the sale cannot proceed without a court order. Unjustifiable opposition could be penalised by costs and liability for any loss, although this is most unlikely in the common case of a genuine dispute as to sale.

---

[119] One solution is for the other beneficiaries to buy out the person whose consent is required.

[120] TLATA, s 11(1)(b).

[121] Ibid, s 11(2). It will extend to pre-TLATA trusts if the settlor executes a deed to that effect: s 11(3).

[122] They applied to the positive exercise of powers and not, e.g., failure to continue a periodic tenancy: *Crawley BC v Ure* [1996] QB 13, applied to s 11 in *Notting Hill Housing Trust v Brackley* [2002] HLR 212. Note, however, the criticism of Pascoe [2004] Conv 370.

[123] TLATA, s 15(3).

[124] See p 341 below.

[125] *Re Brockbank* [1948] Ch 206, though the result of this case (relating to appointment of trustees) is reversed by Part II of TLATA.

[126] Ferris and Battersby [2009] Conv 39, suggesting that s 6(5) could play this role.

In any event, trustees' powers must be exercised unanimously: there is no principle of majority voting.[127] This ties in with the rule that joint tenants and tenants in common must act together to bind the land (as opposed to their individual shares). *Hounslow LBC* v *Pilling*[128] concerned a break clause in a lease, a clause that enabled the joint tenants of the lease to terminate it prematurely. It was held that the joint tenants had to act together to give notice: one of them acting alone could affect only his or her share.[129]

Whilst also stressing unanimity, the earlier House of Lords decision in *Hammersmith and Fulham LBC* v *Monk*[130] provides a contrast. Two joint tenants held a weekly tenancy which enjoyed statutory protection against termination by the landlord. The House of Lords held that one of the joint tenants could terminate the weekly tenancy. The nature of a weekly tenancy was said to be such that both joint tenants had to agree to continue it. Unlike a lease containing a break clause, it could not be treated as a longer arrangement that was being cut short. This was supported by authority,[131] although the result has been criticised.[132] For present purposes, however, both cases support the proposition that co-owners must act together in exercising powers.

(iv) *Court applications*

Unless the trustees are unanimous in wanting to sell, there must be an application to court if sale is to take place. Such applications are common in concurrent interest trusts, as the beneficiaries and trustees are usually the same persons. Most concurrent interests involve spouses or cohabitants. If their relationship breaks down, it is probable that one party will leave the family home and that party may well want the property to be sold.

TLATA, s 14 confers a wide jurisdiction on the court to deal with disputes, certainly not limited to questions of sale. An application may be made by a trustee or a person who has an interest in the trust property; the court may make such order as it thinks fit 'relating to the exercise by the trustees of any of their functions'.[133]

In addition to disagreements between trustees, beneficiaries can seek to overturn unanimous decisions by the trustees; for example, to sell or not to sell. One point might be added here. Nearly all the cases involve trustees and beneficiaries being the same persons. Where there are independent trustees, the courts are generally reluctant to interfere with their decisions, provided they are taken in good faith and not plainly unreasonable.[134] Although s 14 clearly confers jurisdiction to interfere in all trusts of land, one would expect the courts to be more reluctant to interfere with independent trustees.

---

[127] *Re 90 Thornhill Road* [1970] Ch 261. The unanimity requirement was applied to estoppel claims against trustees in *Fielden* v *Christie-Miller* [2015] WTLR 1165. The trust can always provide for majority voting; charitable trusts recognise majority voting.

[128] [1993] 1 WLR 1242.

[129] *Annen* v *Rattee* [1985] 1 EGLR 136 appears to have overlooked creation of rights out of a co-owner's share: Slatter (1985) 135 NLJ 885. Cf *U-Needa Laundry Ltd* v *Hill* [2000] 2 NZLR 308; *Pitt* v *Baxter* (2007) 34 WAR 102 and Pawlowski (2005) 9 L&T Rev 161.

[130] [1992] 1 AC 478; see also *Crawley BC* v *Ure* [1996] QB 13.

[131] *Doe d Aslin* v *Summersett* (1830) 1 B&Ad 135 (109 ER 738) (joint tenants as lessors) being the seminal case.

[132] See p 401 below in the leases context.

[133] The court may also declare the nature or extent of a person's interest in the land: TLATA, s 14(2)(b).

[134] See n 107 above.

Apart from trustees and beneficiaries, who else can apply? Plainly, a trustee in bank-ruptcy of a beneficiary can apply, as the beneficial interest is vested in him. The wording was chosen so that secured creditors of beneficiaries can apply.[135] The wording implies that anybody can apply for an order if they have an interest in the land. This could cover mort-gagees, lessees or holders of easements, whether or not their interests pre-date the trust. Fortunately, it appears that this implication will not be accepted[136]: applications will be limited to trustees, beneficiaries and persons with rights in a beneficiary's interest. It may be noted that the settlor has no standing to apply.

Let us turn to the extent of the jurisdiction. As regards trusts which include both land and other assets, one might suppose that the section is intended to apply only in relation to land. However, the wording suggests a wider scope.[137] What disputes are covered? The jurisdiction is to make an order relating to the exercise of trustees' functions. It has already been seen that it applies to issues relating to occupation and can relieve trustees of the need to get consents. Section 14 clearly enables the court to intervene where the trustees have a power to do an act or, indeed, an obligation to do so.

However, one crucial question is whether the court can make an order in matters in which the trustees have no duty or discretion. The question is not made easier by the statutory reference to trustees' *functions*. This appears to mean duties and powers.[138] Some useful guidance is provided by the Court of Appeal in *Bagum* v *Hafiz*.[139] It lies outside the trustees' powers to order one beneficiary to sell his or her beneficial interest to another and the court has no greater power. However, once a proposal lies within the functions of the trustees, the court has the 'widest discretion', and rules which might constrain the trustees (such as getting the best price) do not limit the jurisdiction of the court.

One particular question concerns a beneficiary who is entitled to occupy under s 12. Does the court possess jurisdiction to order the beneficiary to give up occupation? This is especially significant if the law adopts the 'snapshot' interpretation of the conditions for entitlement[140] and might also have great importance if sale is sought by a secured creditor of another co-owner.[141] The trustees have no power to force the occupying beneficiary out in breach of a s 12 right to occupy,[142] so it might be thought that the court cannot do so, either. Yet, this would mean that, in practice, the land could not be sold: few purchasers will be prepared to proceed in the face of an occupier who refuses to leave, even if the occupier's rights would be overreached on sale.

---

[135] 570 HL Deb col 1543 (Lord Mackay LC).

[136] *Menelaou* v *Bank of Cyprus UK Ltd* [2016] EWHC 2656 (Ch) at [27].

[137] Section 14 refers to 'functions' whilst some other sections are more carefully limited. An example is s 9(1) on delegation: 'functions as trustees which relate to the land'. After sale of land, s 14 applies to trusts which include the proceeds: s 17(2), (3).

[138] *Notting Hill Housing Trust* v *Brackley* [2002] HLR 212 at [15]. Sections 6 (powers), 7 (partition) and 9 (delegation) come under the heading in the Act of 'Functions of trustees of land'. This is of limited use: s 13 decisions (occupation) are outside this heading but are assumed by s 15(2) to be 'functions'.

[139] [2016] Ch 241 (order for pre-emptive right for a beneficiary to purchase the property); see also p 345 below.

[140] See p 328 above.

[141] See p 350 below.

[142] Note that s 13 provides discretion where there is more than one entitled beneficiary. Although this explicitly prevents exclusion of all beneficiaries, it permits the exclusion of the co-owner who opposes sale: *Miller Smith* v *Miller Smith* [2010] 1 FLR 1402 at [23] and *BR* v *VT* [2016] 2 FLR 519.

Perhaps the most likely outcome is that the courts will hold that they can order sale and, as giving vacant possession is an essential aspect of sale, they must be able to oust the beneficiary.[143] One's confidence in this is reduced by the fact that specific provision is made in s 14(2) for cases where consents are unobtainable, thus implying that the courts cannot normally override rights of the beneficiaries. If the trustees have no power to order a beneficiary out, could the courts do so simply because it is thought inappropriate that occupation should continue? Here, it appears that the answer should be no: it would be wrong to interpret s 14, even with its opaque reference to functions, as a basis for denying statutory rights.

Very similar problems arise where powers have been excluded, as permitted by s 8. If, for example, there is to be no sale during the lifetime of X,[144] then the trustees have no power to sell the land. Can the court order sale? One can see good policy reasons for the court being able to do so, so as to ensure proper management of the land. Nevertheless, it is difficult to say that it is one of the trustees' functions to act in breach of trust and in breach of the terms of TLATA.[145]

(v) *Exercising the court's discretion*

Useful guidance is provided by s 15 (new in TLATA), which lists matters which a court is to take into account. They are:

(a) the intentions of the person or persons (if any) who created the trust,
(b) the purposes for which the property subject to the trust is held,
(c) the welfare of any minor who occupies or might reasonably occupy any land subject to the trust as his home, and
(d) the interests of any secured creditor of any beneficiary.

The court is also to consider the wishes of the majority of the adult beneficiaries with interests in possession.[146]

Paragraphs (b) and, probably, (a) largely represent the law as developed by the courts prior to TLATA. The position as regards the interests of minors was uncertain, and making their welfare relevant is a welcome development. It remains to be seen how this will be balanced as against the other criteria. The introduction of the interests of secured creditors is more dubious. It is far from clear that a charge by one beneficiary[147] deserves greater

---

[143] Possibly supported by the Court of Appeal in *Avis* v *Turner* [2008] Ch 218, where s 14 powers were not limited by an argued breach of TLATA, s 6(6). However, the decision may have been based on a narrow reading of s 6(6).

[144] See, e.g., *Abbey National plc* v *Moss* (1993) 26 HLR 249 (under the old trust for sale regime the exclusion could take effect only as a consent requirement).

[145] Watt [1997] Conv 263 at p 266, though there may be other jurisdiction (particularly under Trustee Act 1925, s 57) to order sale. Contrast Megarry and Wade, *The Law of Real Property* (8th edn), para 12-023.

[146] TLATA, s 15(3), save where the trustees wish to transfer the land to absolutely entitled beneficiaries pursuant to s 6(2). Despite the slightly ambiguous wording of s 15(3), *Mortgage Corpn* v *Shaire* [2001] Ch 743 at p 761 confirms that it applies to all other disputes bar occupation (where those entitled to occupy must be consulted, without any majority provision: s 15(2)).

[147] Read literally that there is no requirement that the security is over the beneficial interest under the trust, but this should be implied.

protection than, say, a sale of his or her interest. In any event, we must remember that s 15 does no more than list relevant criteria and then not exhaustively.[148] For example, the interests of a disabled adult person may be relevant, although not listed in s 15.[149] The real question is likely to be what weight the court places upon each of the criteria. It might be added that the s 15 considerations are inapplicable on bankruptcy; this is separately discussed below.

Pre-TLATA cases

Insofar as the earlier cases (decided under LPA, s 30, the forerunner of s 14) recognised the purpose behind the trust, they may provide a good guide to the operation of paras (a) and (b). Although the old trust for sale involved a preference for sale, the courts placed considerable stress on purposes, enabling the 'right' results to be reached. It is likely that these results will still hold good in most cases today.

Our first case is exceptional in not involving a family home. In *Re Buchanan-Wollaston's Conveyance*,[150] a group of neighbours bought an adjoining strip of land as co-owners. Their object, as made clear by a written agreement, was to enhance the amenity and value of their houses by ensuring that the strip would not be built upon. One of these co-owners sold his house and now sought to have the strip sold, it no longer being of any benefit to him. The Court of Appeal accepted that it had a discretion under s 30 and that sale should be ordered if it is right and proper to do so. In words frequently quoted in later cases, the question was whether the applicant is 'a person whose voice should be allowed to prevail'. On the facts, the parties had entered into a contract, and it would not be proper to order a sale which would be inconsistent with that contract.

This analysis was extended beyond the contractual setting. In *Jones* v *Challenger*,[151] husband and wife were co-owners. The wife had long since left the family home and, following divorce, sought sale. Devlin LJ recognised that there will often be a secondary or collateral purpose behind the creation of a trust for sale. An application to sell will be refused if it defeats that purpose. On the facts, however, the marriage had come to an end and with it the purpose. That purpose was for the house to be their matrimonial home rather than the home of just one of them. Significantly, the court was unimpressed with the argument that the wife's conduct had led to the marriage breakdown. It might be reasonable for the husband to want to stay there, but the decisive point was that it was not inequitable for the wife to wish to realise her share.

Jones v *Challenger* was followed in *Rawlings* v *Rawlings*,[152] where the marriage had broken down but there had been no divorce. The purpose was held to be at an end when the marriage was dead as a matter of fact. Willmer LJ entered a powerful dissent, although this related more to the marriage relationship rather than the principles applicable to

---

[148] Thus, on a mortgagee's application, the court will consider the statutory protection available to mortgagors on a possession action: *Bank of Baroda* v *Dhillon* [1998] 1 FLR 524 at p 530.

[149] *First National Bank plc* v *Achampong* [2004] 1 FCR 18 at [65].

[150] [1939] Ch 738. Contractual restraints on alienation are normally void, but not if supporting a valid collateral purpose: *Elton* v *Cavill (No 2)* (1994) 34 NSWLR 289.

[151] [1961] 1 QB 176.

[152] [1964] P 398. See also *Jackson* v *Jackson* [1971] 1 WLR 1539, where the house was too large for one person and the proceeds would enable each to purchase suitable accommodation.

collateral purposes. It should be noted that the collateral purposes cases apply in just the same way to unmarried couples.[153]

The operation of purposes

The above cases show how purposes usually end when the relationship ends. A related question is whether the purpose survives the death of one of the parties. No problem will arise if the survivor inherits the entire property, whether by survivorship or under a will or intestacy. The difficulty is when the deceased's share in a tenancy in common passes to a third party. Can the third party obtain sale? *Jones* v *Challenger* itself supports the idea that the purpose has come to an end, and more recently, Neuberger J in *Mortgage Corpn* v *Shaire*[154] was dubious whether the family home purpose survived death. However, the Court of Appeal in *Stott* v *Ratcliffe*[155] permitted the survivor to continue to occupy, and this seems most preferable as being closer to the likely intentions of the parties. We should also bear in mind that, since TLATA, purposes are less determinative of the outcome (they are just one of the matters to be considered), so the absence of a purpose does not necessarily mean that sale will follow.

It takes little imagination to realise that purposes rarely prevented sale in the family home context. The family home purpose is scarcely likely to be continuing when the parties have split up and are litigating as to sale.[156] Today, this is confirmed by the use of the present tense 'is held' in para (b). Although purposes arising after purchase may suffice,[157] para (b) excludes purposes which have ceased to operate because of a breakdown in the relationship between the parties.[158]

A more sophisticated analysis is required if sale is to be prevented. Some cases recognise that there may be more than one purpose. Despite the termination of the family home purpose, another purpose may survive and deny sale. One example, formerly somewhat controversial, is to provide a home for children. Today, the welfare of minors is a relevant factor under TLATA, s 15 and it is unlikely that we will need to consider whether there is a purpose for their occupation. In some family relationships, it may be easy to persuade the court that a continuing purpose is dominant. Thus, in *Charlton* v *Lester*,[159] the mother was a protected tenant of a house. Her daughter and son-in-law encouraged her to purchase the freehold, to which they contributed, and all three lived in the house. When the daughter and son-in-law purchased a separate house for themselves, they wanted the mother's house sold. Oliver J rejected the claim: the purchase had been on the understanding that

---

[153] *Re Evers' Trust* [1980] 1 WLR 1327.

[154] [2001] Ch 743 at p 762. See also the idea that the purpose ends if one of them parts with his or her interest (p 347 below), although that idea is itself questionable.

[155] (1982) 126 SJ 310; see also *Harris* v *Harris* (1995) 72 P&CR 408 (father and son; the collateral purpose was intended to cover occupation by either and so was not affected when the father moved elsewhere a year before his death).

[156] In exceptional cases, there may be evidence of a purpose of a home for one of them: *Chan* v *Leung* [2003] 1 FLR 23 (purposes in the occupation context), *Holman* v *Howes* [2008] 1 FLR 1217 (applying estoppel).

[157] *Rodway* v *Landy* [2001] Ch 703 at [26]; *White* v *White* [2004] 2 FLR 321 at [24].

[158] *Rodway* v *Landy* [2001] Ch 703 at [26] (breakdown of medical partnership). *Bank of Ireland Home Mortgages Ltd* v *Bell* [2001] 2 FLR 809 interprets para (a) in a similar manner.

[159] [1976] 1 EGLR 131; also see *Harris* v *Harris* (1995) 72 P&CR 408 (father and son) and *Chan* v *Leung* [2003] 1 FLR 23 (unmarried couple).

the mother would be able to keep her existing home. This purpose can be seen to be more significant than that of using the house as a home for all of them.

Turning to other purposes, a well-known case is *Bedson* v *Bedson*,[160] in which the property was used both as a drapery business run by the husband and as a home for the family. The co-owning wife, who had not put any money into the purchase, left with the children and sought sale. The Court of Appeal was clearly unhappy with the idea that the property should be sold, bearing in mind the funding of the purchase by the husband, the wife's conduct and any possibility of future reunion. The one ground upon which *Rawlings* could be safely distinguished, however, was that one of the purposes for the purchase in *Bedson* was to establish the husband's drapery business. That purpose could still be achieved, and it would be wrong to order sale in order to defeat it. The wife's financial interest was recognised by requiring the husband to pay rent.

Estoppel analyses may provide an alternative route to the same result. Where a person contributes to the purchase of property on the understanding that he or she will be entitled to occupy the land, the courts may hold that the detriment suffered by the contributor justifies an order preventing sale. An example is provided by *Jones* v *Jones*,[161] in which a father bought a house for his son. The son gave up his job to move to the house and to be close to his father, provided part of the purchase money and worked on the house. On the father's death, his widow (stepmother of the son) sought sale. The son was held to have a quarter share under a tenancy in common and to be protected by estoppel against sale. Lord Denning MR noted the link with the collateral purpose approach:[162] 'The two doctrines go hand in hand to show that no order should be made so as to disturb the son in his possession of the house . . .'.

Should sale be ordered?

Apart from purposes, the s 30 cases had relatively little to say about the discretion to order sale. It might be thought reasonable that a co-owner should wish to gain access to capital locked up in the house. However, the modern trend is to play down the significance of this. It is commonly stated that purchasing a home is not an investment, certainly not of the nature that the money can be recovered at will. To quote Ormrod LJ,[163] it 'is the least liquid investment that one can possibly make'.

There is a good deal of truth in this, but it should not be allowed to hide the fact that the parties are happy to sink money into their home on the basis that it remains their home. Once it ceases to be their joint home, everything changes. It seems odd if one of the parties enjoys the luxury of the former family home, whilst the other, deprived of capital resources, has to accept inferior accommodation.[164] This reveals, as so often in legal solutions, a preference for an all-or-nothing approach. However, the refusal to sell can of course be justified where there are minor children living in the house. Most people would agree that the desire to recover a share in the value of the house is outweighed by the need to avoid disruption in the housing arrangements for the children, especially when sale is likely to result in unsatisfactory accommodation for them.

---

[160] [1965] 2 QB 666.
[161] [1977] 1 WLR 438; also *Holman* v *Howes* [2008] 1 FLR 1217.
[162] *Jones* at p 442. We have seen that the estoppel can be overreached: p 221 above.
[163] *Browne* v *Pritchard* [1975] 1 WLR 1366 at p 1371. See also *Re Evers' Trust* [1980] 1 WLR 1327.
[164] This appears to have been the position in *Browne* v *Pritchard* [1975] 1 WLR 1366. See Gray [1982] CLJ 228.

We should consider another way of resolving the problem. A simple order for sale means that neither party can use the house. However, if the occupying party is able to buy out the applicant, then a far more satisfactory result is obtained. The occupier keeps occupation of the property and the applicant gains access to his or her financial interest. It is preferable to the alternative of paying rent to the applicant, both because it unlocks the capital and because it produces a more satisfactory clean break. Yet, in many cases it is financially unrealistic.[165] It will be unusual for the occupier to have the necessary money, and it may not be feasible to increase the mortgage if the occupier is at home with young children. Where buying out is feasible, the courts encourage it. In appropriate cases, the court may put pressure on the occupier by indicating that sale will be ordered unless agreement is reached.[166] More directly, the court can provide that a beneficiary shall have a right to purchase the property at a price determined by the court.[167] The order is likely to provide for sale if the right is not exercised.

Changes in TLATA

When considering the modern application of TLATA, four factors need to be stressed. The first is that purpose is but one factor to be considered in s 14 applications; this may lead to a rather more flexible approach than under the old law. In particular, it may make it easier to deal with cases where there are a number of different purposes, some of which are still operating. To say that there should be sale if any one purpose ends is as untenable as arguing that sale should be refused as long as any single purpose remains. The courts must ask whether the ending of one purpose is sufficiently serious to terminate the basis upon which the house was bought. It cannot be pretended that this is anything other than an extremely difficult judgment, especially where the proceeds will be insufficient to allow either co-owner to purchase alternative housing with their share.

The second, and more specific, factor is that it is now clear that interests of minors (who need not be children of the co-owners)[168] must be taken into account. In many broken relationships, there will be children and this may point against sale. However, the courts have shown a reluctance to give much emphasis to the interests of children unless there is evidence of how they will be adversely affected,[169] even though downsizing will result and they will have to share a room.[170] The third factor is that we no longer have a trust for sale. This played little practical role in the pre-TLATA cases, but it is certainly true that today there is no automatic leaning towards sale.[171] The final factor is that the interests of secured creditors must be considered: this is separately studied below.[172]

---

[165] Although the value of the shares net of the mortgage may well be quite small, especially in times of low house price inflation.

[166] *Bernard* v *Josephs* [1982] Ch 391.

[167] *Bagum* v *Hafiz* [2016] Ch 241. It was recognised that this has the same practical result as a sale of the other co-owner's beneficial interest, which cannot be ordered.

[168] *First National Bank plc* v *Achampong* [2004] 1 FCR 18 (grandchildren).

[169] *First National Bank plc* v *Achampong* [2004] 1 FCR 18 at [65] (claim by secured creditor). But note the more sympathetic approach in *Edwards* v *Lloyds TSB Bank plc* [2005] 1 FCR 139, p 352 below.

[170] *White* v *White* [2004] 2 FLR 321 at [14]–[15].

[171] *Mortgage Corpn* v *Shaire* [2001] Ch 743 at p 758.

[172] See pp 350–352.

(vi) *Interplay between s 14 and family law jurisdiction*[173]

As regards husband and wife (and civil partnerships), the court has since 1973 possessed a wide discretion to vary property rights on divorce.[174] This valuable family jurisdiction is frequently used to ensure that the party looking after the children can keep occupation of the home, at least until the children leave home.[175] The rights of the other party may, where appropriate, be recognised by the payment of some form of rent.[176] The exercise of this jurisdiction does not depend upon property rights, and it enables the court to take full account of the needs of the parties.

What is particularly important to us is that this jurisdiction seems far more appropriate than TLATA: it is, of course, designed for the marriage breakdown scenario. This was confirmed by the Court of Appeal in *Miller Smith* v *Miller Smith*,[177] describing the family law jurisdiction as 'in principle far more desirable'. Section 14 of TLATA should be applied only where it is not reasonable to wait for the family law jurisdiction. The case itself was such an exception: the wife's delaying of divorce proceedings coupled with unusually onerous costs of maintaining the property meant that it was not tolerable to wait until the divorce proceedings were completed. However, the family jurisdiction does not apply to cohabiting couples, for whom the factors in s 15 of TLATA will operate. Prior to TLATA, *Re Evers' Trust*,[178] whilst holding that different principles apply in the s 30 and family jurisdiction areas, plainly strove to develop s 30 so as to reach much the same result in each area. This may be somewhat easier today, given that the s 15 factors are wider than the old collateral purposes. Yet there are limits as to what can be done, not least because TLATA operates only if the cohabitants are co-owners.

The above discussion relates to the discretion to vary ownership. A rather different question relates to the discretion under the Family Law Act 1996 relating to occupation rights of cohabitants.[179] Is it appropriate to consider applications between cohabitants under s 14, given that many such applications will involve the question whether the respondent should remain in occupation? Guidance is provided by Mostyn J in *BR* v *VT*.[180] Section 14 can be used to order possession (so as to enable sale), but only when an occupation order could have been made under the Family Law Act.

(vii) *Bankruptcy of a co-owner*

When one of the beneficiary co-owners becomes bankrupt, it is common for the trustee in bankruptcy to seek sale so that the value of the bankrupt's share can be realised and

---

[173] In addition to the jurisdiction discussed in the text, there is power under Children Act 1989, Sched 1, para 1(2) (d), (e), to order settlements and transfers of property for the benefit of children. *White* v *White* [2004] 2 FLR 321 stresses the importance of this jurisdiction and the need to deal with it and any TLATA application together.

[174] Matrimonial Causes Act 1973, s 24. The criteria, listed in s 25, are much wider than those in TLATA, s 15.

[175] The more recent cases show a greater reluctance to order such a delayed sale and seek a clearer resolution of the property issues: Cretney, *Principles of Family Law* (8th edn), paras 13.110–13.117.

[176] *Harvey* v *Harvey* [1982] Fam 83.

[177] [2010] 1 FLR 1402 at [18], following earlier cases.

[178] [1980] 1 WLR 1327; Thompson [1984] Conv 103.

[179] See p 331 above. *Fred Perry (Holdings) Ltd* v *Genis* [2015] 1 P&CR D10 holds that the family homes criteria in the Family Law Act are unlikely to affect the normal preference for sale when sought by secured creditors (discussed below).

[180] [2016] 2 FLR 519 (rejecting a concession made and accepted in *Miller Smith*).

creditors lose as little as possible. It is important to note that the matrimonial jurisdiction is not applicable against the trustee in bankruptcy[181] and, therefore, the s 14 jurisdiction will operate. The principles for ordering sale are, however, regulated by the Insolvency Act 1986, which displaces the normal s 15 considerations.[182] It is first necessary to look at the pre-1986 approach of the courts, as this influenced the 1986 Act.

The courts accepted that the duty of the trustee in bankruptcy to realise the assets for the benefit of creditors overrode any collateral purpose, whether or not the co-owners were still living together. This was confirmed by *Re Citro*,[183] holding that the collateral purpose terminated on bankruptcy. But why should purposes so terminate? One could understand why sale should be ordered if the house had been bought after the debts had been incurred, but in most cases it has been purchased many years earlier: the purpose was operative when the debts were incurred. It is instructive that the Court of Appeal in *Abbey National plc* v *Moss*[184] viewed *Citro* with little enthusiasm. However, TLATA, s 15(4) makes it clear for the future that purposes do not operate on bankruptcy.

The principles upon which sale should be ordered on bankruptcy are now regulated by ss 335A–337 of the Insolvency Act 1986.[185] Where the property is co-owned, temporary protection for the family is available under s 335A, the court making a 'just and reasonable' order. The relevant factors are stated to be (a) the interests of the creditors, (b) where the house has been the home of the bankrupt or the bankrupt's spouse, the conduct of the spouse as regards the bankruptcy, the needs and resources of the spouse, and the needs of any children,[186] (c) all the circumstances of the case other than the needs of the bankrupt. Unmarried cohabitants fall outside (b), although civil partnership is treated the same as marriage.

Section 337 provides similar protection where there are children living with the bankrupt. This requires the needs of the children to be taken into account (independently of co-ownership), though again not the needs of the bankrupt.[187] Finally, s 336 provides protection where there are statutory occupation rights.[188] This is almost identical to the s 335A protection in cases of co-ownership.

A very important qualification upon each of these provisions is that, after one year, the interests of the creditors are to be assumed to outweigh all other considerations unless the circumstances of the case are exceptional.[189] Protection for one year, never automatic, is unlikely to be significant. Nearly all the older cases involve applications well after a year from the date of bankruptcy. So when are circumstances 'exceptional' so as to justify postponing sale beyond a year? *Re Citro*[190] accepted that this test of exceptional circumstances is based upon the pre-1986 law.

---

[181] *Re Holliday* [1981] Ch 405 at p 419.
[182] TLATA, s 15(4). Cases are heard in the court having jurisdiction in bankruptcy: Insolvency Act 1986, s 335A(1).
[183] [1991] Ch 142.
[184] (1993) 26 HLR 249 (Peter Gibson LJ at p 257 and, especially, Ralph Gibson LJ at p 262).
[185] Implementing, in part, the recommendations of the Cork Committee on Insolvency Law and Practice (1982) Cmnd 8558. The Committee had recommended greater court discretion: Cretney (1991) 107 LQR 177. The provisions were recast by TLATA, but there was no significant change.
[186] 'Needs' covers all sorts of needs (not just financial): *Everitt* v *Budhram* [2010] Ch 170.
[187] Insolvency Act 1986, s 337(5).
[188] Under Family Law Act 1996, s 30.
[189] Insolvency Act 1986, ss 335A(2), 336(5), 337(6).
[190] [1991] Ch 142. See Cretney (1991) 107 LQR 177; Brown (1992) 55 MLR 284.

At the time of *Re Citro*, *Re Holliday*[191] was the only fully reported case in which sale had been postponed. There were three children, the youngest aged 12, and sale was post-poned for five years. It was relevant that the non-bankrupt wife would have had difficulty in finding accommodation in the area with her share of the proceeds of sale. However, such factors failed to impress the majority of the Court of Appeal in *Re Citro*. The circumstances might be distressing but not exceptional: 'the melancholy consequences of debt and improvidence with which every civilised society has been familiar', as Nourse LJ put it.[192]

Not everybody would agree. The Court of Appeal in *Re Holliday* had been more sym-pathetic, and in *Re Citro*, Bingham LJ thought the trend in the law was to give greater preference to personal claims over property rights. Nevertheless, the legislation adopts the strict 'exceptional' test, and Bingham LJ accepted that a more generous approach could not be reconciled with the legislation. Returning to *Re Holliday*, *Re Citro* explained it on the basis that the bankrupt spouse had lodged the bankruptcy petition. Not only were the creditors not seeking bankruptcy, but their debts were covered by the bankrupt's assets. True, they would have to wait until the house was sold in order to get their money, but it was entirely safe. This is quite different from the other cases, in which the family can be seen as continuing to occupy the home at the expense of the creditors.

The meaning of exceptional circumstances

It is plain that the loss of the family home and interruption of children's schooling will not be enough. Those who wish to be hard-hearted may observe that children frequently have to change school when their parents move houses and doubt whether the families of bank-rupts have any better right to continue to live in pleasant houses in attractive neighbour-hoods than the less fortunate members of society. Further, mortgagees can sell the land without children's interests being considered.[193] It is not as if the family will be penniless in the typical case, as the non-bankrupt spouse or partner (if a co-owner) will keep their share in the proceeds of sale: a better outcome than on mortgage default. Sale will not take place immediately, and there will be no question of sudden eviction in the midst of GCSE or A-level examinations.

Some examples of exceptional circumstances are found in the cases. Sale may be postponed beyond the standard year if the period falls within a particularly sensitive part of a child's education leading up to examinations.[194] However, the courts require evi-dence that significant harm will result from sale: the mere existence of special educational needs has been held insufficient.[195] Another example may be if the home has been spe-cially adapted for a disabled child[196] or spouse.[197] A number of fairly recent cases have shown that severe ill health of the bankrupt's spouse or child may justify postponement.

---

[191] [1981] Ch 405. A similar argument failed in *Donohoe* v *Ingram* [2006] 2 FLR 1084, when it was less certain whether repayment would be made.

[192] *Re Citro* [1991] Ch 142 at p 157; see also *Re Lowrie* [1981] 3 All ER 353.

[193] The contrast with TLATA, s 15 is noted in *Pickering* v *Wells* [2002] 2 FLR 798 (but contrast *Fred Perry (Holdings) Ltd* v *Genis* [2015] 1 P&CR D10 at [5]). Nield and Hopkins (2013) 33 JLS 431 suggest that the mortgage rule could be challenged on human rights grounds, but see p 614 below.

[194] *Re Lowrie* [1981] 3 All ER 353 at p 356.

[195] *Barca* v *Mears* [2005] 2 FLR 1.

[196] *Re Bailey* [1977] 1 WLR 278.

[197] *Claughton* v *Charalamabous* [1999] 1 FLR 740.

Indefinite postponement was ordered where there was renal failure and chronic osteoarthritis restricting mobility[198] and where chemotherapy treatment required the avoidance of stress (although the outcome was expected to be known within six months).[199] However, *Grant* v *Baker*[200] stresses that, even in exceptional circumstances (severe mental disability of adult child of bankrupt), postponement should normally be measured in terms of months: 12 months were allowed. A similar postponement was also allowed where there was paranoid schizophrenia which could be seriously affected by a move to smaller accommodation away from the family.[201]

On the other hand, it is unlikely that distress and nervous illness will postpone sale unless there is a temporary reason for delay.[202] It must be remembered that the needs of the bankrupt are not relevant.[203] Even so, when an elderly spouse (aged 74) was caring for a terminally ill bankrupt (aged 79) with a life expectancy of six months, it was held that the spouse had needs in these exceptional circumstances which justified postponing sale for three months after the bankrupt's death.[204]

Human rights?

It is possible that the narrow exceptional circumstances test, as applied in the cases, could be attacked as being incompatible with the European Convention on Human Rights and, in particular, the Article 8 right to respect for family life and home.[205] In *Barca* v *Mears*,[206] Strauss QC considered the validity of the test to be 'questionable' and preferred an approach which would take into account severe consequences of a usual kind. The real issue (as Strauss QC recognised) is whether the law as established in the legislation and *Re Citro* provides a proportionate response to the rival claims of creditors and family. However, it was not necessary to reach a conclusion, as the facts readily justified sale.

Earlier, Paul Morgan QC[207] had held that the test was compatible with Article 8, though he may have adopted a relatively generous interpretation of exceptional: 'out of the ordinary course, or unusual, or special, or uncommon'. Nevertheless, the application of Article 8 remains unsettled.[208]

---

[198] Ibid.

[199] *Judd* v *Brown* [1998] 2 FLR 360 (not considered on appeal: [1999] 1 FLR 1191); cf *Re Haghighat* [2009] 1 FLR 1271 (seriously disabled child: three years).

[200] [2016] EWHC 1782 (Ch); two and a half years had already passed since bankruptcy. It was not a case where the property had been specially adapted.

[201] *Re Raval* [1998] 2 FLR 718; cf *Everitt* v *Budhram* [2010] Ch 170.

[202] *Re Densham* [1975] 1 WLR 1519; *Barclays Bank plc* v *Hendricks* [1996] 1 FLR 258.

[203] *Everitt* v *Budhram* [2010] Ch 170 at [53].

[204] *Re Bremner* [1999] 1 FLR 912.

[205] Outside bankruptcy, the s 15 factors will normally satisfy Article 8: *National Westminster Bank plc* v *Rushmer* [2010] 2 FLR 362 at [50].

[206] [2005] 2 FLR 1 (Dixon [2005] Conv 161), adopting a suggestion in Rook, *Property Law and Human Rights*, pp 203–205. *Barca* was discussed in *Donohoe* v *Ingram* [2006] 2 FLR 1084, but the point was not decided.

[207] *Hosking* v *Michaelides* [2006] BPIR 1192 at [70]. The same judge later held in *Nicholls* v *Lan* [2007] 1 FLR 744 that the application of s 335A, once exceptional circumstances have been proved, is human rights compliant. This seems well justified.

[208] In *Ford* v *Alexander* [2012] BPIR 528, Peter Smith J considered s 335A itself to be consistent with Art 8, though *Barca* was not cited. The earlier cases are fully considered by Baker [2010] Conv 352; cf Thompson [2011] Conv 421 at p 439.

Family home protection

Before leaving bankruptcy, it might be noted that some countries protect the family home against bankruptcy of one of the parties.[209] Thus, New Zealand[210] gives protection against creditors, at least up to around £50,000. If the house (less any mortgage) is worth more than this, then the court may order sale unless the co-owners raise the balance. This is useful to prevent disruption of the family home where the house has a small value in the first place, although many houses in England have a net value exceeding £50,000. Although it may be seen as a reasonable compromise, its repeal has been recommended.[211]

The Enterprise Act 2002 introduced two protections for the residence of the bankrupt. First, sale is to be refused if the interest is worth less than £1,000 (after mortgage and sale costs).[212] The object is to prevent sale where no substantial benefit is obtained by creditors.[213] This is, of course, much less generous than the New Zealand approach. Secondly, if the property has not been realised, then it normally reverts to the bankrupt after three years from bankruptcy.[214] Whilst s 335A provides protection against sale for up to one year, the policy is that the effects of bankruptcy should not linger on for a lengthy period. Although the court can extend this period, one side effect was seen in *Grant* v *Baker*[215] – the courts are even more reluctant to postpone sale for an extended period.

Human rights arguments may be used to articulate similar policies. In Northern Ireland, it has been held that a delay for 12 years lulled the occupiers into a false sense of security, encouraging expenditure on the properties. For a sale to take place after house prices had caused the bankrupt's interest to become valuable would be a breach of Articles 6 and 8: the circumstances counted as exceptional.[216]

(viii) *The operation of s 14 as regards successors in title*

Can a successor in title (i.e. successor to one of the co-owners) force sale on the other co-owner who wishes to retain occupation? Although a purchaser from a co-owner would be a successor, virtually all the cases have involved secured creditors. This, of course, triggers s 15(1)(d): the interests of secured creditors must be considered. Two initial points may be made. First, the fact that the occupying co-owner (not the debtor) has an overriding interest does not exclude the operation of s 14.[217] This is inevitable, as any original co-owner can apply to the court (although it is most unlikely that the application would be successful

---

[209] Fox (2005) 25 LS 201 explores the concepts of family home and home in the context of protection against creditors. More generally (home can be relevant in numerous settings), see Fox, *Conceptualising Home* (2007) and contrast the more sceptical views of Bevan in *Modern Studies in Property Law*, Vol 8 (ed Barr), Chapter 11.

[210] Joint Family Homes Act 1964, especially ss 16–18. The limit is NZ$103,000 (as of 2016). The Saskatchewan protection of Can $32,000 (approximately £20,000) is discussed in *Monteith* v *Monteith* (2004) 240 DLR 4th 506.

[211] LCNZ R77 (2001); Omar [2006] Conv 157 at pp 174–176.

[212] Insolvency Act 1986, s 313A; SI 2004 No 547.

[213] It may be noted that the value of the bankrupt's share is in issue, not the land.

[214] Insolvency Act 1986, s 283A.

[215] [2016] EWHC 1782 (Ch).

[216] *Official Receiver for Northern Ireland* v *Rooney* [2009] 2 FLR 1437. For a more generous view of similar delays, compare *Holtham* v *Kelmanson* [2007] WTLR 285.

[217] *Bank of Baroda* v *Dhillon* [1998] 1 FLR 524, decided on LPA, s 30.

if it would defeat a collateral purpose). But this is qualified by the second point: it is clear that successors in title are bound by any continuing collateral purpose. Thus in *Abbey National plc* v *Moss*[218] a chargee from one co-owner was refused sale on an LPA, s 30 application. It remains to be seen how far this result is affected by including the interests of secured creditors within s 15.

However, that is only the beginning of the difficulties. The pre-TLATA cases on successors in title were influenced by the bankruptcy cases. In *Re Citro*, it was stated that, where joint occupation is the purpose, this is based on the parties' joint ownership. On bankruptcy, that joint ownership is shattered and with it the collateral purpose. Although one might have expected that this very technical analysis would be restricted to the bankruptcy setting, it was extended to charges.[219] It was avoided in *Moss* only because there the purpose was, unusually, the occupation of just one of the co-owners (the mother of the chargor).

However, the termination of purposes is less conclusive now that s 15 provides a wider range of criteria for the courts to consider, as held by Neuberger J in the important case of *Mortgage Corpn* v *Shaire*.[220] Although the earlier cases had held that sale should be ordered unless there were exceptional circumstances (the test for bankruptcy), Neuberger J held that this test no longer operates. TLATA provides separately for bankruptcy (the normal s 15 criteria are excluded, so purposes become irrelevant), and s 15 introduces the interests of secured creditors as a material consideration outside bankruptcy. These factors point to there no longer being any rule that a secured creditor automatically succeeds. In addition, TLATA was intended to make changes and to remove the emphasis on sale.

Although sale is no longer automatic, this leaves open the question as to what the courts will do. An obvious problem is that the financial needs of creditors are so different from the other criteria (which are purpose and family based) that it is very difficult to balance them. It is highly significant that Neuberger J accepted that there would be substantial disadvantage to the creditor if its debt was indefinitely tied up in the property. The defendant occupier had a 75% share and the creditor had, effectively,[221] the remaining 25%. This made it feasible for the defendant to buy the creditor out, converting the creditor's 25% share into a secured loan (funding the purchase) upon which interest would be payable. This solution was fair on the creditor, whose business after all was to lend money. So far as the defendant was concerned, if she was not agreeable to this (or could not afford the interest), then the house would have to be sold – despite taking the defendant's majority beneficial interests into account under s 15(3).

This ingenious solution looks after the interests of both creditor (return on its money) and defendant (occupation). It is, nevertheless, viable only because the occupier started with a large share; frequently, it will not be feasible. When such arrangements are not

---

[218] (1993) 26 HLR 249; Hirst LJ dissented. See Clarke [1994] Conv 331; Harwood [1996] Fam Law 293. However, sale was ordered by Judge Behrens in *Begum* v *Issa* [2014] 5 November (Dixon [2015] Conv 97 at pp 100–101).

[219] *Lloyds Bank plc* v *Byrne & Byrne* (1991) 23 HLR 472 and *Barclays Bank plc* v *Hendricks* [1996] 1 FLR 258 applied it to holders of charging orders; see also *Mortgage Corpn* v *Shaire* [2001] Ch 743.

[220] [2001] Ch 743, cited with approval in *Bank of Ireland Home Mortgages Ltd* v *Bell* [2001] 2 FLR 809.

[221] All the 25% share would be required to pay the creditor.

viable, the Court of Appeal has shown no hesitation in ordering sale,[222] regarding 'proper recompense' for the creditor as crucial.

The conclusion may be reached that secured creditors have little to fear from *Shaire*.[223] Either the occupier has to accept a charge over the legal title (valued by reference to the value of the secured charge over the debtor's share) or, more likely, the land will be sold. Two further points deserve attention. The first is that it might be different if there are minor children. This came nowhere close to preventing sale in *First National Bank plc v Achampong*,[224] although it was a relevant factor in *Edwards v Lloyds TSB Bank plc*.[225] The facts in *Edwards* were special in that the value of the debtor's share comfortably exceeded the debt. It followed that the creditors would not, at the end of the day, lose money if sale were delayed. Sale was postponed for five years (until the children ceased to be minors) with the possibility of further postponement. The second and very different point is that a creditor who fails in obtaining an order for sale can nearly always bankrupt the debtor, leading to the almost inevitable sale of the property.[226]

B. Partition and termination of trusteeship

Before 1925, any co-owner could have the land physically partitioned between them so that each would become sole owner of part, regardless of the sense of doing so.[227] By 1868, the courts had power to order sale if it was more beneficial, but any co-owner could insist on there being sale or partition. Since 1925, partition has required agreement of all the trustees and beneficiaries, and this is repeated in TLATA.[228] Strangely, it applies only if there is a tenancy in common, but beneficiaries who agree to partition can easily agree to sever any equitable joint tenancy. Under s 14, the court can order partition if consent is refused, but such orders are rare.[229]

Somewhat different is the power of the trustees under s 6(2) to convey the land to the beneficiaries, if the beneficiaries are of full age and capacity and absolutely entitled. In such cases, co-ownership and the trust of land will continue, but the existing trustees can relieve themselves of any further role. This does not require the agreement of the beneficiaries.[230]

---

[222] *Bank of Ireland Home Mortgages Ltd v Bell* [2001] 2 FLR 809, where there were debts of £300,000 and the occupier had a mere 10% beneficial interest (Probert [2002] Conv 61); *First National Bank plc v Achampong* [2004] 1 FCR 18 (Thompson [2003] Conv 314; Radley-Gardner [2003] 5 Web JCLI). See, generally, Pawlowski and Brown [2012] Fam Law 64, 180.

[223] Including secured creditors of a beneficiary with an interest in remainder: *Pritchard Englefield v Steinberg* [2004] EWHC 1908 (Ch).

[224] [2004] 1 FCR 18.

[225] [2005] 1 FCR 139. Fox (2005) 25 LS 201 at p 214 notes that children's interests receive no protection against mortgagees if the property is not jointly owned. In *Conceptualising Home*, Chapter 9, she welcomes *Edwards* and argues for a greater role for children's interests in resolving disputes involving creditors.

[226] *Alliance and Leicester plc v Slayford* (2000) 33 HLR 743; see p 591 below.

[227] *Turner v Morgan* (1803) 8 Ves 143 (32 ER 307) upheld an award of 'the whole stack of chimneys, all the fire-places, the only staircase in the house, and all the conveniences in the yard'.

[228] TLATA, s 7.

[229] *Ellison v Cleghorn* [2013] EWHC 5 (Ch) provides a recent example (plot bought by two friends for construction of two houses).

[230] Emphasised by excluding consultation: TLATA, ss 11(2)(b), 15(3). The drafting of s 6(2) is a 'nightmare': Whitehouse and Hassall, *Trusts of Land, Trustee Delegation and the Trustee Act 2000* (2nd edn), paras 2.44–2.51.

C. Delegation

The trustees may delegate any of their powers (including sale) to one or more beneficiaries with interests in possession. This power is most likely to be significant for successive interest trusts, where beneficiaries are less likely to be trustees. Full discussion will take place in the following chapter.

4. Protecting purchasers: overreaching[231]

A major objective of the 1925 legislation was that purchasers should be safe in dealing with a small number of legal owners (joint tenants) without any need to look into the details of the equitable interests under the trust. The first point is covered by imposing a maximum of four trustees of land.[232] As to the second point, purchasers should not be concerned with such interests as life interests, remainder interests, equitable joint tenancies and tenancies in common. Overreaching is effective to achieve this.[233] It is the principle whereby on an authorised sale (or other transaction), the trusts are transferred from the land to the proceeds of sale. The purchaser is not bound by the trusts and need not investigate them, although good faith is still required.[234]

Overreaching establishes the curtain principle, whereby a curtain is drawn between purchasers and the beneficial interests. The purchaser is not concerned with the beneficial interests at all.[235] This is enhanced in registered land because the most a purchaser will see is a restriction requiring any sale to be by two trustees.[236]

Nevertheless, beneficiaries are not left completely unprotected. It has already been seen that beneficiaries can exert a degree of control by virtue of consultation and (if relevant) consent requirements, not to mention applications under TLATA, s 14. It should always be remembered that the purchase money will be held on trust for the beneficiaries, who should not lose out financially on sale. However, dangers remain if the trustees spend the money or abscond with it.

It is worth noting exactly what interests are overreached. Most obviously, all beneficial rights operating under the trust are overreached. A borderline case might be thought to be a right to set aside a transfer to two persons for unconscionability. This has been held to be capable of being overreached.[237] Claims to interests predating the trust (such as an equitable easement) are outside the overreaching powers of trustees. However, there can

---

[231] Harpum [1990] CLJ 277; Ferris and Battersby (2002) 118 LQR 270; (2003) 119 LQR 94. Mortgagees and lessees are also protected by overreaching. More surprising (*Dixon* [2017] Conv 1) is the protection of grantees of easements in *Baker* v *Craggs* [2016] EWHC 3250 (Ch).

[232] Trustee Act 1925, s 34(2).

[233] See LPA, s 2(1)(ii), though this depends upon the interests 'being capable of being overreached'. This condition appears satisfied by TLATA, s 6 and, possibly, LPA, s 27(1). Doubts expressed by Hopkins [1997] Conv 81 ('based upon a fundamental misunderstanding': Harpum (2000) 116 LQR at p 343) seem to be answered by these provisions. In any event, overreaching does not require statutory authority where trustees act pursuant to a trust or power.

[234] *HSBC Bank plc* v *Dyche* [2010] 2 P&CR 58 (criticised by Dixon [2010] Conv 1, Gravells [2010] Conv 169 and Thompson, *Landmark Cases in Land Law* (ed Gravells), pp 173–174). There was clear fraud: the purchaser was one of the trustees.

[235] LPA, s 27(1).

[236] The restriction should also refer to any limits on trustees' powers and any need to obtain consents.

[237] *Mortgage Express* v *Lambert* [2017] Ch 93 at [36] (criticised by Televantos [2016] CLJ 458) and Lees [2017] Conv 71; see also *Birmingham Midshires Mortgage Services Ltd* v *Sabherwal* (1999) 80 P&CR 256 (estoppel claim to a share of land held by sons of claimant).

be an 'ad hoc trust' which operates to overreach some prior equitable interests, generally only those of a financial nature.[238] There will be an ad hoc trust if the trustees are court approved or a trust corporation.[239]

A. The need for two trustees

A very important protection for beneficiaries is that LPA, s 27(2) (which survives TLATA) requires capital monies (purchase money) to be paid to at least two trustees or a trust corporation; any attempt to exclude it is invalid. Its purpose is to protect against the risk of fraud on the part of a single trustee, for whom the temptation of receiving a large sum of money may be too great. Fortunately, examples of misappropriation by two trustees are rare.[240]

However, overreaching does not require that there be any capital monies. The Court of Appeal in *State Bank of India* v *Sood*[241] confirmed this. A mortgage had been granted to secure an existing debt: this overreached the beneficiaries' interests. *Sood* seems unquestionably correct. The trustees may, quite properly, have borrowed money for the trust, and the opportunity may arise to obtain a better interest rate (or to avoid repayment of the loan) by securing the loan. In *Sood* itself, the security was in respect of personal obligations of the trustees, unrelated to the trust. Mortgaging the land was a breach of trust which could only damage the beneficiaries. The mortgagee did not know this and overreaching was therefore appropriate, though Peter Gibson LJ supported reforming the law for the better protection of beneficiaries. If there is no receipt of capital monies, then a single trustee can enter into an overreaching transaction. There may still be full consideration: a lease at a market rent provides a good example.

Sale by a single trustee

The cases reveal that it is very unusual for purchasers to obtain a bad title when purchasing from two trustees. However, purchase from a single trustee is very different. A common scenario is the joint purchase of a home by two persons, when the legal title is vested in one of them. That person holds on trust for the two of them. The single trustee should not, of course, sell without appointing a second trustee.[242] What happens if the single trustee in fact conveys the land to a bona fide purchaser who is quite unaware of the trust? The problem for the purchaser is that neither the trust nor the co-ownership is likely to be disclosed on the title deeds or register of title. Overreaching certainly cannot take place: LPA, ss 2(1)(ii) and 27(2) make it clear that overreaching depends upon there being two trustees. This means that we are thrown back on priority principles. In registered land, a purchaser will be bound if there is an entry on the register or an actual occupation

---

[238] LPA, s 2(2), (3), (5). It was considered in the Court of Appeal in *Shiloh Spinners Ltd* v *Harding* [1972] Ch 326 at pp 340–341, 352, 355–356 (reversed [1973] AC 691, see at pp 720–721).

[239] For definition, see LPA, s 205(1)(xxviii); Law of Property (Amendment) Act 1926, s 3; Pettit, *Equity and the Law of Trusts* (12th edn), pp 394–395. Companies formed to act as trustees and with substantial financial backing are included (SI 1975 No 1189).

[240] But they do exist: *City of London BS* v *Flegg* [1988] AC 54.

[241] [1997] Ch 276 (there were two trustees); Thompson [1997] Conv 134.

[242] An injunction stopping conveyance may be obtained: *Waller* v *Waller* [1967] 1 WLR 451.

overriding interest.[243] Otherwise, the purchaser (once registered) will take free of the beneficial interests.[244]

Co-ownership interests should be protected by restriction.[245] Pre-TLATA, a difficult question was whether they were also overriding interests as 'An interest belonging . . . to a person in actual occupation.'[246] *Williams & Glyn's Bank Ltd* v *Boland*[247] held that this applies to trusts of land, a conclusion that is beyond question today. The result is that a beneficiary in actual occupation has an overriding interest binding a registered transferee from a single trustee. The context of these cases is usually that of a registered charge rather than sale, with the proprietor having defaulted on the mortgage payments. If the proprietor is made bankrupt as a result, then (despite success under *Boland*) possession of the land will usually be lost on a sale by the trustee in bankruptcy.[248]

Sale by two trustees

In *City of London BS* v *Flegg*,[249] it was argued that a purchaser is also bound by an overriding interest where there are two trustees. A husband and wife purchased a house with a significant contribution from the wife's parents; all four thereby obtained interests under a trust. The husband and wife became the registered proprietors, but the register contained no mention of the parents' interests. The husband and wife subsequently mortgaged the house without the knowledge of the parents. The parents argued that they were in actual occupation (they lived in the house) and had an overriding interest.[250] This argument was accepted by the Court of Appeal. If correct (it was in fact rejected by the House of Lords), it would have had a significant effect on the entire 1925 scheme of purchaser protection. It would have meant that purchasers could no longer rely on dealing with two trustees and would have had to investigate the beneficial interests.

Part of the parents' argument was based upon land registration principles; this has already been discussed and dismissed.[251] An argument more specific to concurrent interests was that beneficiaries in occupation are protected against overreaching by LPA, s 14: 'This Part of this Act [which contains the overreaching provisions] shall not prejudicially affect the interest of any person in possession . . .'. It has never been clear what the purpose or effect of s 14 is. It had been relied upon in *Bull* v *Bull*[252] to emphasise that rights of occupation are not taken away by the 1925 legislation; this was approved by Lord Wilberforce in *Boland*. However, the House of Lords in *Flegg* declined to interpret s 14 so as to limit overreaching. Whatever its precise effect, it does not operate so as to qualify

---

[243] In unregistered land, it depends on whether there is notice: *Caunce* v *Caunce* [1969] 1 WLR 286.
[244] Confirmed by *Haque* v *Raja* [2016] EWHC 1950 (Ch) at [44] (based on LRA, s 29).
[245] Land Registration Act 2002 (hereafter LRA), s 40. A notice is not available: s 33(a).
[246] The current wording: LRA, Sched 3, para 2.
[247] [1981] AC 487. Problems caused by the doctrine of conversion (abolished by TLATA: p 362 below) no longer need to be considered.
[248] *Alliance and Leicester plc* v *Slayford* (2000) 33 HLR 743 (discussed at p 591 below). Dixon in *Modern Studies in Property Law*, Vol 4 (ed Cooke), Chapter 2, argues that the courts have, to protect mortgagees, denuded beneficial interests of much of their proprietary status.
[249] [1986] Ch 605 (CA); [1988] AC 54. See Hopkins in *Landmark Cases in Land Law* (ed Gravells), Chapter 9.
[250] Overreaching was of little value to the parents as the loan had been dissipated and the trustees were bankrupt.
[251] See p 265 above.
[252] [1955] 1 QB 234.

this fundamental principle of purchaser protection. This fits in well with the perceived intention of the legislation. It appears that these principles are unaffected by TLATA.[253]

B. Reform

The overreaching rules work well in protecting purchasers. The problem of the hidden trust in *Boland* and *Flegg* is one that would be difficult to resolve whatever form of land-holding structure is employed: most cases involve two innocent parties. Nevertheless, should the policy of the law be to continue the protection of purchasers from two trustees? Some modern thinking is that a purchaser who fails to inquire about the rights of occupiers is the less deserving of the two innocent parties[254] and that the law currently fails to give adequate protection to beneficiaries.

From a financial angle, the protection of beneficiaries is reasonably good. Exceptions are fortunately rare, although *Flegg* is one. It is sometimes suggested that a single trustee could appoint an accomplice and thereby sell and defraud a beneficiary. In theory, this is indeed possible. However, few fraudulent single trustees will know about the need to appoint a second trustee, and even fewer will know how to do so.[255] Furthermore, the appointment of a second trustee by an apparently sole owner would be suspicious to lawyers involved in the sale or mortgage.

Even if reasonable financial security is provided, should two trustees be free to sell a family home? We need to remember that the property is a home rather than an investment. If the trustees decide to sell, then this necessarily results in the loss of the beneficiaries' home. Yet, the problem is often exaggerated. In most cases, trustees and beneficiaries will be the same persons. There is no way in which one or more trustees can act against the wishes of the others without a court order: they must all sign any transfer. However, problems can arise where a beneficiary is not a trustee. Even then, it would be difficult to sell so as to defeat occupying beneficiaries, as few purchasers would buy the land in the face of an objecting and occupying beneficiary. More troublesome are mortgages, as in *Flegg*, because occupation is less likely to inhibit the transaction.

The Law Commission considered these questions in the 1980s and concluded[256] that beneficiaries in actual occupation should have to consent before overreaching can operate. Since *Boland*, purchasers have become used to the idea that inquiries should be made of beneficiaries in occupation and it would not be too onerous to extend this to purchasers from two trustees. These reforms are not implemented by TLATA and have not been accepted by the government.[257] More recently, questions have been asked whether overreaching is consistent with human rights and, in particular, the Article 1 (First Protocol) right to peaceful enjoyment of possessions and the right to respect for the home in Article 8.[258] Differing views have been expressed, and it is difficult to predict the likely outcome.

---

[253] *Birmingham Midshires Mortgage Services Ltd* v *Sabherwal* (1999) 80 P&CR 256; Dixon [2000] Conv 267.
[254] Law Com No 158, paras 2.54 et seq.
[255] Forgery, as in *Ahmed* v *Kendrick* (1987) 56 P&CR 120, is a more common problem.
[256] Law Com No 188; see especially paras 3.5, 4.1–4.3. See the criticism of Harpum [1990] CLJ 277 at pp 328 et seq. Note also the somewhat different proposals of Owen and Cahill [2017] Conv 26.
[257] (1998) 587 HL Deb WA213.
[258] See Goymour in *The Impact of the UK Human Rights Act on Private Law* (ed Hoffmann), Chapter 12, pp 287–288 and 297–298.

C. Consent requirements

It has been seen that the consent of stipulated persons may be required before trustees' powers are exercised.[259] Purchasers must ensure that consents are given, but TLATA, s 10 protects purchasers if the consent of at least two such persons has been obtained or they are infants. The trustees remain under a duty to obtain consent of all such persons (or, if infants, their parents or guardians).

D. Protection against irregularities

Purchasers face the danger that an irregularity in a sale might render them open to attack. It has been controversial as to which irregularities might have this effect. Following the analysis by Harpum,[260] the generally accepted test for the scope of overreaching is whether the trustees are acting intra vires.[261]

Ultra vires is clear if the trustees have no power to enter into the transaction (as when the trust deed excludes powers) or where a necessary consent has not been obtained. One of the problems is that TLATA, s 6 imposes duties on trustees, and it has been argued that this extends the scope of ultra vires.[262] This is especially problematic for cases of misuse of powers, such as raising money for the personal benefit of the trustees as in *Flegg* and *Sood*.[263] It is probable that the scope of ultra vires, with its attendant risks for purchasers, will be kept as narrow as possible. For other irregularities, it has been argued that LPA, s 2 confers protection[264] and that the purchaser will be liable only on the basis of knowing assistance in the breach (or unconscionable receipt). However, a preferable analysis may be that purchasers face no liability (even without s 2) as regards intra vires irregularities, at least without knowing assistance.

TLATA, s 16 is the source of a number of useful protections, some of which did not previously exist.[265] These are considered below. An initial observation is that s 16 does not apply to registered land; given the limited significance of unregistered land today, it is surprising to see so much detailed treatment in s 16. As will be seen, purchasers of registered land can rely upon the much more general provision in LRA, s 26 protecting against limitations which affect the validity of dispositions.

---

[259] TLATA, s 8(2).

[260] [1990] CLJ 277; approved by Peter Gibson LJ in *State Bank of India* v *Sood* [1997] Ch 276 at p 281.

[261] Morritt V-C in *National Westminster Bank plc* v *Malhan* [2004] EWHC 847 (Ch) at [43] seems to rely simply upon LPA, s 2 to justify overreaching. However, this was largely unreasoned and would render TLATA, s 16 largely redundant.

[262] Ferris and Battersby (2003) 119 LQR 94 at pp 98–108. This appears fully justified in the case of breach of s 6(8) (statutory restrictions on powers). There is some argument for its applying to s 6(6) (contravention of rules of statute, law or equity), but the approach in *Bagum* v *Hafiz* [2016] Ch 241 at [21] (in the s 14 context of 'functions') renders it very unlikely. The authors accept that breaches of s 6(5) (considering beneficiaries' rights) and (9) (taking care) do not cause ultra vires.

[263] A post-TLATA example might be *HSBC Bank plc* v *Dyche* [2010] 2 P&CR 58 (Gravells [2010] Conv 169), although the point is not developed.

[264] Ferris and Battersby (2002) 118 LQR 270. It is not clear whether LRA, s 26 (discussed below) applies to these irregularities: RJ Smith, *Plural Ownership*, pp 198–200.

[265] The wording of s 16 is justifiably criticised by Pascoe [2005] Conv 140.

(i) *Limitations on powers; consent requirements*

The trustees have a duty, under s 16(3), to bring such limitations (such as exclusion of the power of sale) and requirements to the attention of the purchaser. They do not invalidate any conveyance to a purchaser who does not have actual notice[266] of the limitation or requirement. This provision is needed because there would otherwise be a trap for purchasers, who might be unaware of any problem.[267] It is a new and useful form of purchaser protection. We have already seen that s 10 protects purchasers as regards multiple consents and consents required from minors.

(ii) *Consultation and other requirements*

Purchasers are under no obligation to check whether consultation requirements have been satisfied.[268] This repeats the previous law[269]; it makes sense because questions of consultation and taking beneficiaries' views into account can be very difficult for purchasers to assess.

The same protection is given in respect of trustees' duties to have regard to beneficiaries' rights (s 6(5)) and to obtain beneficiaries' consent prior to partition (s 7(3)).

(iii) *Contravention of other rules*

This applies as regards contravention of statutory or other rules (s 6(6)) or statutory restrictions on trustees in other legislation (s 6(8)). Purchasers are protected against invalidity of the conveyance unless they have actual notice of a contravention by the trustees.[270]

(iv) *Deeds of discharge*

The deed of discharge, introduced by TLATA,[271] is designed to deal with a problem which can occur after the trust is apparently at an end. Suppose that a trust provides for land to be held for a widow for life until remarriage and thereafter for the testator's son. If the widow remarries, the trustees will quite properly transfer the legal estate to the son. How can a purchaser from the son be sure that the widow had remarried so that the son is absolutely entitled? If there were no remarriage, then the trust would continue and the sale would have to be by two trustees. Requiring purchasers to delve into details of the beneficial interests would be inconsistent with the policy of the 1925 legislation that such interests should be hidden behind the curtain.

Fortunately, when trustees convey land on the termination of the trust, s 16(4) imposes a duty on them to execute a deed declaring that they are discharged from the trust.

---

[266] There is a strong case for 'actual notice' to include imputed notice: Ferris and Battersby [1998] Conv 168 at p 178.
[267] E.g. if the trusts are declared in a separate document from the conveyance to the trustees, or a consent requirement is implied.
[268] TLATA, s 16(1).
[269] LPA, s 26(3).
[270] TLATA, s 16(2).
[271] Its origins lie in the Settled Land Act 1925.

Purchasers who rely on such a deed are protected by s 16(5) against the possibility that the trust might still be continuing, provided that there is no actual notice of its continuing.

(v) *Termination of joint tenancy on death of a joint tenant*

A very similar problem arises on the termination of the trust on the death of one of two joint tenants. Suppose A and B are joint tenants. Following B's death, A wishes to sell the land. In principle, A can do so because survivorship operates on B's death: A is now the sole owner and the trust has come to an end.[272] Nevertheless, this depends upon B's not having severed the joint tenancy. In the nature of things, proving such a negative (no severance) is next to impossible; it was often necessary to appoint a second trustee to permit any necessary overreaching.

This needless complexity led to the Law of Property (Joint Tenants) Act 1964, which deemed the survivor to be solely and beneficially interested.[273] If there is a severance, then a memorandum of severance should be entered on the title deeds, in which case the statutory protection ceases to operate. If there is severance where title is registered, a restriction should be entered on the register. As with s 16, the 1964 Act does not apply to registered land (see s 3) and, unless warned by a restriction, purchasers are at risk of being bound by an overriding interest of a claimant in actual occupation.[274]

(vi) *The effect of purchaser protection*

Section 16 provides, as regards the limitations on powers and contravention of rules categories discussed above, that the irregularity does not 'invalidate the conveyance' where the purchaser does not have actual notice.

It is to be noted that the protection is given only to the purchaser from the trustees. Subsequent purchasers will, of course, be able to rely upon the first purchaser's protection. However, they are apparently given no protection where the initial purchaser had actual notice. This could have unfortunate consequences. Most obviously, a second purchaser (or mortgagee) may feel it necessary to make inquiries as to the circumstances of the first purchase.

As regards deeds of discharge, the purchaser is entitled to assume that the land is no longer subject to the trust. Should the trust in fact be continuing, presumably this means that a purchaser without actual notice takes free of it.[275] This protection applies to both first and subsequent purchasers. The consultation protection (s 16(1)) is that purchasers 'need not be concerned to see' that the requirements have been satisfied; it appears to give full protection to purchasers.

---

[272] *Re Cook* [1948] Ch 212.

[273] *Grindal* v *Hooper* (1999) 96/48 LS Gaz 41 (see Gravells [2000] Conv 461) holds that actual notice of the severance defeats the purchaser. Earlier views had been to the contrary: Jackson (1966) 30 Conv 27.

[274] Cooke [2004] Conv 41.

[275] Compare similar wording found in the Settled Land Act 1925: Stone [1984] Conv 354 at pp 356–358; Megarry and Wade, *The Law of Real Property* (8th edn), para A-013.

(vii) *At what stage does protection commence?*

If there is an irregularity, a beneficiary can prevent the proposed future sale or other transaction. Examples would be where a single trustee is intending to sell,[276] a consent requirement has been overlooked[277] or the statutory duty to consult beneficiaries has been flouted.[278] Let us assume that TLATA, s 16 would provide protection for the purchaser after conveyance. Does this protection operate on entry into a contract to buy, or only on the subsequent conveyance? Prior to TLATA, *Waller* v *Waller*[279] seems to have assumed that there is no protection until conveyance; apparently, the point was not argued. Presumably the same applies under TLATA; for irregularities covered by s 16(2) and (3) (limitations on powers, consents and contravention of other rules), this is confirmed by the statutory references to 'conveyance'.

(viii) *Registered land*

Although s 16(7) provides that the s 16 protections are inapplicable to registered land, LRA, s 26 protects purchasers against 'any limitation affecting the validity of a disposition'. Unsurprisingly, this is subject to any entry on the register.[280] Prior to s 26, it was thought that a beneficiary in actual occupation had an overriding interest which would defeat a purchase in contravention of a limitation. *Williams & Glyn's Bank Ltd* v *Boland*[281] provides an example in the context of purchase from a single trustee. It is very significant that s 26 contains no exception for overriding interests, so the danger for purchasers is greatly reduced.[282]

We must consider the scope and effect of s 26. The Law Commission makes it very clear that it is intended to cover such problems as restrictions on powers and consent requirements.[283] This seems uncontroversial. Does it apply to other problems, such as failure to consult or breach of other rules? The drafting of s 26 indicates that the limitations need not be imposed by the trust itself.[284] If so, it seems that the full range of irregularities covered by TLATA, s 16 is within the scope of s 26.[285]

Much more controversial is the possibility that the requirement of two trustees is a 'limitation' within s 26. If it is, then a purchaser from a single trustee could conclude that there are no limitations upon the powers of that proprietor. A reply that the limitation relates to the manner of disposal rather than the ultimate power to dispose appears unjustified: the same is true of both the two-trustee requirement and a consent requirement.

---

[276] *Waller* v *Waller* [1967] 1 WLR 451.

[277] *Re Herklots' Will Trusts* [1964] 2 All ER 66.

[278] *Waller* v *Waller* [1967] 1 WLR 451.

[279] [1967] 1 WLR 451. Compare sales under mortgagees' powers (p 617 below).

[280] A restriction would be normal, as notices are unavailable for interests under trusts of land: LRA, s 33(a).

[281] [1981] AC 487.

[282] *Mortgage Express* v *Lambert* [2017] Ch 93 at [28]. The context was unusual – the limitation seems to have resulted from an earlier transfer being capable of being set aside for unconscionability.

[283] Law Com No 271, paras 4.8–4.11. See Cooke [2002] Conv 11 at pp 23–25. Law Com CP 227, para 5.63 proposes strengthening s 26.

[284] Because s 26 expressly does not apply to limitations imposed by the Land Registration Act, the inference is that other statutory limitations are covered.

[285] This avoids the problems about the scope of ultra vires: p 357 above, especially n 262.

Yet such a wide interpretation of s 26 would overturn *Boland* and is universally rejected by commentators.[286] It was clearly not intended by the Law Commission, and it would be very surprising if the courts were to accept such a radical unplanned change.

Next, we must consider the effect of s 26. An initial point is that it protects only purchasers: no licence is given to trustees to commit breaches of trust. It provides a much simpler protection than s 16: the single relevant factor for s 26 is whether there is an entry on the register.[287] The complex provisions of s 16 deal differently with various irregularities. This is partly because, as protection on the register is not possible, the only viable control available for unregistered land is the knowledge of the purchaser.

Unlike s 16, LRA, s 26 makes no reference to actual notice. However, the Law Commission recognises[288] that a purchaser who is aware of a breach of trust may be liable for knowing receipt of trust property. This produces some sort of equivalent to the effect of s 16, but the clarity of s 16 is surely preferable to reliance upon general principles such as knowing receipt.

5. Trusts for sale

It has already been seen that many existing trusts for sale were converted into simple trusts by TLATA, though express trusts for sale retain that status. Trusts for sale are no longer implied by statute, and one expects that their express creation will be infrequent. In this section, we will investigate how far the remaining trusts for sale (old or new) differ from simple trusts of land.

It must be remembered that the TLATA management structure, described in this chapter, applies to trusts for sale. The major difference appears to lie in the very nature of the trust for sale. There is a trust (an obligation) to sell with a power to postpone sale.[289] If the trustees disagree as to whether to sell, then their lack of unanimity means that the power to postpone has not been exercised. It follows that the land should be sold.[290] By way of contrast, disagreement as to exercise of a power to sell means that the power has not been exercised.[291]

In many cases, this will not be of great significance once the court comes to consider an application under TLATA, s 14. However, if there are independent trustees and they have considered all the relevant factors, then the court may be reluctant to interfere with the normal application of equitable principles. A somewhat separate point is that the choice of a trust for sale after 1996 may well be a pointer to the fact that a sale really was intended by the settlor. This may make the court more reluctant to find a purpose for the trust and, accordingly, make sale more likely.

Probably the most controversial aspect of the trust for sale before TLATA lay in the doctrine of conversion.[292] The doctrine of conversion regarded the beneficiaries as having

---

[286] Ferris and Battersby (2003) 119 LQR 94 at p 121; Ferris in *Modern Studies in Property Law*, Vol 2 (ed Cooke), Chapter 6; Cooke, *The New Law of Land Registration*, p 59.

[287] There is no requirement of a transfer or of registration, although a purchaser who becomes aware of an irregularity between contract and transfer may be subject to knowing receipt liability.

[288] Law Com No 271, para 4.11.

[289] Under TLATA, s 4(1) this power cannot be excluded: n 110 above.

[290] *Re Mayo* [1943] Ch 302.

[291] *Re 90 Thornhill Road* [1970] Ch 261 (settled land power).

[292] Anderson (1984) 100 LQR 86; Warburton [1986] Conv 415.

interests in money (the future proceeds of sale) rather than in land. The idea was that equity treats as done that which ought to be done (sale). When the doctrine of conversion is applied to the typical family home, it is not difficult to see its artificiality: the co-owners would be startled to learn that they are interested merely in the proceeds of sale of the home they have just bought! Fortunately, the courts did not take the doctrine of conversion to all its logical conclusions; for example, they recognised beneficiaries' rights to occupy.

Following sustained criticism of the doctrine, TLATA virtually abolishes it for trusts for sale. Section 3 retrospectively provides that the land is not to be regarded as personal property. In particular, statutes referring to land will be construed so as to include beneficial interests under trusts of land, unless the legislation specifically states otherwise.[293] It should be stressed that conversion was never the basis for overreaching on sale by two trustees, notwithstanding a few misconceived dicta[294] to the contrary.

Further reading

Baker, A [2010] Conv 352: The judicial approach to 'exceptional circumstances': the impact of the Human Rights Act 1998.

Barnsley, D G [1998] CLJ 123: Co-owners' rights to occupy trust land.

Bright, S J [2009] Conv 378: Occupation rents and the Trusts of Land and Appointment of Trustees Act 1996: from property to welfare?

Ferris, G and Battersby, G (2003) 119 LQR 94: The general principles of overreaching and the modern legislative reforms, 1996–2002.

Fox, L (2005) 25 LS 201: Creditors and the concept of 'family home' – a functional analysis.

Harpum, C [1990] CLJ 277: Overreaching, trustees' powers and the reform of the 1925 legislation.

Watt, G [1997] Conv 263: Escaping section 8(1) provisions in 'new style' trusts of land.

---

[293] As in TLATA, Sched 3, para 12(3).

[294] *Irani Finance Ltd* v *Singh* [1971] Ch 59 at p 80, approved by Lord Oliver in *City of London BS* v *Flegg* [1988] AC 54 at pp 82–83. For devastating criticism, see MJ Prichard [1979] CLJ 251; Harpum [1990] CLJ 277 at pp 278–279.

17

Successive interests

Introduction

This chapter will concentrate upon management structures for land subject to successive interests, rather than details of individual successive interests. The law recognises the life interest and the fee simple as the two basic freehold estates capable of creation today (see Chapter 5). They can exist in possession, in remainder and in reversion. It is also possible for interests to be cut short artificially ('to Adrian on condition that he never smokes') and to be contingent ('to Bridget if she passes her driving test by the age of 20'). It may be said that there will be successive interests whenever the land is not held for a fee simple absolute in possession or a term of years absolute.

1. The rule against perpetuities

Before dealing with management structures, the topic of perpetuities requires brief mention. The ability of the settlor to determine who is to have rights to the land in the distant future has long been regulated by complex perpetuity rules. The purposes behind these rules are mixed.[1] In part, the existence of such distant interests renders the land difficult to sell or otherwise deal with. This was a problem when purchasers had to deal with all those with interests in the land, an obvious stumbling block if they included infants or unborn persons. This concern is largely met by trusts of land legislation designed to ensure that land can be managed by trustees, with the beneficial interests hidden behind the curtain.

Another factor is that the settlor's freedom to specify future interests confers undue control in the hands of a past generation (the dead hand rationale). The law needs to find a balance between the understandable wishes of donors and testators to determine what will happen to their property and, on the other side, preventing undue restriction of later generations. There is also an economic argument that property[2] tied up in this way is likely to be used in an overly conservative manner and, therefore, not to its full potential. These problems were most acute in past centuries when much of the land in the country was held under settlements, ensuring that it remained in the settlor's family. In modern society, it is relatively unusual to seek to tie up property for a long period. This change in the use of future interests has resulted in debate as to whether the rule is still justified. Indeed, some jurisdictions have abolished it.

---

[1] Morris and Leach, *The Rule Against Perpetuities* (2nd edn), pp 13–18; Maudsley, *The Modern Law of Perpetuities*, Chapter 9; Deech (1984) OxJLS 454.

[2] This argument concerns not so much specific assets (which may be sold) but rather the fund that it represents.

The nature of the perpetuity rules is that they control how far distant an interest can validly vest in interest. Vesting in interest takes place when all that stands between the interest holder and full enjoyment is a prior interest. It cannot be so vested if the beneficiary is unborn or undetermined, or some condition needs to be satisfied. An example may help. Suppose I leave property to Andrew for life, remainder to the first child of Brian to marry. If Brian has no children at the time of the gift, the remainder cannot be vested: the beneficiary is unborn. Even when there are children, we do not know which of them will marry first, and therefore, the gift is still not vested as the beneficiary is undetermined.[3] Once a child has married, then he or she will have a vested interest, even though Andrew is still alive and enjoying the property. On the death of Andrew, the child's interest will vest in possession (denoting current enjoyment), but the date of vesting in possession is of no concern to perpetuities.

The traditional perpetuity requirement was that every gift must vest in interest within the period of a life in being (that is, anybody alive at the date of the gift) plus 21 years. This formula was designed to validate gifts to children (of persons dead or alive) at the age of 21. At common law, the slightest possibility of vesting outside this period would render the gift void. The operation of perpetuities was complex and prone to disallow gifts that would probably vest in the relatively near future. Without careful drafting, many future gifts were at risk of invalidity. In 1964, legislation[4] relaxed the rules so as to validate gifts that in fact vest in interest during the perpetuity period: the 'wait and see' principle.

The Law Commission reviewed perpetuities and concluded[5] that some control should be retained, largely to limit 'the power of one generation to dictate the devolution of property'. Following their recommendations, the present perpetuity periods and, in particular, the stress on lives in being have been swept away (for new wills and instruments) by the Perpetuities and Accumulations Act 2009. Instead, there is a requirement that gifts should vest within 125 years. The law permits us to wait and see the extent to which this in fact occurs. This should be much simpler to apply.

2. The nineteenth-century need for reform of successive interests

The person who had a legal interest vested in possession (usually called the life tenant)[6] would manage the land and take the net proceeds (principally rent) as income. Where a house was part of the assets, the life tenant could possess it. On a day-to-day basis, this person would be perceived as the owner of the land. However, the life tenant could do nothing that bound the land after the end of the interest.

The restriction on what the life tenant could do caused severe problems.[7] Its significance was great because a very large proportion of land was held under settlements in the

---

[3] The gift 'to Bridget if she passes her driving test by the age of 20' is an example where some condition has to be fulfilled, though the identity of the beneficiary is certain: the gift is contingent, not vested.

[4] Perpetuities and Accumulations Act 1964. It contained numerous changes to the common law rules.

[5] Law Com No 251, welcomed by Sparkes (1998) 12 *Trust Law International* 148, although the reasoning is criticised by Gallanis [2000] CLJ 284.

[6] The life tenant may have an estate other than a life estate.

[7] See Simpson, *A History of the Land Law* (2nd edn), pp 239–240.

nineteenth century. If the life tenant could not sell the land, this might impede proper development, especially where land was required for housing or industrial use. Improvement of land is also made difficult. Life tenants might be reluctant to spend their own money on improvements when different generations (or different branches of the family) would benefit. Although the problems could be avoided by drafting settlements conferring the necessary powers, this was by no means always done. Problems could also be removed by a private Act of Parliament allowing a sale or other transaction, but this was no substitute for getting the settlement structure right to begin with.

The pressure for reform in the nineteenth century came up against the inertia of the powerful landed classes. It is important to appreciate that land had for centuries been the source of wealth and power. Any tampering with the landholding of powerful families was prone to be viewed with hostility, despite the fact that reform was required in the interests of those families as well as the country as a whole. A century and a half later, so much has changed that it is difficult to appreciate the earlier controversy. The idea that land should be concentrated in the senior male member of the family as the life tenant took a battering in the slaughter of the First World War, as well as by death duties that both diminished and discouraged the traditional large settlements. Quite apart from these factors, land is no longer the dominant source of wealth it once was: other assets (especially shares) are more significant today.

These changes must not blind us to the very real need for reform in the mid-nineteenth century, reform which culminated in the 1925 legislation.

3. The strict settlement and the Settled Land Act 1925

The most important change came in 1882, when the life tenant was given power to sell and otherwise deal with the land. It was natural to choose the life tenant (designated the tenant for life) because he (or, more rarely, she) would already be managing the land. The Settled Land Act 1925 took this a stage further by ensuring that the tenant for life had the legal fee simple absolute in possession. The legal estate is held as trustee. There are also separate trustees (a minimum of two) of the settlement, whose principal role is to hold capital money arising from sale. Whilst it might be safe for the tenant for life to hold the land and exercise powers, holding a large sum of money might provide too much of a temptation.

Purchasers are protected by overreaching the beneficial interests onto the proceeds of sale, provided that purchase money is paid to the trustees of the settlement. In addition, the purchaser does not need to read complex trust deeds in order to confirm the identity of the tenant for life and trustees. Instead, the purchaser can rely (indeed, has to rely) on what is known as the vesting deed, a document drawn up so as to include only the information that purchasers need to know. Technically, the strict settlement[8] under the Settled Land Act 1925 is a masterpiece. The old problems are solved in an elegant manner by giving both powers and legal title to the tenant for life, whilst the protection of purchasers is comprehensive.[9] The policy that the land should always be capable of being sold or otherwise dealt with is emphasised by striking down any attempt to limit the powers of the tenant for

---

[8] The term 'strict settlement' is commonly used to describe a Settled Land Act 1925 (hereafter SLA) settlement. The origin of the term lies in a particular form of nineteenth-century settlement, for which the SLA was especially appropriate.

[9] Despite some minor flaws, most notably illustrated by *Weston* v *Henshaw* [1950] Ch 510.

life.[10] In practice, the scheme became little more than a white elephant. It involves great complexity, not only in statutory drafting but, far more important, in its day-to-day operation. Such complexity breeds not only expense but also error. In any event, the social and settlement structure for which it was designed was destined for rapid and terminal decline. The result reached several decades ago was that strict settlements were rarely used and then often by mistake. Those who still wished to create settlements were likely, often for taxation reasons, to choose settlements involving discretionary trusts,[11] for which the Settled Land Act 1925 was not really designed.

4. Trusts for sale[12]

The 1925 legislation provided settlors with a choice between the strict settlement and the trust for sale. The trust for sale vests control in the trustees, thereby escaping the conveyancing and management problems encountered in strict settlements. Besides, the trust for sale had several positive advantages. It could be more readily used for a mixed settlement of land and other assets, and it offered greater flexibility by permitting the settlor to require consents before sale.

Perhaps the most important contrast with the strict settlement lies in the use of independent trustees to manage the land. Although the powers of the tenant for life in settled land were based upon nineteenth-century practice, to modern eyes it is strange for crucial decisions to be taken by somebody who has a beneficial interest. This is especially so because the interests of a life interest holder and a remainderman may often be opposed.[13] The remainderman may, indeed, be seen as having a greater stake in the property. The idea of the head of the family controlling the family assets, to the virtual exclusion of siblings and adult children, is foreign to today's society.

5. Reform under the Trusts of Land and Appointment of Trustees Act 1996

Dissatisfaction with the structure of the law had been expressed for decades.[14] Strict settlements and trusts for sale had quite different rules and procedures, producing an unduly complex legal structure and ample scope for confusion. There might be some real differences (strict settlements being designed for beneficiary control and trusts for sale for trustee control), but they scarcely justified two forms of settlement.

Following Law Commission recommendations,[15] the Trusts of Land and Appointment of Trustees Act 1996 (hereafter TLATA) enacts that no future strict settlements can be created,[16] though pre-TLATA strict settlements continue to be governed by the Settled

---

[10] SLA, s 106. The modern trust of land permits restrictions on powers: Trusts of Land and Appointment of Trustees Act 1996, s 8.
[11] Whereby trustees allocate income amongst a class of beneficiaries on a discretionary basis.
[12] Lightwood (1927) 3 CLJ 59.
[13] Principally in terms of the merits of obtaining the highest income possible, as opposed to long-term capital appreciation.
[14] Lewis (1938) 54 LQR 576; Potter (1944) 8 Conv NS 147; Grove (1961) 24 MLR 123.
[15] Law Com No 181
[16] TLATA, s 2.

Land Act 1925.[17] Trusts for sale can still be created,[18] although we have seen that in Chapter 16, they are a species of trusts of land and subject to the management structure for trusts of land. It is interesting that virtually none of the special features of the strict settlement have been thought worthy of adoption.[19]

One point is worth reiterating. Section 8 permits the settlor to exclude any of the trustees' powers. This means that a settlor could take away the power of sale and tie the land up for as long as the rule against perpetuities permits. In earlier times, the absence of powers (especially to sell) necessitated the reforms from the nineteenth century onwards. The change in the use of settlements over the past century and a half has been such that the risk of exclusion of powers of sale is no longer perceived to be significant: it is revealing that the proposal leading to s 8 merited only fleeting mention by the Law Commission. It is, perhaps, the mark of a mature system that it provides a comprehensive structure for the operation of trusts of land, without feeling the need to impose compulsory provisions on settlors. However, it remains to be seen how many settlors will use their new-found freedom. It seems likely that there will be few.

Section 6 confers unlimited powers of management on trustees (subject to restriction under s 8); see Chapter 16. This does not mean that the settlor cannot confer other powers or duties on the trustees. Subject to the normal constraints of the law of trusts, the settlor can insert whatever terms are appropriate. These will generally relate to the beneficial interests but might include a direction to sell (the traditional trust for sale), lease or, probably, delegate management powers.

6. Beneficiary control over management

A distinctive feature of the strict settlement is that the land is managed by the life interest holder. Such management will sometimes be appropriate for trusts set up today: it is not restricted to nineteenth-century-style settlements. Take a modern example. Caroline owns the large house in which she and David live. She wishes David to have the house for life on her death and their children to have it thereafter. The idea that separate trustees could dictate how and when the house should be sold is repugnant to both Caroline and David. They wish him to live there as long as he wishes. If the house is too large for him, then he should take the decision to sell, and it should not be open to the trustees to say that it is a bad time to sell large houses and that he should stay there for a few more years. Of course, most trustees are likely to give great weight to the settlor's wishes in the exercise of their discretion, but Caroline may still wish the decision to lie in David's hands.

There are a number of ways in which David, as a beneficiary, may be given a role. Most obviously, he may be made a trustee, although it would be unwise to have a single trustee and appointment of others will water down David's control. A certain amount can also be achieved by requiring the consent of David to sale and other transactions. Again, this has some effect, but it does not, for example, permit David to require that the land should be sold. Rather differently, it is possible to provide that David has a right to reside.

---

[17] Ibid, ss 1(3), 2(1).
[18] Ibid, ss 1, 4.
[19] One exception is the deed of discharge, which protects purchasers when the trust has come to an end: see p 358 above.

Most importantly, however, TLATA, s 9 permits the trustees to delegate management of the property to David. The power to delegate was described by Lord Mackay LC[20] as designed 'to reproduce the functional equivalent of a strict settlement'. This power is strengthened by TLATA, in that (unlike the previous law)[21] it extends to selling the land. Today, trustees can delegate any of their functions relating to the land to a beneficiary of full age entitled to an interest in possession. Delegation under s 9(1) is discretionary, but can the settlor direct the trustees to delegate? Unless s 9 is treated as an exhaustive code for delegation, the answer would appear to be yes.[22] In any event, if the trustees refuse to delegate, then an application may be made to court for the exercise of its statutory discretion under TLATA, s 14, and the intentions of the settlor provide a relevant consideration.

Delegation should be by power of attorney executed by all the trustees.[23] The power of attorney may be relied upon by purchasers as proof that the trustees were entitled to delegate to that person.[24] The power may be revoked by a single trustee and terminates automatically on the appointment of a new trustee or the beneficiary's ceasing to have an interest in possession.[25] It should be noted that persons dealing with holders of powers of attorney are protected against unknown revocation of the power.[26] The beneficiary has the duties and liabilities of a trustee, but does not have powers of sub-delegation and cannot be the recipient of capital money.[27]

An important consideration is whether the trustees are liable for the acts and defaults of the beneficiary to whom powers are delegated. Too wide a liability could lead to a reluctance to exercise the power to delegate.[28] The Trustee Act 2000 restructured the duty of care of all trustees, whether or not there is a trust of land. TLATA, s 9A (inserted by the 2000 Act) applies the new statutory duty of care to decisions relating to delegation and to keeping it under review: clearly, there may now be a breach if trustees ignore warning signs that the beneficiary in question may act improperly. Otherwise, trustees are not liable for default by the beneficiary.[29]

Further reading

Gallanis, T P [2000] CLJ 284: The rules against perpetuities and the Law Commission's flawed philosophy.

Sparkes, P (1998) 12 *Trust Law International* 148: Perpetuities reform.

---

[20] 570 HL Deb col 1535.

[21] Law of Property Act 1925, s 29.

[22] Cf Whitehouse and Hassall, *Trusts of Land, Trustee Delegation and the Trustee Act 2000* (2nd edn), para 2.85. See also p 336, n 110, above.

[23] TLATA, s 9(1), (3). A deed is required: Powers of Attorney Act 1971, s 1, as amended by Law of Property (Miscellaneous Provisions) Act 1989, Sched 1, para 6.

[24] TLATA, s 9(2).

[25] Ibid, s 9(3), (4) (different rules apply where there is delegation to two or more beneficiaries jointly).

[26] Powers of Attorney Act 1971, s 5; there is similar protection for the holder of the power.

[27] TLATA, s 9(7).

[28] This argument caused the rejection of the Law Commission's proposal for wide liability.

[29] TLATA, s 9A(6).

18

Leases: types and requirements

Introduction

The essence of the lease is readily grasped: the use of another's land, usually for a specific time in return for the payment of rent. The Law Commission has described it as temporary property ownership.[1] The lease is tremendously important because it enables land to be enjoyed without the capital cost and commitment involved in owning it. Most homes used to be held under leases, but the growth of home ownership has changed the picture quite considerably. Nevertheless, millions of homes are still held under leases from private landlords or local authorities; the legal regulation of this area remains of great importance.

So far as commercial property is involved, it is usual for shops, offices and factories to be leased. Very often, the lessee will not have adequate resources to purchase the premises, and the lease gives added flexibility in moving to different premises later on. Similar points apply to agricultural land: it has long been common for land to be farmed by tenant farmers, frequently lacking the resources to purchase the freehold.

It is easy to comprehend the great social and economic importance of leases. The tenant is generally regarded as having a more significant stake in the land than the courts have recognised. The result has been statutory intervention to improve the position of tenants. Intervention has commonly taken the form of control over rent levels and restricting the landlord's ability to terminate the lease, even where it has ended according to its terms. Obligations to keep the property in good repair are also found, as is the right in certain cases for tenants to purchase the freehold. Intervention operates differently according to the type of property involved: it is more invasive of landlords' rights in residential tenancies than in agricultural and business tenancies. Details of these statutory provisions lie outside this text, but their importance should not be underestimated.

Lengths and types of leases

The lease is found in many different forms: it has sufficient flexibility to render it suitable for a wide range of circumstances. One might take an example of a 10-year lease of shop premises at a full rent.[2] Such leases are very common and fit most people's ideas as to what a lease is. Very different is a 999-year lease in return for a substantial capital sum (a premium, or fine) and a nominal rent. Strictly speaking, there is no need for any rent, but it is usual to stipulate for a nominal sum, or else one peppercorn (hence the term 'peppercorn

---

[1] Law Com No 174, para 3.26.
[2] An average rent would be around 3.5–5.2% of the value of retail and office premises.

rent'). The economic effect of such a lease is virtually identical to a fee simple: the lease is likely to be chosen because covenants are more easily enforced in a lease than on a grant of the fee simple. Halfway between these examples would be a 99-year lease with a mix-ture of rent[3] and premium. This may be seen as a useful tool by a landlord who can foresee the need to redevelop the site in the future.

A feature of all leases is that they can be sold and assigned to purchasers, even though invariably the landlord's consent is required. If there is a premium, the lease is likely to have a high commercial value. Where there is a full rent, the value of the lease will depend upon the extent to which the rent differs from the current market rent. If a lease has a rent above current levels, then it will have a negative value: a 'purchaser' of the lease will demand a payment in return for having to pay an uneconomic rent.[4]

In contrast to these long leases, a weekly tenant holds land on exactly that basis: either party can give a week's notice terminating the tenancy. Such 'periodic tenancies' are highly flexible because the lease may in fact continue for many years. They may also be monthly, quarterly or yearly. The periodic tenancy is of particular value where the parties are reluctant to commit themselves to a specific period: its inherent flexibility also avoids the need for renewals as required for fixed-term leases. Many residential leases were peri-odic until the mid-twentieth century. As we shall see,[5] periodic tenancies can be implied by the courts where a person has been allowed into possession and pays rent. One result is that some notice has to be given to the tenant before eviction can take place,[6] although one cannot pretend that the courts provided tenants with more than very limited protection.

The history of leases

The lease has had a strange history as a proprietary interest.[7] Originally a mere contractual right, actions were developed by the end of the fifteenth century to give it full protection. The nature of those actions was different from those for freehold interests, and this led to its having the strange status as a form of chattel, a 'chattel real'. This had consequences for inheritance rules, fortunately no longer relevant today. Paradoxically, the new lease-hold actions had such advantages that (with the help of fictions) they were later used to protect freehold interests. A further point is that, because the lease did not involve freehold tenure, it was not subject to the rules[8] prohibiting the creation of new tenurial (landlord and tenant) relationships.

Fortunately, little of this history has much impact on the modern law. The lease can be regarded as constituting, in most cases, an estate in the land on a par with freehold estates, although obviously with special rules.[9] Nevertheless, the continued existence of the

---

[3] Inflation has a dramatic effect on the rent payable. It is usual for modern leases (unless shorter than about five years) to contain terms allowing for rent to be increased periodically.

[4] The lessee's position is analogous to an owner whose property value has dropped below the amount of a mortgage and who therefore has a 'negative equity'.

[5] See p 397 below.

[6] The yearly tenancy was especially valuable to agricultural tenants because it recognises the right to remain on the land for the entire growing season: Lord Kenyon CJ in *Doe d Martin & Jones* v *Watts* (1797) 7 TR 83 at p 85 (101 ER 866 at pp 867–868).

[7] Simpson, *A History of the Land Law* (2nd edn), pp 71–78, 92–93.

[8] Statute Quia Emptores 1290.

[9] Harwood (2000) 20 LS 503 criticises the law's approach to leases, especially the chattel real concept.

tenurial relationship between landlord and tenant has some consequences. It explained the right of the landlord to distrain for unpaid rent; that is, seize goods of the tenant on the land. Today, this has been replaced by commercial rent arrears recovery.[10]

Tenancies and estates

Leases can be viewed as relationships as much as estates. Our concept of an estate is enjoyment by time, whether a specified period (leases) or indeterminate (freeholds). There are two forms of tenancy that are not enjoyed by reference to time: they are tenancies rather than estates.

The first and most significant is the tenancy at will. If the owner of land allows another into possession without stipulating any period, then the courts regard the possessor as a tenant at will. This means that the possessor is not a trespasser; it enables the landlord to exercise commercial rent arrears recovery and the tenant to sue third parties in trespass. The tenancy at will cannot be considered as an estate, as its nature is that either party may determine it without prior notice; there is no right that can survive sale of the land.

The second such tenancy is the tenancy at sufferance. This is designed for the case where a tenant 'holds over' on the termination of a lease. If the landlord objects to holding over, then the former tenant is a trespasser. If the landlord consents, then there will be a tenancy at will or periodic tenancy. The tenancy at sufferance therefore operates where consent has neither been given nor refused: it avoids treating a tenant under an expired lease as a trespasser. As with tenancies at will, it can be terminated by either party without prior notice.

The lease is one of the two legal estates recognised by s 1 of the Law of Property Act 1925. The reason for this is plain: the essence of the lease is use of the land. This would be impracticable if the lease did not bind purchasers.[11] Tenancies at will and at sufferance are not estates and therefore outside the limits imposed by s 1. They can therefore continue as legal tenancies, although this will rarely be of any significance.

1. Requirements of leases

A. Certainty requirements: rent, commencement and length

That there are certainty requirements for leases comes as no surprise: certainty is required for most legal transactions. It may be observed that a lease also constitutes a contract between the parties, so that the law of contract provides a natural source of rules for leases.[12] However, the lease certainty rules differ from contractual rules in some crucial respects.

Rent

Taking rent first, it should be noted that a lease can exist without rent. Although doubts had occasionally been expressed,[13] the rule was unambiguously confirmed by the Court of

---

[10] Tribunals, Courts and Enforcement Act 2007, p 445 below.

[11] See Chapter 6 above. Leases over seven years have to be registered: most shorter leases are overriding interests (Land Registration Act 2002 (hereafter LRA), ss 4(1)(c)–(f), 27(2)(b), Sched 3, para 1).

[12] A good example is provided by frustration: *National Carriers Ltd v Panalpina (Northern) Ltd* [1981] AC 675 (p 410 below).

[13] *Scrimgeour v Waller* [1981] 1 EGLR 68 at p 69. See also p 395 below.

Appeal in *Ashburn Anstalt* v *Arnold*.[14] Given that the statutory definition[15] of terms of years absolute stipulates 'whether or not at a rent', this is scarcely surprising. As regards certainty, problems may arise if the parties specify that the rent shall be as agreed in the future. This is especially likely where there is provision for increasing the rent, or for renewal of the lease at a different rent. Can the clause be attacked as being merely an agreement to agree? Some points are quite clear. The courts will give effect to a clause which produces a formula that can be applied. For example, a reference to market value will suffice.[16] Nor is it a problem that the rent may vary from year to year.[17]

Agreements which simply provide that the rent shall be at a figure to be agreed cause greater difficulty. Where the lease is already running, such a term in a rent review clause has been upheld, the courts relying on cases from other contractual contexts.[18] It is more difficult where such a provision governs the initial rent. Despite some authority[19] that rent is such a crucial factor that the level must be specified, it seems that such provisions will be enforced.[20]

Commencement

A long-established requirement is that leases must have a certain beginning and a certain end.[21] So far as the date of commencement is concerned, it should be noted that a lease may commence either immediately or at such future date (up to 21 years)[22] as the parties stipulate. A lease commencing at a future date may be seen as a form of future interest; it is exceptional after 1925 as being a future legal estate.[23] Because this constitutes a trap for purchasers, the Land Registration Act 2002 now requires such leases (for whatever length) to be registered.[24] So far as certainty is concerned, many problems will be solved by the presumption that leases take effect immediately.[25] Further, any initial uncertainty can be cured if there is a formula which produces certainty before the lease is to take effect.[26]

Contracts for leases provide greater difficulty. First, it should be noted that a contract to grant a lease in more than 21 years' time is unaffected by the statutory requirement for leases to take effect within 21 years. This requirement applies only if the lease itself, when granted, is to take effect within 21 years from that grant.[27] This may be illustrated by two examples. A contract in 2018 to grant a lease in the year 2020, to be effective in 2045, is void: there is to be a gap of 25 years between grant and taking effect. In the second

---

[14] [1989] Ch 1. See also *Knight's Case* (1588) 5 Co Rep 54b at p 55a (77 ER 137 at p 138); *Canadian Imperial Bank of Commerce* v *Bello* (1991) 64 P&CR 48; *Skipton BS* v *Clayton* (1993) 66 P&CR 223.

[15] Law of Property Act 1925 (hereafter LPA), s 205(1)(xxvii).

[16] *Brown* v *Gould* [1972] Ch 53; *Sudbrook Trading Estate Ltd* v *Eggleton* [1983] 1 AC 444.

[17] *Ex p Voisey* (1882) 21 Ch D 442.

[18] *Beer* v *Bowden* [1981] 1 WLR 522.

[19] *King's Motors (Oxford) Ltd* v *Lax* [1970] 1 WLR 426 (Burgess V-C).

[20] *Corson* v *Rhuddlan BC* (1990) 59 P&CR 185; Martin [1990] Conv 288. The provision was treated as a condition precedent and unenforceable in *BJ Aviation Ltd* v *Pool Aviation Ltd* [2002] 2 P&CR 369, but not because rent possesses any special status.

[21] Co Litt 45b.

[22] LPA, s 149(3).

[23] See the definition of term of years absolute in LPA, s 205(1)(xxvii).

[24] See pp 244 and 274 above for more detail.

[25] *Doe d Phillip & Walters* v *Benjamin* (1839) 9 Ad&E 644 (112 ER 1356).

[26] Co Litt 45b: id certum est quod certum reddi potest.

[27] *Re Strand & Savoy Properties Ltd* [1960] Ch 582.

example, a contract in 2018 to grant a lease in 2040, to be effective in 2045, is valid: there is a gap of only five years between grant and taking effect.

Whilst it seems difficult to perceive any rational policy explaining those examples, the convenient result is that covenants to renew long leases are valid. A covenant to renew a lease exceeding 21 years will almost invariably be exercised more than 21 years from the date of the covenant. For such covenants to be void would be highly inconvenient and difficult to justify.

If a contract for a lease fails to specify the date upon which the lease is to be granted, it is void. By contrast, in a contract to sell land, it can be implied that completion will take effect within a reasonable time.[28] In *Harvey* v *Pratt*,[29] the Court of Appeal declined to apply similar reasoning to agreements for leases: authority requiring a commencement date was too strong.[30] Whilst this is reasonable if the parties leave the date wholly indeterminate, it is difficult to comprehend if the delay is simply to allow the detailed terms of the lease to be settled. It is incomprehensible that an agreement to sell land is valid without stipulating the date of completion, whilst a similar agreement to grant a 999-year lease is invalid.[31]

The rule was explained by Davies LJ in *Harvey*[32] on the basis that the commencement date is crucial to the length of the lease, whereas with a sale of the freehold, there is no uncertainty as to what is being sold. This doubtless is a distinction, but it scarcely justifies the rule. At least in the modern law, it appears little more than a technical trap, not required for any good reason. Its technicality is demonstrated by the alacrity with which judges accept licences to commence at an unstated time.[33] If there were a serious certainty problem, this would infect licences just as much as leases. It is pleasing to add that Neuberger J in *Liverpool CC* v *Walton Group plc*[34] was prepared to find certainty by implying that the lease would commence on execution of the lease, which the agreement provided to be six weeks after a 'decision notice' that the tenant had complied with conditions precedent. In the context of a 999-year lease, following substantial advance expenditure by the tenant, the result makes good sense.

Length

The most controversial certainty issue concerns the length of the lease. The parties can agree on a lease for any period, however long or short. However, the period must be certain at the time the lease takes effect. Uncertainty at the time of grant is not fatal if it is cured before the lease takes effect. Thus, a lease is valid if it is to take effect in a year's time for the same period as for a lease of adjoining property, to be obtained by the lessee in the meantime.[35]

[28] *Johnson* v *Humphrey* [1946] 1 All ER 460.
[29] [1965] 1 WLR 1025.
[30] See especially *Marshall* v *Berridge* (1881) 19 Ch D 233, although a condition precedent may have prevented such an implication.
[31] *McQuaid* v *Lynam* [1965] IR 564 at p 574.
[32] [1965] 1 WLR 1025 at p 1027; see also Megarry J in *Brown* v *Gould* [1972] Ch 53 at p 61.
[33] *James* v *Lock* [1978] 1 EGLR 1; *Secretary of State for Social Services* v *Beavington* [1982] 1 EGLR 13.
[34] [2002] 1 EGLR 149; Butt (2002) 76 ALJ 86.
[35] Blackstone, *Commentaries on the Laws of England*, Vol ii, p 143.

Two elements of the certainty rule should be noted. First, the law is concerned with *maximum* duration. Most leases may be cut short by forfeiture if there is a breach, but this has never caused certainty problems. The same applies to clauses allowing the lease to be terminated on the happening of an uncertain event.[36] The second element is that periodic tenancies do not fall foul of the law. The point is not that periodic tenancies are outside the rule,[37] but rather that at any point in time, the maximum period is certain: each party has power to determine it. The fact that failure to give notice will cause it to be prolonged indefinitely does not detract from this.[38]

The operation of the certainty requirement is well illustrated by *Lace v Chantler*.[39] The parties agreed that the lease should last for the duration of the Second World War. The Court of Appeal held this to be void. Because such leases were common, the result was inconvenient and led to remedial legislation for wartime leases.[40] It is important to note that *Lace* does not rely upon contractual uncertainty reasoning: it is not suggested that the courts cannot decide what the ending of the war means.[41] Rather, there is a long-established rule that the maximum duration must be specified and certain at the date the lease takes effect.

Lace was approved by the House of Lords in *Prudential Assurance Co Ltd v London Residuary Body*,[42] rejecting an attempt to use a periodic tenancy analysis to circumvent the rule.[43] This should not invalidate a restriction on termination of a periodic tenancy for a certain maximum time.[44] In an attack on the conclusion he felt compelled to reach, Lord Browne-Wilkinson observed in *Prudential*[45] that 'No one has produced any satisfactory rationale for the genesis of this rule. No one has been able to point to any useful purpose that it serves at the present day.' It is, of course, a trap for the unwary. A competent drafts-man can simply create a lease for a term of years terminable on the relevant event.

The issue went to the Supreme Court in *Mexfield Housing Co-operative Ltd v Berrisford*,[46] in which the lease was to last until the tenant failed to pay the rent. With seven justices sitting, one might have expected *Lace* and *Prudential* to be challenged. However (to the evident disappointment of some of the justices), the appeal was argued and decided on narrower grounds. Relying on old authority,[47] a lease for an uncertain period would be treated as a lease for life. Provided that there is consideration, this is then converted by s 149(6) of the Law of Property Act 1925[48] into a lease for 90 years

---

[36] *Bass Holdings Ltd v Lewis* [1986] 2 EGLR 40; see also p 406 below.
[37] *Prudential Assurance Co Ltd v London Residuary Body* [1992] 2 AC 386; criticised by Kohler (1993) 46 CLP Part I, pp 69–81.
[38] Ibid, at p 394.
[39] [1944] KB 368.
[40] Validation of War-time Leases Act 1944. The legislation fitted such leases into the conventional structure of a lease for 10 years, determinable on notice following the end of the war.
[41] It was recognised that a lease for 99 years determinable on the ending of the war would have been valid.
[42] [1992] 2 AC 386; Bright (1993) 13 LS 38.
[43] *Re Midland Railway Company's Agreement* [1971] Ch 725, applied in *Ashburn Anstalt v Arnold* [1989] Ch 1.
[44] *Breams Property Investment Co Ltd v Stroulger* [1948] 2 KB 1 (maximum of three years on the facts); see also *Wallis v Semark* [1951] 2 TLR 222.
[45] [1992] 2 AC 386 at p 396; it was 'difficult to think of a more unsatisfactory outcome'. Sparkes (1993) 109 LQR 93 defends the rule.
[46] [2012] 1 AC 955; Bright (2012) 128 LQR 337.
[47] This has been criticised by Low (2012) 75 MLR 401, Butt (2012) 86 ALJ 515 and Roche [2016] Conv 302.
[48] See p 406 below.

terminable on death and on the failure to pay rent. In *Mexfield*, this ensured that there was an effective lease. This is an ingenious solution but gives rise to problems. As recognised by the Supreme Court, it does not apply to leases to companies (which do not have lives) and problems are quite likely to arise because there is a 90-year term. Most obviously, formality and registration rules will have to be complied with.

The impact of *Mexfield* may be significantly limited by *Southward Housing Co-operative Ltd v Walker*.[49] Hildyard J raised the question (left open in *Mexfield*) whether a contrary intention would preclude a life interest. He concluded that it was not necessary to prove an intention that there be a life interest, but that an intention that there should not be such a right would be fatal. Even if this is permissible reading of *Mexfield*,[50] was the fact that *Southward* was set up as a weekly tenancy (with its provisions relating to notice to quit rather than forfeiture) really enough to prove such a contrary intention? It comes perilously close to limiting *Mexfield* to its facts, something that would be surprising on reading *Mexfield*.

The Supreme Court[51] in *Mexfield* was also prepared to adopt a contractual analysis. If it cannot take effect as a lease, the agreement can be treated as a contractual licence: this was thought more faithful to the parties' intentions than finding a periodic tenancy free of the termination restriction. It can then be enforced as a matter of contract. The contractual solution would, of course, be of no use if the land were to be sold (licences do not bind purchasers), nor would it appear to attract the many rules applying to leases.

Criticism of the rules relating to length

Like Lord Browne-Wilkinson, several of the justices in *Mexfield* expressed unease with the certainty rule. Is there any way in which it can be explained? Perhaps the only answer lies in the core of our thinking as to freehold and leasehold estates.[52] The nature of a freehold estate is that it lasts for an indeterminate time. This may be for life (life estate), indefinitely (fee simple absolute) or until some uncertain time (conditional or determinable interest). The lease is fundamentally different as being based upon a specific period. This underpins, of course, the old rule treating leases for uncertain periods as leases for life. The problem in each of *Lace*, *Prudential* and *Mexfield* is that the parties were intending, despite the uncertain period, to create leases rather than anything else. Where it applies, the s 149(6) analysis enables this to be achieved. For leases to companies, a freehold analysis (based on a determinable fee simple) would look quite inappropriate. Indeed, since 1977, it has been impossible to attach a rent to a freehold interest.[53]

---

[49] [2016] Ch 443; Roche [2016] Conv 302. The decision seems to have been influenced by the problems (Hildyard J discusses them in detail) in operating forfeiture if *Mexfield* were to apply. The lease did not contain provisions relating to forfeiture, though Hildyard J was eventually able to make forfeiture work.

[50] A proposition which Lees and Petrenko deny: [2015] L&T Rev 212.

[51] Baroness Hale preferred not to express any opinion. This analysis was applied in *Southward*; prolonged failure to pay rent meant that it was of no use to the occupier.

[52] Williams [2015] CLJ 592 explains it in terms of the doctrinal basis for estates, in particular that no estate is recognised as lasting forever.

[53] Rentcharges Act 1977. There are exceptions, but none is applicable to a straightforward rent for the use of property.

B. Exclusive possession

(i) *Early developments*

The role of exclusive possession provides the starting point for some of the most difficult and controversial property analyses in recent decades. One relatively clear proposition is that every lease must involve exclusive possession. Indeed, it may be argued that it is the single factor lying at the core of all landlord and tenant relationships. If we consider tenancies at will and at sufferance, it can be seen that other factors such as a term and rent may be absent: all we find is exclusive possession.

The rule is well illustrated by *Clore* v *Theatrical Properties Ltd*.[54] The 'lessee' had 'front of the house' rights at a theatre, that is, the right to sell refreshments and programmes and to manage cloakrooms. Despite the arrangement being worded as a lease, it was held to be no more than a licence to enter the land for the specified purposes. That the right was exclusive, in the sense that nobody was to compete, was insufficient to give exclusive possession. In an earlier case,[55] a simple point had been used to illustrate the distinction. If there were a problem with the lights, then it would be put right by the grantor. If there were exclusive possession, then the grantor would have no right to enter and such work would have to be undertaken by the lessee. Another clear example of a right not amounting to exclusive possession was the use for 13 hours a day of a stall at Buffalo Bill's Wild West exhibition.[56]

The requirement of exclusive possession is so fundamental that it has been rarely challenged. It can be seen as the means of drawing the line between leasehold interests and rights such as easements and profits.[57] The many cases dealing with what counts as exclusive possession will be considered below.

Is exclusive possession conclusive of a landlord and tenant relationship?

This question is far more controversial. There are some obvious examples where exclusive possession is not conclusive, as where the possession is attributable to a freehold estate or where it is without permission (adverse possession). Otherwise, the common law approach was to find a tenancy whenever there was exclusive possession.[58] This was even extended to situations where no rent was being paid and the relationship did not have the feel of a tenancy. For example, a purchaser allowed into occupation before completion would be a tenant at will,[59] as would be a relative permitted to live in a house.[60]

As between landlord and tenant, up to a century ago the common law consequences of there being a tenancy rather than a licence were limited as regards short-term agreements. The landlord would have the power to distrain for arrears of rent, whilst the tenant would have the right to sue third parties in trespass and, if there were a periodic tenancy or term of years, to retain possession until the necessary notice was given or the term expired. The question whether there was a lease or licence was usually litigated in very different

---

[54] [1936] 3 All ER 483.
[55] Rigby LJ in *Daly* v *Edwardes* (1900) 83 LT 548 at p 551, upheld (1901) 85 LT 650.
[56] *Rendell* v *Roman* (1893) 9 TLR 192.
[57] See p 520 below.
[58] See, e.g., *Glenwood Lumber Co Ltd* v *Phillips* [1904] AC 405.
[59] *Doe d Tomes* v *Chamberlaine* (1839) 5 M&W 14 (151 ER 7).
[60] *Doe d Groves* v *Groves* (1847) 10 QB 486 (116 ER 185).

contexts, often relating to the right to vote or liability for various forms of taxation. The parties themselves would very rarely bother whether there was a lease or a licence. That is not to say that it was never significant,[61] rather that there was no reason to negotiate for one rather than the other. The landlord who wanted to create merely a transient interest would be perfectly happy with a periodic tenancy or tenancy at will.[62]

Twentieth-century developments

The effect of there being a lease has become very different. Statutory regulation of the landlord and tenant relationship restricted the rights of landlords, especially the right to regain possession. This produced two principal effects relevant to the present discussion. Initially, the courts were reluctant to apply the full panoply of statutory regulation where the relationship was not the archetypal lease: an arm's-length agreement for the payment of rent in return for exclusive possession.

In *Booker* v *Palmer*,[63] an owner agreed that his cottage could be occupied rent-free by persons made homeless by wartime bombing. The Court of Appeal held that this created a mere licence, terminable by the owner at any time. There was a similar result where a landlord allowed the daughter of a deceased tenant (the daughter and tenant had both lived in the premises) to stay temporarily after her mother's death, whilst refusing a new tenancy.[64] The court obviously thought it wrong for the landlord to have to evict the daughter immediately on the mother's death in order to avoid a tenancy protected by the legislation. The courts also found licences where exclusive possession was given in a family arrangement[65] and, less obviously, where an employee was given possession for the greater convenience of his work.[66]

Accompanying these cases, an analysis developed that exclusive possession was not determinative of leasehold status, a development in which Denning LJ was to the fore. As soon as it became apparent that exclusive possession might not be conclusive, the second effect of the legal regulation began to take centre stage. If exclusive possession is not conclusive, then why should the landlord not avoid the statutory regulation by creating a licence? This would be a very simple way of avoiding the tiresome restraints on regaining possession and increasing rent.[67] The courts were alive to this danger right from the beginning. In 1952, Denning LJ stressed the special features present in the licence cases: it was not enough to apply the label of licence to a transaction that was in substance a lease.[68] Subsequent cases took a similar approach.[69]

---

[61] See also pp 502–505 below.
[62] *Doe d Bastow* v *Cox* (1847) 11 QB 122 (116 ER 421).
[63] [1942] 2 All ER 674.
[64] *Marcroft Wagons Ltd* v *Smith* [1951] 2 KB 496.
[65] *Errington* v *Errington* [1952] 1 KB 290; *Cobb* v *Lane* [1952] 1 All ER 1199; for an example of a licence in a commercial setting, see *Isaac* v *Hotel de Paris* [1960] 1 WLR 239.
[66] *Torbett* v *Faulkner* [1952] 2 TLR 659, followed in *Crane* v *Morris* [1965] 1 WLR 1104. An employee required to live in accommodation for the better performance of the duties had never been a tenant: *Glasgow Corporation* v *Johnstone* [1965] AC 609.
[67] This applies to residential property. For business lettings, a tenancy at will avoids the Landlord and Tenant Act 1954 (*Wheeler* v *Mercer* [1957] AC 416). In contrast, agricultural licences were subject to the same regime as leases until the Agricultural Tenancies Act 1995: Agricultural Holdings Act 1986, s 2(2)(b).
[68] *Facchini* v *Bryson* [1952] 1 TLR 1386.
[69] *Addiscombe Garden Estates Ltd* v *Crabbe* [1958] 1 QB 513; *Bracey* v *Read* [1962] 3 All ER 472 (omitted from the report in [1963] Ch 88).

The scene was now set for combat between draftsmen and the courts. Those drafting agreements attempted to use language and terms that were more consistent with the 'personal privilege' that Denning LJ identified as being at the heart of a licence,[70] as opposed to the 'stake' in the land[71] that epitomised the lease. The result was that cases involved detailed examination of the terms of agreements, assessing which of them was indicative of a lease and which was indicative of a licence.[72] A draftsman would fall into a trap if he inserted rights normally possessed by a licensee: the courts would reply that the rights would not have needed insertion if it was truly a licence.[73] The merits of this reasoning are far from clear, at least if one shuts one's eyes to the draftsman's attempt to circumvent legislation protecting tenants.

The problems became more severe in the 1970s, as draftsmen became more aggressive in finding ways to create licences.[74] The courts appeared to give encouragement, saying in *Somma* v *Hazelhurst*[75] that parties were free to create licences involving exclusive possession, so long as they were not leases masquerading as licences. Although lip service was still paid to the principle that the label is not conclusive, the courts increasingly upheld licence agreements.[76]

(ii) *Street* v *Mountford*

The decision of the House of Lords in *Street* v *Mountford*[77] in 1985 represented a sea change in the approach of the courts. Delivering the only speech, Lord Templeman was emphatic that exclusive possession is conclusive. Almost all the earlier cases were analysed in such a way as to accommodate their results, but doing substantial violence to their reasoning. Exceptions were recognised, in particular that there will be no tenancy where there is no intention to enter into legal relations. This explains several of the early cases, where family relationships or charity were involved. It was found necessary to overrule only three Court of Appeal decisions.[78]

It is easy to see the decision as a return to orthodoxy: numerous early cases treat it as axiomatic that exclusive possession leads to a tenancy. Furthermore, the analysis has the significant support of the High Court of Australia in the 1959 case of *Radaich* v *Smith*.[79] Windeyer J had emphasised that the intention that was relevant was the intention to give exclusive possession: any intention that this should not result in a lease was self-contradictory. Lord

---

[70] E.g. *Errington* v *Errington* [1952] 1 KB 290; *Shell-Mex & BP Ltd* v *Manchester Garages Ltd* [1971] 1 WLR 612.

[71] *Marchant* v *Charters* [1977] 1 WLR 1181 at p 1185.

[72] The complexity is well brought out by Waite (1980) 130 NLJ 939, 959.

[73] *Facchini* v *Bryson* [1952] 1 TLR 1386 is an early example.

[74] The extension of the Rent Acts to furnished accommodation in 1974 was one material factor: *Marchant* v *Charters* [1977] 1 WLR 1181 (Lord Denning MR).

[75] [1978] 1 WLR 1014.

[76] *Aldrington Garages Ltd* v *Fielder* (1978) 37 P&CR 461; *Sturolson & Co* v *Weniz* [1984] 2 EGLR 121; *Matchams Park (Holdings) Ltd* v *Dommett* [1984] 2 EGLR 143.

[77] [1985] AC 809; adopted in New Zealand in *Fatac Ltd* v *CIR* [2002] 3 NZLR 648. Its role is considered by Bright in *Landlord and Tenant Law: Past, Present and Future* (ed Bright), Chapter 2 and Bridge in *Landmark Cases in Land Law* (ed Gravells), Chapter 8.

[78] *Somma* v *Hazelhurst* [1978] 1 WLR 1014; *Aldrington Garages Ltd* v *Fielder* (1978) 37 P&CR 461; *Sturolson & Co* v *Weniz* [1984] 2 EGLR 121.

[79] (1959) 101 CLR 209.

Templeman adopted this reasoning. He also used an everyday analogy[80]: 'The manufacture of a five-pronged implement for manual digging results in a fork even if the manufacturer, unfamiliar with the English language, insists that he intended to make and has made a spade.'

This must now be taken as representing the current state of the law, although one may question whether it was really inevitable. Whilst parties cannot utilise legal categories without conforming to the requirements of those categories (for example, no lease is possible without exclusive possession), it does not follow that categories catch people who do not wish to be within them. Is there any good reason why people should be forced to have an interest in land rather than a personal right? In *IDC Group Ltd* v *Clark*,[81] it was held that the parties could choose to create a licence rather than an easement, even though the legal requirements for an easement were satisfied. In terms of legal principle, it is inexplicable that different reasoning should apply to leases and easements. Lord Templeman considers that, without his analysis, it would be impossible to distinguish leases and licences, yet no such impossibility is found for easements.

Whilst it is certainly true that Lord Templeman is supported by earlier cases, these belong to an era when it was realistic to expect the parties to intend to create a lease whenever possible: it is only in more recent decades that parties[82] will have wanted to create licences. Furthermore, if Lord Templeman were really to follow those earlier cases, then there would be a tenancy at will in many of the exceptions recognised by Lord Templeman, not a licence as he states. Lord Templeman is forced to this conclusion in order to avoid overruling a large number of more recent authorities in favour of licences. The conclusion may be convenient, but it compromises the authority of his analysis.

It is difficult to resist the conclusion that the real reason for the analysis is to stop parties from contracting out of the Rent Acts. Such an analysis would have much justification,[83] although Lord Templeman explicitly disclaimed it in *Street*. It is interesting that Lord Templeman relied far more on the policy of the legislation in later cases.[84] The principal difference between the two approaches is that the broad conceptual analysis in *Street* must apply to leases of commercial property, where there are no Rent Act overtones. The entire area is somewhat ironic in that *Street* was decided shortly before Parliament started to dismantle much of the protection of tenants in the Housing Act 1988.[85] This means that there is far less incentive today for landlords to avoid the use of leases[86]: relatively few cases involving private landlords have been litigated in recent years.

A few cases after *Street* continued to emphasise the intentions of the parties,[87] but the House of Lords reaffirmed the dominance of exclusive possession in *AG Securities* v

---

[80] [1985] AC 809 at p 819.

[81] (1992) 65 P&CR 179; Hill (1996) 16 LS 200 at pp 200–208.

[82] In practice, this means the landlord: the tenant has no choice but to agree if the agreement is to go ahead. See Stephenson LJ in *Aldrington Garages Ltd* v *Fielder* (1978) 37 P&CR 461 at p 476.

[83] Hill (1996) 16 LS 200 at pp 212–214, 217. Cf Bright [2002] CLJ 146, especially at pp 160–166.

[84] *AG Securities* v *Vaughan* [1990] 1 AC 417 at p 458.

[85] The development of the law is usefully summarised in *McDonald* v *McDonald* [2016] 3 WLR 45 at [11]–[19].

[86] Law Com No 297, para 2.2 would include licences in the Law Commission's new statutory regime for residential tenancies. The report has been rejected by the government.

[87] Especially *Dresden Estates Ltd* v *Collinson* (1987) 55 P&CR 47; see also *Smith* v *Northside Developments Ltd* (1987) 55 P&CR 164, *Ogwr BC* v *Dykes* [1989] 1 WLR 295. See also *Mehta* v *Royal Bank of Scotland* (1999) 32 HLR 45.

Vaughan.[88] One initially uncertain point was how far *Street* would be applied to business leases, where the statutory framework is very different. In particular, parties can contract out of statutory protection provided that the requisite notice is given[89] and the parties may create a tenancy at will falling outside the protection.[90] It soon became apparent that *Street* applied to all forms of tenancies, as was to be expected from the reasoning it employed.[91] Nevertheless, we shall see that commercial arrangements sometimes offer greater scope for denying exclusive possession; in this context, the courts place stress on the parties' statement that a licence is intended.[92] Although *Street* retains its status as the leading authority, it may underplay the extent to which intentions can still be taken into account.[93]

A rather different aspect of *Street* concerns the treatment of terms that are inserted in order to deny exclusive possession. An excellent example is found in the earlier case of *Somma v Hazelhurst*,[94] involving a 'licence' to a couple to occupy a single room. The owner reserved a right to occupy the room, together with a right to put in a new person if one of the couple were to leave. The Court of Appeal held that this precluded exclusive possession, but this was overruled in *Street*. Lord Templeman[95] emphasised that: 'the court should, in my opinion, be astute to detect and frustrate sham devices and artificial transactions whose only object is to disguise the grant of a tenancy and to evade the Rent Acts'. The nature and effect of shams will be considered later in this chapter.

(iii) *Lodgers*

> In the case of residential accommodation there is no difficulty in deciding whether the grant confers exclusive possession. An occupier of residential accommodation at a rent for a term is either a lodger or a tenant. The occupier is a lodger if the landlord provides attendance or services which require the landlord or his servants to exercise unrestricted access to and use of the premises.

In these words, Lord Templeman summarised the way in which future disputes would be resolved.[96]

The lodger category has not provided too much difficulty. Although it is an obvious route to obtain a licence, not every landlord will wish to provide the services involved. *Aslan v Murphy*[97] is an instructive case. In order to make the occupier look like a lodger, he was required to vacate the premises for 90 minutes each day; the owner retained a key and was to clean the room and provide bed linen. The Court of Appeal had no doubts in

---

[88] [1990] 1 AC 417, considered below in the context of joint occupation.

[89] Landlord and Tenant Act 1954, s 38A (SI 2003 No 3096).

[90] *Hagee (London) Ltd v AB Erikson & Larson* [1976] QB 209. Tenancies at will of residential accommodation may attract statutory protection.

[91] *London & Associated Investment Trust plc v Calow* [1986] 2 EGLR 80; *Colchester BC v Smith* [1991] Ch 448 at p 484 (upheld [1992] Ch 421 on other grounds). Other cases have assumed that *Street* applies: *University of Reading v Johnson-Houghton* [1985] 2 EGLR 113; *Dellneed Ltd v Chin* (1986) 53 P&CR 172.

[92] *National Car Parks Ltd v Trinity Development Co (Banbury) Ltd* [2002] 2 P&CR 253; *Clear Channel UK Ltd v Manchester City Council* [2006] L&TR 93 at [29]; see p 383 below.

[93] See Bright, op cit, n 77 in this chapter. See also *Vesely v Levy* [2008] L&TR 153 (residential premises, but no rent).

[94] [1978] 1 WLR 1014.

[95] [1985] AC 809 at p 825.

[96] Ibid, at pp 817–818; see also p 827.

[97] [1990] 1 WLR 766.

holding that the term about vacating the room was not intended to be acted upon and was to be ignored as a sham. As regards the retention of a key, this of itself proved little. That a key enables unrestricted access is not inconsistent with exclusive possession. What was far more important was the reason why the key was retained. It might be intended for emergency access to comply with repairing obligations: obviously consistent with a lease. It was only if the landlord used the key for 'frequent cleaning, daily bed-making, the provision of clean linen at regular intervals and the like' that the occupier would be a lodger. On the facts, the services were minimal and there was a lease.

It is significant that *Aslan* treats the actual provision of services as more important than the terms of the agreement. Before *Street*, it had been held that there would be a licence if the services were refused by the occupier.[98] *Aslan* may be authority for the proposition that, after *Street*, the factual absence of services is inconsistent with the occupier's being a lodger.[99] However, the better view is that the test is as to whether the services were intended to be provided or whether their insertion in the agreement was a sham.[100] What if the agreement genuinely contemplates services but the parties subsequently decide that those services will not be provided for the time being? In *Huwyler* v *Ruddy*,[101] the parties reached such a decision several years after the initial agreement. It was held that the occupier remained a lodger, provided that he was still at liberty to insist on the services. Whether the result would have been different if the services had never been provided is unclear.

Markou v *Da Silvaesa*,[102] decided before *Aslan*, involved a very similar agreement. The court stressed that there must be unrestricted access in order to show that the occupier was a lodger. Service and attendance by themselves would not be sufficient: they must be such as to justify unrestricted access at the owner's convenience. The court was suspicious because of a very artificial clause purporting to require the tenant to vacate the premises for 90 minutes each day. The case provides a nice example of suspicion being aroused because the draftsman has inserted patently unworkable terms. However, the significance of 'unrestricted access' was played down by *Huwyler*. Perhaps surprisingly, it was there held that 20 minutes' access for cleaning each week (with provision of bed linen) sufficed. A key was retained for this purpose, with entry in practice being at a time convenient for both parties.

Exclusive possession and exclusive occupation

Although the lodger category has not caused undue difficulty, some aspects of it have given rise to debate. One concerns the difference between exclusive possession and exclusive occupation. Exclusive occupation, in the sense that the occupier is the only person living there and the only person entitled to do so, has never been conclusive of a lease. The lodger is the best example of a person who has exclusive occupation but who, because of the control retained by the owner, does not have exclusive possession. The same might be said of a caretaker living in a flat on the premises (a service occupier). In other words, these cases are a working out of the exclusive possession test rather than exceptions.

---

[98] *Marchant* v *Charters* [1977] 1 WLR 1181 at p 1186.
[99] Evans [1990] JSWL 128.
[100] See *Markou* v *Da Silvaesa* (1986) 52 P&CR 204 (Ralph Gibson and Purchas LJJ).
[101] (1995) 28 HLR 550.
[102] (1986) 52 P&CR 204.

There is much to be said for distinguishing exclusive possession and exclusive occupation in this way,[103] but it must be recognised that the courts have not used this terminology at all consistently.[104] Lord Templeman in *Street* and *AG Securities* appears to treat exclusive possession and exclusive occupation as interchangeable terms.[105] It follows that one cannot read much, if anything, into the language used in the cases. One potential significance of adopting the distinction between exclusive possession and exclusive occupation is that it opens up the possibility of distinguishing *Street* by finding further examples of exclusive occupation.

The extent of the lodger category

In particular, what is the role of attendance or services? Although not a crucial aspect of the common law conception of lodgers, attendance or services was required by Lord Templeman in *Street*. This was adopted in *Markou*. However, a person who shared a house with the owner has been treated as a lodger even in the absence of service and attendance.[106]

It is clear that the lodger category extends to hotel guests[107] and hostel occupiers. *Westminster City Council* v *Clarke*[108] is a useful case. The claimant's 31-room hostel for single homeless men had a warden. A team of social workers assisted the occupiers, many of whom had severe problems of one kind or another. The claimants operated an 11 pm curfew and reserved power to move the occupiers from room to room and to enforce sharing. The House of Lords held that these terms were essential for the Council to discharge its duties to the homeless and to maintain control over the activities of the occupiers. Accordingly, they were lodgers and not tenants. It is interesting to note that little stress is placed upon attendance and services, and this may support a broader view of lodger than was taken by *Markou*. However, the public sector background was crucial: Lord Templeman emphasised that a private landlord could not create a licence by inserting such terms.[109]

Similarly, occupiers of an old people's home run by a charity, with the extensive provision of services, will be licensees.[110] Rather more questionable is the willingness of Millett J in *Camden LBC* v *Shortlife Community Housing Ltd*[111] to take the circumstances of a grant by a local authority to a housing association into account. Although the extent of the rights of the occupier is important, it is far from clear that factors such as the intention to redevelop the premises in the near future should be relevant after *Street*.

---

[103] See, e.g., Tromans [1985] CLJ 351; Hoath [1986] JSWL 46; Hill (1989) 52 MLR 408.
[104] Thus a lodger was described as being in exclusive possession in *Vesely* v *Levy* [2008] L&TR 153 at [43]. Notable exceptions are provided by Lord Denning in *Luganda* v *Service Hotels Ltd* [1969] 2 Ch 209; Windeyer J in *Radaich* v *Smith* (1959) 101 CLR 209 and Chadwick LJ in *Parkins* v *Westminster CC* (1997) 30 HLR 894.
[105] Lord Templeman (*Street* at p 818) quotes a well-known dictum of Blackburn J in *Allan* v *Liverpool Overseers* (1874) LR 9 QB 180 at pp 191–192, in which the terminology is 'exclusive use'.
[106] *Monmouth BC* v *Marlog* [1994] 2 EGLR 68 (there is surprising stress on intention). Note that it is not necessary for the leased property to include cooking facilities: *Uratemp Ventures Ltd* v *Collins* [2002] 1 AC 301.
[107] *Appah* v *Parncliffe Investments Ltd* [1964] 1 WLR 1064 and *Luganda* v *Service Hotels Ltd* [1969] 2 Ch 209 are examples of licences despite the 'hotel' changing into more of a lodging house.
[108] [1992] 2 AC 288; *Brennan* v *Lambeth LBC* (1998) 30 HLR 481 is similar.
[109] A power to move occupiers was not conclusive in *Markou*, although in the commercial context it was seen as important in *Dresden Estates Ltd* v *Collinson* (1987) 55 P&CR 47.
[110] *Abbeyfield (Harpenden) Society Ltd* v *Woods* [1968] 1 WLR 374; *Watts* v *Stewart* [2017] HLR 109 (almshouses).
[111] (1992) 25 HLR 330; Cowan [1993] Conv 157.

Application to the business setting

Analogous problems can arise, although we do not employ the lodger terminology. In *Vandersteen* v *Agius*,[112] the resident owner provided cleaning and secretarial services. It was accepted that services provided as owner could result in a licence, just as with the lodger. On the facts, however, the owner was doing no more than a person unconnected with the land could have contracted to do: she was treated as acting as paid[113] assistant rather than as owner. In other contexts, the control of the owner over units in a market may justify a licence,[114] and the owner of a service station may retain sufficient control to render the operator no more than a licensee.[115]

Generally, a manager of a business will be a licensee, although a lease would be appropriate if the manager is given extensive rights. Such a case was *Dellneed Ltd* v *Chin*,[116] in which the parties adopted a Chinese custom whereby an inexperienced person would run a restaurant for a period (three years), with the owner giving advice as necessary. Millett J found that this was more than mere management on the owner's behalf: exclusive possession was granted, resulting in a lease. It was stressed that the owner did not retain keys and could enter only with the agreement of the occupier. It is also significant that the occupier, although using the owner's equipment and goodwill, was trading on his own account: making a profit or loss according to his success. The contract had been drafted so as to make it appear like a mere licence, but the reality of the transaction was quite different.

These examples all show that it is simplistic to look at the fact of occupation. Notwithstanding what is said in *Street*, it is necessary to look at the terms upon which occupation is taken to see whether there is true exclusive possession. In the business context, it is relatively common to find arrangements that fall short of exclusive possession. Two examples may be given. First, an exclusive right to use a site for depositing waste has been held not to confer exclusive possession and therefore not to amount to a lease.[117] Second, *Clear Channel UK Ltd* v *Manchester City Council*[118] involved the right to erect advertising hoardings. As this was expressed in terms of areas larger than the concrete bases, it constituted a licence.

(iv) *Shams, artificial transactions and pretences*

Ever since *Street*, it has been clear that the courts will not take the terms of the written agreement at face value. In the words of Lord Templeman,[119] 'the court should, in my opinion, be astute to detect and frustrate sham devices and artificial transactions whose

[112] (1992) 65 P&CR 266. The alternative approach of playing down the role of exclusive possession (*Dresden Estates Ltd* v *Collinson* (1987) 55 P&CR 47) is less persuasive: PF Smith [1987] Conv 220.
[113] In the form of free telephone use.
[114] *Smith* v *Northside Developments Ltd* (1987) 55 P&CR 164; *Essex Plan Ltd* v *Broadminster* (1988) 56 P&CR 353.
[115] *Esso Petroleum Co Ltd* v *Fumegrange Ltd* [1994] 2 EGLR 90; see also *National Car Parks Ltd* v *Trinity Development Co (Banbury) Ltd* [2002] 2 P&CR 253 (operating car park).
[116] (1986) 53 P&CR 172; Bright [2005] Conv 352.
[117] *Hunts Refuse Disposals Ltd* v *Norfolk Environmental Waste Services Ltd* [1997] 1 EGLR 16.
[118] [2006] L&TR 93. Earlier, see *Provincial Bill Posting Co* v *Low Moor Iron Co* [1909] 2 KB 344; *Kewal Investments Ltd* v *Arthur Maiden Ltd* [1990] 1 EGLR 193.
[119] [1985] AC 809 at p 825.

only object is to disguise the grant of a tenancy and to evade the Rent Acts'. The Court of Appeal[120] has applied the definition of sham by Diplock LJ in *Snook* v *London & West Riding Investments Ltd*[121]: 'acts done or documents executed by the parties to the "sham" which are intended by them to give to third parties or to the court the appearance of creating legal rights and obligations that are different from the actual between the parties legal rights and obligations (if any) which the parties intend to create'.

A term inserted in order to negate exclusive possession will be a sham if neither party intends that term to be acted upon. A good illustration is provided by *Antoniades* v *Villiers*.[122] Two occupiers were living together as husband and wife: the flat had a single bedroom and a sitting room that was unsuitable as permanent sleeping accommodation. The owner had insisted upon a term whereby he could introduce other licensees or live there himself. The House of Lords refused to accept that it was intended that anybody other than the two occupiers should live there: there was a lease. The courts are very suspicious of clauses of this nature, particularly when the physical arrangement of the accommodation renders it practically impossible.[123] The result in *Antoniades* is not surprising given that *Street* had overruled *Somma* v *Hazelhurst*,[124] in which the facts were similar and a licence had been found by the Court of Appeal.

Another example of a sham is the term in *Aslan* v *Murphy* requiring the occupier to leave for 90 minutes each day. In the leasehold context, the intention to deceive is essentially that of the owner (rather than both parties), but this does not affect the operation of the principle. One point to stress is that the courts are free to look at the operation of the agreement as a guide as to whether the terms are shams. The normal principle is that an agreement cannot be interpreted by the manner of its performance, but this is inapplicable to the detection of shams.[125]

The main question is whether the courts are prepared to go further than the *Snook* concept of shams. Lord Templeman, it will be recalled, also referred to 'artificial transactions'. In *Antoniades*, Lord Templeman expressed a preference for the term 'pretence' over his own words in *Street*, although without explaining the difference. Lord Oliver spoke in terms of shams,[126] though his overall inquiry was as to the 'true nature of the arrangement'.

Despite some suggestions that the application of the sham test is discredited by *Antoniades*,[127] most subsequent cases have continued to use the sham language, assuming that pretence has the same meaning,[128] and Sir Thomas Bingham MR has referred

---

[120] *Markou* v *Da Silvaesa* (1986) 52 P&CR 204; *Hadjiloucas* v *Crean* [1988] 1 WLR 1006 at p 1013.

[121] [1967] 2 QB 786 at p 802.

[122] [1990] 1 AC 417.

[123] It will be even more difficult to persuade the court that the clause is genuine where there is a single occupier and the property is appropriate only for single occupation. An extreme example is *Aslan* v *Murphy* [1990] 1 WLR 766, involving a single room measuring 4' 3″ by 12' 6″.

[124] [1978] 1 WLR 1014; also *Aldrington Garages Ltd* v *Fielder* (1978) 37 P&CR 461 and *Sturolson & Co* v *Weniz* [1984] 2 EGLR 121, all disapproved in *Street*.

[125] Lords Oliver and Jauncey in *Antoniades* [1990] 1 AC 417 at pp 469 and 475.

[126] [1990] 1 AC 417 at p 466: see also Lord Jauncey. Lord Ackner considered the 'substance and reality of the transaction'.

[127] Sparkes (1989) 52 MLR 557; Bright (1991) 11 OxJLS 136 (but contrast her position in [2002] CLJ 146); see also Rodgers [1989] Conv 196; *Bankway Properties Ltd* v *Pensfold-Dunsford* [2001] 1 WLR 1369 at [43]. Cf *KJRR Pty Ltd* v *CSR* [1999] 2 VR 174, especially at [16].

[128] *Stribling* v *Wickham* [1989] 2 EGLR 35; *Nicolaou* v *Pitt* (1989) 21 HLR 487; *Mikeover Ltd* v *Brady* [1989] 3 All ER 618; *Kaye* v *Massbetter Ltd* (1990) 62 P&CR 558.

to 'doing one thing and saying another'.[129] Whilst the overall investigation is said to be directed towards the 'realities of the transaction' or 'true bargain', this investigation is conducted by asking whether the terms are shams. Even in *Aslan*, where greater stress is placed on the actual situation resulting from the agreement,[130] sham and pretence appear to be intertwined.[131] The reality may be that sham was thought not to apply if the intention to mislead is the intention of just one of the parties (almost invariably the landlord): pretence is employed to make it clear that the term can still be attacked by the tenant.[132]

Company lets

One specific type of case has arisen in which a wider approach would be valuable to the occupier. The context is not so much a lease/licence dispute as one relating to the legislation protecting tenants. Owners are aware that certain types of leases are outside the legislation protecting tenants. If these leases can be deployed, then the legislation may be avoided. The best-known example is that of leases to companies, which do not enjoy the protection accorded to residential leases. Schemes have developed whereby owners have insisted that prospective occupiers create companies to act as tenants,[133] although everybody knows that the land will actually be occupied by the individual. Attacks on these schemes as shams have generally failed[134]: it is not difficult to show that the company does have an independent role and that it is the company which has liability to pay rent.

On the other hand, it could be argued that these schemes involve artificial transactions. This is evidenced by the facts that the land is occupied by the individual (as stipulated in the company lease in many cases) and that the company's sole source of money is that individual. Further, it is common to require the individual to guarantee the payment of rent.[135] At one time, such transactions might have been susceptible to an attack based on a development in taxation law, whereby steps inserted into transactions with no commercial purpose may be overlooked even where they have a commercial effect.[136] On this analogy, one could argue that the lease to the company has no commercial purpose and should be overlooked, leaving the individual and the owner as the parties to the lease.[137]

---

[129] *Belvedere Court Management Ltd* v *Frogmore Developments Ltd* [1997] QB 858 at p 876.

[130] Evans [1990] JSWL 128.

[131] McFarlane and Simpson in *Rationalizing Property, Equity and Trusts* (ed Getzler), Chapter 8, are highly critical of an extended meaning of sham that encompasses cases where a party does not intend to enforce a contractual term: such terms are common and valid in many commercial contracts. Vella [2008] LMCLQ 488 argues to the contrary where the parties share an intention not to enforce.

[132] Bright [2002] CLJ 146, doubting whether sham is so limited; Sparkes [1989] JSWL 293 at p 296. Vella [2008] LMCLQ 488 is highly critical of any expansion to pretence, arguing that *Antoniades* itself can be explained as a sham.

[133] This is neither difficult nor expensive.

[134] *Estavest Investments Ltd* v *Commercial Express Travel Ltd* [1988] 2 EGLR 91 (the argument was weak: the company already existed and had a real independent financial role); *Hilton* v *Plustitle Ltd* [1989] 1 WLR 149; *Kaye* v *Massbetter Ltd* (1990) 62 P&CR 558. *Gisborne* v *Burton* [1989] QB 390 (analogous, although not a company let) is an exception, but there the head tenant was treated as the owner's agent.

[135] *Kaye* v *Massbetter Ltd* (1990) 62 P&CR 558; in *Hilton* v *Plustitle Ltd* [1989] 1 WLR 149, the guarantor was the individual's brother.

[136] The leading cases at that time were *WT Ramsay* v *IRC* [1982] AC 300 and *Furniss* v *Dawson* [1984] AC 474; see also *Craven* v *White* [1989] AC 398.

[137] Dillon LJ in *Gisborne* v *Burton* [1989] QB 390 (agricultural property). Ralph Gibson LJ dissented and Russell LJ used a sham analysis.

Hilton v *Plustitle Ltd*[138] undertook a full analysis of the area and found that there was no sham: the scheme succeeded. More explicitly, the Court of Appeal in *Belvedere Court Management Ltd* v *Frogmore Developments Ltd*[139] confirmed that the taxation principles are inapplicable to real property transactions which appear effective on their face and confer an interest in land. In any event, the modern taxation cases are based upon statutory interpretation.[140] This shows that they cannot be an explanation for *Street* v *Mountford*, as Lord Templeman overtly treated the question as being one of principle rather than of statutory interpretation.

Conclusions

It is fair to say that tests such as artificial transactions and pretences are not easily applied. It would be simplistic to suggest that a transaction is caught merely because it was entered into as a response to the statutory protection of tenants. People invariably adjust their conduct in the light of statutory regulation. An obvious example is a genuine lodging agreement, where the services would not have been contracted for and provided but for statutory regulation of leases.

What is not allowed is to use the written agreement as a smokescreen, hiding the reality of the transaction. Thus, in *Bankway Properties Ltd* v *Pensfold-Dunsford*,[141] it was held that a term increasing rent from under £5,000 to £25,000 was ineffective. This was not a genuine increase of rent because the landlord knew it could not be paid: it was an attempt to avoid the statutory protection of assured tenants. The analysis uses a mixture of sham concepts and a rejection of terms which attempt to evade statutory rights.

(v) *Exceptional categories*

Lord Templeman recognised that in certain cases, there will not be a lease, notwithstanding exclusive possession. Before investigating the individual cases, the general role of these exceptions should be considered. It was suggested by May LJ in *Bretherton* v *Paton*[142] that they are not exceptions at all but rather part of the working out of exclusive possession. This may be true of some cases, but it runs the danger of treating exclusive possession as a very fluid concept, with the potential for extending the range of circumstances giving rise to licences. It may be preferable to say that, although the list of exceptions may not be closed, the courts should be very reluctant to extend the list.[143]

---

[138] [1989] 1 WLR 149; see also *Kaye* v *Massbetter Ltd* (1990) 62 P&CR 558; *Eaton Square Properties Ltd* v *O'Higgins* [2001] L&TR 165 (use of company at T's request: no sham).

[139] [1997] QB 858; followed by Neuberger J in the lease context in *National Westminster Bank plc* v *Jones* [2001] 1 BCLC 98 (not relevant on appeal: [2002] 1 BCLC 55).

[140] See especially *Barclays Mercantile Business Finance Ltd* v *Mawson* [2005] 1 AC 684. The relationship between the leases cases and the taxation principles is fully considered by McFarlane and Simpson, op cit, n 131 above.

[141] [2001] 1 WLR 1369 (not a case on the lease/licence distinction); Pill LJ prefers an analysis based on internal inconsistency within the lease. Bright [2002] CLJ 146 argues that the term was genuine (if artificial) and that the court employs a new and indeterminate test.

[142] [1986] 1 EGLR 172. See also Taylor and Windeyer JJ in *Radaich* v *Smith* (1959) 101 CLR 209 at pp 220, 223.

[143] *Dellneed Ltd* v *Chin* (1986) 53 P&CR 172.

In addition to the categories considered below, it is agreed that there will be no tenancy if leasing lies outside the powers of the landlord.[144] However, this is limited to bodies acting ultra vires. In *Bruton* v *London & Quadrant Housing Trust*,[145] the House of Lords held that it does not matter whether or not the landlord has an estate to support a lease binding on third parties. On the facts, the landlord had a mere licence. This did not stop an agreement (worded as a licence), under which exclusive possession was enjoyed, from creating the relationship of lease or tenancy as between the landlord and the possessor.

(a) Owners, mortgagees and trespassers

These possessors are plainly not lessees. The same would be true of some beneficiaries under trusts, although they are not mentioned by Lord Templeman.

Although trespassers are obviously not lessees (their possession is not consensual), three points should be noted. First, the owner may claim compensation for use and occupation pending actual eviction. Local authorities commonly make such claims when their property has been occupied by squatters. In *Westminster City Council* v *Basson*,[146] the council discovered that a friend of a former tenant was living in the premises. The council claimed and received money for use and occupation, whilst denying any tenancy or licence. Possession proceedings were not taken for over a year. It was held that the occupier remained a trespasser, perhaps a rather harsh decision given the extended tolerance of her possession.[147] On the other hand, a contrary result may be reached if the occupier has claimed the land and paid rent over many years.[148]

The second point is that a lease obtained by misrepresentation can be rescinded so as to prevent there being a tenancy protected by statute.[149] This can be seen as producing the same effect as if permission to enter had never been given: the occupier is a trespasser. Finally, the much-criticised concept of tolerated trespasser evolved to explain the position where a former tenant retains occupation after a possession order.[150] Fortunately, this category has been swept into oblivion.[151]

(b) Purchasers in possession prior to completion

The traditional approach was to regard such purchasers as tenants at will.[152] However, in order to bolster his argument that exclusive possession is not conclusive in favour of a tenancy, Denning LJ treated the purchaser as a licensee in *Errington* v *Errington*.[153] This

---

[144] *Street* v *Mountford* [1985] AC 809 at p 821; see also *Gray* v *Taylor* [1998] 1 WLR 1093 at p 1099 (charity trustees).

[145] [2000] 1 AC 406. This is controversial: see p 413 below.

[146] (1990) 62 P&CR 57. In *Southwark LB* v *Logan* (1995) 29 HLR 40, nine years' occupation as a trespasser did not suffice.

[147] Martin [1992] Conv 111. The fact that she was by mistake given a 'rent book' was – correctly, it is submitted – given little weight. See also *Leadenhall Residential 2 Ltd* v *Stirling* [2002] 1 WLR 499, where the occupier had originally been a tenant.

[148] *Tower Hamlets LB* v *Ayinde* (1994) 26 HLR 631.

[149] *Killick* v *Roberts* [1991] 1 WLR 1146; criticised by Tee [1992] CLJ 21.

[150] *Burrows* v *Brent LBC* [1996] 1 WLR 1448.

[151] Housing and Regeneration Act 2008, Sch 11 and *Knowsley* v *White* [2009] AC 636 (Bridge [2009] Conv 268).

[152] *Doe d Tomes* v *Chamberlaine* (1839) 5 M&W 14 (151 ER 7).

[153] [1952] 1 KB 290.

was accepted in a few cases (especially where the contract provided for a licence),[154] despite authoritative criticism of the licence analysis.[155] It is, then, surprising that Lord Templeman thought it necessary to include this category of licensees.

Ramnarace v *Lutchman*[156] brings some clarity to the area. Where possession is allowed in the course of negotiations, then there will normally be a tenancy at will.[157] On the other hand, where possession is taken pursuant to a contract, then the possession is referable to the contract and there is no tenancy. Whether it makes sense to switch from tenancy to licence when a sale contract is entered into might well be questioned. Hoffmann J extended the licence category in *Essex Plan Ltd* v *Broadminster*[158] to apply where the possessor held an option. The extension from purchasers to option holders is, as Hoffmann J accepted, significant. An option holder has no right to possession[159] and, it might be thought, no real interest in taking possession prior to exercising the option.

(c) Service occupiers

It has long been recognised that where an employee is required to live in the employer's premises for the better performance of his or her duties, or living there is necessary for the performance of the duties, there is a licence and not a tenancy.[160] The occupation by the employee is treated as being on behalf of the employer,[161] and the situation might be viewed as one in which there is no exclusive possession. The category most obviously applies to caretakers, but extends to separate accommodation such as farm workers' cottages.[162] It is important to note that simply rewarding the employee by providing accommodation close to the place of work is insufficient to create a licence.[163]

The service occupier category is an old one, although the courts in the period before *Street* did recognise some broadening so as to cover occupation which is beneficial to the performance of duties.[164] Since *Street*, it seems clear that this broadening is unacceptable.[165] To be a service occupier (and therefore a licensee), it will be necessary to satisfy the rules summarised in the previous paragraph. However, the requirements are not applied in an unreasonably harsh manner. Where accommodation is provided in anticipation of a change of duties in the near future, then no objection can be taken that the present duties do not require the accommodation.[166] Nor is it an objection that there

---

[154] *Euston Centre Properties Ltd* v *H&J Wilson Ltd* [1982] 1 EGLR 57 (conditional contract); *Hyde* v *Pearce* [1982] 1 WLR 560; *Sopwith* v *Stutchbury* (1983) 17 HLR 50.
[155] Viscount Simonds LC in *Wheeler* v *Mercer* [1957] AC 416 at p 425; *Radaich* v *Smith* (1959) 101 CLR 209 at p 219 (Taylor J).
[156] [2001] 1 WLR 1651 (PC).
[157] See also *Bretherton* v *Paton* [1986] 1 EGLR 172; *Javad* v *Aqil* [1991] 1 WLR 1007 (see p 398 below).
[158] (1988) 56 P&CR 353 (option for a long lease).
[159] Nor does a purchaser prior to completion.
[160] *Glasgow Corporation* v *Johnstone* [1965] AC 609.
[161] Ibid, at p 626 (Lord Hodson).
[162] *Ramsbottom* v *Snelson* [1948] 1 KB 473.
[163] *Smith* v *Seghill Overseers* (1875) LR 10 QB 422.
[164] *Torbett* v *Faulkner* [1952] 2 TLR 659; *Crane* v *Morris* [1965] 1 WLR 1104. Contrast *Facchini* v *Bryson* [1952] 1 TLR 1386.
[165] *Royal Philanthropic Society* v *County* [1985] 2 EGLR 109.
[166] *Norris* v *Checksfield* [1991] 1 WLR 1241.

is a deduction from salary on account of the accommodation, rather than its being provided free.[167]

(d) An object of charity

Several of the pre-*Street* cases were decided on this basis. Some of them even involved the payment of rent,[168] although such cases are likely to be rare and to involve short-term arrangements. The *Street* analysis is that there is no contract in these charity cases. The indications since *Street* are that the category will not be extended: payment of rent will normally be taken as showing that there is a contract.[169] Where a person occupies as an object of a charitable trust (most frequently encountered for almshouses), then there is no lease even if a maintenance charge is payable.[170]

A rather different point is that there is no special category of letting by charities. If no rent is payable, then there will not be a lease.[171] However, there is no exemption simply because the landlord is a charity; this may cause problems for charity trustees.[172]

Even where family arrangements are concerned, *Nunn* v *Dalrymple*[173] shows that the courts are prepared to find that there is a contract. Parents-in-law were allowed to renovate a cottage, on the understanding that they would give up their council house, live in the cottage and make payments of rent. The Court of Appeal had little hesitation in holding that the family relationship did not preclude there being a contract and a tenancy. The result is readily supportable in circumstances where secure accommodation had been given up and work undertaken on the cottage.

Arrangements whereby a house is shared are far more likely to give rise to licences. The courts will be reluctant to treat the sharing of household expenses as an arrangement for the payment of rent. Nor will it be inferred that the occupation is by virtue of a contract.[174] In any event, the circumstances may well negate exclusive possession of any part of the house.[175]

(e) Possession given under statutory duties

Local authorities have duties towards the homeless.[176] This frequently involves emergency short-term occupation, which local authorities prefer to be by licence rather than lease in order to avoid the secure tenancy provisions protecting tenants. The Court of Appeal in

---

[167] Ibid; it would be difficult to justify a distinction between making a deduction from salary and paying a lower basic salary. Contra: *Warner Pty Ltd* v *Williams* (1948) 73 CLR 421 (High Court of Australia), relying on *R* v *Jarvis* (1824) 1 Mood 7 (168 ER 1163).

[168] *Marcroft Wagons Ltd* v *Smith* [1951] 2 KB 496; p 377 above.

[169] *Royal Philanthropic Society* v *County* [1985] 2 EGLR 109. See also *Bretherton* v *Paton* [1986] 1 EGLR 172. The category was applied in *Colchester BC* v *Smith* [1991] Ch 448 (temporary rent-free possession of agricultural land; upheld on other grounds [1992] Ch 421).

[170] *Gray* v *Taylor* [1998] 1 WLR 1093, upheld by *Watts* v *Stewart* [2017] HLR 109 (also rejecting human rights arguments).

[171] *Gray* v *Taylor* [1998] 1 WLR 1093.

[172] Barr in *Modern Studies in Property Law*, Vol 1 (ed Cooke), Chapter 14; cf the statutory duties category below.

[173] (1989) 59 P&CR 231.

[174] *Bostock* v *Bryant* (1990) 61 P&CR 23, followed in *Vesely* v *Levy* [2008] L&TR 153.

[175] See Roskill LJ in *Heslop* v *Burns* [1974] 1 WLR 1241 (a separate house, but the owner was a frequent visitor); *Armstrong* v *Armstrong* [1970] 1 NSWR 133.

[176] Housing Act 1996, Part VII.

Family Housing Association v *Jones*[177] rejected the argument that there should be an exception to *Street* in such circumstances. However, since the Housing Act 1996,[178] leases granted pursuant to the statutory duties have ceased to be secure tenancies. We have also seen that some types of housing may not involve exclusive possession, necessarily result-ing in a licence.[179]

(vi) *Joint occupiers*

Street has worked pretty well for sole occupiers of residential property, despite the diffi-culties discussed above. Lord Templeman may be seen as having succeeded in replacing the previous complex law with a simple and historically justifiable test. Unfortunately, the verdict on the impact of *Street* where there is multiple occupation must be less favourable.

The simple alternatives of lodger and tenant were soon seen as being simplistic. In many cases, a house or flat is occupied by a shifting population of occupiers. How can any of them be said to be in exclusive possession? In appropriate cases, there might be exclu-sive possession of an individual room within the premises, but frequently this is neither the form nor the substance of the agreement: it is left to the occupiers to agree who is to occupy which room. As a result, attention has often been focused upon the premises as a whole. Quite soon after *Street*, the Court of Appeal felt compelled to decide that joint occupiers (as licensees) constituted a third category alongside lodgers and tenants.[180]

This led to two linked appeals to the House of Lords: *AG Securities* v *Vaughan* and *Antoniades* v *Villiers*.[181] The facts of the cases were quite different, although each involved joint occupation. In *AG Securities*, a flat was occupied by four persons, each having their own room. As one left, a newcomer would enter into a new six-month agreement with the owner. The result was each of the four had entered into agreements at different times, terminating at different times, and with a right to share with three others. As succinctly described by Parker LJ in a later case,[182] 'The flat was suitable for use by a multiple but shifting occupation and was so used.' It followed that no individual occupier could be treated as enjoying exclusive possession of the flat, nor was it possible to regard all four as jointly enjoying exclusive possession. The House of Lords held them to be licensees. It follows that the inaccuracy of the *Street* tenant/lodger dichotomy is accepted by the House of Lords[183]: joint licensees can provide a third category.

One particular aspect of *AG Securities* was that the four unities, required before there can be a joint tenancy, were lacking. Even if there were unity of possession,[184] there was no unity of interest (different rents were paid), no unity of title (genuinely separate agreements were entered into with each of them) and no unity of time (the agreements were entered into

---

[177] [1990] 1 WLR 779, approved by the House of Lords on this point in *Bruton* v *London & Quadrant Housing Trust* [2000] 1 AC 406.

[178] Schedule 17, para 3, substituting Housing Act 1985, Sched 1, para 4.

[179] *Westminster City Council* v *Clarke* [1992] 2 AC 288.

[180] *Brooker Settled Estates Ltd* v *Ayers* (1987) 54 P&CR 165; *Hadjiloucas* v *Crean* [1988] 1 WLR 1006.

[181] [1990] 1 AC 417.

[182] *Stribling* v *Wickham* [1989] 2 EGLR 35 at p 37.

[183] See Lord Templeman [1990] 1 AC 417 at pp 459–460.

[184] Doubted by Sir George Waller in the Court of Appeal at p 436 (his dissenting judgment was upheld by the House of Lords); see also Lords Oliver and Jauncey at pp 472, 474.

at different times). The Court of Appeal had reasoned that each time a newcomer arrived, a fresh agreement was entered into with all four. The House of Lords rejected this: quite apart from its complexity, it was quite inconsistent with the reality of the situation.

The second case, *Antoniades*, likewise involved a sharing arrangement. We have seen that the two occupiers were living together as husband and wife in a flat with a single bedroom. The owner entered into separate agreements (described as licences) with each of them. The House of Lords found that there was a lease: the agreements were interdependent in that they were entered into together, and it was inconceivable that a stranger could be introduced if one of the occupiers were to leave.

Two initial questions may be identified where there is multiple occupation. The first is whether it is possible to construe the facts as involving a joint letting to the individuals concerned. This was plainly impossible in *AG Securities*,[185] but appropriate in *Antoniades*. The simple ploy of entering into separate agreements will not succeed where the reality is a joint letting.

The second question applies where there is a joint letting. Does a right to put others into possession (assuming it is not a sham) mean that the current possessors viewed together do not have exclusive possession? Lord Templeman considers that, where the parties have exclusive possession in fact, even a valid power to force sharing will be inconsistent with the statutory protection of tenants and therefore void. This 'bizarre'[186] analysis is not adopted by Lord Oliver, who also delivered a full speech. Indeed, Lord Oliver recognises that terms genuinely giving the right to disturb exclusive possession will be effective.[187] In *Aslan* v *Murphy*,[188] Lord Donaldson MR attempts a compromise by asking whether the true bargain is for exclusive possession until sharing is required (lease) or for sharing but with de facto exclusive occupation for the time being (licence). It is not easy to see how this line is to be drawn, although it is possible that a postponed obligation to share would create an immediate lease. Other cases instinctively adopt Lord Oliver's analysis.[189]

Borderline cases

AG Securities and *Antoniades* are at different ends of the factual spectrum of joint occupation. *Stribling* v *Wickham*[190] is a more difficult middle case. The facts were similar to *AG Securities*, but the original agreements were entered into by three friends who took the flat together. In the course of time, some moved out and others took their place. Though the initial three took the flat together, the reality was that, when one moved out, the others' rights were unaffected. If they had a joint interest, then it would be inexplicable for one to be able to get out of the agreement and for a new occupier to be chosen by the owner. In other words, the circumstances under which the flat was initially chosen by the occupiers

---

[185] Also in *Parkins* v *Westminster CC* (1997) 30 HLR 894

[186] Hill (1989) 52 MLR 408 at p 410.

[187] [1990] 1 AC 417 at pp 468–469; Lord Jauncey appears to agree.

[188] [1990] 1 WLR 766. See also the discussion of shams at 383 above.

[189] *Stribling* v *Wickham* [1989] 2 EGLR 35; *Kaye* v *Massbetter Ltd* (1990) 62 P&CR 558; *Camden LBC* v *Shortlife Community Housing Ltd* (1992) 25 HLR 330; *Parkins* v *Westminster CC* (1997) 30 HLR 894. *Gray* v *Brown* [1993] 1 EGLR 119 contains the clearest dicta, albeit in a statutory context: 'It is not necessary that he should actually exercise that right, nor have a clear intention to do so, so long as the possibility of moving into the premises is genuinely within his contemplation at the time of the tenancy agreement . . .' (Butler-Sloss LJ at p 120).

[190] [1989] 2 EGLR 35.

was only part of the story: their contemplation was that they would not stay there together indefinitely. The result was a licence.

The earlier and similar case of *Hadjiloucas* v *Crean*[191] poses greater difficulty. Two ladies took an unfurnished flat together, there being separate agreements with each of them. After a few months, one of them left and her place was taken by somebody she introduced to the owner. The Court of Appeal considered that the facts could justify a licence but sent the case back for a more detailed investigation. In *Antoniades*, Lord Templeman (the only judge to discuss *Hadjiloucas*) said that there should have been a tenancy because they applied for and obtained exclusive possession. Yet, *Stribling* seems very similar to *Hadjiloucas*.

Two points may be added. First, in each of *Hadjiloucas* and *Stribling*, there were six-month agreements with similar termination dates for each of the occupiers: a newcomer took over the balance of the period. This makes it easier to contemplate a joint lease than in *AG Securities*, where the various licences had different start and finish dates. The second point is that in *Hadjiloucas*, but not *Stribling*, each of the two occupiers had made herself liable for the entire rent. This factor (unusual in such arrangements) may be a strong indication of a joint arrangement leading to a lease: in separate licences, it would be extraordinary to agree to pay the rent due from the others.[192]

Cases such as *Stribling* are properly treated as creating licences. It surely cannot make a difference that an advertisement is replied to by four friends rather than four strangers. So long as the intention is that others may come in their place, it is difficult to treat the agreement as truly joint. This seems to fit the mobility that is inherent in flat-sharing schemes. That said, it is not entirely clear why statutory protection should be denied to flat sharers when those in self-contained units, or with exclusive possession of their own room, are protected. The reality is surely that a mobile young population utilises a range of types of arrangements, only some of which are outside the statutory protection. Nor should mobility be exaggerated: the facts of *AG Securities* reveal that some of the occupiers had been there for five years.

It remains to be seen whether *Stribling* will be extended to a case where, as in *Antoniades*, a couple living together take a flat. Where the flat is unsuitable for two people unless they are living together as a couple, then it is very easy to conclude that they are taking the flat together and that it must be a lease. More difficult is the flat which could be occupied by two strangers, especially where it has previously been so occupied. Does the fact that it is taken by a couple convert two licences into a lease? From the owner's point of view, the relationship between the occupiers is of limited significance: those living together can fall out or wish to move to take up a new job in the same way as the friends in *Stribling*. From the point of view of the couple, they more obviously see themselves as taking the property together. The problems of another person being forced upon the remaining occupier after the other has left are sometimes stressed,[193] but the facts of *Hadjiloucas*, *AG Securities* and *Stribling* demonstrate that finding new occupiers causes few problems, with owners often happy to agree to suggestions by the occupiers themselves.

---

[191] [1988] 1 WLR 1006.

[192] Joint liability for the full rent in a single document with both occupiers clearly results in a joint tenancy: *Nicolaou* v *Pitt* (1989) 21 HLR 487.

[193] See Lord Templeman's comments in *Antoniades* [1990] 1 AC 417 at p 465 on *Hadjiloucas* that the right to put strangers in was a pretence. This is barely comprehensible given that it is what actually occurred! See Barton (1990) 106 LQR 215 at p 217.

The role of the four unities

It has been noted that *AG Securities* placed some stress on the four unities that are essential for a joint tenancy. This point was developed in *Mikeover Ltd v Brady*.[194] The facts were rather similar to *Antoniades*, there being two separate licences, although this time without any right to put others in. The flat was of such a size as to be suitable only for those 'personally acceptable to each other'. One would have thought that this was a fairly clear example of a lease, but the Court of Appeal held that the occupiers could not hold jointly because there was no unity of interest. The specific problem was that each of the occupiers had agreed to pay half the total rent. This could not be attacked as a sham, because one of the couple had left and the owner refused to accept more than the half share due from the other. The absence of a joint obligation to pay the rent was fatal to unity of interest, and in turn, this was fatal to a joint tenancy.

In the light of *Antoniades*, this is difficult to comprehend. The Court of Appeal had there argued that separate obligations to pay rent rendered the situation inconsistent with a joint tenancy. In the House of Lords, Lord Oliver delivered a scathing response.[195] If the real transaction was one under which the couple became joint tenants with exclusive possession, then it would follow that each would be liable for the rent: the form of the documents as two separate transactions constituted a sham. The *Mikeover* analysis might be justified if the two occupiers' rights are not interdependent,[196] but they were in *Mikeover*. The occupiers took the flat as a couple; it was unsuitable for two people unless they constituted a couple or were very close friends.

Nevertheless, *Mikeover* illustrates the possibility of creating licences by negating one of the four unities. Charging different rents to the two occupiers might emphasise that there is no unity of interest, as would insisting that the agreements are entered into a week apart. Such cases might be more obvious examples of licences than *Mikeover*, although it is far from clear that either Lord Templeman or Lord Oliver would have been deflected from treating the substance of the transaction as joint exclusive possession. How far, indeed, have we returned to a duel between draftsmen and the courts?

Some awkward questions

These cases on joint occupation are interesting as much for what is assumed as for what they say. One initial question is whether it is essential for a joint tenancy that obligations (including payment of rent) be undertaken jointly. It might be argued that unity of interest requires merely that the interest of each be identical: obligations are collateral to the interest and need not be identical. It is plain that either party can enter into separate obligations relating to their interests after the lease has been granted. Is it the case that rent is so central to a lease that, like the term of years itself, liability must be joint before there can be unity of interest? The modern approach is to treat rent as a contractual obligation rather than a specialised obligation with special rules.[197] This may render it easier to argue that separate rent obligations are consistent with unity of interest, even though a joint obligation would be normal where there is a joint tenancy.

---

[194] [1989] 3 All ER 618.
[195] [1990] 1 AC 417 at p 469.
[196] As in *Stribling* (relied upon in *Mikeover*), where Parker LJ stressed the separate liability for rent.
[197] *United Scientific Holdings Ltd v Burnley BC* [1978] AC 904.

So far as authority on joint obligations is concerned, the issue has been raised in relatively few cases, all of them recent. Prior to *AG Securities*, the cases were mixed.[198] In *AG Securities*,[199] Lord Templeman appears to accept that separate obligations are consistent with a joint tenancy, although Lord Oliver seems to assume that a joint tenancy entails joint liability for rent. Although the authorities are scarcely overwhelming, the requirement of joint rent liability seems settled below the Supreme Court.

A more fundamental question is as to why the four unities should have any relevance. Their normal role is to distinguish between joint tenancies and tenancies in common, yet cases such as *AG Securities* and *Mikeover* use the four unities to distinguish between joint leases and licences. This is very puzzling. Any suggestion that there cannot be a tenancy in common of a lease is plainly wrong: the books contain standard precedents for such agreements.[200] So why, in cases such as *Mikeover*, is there not a tenancy in common?

The answer may be linked to the fact that there cannot be a legal tenancy in common since 1925.[201] The normal consequence of a tenancy in common is that the co-owners hold as joint tenants on a trust of land, enabling the tenancy in common to exist in equity.[202] Unfortunately, this analysis may not fit cases such as *Mikeover*, as a legal joint tenancy is not intended (it would require joint liability for rent). If it should be true that the 1925 legislation renders a tenancy in common of such leases impossible, even in equity, this would be a terrible indictment of the legislation.

Is a licence justified because none of these 'lessees' enjoys exclusive possession? It seems to be assumed in the recent cases that exclusive possession is negated by the fact that others may also be permitted to occupy. Yet, is this what the concept of exclusive possession is stressing? There is a strong argument that exclusive possession is based upon the right to prevent the owner from entering at will, rather than the owner's having no right to introduce other occupiers. Certainly, that was the focus of the earlier cases. Insofar as there is a right to exclude third parties, this is as a result of there being a tenancy and not the reason for there being a tenancy. This is well illustrated by the lodger. The owner normally has no right to put others in with the lodger and any attempt to do so would be a breach of contract. However, the lodger is merely a licensee and it is uncertain when an action will lie against the third party.[203]

One might conclude that *AG Securities* is not as well rooted in property theory as at first sight appears. However, most of the points raised in this section fly in the face of authority. Although they show that the law may have developed along dubious lines, it would be optimistic to expect significant changes.

---

[198] No unity of interest where separate obligations: *Somma* v *Hazelhurst* [1978] 1 WLR 1014, *Aldrington Garages Ltd* v *Fielder* (1978) 37 P&CR 461 and *Sturolson & Co* v *Weniz* [1984] 2 EGLR 121 (all overruled in *Street*). For unity of interest: *Demuren* v *Seal Estates Ltd* [1979] 1 EGLR 102 at p 105.

[199] [1990] 1 AC 417 at pp 461, 469. Lord Jauncey at p 473 describes joint liability as one of the 'normal attributes' of a joint tenancy.

[200] *Encyclopaedia of Forms and Precedents* (1st edn, 1905), Vol 7, p 662. Cf *Malayan Credit Ltd* v *Jack Chia-MPH Ltd* [1986] AC 549; Sparkes (1989) 18 Anglo-American LR 151. See also RJ Smith, *Plural Ownership*, pp 24–26.

[201] LPA, s 1(6); Barton (1990) 106 LQR 215. Bright (op cit, n 77 above) suggests at pp 34–35 that there is no true unity of possession.

[202] LPA, s 34(2); *Bull* v *Bull* [1955] 1 QB 234, discussed at p 325 above.

[203] *Allan* v *Liverpool Overseers* (1874) LR 9 QB 180 at p 192; *Street* at p 816; see also p 502 below.

(vii) *At a rent for a term*

One feature of the transactions discussed in the cases since *Street* is that most of them look like leases. When we consider licences cases (in Chapter 22), it will be seen that very few resemble the cases dealt with in this chapter. Some licences cases do not involve exclusive possession and so plainly cannot be leases. Many, however, do involve exclusive possession, but for indeterminate periods and usually without any rent or other annual payment.

Because *Street* requires a rent and a term, this reinforces the distinction between leases and licences. However, subsequent cases have cast doubt on these requirements, causing us to consider whether some licences cases should be recategorised as leases.[204] *Ashburn Anstalt* v *Arnold*[205] held that rent is not required for a lease: a proposition which seems clearly correct.[206] However, this does not mean that a lease necessarily results where there is exclusive possession but no rent. It is one thing to say that a lease does not require rent, but quite another to say that there must be a lease if there is a term but no rent. It is interesting that in *AG Securities*, subsequent to *Ashburn Anstalt*, Lord Templeman repeated the requirement of periodical payments. One factor should be added: in the absence of both rent and any other consideration, there will be no contract, and therefore the arrangement is likely to fall within the exceptions to *Street*.

So far as the length of the lease is concerned, the requirement of a certain maximum term was accepted by the Supreme Court in *Mexfield Housing Co-operative Ltd* v *Berrisford*.[207] Earlier, *Prudential Assurance Co Ltd* v *London Residuary Body*[208] had implied a yearly tenancy from the payment of rent. In *Mexfield*, three possibilities were identified had the lease been void: a periodic tenancy, a contractual licence and a periodic tenancy with a contractual restriction on termination. Although the case was decided on the basis of a lease for life, the Supreme Court considered that the contractual licence would best have given effect to the parties' intentions had the term been void (as it would have been in a lease to a company). As will be seen later,[209] this would have protected against attempts to revoke the licence.

The possibility of a contractual restriction on a periodic tenancy was left open.[210] Agreements for leases provide an analogy: possession under the agreement gives rise to a periodic tenancy (tenancy at will if there were no rent). Equity does not allow that legal tenancy to be terminated so as to break the contract.[211] However, the point remains very unclear.

Tenancy at will or licence?

Will the courts hold there to be a tenancy at will, rather than a licence, where there is neither a rent nor a term? The absence of rent will render it impossible to imply a periodic

---

[204] Sparkes (1993) 109 LQR 93 at pp 107–110.
[205] [1989] Ch 1, noting that rent was not required in *Radaich* v *Smith* (1959) 101 CLR 209, a case relied upon in *Street*.
[206] See p 371 above.
[207] [2012] 1 AC 955.
[208] [1992] 2 AC 386; a similar result had been reached in *Lace* v *Chantler* [1944] KB 368.
[209] See pp 486–489 below.
[210] Lord Neuburger at [69]; see also Lord Mance at [104]. Low (2102) 75 MLR 401 argues persuasively that this would best give effect to the parties' intentions.
[211] *Browne* v *Warner* (1808) 14 Ves 156, 409 (33 ER 480, 578); see p 403 below.

tenancy. Where there is no consideration at all, then we have seen that *Street* is unlikely to apply.[212] The reluctance to apply the tenancy at will in this situation may be a pointer to a reluctance to apply it in other situations. It is significant that the exceptional categories permitted by *Street* result in a licence rather than a tenancy at will.

Although the authorities tend against the tenancy at will, the rationale for this is not clear. Exclusive possession had for centuries led to a tenancy at will, regardless of rent or term. The tenancy at will explained the occupier's presence and enabled the occupier to sue in trespass: there was no need to develop a licence analysis. It is only to a modern lawyer that licences constitute a natural explanation in the absence of rent or term. Lord Denning frequently referred to licences as applying where the occupier had a personal privilege with no stake in the land.[213] Yet, in 1957, the tenancy at will was described by the House of Lords[214] as involving a personal relationship.

In *Street*, Lord Templeman fails to explain why the movement away from the tenancy at will still survives. *Ramnarace* v *Lutchman*[215] attempts to resolve this difficulty by explaining that there cannot be a tenancy at will if there is no intention to enter into legal relations. This will cover many of the exceptions to *Street*, though (perhaps surprisingly) there can be a tenancy at will where the parties are negotiating for an interest.

If there is a tenancy at will, can the parties contract so as to restrict the normal right to terminate it? Although a tenancy at will can be set up by contract, with rent being payable,[216] it is generally thought impossible to restrict rights to terminate.[217] Nevertheless, there is some support for applying a contractual analysis alongside the tenancy at will.[218] This raises questions very similar to those where there is a periodic tenancy, left open in *Mexfield*. If the courts were to take a more receptive stance towards collateral agreements as to revocation, then a movement back towards recognising more tenancies at will could be accommodated with relatively little difficulty.

2. Types of tenancies

A. Term of years absolute

The lease for a term of years is the standard form of tenancy. The period may be as short or as long as the parties choose to stipulate. This form of lease gives rise to few special problems beyond the certainty issues considered above.

---

[212] This will be relevant for many estoppel licences.

[213] See, e.g., *Cobb* v *Lane* [1952] 1 All ER 1199. Hostility to the tenancy at will was increased because a tenant at will could claim the fee simple by adverse possession after 13 years (Limitation Act 1939, s 9(1)). This provision was dropped from the Limitation Act 1980.

[214] *Wheeler* v *Mercer* [1957] AC 416 at p 427.

[215] [2001] 1 WLR 1651 (PC), especially at [17].

[216] *Doe d Bastow* v *Cox* (1847) 11 QB 122 (116 ER 421); *Manfield & Sons Ltd* v *Botchin* [1970] 2 QB 612; *Hagee (London) Ltd* v *AB Erikson & Larson* [1976] QB 209.

[217] *Errington* v *Errington* [1952] 1 KB 290 (Denning LJ); *Binions* v *Evans* [1972] Ch 359 (Lord Denning MR and Megaw LJ); *Colchester BC* v *Smith* [1991] Ch 448 at p 483.

[218] *Landale* v *Menzies* (1909) 9 CLR 89 (contrast Dixon J in *Amad* v *Grant* (1947) 74 CLR 327 at p 345); *Foster* v *Robinson* [1951] 1 KB 149 at p 156; left open by Stephenson LJ in *Binions* v *Evans* [1972] Ch 359. The strongest exponent of this analysis is Hargreaves (1953) 69 LQR 466.

B. Periodic tenancies

The nature of the periodic tenancy is that it extends automatically from one period to another. Unless either party gives notice to terminate it, it will continue. It may be regarded as an arrangement which is open-ended, although with protection against termination without adequate notice. Many periodic tenancies are implied from the payment of rent. This means that the courts have also had to imply other terms: for example, the length of notice required.

The nature of every periodic tenancy is that it constitutes a single continuing term.[219] Taking the example of a yearly tenancy, it is not regarded as a series of leases each lasting one year. Looking backwards, it may have lasted 20 years; looking forwards, it will termi-nate at the end of the current year if either party gives notice. An express provision requir-ing annual renewal is inconsistent with a periodic tenancy.[220]

The periodic tenancy, whether express or implied, constitutes a legal estate.[221] Leases exceeding three years must be created by deed, but periodic tenancies at the best rent tak-ing effect immediately are valid without writing, however long they in fact last.[222]

(i) *Creation*

The origins of periodic tenancies lie in the sixteenth century. Whether expressly created or implied by the courts, they protected tenants (otherwise tenants at will) against arbitrary immediate eviction.[223] The periodic tenancy is especially useful where the parties have reached agreement, but for some reason it cannot govern the relationship. There are two groups of examples. The first is where a lease is void for not being by deed, or else has not proceeded beyond the contract stage, but the tenant has entered and paid rent.[224] The sec-ond is where the lease has terminated, but the tenant is allowed to stay in possession, pay-ing rent as before.[225]

The common factor in these cases is the payment of rent: this distinguishes the periodic tenancy from the tenancy at will.[226] Indeed, in earlier times, the payment of rent almost always gave rise to an implication of a periodic tenancy. Provision of services would also suffice.[227] The hardship to the lessor was limited, bearing in mind that notice of at most a year could be given to terminate the tenancy.[228] The position changed in the twentieth century because of the statutory protection of tenants. For example, the protection of

---

[219] *Legg* v *Strudwick* (1709) 2 Salk 414 (91 ER 359); *Gandy* v *Jubber* (1865) 9 B&S 15 (122 ER 914); *Bowen* v *Anderson* [1894] 1 QB 164. This might be important as regards priorities, if an equitable interest is created or protected on the register whilst a periodic tenancy is running.

[220] *Gray* v *Spyer* [1922] 2 Ch 22.

[221] Simpson, *A History of the Land Law* (2nd edn), pp 252–255; *Jones* v *Mills* (1861) 10 CBNS 788 (142 ER 664).

[222] LPA, s 205(1)(xxvii).

[223] LPA, s 54(2); p 112 above. The yearly tenancy marks the longest period commonly found.

[224] E.g. *Doe d Warner* v *Browne* (1807) 8 East 165 (103 ER 305); *Martin* v *Smith* (1874) LR 9 Ex 50.

[225] E.g. *Cole* v *Kelly* [1920] 2 KB 106 (Atkin LJ at p 132); *Adler* v *Blackman* [1953] 1 QB 146.

[226] *Roe d Bree* v *Lees* (1777) 2 Wm Bl 1171 (96 ER 691); *Braythwayte* v *Hitchcock* (1842) 10 M&W 494 (152 ER 565).

[227] *Doe d Tucker* v *Morse* (1830) 1 B&Ad 365 (109 ER 822).

[228] Save where there is an enforceable agreement for a lease: equity will prevent the owner from acting upon the determination of the legal periodic tenancy: *Browne* v *Warner* (1808) 14 Ves 156, 409 (33 ER 480, 578).

business tenants applies to periodic tenancies but not to tenancies at will.[229] The result is that a periodic tenancy could be disastrous to the landlord.

There is no difficulty in saying that an express agreement for a tenancy at will precludes any periodic tenancy,[230] but will a periodic tenancy still be presumed today where the occupier is simply allowed to go in and pay rent? In *Longrigg, Burrough & Trounson* v *Smith*,[231] the tenant remained in possession and paid rent after the end of the lease. The landlord wished to evict the tenant but was unable to act until the tenant's claim to statutory security of tenure had been rejected. The Court of Appeal held that there was no periodic tenancy: the payment of rent was attributable more to the tenant's refusal to leave than to a contractual tenancy. Significantly, Ormrod LJ said that the presumption of a periodic tenancy is 'unsound and no longer holds'.

The Court of Appeal returned to the question in *Javad* v *Aqil*,[232] in which the defendant had been allowed into occupation, paying rent, in anticipation of a lease. Subsequently, disagreements as to the detailed terms caused negotiations to break down. The defendant argued that a periodic tenancy should be implied from the payment of rent, there being no express contrary agreement. This was rejected. The fundamental question is whether a tenancy was intended; this requires a consideration of all the circumstances, payment of rent being very material. The court did not find it necessary to decide whether the presumption of periodic tenancy survives to the present day: if it does, then it operates so rarely as to be insignificant. There will nearly always be other circumstances pointing in one direction or another. In *Javad*, the parties could not be taken to have agreed upon a periodic tenancy when they had not reached agreement as to the basis on which the defendant was to occupy.

The upshot of these cases is that simple payment of rent is no longer such a strong pointer to a periodic tenancy. It is necessary to consider all the circumstances to see whether such a tenancy is really intended. Relevant factors are likely to include the statutory consequences of there being a periodic tenancy (particularly important for business tenants), how long rent has been paid and the reasons why there is no full legal lease.[233] It may be easiest to argue a periodic tenancy where full agreement as to the terms has been reached, but a lease has either not yet been executed or else fails to satisfy formality requirements.[234] What if rent continues to be paid following the expiry of a term? It appears that a periodic tenancy will not be found whilst there are negotiations for the renewal of the lease.[235]

---

[229] *Wheeler* v *Mercer* [1957] AC 416 (implied tenancy at will); *Hagee (London) Ltd* v *AB Erikson & Larson* [1976] QB 209 (express tenancy at will). *Hagee* stresses that a normal lease cannot simply be dressed up as a tenancy at will. Presumably this means that it must genuinely be terminable by either party at any time.

[230] *Doe d Bastow* v *Cox* (1847) 11 QB 122 (116 ER 421); *Hagee (London) Ltd* v *AB Erikson & Larson* [1976] QB 209.

[231] [1979] 2 EGLR 42.

[232] [1991] 1 WLR 1007. See also *Cardiothoracic Institute* v *Shrewdcrest Ltd* [1986] 1 WLR 368; *D'Silva* v *Lister House Development Ltd* [1971] Ch 17; *London Baggage Company (Charing Cross) Ltd* v *Railtrack plc* [2000] L&TR 439.

[233] It is especially difficult to prove a periodic tenancy where the occupier entered as a trespasser, even if the owner is prepared to grant a lease: *Brent LB* v *O'Bryan* (1992) 65 P&CR 258 and p 387 above. See, generally, Morgan in *Modern Studies in Property Law*, Vol 6 (ed Bright), Chapter 6.

[234] *Walji* v *Mount Cook Land Ltd* [2002] 1 P&CR 163; *Hutchison* v *B&DF Ltd* [2009] L&TR 206 at [71]. Even here, a periodic tenancy is unlikely if the legal lease was intended to gain exemption from statutory protection.

[235] *Barclays Wealth Trustees (Jersey) Ltd* v *Erimus Housing Ltd* [2014] 2 P&CR 85.

Is it relevant that the owner has accepted rent in ignorance of a relevant fact? The earlier cases recognised a periodic tenancy,[236] at least where the tenant was not responsible for the mistake.[237] Subsequent indications[238] are that a periodic tenancy will less readily be implied: this fits the movement away from a strong presumption based upon payment of rent.

(ii) Terms

An initial question for implied periodic tenancies is whether the period is a week, month, quarter, year or (exceptionally) something different. It seems that the origin of the periodic tenancy lies in the yearly tenancy,[239] probably explicable by its application to agricultural land, where possession for a growing season is important. The choice of period has long been determined by the basis upon which rent is calculated. *Adler* v *Blackman*[240] confirms that the frequency of payment is not the test. If a rent of £6,000 per annum is charged, the fact that £500 is paid each month does not prevent the tenancy from being yearly. In Australia, *Moore* v *Dimond*[241] supports an argument that a yearly tenancy should be implied whenever there is possession under a void lease or an agreement for a lease, regardless of the basis upon which rent is calculated. This has the merit of giving the greatest possible protection to the tenant, although it is unclear that English courts would take a similar approach.[242]

Turning away from the period, what other terms will be implied? The courts will look to any agreement between the parties for relevant terms, whether it be a void lease,[243] an agreement for a lease or a lease that has expired.[244] As early as 1793, Lord Kenyon CJ[245] stated that a void lease: 'must regulate the terms on which the tenancy subsists in other respects, as to the rent, the time of the year the tenant is to quit, &c'. Terms will be implied only when they are consistent with a periodic tenancy. For example, the courts will not imply terms which prohibit the giving of notice.[246]

How does this apply to repairing obligations? A term in a 21-year lease requiring the tenant to undertake significant repairs at the beginning would look very odd in a monthly tenancy. However, *Martin* v *Smith*[247] illustrates a pragmatic approach. A void seven-year lease contained a covenant to redecorate in the final year. Applying this to a yearly tenancy

---

[236] *Doe d Martin & Jones* v *Watts* (1797) 7 TR 83 (101 ER 866) (owner's ignorance of own title); *Doe d Tucker* v *Morse* (1830) 1 B&Ad 365 (109 ER 822) (owner unaware of invalidity of lease granted by predecessor).
[237] *Doe d Lord* v *Crago* (1848) 6 CB 90 (136 ER 1185).
[238] *Ladies' Hosiery & Underwear Ltd* v *Parker* [1930] 1 Ch 304 (Maugham J).
[239] *Roe d Bree* v *Lees* (1777) 2 Wm Bl 1171 (96 ER 691); *Richardson* v *Langridge* (1811) 4 Taunt 127 (128 ER 277).
[240] [1953] 1 QB 146. See also *Ladies' Hosiery & Underwear Ltd* v *Parker* [1930] 1 Ch 304 (Maugham J); *EON Motors Ltd* v *Secretary of State for the Environment* [1981] 1 EGLR 19.
[241] (1929) 43 CLR 105 (High Court).
[242] The operation of the equitable lease arising from the agreement will often render the choice of period irrelevant (*Walsh* v *Lonsdale* (1882) 21 Ch D 9). In *Moore* v *Dimond*, there had been no final agreement as to the terms of the lease.
[243] *Doe d Rigge* v *Bell* (1793) 5 TR 471 (101 ER 265); *Martin* v *Smith* (1874) LR 9 Ex 50.
[244] *Thomas* v *Packer* (1857) 1 H&N 669 (156 ER 1370).
[245] *Doe d Rigge* v *Bell* (1793) 5 TR 471 at p 472 (101 ER 265 at p 266).
[246] *Doe d Warner* v *Browne* (1807) 8 East 165 (103 ER 305).
[247] (1874) LR 9 Ex 50; some of the reasoning is more appropriate to equitable leases. Contrast *Pinero* v *Judson* (1829) 6 Bing 206 (130 ER 1259).

is not straightforward, as it cannot be supposed to last more than a year. Nevertheless, the court implied a term that, if the yearly tenancy in fact lasted for seven years, redecoration would be undertaken in that year.

Straightforward examples of implied terms have been payment of rent in advance,[248] arbitration clauses[249] and forfeiture clauses.[250] A rather different implication is that the periodic tenancy will terminate automatically at the end of the period of the void lease or agreement for a lease, without the normal need to give notice.[251]

One troublesome point on the operation of periodic tenancies should be noted. Suppose the landlord wishes to increase the rent; how can this be done? The problem is that whilst the lease continues, the original rent applies. The landlord has no power to increase it, even by giving the same notice of the increase as is required to terminate the tenancy. Instead, the landlord must actually give notice to terminate the lease, offering a new tenancy at the increased rent.[252] Fortunately for both parties, this cumbersome and alarming procedure can be circumvented by an express term permitting rent increases.

(iii) *Termination*

The development of periodic tenancies lay in the desire to prevent the eviction of tenants without notice. The parties can, of course, stipulate whatever period of notice they wish,[253] provided it satisfies the certainty rules for leases. In the absence of specific agreement, the courts have laid down acceptable periods for each form of periodic tenancy. For a yearly tenancy, there must be six months' notice, whilst for shorter periods, the entire length of the period is required. Of course, these are minimum periods: a longer notice will be valid.

Perhaps the core principle is that reasonable notice must be given,[254] but the six-month period for yearly tenancies was settled by the early sixteenth century.[255] Although the position may be less settled for other periodic tenancies,[256] the modern approach is to prefer the certainty of a specific period to the uncertainty of reasonable notice.[257]

A significant trap for landlords is that the notice must expire at the end of a period: at the end of the week, month, quarter or year.[258] It follows that, in a yearly tenancy, being a day late results in the lease being prolonged for a further year. Once a period starts, it cannot be cut short by a notice: it must continue until its natural conclusion. Not knowing when a period expires may be a real problem, particularly for tenancies created many years

---

[248] *Lee v Smith* (1854) 9 Exch 662 (156 ER 284).
[249] *Morgan v William Harrison Ltd* [1907] 2 Ch 137.
[250] *Thomas v Packer* (1857) 1 H&N 669 (156 ER 1370).
[251] *Doe d Bromfield v Smith* (1805) 6 East 530 (102 ER 1390); *Doe d Davenish v Moffatt* (1850) 15 QB 257 (117 ER 455).
[252] *GLC v Connolly* [1970] 2 QB 100.
[253] *Breams Property Investment Co Ltd v Stroulger* [1948] 2 KB 1; formality requirements may be triggered if the lease is to last more than three years.
[254] *Doe d Martin & Jones v Watts* (1797) 7 TR 83 (101 ER 866).
[255] *Jones v Mills* (1861) 10 CBNS 788 at p 799 (142 ER 664 at p 668); *Prudential Assurance Co Ltd v London Residuary Body* [1992] 2 AC 386 at p 393.
[256] Note the differing views expressed in *Jones v Mills* (1861) 10 CBNS 788 (142 ER 664). Cooke [1992] Conv 263 argues that 28 days should suffice for monthly leases, although they are held on a calendar-month basis.
[257] *Queen's Club Gardens Estates Ltd v Bignell* [1924] 1 KB 117, observing at pp 123–124 that expressly giving 'reasonable notice' would be ineffective.
[258] Ibid; *Lemon v Lardeur* [1946] KB 613.

earlier by a predecessor in title. This can be overcome by issuing a notice expressly effective at the next 'proper day of expiry'.[259] In a weekly tenancy, this means that the landlord needs to wait for two weeks after giving notice before insisting upon possession. In an express periodic tenancy, the landlord can avoid the problem by stipulating that the tenancy shall end on the expiry of notice at any time.

A problem which has provoked much controversy in recent years concerns the giving of notice where joint tenants hold a periodic tenancy. It was held by the House of Lords in *Hammersmith and Fulham LBC v Monk*[260] that a notice by one of two joint tenants is effective to terminate the periodic tenancy. The essence of the reasoning is that joint tenants must act together; this is unobjectionable. Nevertheless, the nature of a periodic tenancy is that it continues unless notice is given. It is not as if each new period is a separate lease, and not as if the parties need take any steps if they wish the tenancy to continue. Against this background, one would have thought that giving notice would have required the participation of both joint tenants: it is a positive step changing what would otherwise be the legal position. The answer of Lord Bridge[261] to this argument was that 'the substance of the matter is that it is by his omission to give notice of termination that each party signifies the necessary positive assent to the extension of the term for a further period'.

Although authority favoured the result reached,[262] the result is unattractive.[263] It means that one joint tenant can effectively deprive the other of a valuable property right. Furthermore, it cannot be avoided by reliance on the status of the joint tenant as a trustee,[264] and even an injunction under the Family Law Act 1996 preventing notice is unlikely to affect a landlord unaware of it.[265] It has been argued that, without questioning the principle in *Monk*, the automatic eviction by a local authority of the occupying joint tenant is subject to a human rights challenge, based on the Article 8 right to respect for homes. Though the application of Article 8 was rejected by a majority of the House of Lords in *Harrow LBC v Qazi*,[266] the European Court of Human Rights found in favour of the tenant in *McCann v UK*.[267] Subsequently, as was seen in Chapter 3, the approach to Article 8 in *Qazi* and other similar cases was rejected by the Supreme Court in *Manchester City Council v Pinnock*.[268] It is now apparent that a proportionality test applies in all cases.

---

[259] *Queen's Club Gardens Estates Ltd v Bignell* [1924] 1 KB 117 at p 126.

[260] [1992] 1 AC 478 (see p 339 above).

[261] [1992] 1 AC 478 at pp 490–491. The House of Lords adopts a contractual analysis to help explain the result: Dewar (1992) 108 LQR 375.

[262] *Doe d Aslin v Summersett* (1830) 1 B&Ad 135 (109 ER 738) (joint tenants as lessors); *Leek & Moorlands BS v Clark* [1952] 2 QB 788.

[263] Webb [1983] Conv 194; Dewar (1992) 108 LQR 375; Tee [1992] CLJ 218; Goulding [1992] Conv 279; Shorrock [1995] Conv 424.

[264] *Hammersmith and Fulham LBC v Monk* [1992] 1 AC 478 at p 493; *Crawley BC v Ure* [1996] QB 13; *Notting Hill Housing Trust v Brackley* [2002] HLR 212.

[265] *Harrow LBC v Johnstone* [1997] 1 WLR 459 at p 471 (Lord Hoffmann, supported by Lord Mustill, though Lord Browne-Wilkinson left the point open).

[266] [2004] 1 AC 983 (Howell [2004] Conv 406; Bright (2004) 120 LQR 398); all the judges agreed that the Article 8 defence failed on the facts. *Qazi* was confirmed by the House of Lords in *Kay v Lambeth LBC* [2006] 2 AC 465.

[267] [2008] 2 FLR 899, described by Lord Scott as 'quite astonishing' in *Doherty v Birmingham CC* [2009] AC 367 at [86].

[268] [2011] 2 AC 104; see p 22 above.

This does not mean that the tenant necessarily wins. *Wandsworth LBC* v *Dixon*[269] held (before *Pinnock*) that *McCann* applies only where the local authority engineers the giving of notice so as to bypass the tenant's statutory protection. Although, following *Pinnock*, the local authority must be prepared to justify the loss of the home in all cases, the facts may render this more or less difficult. As it is not easy to challenge the local authority decision when the local authority has no role other than as recipient of the notice, a renewed human rights attack was mounted on *Monk* itself in *Sims* v *Dacorum BC*.[270] However, the Supreme Court rejected this attack, whether based on Article 1, Protocol 1, or Article 8. It was stressed that the loss of the property resulted from the exercise of a term of the lease. It would be surprising if the result were to be different if the lease had been silent as to notice, so that Monk provided the only basis for giving notice. However, the Law Commission has recommended that a joint tenant of a residential tenancy should be able to give notice to leave the joint tenancy without terminating the lease.[271]

C. Tenancy at will

Much of the law relating to tenancies at will has already been considered above. We have seen that its role has been diminished by the expansion of the licence category, though *Street* v *Mountford* and *Ramnarace* v *Lutchman* may restore it somewhat.[272] It may also be created expressly, even if rent is payable.[273]

The principal feature of the tenancy at will is that either party can terminate it without prior notice.[274] Even where the tenant needs to remove goods or crops from the land, this does not delay the ending of the tenancy; there is merely a right to enter to remove them.[275] Its personal nature is shown by the fact that it terminates when either party assigns[276] or on the death of either party.[277] We have seen that it is uncertain whether there can be a contractual limit on termination.[278]

D. Tenancy at sufferance

The tenancy at sufferance is reserved for a tenant who holds over on the termination of a lease: to someone who 'entreth by a lawfull lease, and holdeth over by wrong'.[279] It has the effect that the tenant does not become a trespasser (and cannot claim by adverse possession), although the tenancy can be terminated at any time.

---

[269] [2009] L&TR 503 (Judge Bidder QC); Davis and Hughes [2010] Conv 57. The later Strasbourg cases (cited in *Pinnock*) place more stress on the home (*R (Coombes)* v *SSCLG* [2010] 2 All ER 940 at [42]–[45]) and *Chesterfield BC* v *Bailey* [2011] EW Misc 18 (CC) indicates a slightly more generous approach.

[270] [2015] AC 1336.

[271] Law Com No 297, paras 2.44, 4.12.

[272] See p 396 above; *Heslop* v *Burns* [1974] 1 WLR 1241 (especially Scarman LJ at p 1253).

[273] *Hagee (London) Ltd* v *AB Erikson & Larson* [1976] QB 209 (see n 229 above).

[274] Conduct may suffice: quarrying by the landlord (*Doe d Bennett* v *Turner* (1840) 7 M&W 226 (151 ER 749)) and voluntary waste by tenant (*Countess of Shrewsbury's Case* (1600) 5 Co Rep 13b (77 ER 68)).

[275] Co Litt 55a.

[276] Provided that the other party has notice: *Doe d Davies* v *Thomas* (1851) 6 Exch 854 (155 ER 792) (landlord's assignment); *Pinhorn* v *Souster* (1853) 8 Exch 763 at p 772 (155 ER 1560 at pp 1564–1565) (tenant's assignment). The normal rule is that leases can be assigned, even where to do so is a breach of covenant.

[277] *James* v *Dean* (1805) 11 Ves 383 (32 ER 1135).

[278] See p 396 above.

[279] Co Litt 57b.

If the landlord assents to the holding over,[280] then the relationship will become that of tenancy at will, or periodic tenancy on the payment of rent. On the other hand, a tenant who retains possession in the face of positive objection by the landlord will become a trespasser.[281] Furthermore, the former tenant may be liable for double rent after a notice to quit.[282]

E. Equitable leases

For centuries, equity has recognised the rights of 'lessees' under contracts for leases and endeavoured to equate their position with that of legal tenants. The most important application of this is where a purported lease is void because it is not by deed: equity treats it as an agreement for a lease and enforces it as such. We should note one significant limit in the modern law: contracts for leases have to be in writing signed by both parties. Failure to comply with this formality requirement will preclude the equitable lease analysis.[283]

A clear example of equity's role is found in *Browne* v *Warner*.[284] A lease was void because of lack of formalities, but the tenant entered into occupation and paid rent; this gave rise to a periodic tenancy. The landlord gave the necessary notice to terminate the periodic tenancy, although in breach of the void lease. The landlord succeeded in the common law courts,[285] but equity recognised an agreement for a lease (arising from the void lease) and granted an injunction to prevent enforcement of the common law judgment. The final result was that the tenant was protected as well as if there had been a legal lease. Some years later, it was argued in *Parker* v *Taswell*[286] that the legislation rendering informal leases void had the additional effect of precluding equity from treating them as effective contracts. That argument was rejected; the role of the equitable lease in these cases has never since been seriously challenged.

The role of the equitable lease was enhanced by the Judicature Acts 1873 and 1875, whereby the old courts of law and equity were replaced by the High Court. In any conflict between rules of law and rules of equity, the rules of equity were to prevail.[287] Within a few years, the question arose whether the legal remedy of distress (seizure of the tenant's goods for unpaid rent)[288] could be used by an equitable lessor. In *Walsh* v *Lonsdale*,[289] Sir George Jessel MR uttered a famous dictum:

> There are not two estates as there were formerly, one estate at common law by reason of the payment of rent from year to year, and an estate in equity under the agreement. There is only one

[280] Readily implied: *Canterbury Cathedral* v *Whitbread* (1995) 72 P&CR 9 (negotiations for renewal) and *Banjo* v *Brent LBC* [2005] 1 WLR 2520. Receipt of 'rent' is not enough if the landlord objects to the holding over and views it as a form of compensation: *Vaughan-Armatrading* v *Sarsah* (1995) 27 HLR 631.
[281] *Remon* v *City of London Real Property Co Ltd* [1921] 1 KB 49 (Scrutton LJ).
[282] For details, see Megarry and Wade, *The Law of Real Property* (8th edn), paras 17-110 et seq. This liability applies only if the landlord treats the tenant as a trespasser: *Oliver Ashworth (Holdings) Ltd* v *Ballard (Kent) Ltd* [2000] Ch 12.
[283] Law of Property (Miscellaneous Provisions) Act 1989, s 2; *United Bank of Kuwait plc* v *Sahib* [1997] Ch 107 at p 140.
[284] (1808) 14 Ves 156, 409 (33 ER 480, 578).
[285] *Doe d Warner* v *Browne* (1807) 8 East 165 (103 ER 305).
[286] (1858) 2 De G&J 559 (44 ER 1106), based upon Real Property Act 1845.
[287] Section 25(11) of the 1873 Act.
[288] Today, commercial rent arrears recovery.
[289] (1882) 21 Ch D 9 at pp 14–15. For consideration as to how far the result went beyond the earlier law, see Sparkes (1988) 8 OxJLS 350.

Court, and the equity rules prevail in it. The tenant holds under an agreement for a lease. He holds, therefore, under the same terms in equity as if a lease had been granted, it being a case in which both parties admit that relief is capable of being given by specific performance.

The result was that the distress was lawful, even though the lease was merely equitable.

For the *Walsh* v *Lonsdale* principle to apply, specific performance of the agreement must be available.[290] The major significance of this is that breach of the terms of the agreement may result in refusal of the discretionary remedy of specific performance.[291] This is a troublesome point, because legislation sometimes protects tenants against forfeiture for breaches of covenants. Although a technical breach will not preclude specific performance,[292] there is a danger that a harsher attitude will be adopted by equity than applies in exercising the statutory protection.[293] The legislation extends expressly to agreements for leases,[294] and the better view is that it is not constrained by the old specific performance rules.[295] The specific performance requirement may also pose problems where the contract is disputed[296] or there are conditions precedent to the grant of a legal lease.[297] Despite the fact that the lease has terminated by forfeiture, the *Walsh* principle applies so as to regulate obligations arising before forfeiture.[298]

Assuming that specific performance is available, just how great is the effect of *Walsh* v *Lonsdale*? The question is whether 'an agreement for a lease is in all respects as good as a lease', a proposition denied by Maitland.[299] Although the dicta of Sir George Jessel MR are indeed famous, it should not be overlooked that other judges adopted a far more cautious approach. In *Walsh* v *Lonsdale* itself, neither Cotton LJ nor Lindley LJ adopted such a broad analysis. A few years later, Lopes LJ was distinctly hostile to the idea that an equitable lease was equivalent to a legal lease.[300] On the other hand, several judges soon favoured the approach of Sir George Jessel MR.[301] This is also the trend in more recent cases.[302]

As between the lessor and lessee, the cases justify the conclusion that there is little difference. Nevertheless, they are not identical. One statutory point is that certain easements

---

[290] Gardner (1987) 7 OxJLS 60 is critical of the continued stress on specific performance, arguing that recognition of agreements for leases should be no more discretionary than any other proprietary interest and that the movement is towards applying common rules to legal and equitable leases.

[291] *Coatsworth* v *Johnson* (1886) 55 LJQB 220; *Swain* v *Ayres* (1888) 21 QBD 289; cf *Australian Hardwoods Pty Ltd* v *Commissioner for Railways* [1961] 1 WLR 425 (PC).

[292] *Parker* v *Taswell* (1858) 2 De G&J 559 (44 ER 1106).

[293] See *Baxton* v *Kara* [1982] 1 NSWLR 604.

[294] LPA, s 146(5)(a).

[295] Woodfall, *Landlord and Tenant*, para 17.125; *Sport Internationaal Bussum BV* v *Inter-Footwear Ltd* [1984] 1 WLR 776 at p 790.

[296] *Gray* v *Spyer* [1922] 2 Ch 22.

[297] *Cornish* v *Brook Green Laundry Ltd* [1959] 1 QB 394; *Euston Centre Properties Ltd* v *H&J Wilson Ltd* [1982] 1 EGLR 57.

[298] *Darjan Estate Co plc* v *Hurley* [2012] 1 WLR 1782, applying *Gilbey* v *Cossey* (1912) 106 LT 607.

[299] *Equity* (2nd edn), p 158.

[300] (1888) 21 QBD 289 at p 297.

[301] *Swain* v *Ayres* at p 293 (Lord Esher MR); *Re Maughan* (1885) 14 QBD 956 (Field J); *Lowther* v *Heaver* (1889) 41 Ch D 248 (Cotton LJ).

[302] *Industrial Properties (Barton Hill) Ltd* v *AEI Ltd* [1977] QB 580 (applying *Walsh* v *Lonsdale* where equitable enforceability of two agreements necessary); *Tinsley* v *Milligan* [1994] 1 AC 340.

implied into legal leases will not be implied into equitable leases.[303] Other statutory provisions, particularly those applying to 'conveyances', likewise differentiate between legal and equitable leases.[304]

However, it is with third parties that the differences become most acute. For a start, priority rules for legal and equitable interests are very different: legal interests bind purchasers far more readily. One example is that, for registered land, legal leases not exceeding seven years are overriding interests, but not equitable leases (absent actual occupation).[305] There may also be differences as regards the running of covenants. Farwell J[306] was emphatic that legal and equitable leases are not equated by *Walsh v Lonsdale*: 'the doctrine is applicable only in those cases where specific performance can be obtained between the same parties in the same court, and at the same time as the subsequent legal question falls to be determined'. These points show that it is simplistic to think that legal and equitable leases have been equated, though doubtless the trend is towards minimising the differences.[307]

Is it in any event correct, as Sir George Jessel MR indicated, to say that there is no longer a legal periodic tenancy where there is an agreement for a lease? Undoubtedly, it is irrelevant in the huge majority of cases, but cannot the tenant fall back on the periodic tenancy if the equitable lease fails? Suppose the equitable lease is unenforceable against a purchaser, not having been protected on the register. Surely the tenant could assert a legal periodic tenancy against the purchaser? It could be a point of great significance, bearing in mind that statutory protection could render the periodic tenancy safe against termination.[308]

F. Tenancies by estoppel

This area will be considered in outline only.[309] It sometimes happens that the lessor does not possess a legal estate at the time of granting the lease, often because of a mere technical problem which is unlikely to prejudice anyone. This does not stop there being a tenancy as between the parties,[310] though it might be thought to have an effect on the enforcement of some of its provisions. So long as the tenant's possession has not been disturbed by a third party, there is a rule that the tenant is estopped from denying the landlord's title.[311] In other words, so long as the tenant is enjoying

---

[303] *Borman v Griffith* [1930] 1 Ch 493 (LPA, s 62).

[304] *Long v Tower Hamlets LBC* [1998] Ch 197 (Limitation Act 1980, Sched 1, para 5), criticised by Perkins (1997) 113 LQR 394.

[305] *City Permanent BS v Miller* [1952] Ch 840 (see now LRA, Sched 3, para 1).

[306] *Manchester Brewery Co v Coombs* [1901] 2 Ch 608 at p 617; see also *Purchase v Lichfield Brewery Co* [1915] 1 KB 184.

[307] See *Boyer v Warbey* [1953] 1 QB 234 in the context of covenants; also Landlord and Tenant (Covenants) Act 1995, s 28(1).

[308] Adams [1988] Conv 16.

[309] See generally Martin (1978) 42 Conv 137.

[310] '[I]t is not the estoppel which creates the tenancy, but the tenancy which creates the estoppel': Lord Hoffmann in *Bruton v London & Quadrant Housing Trust* [2000] 1 AC 406 at p 416, criticised by Routley (2000) 63 MLR 424. *Bruton* is considered at p 413 below.

[311] It does not apply if the landlord's title terminates after the grant: *National Westminster Ltd v Hart* [1983] 1 QB 773.

possession, neither the lease nor obligations under it can be escaped because of a defect in the landlord's title.[312]

Of course, if the landlord possesses no estate in the land, then the tenant cannot have an estate binding on third parties. However, the concept of feeding the estoppel does have a proprietary effect. If (as commonly happens) the landlord subsequently acquires the legal estate, then the tenant is treated as having a legal estate from that time: the estoppel is said to be fed.[313] This may be of significance where there is a priority dispute between the tenant and, say, a subsequent mortgagee from the landlord.

G. Special cases

(i) Leases for life

Leases for life are curious in that they form a hybrid between freehold life estates and terms of years. In the nineteenth century, the lease for life was always a freehold estate, whether it was part of a settlement or more like a lease with rent being payable.[314] The modern regulation of settlements, now found in the Trusts of Land and Appointment of Trustees Act 1996, applies wherever there is a life interest. It is quite unsuitable for commercial leases for life.

The legislative response has been to distinguish between leases for life where there is a rent or capital payment and those where there is neither. Where they are lacking, the lease for life appears to fall within the 1996 Act. Where there is rent or capital payment,[315] this is taken as the hallmark of a commercial relationship that should be treated like any other lease. In order that it satisfies normal leasehold certainty rules, s 149(6) of the Law of Property Act 1925 converts it into a 90-year lease, terminable on notice given after death.[316]

This approach is also adopted for a lease for years terminable on death.[317] Where there is rent or capital payment, it is converted into a lease for 90 years terminable on notice after death. This provision could have the effect of creating a longer lease than agreed by the parties. For example, a lease at a rent for three years terminable on death inexplicably becomes a lease for 90 years terminable on notice after death.[318] If there is no rent or capital payment then, despite the existence of a certain maximum duration, it will not be legal: legal leases cannot be made terminable on death.[319]

---

[312] Applicable even after the lease has come to an end: *Industrial Properties (Barton Hill) Ltd* v *AEI Ltd* [1977] QB 580.

[313] The principles apply similarly to the grants of other interests: see *First National Bank plc* v *Thompson* [1996] Ch 231 (charge) for a full discussion.

[314] Challis, *Real Property* (3rd edn, Sweet), p 340.

[315] Or connected sale to the landlord at a clear undervalue: *Skipton BS* v *Clayton* (1993) 66 P&CR 223.

[316] Similar provisions apply to leases terminable on marriage.

[317] Leases terminable on notice after death are outside s 149(6) and can be legal leases: *Bass Holdings Ltd* v *Lewis* [1986] 2 EGLR 40 (approved by Lord Walker in *Mexfield Housing Co-operative Ltd* v *Berrisford* [2012] 1 AC 955 at [84]; see also Lord Neuberger at [51]).

[318] A result narrowly avoided in *Bass Holdings Ltd* v *Lewis* [1986] 2 EGLR 40 because the lease was not technically terminable on death.

[319] LPA, s 205(1)(xxvii).

(ii) *Perpetually renewable leases*

Leases quite commonly contain an option for the tenant to renew the lease. The courts presume that the renewed lease will not include a renewal clause, so that the maximum length is two terms.[320] However, the original lease may explicitly provide that the renewed lease shall include the renewal option. This has the result that each renewed lease contains an option to renew,[321] and the leases may carry on if the tenant continues to exercise the option.

The 1925 legislation provides for such a scenario by converting it into a 2,000-year lease, with a right for the tenant to terminate it at any of the former renewal dates.[322] This has the merit of eliminating renewal costs and also the risk of forgetting to renew.

A number of cases have had to deal with the question whether a lease is perpetually renewable. The basic position is that, following pre-1925 principles, it is not necessary to provide explicitly that the lease is perpetually renewable.[323] On the other hand, the courts believe that the parties are unlikely to intend a perpetual lease. They will clutch at straws to construe the lease so that the option is to be inserted in only the first renewal,[324] resulting in a maximum length of three terms (original and two renewals).

(iii) *Discontinuous leases*

It is possible to create leases that do not involve continuous possession. Thus, one may let property for three successive bank holidays. This is a single lease, rather than three separate leases.[325] Such leases could be used for timeshare schemes,[326] although it is not the favoured way of structuring timesharing.[327]

The law on discontinuous leases has not been fully worked out. It appears that the single term analysis means that a 30-year discontinuous lease does not fall foul of the prohibition on leases commencing more than 21 years in the future.[328] It is uncertain whether a lease for one week every year for 10 years is a lease exceeding 3 years so as to require a deed.[329]

---

[320] *Caerphilly Concrete Products Ltd* v *Owen* [1972] 1 WLR 372 at p 374 (Russell LJ).

[321] *Hare* v *Burges* (1857) 4 K&J 45, especially at p 56 (70 ER 19 at p 24).

[322] LPA 1922, s 145, Sched 15 (see especially paras 5, 10–12). Pawlowski and Brown [2014] Conv 482 are critical of the outcome, noting that it will rarely be intended by the parties.

[323] *Parkus* v *Greenwood* [1950] Ch 644, followed in *Caerphilly Concrete Products Ltd* v *Owen* [1972] 1 WLR 372 (Sachs LJ expressing reluctance).

[324] *Marjorie Burnett Ltd* v *Barclay* (1980) 125 SJ 199 (the suggestion that seven-year rent reviews are inimical to 2,000-year leases is puzzling).

[325] *Smallwood* v *Sheppards* [1895] 2 QB 627.

[326] A typical example is where the tenant has the use of a holiday home for a particular week each year. They are regulated by the Timeshare Act 1992; Timeshare Regulations 1997 (SI 1997 No 1081).

[327] Edmonds, *International Timesharing* (3rd edn), pp 27 et seq.

[328] *Cottage Holiday Associates Ltd* v *Customs & Excise Commissioners* [1983] QB 735 (LPA, s 149(3); see p 372 above).

[329] *Cottage Holiday Associates Ltd* v *Customs & Excise Commissioners* [1983] QB 735 might suggest not, although the issues in that case were very different. Discontinuous leases of any length constitute registrable dispositions: LRA, s 27(2)(b)(iii).

Further reading

Bright, S [2002] CLJ 146: Avoiding tenancy legislation: sham and contracting out revisited.

Gardner, S (1987) 7 OxJLS 60: Equity, estate contracts and the Judicature Acts: *Walsh* v *Lonsdale* revisited.

Hill, J (1996) 16 LS 200: Intention and the creation of property rights: are leases different?

Low, K (2012) 75 MLR 401: Certainty of terms and leases: curiouser and curiouser.

McFarlane, B and Simpson, E F (2003) 'Tackling avoidance' in *Rationalizing Property, Equity and Trusts*, (ed J Getzler), OUP Oxford, Chapter 8.

Sparkes, P (1993) 109 LQR 93: Certainty of leasehold terms.

Williams, I [2015] CLJ 592: The certainty of terms requirement in leases: nothing lasts forever.

19
Leases: obligations and remedies

Introduction

The relationship between landlord and tenant involves obligations on each side, continuing for the duration of the lease. Given the millions of leases and their economic and social significance, it is not surprising that a substantial body of legal rules regulates the landlord–tenant relationship. In part, these rules spell out the terms implied into leases and how they are to be interpreted. However, they also place limits on what terms the parties may insert in leases and govern their enforcement.

There has long been statutory regulation of leases, especially of residential leases. This regulation has included control over the terms of leases (especially repairing obligations), control over termination of leases and control over rent levels.[1] Housing law has been reviewed by the Law Commission in a major project.[2] This impacts on some of the material dealt with in this chapter, although it is mostly outside the scope of the topics we consider. So far as landlords' obligations are concerned, this chapter will concentrate upon the tenant's right to enjoy the land and obligations regarding repair. Tenants' obligations are generally spelt out in individual leases: little is implied other than a duty to take care of the premises. Our major interest regarding their obligations will lie in landlords' rights to forfeit leases in the event of breach.

1. The operation of contract principles

One initial point concerns the extent to which leases are subject to normal contract rules. It has long been recognised that leases are almost invariably contracts, albeit special in that a proprietary interest is conferred on the tenant (T). Nevertheless, many leases rules constitute exceptions to normal contract rules. In part, this is because the contract rules are relatively modern, developed after the leasehold relationship had already been worked out.[3]

In recent decades, the courts have been more inclined to apply normal contract rules. Perhaps the best-known example of the invasion of contract rules is the application of

---

[1] This threefold division is by no means comprehensive. Thus, landlords owe duties to provide certain information to tenants: Landlord and Tenant Act 1985, ss 1–7; Landlord and Tenant Act 1987, ss 46–48, 50.
[2] Law Com No 297: *Renting Homes*; see Partington in *Modern Studies in Property Law*, Vol 4 (ed Cooke), Chapter 1.
[3] See Bradbrook (1976) 10 MULR 459 at p 464.

frustration. In *National Carriers Ltd* v *Panalpina (Northern) Ltd*,[4] the landlord (L) argued that the lease had been effective to vest an estate in T and therefore was not amenable to frustration. The House of Lords resolved a long-standing question by holding that frustration can apply to leases. On the other hand, it remains difficult to prove frustration. *Panalpina* involved lack of access to the premises for 20 months out of a 10-year lease: the House unanimously decided that this did not frustrate the lease.

It is plain that leases are more than contracts, in that they involve proprietary interests. This was emphasised by Millett LJ in *Ingram* v *IRC*.[5] Whilst it cannot be doubted that most leases do constitute contracts and that many contract rules will apply, it does not follow that we can simply treat leases as if they were contracts and no more. As Millett LJ observed, 'It is easy to make too much of the contractual nature of the relationship.'[6] There may be particular issues (as yet unexplored) when the landlord and tenant are assignees, so that there is no contract between them.[7]

Repudiatory breach

Contractual methods of terminating leases on breach have been prominent in litigation. Breach by T usually enables L to terminate the lease under a forfeiture clause. Repudiation under general contract principles might remain useful in two respects. First, it might operate in the absence of an express forfeiture clause,[8] as is required for forfeiture.[9] Next, the old forfeiture rule was that T's liability to pay rent ceased on forfeiture.[10] If future rent can be claimed following repudiatory breach, this would be important.

In 1985, the High Court of Australia recognised that T's repudiatory breach entitled L to terminate the lease under normal contract principles.[11] This enabled L to claim damages for rent payable after termination. Some English cases lend support to the repudiatory breach analysis.[12] However, the application of repudiatory breach to breaches by T was

---

[4] [1981] AC 675 (Lord Russell disagreeing). Performance of covenants may be excused by intervening circumstances: *John Lewis Properties plc* v *Viscount Chelsea* [1993] 2 EGLR 77.

[5] [1997] 4 All ER 395: dissenting, but upheld and approved in the House of Lords [2000] 1 AC 293. Brown and Pawlowski (2009) 13 L&T Rev 145 at p 147 observe that contract analyses may operate only as between the original landlord and tenant, but see *Gumland Property Holdings Pty Ltd* v *Duffy Bros* (2008) 234 CLR 337, [66]–[86]. Such a restriction might well be inconvenient.

[6] Ibid, at p 422. It was argued that a nominee cannot lease to his beneficiary, as this would involve contracting with oneself. In the House of Lords, Lord Hoffmann considered that such a lease involves real obligations: [2000] 1 AC 293 at p 305.

[7] Cf Wonnacott (2014) 130 LQR 635 at p 644.

[8] The contrary view was taken by Brennan J in *Progressive Mailing House Pty Ltd* v *Tabali Pty Ltd* (1985) 157 CLR 17 at pp 42–43.

[9] *Total Oil Great Britain Ltd* v *Thompson Garages (Biggin Hill) Ltd* [1972] 1 QB 318 (Lord Denning MR at p 324).

[10] *Walls* v *Atcheson* (1826) 11 Moore CP & Exch Rep 379; *Jones* v *Carter* (1846) 15 M&W 718 at p 726 (153 ER 1040 at p 1043); *Canas Property Co Ltd* v *KL Television Services Ltd* [1970] 2 QB 433. If T remains in possession, there is liability for mesne profits (the use value of the land): *Moore* v *Assignment Courier Ltd* [1977] 1 WLR 638. See also Mason J in *Progressive Mailing* (1985) 157 CLR 17 at pp 31–32.

[11] *Progressive Mailing House Pty Ltd* v *Tabali Pty Ltd* (1985) 157 CLR 17; Carter and Hill [1986] Conv 262; Effron (1988) 14 Monash LR 83. See also *Gumland Property Holdings Pty Ltd* v *Duffy Bros* (2008) 234 CLR 237.

[12] *WG Clark (Properties) Ltd* v *Dupre Properties Ltd* [1992] Ch 297 (T's disclaimer of lease as repudiation); *Re Park Air Services plc* [1997] 1 WLR 1376 at pp 1385–1386; *Abidogun* v *Frolan Health Care Ltd* [2002] L&TR 275.

subsequently questioned by the Court of Appeal in *Reichman* v *Beveridge*.[13] In particular, it was thought that claims for future rent could not be brought. *Reichman* stands in contrast to the general move towards adopting contractual analyses. However, it is important that we should not countenance the use of repudiation to avoid forfeiture rules which are designed to protect tenants. Indeed, the earlier cases had held that these rules apply to repudiatory breach.[14]

Turning to breach by L, it is unusual for the lease to allow T to resile from the lease.[15] In *Hussein* v *Mehlman*,[16] Assistant Recorder Sedley QC held that T was held justified in leaving the premises after 15 months of a three-year lease, because of L's serious and continuing failure to repair. This application of repudiatory breach seems generally accepted.[17]

Other applications of contract principles

In what other contexts have contract rules been applied? It is not surprising that normal rules as to entering into contracts, including misrepresentation and mistake,[18] are applied to the creation of leases.[19] Rent has been viewed as a contractual payment rather than a service issuing out of the land.[20] A notice by one joint tenant to terminate a periodic tenancy has been viewed in contractual terms by the House of Lords in *Hammersmith and Fulham LBC* v *Monk*,[21] although it is interesting that commentators have expressed reservations.[22]

Another significant development is the courts' willingness to imply terms on normal contractual principles.[23] This appears to follow from *Liverpool City Council* v *Irwin*,[24] in which the House of Lords implied an obligation on the landlord of a block of flats to maintain common access facilities. This approach may enable the courts to imply obligations on landlords more readily,[25] although it is unlikely to produce markedly different results.

---

[13] [2007] 1 P&CR 358 at [26]–[27], [42] (Morgan [2008] Conv 165 and *Modern Studies in Property Law*, Vol 5 (ed Dixon), Chapter 17; Pawlowski (2010) 126 LQR 361).

[14] *Abidogun* v *Frolan Health Care Ltd* [2002] L&TR 275 (Pawlowski [2002] Conv 399). It is otherwise in Australia: *Apriaden Pty Ltd* v *Seacrest Pty Ltd* [2005] VSCA 139 (Dowling (2006) 10 L&T Rev 12).

[15] Many leases are valuable to tenants, so any right in T to terminate would be an illusory advantage.

[16] [1992] 2 EGLR 87; Bright [1993] Conv 71; Harpum [1993] CLJ 212; Pawlowski [1995] Conv 379. See also *GS Fashions Ltd* v *B&Q plc* [1995] 1 WLR 1088; *Chartered Trust plc* v *Davies* (1997) 76 P&CR 396.

[17] Law Com No 297, para 4.14 proposes giving it statutory effect for residential tenancies.

[18] Misrepresentation Act 1967, s 1(b); *Killick* v *Roberts* [1991] 1 WLR 1146 (misrepresentation by T); *Nutt* v *Read* (1999) 32 HLR 761 (mistake).

[19] *London Baggage Company (Charing Cross) Ltd* v *Railtrack plc* [2000] L&TR 439 (intention tested objectively); *Boustany* v *Pigott* (1993) 69 P&CR 298 (unconscionability by T, equally applicable to conveyances of the fee simple).

[20] *CH Bailey Ltd* v *Memorial Enterprises Ltd* [1974] 1 WLR 728 (rent review can be retrospective), approved in *United Scientific Holdings Ltd* v *Burnley BC* [1978] AC 904.

[21] [1992] 1 AC 478; discussed p 401 above.

[22] Especially Dewar (1992) 108 LQR 375; Goulding [1992] Conv 279.

[23] Contrast the category of usual covenants, which the parties can have inserted into leases although the contract makes no express provision. *Chester* v *Buckingham Travel Ltd* [1981] 1 WLR 96 employs an 'occurring in ordinary use' test (criticised by Crabb [1992] Conv 18).

[24] [1977] AC 239. The obligation was one of care; it was not absolute.

[25] *Barrett* v *Lounova (1982) Ltd* [1990] 1 QB 348, especially at p 356 (but see p 417 below).

Most commercial leases impose detailed obligations on the parties, whilst landlords of modern residential leases will be subject to statutory repair obligations.

A very different issue concerns mitigation of loss. *Reichman* v *Beveridge*[26] recognises that mitigation can apply, but that its operation will be very limited. In particular, a landlord is under no obligation to mitigate losses by reletting the premises if T leaves before the end of the lease.[27]

A traditional leases rule is that covenants are treated as independent: this means that a person in breach of covenant can still sue for a breach by the other party. This independence of covenants contrasts with normal contract rules.[28] The development of contractual repudiatory breach concepts in cases such as *Hussein* may well limit the independence rule, although only as regards serious breaches which can be regarded as repudiatory. Independence means that L's failure to repair[29] (unless very serious, as in *Hussein*) or to prevent improper parking[30] does not entitle T to refuse to pay rent, whilst T's failure to pay rent is no defence to an action for L's failure to repair.[31] These results may be justified because leases involve a long-term relationship with numerous obligations on each party. It is difficult to argue that any one duty is dependent upon the other party's performing all their duties.

Statutory contract rules also apply to leases. One prime example is the Consumer Rights Act 2015.[32] A fairly recent example is that a unilateral power for a landlord (a reputable registered social landlord) to vary terms was found unfair.[33]

Assessing the role of contract

Standing back from these detailed points, is it desirable to develop contractual rules within leases? Although it is very tempting to adopt general principles, it is important not to lose sight of the fact that leases principles have been developed over many years to produce a well-understood system for allocating risks and duties. Where it is generally thought that the law on leases has made a wrong turning, then, of course, contractual principles provide a basis for useful reform. Across the board, one may feel that the old leases principles are overly weighted towards landlords, so that contract provides a useful antidote. Yet, the danger is that change may not have this intended effect and may further enhance the landlord's position.[34]

---

[26] [2007] 1 P&CR 358, applying *White & Carter (Councils) Ltd* v *McGregor* [1962] AC 413 and asking whether the landlord was acting 'wholly unreasonably'.
[27] *Boyer* v *Warbey* [1953] 1 QB 234 at pp 244–245, 247; cf *BG Preeco 3 Ltd* v *Universal Explorations Ltd* (1987) 42 DLR 4th 673.
[28] Treitel, *The Law of Contract* (14th edn), pp 908–910.
[29] *Melville* v *Grapelodge Developments Ltd* (1978) 39 P&CR 179. However, T may be entitled to set off loss from L's breach against rent due.
[30] *Nynehead Developments Ltd* v *RH Fibreboard Containers Ltd* [1999] 1 EGLR 7.
[31] *Taylor* v *Webb* [1937] 2 KB 283 at p 290 (Du Parcq J); likewise, L's breach of the covenant for quiet enjoyment: *Edge* v *Boileau* (1885) 16 QBD 117.
[32] Replacing the Unfair Terms in Consumer Contracts Regulations 1999 (SI 1999 No 2083, p 601 below); *R (Khatun)* v *Newham LBC* [2005] QB 37.
[33] *Peabody Trust Governors* v *Reeve* [2009] L&TR 94 (Moss QC).
[34] Barr in *Contemporary Property Law* (eds Jackson and Wilde), Chapter 15.

Leases as contracts without property?

A rather different point arises from the much criticised decision in *Bruton* v *London & Quadrant Housing Trust*,[35] which recognised a lease where the landlord had no estate in the land, being merely a licensee. This may be thought to recognise a contractual tenancy, without the tenant's holding an estate. Many view the essence of a lease as being an estate in land; *Bruton* flies in the face of this. Although tenancies at will and at sufferance provide analogies because they involve no estate, a contractual tenancy would be largely novel in English law and its incidents would be difficult to ascertain.

Thus, it is not clear which statutory provisions would apply to it. *Bruton* decided that repairing obligations under s 11 of the Landlord and Tenant Act 1985 applied, but it would seem improbable that the lease (if possessing the required duration) could be registered under the Land Registration Act 2002. It seems increasingly likely that Lord Hoffmann simply intended to stress that there need not be an estate which can be enforced as against those with a better title than the landlord,[36] so that it is not enforceable against the licensor (i.e. to the landlord) or any successor in title to the licensor. The House of Lords in *Kay* v *Lambeth LBC* emphatically held that the *Bruton* lease is not a property interest capable of affecting the licensor, Lord Scott describing it as a 'non-estate tenancy'.[37]

2. Interference with the tenant's holding and use of the land

A covenant whereby the tenant is entitled to quiet enjoyment is implied into every lease.[38] The covenant's name is misleading: it has little to do with noise.[39] Rather, its essence lies in L's fundamental obligation to ensure that T can enjoy the property for the duration of the lease. A fuller description by Lord Millett is that there is liability 'if the landlord or somebody claiming under him does anything that substantially interferes with the tenant's title to or possession of the demised premises or his ordinary and lawful enjoyment of the demised premises.'[40]

Quiet enjoyment will be absent if T does not get possession of all the premises,[41] if there is subsidence caused by L's activities[42] or if a neighbour's easement prevents full

---

[35] [2000] 1 AC 406 (see pp 387, 405 above). See criticism by Bright (2000) 116 LQR 7; Barr in *Modern Studies in Property Law*, Vol 1 (ed Cooke), pp 249–252; Dixon [2000] CLJ 25; Routley (2000) 63 MLR 424; Pawlowski and Brown (2000) 4 L&T Rev 119; Bridge in *Land Law: Issues, Debates, Policy* (ed Tee), pp 116–120; Pawlowski [2002] Conv 550. Lower [2010] Conv 38 summarises the views adopted.

[36] This relativity analysis is supported by Lord Neuburger MR in *Mexfield Housing Co-operative Ltd* v *Berrisford* [2012] 1 AC 955 at [65]. Earlier, see Hinojosa [2005] Conv 114; cf Harwood (2000) 20 LS 503 at pp 511–513 and Lewison [2009] Conv 433 at p 434. Recent writings support this idea: Roberts [2012] Conv 87, Goymour in *Landmark Cases in Property Law* (eds Douglas, Hickey and Waring), Chapter 7; RJ Smith in *The Jurisprudence of Lord Hoffmann* (eds Davies and Pila), Chapter 17. A more sceptical note is struck by Baker [2014] Conv 495, but that depends upon seeing the landlord as having a relativity based estate: *Bruton* may instead depend upon the tenant having an estate relative to the landlord.

[37] [2006] 2 AC 465 at [138]–[148]; all the judges agreed on this point. See also *London Development Agency* v *Nidai* [2009] EWHC 1730 (Ch); [2009] 2 P&CR D62 (Griffiths [2010] Conv 87), involving a successor in title.

[38] It does not require the use of specific language such as 'demise': *Markham* v *Paget* [1908] 1 Ch 697.

[39] For residential agreements, the Law Commission plans to change the title to protection of the right to occupy: Law Com No 297, para 11.4.

[40] *Southwark LBC* v *Mills* [2001] 1 AC 1 at p 23.

[41] *Line* v *Stephenson* (1838) 4 Bing NC 678 (132 ER 950); *Dawson* v *Dyer* (1833) 5 B&Ad 584 (110 ER 906).

[42] *Markham* v *Paget* [1908] 1 Ch 697.

use of the property.[43] Even then, L is not liable unless the interference is caused by L[44] or somebody to whom L has granted rights.[45] The question of liability gives rise to much litigation. It extends, for example, to liability for scaffolding which restricts access to business premises[46] and for serious damage caused by water from L's land.[47]

A controversial question has been whether the covenant can be used when its practical effect would be to require L to improve the premises (going beyond any repairing obligation). This arose in *Southwark LBC* v *Mills*[48] in the context of soundproofing between flats, which was wholly inadequate by modern building standards. Though accepting that the covenant can apply to intangible interferences with enjoyment of the premises, the House of Lords was emphatic that it could not be used to impose obligations which go beyond duties to repair accepted by the parties or imposed by statute. This was rationalised by stressing that, at least as regards the physical condition of the land, the covenant has only prospective effect: the tenant has to accept the state of the land at the time of the lease.

Threatening conduct

In recent decades, the covenant has been used where L has taken steps to persuade T to leave the premises. Threats of physical eviction, coupled with knocking on the door and shouting, have been held to constitute a breach,[49] as has cutting off electricity and gas.[50]

One major limitation on the use of the covenant in this last type of case is that damages are likely to be low: exemplary damages are not available,[51] nor are damages for mental distress.[52] However, the law of torts may provide a remedy for some types of misconduct, and then substantial exemplary damages may be awarded.[53] Apart from personal violence,[54] there may be a trespass to the land[55] or to T's possessions[56] or nuisance.[57]

---

[43] *Celsteel Ltd* v *Alton House Holdings Ltd (No 2)* [1987] 1 WLR 291.
[44] But not for interference by title paramount, including another tenant of adjoining property: see *Celsteel* and *Brennan* v *Kettell* [2004] 2 P&CR 47.
[45] *Markham* v *Paget* [1908] 1 Ch 697. There is no liability if the action complained of is not authorised by L (*Malzy* v *Eichholz* [1916] 2 KB 308), at least where L has no right to control the other person (*Chartered Trust plc* v *Davies* (1997) 76 P&CR 396).
[46] *Timothy Taylor Ltd* v *Mayfair House Corpn* [2016] 2 P&CR 209 (where all reasonable steps to avoid disturbance have not been taken by L).
[47] *Booth* v *Thomas* [1926] Ch 397. See also *Anderson* v *Oppenheimer* (1880) 5 QBD 602 and *Gordon* v *Selico Co Ltd* [1985] 2 EGLR 79 at p 83 (upheld (1986) 18 HLR 219).
[48] [2001] 1 AC 1 (a claim in nuisance failed as there was ordinary use of the land): Davey [2001] Conv 31.
[49] *Kenny* v *Preen* [1963] 1 QB 499.
[50] *Perera* v *Vandiyar* [1953] 1 WLR 672.
[51] *Kenny* v *Preen* [1963] 1 QB 499 (damages accordingly reduced from £100 to £2).
[52] *Branchett* v *Beaney* [1992] 3 All ER 910.
[53] *Drane* v *Evangelou* [1978] 1 WLR 455, but not against those who act on L's behalf: *Ramdath* v *Daley* (1993) 25 HLR 273 (L's son).
[54] *McMillan* v *Singh* (1984) 17 HLR 120.
[55] *Lavender* v *Betts* [1942] 2 All ER 72 (removal of doors and windows).
[56] *Drane* v *Evangelou* [1978] 1 WLR 455.
[57] *Guppys (Bridport) Ltd* v *Brookling* [1984] 1 EGLR 29. For liability for the conduct of other tenants, see *Hussain* v *Lancaster CC* [2000] QB 1 and *Lippiatt* v *South Gloucestershire Council* [2000] QB 51; Morgan [2001] CLJ 382.

Furthermore, legislation has stepped in to protect tenants against such conduct. It is an offence under the Protection from Eviction Act 1977[58] if a person 'does acts likely to interfere with the peace or comfort of the residential occupier . . . or persistently withdraws or withholds services reasonably required for the occupation of the premises as a residence' with the intent of causing possession to be given up or a remedy not to be pursued.[59] Whether or not the defendant has a property right, s 6 of the Criminal Law Act 1977 renders criminal the use or threatening of violence to secure entry to premises, when a person opposed to that entry is present there.

A powerful civil remedy is given by ss 27 and 28 of the Housing Act 1988. If T is deprived of occupation unlawfully or leaves as a result of conduct within the Protection from Eviction Act 1977, then compensation is payable. It is calculated by reference to any increase in the value of the premises as a result of the ending of the lease. The significance of this is that the value of premises with vacant possession is usually very much higher than where T enjoys statutory security of tenure,[60] although the difference is reduced by the much more limited security in recent lettings.[61] There is a defence if T is reinstated,[62] but not if L simply provides a key to a wrecked room,[63] and T's conduct may reduce damages.[64] Finally, the Protection from Harassment Act 1997 creates the tort (and crime) of unreasonable harassment.

Derogation from grant

A rather different case is where T complains that L's conduct prevents the use of the premises for the purposes contemplated. This brings into play the principle that a grantor (L) cannot derogate from the grant. The non-derogation principle applies throughout property law.[65] In many respects, it can be seen as underpinning the implication of covenants for quiet enjoyment. Indeed, Lord Millett has suggested that there is 'little if any difference' between the two forms of liability.[66]

---

[58] Section 1(3) (as amended by Housing Act 1988, s 29); unlawful deprivation of possession is made illegal by s 1(2). See Ashworth [1979] JSWL 76. There is no civil liability: *McCall* v *Abelesz* [1976] QB 585. See Cowan [2001] Conv 249 for a study of decisions to prosecute (relatively infrequent).

[59] The intention might include persuasion of a tenant to leave temporarily whilst work is undertaken: *Schon* v *Camden LB* [1986] 2 EGLR 37.

[60] A standard discount of 25% on the vacant possession value was recognised in *Murray* v *Lloyd* [1989] 1 WLR 1060. Damages of over £90,000 were awarded in *Loveridge* v *Lambeth* LBC [2014] 1 WLR 4516, though the Supreme Court had doubts as to whether this was appropriate for a local authority landlord that neither intended to make nor in fact made any profit.

[61] *Melville* v *Bruton* (1996) 29 HLR 319.

[62] Housing Act 1988, s 27(6); an unreasonable refusal of reinstatement may reduce damages (s 27(7)).

[63] *Haniff* v *Robinson* [1993] QB 419.

[64] *Regalgrand Ltd* v *Dickerson & Wade* (1996) 74 P&CR 312: reduced from £12,000 to £1,500 where there were rent arrears and T had virtually ceased to reside following a notice to quit; *Osei-Bonsu* v *Wandsworth LBC* [1999] 1 WLR 1011 (matrimonial violence and mistaken belief that the lease had been terminated by the wife's notice).

[65] See Elliott (1964) 80 LQR 244. It is sometimes seen as operating by implying a term (*Harmer* v *Jumbil (Nigeria) Tin Areas Ltd* [1921] 1 Ch 200), sometimes as a free-standing legal principle (Lord Denning MR in *Molton Builders Ltd* v *City of Westminster LBC* (1975) 30 P&CR 182 at p 186).

[66] *Southwark LBC* v *Mills* [2001] 1 AC 1 at p 23; see also *Robinson* v *Kilvert* (1889) 41 Ch D 88 at p 95 (Lindley LJ).

Nevertheless, the leading case of *Harmer* v *Jumbil (Nigeria) Tin Areas Ltd*[67] shows how non-derogation can play a distinct role. T took a lease of land for use as an explosives magazine, both parties being aware of the need for explosives licences, which would require there to be no buildings within a certain radius. A subsequent lessee of L's adjoining land was held unable to build so as to endanger the licence.[68] This was a clear case in which the defendant's conduct threatened the very purpose for which the lease was, to the knowledge of both parties, granted.

Three possible advantages relative to the covenant for quiet enjoyment may be mentioned. First, it was sometimes thought that quiet enjoyment requires physical interference with T's possession.[69] However, *Southwark LBC* v *Mills*[70] rejected that limitation. Secondly, it may be better able to cover special uses of the leased property, as seen in *Harmer* itself. Thirdly, it may be useful if the implied covenant for quiet enjoyment is excluded by a narrowly drafted express covenant.[71]

Although the non-derogation principle is universally accepted, its operation is kept within fairly narrow limits. It cannot generally be used to stop L from competing with T's business.[72] Competition has an effect on the profitability of the leased premises, but it does not prevent their use as intended. On the other hand, it may be different if the lease is for a very specific purpose when competition would be seen as inconsistent with what the parties intended.[73] Nor is it wrong for L to develop retained land in such a way as to diminish the value of the leased property.[74] Again, however, one has to look at the detailed facts. If the premises are let as part of, say, a shopping mall, then duties may be owed to maintain the character of the area.[75] Although one should not expect too much of non-derogation, it can provide a useful argument for tenants.

3. Repairing obligations

This section is primarily concerned with obligations that are implied by the courts or statute. Most leases (especially commercial leases) make extensive provision for repair, but little will be said about the construction of these provisions.

The law's starting point is that L is under no general obligation to repair the premises: it is up to the parties to stipulate who (if anyone) should repair.[76] Very occasionally,[77] obligations to repair are implied. One well-known example is that a landlord of a block of flats may be responsible for taking care to maintain common access areas: *Liverpool City*

---

[67] [1921] 1 Ch 200. See also *Aldin* v *Latimer Clark, Muirhead & Co* [1894] 2 Ch 437 (timber drying sheds entitled to free flow of air).
[68] The principle creates a property right that binds successors in title.
[69] The background to *Harmer*: see Eve J [1921] Ch 200 at p 213; Russell (1977) 40 MLR 651.
[70] [2001] 1 AC 1; Rook [2000] Conv 161.
[71] *Grosvenor Hotel Company* v *Hamilton* [1894] 2 QB 836.
[72] *Port* v *Griffith* [1938] 1 All ER 295; *Romulus Trading Co Ltd* v *Comet Properties Ltd* [1996] 2 EGLR 70.
[73] *Oceanic Village Ltd* v *Shirayma Shokussan Co Ltd* [2001] L&TR 478 (London Aquarium shop).
[74] *Birmingham, Dudley & District Banking Company* v *Ross* (1888) 38 Ch D 295 (reducing light).
[75] *Chartered Trust plc* v *Davies* (1997) 76 P&CR 396; *Petra Investments Ltd* v *Jeffrey Rogers plc* (2000) 81 P&CR 267.
[76] *Gott* v *Gandy* (1853) 2 El&Bl 845 (118 ER 984); *Duke of Westminster* v *Guild* [1985] QB 688.
[77] *Habinteg Housing Association* v *James* (1994) 27 HLR 299 rejected an implied term to eradicate cockroaches, in the context of an estate of 91 leased dwellings.

Council v *Irwin*.[78] This was based upon such liability being necessary for the business efficacy of the transaction, not Lord Denning MR's broader analysis based upon the reasonableness of such a term. However, such implications are inappropriate where the lease makes express provision for repairs.[79]

In 1988, the Court of Appeal implied an obligation on L to repair the exterior of a dwelling house in *Barrett* v *Lounova (1982) Ltd*.[80] Although this appeared to go beyond previous cases,[81] it was necessary in order to make sense of T's express obligation to maintain the interior. Although it may be useful to avoid gaps in obligations where there are provisions for repair,[82] it seems unlikely to herald a radical new approach to implying repairing obligations. It was distinguished in *Adami* v *Lincoln Grange Management Ltd*,[83] and the House of Lords in *Southwark LBC* v *Mills*[84] displayed marked reluctance to go beyond the statutory repairing obligations.

Standing back from the cases, can we justify the current stance that L is under no duty to repair? This absence of duty may have been suitable for agricultural leases centuries ago. For modern leases of buildings, some repair is inevitable during any but the shortest lease. Especially where there is a lease of part of a building (whether as a residential flat or offices) or a short lease, it is unrealistic to expect the tenant to undertake the repair; the only credible solution is repair by the landlord.[85] However, when an obligation is expressly imposed on L, leases commonly provide for the cost to be charged to the tenants.[86]

Part of the problem is that so much depends upon the nature of the premises, the purpose for which the tenant intends to use them and the length of the lease.[87] Although legislation can lay down clear and definite rules, one can appreciate that it is difficult for courts to imply obligations without causing considerable uncertainty as to when implications will be made and what the extent of any liability may be.

A. Obligations on tenants

These have been traditionally expressed in the language of waste. All tenants are liable for voluntary waste: causing damage to the property. The traditional view is that tenants for years are liable for permissive waste: failure to maintain the property in its state at the time

---

[78] [1977] AC 239. An attempt to extend this to an inefficient heating system was rejected in *Collins* v *NIHE* (1984) 17 NIJB. For obligations relating to damage caused by L's adjoining premises, see *Gavin* v *One Housing Group* [2013] 2 P&CR 332.

[79] *Gordon* v *Selico Co Ltd* (1986) 18 HLR 219.

[80] [1990] 1 QB 348.

[81] PF Smith [1988] Conv 448; contrast [2003] Conv 112 at pp 117–118.

[82] There is also pressure to avoid overlapping duties on both landlord and tenant to repair, which can be 'deeply impractical': *Petersson* v *Pitt Place (Epsom) Ltd* (2001) 82 P&CR 276.

[83] (1997) 30 HLR 982; the case for such an obligation was weak given the length of the lease (260 years) and the fact that the lessor was a management company owned by the tenants. See also *Demetriou* v *Poolaction Ltd* [1991] 1 EGLR 100 (premises were non-residential and there was no correlative obligation on T); *Crédit Suisse* v *Beegas Nominees Ltd* [1994] 4 All ER 803 at p 819; *Gavin* v *One Housing Group* [2013] 2 P&CR 332 at [42] (provision by way of insurance).

[84] [2001] 1 AC 1.

[85] Arguments employed in *Barrett*; see also *Siney* v *Corporation of Dublin* [1980] IR 400.

[86] *New England Properties* v *Portsmouth New Shops* (1993) 67 P&CR 141.

[87] In *Adami*, the fact that there was a 260-year lease with a nominal rent made any obligation on the landlord unrealistic.

the lease commenced.[88] The courts appear to treat this as an obligation to prevent damage resulting from, for example, wind and water.[89] The extent to which this can be treated as a general obligation to repair is unclear: Lord Denning MR certainly denied any such duty.[90] Most modern litigation concerns express terms or the obligations owed by periodic tenants. As Dillon LJ has observed: 'Waste is a somewhat archaic subject, now seldom mentioned; actions in respect of disrepair are now usually brought on the covenant.'[91]

So far as periodic tenants are concerned, it is often said that they owe an obligation to keep the property wind and water tight[92] and probably to leave the property in the same state as it was demised (making allowance for fair wear and tear).[93] This does not entail liability for permissive waste or a general duty to repair.[94] The Court of Appeal considered the position in *Warren v Keen*,[95] which involved water damage to walls and windows during a weekly tenancy. The court held that a weekly tenant could not be expected to undertake the sort of work required to eradicate these problems. Lord Denning MR required simply that the tenant use the property in a tenant-like manner. This would include unblocking drains, cleaning the chimney and windows and draining the water to avoid burst pipes whilst away in winter.[96] The duty owed by a yearly tenant might be a little more demanding.

B. Obligations on landlords

(i) *Fitness for habitation*

The landlord has long been liable for the state of furnished accommodation: the property must be in a 'state fit for decent and habitable occupation'. This was held by *Smith v Marrable*[97] in 1843, where infestation[98] by bugs was held to justify the tenant's giving up the property.[99] This liability is well established today, although it originally had a mixed reception and has been quite narrowly confined. Any idea that it recognised a general fitness for purpose concept was squashed by its immediate restriction to furnished accommodation.[100] Just as importantly, the obligation applies only as to the initial state of the premises: there is no duty to keep them fit for human habitation.[101]

---

[88] *Yellowly v Gower* (1855) 11 Exch 274 at pp 293–294 (156 ER 833 at p 842).
[89] *Proudfoot v Hart* (1890) 25 QBD 42.
[90] *Warren v Keen* [1954] 1 QB 15 at p 20.
[91] *Mancetter Developments Ltd v Garmanson Ltd* [1986] QB 1212 at p 1218. But contrast the somewhat surprising use of waste in *Dayani v Bromley LBC* [1999] 3 EGLR 144.
[92] *Wedd v Porter* [1916] 2 KB 91.
[93] *Marsden v Edward Heyes Ltd* [1927] 2 KB 1.
[94] *Gott v Gandy* (1853) 2 El&Bl 845 (118 ER 984); *Yellowly v Gower* (1855) 11 Exch 274 (156 ER 833).
[95] [1954] 1 QB 15.
[96] Excepting short absences: *Wycombe HA v Barnett* [1982] 2 EGLR 35.
[97] (1843) 11 M&W 5 (152 ER 693).
[98] Surprisingly, this requires breeding on the premises rather than incursion from outside: *Stanton v Southwick* [1920] 2 KB 642 (rats from sewer).
[99] At least in short leases, the property must be fit from the beginning: *Wilson v Finch Hatton* (1877) 2 Ex D 336.
[100] *Sutton v Temple* (1843) 12 M&W 52 (152 ER 1108) (inapplicable to 'eatage' of grazing land); *Hart v Windsor* (1843) 12 M&W 68 (152 ER 1114) (inapplicable to unfurnished lettings); confirmed by *Southwark LBC v Mills* [2001] 1 AC 1 at p 7.
[101] *Sarson v Roberts* [1895] 2 QB 395.

(ii) *Statutory duties*

The common law has long been recognised as unsatisfactory. In particular, the weakness of landlords' obligations in leases of dwelling houses is at odds with the reasonable expectations of tenants. A long-standing requirement, currently s 8 of the Landlord and Tenant Act 1985, is that the landlord shall keep the house fit for human habitation[102] during the lease. The section does not apply to leases for more than three years, if the tenant is to put the premises into repair. More importantly, there is a maximum rent limit (unchanged since 1957) of £52 pa (£80 pa in London). This pathetically low figure ensures that the section virtually never applies to a modern lease.[103] It is not worth considering further.[104]

Much more important is s 11 of the 1985 Act, which imposes specific repairing obligations. It applies to leases of dwelling houses for less than seven years (no such limit applies to public sector leases)[105] and, as one would expect, cannot be excluded.[106] There are three heads of duty. The first is to keep the structure and exterior in repair, including drains, gutters and external pipes. This excludes interior decorations, although ceilings and plasterwork (for example) are covered.[107] As regards the exterior, problems can arise where part of a building is leased. Legislation has extended the repairing obligation to parts of the building over which the landlord has an estate or interest,[108] where the disrepair affects the enjoyment of the part leased.[109] The Supreme Court has declined to give this a wide application: it does not include necessary access to the building.[110] Garden steps are clearly not covered,[111] nor is the garden itself or items such as fences.

The second head of duty is to repair and keep in proper working order installations for the supply of water, gas, electricity and sanitation.[112] This includes basins, baths and toilets but not other fittings and facilities using water, gas or electricity. It follows that cookers, washing machines and refrigerators are not covered. The third head of duty is to repair and keep in proper working order installations for space heating and water heating. This forms an exception to the normal rule that electrical and gas appliances are not covered.

---

[102] The relevant factors are listed in s 10. They include repair, stability, freedom from damp, internal arrangement, lighting and ventilation, water supply, drainage and sanitary conveniences, facilities for food preparation and cooking.

[103] Commented upon in several cases, including *Quick* v *Taff Ely BC* [1986] QB 809 at pp 816–817, 821.

[104] Leading cases include *Summers* v *Salford Corporation* [1943] AC 283 (liability for injury caused by broken sash cord) and *McCarrick* v *Liverpool Corporation* [1947] AC 219 (no liability before notice of defect is given). For reform suggestions, see PF Smith [1998] Conv 189.

[105] Landlord and Tenant Act 1985, s 13, extended by Localism Act 2011, s 166 for public sector housing.

[106] Ibid, ss 11(4)–(5), 12.

[107] *Hussein* v *Mehlman* [1992] 2 EGLR 87; *Grand* v *Gill* [2011] 1 WLR 2253.

[108] *Edwards* v *Kumarasamy* [2016] AC 1334 holds that an easement held by the landlord suffices; s 11(3A) provides a defence where the landlord cannot obtain permission to undertake repairs.

[109] Section 11(1A), (1B), (3A), added by Housing Act 1988, s 116.

[110] *Edwards* v *Kumarasamy* [2016] AC 1334, approving *Hopwood* v *Cannock Chase DC* [1975] 1 WLR 373 (steps providing secondary access not covered).

[111] Conceded in *McAuley* v *Bristol City Council* [1992] QB 134.

[112] *Niazi Services Ltd* v *van der Loo* [2004] 1 WLR 1254 (criticised by Potts [2004] Conv 330) interprets s 11(1A) as not covering installations in parts over which the landlord has no interest, unless there is ownership or control of the installation itself.

The meaning of repair

Difficult questions have arisen as to what it means to keep in repair.[113] The standard of repair is, under s 11(3), to be determined by reference to the locality,[114] together with the age, character and prospective life of the dwelling house.[115] The major problem lies in determining the line between repair and improvement, the latter not being required. A good example is provided by *Wainwright* v *Leeds City Council*.[116] Terraced houses had been built many decades ago without a damp-course. The Court of Appeal was adamant that complaints about damp involved improvement of the property rather than repair.

Similar principles have been applied to excess condensation, a common housing problem. *Quick* v *Taff Ely BC*[117] stresses that 'disrepair is related to the physical condition of whatever has to be repaired, and not to questions of lack of amenity or inefficiency'. The court accepted that repairing obligations must be construed in the same way whether they are statutory or contractual obligations, or on L or on T. It would be unfortunate, on this reasoning, to have a broad concept of repair which would operate harshly on tenants with repairing duties. However, one may doubt whether it is necessary to interpret all repairing obligations in an identical manner. Surely landlords' statutory duties in leases of dwelling houses could be distinguished from express tenants' duties in commercial leases?[118]

A challenge to *Quick* on human rights grounds (Article 8: respect for homes) was made in *Lee* v *Leeds City Council*,[119] but failed as no general and unqualified obligation is thereby imposed on local authorities in relation to the condition of their housing.

One concession to the approach in *Wainwright* and *Quick* has, nevertheless, been accepted where the defect has caused disrepair. If the only sensible action is to correct the initial defect (an improvement) in order to prevent rapid recurrence of the disrepair, then there will be a duty to undertake that improvement. Two examples may be given. In *Ravenseft Properties Ltd* v *Davstone (Holdings) Ltd*,[120] external cladding became dangerous as a result of the lack of expansion joints. Forbes J asked[121] whether a 'wholly different thing' would be provided if a repair involving expansion joints was carried out. Bearing in mind that just 10% of the cost was attributable to the joints and there was no other way of reinstating the cladding, the work fell within T's covenant to repair.

---

[113] See the useful analysis by PF Smith [2003] Conv 112.

[114] *Stent* v *Monmouth DC* (1987) 54 P&CR 193 (exposed position demanded more weather-resistant door).

[115] Useless repairs to a building at the end of its life will not be required: *Newham LB* v *Patel* (1978) 13 HLR 77. See also *Kenny* v *Kingston upon Thames Royal LBC* [1985] 1 EGLR 26. *McDougall* v *Easington DC* (1989) 58 P&CR 201 may suggest that T is not entitled to have the property put in a better state than at the time of the lease. This would emasculate the section when there was disrepair right from the beginning. In any event, there is liability where the disrepair was unknown to the parties: *Ladbroke Hotels Ltd* v *Sandhu* (1995) 72 P&CR 498.

[116] [1984] 1 EGLR 67. See also *Eyre* v *McCracken* (2000) 80 P&CR 220 (T's covenant).

[117] [1986] QB 809 at p 818; approved by *Southwark LBC* v *Mills* [2001] 1 AC 1 (improvements not covered). See Brown and Pawlowski [2001] Conv 184 for responses to condensation problems. *Quick* was applied to safety-related standards in *Alker* v *Collingwood Housing Association* [2007] 1 WLR 2230 (glass in door).

[118] The more recent cases provide some support for this: PF Smith [2001] Conv 102.

[119] [2002] 1 WLR 1488, upholding *Quick* and denying any implied term more onerous than s 11 (see Thompson [2002] Conv 84).

[120] [1980] QB 12, approved in *Quick* v *Taff Ely BC* [1986] QB 809.

[121] [1980] QB 12 at p 21. Contrast gutting buildings for structural work: *McDougall* v *Easington DC* (1989) 58 P&CR 201.

Stent v *Monmouth DC*[122] provides the second example. A house built in 1953 suffered from water penetration through the front door. Various repairs, including a new door, were ineffectual. Finally, a sealed aluminium door unit was fitted and proved successful. Although the inadequacy of the door was not itself a defect within s 11 (it was an example of an initial design defect), water ingress led to its being damaged (the disrepair). This made replacement by an effective door unit sensible, practicable and necessary; fitting it could not be regarded as substantial rebuilding. *Stent* is interesting because it recognises, more clearly than *Ravenseft*, that preventative work may be required even where it could be seen as separate from correcting the disrepair.[123]

Notice to L required?

An important defence is that notice of the defect must first have been given to L. These rules are particularly important where T wishes to claim damages for personal injuries or damage. Notice has long been required for s 8, and this was extended to s 11 by the House of Lords in *O'Brien* v *Robinson*.[124] Indeed, the House of Lords went one step further and held notice necessary even for latent defects (a ceiling collapse). Although s 11(6) gives L a right of entry to inspect the property, *O'Brien* rules that L has no obligation to discover defects.[125]

It is arguable that T will be in the best position to know of some defects, so that it is reasonable that T should notify L. Nevertheless, it does seem unfortunate to reduce the incentive for landlords to check that their premises are in good repair.[126] Subsequent cases have indicated unease over this restriction[127] and have readily held L bound if notice of defects has been gained either in other contexts or from sources other than T.[128] It will be seen later that statute sometimes permits an action for personal injuries or property damage despite the absence of notice[129]; this significantly reduces the effect of *O'Brien*.

The analysis above applies where the defect arises on the leased land. Where the defect arises on land outside the lease, L is liable[130] regardless of notice being given or prompt repair.[131] This was confirmed by the Supreme Court in *Edwards* v *Kumarasamy*.[132] However, this is qualified by the holding that, as regards defects on land leased to another tenant, L is liable only if he has notice of the defect.

---

[122] (1987) 54 P&CR 193; see also *Crédit Suisse* v *Beegas Nominees Ltd* [1994] 4 All ER 803 and *Uddin* v *Islington LBC* [2015] HLR 584 at [4]–[9] (absence of damp course).
[123] But there will not be liability without disrepair: *Post Office* v *Aquarius Properties Ltd* [1987] 1 All ER 1055 (water in basement, but no damage).
[124] [1973] AC 912.
[125] See also *Morgan* v *Liverpool Corporation* [1927] 2 KB 131, affirmed by *McCarrick* v *Liverpool Corporation* [1947] AC 219.
[126] Reynolds (1974) 37 MLR 377; cf Robinson (1976) 39 MLR 43.
[127] *McGreal* v *Wake* [1984] 1 EGLR 42, noting the seemingly clear statutory wording 'keep in repair'.
[128] See, e.g., *Dinefwr BC* v *Jones* [1987] 2 EGLR 58.
[129] See p 426 below.
[130] Provided that the obligation is, as in s 11, 'to keep in repair': *British Telecommunications plc* v *Sun Life Assurance Society plc* [1996] Ch 69.
[131] *Earle* v *Charalambous* [2007] HLR 93 at Addendum [10] suggests that immediate liability in long residential leases may need reconsideration, given that L must normally consult T, who will be ultimately liable under a service charge.
[132] [2016] AC 1334.

C. Enforcing repairing obligations

How do T and L ensure that repairing obligations are fulfilled? Actions by L are regulated by statute. Section 18 of the Landlord and Tenant Act 1927 restricts damages to the reduction in the value of the landlord's reversion[133] and precludes damages altogether if the premises are to be pulled down or so altered as to render the repairs valueless. This is to prevent oppressive enforcement of repairing obligations. It might be noted that these restrictions apply even if reasonably necessary repairs are in fact carried out by L.[134] The Leasehold Property (Repairs) Act 1938 also imposes limitations; these will be considered below in the context of forfeiture.

Turning to L's liability[135] for damages, an initial question is whether the claim is for loss of amenity or discomfort, inconvenience and distress. This was relevant in *Moorjani* v *Durban Estates Ltd*,[136] as only the former would compensate the tenant who had (quite separately) chosen not to live in the property. The Court of Appeal held that the tenant could recover but reduced the award by 50% to take account of the fact that the tenant had chosen to live elsewhere. Leaving that point aside, loss must be proved and damages may well be low. *Wallace* v *Manchester CC*[137] held that the judge can choose to award a proportion of the rent or a global sum (or a mixture). If the latter is chosen, it should be checked against the rent for the period. Although sums up to £3,000 pa represent the normal maximum, it may be most appropriate to take a proportion of the rental value for long residential leases – this reflects the distress resulting from interference with the enjoyment of the tenant's long-term home.[138] The maximum that will be awarded is the rent for the period of breach, unless there are special circumstances.[139] Consequential ill health can trigger higher awards: £50,000 in *Brent LBC* v *Carmel*.[140]

Interestingly, T can get an order for specific performance[141] despite its being unusual to grant specific performance of building contracts.[142] There is an overlapping statutory rule that specific performance of landlords' repairing obligations is available in non-commercial

---

[133] A recent example is provided by *Hammersmatch Properties (Welwyn) Ltd* v *Saint-Gobain Ceramics & Plastics Ltd* [2013] 2 P&CR 351: repair costs over £3m, but damages limited to £0.9m. In many cases, however, it may be inferred that the reduction in value equates to the repair costs: *Sunlife Europe Properties Ltd* v *Tiger Aspect Holdings Ltd* [2014] 1 EGLR 30 at [15]–[16].

[134] PF Smith [1990] Conv 335 at pp 342–344.

[135] See PF Smith in *The Reform of Property Law* (eds Jackson and Wilde), Chapter 6; Madge (1999) 149 NLJ 1643.

[136] [2016] 1 WLR 2265. The successful 50% claim related to part only of the rent (see below).

[137] (1998) 30 HLR 1111.

[138] *Earle* v *Charalambous* [2007] HLR 93: 50% of rental value when severe water penetration. Varying lesser degrees of disrepair in *Moorjani* v *Durban Estates Ltd* [2016] 1WLR 2265 resulted in 5% and 20% of the rent being appropriate amounts.

[139] *Shine* v *English Churches Housing Group* [2004] HLR 727: 75% of the rent thought appropriate for periods involving very poor conditions.

[140] (1995) 28 HLR 203.

[141] *Jeune* v *Queens Cross Properties Ltd* [1974] Ch 97; *Peninsular Maritime Ltd* v *Padseal Ltd* [1981] 2 EGLR 43; *Hammond* v *Allen* (1992) 65 P&CR 18 at p 25.

[142] Treitel, *The Law of Contract* (14th edn), para 21-043. Note the discussion of principle in *Co-operative Insurance Society Ltd* v *Argyll Stores (Holdings) Ltd* [1998] AC 1 at pp 13–14 (specific performance of a tenant's obligation to trade refused, though covenants to repair were distinguished).

leases.[143] *Rainbow Estates Ltd* v *Tokenhold Ltd*[144] extended specific performance to breaches by T, notwithstanding long-standing doubts.[145] However, forfeiture or L's under-taking the work under contractual powers will normally be more appropriate where T is in breach. Specific performance against T will be rare and will not be allowed to be used to harass tenants, though the statutory protections applicable to damages actions are not directly applicable.[146]

Where L fails, in breach of covenant, to repair, T has a well-established right to under-take the necessary work.[147] T can then either sue for the cost[148] or have a defence to an action for rent.[149] The law was reviewed by Goff J in *Lee-Parker* v *Izzet*,[150] confirming the common law right for T to recoup properly incurred expenditure out of future rent.

In *Melville* v *Grapelodge Developments Ltd*,[151] Neill J took the further and significant step of allowing an equitable set-off against rent even though T had not carried out the repairs. The only limitation for such set-off was that the two claims should be sufficiently closely connected. This may well be a useful weapon for tenants, but Neill J emphasised that T cannot simply refuse to pay rent. In many cases, T's claim for damages for breach will be small and not justify a significant withholding of rent. Forbes J similarly allowed an equitable set-off in his fully reasoned judgment in *British Anzani (Felixstowe) Ltd* v *International Marine Management (UK) Ltd*,[152] and it now seems well recognised.[153] It can be excluded by express provision in the lease,[154] but simply saying that rent shall be paid 'without deductions' is insufficient.[155]

Other types of remedies

A number of other remedies deserve brief mention. Where T is paying a significant sum as rent or for repairs, the court may appoint a receiver to receive those sums and undertake the necessary work.[156] Where a building is divided into flats, there is a statutory right to apply to court for the appointment of a manager[157] and, in certain cases, for compulsory acquisition of the landlord's interest.[158] Secure tenants (mainly residential tenants of local

---

[143] Landlord and Tenant Act 1985, ss 17, 32. See *Parker* v *Camden LBC* [1986] Ch 162.
[144] [1999] Ch 64.
[145] Based on *Hill* v *Barclay* (1810) 16 Ves 402 at p 405 (33 ER 1037 at p 1038).
[146] *Rainbow* at pp 72–73.
[147] Including an implied licence over L's land. However, this right will not apply where L is proceeding to have the work done: *Metropolitan Properties Co Ltd* v *Wilson* [2003] L&TR 226.
[148] *Loria* v *Hammer* [1989] 2 EGLR 249.
[149] *Taylor* v *Beal* (1591) Cro Eliz 222 (78 ER 478); *Waters* v *Weigall* (1795) 2 Anst 575 (145 ER 971) (emergency repairs).
[150] [1971] 1 WLR 1688. See Rank (1976) 40 Conv 196; Waite [1981] Conv 199.
[151] (1978) 39 P&CR 179.
[152] [1980] QB 137.
[153] For its application to commercial rent arrears recovery (p 445 below), see Tribunals, Courts and Enforcement Act 2007, s 77(7).
[154] *Hongkong & Shanghai Banking Corporation* v *Kloeckner & Co AG* [1990] 2 QB 514; conceded in *Electricity Supply Nominees Ltd* v *IAF Group Ltd* [1993] 1 WLR 1059. Cf [2002] Conv 99 at p 100.
[155] *Connaught Restaurants Ltd* v *Indoor Leisure Ltd* [1994] 1 WLR 501.
[156] *Hart* v *Emelkirk Ltd* [1983] 1 WLR 1289; *Daiches* v *Bluelake Investment Ltd* [1985] 2 EGLR 67.
[157] Landlord and Tenant Act 1987, Part II, as amended by Housing Act 1996 (see Sched 5).
[158] Landlord and Tenant Act 1987, Part III (see especially s 29), as amended by Leasehold Reform, Housing and Urban Development Act 1993.

authorities) have a statutory right to have certain work done promptly at L's expense,[159] but the generosity of the scheme is restricted by a right to limit it where costs will exceed £250.[160]

Other remedies do not depend upon specific repairing obligations. Local authorities may serve a notice requiring abatement of a statutory nuisance upon the owner (for structural defects) or person responsible, in particular where the premises are in a state prejudicial to health.[161] This remedy, being based upon health considerations, is available whether or not there is a breach of repairing obligations.[162] Although it is tested by modern standards (even for elderly buildings), it does not cover the building layout.[163] Although compensation may be awarded in criminal proceedings, there is no independent action for damages.[164]

The Housing Act 2004[165] makes new provision for assessing housing standards for dwelling houses, based on an assessment of hazards. A number of courses are open to a local housing authority as regards hazards counting as level 1 and level 2 hazards.[166] For example, improvement notices may be served by the local housing authority on persons with control.[167] Where there is an imminent risk of serious harm to the health or safety of occupiers, the housing authority may carry out emergency remedial action itself and recoup its expenses.[168] Prohibition and emergency prohibition orders can restrict the use of the premises.[169] Most dramatically, a demolition order may be made.[170] Paradoxically, the housing authority may still purchase such property and use it for temporary housing.[171]

Rather different problems arise where landlords are inefficient in carrying out repairing obligations, particularly where the lease provides for the tenants to pay the cost. It has already been seen that the court may appoint receivers or managers and order compulsory acquisition of the landlord's interest. There is also control over the amount of management charges passed on to tenants[172] and the ability of landlords to forfeit where charges are

---

[159] Housing Act 1985, s 96, as substituted by Leasehold Reform, Housing and Urban Development Act 1993; L must nominate a contractor to do the work. See also SI 1994 No 133.

[160] SI 1994 No 133, art 4.

[161] Environmental Protection Act 1990, ss 79–82. A significant restriction is that physical dangers are not included: *R v Bristol CC, ex p Everett* [1999] 1 WLR 1170.

[162] *Birmingham DC v Kelly* (1985) 17 HLR 572. Nor does a breach of covenant necessarily justify a notice: *Salford City Council v McNally* [1976] AC 379.

[163] *Birmingham CC v Oakley* [2001] 1 AC 617.

[164] *Issa v Hackney LBC* [1997] 1 All ER 999.

[165] Part I. The previous law was couched in terms of fitness for habitation and disrepair. Regulations provide details.

[166] Summarised in Housing Act 2004, s 1(3).

[167] See ibid, Sched 1 for further detail. For leased premises, this will generally be L (not T, if paying a full rent): *White v Barnet LBC* [1990] 2 QB 328.

[168] Ibid, ss 40–42.

[169] Ibid, ss 20–27, 43–45.

[170] Housing Act 1985, s 265. For an earlier case on the choice between repair and closure, see *R v Southwark LBC, ex p Cordwell* (1994) 27 HLR 594.

[171] Housing Act 1985, s 300. In *Salford City Council v McNally* [1976] AC 379 this lasted for seven years, despite there being a statutory nuisance.

[172] Landlord and Tenant Act 1985, ss 18 et seq (as amended by Landlord and Tenant Act 1987, ss 41–42; Housing Act 1996, s 83; and Commonhold and Leasehold Reform Act 2002 (hereafter CLRA), Sched 9). The costs must be reasonably incurred and the work done to a reasonable standard. Any significant work requires a minimum of two estimates and notice to be given to tenants.

disputed.[173] Tenants may have a 'management audit' conducted by an accountant or surveyor,[174] and a tenants' association may appoint a surveyor with powers to inspect the land and documents.[175]

Rights to manage

It may be doubted whether any of the remedies just discussed regarding management is really effective. As well as strengthening some of them, the response of the Commonhold and Leasehold Reform Act 2002[176] (hereafter CLRA) was to confer a right on tenants of longer leases to take over management. Unlike other remedies, it does not depend upon any breach by L. Instead, the requirements for its exercise are essentially the same as for the right to enfranchisement. Tenants can choose whether to buy out the landlord or to take over management. The fundamental requirements[177] are that two-thirds of the flats (a minimum of two) are held by qualifying tenants (generally whose leases exceed 21 years) and that at least half of these tenants participate; no more than 25% of the property can be commercially let.

This right to manage has to be exercised by an RTM company, which may be seen as analogous to the RTE company used for enfranchisement. Once the RTM company (whose members will be the participating tenants and L) has taken over management, then it exercises functions relating to 'services, repairs, maintenance, improvements, insurance and management', though not forfeiture, or functions relating solely to units held by non-qualifying tenants.[178] It might be noted that these powers extend to giving consents to assignments and other activities requiring permission, although notice must be given to L. L has a power to object if he would have had grounds for refusing permission.[179]

For most purposes, it seems appropriate to treat the RTM company as if it were an assignee of the reversion as regards the role it plays. This means that it is liable for any default as regards management, which would include liability for disrepair and injury. L will cease to be liable, at least for any defaults after the right to manage is exercised. This has to be remembered when considering liability of L as described in this and the following chapter.[180]

D. Liability for personal injuries

If L's breach of a repairing obligation causes injury to T, L is clearly liable provided that remoteness rules are satisfied.[181] What about injuries to other persons? If L is under no obligation to repair, the common law position is encapsulated in the oft-quoted proposition

---

[173] Housing Act 1996, s 81, as amended by CLRA: see p 430 below.
[174] Leasehold Reform, Housing and Urban Development Act 1993, Chapter V.
[175] Housing Act 1996, s 84.
[176] Part 2, Chapter 1, described by Roberts (2002) 152 NLJ 338 as 'one of the most difficult and controversial reforms to operate'.
[177] For more detail, see CLRA, ss 72, 75, 79(5), Sched 6.
[178] Ibid, s 96.
[179] Ibid, ss 98–99.
[180] Ibid, Sched 7 amends provisions in other legislation to produce this result: examples are repairing obligations (Landlord and Tenant Act 1985, s 11) and liability for personal injuries (Defective Premises Act 1972, discussed below).
[181] *Berryman* v *Hounslow LBC* (1996) 30 HLR 567.

that 'fraud apart, there is no law against letting a tumble-down house'.[182] This principle applies just as strongly today.[183]

Even where L is under a duty to T to repair, the courts have insisted that the tort of negligence does not enable other persons to sue.[184] The question is how far this rule survives *Donoghue* v *Stevenson*.[185] It seems plain that the landlord will today be liable where the defect results from work he or she carried out.[186] Despite some criticism,[187] it seems likely that breach of a duty to repair remains insufficient by itself to ground liability to anybody other than T at common law.

This result, however, has been overtaken by s 4 of the Defective Premises Act 1972.[188] This makes it clear that a landlord's breach of a repairing obligation may result in negligence liability to anybody who can reasonably be expected to be affected by the defect. Although L will not usually be in breach of a repairing obligation unless T has given notice of the defect, for the purposes of liability under s 4, no notice is necessary where L ought to have known of the defect.[189]

Also important is the extension to landlords who have no duty to repair but merely a right to enter premises to carry out repairs.[190] This will, for example, apply to defects within gardens, which fall outside the statutory repairing obligations for dwelling houses.[191] A right to enter to repair is readily implied into periodic tenancies which do not contain full repairing obligations,[192] although the implication will not be made in commercial leases which impose repairing obligations on T.[193]

It must always be remembered that there must be a state of disrepair for s 4 to operate: it does not mean that there is a general duty to make the premises safe.[194] A further point is that a tenant who is in breach of a valid repairing obligation cannot sue if liability is based on the landlord's right to enter.

---

[182] *Robbins* v *Jones* (1863) 15 CBNS 221 at p 240 (143 ER 768 at p 776) (Erle CJ). See also *Lane* v *Cox* [1897] 1 QB 415.

[183] *McNerny* v *Lambeth LB* (1988) 21 HLR 188. Similarly, nuisance claims cannot be based on the state of the premises at the time of the lease: *Southwark LBC* v *Mills* [2001] 1 AC 1.

[184] *Cavalier* v *Pope* [1906] AC 428; *Boldack* v *East Lindsey DC* (1998) 31 HLR 41; *Dodd* v *Raebarn Estates Ltd* [2016] HLR 223 at [67]–[69].

[185] [1932] AC 562.

[186] *Anns* v *Merton LBC* [1978] AC 728; *Rimmer* v *Liverpool City Council* [1985] QB 1. This survives the rejection of *Anns* by *Murphy* v *Brentwood DC* [1991] 1 AC 398: *Targett* v *Torfaen BC* [1992] 3 All ER 27.

[187] E.g. *Greene* v *Chelsea BC* [1954] 2 QB 127 at p 138 (Denning LJ). Other jurisdictions recognise liability: *Northern Sandblasting Pty Ltd* v *Harris* (1997) 188 CLR 313; *Basset Realty Ltd* v *Lindstrom* (1979) 103 DLR 3d 654.

[188] Replacing the Occupiers' Liability Act 1957, s 4; it extends to property damage.

[189] *Sykes* v *Harry* [2001] QB 1014. *Lafferty* v *Newark and Sherwood DC* [2016] HLR 243 confirms that this is a negligence (not strict) liability.

[190] Defective Premises Act 1972, s 4(4). The right must relate to the claimed defect: in *Boldack* v *East Lindsey DC* (1998) 31 HLR 41, repair did not include removing a paving slab.

[191] *Smith* v *Bradford MC* (1982) 4 HLR 86.

[192] *Mint* v *Good* [1951] 1 KB 517; see also *McAuley* v *Bristol City Council* [1992] QB 134 (implied right to repair council house garden).

[193] *Stocker* v *The Planet BS* (1879) 27 WR 877; *Regional Properties Ltd* v *City of London Real Property Co Ltd* [1981] 1 EGLR 33.

[194] *Alker* v *Collingwood Housing Association* [2007] 1 WLR 2230 (no liability for glass in door not complying with modern construction standards). *Alker* was applied to the absence of a handrail on stairs in each of *Sternbaum* v *Dhesi* [2016] 2 P&CR 112 (CA) and *Dodd* v *Raebarn Estates Ltd* [2016] HLR 223.

E. Reform

In 1996, the Law Commission issued a Report[195] on *Responsibility for State and Condition of Property*. The fitness for human habitation requirement for dwelling houses would be reinvigorated by removing the rent limits, extending it to all leases of dwelling houses under seven years and requiring the property to be kept fit during the tenancy. This, rather than changing the concept of 'repair' in s 11, is seen as the best answer to the problems exemplified by *Quick*.

For most other leases, there would be a residual liability on L to keep the premises in repair, although it could be excluded and would not apply if there were express repairing obligations on L or T. The outdated waste rules would be replaced by new obligations on T, for example, to take proper care of the premises and to make good wilful damage.

4. Forfeiture

Virtually every lease contains a covenant permitting L to forfeit the lease on T's failure to comply with the covenants. This can be a powerful weapon in L's hands. Where a lease has been granted in return for a capital sum, a very valuable asset will be lost if there is forfeiture. In other cases, the rent may be lower than the current annual value of the property, again with the result that the lease will be worth a considerable amount. On the other hand, if the rent is above current market rates, then forfeiture will be an empty threat.[196] It should be added that the security of tenure enjoyed by certain lessees of dwelling houses operates to the exclusion of the forfeiture rules.[197]

Although forfeiture clauses are almost invariably inserted in leases, it is still necessary to do so expressly.[198] There is no automatic right to forfeit for breach of covenant,[199] with the sole and outmoded exception that T cannot deny L's title.[200] These rules apply to legal leases. By contrast, a forfeiture clause is a 'usual covenant' that will be implied into agreements for leases.[201] Turning to T's rights, it is very unusual for T to be given a right to terminate for L's breach. Modern repudiatory breach principles may, of course, qualify the above analysis.[202]

The drastic effect of forfeiture is such that equity has for centuries given relief to T. Forfeiture has been seen as mere security for the payment of rent and cannot be insisted upon if T pays off the arrears.[203] By far the greatest part of the law on forfeiture relates

---

[195] Law Com No 238; Bridge [1996] Conv 342. Law Com No 297 endorses these reforms, as well as modernising the language of s 11, but the proposals are not being implemented.

[196] There is no rent liability after forfeiture: p 410 above. In *GS Fashions Ltd v B&Q plc* [1995] 1 WLR 1088, L unsuccessfully attempted to argue that its own forfeiture was improper!

[197] Housing Act 1988, ss 5, 7 (assured tenancies); Rent Act 1977, s 98 (protected and statutory tenancies). For secure tenancies, see Housing Act 1985, s 82.

[198] Making a lease conditional on the performance of covenants suffices: *Doe d Henniker v Watt* (1828) 8 B&C 308 (108 ER 1057).

[199] *Doe d Willson v Phillips* (1824) 2 Bing 13 (Best CJ at p 15) (130 ER 208 at p 210).

[200] *WG Clark (Properties) Ltd v Dupre Properties Ltd* [1992] Ch 297 and *Abidogun v Frolan Health Care Ltd* [2002] L&TR 275 (applying the procedure in Law of Property Act 1925 (hereafter LPA), s 146).

[201] *Chester v Buckingham Travel Ltd* [1981] 1 WLR 96 (previously limited to forfeiture for non-payment of rent).

[202] *Hussein v Mehlman* [1992] 2 EGLR 87; p 411 above.

[203] See, e.g., *Sanders v Pope* (1806) 12 Ves 282 at p 289 (33 ER 108 at p 110); *Bowser v Colby* (1841) 1 Hare 109 (66 ER 969).

to relief. Unfortunately, the law is notoriously complex and riddled with traps and gaps. However, the law has adopted a broad attitude to what counts as forfeiture, in order to give a reasonably wide scope to relief rules. Thus, a right to give notice of termination on breach[204] and a right to insist upon surrender on breach[205] are both examples of forfeiture.[206]

A rather different point is that L is able to seek forfeiture of part of the leased premises, at least where that part is physically separated and capable of being separately let.[207] This may be useful where part of the premises has been sublet and L wishes to restrict forfeiture to the 'guilty' party (whether that be T or the sublessee).

A. The operation of forfeiture

One initial point is that the lease is rendered voidable, rather than void, by the breach.[208] This means that L has a choice whether or not to forfeit. The decision to forfeit is usually taken in one of two ways: by actual peaceable re-entry or bringing a claim seeking possession.[209] It is to be noted that, in both cases, it is L who forfeits the lease rather than the court. All the court does in a possession claim is to order possession because the lease has already been forfeited. This principle sits awkwardly with the linking of many of the rules on relief with court proceedings, as will be seen later.

The entire procedure is very clumsy, not least because T is not in possession under the lease in the period after L claims forfeiture and before the court order (assuming no relief). Indeed, Lord Neuberger has described it as 'anomalous and archaic'.[210] It follows that T is liable to pay mesne profits (rental value of the land) rather than rent[211] and is not subject to the covenants. Pending resolution of any dispute regarding forfeiture and relief, however, the lease retains a shadowy existence, and this enables the tenant to rely upon covenants in the lease[212] and the statutory rights of tenants.[213] The problems are further illustrated if L wishes to discontinue the forfeiture proceedings and rely on the lease. It has been held that the lease is then restored to its initial force, at least where T has opposed forfeiture.[214] On the other hand, once T has accepted the forfeiture, it is too late for L to deny forfeiture.[215]

---

[204] *Richard Clarke & Co Ltd v Widnall* [1976] 1 WLR 845.

[205] *Badley v Badley* (1982) 138 DLR 3d 493.

[206] See also LPA, s 146(7).

[207] Similarly, relief relating to a part can be given (*GMS Syndicate Ltd v Gary Elliott Ltd* [1982] Ch 1), although the courts may be reluctant to split the leased property: *Clifford v Personal Representatives of Johnson, deceased* [1979] 2 EGLR 41.

[208] *Bowser v Colby* (1841) 1 Hare 109 (66 ER 969); *Jones v Carter* (1846) 15 M&W 718 at pp 724–725 (153 ER 1040 at p 1043); *Jardine v Att-Gen for Newfoundland* [1932] AC 275 at p 286. Forfeiture may operate on events other than breach, in particular T's bankruptcy.

[209] Reiterated by Lord Templeman in *Billson v Residential Apartments Ltd* [1992] 1 AC 494 at p 535.

[210] *Knowsley Housing Trust v White* [2009] AC 636 at [81].

[211] *Moore v Assignment Courier Ltd* [1977] 1 WLR 638. If the rent is low, mesne profits will be more attractive to L: *Viscount Chelsea v Hutchinson* (1994) 28 HLR 17. *Serjeant v Nash, Field & Co* [1903] 2 KB 304 held distress to be unavailable, and presumably this applies to commercial rent arrears recovery.

[212] *Peninsular Maritime Ltd v Padseal Ltd* [1981] 2 EGLR 43.

[213] *Twinsectra Ltd v Hynes* (1995) 71 P&CR 145.

[214] *Mount Cook Land Ltd v Media Business Centre Ltd* [2004] 2 P&CR 477; Cockshutt (2006) 175 PLJ 19.

[215] Even if L's forfeiture claim was irregular: *GS Fashions Ltd v B&Q plc* [1995] 1 WLR 1088; *Rother District Investments Ltd v Corke* [2004] 2 P&CR 311.

Peaceable re-entry is relatively uncommon, unless T has simply left the premises. It carries the danger of committing several criminal offences. Section 6 of the Criminal Law Act 1977[216] enacts the crime of using or threatening violence to property or to a person in order to secure entry, where the defendant knows that a person opposed to the entry is present on the premises. This means that it is very dangerous to take possession where T is on the premises.

Greater protection is given to residential occupiers by the Protection from Eviction Act 1977. It is unlawful to enforce a right to forfeit a lease of a dwelling house (or to enforce rights to possession on expiry of leases) other than by court proceedings and an offence to deprive such occupiers of their occupation by unlawful means.[217] The sole exception is where nobody is residing on the premises. It follows that peaceable re-entry of dwelling houses is virtually never feasible.[218] A further and rather different rule is that notices to quit dwelling houses must be in writing and be given at least four weeks in advance.[219]

Peaceable re-entry commonly takes the form of entry and changing of the locks so as to exclude T.[220] What happens if T has sublet to S? Forfeiture will destroy S's sublease, so re-entry needs to be such as to deny the rights of both T and S. Continued recognition of S is inconsistent with forfeiture, unless the parties contemplate that S will have a new lease directly from L. Simply changing the locks and telling S to pay rent directly to L will not suffice.[221]

Peaceable re-entry was once attractive to landlords because of the possibility that it might preclude relief against forfeiture. As will be discussed below, relief is now available in all cases of peaceable re-entry.[222] This avoids the unpalatable possibility that L could be better off taking the 'dubious and dangerous method'[223] of peaceable re-entry rather than seeking a court order. There is also a slight chance that it might fall foul of human rights legislation.[224]

B. Protection for residential tenants

In recent years, there has been concern that tenants of long residential leases have been unfairly threatened with forfeiture and that, in some cases, they have lost a valuable asset when forfeiture has taken place. Shorter residential leases are less likely to suffer from this problem because they are more likely to be at a full market rent (and hence have much less capital value) and sometimes protected by statutory provisions restricting termination. Commercial tenants, as well as being more likely to be in receipt of legal advice, are much more likely to be paying a full market rent and therefore less likely to suffer a large capital loss on forfeiture.

---

[216] Replacing the Forcible Entry Acts 1381–1623.
[217] It has already been seen that conduct designed to force tenants out may be an offence: p 415 above.
[218] If there is a breach of these provisions, the purported re-entry is ineffective: *Belgravia Property Investment and Development Co Ltd v Webb* [2002] L&TR 481 at [13].
[219] Protection from Eviction Act 1977, s 5.
[220] See, e.g., *Fuller v Judy Properties Ltd* (1991) 64 P&CR 176.
[221] *Ashton v Sobelman* [1987] 1 WLR 177.
[222] *Billson v Residential Apartments Ltd* [1992] 1 AC 494 (see p 440 below).
[223] Ibid, at p 536 (Lord Templeman). The case involved the 'farce' of L's entry and changing the locks at 6 am, followed by T's employees breaking back in later that morning.
[224] Bruce (2000) 150 NLJ 462 is sceptical: the availability of relief is a significant factor.

These concerns led to a range of protections being inserted in the Commonhold and Leasehold Reform Act 2002.[225] They all relate to long residential leases. To simplify,[226] these are leases exceeding 21 years. These protections may be grouped as follows:

(1) ensuring that a clear breach has taken place prior to forfeiture;
(2) restricting thereafter when forfeiture can take place;
(3) establishing publicity and procedural requirements to protect tenants.

(i) *Is there breach?*

One danger is that L seeks to forfeit as a heavy-handed way of enforcing a liability which is disputed by T. The threat of forfeiture may place undue pressure on T to comply with L's view of liability. Therefore, liability has to be clearly established before forfeiture can proceed. Where there are arrears of rent, s 166 requires L to notify T of the sum due and the date it is due. The notice must specify a date for payment within 30–60 days of the notice. Without a notice, the rent is not due.

Other breaches (failure to repair or unauthorised user are likely examples) are more likely to be disputed. Accordingly, s 168 requires L to make an application to a leasehold valuation tribunal for a determination that there is a breach before the statutory notice preceding forfeiture can be issued. There are exceptions if T admits the breach or a court has determined that there is liability.

Service charges are generally treated as rent liability for forfeiture purposes. They have long been a source of concern because of the danger of inflated and unjustified bills being passed on to tenants. Accordingly, CLRA, s 170, amending previous provisions, provides rules similar to s 168 for non-rent breaches.

(ii) *Restrictions on forfeiture*

To avoid hasty action where small sums are due, CLRA, s 167 requires either that at least £350 is due or that the sum has been unpaid for more than three years.[227] This provides useful protection where trivial sums are involved, but obviously greater sums will be due in many cases. It does not apply unless the breach consists of a failure to pay rent or service charges.

(iii) *Publicity and procedural requirements*

CLRA, s 171 rather opaquely authorises regulations which must be met before forfeiture can proceed (there are none as yet). It was explained in the House of Commons[228] that this

---

[225] The need for protection is recounted in *Commonhold and Leasehold Reform* (DETR) (2000) Cm 4843, Section 4.6 and (2002) 381 HC Deb cols 956–957. A danger for tenants is that the protection may involve extra costs, ultimately chargeable to them: *Freeholders of 69 Marina, St Leonards-on-Sea* v *Oram* [2012] HLR 166.

[226] CLRA, ss 76–77. 'Residential lease' is not a statutory term: the provisions cover dwellings which are not business and agricultural tenancies (e.g. s 167(4)).

[227] Rights of Re-entry and Forfeiture (Prescribed Sum and Period) (England) Regulations 2004 (SI 2004 No 3086). Under s 167, the prescribed sum may be up to £500; 'administration charges' within Sched 11, Part 1, are ignored.

[228] (2002) 381 HC Deb col 960.

is intended to protect vulnerable tenants who do not respond to notices and demands. It may include a duty to investigate T's circumstances.

C. Waiver

That L possesses a choice as to whether to forfeit has the very important result that there may be waiver of the right. Just as bringing a claim constitutes a final decision to forfeit,[229] so other conduct may operate as a final decision to continue the lease. The courts have been exceptionally generous to tenants in holding that such waiver has taken place. This generosity was an antidote to the overly powerful remedy of forfeiture. Now that there are greater controls over forfeiture, doubts are being expressed as to whether the waiver rules can be justified.[230]

For waiver to operate, L must both have notice of the breach[231] and act in such a way as to indicate that the lease is treated as continuing. There is a danger that steps taken to ascertain the circumstances of a breach might occasionally themselves constitute waiver.[232] L cannot argue that he did not realise that forfeiture proceedings could be brought,[233] although L can rely upon T's own representations as to the facts.[234]

The most common form of waiver is by receipt of rent due after the relevant breach. The courts' analysis is that such rent is payable only if the lease is continuing. It follows that the receipt of rent recognises that the lease is continuing.[235] Three criticisms may be made of this rule. First, one must feel sympathy for the position of L, who can claim neither rent nor mesne profits until the action is heard.[236] Second, rent is usually accepted because of some mistake within L's offices: it is not as if a conscious decision has been made to keep the lease alive.[237] Third, and most damning, it does not matter that T is well aware that L has no intention of waiving the forfeiture.[238] The rule has even been extended to claiming rent without receiving it.[239] Nor can a landlord who wishes to avoid waiver simply accept the payment 'without prejudice'.[240] However, receipt of a sum genuinely

[229] It precludes subsequent waiver (*Civil Service Co-operative Society Ltd v McGrigor* [1923] 2 Ch 347), though we have seen that the claim can be discontinued.

[230] *Segal Securities Ltd v Thoseby* [1963] 1 QB 887; *Greenwich LBC v Discreet Selling Estates Ltd* (1990) 61 P&CR 405.

[231] Awareness by L's porter suffices: *Metropolitan Properties Co Ltd v Cordery* (1979) 39 P&CR 10.

[232] *Cornillie v Saha* (1996) 72 P&CR 147.

[233] *David Blackstone Ltd v Burnetts (West End) Ltd* [1973] 1 WLR 1487 at p 1501; *Van Haarlam v Kasner* (1992) 64 P&CR 214.

[234] *Chrisdell Ltd v Johnson* (1987) 54 P&CR 257.

[235] Receipt of rent due on or before the breach does not constitute waiver. Nor is there waiver if the rent is payable in advance, due on or before breach for a period ending after the breach: *Re A Debtor* [1995] 1 WLR 1127.

[236] *Moore v Assignment Courier Ltd* [1977] 1 WLR 638.

[237] *Central Estates (Belgravia) Ltd v Woolgar (No 2)* [1972] 1 WLR 1048.

[238] Ibid; *Thomas v Ken Thomas Ltd* [2007] L&TR 326.

[239] The cases, especially *Segal Securities Ltd v Thoseby* [1963] 1 QB 887 and *David Blackstone Ltd v Burnetts (West End) Ltd* [1973] 1 WLR 1487, are considered in *Greenwood Reversions Ltd v World Environmental Foundation Ltd* [2008] HLR 486 at [26], where it is observed that there is no binding Court of Appeal authority.

[240] *Davenport v The Queen* (1877) 3 App Cas 115; *Matthews v Smallwood* [1910] 1 Ch 777; *Segal Securities Ltd v Thoseby* [1963] 1 QB 887. It seems unlikely that waiver can be excluded by the terms of the lease: Adams [1991] Conv 79.

other than as rent will not amount to waiver.[241] Levying distress[242] depended upon rent being due. Not surprisingly, it was treated as constituting waiver in the same way as claiming or receiving rent.[243]

Leaving aside rent receipts and demands, an unequivocal act of waiver is required.[244] Simply delaying a decision as to forfeiture is no waiver.[245] Nor will there be waiver unless the decision is communicated to T or has an impact on T.[246] A rather different aspect of the waiver rules, one that operates in L's favour, is that LPA, s 148 provides that waiver is not treated as extending to future breaches. Thus, waiver of a failure to pay rent cannot be relied upon as regards any future default. Some breaches are continuing in nature, as with a covenant to repair property[247] or a covenant restricting user of it.[248] In these instances, forfeiture proceedings can still be brought if the breach continues after the waiver.[249] Care needs to be taken in deciding whether breach of any particular covenant is continuing or not: the wording of the covenant is all-important.[250]

D. Relief: non-payment of rent

One of the factors complicating relief against forfeiture is that different rules apply to rent breaches as opposed to other breaches. This is largely a consequence of the nineteenth-century rule that equity would relieve only against rent breaches.[251] The result has been that relief for rent breaches can still be based upon equitable principles, although there has been extensive statutory intervention. On the other hand, relief for non-rent breaches is statutory in origin and, as will be seen, it is unlikely that equitable rights to relief can be asserted.

(i) *Formal demands*

Before forfeiture can proceed for unpaid rent, L must make a formal demand for the rent due. The rules are absurdly archaic: there must be demand on the premises before sunset on the day the money is due.[252] Section 210 of the Common Law Procedure Act 1852

---

[241] *Croft v Lumley* (1858) 6 HLC 672 (10 ER 1459). For cheques covering rent and other debts, see *Osibanjo v Seahive Investments Ltd* [2009] 2 P&CR 9.

[242] Seizing T's property to cover arrears; now commercial rent arrears recovery (see below, p 445).

[243] *Doe d Flower v Peck* (1830) 1 B&Ad 428 (109 ER 847).

[244] *Matthews v Smallwood* [1910] 1 Ch 777.

[245] *Van Haarlam v Kasner* (1992) 64 P&CR 214. See also *Perry v Davis* (1858) 3 CBNS 769 (140 ER 945).

[246] *London & County (A&D) Ltd v Wilfred Sportsman Ltd* [1971] Ch 764 at p 782 (grant of reversionary lease).

[247] *Penton v Barnett* [1898] 1 QB 276.

[248] *Segal Securities Ltd v Thoseby* [1963] 1 QB 887.

[249] Somewhat generously, L can still rely on a notice (notices are required by LPA, s 146) issued before the waiver: *Penton v Barnett* [1898] 1 QB 276; *Greenwich LBC v Discreet Selling Estates Ltd* (1990) 61 P&CR 405.

[250] *Doe d Flower v Peck* (1830) 1 B&Ad 428 (109 ER 847) (to keep insured is continuing, to effect an insurance policy not). A covenant to build (unlike a covenant to keep in repair) is not continuing: *Stephens v Junior Army & Navy Stores Ltd* [1914] 2 Ch 517. See also Pawlowski (2005) 9 L&T Rev 16.

[251] *Hill v Barclay* (1810) 16 Ves 402 (33 ER 1037) (possibly also in respect of other payments: *Sanders v Pope* (1806) 12 Ves 282 (33 ER 108)).

[252] 1 Wms Saund 287 (being note 16 to *Duppa v Mayo*) (85 ER 374).

provides that a formal demand is not necessary[253] if there are six months' arrears.[254] The rules are unimportant because virtually every lease excludes the need for a formal demand.[255]

(ii) *Relief before trial*

Section 212 of the Common Law Procedure Act 1852 confers an absolute right to relief where arrears and costs are paid before trial.[256] Even where there is an appalling payment record and the money is tendered at the very last minute, relief is automatic.[257] Very strangely, this right to relief applies only where the lease falls within s 210: in other words, a minimum of six months' arrears.[258] It is strange because it means that the greater the arrears due, the greater the right to relief! Further details are provided by ss 138–140 of the County Courts Act 1984.

One unwelcome characteristic of the relief legislation is that separate provision is made for the county court, sometimes differing from relief in the High Court. Section 138 enacts that, in the county court, possession is to be deferred for a minimum of four weeks and that T is entitled to relief if arrears[259] and costs are paid during that time, without any requirement of six months' arrears. It should be noted that, since 1991, county courts have unlimited jurisdiction in actions for forfeiture and relief.[260]

(iii) *Other relief*

Equity gave relief before the 1852 Act and this jurisdiction survives today.[261] Most commonly, this means that T can get relief even after a court has ordered possession in favour of L. Section 210 of the 1852 Act imposes a time limit of six months after L has taken possession.[262] In county courts, there is a similar six-month limit.[263] Equitable relief also has a role where L re-enters peaceably. Section 210 does not apply, but the courts readily

---

[253] For the purposes of forfeiture by action in court. See also County Courts Act 1984, s 139(1).
[254] This probably means the amount of arrears (even if in arrears for only one day) rather than the period of arrears: Megarry (1962) 78 LQR 168. A further condition is that there are insufficient goods for commercial rent arrears recovery (p 445 below): s 210A of the 1852 Act.
[255] *Van Haarlam v Kasner* (1992) 64 P&CR 214 at p 224.
[256] Inapplicable if T is also in breach of other covenants: *Wadman v Calcraft* (1804) 10 Ves 67 (32 ER 768). Payment cannot be made by third parties (unless sublessees or chargees from T, or an agent): *Matthews v Dobbins* [1963] 1 WLR 227.
[257] *Gill v Lewis* [1956] 2 QB 1 (relief would have been given on a discretionary basis anyway).
[258] *Standard Pattern Co Ltd v Ivey* [1962] Ch 432, criticised by Megarry (1962) 78 LQR 168. Equitable relief was given.
[259] Arrears up to this time, not merely the date the claim is brought: *Maryland Estates Ltd v Joseph* [1999] 1 WLR 83.
[260] High Court and County Courts Jurisdiction Order 1991 (SI 1991 No 724), art 2.
[261] The jurisdiction of the High Court is preserved by Senior Courts Act 1981, s 38.
[262] Oddly, this limitation applies only if there are six months' arrears: *Billson v Residential Apartments Ltd* [1992] 1 AC 494 at p 529 (Nicholls LJ).
[263] County Courts Act 1984, s 138(9A)–(9C), inserted by Administration of Justice Act 1985, s 55. L may be estopped from relying on the limit if re-entry is hidden from a mortgagee: *Target Home Loans Ltd v Iza Ltd* [2000] 1 EGLR 23.

asserted the equitable jurisdiction.[264] The absence of a six-month limit was not regarded as a reason for holding otherwise. It is unsurprising that a few days beyond six months have been held not to preclude relief.[265] More surprising is that a delay of 14 months has been accepted.[266] This may be best understood as a reaction to the prospect of the loss of a very valuable lease: a windfall gain for the landlord.

Once there is jurisdiction to give relief, what principles operate in the exercise of the discretion? Because the right to forfeit is viewed as a form of security, the general approach is to grant relief if the arrears are paid, save in very exceptional cases. This was adopted by the Court of Appeal in *Gill v Lewis*.[267] It was irrelevant that T had a poor payment record; nor was conviction for an isolated indecent assault committed on the premises enough to deny relief, although conduct giving the property a bad name might do so. Even an earlier contumacious failure to pay is unlikely to deny relief.[268]

Relief is more likely to be denied where T delays in seeking relief and L either disposes of the property or otherwise changes his position.[269] Disposition to a third party does not preclude relief,[270] although when combined with delay, it may tip the balance against relief.[271] Relief will not be given to the detriment of a third party who is a registered proprietor (for unregistered land, a bona fide purchaser without notice).[272] When considering the terms on which relief is given, the object is to put the parties in the same position as if there had been no forfeiture. Where L has re-entered, this means that L must account for a full occupation rent.[273]

(iv) *The effect of relief*

In all cases, the effect of relief is that T holds under the original lease.[274] There is no need for a new lease.

(v) *Sub-tenants and mortgagees*

If a lease is forfeited, then any subordinate property rights fall with it.[275] This will be disastrous for both sub-tenants and mortgagees. The result is that such persons will be anxious to claim relief, especially where T either does not want to claim or else is unlikely to succeed. Sections 210 and 212 of the Common Law Procedure Act 1852 apply

---

[264] *Howard v Fanshawe* [1895] 2 Ch 581; *Lovelock v Margo* [1963] 2 QB 786.

[265] *Thatcher v CH Pearce & Sons (Contractors) Ltd* [1968] 1 WLR 748 (T normally a good payer, but had problems because temporarily in prison).

[266] *Pineport Ltd v Grangeglen Ltd* [2016] L&TR 453 (there were some mitigating circumstances).

[267] [1956] 2 QB 1, approved in *Bland v Ingrams Estates Ltd* [2001] Ch 767 at [39].

[268] *Di Palma v Victoria Square Property Co Ltd* [1984] Ch 346 (service charge).

[269] *Stanhope v Haworth* (1886) 3 TLR 34; *Newbolt v Bingham* (1895) 72 LT 852.

[270] *Ashton v Sobelman* [1987] 1 WLR 177.

[271] *Silverman v AFCO (UK) Ltd* (1988) 56 P&CR 185 (originally, T had not contested forfeiture).

[272] *Fuller v Judy Properties Ltd* (1991) 64 P&CR 176 (Martin [1992] Conv 343); *Bank of Ireland Home Mortgages v South Lodge Developments* [1996] 1 EGLR 91.

[273] *Bland v Ingrams Estates Ltd (No 2)* [2002] Ch 177 (see [12]–[15] for the principles).

[274] Common Law Procedure Act 1852, s 212; Senior Courts Act 1981, s 38(2) (equitable relief); County Courts Act 1984, s 138(5), (9B).

[275] See, e.g., *Great Western Railway Co v Smith* (1875) 2 Ch D 235; *Dewar v Goodman* [1909] AC 72.

to mortgagees[276] and to sublessees.[277] For the county court, the statutory provisions have been construed in a similar fashion[278] and also include equitable chargees.[279]

In *Bland v Ingrams Estates Ltd*,[280] equitable chargees claimed relief under the High Court's inherent jurisdiction (peaceable re-entry). Although a direct claim for relief by the chargee was denied (largely because of the weak property status of the charge), it was held that the chargee could indirectly assert T's claim for relief by joining T. As observed above, equitable charges can claim direct relief in the county court.

It will be seen below[281] that holders of subordinate rights can claim relief for both rent and non-rent breaches under LPA, s 146(4). This is the most common basis for seeking discretionary relief today. The section probably has the effect of excluding the equitable relief previously available to sub-tenants and mortgagees.[282]

E. Relief: non-rent breaches

It has been noted that equity did not generally give relief. An exception for fraud, accident or mistake was narrowly applied.[283] This resulted in statutory control, now embodied in LPA, s 146.[284] It will be seen later that a slight doubt remains as to whether the modern law recognises a residual equitable jurisdiction to grant relief.

The essence of the s 146 scheme (which is limited to non-rent breaches)[285] may be summarised as follows. L must give T[286] a notice specifying the breach and (as relevant) demanding remedy of it and damages. If T remedies the breach within a reasonable time, then there is a right to relief. In other cases, the court has a discretion as to whether to grant relief. Where relief is given, the effect is to continue the original lease.[287] Once L has taken possession after a court order, it is no longer possible to seek relief under the section.[288]

---

[276] *Ladup Ltd v Williams & Glyn's Bank plc* [1985] 1 WLR 851 would include equitable chargees, although this is dubious in the light of *Bland v Ingrams Estates Ltd* [2001] Ch 767.

[277] *Doe d Wyatt v Byron* (1845) 1 CB 624 (135 ER 685).

[278] *United Dominions Trust Ltd v Shellpoint Trustees Ltd* [1993] 4 All ER 310 (the effect was to bar relief when a mortgagee failed to comply with the statutory time limits). County Courts Act 1984, s 138(9C), expressly provides for persons with derivative interests to apply within six months of L's taking possession.

[279] *Croydon (Unique) Ltd v Wright* [2001] Ch 318. Probably the same applies if there has been peaceable re-entry: *Bland v Ingrams Estates Ltd* [2001] Ch 767 at [62], [83].

[280] [2001] Ch 767. Hale LJ expressed doubts about the absence of a direct claim. In contrast, *Test Valley BC v Minilec Engineering Ltd* [2005] 2 EGLR 113 allowed an equitable assignee to seek relief.

[281] See p 441 below. It does not apply to equitable chargees.

[282] See p 441 below. For the previous relief, see *Abbey National BS v Maybeech Ltd* [1985] Ch 190 at p 200.

[283] *Barrow v Isaacs & Son* [1891] 1 QB 417; the exception was recognised in *Shiloh Spinners Ltd v Harding* [1973] AC 691 at p 722.

[284] It cannot be excluded: s 146(12). For its application to equitable leases, see p 404 above.

[285] LPA, s 146(11). For dwellings, s 146 applies despite a term that service charges shall be treated as rent: *Freeholders of 69 Marina, St Leonards-on-Sea v Oram* [2012] HLR 166 (criticised by Lees [2012] Conv 498 as inconsistent with previous thinking and with *Escalus Properties Ltd v Robinson* [1996] QB 231).

[286] Notice is given to T as the person obliged to remedy the breach and compensate L, even if T's mortgagee has taken possession: *Smith v Spaul* [2003] QB 983.

[287] *Dendy v Evans* [1910] 1 KB 263.

[288] *Quilter v Mapleson* (1882) 9 QBD 672; *Rogers v Rice* [1892] 2 Ch 170; *Egerton v Jones* [1939] 2 KB 702; *Ladup Ltd v Williams & Glyn's Bank plc* [1985] 1 WLR 851; confirmed by *Billson v Residential Apartments Ltd* [1992] 1 AC 494 at pp 538, 542.

(i) *The notice*

The validity of notices has been a constant source of litigation. If the notice is inadequate, then T can frustrate the forfeiture and, at least, buy time whilst a new notice is issued. The general role of the notice was stated in *Horsey Estate Ltd* v *Steiger*[289] as being 'to give to the person whose interest it is sought to forfeit the opportunity of considering his position before an action is brought against him'. T will wish to decide whether to admit the breach, remedy it and compensate L, and whether to apply for relief.

The notice must specify the particular breach, and this means that T must be able to 'understand with reasonable certainty what it is which he is required to do'.[290] Thus in *Akici* v *LR Butlin Ltd*[291] a notice asserting that T had parted with possession was bad when the relevant breach was sharing possession. The courts have consistently held that L can decide to forfeit without claiming compensation.[292] This is sensible, although difficult to justify from the wording of the legislation ('in any case, requiring the lessee to make compensation').[293]

Remediable breaches

The really difficult question has been as to what breaches are remediable: the notice need not require remedy where remedy is impossible. The remediability question is more important than simply deciding the validity of the notice, as it determines whether T is entitled to relief by remedying the breach. Yet, we should remember that discretionary relief can always be given: holding a breach to be irremediable may well not determine the final outcome.[294] If L is unsure as to whether the breach can be remedied, the easy answer is to require the breach to be remedied 'if it is capable of remedy'.[295] Problems arise where the notice has failed to mention remedying the breach.

The debate has centred around two ideas: that a breach resulting in a stigma to the premises cannot be remedied and (more widely) that no breach of a negative covenant can be remedied. The best-known stigma case is *Rugby School (Governors)* v *Tannahill*.[296] The leased premises had been used for prostitution, in breach of a standard covenant preventing illegal or immoral use. It was found that the breach 'would be known all over the neighbourhood and seriously affect the value of the premises'.[297] The result was that stopping the use would not remedy it: a continuing stigma would affect the premises.[298] Accordingly, the breach was irremediable and a notice was valid despite not requiring remedy.

---

[289] [1899] 2 QB 79 at pp 91–92.
[290] *Fletcher* v *Nokes* [1897] 1 Ch 271 at p 274.
[291] [2006] 1 WLR 201.
[292] *Lock* v *Pearce* [1893] 2 Ch 271; *Rugby School (Governors)* v *Tannahill* [1935] 1 KB 87.
[293] Recognised by Russell J in *Civil Service Co-operative Society Ltd* v *McGrigor* [1923] 2 Ch 347 at p 356.
[294] See Kerr LJ in *Bass Holdings Ltd* v *Morton Music Ltd* [1988] Ch 493 at p 527.
[295] *Glass* v *Kencakes Ltd* [1966] 1 QB 611 at p 629.
[296] [1935] 1 KB 87.
[297] Ibid, at p 91.
[298] Cesser of the stigma would take much longer than the reasonable time contemplated by s 146(1): *Egerton* v *Esplanade Hotels, London Ltd* [1947] 2 All ER 88 at p 91.

Rugby School has been repeatedly followed in subsequent cases and is not limited to prostitution.[299] One factor stressed in these cases is that the breach in *Rugby School* continued over an extensive period. It is far from clear that an isolated act, even if illegal, would have been similarly treated. It is also interesting that, in virtually every case, the court has gone on to hold that relief should not be given on a discretionary basis. One exception is *Central Estates (Belgravia) Ltd* v *Woolgar (No 2)*,[300] which involved a valuable lease, a breach for a relatively short period, no damage to the value of the premises and an elderly and ill tenant. Even then, granting relief was not straightforward, and Buckley LJ in particular expressed doubts.

Great difficulty has been encountered where a breach of this type is caused by a subtenant. If it was encouraged by T, then the courts have no difficulty in saying that the breach is irremediable.[301] In other cases, T is likely to be in breach despite being quite unaware of the conduct complained of. Can T's breach be remedied by prompt eviction of the guilty sub-tenant? This issue was fully discussed by Paull J in *Glass* v *Kencakes Ltd*.[302] The judge was unwilling to hold that the breach was automatically irremediable, the more so as it could have severe effects where there are many subleases (as with a lease of a block of flats). The question should be treated as a question of fact: in *Glass*, there was no significant effect on the value of the premises, given the prompt response by T.[303] Although this decision seems compatible with the earlier authorities, it accepts that some breaches of negative covenants can be remedied. It is to this that we now turn.

Positive and negative covenants

As judges have stressed, failure to comply with covenants can never, strictly, be remedied. No remedy can remove the fact that there has been a breach. Nevertheless, s 146 obviously contemplates that breach of some covenants can be remedied.[304] The Court of Appeal in *Expert Clothing Service & Sales Ltd* v *Hillgate House Ltd*[305] accepted that most breaches of positive covenants can be remedied[306]: the question is whether harm resulting from the breach can be undone. In any event, the remedy must be capable of being undertaken within a reasonable time. On the facts, a breach of a covenant to undertake building work was held remediable.

---

[299] *Egerton* v *Esplanade Hotels, London Ltd* [1947] 2 All ER 88 (immoral use of hotel); *Hoffmann* v *Fineberg* [1949] Ch 245 (gambling); *Ali* v *Booth* (1966) 110 SJ 708 (restaurant, breach of health regulations); *Central Estates (Belgravia) Ltd* v *Woolgar (No 2)* [1972] 1 WLR 1048 (prostitution); *Dunraven Securities Ltd* v *Holloway* [1982] 2 EGLR 47 (illegal pornography); *British Petroleum Pension Trust Ltd* v *Behrendt* (1985) 52 P&CR 117 (prostitution); *Van Haarlam* v *Kasner* (1992) 64 P&CR 214 (spying).

[300] [1972] 1 WLR 1048.

[301] *Rugby School (Governors)* v *Tannahill* [1935] 1 KB 87; *Borthwick-Norton* v *Romney Warwick Estates Ltd* [1950] 1 All ER 798; *British Petroleum Pension Trust Ltd* v *Behrendt* (1985) 52 P&CR 117 (the last two cases involve T's shutting eyes to what was going on).

[302] [1966] 1 QB 611.

[303] This more lenient approach is not applied when T is implicated in the breach: *British Petroleum Pension Trust Ltd* v *Behrendt* (1985) 52 P&CR 117. Cf *Patel* v *K&J Restaurants Ltd* [2010] EWCA Civ 1211 (delay by L in taking action caused the breach to be irremediable, but discretionary relief was granted).

[304] See *Hoffmann* v *Fineberg* [1949] Ch 245 at p 253; *Akici* v *LR Butlin Ltd* [2006] 1 WLR 201 at [64].

[305] [1986] Ch 340. The court rejected an argument based upon *Scala House & District Property Co Ltd* v *Forbes* [1974] QB 575 that 'once and for all' breaches of positive covenants cannot be remedied.

[306] One exception would be a failure to insure, if the property has burnt down: Slade LJ [1986] Ch 340 at p 355.

The position regarding negative covenants has been more controversial. MacKinnon J had suggested at first instance in *Rugby School*[307] that no breach of a negative covenant could be remedied: one can never remove the fact that T has done something that should not have been done. However, that suggestion was rejected by the Court of Appeal, which applied the narrower stigma test.

Scala House & District Property Co Ltd v Forbes[308] (decided a decade before *Expert Clothing*) returned to the question. The breach was entering into a sublease without obtaining L's consent. The Court of Appeal adopted the analysis that the subletting constituted a once-and-for-all breach: it was thereafter impossible to wipe the slate clean. Much of the reasoning was based upon the proposition that, had the sublease ended before the s 146 notice, the breach could not be remedied. It would then be strange if T could remedy the breach by terminating the sublease after the notice. Such a distinction would indeed be strange, but it is quite unclear why termination of the sublease *before the notice* should not have remedied the breach.

In *Expert Clothing*, O'Connor LJ explicitly rejected the reasoning in *Scala* and limited its effect to covenants not to sublet (or assign).[309] This wider view of remediability has been twice adopted by the Court of Appeal: in *Savva v Hussein*[310] and *Akici v LR Butlin Ltd*.[311] In *Akici*, Neuberger LJ observed that the reasoning in *Scala* was 'demonstrably fallacious and inconsistent with common sense and many cases'. He considered that the great majority of breaches would be remediable, including (on the facts) parting with or sharing possession.

O'Connor LJ in *Expert Clothing* regards it as absurd that a trivial breach (he gives the example of the wrongful removal of a window box) should be irremediable. At first sight, the approach of O'Connor LJ seems far preferable to the draconian stance in *Scala*. However, it needs to be remembered that *Scala* does not hold that relief should not be given, rather that it is not automatic. In fact, the court in *Scala* granted discretionary relief. Furthermore, the *Glass* approach that certain breaches can be remedied provides a trap for L if the statutory notice fails to mention remedy. It may be argued that these issues are best resolved not by the technicality of striking down notices, but rather by the exercise of discretion as to whether there should be relief.

The approach in *Rugby School*, *Expert Clothing*, *Savva* and *Akici* was approved by the Supreme Court in *Wickland (Holdings) Ltd v Telchadder*.[312] However, a new issue was raised: what happens if the breach of a negative covenant has no continuing effect (anti-social behaviour in the facts)? This cannot be remedied in a traditional fashion. However, all the justices considered that this was no bar to remediability: the mischief may (if not too serious) be capable of being redressed by the notice requiring the tenant not to repeat the breach for a reasonable period. A majority held that this period was less than the duration of the lease: after a gap of three years, the notice could no longer be relied upon.

---

[307] [1934] 1 KB 695. It has the advantage of clarity, causing Harman J in *Hoffmann v Fineberg* [1949] Ch 245 at p 254 to regret its rejection by the Court of Appeal.
[308] [1974] QB 575.
[309] [1986] Ch 340 at p 364 (obiter, as the covenant in *Expert Clothing* was positive).
[310] (1996) 73 P&CR 150.
[311] [2006] 1 WLR 201 at [71]–[74].
[312] [2014] 1 WLR 4004; the case involved mobile homes legislation, which was similar to s 146. All the justices held that the notice could not be relied upon on the facts, the minority finding that there was insufficient 'causal or temporal link' between the notice and later breach.

Further issues

Before leaving the requirements for a valid notice, a few specific points should be added. There are certain exceptions to the requirement of notice, including some cases of T's bankruptcy.[313] Rather generously, no new notice is required if a breach is continued after waiver.[314] Again generously, it appears that L can give notice after taking possession: this will regularise earlier improper actions.[315] If the notice includes allegations that are not in fact breaches, it appears that the notice remains valid as regards the actual breaches.[316]

(ii) *The position after the notice*

It has been seen that T is entitled to relief if the breach is remedied within a reasonable time. What is a reasonable time will depend upon the nature of the breach and the length of the lease remaining.[317] Where the breach is not remediable, it seems that L must still allow a short period before proceeding to forfeit the lease: 14 days is adequate.[318]

The court has a discretion to grant relief where the breach is not remedied. Relief is likely where the effect of the breach on L is limited, at least if there are no deliberate and continuing breaches by T. Relief is available for even deliberate breaches, although the tenant's conduct will be taken into account – deliberate breaches causing significant prejudice to the landlord are likely to lead to the termination of the landlord/tenant relationship.[319]

A particular problem arises in longer leases, which commonly have a significant value (the rent in such leases is commonly nominal). Forfeiture will cause real loss to the tenant and give the landlord a windfall profit. This raises issues of proportionality, bearing in mind that forfeiture is designed to provide security for the landlord and not to penalize the defaulting tenant.[320] Though the breach may render it inappropriate for the relationship between the parties to continue, the lease may be sold and the proceeds, net of any obligation to L, paid to T.[321] This both gets rid of the defaulting tenant and avoids unnecessary loss (or windfall profit).

(iii) *Peaceable re-entry*

Section 146 makes it clear that notice must be given before peaceable re-entry.[322] More difficult has been the question whether relief is available after peaceable re-entry. Although

---

[313] LPA, s 146(8)–(10).

[314] See n 249 above.

[315] *Fuller v Judy Properties Ltd* (1991) 64 P&CR 176.

[316] *Pannell v City of London Brewery Co* [1900] 1 Ch 496, approved by *Fox v Jolly* [1916] 1 AC 1 at p 15.

[317] *Expert Clothing Service & Sales Ltd v Hillgate House Ltd* [1986] Ch 340 at pp 357–358. It was said in *Bhojwani v Kingsley Investment Trust Ltd* [1992] 2 EGLR 70 at p 73 that three months is generally thought to be adequate for repair. For breaches of negative covenants (by T's licensee), a month was thought more than enough in *Albany Holdings Ltd v Crown Estate Commissioners* [2003] EWHC 1480 (Ch). See, generally, Pawlowski (2004) 8 L&T Rev 131.

[318] *Scala*. Seven days from receipt of the notice may suffice: *Fuller v Judy Properties Ltd* (1991) 64 P&CR 176.

[319] *Freifeld v West Kensington Court Ltd* [2016] 1 P&CR 83.

[320] *Magnic Ltd v Ul-Hassan* [2015] EWCA Civ 224 at [50]; *Freifeld* at [43]. Duckworth and Sissons [2016] Conv 286 argue that the cumulative effect of tenant protections renders forfeiture unduly slow and difficult.

[321] *Khar v Delmounty Ltd* (1996) 75 P&CR 232 (maintenance charge arrears); *Freifeld* (tenant allowed six months to sell the lease).

[322] *Re Riggs, ex p Lovell* [1901] 2 KB 16.

s 146(2) makes it clear that T can seek relief before re-entry (whether or not L is taking court proceedings),[323] it was long thought that relief was no longer available after re-entry was complete. Thereafter, it is difficult to argue that L, in the language of the section, 'is proceeding' to enforce the forfeiture.[324] By analogy, relief is not available under s 146(2) after L has taken possession under a court order.

The House of Lords in *Billson v Residential Apartments Ltd*[325] overturned that line of thinking. Lord Templeman noted that forfeiture is complete when L brings a claim, yet it has always been the law that relief can be given in the resulting proceedings. Although s 146 uses the present tense 'is proceeding', the jurisdiction cannot be restricted to cases where forfeiture is technically incomplete. Just as T can claim relief after L forfeits by bringing a claim, so also where L has peaceably re-entered. If the words 'is proceeding' are troublesome, they should be interpreted as meaning 'proceeds'.

Any idea that L could avoid discretionary relief by taking peaceable re-entry was regarded as unacceptable.[326] The policy of the law is to limit such self-help remedies, and it would be most unfortunate if s 146 were to favour landlords utilising self-help. The somewhat strained interpretation of the section seems justified by these considerations.[327]

It might be added that a majority of the Court of Appeal in *Billson* denied any equitable jurisdiction to grant relief. Section 146 was considered to provide a comprehensive code for non-rent breaches, thereby excluding any equitable jurisdiction. The House of Lords did not need to consider this question in the light of their broad interpretation of s 146. If anything, that interpretation makes it even more difficult to argue in favour of the equitable jurisdiction today. It would be relevant once L has taken possession under a court order, when there is no statutory relief. This may be contrasted with the position for rent breaches, where the equitable jurisdiction survives (given the absence of comprehensive legislation) and T has six months in which to seek relief.

(iv) *Sub-tenants and mortgagees*[328]

There appear to be two routes available. The Court of Appeal held in *Escalus Properties Ltd v Robinson*[329] that the discretion to grant relief under s 146(2) extends to sub-tenants and mortgagees.[330] This relief involves continuation of the existing lease and the attraction of the *Escalus* route is that relief is therefore retrospective. The implications of this approach have not yet been clarified. For example, how would it operate when T is not qualified for relief?

---

[323] *Pakwood Transport Ltd v 15 Beauchamp Place Ltd* (1977) 36 P&CR 112.
[324] See the Court of Appeal in *Billson v Residential Apartments Ltd* [1992] 1 AC 494.
[325] [1992] 1 AC 494.
[326] It is not an adequate response that T could seek relief before re-entry. It cannot be incumbent upon every tenant to seek relief on receipt of a s 146 notice, simply in order to guard against peaceable re-entry.
[327] County Courts Act 1984, s 139(2) provides a useful six-month limit on county court applications.
[328] See the useful discussion by Tromans [1986] Conv 187.
[329] [1996] QB 231.
[330] Equitable assignees are also within s 146(2): *High Street Investments Ltd v Bellshore Property Investments Ltd* (1996) 73 P&CR 143.

Traditionally, applications have been brought under the second route: s 146(4). This, unlike the rest of s 146, covers both rent and non-rent breaches.[331] It makes specific provision for relief to be given to sub-tenants but also applies to mortgagees.[332] The jurisdiction applies where relief is sought either before re-entry or after peaceable re-entry. The sub-tenant is normally in possession and is likely to be aware of the circumstances and be made a party to L's proceedings for possession.

However, there is a distinct danger that mortgagees may be unaware of the forfeiture proceedings. There is clear authority that mortgagees cannot rely upon s 146(4) once possession has been obtained under a court order against T.[333] *Billson* approved that proposition, which appears to render it impregnable. The position of the mortgagee may, however, be ameliorated by the jurisdiction to set aside the order in order to permit a claim to relief to proceed, although a person who had been given notice of the action is most unlikely to succeed on this basis.[334]

Equitable relief

This conclusive effect of the court order as regards statutory relief makes it important to know whether equitable relief is available. It has been seen that equitable jurisdiction was recognised for rent breaches. For non-rent breaches, jurisdiction to grant relief was not generally recognised (even for T) in the nineteenth century. It was only with the decision of the House of Lords in *Shiloh Spinners Ltd* v *Harding*[335] in 1972 that equitable relief was allowed a broader scope. *Shiloh* involved a forfeiture of an assignment of a lease, not the forfeiture of the lease itself. Two questions need to be addressed in the present context. The first is whether this broader jurisdiction extends to non-rent covenants in leases. This appears very likely. The second and more difficult question is how far this jurisdiction is excluded by the statutory scheme for relief in s 146.

In *Shiloh*,[336] Lord Wilberforce considered that 'particular legislation in a particular area' leaves unaffected a general principle of law or equity operating outside that area. The question is how broadly we should interpret a 'particular area'. Section 146 makes provision for relief for both tenants (non-rent breaches) and sub-tenants and mortgagees (all breaches). It appears most likely that this excludes equitable relief in both these areas.[337] Nicholls J had taken the contrary view in *Abbey National BS* v *Maybeech Ltd*,[338] being reluctant to treat s 146(4) as a complete code. Nevertheless, the Court of Appeal in *Billson*[339] rejected any equitable jurisdiction. Although *Billson* dealt with the relief

---

[331] For rent breaches, see also p 434 above.

[332] *Grand Junction Co Ltd* v *Bates* [1954] 2 QB 160. *Bland* v *Ingrams Estates Ltd* [2001] Ch 767 at [14], [60] denies its application to equitable chargees or holders of charging orders.

[333] *Egerton* v *Jones* [1939] 2 KB 702, Greene MR at p 707, unhelpfully describing this as 'one of the risks of the game'.

[334] *Rexhaven Ltd* v *Nurse* (1995) 28 HLR 241 (Chancery Division: Judge Colyer QC).

[335] [1973] AC 691.

[336] [1973] AC 691 at p 725.

[337] But not rent breaches by tenants. This jurisdiction is recognised in many cases, including *Silverman* v *AFCO (UK) Ltd* (1988) 56 P&CR 185.

[338] [1985] Ch 190, followed in *Ladup Ltd* v *Williams & Glyn's Bank Ltd* [1985] 1 WLR 851.

[339] Nicholls LJ dissented. The majority preferred the reasoning in *Official Custodian for Charities* v *Parway Estates Developments Ltd* [1985] Ch 151 and *Smith* v *Metropolitan City Properties Ltd* [1986] 1 EGLR 52.

available to tenants, it seems clear[340] that s 146(4) was perceived as having an identical effect upon sub-tenants and mortgagees. Accordingly, the current position must be that there is no equitable relief for sub-tenants and mortgagees.[341] Whether this is satisfactory appears to depend upon JR the scope for setting the order aside, discussed above.

The grant of relief

Where there is jurisdiction to grant relief to sub-tenants and mortgagees, how readily will relief follow? Unlike s 146(2), relief under s 146(4) involves a new lease,[342] and this has led to dicta that the jurisdiction will be sparingly exercised.[343] However, at least where T rather than the claimant for relief is in the wrong, the cases indicate that relief is in fact readily granted. Indeed, relief will be granted even if T is guilty of the sort of breach that leads to stigma.[344]

Because there will be a new lease, the question arises as to the terms upon which that lease will be granted. So far as mortgagees are concerned, the expectation is that the mortgagee will hold a lease on identical terms to the original lease, but it will be held as security with T having the equity of redemption. This may have the practical effect of giving relief to T even where an application by T would have been rejected.[345]

Deciding the appropriate relief for sub-tenants causes more difficult problems. A sub-lease may be of part of the premises, for a much shorter length than the head lease and at a greater or lesser rent. What terms are appropriate when relief is given?[346] Section 146(4) enacts that S is not entitled to a longer lease than the sublease but otherwise leaves the terms to the court. Where S has a sublease of part of the premises, relief will be limited to that part. S will invariably be required to make good breaches by T, but *Chatham Empire Theatre (1955) Ltd* v *Ultrans Ltd*[347] establishes that this will normally apply only to the part sublet. This is a sensible rule, as it would be oppressive to require a sub-tenant of one of a large number of flats in a building to be responsible for the arrears due under a head lease of the entire building. However, S will have to pay T's arrears of rent on the part sublet, even if S has already paid rent to T.

As regards the amount of rent in the new lease, it appears from *Ewart* v *Fryer*[348] that L is entitled to the higher of the rent under the head lease (for the part sublet) and the rent under the sublease.[349] It is inevitable that differing rent levels necessitate that one person will benefit or the other person will lose. The case for favouring L can only be that it is S who is claiming a discretionary remedy.

---

[340] [1992] 1 AC 494, especially at pp 517, 522.

[341] Subject to the narrow equitable jurisdiction to relieve against fraud, accident or mistake: Sir Nicolas Browne-Wilkinson V-C in *Billson* [1992] 1 AC 494 at pp 518–519.

[342] *Cadogan* v *Dimovic* [1984] 1 WLR 609; *Official Custodian for Charities* v *Mackey* [1985] Ch 169.

[343] See, e.g., *Fivecourts Ltd* v *JR Leisure Development Co Ltd* [2001] L&TR 47 at pp 55–56.

[344] *Grand Junction Co Ltd* v *Bates* [1954] 2 QB 160.

[345] *Chelsea Estates Investment Trust Co Ltd* v *Marche* [1955] Ch 328 at pp 338–339. The Law Commission considers that the best solution would be for the lease to be sold to provide funds for the mortgagee: Law Com No 303, para 6.123.

[346] See Tromans [1986] Conv 187 at pp 198–210.

[347] [1961] 1 WLR 817.

[348] [1901] 1 Ch 499 (see especially Romer LJ at p 516).

[349] *Chatham* and *Ewart* illustrate that the figures will take into account any premium payable and other terms affecting rent levels.

(v) *Repairing covenants*

Extra controls are found in the Leasehold Property (Repairs) Act 1938,[350] which applies both to forfeiture and to actions for damages. The mischief against which the legislation is directed is the buying of reversions by speculators, who then try to force tenants out by enforcing repairing covenants. The resultant vacant possession would lead to windfall profits.[351]

The Act applies to repairing covenants in non-agricultural leases exceeding seven years, where more than three years remain unexpired. A s 146 notice must inform T of the right to serve a counter notice under the 1938 Act. When such a counter notice is served, forfeiture is blocked unless the court orders otherwise. The 1938 Act[352] stipulates when the court may allow the covenant to be enforced: the circumstances may be summarised as being where they necessitate the immediate remedying of the lack of repair.

The general perception is that it takes exceptional circumstances to persuade the court to give leave.[353] The House of Lords has held that it is not enough to prove an arguable case: it is necessary to prove the factors relied upon.[354] Although the legislation serves a useful purpose, it contains at least one flaw: leave cannot be given after the repairs have been carried out. This means that if L undertakes even emergency work (under powers reserved in the lease), it may be impossible to recoup the costs.[355] However, such powers nearly always go on to state that the cost is to be borne by T. Enforcement of such a clause (being an action for debt rather than for damages for breach of covenant) is outside the 1938 Act.[356] This avoids the injustice identified above. Although it limits tenants' protection, the mischief against which the Act is directed is less likely where L has had to expend money on the repairs.[357]

F. Reform

In a major report in 1985,[358] the Law Commission recommended wide-ranging reforms. The complexity of the present law was severely criticised:[359] the reforms would remove many of the present distinctions and technical rules. In particular, rent and non-rent breaches should be treated in the same way. We now have a 2006 Report, updating the proposed reforms.[360]

---

[350] Extended by the Landlord and Tenant Act 1954, s 51. See, generally, PF Smith [1986] Conv 85.
[351] *National Real Estate & Finance Co Ltd v Hassan* [1939] 2 KB 61 at p 78.
[352] Section 1(5).
[353] *Sidnell v Wilson* [1966] 2 QB 67.
[354] *Associated British Ports v CH Bailey plc* [1990] 2 AC 703.
[355] *SEDAC Investments Ltd v Tanner* [1982] 1 WLR 1342. The result is criticised in Law Com No 142, para 8.46.
[356] *Jervis v Harris* [1996] Ch 195.
[357] Contra: Bickford-Smith (1984) 270 EG 908.
[358] Law Com No 142.
[359] See the catalogue of flaws in Bignell (2007) 11 L&T Rev 140.
[360] Law Com No 303, usefully summarised by Pawlowski (2007) 11 L&T Rev 9 and Bridge (2007) 11 L&T Rev 145. Residential leases for less than 21 years would be subject to the different rules proposed in Law Com No 297.

Generally, termination of leases for breach would require a court order. Instead of the court's being asked to enforce an existing forfeiture by L as at present, the court would make the 'termination order'. Many of the features of the present law will disappear. No forfeiture clause would need to be included (though denial of title would no longer justify termination without an express term) and formal demands would disappear. A tenant default notice would be required in all cases: this would identify the breach, the response L requires from T and the period allowed. The minimum period would be seven days even if no response is requested, but an unreasonably short period might be very relevant when the court comes to exercise discretion (see below).

Thereafter, L could apply for a termination order, whether or not T acts on the notice. This recognises the inequity of T's constantly acting in breach of covenants and yet avoiding forfeiture by remedying the breaches at the last minute. Questions of remediability are thus replaced by the exercise of discretion by the court. The court might decide that T had done enough to justify relief, issue a termination order or make a remedial order. If there is a remedial order, L's application would be stayed for three months after specified work should be completed. If L wants a termination order, then it would be necessary to apply within that period to lift the stay. An interesting proposed new power is to order sale of the lease – especially useful if it has a high value.

Waiver would be abolished. If L actively leads T to suppose that there will be no application for a termination order, this could be considered as part of the court's discretion. A related point is that L would have to issue the tenant default notice within six months from knowledge of the breach, with the court application being no more than six months after the period specified in that notice.

It would no longer be possible to terminate by peaceable re-entry. However, a special procedure is proposed for many straightforward cases – an obvious example is where the tenant has abandoned the premises. The landlord could issue a summary termination notice, somewhat similar to the tenant default notice. It would identify the breach and state that it will be effective after one month. Unless the tenant applied to court within that period, the lease would terminate without any court proceedings (though the tenant could still apply to court within the following six months). The procedure would be limited to cases where the tenant has no reasonable prospect of resisting termination – otherwise, the tenant's court application within the one-month period would succeed.

The court would have a broad jurisdiction to deal with derivative interests, described as 'qualifying interests' in the scheme. Sub-tenants, mortgagees and chargees (legal or equitable) are included. L would have a duty to discover qualifying interests (from the register or from being informed about them) and issue tenant default notices to their holders.

5. Distress and commercial rent arrears recovery

If rent is in arrears, an ancient remedy of landlords was to seize tenants' goods on the land and then sell them. The sums received were likely to be so low as to make distress more of a potent threat to tenants than a realistic manner of raising significant sums of money. An especially powerful element of distress was that L could seize other persons' goods found on the premises.

Distress was encrusted with large numbers of technical and peculiar rules.[361] More importantly, it was regarded as being inconsistent with modern ideas of obligation enforcement. Not only was it a rare example of a self-help remedy, but it operated so as to prefer landlords to other creditors. Perhaps unsurprisingly, there were doubts as to its compliance with human rights legislation.[362]

Fortunately, it was abolished by the Tribunals, Courts and Enforcement Act 2007.[363] A replacement procedure is introduced but only for commercial leases. This commercial rent arrears recovery scheme[364] applies only to the tenant's goods. The major problems of the old law are ameliorated by requiring notice and permitting the tenant to ask the court to intervene. Any attempt to assert an express right to seize goods is ineffective. The scheme possesses numerous details protecting tenants, but these lie outside the scope of this text.

Further reading

Elliott, D W (1964) 80 LQR 244: Non-derogation from grant.

Goymour, A (2015) 'Relativity of title, and the regulation of the "proprietary underworld"' in *Landmark Cases in Property Law* (eds S Douglas, R Hickey and E Waring).

Harwood, M (2000) 20 LS 503: Leases: are they still not really real?

Morgan, J (2009) 'Leases: property, contract or more?', in *Modern Studies in Property Law*, Vol 5 (ed M Dixon), Chapter 17.

Reynolds, J I (1974) 37 MLR 377: Statutory covenants of fitness and repair: social legislation and the judges.

Roberts, N [2012] Conv 87: The Bruton tenancy: a matter of relativity.

Smith, P F [2003] Conv 112: Disrepair and unfitness revisited.

Tromans, S [1986] Conv 187: Forfeiture of leases: relief for underlessees and holders of other derivative interests.

---

[361] Arden [1979] LAG Bull 79.
[362] *Fuller v Happy Shopper Markets Ltd* [2001] 1 WLR 1681 at [27]; Walton [2000] Conv 508 at pp 522–526.
[363] Section 71; see also Law Com No 5; Law Com No 194 (1991).
[364] Tribunals, Courts and Enforcement Act 2007, Part 3, Chapter 2 and Sched 12; Shea (2008) 12 L&T Rev 126; Tanguay (2014) 320 PLJ 7.

20

Leases: parties and the running of covenants

Introduction

One very important characteristic of a lease is that both the lease and the freehold reversion may be assigned (transferred); the covenants in the lease can then be relied upon by and against the assignees.[1] The running of the burden is particularly significant: in contract law, it is very unusual for obligations to be enforced against anyone except the original contracting party.[2] Where freehold land is concerned, positive covenants do not bind purchasers of the burdened land,[3] although the restrictive covenant has been recognised since the nineteenth century as a proprietary interest binding purchasers.[4] The benefit of freehold covenants relating to land is capable of running,[5] so the running of the benefit of covenants in leases comes as no surprise.

The relationship of parties to a lease is commonly portrayed in diagrammatic form:

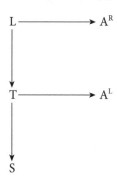

In this example, the landlord (L) has sold the freehold reversion to A^R and the tenant (T) has sold the lease to A^L. The covenants in the lease can be enforced between A^R and A^L as if they were the original landlord and tenant. For pre-1996 leases, this is subject to one

[1] See, generally, Thornton (1991) 11 LS 47.
[2] Witness the controversy surrounding *De Mattos* v *Gibson* (1859) 4 De G&J 276 (45 ER 108): Gardner (1982) 98 LQR 279.
[3] *Haywood* v *Brunswick Permanent Benefit BS* (1881) 8 QBD 403.
[4] See Chapter 24. The contrast with leases is discussed at p 553.
[5] *Smith and Snipes Hall Farm Ltd* v *River Douglas Catchment Board* [1949] 2 KB 500; *Kumar* v *Dunning* [1989] QB 193.

major qualification: the covenants must, in the traditional property law terminology, touch and concern the land. This was the test used to distinguish those covenants that relate to the landlord and tenant relationship from those that do not.

Why do covenants run?

It has already been observed that the running of covenants in leases constitutes a special rule. It may be justified by the combination of two factors. The first is that assignments of the reversion and of the lease are common. So far as the reversion is concerned, it is obvious that the landlord may wish to sell what may be a valuable asset: there is a large market in freehold reversions. The tenant will frequently wish to assign the lease, especially where it is for a moderately long period. Take a lease of a shop: the trader may find after 5 years of a 21-year lease that new and larger premises are needed. Theoretically, the tenant could surrender the lease to the landlord, but in many cases, the lease will have a value that can be realised only by selling to an assignee.[6] Where the lease has no value,[7] the landlord will prefer that the tenant should find a new possessor.

The second factor is that a lease necessarily involves obligations which must bind successors in title in order for the landlord–tenant relationship to remain viable. Most obviously, A^L must be liable on the covenant to pay rent. The running of repairing covenants is also essential, whether the obligation is placed upon the landlord or the tenant. In short, the continued enforceability of covenants is 'necessary for the effective operation of the law of landlord and tenant'.[8]

Another way of looking at the issues is to ask whether the original landlord and tenant expect to remain liable after assignment of the reversion or the lease. Their purpose in assigning is to sever all connection with the land. Continued liability is neither an efficient method of enforcing covenants (how could the original landlord or tenant repair after assigning?), nor is it what the parties desire. Nevertheless, it will be seen below that, in pre-1996 leases, both landlord and tenant may remain *contractually* liable after assignment.[9]

Subleases and privity of estate

The above diagram also involves a sublease (or underlease) created by T in favour of S. It is important to appreciate that a tenant can create a lease just as a freeholder can. The result is to create a second and entirely separate leasehold relationship. Indeed, the terms of the two leases may be quite different. The sublease may be for a much shorter term, and the rent may be quite different. An immediate question is as to the relationship between L (or A^R) and S. The short answer is that the law recognises no relationship between them at all: covenants, whether in the head lease or the sublease, cannot be enforced between L (or A^R) and S.[10]

This contrast between the assignee and the sublessee is expressed in legal terminology by saying that A^L is in *privity of estate* with A^R, whereas S is not.[11] The running of leasehold

---

[6] This will most obviously occur where T has paid a premium (capital sum) for the lease.

[7] In times of falling rents, many leases have a negative value; a landlord will not accept a surrender unless substantial compensation is paid.

[8] Lord Templeman in *City of London Corporation* v *Fell* [1994] 1 AC 458 at p 464.

[9] The original landlord or tenant can recoup any liability from the relevant assignee: *Moule* v *Garrett* (1872) LR 7 Ex 101.

[10] For some qualifications, see p 471 below.

[11] See, e.g., *Ewart* v *Fryer* [1901] 1 Ch 499 at p 512.

covenants depends upon privity of estate. This concept of privity of estate is easily explained. The persons who currently hold the lease and the reversion on the lease are in privity of estate. In the above example, A^L and A^R are in privity of estate, as are S and A^L as regards the sublease. L and T were in privity of estate before either assigned, although this is of little significance because of their contractual relationship.

Why should sublessees not be bound by the covenants? The distinction between sub-leases and assignments may be 'very nice and technical',[12] but it is convenient for T to have two ways of dealing with the lease.[13] By assignment, T terminates all relationship with the lease and becomes a 'stranger to the land'.[14] A^L takes over the obligations and benefits. However, a sublease enables T to retain the head lease and to impose different obligations on the sub-tenant.

Take this example of shop premises. Suppose the head lease is for 99 years, T having paid a substantial premium and the rent being nominal. As one would expect in such a long lease, T is under an obligation to repair. T subleases the shop to S for three years at the current annual market rent of £30,000. Bearing in mind the short period of the sublease, T undertakes to repair. In this setting, it is plain that the two leases are entirely different. If L could sue S on the covenants in the head lease, it could have the disastrous consequence of rendering S liable for very expensive repairs. So far as the rent is concerned, it is obvi-ous that only T is entitled to the £30,000: a continuing relationship is intended between T and S and in no way is T receiving money on behalf of L.

What is the position of S should T's head lease terminate? The normal rule is that sub-leases fail if the head lease is brought to an end.[15] However, if T surrenders the head lease, then the sublease survives and its covenants are enforceable by and against L.[16] This sur-vival does not apply where the head lease is a periodic tenancy and either L or T gives notice of termination: any sublease automatically fails,[17] whether or not L and T act consensually.[18]

This failure of subleases may be justified on the basis that it would be contrary to prin-ciple for T to be able to create a right binding L, where that right might be more onerous than T's own lease. In addition, covenants would not be enforceable against S.[19] Similarly, subleases are defeated by the exercise of a break clause in the head lease which permits termination of a fixed-term lease.[20] Perhaps surprisingly, it is not open to L and T to oust this principle by express provision in the lease.[21]

---

[12] Lindley LJ in *Hall* v *Ewin* (1887) 37 Ch D 74 at p 81.

[13] The existence of choice is illustrated by the fact that the sublease may be for just one day less than the lease. However, a sublease is the only option if T wishes to part with the land for a shorter period than the head lease.

[14] Lord Greene MR in *Milmo* v *Carreras* [1946] KB 306 at p 310.

[15] This is most relevant if the head lease is forfeited (as seen in Chapter 19).

[16] *St Marylebone Property Co Ltd* v *Fairweather* [1963] AC 510 at pp 546–547; Law of Property Act 1925 (hereafter LPA), s 139.

[17] *Pennell* v *Payne* [1995] QB 192, approved in *Barrett* v *Morgan* [2000] 2 AC 264.

[18] *Barrett* v *Morgan* [2000] 2 AC 264; Dawson [2000] Conv 344. Subject to qualifications, this would be changed for residential tenancies by Law Com No 297, para 6.23.

[19] LPA, s 139 applies only on surrender or merger, even though human rights considerations may enable the leg-islation to be interpreted to avoid this result: *PW & Co* v *Milton Gate Investments Ltd* [2004] Ch 142 at [134].

[20] *PW & Co* v *Milton Gate Investments Ltd* [2004] Ch 142 (earlier assumed by the Court of Appeal in *Pennell,* but criticised by Luxton and Wilkie [1995] Conv 263).

[21] *PW & Co* v *Milton Gate Investments Ltd* [2004] Ch 142 (Neuberger J).

Landlord and Tenant (Covenants) Act 1995

The law relating to the running of covenants has been changed and codified by the Landlord and Tenant (Covenants) Act 1995 (hereafter the 1995 Act).[22] The general structure of the law remains as described above, but many of the detailed rules are amended and, in any event, now have a statutory source. Although the legislation was introduced to deal with the contractual liability of tenants after assignment of the lease, the opportunity was taken to produce a statutory code governing the running of leasehold covenants. Although most of the principles are now enshrined in this legislation, it appears that the basic principles (privity of estate; privity of contract) are still in place. It follows that the 1995 Act fails to establish an exhaustive code.[23]

The 1995 Act is to be welcomed, but it applies only to 'new tenancies' entered into from 1 January 1996.[24] This has the unfortunate consequence that we now have two separate sets of rules for leasehold covenants. It is particularly troublesome because leases are often entered into for extended periods[25]; the old rules will continue to operate for decades, and in some cases centuries, in the future.

Most leases encountered today will have been created since 1996. Accordingly, the treatment of the law in this chapter will be based on the 1995 Act. The position regarding old tenancies will be considered briefly, although it is sometimes important in explaining the need for provisions in the legislation.

1. Assignment and subletting

In this section, we will look at the powers of the parties to assign or sublet. Nearly all the material relates to assignment and subletting by T; it is very unusual for a lease to contain restrictions on assignment of the reversion by L.[26]

A. The power to assign and sublease

Apart from tenancies at will, any lease can be assigned or sublet. Although it is common for a lease to contain restrictions on such dispositions, the assignment or sublease is valid even if it is executed in breach of covenant.[27] This is confirmed by s 26 of the Land Registration Act 2002 (hereafter LRA), although placing a restriction on the register (s 40 of that Act) would prevent any assignment or sublease being entered on the register.

However, this does not mean that restrictions in leases can be ignored. Their breach will normally be a ground for forfeiture. Forfeiture proceedings must be taken against A^L,[28] the lease now being in A^L's hands (assuming no restriction preventing its registration). Failure

---

[22] See Bridge [1996] CLJ 313; Davey (1996) 59 MLR 78; Clarke [1996] CLP Pt 1, pp 97–114.

[23] Dixon [2006] Conv 79, commenting on *London Diocesan Fund v Phithwa* [2005] 1 WLR 3956.

[24] 1995 Act, s 1(1); SI 1995 No 2963. A few provisions do apply to old leases.

[25] A right to extend an existing lease will not create a new tenancy: 1995 Act, s 1(6).

[26] If the premises are divided into two or more flats, a majority of the tenants may possess a right to purchase if L intends to assign: Landlord and Tenant Act 1987, Part I.

[27] The leading modern case is *Old Grovebury Manor Farm Ltd v W Seymour Plant Sales & Hire Ltd (No 2)* [1979] 1 WLR 1397, followed in *Governors of the Peabody Donation Fund v Higgins* [1983] 1 WLR 1091. For subleases, see *Dellneed Ltd v Chin* (1986) 53 P&CR 172.

[28] *Old Grovebury Manor Farm Ltd v W Seymour Plant Sales & Hire Ltd (No 2)* [1979] 1 WLR 1397.

to obtain consent will also result in liability for losses resulting from the assignment or sublease. In particular, T will be liable for rent unpaid by the assignee.[29]

B. Assignment or sublease?

The question sometimes arises as to whether a particular transaction takes effect as an assignment or sublease. It is clear that any attempt to assign for a period less than T's lease can only create a sublease. However, there has been litigation regarding attempts to create a sublease for a period as long as (or longer than) T's lease.

Milmo v *Carreras*[30] held that such transactions take effect only as assignments, regardless of both of the label given to them and of the parties' intentions. The analysis is that T has parted with the entire leasehold estate and that this necessarily constitutes an assignment. A partial exception is that a periodic tenant is allowed to sublease for a term longer than the current period.[31] This may be justified because periodic tenancies continue indefinitely unless notice is given.

This insistence upon there being an assignment is unfortunate in a number of respects. Even if the intended sublease is longer than the head lease, there may be an expectation that T's lease may be renewed or that T will be allowed to hold over as a periodic tenant.[32] That it is unrealistic to regard T's interest as being limited to the strict length of the present term is already recognised in the rule for periodic tenancies. Furthermore, the landlord–tenant relationship does not require L to have an estate in the land.[33]

Especially troubling is that the terms of a sublease are likely to be different from those in the assigned lease: it may be difficult to give effect to the parties' intentions where an assignment is forced upon them. The most obvious example concerns rent. The sublease may well be at a rent greater than that being paid by T.[34] Because it constitutes an assignment, the rent (up to the amount payable by T) should be paid directly to L. The assignee is at risk if it is paid to T and T fails to pay L. Perhaps more serious is the position of the additional rent. This is payable to T, but not as rent on a lease: T and A^L are not landlord and tenant. Instead it appears to be a rentcharge, in a form rendered void by the Rentcharges Act 1977. If T and the assignee had realised that they were entering into an assignment then, instead of extra rent being payable by the assignee, there might have been a capital payment to T.

The rule is likely to catch only the unwary. If T wishes to create a sublease for the remainder of the term, this can in substance be achieved by providing that it shall be for a few days less than T's lease.[35] This common, if technical, device ensures that no assignment takes effect, whilst effectively giving possession to the sublessee for the remainder of the term. It may be questioned whether the rule converting subleases into assignments

---

[29]   1995 Act, s 11; earlier, *Williams* v *Earle* (1868) LR 3 QB 739.

[30]   [1946] KB 306. The rule goes back to *Hicks* v *Downing* (1696) 1 Ld Raym 99 (91 ER 962). For subleases which are the same length as T's lease, see *Parmenter* v *Webber* (1818) 8 Taunt 593 (129 ER 515); *Beardman* v *Wilson* (1868) LR 4 CP 57; *Hallen* v *Spaeth* [1923] AC 684 (PC).

[31]   *Oxley* v *James* (1844) 13 M&W 209 (153 ER 87).

[32]   *Milmo* v *Carreras* [1946] KB 306; Morton LJ regretted the court's decision.

[33]   *Bruton* v *London & Quadrant Housing Trust* [2000] 1 AC 406; pp 387, 405, 411 above.

[34]   It still operates as an assignment: *Wollaston* v *Hakewill* (1841) 3 Man&G 297 (133 ER 1157).

[35]   See Harman J in *Centrovincial Estates plc* v *Bulk Storage Ltd* (1983) 46 P&CR 393 at p 398.

is necessary. Although the label by itself should not be conclusive, it is difficult to see what harm would be done by allowing a sublease for the length of T's lease. Indeed, the Law Commission would reverse it for residential tenancies.[36] Nevertheless, the rule is so well established as to appear free from attack in the courts.[37]

C. Common restrictions

Virtually every lease contains a covenant restricting assignment and subletting. Nevertheless, such a covenant will not be implied; nor is it within the category of 'usual' covenants, implied into contracts for leases.[38] The landlord's interest in the identity of the assignee is obvious, for the assignee bears the primary responsibility for complying with the terms of the lease. The identity of the sublessee is less obviously important, but the landlord may be concerned that a particular occupier may damage the property or behave in such a way as to make the property appear less desirable, with a consequent diminution in value. The landlord also needs to remember that, should the lease be forfeited, it is quite likely that relief will result in the sublessee becoming a direct tenant.

The lease may simply provide that there shall be no assignment or subletting. Such an absolute prohibition is unusual, although consent can still be given.[39] Furthermore, the lease can validly specify circumstances in which consent may be sought.[40] A qualified prohibition, whereby T shall not assign or sublease without L's consent, is much more common. This protects L's interests and, by recognising T's vital interest in being able to realise the value of the lease, enables L to negotiate a higher rent (or premium). Recent attention has been focused on 'virtual assignments', under which the economic benefits and burdens are transferred without any assignment. These are not covered by standard restrictions on assignment.[41]

Statutory controls

This qualified prohibition is regulated by the Landlord and Tenant Act 1927: L cannot refuse consent without reasonable cause.[42] It may be noted that actual assignment or subletting does not prevent T from arguing that refusal is unreasonable,[43] at least where L's consent has been sought in advance.[44] The procedure for giving consents is regulated by

---

[36] Law Com No 297, para 6.17. Recent analyses have been very critical of the decision: Wonnacott [2013] L&T Rev 167; Hill-Smith [2013] Conv 509.

[37] Its status as a rule of law provides exemption from formality requirements: *Parc Battersea Ltd* v *Hutchinson* [1999] 2 EGLR 33.

[38] *Church* v *Brown* (1808) 15 Ves 258 (33 ER 752); *Hampshire* v *Wickens* (1878) 7 Ch D 555; *Chester* v *Buckingham Travel Co* [1981] 1 WLR 96.

[39] *Re Robert Stephenson & Co Ltd* [1915] 1 Ch 802.

[40] *Crestfort Ltd* v *Tesco Stores Ltd* [2005] L&TR 413 shows how this avoids looking at issues of reasonableness, discussed below; see also *Level Properties Ltd* v *Balls Brothers Ltd* [2008] 1 P&CR 1.

[41] *Clarence House Ltd* v *National Westminster Bank plc* [2010] 1 WLR 1216. There was no sharing of possession (prohibited by the lease) as the property was sublet and the 'assignee' could claim the rent as agent for the tenant.

[42] Section 19(1). This cannot be excluded by the lease, although absolute prohibitions fall outside the statute: *Bocardo SA* v *S & M Hotels Ltd* [1980] 1 WLR 17 at p 22.

[43] *Bromley Park Garden Estates Ltd* v *Moss* [1982] 1 WLR 1019 is one example.

[44] This qualification was required by *Eastern Telegraph Co Ltd* v *Dent* [1899] 1 QB 835, but not strictly applied in *Leeward Securities Ltd* v *Lilyheath Properties Ltd* (1983) 17 HLR 35 (no formal approach to L). In any event, relief against forfeiture is likely if refusal of consent would have been unreasonable.

the Landlord and Tenant Act 1988, requiring decisions to be made within a reasonable time and reasons to be given for refusing consent.[45]

The cases establish that a reasonable period will be counted in weeks rather than months. It has been said that a decision should be made within a week of having the relevant information,[46] although a slightly longer period may be reasonable when there is no suggestion of urgency.[47] Three weeks has been held to be reasonable for applications that raise complex legal or estate management issues.[48] The tenant has a tort action for breach of the statutory requirements and in particular for unreasonable refusal of consent; L has a duty to prove reasonableness.[49] Where L deliberately delays in order to sabotage the transaction and to gain from a likely surrender by T, then exemplary damages may be payable.[50]

The 1995 Act introduced some changes favouring landlords. This was a quid pro quo for the abolition of the tenant's contractual liability after assignment.[51] That abolition obviously makes it even more important for L to be satisfied as to the ability of A^L to pay the rent and observe the covenants. The principal change[52] is that the parties may agree in advance the circumstances in which consent may be withheld and conditions upon which consent may be given. The latter may include T's agreeing to guarantee A^L's compliance with the covenants.[53] It is provided that L's acting upon the agreement will not constitute unreasonable refusal of consent.

Reasonable cause

The meaning of 'reasonable cause' for the purposes of the Landlord and Tenant Act 1927 has given rise to extensive litigation.[54] The starting point is that consent should be given to an assignment to a person able to pay the rent and likely to observe the covenants.[55] It may come as a surprise that it took a decision of the House of Lords to establish that it may be (and usually will be) reasonable to refuse consent where it is reasonably thought that the assignee will act in breach of the covenants.[56] The modern approach is to treat the

---

[45] Based on Law Com Nos 141 and 161, largely designed to avoid delays in assigning and subletting. The operation of the legislation is reviewed by Sandham [2004] Conv 453 and Fancourt [2006] Conv 37.

[46] *Go West Ltd v Spigarolo* [2003] QB 1140 at [73]; *Blockbuster Entertainment Ltd v Barnsdale Properties Ltd* [2004] L&TR 239 at [22]–[23].

[47] *E.ON UK plc v Gilesports Ltd* [2013] 1 P&CR 51 (11 working days reasonable).

[48] *NCR Ltd v Riverland Portfolio No 1 Ltd* [2005] 2 P&CR 463 at [19]–[25].

[49] Landlord and Tenant Act 1988, ss 4, 2(6), 3(5).

[50] *Design Progression Ltd v Thurloe Properties Ltd* [2005] 1 WLR 1; £25,000 was awarded, a quarter of the rent, in addition to losses incurred.

[51] '[A] hard bargain indeed': Bridge [1996] CLJ 313 at p 356.

[52] 1995 Act, s 22, inserting s 19(1A)–(1E) into the Landlord and Tenant Act 1927. It applies only to new non-residential tenancies.

[53] Permitted by 1995 Act, s 16. There is a slight doubt whether such guarantees can be required in all cases: *K/S Victoria Street v House of Fraser Ltd* [2012] Ch 497 at [50] (Dollar [2012] L&T Rev 63).

[54] *International Drilling Fluids Ltd v Louisville Investments (Uxbridge) Ltd* [1986] Ch 513 contains a useful summary of the current law at pp 519–521. Apart from the burden of proof, this survives the Landlord and Tenant Act 1988: *Air India v Balabel* [1993] 2 EGLR 66. *Iqbal v Thakrar* [2004] 3 EGLR 21 at [26] contains a more recent restatement of the principles.

[55] *West Layton Ltd v Ford* [1979] QB 593 at p 606 (Lawton LJ).

[56] *Ashworth Frazer Ltd v Gloucester CC* [2001] 1 WLR 2180. Relatively insignificant breaches by the assignor do not make refusal reasonable: *Singh v Dhanji* [2014] EWCA Civ 414.

question of reasonableness as essentially factual, the cases being merely illustrative.[57] Leases usually require T to pay L's expenses, although this should be limited to reasonable expenses.[58]

If L takes facts into account that are collateral to the leased property, then refusal of consent will be treated as unreasonable.[59] Unsurprisingly, L cannot insist upon conditions which would improve his or her position under the lease.[60] It is insufficient for L to rely on financial or investment plans where these do not relate specifically to the leased property.[61] On the other hand, other decisions are more favourable to L, especially where competition with L's activities on other land is involved.[62]

A significant change consequential upon the Landlord and Tenant Act 1988 is that L can rely only on reasons which are given in writing within the reasonable period allowed for considering consent.[63] Once consent has been unreasonably refused, that is final. It is not possible to avoid liability by later qualifying the refusal or giving additional reasons, even within what might originally have been a reasonable period.[64]

One difficult question has concerned the effect of statutory protection (especially security of tenure and rent control) which will be enjoyed by the assignee. This does not justify refusal where such protection is already enjoyed by the assignor.[65] Where the statutory protection applies only to the assignee, the courts initially distinguished between normal assignments and abnormal assignments. The latter were those entered into specifically to obtain the statutory protection: consent could reasonably be refused. Later cases[66] rejected this distinction, in line with the stress on reasonableness being a case by case factual decision. It became common to uphold refusal of consent when it is based upon Rent Act protection.[67]

Generally, L need consider only his or her interests. However, there will be occasions when refusal of consent will have a disproportionately greater effect upon T. The most obvious example is where T will be unable to assign at all and hence unable to derive any benefit from the premises. In such cases, the courts may hold L's refusal unreasonable despite L's having otherwise valid reasons for refusing consent.[68]

---

[57] *Bickel v Duke of Westminster* [1977] QB 517, approved in *Ashworth Frazer.*
[58] *Dong Bang Minerva (UK) Ltd v Davina Ltd* (1996) 73 P&CR 253.
[59] *Houlder Brothers & Co Ltd v Gibbs* [1925] Ch 575 (assignee was a yearly tenant of the same landlord and would vacate this property on an assignment; difficulty in reletting this property was not a reasonable ground for refusing consent).
[60] *Mount Eden Land Ltd v Straudley Investments Ltd* (1996) 74 P&CR 306 (payment of rent under sublease jointly to L and T); *Jaison Property Development Ltd v Roux Restaurants Ltd* (1996) 74 P&CR 357 (contribution to maintenance costs).
[61] *Bromley Park Garden Estates Ltd v Moss* [1982] 1 WLR 1019 (effect on the building in which the leased flat was situated).
[62] *Sportoffer Ltd v Erewash BC* [1999] 3 EGLR 136.
[63] *Norwich Union Life Insurance Society v Shopmoor Ltd* [1999] 1 WLR 531; *Footwear Corporation Ltd v Amplight Properties Ltd* [1999] 1 WLR 551 (approved in *Go West Ltd v Spigarolo* [2003] QB 1140).
[64] *Go West Ltd v Spigarolo* [2003] QB 1140.
[65] *Bromley Park Garden Estates Ltd v Moss* [1982] 1 WLR 1019.
[66] *West Layton Ltd v Ford* [1979] QB 593; *International Drilling Fluids Ltd v Louisville Investments (Uxbridge) Ltd* [1986] Ch 513.
[67] *West Layton Ltd v Ford* [1979] QB 593; *Leeward Securities Ltd v Lilyheath Properties Ltd* (1983) 17 HLR 35. Earlier cases had upheld refusal in the context of rights to enfranchisement under the Leasehold Reform Act 1967: e.g. *Bickel v Duke of Westminster* [1977] QB 517.
[68] *International Drilling Fluids Ltd v Louisville Investments (Uxbridge) Ltd* [1986] Ch 513.

D. Concurrent leases[69]

The above analyses deal with dispositions by T. What happens if L creates a second lease, in favour of T2? Almost invariably, T's lease (being legal and first in time) will have priority, and T2 will have no right to possession for the duration of T's lease. However, the effect of T2's lease (the concurrent lease, or lease of the reversion) is to make T2 the landlord to T for as long as both leases last.[70] The effect of a concurrent lease may be shown diagrammatically as follows:

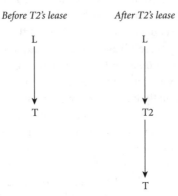

It follows that T2 can enforce the covenants in the lease and, in particular, collect rent from T. T2's liability to L depends upon the terms of their lease. Although the diagram illustrates the privity of estate results, it should be noted that T's lease is not in fact a sublease. It is an original lease from L and does not depend upon T2's lease. It follows that forfeiture of T2's lease would have no effect upon T.

2. Enforcing covenants after assignment

A. Privity of estate: general rules

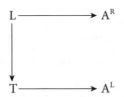

We have seen that those parties in privity of estate (A^L and A^R: the current tenant and the current holder of the reversion) can sue and be sued on the covenants. Section 3 of the 1995 Act provides for the running of covenants on the assignment of lease or reversion. The benefit and burden pass, provided that they relate to demised premises included in the assignment[71] (and provided that the covenant has not been released). Section 4 enacts that forfeiture clauses run.

---

[69] The 'overriding lease' created under the 1995 Act, s 19 (p 464 below) creates a concurrent lease.

[70] *Birch* v *Wright* (1786) 1 TR 378 at p 384 (99 ER 1148 at p 1152); *Burton* v *Barclay* (1831) 7 Bing 745 (131 ER 288); *Cole* v *Kelly* [1920] 2 KB 106. Because T2's lease operates as a grant of the reversion, it appears that it cannot take advantage of the relaxation of formality requirements for short leases: *Neale* v *Mackenzie* (1836) 1 M&W 747 (150 ER 635).

[71] 1995 Act, s 3(2), (3); for old tenancies, see *Smith* v *Jafton Properties Ltd* [2012] Ch 519.

It should be noted that it is not necessary for the covenants to be in the lease itself: obligations in a collateral agreement will also run.[72] This presents an obvious source of danger to assignees if that agreement is not disclosed.

Old tenancies

Covenants run in a broadly similar manner. On the assignment of the lease, this is generally attributed to *Spencer's Case*[73] in 1583, where the touching and concerning requirement was analysed. So far as assignment of the reversion is concerned, it was enacted by the Grantees of Reversions Act 1540 that the benefit and burden should run. The 1540 Act was re-enacted in LPA, ss 141 (benefit) and 142 (burden).

The single significant difference for old tenancies is that covenants run only if they touch and concern the land ('having reference to the subject matter of the lease' in the language of ss 141, 142).[74] This is explained below.

B. Which covenants run?

Although it seems sensible to say that only covenants relating to the land (the essence of touching and concerning) should run, we shall see below that the old law led to very fine distinctions and much litigation. As Lord Nicholls has observed, the distinction was 'long criticised as illogical and not easily drawn'.[75] Accordingly, the 1995 Act removes the touching and concerning requirement.[76] Section 3 applies to 'tenant covenants' and 'landlord covenants'. These are defined[77] as covenants falling to be complied with by the tenant or landlord, respectively. On the face of it, it seems that every covenant will pass on assignment.[78]

Limits in the 1995 Act

There is an exception for covenants personal to L or T. This is based upon the definition of landlord and tenant in s 28(1), referring to their being landlord or tenant 'for the time being'. These words were seized upon by the Court of Appeal in *BHP Petroleum Great Britain Ltd* v *Chesterfield Properties Ltd*[79] to show that a covenant that was expressed to be personal to L was not a landlord covenant. Because a landlord covenant has to be complied with by the landlord for the time being, it cannot apply where the lease provides otherwise. On a different point, in *Oceanic Village Ltd* v *United Attractions Ltd*, Neuberger J held, unsurprisingly, that a landlord covenant need not relate to the demised land: a covenant not to use adjoining land for competition with T was held to be a landlord covenant.[80]

---

[72] 1995 Act, s 28(1); *System Floors Ltd* v *Ruralpride Ltd* [1995] 1 EGLR 48.

[73] 5 Co Rep 16a (77 ER 72).

[74] *Hua Chiao Commercial Bank Ltd* v *Chiaphua Industries Ltd* [1987] AC 99 (PC) confirms that this means the same as touching and concerning.

[75] *London Diocesan Fund* v *Phithwa* [2005] 1 WLR 3956 at [26].

[76] 1995 Act, s 2(1)(a); Law Com No 174, para 4.46.

[77] 1995 Act, s 28(1).

[78] Adams and Williamson [1989] 47 EG 24; 48 EG 22. But in an agreement for a lease, conditions precedent are not landlord or tenant covenants: *Ridgewood Properties Group Ltd* v *Valero Energy Ltd* [2013] Ch 525 at [55].

[79] [2002] Ch 194; approved by the House of Lords in *London Diocesan Fund* v *Phithwa* [2005] 1 WLR 3956.

[80] [2000] Ch 234 at p 244. This did not mean that an assignee from L of the land affected was liable. Section 3(1) imposes liability only on assignees of the reversion; restrictive covenant liability under s 3(5) was held to require the defendant to own or occupy the premises leased by T. For competition law implications, see Butterworth [2011] Conv 486 and p 597 below.

Even if a covenant is a landlord or tenant covenant, s 3(6)(a) enacts that the benefit or burden will not pass if 'expressed to be personal to any person'. To fall within this exception, explicit words are not required; it is enough that the circumstances indicate that the covenant was intended to be personal.[81] It is difficult to see what role this provision can have, following the *BHP* decision that personal covenants are not landlord or tenant covenants in the first place.

Why is *BHP* significant, given the existence of s 3(6)(a)? The answer is that several provisions in the 1995 Act refer to landlord and tenant covenants. A major example concerns the liability of the original landlord or tenant following assignment, the issue in *BHP* itself.

How readily will a covenant be construed as being personal to L or T? Suppose that T covenants not to build on her freehold land which adjoins the demised land. Would A^L (not owning this adjoining freehold land) be bound by this covenant?[82] A^L might argue that the covenant is not one intended to be complied with by the person for the time being entitled to the term.[83] One can see the attraction of this, but it runs the danger of returning to the touching and concerning rule.[84] It is interesting that, in *Oceanic Village*, Neuberger J was reluctant to adopt an interpretation of landlord covenants which would reintroduce the old law.

The new rules might encourage the use of some covenants that would be surprising to see run. A covenant, for example, that the occupier should buy merchandise from a particular shop would bind assignees. Although such covenants are rare at present, the greater freedom to enforce covenants may tempt landlords to insert them. It is arguable that the law should continue to act as a filter for covenants which are suitable for binding purchasers,[85] even if the touching and concerning rules are not ideal.

The impact of registration rules

A final question is whether a covenant can be enforced as a leasehold covenant if it falls foul of registration requirements. This will be relevant when the covenant also constitutes an interest in land: options to renew leases and restrictive covenants provide the best examples. Unprotected rights do not normally bind registered transferees (assignees of the reversion or lease). Can s 3 liability (privity of estate) still operate? Section 3(6)(b) explicitly provides that registration rules are not affected by the 1995 Act, so the older material remains relevant.

Problems will not normally arise where registered land is involved. If the lease is registered, this may be taken to constitute registration of landlord and tenant covenants. This will protect the tenant on assignment of the freehold. Leases for seven years or less are overriding interests. Their overriding status presumably extends to landlord and tenant

---

[81] *First Penthouse Ltd v Channel Hotels and Properties (UK) Ltd* [2004] L&TR 274 at [49] (Lightman J; not considered on appeal [2004] L&TR 467).

[82] Note that the exception for demised premises not comprised in the assignment (s 3(3)) is inapplicable here.

[83] It may not be personal to T within s 3(6)(a), as a purchaser of both the leased and the adjoining land would be bound.

[84] Or something similar: *BHP* properly observed that personal is not the antithesis of touching and concerning.

[85] Berger (1970) 55 Minnesota LR 167; Stake [1988] Duke LJ 925; contrast Epstein (1982) 55 S Cal LR 1353 and American Law Institute, *Restatement of the Law of Property (Servitudes)*, Tentative Draft No 2, pp 20–26.

covenants. One exception is that a covenant to renew will not be protected if it can cause the overall transaction to exceed seven years.[86] What about assignment of the lease, as regards covenants benefiting the landlord (covenants restrictive of the use of the land provide the best example)? It is enacted that they bind assignees of leases, whether the lease is registered or overriding.[87] It might be added that restrictive covenants in leases cannot be protected when they relate to the leased premises[88]; this has no effect on their enforceability.

Turning to unregistered land, it has been held that renewal covenants must be registered, despite the fact that they would bind a purchaser even if they were not interests in land.[89] The legislation renders unregistered interests void,[90] and this was held to be too strong to permit their enforcement under privity of estate rules. The result may be regarded as an unnecessary trap for lessees, given that A^R will almost invariably be aware of the lease and its covenants.[91] By way of contrast, restrictive covenants in leases do not require registration[92] and attract the doctrine of notice.

The analyses in the previous two paragraphs apply to landlord and tenant covenants. Could problems arise for personal covenants? Here, the very fact that they are personal means that they will not run under s 3. There will be no clash with registration rules.

Old tenancies: touching and concerning

It has been seen that covenants must touch and concern the land before they can run in old tenancies. The test involves many complex cases, which we will consider only in outline. It should be added that touching and concerning remains a requirement for freehold covenants (Chapter 24), although it has given rise to much less difficulty in that context.

Before considering the meaning of touching and concerning, it should be noted that covenants may fall into three categories. First, there are covenants that touch and concern; these are enforceable whenever there is privity of estate. Next, at the opposite extreme, there are covenants that are obviously personal to the parties and incapable of applying to anybody else. Thus, a tenant's covenant to provide nursing facilities for an elderly landlord would apply only to the two parties. Today, these are likely to be personal covenants outside s 3 of the 1995 Act.

The third category falls in the middle: covenants that are not personal to the parties, but yet do not touch and concern. An example is an option to purchase L's interest. We will see that this does not touch and concern the land, but clearly its benefit can be assigned.[93] Indeed, it is a form of estate contract constituting an interest in land: the burden of this particular covenant can bind purchasers (A^R), provided it has been protected on the register.

---

[86] *Markfaith Investment Ltd* v *Chiap Hua Flashlights Ltd* [1991] 2 AC 43 (PC).

[87] LRA, s 29(2)(b), (4): see p 250 above.

[88] LRA, s 33(c).

[89] *Beesly* v *Hallwood Estates Ltd* [1960] 1 WLR 549, confirmed by the Court of Appeal in *Phillips* v *Mobil Oil Co Ltd* [1989] 1 WLR 888. The arguments are rehearsed in *Taylors Fashions Ltd* v *Liverpool Victoria Trustees Co Ltd* [1982] QB 133 at pp 142–143. Registration is required by s 2(4), Class C(iv).

[90] Land Charges Act 1972, s 4(6).

[91] Thompson (1981) 125 Sol Jo 816.

[92] Land Charges Act 1972, s 2(5), Class D(ii), even if the covenant burdens land other than that leased: *Dartstone Ltd* v *Cleveland Petroleum Co Ltd* [1969] 3 All ER 668.

[93] *Griffith* v *Pelton* [1958] Ch 205.

It is difficult to articulate and apply tests for deciding which covenants touch and concern the land. The problem is that the most commonly used tests are too vague to provide much guidance for the resolution of difficult cases. In practice, common covenants are covered by authority, but the distinctions drawn in the cases are sometimes difficult to justify. Romer LJ expressed his opinion in strong words[94]: 'The established rules . . . are purely arbitrary, and the distinctions, for the most part, quite illogical.'

The test and its application

The most frequently cited test derives from Bayley J in *Congleton Corporation* v *Pattison*[95]:'the covenant must either affect the land as regards mode of occupation, or it must be such as per se, and not merely from collateral circumstances, affects the value of the land'. A more general expression of the test is whether the covenant 'affects the landlord in his normal capacity as landlord or the tenant in his normal capacity as tenant'.[96]

It is easy to appreciate that covenants having a physical effect upon the land will touch and concern. Most obviously, a covenant to repair or build on the land passes the test,[97] as will landlords' covenants to provide services to the land.[98] A covenant restricting assignment and subletting affects the identity of the user of the land and therefore touches and concerns.[99] Covenants restricting the use of the land also touch and concern: nearly all leases specify permitted or prohibited uses. Insofar as this is intended to maintain the quality and value of the leased land, it is plainly correct. Even if the covenant is inserted in order to prevent competition with the landlord's business on adjoining land, or to force the tenant to purchase products from the landlord for sale on the premises, it has been held to touch and concern.[100]

However, not every covenant relating to use of the land necessarily touches and concerns. Two cases may be contrasted. *Congleton Corporation* v *Pattison*[101] itself concerned a covenant not to employ persons from outside the parish. The purpose was to reduce parish expenses, rather than to affect the land as such. It was held not to touch and concern. By contrast, in *Lewin* v *American & Colonial Distributors Ltd*[102] there was a covenant that a particular person should not be involved in the management of a restaurant. This was held to touch and concern: the identity of managers was relevant to the continuation of a licence to sell alcohol.

Tenants' covenants to perform acts (or refrain from doing so) on other land are unlikely to touch and concern. Thus, a covenant to build on adjoining land of the landlord will not touch and concern.[103] Particular problems have arisen with respect to covenants to pay

---

[94] *Grant* v *Edmondson* [1931] 1 Ch 1 at p 28.
[95] (1808) 10 East 130 at p 138 (103 ER 725 at p 728), as paraphrased by Farwell J in *Rogers* v *Hosegood* [1900] 2 Ch 388 at p 395.
[96] Cheshire and Burn's *Modern Law of Real Property* (18th edn), p 304, adopted by the Privy Council in *Hua Chiao Commercial Bank Ltd* v *Chiaphua Industries Ltd* [1987] AC 99 at p 107.
[97] *Matures* v *Westwood* (1598) Cro Eliz 599 (78 ER 842).
[98] *Jourdain* v *Wilson* (1821) 4 B&Ald 266 (106 ER 935) (water).
[99] *Williams* v *Earle* (1868) LR 3 QB 739; *Re Robert Stephenson & Co Ltd* [1915] 1 Ch 802.
[100] *Clegg* v *Hands* (1890) 44 Ch D 503; *Caerns Motor Services Ltd* v *Texaco Ltd* [1994] 1 WLR 1249.
[101] (1808) 10 East 130 (103 ER 725).
[102] [1945] Ch 225.
[103] *Spencer's Case* (1583) 5 Co Rep 16a at p 16b (77 ER 72 at p 74), unless the buildings are ancillary to the use of the demised land: *Sampson* v *Easterby* (1829) 9 B&C 505 (109 ER 188) (mine and smelting mill).

money. Payment of rent has, obviously, always touched and concerned.[104] However, rent payable to a third party fails the test,[105] as do other monetary payments to the landlord.[106] Yet it would be wrong to write off all such payments. In *Vernon v Smith*,[107] a covenant to maintain fire insurance was held to touch and concern. There is here an obvious link with the leased property, as the insurance proceeds would have to be used for rebuilding.

Most of the cases so far discussed involve covenants by tenants. As regards landlords' covenants, obligations to repair or provide services obviously touch and concern. What is the status of covenants by the landlord which relate to other land? *Ricketts v Enfield Churchwardens*[108] demonstrates that this is no absolute bar to touching and concerning. A covenant not to build on adjoining land was held to touch and concern the leased land, the outlook of which would be affected. Yet in *Thomas v Hayward*,[109] a landlord's covenant not to compete with the leased public house was held not to touch and concern: it did not have any physical effect on the land, although it did affect its value.

A similar stress on the need for physical effect is found in the controversial decision of the House of Lords in *Dewar v Goodman*.[110] T, who held 211 houses under a head lease, sublet two of them to S. T covenanted in the sublease to keep all the houses in repair, against the background that failure to do so would trigger a forfeiture of the head lease and the consequent destruction of the sublease. The emphatic response was that this did not affect the land: there was no authority that affecting the leasehold estate rather than the land would suffice.[111] Sir Nicolas Browne-Wilkinson V-C in *Kumar v Dunning*[112] criticised this as inconsistent with authority[113] and the *Congleton* test; he also thought *Thomas v Hayward* to be a hard decision. The approval of *Kumar* by the House of Lords in *P & A Swift Investments v Combined English Stores Group plc*[114] may signify the rejection of *Dewar v Goodman*. The courts now appear to take a more realistic view in asking whether the lease (not merely the land) is benefited by the covenant.

More modern approaches

This analysis of the touching and concerning rules demonstrates that they are complex and unpredictable in application. However, some more recent cases take a less technical approach. In *P & A Swift Investments v Combined English Stores Group plc*,[115] Lord Oliver proposed four tests: (1) whether the covenant ceases to be of benefit if it does not pass to the assignee; (2) whether the covenant affects the nature, quality, mode of user or

---

[104] *Parker v Webb* (1693) 3 Salk 5 (91 ER 656).

[105] *Mayho v Buckhurst* (1617) Cro Jac 438 (79 ER 374).

[106] *Spencer's Case* (1583) 5 Co Rep 16a at p 16b (77 ER 72 at p 74).

[107] (1821) 5 B&Ald 1 (106 ER 1094) (Best J; the other judges are more guarded).

[108] [1909] 1 Ch 544. As in *Vyvyan v Arthur* (1823) 1 B&C 410 (107 ER 152), land other than that demised is involved.

[109] (1869) LR 4 Ex 311.

[110] [1909] AC 72.

[111] Yet landlords' covenants for quiet enjoyment do touch and concern: *Celsteel Ltd v Alton House Holdings Ltd (No 2)* [1986] 1 WLR 666 at p 672.

[112] [1989] QB 193 at pp 205–206.

[113] *Dyson v Forster* [1909] AC 98 (not a landlord and tenant case).

[114] [1989] AC 632.

[115] [1989] AC 632 at p 642; see also *Coronation Street Industrial Properties Ltd v Ingall Industries plc* [1989] 1 WLR 304; *Harbour Estates Ltd v HSBC Bank plc* [2005] Ch 194.

value of the land of the reversioner; (3) that the covenant is not expressed to be personal; (4) in the case of a covenant to pay money, whether (in addition to the above) it is connected with something to be done on, to or in relation to the land. The first test is satisfied by covenants to insure or to guarantee rent payments. These are of no use to a landlord after assignment of the reversion: they are of value only to the assignee and therefore touch and concern.

These tests may make it easier to decide future cases, although they were soon held not to replace the old *Congleton* test.[116] *Swift* was not a case on privity of estate, and it does not do justice to the established principle that a covenant touches and concerns if it 'affect[s] the land as regards mode of occupation'. What *Swift* does well is to explain the status of those covenants which are unrelated to occupation and use.

Other issues

One particular pair of covenants has caused difficulty: covenants to renew leases and those giving T an option to purchase the reversion (usually the freehold). Covenants to renew have long been treated as touching and concerning the land[117]: it would scarcely make sense for T to be able to claim renewal after the lease has been assigned. On the other hand, options to purchase the reversion were settled not to touch and concern in *Woodall* v *Clifton*.[118] The distinction appears to be that such options create a quite different relationship: that of vendor and purchaser.

One final question must be considered. Is a forfeiture clause enforceable against A^L as regards covenants that do not touch and concern? An obvious requirement is that the forfeiture clause is drafted so as to apply to such covenants; the following discussion presumes that it is. One point in favour of forfeiture is that, outside the leases context, there is no need for any breach of duty before a property right can be made terminable.[119] Earlier cases indicated that, in leases, the law limits forfeiture to touching and concerning covenants.[120] However, the House of Lords in *Shiloh Spinners Ltd* v *Harding*[121] distinguished and criticised those cases; their status today is unclear. If forfeiture is available, this is likely to place overwhelming pressure on the assignee to comply with the covenant.

C. Breaches committed after assignment

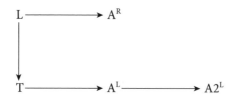

---

[116]   *Caerns Motor Services Ltd* v *Texaco Ltd* [1994] 1 WLR 1249 (Judge Paul Baker QC; Chancery Division).
[117]   *Roe d Bamford* v *Hayley* (1810) 12 East 464 (104 ER 181).
[118]   [1905] 2 Ch 257. See also *Batchelor* v *Murphy* [1926] AC 63, especially at p 67.
[119]   A standard example is a gift to a widow on condition that she does not remarry: there is no obligation not to remarry.
[120]   *Stevens* v *Copp* (1868) LR 4 Ex 20; *Horsey Estate Ltd* v *Steiger* [1899] 2 QB 79.
[121]   [1973] AC 691 at p 717. See also *Dalegrove Pty Ltd* v *Isles Parking Station Pty Ltd* (1988) 12 NSWLR 546.

The current assignee of the lease or reversion is liable on the covenants: such liability was discussed above. In this section, we will consider the liability of T and A^L for breaches committed after their respective assignments. For example, is T liable if A^L fails to pay rent? The liability of L after assignment to A^R will also be considered, although this arises less frequently.

(i) *Privity of estate*

The normal rule is that liability of both T and A^L ceases on assignment by them: 1995 Act, s 5. However, s 11 of the 1995 Act provides for an exception if the assignment is in breach of covenant or by operation of law (bankruptcy is the best example). It is discussed below in the context of contractual liability.

Old tenancies

The same normal rule applies. One application of this is that A^L ceases to be liable once there is a further assignment of the lease to $A2^L$.[122] This applies even though there is an assignment deliberately to avoid liability,[123] although in many cases there would be liability on a covenant not to assign without L's consent.

(ii) *Contractual liability: original landlord and tenant*

(a) The development of the law up to 1995

The privity of estate rules lead one to expect that neither landlord nor tenant would be liable for breaches by their assignees. However, this never represented the law. Leases have always been interpreted so that each original party remains liable for the entire period of the lease. This liability is contractual in nature. It is mainly significant as regards the liability of T to pay rent.

The original reason for this liability is fairly clear. Without it, the tenant could avoid future liability on an onerous lease by assigning it to a pauper. For example, a lease with an obligation to return the premises in good repair could be assigned in poor condition to a pauper just a day before the lease ends, with consequent avoidance of liability. Since the sixteenth century, the courts have sought to avoid this.[124] The liability also means that, if the assignee turns out to be insolvent and unable to pay rent, then the loss falls upon the original tenant. Having undertaken to pay rent for a specified period, it is the tenant's responsibility to ensure that any assignee is able to pay. T's liability applies not only as regards A^L but also as regards $A2^L$, despite the fact that T is unlikely to have any say in the identity of $A2^L$.

Several factors combined to make this area controversial in the years leading up to the 1995 Act. First, the effects of economic recession rendered many assignees insolvent and

---

[122] *Pitcher* v *Tovey* (1692) 4 Mod 71 (87 ER 268).
[123] *Onslow* v *Corrie* (1817) 2 Madd 330 at p 340 (56 ER 357 at p 360): 'The liability of an Assignee of a Lease, begins and ends with his character of Assignee' (Plumer V-C); *Beardman* v *Wilson* (1868) LR 4 CP 57.
[124] *Walker's Case* (1587) 3 Co Rep 22a (76 ER 676); *Barnard* v *Godscall* (1612) Cro Jac 309 (79 ER 269).

unable to pay rent. Because rent levels had dropped, forfeiture was less attractive for land-lords (a new lease would have a lower rent). This led to many original tenants being pur-sued for unpaid rent, often years after they had assigned the lease. The second factor is that the extent of the liability was, at least initially, far wider than one might suppose. More specifically, the liability may be for a greater rent than initially agreed and for a longer period than anticipated.

The greater rent is possible because T will be liable for increased rent under rent review clauses found in most leases.[125] This is fair enough if the increase is to take account of inflation, but it was extended to cases where the increase takes account of a change in the premises or their use.[126] As regards length of liability, T will be liable for the duration of any renewal under the provisions of the lease.[127] With respect to both of these factors, T may feel that liability is very hard given the absence of any say in the increase of the rent or the renewal of the lease.

A third factor is that T's liability is broader than that of a guarantor. Even though the expectation is that A^L will pay the rent, the liability of T is unlimited and L can choose who to sue.[128] More significantly, T is not protected by the rules protecting guarantors against changes which may affect their liability.[129] T's liability is unaffected by the dis-claimer of the lease on A^L's bankruptcy[130] or voluntary arrangements on insolvency.[131] However, releasing A^L from liability to pay all or part of the rent will release T,[132] as will the exceptional case where the variation operates as a surrender and regrant.[133]

A final and vitally important factor is that virtually every modern lease contains a cov-enant prohibiting assignment without the landlord's consent. This means that landlords seek evidence that assignees are capable of complying with the covenants: there is no question today of the tenant's simply assigning to a pauper.[134] Once the assignee's finan-cial status has been approved by the landlord, the tenant is likely to feel that any loss caused by the assignee should fall on the landlord.[135]

It should be added that this contractual liability may be enforced not only by L but also by A^R, even though there may never have been privity of estate between A^R and T.[136] The result is that A^R can sue T for rent due both before[137] and after[138] the assignment to A^L.[139]

---

[125] *Centrovincial Estates plc v Bulk Storage Ltd* (1983) 46 P&CR 393.

[126] *Selous Street Properties Ltd v Oronel Fabrics Ltd* [1984] 1 EGLR 50 at pp 55–57.

[127] *Baker v Merckel* [1960] 1 QB 657.

[128] *Norwich Union Life Insurance Society v Low Profile Fashions Ltd* (1991) 64 P&CR 187.

[129] *Baynton v Morgan* (1888) 22 QBD 74 (surrender of part of the leased property by A^L to L); *Allied London Investments Ltd v Hambro Life Assurance Ltd* [1984] 1 EGLR 16 (release of guarantor of A^L).

[130] *Hindcastle Ltd v Barbara Attenborough Associates Ltd* [1997] AC 70 applies the same rule to guarantors.

[131] *RA Securities Ltd v Mercantile Credit Co Ltd* [1995] 3 All ER 581; *Mytre Investments v Reynolds* [1995] 3 All ER 588.

[132] *Deanplan Ltd v Mahmoud* [1993] Ch 151.

[133] Bright in *The Reform of Property Law* (eds Jackson and Wilde), at pp 75–79.

[134] Should the tenant do so, there would be liability on the covenant not to assign without consent: *Williams v Earle* (1868) LR 3 QB 739.

[135] L owes no duty of care in approving assignees: *Norwich Union Life Insurance Society v Low Profile Fashions Ltd* (1991) 64 P&CR 187.

[136] An early example is *Brett v Cumberland* (1619) Cro Jac 521 (79 ER 446).

[137] *Arlesford Trading Co Ltd v Servansingh* [1971] 1 WLR 1080.

[138] *Brett v Cumberland* (1619) Cro Jac 521 (79 ER 446); *Parker v Webb* (1693) 3 Salk 5 (91 ER 656); *Centrovincial Estates plc v Bulk Storage Ltd* (1983) 46 P&CR 393.

[139] For old tenancies, this includes rent due before the assignment to A^R.

It is unsurprising that the original tenant's liability came in for much criticism. Although this contractual liability invariably arises in commercial leases,[140] it remains true that the landlord is generally in a position to dictate the terms of the lease. Tenants are frequently unaware of the significance of contractual liability on subsequent assignments. Accordingly, the Law Commission proposed the abolition of contractual liability for breaches after assignment.[141]

(b) Tenant protection under the 1995 Act

Section 5 of the 1995 Act abolishes T's liability for breaches after assignment. The prima facie result is that, after assignment, only A^L is liable on the tenant covenants. There are two qualifications. The first is that, under s 11, T remains liable on the covenants if the assignment is in breach of covenant or is by operation of law (as on bankruptcy).[142] The reason for this is that L has had no opportunity to be satisfied as to the standing of A^L as a future tenant. L remains at risk if there is no covenant restricting assignment, but that is rare.

The second qualification is that T can enter into an 'authorised guarantee arrangement' within s 16. This guarantee is likely to be imposed on T as part of the process of L's giving consent to the assignment; its imposition must satisfy the reasonableness requirements of the Landlord and Tenant Act 1927.[143] Given that most leases will require a guarantee as a condition of consent (permitted by the 1995 Act) and that in any event the reasonableness requirement is not difficult to satisfy,[144] virtually all assignors will be required to enter into guarantees. This means that T has to take care in choosing the assignee. However, it is important to note that the guarantee must terminate on a subsequent assignment to $A2^L$.[145] At that point, A^L (but not T) may be required to act as guarantor of $A2^L$. A further point is that because liability is as guarantor,[146] the courts will be more likely to hold that any change affecting A^L's liability discharges the guarantee.

Further protections

The 1995 Act provides three further protections for tenants facing liability under authorised guarantee arrangements. These are intended to counter some of the specific problems discussed above.

First, s 18 deals with the problem of variations of leases which impose more extensive obligations on T. It provides that T is not to be liable to the extent of any post-assignment variation of the lease which L has an absolute right to refuse. A^L's exercise of an option to renew a lease does not free T from liability as L has no right to refuse renewal. For rent review clauses, the theory must be that their operation does not represent a variation of the

---

[140] It is excluded on the transfer of a tenancy under the Family Law Act 1996, Sched 7, para 7(2).

[141] Law Com No 174.

[142] Applied in *E.ON UK plc* v *Gilesports Ltd* [2013] 1 P&CR 51. *UK Leasing Brighton Ltd* v *Topland Neptune Ltd* [2015] 2 P&CR 36 considers the position if A^L assigns back to T: T and any guarantor are liable under the covenants.

[143] *Wallis Fashion Group Ltd* v *CGU Life Assurance* (2000) 81 P&CR 393 at p 398. See also n 53 above.

[144] See p 452 above; *Wallis Fashion Group Ltd* v *CGU Life Assurance* (2000) 81 P&CR 393 at p 402.

[145] The liability of any guarantor (G) of T is terminated on T's assignment: 1995 Act, s 24(2). *K/S Victoria Street* v *House of Fraser Ltd* [2012] Ch 497 holds (applying s 25) that this cannot be avoided by G's entering into a new guarantee of A^L's liability, although there can be a guarantee of T's authorised guarantee liability. Nor (controversially: Williams [2016] L&T Rev 84) can it be avoided by assigning the lease to G: *EMI Group Ltd* v *O&H Q1 Ltd* [2016] Ch 586 (the assignment is wholly void) the assignment is wholly void.

[146] 1995 Act, s 16(8).

terms of the lease. It is ironic that, at the same time as s 18 was enacted (but before it was in effect), the Court of Appeal in *Friends' Provident Life Office* v *British Railways Board*[147] limited the liability to variations provided for by the lease. These would include the operation of rent review and renewal clauses. *Friends' Provident* may well be the wider of the two protections,[148] given that it may apply to circumstances where an increased rent is attributable to changes undertaken by A^L.[149] Care must be taken by L even as regards rent review clauses. In *Beegas Nominees Ltd* v *BHP Petroleum Ltd*,[150] the review resulted in stepped rent increases (£10,000 extra pa). It was held that such an outcome was not within the rent review clause, which contemplated a single rent for the next five years; not even the increased rent in the first year was binding on T.

Next, s 17 is intended to avoid T's being surprised by a sudden and enormous demand for arrears that have been building up over several years. Where L wishes to sue T in respect of rent or service charge liability,[151] s 17 requires that T should have been served with a notice of intention to recover the specified sum.[152] The notice must be served within six months of the sum becoming due. It should be noted that there is no time limit for L's recovery of the sum (once notice has been given) and that successive six-monthly notices could be given, enabling arrears to pile up. Although a useful reform, s 17 provides limited benefit. *Scottish and Newcastle plc* v *Raguz*[153] deals with the situation where a rent review is in progress which may increase the rent for the period in question. The issue that arose was whether the notice needs to include sums that will become payable following the revision (backdated to that period). The House of Lords held that only sums currently payable are within s 17, avoiding the 'remarkably silly' need for a notice even if there are no arrears.

Finally, once T has made full payment (in accordance with the notice provisions), there is a right to be granted an 'overriding lease'.[154] This is to be on the same terms and of the same length as the original lease; it takes effect as a concurrent lease.[155] It has the effect of making T the landlord of A^L for the duration of the lease. It is very important because it enables T to control A^L: either T can take steps to ensure that A^L complies with the covenants, or else T can forfeit A^L's lease and regain control over the premises.[156] In most cases, it should have a limited effect on L, although it might remove the possibility of L's forfeiting A^L's

---

[147] [1996] 1 All ER 336; Bright in *The Reform of Property Law* (eds Jackson and Wilde), Chapter 5. Although it is a matter of construction of T's contractual obligations, the House of Lords held that liability does not normally extend to an extension of a lease by force of statute: *City of London Corporation* v *Fell* [1994] 1 AC 458.

[148] Bridge [1996] CLJ 313 at p 335.

[149] Sir Christopher Slade thought *Selous Street Properties Ltd* v *Oronel Fabrics Ltd* [1984] 1 EGLR 50 (n 126 above) of dubious authority, although Beldam LJ was prepared to say that the increase fell within the rent review clause. No question of variation or of L's permission arose.

[150] (1998) 77 P&CR 14.

[151] 1995 Act, s 17(6); also liability for liquidated sums.

[152] A prescribed form must be used: s 27; see also SI 1995 No 2964. If sent by recorded delivery to the last known address, it is valid even if known not to have been delivered: *Commercial Union Life Assurance Co Ltd* v *Moustafa* [1999] 2 EGLR 44.

[153] [2008] 1 WLR 2494. The minority would have required rent review sums to be included only if there were arrears.

[154] 1995 Act, s 19.

[155] See p 454 above. Section 15(1)(a) of the 1995 Act permits T, as holder of the concurrent lease, to sue A^L.

[156] When considering whether to claim an overriding lease, T should bear in mind that liability might last longer (the entire length of the lease) than under the guarantee.

lease.[157] The utility to T of this protection is limited by the fact that T is not entitled until payment is made to L: it does not apply on the service of a notice of intention to recover from T.[158]

Anti-avoidance

The 1995 Act protection cannot be contracted out of: s 25 contains comprehensive anti-avoidance provisions. On the other hand, it is possible for one party to release the other from liability.[159] It should also be remembered that s 5 applies only to landlord and tenant covenants. We have seen that the parties can enter into personal covenants,[160] and these may continue after assignment.[161]

Old tenancies

The contractual liability of T continues as before. However, the protections in ss 17–19 (notices, variation, overriding leases) apply to old tenancies.[162] These sections are exceptional in applying to old tenancies: they reflect the concern regarding contractual liability.

(iii) *Contractual liability: assignees of the lease*

The effect of s 5 is that A^L cannot be made liable after a further assignment, save under an authorised guarantee agreement. All the same protections and provisions applicable to T extend to A^L.

Old tenancies

It has been seen that L normally has to consent to an assignment. As part of the consent process, it is common for L to require a direct covenant from A^L to comply with the terms of the lease. This changes the normal leasehold covenant rules in that A^L undertakes contractual liability for the breaches of subsequent assignees, almost identical to T's liability.[163] It also has the effect that A^L may be made liable for the breach of all covenants, regardless of whether they touch and concern.[164] This contractual liability of A^L is treated in the same way as that of T: ss 17–19 apply.

(iv) *Recovery in respect of contractual liability*

The background here is that T (or A^L) has been made liable under an authorised guarantee arrangement for breaches after assignment. Liability of T as guarantor necessarily involves

---

[157] T has no right to an overriding lease if L has already forfeited A^L's lease: s 19(7).
[158] It would not appear that T can volunteer to pay the arrears. Section 19 refers to T's being 'duly required to pay', whereas the s 17 notice is merely of an intention to recover.
[159] Ibid, s 26(1)(a).
[160] See p 455 above.
[161] [2007] Conv 1 explains how this could be exploited to avoid the intended effect of s 5, but Slessenger [2007] Conv 198 expresses some doubts.
[162] 1995 Act, s 1(2).
[163] See, e.g., *Estates Gazette Ltd* v *Benjamin Restaurants Ltd* [1994] 1 WLR 1528; *Selous Street Properties Ltd* v *Oronel Fabrics Ltd* [1984] 1 EGLR 50; *J Lyons & Co Ltd* v *Knowles* [1943] 1 KB 366. Roberts (2015) 165 NLJ 20 November p 12 notes that direct covenants are still found in assignment of new leases, although they appear to achieve nothing.
[164] Law Com No 174, para 2.3.

a right to recover against A^L, the primary debtor. It should also be remembered that there is a right to an overriding lease.

Old tenancies

The position is a little more complex. First, there is a restitutionary[165] remedy available to T or A^L against the current tenant,[166] reflecting that person's primary obligation. In addition, each of T and A^L may have a contractual remedy against their immediate assignee. In other words, T may be able to sue A^L and A^L may in turn be able to sue A2^L, regardless of any further assignment to A3^L. This contractual remedy is based on a term implied into every assignment of a lease[167] and appears to apply even if notice has not been given to A^L (or A2^L) under s 17 of the 1995 Act.[168] It may be noted that there is no possibility of such chains of liability under authorised guarantee arrangements, as liability terminates on any subsequent assignment.

(v) *Assignment of the reversion*

So far, we have been considering the assignment of the lease. Similar principles are applied by the courts on assignment of the reversion. L remains liable on the covenants,[169] although the courts have on occasion been less harsh on L than they are on T.[170] It might be observed that there are fewer dangers of assignment of the reversion to a pauper: a freehold reversion will normally be a valuable asset and it would be madness to give it away. However, if the reversion is a head lease, then it may well be worthless. This came to the fore in *London Diocesan Fund* v *Phithwa*,[171] in which the sublessee lost out badly because the assignee of the head lease had disappeared and the sublease excluded the contractual liability of the sublessor (assignor).

The 1995 Act seeks to produce similar results to assignments of leases, namely that L should drop out of the picture on assignment to A^R. However, it is not possible to replicate the position on the assignment of leases. It is very unusual for T to have to consent to an assignment by L, and it would be wrong for L to be able to escape liability by the simple expedient of assignment.[172]

There is no authorised guarantee arrangement. Instead, it is enacted[173] that L will be released from liability[174] if notice of the assignment is given to T and either T does not

---

[165] Some cases use an analysis of subrogation to L's claim: *Re Downer Enterprises Ltd* [1974] 1 WLR 1460; *Kumar* v *Dunning* [1989] QB 193.

[166] *Moule* v *Garrett* (1872) LR 7 Ex 101. A guarantor of the current tenant can also be sued: *Selous Street Properties Ltd* v *Oronel Fabrics Ltd* [1984] 1 EGLR 50; *Kumar* v *Dunning* [1989] QB 193; *Becton Dickinson UK Ltd* v *Zwebner* [1989] QB 208.

[167] LPA, s 77(1)(C); Sched 2, Part IX. For registered land, LRA, Sched 12, para 20. See *Johnsey Estates Ltd* v *Lewis & Manley (Engineering) Ltd* (1987) 54 P&CR 296. Exclusion of the contractual term does not exclude the restitutionary remedy: *Re Healing Research Trustee Co Ltd* [1992] 2 All ER 481.

[168] Stevens [1999] 20 EG 152.

[169] *Stuart* v *Joy* [1904] 1 KB 362; *Celsteel Ltd* v *Alton House Holdings Ltd (No 2)* [1986] 1 WLR 666 at pp 672–673 (supported on appeal: [1987] 1 WLR 291 at p 296); *City & Metropolitan Properties Ltd* v *Greycroft Ltd* [1987] 1 WLR 1085.

[170] *Bath* v *Bowles* (1905) 93 LT 801.

[171] [2005] 1 WLR 3956; Martin (2010) 253 PLJ 9 discusses its impact.

[172] If L is liable, recovery against A^R may be possible, just as A^L is liable to T: *Eagon* v *Dent* [1965] 3 All ER 334.

[173] 1995 Act, ss 6–8 (Riley [2015] L&T Rev 139). This applies only to landlord covenants: *BHP Petroleum Great Britain Ltd* v *Chesterfield Properties Ltd* [2002] Ch 194 (p 455 above).

[174] Very oddly, s 6(2)(b) also provides for L to cease to be entitled to the *benefit* of tenant covenants thereafter. The benefit of tenant covenants is vested in A^R by s 3(3)(b) from the time of assignment.

object or the court declares that it is reasonable for L to be released. The notice must be in the prescribed form[175] and be given within four weeks after the assignment, although L has a further opportunity to give notice on the occasion of a further assignment by A^R. Perhaps surprisingly, the lease can provide that L's liability ceases when the reversion is assigned. Because this restricts liability after assignment, it is regarded as consistent with the policy of the legislation and is not caught by s 25 of the 1995 Act.[176]

What is the position of A^R on a subsequent assignment of the reversion? Unlike the law on old tenancies, A^R remains liable unless there is a release of liability as discussed above for L. The justification for this new liability is unclear.[177]

D. Breaches committed before assignment

(i) Obligations

The position here is quite straightforward. Neither A^R nor A^L is liable for breaches before the date of their assignment.[178] As one would expect, liability in L or T for a past breach continues notwithstanding their assignment.[179]

Two complications will be mentioned. The first is that some covenants will be of a continuing nature; covenants to repair provide a good example. Although the leased property may already be in disrepair at the time of assignment, a covenant to keep it in repair will be enforceable against the assignee.[180] Secondly, forfeiture proceedings can be brought in respect of breaches prior to assignment, although prospective assignees generally seek assurance that the covenants have been complied with.[181]

Old tenancies

Similar rules apply.[182]

Set-off claims

Suppose that A^R sues T for rent (the lease has not been assigned). Can T assert a set-off, in respect of breaches by L before the assignment A^R? Such a set-off would have the practical effect of enforcing liability against A^R in respect of pre-assignment breaches, which is not normally possible. Set-off was allowed as regards rent arrears predating assignment in *Muscat* v *Smith*,[183] but *Edlington Properties Ltd* v *JH Fenner & Co Ltd*[184] held that rent accruing after assignment is free of any such set-off. This can be explained on the basis

---

[175] 1995 Act, s 27.
[176] *London Diocesan Fund* v *Phithwa* [2005] 1 WLR 3956 (HL, Lord Walker dissenting); Dixon [2006] Conv 79.
[177] Thornton (1991) 11 LS 47 at p 67.
[178] 1995 Act, s 23(1).
[179] *Harley* v *King* (1835) 2 CrM&R 18 (150 ER 8).
[180] *Granada Theatres Ltd* v *Freehold Investment (Leytonstone) Ltd* [1959] Ch 592 at p 606.
[181] Illustrated by *Arlesford Trading Co Ltd* v *Servansingh* [1971] 1 WLR 1080.
[182] Reversion: *Duncliffe* v *Caerfelin Properties Ltd* [1989] 2 EGLR 38; *Muscat* v *Smith* [2003] 1 WLR 2853. Lease: *Grescot* v *Green* (1700) 1 Salk 199 (91 ER 179); *Churchwardens of St Saviour's Southwark* v *Smith* (1762) 3 Burr 1271 (97 ER 827). Rent is apportioned from the date of assignment: *Parry* v *Robinson-Wyllie Ltd* (1987) 54 P&CR 187.
[183] [2003] 1 WLR 2853.
[184] [2006] 1 WLR 1583.

that A^R's claim in *Muscat* is based on a chose in action, whereas it is an incident of the reversion in *Edlington*. As seen below, A^R cannot normally sue for arrears predating assignment after the 1995 Act, so this set-off is principally relevant for old tenancies.

(ii) *Rights to sue*

Problems are most likely to arise with assignments of the reversion, when arrears of rent are due at the time of assignment. If the assignment of the reversion expressly includes rent arrears, there is no problem in allowing A^R to sue,[185] but what is the position if the assignment is silent? Section 23 of the 1995 Act enacts that an assignee enjoys no rights in relation to any time before the assignment, save that forfeiture proceedings can be brought for pre-assignment breaches. This provides a simple and clear solution, applicable both to A^R and A^L. It might be noted that if there is a continuing breach (as with failure to repair), then both assignor and assignee can sue for their respective periods as landlord or tenant.

Old tenancies

Re King[186] held that only A^R could sue on a tenant's liability to repair and reinstate: L's rights had passed on the assignment (based on the wording of LPA, s 141). This approach has been applied to arrears of rent.[187] The result is that any action on a touching and concerning covenant must be brought by A^R: the price paid for the assignment will reflect this.

Similar questions may arise on assignment of the lease, where the most likely liability is for L's failure to repair. *City & Metropolitan Properties Ltd v Greycroft Ltd*[188] reached a very different conclusion to that in *Re King*: the assignor was allowed to sue. The reasoning was that s 142 (dealing with covenants benefiting the tenant) is differently worded from s 141. The contrast with *Re King* may be regarded as unfortunate. We may therefore welcome the s 23 rules (for new tenancies) which apply to assignments both of leases and reversions.

E. Equitable leases and equitable assignments

So far, we have been considering the running of covenants in legal leases, where there have been legal assignments. In the past, problems arose when there was an equitable lease or equitable assignment.

Old tenancies[189]

Equitable leases

The running of the benefit should not pose too much of a problem: the benefit of promises can always be assigned and an assignment of a lease or a reversion may be taken as including the benefit of covenants.[190] Problems have arisen as regards the burden of positive covenants, which do not run on assignment unless the privity of estate rules apply. Given

---

[185] 1995 Act, s 23(2).
[186] [1963] Ch 459.
[187] *London & County (A & D) Ltd v Wilfred Sportsman Ltd* [1971] Ch 764.
[188] [1987] 1 WLR 1085 (Mowbray QC in the Chancery Division).
[189] See RJ Smith [1978] CLJ 98.
[190] *Manchester Brewery Co v Coombs* [1901] 2 Ch 608 (reversion).

the *Walsh* v *Lonsdale*[191] approach of equating legal and equitable leases, one would have expected that covenants would run in equitable leases in the same way as in legal leases. Nevertheless, *Purchase* v *Lichfield Brewery Co*[192] stressed the absence of legal privity of estate and opposed the running of the burden of covenants.

There are, perhaps, two principal ways of looking at the problem. The first, applying *Walsh* v *Lonsdale*, is to treat equitable leases as being little different from legal leases. Equity should allow covenants to run in just the same way as in legal leases. The second approach has a more contractual flavour. Although the assignee of the lease is entitled to seek specific performance, it does not follow that any remedy is available against an assignee who chooses to walk away from the assignment and give up any right to the land. The argument based upon *Walsh* v *Lonsdale* is rebutted by limiting its application to a two-party setting. Once an assignee comes into the picture, the crucial question is whether specific performance is available against that person.[193]

The contrast between these two analyses may be thought to reflect the difference between two forms of equitable leases. Where the equitable lessee has taken possession, then the situation looks more like a legal lease than a contract.[194] It is in this scenario that one expects the assignee to be bound by the covenants. On the other hand, where there is merely an executory agreement for a lease, then it is far less clear that this 'equitable lease' should be treated as if there were a legal lease. The problem, however, is that both situations are analysed on the basis of an agreement for a lease.[195]

At least where the equitable lease falls into the first category, one modern approach is to say that the covenants run. This was the analysis of Denning LJ in *Boyer* v *Warbey*.[196] It produces a clear and justifiable rule.

Supposing that *Boyer* v *Warbey* is not adopted, there are several routes whereby the assignee may still be open to attack.[197] Most obviously, an assignee cannot enforce the contract for the lease (equitable lease) without being prepared to accept liability on the covenants.[198] Equally clearly, any serious breach of the covenants is likely to mean that the assignee cannot claim specific performance.[199] An assignee who takes possession is likely to be liable for use and occupation: for most practical purposes, this means liability to pay rent. These clear propositions leave significant gaps – for example, an obligation to repair where the equitable lease has come to an end. The growing practice of requiring assignees to enter into express contracts with the landlord, as a condition of consenting to assignment, provides a likely basis for liability. A distinct merit of the *Boyer* v *Warbey* analysis is that it side-steps all these complex points.

---

[191] (1882) 21 Ch D 9.

[192] [1915] 1 KB 184.

[193] *Manchester Brewery Co* v *Coombs* [1901] 2 Ch 608, considered at p 405 above.

[194] Note the reluctance of Lord Browne-Wilkinson in *Tinsley* v *Milligan* [1994] 1 AC 340 at pp 370–371 to treat such leases as executory agreements, even though they are technically analysed as based upon a contract to grant a lease.

[195] See p 403 above.

[196] [1953] 1 QB 234. The running of covenants in equitable leases was relied upon to support the conclusion that covenants run in legal leases not under seal. Romer LJ agreed with Denning LJ on this point; Evershed MR appeared to rely on the assignee's possession. See also *Goldstein* v *Sanders* [1915] 1 Ch 549.

[197] For details, see RJ Smith [1978] CLJ 98 at pp 105–111.

[198] *Goldstein* v *Sanders* [1915] 1 Ch 549.

[199] See p 404 above.

So far, we have concentrated upon the assignment of the equitable lease. The position on assignment of the freehold reversion turns upon the interpretation of LPA, ss 141 and 142. These sections are treated as applying to reversions to equitable leases.[200] The result is that both the benefit and burden of covenants run on the assignment of the reversion.

Equitable assignments of legal leases[201]

Here, the 'fault' lies in the assignment rather than the lease itself. Every legal assignment of a lease, regardless of its duration, requires a deed.[202] The absence of a deed means that the assignment can take effect only in equity. The running of the benefit will pose no problem: the assignee will be able to sue as an assignee of a contract.

So far as the liability of the equitable assignee is concerned, the cases are strongly against liability.[203] The problem, of course, is that liability on a contract does not pass on assignment. Although *Boyer* v *Warbey* signals similar treatment of legal and equitable leases, it would not seem to apply to the analogous area of equitable assignments. The cases denying liability are probably too strong to be discarded. In support of these cases, it might be observed that the landlord can sue the assignor, being the current legal tenant. If the equitable assignee were to be liable, this would enable two different persons to be sued on privity of estate (the assignor and assignee). This might be regarded as overly generous to the landlord.

As with equitable leases, various techniques can be employed in order to render the equitable assignee liable.[204] The assignee will usually risk forfeiture of the lease if there is a breach. Another possibility lies in finding an estoppel. The landlord normally has to consent to an assignment; such consent would normally be given only for a legal assignment. Should the subsequent assignment be equitable, the assignee's payment of rent to the landlord might well contain a representation that there had been a legal assignment within the terms of the consent. This estoppel analysis was adopted by the Court of Appeal in *Rodenhurst Estates Ltd* v *WH Barnes Ltd*.[205] It will apply widely,[206] as consent to assignment is almost invariably required.

Given that equitable leases and equitable assignments are not uncommon, it is disappointing that the law is so uncertain and complex. There are strong arguments for applying the normal privity of estate rules, at least where possession has been taken under the lease or assignment.

[200] *Cole* v *Kelly* [1920] 2 KB 106; *Rye* v *Purcell* [1926] 1 KB 446 at p 452.

[201] Similar problems arise on the equitable assignment of the reversion, which may be most likely where a transfer has not been registered. Although the assignee may be entitled to forfeit for breach (Scribes *West Ltd* v *Relsa Anstalt (No 3)* [2005] 1 WLR 1847), it may not be possible to exercise powers depending on privity of estate (*Stodday Land Ltd* v *Pye* [2017] 1 P&CR 56 especially [30]–[32]: notice to quit). Further, it appears that the assignee cannot rely on s 141 for the assignment of arrears of rent: *Rother District Investments Ltd* v *Corke* [2004] 2 P&CR 311.

[202] *Crago* v *Julian* [1992] 1 WLR 372.

[203] *Moores* v *Choat* (1839) 8 Sim 508 (59 ER 202); *Robinson* v *Rosher* (1841) 1 Y&CCC 7 (62 ER 767); *Moore* v *Greg* (1848) 2 Ph 717 (41 ER 1120); *Cox* v *Bishop* (1857) 8 De GM&G 815 (44 ER 604). A contrary argument based on *Walsh* v *Lonsdale* was rejected in *Chronopoulos* v *Caltex Oil (Australia) Pty Ltd* (1982) 45 ALR 481.

[204] RJ Smith [1978] CLJ 98 at pp 116–119.

[205] [1936] 2 All ER 3, subject to problems in proving reliance: *Brown & Root Technology Ltd* v *Sun Alliance and London Assurance Co Ltd* [2001] Ch 733.

[206] Unless L is aware of the lack of a legal assignment: *Chronopoulos* v *Caltex Oil (Australia) Pty Ltd* (1982) 45 ALR 481.

Tenancies under the 1995 Act

It is pleasing that all these problems melt away. Agreements for leases are treated in the same way as legal leases (it appears that specific performance need not be available) and equitable assignments in the same way as legal assignments.[207] It might be added that special provision is made for mortgages and charges (whether of the lease or the reversion). The mortgagee or chargee has the benefit and the burden of covenants if, but only if, in possession of the premises or the reversion.[208]

3. Subleases

It has already been explained that a sublessee is not in privity of estate with the head lessor.[209] It follows that, under the privity of estate rules, the sublessee can neither enforce covenants in the head lease[210] nor be sued for breach of them.

The sublessee's immunity from liability does not mean that the covenants can be ignored. Most leases contain a forfeiture clause, so that the head lease can be forfeited if there is breach of covenant. The effect of forfeiture will be to destroy the sublease,[211] and the threat of forfeiture is a powerful tool in the hands of the landlord. The sub-tenant may be entitled to relief against forfeiture, but compliance with the covenants is likely to be a condition of relief.[212]

Although privity of estate does not apply as between head landlord and sub-tenant, covenants may be enforced on other grounds. Thus s 3(5) of the 1995 Act imposes liability under restrictive covenants[213] on those occupying the land – this will include S. This replicates the results previously reached using an equitable restrictive covenant analysis.[214] Restrictive covenants normally require benefited land, but for leases, the freehold reversion suffices: it is not necessary for the landlord to have adjoining land benefited by T's covenant.[215]

Controversially, *Hemingway Securities Ltd* v *Dunraven Ltd*[216] held S liable under a covenant restricting subletting; S was required to surrender the sublease. If restrictive covenants apply in this way, they might evade the right to relief against forfeiture. In any event, it is not clear whether the *Hemingway* liability survives s 3(5).

---

[207] 1995 Act, s 28(1) (seemingly overlooked in the dicta in *Lankester & Son Ltd* v *Rennie* [2014] EWCA Civ 1515 at [25]. This does not extend to options for lease: *Ridgewood Properties Group Ltd* v *Valero Energy Ltd* [2013] Ch 525.
[208] Ibid, s 15.
[209] See p 447 above.
[210] Possibly, the sublessee could enforce the benefit of covenants by virtue of LPA, s 78. Lessees can enforce covenants when a freehold landlord is the covenantee (*Smith and Snipes Hall Farm Ltd* v *River Douglas Catchment Board* [1949] 2 KB 500, p 556 below), so perhaps sublessees can enforce covenants in favour of a leasehold landlord.
[211] See, e.g., *Great Western Railway Co* v *Smith* (1875) 2 Ch D 235; *Dewar* v *Goodman* [1909] AC 72. Contrast surrender: p 448 above.
[212] LPA, s 146(4): see p 442 above.
[213] This includes landlord covenants, although without much effect: *Oceanic Village Ltd* v *United Attractions Ltd* [2000] Ch 234 at pp 246–247 (see p 455 above).
[214] *Hall* v *Ewin* (1887) 37 Ch D 74; *Teape* v *Douse* (1905) 92 LT 319.
[215] *Regent Oil Co Ltd* v *JA Gregory (Hatch End) Ltd* [1966] Ch 402.
[216] (1994) 71 P&CR 30; Luxton & Wilkie [1995] Conv 416 (see p 562 below). *Crestfort Ltd* v *Tesco Stores Ltd* [2005] L&TR 413 reaches a similar result by reliance on the tort of inducing breach of contract; see also *Test Valley BC* v *Minilec Engineering Ltd* [2005] 2 EGLR 113.

Contract provides another possible basis for liability between L and S. Although they are not in privity of contract, the Contracts (Rights of Third Parties) Act 1999 might apply if S covenants with T in favour of L. This has yet to be tested.[217] Similar arguments could arise as regards covenants between L and T, in favour of S.

Finally, in the distant past, L had a right to distrain (seize) sub-tenants' goods on the land for unpaid rent. That right was replaced in 1908 by a statutory right to claim arrears of rent directly from the sub-tenant after service of a notice.[218]

Further reading

Bridge, S [1996] CLJ 313: Former tenants, future liabilities and the privity of contract principle: the Landlord and Tenant (Covenants) Act 1995.

Clarke, A [1996] CLP Pt 1, pp 97–114 [on the Landlord and Tenant (Covenants) Act 1995].

Fancourt, T [2006] Conv 37: Licences to assign: another turn of the screw?

Riley, A [2015] L&T Rev 109, 139, 190: The Landlord and Tenant (Covenants) Act 1995 – 20 years on.

---

[217] See p 557 below. *Amsprop Trading Ltd* v *Harris Distribution Ltd* [1997] 1 WLR 1025 rejected an argument based upon LPA, s 56: this would require S to purport to covenant *with* L.

[218] Law of Distress Amendment Act 1908, s 6, replaced by Tribunals, Courts and Enforcement Act 2007, ss 81–84. The modern right is limited to commercial leases.

21
Commonhold

1. Nature and origins

Part III of this book (containing this chapter) deals with freehold and leasehold estates. Where does commonhold fit in? Introduced in 2002, commonhold is both a new term[1] and a new concept in English law.[2] It is best seen as a way of holding an area of land (or building) that is split into a number of units – the most obvious example being a block of flats.

To avoid confusion, it should be stressed that commonhold is designed only for situations where the occupiers will pay the full capital value of the flats. If a person is taking a one-year lease of a flat, then the lease is the only way of proceeding.

Flats have long caused problems for English law. The nature of flats is that the units are physically interdependent: this makes it essential to have obligations to repair and to contribute towards the cost of repair (especially for central facilities such as stairs and lifts). Normal freehold ownership is not viable because, as will be seen in Chapter 24, positive covenants do not bind purchasers. Indeed, these problems mean that mortgage lenders do not normally accept freehold flats as security. Instead, such flats are generally held under long leases, with either the developer or a company controlled by the tenants as the landlord. With a lease, both positive and restrictive covenants can be enforced against purchasers. This use of leases was thought to be unsatisfactory, partly because many people prefer to be owners rather than tenants (leases are inherently less secure)[3] and partly because management of flats by landlords has often been inefficient and a cause of friction.

Commonhold enables the holders of individual units to enjoy fee simple ownership, even though the incidents of this fee simple make it look like a new type of estate.[4] As one might expect, positive obligations can be enforced against purchasers of units – an essential factor if the move away from leasehold estates is to be successful. However, this is a minor element of commonhold: the legislation concentrates upon land management structures, relating both to the units and to the common areas. This constitutes its greatest practical significance. It might be added that we will see at the end of this chapter that the use of commonhold has been minimal – long leases are still invariably used.

---

[1] Roberts [2002] Conv 341 describes the evolution of the term.
[2] See the useful analysis by Clarke [2002] Conv 349. The new system is well described by van der Merwe and Smith in *Modern Studies in Property Law*, Vol 3 (ed Cooke), Chapter 11.
[3] Although this has been rendered less important by other developments: PF Smith in *Property Law: Current Issues and Debates* (eds Jackson and Wilde) at pp 120–121.
[4] An analysis developed by Clarke (1995) 58 MLR 486.

Other common law countries have for decades employed concepts similar to commonhold (referred to as condominiums in North America and strata titles in Australia). In England, the first proposals came from the Aldridge Committee in 1987.[5] Commonhold was enacted in the Commonhold and Leasehold Reform Act 2002 (hereafter CLRA).

Before looking at some of the principles (space permits only a brief summary of a highly complex structure), some of the terminology and ideas will be mentioned. The commonhold will encompass both individual units and the common parts (including staircases, roadways and recreation areas). There will be a commonhold association (CA), which will be a company limited by guarantee,[6] with all the unit-holders members of it. The common parts will be vested in the CA. The individual units will be held in fee simple by their owners. There will be a commonhold community statement (CCS) which will determine the rights and duties of both the CA and unit-holders. Its enforcement involves positive obligations binding purchasers of units. One rather different point is that the Commonhold Regulations 2004[7] (hereafter CR) spell out much of the detail, the legislation providing merely a general framework.

2. Principal commonhold rules

A. Becoming commonhold land

Only freehold land can be commonhold land. It must be registered as a freehold estate in commonhold land; the Land Registry plays a role in ensuring that the statutory requirements are satisfied.[8] There must also be a CA and CCS.[9] Although commonhold is really designed for residential flats, it can apply to separate houses (especially useful where there are common areas), commercial property and any mixture of these, although not agricultural land. There is no reason why the commonhold should not include separate plots of land (garages for a block of flats might be separated from the flats, for example), although flying freeholds[10] are excluded. The flexibility of commonhold is demonstrated by the fact that there need be no more than two units.[11] Thus, a normal house split into two flats would qualify.

New commonhold developments will almost always be registered as commonhold prior to the disposal of units. Provision is made for this by CLRA, ss 2, 7; it should be noted that the consent of all freeholders, long leaseholders (over 21 years) and chargees is required.[12]

As regards existing flats, things are more complex. They are likely to be held under long leases. Before a commonhold can be created, it is necessary for the tenants to acquire the freehold by enfranchisement. CLRA has rendered this more straightforward for long (over

---

[5] (1987) Cm 179.

[6] The guarantee is a nominal £1: CLRA, s 34(1)(b). Potential problems with the CA and CCS are identified by Wong [2006] Conv 14.

[7] SI 2004 No 1829. The CA constitution is found in Schedules 1 and 2 and the CCS in Schedule 3. Most of the provisions are mandatory, but with provision for details relevant to the specific commonhold (to be inserted in Annexes to the CCS) and for additional provisions.

[8] CLRA, s 6 makes provision for the court to determine what is to happen if it transpires that the requirements were not satisfied. It is intended that the commonhold should continue wherever possible: *Commonhold and Leasehold Reform* (DETR) (2000) Cm 4843, Section 4.

[9] CLRA, s 1.

[10] See p 42 above; CLRA, Sched 2 details when commonhold is not available.

[11] Ibid, s 11(2).

[12] Ibid, s 3.

21 years) residential tenants, though cost will be involved.[13] However, the main stumbling block is that the consent of every unit-holder is required for a commonhold application. In a medium or large development, this is likely to prove impossible, and it was recognised that conversion to commonhold will be distinctly unusual.[14]

When a commonhold commences, existing leases and (as regards the common parts) charges are extinguished.[15] One need not quarrel with this for leases exceeding 21 years and charges, as their holders' consents are required for a valid commonhold application.[16] However, the insistence in the primary legislation of clearing out shorter leases appeared pernicious and arguably difficult to square with the Human Rights Act 1998.[17] Fortunately, CR, reg 3(1)(d) and (2) establish the need for tenants of short leases to consent, unless the tenant is entitled to a replacement lease.[18]

B. Commonhold association and commonhold community statement

These are the core constitutional elements of commonhold and receive detailed attention in CLRA. The CA[19] is based upon the normal company law structure for companies limited by guarantee. It may be worth noting that all unit-holders are entitled to be members and that nobody else can become a member: membership is lost on sale of the unit.[20] All members must be given the opportunity to vote.[21]

The CCS will vary considerably from one case to another; it contains the obligations (positive and negative) of the CA and individual unit-holders. In addition to some requirements found in CLRA, CR make provision as to its content and amendment.[22] Some of the contents will be mentioned in the following sections. The one area to stress now is that the CCS must provide for the percentage of the CA's income-raising which is to be allocated to each unit: this is obviously one of the most crucial elements of the commonhold. Most major expenditure will be undertaken by the CA and there must be clear provision for raising that money from the unit-holders in agreed proportions: there is no other source of income!

C. Common parts

The common parts (essentially, all the commonhold except for the units) are vested in the CA, which will inevitably have responsibility for them. This is confirmed by s 26, which requires the CCS to oblige the CA to insure, repair and maintain the common parts. Provision must be made as to use of the common parts and this may involve limited use

---

[13] See p 425 above in the context of the similar rules applied to rights to manage.

[14] *Commonhold and Leasehold Reform* (DETR) (2000) Cm 4843, para 2.2.3. The position is criticised by Clarke [2002] Conv 349 at pp 359–362.

[15] CLRA, ss 7(3), (4), 9(3)(f), (4) (leases), 28(3) (charges). It will be seen below that charges over common parts are prohibited. See Smith [2004] Conv 194 at pp 199–200.

[16] Ibid, s 3 (where the holder is registered).

[17] Compensation is payable (normally by the landlord): ibid, s 10. The provisions are described by Clarke [2002] Conv 349 at p 356 as 'startlingly draconian'.

[18] Such leases are authorised by CR, reg 11(2); the normal seven-year limit on leases does not apply.

[19] CLRA, ss 34–36, 43–56 (termination) and Sched 3.

[20] Ibid, Sched 3, paras 7–8, 10–13 (different rules apply before the first unit is registered).

[21] Ibid, s 36.

[22] Ibid, ss 32–33; CR, reg 15, Sched 3, CCS para 4.11.

of certain areas[23]: examples might be car parking for unit-holders without a garage or play areas restricted to young children.

Perhaps surprisingly, the CA has power to dispose of, or create other interests (but not charges) in, the common parts. This would be exceptional, but it might be desirable to sell a small and unused piece of land to a neighbour, or to exchange land with a neighbour to the benefit of all.

D. Units

Each unit is held in fee simple. A major question is how far this varies from a normal fee simple. The very fact that virtually every commonhold involves interdependency between unit-holders means that obligations are essential if proper management of the land is to be achieved. Obligations might be placed in two categories. The first relates to limits on the use of the land. These are equivalent to restrictive covenants, and it comes as no surprise that they are permitted in the CCS.[24]

More interesting are positive obligations, as these are not recognised as running with freehold land. It is clear from s 16 that, on transfer, the new unit-holder is liable on the CCS obligations, to the exclusion of the transferor.[25] Section 14(2) requires the CCS to make provision regarding insurance, repair and maintenance, though the obligations may be placed on the CA[26] or unit-holder. The purpose is to ensure that these core obligations are located somewhere. For example, it would be financially disastrous if a block of flats was not fully insured, nobody being obliged to insure, and then destroyed by fire. Further obligations may be imposed by the CCS.[27]

Given the real possibility of default by unit-holders, the question of enforcement arises.[28] Two points may be mentioned. First, enforcement may (in appropriate cases) be by other unit-holders. This may be seen as similar to the operation of building schemes for restrictive covenants. It may be most useful as regards negative obligations but is not so limited. The second point is that the CCS cannot provide for transfer or loss of the unit on default.[29] This barring of forfeiture marks a contrast with leasehold tenure. Nevertheless, failure to pay may result in a charge being placed on the unit and, ultimately, its sale to realise the amount owed to the CA.[30]

Section 35 makes it clear that the directors of the CA must exercise their powers to ensure compliance by unit-holders. However, this can be overlooked if 'in the best interests of establishing or maintaining harmonious relationships between all the unit-holders'. It is easy to appreciate that disputes may arise regarding other issues, especially as regards work which some unit-holders regard as unnecessary or which benefits only some units.[31]

---

[23] CLRA, s 25.

[24] Ibid, s 31(5).

[25] This freedom from liability cannot be varied: it provides greater freedom than is found in leasehold or other freehold estates.

[26] Compulsory for the common parts: CR, Sched 3, CCS para 4.4.1.

[27] Section 31.

[28] CLRA, s 37 (also covering enforcement against the CA); CR, reg 17.

[29] CLRA, s 31(8).

[30] Transferees of units are liable for unpaid assessments: CCS (CR, Sched 3), para 4.7.3.

[31] See PF Smith in *Property Law: Current Issues and Debates* (eds Jackson and Wilde), p 129.

Moving away from the CCS, the legislation makes provision for what the unit-holder can do.[32] Most importantly, the unit can be transferred or charged, and any attempt to fetter that freedom is void.[33] Leases of residential units not exceeding seven years are permitted, provided no premium is payable.[34] This limit on leasing is justified by the need to avoid freehold and long leasehold overlapping in the same development.[35] However, there is no limit on leases of non-residential units, unless the CCS provides otherwise.[36] There is provision for the creation of other interests, if of a kind prescribed by regulations, to require approval of the CA.[37]

3. How successful is commonhold?

A. The use of commonhold so far

Conversion of existing developments to commonhold was always likely to be uncommon. For new developments, it was thought that commonhold would become very common, at least as regards residential flats. However, progress over the first few years was minimal.[38] Even worse, the evidence is that commonhold has almost completely stalled over the past decade.[39] This may be because commonhold is radically different from existing land ownership structures: it has not been embraced by lawyers or developers. One major issue is that half of lenders will not lend on commonhold.

B. Overview

The use of freehold tenure in place of long leasehold may be warmly welcomed. Nevertheless, it may be optimistic to expect that management will suddenly be much improved by commonhold. There are equally great dangers if the unit-holders are either apathetic or incompetent (so necessary work is not done)[40] or over-enthusiastic (so that other unit-holders are faced with large and unwelcome bills). Indeed, unit-holders do not receive the extensive protection accorded to tenants as regards management by landlords. A further factor is that commonhold involves a significant bureaucratic structure, which will itself involve expense.

The evidence appears to be that, in the tiny number of commonholds today, the scheme works quite well.[41] Problems in selling units (especially because of the availability of mortgage finance) are, however, very troubling. It is scarcely surprising that commonhold is pretty well moribund. The scheme may be seen as an irrelevance and often as a disaster for those using it.

---

[32] CLRA, ss 21–22 restrict dispositions of parts of units: e.g. transfer of part requires CA approval.

[33] Ibid, ss 15, 20(1). Roberts (2002) 152 NLJ 338 at p 339 observes that this might discourage the adoption of commonhold where greater control of identity of unit-holders is desired, e.g. to ensure owner occupation.

[34] CLRA, s 17 (see s 18 for other units); s 19 authorises regulations imposing (or permitting) obligations on tenants. See CR, reg 11; Sched 3, CCS paras 4.7.11–4.7.20.

[35] *Commonhold and Leasehold Reform* (DETR) (2000) Cm 4843, para 2.4.2.

[36] CLRA, s 18.

[37] CLRA, s 20(3)–(6): 75% approval is required.

[38] Only 14 commonhold titles had been registered by early 2008: Law Com CP 186, para 11.4.

[39] Xu in *Modern Studies in Property Law*, Vol 8 (ed Barr), Chapter 18. The number of active commonholds was 16 in 2014 and the total number of units a paltry 141.

[40] Stressed by PF Smith in *Property Law: Current Issues and Debates* (eds Jackson and Wilde), Chapter 7.

[41] Xu in *Modern Studies in Property Law*, Vol 8 (ed Barr), Chapter 18. It is recommended that unless it can be revived (which appears improbable), there be no new commonholds.

Further reading

Clarke, D [2002] Conv 349: The enactment of commonhold: problems, principles and perspectives.

Roberts, N [2002] Conv 341: Commonhold: a new property term – but no property in a term?

Smith, P F [2004] Conv 194: The purity of commonholds.

van der Merwe, C G and Smith, P (2005) 'Commonhold – a critical appraisal' in *Modern Studies in Property Law*, Vol 3 (ed E Cooke), Chapter 11.

Xu, L (2015) 'Commonhold developments in practice' in *Modern Studies in Property Law*, Vol 8 (ed W Barr), Chapter 18.

Part IV
Other interests in land

22

Licences

Introduction

Licences provide many difficulties for property lawyers. The conventional analysis is that they do not constitute interests in land. Plainly, I can invite a friend to my home for a meal without having to create an interest in land to explain his presence on my land. Technically, we say that the friend has a licence to be on my land and this means that he is not a trespasser. If the law stopped there, there would be relatively little to say about licences and every justification for leaving them out of a book on property. However, licences have developed some of the characteristics of proprietary interests. To be more precise, some types of licences are gaining recognition as rights that may bind purchasers, although others are still regarded as purely personal rights. Some analyses upgrade licences into hybrid rights that, whilst not full interests in land, have some of their characteristics. Licences represent one of the most fluid areas of property law over the past decades.

There are several forms of licences; it is not feasible to consider them as a single category. We shall see that bare licences (simple gratuitous permission), contractual licences, estoppel licences and licences coupled with an interest attract quite different rules, especially as to when purchasers may be affected. In addition, licences may bind a purchaser by way of a constructive trust in some situations. The distinctions between these forms of licences lie in the route to legal protection (contract, estoppel, trust).

Another way in which to consider licences is by the substance of the rights enjoyed under the licence. It is important to realise that licences form a residual category in property law. In other chapters, we investigate rights such as life interests and remainders, concurrent interests, leases and easements. Each of these has its own rules as to what counts as such an interest and how it is created. If these rules are not complied with, then the interest will not exist. Take one example.[1] A agrees with B that B has an exclusive right to hire out boats on A's lake. This is not a lease of the lake as B has only a limited right over the lake. Equally clearly, it is not an easement, as such a commercial right is difficult to classify as an easement. Yet, it is obvious that B is not trespassing when exercising his rights; he is said to have a licence.

Any right to enter land that does not fit into one of the recognised property categories will be a licence. The licensee may be enjoying rights similar to those of a lessee or estate owner. For example, I may tell a relative that they can live in a house I own until they can find a house of their own. This is unlikely to be a lease (partly because there is no maximum period

---

[1] Based upon *Hill* v *Tupper* (1863) 2 H&C 121 (159 ER 51).

stated and partly because there is no contractual relationship), and it seems too personal and restricted to be a full life interest.[2] It is a licence. In other cases, there may be rights more in the nature of easements and profits (as in the boating example). However, huge numbers of licences involve situations that seem far removed from property law, such as the friend I invited for a meal or those who buy tickets for a football match or cinema.

The above examples are ones where the rights do not fit any of the categories of proprietary interests. Licences also exist where the right is of a proprietary nature, but the necessary formalities have not been satisfied. If A tells his daughter that he is giving her a plot of land on which to build a house and signs a document saying the land is hers, then the daughter will be a licensee. A conveyance or transfer of land has to be by deed: the written document is ineffective. It follows that the rights enjoyed under licences may overlap with property rights, although the licence (unlike a property right) may often be terminated by the licensor and is much less likely to bind purchasers. Quite apart from such overlap in cases where formalities are lacking, the parties to a transaction may stipulate for a licence if they do not wish the proprietary consequences of interests such as easements.[3]

These huge differences in the types of rights enjoyed under a licence provide one reason why it is difficult to consider licences as a single category. This, coupled with difficulties in enforcement in many forms of licences,[4] helps explain why it is difficult to accord proprietary status to licences. So far, licences cases have not sought to differentiate according to the types of rights involved. Yet it is certainly arguable that one way forward is to give greater protection to a certain range of licences, in particular those involving exclusive possession. The justification for protecting a person's continued residence in the licensor's house may be quite different from that in other licences.[5]

In the unlikely scenario that all licences were accepted as proprietary interests, it is arguable that this would do away with the need for specific property interests such as leases and easements. They could all fit within the new interest called licences. Too much should not be made of this, as specific interests have developed their own rules (a good example being the way easements can be implied) and it is most unlikely that these rules would be affected by the development of licences as proprietary interests. The fact remains, however, that licences form an immensely wide category. The law has long sought to control the range of proprietary interests, insisting that it is not open to the owner of land to create new types of interests. Should licences ever be accepted as proprietary interests, that control would be almost totally abdicated.

Before leaving these issues, it may be asked whether licences cover the entire range of property rights, given their wide scope. The clear answer is that they do not. Covenants form a good example of rights that cannot be seen as licences.[6] The essence of a covenant is a right to force another to do something or (for restrictive covenants) not to do something, rather than a right to do something oneself.

[2] Sparkes (1993) 109 LQR 93 argues that many of the cases analysed as licences might be regarded as freehold interests or leases.
[3] *IDC Group Ltd* v *Clark* (1992) 65 P&CR 179. This is not possible for leases: *Street* v *Mountford* [1985] AC 809.
[4] Bright in *Land Law: Themes and Perspectives* (eds Bright and Dewar), p 541.
[5] As well as posing fewer problems for purchasers in discovering licences: Maudsley (1956) 20 Conv 281.
[6] Mortgages may provide another example. The hallmark of a security interest such as a mortgage is the right to realise the security, especially by sale, if the debt is not repaid.

1. Forms of licences

Virtually any permission to do something can be a licence. In the huge majority of cases, the right is to do something on the licensor's land. It is also quite possible for there to be a licence to do something (otherwise wrongful) on one's own land. A simple example would be the erection of a building that interferes with a neighbour's easement of light. The neighbour may give prior permission for the building and cannot thereafter object to it.[7] This form of licence will not be discussed.

A. Bare licences

A bare licence is a simple permission to enter land. It has always been clear that it can be terminated by telling the licensee to leave. Granting a licence by deed makes no difference.[8] There is no need to give much thought to the position of purchasers. The licensor can readily terminate the licence, and so can the purchaser. Indeed, it is likely that sale by the licensor will be treated as an implicit termination of the licence.[9]

The one point to observe is that the licensee must be allowed a reasonable time to leave. This might vary from a matter of seconds (at most, minutes) for a police officer who is told to leave a house,[10] to weeks (very occasionally a year or more) where a licensee's home is involved.[11] It is only after that time that the licensee becomes a trespasser. However, the better view is that there is no added requirement of reasonable notice: providing for a packing-up period (sometimes generously calculated) suffices.[12]

Before leaving bare licences, it should be noted that they may subsequently become protected by an estoppel or constructive trust. This will not be the effect of the bare licence itself, but rather of other circumstances.

B. Licences coupled with an interest

Proprietary interests frequently require access on to land in order to be effective. The best example is found in profits: rights to take things from another's land (fish, for example). It is plain that access on to that land is essential for the profit to be exercised: a licence to enter is implied. The law has always regarded this licence as having the same enforceability as the profit or other right to which it is attached. Even the earlier cases, whilst stressing that licences created merely personal rights, allowed an exception for licences coupled with an interest.[13] This is obvious common sense where the licence is coupled with a

---

[7] See Cullity (1965) 29 Conv 19. A number of the earlier cases can be explained on this basis: Wade (1948) 64 LQR 57 at p 59. *Lester* v *Woodgate* [2010] 2 P&CR 359 provides a recent example.

[8] *Wood* v *Leadbitter* (1845) 13 M&W 838 (153 ER 351). There might be an action for damages for breach of covenant.

[9] Compare the similar rule for tenancies at will: *Doe d Davies* v *Thomas* (1851) 6 Exch 854 (155 ER 792). Not all dispositions would have this effect: a mortgage, for example, would not terminate the licence. Should a licensor mortgage her house to secure a loan, this would not terminate the licence of her boyfriend.

[10] *Robson* v *Hallett* [1967] 2 QB 939.

[11] *Gibson* v *Douglas* [2016] EWCA Civ 1266 at [21].

[12] Hill [2001] CLJ 89, noting that deserving licensees may often be able to rely on estoppel.

[13] *Thomas* v *Sorrell* (1673) Vaugh 330 at p 351 (124 ER 1098 at p 1109); *Wood* v *Leadbitter* (1845) 13 M&W 838 (153 ER 351).

proprietary interest such as a profit. Unfortunately, the courts have sometimes talked about licences coupled with interests despite there being no conventional proprietary interest. This may in part be explicable because the boundaries of proprietary interests were not so clear at the time of these nineteenth-century dicta.[14]

It seems clear that the interest may be in a chattel on the land rather than the land itself. This idea is very old, going back to *Webb* v *Paternoster* in 1619.[15] It has been applied in many cases stretching to the twentieth century.[16] In most of the cases, the chattel has originally been part of the land: crops or timber. Although this may help explain why the courts were so willing to recognise a licence coupled with an interest in these cases, the principle does not seem to be limited to such situations. The courts appear to welcome the idea that there is a right to go on to another's land to recover property that has been placed or left there with the landowner's permission.

Hurst v *Picture Theatres Ltd*[17] contains the most controversial invocation of the principle of the licence coupled with an interest. The claimant was watching a film in the defendant's cinema, having bought a ticket. The defendant evicted him in breach of contract, and the claimant brought an action for assault. For this action to succeed, he had to show a right to be on the premises. The Court of Appeal held that he had such a right by virtue of a licence coupled with an interest. It was immaterial that there was no deed, as equity will enforce agreements. However, as has been pointed out on many occasions, there was simply no proprietary interest for the licence to be coupled with in *Hurst*. There was a contractual right to watch the film, but this can scarcely be said to be an interest in property. The dissent by Phillimore LJ is convincing and has been regarded as unanswerable. Whilst *Hurst* has never been overruled, it has received criticism[18] and not been followed in Australia[19] and New Zealand.[20] More recent English cases have considered similar facts to *Hurst* from a contractual standpoint.

C. Contractual licences

The effect of licences created by a contract has given rise to much debate and difficulty. The availability of equitable remedies for breach of contract has fuelled the argument that contractual licences may have a greater effect than the mere revocable personal permission recognised by the common law. A significant analogy lies in the history of restrictive covenants: it was the willingness of the courts to give equitable remedies that lay at the heart of their recognition as proprietary interests in *Tulk* v *Moxhay*.[21]

---

[14] *Cowell* v *Rosehill Racecourse Co Ltd* (1937) 56 CLR 605 at pp 630, 636.
[15] Popham 151 (79 ER 1250); 2 Rolle 143 (81 ER 713, 719), 152; Palm 71 (81 ER 983). The case is not easy to interpret: see the analyses in *Wood* v *Leadbitter* (1845) 13 M&W 838 (153 ER 351) and *Re Solomon* [1967] Ch 573.
[16] *James Jones & Sons Ltd* v *Earl of Tankerville* [1909] 2 Ch 440.
[17] [1915] 1 KB 1. See also the strange case of *Vaughan* v *Hampson* (1875) 33 LT 15.
[18] *Winter Garden Theatre (London) Ltd* v *Millenium Productions Ltd* [1946] 1 All ER 678 (Lord Greene MR); [1948] AC 173 (Lord Uthwatt); *Hounslow LBC* v *Twickenham Garden Developments Ltd* [1971] Ch 233; Evershed (1954) 70 LQR 326. *London Development Agency* v *Nidai* [2009] EWHC 1730 (Ch); [2009] 2 P&CR D62 does not cite *Hurst*, but declines to apply a 'licence coupled' analysis.
[19] *Cowell* v *Rosehill Racecourse Co Ltd* (1937) 56 CLR 605.
[20] *Mayfield Holdings Ltd* v *Moana Reef Ltd* [1973] 1 NZLR 309.
[21] (1848) 2 Ph 774 (41 ER 1143).

Most of the cases do not involve the issue of proprietary status: they are disputes between licensor and licensee. If licensors can revoke licences, then this obviously precludes any development of proprietary status. The orthodox nineteenth-century approach, exemplified by *Wood* v *Leadbitter*,[22] was that a licensor could terminate a licence even if doing so was a breach of contract. The licence was regarded as separate from the contract. Not being an interest in land, it did not justify the licensee's remaining in possession once it was terminated. The licensee might have a remedy for breach of contract, but that was all. It may be observed that it was all or nothing for the licensee. Either there was an interest in land binding on purchasers, or else a mere personal permission that could be revoked by the licensor at any time. It was not until the twentieth century that a contract-based equitable right to remain was developed. Consideration of this right needs to be split into two parts: enforcement against the licensor and enforcement against purchasers.

First, however, a couple of comments should be made as to when there will be a contractual licence. In the leases context, it was seen that great ingenuity has been employed in creating licences rather than leases, almost invariably to avoid legislation benefiting tenants. It might be thought that this would lead to these licence cases causing problems as contractual licences. In reality, this has not happened. The obvious explanation is that the huge majority of these cases involve short-term agreements. They are rarely worth enforcing by legal action and will nearly always expire before a case can be brought to court. Licence cases have generally involved either licences not involving exclusive possession or exclusive possession licences in the family setting. Leases are frequently unsuitable in the family setting; apart from any other considerations, there will rarely be the required formalities.

A second comment concerns family licences. There have been several cases in which the courts have analysed a family arrangement as a contractual licence. It is far from clear that this analysis is appropriate. It is, of course, difficult to reconcile with the general reluctance to find contracts in the family setting.[23] Where one partner tells the other that he or she will be entitled to live in a house if they move into it and look after children there,[24] it seems especially difficult to justify the parties' being bound by contractual obligations. It is interesting that in a case in which a contract was more justifiably found, the Court of Appeal held that a seemingly indefinite licence was terminable on a year's notice.[25] In other cases, parents and children have made arrangements whereby the parents have bought houses for their children to live in, the children making some sort of contribution. The courts have been ready to find a contract under which there is an unlimited right of occupation.

One example is *Hardwick* v *Johnson*,[26] in which a mother allowed her son and daughter-in-law to occupy a house in return for paying £7 per week towards the purchase price. This

[22] (1845) 13 M&W 838 (153 ER 351).
[23] *Balfour* v *Balfour* [1919] 2 KB 571.
[24] The facts of *Tanner* v *Tanner* [1975] 1 WLR 1346 (contract), distinguished in *Horrocks* v *Forray* [1976] 1 WLR 230 and convincingly criticised in *McGill* v *LS* [1979] IR 283.
[25] *Chandler* v *Kerley* [1978] 1 WLR 693. The licensee had been an original co-owner of the house who had sold to the licensor for two-thirds of the asking price on the basis of a licence to remain there. It is easy to see that a contract was properly found here, although one year's occupation was poor recompense for the reduction in the price.
[26] [1978] 1 WLR 683; see also *Errington* v *Errington* [1952] 1 KB 290.

sum amounted to a return of little more than 3% on the purchase price. The Court of Appeal held that the mother could not regain possession when her son left the pregnant daughter-in-law. By any test, the licensees had a remarkably good bargain and there seems little legal justification (in the absence of an explicit contract) for forcing it to continue indefinitely. There is a particular irony in the case, as the licensor had deliberately created a licence in order to avoid problems that had arisen on the break-up of her son's earlier marriage. Whilst it would be wrong to reject any possibility of a contract in the family setting, most of these cases would seem better analysed as estoppel licences, benefiting from the greater flexibility in that area.

(i) *Licensor and licensee*

If a licence is to have any chance of being a proprietary interest binding purchasers, it must first be irrevocable by the licensor. Therefore, our first question must concern the licensor's right to revoke. Quite apart from its importance for the proprietary status of licences, the position as between licensor and licensee is both significant in its own right and disputed.

The orthodox nineteenth-century approach in *Wood* v *Leadbitter*[27] was that a licensor could always terminate a contractual licence, even if contractual liability resulted. It has been seen that *Hurst* used a licence coupled with an interest analysis to render a contractual licence irrevocable. However, Buckley LJ at the end of his judgment makes a brief observation that the case could also be analysed as a licence with an agreement not to revoke it. Equity will intervene in one of two ways. First, there may be specific performance of the contract, and second, equity will prevent the licensor from revoking the licence in breach of contract. Either way, equity will ensure that the licensee is not evicted. The next step in the reasoning is less straightforward. Because an equitable remedy is available, equity will treat the licensee as being entitled to remain in possession. Should the licensor actually evict the licensee, equity considers that the licensee had a right to remain. The licensor is, accordingly, acting wrongfully in evicting the licensee and will be liable for assault. This provides the basis upon which *Hurst* is generally explained today, distinguishing *Wood* v *Leadbitter* as a pre-Judicature Acts decision of a common law court.

A possible problem with this analysis is that equity is acting retrospectively. Unless Mr Hurst had a judge as his companion, he had no opportunity of seeking a remedy before his eviction.[28] Even so, equity will treat him in the same way as if he had obtained an injunction preventing eviction. This has always been the approach of equity when there has been an agreement for an interest in land,[29] and there is little reason why a similar analysis should not be applied where there is a licence: in each case, equity treats as done what ought to be done.[30]

The leading case today is *Winter Garden Theatre (London) Ltd* v *Millenium Productions Ltd*.[31] The licensor purported to revoke a licence to produce plays in the licensor's theatre.

---

[27] (1845) 13 M&W 838 (153 ER 351).
[28] See Phillimore LJ in *Hurst* v *Picture Theatres Ltd* [1915] 1 KB 1; Bandali (1973) 37 Conv 402 at pp 404–405.
[29] The best-known case is *Walsh* v *Lonsdale* (1882) 21 Ch D 9; see also *Gilbey* v *Cossey* (1912) 106 LT 607.
[30] Supported by *Cowell* v *Rosehill Racecourse Co Ltd* (1937) 56 CLR 605, although in fact the court refused to give an equitable remedy.
[31] [1946] 1 All ER 678 (Court of Appeal); [1948] AC 173 (House of Lords).

The fullest analysis is provided by Lord Greene MR in the Court of Appeal. He stressed that the licence should not be regarded as an entity separate from the contract, but rather as a contractual right and subject to normal contractual rules.[32] On the facts, he found that the licence was intended to be irrevocable and, as a necessary consequence, there was an undertaking not to revoke.[33] The court would give effect to this undertaking, and it did not matter that the licence had been purportedly revoked by the time the case came to court.[34] The House of Lords concluded that the particular licence was intended to be revocable. However, this disagreement as to the construction of the contract does not remove the authority of Lord Greene's analysis of licences. Indeed, Viscount Simon went out of his way to approve of the result of *Hurst* and Lord Uthwatt expressed his agreement with Lord Greene's analysis, whilst Lord Porter more cautiously thought that licences once acted upon were irrevocable.

The next case to contain a full analysis of the issues is *Hounslow LBC* v *Twickenham Garden Developments Ltd.*[35] The claimant landowner entered into a building contract with the defendants, who commenced building work. The claimant, dissatisfied with the defendants' progress, sought to terminate the building contract and applied for an order that the defendants leave the premises. Megarry J held that the claim failed. The claimant would succeed if the defendants had broken the contract, but this was hotly disputed and as yet unresolved. Megarry J thought that specific performance of the contract might well be available to the defendant, but in any event, equity would not help the landowner to break a contract. This shows a rather different way in which equity recognises a licence, by declining to assist the licensor.

In *Verrall* v *Great Yarmouth BC*,[36] the National Front had contracted to hold their annual conference in the defendant's Wellington Pier pavilion. When the Labour Party took control of the council, the licence was purportedly revoked. Unlike the earlier cases, the licensee had not entered into possession and the only possible equitable remedy was specific performance. The Court of Appeal had little hesitation in holding that specific performance should be ordered, noting that damages would be inadequate as the National Front had been unable to find an alternative venue for its conference. Although much of the case's interest lies in its political setting, it is a good example of equity's enforcing a contractual licence.

Are all contractual licences irrevocable?

Although many other cases have held or assumed that licensees cannot be evicted in breach of contract,[37] the twentieth-century cases were not all in one direction. A contrasting

---

[32] He added that, even if the licence was to be treated as a separate entity, equity would treat it as irrevocable and prevent revocation.

[33] The idea of a promise not to revoke is rather odd. Its origin lies in the greater ease with which an injunction to prevent breach of a negative promise will be given as contrasted with specific performance: *Lumley* v *Wagner* (1852) 1 De GM&G 604 (42 ER 687). However, that type of case involves a negative promise that is different from the positive contractual obligation. In the licences context, the negative and positive promises are identical: the promise not to revoke seems superfluous.

[34] Contrast the very different view expressed by Lord Greene MR four years earlier in *Booker* v *Palmer* [1942] 2 All ER 674.

[35] [1971] Ch 233.

[36] [1981] QB 202.

[37] *Foster* v *Robinson* [1951] 1 KB 149; *Ivory* v *Palmer* [1975] ICR 340; *Hardwick* v *Johnson* [1978] 1 WLR 683; *Chandler* v *Kerley* [1978] 1 WLR 693; see also the cases on licensees and purchasers.

decision is to be found in *Thompson* v *Park*,[38] involving an agreement by two headmasters to share the school of one of them (the licensor). Disagreements arose and the licensor purported to terminate the licence during a holiday. The licensee forced his way back into the school, whereupon the licensor sought a court order to evict him. The Court of Appeal was emphatic that the licensee had no right to return to the school once the licence had been revoked, whether lawfully or not.

Three possible justifications for this decision may be noted. First, Goddard LJ said that licensors are able to revoke licences in breach of contract, subject only to having to pay contract damages. This dictum seems inconsistent with *Winter Garden*, decided a few years later, and is regarded as bad law.[39] Second, and more defensible, is the observation that 'the court cannot specifically enforce an agreement for two people to live peaceably under the same roof'. It is important to remember that equitable remedies are not available automatically. Third, Megarry J observed in *Twickenham Garden* that the court was undoubtedly influenced by the high-handed conduct of the defendant, described as a riot. In particular, the defendant could not improve his position by forcible entry and so should be treated as if not in possession.

Interestingly, Australian and New Zealand courts have taken a different approach from that adopted in England. The leading case is *Cowell* v *Rosehill Racecourse Co Ltd*[40] in the High Court of Australia. It is regrettable that it was not cited in *Winter Garden*, decided some 10 years later. The Australian approach is to accept the general thrust of the English contractual analysis. The principal contrast is that the Australian courts are far less willing to give equitable remedies. In particular, they will not assist the licensee in entertainment contracts (as in *Cowell*: horse-racing) or building contracts.[41] In New Zealand, a similar approach was taken by Mahon J in *Mayfield Holdings Ltd* v *Moana Reef Ltd*,[42] a building contract case.

There is much to be said for this more restrictive approach. It has to be remembered that specific performance (like other equitable remedies) is a discretionary remedy and it is proper to be cautious in giving such remedies outside contracts for conventional proprietary interests. If a landowner loses confidence in his builder, is it right to force the landowner to continue to employ him? Building contracts are not, in general, specifically enforceable. It does seem odd to say that the builder can insist on performing the remainder of the contract once possession of the land has been taken. To the argument that the builder will have made a large investment by entering into sub-contracts and buying materials,[43] the answer is that these matters can be dealt with by contract damages.

So far as entertainment contracts are concerned, is it really the case that equity would enforce a right to enter a cinema for two hours? The English analysis is that equity will enforce agreements for short-term interests.[44] This is indeed correct, but it fails to deal with the peculiar issues involved in these contracts: it is the nature of the right rather than its

---

[38] [1944] KB 408.
[39] See *Verrall* v *Great Yarmouth BC* [1981] QB 202 (Lord Denning MR).
[40] (1937) 56 CLR 605.
[41] *Graham H Roberts Pty Ltd* v *Maurbeth Investments Pty Ltd* [1974] 1 NSWLR 93.
[42] [1973] 1 NZLR 309.
[43] Stressed by Megarry J in *Twickenham Garden*.
[44] See Lord Denning MR in *Verrall*; Evershed (1954) 70 LQR 326.

length that counsels caution in equitable intervention. Australian courts have been alive to the problems of management that the licensor faces: it will sometimes be necessary to order licensees to leave, an example being where evacuation is dictated by safety considerations. Whilst it is entirely reasonable for the licensor to be liable in contract damages if the eviction is not justified, it is arguably unreasonable to open up the possibility of damages for trespass, let alone the dangers of violence if entrants are entitled to use force to object to an unlawful eviction. Underpinning the Australian analysis is a greater inclination to give the licensor control over his own land. Whilst this factor should not be pressed too far, it may reflect the expectations of society better than some of the English cases.

A final point in relation to *Hurst* concerns an argument that assault will in any event be committed if the evicted licensee has a contractual right to remain. Lord Greene thought in *Winter Garden* that an assault might be committed even if equity would not enforce the contract, and this is supported by Professor Wade.[45] The reasoning is that the contract will continue to exist notwithstanding any purported termination by the licensor.[46] However, Megarry J was reluctant to accept this idea in *Twickenham Garden*, and it is submitted that he was right. It is not appropriate to allow the licensee to insist on completing the contract when some co-operation by the licensor is required and equity will not assist the licensee.

(ii) *Licensee and purchaser*

It has been seen that most contractual licensees can assert a right to remain on the land as regards the licensor. However, to say that a purchaser is bound is another matter. As a matter of contract law, only the parties to it are bound: there is no privity of contract with a purchaser from the licensor. If the purchaser is to be bound, it must be through some form of equitable interest. Some cases have suggested that the purchaser is bound, although the modern authorities are against according proprietary status to the contractual licence.[47]

Early decisions
Leaving the pre-Judicature Act cases on one side, two early leading cases deny that contractual licences bind purchasers. In *King* v *David Allen & Sons, Billposting, Ltd*,[48] the House of Lords held that a licence to place an advertisement on the walls of a building (yet to be constructed) did not bind a lessee from the licensor. It created no estate or interest in the land. *Clore* v *Theatrical Properties Ltd*[49] involved a 'lease' of front of the house rights (to sell refreshments and programmes) at the Prince of Wales Theatre. The Court of Appeal held that this constituted a licence rather than a lease, and as a personal contract it was not binding on the licensor's assignee.

---

[45] (1948) 64 LQR 57. It is inconsistent with *Cowell* and difficult to reconcile with *Wood* v *Leadbitter*.

[46] Compare the principle in *White & Carter (Councils) Ltd* v *McGregor* [1962] AC 413 that the 'innocent' party can continue to perform a contract after purported rescission by the other party.

[47] The purchaser might still be bound if the facts give rise to an estoppel or constructive trust, but our present concern is with the question of whether the contractual licence itself binds purchasers.

[48] [1916] 2 AC 54. The licensee was suing the licensor, who would have escaped liability if the lessee had been bound.

[49] [1936] 3 All ER 483.

These two cases stand as high authority that contractual licences do not bind purchasers. Two aspects of them, nevertheless, stand out as weaknesses. First, neither of them involves full or exclusive possession of the land. It has been argued that cases of exclusive possession are more deserving of proprietary status, being both close to the conventional category of leases and being readily discoverable by purchasers.[50] Secondly, both cases pre-date *Winter Garden*. *Clore*, in particular, contains dicta suggesting that the licensor could have revoked the licence. In that environment, it is scarcely surprising that any suggestion of purchasers being bound was quickly rejected.

Mid-twentieth-century developments

The Court of Appeal surprised lawyers by holding in *Errington* v *Errington*[51] that a successor in title was bound. The licensor bought a house for his son and daughter-in-law and told them that they would own it, provided that they paid the mortgage instalments (the mortgage was for two-thirds of the purchase price). The licensor died, and his widow was now the legal owner. When the son deserted the daughter-in-law, the widow sought to obtain possession. Her claim failed. It is commonly thought that the court could have held that there was an estate contract under which there was a future entitlement to the legal estate. The licence could be linked with this proprietary interest and thus made irrevocable and binding on successors in title. Alternatively, the payments by the son and daughter-in-law could be seen as giving rise to an estoppel in their favour, although it may be observed that the modern development of estoppel came after 1951.

However *Errington* might have been decided, the court in fact held that the contractual licence bound the widow. Denning LJ[52] was most explicit: 'This infusion of equity [from cases such as *Winter Garden*] means that contractual licences now have a force and vitality of their own and cannot be revoked in breach of contract. Neither the licensor nor anyone who claims through him can disregard the contract except a purchaser for value without notice.' It will be noted that this simply asserts that the purchaser is bound: no explanation or authority is given. Probably the fullest explanation was provided by Denning LJ six months later in the deserted wife's equity[53] case of *Bendall* v *McWhirter*.[54] His analysis is that the equitable remedy available against the licensor binds the purchaser, just as it does in the restrictive covenant.

That remedy analysis was comprehensively rejected by the House of Lords in *National Provincial Bank Ltd* v *Ainsworth*[55] in the course of denying any deserted wife's equity. It was stressed by Lord Upjohn and Lord Wilberforce that equitable remedies do not bind purchasers unless there is a proprietary interest; the development of restrictive

---

[50] Maudsley (1956) 20 Conv 281.

[51] [1952] 1 KB 290.

[52] Ibid, at p 299.

[53] This equity was a claim that a deserted wife had a proprietary right to remain in the matrimonial home, binding purchasers from the husband. It was, in part, modelled on the rights of a contractual licensee.

[54] [1952] 2 QB 466. Denning LJ also observes that earlier cases use the language of a licence acted upon and that this form of analysis has dropped out of view. See *Armstrong* v *Sheppard & Short Ltd* [1959] 2 QB 384; Cullity (1965) 29 Conv 19; Crane (1952) 16 Conv NS 323 at p 328; Hill [2001] CLJ 89 at pp 93–95. These earlier cases are explicable on estoppel grounds.

[55] [1965] AC 1175.

covenants shows that several tests have to be satisfied before a purchaser will be bound. The availability of remedies against the original covenantor is quite insufficient by itself. Although it was not said that contractual licences could not be (or become) proprietary interests,[56] it was clear that the ground had been cut from under the feet of the argument for contractual licences binding purchasers.

Since *Ainsworth*, the major developments of licences have centred upon estoppel, although Lord Denning MR relied upon a contractual licence as a proprietary interest in *Binions* v *Evans*[57] and, surprisingly, Goff LJ applied *Binions* in *DHN Food Distributors Ltd* v *Tower Hamlets LBC*.[58] Otherwise, support for contractual licences as proprietary interests was limited to the odd throw-away comment[59] and assumption.[60]

Ashburn Anstalt v Arnold

The Court of Appeal reviewed the authorities in *Ashburn Anstalt* v *Arnold*.[61] The licensee had sold his shop to a developer subject to a licence to retain the shop rent-free until redevelopment took place. Fox LJ, delivering the judgment of the court, considered that contractual licences could not affect successors in title. *Errington* was regarded as the only authority supporting the contrary view, but Fox LJ observed[62] that 'The far-reaching statement of principle in *Errington* was not supported by authority, not necessary for the decision of the case[63] and per incuriam in the sense that it was made without reference to authorities which, if they would not have compelled, would surely have persuaded the court to adopt a different ratio.' Whilst this might well be regarded as a rather harsh treatment of the argument for contractual licences as proprietary interests, it is difficult to deny that the authority in their favour was pretty meagre and that the writing had been on the wall since *Ainsworth*. Although most judges had chosen not to comment on Lord Denning's contractual licence analyses, Russell LJ in the Court of Appeal in *Ainsworth*[64] had laid bare the inadequacies of Lord Denning's arguments. In particular, he had ridiculed attempts to distinguish *King* and *Clore*.

Subject to a point made later regarding registered land, *Ashburn Anstalt* seems to close the argument, at least below the Supreme Court. It might be objected that Fox LJ's dicta were obiter (the licence was in fact held to be a lease),[65] but this would be to overlook the

---

[56] Any analogy between contractual licences and the wife's right of occupation was denied: the wife was not to be regarded as a licensee.

[57] [1972] Ch 359.

[58] [1976] 1 WLR 852 (Shaw LJ agreed). There is particular surprise because Goff LJ had been very sceptical of *Errington* in *Re Solomon* [1967] Ch 573 (first instance).

[59] *Re Webb's Lease* [1951] Ch 808 at pp 821, 830; *Tanner* v *Tanner* [1975] 1 WLR 1346 (Lord Denning MR).

[60] *Midland Bank Ltd* v *Farmpride Hatcheries Ltd* [1981] 2 EGLR 147. A successor in title was held not to have notice of the licence, but there was no discussion as to how a contractual licence could bind the successor even with notice. Cf *Jones* v *Jones* [2001] NI 244 (none of the relevant cases were cited).

[61] [1989] Ch 1; Hill (1988) 51 MLR 226.

[62] [1989] Ch 1 at p 22.

[63] As well as estate contract and estoppel possibilities, Fox LJ thought that there might have been a constructive trust based on *Gissing* v *Gissing* [1971] AC 886.

[64] Sub nom *National Provincial Bank Ltd* v *Hastings Car Mart Ltd* [1964] Ch 665. Russell LJ dissented, but the majority was reversed by the House of Lords.

[65] It was overruled on the lease aspect by the House of Lords in *Prudential Assurance Co Ltd* v *London Residuary Body* [1992] 2 AC 386.

very full consideration given to the licence question.[66] At least for the time being, contractual licences must be regarded as having no impact on successors in title.

This might also be argued to gain some support from the proviso to s 4(1) of the Law of Property Act 1925: 'an equitable interest in land shall only be capable of being validly created in any case in which an equivalent equitable interest in property real or personal could have been validly created' before the 1925 Act. This has been said to limit the power of the courts to develop new proprietary interests,[67] but it seems preferable to regard it as dealing with the effect of the 1925 legislation. In other words, it ensured that conventional rights alone were recognised in the immediate aftermath of the legislation, rather than inhibiting all development for the indefinite future.

Land Registration Act 2002, s 116

Section 116 provides a possible route for attacking *Ashburn Anstalt*. It enacts, 'for the avoidance of doubt', that a 'mere equity' is capable of binding purchasers. Because of the equitable remedy available to many contractual licensees, this supports an argument that a contractual licence is a mere equity binding purchasers: it would restore the equitable remedy analysis which was rejected by *Ainsworth*. However, it was seen in Chapter 4[68] that it is highly questionable whether such a wide interpretation will be given to s 116: it would scarcely be for the avoidance of doubt!

D. Constructive trusts

Any form of licence may be protected by a constructive trust, but it has been most influential in the context of contractual licences. The constructive trust in this area is based on *Binions* v *Evans*.[69] A purchaser had agreed to buy land subject to the licensee's rights and, accordingly, paid a reduced purchase price. Lord Denning MR imposed a constructive trust on the purchaser, and this was approved by the Court of Appeal in *Ashburn Anstalt*. The attraction of the constructive trust is that it gets around the authorities of *King* and *Clore*. It is not necessary to ask whether an existing interest binds a purchaser; instead, a fresh trust arises at the time of the sale by virtue of the purchaser's promise.[70]

When will such a constructive trust be imposed? This issue was discussed in the formality context[71]: the essential requirement is that the purchaser must promise to give effect to the licence. One point worthy of note is that there was at one time a suggestion that a constructive trust might be imposed on the licensor. This idea was promoted by Lord Denning

---

[66] *Ashburn Anstalt* has been accepted in *IDC Group Ltd* v *Clark* [1992] 1 EGLR 187 (Sir Nicolas Browne-Wilkinson V-C at first instance upheld 65 P&CR 179); *Canadian Imperial Bank of Commerce* v *Bello* (1991) 64 P&CR 48; *Camden LBC* v *Shortlife Community Housing Ltd* (1992) 25 HLR 330; *Nationwide BS* v *Ahmed & Balakrishnan* (1995) 70 P&CR 381; *Lloyd* v *Dugdale* [2002] 2 P&CR 167.

[67] *Hanchett-Stamford* v *Att-Gen* [2009] Ch 173 at [31]; Briggs [1983] Conv 285 at pp 290–291. Numerous commentators have noticed s 4, though they are generally unwilling to treat it as conclusive evidence against the contractual licence being a proprietary interest.

[68] See p 37 above.

[69] [1972] Ch 359. *Pritchard Englefield* v *Steinberg* [2004] EWHC 1908 (Ch) is somewhat similar, though the occupier appears to receive a life interest under the trust.

[70] If the purchaser declares a trust in writing, then there would be an express trust.

[71] See pp 143–146 above.

MR in *DHN Food Distributors Ltd* v *Tower Hamlets LBC*[72] and Browne-Wilkinson J in *Re Sharpe*.[73] Neither case explained how the constructive trust could be justified, or appreciated that it is different from imposing the trust on the purchaser in *Binions*. If adopted, these cases might have had the effect of giving all contractual licences the status of interests in land, by the back door method of constructive trust. This unjustified use of the constructive trust was condemned by the Court of Appeal in *Ashburn Anstalt*[74] and now seems unarguable.

The constructive trust in *Binions* poses particular problems because the beneficial right under the trust is not an interest in land. One generally expects beneficial rights under trusts to be of a proprietary nature. Unfortunately, the law of trusts is not so straightforward. It is possible to set up purpose trusts and discretionary trusts, at least so long as there are identifiable human beneficiaries.[75] Take a trust under which the trustees have power to provide for the education of B, a beneficiary. It is difficult to define B's interest in terms of conventional interests such as a fee simple or life interest. Closer to our present context, it may be possible to create a trust to enable a person to reside in a house, without creating a life interest.[76]

Is it, then, possible to create any form of licence behind a trust? Once there is a trust, it might be thought to be an inevitable consequence that a purchaser will be bound: it is natural to think of trusts binding purchasers, rather than of particular interests under trusts doing so. Yet if we were to go this far, the law's control over what can be a proprietary interest would be lost. For example, the law has long refused to recognise easements unless there is a dominant tenement. Could this be evaded by the simple expedient of the owner's declaring a trust of the land in order to give effect to a right of way in favour of an individual? Indeed, can *Ashburn Anstalt* be circumvented by the simple expedient of the licensor declaring himself a trustee?

At this point, we may need to distinguish two questions. The first question is whether there can be a trust where there is a non-proprietary beneficial interest. Both the purpose trust cases and *Binions* suggest a positive answer. The second question is more difficult. Does that constructive trust bind subsequent purchasers? We cannot simply say that constructive trusts based on unconscionable conduct do not bind purchasers: that would be inconsistent with countless cases involving trusts of the family home. Nor is it thought that purpose trusts are unenforceable against purchasers. However, problems become severe when we consider licences.

Consider this example. A creates a contractual licence in favour of B. Purchasers from A (the licensor) will not be bound: *Ashburn Anstalt*. However, should a purchaser, C, agree to give effect to B's licence, then *Binions* is authority that there may be a constructive trust.

---

[72] [1976] 1 WLR 852.

[73] [1980] 1 WLR 219.

[74] See also Sir Nicolas Browne-Wilkinson V-C at first instance in *IDC Group Ltd* v *Clark* [1992] 1 EGLR 187 (upheld 65 P&CR 179).

[75] See especially *Re Denley's Trust Deed* [1969] 1 Ch 373. Note the analysis of Parkinson [2002] CLJ 657 of trusts as based on obligations rather than identifiable equitable interests.

[76] See the useful analysis by Hornby (1977) 93 LQR 561, but contrast Hill (1991) 107 LQR 596 at p 598. More recently, cf *Dent* v *Dent* [1996] 1 WLR 683, *Pritchard Englefield* v *Steinberg* [2004] EWHC 1908 (Ch) and *Clowes Developments (UK) Ltd* v *Walters* [2006] 1 P&CR 1 at [44].

Suppose that C then sells on to D, who says nothing about taking subject to it. If the constructive trust does bind purchasers, this will mean that D is bound by the licence (provided that B is in actual occupation). It is incomprehensible that D should be bound when he buys from C, but not if he had bought directly from A. The puzzle would be why such proprietary consequences should flow from a purchaser's promise but not from that of the licensor.

Every instinct suggests that it is not permissible to use express or constructive trusts to bind purchasers such as D where the trust gives effect to a licence.[77] Of course, this does not preclude the constructive trust in *Binions* itself: it can be justified by the purchaser's promise to respect the licence. Part of the problem is that the courts seem willing to accept constructive trusts to give effect to licences, without pausing to consider the nature of the trust and whether it fits conventional principles as to trust interests. Relatively early, there were suggestions that the *Binions* constructive trust might not bind subsequent purchasers.[78]

Chattey v *Farndale Holdings Inc*[79] considers subsequent purchasers, even though the constructive trust in *Chattey* protected an estate contract rather than a licence. The Court of Appeal held that the subsequent purchaser was not bound by the constructive trust, as it had not promised to respect the estate contract. Unfortunately, this is not as conclusive as at first sight appears. Even if the trust could bind purchasers, on the facts, the purchaser could not be affected by it because there was no entry on the register (there was no possibility of an actual occupation overriding interest on the facts). Indeed, the very fact that the court gave prominence to the protection accorded by registration could be used to argue that the court assumed that purchasers would normally be bound by the constructive trust. The issue clearly remains open.

E. Estoppel licences

The role of estoppel has already been considered in the context of formalities. Although it is not essential,[80] the claimant will generally be a licensee prior to seeking an estoppel remedy. The normal case is where C is occupying or exercising rights over land in the belief that there is a right to do so. If C acts to his detriment and the owner, O, is aware of the circumstances, equity will give a remedy to C.

Most estoppel cases involve C's assumption or expectation of a conventional property right, such as a fee simple or easement. When estoppel operates in these cases to give effect to the assumption or expectation, it is arguable that it has little to do with licences. The licence is merely a way of describing the status of C before a remedy is given. Moriarty[81] has argued that the courts can be seen as doing little more than avoiding formality rules in recognising the conventional property right. This analysis has already been criticised, but what is of importance in the present context is that it fails to recognise that estoppel may protect true licences. This has two elements, often intertwined.

---

[77] Jackson [1983] Conv 64 at p 65; Hill (1988) 51 MLR 226 at p 232; McFarlane (2004) 120 LQR 667 at p 679.
[78] It was left open in *Re Sharpe* [1980] 1 WLR 219 at p 226. See Hardingham (1980) 12 MULR 356 at p 387.
[79] (1996) 75 P&CR 298 at pp 313–317. See also *Halifax plc* v *Curry Popeck* [2008] EWHC 1692 (Ch) at [51], in which unprotected rights binding a fraudulent registered transferee were held merely personal. However, this relates to the mode of creation rather than the substance of the right claimed.
[80] *JT Developments Ltd* v *Quinn* (1990) 62 P&CR 33.
[81] (1984) 100 LQR 376; see p 164 above.

First, the right that is assumed or expected may be of the nature of a licence. Examples are where there is a right not involving exclusive possession, as in *King* and *Clore*, and where there is no term or rent (especially common in the family setting). The second element is that the court may give a licence as a remedy. There are estoppel cases on the assumption (or expectation)[82] and the remedy[83] being licences. In addition, there are several cases in which contractual and estoppel licence issues are seen to overlap.[84] Indeed, it is commonly argued that *Errington* v *Errington*[85] could have been decided upon an estoppel basis, an argument which receives support from *Ashburn Anstalt* v *Arnold*.[86]

Are purchasers bound?

This has been the most difficult question regarding estoppel licences. It has already been seen that s 116 of the Land Registration Act 2002 provides that estoppels are capable of binding purchasers of registered land and that this probably confirms the position for unregistered land.[87] Even for unregistered land, the indications are that this extends to licences protected by estoppel.[88] Indeed, Fox LJ in *Ashburn Anstalt* makes this clear when he suggests that the successor in title in *Errington* could have been bound on an estoppel analysis. However, the weight of authority was not great and there were contrary suggestions.[89] Proprietary status for estoppel licences represents a sharp contrast with contractual licences, a contrast which has been criticised by some commentators.[90] In principle, there is a strong argument that estoppel should have no greater effect than contract.

When analysing the effect of estoppel licences, it is common to distinguish two stages: inchoate (before the court determines the remedy) and after the court order. Nearly all the cases involve disputes arising at the inchoate stage. In this context, s 116 appears clear that, for registered land, purchasers can be bound.[91]

What is the position after a remedy is given? Does a licence as a remedy bind purchasers? *Williams* v *Staite*[92] was decided on the basis that it does, but *Maharaj* v *Chand*[93] appears to indicate the contrary. Given the reluctance to recognise licences as proprietary interests, it would seem difficult to justify a licence ordered by the court as having proprietary

---

[82] *Plimmer* v *Mayor of Wellington* (1884) 9 App Cas 699; *Inwards* v *Baker* [1965] 2 QB 29 (although *Dodsworth* v *Dodsworth* (1973) 228 EG 1115 suggests there may have been a life interest); *Williams* v *Staite* [1979] Ch 291; *Coombes* v *Smith* [1986] 1 WLR 808 (claim failed); *Greasley* v *Cooke* [1980] 1 WLR 1306; *Bostock* v *Bryant* (1990) 61 P&CR 23 (claim failed); *Matharu* v *Matharu* (1994) 68 P&CR 93.

[83] In addition to the cases in the preceding footnote, see *Maharaj* v *Chand* [1986] AC 898 (PC).

[84] *National Provincial Bank Ltd* v *Ainsworth* [1965] AC 1175; *Re Sharpe* [1980] 1 WLR 219; *Ashburn Anstalt* v *Arnold* [1989] Ch 1.

[85] [1952] 1 KB 290.

[86] [1989] Ch 1.

[87] See p 171 above.

[88] *Inwards* v *Baker* [1965] 2 QB 29.

[89] Peter Gibson LJ in *Habermann* v *Koehler* (1996) 73 P&CR 515 at p 523 noted 'much controversy' and left the point open.

[90] Battersby [1991] Conv 36; Baughen (1994) 14 LS 147.

[91] McFarlane [2003] CLJ 661 at pp 694–695 argues otherwise, but his analysis is very different from that of the Law Commission and requires (as he admits) a strained interpretation.

[92] [1979] Ch 291.

[93] [1986] AC 898 (PC), although it might be argued that on the facts, a non-proprietary licence had been ordered.

effect.[94] Is this affected by s 116? It depends upon whether the remedy is within the words 'equity by estoppel'. The better view is that it is not: the section naturally applies to the inchoate equity rather than the remedy subsequently awarded.[95] This, in turn, supports the argument that the licence as a remedy did not, prior to the Land Registration Act 2002, bind purchasers and therefore will not do so in the future.

McFarlane has suggested[96] that it is wrong to distinguish the two stages. We should look at the nature of the right and determine property status on that basis. This might seem an attractive argument, but the development of discretion in determining estoppel remedies poses a considerable objection to it (quite apart from its being inconsistent with s 116). This discretion means that it is difficult to identify true licence status prior to the court order.

Leaving that argument aside, estoppel licences now seem accepted as being proprietary at the inchoate stage. Nevertheless, two issues arise. First (and most difficult), why do estoppel licences bind purchasers when contractual licences do not? The second issue concerns the interrelationship of estoppel and contractual licences: how readily can one rely upon an estoppel when there is already a contract?

Why should purchasers be bound?

On the first issue, it is not easy to comprehend why estoppel licences should bind purchasers when contractual licences do not. Both estoppel and contract may be seen as routes to the creation of interests. This works well when proprietary interests are involved. However, we do not accept that contracts as such bind purchasers, so why should estoppels do so? Moriarty demonstrates that the consideration rules for contracts are generally more demanding than detriment for estoppel: consideration requires a request that the detriment be undertaken. Estoppel places emphasis on the fact of detriment, against a background of an assumption or expectation. On the other hand, estoppel rules require more than contract as regards the nature of the detriment. Contract recognises an obligation to act as being effective consideration (as in the standard executory contract), whereas the act itself must be undertaken for there to be detriment in estoppel.

Perhaps the underlying problem is that orthodox contract theory states that detriment will not suffice as the source of a contractual obligation. Estoppel has weaker effects than contract, operating as a shield rather than as a sword; as a defence rather than as a cause of action in itself.[97] In the property context, estoppel has long been recognised as giving rise to a cause of action, although the remedy is discretionary. This may be just about acceptable, putting it much on a par with contract.[98] When the further step of binding purchasers is

---

[94] RJ Smith in *Consensus ad Idem* (ed Rose), pp 248–249; Battersby in *Land Law: Themes and Perspectives* (eds Bright and Dewar), Chapter 19.

[95] Law Com No 271, paras 5.4 (n 12), 5.30.

[96] [2003] CLJ 661 The *Law of Proprietary Estoppel*, paras 8.101 et seq, 8.113. This argument would be most relevant for the increasing number of cases where a monetary remedy is given: Bright and McFarlane [2005] CLJ 449. His argument may be supported by dicta of Lord Collins in *Mortgage Business plc* v *O'Shaugnessy* [2015] AC 385 at [58]–[59], but those dicta are best read as referring to the ability of the owner to create proprietary interests (the issue in the case).

[97] *Combe* v *Combe* [1951] 2 KB 215, but see the more flexible analysis of Robert Goff J in *Amalgamated Investment & Property Co Ltd* v *Texas Commerce International Bank Ltd* [1982] QB 84.

[98] Some estoppel analyses use a contract to bind the owner: *Dillwyn* v *Llewelyn* (1862) 4 De GF&J 517 (45 ER 1285) is a good example.

taken, however, a very odd situation results. Estoppel is weaker than contract in establishing causes of action generally, yet it is stronger in the binding of purchasers. How can this be?

It might be argued that the law is placing greater emphasis on actual detriment than on promises. Professor Atiyah,[99] amongst others, argued this and it may be so, although one may doubt whether the courts have been consciously adopting such a stance. It is more likely that two different factors have been influential. The first is that the earlier cases involved claims to recognised interests in land. If, as in *Dillwyn* v *Llewelyn*,[100] the claim is to the fee simple, then it is not at all surprising that it binds a successor in title. This is, of course, the more understandable in the period before the full development of the discretionary nature of the remedy. The extension from proprietary interest claims to licence claims is not stressed at all in the cases[101]: emphasis is placed on the fact that there is an estoppel rather than the nature of the assumption or expectation. In other words, the development may be regarded as almost accidental.

The second factor concerns the state of the authorities. We have seen that *King* and *Clore* provide a very distinct stumbling block for any development of contractual licences as proprietary interests. There are no cases denying proprietary effect to estoppel licences. Even if there is no very good reason for the two types of licence to be treated differently, the absence of authorities may have enabled the development of the estoppel licence.

By themselves, however, these factors are not at all satisfying. They do not explain why the instinct of the courts has been to reject contractual licences whilst they have been perfectly happy to enforce estoppel licences against purchasers. Professor Maudsley has noted that the contractual licensee will have a remedy against the licensor even after sale,[102] whereas an estoppel licensee may have no remedy against anyone save the purchaser. This is an interesting observation, but it has been convincingly argued that more recent developments in estoppel support the existence of a remedy against the licensor even after sale.[103]

More significant is the remedy in contract and estoppel licences. If the courts were to allow specific performance of contractual licences to bind purchasers, this would enable licensors to decide the scope of proprietary interests in many cases. The result would be inconsistent with the long-standing principle that the parties cannot create new forms of proprietary interests. Reasons for the principle are not hard to discover. One of the most potent has been the problems that such extended rights would pose for purchasers. Purchasers are at present aware of the sorts of claims (leases, easements and profits, especially) to look out for. If any type of right could be entered into, this would render investigation of title by purchasers unduly difficult. In addition, the ownership of land is being further encumbered. Although the policy of the law is to allow owners to encumber the land where this is generally beneficial (rights of way are more

---

[99] See, e.g., *Rise and Fall of Freedom of Contract*, Chapter 22; *Essays on Contract*, Essay 8.

[100] (1862) 4 De GF&J 517 (45 ER 1285).

[101] Note that in virtually all cases, there will be a licence before the detriment occurs: it is the nature of the assumption or expectation that may or may not be proprietary.

[102] (1956) 20 Conv NS 281; *King* v *David Allen & Sons, Billposting, Ltd* [1916] 2 AC 54 is one example of such an action.

[103] Bright and McFarlane [2005] Conv 14, relying on the growth of monetary remedies. Less persuasive is their suggestion that this calls into question estoppel's proprietary effect.

likely to benefit the dominant land than to harm the servient land), unlimited freedom to create proprietary interests might lead to obligations being imposed that are too restrictive of the landowner. Nobody doubts that a landowner may bind himself by contract in any way he chooses, but it is another thing to allow successors to be bound for all time.

By way of contrast, an estoppel does not give effect to expectations as a matter of right. Instead, the court has at least some choice as to the remedy. This enables the court to keep a much stricter control over developments, most especially where purchasers are involved. There is less temptation for people to go out of their way to try to create novel rights when the courts may not give a remedy. Many commercial licences are in consideration of an annual payment, and it is difficult to see the courts giving, as a matter of course, a remedy that will stretch indefinitely into the future. Estoppel licences are most likely to be effective in the informality of the family setting, where a licence to reside for life is frequently intended.[104]

However, some of the fears engendered by contractual licences may be applicable to estoppel. Purchasers may find an estoppel licence at least as difficult to discover as a contractual licence. At least a contractual licence is more likely to be in writing! However, it is arguable that the problems facing purchasers have been exaggerated for both forms of licences. Now that the great majority of land is registered, a purchaser will be affected by an interest only if it is entered on the register (when there is no excuse for failing to discover it) or else if it is an overriding interest protected by actual occupation. All purchasers should make inquiries of persons in actual occupation in order to avoid running a significant risk of taking a bad title. Once inquiries are made, it is as easy for the occupier to disclose a licence as it is for any other interest (most occupiers will be unaware of the niceties of lawyers' categories of interests in land).[105]

The purchaser may, nevertheless, face problems as a result of the wide scope of licences. It may be difficult to sort out what exactly is being claimed and its implications. To take one example, if there is a licence for life, does the licensor have an obligation to keep the premises in repair? Given the huge variety of licences, it may not be easy to answer this sort of query. For conventional interests, of course, the law gives much more guidance in rules developed over centuries.

The overlap with contractual licences

The second issue for consideration is how far contractual licences and estoppel licences may both apply to the same facts. At one time, it might have been argued that the two are quite different. The assumption or expectation that lies at the heart of an estoppel is different from a promise. To believe that one has a right is different from being promised a right.[106] Yet it has been seen that estoppels have expanded in the past few decades and now operate so as to give effect to promises relating to land.[107]

---

[104] See *Inwards* v *Baker* [1965] 2 QB 29; *Williams* v *Staite* [1979] Ch 291.
[105] When the House of Lords in *National Provincial Bank Ltd* v *Ainsworth* [1965] AC 1175 rejected the deserted wife's equity, it stressed the difficulty of inquiring as to the state of the marriage. This is a significant point for that particular right, but seems inapplicable to licences generally.
[106] Briggs [1981] Conv 212.
[107] See *Thorner* v *Major* [2009] 1 WLR 776, pp 155, 163 above.

Overlap between contracts and estoppel is encouraged by the suggestion in *Ashburn Anstalt* that *Errington* may be looked at as a case on estoppel. However, *Lloyds Bank plc v Carrick* casts some doubt on this.[108] The defendant had an estate contract which failed because it was not registered, but sought to argue that she could rely on an estoppel so as to bind a purchaser. The Court of Appeal rejected this suggestion, essentially on the basis that she already had what she was claiming under the estoppel: the need to register the estate contract was no reason for also recognising an estoppel (not registrable under the Land Charges Act 1972). This is not a case on contractual licences, but it displays a marked reluctance to allow contract and estoppel to overlap. It remains to be seen how broadly it will be applied. In contrast, *ER Ives Investment Ltd v High*[109] had recognised an estoppel where an equitable (contractual) easement had failed for non-registration. It may be that the easement had failed in *Ives* before the estoppel arose and that it is therefore distinguishable.

Both *Carrick* and *Ives* involve detriment which is separate from the contractual consideration. It is probably more difficult to argue for an estoppel licence where the detriment incurred is the same as the contractual consideration. Such cases are likely to be rare, simply because of the small number of cases involving contractual licences and purchasers.[110] However, if *Errington* were explained on estoppel grounds, this would show how contractual consideration (the payment of mortgage instalments) may be seen as detriment for estoppel. Other cases seem to support this, although not so explicitly.[111] If this is correct, then very many contractual licences will become enforceable by estoppel. This should not be surprising when the close relationship between estoppel detriment and contractual consideration is recalled. Yet, the existence of contractual consideration by itself is not enough. Most obviously, a promise (executory consideration) will not suffice for estoppel. It is only when the promise has been carried out that estoppel may become arguable.

It must always be remembered that the estoppel remedy is discretionary. If the consideration (and detriment) takes the form of rent, then it is most unlikely that the court would consider it proper to give a long-term remedy: the licensee will get no more than what has been paid for. Even so, some contractual licences would be given added force as against third parties. Indeed, one startling question is as to why estoppel was not applied on the facts of *Ashburn Anstalt* itself. The licensee had sold his land to the licensor on the faith of the licence: surely parting with one's land suffices for detriment? Strangely, this point seems not to have been considered by the Court of Appeal despite the suggestion that *Errington* might have been decided on estoppel grounds.

---

[108] [1996] 4 All ER 630; Ferguson (1996) 112 LQR 549; Thompson [1996] Conv 295. Cf *Birmingham Midshires Mortgage Services Ltd* v *Sabherwal* (1999) 80 P&CR 256 at p 263 (overreaching cannot be avoided by use of estoppel instead of a resulting trust).

[109] [1967] 2 QB 379. The case involves a right in the nature of an easement rather than a licence, but there is no reason why this should affect the relationship between contract and estoppel.

[110] Contractual rights to proprietary interests will bind purchasers as estate contracts unless, as in *Ives*, there are registration problems.

[111] *Siew Soon Wah* v *Yong Tong Hong* [1973] AC 836; *Tanner* v *Tanner* [1975] 1 WLR 1346 (Lord Denning MR); *Jones* v *Jones* [1977] 1 WLR 438; *Re Sharpe* [1980] 1 WLR 219; *Pennine Raceway Ltd* v *Kirklees MBC* [1983] QB 382 (Eveleigh LJ at p 390).

Quite apart from *Carrick*, this failure to grasp the issue in *Ashburn Anstalt* raises doubts as to the extent of the overlap between contract and estoppel. Briggs[112] has observed that the House of Lords in *Secretary of State for Employment* v *Globe Elastic Thread Co Ltd*[113] refused to apply estoppel in a contractual setting. That, however, was a case of promissory estoppel as between promisor and promisee. There is every reason why estoppel should not be seen as relevant in this relationship: the remedies are as provided for by the contract and not dependent upon the court's discretion. It is quite different where a purchaser is involved, as the contract no longer operates and the estoppel can come into its own.[114]

The arguments seem finely balanced. Apart from *Carrick*, the case for recognising an overlapping estoppel licence seems quite strong. However, despite not being exactly in point, *Carrick* certainly casts doubt on this. If the overlap is recognised, this renders it even more difficult to justify the differences in proprietary effect between contractual and estoppel licences.

F. Other analyses

When considering whether a purchaser may be bound by a licence, it is important to remember that a variety of analyses may be employed. The constructive trust provides a good example of a licence binding a purchaser without reference to a proprietary interest, as may also the benefit and burden doctrine.[115] Mention will now be made of another analysis: economic torts.[116]

It is well known that it is a tort to induce a person to break a contract. The application of this tort in the property context is supported by a small number of cases (usually as a subsidiary issue)[117] and dicta,[118] although the implications of the principle have not been thought through. Most property rights and many licences are based upon contract. It follows that the scope for holding that a purchaser has induced a breach of contract is quite substantial. Difficulties arise because we have well-established rules as to what constitutes an interest in land capable of binding purchasers. It would be odd if the economic torts were to produce a different set of answers. There can be no objection to one legal analysis

---

[112] [1983] Conv 285.

[113] [1980] AC 506 at p 518: 'it would be a strange doctrine, that a contract gives rise to an estoppel'. The argument in the text is not, of course, that the contract itself gives rise to an estoppel, but rather a combination of O's contractual promise and subsequent actions (which may, perhaps, include C's carrying out a contractual obligation).

[114] An analogy can be seen in the relationship between a legal periodic tenancy and a coexisting equitable lease. It is generally said that a court will look only to the equitable lease: *Walsh* v *Lonsdale* (1882) 21 Ch D 9. Yet everything changes once a purchaser is introduced. The purchaser might not be bound by the equitable lease and yet quite clearly will be bound by the legal lease.

[115] See p 175 above and especially *ER Ives Investment Ltd* v *High* [1967] 2 QB 379.

[116] Developed in greater detail in [1977] Conv 318; see also Gardner (1982) 98 LQR 279, especially pp 289–293.

[117] *Sefton* v *Tophams Ltd* [1965] Ch 1140; *Esso Petroleum Co Ltd* v *Kingswood Motors (Addlestone) Ltd* [1974] QB 142; *Pritchard* v *Briggs* [1980] Ch 338 at pp 409–417 (Goff LJ, relying on conspiracy); *Hemingway Securities Ltd* v *Dunraven Ltd* (1994) 71 P&CR 30; *Crestfort Ltd* v *Tesco Stores Ltd* [2005] L&TR 413.

[118] *Binions* v *Evans* [1972] Ch 359 at p 371; *Smith* v *Morrison* [1974] 1 WLR 659; see also *Swiss Bank Corporation* v *Lloyds Bank Ltd* [1979] Ch 548 at pp 569–575, 579–580 (reversed on other grounds: [1982] AC 584).

reaching a different conclusion to another, but it would be extraordinary for the side-wind of a tort analysis effectively to defeat common law and statutory rules carefully developed over many years.[119] Nor is it any answer to say that tort liability sounds in damages: injunctive relief has been awarded against tortfeasors.[120]

The paucity of the authorities renders the state of the current law unclear. The most that can be said is that there is some scope for arguing that a purchaser has induced a breach of contract. This has, of course, great significance for contractual licences. Although a purchaser would not commit the tort if there is mere constructive notice, one who knows about the licence may be at risk. The tort has never been fully discussed in the licences context, although Megaw LJ made a brief reference to it in *Binions v Evans*. It might be observed that, although the purchaser was aware of the licence in *Ashburn Anstalt*, the Court of Appeal was emphatic that the purchaser was not bound. It would be extraordinary if the court could have come to the contrary conclusion on the incantation of the magic words 'economic torts'.

If the tort does apply, then one of the major problems is likely to centre on the defence of justification. Although this defence has a limited role in the tort generally, there is some indication that it may have a somewhat greater role to play in the property context.[121]

A rather different point is that the parties may, apparently, agree that a restriction should be entered on the licensor's registered title, limiting the power to sell.[122] Although this does not as such mean that licences bind purchasers, it may mean that purchasers have to agree to respect the licence. In this respect, the restriction would be used in a similar fashion as in positive covenants.[123]

2. Creation and transfer of licences

If, as seems likely, contractual licences are not proprietary interests binding purchasers, then there are no formality requirements for their creation. The implication of contractual licences in the family setting has already been noted and criticised. No more need be said about these issues.

The transfer of the benefit of licences provides a more difficult problem. One objection to the licence as a proprietary interest is that it is said to be personal to the licensee.[124] The validity of this objection may be doubted. Transferability is a normal attribute of proprietary interests, although there seems to be little reason to say that proprietary status cannot exist without it.[125] Whatever one's views on that question, are licences assignable? Of

---

[119] Comparisons can be made with the use of economic torts and constructive trusts to avoid registration requirements: p 257 above.

[120] *Esso Petroleum Co Ltd v Kingswood Motors (Addlestone) Ltd* [1974] QB 142; *Hemingway Securities Ltd v Dunraven Ltd* (1994) 71 P&CR 30; *Crestfort Ltd v Tesco Stores Ltd* [2005] L&TR 413.

[121] *Edwin Hill & Partners v First National Finance Corporation plc* [1989] 1 WLR 225; O'Dair (1991) 11 OxJLS 227.

[122] *Donington Park Leisure Ltd v Wheatcroft & Son Ltd* [2006] EWHC 904 (Ch) at [45]; criticised by Dixon [2006] Conv 374.

[123] Described at p 252 above.

[124] Maudsley (1956) 20 Conv 281 observes that this renders the licence less like recognised proprietary interests.

[125] See p 14 above.

course, very many licences will be personal to the licensee, especially in the family setting with licences to reside for life. Commercial licences are less likely to be personal, and *Clore* v *Theatrical Properties Ltd* confirms that they can be assigned.[126] The central problem in the case, of course, lay in the fact that the defendant was the assignee of the licensor: burdens of contractual rights cannot be assigned. The only sensible conclusion is that there is no universal restriction on the right to assign, but that the nature of the individual licence has to be considered carefully.[127]

As regards formalities, assignments should follow the rules for the assignment of choses in action. As contractual licences are not interests in land, there are no special formality requirements for their assignment. What is required for assignment of an estoppel licence? Such an assignment would be unusual, but it is probable that writing is required both because the right is equitable and because it is usually an interest in land.[128]

3. The relationship constituted by the licence

The range of different licences (both in method of creation and type of right given) is so great that it is difficult to make useful statements as to the nature of the licence relationship. An obvious point is that the terms of the particular licence are all-important. Discussion will be limited to two more specific areas.

A. Trespass and nuisance

The orthodox view has been that a licensee cannot rely on either trespass or nuisance. These property-based remedies have been regarded as inapplicable because of the non-proprietary nature of the licence. It has been seen that licences have become much better protected over the past century, at least as against licensors. The awkward question is whether the developments in licences have had any effect on these remedies. Although there have been quite recent cases on the remedies, they have paid little attention to developments within licences.

Taking trespass first, this is the primary remedy against those who interfere with occupation of land. There will be an action in contract if a licensor under a contractual licence interferes with the licensee's possession; it would not normally be necessary to rely on trespass.[129] It is as against third parties (other than successors in title to the licensor) that the availability of trespass becomes important. One thing is clear: a licence which does not confer possession cannot be the basis of trespass. This was decided in *Hill* v *Tupper*,[130] where an exclusive right to put boats on a canal could not be enforced against a third party by way of trespass. This comes as no surprise, as even easements do not give rise to a

---

[126] [1936] 3 All ER 483 at p 490. The licensor had consented, as required by the agreement.
[127] See Anderson (1979) 42 MLR 203 at p 207. For estoppel claims, see p 174 above.
[128] Law of Property Act 1925, s 53(1)(a), (c). The proprietary status of the estoppel before a remedy is given is discussed at p 171 above.
[129] If the licensor evicts the licensee, then there may be trespass to the person (*Hurst* v *Picture Theatres Ltd* [1915] 1 KB 1); but this is not the same as trespass to land.
[130] (1863) 2 H&C 121 (159 ER 51).

remedy in trespass.[131] So far as licensees in occupation are concerned, it was suggested by Lord Upjohn in *National Provincial Bank Ltd* v *Ainsworth*[132] that the deserted wife could sue in trespass, and this supports the view that a licensee in possession (at least if in exclusive possession) can bring an action in trespass.

A remedy in trespass has the merit of giving full protection to the licensee in possession. The licensee's position would be precarious if a third party could take possession of the land and deprive the licence of all value. It is not even clear that the licensee would have any remedy against the licensor in respect of such third-party conduct.[133] The licensor would still be able to sue in trespass, but may not wish to do so. It must be stressed that a third party who is a successor in title to the licensor will not be liable to trespass. In this case, the successor can rely on his title to the land to justify entry on the land.[134]

More difficult is the question whether the licensee who has never been in possession can seek possession against a trespasser. The Court of Appeal in *Manchester Airport plc* v *Dutton*[135] gave such a remedy, showing a marked reluctance to be restricted by rules attaching to old remedies. However, this has been criticised by commentators.[136] Although *Dutton* has been accepted by later cases,[137] it is limited to occupation licences conferring effective control: a licence merely allowing access is outside *Dutton*.[138] All the judges in *Dutton* agreed that a licensee could rely on trespass if in possession; this probably lays to rest any lingering doubts on that point.

Turning to nuisance, there is a more substantial body of authority against an action by the licensee.[139] This is particularly significant for non-possessory licences. No trespass action can lie to protect such licences. If there were to be any remedy for third-party interference with the licence, it would have to be in nuisance, just as nuisance provides a remedy for interference with easements.

The reason most commonly given for not allowing an action in nuisance (other than simply the absence of a proprietary interest) is based on the fact that most nuisances involve a continuing interference with the use of land. If the licensor says that he does not object to the interference, then the licensee should not be able to maintain a separate action.[140] Although there is merit in this argument, two weaknesses should be noted. The

---

[131] Profits can, however, lead to an action in trespass: Jackson, *The Law of Easements and Profits*, pp 210–212.

[132] [1965] AC 1175 at p 1232; relied upon by Dawson and Pearce, *Licences Relating to the Occupation or Use of Land*, pp 170–171. Also supported by *Harper* v *Charlesworth* (1825) 4 B&C 574 (107 ER 1174); contra *Allan* v *Liverpool Overseers* (1874) LR 9 QB 180 at p 192.

[133] The licensor would be liable if the third party is a successor in title (*King* v *David Allen & Sons, Billposting, Ltd* [1916] 2 AC 54), as the licensor has put performance of the licence outside his control.

[134] This assumes that the licence does not bind the successor; estoppel licences most likely do so.

[135] [2000] QB 133 (Chadwick LJ dissenting as there was no right to exclusive possession); Paton and Seabourne [1999] Conv 535.

[136] E.g., Hill, *Modern Studies in Property Law*, Vol 1 (ed Cooke), Chapter 2, argues persuasively that what binds third parties is the possession and that *Dutton* appears inconsistent with the non-proprietary status of licences; Swadling (2000) 116 LQR 354. Baker in *Modern Studies in Property Law*, Vol 8 (ed Barr), Chapter 6, is more welcoming.

[137] Though Lord Neuberger MR saw 'real force' in the criticisms in *Mayor of London* v *Hall* [2011] 1 WLR 504 at [26], his later comments indicate support for *Dutton*; *Vehicle Control Services Ltd* v *RCC* [2013] RTR 313.

[138] *Countryside Residential (North Thames) Ltd* v *A Child* (2000) 81 P&CR 10; cf *Vehicle Control Services Ltd* v *RCC* [2013] RTR 313 at [41].

[139] *Malone* v *Laskey* [1907] 2 KB 141; *Cunard* v *Antifyre Ltd* [1933] 1 KB 551; *Metropolitan Properties Ltd* v *Jones* [1939] 2 All ER 202.

[140] *Malone* v *Laskey* [1907] 2 KB 141; *Cunard* v *Antifyre Ltd* [1933] 1 KB 551.

first is that nuisance lies for interference with an easement, irrespective of what the owner of the servient land might have permitted. It is arguable that at least an interference which frustrates a licence should give a remedy. The second weakness is that none of the cases involves a licensee in exclusive possession and with a right (against the licensor) to remain in possession. It is suggested that the licensor should not then be free to authorise the nuisance. If the exclusive possession had been held under a lease, then the permission of both lessor and lessee would be required.

In *Hunter* v *Canary Wharf Ltd*,[141] a majority of the House of Lords confirmed that licensees generally cannot sue for nuisance. However, the case did not involve licensees in exclusive possession and Lords Goff and Hope[142] accepted that such licensees could sue in nuisance. It follows that it would be too sweeping an assertion today to state that a licensee can never sue in nuisance, although there seems little hope of success unless there is exclusive possession.

B. Comparisons with leases

It has been seen in the leases context that landlords have frequently attempted to create licences rather than leases in order to avoid the application of statutory protection of tenants. That this protection does not apply to licences is the most important practical difference between licences and leases. There are many statutory provisions applicable only to leases, most of them favouring the tenant.

More instructive at a theoretical level is the question whether common law rules are different. Both leases and licences are contractual in origin. Many of the differences between them depend upon how far the courts are willing to introduce modern contractual ideas into leases.[143] Over the years, the rules as to leases have been formulated in ways which differ from contract principles. Licences, on the other hand, are governed by contract principles. Two examples may be given.

The first concerns frustration. It has long been accepted that the doctrine of frustration applies to licences. It follows that a licence to use a room to view a spectacle (such as a procession) may be frustrated if the spectacle is cancelled.[144] The House of Lords has held in *National Carriers Ltd* v *Panalpina (Northern) Ltd*[145] that frustration may apply to leases, though only in exceptional cases. It is interesting that one of the principal arguments for recognising frustration was that it would be unsatisfactory to have to draw a distinction between leases and licences.

The second example concerns obligations on the landlord or licensor in respect of the state of the premises. The common law is notoriously reluctant to imply such obligations in leases. This has led to complex statutory provisions, themselves applicable only to

---

[141] [1997] AC 655 (Lord Cooke dissented); Kidner [1998] Conv 267; Ghandhi [1998] Conv 309. See also *Butcher Robinson & Staples Ltd* v *London Regional Transport* (1999) 79 P&CR 523.

[142] Ibid, at pp 692, 724 (Lord Hope refers to exclusive occupation). Lord Lloyd at p 695 is consistent with this, although Lord Hoffmann might place more stress on proprietary status.

[143] This is more fully discussed in the leases context: p 409 above.

[144] *Krell* v *Henry* [1903] 2 KB 740 (coronation procession).

[145] [1981] AC 675 (see p 410 above).

leases. Yet, in *Wettern Electric Ltd* v *Welsh Development Agency*,[146] a term was implied into a licence that the property was suitable for the licensee's use, despite the fact that there would have been no such term had there been a lease. Whilst it is difficult to quarrel with the reasonableness of the implication on the facts of *Wettern Electric*, it does seem to open up a contrast with leases. That contrast is difficult to justify. One may observe that the courts are rather more prepared to imply obligations into leases today[147] and suggest that, following the lead in *National Carriers*, a term as to suitability (similar to *Wettern Electric*) should be implied into leases.[148]

Further reading

Battersby, G [1991] Conv 36: Contractual and estoppel licences as proprietary interests in land.

Baughen, S (1994) 14 LS 147: Estoppels over land and third parties: an open question?

Briggs, A [1983] Conv 285: Contractual licences: a reply.

Evershed, Sir Raymond (1954) 70 LQR 326: Reflections on the fusion of law and equity after 75 years.

McFarlane, B [2003] CLJ 661: Proprietary estoppel and third parties after the Land Registration Act 2002.

---

[146] [1983] QB 796.

[147] *Liverpool City Council* v *Irwin* [1977] AC 239 (implied obligations as regards common parts of a block of flats); pp 411, 416 above.

[148] Wilkinson (1983) 80 LS Gaz 2195.

23

Easements and profits

Introduction

Most of the rights considered in earlier chapters entitle the holder to possess land. Some may not give an immediate right to possession (as in the case of future interests or the freehold reversion subject to a long lease), but ultimately they are rights which may involve possession of the land. Easements and profits fit within the old category of incorporeal hereditaments. Even more than estates, this category places greater stress upon the right than upon the underlying property. In the words of Blackstone,[1] 'Their existence is merely in idea and abstracted contemplation; though their effects and profits may be frequently objects of our bodily senses.' Just as one can have an estate in the freehold (a corporeal hereditament), one can have an estate (e.g. a life interest) in an incorporeal hereditament. A right of way for life provides a good example.

Incorporeal hereditaments were very important to earlier generations of lawyers, but few forms of them are significant today. Though the terminology of incorporeal hereditaments feels outmoded, easements and (to a lesser extent) profits remain extremely common. They are property rights in that they may bind purchasers of the land adversely affected.

That incorporeal hereditaments confer rights less than freehold or leasehold estates is well illustrated by the best-known easement: a right of way over another's land. Profits may involve rather broader rights – for example, the right to fish on another's land – but the rights are still limited. There is another factor that is vitally important for all easements and some profits. The right must benefit the claimant's adjoining land. From this we talk about the dominant land or tenement (that which has the benefit) and the servient land or tenement (that which has the burden).

The category of easements is very old, for the obvious reason that effective land use often requires that landowners have rights over adjoining land. This is equally true whether the land is used for agricultural or building purposes. Economic efficiency demands that easements be recognised as proprietary interests, far more so than rights where there is no benefited land. Indeed, it can be said that easements as a whole bring far more benefit to dominant land than harm to servient land.[2] For example, a right of way may provide essential access to dominant land.

---

[1] *Commentaries on the Laws of England*, Vol ii, p 20.
[2] Prichard [1987] Conv 328 argues that the utility of easements is such that registration rules should not readily defeat them.

Beneficial as they are, easements and profits had never been comprehensively reviewed until a lengthy 2011 report of the Law Commission.[3] Although it is not proposed to codify the law relating to easements, most of the controversial issues considered in this chapter are reviewed; reform of many of them is recommended. The major proposals will be discussed alongside the relevant topics within easements.

Easements and profits pose several difficult questions, two of which will be concentrated upon in this chapter. The first question concerns the rules relating to the types of rights within the category of easements and profits. Because the area is so old, there are set requirements to be satisfied and many examples of acceptable and unacceptable rights. The second question concerns the creation of these rights. Easements and profits are special in that it is quite easy for them to arise by implication or long user (prescription). In general terms, this may be explained by the utility of the rights: the law is inclined to find that they exist whenever it is reasonable to do so.

Another common question concerns the extent of easements. If a person has a right of way to his house, can it be used for access by coaches or by a multitude of cars if the house is converted to use as a hotel? This type of question is ultimately a question of interpretation of the easement and, because few significant issues of principle are involved, will receive only a brief discussion.

1. Similar rights

Before beginning with the requirements for easements and profits, it is worth considering similar rights, which to a certain extent overlap with easements and profits.

A. Restrictive covenants

It is plain that not all rights as between adjoining landowners fit into the category of easements. Where a covenant limits the use of land for the benefit of neighbouring land, this restrictive covenant has, since *Tulk* v *Moxhay* in 1848,[4] been recognised as an interest in land. Although they might be thought to be a branch of easements,[5] restrictive covenants have their own rules. Not only are they merely equitable interests (easements and profits can be legal), but restrictive covenants do not share the rules of implication and prescription. In addition, they are subject to a special statutory regime for modification in certain circumstances.

The similarities between easements and covenants have led to ideas that the categories should be merged. However, the Law Commission[6] considers that the differences between

---

[3] Law Com No 327. The report also covers covenants: see p 573 below. Law Com No 356 reviews aspects of the easement of light, an area of great practical importance as it can impede land development.

[4] 2 Ph 774 (41 ER 1143).

[5] Jessel MR, in an oft-quoted passage, observes that one way of looking at restrictive covenants is as 'an extension in equity of the doctrine of negative easements' (*London & South Western Ry* v *Gomm* (1882) 20 Ch D 562 at p 583). As Simpson, *A History of the Land Law* (2nd edn), observes at p 260, this was not the reasoning employed in *Tulk* v *Moxhay*.

[6] Law Com CP 186, influenced by a desire not to introduce a statutory code for easements. See also Cooke [2009] Conv 448 at pp 465–472.

them justify keeping them separate. Nevertheless, reform may well bring the categories closer together – a good example being the extension to easements of the powers[7] to modify covenants.

Most easements are positive in the sense that they entitle the dominant owner to do something. However, some well-established easements are negative in character (similar to restrictive covenants), because they prevent the servient owner from doing something. The best example is the right to light. In substance, this is a right to stop a neighbour from building so as to interfere with the light to one's windows. As will be seen, the courts are reluctant to recognise new negative easements, believing that they fit better within restrictive covenants.

B. Natural rights[8]

Every landowner has rights against neighbours, recognised by the law without any form of creation. Virtually all the law of nuisance is of this nature.[9] The obligation not to create an unreasonable amount of noise is not, of course, based on any right granted by one landowner to another. However, some natural rights look almost identical to easements. The best example is the natural right to support. This prevents a neighbour from interfering with the support for one's land. If my neighbour digs a trench so close to the boundary that it causes my land to collapse, then I can sue. However, one very important qualification is that I have no right if my land collapses because of a building on it[10]: the natural right is limited to such support as would be necessary for land without the extra weight of buildings.[11] Similarly, there is no natural right of support from a neighbouring building, a proposition which is very significant for semi-detached and terraced houses.[12] If I want my building to depend upon support from my neighbour's land or building, then it is essential to negotiate with my neighbour for an easement to support my building.

People frequently build up to the boundaries of their land, most especially in large cities, without taking the precaution of negotiating easements of support. There is some sense in not protecting such builders automatically. Otherwise, the builder could render development of the neighbour's land more difficult or expensive: this appears to be unfairly oppressive of the neighbour. Yet, it remains odd that the neighbour is entirely free to excavate such as to cause the collapse of the building.[13] Indeed, there appears to be no way

---

[7] Law Com No 327, para 7.53 (extended to existing easements by Law Com No 356); see p 571 below.

[8] For details of these and the following rights, see Megarry and Wade, *The Law of Real Property* (8th edn), paras 27-027–27-042, 27-049–27-054, 27-058–27-063, 27-069–27-072.

[9] A ready source of confusion is that an action in nuisance is brought in order to complain of an interference with an easement. The nature of the action is therefore of no assistance in drawing the line between natural rights and easements.

[10] Confirmed by *Dalton* v *Angus & Co* (1881) 6 App Cas 740 (criticised by Wu [2002] Conv 237).

[11] An action for building damage lies if the land would have collapsed anyway: *Brown* v *Robins* (1859) 4 H&N 186 (157 ER 809); *Stroyan* v *Knowles* (1861) 6 H&N 454 (158 ER 186); see also *Ray* v *Fairway Motors (Barnstaple) Ltd* (1968) 20 P&CR 261.

[12] *Peyton* v *Mayor of London* (1829) 9 B&C 725 (109 ER 269). Usually, the houses will have been built by one person and easements will be implied on the sale of the individual houses: Bodkin (1962) 26 Conv 210.

[13] The Party Wall etc Act 1996 makes provision for the building of, and work relating to, party walls and structures close to the boundary. This enables the builder to strengthen foundations of adjoining buildings, but does not restrict liability which would otherwise exist (see especially ss 6(10) and 9).

of preventing the neighbour from excavating out of pure malice.[14] Nevertheless, the leading case of *Dalton v Angus & Co*[15] demonstrates how an easement of support will arise by prescription after the building has stood for 20 years. This diminishes the significance of the rule that the natural right of support does not extend to buildings. There is a case for saying that buildings should automatically enjoy a right of support.[16]

Apart from the protection of buildings, the natural right of support and the easement of support seem virtually identical in nature. There is, of course, a contrast as to when they exist. The natural right arises automatically, whilst the easement requires creation by one of the normal methods for easements. For both natural rights and easements, there is no right to prevent the servient owner from removing support. Rather, the essence of the right is not to have one's land collapse because of removal of support.[17] The neighbour is at liberty to remove the original support as part of building operations,[18] and no objection can be raised to the provision of substitute support. The person with the right of support can sue only if subsidence occurs[19] and has no right to charge the cost of preventative work to the neighbour.[20] However, there may be a right to an injunction to require restoration of support where there is a very strong probability of serious damage.[21]

The intertwined nature of nuisance and easements may raise questions as to the interplay between the principles applied in each. In recent years, it has been recognised that nuisance may require a landowner to take limited steps to avoid damage to neighbouring land. In *Holbeck Hall Hotel Ltd v Scarborough BC*,[22] a landslip had destroyed the claimant's hotel. The Court of Appeal applied this nuisance duty to the claimant's natural right of support. The court relied on cases involving the easement of support. Although the normal easement principle is that servient owners are not subject to any positive obligations, this reasoning indicates that a tort duty similar to that in *Holbeck Hall* may apply in at least some easements.[23]

Another natural right is to water flowing in a river or channel. This is subject to rights of upper riparian landowners. Although landowners have unrestricted rights to take percolating water,[24] water flowing in a channel can be used only for domestic or commercial purposes on the land. Abstraction for commercial use must be reasonable and not diminish the flow.[25] More extensive rights to take water may exist by virtue of an easement. Water rights have been significantly affected by legislation and form a complex area of law, outside the scope of this text.

---

[14] An action in negligence was dismissed in *Ray v Fairway Motors (Barnstaple) Ltd* (1968) 20 P&CR 261; supported by the analogy of negligent abstraction of water: *Stephens v Anglian Water Authority* [1987] 1 WLR 1381.

[15] (1881) 6 App Cas 740.

[16] Law Com WP 36, paras 45–82. The ensuing report (Law Com No 127) was limited to covenants.

[17] Wind suction damage arising from removal of support is actionable: *Rees v Skerrett* [2001] 1 WLR 1541.

[18] *Bonomi v Backhouse* (1859) El Bl&El 622 at p 655 (120 ER 643 at p 655) (Exchequer Chamber).

[19] *Backhouse v Bonomi* (1861) 9 HLC 503 (11 ER 825); *West Leigh Colliery Co Ltd v Tunnicliffe & Hampson Ltd* [1908] AC 27. The person who removed the support remains liable even after the land has been sold.

[20] *Midland Bank plc v Bardgrove Property Services Ltd* (1992) 65 P&CR 153.

[21] The leading case is *Redland Bricks Ltd v Morris* [1970] AC 652.

[22] [2000] QB 836: there was no breach of that duty on the facts (Thompson [2001] Conv 177).

[23] In *Ward v Coope* [2015 1 WLR 4081, the Court of Appeal stresses that the duty lies in tort and is separate from the question whether there is an easement of support.

[24] *Chasemore v Richards* (1859) 7 HLC 349 (11 ER 140); *Palmer v Bowman* [2000] 1 WLR 842 recognises an obligation to accept water from higher land.

[25] *Swindon Waterworks Co Ltd v Wilts & Berks Canal Navigation Co* (1875) LR 7 HL 697.

C. Public rights

Certain rights similar to easements and profits are enjoyed by the public. They will not be dealt with in detail as we are principally interested in rights held by individuals. The most obvious example is a public right of way. Similarly, there may be a public right to navigate a river. The public has a natural right to fish and navigate on the foreshore, but this does not extend either to beachcombing[26] or to inland waters.[27] Rather surprisingly, it is unclear whether there is any public right to use beaches (the foreshore) for bathing.[28] Turning to statutory material, the Countryside and Rights of Way Act 2000 provides for rights of access over common land and 'open country', whilst coastal access is dealt with by the Marine and Coastal Access Act 2009.

D. Rights of fluctuating bodies

Generally speaking, rights must be held by an individual or a company (whether or not as owner of land) or be public. A fluctuating body (such as the residents of a particular locality) cannot enjoy rights, whether of a public or private proprietary nature. There are two exceptions to this, although they both have a distinctly old-fashioned flavour and will rarely apply today.

The first exception is that rights, including those in the nature of an easement, may be enjoyed by custom, provided that they are certain and reasonable.[29] The major restriction is that rights shown to have arisen since 1189 are excluded,[30] although it does not matter that the form of enjoyment of the right has changed. Thus, a right to play cricket may be recognised as a form of a right to play games, although cricket was unknown in 1189 and for many years after.[31] It will be obvious that few rights will qualify and even fewer will be significant for twenty-first-century society. That said, they may have surprising effects. In *Wyld* v *Silver*,[32] a right to hold a market had been in disuse for some 160 years. The owner of the land affected wished to build on it and obtained planning permission to do so. The claimants were able to prove the right to hold a market, and this was sufficient to obtain an injunction to prevent building. Once proved, a customary right can be lost only by statute.

The second exception is especially important for rights in the nature of a profit: rights to take things from another's land. These rights cannot be acquired by custom.[33] Nevertheless, the courts have been reluctant to strike down rights exercised for centuries[34] and have found two ways of giving effect to them. Both depend upon the idea that a profit

---

[26] *Alfred F Beckett Ltd* v *Lyons* [1967] Ch 449.

[27] *Toome Eel Fishery (Northern Ireland) Ltd* v *Cardwell* [1966] NI 1.

[28] *R (Newhaven Port & Properties Ltd)* v *East Sussex CC* [2015] AC 1547 at [26]–[50], [108]–[136].

[29] See Farwell J in *Mercer* v *Denne* [1904] 2 Ch 534 at pp 551–552, upheld [1905] 2 Ch 538.

[30] *Simpson* v *Wells* (1872) LR 7 QB 214: could not have pre-dated the fourteenth century.

[31] *Fitch* v *Rawling* (1795) 2 H Bl 393 (126 ER 614), as explained in *Mercer* v *Denne* [1904] 2 Ch 534 at p 553 (Farwell J), [1905] 2 Ch 538 at p 586 (Cozens-Hardy LJ).

[32] [1963] Ch 243.

[33] *Gateward's Case* (1607) 6 Co Rep 59b (77 ER 344); *Lord Chesterfield* v *Harris* [1908] 2 Ch 397, [1911] AC 623; *Alfred F Beckett Ltd* v *Lyons* [1967] Ch 449.

[34] This reluctance (seen also in customary easements) applies generally in the law: it is material in the recognition of easements and profits by prescription or long use: see p 537 below.

may be held by an incorporated body (a company).[35] The first supposes that the Crown incorporated the fluctuating body and granted the profit to it. The second supposes that there was a grant to an existing corporation (generally a local authority) on a charitable trust for the fluctuating body.[36] It is obvious that a high level of inventiveness is involved in these analyses; they have limited application.[37]

There are also rights of common. Today, these can be asserted only if registered under the Commons Act 2006 (replacing the Commons Registration Act 1965), registration being conclusive. Rights of common can still be created by express grant, but not by prescription after the 2006 Act. Town and village greens are included within the Act; they may still be registered if there has been 20 years' user.[38]

2. What can be an easement or profit?

A. Profits

Profits present the fewest problems and will be dealt with first. A profit is the right to take something from a neighbour's land.[39] It may be a right to allow animals to graze (pasture),[40] to fish (piscary) or take game, to cut turf (turbary), to take timber (estovers) or to take minerals. Although some of these are distinctly archaic, others (especially the right to fish and the right to minerals) have great economic importance. It may be observed that profits provide a way of splitting ownership by way of substance. Whilst freehold and leasehold interests split ownership by time, profits enable the present enjoyment to be split by way of differing benefits.

A distinct feature of profits is that they may be expressed to exist either for the benefit of specific neighbouring land (appurtenant) or for the benefit of individuals (in gross). It is important to stress that profits appurtenant can be exercised only for the benefit of the dominant land. It follows that a profit appurtenant to take fish does not allow the dominant owner to sell fish: the right is limited to what is required for consumption on the land.[41] By way of contrast, a profit in gross can exist without limit, although in many cases, the grant of the profit will contain express restrictions. Whether a profit is appurtenant or in gross need not be permanent. Thus, the dominant owner may convert a profit appurtenant (if limited in extent) into a profit in gross with the same limit.[42]

It would appear at first sight that a profit in gross, especially if unlimited in extent, is far more beneficial to the dominant owner. So it is, but there are drawbacks which may cause the holder to argue for a profit appurtenant. First, profits quite frequently arise from

---

[35] A profit does not require benefited land.
[36] *Goodman* v *Mayor of Saltash* (1882) 7 App Cas 633; *Peggs* v *Lamb* [1994] Ch 172.
[37] *Lord Chesterfield* v *Harris* [1911] AC 623.
[38] Leading cases under the 1965 Act include *R* v *Oxfordshire CC, ex p Sunningwell PC* [2000] 1 AC 335 and *Oxfordshire CC* v *Oxford City C* [2006] 2 AC 674.
[39] The thing must be part of the land or else a wild animal. For application to water, see Fiennes (1938) 2 Conv NS 203.
[40] Such rights must be registered: see Commons Act 2006, s 61(1).
[41] *Bailey* v *Stephens* (1862) 12 CBNS 91 (142 ER 1077); *Lord Chesterfield* v *Harris* [1908] 2 Ch 397, [1911] AC 623; *Staffordshire & Worcestershire Canal Navigation* v *Bradley* [1912] 1 Ch 91.
[42] *Bettison* v *Langton* [2002] 1 AC 27.

long use (prescription). In many prescription claims, the claimant has to rely upon user by the previous owner of his land. To do this, it is necessary to show a profit appurtenant (with use limited to what is required for the dominant land). A second point is that a profit appurtenant will pass automatically on the conveyance of the benefited land, whereas a profit in gross requires a specific assignment of the profit.[43]

B. Easements

An easement is usually a right to do something on the servient land or (in a few cases) to prevent something from being done on the servient land.[44] Common examples are rights of way, rights to run drains across the servient land, rights of light (preventing the servient owner from building so as to block light to windows) and rights of support. However, there is no finite list of easements: rights as varied as storage,[45] use of chimney flues,[46] putting up a clothes line[47] and use of a lavatory[48] have been accepted.

Whilst one can get a feel for the nature of easements from these examples, it is less easy to define their requirements. It is normal to take the four characteristics accepted by the Court of Appeal in *Re Ellenborough Park*.[49] These are:

(1) there must be a dominant and a servient tenement;
(2) the easement must accommodate the dominant tenement;
(3) the dominant and servient owners must be different persons; and
(4) the right must be capable of forming the subject matter of a grant.

Useful as these tests are, they scarcely answer the question as to whether a particular right will be accepted. There are further rules to be considered. In particular, obligations of a positive nature cannot normally be imposed on the servient owner. The right of the dominant owner must usually be to do something: a negative obligation limiting what the servient owner can do is the province of the restrictive covenant. Furthermore, there cannot be a right to exclusive use of the servient land. The four characteristics from *Re Ellenborough Park* and the further rules will now be considered in turn.

(i) Dominant and servient tenements

The nature of all incorporeal hereditaments is that there must be land adversely affected by the right: the servient land. What is more significant for easements is that there must also be land which is benefited by the right: the dominant land. There is no conclusive reason for this rule. Many rights naturally do benefit land; most rights of way and support provide good examples. Yet, I could have a right to cross someone's land to reach a beach,

---

[43] *Anderson* v *Bostock* [1976] Ch 312. See also *Lovett* v *Fairclough* (1990) 61 P&CR 385.
[44] There can also be an easement to do an act on the dominant land which would otherwise be a nuisance.
[45] *Att-Gen of Southern Nigeria* v *John Holt & Co (Liverpool) Ltd* [1915] AC 599.
[46] *Jones* v *Pritchard* [1908] 1 Ch 630.
[47] *Drewell* v *Towler* (1832) 3 B&Ad 735 (110 ER 268); *Pallister* v *Clark* (1975) 30 P&CR 84.
[48] *Miller* v *Emcer Products Ltd* [1956] Ch 304.
[49] [1956] Ch 131 at p 163. Cooke in *Landmark Cases in Land Law* (ed Gravells), Chapter 3.

or a right to land my helicopter on a particular landing pad in London: in each of these cases, I might have no land benefited by the right. The rights will be no more than contractual licences.

The rule is almost universally assumed to have existed for centuries.[50] This helps to explain why authority to support it is thin on the ground: few counsel would waste their breath (and litigants' money) in arguing the contrary. Apart from *Re Ellenborough Park*, the rule is referred to in a considerable number of cases[51] and has been said by the Court of Appeal to be trite law.[52] Dicta can be found to support the concept of easements in gross,[53] but they run counter to the overwhelming weight of authority and opinion.

It is more questionable whether there is sufficient policy justification for the rule.[54] It may be argued that economically valuable rights could be created as easements in gross. It seems unlikely that this would make the title to the servient land either unduly difficult to investigate or so encumbered by adverse claims as to deter purchasers or mortgagees. Nevertheless, the courts have always been reluctant to allow landowners to create new forms of interests,[55] illustrated by the rejection of the contractual licence as an interest in land.[56]

Although there must be a dominant tenement, there is no requirement that it be identified by the document creating the easement. The courts are prepared to look to the surrounding circumstances in order to discover the benefited land.[57] Very many easements are created by implication on the sale of land and, inevitably, there is no explicit identification of the benefited land. However, the implication is nearly always in favour of the purchaser (as will be seen later), and the benefited land will be the land sold: identification causes few problems.

It remains good practice to identify the benefited land; this avoids subsequent uncertainty. Many years later, it may be very difficult to work out what land was intended to be benefited.[58] In particular, there is a real risk that the courts will hold that the easement operates for the benefit of only one of two plots owned by the dominant owner. Thus, in *Nickerson* v *Barraclough*[59] a right of way was implied into a conveyance of land. The purchaser already owned land adjacent to that purchased, to which the right of way would provide vitally important access. It was held that the right of way operated so as to benefit only the land purchased and could not be used for access to the adjacent land.

---

[50] Lawson in *Land Law: Issues, Debates, Policy* (ed Tee), p 70 observes that it did not 'fully crystallise' until the mid-nineteenth century.

[51] Examples are *Todrick* v *Western National Omnibus Co Ltd* [1934] Ch 561; *Re Salvin's Indenture* [1938] 2 All ER 498 at p 506.

[52] *London & Blenheim Estates Ltd* v *Ladbroke Retail Parks Ltd* [1994] 1 WLR 31 at p 36.

[53] See especially *Johnstone* v *Holdway* [1963] 1 QB 601.

[54] Sturley (1980) 96 LQR 557.

[55] *Keppell* v *Bailey* (1834) 2 My&K 517 (39 ER 1042); *Ackroyd* v *Smith* (1850) 10 CB 164 (138 ER 68) (rejecting ways in gross); *Hill* v *Tupper* (1863) 2 H&C 121 (159 ER 51).

[56] *Ashburn Anstalt* v *Arnold* [1989] Ch 1.

[57] *Thorpe* v *Brumfitt* (1873) 8 Ch App 650; *Re Salvin's Indenture* [1938] 2 All ER 498; *Johnstone* v *Holdway* [1963] 1 QB 601; *The Shannon Ltd* v *Venner Ltd* [1965] Ch 682.

[58] The problem has a higher profile in the law relating to restrictive covenants and is more fully considered in that context.

[59] [1981] Ch 426.

(ii) *The easement must accommodate the dominant tenement*

It is no surprise that not only must there be a dominant tenement, but that it must be benefited (accommodated) by the easement.[60] The nature of the requirement is that the easement must affect the land directly (rights of light and support are good examples) or the manner in which the land is used (rights of way giving access to the land, for example). The crucial point to stress is that it must be the land that benefits, rather than the individual owner of the land.

This contrast may be illustrated by the following two examples. Suppose I live in Liverpool and negotiate an agreement with Liverpool Football Club that the owners of my house can enter to watch all Liverpool's home matches for free. This promise does not accommodate the land I own: it merely operates for the benefit of the individual owners of my house. Doubtless it would increase the value of my house, but that is not enough. It does not affect the way in which the house itself is enjoyed. In the second example, my neighbour owns land between the bottom of my garden and a road. I negotiate for a right of access over my neighbour's land. This right of way, making my use of the house more convenient, clearly accommodates my land.

Whether a recognised easement (such as right of way) benefits land in a particular case is a question of fact. There is no requirement that servient and dominant land be adjacent to one another.[61] For example, a right of way may pass over an immediate neighbour's land and then over the servient land before reaching the highway.[62] Rights to light often involve servient land separated from the dominant land by a road.[63] Furthermore, there is no requirement that the right be reasonably necessary[64]: that is the province of rules on the implication of easements.

Business use

It is no objection that the easement relates to a business of the dominant owner. In the well-known case of *Moody* v *Steggles*,[65] the dominant owner had a right to advertise his public house on the servient land. This was readily treated as accommodating the dominant land, bearing in mind the way in which it was used. It does not follow that an advertisement placed miles away will suffice. In *Moody*, the servient land was situated in front of the public house, and the advertising sign was an indication of its existence.

An equally well-known case on the other side of the line is *Hill* v *Tupper*.[66] It involved an exclusive right to put boats on a canal, on the bank of which the claimant had land. It

---

[60] If, after valid creation, the dominant land ceases to be accommodated, then the easement probably terminates: *Huckvale* v *Aegean Hotels Ltd* (1989) 58 P&CR 163. However, the Court of Appeal stressed that this is most unlikely: the strict requirements for abandonment (p 549 below) cannot readily be circumvented by such an analysis.

[61] *Todrick* v *Western National Omnibus Co Ltd* [1934] Ch 561; *Pugh* v *Savage* [1970] 2 QB 373.

[62] A more extreme example is *Re Salvin's Indenture* [1938] 2 All ER 498, in which a right to have water pipes on the servient land accommodated a reservoir (as part of the dominant owner's 'undertaking'). Pipes and cables will generally be laid under statutory powers.

[63] The leading case of *Colls* v *Home & Colonial Stores Ltd* [1904] AC 179 provides an example.

[64] *Polo Woods Foundation* v *Shelton-Agar* [2010] 1 All ER 539, especially at [39].

[65] (1879) 12 Ch D 261.

[66] (1863) 2 H&C 121 (159 ER 51).

was held that this was not a right known to the law: the parties were not free to create novel forms of interests. It is difficult to tell exactly why the court thought this right impermissible. It appears that counsel argued that it was a form of profit in gross and the judgments have to be considered against this background. Two factors may be thought to be crucial to its not being an easement. First, the whole point of the right was to set up a boating business rather than to benefit an existing business; to put it another way, the claimed easement was the business. It might be contrasted with a right of a hotel owner to put boats on a canal as part of the hotel business, which is accepted as an easement.[67] The second factor is that the right purported to be exclusive.[68] Whilst a right to put boats on a canal might be an easement, an exclusive right smacks too much of a commercial agreement. It is not so much a right to do something as it is a right to stop others from competing with the dominant land. Apart from being negative in character, this is too purely commercial in nature to be accepted.

Gardens and similar rights

Another controversial case is *Re Ellenborough Park*[69] itself. Building plots had been sold around an open area (the park) with rights to use the park. One question facing the Court of Appeal was whether this sufficiently accommodated the building plots (long since built upon). It was accepted that merely increasing the value of the plots was insufficient: it would be fatal if the right were 'extraneous to, and independent of, the use of a house as a house'.[70] On the facts, the right was recognised: it passed the test that 'the park should constitute in a real and intelligible sense the garden (albeit the communal garden) of the houses to which its enjoyment is annexed'.[71]

The crucial element in the decision might be thought to be that houses normally have gardens. The park was a form of garden substitute.[72] Could the same reasoning apply to the use of a swimming pool, given that houses in England do not normally have swimming pools? This was the issue raised in *Regency Villas Ltd* v *Diamond Resorts (Europe) Ltd*,[73] in which timeshare owners claimed a right to use a swimming pool and other recreational facilities. Judge Purle QC held that such a right was recognised: it was a 'relatively small step' from *Re Ellenborough Park*. Although there was no English authority in point, this was supported by Canadian and Australian cases. Doubts had been expressed by Lord Scott in *Moncrieff* v *Jamieson*,[74] but these were swept aside as being applicable to cases involving normal neighbours – in contrast to the more commercial context of *Regency Villas*. However, it seems unlikely that such an easement would be recognised in that context but not in the domestic context.

---

[67] Cf *P&S Platt Ltd* v *Crouch* [2004] 1 P&CR 242 (use of river moorings).

[68] This was crucial to the action. The claimant complained that somebody else was putting boats on the canal, not that he was prevented from doing so. Exclusive easements may occasionally be recognised: *Simmons* v *Midford* [1969] 2 Ch 415 (use of drains).

[69] [1956] Ch 131. See also *George Wimpey & Co Ltd* v *Sohn* [1967] Ch 487; *Jackson* v *Mulvaney* [2003] 1 WLR 360 (prescriptive or implied right).

[70] [1956] Ch 131 at p 174.

[71] Ibid, at p 175.

[72] But the existence of an adequate garden is no objection: *Riley* v *Penttila* [1974] VR 547.

[73] [2016] 4 WLR 61 (subject to appeal).

[74] [2007] 1 WLR 2620 at [47]. Those doubts concerned there being a positive obligation. *Regency Villas* is considered further in that context: p 518 below.

(iii) *Dominant and servient owner different persons*

It is pretty obvious that a person cannot have an easement over his or her own land. However, it is not fatal that the same person holds the fee simple in both plots. It is common for a tenant to have an easement over the landlord's adjoining land.[75] In order to aid land development, the Law Commission[76] would allow the owners (and occupiers) to be the same if the plots have different registered titles.

(iv) *The right must be capable of being the subject matter of a grant*

This is the most difficult requirement. At first sight, it appears distinctly unhelpful: it simply says in a circular manner that a right can only be an easement if recognised as such. It is widely accepted that the list of easements is not closed. So long as a novel right fits within the requirements currently being discussed, there is no bar to its recognition. This was made clear by the Privy Council in *Att-Gen of Southern Nigeria* v *John Holt & Co (Liverpool) Ltd*[77] when recognising a right of storage. The statement in *Hill* v *Tupper* that parties cannot create new forms of interests must be taken as meaning forms of interests falling outside the requirements for easements.

As one would expect, the right must be capable of clear definition. This may help to explain why rights to a view,[78] to privacy,[79] for water to percolate on to lower ground[80] and to the natural flow of air[81] have never been recognised. In more modern cases, the right to television reception has been doubted,[82] even though a right to create noise is recognised.[83] Counsel in *Re Ellenborough Park*[84] argued that the right to use the communal garden was a form of ius spatiendi, a right to wander over another's land, and that such rights were not proprietary interests. Some such rights might be too uncertain, but the court had no hesitation in holding that, on the facts, the right had been sufficiently defined.

But what of the ius spatiendi argument? It was held that the right to a garden should not be regarded as a ius spatiendi, despite the fact that it involved wandering around the communal garden. To the objection that a right involving 'mere recreation and amusement' could not be an easement,[85] the reply was that the cases did not clearly establish any such rule, and in any event a right to a garden was more than recreation and amusement. A right to a garden was an attribute of a house, having many uses in connection with

---

[75] There are countless cases of easements being implied into leases: *Wright* v *Macadam* [1949] 2 KB 744 is one example.

[76] Law Com No 327, para 4.44.

[77] [1915] AC 599.

[78] *William Aldred's Case* (1610) 9 Co Rep 57b (77 ER 816).

[79] *Browne* v *Flower* [1911] 1 Ch 219.

[80] *Palmer* v *Bowman* [2000] 1 WLR 842, though there is a natural right to the same effect.

[81] *Webb* v *Bird* (1863) 13 CBNS 841 (143 ER 332). There can be a right to air through a defined channel: *Bass* v *Gregory* (1890) 25 QBD 481.

[82] *Hunter* v *Canary Wharf Ltd* [1997] AC 655 at pp 709, 727, stressing how wide liability would be.

[83] *Lawrence* v *Fen Tigers Ltd* [2014] AC 822 at [33]. Despite some practical problems relating to noise levels, prescription is possible: see [35]–[41]. See Dixon [2014] Conv 79.

[84] [1956] Ch 131.

[85] *Mounsey* v *Ismay* (1865) 3 H&C 486 at p 498 (159 ER 621 at p 625).

enjoyment of the house. The court further held that it would be no objection if it did constitute a ius spatiendi.[86]

It is unclear how far this goes. Even though the label of ius spatiendi is no longer an absolute bar, a general right to wander over another's land was regarded as being too uncertain to be accepted. Whilst *Re Ellenborough Park* and *Regency Villas* reject some of the former restrictive rules, it would be unwise to assume that all rights of a recreational nature will be accepted.[87] It seems probable that many would be regarded as being either personal to the parties or uncertain.

Next, we can consider the further principles which operate to limit the range of easements.

(a) No positive obligation on the servient owner

The nature of an easement is that it places no positive obligation on the servient owner.[88] Positive obligations can, of course, be imposed by contract or covenant, but these will not bind purchasers.[89] The rule, together with its limits, is illustrated by *Rance v Elvin*.[90]

The claimant asserted, under an express covenant, a right to a flow of fresh water in pipes leading to his land. The defendant, a purchaser of the servient land, argued that this was a positive obligation which did not bind him. The Court of Appeal accepted that a positive obligation was incompatible with an easement. However, on the face of the covenant, there was no positive obligation. The obligation was not to interfere with the flow of water (under pressure) through the pipes; there was no obligation to provide water. Nevertheless, the defendant had a more subtle argument. He had to pay the water authority for the water supplied, the supply being metered as it entered his land. It followed that the claimant's use of water would involve him in expenditure. The court rejected this argument. The nature of the claim was limited to the passage of water: there was no obligation on the defendant to pay for the water supply, nor to ensure a supply of water. Thus if the supply were cut off because the defendant failed to pay,[91] there would be no breach of any obligations under the easement. What the defendant could not do was to interfere with the supply. To the objection that the defendant would be out of pocket on the water bills, the reply was that the claimant had to pay for his share of water used.

The result is a convenient one, even if it does stretch the rules somewhat.[92] It remains to be seen how far it goes. It had previously been said in *Regis Property Co Ltd v Redman*[93]

---

[86] Rejecting dicta of Farwell J in *International Tea Stores Co v Hobbs* [1903] 2 Ch 165 and *Att-Gen v Antrobus* [1905] 2 Ch 188. However, *Beech v Kennerley* [2012] EWCA Civ 158 held that a right of way that failed (it did not lead anywhere) could not be saved on this basis.

[87] Baker [2012] Conv 37 argues in favour of a limited recognition of recreational easements (alongside the more clearly recognised 'pleasure ground' cases).

[88] Thus, the servient owner has no obligation to repair a right of way (see p 547 below). A recent authority is *William Old International Ltd v Arya* [2009] 2 P&CR 362.

[89] Save where it runs as a covenant in a lease (the lease being the dominant tenement); see *Liverpool CC v Irwin* [1977] AC 239.

[90] (1985) 50 P&CR 9.

[91] This was unlikely, as there was a single supply for both claimant and defendant.

[92] Compare the test for restrictive covenants, where it is fatal if the servient owner has to dip into his own pocket: *Haywood v Brunswick Permanent Benefit BS* (1881) 8 QBD 403 at pp 409, 410.

[93] [1956] 2 QB 612. *Dikstein v Kanevsky* [1947] VLR 216 held that the use of a lift could not be an easement, as it was meaningless without positive obligations such as servicing and repair.

that the supply of hot water for central heating was merely the performance of services, not an easement. Whilst an *obligation* to provide hot water could not be an easement, could there be a right to the supply of such hot water as flows through the pipes? Suppose the dominant owner has a flat in the servient owner's building. If the flat is connected to the servient land's central heating system, then hot water will flow automatically unless steps are taken to cut the flow of water. Presuming that the servient owner will continue to heat his or her own property, can the dominant owner take the benefit of this, paying a share of the costs? *Rance* v *Elvin* was extended to electricity cables in *Duffy* v *Lamb*,[94] and this indicates that higher costs do not bar such an easement. It remains to be seen whether the servient owner's greater control over a heating system would prevent any application of *Rance* v *Elvin* to hot water.

Lord Scott in *Moncrieff* v *Jamieson*[95] considered, obiter, that use of a swimming pool involves too many positive duties to be acceptable. On the other hand, *Regency Villas Ltd* v *Diamond Resorts (Europe) Ltd*[96] has subsequently recognised such an easement (neither case cited *Rance*). The outcome in *Regency Villas* provides some cause for concern. There was no provision for payment by the dominant owner, so the facilities (of which the swimming pool was one part) were obtained for free. The servient owner maintained the facilities for use by the public as a profit-making venture, such that there was no practical choice other than to spend significant sums maintaining the facilities: none of this cost could be charged to the dominant owners.

Fencing

This provides an anomalous exception to the no positive obligation rule. This is an ancient area of law, linked with cattle trespass: very often, an obligation to fence is asserted as a defence to an action for cattle trespass. It was considered in several cases some decades ago. In *Jones* v *Price*,[97] the Court of Appeal recognised the right, even if unsure whether it was properly called an easement. It could in any event be created by prescription. A few years later, *Crow* v *Wood*[98] recognised the right with fewer qualms. It was held to be capable of grant, and Lord Denning MR, at least, described it as an easement albeit in a spurious form.

Although anomalous, this spurious easement can be justified because fences are normally maintained by one of two adjoining landowners. It would be both odd and inefficient if the law were to oblige each of them to maintain a stock-proof fence. It is far more efficient to place the obligation upon the landowner who, on the facts, has accepted it. This is even more the case when (as in several of the cases, including *Crow* v *Wood*) the dominant and servient tenements each adjoin common land or moorland, upon which sheep or cattle are grazed. It would be extraordinary if each person grazing animals were to be under an obligation to fence all the boundaries of the common land in order to avoid cattle trespass liability. It is sensible for the law to enforce a custom or understanding that each farm adjoining the common land should be responsible for fencing its own boundaries.

---

[94] (1997) 75 P&CR 364; the servient owner paid for the electricity and charged the dominant owner.
[95] [2007] 1 WLR 2620 at [47] (obiter).
[96] [2016] 4 WLR 61; p 515 above.
[97] [1965] 2 QB 618 at pp 633, 639. See also *Egerton* v *Harding* [1975] QB 62.
[98] [1971] 1 QB 77.

Nevertheless, the Law Commission has recommended that it should be capable of existing only as a land obligation.[99]

(b) No new negative easements

As has just been seen, virtually all easements are negative in the sense that they impose no obligation upon the servient land. The positive/negative distinction can also be applied in a different sense. In the vast majority of cases, the dominant owner has a right to do either something directly on the servient land or something that affects the servient land[100]: positive easements. Other easements do not involve any positive conduct on the part of the dominant owner, but simply inhibit the servient owner from acting in a certain way. These are negative easements. The best example is the right to light. This easement does not involve the dominant owner doing anything, but rather prevents the servient owner from building so as to block light.

The courts are reluctant to recognise new negative easements.[101] The leading case is *Phipps* v *Pears*.[102] The owner of two adjoining houses pulled one (house 1) down and rebuilt it right up to house 2. The result was that the rebuilt wall next to house 2 was not weatherproof. This did not matter so long as house 2 was there to provide protection against the weather. Later, however, house 2 (now in separate ownership) was pulled down. As a consequence, water penetrated the newly exposed wall of the rebuilt house 1. The Court of Appeal was faced with the question as to whether there could be an easement to be protected against the weather.

The court, noting that the law is very wary of recognising new negative easements, held that no such easement could exist. It was observed that a number of other possible negative rights (rights to air, to a view) were not permitted, although these may also fail as being too uncertain. Underlying the court's approach is the nineteenth-century development of restrictive covenants. In essence, *Phipps* is saying that future development of negative rights should be within the sphere of covenants. A crucial difference between easements and covenants is that covenants cannot be acquired by prescription and will virtually never be implied: in *Phipps*, the claimant relied upon these modes of acquisition.

Other analyses might sometimes be employed to establish liability on facts similar to *Phipps*. Often, the removal of the house will be inconsistent with a right to support and the damage regarded as related to that right.[103] More significantly, developments in torts are such that there may be liability in nuisance or negligence where there is fault, regardless of support rights.[104]

Whether the law's distinction between positive and negative easements is justified may be doubted.[105] It should be noted that the distinction is not easily made. A right to support

---

[99] Law Com No 327, para 5.94.
[100] The latter category will cover a right to do something that would otherwise be a nuisance.
[101] On negative easements, see Dawson and Dunn (1998) 18 LS 510.
[102] [1965] 1 QB 76.
[103] *Bradburn* v *Lindsay* [1983] 2 All ER 408 (dry rot); *Rees* v *Skerrett* [2001] 1 WLR 1541 (wind suction). Further, local authorities may require weatherproofing when demolition is undertaken: Building Act 1984, ss 80–82.
[104] *Rees* v *Skerrett* [2001] 1 WLR 1541 at pp 1551–1555.
[105] See Megarry (1964) 80 LQR 318; also Law Reform Committee (14th Report (1966) Cmnd 3100). However, Law Com No 327 makes no recommendations on this (para 5.99).

looks negative, although the House of Lords has regarded it as positive[106] and *Phipps* viewed it as mixed. A right to have fresh or waste water pass through pipes is not easily seen as positive, especially when the right is to a flow of water to the dominant land, as in *Rance* v *Elvin*.[107] Nevertheless, its status as an easement is beyond doubt.

Finally, it should be added that Oliver J thought it possible that there might be an easement to be protected by premises above the dominant land.[108] This would apply to flats, although the dominant land will usually be leased and the law of leasehold covenants will then apply.

(c) No claim to possession

Another troublesome limit is that any claim to exclusive or joint occupation is inconsistent with an easement. Such claims tend to confuse easements with interests such as leases and the fee simple. One cannot disguise such interests as easements in order to take advantage of their generous modes of acquisition.

A decade ago, the area was considered, obiter, by the House of Lords in *Moncrieff* v *Jamieson*.[109] Lord Scott, in particular, thought that some earlier cases applied far too strict an approach. However, there was no definite ruling and it remains necessary to study the earlier cases. We will return to *Moncrieff* once the earlier cases have been discussed.

The earlier cases

The seminal modern case is *Copeland* v *Greenhalf*,[110] in which a wheelwright claimed a right to store vehicles on an eight-foot-wide part of a strip of land (itself varying in width between 15 and 35 feet). Upjohn J was clear that this claim went beyond any normal conception of easements and was unsupported by authority.[111] If it was to succeed, it had to be as an adverse possession claim to the fee simple. One form of easement must be distinguished. It has been accepted ever since *Att-Gen of Southern Nigeria* v *John Holt & Co (Liverpool) Ltd*[112] that there may be an easement to store goods on the servient land. In *Copeland*, Upjohn J thought the easement to store quite different from the claim before him. A right to store on the servient land is acceptable so long as it does not allocate a specific area to the sole use of the dominant owner. Even so, it is difficult to avoid the impression of joint user that Upjohn J thought objectionable.[113]

Somewhat analogous is a claim to use an area as a garden. If the claimant is doing the gardening (rather than visiting the garden, as in *Re Ellenborough Park*), then it might look as if the owner is excluded. However, such a claim was recognised in *Jackson* v *Mulvaney*.[114] This may be explained because it was not a claim to cultivate a specific area,

---

[106] *Dalton* v *Angus & Co* (1881) 6 App Cas 740 at pp 793, 831 (Lords Selborne, Watson).
[107] Insofar as the positive/negative distinction was taken in Roman law, there was a broader view as to what was negative: Buckland, *Textbook of Roman Law* (3rd edn), pp 262, 267.
[108] *Sedgwick Forbes Bland Payne Group Ltd* v *Regional Properties Ltd* [1981] 1 EGLR 33.
[109] [2007] 1 WLR 2620; Goymour [2008] CLJ 20, Haley [2008] Conv 244.
[110] [1952] Ch 488. The decision was expressly limited to prescription, but it is difficult to understand how the rules for grant could differ. See also *Thomas W Ward Ltd* v *Alexander Bruce (Grays) Ltd* [1959] 2 Ll Rep 472.
[111] This was linked with the claim's being uncertain: Luther (1996) 16 LS 51.
[112] [1915] AC 599 (PC).
[113] Spark [2012] Conv 6 criticises the joint possession point, though easements generally allow a specific use of the land, rather than unlimited joint use.
[114] [2003] 1 WLR 360; Thompson [2002] Conv 571.

but rather a claim to use an area generally as a garden: the servient owner was entitled to put in a gravelled driveway across it.

Despite *Copeland*, it is no objection that the servient owner may be precluded from some uses of the land, or may be temporarily ousted from part of the land whilst an easement is being exercised. To take a straightforward example, the servient owner cannot build on the route of a right of way. Slightly more difficult is an easement to use the servient land for access when maintaining and repairing buildings on the dominant land. Whilst the dominant owner is using ladders and other equipment, the servient owner is effectively ousted from the relevant part of the servient land. However, the nature of the user (short and intermittent) permits it to exist as an easement.[115]

A very different sort of right is the right to use lavatories on the servient land. This was recognised as an easement by the Court of Appeal in *Miller* v *Emcer Products Ltd*.[116] It was regarded as no objection that the servient owner was excluded whilst the right was being exercised, for this is a feature of many easements. The court saw the right to share the use of a kitchen[117] as an analogy. However, such claims may be thought not to sit easily with *Copeland*.[118] Unlike access for maintenance, they are likely to be exercised frequently. Perhaps more importantly, they enable the dominant owner to use the land in the same way as the servient owner. Rather different forms of accepted easements involve projections over the servient land[119] and rights to run pipes or drains under the servient land[120] or an aqueduct over it.

A more difficult case is *Wright* v *Macadam*,[121] in which the Court of Appeal viewed the right to use a coal shed as an easement. Whilst it might appear to be an example of a right to store, the problem is that the servient owner seems to be excluded. The point was not discussed and, unfortunately, the case was not cited in *Copeland*. Several subsequent decisions shed some light on pre-*Moncrieff* judicial attitudes.

In *Grigsby* v *Melville*,[122] the servient land had a cellar underneath it. Access to the cellar was from the adjoining land, originally in common ownership with the servient land. The servient land was sold. It was held that the purchaser owned the cellar,[123] but the vendor, who as adjoining landowner had the sole means of access, claimed an easement to use it. Brightman J followed *Copeland* and rejected this claim, on the basis that it involved the whole beneficial user of the cellar. *Wright* v *Macadam* was distinguished as the facts of that case were not clear. It may have been that the right was limited to part of the coal shed.

The suggestion that it is largely a matter of degree was taken up in *London & Blenheim Estates Ltd* v *Ladbroke Retail Parks Ltd*.[124] Judge Paul Baker QC considered *Copeland*

---

[115] *Ward* v *Kirkland* [1967] Ch 194. In the absence of an easement, the court has power to order access for such purposes: Access to Neighbouring Land Act 1992.

[116] [1956] Ch 304.

[117] *Heywood* v *Mallalieu* (1883) 25 Ch D 357 (not a normal domestic kitchen).

[118] Megarry (1956) 72 LQR 172.

[119] *Suffield* v *Brown* (1864) 4 De GF&S 185 (46 ER 888); *Harris* v *De Pinna* (1886) 33 Ch D 238.

[120] *Goodhart* v *Hyett* (1883) 25 Ch D 182 (water pipes); *Pyer* v *Carter* (1851) 1 H&N 916 (156 ER 1472); *Ward* v *Kirkland* [1967] Ch 194 (drains).

[121] [1949] 2 KB 744.

[122] [1972] 1 WLR 1355 (upheld [1974] 1 WLR 80 on other grounds).

[123] Brightman J observed ([1972] 1 WLR 1355 at p 1360) that a purchaser does not expect the vendor to live mole-like under the lounge.

[124] [1992] 1 WLR 1278 at p 1286; not considered on appeal [1994] 1 WLR 31.

and *Wright* v *Macadam* to be consistent with one another: 'A small coal shed in a large property is one thing. The exclusive use of a large part of the alleged servient tenement is another.' This may be a convenient way of dealing with the cases, although the retreat from principle may raise awkward questions. Is it really the law that the right to use a coal shed is acceptable only so long as it forms part of a large house?[125] Subsequently, the Court of Appeal in *Batchelor* v *Marlow*[126] concentrated on the land over which the right was asserted, rather than the entire area owned by the servient owner. Most importantly, in *Moncrieff*,[127] Lord Scott was dismissive of the *London & Blenheim* analysis.

Parking cars

Rights to park cars have received a good deal of interest; they are somewhat analogous to the right claimed in *Copeland*. Several cases have touched upon this area, but the earlier ones are of low authority and briefly reported. It was accepted by all three English law lords in *Moncrieff* (a Scottish case) that a right to park can be an easement, and this now seems settled. It fits well with the right to store and with cases such as *Miller* v *Emcer Products Ltd*.

The only significant problem today relates to the extent of rights to park. Fifteen years before *Moncrieff*, Judge Baker QC in *London & Blenheim* had accepted the right to park cars on a car park. Not only was the area over which the right was to be exercised clearly defined, but also it did not fall foul of the objection that it left the servient owner 'without any reasonable use of his land, whether for parking or anything else'.[128]

The right to park in *London & Blenheim* was exercisable over what appears to have been a large car park. It also seems that a right to park in common with others (typically, flat occupants) in specified areas can be an easement.[129] Even though the owner may effectively be excluded, this is not by virtue of a right held by any individual claimant. Can an individual's right to park in a specific place (most especially in a normal domestic garage) be an easement? Certainly some such rights could be formulated as a lease or fee simple. This question arose in *Batchelor*, in which there was a claim to park six cars on the verge of a road (which would be exclusive of anybody else seeking to park there). The Court of Appeal had no hesitation in holding that this left the servient owner without any reasonable use for the land. The court was unimpressed that the claim was limited to nine and a half hours a day (daytime), Monday to Friday. This was regarded as leaving the servient owner with no reasonable use. It might be observed that it is unusual to see an analysis which concerns itself with the number of useful hours in a week. The cases normally concentrate on the quality of the user rather than the period involved.

Batchelor appears to mean that a claim to use a normal domestic garage would fail. But it is possible that the servient owner keeps his own property in the garage (garages frequently contain far more than cars, even if space is tight) – this might demonstrate a reasonable (if distinctly limited) use for the garage. Finally, it may be presumed that a right to park

---

[125] Further, what would happen if, in *Wright* v *Macadam*, a large part of the servient land (excluding the land on which the coal shed stood) were to be sold?

[126] [2003] 1 WLR 764, criticised by Hill-Smith [2007] Conv 223. Earlier, see Luther (1996) 16 LS 51.

[127] [2007] 1 WLR 2620 at [57].

[128] [1992] 1 WLR 1278 at p 1288.

[129] *Montrose Court Holdings Ltd* v *Shamash* [2006] EWCA Civ 251.

one car in a double garage would in any event be acceptable because there is no exclusive claim to the garage as a whole: this follows from the principles applicable in easements to store. It may result in a rather uncomfortable distinction between single and double garages.

Moncrieff v Jamieson

As already observed, the discussion of the issue in *Moncrieff*[130] was obiter; it was not fully argued. Nevertheless, Lord Scott considered that the range of easements accepted (including rights of storage, rights to use aqueducts and the coal shed in *Wright v Macadam*) was such as to reject any rule that sole use of land was fatal to an easement. Before problems could arise, there would be a need for the dominant owner to be claiming exclusive possession and control. This would be unusual, as relatively minor uses by the servient owner (such as storing things in a garage) would be consistent with an easement. An example where a claim to an easement would fail would be a claim to use a garage, where the dominant owner was given the only keys to the garage. One great advantage of this approach is that there would be no gap between claims to the fee simple (or a lease) and claims to easements.

In relation to the earlier cases, Lord Scott considered that the statement of principle in *Copeland* was correct, although he was uncertain whether the claim was really one to exclusive possession. However, the 'no reasonable use' test found in *London & Blenheim* and *Batchelor* was rejected; *Batchelor* was thought to be wrongly decided.

Although Lord Neuberger expressed himself to be impressed by Lord Scott's analysis, three factors persuaded him not to express a firm conclusion. First, it will still be necessary to assess the degree of ouster of the servient owner that will defeat the claim. Next, the point was obiter and not fully argued. Finally, he feared that Lord Scott's analysis might lead to occupational licences becoming proprietary. The third English judge, Lord Mance, did not address the question.

Batchelor has been held to remain binding on lower courts.[131] However, it has been applied in a way that reflects the reasoning in *Moncrieff*. Thus, *Kettel v Bloomfold Ltd*[132] recognised a sole right of parking in a designated space. The judge relied upon rights to use the airspace above the surface and the soil beneath, together with rights to cross the land if there were no car there to show that the servient owner retained reasonable use. The outcome looks appropriate, if almost impossible to square with the actual result in *Batchelor*. The Law Commission[133] proposes the abolition of the 'prevents . . . any reasonable use' test. This is designed to permit a generous approach to the recognition of such easements, provided that they do not amount to claims to exclusive possession. This would place more stress on the nature of the right rather than (as Lord Scott thought) the impact on the servient owner.

3. The creation and transfer of easements and profits

Express creation calls for little comment. As easements and profits are interests in land, a deed is required for a legal interest and writing for an equitable interest. Assuming that

---

[130] [2007] 1 WLR 2620.

[131] *Polo Woods Foundation* v *Shelton-Agar* [2010] 1 All ER 539 at [121] (Warren J).

[132] [2012] L&TR 514; *Virdi* v *Chana* [2008] EWHC 2901 (Ch) is very similar.

[133] Law Com No 327, paras 3.188–3.209 (criticised by Xu [2012] Conv 291 as having too wide an impact and being unnecessary after recent cases on parking).

title to the servient land is registered, entry of a notice is required; to be legal, an easement or profit must also be registered on the title to the dominant land (if that title is registered). As for transfer, the main point to note is that easements, like profits appurtenant, pass automatically on the transfer of the dominant land.[134] Furthermore, no problem is caused because the transfer is merely of part of the dominant land.[135]

A. Implied easements[136]

Very many easements are implied rather than express. There is a substantial body of law regarding the circumstances in which an implication will be allowed. One initial point to note is that an implied easement takes effect as a legal easement, provided that it is implied into a deed of conveyance or lease: the easement has the same effect as if it were spelt out in the relevant document. However, we have seen that it is not subject to the registration requirements applicable to express easements.[137]

The context in which implication nearly always takes place is that of a common owner of two or more plots (the grantor) selling or leasing one of them to the grantee.[138] The law draws a crucial distinction between the implied grant of easements in favour of the grantee (purchaser) and the implied reservation of easements in favour of the grantor (vendor). The general rule, established in *Wheeldon* v *Burrows*,[139] is that implied reservation will be recognised only in exceptional cases. It follows that the lion's share of implications take effect in favour of the grantee.

The reason for this is related to the rule that a grantor shall not derogate from his grant. This principle, which operates throughout the law of property, means that the grantor cannot act so as to detract from what has been granted. It reflects the fact that the grantor is generally able to dictate the terms on which land is sold or leased. If the grantor wishes to retain any benefit over the land sold, then it is the grantor's duty to spell this out explicitly.

Contemporaneous sales

If a common owner sells both of two adjoining plots, how do the grant and reservation rules apply? On a strict interpretation of the principles, one might expect that the first purchaser would gain the wider easements permitted under the implied grant rules. The vendor would obtain very restricted easements by implied reservation. The second purchaser would have only these reserved easements: it is then too late to create fresh easements over the plot that has already been sold.

---

[134] *Godwin* v *Schweppes Ltd* [1902] 1 Ch 926 at p 932; Law of Property Act 1925 (hereafter LPA), s 62.

[135] *Laurie* v *Winch* [1952] 4 DLR 449; *Newcomen* v *Coulson* (1877) 5 Ch D 133, pp 141–142, subject to the qualification that there is no excessive user of the easement (discussed below at p 545).

[136] These rules also apply to profits (for implication by LPA, s 62, see *White* v *Williams* [1922] 1 KB 727 and *Anderson* v *Bostock* [1976] Ch 312), although nearly all the cases concern easements. Under the Law Commission proposals in No 327, profits will be capable of being created only by express words: para 3.9.

[137] See p 248 above.

[138] *Collins* v *Collins (No 2)* [2016] 2 P&CR 127 grapples with the implication of easements on a declaration of trust (easement of access allowed over settlor's adjoining land)

[139] (1879) 12 Ch D 31, following *Suffield* v *Brown* (1864) 4 De GJ&S 185 (46 ER 888). Several earlier cases, including *Pyer* v *Carter* (1857) 1 H&N 916 (156 ER 1472), are not good law.

However, contemporaneous sales are treated so that each purchaser obtains rights as against the other under the more generous implied grant rules.[140] This will generally apply when the properties are sold by auction. It does not matter that the conveyances may be executed at different times: it is the time of contract that is crucial.[141] It is not sufficient, however, that the sales are close together. In *Wheeldon v Burrows*[142] itself, the two properties were auctioned together. The alleged dominant tenement was not sold, but a buyer was found for it a month later. The court rejected an argument that the sales were contemporaneous.

(i) *Implied reservation*

Implied reservation is recognised where there is necessity.[143] In such cases, both grantor and grantee may benefit from an implication, but the exceptional nature of reservation means that its operation in favour of the grantor is the most interesting.

The terminology of easement of necessity is ambiguous: there are two very different types of necessity. Strictly, an easement of necessity is an easement without which the dominant land cannot be used. In this form, it is probably limited to a right of way to land which is otherwise landlocked or, in other words, has no access. A wider sense of necessity is that an easement will be implied whenever required to give effect to the intention of the parties as to the use of the land.

Necessity in its narrow sense
It has long been accepted that there should be access to a plot that is left landlocked.[144] This does not mean that every landlocked plot necessarily has a right of access: there must be a transaction into which a right of way may be implied.[145]

The existence of another form of access is fatal to the implication, even if the access is by water[146] or is inconvenient.[147] However, there are some indications of a more generous approach.[148] Where the alternative access is based upon a revocable licence, then this does not prevent an implication of a way of necessity.[149] Nor was it held fatal when access was possible, but only if a building were to be demolished.[150]

---

[140] *Swansborough v Coventry* (1832) 9 Bing 305 (131 ER 629); *Allen v Taylor* (1880) 16 Ch D 355; *White v Taylor (No 2)* [1969] 1 Ch 160. Consideration is not required: the rule applies to devises by will: *Phillips v Lowe* [1892] 1 Ch 47. In Australia, *McGrath v Campbell* (2006) 68 NSWLR 229 requires an intention that the first purchaser should be bound, or else an implied term to that effect.
[141] The order of contracts that is also crucial where the sales are not contemporaneous. If V contracts to sell one plot to A and later another plot to B, but conveys B's plot first, then B cannot acquire rights over A's land: *Beddington v Attlee* (1887) 35 Ch D 317.
[142] (1879) 12 Ch D 31. A 15-day gap was fatal in *Beddington v Attlee* (1887) 35 Ch D 317.
[143] See Jackson (1981) 34 CLP 133.
[144] *Pomfret v Ricroft* (1669) 1 Wms Saund 321 at p 323 (85 ER 454 at pp 460–462); *Pinnington v Galland* (1853) 9 Exch 1 (156 ER 1).
[145] *Wilkes v Greenway* (1890) 6 TLR 449 (adverse possession), seemingly overlooked in *Williams v Usherwood* (1981) 45 P&CR 235. *Williams v Usherwood* is difficult to reconcile with *Nickerson v Barraclough* [1981] Ch 426.
[146] *Manjang v Drammeh* (1990) 61 P&CR 194 (PC).
[147] *Titchmarsh v Royston Water Co Ltd* (1899) 81 LT 673; *MRA Engineering Ltd v Trimster Co Ltd* (1987) 56 P&CR 1, in which Dillon LJ thought reconsideration of the rules desirable.
[148] In *Sweet v Sommer* [2004] EWHC 1504 (Ch) at [30] (left open on appeal: [2005] EWCA Civ 227), Hart J thought vehicular access necessary for a house.
[149] *Barry v Hasseldine* [1952] Ch 835.
[150] *Sweet v Sommer* [2004] 4 All ER 288 (left open on appeal: [2005] EWCA Civ 227).

Nickerson v *Barraclough* considered how necessity operates.[151] The two competing views were, first, that the easement is implied as a result of the presumed intention of the parties, and second, that it is implied because of public policy. After reviewing the cases, the Court of Appeal concluded that the easement is based on the parties' presumed intention. It followed that a clause denying a right of way[152] could not be attacked as being contrary to public policy.

It seems unlikely that anything other than access will be treated as necessity. *Union Lighterage Co* v *London Graving Dock Co*[153] involved a dock, the wooden walls of which were held in place by tie-rods in the servient land. It was held that there was no easement of necessity to prevent removal of the tie-rods. Stirling LJ[154] limited the category to 'an easement without which the property retained cannot be used at all, and not merely necessary to the reasonable enjoyment of that property'. Although some cases have suggested a broader category,[155] any extension beyond rights of way is difficult to support on the current state of the authorities.

What happens if the dominant owner acquires other land providing an alternative access, so that the right of way ceases to be necessary? It was suggested in *Holmes* v *Goring*[156] that the easement of necessity would terminate in these circumstances. This has been criticised[157] and seems difficult to reconcile with the modern basis of presumed intention at the time of the grant.

Necessity in a wider sense

This involves looking at the intended use of the dominant land. If a particular use is both intended and requires some right over the servient land, then the courts are willing to imply such a right. An excellent example is provided by *Wong* v *Beaumont Property Trust Ltd*.[158] A lease of cellars specified that they should be used as a restaurant. As the business prospered, it became apparent that, for continued lawful use of the restaurant, there would need to be a ventilation system with a duct fixed to the landlord's property. The Court of Appeal held that the fixing of the ducting was necessary if the restaurant was to continue. As restaurant use was the only possible user under the lease, there was an easement of necessity to fix the ducting. This can be justified given the specific terms of the lease.

The classic test (rehearsed in *Wong*) had been laid down by Lord Parker in *Pwllbach Colliery Co Ltd* v *Woodman*[159]: 'The law will readily imply the grant or reservation of such easements as may be necessary to give effect to the common intention of the parties to a

---

[151] [1981] Ch 426, cited with approval by the Privy Council in *Manjang* v *Drammeh* (1990) 61 P&CR 194, but criticised by Lawson in *Land Law: Issues, Debates, Policy* (ed Tee), pp 78–81.

[152] Such a clause would rarely be inserted in order to prevent any access at all. It is more likely that, as in *North Sydney Printing Pty Ltd* v *Sabemo Investment Corporation Pty Ltd* [1971] 2 NSWLR 150, the parties erroneously believe that there is an acceptable alternative access.

[153] [1902] 2 Ch 557.

[154] Ibid, at p 573.

[155] See *Williams* v *Usherwood* (1981) 45 P&CR 235, especially at p 254 (access for repair of dominant land); *Walby* v *Walby* [2013] 1 EGLR 111, [2012] EWHC 3089 (Ch) at [32].

[156] (1824) 2 Bing 76 (130 ER 233).

[157] See especially *Proctor* v *Hodgson* (1855) 10 Exch 824 *arguendo* at p 828 (156 ER 674 at p 675) and *Deacon* v *South-Eastern Ry Co* (1889) 61 LT 377.

[158] [1965] 1 QB 173 (implied grant).

[159] [1915] AC 634 at pp 646–647.

grant of real property, with reference to the manner or purposes in and for which the land granted or some land retained by the grantor is to be used.' It is necessary to stress the limits to this principle. As Lord Atkinson stated,[160] it is insufficient that the right claimed is 'what is convenient, or what is usual, or what is common in the district, or what is simply reasonable'; it must be '*necessary* for the use and enjoyment, in the way contemplated by the parties'. It appears that the use need not be certain at the time of the grant, so long as it is then a contemplated use.[161]

This principle had earlier been applied, so as to imply a reservation, in *Lyttleton Times Co Ltd v Warners Ltd*.[162] The parties had agreed that, when the defendant rebuilt its printing house, the claimant would take a lease of the upper floors for its hotel. It was held that the claimant could not complain about the noise from the printing house: the defendant was entitled to use it as contemplated by the agreement.

A recent example in favour of a purchaser is provided by *Donovan v Rana*.[163] A plot having been sold for building a house on, it was held that there was an implied right to connect to mains services (electricity, drains, etc) through the vendor's retained land. Whilst it might have been the case that the land could have been used without this right, it could not have been used in the manner contemplated. This slight relaxation, placing emphasis upon what the parties intended, seems very welcome. Yet *Re Webb's Lease*[164] illustrates the limits to the doctrine, at least as regards reservation. A landlord had advertisements on the outside of the leased premises. Indeed, they had been there throughout the tenants' occupation prior to their current lease. The Court of Appeal had little hesitation in rejecting any reservation of a right to advertise on the walls. It was not enough that the advertisement had existed before the present lease and that the tenant was well aware of it. There was no necessity for the advertisement in order that the landlord's business as a butcher be carried on and there was no proof of a common intention of a right to keep the advertisements. *Re Webb's Lease* shows that even where the grantor openly exercises a right, it may well not survive a sale or lease. Yet, it appears that a more generous approach may occasionally be taken where the reservation is for the benefit of other tenants of the retained land, rather than the grantor personally.[165]

There are a very few circumstances in which an implied reservation is more readily accepted. The clearest example is where there is a reciprocal right as between the two tenements. This is most obvious where two houses each support each other.[166]

---

[160] Ibid, at p 643.

[161] *Stafford v Lee* (1992) 65 P&CR 172 (woodland with contemplated use for housing).

[162] [1907] AC 476 (PC), distinguished in *Pwllbach* because there it was not shown that the conduct complained of (dust from coal screening) was an inevitable consequence of the contemplated mining use. The application of *Pwllbach* to reservations met with a cautious response from Scrutton LJ in *Aldridge v Wright* [1929] 2 KB 115 at pp 155–156.

[163] [2014] 1 P&CR 374. See also *Linvale Investment Ltd v Walker* [2016] 2 P&CR 269 (emergency fire exit).

[164] [1951] Ch 808; see also *Chaffe v Kingsley* (1999) 79 P&CR 404.

[165] *Peckham v Ellison* (1998) 79 P&CR 276 (Fox [1999] Conv 353); on the facts, the grantee expected to be bound by the right. Neuberger J has distinguished it as 'a case turning on its own special facts': *Holaw (470) Ltd v Stockton Estates Ltd* (2000) 81 P&CR 404 at p 429.

[166] *Richards v Rose* (1853) 9 Exch 218 (156 ER 93), approved in *Wheeldon v Burrows*. A right to support might squeeze into the narrower necessity category: *Shubrook v Tufnell* (1882) 46 LT 886.

(ii) *Implied grant*

The purchaser or lessee can, of course, take advantage of the necessity rules. However, there are two more generous bases upon which easements may be implied: the rule in *Wheeldon* v *Burrows* and LPA, s 62 (the 'general words'). The Court of Appeal in *Kent* v *Kavanagh*[167] explained that *Wheeldon* applies where the same person occupies both plots prior to the sale or lease, whereas s 62 applies if there is diversity of occupation. This neat explanation of the principles is by no means straightforward and will be further discussed below.

(a) The rule in *Wheeldon v Burrows*

Certain continuous and apparent easements will be implied in favour of the grantee (but not the grantor). The rule in *Wheeldon* v *Burrows*[168] was formulated by Thesiger LJ:

> on the grant by the owner of a tenement of part of that tenement as it is then used and enjoyed, there will pass to the grantee all those continuous and apparent easements (by which, of course, I mean quasi easements), or, in other words, all those easements which are necessary to the reasonable enjoyment of the property granted, and which have been and are at the time of the grant used by the owners of the entirety for the benefit of the part granted.

It will be seen that the crucial elements are that the easement is continuous and apparent and that it is necessary for reasonable enjoyment. The term 'quasi easements' is used to signify a right which is of the nature of an easement. Before the grant, it cannot be an actual easement because the grantor owns both tenements.

Continuous and apparent

Several forms of easement easily fulfil the continuous and apparent requirement. Clear examples are rights to light,[169] rights to run drains through the servient land[170] and rights to support.[171] Rather more surprisingly, rights of way over made-up roads or tracks[172] have long been held to satisfy the test.[173] Maugham J in *Borman* v *Griffith*[174] stated that an easement will be implied 'where a plainly visible road exists over the one [property] for the apparent use of the other, and that road is necessary for the reasonable enjoyment of the property'. Maugham J recognised that, although such a right is apparent, its use is scarcely continuous. Although it remains essential to show use of the access,[175] Lewison LJ has recently observed[176] that the word continuous is 'all but superfluous'.

---

[167] [2007] Ch 1.
[168] (1879) 12 Ch D 31 at p 49.
[169] *Swansborough* v *Coventry* (1832) 9 Bing 305 (131 ER 629). *Wheeldon* v *Burrows* itself involved an unsuccessful claim to a right to light by implied reservation.
[170] *Pyer* v *Carter* (1851) 1 H&N 916 (156 ER 1472). It is no objection that they are not immediately visible: *Schwann* v *Cotton* [1916] 2 Ch 120 (upheld at p 459).
[171] *Scouton & Co (Builders) Ltd* v *Gilyott & Scott Ltd* (1971) 221 EG 1499.
[172] Any form of track will suffice, so long as it indicates access to the dominant tenement: *Hansford* v *Jago* [1921] 1 Ch 322.
[173] Earlier cases include *Bayley* v *Great Western Ry Co* (1884) 26 Ch D 434 and *Brown* v *Alabaster* (1887) 37 Ch D 490. The existence of a road is not enough. It must lead to the dominant land so as to indicate use for that purpose: *Titchmarsh* v *Royston Water Co Ltd* (1899) 81 LT 673.
[174] [1930] 1 Ch 493 at p 499.
[175] *Linvale Investment Ltd* v *Walker* [2016] 2 P&CR 269.
[176] *Wood* v *Waddington* [2015] 2 P&CR 195 at [15].

This application of the continuous and apparent test was discussed by the Court of Appeal in *Wood* v *Waddington*.[177] It is generously developed in two ways. First, there need not be a made-up road – it suffices that it is apparent that there is access over the land. Next, it is not necessary for it to be apparent that the enjoyment is for the benefit of the dominant land[178] – it is enough that the use is continuous and apparent. This might be thought to be unduly generous.[179]

In *Ward* v *Kirkland*,[180] the grantee claimed a right to enter the servient land to enable access to his buildings for maintenance. Ungoed-Thomas J required[181] 'a feature which would be seen on inspection and which is neither transitory nor intermittent'. The right failed this test: it would only be seen whilst being exercised, and it was insufficient that a person looking at the land would realise that there would need to be entry for the buildings to be maintained.[182] Similarly, a right to have occasional projections into the airspace of the servient tenement fails the test.[183]

The upshot of this appears to be that a right will be continuous and apparent if either (1) it is of a continuous and obvious nature, as with a right to light; or (2) although used intermittently, there is some feature on the servient land which indicates that there is a right, as with a right of way over a road.

Necessity for reasonable enjoyment

The element of necessity is much weaker than in easements of necessity.[184] The way in which it is interpreted is illustrated by a number of cases involving a secondary access to the dominant land. Such access could never, of course, be a strict way of necessity.

Borman v *Griffith*[185] is one such case. There was a right of way to the rear of the dominant tenement, but the lessee used a drive passing the front of it. Not only was his front door inaccessible save from this drive, but it was the only practicable access for heavy vehicles involved in his business use. These circumstances sufficed to satisfy *Wheeldon* v *Burrows*. Another straightforward example is provided by terraced houses which have a right of access to their front and a secondary access to their rear gardens from a track running across the bottoms of the gardens. If the only other access to the rear gardens is through the houses, the courts have been very ready to hold the test of necessity satisfied for a right of way over the track at the rear.[186]

However, it is not sufficient that an alternative access is simply more convenient.[187] In *Goldberg* v *Edwards*,[188] access to an annex to a house was reached by a right of way along

---

[177] [2015] 2 P&CR 195; see p 535 below.
[178] Ibid, [30]–[35].
[179] Especially when (as in *Wood* v *Waddington*) the test is being applied in the s 62 context, where the right must be enjoyed with the land.
[180] [1967] Ch 194.
[181] Ibid, at p 225.
[182] The claim nevertheless succeeded under the implied general words.
[183] *Suffield* v *Brown* (1864) 4 De GJ&S 185 (46 ER 888): ships' bowsprits projecting from the dominant land's dock.
[184] *Union Lighterage Co* v *London Graving Dock Co* [1902] 2 Ch 557 (Stirling LJ).
[185] [1930] 1 Ch 493.
[186] *Brown* v *Alabaster* (1887) 37 Ch D 490; *Hansford* v *Jago* [1921] 1 Ch 322.
[187] The test of 'convenient and comfortable enjoyment', approved in *Schwann* v *Cotton* [1916] 2 Ch 459 at p 469, must now be regarded as too generous.
[188] [1950] Ch 247; the right was held to have been created under the general words. See also *Wheeler* v *JJ Saunders Ltd* [1996] Ch 19.

an outside passage. The lessee of the annex claimed to continue a practice of obtaining access through the house. The Court of Appeal held there was no necessity for access through the house, as shown by the fact that earlier tenants had used only the outside passage. A more difficult case is *Horn* v *Hiscock*.[189] The dominant land (a farm) had a right of way, but one that was difficult for heavy vehicles and in adverse weather. Goulding J expressed uncertainty as to whether an alternative access could be said to be necessary for the reasonable enjoyment.

Must the easement be both continuous and apparent *and* necessary for reasonable enjoyment?

This question has caused much difficulty. Do both tests have to be satisfied, or are they alternatives? *Wheeldon* v *Burrows* itself is ambiguous, especially with the statement 'in other words'. Later cases may be cited to support either view and the issue has never been satisfactorily resolved. Assessment of these cases is rendered awkward because the presence of any difficulty is rarely alluded to.[190] Whenever judges show awareness of there being a problem, they are frequently wise enough to say relatively little.[191]

The history of the tests renders it easier to understand the problem, although not necessarily to solve it. The test of necessity for reasonable enjoyment derives from the old idea that a grantor shall not derogate from his grant. The continuous and apparent test was imported from the French law.[192] What *Wheeldon* v *Burrows* achieved was a formulation that incorporated both tests. No wonder then that there are problems in sorting out the resulting mess.

The question was discussed by Ungoed-Thomas J in *Ward* v *Kirkland*,[193] together with the suggestion that the necessity test was referable to negative easements. The one clear conclusion was that positive easements (such as the claim to access for maintenance) must always satisfy the continuous and apparent test. Overall, the cases do seem to support the view that both tests must be satisfied; otherwise, it would be unnecessary to discuss both tests where one is satisfied.[194] Even so, there are cases that apply *Wheeldon* v *Burrows* with mention of only one of the tests.[195]

Perhaps the answer may be found by reference to the modern basis for the rule. The predominant view is that it is based upon the principle of non-derogation from grant.[196] This being so, it may be wrong to treat the tests in *Wheeldon* v *Burrows* as if they constituted a statutory formulation. Rather, they are guidelines as to when denial of an easement

---

[189] (1972) 223 EG 1437. See also *Costagliola* v *English* (1969) 210 EG 1425.

[190] For this reason, it is difficult to agree with Harpum [1977] Conv 415 that dicta of Lords Wilberforce and Edmund-Davies in *Sovmots Investments Ltd* v *SSE* [1979] AC 144 decide that the tests are cumulative.

[191] E.g. Oliver LJ in *Squarey* v *Harris-Smith* (1981) 42 P&CR 118.

[192] See Simpson (1967) 83 LQR 240. Gale, *Easements*, was largely responsible for this. It is interesting that Gale (5th edn, 1876, pp 97–104) relies on the operation of continuous and apparent easements *in favour of grantors* to contrast them with non-derogation from grant. Since *Wheeldon* v *Burrows*, of course, it has been clear that continuous and apparent easements operate only in favour of grantees.

[193] [1967] Ch 194.

[194] See, e.g., *Wheeler* v *JJ Saunders Ltd* [1996] Ch 19 (especially Peter Gibson LJ); *Millman* v *Ellis* (1995) 71 P&CR 158. *Wood* v *Waddington* [2015] 2 P&CR 195 at [36] is recent supporting authority.

[195] See, e.g., Fox LJ in *Simmons* v *Dobson* [1991] 1 WLR 720 at p 722, not mentioning necessity.

[196] Lords Wilberforce and Edmund-Davies in *Sovmots Investments Ltd* v *SSE* [1979] AC 144 at pp 168, 175.

will derogate from grant. It is difficult to see why a frivolous right should be implied, however continuous and apparent it may be. On the other hand, it may be proper to imply a right that is reasonably necessary even if it is not strictly continuous and apparent,[197] the more so as the necessity becomes more pressing. Of course, the greater the necessity, the more likely it is to fit within the necessity test in *Pwllbach Colliery Co Ltd* v *Woodman*.[198]

Time of exercise; contrary intention

The requirement that the right be exercised at the time of the grant need not be taken literally. If the right has been exercised in the recent past, so that it may be expected to continue after the grant, that is sufficient. Thus, it has been held immaterial that the right was not exercised during a 10-month gap between the owner's leaving the premises and subsequently selling them.[199]

As one might expect, the rule in *Wheeldon* v *Burrows* yields to a contrary intention. A contrary intention need not be in the conveyance itself. In *Squarey* v *Harris-Smith*,[200] the contract contained a standard form term which would exclude a claimed right of way. The conveyance was silent as to any right. Could the right of way be implied into the conveyance? The Court of Appeal held that the effect of the contract was to show that the right was not intended to pass, despite the fact that it was a standard term to which neither party had given any thought. Accordingly, no easement was implied. *Millman* v *Ellis*[201] shows that the presence of an express right of way need not preclude the implication of a wider right under *Wheeldon* v *Burrows*. On the facts, the right of way was extended to an area of land required (and previously used) for safe access to the highway.

(b) Implication under the general words (Law of Property Act 1925, s 62)[202]

Conveyancers have long inserted words into conveyances, describing what rights pass to the purchaser (or lessee). Today, s 62 implies such words (the general words) into conveyances and leases. Section 62(1) provides:

> A conveyance of land shall be deemed to include and shall by virtue of this Act operate to convey, with the land, all . . . ways, waters, watercourses, liberties, privileges, easements, rights, and advantages whatsoever, appertaining or reputed to appertain to the land, or any part thereof, or, at the time of conveyance, demised, occupied, or enjoyed with . . . the land . . .

It is obvious that these words suffice to pass existing easements exercised by the grantor over another person's land, although they would pass anyway.[203] However, their real

---

[197] Admittedly, this is difficult to square with *Ward* v *Kirkland* [1967] Ch 194 and the modern thinking (*Wood* v *Waddington*) that s 62 leaves *Wheeldon* with no useful role. Taylor (2012) 38(2) Monash ULR 128 is critical of any role for continuous and apparent.

[198] [1915] AC 634.

[199] *Costagliola* v *English* (1969) 210 EG 1425; *Wood* v *Waddington* [2015] 2 P&CR 195 (use once a month sufficient). However, a two-year gap (when the dominant land was unused) was fatal in *Linvale Investment Ltd* v *Walker* [2016] 2 P&CR 269.

[200] (1981) 42 P&CR 118.

[201] (1995) 71 P&CR 158.

[202] See Jackson (1966) 30 Conv 340. Section 62 re-enacts Conveyancing Act 1881, s 6(1). 'Conveyance' is defined by LPA, s 205(1)(ii) so as to include leases. This applies despite the absence of a deed (*Wright* v *Macadam* [1949] 2 KB 744) but does not extend to oral leases (*Rye* v *Rye* [1962] AC 496).

[203] *Godwin* v *Schweppes Ltd* [1902] 1 Ch 926 at p 932.

significance lies in their ability to create new easements on the conveyance of one of two plots. If a right (generally in the form of a licence) has earlier been exercised by the occupier of the plot conveyed, it will blossom into a full easement on conveyance.

This application of s 62 has been accepted ever since it was first clearly articulated by Farwell J in *International Tea Stores Co* v *Hobbs*.[204] The facts illustrate the operation of the section. Whilst the claimant was tenant of the defendant's house, he was allowed access over the defendant's adjoining yard to reach the back door. After the claimant bought the freehold to the house, it was held that the permission to cross the yard had been turned into an easement: the original revocable permission had become permanent on the conveyance. This may be seen as a warning to grantors not to be generous to occupiers: any subsequent sale or renewal of a lease[205] will convert licences into proprietary rights. Indeed, some situations can be more remarkable still. Tenants are frequently let into possession before leases are granted. Any permission given in the intervening period may become an easement.[206]

Comparisons with the rule in *Wheeldon* v *Burrows* will be made later, but it is worth stressing that s 62 does not require that the easement be continuous and apparent, nor any element of necessity. The single restriction is that there must normally be diversity of occupation prior to the conveyance. It follows that the operation of s 62 is remarkably wide. Not surprisingly, this has led to doubts about the state of the law[207] and attempts to limit it.

An unsurprising requirement is that the right must be capable of being an easement or profit.[208] This means that we must look at the nature of the user. If it depends on permission by the servient owner on each occasion, then the right does not fit within the category of easements. It was on this ground that the claim failed in *Green* v *Ashco Horticulturist Ltd*.[209] The claimed right of access was through wooden doors. Whenever the lessee of the dominant land wanted to gain access, the servient owner would allow the doors to be opened, provided it was not inconvenient. Cross J held that this continued control over access was incompatible with an easement: the facts did not indicate that an easement existed.

Restricting the permission

The best example is provided by *Goldberg* v *Edwards*.[210] The dominant land was an annex to the defendant's house; secondary access through the house was claimed. This access had been used by the claimant before the execution of the lease to him. The Court of Appeal found that the claimant had been allowed unrestricted personal access for the

---

[204] [1903] 2 Ch 165, supported by earlier cases such as *Kay* v *Oxley* (1875) LR 10 QB 360 and *Barkshire* v *Grubb* (1881) 18 Ch D 616.

[205] *Wright* v *Macadam* [1949] 2 KB 744. Section 62 similarly applies if the initial lease permits the use, but it is not mentioned in the later sale or renewal: *Wall* v *Collins* [2007] Ch 390 at [27].

[206] *Goldberg* v *Edwards* [1950] Ch 247; *Baron Hamilton* v *Edgar* (1953) 162 EG 568; *Lyme Valley Squash Club Ltd* v *Newcastle under Lyme BC* [1985] 2 All ER 405 (purchaser let into possession before conveyance).

[207] *Wright* v *Macadam* [1949] 2 KB 744 (Tucker LJ); *Green* v *Ashco Horticulturist Ltd* [1966] 1 WLR 889 (Cross J); *Hair* v *Gillman* (2000) 80 P&CR 108 (Chadwick LJ).

[208] *Le Strange* v *Pettefar* (1939) 161 LT 300; *Phipps* v *Pears* [1965] 1 QB 76.

[209] [1966] 1 WLR 889.

[210] [1950] Ch 247; the use of the house for business purposes makes the facts seem less odd.

length of the lease and that this fell within s 62. However, permission for the claimant's customers to use the access was only for as long as the landlord retained possession of the house. Now that the landlord had leased the house, the temporary permission had ended, and counsel conceded that s 62 could not assist the claimant.

In this last respect, *Goldberg* is similar to *Birmingham, Dudley & District Banking Co v Ross*.[211] In that case, a lessee claimed a right to light in respect of a building. Because it was known that the lessor planned to build on the other side of a 20-foot passage, the Court of Appeal held that it was not intended that the building should continue to enjoy the light it currently received; this rendered s 62 inapplicable. *Goldberg* v *Edwards* viewed this as a temporary right to light, similar to the customers' use of the access.[212]

The problem with this analysis is that it places considerable stress on the nature of the permission. It is not easy to reconcile with the decision in *International Tea Stores* that a revocable permission falls within s 62, nor to reconcile with the wording of the section which refers to the actual enjoyment.[213] It is odd that s 62 may apply if I have allowed somebody to use an access, knowing that I may at any time withdraw that permission, but not if I say that the access may be used for six months and the position reviewed after that time.

More understandable is the comment in *Goldberg* v *Edwards* that a right personal to a particular person may not fall within s 62. If I lease an annex to an aunt and allow her to have a secondary access through my house, it seems plain that the right of access is a personal right for the aunt and not 'enjoyed with . . . the land'. The section has no application on sale of the annex to a stranger.

Section 62(4) allows for a contrary intention to be effective. Could these temporary licences be seen as examples of contrary intention? The problem is that s 62(4) requires it to be 'expressed in the conveyance'. This has been interpreted to require some explicit provision in the conveyance: a prior understanding of the parties will not suffice.[214] In this respect again, s 62 is more powerful than the rule in *Wheeldon* v *Burrows*.[215]

Other points

Some of the principles applicable to the rule in *Wheeldon* v *Burrows* apply also to s 62. Very obviously (but often forgotten), no right can be implied over land that the grantor does not own or has previously sold.[216] However, in the case of contemporaneous sales, each purchaser can take advantage of s 62.[217]

---

[211] (1888) 38 Ch D 295. Other cases have been more reluctant to limit the grantee's rights: *Broomfield* v *Williams* [1897] 1 Ch 602.

[212] [1950] Ch 247 at p 256. See also *Bartlett* v *Tottenham* [1932] 1 Ch 114; *Wright* v *Macadam* [1949] 2 KB 744. The *Goldberg* analysis was approved in *Hair* v *Gillman* (2000) 80 P&CR 108; also *P&S Platt Ltd* v *Crouch* [2004] 1 P&CR 242.

[213] Tee [1998] Conv 115 at p 116 regards these distinctions as 'incoherent' and criticises the effect of s 62.

[214] *Gregg* v *Richards* [1926] Ch 521; *Clark* v *Barnes* [1929] 2 Ch 368; *Green* v *Ashco Horticulturist Ltd* [1966] 1 WLR 889. See also *Wood* v *Waddington* [2015] 2 P&CR 195 at [60]–[68].

[215] For the effect of contract terms inconsistent with the easement, contrast *Lyme Valley Squash Club Ltd* v *Newcastle under Lyme BC* [1985] 2 All ER 405 (s 62) with *Squarey* v *Harris-Smith* (1981) 42 P&CR 118 (*Wheeldon* v *Burrows*).

[216] *Beddington* v *Attlee* (1887) 35 Ch D 317; *MRA Engineering Ltd* v *Trimster Co Ltd* (1987) 56 P&CR 1. See also s 62(5).

[217] *White* v *Taylor (No 2)* [1969] 1 Ch 160. This is despite the fact that, as will be seen, s 62 (unlike *Wheeldon* v *Burrows*) does not apply to contracts. Yet, it is the order of contracts (or the fact that they are contemporaneous) that determines whether the sales are contemporaneous.

As with *Wheeldon*, the right need not be enjoyed right up to the time of the conveyance. *Green* v *Ashco Horticulturist Ltd*[218] provides a good example. A right of access by van was not used at the time of a lease because the grantee had sold the van. Cross J was clear that this temporary interruption of user did not matter. On the other hand, user which stops because permission has been withdrawn will not fall within s 62.[219]

(c) Contracts for the sale of land

So far, we have been considering conveyances of land. Suppose, however, that V contracts to sell land to P. If the contract is silent, what easements can V and P insist on inserting into their conveyance?

Section 62 applies only to conveyances and therefore does not apply to contracts.[220] Nor can the contract be construed as entitling the purchaser to the rights normally implied into conveyances.[221] This provides a trap for purchasers, as it means that the vendor can insist upon excluding s 62 from the conveyance if the contract is silent.[222]

Wheeldon v *Burrows* is less restricted in this respect. Although its origin may lie in the doctrine of non-derogation from grant, the courts have been prepared to imply identical rights into a contract. A revealing example is provided by *Borman* v *Griffith*,[223] in which Maugham J applied *Wheeldon* to a contract after holding s 62 inapplicable.

Can a conveyance be rectified if it implies rights greater than those provided for by the contract (or intended by the parties at the time of contract)? In *Clark* v *Barnes*,[224] the buyer sought to include a right of way in the contract. This was opposed by the seller, and no right of way was included in either contract or conveyance. Nevertheless, the buyer argued that s 62 caused the right of way to be implied into the conveyance, an argument accepted by Luxmoore J. The buyer's victory was evanescent. The judge proceeded to hold that the conveyance should be rectified as the seller was entitled only to a conveyance without the right of way.

The problem lies in knowing how far this goes. On the facts in *Clark* v *Barnes*, it was clear that the parties positively intended that there should be no right of way. Suppose s 62 operates to create easements when, as is normal, the contract confers no rights to easements. Could rectification be relied upon by the grantor so as to reconcile the conveyance with the contract? The answer seems clearly in the negative: it is difficult to say that there has been a mistake if the parties have given no thought as to whether a particular right is covered by the contract.[225] In any event, rectification is a discretionary remedy and will not be awarded if a third party (such as a mortgagee) has taken an interest in the property whilst unaware of the mistake.[226]

---

[218] [1966] 1 WLR 889, somewhat generously applied in *Pretoria Warehousing Co Ltd* v *Shelton* [1993] EGCS 120.

[219] *Le Strange* v *Pettefar* (1939) 161 LT 300. Section 62 might still apply if the grantee (not being the occupier whose user had ceased) was unaware of the withdrawal.

[220] *Borman* v *Griffith* [1930] 1 Ch 493.

[221] Forbes J at first instance in *Sovmots Investments Ltd* v *SSE* [1977] QB 411 at pp 440–442 (this appears not to have been appealed from: Browne LJ at pp 476–477).

[222] *Re Peck & The School Board for London* [1893] 2 Ch 315.

[223] [1930] 1 Ch 493; the facts were summarised at p 529 above.

[224] [1929] 2 Ch 368.

[225] Nor can rectification be based upon a contractual term excluding the right, when the term was a standard term not discussed by the parties and they could be taken to have intended that the right should exist: *Lyme Valley Squash Club Ltd* v *Newcastle under Lyme BC* [1985] 2 All ER 405.

[226] *Lyme Valley Squash Club Ltd* v *Newcastle under Lyme BC* [1985] 2 All ER 405.

A converse problem arises where the contract includes greater rights than are expressed or implied into a conveyance. This arose in *Holaw (470) Ltd* v *Stockton Estates Ltd*,[227] in which Neuberger J distinguished between terms which give a right to reserve an easement in the conveyance and those which state that the transfer shall include the reservation. In the first case, the vendor has to exercise the right and has no claim otherwise, but the latter (more common today) will give a right to rectify if the right is overlooked in the drafting of the transfer.

(d) The role of s 62 and the rule in *Wheeldon* v *Burrows*

Limits on s 62

Section 62 was thought to apply only when there had been prior diversity of occupation of servient and dominant tenements: it would not apply where the grantor has been in ownership and occupation of both tenements. The typical s 62 case is therefore one in which the dominant land has been occupied by a tenant, although the conveyance may be to the tenant or somebody else. If this limitation did not exist, then there would be a danger that all sorts of activities by the grantor might be turned into easements. Take the example of an owner of a house and an orchard who sells the orchard. It would be odd indeed if the seller found himself liable to allow the purchaser to use a lavatory in the house, merely because the seller had done so when tending the orchard.

This limit was first clearly formulated by Sargant J in *Long* v *Gowlett*.[228] It is not obvious from the wording of s 62, although perhaps a right is not 'enjoyed with . . . the land' when it is being exercised by a common occupier. Despite some criticism of the rule,[229] it had the approval of the House of Lords in *Sovmots Investments Ltd* v *SSE*.[230]

Nevertheless, it now appears that s 62 will apply to continuous and apparent easements, even without diversity. Though *Sovmots* and, more recently, *Kent* v *Kavanagh*[231] did not recognise this application of the section, it is supported by dicta in *Long* v *Gowlett*[232] and several fairly recent Court of Appeal decisions.[233] However, none of these cases had regard to the rival authorities and reasoning. The recent decision in *Wood* v *Waddington*,[234] however, did contain a full investigation of the principles and authorities. The Court of Appeal had little hesitation in concluding that continuous and apparent easements do fall within s 62, even without diversity. Of course, diversity remains essential for rights that are not continuous and apparent.

This means that s 62 has a wider application that many had thought – providing more ammunition for its critics. Unlike *Wheeldon*, there is no requirement of reasonable necessity. Indeed, *Wood* v *Waddington* recognises that it will be very rare for a claimant to need to rely upon *Wheeldon*. It has also been argued that *all* s 62 easements should be

---

[227] (2000) 81 P&CR 404 at pp 413–414, 416–417.
[228] [1923] 2 Ch 177.
[229] See especially Jackson (1966) 30 Conv 340.
[230] [1979] AC 144; criticised by P Smith (1978) 42 Conv 449, but welcomed by Harpum (1977) 41 Conv 415, (1979) 43 Conv 113.
[231] [2007] Ch 1 at [46].
[232] Among other earlier cases, see e.g. *Watts* v *Kelsen* (1871) LR 6 Ch App 166.
[233] *P&S Platt Ltd* v *Crouch* [2004] 1 P&CR 242 at [42], [59]; *Alford* v *Hannaford* [2011] EWCA Civ 1099 at [36]. It also has the support of Law Com CP 186, para 4.75.
[234] [2015] 2 P&CR 195. See Gardner (2016) 132 LQR 192 and Lees [2015] Conv 423. *Broomfield* v *Williams* [1897] 1 Ch 602 shows that the right to light was never subject to the diversity requirement.

continuous and apparent,[235] but this seems contrary to the cases.[236] What is more probable is that, in order to satisfy the 'enjoyed with . . . the land' test, the right should be obvious to the purchaser or lessee.[237]

Limits on *Wheeldon v Burrows*

Kent v *Kavanagh*[238] held that *Wheeldon* does not apply if there is diversity of occupation: in the language of Thesiger LJ, the use has to be by the common owner. This is unlikely to prejudice purchasers, as s 62 is (where diversity is proved) much the wider in its application.

However, three factors signal the need for caution. The first is that *Wheeldon* is a common law principle, predating s 62. It would have been strange for it not to apply in cases of diversity, as these situations are ones in which it is more natural for a purchaser to infer that there is an easement. Secondly, several cases have discussed both *Wheeldon* and s 62, assuming that both might apply if there is diversity. Finally, how does *Kent* apply to contracts? Section 62 does not apply to contracts. Accordingly, it appears that no rights can be implied into contracts where there is diversity: that conclusion seems perverse.

The principles compared

Following *Wood* v *Waddington*, it is difficult to see any role for *Wheeldon* and, most specifically, the necessary for reasonable enjoyment test. The sole relevance of *Wheeldon* lies in implying easements into contracts.

(iii) *Reform*

The Law Commission proposes very extensive reform of the implication rules. The present law draws a very significant distinction between implied reservation and implied grant. The Law Commission considers this as difficult to justify. Particular problems are faced by successors in title to two plots sold by a single owner in the distant past, where rights will vary according to which was sold first.[239]

More generally, the entire law of implied easements is thought to be in need of reform. The effect of LPA, s 62 in transforming licences into easements is criticised,[240] and its role in creating easements will survive only as regards easements (not licences) already exercised by tenants on purchasing the freehold. The formulation in *Wheeldon* v *Burrows* would also disappear[241]: all implications should be based upon necessity for reasonable enjoyment (which, of course, encompasses part of *Wheeldon*). Relevant factors will include the present and intended use of the land and relevant physical features on the servient land (analogous to the continuous and apparent test).

---

[235] Harpum (1977) 41 Conv 415.
[236] See, e.g., *Gregg* v *Richards* [1926] Ch 521.
[237] *Ward* v *Kirkland* [1967] Ch 194, stressing that this is not the same as continuous and apparent. The nineteenth-century cases often mixed up the tests for the general words and *Wheeldon* v *Burrows*; *Watts* v *Kelsen* (1871) LR 6 Ch App 166 is one example.
[238] [2007] Ch 1 at [45].
[239] Law Com CP 186, para 4.53; Law Com No 327, paras 3.28–3.30.
[240] See also Tee [1998] Conv 115 and Gardner (2016) 132 LQR 192. Contrast Lees [2015] Conv 423 and (to a more limited extent) Douglas [2015] Conv 13.
[241] Law Com No 327, paras 3.41–3.51 (for s 62, see paras 3.59–3.69). Douglas (2015) 131 LQR 251 is unpersuaded by the need for reform (leaving aside s 62), arguing that the present law is simply based upon intention.

B. Prescription

Many easements and profits are acquired by long use. This bears some similarity to adverse possession of the fee simple for 12 years. However, the law as to prescription is highly technical, artificial and out of date.[242] The essence of the argument in favour of prescription is that, as with adverse possession, the law should give protection to a situation that has been continued for a long time. As with implied grant, the point can be made that easements often enable the most effective use of the benefited land and should be encouraged. In addition, the dominant owner may have relied upon the 'right' in some way, though estoppel may be the preferable way to recognise this. Finally, the effect of prescription may occasionally confirm a claim where there really has been a grant of an easement, but it has been lost.

On the other hand, prescription often arises from neighbourly conduct in not objecting to the claimant's actions. Unlike adverse possession, easements do not involve conduct fundamentally inconsistent with the owner's rights. Prescription therefore penalises and discourages neighbourly conduct. Nevertheless, the Law Commission advocates the retention of prescription, although criticising many of the present rules.[243] They propose a single basis for prescription: 20 years' use.[244]

(i) *Forms of prescription*

Today, there are three methods of prescription. They are all based on the idea that, after a certain time, use of land should be presumed to have a lawful origin.[245] To this end, the courts will assume that a grant of the right was in fact made. This, it must be stressed, is almost always pure invention and fiction; everybody is well aware that in fact no such grant ever existed.

(a) Common law prescription

The theory underlying common law prescription is that there was a grant before 1189, the origin of legal memory.[246] It is not necessary to prove use stretching back to 1189 (invariably impossible). Instead, proof of use for 20 years is sufficient. The major problem is that any evidence that the right could not have existed in 1189 is fatal. In particular, a right connected to buildings constructed since 1189 will fail,[247] and proof of common ownership of the dominant and servient land at any time after 1189 is fatal.[248]

(b) Lost modern grant

In order to remedy this problem, the courts began to presume from 20 years' use that a grant had been made and had been lost. It was, of course, pure fiction. Even proof that

---

[242] For one quite recent analysis, see Burns [2007] Conv 133.

[243] Law Com No 327, paras 3.80, 3.110. After some doubts, Law Com No 356 recommends the retention of prescription for rights to light. See also Bridge in *Modern Studies in Property Law*, Vol 3 (ed Cooke), Chapter 1; Bogusz [2013] Conv 198.

[244] Unlike the Prescription Act 1832, this need not be immediately before the action.

[245] Goymour in *Modern Studies in Property Law*, Vol 4 (ed Cooke), Chapter 8, observes how this masks the policy considerations in recognising easements (and other rights).

[246] Co Litt 114b.

[247] *Duke of Norfolk v Arbuthnot* (1880) 5 CPD 390.

[248] *Tehidy Minerals Ltd v Norman* [1971] 2 QB 528 at p 544.

there had not been a grant was immaterial.[249] This fiction was powerful, but it was still subject to limitations. It would not operate if the owner of the servient land was legally incapable of granting an easement.[250]

As will be seen, the Prescription Act 1832 cured some of the problems of common law prescription. Nevertheless, the legislation contains some distinct traps, and this means that lost modern grant still has a role to play. Cases over the last 50 years have increasingly relied upon lost modern grant and have been untroubled by its fictitious nature.[251]

(c) Prescription Act 1832[252]

This legislation set out to cure the problems of common law prescription. Essentially, prescription no longer needs to relate back to 1189.[253] Instead, s 2 provides that it is sufficient that there has been 20 years' user (30 years for profits: s 1).[254] The Act might appear to supersede the previous law, but there is a major restriction on its application.

Sections 2 and 4 require uninterrupted user for the 20 years prior to the claim in which the right is in issue.[255] It follows that use for 20 years does not by itself give rise to an easement under the Act; it must be the last 20 years' user. The nature of the user is discussed in the leading case of *Hollins v Verney*.[256] Lindley LJ required that 'during the whole of the statutory term (whether acts of user be proved in each year or not) the user is enough at any rate to carry to the mind of a reasonable person who is in possession of the servient tenement, the fact that a continuous right to enjoyment is being asserted, and ought to be resisted'. There is no requirement that the right be exercised literally all the time. Everything depends on the facts of the case, but in *Hollins v Verney*, the use of an access for cutting wood only every 12 years did not constitute continuous user. A temporary non-use is unlikely to be fatal, but non-use for several years immediately before the claim will generally be inconsistent with the user being continuing.[257] Where user has been discontinued or interrupted, common law prescription or lost modern grant may still be relied upon.[258]

---

[249] *Dalton v Angus & Co* (1881) 6 App Cas 740 (see also (1878) 4 QBD 162), as explained in *Tehidy Minerals Ltd v Norman* [1971] 2 QB 528. The development of the fiction is recounted in many cases; *Simmons v Dobson* [1991] 1 WLR 720 provides one example.

[250] *Oakley v Boston* [1976] QB 270. This limitation also applies to other forms of prescription: *Rochdale Canal Co v Radcliffe* (1852) 18 QB 287 (118 ER 108); *Liverpool Corporation v H Coghill & Son Ltd* [1918] 1 Ch 307; *Housden v Conservators of Wimbledon and Putney Commons* [2008] 1 WLR 1172.

[251] *Pugh v Savage* [1970] 2 QB 373; *Tehidy Minerals Ltd v Norman* [1971] 2 QB 528; *Ward (Helston) Ltd v Kerrier DC* (1984) 24 RVR 18; *Bridle v Ruby* [1989] QB 169; *Mills v Silver* [1991] Ch 271; *Simmons v Dobson* [1991] 1 WLR 720.

[252] The legislation is very complex and has given rise to numerous problems. See Megarry and Wade, *The Law of Real Property* (8th edn), paras 28-066 et seq for a fuller analysis.

[253] Several cases stress this limited effect of the legislation: see, e.g., *Sturges v Bridgman* (1879) 11 Ch D 852 and *Gardner v Hodgson's Kingston Brewery Co Ltd* [1903] AC 229. Some provisions (especially s 3 as to rights of light) have greater effect.

[254] There is separate provision for use for 40 years (60 for profits), but with limited practical effect. Profits in gross are not covered: *Shuttleworth v Le Fleming* (1865) 19 CBNS 687 (144 ER 956).

[255] The date of bringing the claim is crucial: *Davies v Du Paver* [1953] 1 QB 184.

[256] (1884) 13 QBD 304 (see especially p 315), approved in *Mills v Silver* [1991] Ch 271.

[257] *Parker v Mitchell* (1840) 11 Ad&E 788 (113 ER 613), approved in *Hollins v Verney* (1884) 13 QBD 304 at p 312.

[258] Modern cases include *Tehidy Minerals v Norman* [1971] 2 QB 528 (prescription and lost modern grant); *Mills v Silver* [1991] Ch 271 (lost modern grant). It is similar if there has been unity of possession in the 20 years prior to the claim: *Hulbert v Dale* [1909] 2 Ch 570 (lost modern grant).

Interruptions to user

Section 4 provides that an interruption shall be disregarded unless it is acquiesced in or submitted to for a period of a year. Litigation frequently arises because the servient owner has prevented the exercise of the right. Necessarily in those circumstances, the easement will not be exercised at the time the claim is brought. This does not matter, provided that not more than a year passes before the dominant owner brings the claim.[259] Several cases have involved a gap exceeding a year, and these give rise to the question whether the interruption has been submitted to or acquiesced in.

Davies v Du Paver[260] involved a dominant owner who protested vigorously when fencing prevented the exercise of the right to graze sheep on the servient land. There was a gap of a little over 13 months between the last correspondence (contemporaneous with the completion of the fencing) and the claim being brought. A majority of the Court of Appeal held that the judge was justified in finding that there had been no acquiescence or submission. As Morris LJ observed,[261] 'The parties were breathing fury on each side of a newly erected fence.' In the different scenario where the parties are actively negotiating, it is again unlikely that there will be an interruption.[262]

Dance v Triplow provides a contrast.[263] There was a two-year gap between the blocking of light to the dominant owner's windows and the taking of legal advice. The claim was brought after a further two and a half years. The Court of Appeal thought that some delay would not be fatal if complaints had been maintained strongly up to the time of seeking legal advice, but that it was essential for the dominant owner to show continuing objections. On the facts, this had not been shown and there was no prescription. It is not enough to be unhappy with what the servient owner does and to grumble about it: the impression must be given that the dominant owner intends to do something about it.[264]

Stopping time running

The servient owner who wishes to challenge a claim before the statutory 20 years' period has expired can normally take the simple step of denying entry to the dominant owner. This will stop time from running, and any attempt by the dominant owner to use force to enforce the claim will result in its failure.[265] This, however, is not feasible for all easements. In particular, a claimant to a right of light is not doing anything on the servient land and is perfectly entitled to have whatever windows are desired. All the servient owner can do to stop time running is to put up hoarding so as to block light to the windows.

This absurd situation has been ameliorated by the Rights of Light Act 1959. The servient owner can register a notice,[266] which acts as an interruption for all types of prescription.

---

[259] It follows that the use may be for less than 20 years, provided that the interruption has taken place within the last year and the use commenced 20 years before the claim is brought: *Flight v Thomas* (1840) 11 Ad&E 688 (113 ER 575), upheld (1841) 8 Cl&F 231 (8 ER 91). However, a claim brought by the servient owner during the 20th year of user will succeed: *Reilly v Orange* [1955] 1 WLR 616.

[260] [1953] 1 QB 184.

[261] Ibid, at pp 207–208.

[262] *Smith v Brudenell-Bruce* [2002] 2 P&CR 51.

[263] (1991) 64 P&CR 1.

[264] *Glover v Coleman* (1874) LR 10 CP 108.

[265] *Newnham v Willison* (1987) 56 P&CR 8.

[266] Registration is in the local land charges register maintained by the local authority. Law Com No 356 would replace the 1959 Act by a simpler procedure.

There are provisions ensuring that notice is given to the dominant owner, who is deemed to acquiesce in the interruption unless a claim is brought to assert a right of light. The registration is valid for one year only, but this statutory interruption will protect the servient owner for a further 20 years (until a fresh period has run its course).

Similar problems may arise with other easements of a negative character: this may help explain the reluctance to recognise new negative easements. Consider the right of support of a building. The servient owner cannot say 'Stop pressing on my land', for the dominant owner is doing no wrong. Unlike the right to light, no registration is possible to interrupt this easement. The servient owner could excavate his land in order to undermine the building, but this is an extraordinary suggestion for somebody who simply wishes to prevent prescription.

(ii) *Requirements for all forms of prescription*

Simple use for the required period is not enough. There must be use as of right: it must appear as if the claimant is exercising a legal right, although it is not necessary for the claimant to believe that there is a legal right.[267] The test for this is that the use must not be by force, stealth or permission (nec vi, nec clam, nec precario).[268] Recent authorities indicate that this test does not leave any scope for a separate test that the servient owner should have realised that a right was being claimed.[269] In particular, there is no defence that the exercise of the right showed 'deference' to the rights of the servient owner.

Acquiescence by the servient owner lies at the heart of prescription,[270] and *Sturges* v *Bridgman*[271] provides a well-known example. The defendant had for many years conducted the business of a confectioner. He used a large pestle and mortar connected to a wall as part of his activities. The claimant was a neighbouring doctor, who complained about the noise caused by the pestle and mortar. Until recently, this had not been a problem, as the doctor had been using buildings at the other end of his land. He had recently built consulting rooms right up to the wall to which the pestle and mortar were fixed. Only then had the noise and vibration become intolerable to him; he brought an action for nuisance. The confectioner argued that he had acquired an easement to create the noise and vibration by prescription. The Court of Appeal held that there had been no actionable nuisance until the consulting rooms had been built. Therefore, only then could the prescription period begin to run: there was nothing that the servient owner could have done earlier to prevent the noise and he could not be said to have acquiesced.

The stress on acquiescence raises the point that prescription may be similar to estoppel. However, the two doctrines are quite separate. Thus, acquiescence coupled with detrimental reliance on the part of the dominant owner may give rise to a proprietary estoppel

[267] *R* v *Oxfordshire CC, ex p Sunningwell PC* [2000] 1 AC 335.
[268] See, e.g., Lord Lindley in *Gardner* v *Hodgson's Kingston Brewery Co Ltd* [1903] AC 229 at p 239. Unity of possession excludes use as of right: *Battishill* v *Reed* (1856) 18 CBNS 696.
[269] *R (Lewis)* v *Redcar and Cleveland BC (No 2)* [2010] 2 AC 70 (right of commons); Suggett and Riddall [2013] Conv 416. Nor need the servient owner be aware that permission has terminated: *London Tara Hotel Ltd* v *Kensington Close Hotel Ltd* [2012] 2 All ER 554.
[270] *Dalton* v *Angus & Co* (1881) 6 App Cas 740 at p 773 (Fry J); *Oakley* v *Boston* [1976] QB 270.
[271] (1879) 11 Ch D 852. Followed by the majority of the Court of Appeal in *Miller* v *Jackson* [1977] QB 966 (Lord Denning MR's dissent was more on the law of nuisance than on prescription).

without any period of user being necessary.[272] On the other hand, prescription does not require detrimental reliance. The Law Commission would adopt most of the 'as of right' rules, though removing acquiescence from its central role.[273]

Before going into the rules, it should be noted that statutory prescription of rights to light is exceptional in not requiring use as of right.[274] Such prescription is, however, excluded by written consent or interruption for one year. Although prescription of negative easements is allowed, it does cause difficulty[275] – it is not easy to apply acquiescence principles where the dominant owner is not doing anything.[276]

(a) Force

It is unusual for rights to be asserted by force, although force is sometimes used after the right has been challenged by the servient owner. If the claimant removes barriers placed by the servient owner, then *Newnham* v *Willison*[277] establishes that the following period of user will not be counted for prescription purposes.

Somewhat similar is 'contentious user'. An early leading case is *Eaton* v *Swansea Waterworks Co*,[278] in which the claimant had been prosecuted for interference with a watercourse. It was held that his conduct could not be said to be as of right. Subsequent cases have explained this as an example of contentious user, which is fatal to prescription.[279] This has recently been extended to notices prohibiting the user – so long as the notice indicates that the owner objects to user, then there is no user as of right and no acquiescence.[280] In particular, there is no need to indicate that physical action or legal proceedings will be employed to stop the user.[281]

It was formerly thought that an illegal user could not give rise to prescription.[282] However, this proved very inconvenient in the context of commons, where use unauthorised by the owner is illegal. It followed that even very long use could not be relied upon: lack of permission resulted in illegality and permission would be fatal to prescription. The House of Lords in *Bakewell Management Co Ltd* v *Brandwood*[283] rejected that analysis. Although prescription generally cannot give rise to a right which contravenes statute,[284] there is no reason why it cannot operate where the owner's permission removes any illegality.

---

[272] *Crabb* v *Arun DC* [1976] Ch 179.
[273] Law Com No 327, para 3.121; Piska [2009] Conv 349.
[274] Prescription Act 1832, s 3; *Colls* v *Home & Colonial Stores Ltd* [1904] AC 179 at p 205.
[275] Cf *Mason* v *Shrewsbury and Hereford Railway Co* (1871) LR 6 QB 578.
[276] See the celebrated and contentious case of *Dalton* v *Angus & Co* (1881) 6 App Cas 740; Anderson (1975) 38 MLR 641. The role of acquiescence divided the judges.
[277] (1987) 56 P&CR 8. This will not matter if the prescription period has been completed, unless (for statutory prescription) the interruption exceeds a year.
[278] (1851) 17 QB 267 (117 ER 1282).
[279] *Dalton* v *Angus & Co* (1881) 6 App Cas 740 at p 786 (Bowen J); *Hollins* v *Verney* (1884) 13 QBD 304.
[280] *Winterburn* v *Bennett* [2017] 1 WLR 646 (right to park), applying *Betterment Properties (Weymouth) Ltd* v *Dorset CC* [2012] 2 P&CR 32 (upheld [2014] AC 1072, when this point was not appealed).
[281] The contrary suggestion in *Smith* v *Brudenell-Bruce* [2002] 2 P&CR 51 was rejected in *Winterburn*.
[282] *Cargill* v *Gotts* [1981] 1 WLR 441, especially at p 446.
[283] [2004] 2 AC 519 (McNall [2004] Conv 517; Goymour [2005] CLJ 39); cf Fox [2004] Conv 173. The commons owners attempted to use the law to extract extortionate payments from householders, rather than to preserve amenity values.
[284] Such as water abstraction without a water authority licence: *Cargill* v *Gotts* [1981] 1 WLR 441.

(b) Stealth

This does not mean that the dominant owner has deliberately hidden the use from the servient owner. Rather, the question is whether the user should have been obvious: the cases stress the close connection with acquiescence. Romer LJ required that 'the enjoyment has been open – that is to say, of such a character that an ordinary owner of the land, diligent in the protection of his interests, would have, or must be taken to have, a reasonable opportunity of becoming aware of that enjoyment'.[285] There will be stealth if the state of the land does not disclose the claim,[286] or if there is a user at such times of the day as would not be spotted by the servient owner.[287] However, building on one's land is sufficient to indicate support from neighbouring land.[288] Absence of the servient owner may render it difficult to pursue a claim; for example, as regards an infrequently used and non-obvious access through an outlying field.[289]

For common law prescription, it is not necessary that user be continuous.[290] Nevertheless, non-continuous user may not be indicative of an easement.[291] Similar principles apply for all forms of prescription, though only the Prescription Act 1832 requires user for the 20 years preceding the claim.

(c) Permission

One obvious case is where the servient owner receives an annual sum from the claimant. This shows a continuing element of permission, which is destructive of any argument that the user is as of right.[292]

An interesting problem arises if the user is initially permissive, but the dominant land is sold to a person who assumes that there is a legal right. The purchaser will regard the user as being as of right, although it is difficult to argue that the servient owner acquiesces in user as of right. Although a purchaser's prescription claim failed in *Gaved* v *Martyn*,[293] an initial permission does not necessarily govern the entirety of the future user. After some time, the user may become as of right, even if the dominant land has not been sold.[294]

It sometimes happens that dominant and servient owners reach some sort of agreement as to what should happen in the future. In *Davis* v *Whitby*,[295] the route of a claimed right

---

[285] *Union Lighterage Co* v *London Graving Dock Co* [1902] 2 Ch 557 at p 571.

[286] *Union Lighterage Co* v *London Graving Dock Co* [1902] 2 Ch 557 (tie-rods embedded in soil); *Solomon* v *Vintners' Company* (1859) 4 H&N 585 (157 ER 970) (right of support against house not immediately adjacent to dominant land).

[287] *Liverpool Corporation* v *H Coghill & Son Ltd* [1918] 1 Ch 307 (night-time discharge of polluting waste).

[288] *Dalton* v *Angus & Co* (1881) 6 App Cas 740.

[289] *Diment* v *NH Foot Ltd* [1974] 1 WLR 1427.

[290] *RPC Holdings Ltd* v *Rogers* [1953] 1 All ER 1029 at p 1032.

[291] *Mills* v *Silver* [1991] Ch 271 (lost modern grant), approving *Hollins* v *Verney* (1884) 13 QBD 304. Some of the language of the cases may need to be reconsidered after *Redcar* (see p 540 above).

[292] *Gardner* v *Hodgson's Kingston Brewery Co Ltd* [1903] AC 229. The suggestion that the payment was for the upkeep of the right of way was roundly rejected.

[293] (1865) 19 CBNS 732 (144 ER 974). Contrast *London Tara Hotel Ltd* v *Kensington Close Hotel Ltd* [2012] 2 All ER 554: personal licence to vendor.

[294] See Cotton LJ in *Earl de la Warr* v *Miles* (1881) 17 Ch D 535 at p 596; *Healy* v *Hawkins* [1968] 1 WLR 1967 at p 1974. Under the Prescription Act 1832, s 2, user for 40 years is effective unless there is written consent. However, Cotton LJ stresses that such prescription always fails if use is not as of right, as where permission is given from time to time.

[295] [1974] Ch 186. Contrast *Patel* v *WH Smith (Eziot) Ltd* [1987] 1 WLR 853.

of way was changed by agreement. The Court of Appeal held that use of the right of way was still as of right after the agreement. Stamp LJ stressed that the dominant owner at all times asserted a right of way and the only point in issue at the time of agreement was the precise route. It was not a case in which the servient owner had challenged the user. However, time will stop running if the servient owner explicitly gives permission for the continued exercise of the right.[296] Although this has been criticised as too easy a way of stopping time running (permission could be withdrawn later),[297] it has been upheld after a full review of the authorities.[298]

Tolerated user

A number of cases suggested that if the true explanation of the user was that it was tolerated by the servient owner, then this precluded prescription.[299] The issue was fully reviewed by the Court of Appeal in *Mills* v *Silver*.[300] Whilst recognising the use of tolerance in some cases, the court held that it was no defence to prescription. As was pointed out, to hold that tolerance negates acquiescence would mean that prescription could virtually never take place, for how else could the use be explained? This was approved by the Supreme Court in *R (Barkas)* v *North Yorkshire CC*.[301] However, once the use is 'by right' (a statutory right on the facts in *Barkas*), then this precludes use 'as of right'.

In *Jones* v *Price & Morgan*,[302] there was a tacit understanding that the claimant could use a track. This was treated as negating user as of right. Although tolerance was not discussed, the case correctly places stress on the nature of user by the claimant. Tolerance is not therefore a defence to prescription, but it may be a relevant factor in determining the quality of the claimant's user.

Mistake

Is a mistake by the claimant fatal to prescription? In *Earl de la Warr* v *Miles*,[303] the claimant mistakenly believed that an enclosure award of 1693 entitled him to a profit over a common, and in *Bridle* v *Ruby*,[304] the claimant mistakenly believed that there was a right of way in a conveyance. In each case, the user was held to be as of right and prescription operated: the claimant was asserting a proprietary right and not relying upon a mere temporary permission.

It was stressed in *Bridle* that some mistakes may show that the user is not as of right. An example would be where the parties believe mistakenly that there is a right of user in a lease: such a limited right (use for the duration of a lease) is inconsistent with a fee

[296] *Rafique* v *Trustees of the Walton Estate* (1992) 65 P&CR 356.
[297] Wallace [1994] Conv 196, noting that permission would render the Prescription Act inapplicable as there would not have been the necessary user for the last 20 years.
[298] *Odey* v *Barber* [2008] Ch 175.
[299] *Alfred F Beckett Ltd* v *Lyons* [1967] Ch 449 provided the modern origin of the idea.
[300] [1991] Ch 271.
[301] [2015] AC 195: use as of right of a village or town green. See also (earlier) Blohm [2014] Conv 40.
[302] (1992) 64 P&CR 404.
[303] (1881) 17 Ch D 535.
[304] [1989] QB 169. See Kodilinye [1989] Conv 261.

simple prescription.[305] It seems unlikely that mistake by the servient owner will mean that there is no acquiescence such as to deny prescription.[306]

(iii) *Prescription where there is a lease*

The courts have held that prescription operates only in respect of claims that affect the fee simple of the servient and dominant tenements. So far as the dominant land is concerned, this does not cause too much difficulty: the courts are willing to say that a tenant uses and acquires an easement on behalf of the fee simple.[307] However, this does not work where the servient land is owned by the tenant's landlord, for then the landlord would have an easement over his own land, and that is legally impossible.[308]

Problems really multiply when the servient land is subject to a lease. Because the courts insist upon prescription against the fee simple estate, acquiescence by the tenant cannot give rise to prescription.[309] This is a remarkably inconvenient rule, given that many titles are held under long leases. It may have been logical (if silly) for common law prescription which has to date back to 1189, but it is difficult to justify for statutory prescription or lost modern grant. The rule survives despite constant criticism, though Lord Millett recently stated in the Hong Kong Final Court of Appeal that it is unprincipled and might well not survive scrutiny in the House of Lords.[310] Of course, nobody suggests that the fee simple owner should be bound in these cases.[311]

Although many lawyers regard the current state of the law as unsatisfactory, the Law Commission is not recommending any reform.[312] It was thought to raise issues of great complexity and reform would lead to an undesired increase in the role of prescription.

However, prescription is possible if the holder of the fee simple can be said to have acquiesced. This is readily proved if the lease commenced after the prescription period began, for then the fee simple servient owner had the opportunity of objecting to the user.[313] Some cases ask whether the landlord had notice of the user.[314] This becomes important if the landlord has a right to object during the lease. This right is likely to be by virtue of a term in the lease: failure to enforce that term is the acquiescence.[315] In order to dispel

---

[305] *Chamber Colliery Co* v *Hopwood* (1886) 32 Ch D 549. *Thomas W Ward Ltd* v *Alexander Bruce (Grays) Ltd* [1959] 2 Ll Rep 472 at p 477 suggests that 'a claim of right by contract' is insufficiently adverse to ground prescription. This analysis is difficult to reconcile with *Bridle*.

[306] *London Tara Hotel Ltd* v *Kensington Close Hotel Ltd* [2012] 2 All ER 554.

[307] *Pugh* v *Savage* [1970] 2 QB 373 at p 380.

[308] *Gayford* v *Moffatt* (1868) LR 4 Ch App 133; *Kilgour* v *Gaddes* [1904] 1 KB 457.

[309] *Wheaton* v *Maple & Co* [1893] 3 Ch 48; *Simmons* v *Dobson* [1991] 1 WLR 720. An exception was accepted in *Bosomworth* v *Faber* (1992) 69 P&CR 288, where each tenant had the right to enlarge a 2,000-year lease into a fee simple. Turner [2012] Conv 19 argues, contrary to the views of many, that *Simmons* is the sole authority establishing a special rule for leases.

[310] *China Field Ltd* v *Appeal Tribunal (Buildings)* [2009] 5 HKC 231; Merry [2010] Conv 176. For earlier criticism, see Kiralfy (1949) 13 Conv NS 104; Delany (1958) 74 LQR 82; Sparkes [1992] Conv 167.

[311] But note that this is already the position for rights of light: *Frewen* v *Philipps* (1861) 11 CBNS 449 at p 455 (142 ER 871 at p 873), based on Prescription Act 1832, s 3; *Fear* v *Morgan* [1906] 2 Ch 406 (upheld [1907] AC 425); *Willoughby* v *Eckstein* [1937] Ch 167 at p 170.

[312] Law Com No 327, paras 3.144–3.150.

[313] *Pugh* v *Savage* [1970] 2 QB 373.

[314] *Davies* v *Stephens* (1836) 7 C&P 570 (173 ER 251); *Davies* v *Du Paver* [1953] 1 QB 184 (onus on claimant to prove notice).

[315] *Williams* v *Sandy Lane (Chester) Ltd* [2007] 1 P&CR 457; Dixon [2007] Conv 161.

doubt, it should be added that tenants can both grant and be granted easements (whether or not as regards their landlords): problems arise only in the sphere of prescription.

4. The relationship constituted by easements and profits

This topic will be considered very briefly. There are huge numbers of cases dealing with the extent of rights under easements and profits, but they generally turn on the construction of the individual grant.

A. Extent of the right

As one would expect, the servient owner can prevent user going beyond what has been agreed. Unless the excessive user cannot be separated from the lawful user, the easement will not be terminated. In the case of an express grant in unlimited terms, the courts are reluctant to restrict the extent of the user. The courts do sometimes restrict the right according to the physical state of the land at the time of grant,[316] but more typical is *Keefe* v *Amor*.[317] There was a right of way leading to a narrow gap in the servient owner's wall. When the servient owner widened the gap, it was held that the dominant owner had a right to use vehicles that would not have been able to pass through the earlier narrow gap.

Problems most frequently arise when the use of the dominant land changes, resulting in a much heavier use of the right. Generally, the courts take the approach that intensification and change of use are immaterial,[318] but excessive use may persuade the courts to say that it goes beyond what was contemplated and constitutes an unreasonable interference with the servient landowner.[319] Problems have rarely arisen from use of the right by employees or visitors of the dominant owner.[320]

A stricter view is taken where the right is acquired by prescription or implication.[321] In these cases, the use of the dominant land at the time of the prescriptive user or implication controls the extent of the right,[322] although mere increase in intensity of use cannot be objected to.[323] In a useful review, Neuberger J in *Atwood* v *Bovis Homes Ltd*[324] held that change of use is not automatically fatal. What is important is whether it results in a substantial intensification of user or change in its nature. This was in the context of a right of

---

[316] *Todrick* v *Western National Omnibus Co Ltd* [1934] Ch 561 (Butt in *Landmark Cases in Land Law* (ed Gravells), Chapter 2); *White* v *Richards* (1993) 68 P&CR 105.

[318] *White* v *Grand Hotel, Eastbourne Ltd* [1913] 1 Ch 113 (house became part of hotel); *South Eastern Ry Co* v *Cooper* [1924] 1 Ch 211 (sand pit on farm).

[317] [1965] 1 QB 334.

[319] See Lord Denning MR in *Jelbert* v *Davis* [1968] 1 WLR 589 (right of way to farm, now used as large caravan park), applied on less compelling facts in *Bee* v *Thompson* [2010] Ch 412 (Butt (2011) 85 ALJ 134).

[320] *Woodhouse & Co Ltd* v *Kirkland (Derby) Ltd* [1970] 1 WLR 1185. Roberts [2007] Conv 235 raises the interesting question whether such persons can enforce rights of access.

[321] For implied easements, see *Nickerson* v *Barraclough* [1981] Ch 426. Easements of necessity are included: *Corporation of London* v *Riggs* (1880) 13 Ch D 798.

[322] *Williams* v *James* (1867) LR 2 CP 577; *Loder* v *Gaden* (1999) 78 P&CR 223 (change from agriculture to road haulage).

[323] *Cargill* v *Gotts* [1981] 1 WLR 441 (abstraction of water). An exception exists where there is clear excessive use, as where drains overflow as a result: *McAdams Homes Ltd* v *Robinson* [2005] 1 P&CR 520 at [28].

[324] [2001] Ch 379.

surface drainage (where change of use does not increase the burden on the servient land), but it was thought that the same might apply to rights of way – the source of most disputes. The *Atwood* approach was adopted in *McAdams Homes Ltd v Robinson*.[325] Increased foul water drainage resulting from a change from a bakery to two houses marginally justified a finding of a substantial increase in burden terminating the easement.

Rights of light give rise to rather different questions. The dominant tenement is not entitled to all the light that passes through windows, but merely to so much as is 'required for the ordinary purposes of inhabitancy or business'.[326] Although this might seem to indicate a single standard, the courts have been prepared to look at the particular use of the dominant land. The most striking example is *Allen v Greenwood*,[327] in which the Court of Appeal held that a greenhouse could not be deprived of the high level of light necessary for growing plants.

Finally, the courts are inclined to interpret any ambiguity against the grantor. This always has the effect of widening the easement. This is obvious in the case of a grant. In a reservation, the owner of the servient land (the purchaser or lessee) is treated as the grantor.[328] However, the Court of Appeal has said that this rule of interpretation will be applied very rarely.[329] Nearly always, the extent of the right can be gleaned from the terms of the easement and the factual circumstances at the time of grant.

B. User must be limited to dominant tenement

Suppose that there is a right of way to plot A. The dominant owner purchases an adjoining plot B and builds a house on it. Access to the house is through plot A and the right of way. *Harris v Flower*[330] established beyond doubt that the right of way cannot be exercised to reach plot B, for that is not part of the dominant tenement.

Disputes generally centre upon two issues. The first lies in defining the dominant tenement. This is a matter of interpretation of the grant[331] and need not be discussed further save to observe that the dominant tenement is most unlikely to extend to land subsequently acquired.[332] The second issue is whether access is really being sought for the dominant tenement or the further land. There would not be a problem if the dominant owner purchased a small area of land and incorporated it into the garden of the dominant land. Whilst this might appear similar to the example concerning A and B, it is more realistic to say that the right of way is used for access to the dominant land: any benefit to the new land is ancillary to its operation as regards the dominant land.[333]

---

[325] [2005] 1 P&CR 520. The flow was likely at least to quadruple.

[326] *Colls v Home & Colonial Stores Ltd* [1904] AC 179 at p 204.

[327] [1980] Ch 119.

[328] *St Edmundsbury & Ipswich Diocesan Board of Finance v Clark (No 2)* [1975] 1 WLR 468, notwithstanding LPA, s 65. Apart from authority, there is much to be said for the contrary view taken by Megarry V-C at first instance ([1973] 1 WLR 1572).

[329] *St Edmundsbury & Ipswich Diocesan Board of Finance v Clark (No 2)* [1975] 1 WLR 468.

[330] (1904) 74 LJ Ch 127, applied in *Bracewell v Appleby* [1975] Ch 408. It is criticised by Paton and Seabourne [2003] Conv 127, but appears well established.

[331] See p 513 above.

[332] Even an express provision to benefit such land does not create an immediate proprietary interest: *London & Blenheim Estates Ltd v Ladbroke Retail Parks Ltd* [1994] 1 WLR 31.

[333] *Massey v Boulden* [2003] 1 WLR 1792 (addition of two rooms from adjoining premises).

However, this idea of ancillary benefit is limited. It has been held not to allow access by the dominant owner for parking on the new land, even though this is obviously for the benefit of the dominant owner's house.[334] It may be observed that, in this case, the intensity of user is scarcely affected. Rather different is *Macepark (Whittlebury) Ltd v Sargeant*,[335] which involved a right of way to a hotel. The hotel proposed to arrange for guests to drive directly (by a new exit) to the Silverstone motor circuit. Given the benefit to the other land (Silverstone and the land in between in separate ownership) it was held that this was more than ancillary benefit. This does seem surprising, given that the guests would be genuinely visiting the hotel.

Especially difficult problems arise where the use of the two properties is integrated. A good example is storing material, intended for future use on the further land, on the dominant tenement. This may be viewed as either an independent use of the dominant tenement (so that a right of way may be exercised to transport the material)[336] or else a method of obtaining access to the further land (impermissible).[337]

These examples demonstrate the inconvenience and complexity of the principle. The law is easy to justify in the clear case of two separate plots where access is sought for the further plot: there is no reason for the servient owner to have to put up with a use of the right that has not been agreed to. However, the justification is less convincing where the further plot is integrated into the dominant tenement. Perhaps one has to recognise that no entirely logical answer is available and each case does have to be considered on its facts.[338]

C. Repair

We have seen that the servient owner may owe limited positive duties where there is an easement of support.[339] Could this nuisance liability extend to a right of way which has become obstructed? Given that easements cannot impose positive obligations, the lack of any duty to repair a right of way is unlikely to change.[340] One qualification is that since 1984, there may be tort liability as an occupier to a person using a private right of way who is injured by the state of the land.[341]

The dominant owner generally has a right to enter to repair at his or her expense.[342] Further, there may be a contractual duty on the servient owner to repair, and in appropriate

---

[334] *Das v Linden Mews Ltd* [2003] 2 P&CR 58 (direct access to the further land); contra *Shean Pty Ltd v Corinne Court* (2001) 25 WAR 65 and see also *Freestyle Enterprises Ltd v Starfin Group Ltd* [2008] 1 NZLR 266. *Wall v Collins* [2007] Ch 390 supports a more generous view; *Das* was not cited.

[335] [2003] 1 WLR 2284; Bullock (2005) 155 NLJ 1402.

[336] *Williams v James* (1867) LR 2 CP 577 (hay stacked on dominant land included hay from other land); cf *Jobson v Record* (1997) 75 P&CR 375.

[337] *Skull v Glenister* (1864) 16 CBNS 81 (143 ER 1055), stressing that it is essentially a question of fact; see also *Peacock v Custins* [2002] 1 WLR 1815.

[338] The Law Commission has dropped its original idea of abrogating the principle: Law Com No 327, para 2.70 (cf CP 186, para 5.70).

[339] See p 509 above.

[340] *Jones v Pritchard* [1908] 1 Ch 630; *Liverpool City Council v Irwin* [1977] AC 239 at p 259.

[341] Occupiers' Liability Act 1984, s 1.

[342] *Jones v Pritchard* [1908] 1 Ch 630. *Edwards v Kumarasamy* [2016] AC 1334 at [57] stresses that this is a matter of construction: it may not apply if it is not required on the facts. There is no right to improve a right of way: *Mills v Silver* [1991] Ch 271.

cases (especially as between landlord and tenant), this may be implied.[343] In many cases, a right of way is used by both dominant and servient owners. The servient owner will wish to keep it in good condition, and it is quite common for the easement to provide that the dominant owner shall contribute to the cost of repair. Continued use of the easement is likely to be conditional on such contributions being made.[344] Otherwise, the dominant owner can take free advantage of any improvements and repair.[345]

D. Conduct by the servient owner

The servient owner can maintain normal control over the land, so long as there is no unreasonable interference with the exercise of the easement. For example, it may be permissible to install gates across the right of way[346] or speed humps to reduce the speed of vehicles.[347] The servient owner may reduce the width of a right of way, provided that it would be unreasonable for the dominant owner to insist on the unrestricted right.[348] Once the line of a right of way has been established,[349] the servient owner has no right to change it,[350] although it may be that the dominant owner cannot object to a realignment which causes no disadvantage.[351]

E. Enforcement

Conduct of the servient owner inconsistent with an easement is usually thought to constitute a nuisance, although some question whether it is a true example of a nuisance.[352] The use of injunctions to enforce easements involves issues discussed in the following chapter on covenants.

5. Termination of easements and profits

The clearest and most effective method is by deed. Equity recognises other agreements to terminate. Two other possibilities need to be discussed.

[343] *Liverpool City Council v Irwin* [1977] AC 239 (access within a block of flats: the tenants could scarcely be expected to keep lifts in repair). The rules on the running of leasehold covenants ensure that an assignee from the landlord will be bound by the implied term.
[344] *Halsall v Brizell* [1957] Ch 169 (the benefit and burden principle: p 175 above). Although in *Rural View Developments Pty Ltd v Fastfort Pty Ltd* [2011] 1 Qd R 35, a covenant to contribute did not render the easement conditional, most cases are less strict: *Wilkinson v Kerdene Ltd* [2013] EWCA Civ 44; [2013] 2 EGLR 163, especially at [33].
[345] Frequently a catalyst for disputes: *Keefe v Amor* [1965] 1 QB 334.
[346] An example is *Hamble PC v Haggard* [1992] 1 WLR 122.
[347] *Saint v Jenner* [1973] 1 Ch 275.
[348] *Celsteel Ltd v Alton House Holdings Ltd* [1985] 1 WLR 204; *Emmett v Sisson* [2014] 2 P&CR 71. For height, see *VT Engineering Ltd v Richard Borland & Co Ltd* (1968) 19 P&CR 890.
[349] Unless specified by the grant, the servient owner can choose it: *Bolton v Bolton* (1879) 11 Ch D 968.
[350] *Deacon v South Eastern Ry Co* (1889) 61 LT 377.
[351] *Greenwich Healthcare NHS Trust v London & Quadrant Housing Trust* [1998] 1 WLR 1749.
[352] Roberts [2007] Conv 235 at pp 250–254.

A. Common ownership[353]

If the same person becomes the owner and occupier of both dominant and servient tene-ments, then the easement terminates.[354] It will not automatically revive if one of the tene-ments is later sold, although it may, of course, be implied as a fresh easement.[355] This need for fresh creation may constitute a trap for the purchaser on the later sale.

The easement will terminate only if the same person is both owner and occupier of each of the two tenements. If that person owns one but is merely tenant of the other, then the easement is suspended whilst the lease runs.[356] Conversely, the same person may be owner of both tenements, with one or both of them being leased.[357] There is then an easement for the duration of the lease. Indeed, it is common for tenants to have easements over land-lords' adjoining land.

B. Termination of the estate

Where an easement benefits or burdens a leasehold estate, one would expect it to terminate when the lease terminates. What is the position if an easement is held by a tenant who buys the freehold? As the lease terminates, one might expect the easement also to terminate. However, *Wall* v *Collins*[358] provides the convenient, if controversial, result that the ease-ment continues for the length of the lease.

C. Abandonment

Lengthy non-use may terminate easements and profits, just as they may be gained by long use. In this area, however, there are no specified periods of non-use to guide us. The essen-tial question is whether the dominant owner can be said to have abandoned the right. Even centuries of non-use may be insufficient for abandonment to be inferred. It is very different if the servient owner acts to his or her detriment on the basis that the right is no more, for the dominant owner who acquiesces in such detriment will be bound by estoppel.[359] Building upon the servient land in a way inconsistent with the easement provides a good example of detriment. There are strong dicta supporting estoppel as the basis for abandon-ment,[360] although some cases are not readily explained that way.

---

[353] Brooke-Taylor (1977) 41 Conv 107. This would change under the Law Commission's proposals: see p 516 above.

[354] Based on *Tyrringham's Case* (1584) 4 Co Rep 36b at p 38a (76 ER 973 at p 980).

[355] *James* v *Plant* (1836) 4 Ad&E 749 at p 761 (111 ER 967 at p 971).

[356] *Simper* v *Foley* (1862) 2 J&H 555 (70 ER 1179).

[357] *Richardson* v *Graham* [1908] 1 QB 39.

[358] [2007] Ch 390. Ward [2007] Conv 464 finds the result surprising, but contrast Lyall [2010] Conv 300. The Law Commission recommends reversal, but with a simple means of producing the convenient result that the easement can continue (Law Com No 327, para 3.255; Cooke in *Modern Studies in Property Law*, Vol 6 (ed Bright), Chapter 9). *Wall* applies whether or not the servient land is owned by the landlord; if it is, the normal implication rules may create a freehold easement on the acquisition of the freehold.

[359] *Davies* v *Marshall* (1861) 10 CBNS 697 (142 ER 627). The dominant owner must be aware of the circum-stances: *Costagliola* v *English* (1969) 210 EG 1425. Estoppel was applied in *Lester* v *Woodgate* [2010] 2 P&CR 359.

[360] See *Moore* v *Rawson* (1824) 3 B&C 332 (107 ER 756) (right to light); *Cook* v *Mayor & Corporation of Bath* (1868) LR 6 Eq 177 (right of way).

As has been observed, there are no set periods for abandonment. The essential reason for this is that many easements may be unnecessary for the time being and therefore not used for many years. A right of way may provide a secondary access to the dominant land and may remain unexercised until some change to the layout or use of the dominant land renders it advantageous. As the Privy Council held in *James* v *Stevenson*,[361] 'it is one thing not to assert an intention to use a way, and another thing to assert an intention to abandon it'. In that case, a right of way had been used on only one occasion since its creation 50 years earlier, there being no occasion to use it. It had not been abandoned. In *Cook* v *Mayor & Corporation of Bath*,[362] a right of way had not been exercised for 40 years because a doorway on the dominant land had been blocked up. Again there was no abandonment. Somewhat more recently, a right of way unused for 175 years, because there were alternative access routes, has been held not to be abandoned.[363]

The courts have been more willing to allow abandonment where the right is connected with a building on the dominant land that has been demolished and not replaced. The best-known case is *Moore* v *Rawson*.[364] A building enjoying a right of light was pulled down and replaced by one with no windows facing the servient tenement. Fourteen years later, the servient owner built in such a way as to block light to the blank wall. When the dominant owner three years later sought to reassert the right to light by opening a window in the blank wall, the court held it to be too late: the right had been abandoned. A number of factors were significant: the building with the window had been demolished, the replacement building with its blank wall indicated that the right was no longer needed, the servient owner had acted to his detriment in building three years earlier and the gap of 17 years showed that the right was at an end. The judgments are confusing as to what combination of these factors was crucial.[365] In *Crossley & Sons Ltd* v *Lightowler*,[366] it was held that a right to pollute a stream was abandoned when the polluting dye-works were demolished and not replaced for more than 25 years.

Abandonment of rights of way is notoriously difficult to establish. More than simple non-use is required. Abandonment has been accepted where a right of way was never used in the 50 years after it was granted and had been blocked by fences and unlevel ground,[367] and where a redundant access had been blocked up for over 25 years.[368]

This material shows how each case is decided on its own facts. Indeed, it is not clear whether an intention to abandon suffices, or whether the servient owner has to rely on it before the easement will terminate.[369] It is unfortunate that there are no periods that can be

---

[361] [1893] AC 162 at p 168.

[362] (1868) LR 6 Eq 177.

[363] *Benn* v *Hardinge* (1992) 66 P&CR 246; Waring in *Landmark Cases in Property Law* (ed Douglas, Hickey and Waring), Chapter 11.

[364] (1824) 3 B&C 332 (107 ER 756). Contrast *CDC2020 plc* v *Ferreira* [2005] 3 EGLR 15 (right of way).

[365] Malins V-C in *Cook* v *Mayor & Corporation of Bath* (1868) LR 6 Eq 177 thought it crucial that the servient owner acted by building.

[366] (1867) LR 2 Ch App 478.

[367] *Swan* v *Sinclair* [1924] 1 Ch 254.

[368] *Williams* v *Usherwood* (1981) 45 P&CR 235 (the effective abandonment appears to have taken place after just two years); contrast *Williams* v *Sandy Lane (Chester) Ltd* [2007] 1 P&CR 457 (insubstantial fence for 30 years).

[369] Davis [1995] Conv 291.

relied upon as indicators of abandonment. There is an obvious contrast with prescription, where 20-year user provides the key to most cases. The Law Commission suggests a rebuttable presumption of abandonment after 20 years.[370]

Further reading

Baker, A [2012] Conv 37: Recreational privileges as easements: law and policy.

Bridge, S (2005) 'Prescriptive acquisition of easements: abolition or reform?' in *Modern Studies in Property Law*, Vol 3 (ed E Cooke), Chapter 1.

Davis, C [1995] Conv 291: Abandonment of an easement: is it a question of intention only?

Dawson, I and Dunn, A (1998) 18 LS 510: Negative easements – a crumb of analysis.

Spark, G [2012] Conv 6: Easements of parking and storage: are easements non-possessory interests in land?

Sturley, M F (1980) 96 LQR 557: Easements in gross.

Tee, L [1998] Conv 115: Metamorphoses and section 62 of the Law of Property Act 1925.

Turner, P G [2012] Conv 19: Prescription by and against lessees.

---

[370] Law Com No 327, para 3.230 (the period would be five years for rights to light, given that blocking up windows unequivocally points to abandonment: Law Com No 356).

24
Covenants

Introduction

A covenant is an obligation entered into by deed. As such, it may be regarded as part of the law of contract. Land law is concerned with two aspects of covenants. The first (and oldest) is whether the benefit of a covenant passes to the purchaser of land benefited by the covenant. Until the 1870s, it was not possible to assign the benefit of contractual rights at law, but the common law had centuries earlier recognised the passing of the benefit of covenants relating to land. The second concerns the burden of covenants affecting the covenantor's land: do they run on a transfer of that land? Since the mid-nineteenth century, equity has recognised that restrictive covenants (those not involving expenditure) bind purchasers of the burdened land. This created the restrictive covenant as a new form of equitable proprietary interest.

Much of the difficulty today results from confusion as to whether we are dealing with a contractual right (to which contract rules, such as assignment, apply) or a fully fledged property right. This has led to considerable complexity, particularly as regards the passing of the benefit of covenants. For most property rights, the most crucial question is as to the requirements for the burden to run. At least for restrictive covenants, this provides relatively few problems. It is odd that much of this chapter has to be devoted to the running of the benefit of covenants. Significantly, this issue is practically non-existent as regards easements, a comparable category of proprietary interests.

1. Positive covenants

A. Running of the burden

It has long been clear that the burden of positive covenants (those which require expenditure by the covenantor) does not run with any land to which the covenant is attached. This has received modern confirmation by the House of Lords in *Rhone* v *Stephens*,[1] which will be discussed later in this chapter.

A positive covenant may be entered into on a personal basis or in such a way as to purport to bind successors in title of the land affected. An example of a personal covenant was an obligation entered into by a statutory body to maintain river banks.[2] Although this benefited land of the covenantee (the land bordering the river), the covenantor had no land

---

[1] [1994] 2 AC 310; see p 559 below.
[2] *Smith and Snipes Hall Farm Ltd* v *River Douglas Catchment Board* [1949] 2 KB 500.

to which the burden related. No question as to the running of the burden with land could arise. On the other hand, an obligation to keep a road on one's land in repair and to allow public use obviously relates to that land.[3] It is in this second type of case that the question has arisen as to whether a purchaser of the land is bound by the covenant. Early in the nineteenth century, *Keppell* v *Bailey*[4] firmly held that the purchaser is not bound; this has been repeatedly confirmed.[5] The development of liability for breach of restrictive covenants in 1848 led to suggestions that this equitable liability should be extended to positive covenants. As will be seen later, this also has been firmly dismissed.[6]

In recent decades, there has been frequent criticism of this refusal to allow the burden of positive covenants to run. The problems are most acute for flats, where effective property management requires obligations to maintain each unit for the benefit of other flat holders and to share the costs of central facilities such as stairwells. Problems with the enforcement of freehold covenants have meant that lenders are reluctant to lend money on mortgage of freehold flats,[7] a factor contributing to their rarity.

After years of delay, we now have commonhold, a form of ownership under which the burden of covenants can run. However, commonhold (discussed in Chapter 21) has so far been a dismal failure (as well as not being suitable for all situations), and recent reform proposals will be considered at the end of this chapter. The inconvenience of the law relating to positive covenants has led to many suggestions as to how to circumvent it, some of which will now be considered. Those applying to freehold land have been described as 'all inconvenient, of doubtful effectiveness, and are of little or no use for practical purposes'.[8]

(i) *Use of leases*

The law of leasehold covenants permits both positive and restrictive covenants to run. This means that any assignee of the landlord or the tenant is bound by covenants, positive or negative, in the lease. As a consequence, leases are almost invariably used where the imposition of positive covenants is vital, as with blocks of flats.[9] The use of a lease need not mean that there is an obligation to pay rent. It may be for 99 years (or longer) with a nominal rent being due. For most practical purposes, a very long lease is as good as a fee simple.

How effective are such leases? They enable the landlord to enforce the covenants, but they suffer from the disadvantage that others cannot do so. In particular, lessees of other flats will not be able to enforce the covenants.[10] This means that use of leases is less flexible than restrictive covenants, which may be made in such a way as to be enforceable by

---

[3] *Austerberry* v *Oldham Corporation* (1885) 29 Ch D 750.
[4] (1834) 2 My&K 517 (39 ER 1042).
[5] *Austerberry* v *Oldham Corporation* (1885) 29 Ch D 750; *Jones* v *Price* [1965] 2 QB 618; *Rhone* v *Stephens* [1994] 2 AC 310.
[6] *Haywood* v *Brunswick Permanent Benefit BS* (1881) 8 QBD 403; see p 558 below.
[7] Wilberforce Committee on Positive Covenants Affecting Land (1965) Cmnd 2719, para 5.
[8] *Commonhold and Leasehold Reform* (DETR) (2000) Cm 4843, para 1.1.3. See also Law Com No 327, paras 5.21–5.28.
[9] The practice is well described by Clarke in *Land Law: Themes and Perspectives* (eds Bright and Dewar), Chapter 15.
[10] This can be alleviated if the freehold reversion (which may have little or no commercial value) is vested in a company controlled by all the lessees.

anyone who has land benefited by them.[11] In addition, the landlord cannot enforce positive covenants against sub-tenants, there being no privity of estate between them.

Can we justify the difference between freehold and leasehold covenants? This is a difficult question. The point can be made that in the case of a lease, the landlord retains an interest in the land. It is essential for the protection of this interest that, for example, the current tenant may be required to keep the land in repair. When we compare freehold covenants, the covenantee owns adjoining land. It may be less essential that positive obligations are enforced in this context, for the covenantee is often well positioned to do the work himself. However, the application of leasehold covenants for flats constitutes a distortion of the normal leasehold rules. The covenant is not entered into to protect a freehold reversion in 99 or 999 years' time; rather, it is to protect adjoining land of the other lessees. This does not prevent the efficacy of the leasehold covenant, but it does stress its artificiality.

Perhaps more than anything else, what the enforcement of leasehold covenants tells us is that there are no dreadful effects of allowing positive covenants to bind purchasers.[12] On the contrary, problems arise because the burden of positive covenants does not run.

(ii) *Chains of covenants*

Where the covenant relates to land, it will normally provide that the covenantor will be liable if he sells the land and the purchaser fails to comply with the covenant.[13] Accordingly, it is wise (and common) for the covenantor to require the purchaser to comply with the covenant. If the purchaser fails to comply, then the covenantee will sue the covenantor, who will in turn sue the purchaser. The purchaser will extract similar promises when subsequently selling the land. This chain of covenants suffers from the obvious problem that the chain is liable to be broken. If any covenantee or intermediate purchaser has disappeared or died, then the chain fails to impose liability on the current owner. The most that can usually be hoped for is that the current owner performs the obligation in the mistaken belief that the covenant has to be complied with.

It is, however, possible that the Contracts (Rights of Third Parties) Act 1999[14] will enable the original covenantee to sue on the promise by the present owner of the land, although this will depend upon whether the parties to that promise did indeed 'intend the term to be enforceable by the third party [the original covenantee]'.

(iii) *Requiring the covenantee's consent before sale by covenantor*

This enables the covenantee to require the purchaser to undertake a direct and fresh obligation as a condition of giving consent. In registered land, sale in breach of the requirement may be prevented by the entry of a restriction.[15] Although this may be effective in ensuring purchasers are bound, it is cumbersome in operation. There is no equivalent in unregis-

---

[11] See also Clarke (1995) 58 MLR 486.
[12] But cf p 559 below.
[13] It is impliedly made on behalf of successors in title (Law of Property Act 1925 (hereafter LPA), s 79); this means liability for successors in title.
[14] Discussed below, p 557.
[15] Law Com No 254, para 6.36 and Law Com No 271, para 6.40. See p 252 above.

tered land, unless it is stipulated that the covenantee's fee simple will terminate if consent is not sought. That uses a sledgehammer to crack a nut and is likely to be unacceptable.

(iv) *Benefit and burden*

It may be possible to bind a purchaser where (as is common) the covenant is the counterpart of rights being enjoyed by the purchaser. The purchaser cannot enjoy the benefit of a right without accepting the correlative covenanted burden. For example, the purchaser cannot use a private road without complying with a positive covenant to contribute towards its upkeep.[16] *Rhone* v *Stephens*[17] has shown that the principle will not apply unless performance of the covenant is a condition of the exercise of rights: this will generally require a distinct element of reciprocity between the covenant and the right. It is insufficient just to insert a covenant into a conveyance to the covenantor.

(v) *Other devices*

A number of technical devices have been suggested, but none has been shown to work in practice.[18] Statute permits tenants to convert certain very long leases into freeholds, whereupon covenants will continue to run as if the covenantee were still a landlord. It has been suggested that a covenantee (as intending vendor) could grant a long lease, which is almost immediately converted into a fee simple. Quite apart from the fact that leasehold covenants fail to solve all the problems, there may be drawbacks to such an artificial analysis.[19] It has also been suggested that covenants might be attached to rentcharges,[20] but there is great complexity in the analysis and no guarantee that courts would accept it.

B. The benefit of positive covenants

As will be seen a little later, running of the benefit has caused awful problems for restrictive covenants. So far as positive covenants are concerned, the cases are too few in number to extract useful principles. Although it became common for commentators to separate the positive covenant rules from the restrictive covenant rules, most cases seem to treat the principles as being substantially the same.[21] Sometimes, the equitable rules for restrictive covenants are today more relaxed than the old common law rules.[22] However, more recent tightening[23] of the rules for restrictive covenants may increase the risk of there being two sets of rules.

[16] *Halsall* v *Brizell* [1957] Ch 169, discussed above p 175.
[17] [1994] 2 AC 310.
[18] See Prichard (1973) 37 Conv 194.
[19] Taylor (1958) 22 Conv 101, perhaps too alarmist.
[20] Bright [1988] Conv 99. Such estate rentcharges can still be created after the Rentcharges Act 1977.
[21] Hurst (1982) 2 LS 53. *Westhoughton UDC* v *Wigan Coal & Iron Co Ltd* [1919] 1 Ch 159 at p 170 and *Federated Homes Ltd* v *Mill Lodge Properties Ltd* [1980] 1 WLR 594 are examples of authorities being used regardless of their origin in positive or restrictive covenants.
[22] For example, an equitable estate is sufficient: *Rogers* v *Hosegood* [1900] 2 Ch 388 at p 404. Further, there is no problem that the transferee holds just part of the land: *Re Union of London & Smith's Bank Ltd's Conveyance, Miles* v *Easter* [1933] Ch 611 at p 630.
[23] *Crest Nicholson Residential (South) Ltd* v *McAllister* [2004] 1 WLR 2409 (p 564 below); the reasoning is based on factors specific to restrictive covenants, in particular the running of the burden.

It is probably correct to say that a positive covenant will run provided that it 'touches and concerns' the benefited land.[24] This requirement will be considered in the context of restrictive covenants; it is not difficult to satisfy. Whilst there have been suggestions that it is necessary to show that the covenant is intended to run with the land (or, to use the technical term, is annexed to the land), developments in restrictive covenants indicate that it is unnecessary to make express provision in the covenant.[25] There used to be a rule that the claimant must have the same estate as the covenantee, so that a lessee could not enforce a covenant that had been entered into with the landlord. In *Smith and Snipes Hall Farm Ltd* v *River Douglas Catchment Board*,[26] the Court of Appeal held that this rule had been abrogated by LPA, s 78. Although the point was apparently conceded by counsel in *Smith and Snipes*, that case was treated as conclusive by the Court of Appeal in *Williams* v *Unit Construction Co Ltd*.[27] It is generally applauded for getting rid of an artificial and unnecessary rule.

The role of LPA, s 56

A somewhat different point arises from s 56. This provides that a person may take an interest in a covenant, although not named as a party. How can this be used in relation to the benefit of covenants? There are two principal possibilities, applicable to both positive and restrictive covenants. The first is that it might enable purchasers from covenantees to take the benefit of covenants, should the benefit not otherwise run. Although Denning LJ used s 56 to benefit purchasers in *Smith and Snipes*, this seems to be an inappropriate use of the section. There is a strong line of cases[28] holding that the section applies only to existing persons: it cannot apply to future unascertained persons. These cases were not dealt with by Denning LJ; his extension of the section seems plainly erroneous.

The second possibility regarding s 56 is that the covenant may be intended to benefit a neighbouring owner who is not party to the conveyance. For example, a vendor may sell land to A and then subsequently sell neighbouring land to B, taking a covenant from B. The vendor may intend that the covenant should benefit A as well as any land retained by the vendor. In these circumstances, s 56 may be used in order to enable A (and, thereby, A's successors in title) to sue on the covenant. The law of contract tells us that there are privity problems in this situation, but the common law had always allowed persons who were named as parties to a deed to sue upon it, even though they had not executed the deed. Section 56 clearly relaxes the common law requirement for A to be named as a party, but how far? A covenant 'with [the vendor's] assigns, owners for the time being of the lands adjoining or adjacent . . .' clearly falls within s 56[29] because it purports to be made with the vendor's assigns (earlier purchasers). Whether the section applies if the covenantor simply promises the vendor that those assigns will benefit is the contentious question.

Section 56 was considered by the House of Lords in *Beswick* v *Beswick*,[30] which involved the application of s 56 in a contract setting, far away from land law and deeds.

---

[24] *Kumar* v *Dunning* [1989] QB 193.
[25] Based on LPA, s 78: see p 563 below.
[26] [1949] 2 KB 500.
[27] (1951), reported (1955) 19 Conv NS 262.
[28] From *Kelsey* v *Dodd* (1881) 52 LJ Ch 34 (on the predecessor to s 56, s 5 of the Real Property Act 1845) to *Grant* v *Edmondson* [1931] 1 Ch 1.
[29] *Re Ecclesiastical Commissioners for England's Conveyance* [1936] Ch 430 at p 440.
[30] [1968] AC 58.

The House of Lords rejected an attempt by Lord Denning to apply s 56 in a purely contractual context, but left unsettled the role of s 56 in the property setting. Lord Upjohn expressed the opinion that the section applied only where the covenant purported to be with the claimant, in which case it is no longer necessary to name the claimant as a party to the deed. This restricted view of the section had the support of Lord Pearce, although Lord Guest appeared not to agree; Lord Reid left the question open, whilst apparently leaning towards Lord Upjohn. The previous cases[31] support Lord Upjohn, and his approach has been adopted by Neuberger J.[32] It means that it is not enough merely to promise the vendor that adjoining landowners will benefit: there must be a promise to those persons.

Contracts (Rights of Third Parties) Act 1999

Finally, it should be borne in mind that the enforceability of covenants may be affected by the 1999 Act. This enables a person other than the promisee (covenantee) to sue where 'the term purports to confer a benefit on him'. This will overlap with s 56, but without the limitations considered in the previous paragraph. Indeed, it may apply even if the covenant does not touch and concern the land in question, although then it would be unusual for the covenant to be intended to benefit the third party. On the other hand, the new right may sometimes be affected by rescission or variation of the contract[33]; it will sometimes be preferable for the third party to rely on s 56.

It is likely that the 1999 Act can also be used by successors in title to the covenantee. Section 1(3) establishes that it suffices if the third party is a member of a class or answers a particular description, and that the third party need not be alive. However, the rules on the running of the benefit are today sufficiently relaxed that few successors will need to rely on the 1999 Act.

2. Restrictive covenants

A series of nineteenth-century cases established that purchasers from covenantors are bound by restrictive covenants. The leading case is *Tulk* v *Moxhay* in 1848,[34] which involved Leicester Square garden. The reasoning in *Tulk* is not easy to disentangle, something which caused problems in later cases.

The general rationale for enforcing such promises was the fear of inappropriate use of land close to that of the covenantee: without the restrictive covenant, 'it would be impossible to sell part of [the covenantee's land] without incurring the risk of rendering what he retains worthless'. This may be seen as both fulfilling a planning function in limiting the use of land and also encouraging the sale of land at a time when land was required for development. However, the more specific analysis seems to have been that a purchaser who has notice of an obligation cannot ignore it, linked with the proposition that it would

---

[31] *Forster* v *Elvet Colliery Co Ltd* [1908] 1 KB 629 (upheld [1909] AC 98); *Re Ecclesiastical Commissioners for England's Conveyance* [1936] Ch 430; *White* v *Bijou Mansions Ltd* [1937] Ch 610 (upheld [1938] Ch 351). See also *Wiles* v *Banks* (1983) 50 P&CR 80.

[32] *Amsprop Trading Ltd* v *Harris Distribution Ltd* [1997] 1 WLR 1025.

[33] Section 2; note also defences in ss 3, 5.

[34] 2 Ph 774 (41 ER 1143); see McFarlane in *Landmark Cases in Equity* (eds Mitchell and Mitchell), Chapter 7.

be inequitable if the covenantor could purchase the land subject to the covenant one day and be able to sell it free of the restriction the following day.

Tulk v *Moxhay* is the leading authority, although earlier cases had come to the same result.[35] It was just a few years earlier in 1834 that Lord Brougham LC in *Keppell* v *Bailey*[36] denied that new interests in land could be created, but this opinion was soon strictly limited. In *Tulk* v *Moxhay*, Lord Cottenham LC expressly disagreed with *Keppell* v *Bailey*, insofar as it operated to limit the operation of equity. It is telling that counsel for the successful covenantee was not even called upon to argue his case before Lord Cottenham LC.

A. The limitation to restrictive covenants

The covenant in *Tulk* v *Moxhay* was to 'keep and maintain the said piece of ground and square garden . . . in its then form, and in sufficient and proper repair as a square garden and pleasure ground, in an open state and uncovered with any buildings . . .'. This has both a positive content (repair and maintenance) and a negative content (no use for building). Although the remedy given was in fact limited to a negative obligation,[37] the analysis regarding the effect of notice on purchasers was equally applicable to both positive and negative covenants. For a time, there was confusion as to whether the doctrine applied to positive covenants.

The restriction to negative covenants was effectively settled three decades later by *Haywood* v *Brunswick Permanent Benefit BS*,[38] in which it was observed that there had been only one clear example[39] of the application of *Tulk* v *Moxhay* to positive covenants. The reasoning in *Haywood* is difficult to assess,[40] as it seems to be assumed that *Tulk* v *Moxhay* had limited liability to restrictive covenants. In any event, *Haywood* was soon confirmed in *London & South Western Railway Co* v *Gomm*.[41] The language of the judges in *Gomm* demonstrates the uncertainty as to the position before *Haywood*. Whilst Jessell MR and Lindley LJ decline to 'extend' *Tulk* v *Moxhay*, Sir James Hannen treats *Haywood* as a 'restriction' on the doctrine.

Jessell MR made the oft-cited comment in *Gomm*[42] that 'The doctrine of [*Tulk* v *Moxhay*], rightly considered, appears to me to be either an extension in equity of the doctrine of *Spencer's Case* to another line of cases, or else an extension in equity of the doctrine of negative easements.' It might be observed that the comparison with negative easements has been most frequently stressed in later cases.[43] Indeed, if the comparison with the rules for leases in *Spencer's Case* is taken seriously, it is difficult to understand why positive covenants are not enforced just as they are in leases.

---

[35] Particularly *Whatman* v *Gibson* (1838) 9 Sim 196 (59 ER 333) and *Mann* v *Stephens* (1846) 15 Sim 377 (60 ER 665).
[36] 2 My&K 517 (39 ER 1042).
[37] See the proceedings before Lord Langdale MR (1848) 11 Beav 571 (50 ER 937).
[38] (1881) 8 QBD 403.
[39] *Cooke* v *Chilcott* (1876) 3 Ch D 694.
[40] Gardner (1982) 98 LQR 279 at p 293.
[41] (1882) 20 Ch D 562.
[42] Ibid, at p 583. Note the criticism in *Forestview Nominees Pty Ltd* v *Perpetual Trustee WA Ltd* (1998) 193 CLR 154.
[43] Most explicit is Scrutton J at first instance in *Wilkes* v *Spooner* [1911] 2 KB 473 at p 478.

Positive covenants were more recently reconsidered by *Rhone* v *Stephens*,[44] in which the House of Lords emphatically endorsed the earlier cases. The reasoning appears to be that it would be inconsistent with the common law rules on privity of contract for equity to enforce a positive covenant.[45] Given that the claimant was seeking an equitable remedy, it is difficult to comprehend that a positive equitable remedy is a negation of the common law rules[46] whereas a negative remedy is not. The explanation that a negative covenant 'prevents the successor from exercising a right which he never acquired' is little more than a repetition of the fact that a negative covenant is negative!

Are there other, more convincing, reasons for limiting *Tulk* v *Moxhay*? We should remember that the non-running of positive covenants is commonly regarded as inconvenient, especially for flats where they are essential for proper property maintenance. The law was probably based upon problems in giving equitable remedies for positive obligations,[47] together with a fear that positive obligations may render the ownership of land unduly burdensome. Burdening ownership could lead to an undesirable reduction in the alienability of land.

Despite the point that positive covenants are readily enforced in leases,[48] these operate so as to benefit the leased land: covenants benefiting adjoining land may be seen as less reasonable and less necessary. There are also fears that some positive covenants could, without statutory regulation, be enforced in a harsh and burdensome manner.[49] Finally, the telling point can be made in relation to *Rhone* that it would have been wrong to introduce the running of positive covenants when many thousands of people will have dealt with land on the basis of *Haywood* and *Gomm*.

A consequential question is what counts as a restrictive covenant. As *Tulk* v *Moxhay* itself shows, if a covenant imposes both positive and restrictive obligations, then the court will be prepared to enforce the restrictive part.[50] Further, the language of a covenant is not conclusive: *Gomm* stresses that a negative obligation may be found from positive words.[51] The crucial issue revolves around expenditure: whether the covenantor is required to 'put his hand into his pocket'.[52]

B. Dominant tenement

(i) *The requirement of a dominant tenement*

The story of this requirement is similar to that of the limitation to restrictive covenants. It fits in with Lord Cottenham LC's dictum in *Tulk* v *Moxhay* that liability is justified

---

[44] [1994] 2 AC 310.

[45] Convincingly criticised by Gardner [1995] CLJ 60 at pp 63–67.

[46] Lord Templeman feared that it would 'destroy the distinction between law and equity'. The old law of part performance of oral contracts was a good example of enforcement of positive obligations not recognised at law.

[47] Gardner (1982) 98 LQR 279 at p 296; see also Bell [1981] Conv 55 and [1983] Conv 327 and the contrary view of Griffith [1983] Conv 29.

[48] Gardner (1982) 98 LQR 279 at pp 295–296.

[49] See Lord Templeman in *Rhone* [1994] 2 AC 310 at p 321; also O'Connor [2011] Conv 191 in a spirited defence of the present law.

[50] See also *Shepherd Homes Ltd* v *Sandham (No 2)* [1971] 1 WLR 1062 at p 1067.

[51] For a strong example, see *Montross Associated Investments SA* v *Moussaieff* (1990) 61 P&CR 437; 'but will use' was interpreted as an emphatic negative, that no other use would be employed.

[52] Cotton LJ in *Haywood* (1881) 8 QBD 403 at p 409. Provision of services by the covenantor personally would also be positive.

because otherwise it would be dangerous to sell part of one's land. On the other hand, the stress on the purchaser's notice seems to deny the significance of a dominant tenement.

Although some cases initially enforced covenants without a dominant tenement, the requirement was imposed in *Formby* v *Barker*.[53] It was partly based on the *Gomm* rejection of the notice basis for *Tulk* v *Moxhay*. Stress was also placed on the *Tulk* v *Moxhay* dictum about the dangers of selling part of one's land and Jessell MR's comparison with negative easements and leasehold covenants. The earlier cases to the contrary were overlooked, although they were cited in the leading case of *LCC* v *Allen*[54] a few years later. *Allen* held that these cases must be treated as overruled by the later authorities, *Gomm* and *Formby* in particular. The judgment of Scrutton J is most illuminating, as he makes it clear that *Gomm* signalled a departure from the previous law and narrowed the operation of *Tulk* v *Moxhay*. Since that time, the requirement has never been doubted and is a central part of covenants law.[55]

It is not easy to explain why the requirement should exist. It receives support from the analogy with easements. However, the requirement of a dominant tenement in that context is sometimes disputed and it is doubtless inappropriate to push the analogy between the two interests too far. It can be also said that restrictive covenants provide a useful planning function, but that enforcement by a person who does not own neighbouring land could render them too oppressive. Restrictive covenants can be seen as socially useful insofar as they protect other land but otherwise as an unnecessary bar on development.[56] This is confirmed by the growth of public planning control to restrict the undesirable change of use of land. Where the covenantee has a valid interest in enforcing a covenant, statute has provided limited exemptions from the dominant land requirement.[57]

One point should be added. It is not essential that the dominant tenement be a separate plot of land. It was held in *Hall* v *Ewin*[58] that a different estate in the same land will suffice. The significance of this is that a landlord can assert the freehold reversion as the dominant tenement so as to enforce restrictive covenants against a sub-tenant, with whom there is no privity of estate.

(ii) *Touching and concerning the dominant tenement*

It would be pointless to require a dominant tenement if it did not have to be benefited by the covenant. The test is modelled on that for leasehold covenants; in the words of Farwell J in *Rogers* v *Hosegood*,[59] the covenant 'must either affect the land as regards mode of occupation, or it must be such as per se, and not merely from collateral circumstances, affects the

---

[53] [1903] 2 Ch 539.

[54] [1914] 3 KB 642.

[55] Lord Wilberforce, in the course of a dissenting speech, was surprisingly guarded in *Tophams Ltd* v *Sefton* [1967] 1 AC 50 at p 81. No other judge expressed doubts.

[56] See Gardner (1982) 98 LQR 279 at pp 308–310.

[57] Well known examples are s 609 of the Housing Act 1985, relating to local housing authorities (not extending to positive covenants: *Cantrell* v *Wycombe DC* [2009] HLR 225) and the National Trust Act 1937, s 8.

[58] (1887) 37 Ch D 74 (a wild beast exhibition involving lions, gongs and trumpets). Mortgagees may also be liable: *Regent Oil Co Ltd* v *JA Gregory (Hatch End) Ltd* [1966] Ch 402 at pp 432–433.

[59] [1900] 2 Ch 388 at p 395, relying on Bayley J in *Congleton Corporation* v *Pattison* (1808) 10 East 130 at p 138 (103 ER 725 at p 728).

value of the land'. Essentially, it is a question of fact whether the land is benefited and the courts have not been zealous in requiring proof of benefit. In most cases, the covenant is imposed on the sale of part of the covenantee's land: the retained land becomes the dominant tenement. In this context, the retained land is adjacent to the burdened land and clearly benefited by the covenant. However, three problematic issues will be considered.

Large estates

The first issue is whether a very large estate can be said to benefit from a covenant taken on the sale of a small part. The covenant may be taken for the benefit of the retained land as a single unit, though this is unusual today. Despite the retained land being many thousands of acres, the courts in *Marten* v *Flight Refuelling Ltd*[60] and subsequent cases[61] have been willing to accept the opinion of the covenantee that the land is benefited. So long as this opinion can reasonably be held, the courts will not delve into the detailed evidence.

Today, the covenant is far more likely to provide that the benefit will be enjoyed by each part of the estate rather than the estate as a single unit.[62] This raises the question as to whether a sale of a distant part of the retained land will enable that purchaser to enforce the covenant. It seems probable that the courts would decide that the distant part is not benefited. It is one thing to say that a 10,000-acre estate is benefited as an entire entity, but quite a different thing to argue that each individual acre is benefited.

How does this apply where a housing estate is developed under a scheme of development? If the number of houses being built is small, then it is easy to say that each is benefited by the covenant. But this may be more difficult where there is a large building estate of hundreds of houses. Even then, the courts are likely to hold that each householder has an interest in maintaining the amenities and nature of the neighbourhood. This is supported by *Gilbert* v *Spoor*,[63] in which the dominant land was held to benefit from a low housing density and the preservation of a view, even though it was not visible from the dominant land.

Types of covenant

The second issue concerns the nature of the covenant. Most restrictive covenants prevent building or change of use. These will normally benefit adjoining land, although *Cosmichome Ltd* v *Southampton CC*[64] illustrates limits. Such a covenant was found to be designed to obtain part of the profit on a change of use and not in fact to have any effect on adjoining land. What about covenants designed to prevent competition with the covenantee's business on neighbouring land? Despite some criticism,[65] numerous cases accept

---

[60] [1962] Ch 115. *Re Ballard's Conveyance* [1937] Ch 473, which had suggested a stricter approach, was distinguished.
[61] *Earl of Leicester* v *Wells-next-the-Sea UDC* [1973] Ch 110; *Wrotham Park Estate Co Ltd* v *Parkside Homes Ltd* [1974] 1 WLR 798.
[62] *Federated Homes Ltd* v *Mill Lodge Properties Ltd* [1980] 1 WLR 594, discussed fully below.
[63] [1983] Ch 27.
[64] [2013] 1 WLR 2436 (covenants by BBC).
[65] Elphinstone (1952) 68 LQR 353; cf Hayton (1971) 87 LQR 539 at pp 544–545. See also the doubts expressed as to solus ties in *Noakes & Co Ltd* v *Rice* [1902] AC 24 (Lords Macnaghten and Davey).

them as effective restrictive covenants.[66] A fairly recent development is that land agreements have been brought within the competition legislation.[67] This may, in particular, have a significant impact on traders with a significant market share.

It may also be possible to have quite different forms of covenant. Thus, one case has held a covenant restricting disposal of land to be a restrictive covenant, although it does not relate to the manner of use of the land.[68] However, other cases have taken the opposite view.[69]

How far apart?

The third issue is where the covenantee owns properties some distance apart and attempts to impose a restrictive covenant on the sale of one of them. There seems to be every reason for the courts to take a generous view (similar to *Marten* v *Flight Refuelling Ltd*) in assessing whether the retained land is benefited. Greater problems may arise where the covenant is designed to prevent competition. It is obvious that such a covenant may benefit a business conducted on land several miles away. The courts are likely to enforce such covenants against purchasers if the two properties are relatively close together, as in the same street or shopping centre, although long distances may be more problematic.[70]

C. The running of the benefit

The outstanding feature of restrictive covenants in the twentieth century was the number of cases on the running of their benefit. This has, perhaps, been the product of uncertainty as to how far restrictive covenants should be treated as property rights running with the benefited land automatically (in the same way as the benefit of easements runs) or as contractual rights passing by assignment. The result was an explosion of complexity that reflects little credit on the law. Fortunately, the decision of the Court of Appeal in *Federated Homes Ltd* v *Mill Lodge Properties Ltd*[71] in 1980 provided some welcome simplification.

There are three traditional ways in which the benefit may run: annexation, assignment and schemes of development. In addition, we should not forget that the Contracts (Rights of Third Parties) Act 1999 may have an impact.

---

[66] *Wilkes* v *Spooner* [1911] 2 KB 473; *Newton Abbot Co-operative Society Ltd* v *Williamson & Treadgold Ltd* [1952] Ch 286; *Regent Oil Co Ltd* v *JA Gregory (Hatch End) Ltd* [1966] Ch 402; *Re Royal Victoria Pavilion, Ramsgate* [1961] Ch 581; *Williams* v *Kiley* [2003] 1 EGLR 46 (Buxton LJ considered, obiter, the competition legislation). Covenants imposed by sellers and lessors are outside the restraint of trade rules: *Esso Petroleum Co Ltd* v *Harper's Garage (Stourport) Ltd* [1968] AC 269.

[67] See p 597 below.

[68] *Hemingway Securities Ltd* v *Dunraven Ltd* (1994) 71 P&CR 30 (Jacob J; the issue was not fully discussed); Luxton & Wilkie [1995] Conv 416. *Hemingway* was followed in *Test Valley BC* v *Minilec Engineering Ltd* [2005] 2 EGLR 113, although on other grounds.

[69] Megarry J in *Shepherd Homes Ltd* v *Sandham (No 2)* [1971] 1 WLR 1062 at p 1070 and Lightman J in *University of East London Corporation* v *Barking and Dagenham LBC* [2005] Ch 354. In *Caldy Manor Estate Ltd* v *Farrell* [1974] 1 WLR 1303 Russell LJ left the question open, as did Lightman J in *Crestfort Ltd* v *Tesco Stores Ltd* [2005] L&TR 413 at [58] after *Hemingway* had been cited to him.

[70] Finkelstein J in *Baramon Sales Pty Ltd* v *Goodman Fielder Mills Ltd* [2001] FCA 1792 regarded distance as immaterial if benefit could be proved (flour mill: seven miles not a problem). Contrast *McGuigan Investments Pty Ltd* v *Dalwood Vineyards Pty Ltd* [1970] 1 NSWR 686 (properties 17 miles apart: no benefit).

[71] [1980] 1 WLR 594; Gravells in *Landmark Cases in Land Law* (ed Gravells), Chapter 5.

(i) *Annexation*

Annexation is the linking of the covenant to the benefited land, usually by the covenant itself. Once annexed, the benefit passes automatically on the transfer of the land: the purchaser's awareness of the covenant is irrelevant.[72] What is necessary to show an intention to annex? With easements, annexation seems to be automatic and to give rise to virtually no problems. Perhaps because of the contractual origins of the restrictive covenant, the courts have looked for words linking the covenant with the dominant land. This has two interwoven elements: identifying the benefited land and then showing that the covenant is for the benefit of that land.

The leading case is *Rogers* v *Hosegood*,[73] in which annexation resulted from a covenant with the vendors, 'their heirs and assigns, and others claiming under them to all or any of their lands adjoining or near to the said premises'. It will be noted that the covenant itself did not identify the benefited land with precision: extrinsic evidence was required to establish what adjoining or near land was owned.[74] Yet, *Renals* v *Cowlishaw*[75] shows that it is fatal to say nothing at all about the land, and in *Reid* v *Bickerstaff*,[76] a provision that the benefit was for the 'vendors, their heirs and assigns' was insufficient to annex.

The role of LPA, s 78

The major issue that has arisen in recent decades concerns the role of s 78 in annexing restrictive covenants without the need for express words.[77] The section reads: 'A covenant relating to any land of the covenantee shall be deemed to be made with the covenantee and his successors in title and the persons deriving title under him or them . . .'. In *Federated Homes*, the Court of Appeal held that the section effected a statutory annexation. The court brushed aside the conventional view that the section was merely a word-saving provision. Brightman LJ relied on earlier positive covenant cases,[78] despite their failure to give full consideration to the section. Although the decision has received strong and cogent criticism from commentators,[79] *Crest Nicholson Residential (South) Ltd* v *McAllister*[80] confirms it, although with a rather narrower scope than was initially thought.

The principal question is as to what is required for s 78 to operate. It is common ground that the covenant must touch and concern the benefited land or, in the language of the section, relate to it. More importantly, Brightman LJ left open whether it is necessary for the

---

[72] *Rogers* v *Hosegood* [1900] 2 Ch 388.

[73] [1900] 2 Ch 388.

[74] See also *Shropshire CC* v *Edwards* (1982) 46 P&CR 270.

[75] (1878) 9 Ch D 125; (1879) 11 Ch D 866.

[76] [1909] 2 Ch 305.

[77] There has been a separate argument (see Wade [1972B] CLJ 157 at pp 168–169, based on *Marten* v *Flight Refuelling Ltd* [1962] Ch 115) that the courts could imply annexation from the surrounding circumstances, but see the convincing contrary arguments of Ryder (1972) 36 Conv 20 and also *J Sainsbury plc* v *Enfield LBC* [1989] 1 WLR 590. Wade's argument is substantially bypassed by the s 78 analysis.

[78] *Smith and Snipes Hall Farm Ltd* v *River Douglas Catchment Board* [1949] 2 KB 500; *Williams* v *Unit Construction Co Ltd* (1955) 19 Conv NS 262. See also Radcliffe (1941) 57 LQR 203 and Wade [1972B] CLJ 157, although Wade's argument that the predecessor of s 78 (Conveyancing Act 1881, s 58) effected annexation was rejected in *J Sainsbury plc* v *Enfield LBC* [1989] 1 WLR 590.

[79] Newsom (1981) 97 LQR 32, stressing the legislative history of s 78 and the weakness of the cases relied upon by the court; Hayton (1980) 43 MLR 445; Hurst (1982) 2 LS 53.

[80] [2004] 1 WLR 2409; Howell [2004] Conv 507; Moran (2004) 133 Prop LJ 10.

covenant to identify the benefited land.[81] This question was addressed by the Court of Appeal in *Crest Nicholson*.[82] It was firmly held both that the earlier cases required identification of the benefited land (although a general description suffices, as in *Rogers* v *Hosegood*) and that this was unaffected by s 78. It was stressed that it is important that purchasers of the burdened land should be able to identify which land is benefited. *Crest Nicholson* acts as a major restriction upon the scope of statutory annexation. What, then, does s 78 achieve? Following *Federated Homes*, the section renders it unnecessary to state that the covenant is enforceable by successors in title or that the covenant is to run with the land.[83] Nevertheless, a covenant which identifies the land to be benefited might readily be construed (even apart from s 78) as effecting an express annexation.

A separate issue is whether the parties can exclude the effect of s 78. The starting point is that s 78 contains no provision for contrary intention. The question was soon considered by Judge Paul Baker QC in *Roake* v *Chadha*.[84] In that case, the covenant stipulated that the benefit should pass only by assignment: in other words, that there should be no annexation. It was held that annexation may still be excluded by contrary intention, and this was approved by the Court of Appeal in *Crest Nicholson*.[85] The Court of Appeal relied on the wording of s 78, which defines successors in title by reference to land 'intended to be benefited'. This wording supports the significance of intention in annexation and explains why there is no need for any explicit statutory mention of contrary intention.

Section 78 displays several contrasts with its sister provision s 79, which covers the running of burdens. The latter section does allow for contrary intention,[86] though it was explained in *Crest Nicholson* that this is required because there is nothing in s 79 equivalent to the words 'intended to be benefited'. The effect of s 78 as making the benefit run has explicitly not been applied to s 79 to make the burden of covenants (positive and restrictive) run.[87] However, the effect of s 78 is a good deal less radical following *Crest Nicholson*. In any event, the contrasts may be justified by the different drafting of the two sections.

Forms of annexation

A quite separate annexation issue relates to the entity to which the covenant is annexed. Most simply, the covenant may be annexed to each and every part of the land.[88] The consequence of this is that a purchaser of any part of the dominant land can enforce the covenant, provided always that it touches and concerns that part. The alternative is annexation to the whole. It is common for the covenantee to own a large block of land, often a named

---

[81] [1980] 1 WLR 594 at p 604.

[82] [2004] 1 WLR 2409 at [30]–[34].

[83] *Mohammadzadeh* v *Joseph* [2008] 1 P&CR 107 stresses that there is no requirement for the transfer to state that the identified land (retained by the covenantee) is benefited.

[84] [1984] 1 WLR 40. Judge Paul Baker QC was no stranger to these problems: see (1968) 84 LQR 22.

[85] [2004] 1 WLR 2409 at [41]–[44]. See also *Sugarman* v *Porter* [2006] 2 P&CR 274: annexation may be limited until the time the benefited land is sold.

[86] *Morrells of Oxford Ltd* v *Oxford United FC Ltd* [2001] Ch 459 considers the operation of contrary intention in s 79.

[87] *Tophams Ltd* v *Sefton* [1967] 1 AC 50; *Rhone* v *Stephens* [1994] 2 AC 310 at pp 321–322; *Morrells of Oxford Ltd* v *Oxford United FC Ltd* [2001] Ch 459. This failure to use s 79 is attacked by Turano [2000] Conv 377.

[88] *Marquess of Zetland* v *Driver* [1939] Ch 1.

estate such as the Blenheim estate. In cases of this nature, it is natural to think of the benefit as being for the estate as a single entity. This means that a subsequent purchaser of a small part of the estate would not acquire the benefit.[89] If the estate was broken up so that it ceased to exist as an entity, then the annexation would cease to be effective,[90] although there would be no problems in the estate owner's ability to sue if relatively small areas were sold off.[91]

Although the two possibilities of annexation to each and every part and to the whole necessarily add complexity to the law, it can be claimed that they allow the courts to give effect to differing intentions. Unfortunately, there used to be a presumption of annexation to the whole, even in situations where there was little reason to view the dominant land as a single entity. This emerged in a string of cases in the 1960s[92] and resulted in the employment of assignment as an alternative method of passing the benefit.[93] This presumption of annexation to the whole was rejected in *Federated Homes*. Brightman LJ thought annexation to the whole to be 'a difficult conception fully to grasp' and held that annexation to each and every part was to be presumed.[94] This is a welcome conclusion.

(ii) *Assignment*

In the years before *Federated Homes*, assignment became an important method of passing the benefit of restrictive covenants. It was particularly useful when inadequate words of annexation had been used or there had been annexation to the whole. *Federated Homes* solved many of these problems with annexation, and it is unlikely that assignment will be as widely used in the future. Its rules will be summarised. Modern examples of successful assignment commence with *Newton Abbot Co-operative Society Ltd* v *Williamson & Treadgold Ltd* in 1952,[95] although it has earlier roots.[96] Unlike annexation, the covenant need say nothing as to the benefited land. *Newton Abbot*[97] held that it suffices if the land to be benefited can be identified by extrinsic evidence with reasonable certainty.[98] All that is thereafter required is that the sale of the land makes it clear that the purchaser is to get the benefit of the covenant. As has been seen, there can be an assignment whether or not the benefit has been annexed.[99]

---

[89] *Russell* v *Archdale* [1964] Ch 38. One advantage to the covenantee is that he or she would be able to control any relaxation of the covenant and would be able to pocket the whole of any payment for the relaxation.

[90] *Stilwell* v *Blackman* [1968] Ch 508.

[91] *Wrotham Park Estate Co Ltd* v *Parkside Homes Ltd* [1974] 1 WLR 798.

[92] *Russell* v *Archdale* [1964] Ch 38; *Re Jeff's Transfer (No 2)* [1966] 1 WLR 841; *Stilwell* v *Blackman* [1968] Ch 508. *Re Selwyn's Conveyance* [1967] Ch 674 is a lonely exception.

[93] Baker (1968) 84 LQR 22 and Hayton (1971) 87 LQR 539 are critical of the use of assignment in this context, arguing that it brings contractual principles into a property context and subverts the annexation rules.

[94] [1980] 1 WLR 594 at p 606. *Bryant Homes Southern Ltd* v *Stein Management Ltd* [2017] 1 P&CR 65 displays a marked reluctance to depart from that presumption.

[95] [1952] Ch 286.

[96] *Renals* v *Cowlishaw* (1878) 9 Ch D 125; (1879) 11 Ch D 866.

[97] Rejecting the contrary view of Bennett J at first instance in *Re Union of London & Smith's Bank Ltd's Conveyance, Miles* v *Easter* [1933] Ch 611. This relaxation has not gone unchallenged: Elphinstone (1952) 68 LQR 353; Hayton (1971) 87 LQR 539.

[98] Doubtless the covenant could provide that it is personal to the covenantee such that it could not be assigned, but this would be very unusual.

[99] The point is fully discussed in *Stilwell* v *Blackman* [1968] Ch 508.

Two further requirements should be noted. First, the covenant must be assigned at the same time that the land is sold. Once land and covenant have become separated, the covenant ceases to exist as anything more than a contractual right in the covenantee; thereafter, it cannot be assigned to the purchaser. This was established by the Court of Appeal in *Re Union of London & Smith's Bank Ltd's Conveyance*.[100] It may be seen as an aspect of the requirement of a dominant tenement, which is infringed once there is a split between entitlement to the covenant and entitlement to the land.[101]

The second requirement is that there may need to be an assignment every time the dominant land is sold; in other words, a chain of assignments from the original covenantee to the current owner. This was conceded, and accepted by Wynn-Parry J, in *Re Pinewood Estate, Farnborough*[102] and most recent cases assume it to be correct.[103] However, there is a contrary view[104] that the earlier cases permitted the covenantee unilaterally to annex the covenant to the land (after the execution of the covenant). Assignment would be an obvious example of unilateral annexation. If such delayed annexation had been accepted (the authorities requiring a chain are probably too strong), then it would have been necessary only to have an assignment on the first sale: thereafter, the benefit would pass by annexation.

Implied assignment?

It has been argued that assignment may be implied by statute. This is based on LPA, s 62, which deems conveyances to include all 'easements, rights, and advantages whatsoever, appertaining or reputed to appertain to the land'. If this were to apply to covenants, then this would render much of the litigation of the last century unnecessary: there would have been a statutory assignment in virtually every case. This very fact renders it unlikely that the section has any such effect. Farwell J expressed early doubts in *Rogers* v *Hosegood*,[105] although the first instance judge in *Federated Homes* supported the application of s 62.

Roake v *Chadha*[106] contains the only reported full discussion of the issue. Judge Paul Baker QC refused to apply the section, holding that a non-annexed covenant does not appertain to the land and that in any event the section may not apply to rights of an equitable nature. Sir Nicolas Browne-Wilkinson V-C adopted a very similar analysis in *Kumar* v *Dunning*.[107]

Where a trustee[108] or personal representative[109] transfers the dominant land to the beneficiary or legatee, then express assignment is not required. The courts regard the covenant as held for the benefit of the transferee. Plainly, the trustee or personal representative

---

[100] [1933] Ch 611.

[101] *Chambers* v *Randall* [1923] 1 Ch 149.

[102] [1958] Ch 280; supported by the trial judge in *Federated Homes* and, apparently, *Emile Elias & Co Ltd* v *Pine Groves Ltd* [1993] 1 WLR 305 at p 309 (PC).

[103] See Gravells *Landmark Cases in Land Law* (ed Gravells), pp 107–108.

[104] See Hayton (1971) 87 LQR 539 at pp 557 and 565 and the authorities referred to. It may be supported by Proudman J in *Cygnet Healthcare Ltd* v *Greenswan Consultants Ltd* [2009] EWHC 1318 (Ch) at [14].

[105] [1900] 2 Ch 388 at p 398.

[106] [1984] 1 WLR 40. Peter Smith J reached a similar conclusion regarding LPA, s 63 in *Sugarman* v *Porter* [2006] 2 P&CR 274.

[107] [1989] QB 193 at p 198.

[108] *Lord Northbourne* v *Johnston & Son* [1922] 2 Ch 309.

[109] *Newton Abbot Co-operative Society Ltd* v *Williamson & Treadgold Ltd* [1952] Ch 286; *Earl of Leicester* v *Wells-next-the-Sea UDC* [1973] Ch 110.

cannot hold the covenant for their personal benefit. No express assignment is required on the transfer as the transferee was entitled to the benefit of the covenant even before the transfer.

(iii) *Schemes of development*

Suppose land is laid out in plots as part of a scheme of development, building to be undertaken by the owner/developer or by individual purchasers. In such a situation, it is common for identical forms of covenants to be imposed on purchasers. The courts have been prepared to hold that a form of 'local law' applies within the scheme and that restrictive covenants pass without annexation or assignment.

The importance of schemes of development

The most obvious point is that, as has been observed, there is no need for annexation or assignment.[110] Now that *Federated Homes* has permitted statutory annexation, this is less likely to be important. More significant is that owners of plots that have already been sold off can enforce covenants entered into on subsequent sales. This could be achieved by applying LPA, s 56, although this may require careful drafting of the covenant.

So far, we have been considering the liability accepted by the purchaser, but equally important is the liability of the vendor. In many cases, the covenant is drafted simply so as to bind the purchaser, with nothing being said as to any right for the purchaser to control use of the vendor's retained land within the scheme. However, the courts have been ready to imply that the purchaser has such a right. This means that future purchasers from the developer will buy land already burdened by covenants, even if they do not enter into fresh covenants.[111] This is a clear manifestation of the idea behind a scheme of development whereby each plot is intended to be subject to the same covenant regime. Its most telling application lies in the liability of the developer who retains some of the plots and uses them in a manner inconsistent with the covenants.[112]

A quite different effect of a scheme of development is that the 'local law' will survive common ownership and occupation of two or more plots within the scheme. The normal rule is that common ownership and occupation terminates a covenant,[113] just as with easements. If the plots are subsequently separated again, it is necessary to create the covenants afresh. However, the Privy Council held in *Texaco Antilles Ltd v Kernochan*[114] that the covenants in a scheme of development automatically revive when the plots are separated. This is a convenient result because two or more plots frequently come into common ownership, particularly when a builder purchases them for the purpose of building and then

---

[110] There was never any analogy to annexation to the whole, so purchase of a part poses no problems.

[111] See Megarry J in *Brunner* v *Greenslade* [1971] Ch 993. Bailey observed that the peculiarity of schemes of development is 'that the Court will hold that surrounding facts . . . permit the covenant to be read in a wider sense than its bare words would do': (1938) 6 CLJ 339 at p 365.

[112] *Hudson* v *Cripps* [1896] 1 Ch 265; *Newman* v *Real Estate Debenture Corporation Ltd* [1940] 1 All ER 131. Both cases are examples of schemes of development involving the leasing of flats, where it is the landlord who is liable. *Newman* demonstrates that large numbers of plots are not essential: there were just four flats.

[113] *Re Tiltwood, Sussex* [1978] Ch 269. Note the interesting criticism by Bates (1980) 54 ALJ 156, although it is far from convincing.

[114] [1973] AC 609. See also Megarry J in *Brunner* v *Greenslade* [1971] Ch 993.

selling. It would be odd if the purchasers of these plots could not enforce the covenants inter se, the more so as they remain liable on the covenants to all other purchasers within the scheme. It also fits well with the idea of a 'local law' operating within the area of the scheme: whilst an owner of two plots obviously cannot enforce the covenant against himself, there is no reason for the local law not to apply when one of the plots is sold.

When will there be a scheme of development?

Although the origins of schemes lie in nineteenth-century deeds of mutual covenant by purchasers, it is usual today to refer to the tests laid down by Parker J in *Elliston* v *Reacher*.[115] Parker J required proof of four factors:

(1) that both the claimant and defendant derive title from the same common vendor;
(2) that previously to selling the land, the vendor laid out his estate or a defined portion thereof (including the lands purchased by the claimant and defendant, respectively) for sale in lots subject to restrictions intended to be imposed on all the lots, and which, although varying in details as to particular lots,[116] are consistent and consistent only with some general scheme of development;
(3) that these restrictions were intended by the common vendor to be and were for the benefit of all the lots intended to be sold, whether or not they were also intended to be for the benefit of other land retained by the vendor; and
(4) that the lots were purchased from the common vendor upon the footing that the restrictions were to enure for the benefit of the other lots included in the scheme, whether or not they were intended to enure for other lots retained by the vendor.

Although the fourth requirement would readily be inferred, these requirements were so demanding that it is said that until the 1960s, only two litigated schemes had satisfied them.[117] The mood has subsequently changed towards a much less technical approach. Cross J upheld a scheme in *Baxter* v *Four Oaks Properties Ltd*[118] despite the absence of lotting: the vendor intended that there be plots of differing sizes and did not specify details at the start. It is interesting that the covenant was explicit that purchasers should be able to enforce the covenants inter se. A similar problem was encountered in *Re Dolphin's Conveyance*[119]; there was also no common vendor because the original vendor had died during the sales. Stamp J adopted the approach of Cross J and placed emphasis on the parties' common intention and common interest. Without doubt, these cases herald a more flexible approach. In particular, the precise *Elliston* requirements may be relaxed where necessary to avoid undue technicality.[120]

However, it would be unsafe to assume that *Elliston* can be forgotten. It is instructive that the Court of Appeal in *Lund* v *Taylor*[121] considered that the conditions for inferring a

---

[115] [1908] 2 Ch 374 at p 384, approved by the Court of Appeal [1908] 2 Ch 665.
[116] Significant differences, particularly where the plots are of a similar size, are likely to be fatal: *Emile Elias & Co Ltd* v *Pine Groves Ltd* [1993] 1 WLR 305.
[117] Preston and Newsom, *Restrictive Covenants* (10th edn), para 2.81.
[118] [1965] Ch 816.
[119] [1970] Ch 654.
[120] Note the convincing Australian view that it suffices if two different owners combine to develop an area: *Re Mack & the Conveyancing Act* [1975] 2 NSWLR 623 at p 629.
[121] (1975) 31 P&CR 167 at pp 178–179.

scheme of development were fundamentally the same as before. The Privy Council in *Emile Elias & Co Ltd v Pine Groves Ltd*[122] also continued to apply the *Elliston* criteria.

It is probable that there must be some indication as to the extent of the scheme, even if the precise lots are not specified. Without any form of estate plan establishing the extent of the locality and therefore liability, it is difficult to accept the idea of a local law.[123] It will also be essential to prove the common intention that all lots should be subject to the covenants. As Browne-Wilkinson J stressed,[124] 'reciprocity of obligation and the intention to create such reciprocity is a fundamental requirement'. It is here that problems are likely to centre.

Countless cases have held that it is quite insufficient for a common vendor to sell to purchasers with identical covenants: this fails to prove an intention as to reciprocity as regards purchasers inter se.[125] Such was fully accepted in *Dolphin*. It is significant that both *Baxter* and *Dolphin* involved covenants which on their face made it clear that reciprocity was intended. Similarly, in *Williams v Kiley*,[126] interlocking covenants in five leases of shops in a parade demonstrated reciprocity. Although the substance of the obligations varied (each shop had its own and exclusive sphere of business), there clearly was a carefully worked out scheme to benefit each shop. There is much to be said for the view of Newsom[127] that *Elliston* is still of great value where reciprocity is not evident on the face of the covenant.[128]

(iv) *Contract*

Absent any assignment, purchasers of the benefited land cannot rely on traditional contract principles: there is no privity of contract. However, it is possible that they could rely on the Contracts (Rights of Third Parties) Act 1999.[129] This would apply if there were wording in the covenant, perhaps supplied by LPA, s 78, showing that third parties (the purchasers of the benefited land) should have the benefit of the covenant. This would be relevant if the benefited land was not sufficiently identified so as to allow annexation. However, this essentially contractual analysis would not necessarily operate so as to enable purchasers of the benefited land to sue purchasers of the burdened land.

(v) *Conclusions*

It may readily be concluded that the rules as to passing the benefit are quite unnecessarily complex. The law as to schemes of development may be put on one side, as it achieves more

---

[122] [1993] 1 WLR 305.
[123] *Reid v Bickerstaff* [1909] 2 Ch 305; *Jamaica Mutual Life Assurance Society v Hillsborough Ltd* [1989] 1 WLR 1101; *Emile Elias & Co Ltd v Pine Groves Ltd* [1993] 1 WLR 305; *Birdlip Ltd v Hunter* [2016] EWCA Civ 603.
[124] *Kingsbury v LW Anderson Ltd* (1979) 40 P&CR 136 at p 143.
[125] A fairly recent example is *Small v Oliver & Saunders (Developments) Ltd* [2006] 3 EGLR 141.
[126] [2003] 1 EGLR 46. It is the first English case to involve a letting scheme with restrictions on trading. Buxton LJ considered, obiter, competition aspects of the facts.
[127] (1970) 114 SJ 798.
[128] Although there must still be proof of intended reciprocity: *Small v Oliver & Saunders (Developments) Ltd* [2006] 3 EGLR 141.
[129] See p 557 above.

than merely passing the benefit. Otherwise, what do the rules set out to achieve? It has already been observed that they may originate from confusion as to whether a restrictive covenant is a property right passing automatically with the land or a contractual right held by the covenantee. Though it may help to explain the present state of the law, this does not justify it.

Nevertheless, it can be argued that some special rules for covenants are justified. It is instructive that reform proposals have included a tightening up of the rules relating to benefit.[130] This, of course, runs counter to the liberalising developments in each of annexation, assignment and schemes of development. The reform proposals do not propose words of annexation, but it is urged that the land to be benefited should be clearly identified by the covenant in order that the benefit can be registered. Why is this important for restrictive covenants?

Two factors might be identified. First, the nature of a restrictive covenant is such that the dominant land is likely to be uncertain. In part, this is because restrictive covenants commonly benefit the vendor's retained land and that land is frequently not identified in the conveyance. In contrast, most easements are created in favour of the land sold, in which case the benefited land is obvious. In part, it is based upon the nature of a restrictive covenant: an obligation not to do something. It is natural to enter into restrictive covenants without mention of the land to be benefited. Positive rights (whether to require another to spend money or a right, such as an easement, to do something) are far more likely to identify the benefited land. Take the obligation to maintain river banks in *Smith and Snipes*. It is natural in such a case to specify the land benefited. Even if the river banks were on the covenantor's land, the land to be benefited will generally be obvious from the physical facts. So far as easements are concerned, it is difficult to create a right of way, for example, without the facts making it clear what land is benefited. This is not to argue that problems of identifying the benefited land never occur outside restrictive covenants, but rather that they are far less common.

This leads to the second factor: the importance of identifying the benefited land. Whenever a right is being asserted (whether it be a restrictive covenant, positive covenant or easement), it is incumbent on the claimant to prove the passing of the benefit. Whilst holders of servient land have an obvious interest in whether this can be done, it might be thought that the presence of uncertainty does not matter too much to them. It is the servient owner's good fortune if the right cannot be enforced.

However, this argument overlooks the fact that owners of land subject to restrictive covenants frequently wish to develop it in a manner inconsistent with the covenants. The simplest way of doing so is by coming to an agreement with the holders of the benefited land. Agreement will normally be feasible where either there is a trivial breach or sufficiently generous compensation is offered. However, such an agreement is impossible if the benefited land cannot be identified; identification is likely to be especially difficult for successors in title of the burdened land. The holders of land bound by positive covenants and easements are less likely to want to negotiate out of these obligations. One can therefore argue that efficient land management requires the ready identification of the benefited land and that this is particularly important for restrictive covenants.

---

[130] Wilberforce Committee on Positive Covenants Affecting Land (1965) Cmnd 2719, paras 15–17; Law Com No 127, paras 4.10, 8.21–8.24. See now Law Com No 327, paras 6.48–6.51.

The importance of identification was recognised by *Crest Nicholson*, although the lax identification permitted in *Rogers* v *Hosegood* (reference to the vendor's 'adjoining or near' land suffices) is unhelpful to those later dealing with the land. Equally significantly, assignment requires no form of identification in the covenant itself. Generally, much of the development of the rules in the past century has shown a woefully inadequate recognition of the genuine needs of covenantors and their successors in title. It might be admitted that it would be wrong to rule out assignment if annexation is inappropriate or ineffective, but should not the right then be a mere contractual right not binding on successors in title to the covenantor?

D. Modification

Land development proposals are often inconsistent with restrictive covenants. In some cases, agreement with the dominant owner may allow the development to proceed. In others, obsolescent or unreasonable covenants can inhibit economically and socially valuable land use. This has resulted in legislation permitting the discharge or modification of restrictive covenants: LPA, s 84. The jurisdiction has been broadened over the years (especially by LPA 1969) and is currently exercised by the Upper Tribunal, with an appeal to the Court of Appeal on points of law.[131]

In outline, the jurisdiction is based upon four alternative cases.[132] They are that the covenant is obsolete, that reasonable user of the burdened land is being impeded, that there is express or implicit agreement by those entitled to the benefit and that those entitled to the benefit will not be injured. Compensation may be ordered.[133] The most significant head is that of impeding reasonable user. It applies only if, first, the restriction does not secure substantial benefits or is contrary to the public interest, and second, if money can be an adequate compensation. Although planning permission policies (including the development plan for the area) are relevant in this context,[134] it certainly does not follow that discharge of a restrictive covenant will be ordered simply because planning permission has been granted.[135]

County courts enjoy a separate jurisdiction under s 610 of the Housing Act 1985.[136] This applies if it is intended to split premises into two or more dwelling houses (plainly intended to aid the provision of much-needed housing). It is important because the discretion is not constrained by the detailed requirements found in s 84.

Following the introduction of planning permission in 1948, it was widely thought that restrictive covenants would wither away as an unnecessary historical relic. This prediction has been proved wrong. It has been realised that planning permission does not protect

---

[131] Transfer of Tribunal Functions (Lands Tribunal and Miscellaneous Amendments) Order 2009; Tribunals, Courts and Enforcement Act 2007, s 13.

[132] Wilkinson (2000) 150 NLJ 1523, 1623, discusses the operation of the legislation.

[133] There is no entitlement to a share in the profit, as discussed in the following section: *Winter* v *Traditional & Contemporary Contracts Ltd* [2008] 1 EGLR 80.

[134] LPA, s 84(1B).

[135] *Re Martins' Application* (1988) 57 P&CR 119.

[136] *Lawntown Ltd* v *Camenzuli* [2008] 1 WLR 2656.

neighbouring landowners as effectively as restrictive covenants.[137] The result has been the continuing vitality of restrictive covenants, perhaps combined with a greater reluctance to discharge or modify.[138]

3. Enforcement of covenants

Positive covenants will usually be enforced by an award of damages, but restrictive covenants give rise to greater problems.[139] The principles discussed in this section apply in several contexts, including actions for nuisance and breach of easements. However, it should not be assumed that their application will be identical in each area.[140]

It is normal for breach of a restrictive covenant to cause relatively little diminution in value of the benefited land, and the claimant usually seeks an injunction. Injunctive relief is, of course, discretionary. Whilst it is relatively easy to obtain an injunction to prevent future breach of a covenant, it is more difficult to obtain a mandatory injunction requiring the demolition of a building constructed in breach of covenant. Until very recently, the prima facie remedy remained the injunction, likely to be awarded if the defendant deliberately acted in breach of covenant. However, the Supreme Court in *Lawrence* v *Fen Tigers Ltd*[141] (a nuisance case) was critical of too great a readiness to grant injunctions, stressing that the court should exercise a real discretion in each case. Even under the old law, an injunction might be refused as having a disproportionate and oppressive effect.[142] More commonly, the defendant would have built in ignorance of the covenant or else genuinely believe that the covenant is not enforceable. In such situations, the court is very reluctant to order demolition.

The most likely order is for damages in lieu of an injunction,[143] calculated on what the claimant could have required as a proper and fair price for giving permission. In *Wrotham Park Estate Co Ltd* v *Parkside Homes Ltd*,[144] the claimant was awarded 5% of the defendant's anticipated profit. In most other cases, a considerably higher proportion (up to 40%) has been awarded: the test is essentially what sum the parties might have negotiated for.[145]

Such awards, related to the anticipated profit, appeared to differ from the common law measure of damages, leading to their being questioned. However, *Wrotham Park* was

---

[137] See, e.g., Law Com No 11. Law Com CP 186, para 1.3 observes that 79% of titles are subject to restrictive covenants.

[138] See the survey of the legislation by Polden (1986) 49 MLR 195 and, more recently, Sutton [2013] Conv 17.

[139] Martin [1996] Conv 329.

[140] Law Com No 356 proposes a new test based upon proportionality for infringement of rights to light.

[141] [2014] AC 822. The previous law was based upon *Shelfer* v *City of London Electric Lighting Co* [1895] 1 Ch 287 at pp 322–323. The principles articulated in *Shelfer* were not completely rejected but should not be rigidly applied.

[142] *Ketley* v *Gooden* (1996) 73 P&CR 305; especially if the claimant has shown some willingness to be bought out: *Gafford* v *Graham* (1998) 77 P&CR 73.

[143] The jurisdiction originated in Lord Cairns' Act: Chancery Amendment Act 1858.

[144] [1974] 1 WLR 798; followed in the easement context in *Bracewell* v *Appleby* [1975] Ch 408 (no right of way to a newly constructed house).

[145] See *Small* v *Oliver & Saunders (Developments) Ltd* [2006] 3 EGLR 141 at [90]–[96] (35%) and *Tamares (Vincent Square) Ltd* v *Fairpoint Properties (Vincent Square) Ltd (No 2)* [2007] 1 WLR 2167 (33% as a starting point). *Kettel* v *Bloomfold Ltd* [2012] L&TR 514 supports a different approach: giving the developer 25% profit and then dividing the balance equally. See Law Com No 356, Chapter 5 (no reform is recommended at this point).

approved by the Court of Appeal in *Jaggard* v *Sawyer*[146] and the House of Lords in *Att-Gen* v *Blake*.[147] The modern approach is to deny that there are special rules for damages in equity. One explanation of the *Wrotham Park* damages is that the claimant has lost the ability to negotiate a price for consenting to the breach:[148] an interference with a property right. *Blake* accepted a more general analysis that damages for breach of contract can take the form of an account of profits in an exceptional case where justice so demands. This might be more generous to claimants, but it has not been applied in restrictive covenant cases; it operates beyond the scope of property law.

A rather different point is that a claimant who was aware of the breach and did not object may be held to have acquiesced in the breach and so be able to claim neither injunction nor damages. Although the courts are loath to say that claims should be brought at an early stage,[149] acquiescence in building in breach of covenant may render it unconscionable to complain about it thereafter.[150] However, it must be remembered that detriment is usually required before acquiescence can be relied upon: this will usually mean that the alleged acquiescence must operate before substantial building works have been undertaken.[151] Acquiescence in extensive breaches over many years may amount to abandonment of the covenant, so that even fresh breaches cannot be complained of.[152]

4. Reform

The unsatisfactory nature of the law as to covenants is reflected in a large number of proposals for reform. Unfortunately, only the commonhold proposals have been implemented. What follows is a brief summary of the other main proposals.

In 1991, the Law Commission[153] proposed an elaborate scheme for regulating both positive and restrictive covenants as 'land obligations', but this was not implemented. The Law Commission returned to the area in their 2011 Report. This makes significant proposals for the reform of the law of covenants. Unlike the position with easements, a new statutory scheme for covenants is proposed. Although this would replace most of the material in this chapter, the proposals aim to build upon existing principles as far as possible. Perhaps the main focus for reform lies in the status of positive covenants. It has long been clear that the failure to recognise them as property rights binding purchasers causes great problems, particularly as regards flats. As has been observed, leases are commonly used to alleviate these problems, even though the parties would prefer a freehold estate. The implementation of commonhold might be thought to alleviate the most severe problems caused by the present law. However, commonhold is so rarely used that it does not affect the need for reform.

---

[146] [1995] 1 WLR 269. Explaining it on restitutionary principles (Steyn LJ in *Surrey CC* v *Bredero Homes Ltd* [1993] 1 WLR 1361) was rejected.

[147] [2001] 1 AC 268.

[148] *WWF* v *World Wrestling Federation Entertainment Inc* [2008] 1 WLR 445, criticised by Rotherham [2008] LMCLQ 25. Cunnington (2008) 71 MLR 559 argues for a gains-based approach, but one which is different from *Blake*.

[149] *Shaw* v *Applegate* [1977] 1 WLR 970 at p 978.

[150] *Gafford* v *Graham* (1998) 77 P&CR 73, although this was distinguished in *Harris* v *Williams-Wynne* [2006] 2 P&CR 595.

[151] *Jones* v *Stones* [1999] 1 WLR 1739; *Harris* v *Williams-Wynne* [2006] 2 P&CR 595.

[152] *Att-Gen of Hong Kong* v *Fairfax Ltd* [1997] 1 WLR 149.

[153] Law Com No 127 (1984); Polden (1984) 47 MLR 566.

The Law Commission[154] regards the present law as being defective, especially as positive covenants already run in leases; the workarounds to try to get them to affect purchasers are unsatisfactory. It is therefore proposed (following general support on consultation) that a new category of Land Obligations should regulate both restrictive and positive covenants: they would be legal interests in land, modelled on easements. Responding to the problem that positive obligations could be used to impose capricious requirements, it is proposed that they must relate to work done on the servient land (or boundary) or be payments of a reciprocal or apportioning nature (para 5.53). Covenants entered into outside the new Land Obligation scheme would not run with the land (para 5.89).

A significant aspect of Land Obligations is that they must be express and registration requirements must be complied with. As for easements under the present law, entry in the titles of both plots will be required. In practice, this means that both benefited and burdened land must be identified.[155]

Subject to registration, a Land Obligation will run with both benefited and burdened land automatically as appurtenant to the land. Unsurprisingly, this is subject to any provision to the contrary. The new requirement to enter the Land Obligation on the benefited land's registered title will avoid the problems that currently bedevil the law on the running of the benefit. There will be no scope for schemes of development, although a developer will be able to enter land obligations on the register even before the first plot is sold, so that all plots will be able to have the benefit and the burden of the obligations when they are later sold (para 6.84). It is recognised that the burden of positive obligations cannot sensibly bind those with short leases (not exceeding seven years: para 6.115).

Part 7 considers modification and LPA, s 84. Although it is not proposed to change the grounds for modification, the provisions would apply to positive as well as restrictive obligations and also to easements. The Law Commission recognises that positive obligations have the potential to operate oppressively, and additional tests are developed, based upon the obligation's ceasing to be reasonably practicable or becoming disproportionately expensive.[156]

Quite different are problems caused by obsolete restrictive covenants, which can clutter titles for decades after they cease to be relevant. An earlier Law Commission report[157] had proposed that covenants should terminate after 80 years, absent proof of continuing importance. This was severely criticised, and the Law Commission is not now proposing any reform in this area.

A separate Law Commission report[158] deals with conservation covenants. It is recommended that there be a statutory scheme whereby a landowner could enter into covenants with conservation bodies. These may bind purchasers from the landowner, although it is proposed that they be statutory burdens on the land rather than proprietary interests. In contrast with present rules, there would be no need for benefited land, and the covenants could be positive or negative.

---

[154] Law Com No 327, Part 5. Earlier, see the Wilberforce Committee on Positive Covenants Affecting Land (1965) Cmnd 2719.

[155] Law Com No 327, paras 6.46–6.53. Where the servient land is unregistered, land charges registration will be required.

[156] Law Com No 327, para 7.69; Sutton [2013] Conv 17.

[157] Law Com No 201 (1991).

[158] Law Com No 349. Pratt [2014] Conv 328 is critical of conservation covenants not being established as proprietary interests.

Further reading

Gardner, S (1982) 98 LQR 279: The proprietary effect of contractual obligations under *Tulk* v *Moxhay* and *De Mattos* v *Gibson*.

Hayton, D J (1971) 87 LQR 539: Restrictive covenants as property interests.

Newsom, G H (1981) 97 LQR 32: Universal annexation?

O'Connor, P [2011] Conv 191: Careful what you wish for: positive freehold covenants.

Turano, L [2000] Conv 377: Intention, interpretation and the 'mystery' of section 79 of the Law of Property Act 1925.

25
Mortgages

Introduction

Most property rights involve the use of property or else obtaining income or some other continuing benefit from it. We now turn to a very different type of right: security interests. If A is under an obligation to B (normally a debt), then A may secure the obligation by giving rights over property to B. The advantage to B is plain: if A is unable to pay the debt, then B can sell the secured property[1] and use the proceeds to pay off the debt. In turn, A will find it easier to obtain the loan and the rate of interest is likely to be much lower than if the loan were unsecured.

Without security interests, it would be difficult for the vast majority of people to buy a house. Lending, say, £150,000 to a first-time buyer who has limited savings would be a reckless proposition for any lender. What makes the transaction viable is a security interest in the house. So long as the house is worth more than the loan (plus any unpaid interest), then the lender can recover the loan by selling the house in the event of financial disaster striking the purchaser. Although buying a house is the best-known occasion for creating security interests, the security may be for any form of loan or obligation.

Homeowners may also raise money after purchase by creating further security interests. This money may be used to improve the house, buy a car, pay off other debts or any other purpose. It may be observed that people who create such further securities are frequently stretched financially, with the related results that default on the loan is more likely and that the terms imposed by the lender may be harsh.

Funding of companies and small businesses is commonly undertaken by banks. The bank may require security over the business assets, whether or not they are being bought with the loan. In many cases, there will be few business assets and the lender will seek security over assets of the individuals who control the business. Often, this will take the form of security over their houses.[2] The cases demonstrate that failure of small businesses is a common catalyst for mortgage default, one example being *Williams & Glyn's Bank Ltd v Boland*.[3]

Rights to redeem

The dominant form of security interest is the mortgage. The traditional essence of a mortgage is a transfer of a property interest to the lender: in the nineteenth century, the fee

---

[1] Sale is the most commonly exercised remedy; other rights and remedies will be discussed later.
[2] Any earlier security interest created on the purchase of the house has priority.
[3] [1981] AC 487.

simple. This idea of transfer of a property interest is still very influential, although the form of security used today is called a legal charge. Despite the transfer of property, the borrower would virtually always retain possession and would be able to recover full title to the property on repayment of the loan. This right to recover title may be either contractual (legal right to redeem) or equitable (equitable right to redeem).

The traditional nineteenth-century form of mortgage gave a contractual right to redeem after six months. This provision gives the impression that the lender will be the absolute owner if there is no redemption (repayment) after six months, but this is very misleading. At least since the early seventeenth century,[4] equity has allowed redemption regardless of what the mortgage says. This is because, once it has been decided that the nature of the transaction is one of loan, equity regards the borrower as the real owner of the property. Despite the lender's having a proprietary interest (the fee simple before 1925), this is regarded as no more than a security interest limited to the value of the debt. Indeed, this applies even where the mortgage has been obtained by fraud.[5] This intervention of equity in mortgages has spawned rules governing the validity of mortgage terms. These rules, to be considered later, are markedly different from normal contract rules.

Lenders' rights

The rights of the lender may be placed in two categories. First, the lender has all the rights flowing from the interest transferred. Particularly important is the right to possession, most commonly used when the lender intends to exercise the power to sell (discussed below). Moreover, the lender can apply to court to terminate the borrower's equitable right to redeem: a process called foreclosure. After foreclosure, the mortgagee no longer has a mere security interest, but rather a true fee simple, or whatever interest has been mortgaged. The courts permit foreclosure because they are aware that it would be unfair on a lender to insist that the loan should last forever. However, the court gives time to the mortgagor to repay the loan, normally six months. Foreclosure is generally frowned upon because the property may be worth much more than the debt. It is rare today: extensive safeguards for the borrower make it unattractive to most lenders.

Today, the lender is likely to rely upon the second category of rights: remedies conferred by the mortgage. In particular, there is virtually always a power to sell the property. The borrower is entitled to what money is left after payment of the mortgage debt and expenses. If it becomes necessary to enforce the security, it is the power of sale that the lender is most likely to exercise. Today, the most important remedies (including sale) are implied by statute, though the parties can still stipulate for their own express rights.

Terminology

It is worth stressing the terminology used in mortgages. The borrower, who executes the mortgage, is the mortgagor. The lender is the mortgagee. People commonly refer to purchasers as obtaining a mortgage. Technically, this is inaccurate. The purchaser will indeed obtain a loan. However, the mortgage is the security interest, and it is the purchaser (mortgagor) who creates it in favour of the lender (mortgagee).

---

[4] For a brief history of mortgages, see Megarry and Wade, *The Law of Real Property* (8th edn), paras 24-006 et seq.
[5] *Halifax BS* v *Thomas* [1996] Ch 217.

It is apparent that this traditional form of a mortgage is highly misleading. It makes the lender look as if he is an owner, whilst the rights of the borrower are likely to be misrepresented as a right to redeem after six months. As Lord Macnaghten famously observed, 'no one, I am sure, by the light of nature ever understood an English mortgage'.[6] Nevertheless, the law worked quite satisfactorily because as a matter of substance equity treated the mortgagor as owner.[7] The totality of the mortgagor's rights is called the equity of redemption, the most important component of which is the equitable right to redeem. The value of the equity of redemption is simply the value of the land less the amount of the loan currently outstanding. There will be 'negative equity' where the land is worth less than the loan. This will most obviously occur if land values drop. The land is no longer adequate security for the loan, but the borrower remains contractually liable to repay the loan.

Reforming the structure and terminology

The 1925 legislation made the position even more confused. Instead of the fee simple, the mortgagee of land could have no more than a lease: a lease for 3,000 years if no term is specified.[8] One welcome result of this is that the fee simple is retained by the borrower, rendering the title to the land easier to trace. It is wrong to see this as changing the fundamental position of the parties: its consequences on the economic relationship are minimal. The borrower was already regarded as the owner. So far as the lender is concerned, there is still a right to the deeds,[9] a right to sell the fee simple (not merely the lease)[10] and on foreclosure the fee simple is still vested in the lender.[11]

Of greater interest is the introduction in 1925 of the mortgage by legal charge. No property right, such as fee simple or lease, is vested in the lender. Instead, the lender has a pure security right. The simplicity of this is immediately compromised by defining the rights of the chargee as being identical to those if there had been a lease for 3,000 years.[12] It should be added that the legal charge is regarded as a legal interest in property, with the normal consequences that (on registration) it will bind subsequent interests and may defeat earlier unprotected interests.[13] The courts endeavour to ensure that the legal chargee has the same rights as a mortgagee by long lease.[14]

Today, nearly all mortgages are created by legal charge.[15] Indeed, since the Land Registration Act 2002,[16] it is no longer possible to create a mortgage by demise (i.e. lease) in registered land. This encourages us to think of mortgages in terms of security interests rather than as forms of fee simple or lease. Doubtless, the borrower's retention of the fee simple makes it easier (particularly for the non-lawyer) to regard the borrower as the true

---

[6] *Samuel* v *Jarrah Timber & Wood Paving Corporation Ltd* [1904] AC 323 at p 326.
[7] E.g. *Fairclough* v *Marshall* (1878) 4 Ex D 37.
[8] Law of Property Act 1925 (hereafter LPA), s 85.
[9] Ibid, s 85(1).
[10] Ibid, s 101 (assuming that a fee simple is mortgaged).
[11] Ibid, s 88(2) (assuming that a fee simple is mortgaged).
[12] Ibid, s 87; defensible in 1925 as it was necessary to encourage use of the legal charge.
[13] Ibid, s 1(2)(c); Land Registration Act 2002 (hereafter LRA), ss 27, 29.
[14] See, e.g., *Grand Junction Co Ltd* v *Bates* [1954] 2 QB 160 (relief from forfeiture under LPA, s 146(4)). Nevertheless, a charge is not identical to a lease. Thus, a legal charge over a lease will not fall foul of a covenant restricting assignment or subletting.
[15] Described by Wurtzburg and Mills, *Building Society Law* (15th edn), para 5.03 as almost universal.
[16] Section 23(1)(a).

owner. Whatever the value of that ownership (it could be negative), the perception of ownership is important.

It might be said that we are in a transitional stage in the development of a security interest[17] that is independent of conventional interests such as the fee simple or lease. Despite the registered land developments, that reform is incomplete: mortgages by demise still play a vital role in determining the rights of chargees. However, the Law Commission proposed some decades ago that the law of mortgages should be recast so that the mortgage by demise should be abolished and the mortgagee's rights be specified by statute (or the mortgage itself) rather than gleaned from 3,000-year leases.[18]

Equally welcome is the modern drafting of mortgages, accurately stating the rights of the parties. Instead of a vacuous provision for repayment after six months, it is more likely today that the mortgage will spell out when and how repayment will be made. The most prominent choice for borrowers is between fixed and variable interest rates. However, this has little or no significance for legal principles. Somewhat more relevant are the two standard forms of mortgage to finance house purchase.

The *repayment mortgage* provides for a constant monthly payment (subject to interest rate changes) over an agreed period, which may be up to 40 years. The payments will exceed interest on the loan, so that the outstanding capital is gradually reduced to zero at the end of the period.

The *interest-only mortgage* is just that: the borrower has to find some other way of paying off the capital borrowed. In past decades, it was very common to have an *endowment mortgage* – linked to an endowment life assurance policy. The policy, issued by a life assurance company, was designed to produce (in several decades' time) a sum large enough to pay off the sum borrowed; with luck, there should be a surplus for the borrower. Endowment mortgages have fallen out of favour, as falling returns meant that they frequently failed to produce enough money to pay off the debt. However, interest-only mortgages can be linked with any source of repayment, including ISA investments.

In neither form of mortgage is it necessary to provide for payment after six months, although such a term may still be inserted.[19] Lawyers are used to stressing the equitable right to redeem, but it is arguable that no such right ever exists in many modern mortgages: the mortgage will be redeemed according to the contractual provisions. The concern of modern mortgagees is to ensure that the loan is repaid, not to restrict the right to repay. The entire focus of the old law of mortgages seems barely applicable today.

Significance

Mortgages are of immense importance. Not only is business financing facilitated by the availability of security, but the growth in home ownership has been dependent upon the mortgage. At the end of the nineteenth century, over 90% of the population lived in rented

[17] English law has long recognised equitable charges. However, this charge is an inferior form of security, with remedies requiring court orders.
[18] Law Com No 204, especially paras 2.14–2.20, 2.30. The report will not be implemented in its present form: (1998) 587 HL Deb WA213. Watt in *Modern Studies in Property Law*, Vol 4 (ed Cooke), Chapter 4, urges the rejection of the fictions endemic in mortgages law.
[19] The mortgagee's statutory powers depend upon the mortgage money being due. The six months' term is inserted to ensure that those powers apply from a time early in the mortgage.

accommodation. The period since the First World War has seen a steady increase in owner occupation of houses to around 65%. This development, of course, has causes other than the mortgage, but it could not have taken place without an efficient method of borrowing money. At the same time, owner occupation has been accorded advantages in terms of taxation[20] and been actively promoted by the sale of council housing. Most owner occupiers buy with mortgage loans, and the law of mortgages therefore impinges on a very large sector of the population.

1. Forms of mortgages

This chapter will concentrate on the mortgage by legal charge (mortgages by long lease are almost identical). The mortgagor can create successive mortgages over the land. The fact that the legal fee simple is retained after the first mortgage enables these subsequent mortgages to be legal,[21] although it should never be forgotten that what renders such a mortgage attractive to the lender is the value of the equity of redemption on the first mortgage (how far the property value exceeds the loan). Mortgages of leaseholds take the form of subleases or legal charges. Just as mortgages of freeholds cannot take the form of a transfer of the fee simple, so leases cannot today be mortgaged by assignment.[22] Most short leases have little value and therefore are unacceptable as security. Longer leases with a nominal or low rent are those most likely to be mortgaged.

A second form of mortgage is the equitable mortgage. It is encountered where an equitable interest is mortgaged, where there is an agreement to mortgage in the future or where the formalities (including registration) for a legal mortgage have not been satisfied. An equitable mortgagee may not have the same rights and remedies as a legal mortgagee,[23] although a well-drafted equitable mortgage will remedy most deficiencies.

Third, there may be a charge over the land (different from the legal charge already discussed). Equity recognised the charge as a security short of a mortgage. It would enable the court to order sale or to appoint a receiver, although there is no right to take possession and no right to foreclose.[24] The essence of a charge is that property is made liable for the payment of a debt, without there being any property transfer to the chargee.[25] It has been seen that the legal charge has moved the focus of attention in mortgages away from the transfer of property. This may well render it difficult to maintain a clear distinction between mortgages and equitable charges.

Mention should also be made of charging orders. A charging order gives an otherwise unsecured creditor an equitable charge. Any creditor with a court judgment can apply to

---

[20] No capital gains tax is payable on the sale of the home (Taxation of Chargeable Gains Act 1992, ss 222–226); income tax relief on mortgage interest was available before Finance Act 1999, s 38.
[21] Such mortgages require registration, even in unregistered land (Land Charges Act 1972, s 2(4), Class C(i)).
[22] LPA, s 86.
[23] Thus possession depends upon a court order (*Barclays Bank Ltd* v *Bird* [1954] Ch 274, but convincingly criticised by Wade (1955) 71 LQR 204); *Re White Rose Cottage* [1965] Ch 940 at pp 951, 956 supports a power to transfer a legal estate on sale where the mortgage is created by deed. Though doubted by some textbooks, it was followed in *Swift 1st Ltd* v *Colin* [2012] Ch 206 (criticised by Evans [2015] Conv 123).
[24] *Ladup Ltd* v *Williams & Glyn's Bank plc* [1985] 1 WLR 851.
[25] *Swiss Bank Corporation* v *Lloyds Bank Ltd* [1982] AC 584 (especially Buckley LJ at p 595).

the court for the creation of a charging order on the debtor's interest in land.[26] Although it has been said that a charging order will normally be granted,[27] considerable difficulty has arisen where an application against a husband is challenged by a wife who fears that her position on marriage breakdown will be prejudiced. The prejudice lies principally in stultifying any future order for the transfer of property between the spouses. It is likely that the charging order application will be transferred to the Family Division; the most common order is that the wife should keep possession until the education of the children is complete, at which point the charging order can be enforced. If a charging order is made without the non-debtor spouse being aware, an application can be made to the court to set it aside. However, the application is unlikely to succeed unless divorce proceedings were commenced before the charging order.[28]

2. Creation of mortgages

There are two principal requirements for the creation of a legal mortgage by the owner of a legal estate: a deed and an intention to create a mortgage. In addition, registration is almost always essential.[29] Normally, it will be obvious from the deed that a mortgage is intended. However, it is possible that the document may take the old form of an absolute transfer. The courts look to the substance of the transaction to discover whether the apparently absolute transfer was in fact intended as security for an obligation. If the purchase price is in fact a loan and it is intended that the property can be recovered on repayment, then the courts will readily hold that there is a mortgage.[30] On the other hand, it is clearly possible to have a genuine sale coupled with an option to repurchase.[31]

How does such a hidden mortgage fit within the legislation, given that LPA, s 85 debars mortgages other than by lease or legal charge? Section 85(2) provides that an express conveyance of the fee simple on mortgage takes effect as a lease for 3,000 years. It was established by the Court of Appeal in *Grangeside Properties Ltd* v *Collingwoods Securities Ltd*[32] that this subsection applies equally well where the mortgage is proved from extrinsic evidence. Harman LJ was emphatic:[33] 'Once a mortgage, always a mortgage and nothing but a mortgage has been a principle for centuries.'

Section 85(2) no longer applies to registered land now that the proprietor cannot create a mortgage by demise.[34] What effect does this have? The register must be conclusive that the fee simple is vested in the lender, but it would be extraordinary if a clearly intended mortgage took effect as an outright transfer to the lender. *HSBC Bank plc* v *Dyche*[35] held

---

[26] Charging Orders Act 1979.
[27] *First National Securities Ltd* v *Hegerty* [1985] QB 850.
[28] *Harman* v *Glencross* [1986] Fam 81; *Austin-Fell* v *Austin-Fell* [1990] Fam 172.
[29] LRA, ss 27(2)(f) (mortgagor registered), 4(1)(g) (mortgagor unregistered, if a first mortgage).
[30] *England* v *Codrington* (1758) 1 Eden 169 (28 ER 649); *Barnhart* v *Greenshields* (1853) 9 Moo PC 18 (14 ER 204); *Lincoln* v *Wright* (1859) 4 De G&J 16 (45 ER 6) (oral evidence suffices).
[31] *Dutton* v *Davis* [2006] 2 P&CR D51; [2006] EWCA Civ 694. Even a price 40% below market value was insufficient to prove a mortgage: it was explicable by the urgency of the transaction.
[32] [1964] 1 WLR 139.
[33] Ibid, at p 142.
[34] LPA s 85(3), as amended.
[35] [2010] 2 P&CR 58.

that there was a common intention constructive trust binding the lender. This inventive analysis suffers from the disadvantage of introducing trusts of land rules on overreaching into mortgages: a confusing outcome. Alternatively, the borrower should be able to assert a personal claim against the lender, justifying alteration of the register.

Equitable mortgages of legal estates generally take the form of agreements to create mortgages. As such, they must satisfy the requirements applicable to contracts relating to land: writing signed by both parties.[36] One change in 1989 deserves mention. For centuries, equity had recognised that a mortgage results from the simple deposit of title deeds with the lender.[37] The deposit implied a contract to create a mortgage and at the same time counted as part performance of the contract, thus avoiding the Statute of Frauds requirement of writing.[38] Because part performance no longer operates, it follows that mortgages by deposit no longer have this special status,[39] although it may be possible for the lender to rely on estoppel in an appropriate case.[40] Lenders may continue to insist on the deposit of title deeds for unregistered land, but any agreement to create security over the land will require writing signed by both parties.

Following the normal rules for interests in land, a mortgage of an equitable interest and an equitable charge both require writing signed by the landowner.[41] In the future, compulsory electronic conveyancing will require electronic creation for there to be any form of mortgage or charge.

3. Vitiating factors

It is rare for somebody who borrows money for their own use to be able to argue his or her way out of the mortgage. However, problems have frequently arisen when the mortgage (often by a wife) guarantees another person's loan (often the husband's). For convenience, the guarantor (or mortgagor) will generally be termed the wife and the borrower as the husband. The rules are identical if the roles are reversed and, indeed, can apply to other relationships. The mortgagee may be termed the lender.

Plainly, there will be no effective mortgage if a signature is forged[42] or if consent is negated by the defence of non est factum.[43] Most difficult is the case where the document is signed, but there is no full comprehension of its effect. Typically, cases involve mortgages to secure loans to businesses run by the mortgagor's husband or children. The borrower is often desperate to get the money and not keen to spell out the dangers to the mortgagor. Although the mortgagor is aware that a mortgage is involved, there is commonly confusion as to the extent of liability.

---

[36] Law of Property (Miscellaneous Provisions) Act 1989, s 2; see p 101 above.
[37] *Russel* v *Russel* (1783) 1 Bro CC 269 (28 ER 1121); *Re Wallis & Simmonds (Builders) Ltd* [1974] 1 WLR 391.
[38] Until the Land Registration Act 2002, this was applied to the deposit of the land certificate where title was registered: LRA 1925, s 66.
[39] *United Bank of Kuwait plc* v *Sahib* [1997] Ch 107 at pp 135–141; criticised by Robinson (1997) 113 LQR 533.
[40] *Kinane* v *Mackie-Conteh* [2005] WTLR 345, but see p 109 above.
[41] LPA, s 53(1)(a). In *Kinane* v *Mackie-Conteh* [2005] WTLR 345, the question whether s 2 of the 1989 Act must still be satisfied (requiring signature by both parties) was left open.
[42] The cases reveal that husbands seem to forge wives' signatures relatively frequently.
[43] Very difficult to prove: e.g. *Norwich & Peterborough BS* v *Steed* [1993] Ch 116.

There are two routes whereby the mortgage might be attacked.[44] The first is to argue that the mortgagee, usually a bank, owes a direct duty to the wife or parent. This route will rarely succeed: Lord Denning's attempts to develop a principle of inequality of bargaining power[45] were rejected by the House of Lords.[46] Even if the mortgagee negligently advises the mortgagor so that damages are payable, the mortgage itself cannot be challenged.[47] Extreme cases might attract an argument of unconscionability,[48] but this would be rare. In *Portman BS* v *Dusangh*,[49] a barely literate 72-year-old man borrowed money on his house to enable his son to purchase a supermarket. Improvident as the transaction was, it failed to shock the moral conscience of the court: the law will not frustrate such foolish generosity.

The second and more effective route of attack is through the borrower (husband).[50] As developed over the past 20 years, this involves three stages of analysis. The first is whether the conduct of the husband suffices to prove a vitiating factor. The second concerns the circumstances where the lender should be aware of the possibility of such conduct. The final stage concerns the steps which the lender should take to satisfy itself that there was no undue influence.

This basic structure was developed by Lord Browne-Wilkinson in *Barclays Bank plc* v *O'Brien*[51] and remains in place today. However, all three stages gave rise to extensive difficulty and litigation. In *Royal Bank of Scotland plc* v *Etridge (No 2)*,[52] the House of Lords restructured the operation of the principles and gave detailed guidance as to how lenders should act. It follows that *Etridge* provides the basis for modern analysis. The flood of intervening cases can generally be ignored save as far as they illuminate issues not fully developed in *Etridge*.

A. Undue influence

Although misrepresentation will be a vitiating factor, most attention has been on undue influence. The law will be merely summarised, as it extends well beyond property law. It

---

[44] See generally Treitel, *The Law of Contract* (14th edn), Chapter 10.

[45] *Lloyds Bank Ltd* v *Bundy* [1975] QB 326.

[46] *National Westminster Bank plc* v *Morgan* [1985] AC 686. *Barclays Bank plc* v *O'Brien* [1994] 1 AC 180 rejects the 'special equity theory' protecting a wife who is subject to undue influence or misrepresentation by her husband, or who simply has no adequate understanding of the transaction.

[47] *Cornish* v *Midland Bank plc* [1985] 3 All ER 513.

[48] *Credit Lyonnais Bank Nederland NV* v *Burch* [1997] 1 All ER 144 at p 151 (Nourse LJ). Chen-Wishart has argued for an approach based on substantive unfairness: [1997] CLJ 60. Australia has adopted an approach based on unconscionability, although reaching very similar results to those in England: *Garcia* v *National Australia Bank Ltd* (1998) 155 ALR 614 (Gardner (1999) 115 LQR 1; Bryan [1999] LMCLQ 327).

[49] [2000] 2 All ER (Comm) 221.

[50] This was extended in *First National Bank plc* v *Achampong* [2004] 1 FCR 18 to conduct on the part of a third party (the chargor's husband, who was not the borrower). The extension is criticised by Enonchong [2003] LMCLQ 307, but may be supported on the basis that the charge looked odd and the chargor required advice.

[51] [1994] 1 AC 180; see Lehane (1994) 110 LQR 167; Fehlberg (1994) 57 MLR 467; Battersby (1995) 15 LS 35; Lawson [1995] CLJ 280; Cartwright [1999] RLR 1. The modern law is well described by Thompson in *Modern Studies in Property Law*, Vol 2 (ed Cooke), Chapter 7.

[52] [2002] 2 AC 773; Thompson [2002] Conv 174; Oldham in *Land Law: Issues, Debates, Policy* (ed Tee), pp 175–185; O'Sullivan (2002) 119 LQR 337. The lead speech was given by Lord Nicholls, with whom all the Law Lords agreed (see Lord Bingham at [3]) and that will be the basis of the following analysis. Lord Scott gave a separate fully reasoned speech, which produces similar (but possibly not identical) results. Lord Hobhouse delivered a fairly full speech, which may be seen as amplifying some of the elements of Lord Nicholls' analysis.

is commonly said[53] that there are two classes of undue influence. Class 1 is where actual undue influence has been proved. This will apply, for example, if there is proved to be 'overt acts of improper pressure or coercion' as described by Lord Nicholls in *Etridge*.[54] In Class 2, undue influence is presumed. Prior to *Etridge*, Class 2 had two categories. In category A, undue influence would be presumed in certain relationships of trust and reliance.[55] These are generally of a fiduciary nature and do not include husband and wife[56] or parents and children.[57] For category B, it had to be shown that the relationship on the facts of the case involved such reliance that undue influence might be presumed.

Class 2 presumed undue influence has been remodelled by *Etridge*. The vitally important question is whether there is sufficient evidence for the court to conclude that there is undue influence on the facts. The House of Lords recognises that a combination of two factors will provide such evidence. The first is a relationship of trust and confidence and the second is that the transaction is not readily explicable by the relationship of the parties.[58] The old Class 2A situations are clear examples of such a relationship.[59] However, there may be no role for Class 2B, at least in the type of situation typified by *Etridge*.[60] It is simply a question as to whether the facts proved are sufficient evidence to lead to an inference of influence.[61] There are no special categories of relationship here: the principles can apply whatever the relationship.

The second factor ('not readily explicable') relates to the impugned transaction. The House of Lords in *National Westminster Bank plc v Morgan*[62] required manifest disadvantage, but there were widespread doubts as to whether this was truly needed. *Etridge* now explains that it is needed, although it should be remodelled as requiring 'a disadvantage sufficiently serious to require evidence to rebut the presumption that in the circumstances of the parties' relationship, it was procured by the exercise of undue influence'.[63] On the other hand, disadvantage is not required for actual undue influence: no question of inference is involved where undue influence has been proved.[64] Why is it required where there is no actual undue influence? The problem is that a relationship of trust and confidence is

---

[53] *Bank of Credit & Commerce International SA v Aboody* [1990] 1 QB 923, adopted by the House of Lords in *O'Brien*.

[54] At [9].

[55] *Allcard v Skinner* (1887) 36 Ch D 145 (religious influence).

[56] *Bank of Montreal v Stuart* [1911] AC 120 (PC); *Etridge* at [19] (Lord Nicholls).

[57] *Coldunell Ltd v Gallon* [1986] QB 1184.

[58] *Etridge* at [14], [21] (Lord Nicholls, based on *Allcard v Skinner* (1887) 36 Ch D 145), [104] (Lord Hobhouse), [158] (Lord Scott). Lord Nicholls observes at [11] that undue influence is highly flexible and may apply without trust and confidence, especially as regards the highly vulnerable. See, generally, Bigwood (2002) 65 MLR 435.

[59] *Etridge*: Lord Nicholls at [18] and Lord Hobhouse at [104]. Cf Lord Scott at [153].

[60] Treitel, *The Law of Contract* (14th edn), pp 514–516.

[61] As in *Abbey National Bank plc v Stringer* [2006] EWCA Civ 338; [2006] 2 P&CR D38, where the victim mother did not read English and relied on her son when signing a highly disadvantageous charge. Simply proving the necessary relationship does not mean that the influence was *undue*: Thompson in *Modern Studies in Property Law*, Vol 2 (ed Cooke), pp 137–138; Enonchong (2005) 121 LQR 29.

[62] [1985] AC 686.

[63] Lord Nicholls at [25], based on Lord Scarman in *Morgan* at p 704; criticised by Andrews [2002] Conv 456 and Phang and Tjio [2002] LMCLQ 231 at pp 234–236.

[64] *CIBC Mortgages plc v Pitt* [1994] 1 AC 200; *Etridge* at [12] (Lord Nicholls), [156] (Lord Scott).

easily shown: almost every marriage, for example, will qualify.[65] Lots of transactions (including those by parties within Class 2A relationships) are completely innocent and understandable.[66] Undue influence would have far too wide an application if the relationship resulted in a presumption of undue influence.

A typical scenario from the cases is that a wife provides security for her husband's business debt. *Etridge* stresses that this by itself is insufficient to lead to an inference of undue influence. Although from a narrow perspective it is financially disadvantageous, it is exactly the sort of supportive conduct that one expects in such a relationship.[67] As undue influence is a prerequisite for most claims by wives, this may sharply restrict the likelihood of success. This is further emphasised by the warning that hyperbole on the part of the husband should not be taken as misrepresentation.[68] Similarly, parents often make substantial gifts to children, though committing the entire home to one of two children did lead to undue influence being found in *Chater* v *Mortgage Agency Services Number Two Ltd*.[69]

Of course, there may be additional factors which indicate undue influence. It is not unusual for a guarantee to be in the context of a patently failing business and then giving that guarantee looks far more questionable. More generally, in *Hewett* v *First Plus Financial Group plc*,[70] the Court of Appeal stressed that the borrower (once the relationship of trust and confidence is shown) owes a duty of 'candour and fairness'. It was held that this duty was broken when the borrower failed to disclose an affair (he, in fact, later left the wife): the wife agreed to the charge specifically in order to preserve their family home.

B. Is the lender put on inquiry?

The second stage of analysis determines when the lender may be affected by the husband's conduct. Some early cases reasoned that the lender was bound if the borrower could be seen as an agent to obtain the consent and signature of the wife.[71] However, the House of Lords in *O'Brien* established that agency will not apply save in exceptional cases. In truth, the husband is acting on his own behalf in persuading the wife to sign the documents. If the lender leaves it to the husband to get the signature, this does not give rise to an agency under which the lender is liable for wrongs committed by the husband.

The House of Lords in *O'Brien* did, however, provide an important alternative route for protecting the wife; this forms the basis of the modern law. Where the lender has notice (actual or constructive) of the undue influence, then the lender will be subject to the wife's right to set aside the mortgage. The application of constructive notice quickly spawned a

---

[65] *Etridge*: Lord Scott at [159]. However, an exception was found in *Dailey* v *Dailey* [2003] 3 FCR 369 (PC) where the marriage had broken down and the 'victim' was the financially astute party.

[66] Although it is sometimes said that undue influence carries a connotation of 'impropriety' (Lord Nicholls at [32]), the courts seek to protect the transferor rather than to find wrongdoing: *Niersmans* v *Pesticcio* [2004] WTLR 699.

[67] Lord Nicholls at [30], Lord Scott at [162]. But once undue influence affects the decision, it is irrelevant that the transaction would have been entered into anyway: *UCB Corporate Services Ltd* v *Williams* [2003] 1 P&CR 168 at [86].

[68] Lord Nicholls at [32].

[69] [2004] 1 P&CR 28; other factors surrounding the loan assisted this conclusion.

[70] [2010] 2 FLR 177, drawing on *Etridge* at [33].

[71] Based on *Kings North Trust Ltd* v *Bell* [1986] 1 WLR 119.

multitude of cases. It is now recognised that this is an unconventional use of notice. It is not as if the wife has a property right against the husband which is enforceable against the lender. This was fully recognised by the House of Lords in *Barclays Bank plc v Boulter*[72] and in *Etridge*. Although we still ask whether the lender is put on inquiry, it is recognised that this is inaccurate: no inquiries have to be made![73] Yet there is authority for notice to be used in this broader fashion[74] and, more important, it plays a valuable role in balancing the interests of mortgagee and mortgagor. As will be seen below, it triggers the giving of advice which may both dissipate the effects of undue influence and protect the lender.

The crucial question for lenders is when there will be constructive notice. Lord Browne-Wilkinson held in *O'Brien* that there will be notice if, on the facts known to the mortgagee, the mortgage is on its face to the mortgagor's disadvantage and there is a substantial risk that the borrower has committed a legal wrong.

In *Etridge*, Lord Hobhouse[75] explains that a high threshold could be employed for a lender to be put on inquiry, whereupon extensive obligations would be imposed on the lender. The alternative is to employ a lower threshold, with less extensive obligations in individual cases. The latter is preferred because of the practical difficulties in drawing the line. It is worth stressing that the analysis employed by the House of Lords is explicitly intended to produce a system which is both readily operated by lenders and protective of wives.

Lord Nicholls appears to conclude that a lender is put on inquiry whenever there is a non-commercial surety arrangement.[76] Once the lender has established that the arrangement is not commercial, this means that there is no need to consider the nature of the relationship (such as employer and employee in *Credit Lyonnais Bank Nederland NV v Burch*[77]) or whether there is anything suspicious about the transaction. However, Lord Nicholls had earlier articulated a rather narrower test, based on knowledge of the type of relationship between the borrower and surety.[78] Apart from applying to married couples, this would be readily satisfied for unmarried couples; it would not require cohabitation.

The element of disadvantage mentioned in *O'Brien* seems not to be emphasised in *Etridge*.[79] However, a joint loan to husband and wife (or, indeed, a loan to the wife) is not a surety transaction and is not caught. There is here no indication of anything wrong – such loans are commonplace for buying and improving houses.[80] The lender is not affected if in fact the husband diverts the money to his own purposes. It is, unsurprisingly, different if the lender knows of that intention: the lender cannot then rely on the mere form of the

---

[72] [1999] 1 WLR 1919 (so that a different onus of proof applies).
[73] *Etridge* at [44] (Lord Nicholls); see also Lord Scott at [144]: 'They are contractual questions, not questions relating to competing property interests.'
[74] Gardner (1999) 115 LQR 1 at p 5.
[75] At [108].
[76] At [87], but this might be more aspiration: cf [89]. Cf Hopkins (2011) 31 LS 175 at pp 191–192.
[77] [1997] 1 All ER 144.
[78] *Etridge* at [45]–[49]; this has difficulty in coping with the *Burch* facts, a major reason for preferring the more general approach. Lords Hobhouse (at [109]) and Lord Scott (at [147]) deal only with wives.
[79] Previous cases had treated it much like manifest disadvantage (*Bank of Scotland v Bennett* [1999] 1 FLR 1115 at pp 1138–1140, reversed in *Etridge*), and clearly Lord Nicholls wished to get away from the problems that test had caused.
[80] *CIBC Mortgages plc v Pitt* [1994] 1 AC 200 (paying off a small existing mortgage and the purchase of a second home). This was applied to a loan to mother and son in *Chater v Mortgage Agency Services Number Two Ltd* [2004] 1 P&CR 28; there was evidence that such loans are not unusual.

transaction.[81] What happens if the wife is a shareholder or director of the husband's company? Given the problems in assessing the realities of these situations, all such loans now result in notice being imputed.[82]

C. Consequences of being put on inquiry

Huge numbers of transactions will involve the lender being put on inquiry, though only in a tiny proportion will undue influence exist. Neither *O'Brien* nor *Etridge* is content to leave lenders at risk: both set out to provide ways in which the lender can dissipate the risk to the wife and to itself. It is overtly recognised that the financing of many small businesses depends upon using the family home as security and that it is important that the law does not inhibit this.[83] If the appropriate steps are taken then, in the words of Lord Scott,[84] 'it becomes reasonable for the bank to rely on the apparent consent to enter into the transaction and to take no further steps to satisfy itself that she understood the transaction'.

What are the appropriate steps? Lord Browne-Wilkinson in *O'Brien* contemplated[85] that the lender must insist on a meeting with the wife in the absence of the husband. The wife must then be informed as to the nature and extent of the liability undertaken and urged to take independent legal advice. However, subsequent experience showed that banks are not prepared to undertake this role, fearing the consequences of giving this sort of advice.[86] Instead, they insist on advice by a solicitor. In *Etridge*, this is accepted as an alternative route to protection, and much of the analysis is based upon what exactly needs to be done by the bank and the solicitor.

Prior to *Etridge*, there had been considerable concern that wives were being inadequately advised by solicitors, so that all that happened in substance was that the lender received a certificate from the solicitor and was able to rely on it.[87] The House of Lords in *Etridge* sought to produce a workable scheme to ensure that, as far as possible, the wife obtains proper advice: this is the best way to dissipate any effects of undue influence. It may be observed that the structure laid down reads very much as if it were a statutory formulation.

Who can give advice?

A crucial element is that the solicitor must be the wife's solicitor: in advising her, the solicitor is not acting for the lender, the husband or the husband's business. To this end, a

---

[81] *Allied Irish Bank plc v Byrne* [1995] 2 FLR 325; *Northern Rock BS v Archer* (1998) 78 P&CR 65; *Davies v AIB Group (UK) plc* [2012] 2 P&CR 382 at [117].

[82] *Etridge*: Lord Nicholls at [49].

[83] *Barclays Bank plc v O'Brien* [1994] 1 AC 180 at p 188; *Etridge* at [34] (Lord Nicholls). See Pawlowski and Greer [2001] Conv 229 at p 242 for reluctance to lend if there are problems with the wife's consent.

[84] *Etridge* at [148].

[85] [1994] 1 AC 180 at p 196.

[86] *Etridge* at [55] (Lord Nicholls), [113] (Lord Hobhouse). See the survey of lenders' practice by Pawlowski and Greer [2001] Conv 229 at pp 237–238, 241–243. It is noted that the Code of Banking Practice requires independent advice.

[87] See the influential views of Millett (1998) 114 LQR 214 at p 220.

procedure is set up for the appointment of the solicitor.[88] The lender must first write to the wife explaining that a solicitor's confirmation will be required that the solicitor has explained the nature and implications of the documents and that the exercise is in order to prevent her from later objecting to them. She should be asked to nominate a solicitor, although she may be able to use her husband's solicitor. Although this procedure is not in any way regarded as optional, one must wonder whether minor failings will necessarily defeat the lender. One could imagine circumstances where the wife is still properly advised by a solicitor, with whom she is in fact entirely happy.

The bank must in any event disclose to the solicitor details about the transaction, such as the purpose of it, the husband's current indebtedness and overdraft limit and the amount and terms of any new credit facility.[89] It is probable that the lender's awareness of any vulnerability should also be communicated.[90]

Is there any restriction on who may act as the wife's solicitor?[91] The House of Lords gives full consideration to the use of the husband's solicitor. There are patent dangers in this, as the solicitor may be too closely identified with the husband.[92] On the other hand, somebody who knows the family and the loan transaction may be in a position to give better advice; certainly it will be cheaper than employing a solicitor who has to spend considerable time in mastering the circumstances. The House of Lords concludes that it is acceptable to employ the husband's solicitor, whilst being aware that it does involve some danger.[93] It is up to the individual solicitor to decide whether there is a conflict of interest which precludes also acting for the wife.

On past experience, it will be very common for the same solicitor to act for both, though the lender's letter to the wife must make it clear that she has a choice. Lord Scott, however, insists that there must be an independent solicitor if the lender has reason to suspect that there is in fact undue influence or other impropriety.[94] It is unclear whether the other judges accept this.[95] A rather different point is that if the lender knows that the solicitor plays a significant role in the husband's affairs (going beyond normal legal advice, such as being an active company secretary of the husband's company), then it may not be proper to permit him to act for the wife.[96]

Is it a problem that the solicitor also acts for the lender? It is plainly not a problem that the solicitor acts for the lender in undertaking the conveyancing formalities.[97] It appears to be implicit, however, that it is not otherwise appropriate for the lender's solicitor to act.[98]

---

[88] *Etridge*: Lord Nicholls at [79].

[89] Ibid. An 'immaterial inaccuracy' is unlikely to prove fatal: *Leggatt* v *National Westminster Bank plc* [2001] 1 FLR 563 (pre-*Etridge*).

[90] *National Westminster Bank plc* v *Amin* [2002] 1 FLR 735 (inability to speak English).

[91] It is no problem that a legal executive provides the advice: *Etridge* at [292] (appeal in *Barclays Bank plc* v *Coleman*).

[92] Note the dissent of Hobhouse LJ in *Banco Exterior Internacional* v *Mann* [1995] 1 All ER 936.

[93] *Etridge*: Lord Nicholls at [74], Lord Scott at [174].

[94] At [174].

[95] Cf Lord Nicholls at [57] (not obviously directed to this), Lord Hobhouse at [108].

[96] *National Westminster Bank plc* v *Breeds* [2001] Lloyd's Rep Bank 98 (pre-*Etridge*).

[97] *Etridge*: Lord Nicholls at [76], Lord Scott at [173].

[98] Thompson [2002] Conv 174 at p 190; see especially Lord Scott at [173].

The content of the advice

Whilst poor advice is apparent in many of the cases, the House of Lords was anxious not to impose an unrealistic burden. Lord Nicholls[99] articulates the minimum core of the duty. Initially, the solicitor must explain what his role is and that his involvement will be used to counter any later objection by the wife; confirmation that she wishes him to act for her is then required. Obviously, advice has to be given as to the nature of the documents and the effects of default (loss of the home). The seriousness of the risk must be assessed. This involves the purpose, amount and terms of the facility, together with any scope for its being changed. Also relevant are other assets of the husband and wife, which could be used to cover the guarantee. It needs to be stressed that the wife has a choice and this will involve discussion of the risks. Plainly, if the husband's business is failing, then it would be pointless for the wife to guarantee debts. Finally, the wife must give authority for the solicitor to confirm to the lender that the nature and implications of the documents have been explained: it may be that renegotiation of the terms of the transaction is required.

These requirements should go a long way towards ensuring that the wife is properly advised. One important element is that there should be a face-to-face meeting in the absence of the husband, something which has frequently not happened in the past. The terms of the guarantee will, of course, be crucial. One notorious clause is the 'all moneys' clause, under which all debts of the borrower (existing or future) are covered. This clause can lead to unexpectedly extensive liability, and there are indications that the solicitor should object to it.[100] As regards guarantors, the clause is now inconsistent with the Code of Banking Practice.[101]

Despite these obligations, the House of Lords was anxious that unrealistic demands should not be put upon solicitors. Lawyers are not accountants and cannot be expected to undertake deep financial research.[102] This helps explain why the lender has to provide relevant information to the solicitor. An element stressed by Lords Nicholls and Scott[103] is that the solicitor's duty is not to probe undue influence as such. It will occur in few cases, and it would be an impertinence to ask the sort of questions which would relate to it. Nor is it the solicitor's job to decide whether the wife should enter the transaction by refusing to proceed if she ignores his advice.[104] It does not matter that the solicitor believes that it is improvident or that no solicitor could recommend it: these are decisions for the wife, not her advisers. As had been observed earlier,[105] 'But the purpose of advisers is to advise. The recipient of advice does not have to accept it.'

The earlier case of *Credit Lyonnais Bank Nederland NV* v *Burch*[106] illustrates the dangers. An employee, who was friendly with her employer and whose life revolved around

---

[99] At [65]. At [111], Lord Hobhouse considers that Lord Scott's requirements fail fully to reflect that the wife's weakness rather than comprehension is in issue, but contrast Lord Bingham at [3].

[100] Lord Hobhouse at [112].

[101] *Etridge* [1998] 4 All ER 705 at p 716 (CA).

[102] *Etridge*: Lord Scott at [344].

[103] At [53], [182] respectively. This is reflected in the successful appeal of the solicitor in *Kenyon-Brown* v *Desmond Banks & Co*: see [374].

[104] *Etridge*: Lord Nicholls at [61]–[63].

[105] *Banco Exterior Internacional SA* v *Thomas* [1997] 1 WLR 221 at p 229 (Sir Richard Scott V-C).

[106] [1997] 1 All ER 144; Tjio (1997) 113 LQR 10; Hooley and O'Sullivan [1997] LMCLQ 17.

her work, charged her flat to the bank in order to enable her employer to gain an increase of £20,000 in his overdraft limit. The charge was in an all moneys form which covered the entirety of the overdraft and any other sums which might become due. The Court of Appeal regarded this as incredibly harsh: very extensive liability was being undertaken with barely any benefit for the employee. There was no hesitation in striking down the charge. The harshness of the deal seems to have been based partly on the relationship between the employee and her employer (coupled with her lack of benefit) and partly on the basis of the advantage secured by the bank in return for a small increase in the overdraft limit.[107] This is explicable today only in the exceptional circumstances identified in the following paragraph.

In *Burch*, Millett LJ thought that legal advice might not have saved the bank (there was none on the facts). This was on the basis that an adviser would have been bound to advise her not to enter into the transaction and to refuse to act for her if she refused the advice. How can this be reconciled with the *Etridge* analysis? In *Etridge*, Lord Scott thought that further steps might be necessary if the solicitor suspected undue influence,[108] and Lord Nicholls would recognise that the solicitor should withdraw if it 'is glaringly obvious that the wife is being grievously wronged'.[109] It should be borne in mind that the strength of the influence held over the wife may be one reason why the solicitor's advice is ignored. If Millett LJ intended to go beyond this, then his dicta can no longer be supported.

D. The solicitor's certificate

The final piece in the jigsaw is that the solicitor provides the lender with a certificate that the nature and practical implications of the documents have been fully explained. Unless the lender is aware that this is false or is aware of facts suggesting that the appropriate advice has not been received,[110] there will be freedom from any claim of undue influence.[111] This is the crucial point: if the lender follows the rules as laid down in *Etridge*, then the suspicion of undue influence is lifted and the lender will be protected.

It was argued in some earlier cases (and by counsel in *Etridge*), that the lender may be affected by notice of facts discovered by the solicitor, where that solicitor also acts for the lender. The House of Lords roundly rejects this analysis.[112] A most important element of the scheme described above is that the solicitor is acting solely as the wife's solicitor when advising her. In this context, there is no scope for imputing knowledge to the lender. It would be otherwise if the solicitor were not acting as the wife's solicitor,[113] but then the certificate could not in any event be relied upon.

---

[107] See also *Steeples* v *Lea* (1997) 76 P&CR 157: £50,000 security by a 51-year-old receptionist.
[108] *Etridge* at [182]. Lord Nicholls would merely require that the solicitor be told of this: [79]. See Phang and Tjio [2002] LMCLQ 231 at pp 240–241.
[109] At [62].
[110] Lord Nicholls at [57].
[111] Lord Nicholls at [56]. Lord Scott at [172].
[112] Lord Nicholls at [77], Lord Hobhouse at [122], Lord Scott at [178].
[113] *National Westminster Bank plc* v *Amin* [2002] 1 FLR 735, especially at [22].

E. Other factors

What is the position where part only of the loan is subject to attack? *TSB Bank plc* v *Camfield*[114] held that the mortgage will be set aside even if the undue influence or misrepresentation related to the amount of the mortgage (or to one of its purposes): the mortgagor is not bound even as regards the lesser amount genuinely and freely intended. However, this may be qualified in two respects. First, if the mortgage secures separate obligations and only some of these obligations can be attacked under *O'Brien*, then the valid obligations can be severed.[115] Second, where money has been paid to the wife or another benefit received (commonly a share in the property), then restitution of this will be required before relief is given.[116]

Problems may arise where a charge replaces an existing charge and one of the two charges can be avoided because of undue influence. If only the new loan is voidable under *O'Brien*, the lender may be able to claim a charge by subrogation to the extent of the original charge.[117] To that extent, the new charge is not wholly ineffective. The converse situation is where the replacement loan is free from the undue influence which rendered the first voidable. Here, the replacement charge is also vulnerable.[118] However, the scope for this vulnerability is limited: it applies only if the second charge is in favour of the same lender and if there is no independent advice (in accordance with the *Etridge* guidelines) for the second charge.[119]

Finally, a wife or other claimant who has successfully invoked *O'Brien* should bear in mind that they may have won a battle rather than the war. Very often, the most important matter for the wife is retaining possession. The *O'Brien* issue is most likely to be raised when the mortgagee seeks possession as a prelude to sale. Supposing *O'Brien* causes this possession claim to fail, *Alliance and Leicester plc* v *Slayford*[120] illustrates that the lender can still sue the borrower for the sums outstanding (which will usually include the capital) and bankrupt the borrower on the almost inevitable failure to pay. On the principles investigated in Chapter 16,[121] sale will nearly always follow on bankruptcy of a co-owner. The financial value of the wife's interest will be safe, but the home will be lost. One constraining factor is that, as recognised in *Slayford*, the lender will have to give up the security in this procedure, although this will not be significant if the lender is the only major creditor.

4. The relationship constituted by the mortgage

This important topic will occupy the remainder of the chapter. The nature of the mortgage transaction is that the lender is in a position of great power. The borrower is often in

---

[114] [1995] 1 WLR 430; Ferguson (1995) 111 LQR 555; O'Sullivan in *Restitution and Banking Law* (ed Rose), pp 65–69.

[115] *Barclays Bank plc* v *Caplan* (1997) 78 P&CR 153.

[116] *Dunbar Bank plc* v *Nadeem* [1998] 3 All ER 876; see also *Maguire* v *Makaronis* (1997) 71 ALJR 781.

[117] *UCB Group Ltd* v *Hedworth* [2003] 3 FCR 739 (assuming the original charge is valid).

[118] *Yorkshire Bank plc* v *Tinsley* [2004] 1 WLR 2380 (second charge over different land).

[119] Ibid, see [21] (Longmore LJ) and [35] (Peter Gibson LJ) on the first point; [35]–[36] on the second point. See also Thompson [2004] Conv 399 and Gravells [2005] CLJ 42.

[120] (2000) 33 HLR 743; Thompson [2002] Conv 53; Pawlowski and Greer [2001] Fam Law 275. An argument based on abuse of process was roundly rejected.

[121] See p 346 above.

desperate need of money to stave off financial disaster or to enable property to be bought. The cases, particularly in the past, contain plentiful references to the 'impecunious land-owner in the toils of a crafty money-lender'.[122] This, coupled with the interventionist role of equity in mortgages, has led to a wide range of protections for the mortgagor.

The material will be considered under the headings of (A) rules designed to protect the mortgagor and (B) rights and remedies of the mortgagee. The first heading contains much law dating back to the nineteenth century. Parts of this may be thought to have little relevance to most mortgages today, though the modern law contains very significant consumer protection rules. Rights and remedies of the mortgagee are very important today, for this area governs default by mortgagors.

A. Rules protecting the mortgagor

(i) *The right to redeem*

It has been seen that equity gives a right to redeem (pay off the loan and terminate the mortgage) on repayment of the mortgage debt,[123] after the contractual right has expired. In the modern law, the mortgagor keeps the fee simple. This means that it would be more accurate to talk of *discharging* rather than *redeeming*.[124] This equitable right will be defeated only if the mortgagee forecloses (to be considered later) or exercises the power of sale. It is fundamental to the law of mortgages that the right to redeem cannot be excluded.[125]

Can the contractual right to redeem be postponed,[126] bearing in mind that the equitable right commences after the expiry of the contractual right?[127] Patently, a right to redeem in 1,000 years' time would be seen as inconsistent with there being a true right to redeem. In *Knightsbridge Estates Trust Ltd* v *Byrne*,[128] the Court of Appeal had to consider a postponement for 40 years. The parties had bargained so that a lower interest rate was obtained in return for this postponement: the loan replaced a shorter-term loan at a higher interest rate. The court had little doubt in holding that such a freely bargained postponement was perfectly fair and valid. Earlier cases suggesting that a postponement of five to seven years was valid[129] were not regarded as prohibiting all longer postponements.

It should be remembered that the existence of the mortgage does not greatly inhibit the use of the mortgaged property. The mortgagor will normally be in possession[130] and can

---

[122] Lord Macnaghten in *Samuel* v *Jarrah Timber & Wood Paving Corporation Ltd* [1904] AC 323 at p 327. Much earlier, see *Vernon* v *Bethell* (1762) 2 Eden 110 at p 113 (28 ER 838 at p 839).

[123] The mortgagor must pay all sums due, even though actions for them would be time-barred: *Holmes* v *Cowcher* [1970] 1 WLR 834.

[124] Nield in *Modern Studies in Property Law*, Vol 3 (ed Cooke), at p 159.

[125] See, e.g., Lawrence LJ in *Re Wells* [1933] Ch 29 at p 52. In the absence of express provisions, the mortgagor normally has to give six months' notice of redemption or pay interest in lieu: *Smith* v *Smith* [1891] 3 Ch 550; *Centrax Trustees Ltd* v *Ross* [1979] 2 All ER 952 at pp 955–956.

[126] Early payment is allowed for regulated agreements (Consumer Credit Act 1974, s 94): see p 611 below.

[127] *Brown* v *Cole* (1845) 14 Sim 427 (60 ER 424).

[128] [1939] Ch 441. Upheld in the House of Lords on different grounds: [1940] AC 613, leaving open the validity of the Court of Appeal analysis. See Bodkin (1940) 5 Conv NS 178.

[129] Based on dicta in *Teevan* v *Smith* (1882) 20 Ch D 724.

[130] Any attempt by the mortgagee to take possession enables the mortgagor to redeem: *Bovill* v *Endle* [1896] 1 Ch 648.

sell it subject to the mortgage. The real cause of the demand to redeem is likely to be that interest rates have fallen so that the postponement turns out to benefit the mortgagee. This factor relates far more to the terms of the loan than to the security.

A separate point is that the mortgage is sometimes made irredeemable for a considerable period in an attempt to render covenants in the mortgage enforceable for that period. This most commonly applies to solus ties: obligations on mortgagor retailers to sell only the mortgagee's products (usually petrol or beer). Since *Esso Petroleum Co Ltd* v *Harper's Garage (Stourport) Ltd*,[131] it has been clear that the continuation of the mortgage affords no exception from restraint of trade rules. If the tie is void as being in restraint of trade, then the courts are likely to strike down the postponement of redemption as being closely related to the tie.[132] A related point is that there is an old mortgages rule, discussed later, that obligations cannot be enforced against mortgagors after redemption.[133] This is obviously an encouragement to mortgagees to postpone redemption for the intended lifetime of the tie.

Mortgages of leases raise special difficulties. If the lease is for a relatively short term, then any significant postponement of redemption may risk there being little time left after redemption. Such circumstances arose in *Fairclough* v *Swan Brewery Co Ltd*.[134] Redemption was postponed for 17 years, at which point there would be just six weeks of the lease left. The Privy Council regarded this right to redeem as a mere pretence: the intention was that the mortgage should not be redeemed whilst the lease was running. Because in substance the lease was not redeemable, equity stepped in to allow redemption.

It is far from clear that this result is justified. Postponement of redemption does not mean that the property belongs to the mortgagee. The more we adopt the modern view of mortgages as being charges created as security interests, the more it is apparent that the mortgagor is challenging the refusal to accept repayment of the loan. Looked at in this way, is it obvious that a mortgage of a short lease should be subject to different rules from those applying to a mortgage of the fee simple? The strict rules governing the enforceability of terms in mortgages, to which the *Fairclough* principle is related, have come under attack in the years since *Fairclough*. The indications are that the courts may be less inclined to accept *Fairclough* itself.[135]

It should be added that the postponement of redemption may also be challenged as being unconscionable. This is a general ground for attacking terms in a mortgage and will be considered later.

(ii) *Clogs and fetters on the right to redeem*

Because equity treats the right to redeem as inviolable, it has been alert to prevent mortgagees impeding its exercise. This has led to careful scrutiny of the terms of the

---

[131] [1968] AC 269; see p 597 below.
[132] *Esso Petroleum Co Ltd* v *Harper's Garage (Stourport) Ltd* [1968] AC 269 at pp 314, 321, 342.
[133] *Noakes & Co Ltd* v *Rice* [1902] AC 24.
[134] [1912] AC 565. Redemption had been postponed in order to enable the mortgagee to enforce a valid solus tie.
[135] *Kreglinger* v *New Patagonia Meat and Cold Storage Co Ltd* [1914] AC 25 at p 53.

mortgage. Some terms that appear entirely fair are subject to attack as impeding full and free redemption.

Options

An option conferred on a mortgagee to buy the mortgaged land is generally struck down. The result of the exercise of the option would be that the mortgagee becomes the owner of the land: a result that is inconsistent with the right to redeem.

This approach was upheld a century ago, with reluctance, by the House of Lords in *Samuel v Jarrah Timber & Wood Paving Corporation Ltd.*[136] From a modern perspective, it is difficult to comprehend why a freely negotiated option should be struck down by the court. Indeed, the Earl of Halsbury LC expressed himself to be unable to appreciate the 'sense or reason' of the equitable rule and Lord Macnaghten viewed it as based on 'sentiment rather than principle'. The modern stress on the mortgage as a security right further diminishes the justification for striking down freely negotiated options. When the Court of Appeal more recently reviewed the law, Lord Phillips MR observed that the rules constitute 'an appendix to our law which no longer serves a useful purpose'.[137] Nevertheless, the court felt constrained by authority to apply *Samuel*. We will consider below[138] the extent to which options may be saved by rules treating benefits in the mortgage deed as being collateral to the mortgage and therefore valid.

The *Samuel* rule does not apply to an option entered into in a separate transaction. Thus, an agreement two weeks after the mortgage was regarded as separate in *Reeve v Lisle.*[139] However, *Lewis v Frank Love Ltd*[140] demonstrates that it is not enough to put the option in a separate document, executed on the same day as the mortgage. The court considers the question as a matter of substance: is the mortgage dependent upon the grant of the option, so that the two documents are merely part of a single transaction? A more difficult point arises if the option is found in a variation of the mortgage agreement. In *Jones v Morgan*,[141] a majority of the Court of Appeal held that this, like *Lewis*, fell outside the *Reeve* protection.

The separate transaction rule is a welcome, if limited, relaxation. It should be noted that the mortgagor may still be under pressure where the option is separately entered into. The loan may be repayable on demand, and then the borrower will be well aware that repayment will be insisted upon unless the option is agreed to. In other words, the relaxation has as much to do with technical mortgage rules as the need to protect the mortgagor.

Collateral benefits: the earlier cases

Other terms in mortgages have also been attacked because they clog or fetter the right to redeem the property in its original state. Assessing the earlier cases is difficult because of

---

[136] [1904] AC 323.
[137] *Jones v Morgan* [2002] 1 EGLR 125 at [86]; Thompson [2001] Conv 502.
[138] See p 596.
[139] [1902] AC 461, approved in *Samuel*.
[140] [1961] 1 WLR 261. See also *Baker v Biddle* (1923) 33 CLR 188 (option executed before the mortgage, but part of a single transaction).
[141] [2002] 1 EGLR 125.

the usury laws. These limited the interest that could be charged on loans and could not be evaded by providing for collateral benefits. Once the usury laws were repealed in the mid-nineteenth century,[142] leaving the parties free to negotiate the terms of mortgages, the courts were faced with a novel range of problems.

It was established in *Biggs* v *Hoddinott*[143] that collateral advantages are not, per se, invalid. The case involved a solus tie to the mortgagee brewer for five years. The Court of Appeal held that this was valid. It was stressed that the tie was not unconscionable and did not affect the right to redeem. Matters are different where the tie continues to operate after redemption. The courts took the view that one aspect of the right to redeem was that the property, after redemption, must be in the same condition as before the mortgage. In *Noakes & Co Ltd* v *Rice*[144] this meant that a solus tie could not be enforced after redemption. Otherwise, the mortgagor would be recovering a tied property (selling only the mortgagee's beer) when a free property had been mortgaged.

Lindley MR had challenged this invalidity of collateral advantages in *Santley* v *Wilde*.[145] A short lease of a theatre had been mortgaged. Being aware of the weakness of the security, the mortgagee required repayment over five years and also a share in the profits from underleasing the theatre (for 10 years). The court held that the provision for a share in the profits was valid, on the basis that redemption would be postponed until these profits had been repaid.[146] In *Noakes*, this was criticised on the basis that redemption was consequential upon payment of capital and interest: the mortgage could not be kept alive simply to enforce covenants.

The issue returned to the House of Lords a year later in *Bradley* v *Carritt*.[147] The facts were a little different: the mortgage was over shares in a tea company, and the mortgagee was a tea broker. The mortgagor agreed in the mortgage to use his best endeavours to ensure that the broker should act as agent for the sale of the company's tea. The question concerned the enforceability of this term after redemption. The battle lines were clearly defined. On one side, the analysis in cases such as *Noakes* is that a mortgage can be no more than a security: once the loan has been paid off, then the mortgagee can no longer enforce obligations. On the other side, the argument is that businessmen should be free to negotiate fair arrangements and have them enforced by the courts. Insofar as a bargain involves more than security, there is no reason why it should not be enforced after redemption.

This time, the House of Lords split three to two in favour of the *Noakes* analysis: terms cannot be enforced after redemption. It had been argued that *Noakes* could be distinguished because the obligation was a personal one on the mortgagor rather than one affecting the shares. The majority was unimpressed with this argument. It may be observed that the covenant did relate to the shares in a practical sense: there was an obligation to use the votes attaching to them. The result might be different if there were a purely personal obligation, having no reference to the mortgaged property.

---

[142] Usury Laws Repeal Act 1854.
[143] [1898] 2 Ch 307.
[144] [1902] AC 24.
[145] [1899] 2 Ch 474.
[146] As this extended until the end of the mortgagor's lease, it is difficult to reconcile with *Fairclough* v *Swan Brewery Co Ltd* [1912] AC 565.
[147] [1903] AC 253.

Collateral benefits: *Kreglinger*

Despite the *Noakes* rejection of the freedom of contract arguments, the tide was in favour of wider recognition of collateral advantages. Some 10 years later, the issue arose again in the difficult case of *Kreglinger* v *New Patagonia Meat & Cold Storage Co Ltd*.[148] The issue concerned a right of pre-emption over the mortgaged property, exercisable after redemption. It was unanimously held valid. The earlier cases were not rejected, but there was overt hostility to a rigid approach that struck down fair and reasonable bargains. How, then, are these earlier cases distinguished, and how is the line to be drawn for the future? Delivering one of the two full judgments, Lord Parker relied upon a test of repugnancy: whether the term is repugnant to the right to redeem. Whilst this may be appropriate to justify the rules for options, Professor Glanville Williams has convincingly criticised it as a basis for drawing a line between *Noakes* and *Bradley* on one side and *Kreglinger* on the other: more or less any collateral advantage *could* be described as being repugnant to the right to redeem.[149]

More promising is the analysis of Viscount Haldane LC. He is prepared to recognise a 'collateral undertaking, outside and clear of the mortgage'.[150] This does not require a wholly separate agreement. Further, it is no objection that entry into the mortgage is the consideration for the collateral agreement. Essentially, the analysis is that there is a security agreement and a pre-emption agreement. The difficulty is that it is hard to identify exactly when an advantage will be held to be collateral. One suspects that the language of the judgments masks a drastic change of approach, so that virtually any advantage intended to operate after redemption will be labelled collateral.

There has been little useful authority in the decades following *Kreglinger*, so it is difficult to evaluate the position today. Perhaps lenders are less likely to incorporate collateral advantages in modern mortgages: most lending is undertaken by banks and other financial institutions that have less cause to rely on collateral advantages. However, it is interesting that Ungoed-Thomas J held a solus tie to be a collateral undertaking within *Kreglinger*.[151] This is one indication that the pre-*Kreglinger* cases must be treated with great caution.[152]

Collateral benefits: options

Warnborough Ltd v *Garmite Ltd*[153] discusses *Kreglinger* in the context of options. There was a sale of property, in which the unpaid purchase money was secured by mortgaging the property to the seller. The seller had an option to repurchase the property in specified circumstances. The Court of Appeal relied on *Kreglinger* in viewing this option as part of

---

[148] [1914] AC 25. Somewhat similar views had been expressed in *De Beers Consolidated Mines Ltd* v *British South Africa Co* [1912] AC 52.

[149] (1944) 60 LQR 190, also criticising its use for options.

[150] [1914] AC 25 at p 39.

[151] *Re Petrol Filling Station, Vauxhall Bridge Road, London* (1968) 20 P&CR 1.

[152] The High Court of Australia narrowly interpreted *Kreglinger* in *Toohey* v *Gunther* (1928) 41 CLR 181, but this is not typical.

[153] [2003] EWCA Civ 1544; [2004] 1 P&CR D18 (confirmed at the later trial: [2007] 1 P&CR 34). Applied in *Brighton and Hove City C* v *Audus* [2010] 1 All ER (Comm) 343 where in substance a mortgage was not intended at all; both cases are criticised by Tanney [2009] Conv 490.

the sale; as such, it was not part of the mortgage and not subject to the mortgage's rules. This is a most welcome development: it shows how the courts will not apply the mortgage rules when the reality is a different form of commercial transaction.[154]

The facts of *Warnborough* provide a very clear case for saying that the option is not part of the mortgage: there really was a separate sale. It would be unfortunate if, by inference, such circumstances were to be seen as necessary for other collateral advantages to be upheld. In other words, *Warnborough* is better viewed as a restricted application of *Kreglinger* to options, rather than defining the circumstances in which *Kreglinger* applies to other collateral advantages.

Reviewing the rules

It is submitted that modern commercial considerations render the older cases difficult to support.[155] Their attempt to classify mortgages as security transactions and no more is doomed to failure when the reality is more complex. Particularly where the security is inadequate or unsafe, lenders to businesses may require more than a market rate of interest before making a loan. To demand an interest rate that matches the risk would often be destructive of the mortgagor's business. Instead, the lender may quite reasonably want to share in the returns if the business is successful. Traditional mortgage rules are liable to frustrate this. It is interesting that the financing of new ventures frequently takes the form of lending money on security (generally inadequate to support the amount of the loan) and acquiring shares in the company concerned. No clogs and fetters problems arise from this combination of security and shares, but it demonstrates how unreal it is to demand that mortgages must involve no more than lending money.

(iii) *Restraint of trade*

The cases on clogs and fetters on redemption frequently overlap the restraint of trade principle: a term of any contract will be unenforceable if it unreasonably restrains trade.[156] The unreasonableness may be either as between the parties or as regards the public interest. The principle is one of general application: it does not derive from the law of mortgages. Accordingly, its operation in the mortgage context will be merely summarised.

In *Esso Petroleum Co Ltd* v *Harper's Garage (Stourport) Ltd*,[157] the House of Lords established that the principle applies to mortgages in just the same way as it applies to other contracts. Its main operation will be with regard to solus ties of the kind litigated in *Biggs* v *Hoddinott* and *Noakes & Co Ltd* v *Rice*. It may be true that it is reasonable for the tie to continue whilst money is owed to the mortgagor,[158] but what is not permitted is

---

[154] Supported by *Davies* v *Chamberlain* (1909) 26 TLR 138; also by the analyses in *Harper* v *Joblin* [1916] NZLR 895 and *Baker* v *Biddle* (1923) 33 CLR 188.
[155] They have not been accepted by Australian courts, which prefer an unconscionability test: see *Lift Capital Partners Pty Ltd* v *Merrill Lynch International* (2009) 253 ALR 482 at [106]–[137].
[156] Land agreements are now included in the operation of the Competition Act 1998 (SI 2010 No 1709), but this seems unlikely to impact on most solus ties: Butterworth [2011] Conv 486.
[157] [1968] AC 269.
[158] Lord Pearce at p 326, Lord Wilberforce at pp 341–342.

postponement of redemption as part of an attempt to render the tie enforceable for an unusually long period. In the absence of any special factors, it would appear that a solus tie will be regarded as reasonable if it lasts for no more than five years.[159]

The restraint of trade principle will not apply in certain circumstances. The most important is where there is no existing right to trade. It follows that a seller or lessor of land can impose restraints: the purchaser or lessee will normally have no prior right to trade on the land.[160] This was used in *Esso* to explain earlier cases in which restraints relating to land had been enforced. This protection of sellers and lessors will also apply if they lend money on mortgage to finance the transaction.

(iv) *Unfair terms*

Our final equitable rule is that unconscionable terms will be struck down. As with other equitable rules relating to mortgages, equity is more willing to interfere than in other contracts.[161] It was established in *Knightsbridge Estates Trust Ltd v Byrne*[162] that it is not enough for a term to be unreasonable: it must be oppressive or unconscionable. The operation of the rule is illustrated by two first-instance cases.

In *Cityland & Property (Holdings) Ltd v Dabrah*,[163] a mortgage took the form of a promise to pay £4,553 over six years, £2,900 having been lent initially. It will be observed that repayment was by reference to a fixed sum, not a rate of interest.[164] The mortgage contained the common clause that if the mortgagor defaulted on making payments, then the capital would become due. Normally, such a clause would mean the sum lent plus interest to date of repayment. This would be unobjectionable,[165] but in *Cityland* it meant the full £4,553. Default took place after about a year, and the liability to pay £4,553 represented 157% of the loan and an annual interest rate of 38%. Goff J had little hesitation in striking down this liability and substituting interest at 7%. Unfortunately, he appears uncertain whether the test is that of unfair and unconscionable conduct or of unreasonable conduct.

In the second case, *Multiservice Bookbinding Ltd v Marden*,[166] Browne-Wilkinson J stressed that *Knightsbridge* is conclusive that reasonableness is not the test, although the terms in *Cityland* would fail either test. The principal feature in *Multiservice* was that the debt was to be calculated in Swiss francs and to be repayable over 10 years. Given massive

---

[159] In *Esso*, a tie for 21 years was struck down, but one for just under five years upheld. In *Alec Lobb (Garages) Ltd v Total Oil (Great Britain) Ltd* [1985] 1 WLR 173, a tie lasting at least seven years was upheld, but there it was a part of a rescue operation for the garage.

[160] Applied by the High Court of Australia in *Quadramain Pty Ltd v Sevastopol Investments Pty Ltd* (1976) 133 CLR 390. In *Esso* itself, restraint of trade operated when a mortgagee imposed a solus tie on a purchaser. However, the purchaser was a company controlled by the sellers, so it was appropriate to treat the purchaser as having an existing right to trade: *Alec Lobb (Garages) Ltd v Total Oil (Great Britain) Ltd* [1985] 1 WLR 173.

[161] See Treitel, *The Law of Contract* (14th edn), pp 524–525 for contracts generally.

[162] [1939] Ch 441. References to unconscionability are found in earlier cases, but the usury laws then prevented the enforcement of any collateral advantage: *Jennings v Ward* (1705) 2 Vern 520 (23 ER 935), explained by Lindley MR in *Biggs v Hoddinott* and Viscount Haldane LC in *Kreglinger*.

[163] [1968] Ch 166.

[164] Over six years, it was equivalent to 19%.

[165] *Sterne v Beck* (1863) 32 LJCh 682.

[166] [1979] Ch 84.

depreciation of sterling, the original loan of £36,000 had become a debt of £63,000, even after capital repayments of £24,000. Overall, the mortgagor's obligations were equivalent to annual interest of 33% over the life of the mortgage: arguably much more severe than 38% for a year or so in *Cityland*. Nevertheless, Browne-Wilkinson J upheld the arrangement. It was a freely negotiated agreement between businessmen who fully understood what they were doing. Indeed, the value of the land had increased no less than the Swiss franc, and the mortgagor's business had been extremely successful. There was no evidence of sharp practice or taking unfair advantage of a mortgagor desperate for a loan. The mortgagor's strongest point was that the interest rate was related to sterling interest rates. A currency that is weak, as sterling was, nearly always has a high rate of interest: otherwise, nobody will be willing to hold that currency. In other words, the mortgagee obtained both a high interest rate (appropriate to a weak currency) and protection of the real value of the capital (appropriate to a strong currency). Browne-Wilkinson J regarded this as unreasonable, but not unconscionable.

The approach in *Multiservice* was approved by the Court of Appeal in *Jones* v *Morgan*,[167] where it was insufficient that the bargain was 'unwise or improvident'. It was further held that any argument based on the naivety of the borrower is doomed to failure if the borrower is known to be in receipt of legal advice. Amongst other things, *Multiservice* establishes that mortgagees can validly use indices to adjust the sums owed. Schemes have been established taking advantage of this. One interesting use of it is to enable lower interest rates to be charged, in return for uplift of the loan capital relative to (say) inflation.[168] This facilitates the granting of mortgages to low income earners, although such schemes do not appear to have been much used.

Variable interest rates

A feature of many modern mortgages is that the interest rate is variable, sometimes related to external rates, such as the base rate, and sometimes variable by reference to the lender's standard rates. Most building societies and banks adopt the second type of variation clause. This carries the obvious danger that the lender will allow rates to drift upwards. This is especially the case if special low rates or deals are offered to new borrowers to attract their custom. Existing borrowers may find themselves saddled with a rate of interest exceeding that charged by other lenders. In contract law, such a unilateral power to amend a crucial term is, of course, unusual. One justification for the power in mortgages is the unlimited right of the mortgagor to redeem.[169]

In *Paragon Finance plc* v *Nash*,[170] the Court of Appeal considered the power and concluded that there was an implied term preventing its use 'dishonestly, for an improper purpose, capriciously or arbitrarily'. Potentially more significantly, it could not be exercised unreasonably. Crucially, however, this does not preclude an unreasonable interest rate.

---

[167] [2002] 1 EGLR 125.
[168] *Nationwide BS* v *Registry of Friendly Societies* [1983] 1 WLR 1226, perhaps unfairly criticised by Cohen (1984) 134 NLJ 437.
[169] Wurtzburg and Mills, *Building Society Law* (15th edn), para 6.32.
[170] [2002] 1 WLR 685 at [36]–[41], followed in *Paragon Finance plc* v *Pender* [2005] 1 WLR 3412; cf Law Com No 204, paras 6.35 et seq.

Rather, it means that the exercise of the power must be 'in a way that no reasonable lender, acting reasonably, would do'.[171] On the facts, raising rates (increasing margins over other lenders by 3%) because of losses incurred by the lender was held free from challenge.

Statutory controls

Sections 140A–140D of the Consumer Credit Act 1974 enable the courts to provide redress where credit bargains are unfair or have been enforced in an unfair manner. We will see below that its application has been narrowed very significantly. The original wording covered extortionate credit bargains: where the payments were grossly exorbitant or the terms otherwise grossly contravened ordinary principles of fair dealing. The new unfairness test was introduced by the Consumer Credit Act 2006.[172] It may be observed that the previous test looks closer to the equitable unconscionability test, although it was not treated as identical.[173] The new test seems likely to be applied more frequently, although it is too early to predict how great its significance will be.[174]

The legislation applies to both secured and unsecured loans to individuals, whether or not secured. Where a loan is secured, this makes it more likely that the loan will be repaid and the courts will expect less stringent terms.[175] The court is to take into account all relevant factors, including those relating to the borrower (which might include financial pressure) and the lender (which might include financial risk).

Most cases under the original 1974 test involved a challenge to the interest rate. Two problems quickly emerged. Many of the borrowers in the cases are poor credit risks, who would not be able to obtain loans from banks or building societies. This has the twin effects of rendering them vulnerable and meaning that any lender is bound to charge interest at above normal rates in order to cover the risk of default.

The second problem is that many of the loans are short term: often for a matter of months. A rate of interest that would look exorbitant in a five-year mortgage might be quite reasonable in a loan for two months. Quite apart from the element of risk, there will be significant administrative costs that will not vary much with the length of the loan. There is a formula for calculating the annual percentage rate (APR) that is generally used in the cases. It is sobering to note that borrowing £1 for a day from a high street bank will often involve an APR of several thousand per cent, a result of the imposition of a standard charge for overdrawing an account. Yet, it should also be remembered that short-term loans are frequently a route to financial disaster: if the borrower is unable to repay, then another short-term loan will be required, often for a larger sum and at an equally high interest rate.

---

[171] It is recognised that it adds little to the other requirements and to be analogous to unreasonableness as applied in administrative law.

[172] See Brown [2007] Conv 316. The legislation adds numerous other controls over lenders and also requirements designed to protect borrowers.

[173] *Davies* v *Directloans Ltd* [1986] 1 WLR 823 at p 831.

[174] In *Graves* v *Capital Home Loans Ltd* [2014] EWCA Civ 1297, it was argued that sale was unfair when the mortgagor (in a buy to let mortgage) had been suffering from mental incapacity. The court held that it was fair to sell as there were arrears predating the incapacity; a decision to sell where there were arrears would be unfair only in exceptional cases.

[175] *Castle Phillips Finance Co Ltd* v *Williams* [1986] CCLR 13.

Under the original extortionate test, the courts showed little sympathy to the argument that money should not have been lent at all.[176] A lender of last resort, taking a distinct risk, was able to justify a rate of 21.6% over 10 years in *Davies* v *Directloans Ltd*.[177] More surprisingly, interest of 12% for a three-month loan (APR well over 48%) was upheld in *A Ketley Ltd* v *Scott*.[178] This is a useful example of a short loan. It was relevant that the interest charge included expenses and that the money was advanced at very short notice before the lender could make the normal checks of the borrower or the security: the borrower needed the money in order to purchase the house in which he was a protected tenant. On the other hand, courts were highly critical of inflated and unexplained charges by lenders, particularly when coupled with a high interest rate,[179] and of dual interest rates involving unjustifiable extra payments on default.[180]

It is plain that each case must be considered on its full facts. Where there is no sharp practice by the lender and the borrower is fully aware of what is being agreed (especially if legally advised), then the courts have been reluctant to intervene. That may, of course, change with the new unfairness test. There is, of course, a fundamental question to be faced. If such risky loans are to be permitted, then terms such as those in the cases will have to be accepted. If it is thought that such loans are conducive only of financial disaster, then there is a case for prohibiting them altogether. Should that be done, doubtless illegal loans would continue to be made and on even more unfavourable terms.

However, a major limitation on all this is that most mortgage loans to individuals are excluded[181]: these are regulated by the Financial Conduct Authority under the Financial Services and Markets Act 2000. That regulation should ensure that mortgages less frequently contain unfair terms – some of the concerns expressed above (especially relating to affordability of loans) are addressed by the regulation.

A rather different legislative control over mortgage terms is created by the Consumer Rights Act 2015 (replacing the Unfair Terms in Consumer Contracts Regulations 1999).[182] Section 62(4) provides that a term is unfair 'if, contrary to the requirement of good faith, it causes a significant imbalance in the parties' rights and obligations'.[183] Unfair terms are not binding. However, the borrower must be dealing as a consumer and the lender dealing in the course of his business. Furthermore, the term must not have been individually negotiated (most large lenders use standard terms). Perhaps the most important point is that a term cannot be challenged if it relates to the main subject matter of the contract or the

---

[176] *Wills* v *Wood* [1984] CCLR 7. Wadsley [2003] LMCLQ 431 argues that lenders should owe a duty of care.

[177] [1986] 1 WLR 823. The loan was secured; the APR for building society loans at the date of charge was 17.5%; the 21.6% rate was fixed for the 10 years, but the mortgagor could repay earlier.

[178] [1980] CCLR 37; Foster J would in any event have refused relief because of significant non-disclosures by the borrower. See also *Premier Finance Co Ltd* v *Gravesande* [1985] CCLR 1.

[179] *Castle Phillips Finance Co Ltd* v *Williams* [1986] CCLR 13; applied in *Castle Phillips Co Ltd* v *Wilkinson* [1992] CCLR 83.

[180] *Falco Finance Ltd* v *Gough* [1999] CCLR 16.

[181] Consumer Credit Act 1974, s 140A(5). This was significantly extended in 2015 – previously, it was mainly first mortgages that were excluded.

[182] The application of the Regulations to land transactions was confirmed by *R (Khatun)* v *Newham LBC* [2005] 1 QB 37. See generally Treitel, *The Law of Contract* (14th edn), pp 320–342, 1307–1314.

[183] This requires 'fair and open dealing': terms must be expressed clearly and no advantage taken of the weakness of the consumer. See *Director General of Fair Trading* v *First National Bank plc* [2002] 1 AC 481 (Macdonald (2002) 65 MLR 763).

price payable.[184] In the loan context, this includes the rate of interest[185] and charges levied by the lender.[186] Similarly, rights to vary the rate of interest and to call in the loan are protected, subject in each case to there being a 'valid reason'.[187]

It has been seen that the Consumer Credit Act provisions today apply to few mortgages – this may reveal an important role for the 2015 Act. Where the Consumer Credit Act provisions do apply, it might be anticipated that the test of unfairness introduced by the Consumer Credit Act 2006 will provide the main focus for control over mortgages – it provides more tightly focussed control than the 2015 Act, which applies to many different types of contracts.

This section has been considering controls over individual mortgages. However, much recent discussion has centred on the regulation of mortgage lenders, with the objective of ensuring responsible lending. This includes the policing of unfair terms by the Financial Conduct Authority,[188] although the regulation goes well beyond this.[189]

B. Rights and remedies of the mortgagee

(i) *Foreclosure*

A traditional right of the mortgagee is to ask the court to put an end to the equitable right to redeem: to foreclose.[190] Of its nature, this is inapplicable until after the legal date for redemption has passed. The court will give the mortgagor six months to pay off the mortgage. Only if no payment is made will foreclosure be made absolute. This delay will not avail an impecunious mortgagor who is unable to raise the necessary cash.

Although foreclosure appears to be drastic and highly beneficial to the mortgagee (who then owns the property absolutely), it is in fact of little use and is 'almost unheard of today'.[191] Because of the possibility of a large windfall profit for the mortgagee if the property is worth more than the debt, the court has jurisdiction under LPA, s 91 to order sale of the property. The mortgagee will receive the capital, interest and expenses, and the mortgagor is entitled to the balance. This jurisdiction ensures that the mortgagor does not lose the value of the equity of redemption.

In foreclosure, as so often in mortgages, the terminology is misleading. Termination of the equitable right to redeem is not as final as the language of an 'absolute' order indicates. The mortgagor can at any time apply to court to have the foreclosure set aside. Even

---

[184] Consumer Rights Act 2015, s 64. This does not preclude an argument that the contract as whole is unfair.

[185] *Director General of Fair Trading* v *First National Bank plc* [2002] 1 AC 481 (but applying interest to judgment debts was caught, although not unfair on the facts). Cf *Falco Finance Ltd* v *Gough* [1999] CCLR 16 (Bright (1999) 115 LQR 360), involving a challenge to dual interest rates. The somewhat unconvincing challenge in *Falco* to flat rate interest rates is less readily justified.

[186] *Office of Fair Trading* v *Abbey National plc* [2010] 1 AC 696, rejecting any restriction to essential or core terms. Consumer Rights Act 2015, s 64(2) limits this to transparent and prominent terms.

[187] Consumer Rights Act 2015, Sched 2, paras 21, 22.

[188] Consumer Rights Act 2015, ss 62, 70 (and Schedule 3) (previously the Office of Fair Trading); Bright (2000) 20 LS 331.

[189] Nield (2010) 30 LS 610 provides a useful analysis of the issues and challenges; more recently, see Kenna and Lynch-Shally [2014] Conv 294.

[190] The effect of a foreclosure order is to vest the fee simple (or other mortgaged estate) in the mortgagee: LPA, ss 88(2), 89(2).

[191] *Palk* v *Mortgage Services Funding plc* [1993] Ch 330 at p 336.

purchasers from the mortgagee could be ordered to return the land to the mortgagor.[192] Today, the purchaser's title will almost invariably be registered and the purchaser should be safe unless the mortgagor is protected by an entry on the register or actual occupation overriding interest.[193]

A further disadvantage of foreclosure emerges when the property is worth less than the debt. An action for debt for the balance will be allowed only on the basis that the mortgagor can redeem the property.[194] The reason for this is that the mortgagee is not allowed both debt and the property. If the property has been sold following foreclosure, then the mortgagee has lost the power to allow redemption. It follows that a mortgagee's action for debt will be barred: the mortgagee is not allowed simply to credit the mortgagor with the amount realised on sale.

Given the problems surrounding foreclosure and its rarity today, it is not surprising that the Law Commission recommended its abolition.[195]

(ii) *Possession*

The right to take possession is also old, but considerably more important than foreclosure. It is an incident of the estate held by the mortgagee: since 1925, a lease (or rights as if there were a lease). It can be exercised, in the words of Harman J, 'before the ink is dry on the mortgage'.[196] Unlike most remedies, it does not depend upon any default by the mortgagor, nor upon any express provision in the legislation or the mortgage deed. Although we shall see that there are limits on taking possession, especially of dwelling houses, it may be doubted whether such an extensive right is justified today.

(a) The mortgagor's possession

We have seen that the mortgagee's right to possession is exercisable immediately: there is no need for the legal date for redemption to have passed or for default.[197] Yet for well over three centuries, it has been the almost invariable practice for mortgagors to remain in possession. Similarly, if the property is leased, then the mortgagor will normally receive the rents.[198]

It is odd that the mortgagor's possession has never attained legal recognition and that its status has never developed from the rather lame analysis of being that of a mortgagor in possession.[199] Some mortgages do set out to regulate the position and permit the mortgagor to remain in possession until default; many building society mortgages provide examples.

---

[192] *Campbell* v *Holyland* (1877) 7 Ch D 166.

[193] For registration of the mortgagee on foreclosure, see Land Registration Rules 2003, r 112. A collusive sale designed to defeat the mortgagor's rights might well lead to personal liability.

[194] *Lockhart* v *Hardy* (1846) 9 Beav 349 (50 ER 378); *Rudge* v *Richens* (1873) LR 8 CP 358.

[195] Law Com No 204, para 7.27, although sale to the mortgagee would be permitted.

[196] *Four-Maids Ltd* v *Dudley Marshall (Properties) Ltd* [1957] Ch 317 at p 320.

[197] *Doe d Roylance* v *Lightfoot* (1841) 8 M&W 553 (151 ER 1158).

[198] The mortgagor has, in principle, no power to create new leases binding the mortgagee (*Rogers* v *Humphreys* (1835) 4 Ad&E 299 (111 ER 799)). Although statute confers power on the mortgagor to enter into certain leases binding the mortgagee (LPA, s 99), mortgages routinely exclude this power.

[199] *Moss* v *Gallimore* (1779) 1 Dougl 279 (99 ER 182), rejecting analogies of a tenant at will and receiver; *Birch* v *Wright* (1786) 1 TR 378 (99 ER 1148). Indeed, it may result in the mortgagor's being able to claim adverse possession, at least if no payments are made: *Ashe* v *National Westminster Bank plc* [2008] 1 WLR 710.

In the past, it was common for the mortgagor to 'attorn tenant' to the mortgagee, in other words recognise that he or she held as a tenant of the mortgagee. This would not by itself give any right to possession but at least explained it. However, the courts were not inclined to take this tenancy relationship at all seriously.[200] Although it might have some advantages in the running of covenants on assignment by either party,[201] the attornment clause is seen as of little value and obsolescent.[202]

There are several ways in which the law recognises the expectation of the mortgagor to be in possession. First, if not very helpful, the mortgagee who seeks or takes possession must allow the mortgagor to redeem.[203] One consequence of this is that the mortgagor is entitled to redeem before the legal (contractual) date for redemption has passed, when otherwise there would be no immediate right to redeem.

Second, it may be possible to persuade the court to imply a right for the mortgagor to possess the land. This will not be difficult if the mortgage provides for the mortgagee to have a right to possession after default: the implied corollary is that the mortgagor has a right to possession before default.[204] It may be easier to imply a right for the mortgagor to occupy in an instalment mortgage, as it is clear that such mortgages are intended to last for a specific time. However, even here the courts are reluctant to imply such a right unless there are some specific indications that it is intended.[205] Nevertheless, it is exceptional for a mortgagee to seek possession before default, as the power of sale depends upon default and sale is almost always the mortgagee's ultimate objective.

(b) Reasons for mortgagees taking possession

Possession is nearly always sought as a prelude to selling the property. It is usually hopeless for the mortgagee to attempt to sell a house with a mortgagor in it who is refusing to move. As will be seen later, exercise of the power to sell does not require approval by the court. On the other hand, possession is invariably sought by court proceedings (unless the mortgagor voluntarily gives up possession). It is a criminal offence to take possession of premises from another by violence or threat of violence, whether to person or property,[206] and few mortgagees will wish to test the limits of peaceable entry. The court proceedings for possession in substance pose the question whether sale should take place.[207] It is worth adding that a number of protections for residential mortgagors have been instituted, short of actually changing the rights and obligations of the parties. In particular, the Pre-Action

---

[200] Legislation protecting tenants has been held inapplicable: *Peckham Mutual BS* v *Registe* (1980) 42 P&CR 186.

[201] *Regent Oil Co Ltd* v *JA Gregory (Hatch End) Ltd* [1966] Ch 402 (attornment clause in a legal charge). Quaere whether covenants would run anyway by virtue of the leasehold relationship created (or replicated) in all mortgages of legal estates after 1925 or, most simply, as an incident of the mortgage relationship.

[202] Wurtzburg and Mills, *Building Society Law* (14th edn), pp 184–185; Miller (1966) 30 Conv 30.

[203] *Bovill* v *Endle* [1896] 1 Ch 648.

[204] *Birmingham Citizens Permanent BS* v *Caunt* [1962] Ch 883 at p 890. The standard form of building society mortgage in Wurtzburg and Mills, *Building Society Law* (15th edn), Appendix C, is drafted in this way. Any right to possession lost by default will not be revived by clearing the arrears: *Esso Petroleum Co Ltd* v *Alstonbridge Properties Ltd* [1975] 1 WLR 1474.

[205] *Esso Petroleum Co Ltd* v *Alstonbridge Properties Ltd* [1975] 1 WLR 1474; *Western Bank Ltd* v *Schindler* [1977] Ch 1. Neither case involved a normal instalment mortgage of residential premises.

[206] Criminal Law Act 1977, s 6.

[207] One explicit recognition of this is found in *Citibank Trust Ltd* v *Ayivor* [1987] 3 All ER 241.

Protocol for Possession Claims[208] sets out steps (including the giving of information and consideration of proposals from the borrower) which the mortgagee should take before commencing proceedings.

There are other, relatively rare, reasons why the mortgagee might consider taking possession. It is possible that the mortgagor is failing to maintain the property, and so diminishing its value as a security.[209] Alternatively, the mortgagee may wish to exercise the power to lease,[210] with the rent going to pay the mortgage interest, or (more likely) that the rents on existing leases should be received directly by the mortgagee rather than paid to the mortgagor. Once a mortgagee has taken possession, there are onerous duties regarding the use of the land and accounting for receipts. These render taking possession, other than as a prelude to sale, unpopular. It will be seen later that the appointment of a receiver achieves most of the mortgagee's objectives with fewer legal risks.

(c) Jurisdiction to postpone possession

The question whether the court possesses jurisdiction to deny or delay the mortgagee's right to possession proved controversial. The nineteenth-century cases denied any such equitable jurisdiction.[211] However, in the middle of the twentieth century, the courts began to apply a discretion. When this was challenged in the High Court, it was first qualified[212] and then conclusively rejected by Russell J in *Birmingham Citizens Permanent BS* v *Caunt*.[213] It is clear today that any general jurisdiction is dead; the cases prior to *Caunt* need not be considered.

The sole ground for postponement allowed by *Caunt* is to permit redemption. However, the time allowed for the mortgagor to redeem is likely to be no more than two or three months, even where a reasonable prospect of redemption is proved.[214] The court is unlikely to be moved by vague assurances that the debt will be repaid where (as is often the case) possession proceedings are the culmination of a protracted series of demands for payment.[215] It is always possible for the mortgagor to say that he or she is on the point of selling the property to raise money, but the courts are likely to be sympathetic only if the mortgagor 'has entered or is about to enter into a contract' at a price sufficient to pay off the debt.[216]

---

[208] Bailey and Williams (2009) 159 NLJ 221; Greer [2009] Conv 516. Rather differently, the Mortgage Repossessions (Protection of Tenants etc) Act 2010 (O'Neill [2011] Conv 380) enables most tenants to request a two-month postponement of possession. This is designed to protect tenants rather than mortgagors.

[209] *Western Bank Ltd* v *Schindler* [1977] Ch 1.

[210] LPA, s 99(2): see *Berkshire Capital Funding Ltd* v *Street* (1999) 78 P&CR 321 for the operation of the power as regards subsequent mortgagees.

[211] *Cholmondeley* v *Clinton* (1817) 2 Mer 171 at p 359 (35 ER 905 at p 976).

[212] *Four-Maids Ltd* v *Dudley Marshall (Properties) Ltd* [1957] Ch 317.

[213] [1962] Ch 883. For the earlier law, see Rudden (1961) 25 Conv 278.

[214] The entire debt must be repaid: it is insufficient to allege a counterclaim that would cover the debt: *Mobil Oil Co Ltd* v *Rawlinson* (1981) 43 P&CR 221 (applied to set-offs, even where the mortgagor is a guarantor, in *National Westminster Bank plc* v *Skelton* [1993] 1 WLR 72; cf *Ashley Guarantee plc* v *Zacaria* [1993] 1 WLR 62).

[215] *Braithwaite* v *Winwood* [1960] 1 WLR 1257. In *Hastings & Thanet BS* v *Goddard* [1970] 1 WLR 1544, Russell LJ was singularly unmoved by an argument that the unexpected might happen – a win on the pools, for example!

[216] *Royal Trust Co of Canada* v *Markham* [1975] 1 WLR 1416 at p 1420; see also p 612 below.

One further case should, however, be considered. In *Quennell* v *Maltby*,[217] the mortgagor had leased the mortgaged property. The mortgagee was not bound by the statutory protection of the lessees' possession, as the lease was not authorised by the mortgage.[218] In order to evict the tenants, the mortgagor's wife paid off the mortgage loan in return for a transfer of the mortgage; she then sought possession as mortgagee. The Court of Appeal unanimously rejected her claim. It was held that she was not bona fide exercising her rights as mortgagee in order to protect her security.[219] The decision is readily justified because she was acting on her husband's behalf. The real interest lies in Lord Denning MR's insistence that possession must be sought reasonably and subject to such conditions as the court may impose. These dicta hark back to the days before *Caunt*. Whilst the proposition is not unreasonable, it is inconsistent with *Caunt* and has little support.[220] *The Co-operative Bank plc* v *Phillips*[221] illustrates how difficult it is for a mortgagor to rely on *Quennel*. Possession was sought by a second mortgagee not in order to sell (not practical on the facts) or lease, but in order to put pressure on the borrower – in the hope that he or his family would make repayment. This was held to be a proper purpose: obtaining payment.

(d) The statutory discretion

Following *Caunt*, the Payne Committee[222] reported that control over possession applications was desirable, although there were few instances of abuse by building societies. Particular sympathy was felt for those experiencing short-term problems in meeting mortgage payments, especially in cases of illness or unemployment. The Committee thought that postponement of possession for six months would normally be sufficient to allow the arrears to be paid off in these cases. Sections 36–39 of the Administration of Justice Act 1970 gave effect to their proposals.[223] Unfortunately, the drafting of the legislation has given rise to much litigation, especially as to which mortgages and situations are covered.

Before going into these problems, it should be noted that the jurisdiction is limited to mortgages of dwelling houses or of land including a dwelling house.[224] This may contain a trap for mortgagees if a dwelling house is included in a mortgage of substantially business premises. However, relief will depend upon ability to pay off arrears in relation to the entire mortgaged property.[225] It might be added that it is not necessary for the mortgagor to be the person occupying the dwelling house and that the dwelling house requirement relates to the date of the possession proceedings, not the date of the mortgage.[226]

[217] [1979] 1 WLR 318; Pearce [1979] CLJ 257.
[218] *Britannia BS* v *Earl* [1992] 1 WLR 422 confirms that mortgagees are unaffected by the statutory protection of mortgagors' tenants unless the lease is authorised.
[219] Cf the discussion on sale, p 621 below.
[220] It is applied by *Albany Home Loans Ltd* v *Massey* [1997] 2 All ER 609, but in the much more restricted context of preventing orders against only one of two joint mortgagors.
[221] [2014] BPIR 1430 (Morgan J); it involved a mortgage of two farms.
[222] Committee on Enforcement of Judgment Debts (1969) Cmnd 3909, Part IX.
[223] RJ Smith (1979) 43 Conv 266; Tromans [1984] Conv 91.
[224] Applied in *Royal Bank of Scotland plc* v *Miller* [2002] QB 255 (nightclub with flat above).
[225] *Barclays Bank plc* v *Alcorn* [2002] 2 P&CR D19; [2002] EWHC 498 (Ch) (McMurtry [2002] Conv 594).
[226] *Royal Bank of Scotland plc* v *Miller* [2002] QB 255.

Default clauses

The first case on s 36 illustrated its defective drafting. The court is given a power to adjourn the proceedings or suspend or postpone execution of a possession order:

> if it appears to the court that in the event of its exercising the power the mortgagor[227] is likely to be able within a reasonable period to pay any sums due under the mortgage or to remedy a default . . .

In *Halifax BS v Clark*,[228] there were arrears of £100 and a total liability of £1,420. As in nearly all mortgages, there was a clause providing that the entire loan would be immediately repayable on default in paying instalments. It followed that the sums due under the mortgage included the balance of the sum lent (£1,420, a large sum in 1972). There was no prospect of that being repaid within a reasonable period: possession was ordered. The result was to render the jurisdiction useless in the great majority of mortgages. Fortunately, s 8 of the Administration of Justice Act 1973 provided a swift response, whereby if:

> the mortgagor is entitled or is to be permitted to pay the principal sum secured by instalments or otherwise to defer payment of it in whole or in part, but provision is also made for earlier payment in the event of any default by the mortgagor or of a demand by the mortgagee or otherwise, then for purposes of s 36 . . . a court may treat as due . . . only such amounts as the mortgagor would have expected to be required to pay if there had been no such provision for earlier payment.

Types of mortgage caught

There can be no doubt that s 8 covers a repayment mortgage with a default clause[229]: the position in *Clark*. Its application to other mortgages has been clarified by litigation. In *Centrax Trustees Ltd v Ross*,[230] Goulding J held that it applied to the traditional form of mortgage with redemption after six months, where there is no provision for repayment by instalments or endowment policy. The problem with this sort of mortgage is that its length is indeterminate: it will last until either party wishes it to end. It was regarded as implicit in the mortgage in *Centrax* that it would last for more than six months and this sufficed to say that the mortgagor was 'permitted . . . to defer payment'. The right to call in the capital at any time sufficed as a provision for repayment on demand.[231] This may effectively convert a six-month mortgage into one of virtually unlimited duration. Whilst this may be reasonable for financial institutions, it may make individuals reluctant to lend money on mortgages for fear that it may be difficult to get their money back when it is needed.

---

[227] Purchasers from the mortgagor are covered but, perhaps surprisingly, not tenants: *Britannia BS v Earl* [1990] 1 WLR 422 (Bridge [1990] Conv 450).

[228] [1973] Ch 307.

[229] If the mortgagee seeks payment of the capital, the court is likely to exercise its discretion under County Courts Act 1984, s 71(2), to suspend its order in a similar manner to suspending possession: *Cheltenham & Gloucester BS v Grattidge* (1993) 25 HLR 454; *Alliance and Leicester plc v Slayford* (2000) 33 HLR 743 at p 751. However, a suspended judgment may still be advantageous: *Cheltenham & Gloucester BS v Johnson* (1996) 73 P&CR 293.

[230] [1979] 2 All ER 952.

[231] On the facts, there was a default clause (unnecessary in a mortgage of this type), but Goulding J does not seem to have relied upon that clause.

By contrast, a mortgage to secure a bank overdraft was held to be outside the section in *Habib Bank Ltd* v *Tailor*.[232] The Court of Appeal approved *Centrax* (if without enthusiasm) but held that the sum must be due before it can be said to be deferred. In the case of an overdraft, the balance is not payable until the bank demands payment: the equivalent time to the contractual date for redemption in *Centrax*. It follows that, because an overdraft gives no right to defer after demand has been made, s 8 does not apply to overdrafts. This can be justified because an overdraft is understood to be repayable at any time and, unlike other forms of mortgage, cannot be seen as long-term financing.

It may be difficult to decide whether a transaction should be treated as an overdraft. This is because bank mortgages frequently take the simple form of a promise to pay on demand. The repayment or endowment nature of the mortgage (where such exists) appears not from the mortgage deed, but from a prior exchange of letters. It is essential that these letters are taken into account in order to appreciate the true nature of the mortgage.[233]

The final form of mortgage to be considered is the interest-only mortgage, in particular an endowment mortgage whereby repayment of the capital is postponed until the endowment life insurance policy matures. Given that this is a common form of mortgage, with a set length, few would argue that it should be outside the legislation. Nevertheless, interpretation of the legislation posed problems for the Court of Appeal in *Bank of Scotland* v *Grimes*.[234] The first requirement is that 'the mortgagor is entitled or is to be permitted to pay the principal sum secured by instalments or otherwise to defer payment'. There are no instalments of capital in such a mortgage, and *Habib* might indicate that there is no deferment as the capital is not due until the policy matures. The court was emphatic that the discretion must apply to endowment mortgages and sharply distinguished *Habib*. It was held that a fixed future date for repayment provided a right to defer until then. Such a date is unusual in an overdraft.

The satisfactory conclusion is that s 8 applies to all mortgages apart from those securing overdrafts.

The role of arrears

The jurisdiction (whether s 36 or s 8 applies) is based upon ability to pay arrears. The legislation seems to assume that (1) possession will not be sought if there are no arrears and (2) possession will not be sought if arrears have been paid. Neither assumption bears any relationship to the law on possession.[235]

The problem arose in *Western Bank Ltd* v *Schindler*,[236] in which there were, technically, no arrears. Defective drafting of the mortgage resulted in interest not being due until the end of nine years, nor was failure to maintain payments on an endowment policy a breach

---

[232] [1982] 1 WLR 1218.
[233] Tromans [1984] Conv 91. *Citibank Trust Ltd* v *Ayivor* [1987] 3 All ER 241 and *Bank of Scotland* v *Grimes* [1985] QB 1179 took into account such letters, showing there to be endowment mortgages. *Centrax* had refused to consider such letters, but on the facts they did not seem to affect the nature of the mortgage.
[234] [1985] QB 1179, followed in *Royal Bank of Scotland plc* v *Miller* [2002] QB 255.
[235] *Robertson* v *Cilia* [1956] 1 WLR 1502 is an example of possession being sought after arrears have been paid. The power of sale is likely to survive payment of arrears, certainly in the normal case where the capital has become due on default.
[236] [1977] Ch 1.

of any term of the mortgage. The mortgagee was naturally worried when the mortgagor failed to pay interest or policy premiums. The only possible remedy was possession, there being no default to trigger other remedies. The court was faced with three possibilities: that the Administration of Justice Act 1970 had no application, that it applied so that the court had to decide in favour of the mortgagor as there was no default and that the court had a genuine discretion.

By a two-to-one majority, the Court of Appeal held that the 1970 Act did apply. The majority was influenced by the consideration that it would be absurd to protect a mortgagor in default but not one who was up to date with payments: 'irrational and unfair', in the words of Buckley LJ.[237] This was refuted by Goff LJ, dissenting, on the basis that mortgagees almost never seek possession save in order to sell, and sale requires default. Hence, any absurdity is of little consequence. Yet, his argument overlooks the position of the mortgagor who has defaulted but then pays off arrears: the power of sale survives, although it may be a proper case to refuse possession if the Act applies.

The majority further concluded that there was a real discretion. Counsel's argument that the non-defaulting mortgagor was entitled to succeed would abrogate the mortgagee's right to possession and was inconsistent with the discretion conferred by s 36. On the facts, the conduct of the mortgagor persuaded the court that the mortgagee should be given possession. An important consequential issue, irrelevant in *Schindler* because the mortgagee won, is what the form of order would have been, had possession been postponed. The standard order is that possession is postponed to give time for payment of arrears. This is totally inappropriate where there are no arrears.[238]

Does the common law right to possession survive?

In the light of *Schindler*, the argument[239] that s 36 abrogates the mortgagee's common law right to possession seems untenable. This remains so despite the right seeming out of place in a modern law of mortgages. However, more persuasive is the argument, based on Rent Act analogies,[240] that the right to take possession *out of court* is superseded by the legislation.

This question arose in *Ropaigealach v Barclays Bank plc*,[241] which held that the right does survive and that the court then has no s 36 jurisdiction. Although it is an offence to use or threaten violence if another person is present,[242] this does not protect those who are even temporarily absent (for refurbishment in *Ropaigealach*) and gives no civil remedy. It is probably pessimistic to suggest[243] that the decision will have a significant effect, but it does cause a 'curious anomaly' which Clarke LJ accepted only with 'considerable reluctance'.

---

[237] Ibid, at p 15.

[238] Buckley and Scarman LJJ differed as to the proper length of postponement, but *Cheltenham & Gloucester BS v Norgan* [1996] 1 WLR 343 (discussed below) supports Buckley LJ's preference for the full length of the mortgage.

[239] Clarke [1983] Conv 293, discussed by Bamforth [1996] CLP Pt 2 at pp 237–241.

[240] See, e.g., *Remon v City of London Real Property Co Ltd* [1921] 1 KB 49.

[241] [2000] QB 263.

[242] Criminal Law Act 1977, s 6.

[243] Cf Paton (1999) 149 NLJ 614. But could it be challenged on human rights grounds? See Goymour in *The Impact of the UK Human Rights Act on Private Law* (ed Hoffmann), Chapter 12, pp 296–297 and Loveland [2014] Conv 381. The approach of the Supreme Court in *McDonald v McDonald* [2016] 3 WLR 45 (p 24 above) renders this less likely; *Ropaigealach* is cited and assumed to be correct.

Sale without taking possession?

Horsham Properties Group Ltd v *Clark*[244] illustrates a potentially calamitous flaw in the application of s 36. It has been assumed that sale will not take place without first taking possession. However, in *Horsham*, the mortgagee simply sold the land, thereby defeating the proprietary interest of the mortgagor. Possession was then ordered in favour of the purchaser; s 36 did not protect the mortgagor, as it was not an action by a mortgagee.

This led to much criticism, and there are proposals[245] to amend the law so that a court order (with a discretion based on s 36) would be required prior to sale. This would apply to a residential owner-occupier mortgage, unless the mortgagor agrees to the sale or there has been a possession order. It would not apply to buy-to-let mortgages, nor to mortgages for purposes unrelated to the land, such as securing business debts. This restricted proposal would also apply to a sale in the *Ropaigealach* circumstances. This quite timid response would affect almost no cases on the basis of current practice: *Horsham* itself involved a buy-to-let mortgage.

(e) The exercise of the statutory discretion[246]

The courts are nearly always willing to allow postponement if it can be shown that there is a reasonable prospect of the arrears bring paid. A crucial question concerns the period over which the arrears must be paid. By the time cases come to court, there has frequently been default over a protracted period, with the result that the arrears are substantial. A mortgagor who has been struggling to meet current payments will find it difficult to pay arrears as well. This is emphasised by the fact that social security payments will cover interest charges (at least after 13 weeks) but will not cover arrears.[247] This is particularly important in cases where there are arrears and the relationship between a couple living together breaks down. The woman is frequently left in the home with children and is dependent on social security to meet mortgage obligations.[248]

For some time, it was thought that arrears had to be paid within a period of about two years. Unless illness or unemployment had caused a temporary problem, this would frequently be impracticable. However, a far more generous approach was adopted by the Court of Appeal in *Cheltenham & Gloucester BS* v *Norgan*.[249] Postponement was accepted until the end of the mortgage, in line with options stated in the Council of Mortgage Lenders' statement of current practice. This is tremendously important, as even substantial arrears become manageable when, in substance, added to the capital debt. Payment of, say,

---

[244] [2009] 1 WLR 1255; the effect of the sale was conceded, subject to human rights considerations (p 27 above). Earlier, *National Provincial BS* v *Ahmed* [1995] 2 EGLR 127 had assumed that sale would not overreach possession protected by the legislation, but Clarke LJ in *Ropaigealach* v *Barclays Bank plc* [2000] QB 263 at p 285 noted that this 'desirable' result is difficult to justify.

[245] Ministry of Justice CP 55/09 (http://webarchive.nationalarchives.gov.uk/20100403061401/http://www.justice.gov.uk/consultations/mortgages-power-sale.htm); Dixon [2010] Conv 111.

[246] See Whitehouse in *The Reform of Property Law* (eds Jackson and Wilde), Chapter 9.

[247] See Wikeley, Ogus and Barendt, *Law of Social Security* (5th edn), pp 303–308; Nield (2010) 30 LS 610 at p 620. Borrowers are expected to take out mortgage payments protection insurance.

[248] See Nevitt and Levin (1973) 36 MLR 345.

[249] [1996] 1 WLR 343; Thompson [1996] Conv 118. The result is supported by *First Middlesbrough Trading & Mortgage Co Ltd* v *Cunningham* (1974) 28 P&CR 69 (the mortgage had five years to run) and Buckley LJ in *Western Bank Ltd* v *Schindler* [1977] Ch 1.

£10,000 arrears may seem impossible within two years, whereas additional monthly payments of around £70 for the lifetime of the mortgage may be quite a different matter.

However, such long postponement is likely to be permitted only if the value of the property is sufficient to secure both the original loan and arrears. Further, in longer mortgages, it cannot be assumed that the court will in fact postpone for the entire duration. Thus there was an order for payment over about 9½ years in *Bank of Scotland plc* v *Zinda*[250] when the mortgage had a further 23 years to run. In 2009, the Ministry of Justice had stated that the normal period of postponement was for 2–4 years.[251]

One consequence of *Norgan* is that borrowers will be expected to produce a detailed budget to show that they will be able to make repayments: this replaced the previous easy-going system whereby judges permitted postponement very readily but with costs (charged to the mortgagor) mounting alarmingly.[252] In most previous possession cases, there had been a protracted record of default and failure to meet rescheduled payments.[253] Although *Norgan* allows postponement on a generous basis, the court made it clear that any future failure to make payments is likely to result in no further mercy being shown. If this is applied at all strictly, the effect of *Norgan* may well be to favour lenders.

Whatever the period of repayment, the borrower must be able to pay current instalments and arrears. Although social security payments are likely to cover current interest payments, commonly there will be real problems as regards arrears.[254] Now that the borrower must provide a detailed budget, what happens if there is a continuing but temporary difficulty such as illness or unemployment? It will be clear that current income will be insufficient for repayments to be made, but it is to be hoped that the courts will consider the prospect of employment within a reasonable period and, perhaps, adjourn the proceedings for this to be ascertained.

In *First National Bank plc* v *Syed*,[255] there had been prolonged failure to comply with mortgage payments and rearranged terms. Finally, the mortgagor offered a payment below the current interest charge. The Court of Appeal was emphatic that the repayment under the discretionary jurisdiction must cover both current payments and arrears. It is wrong either to order a lesser payment or a payment that the mortgagor patently cannot afford.

Syed is interesting because it contains a reference to the separate jurisdiction under the Consumer Credit Act 1974[256] to amend the terms of debts. A time order enables the court to reschedule the loan so that smaller payments are made over a longer period and the rate of interest may be reduced in consequence of the order.[257] However, most mortgages are

---

[250] [2012] 1 WLR 728; the length of postponement was not in issue in the appeal, but received no comment.

[251] Ministry of Justice CP 55/09 (n 245 above), para 57. Whitehouse in *Modern Studies in Property Law*, Vol 6 (ed Bright), Chapter 7, observes at p 163 that *Norgan* has made little change in practice.

[252] Whitehouse in *Land Law: Themes and Perspectives* (eds Bright and Dewar), Chapter 7, especially pp 183–198.

[253] *LBI HF* v *Stanford* [2015] EWHC 3130 (Ch) is explicit authority that there can be consecutive applications under s 36. It is surprising that there was any doubt regarding this.

[254] *Bristol & West BS* v *Ellis* (1996) 73 P&CR 158. An order which contemplated repayments over 98 years was held to be outside the jurisdiction.

[255] [1991] 2 All ER 250. A far more sympathetic approach was taken in *Cheltenham & Gloucester BS* v *Grant* (1994) 26 HLR 703, in which there was suspension for a year although the chances of payment seemed pretty remote: Thompson [1995] Conv 51.

[256] Section 129; Wilkinson (1991) 141 NLJ 793.

[257] The discretion is fully reviewed in *Southern & District Finance plc* v *Barnes* (1995) 27 HLR 691 (Dunn [1996] Conv 209); it is also considered in *Norgan*.

relatively long-term arrangements, and extending the term would have a very limited effect on the monthly payments. On the facts in *Syed*, the mortgagor could not afford even the interest, so that prolonging the original six-year loan was not a viable option.

Capital repayment

A quite different possibility is that the mortgagor may wish to sell the property and so pay off both arrears and loan. This may be attractive to the mortgagor because a mortgagor's sale may attract a higher price than a forced mortgagee's sale of vacant property.[258] In addition, it is better for the mortgagor if the sale can be made contemporaneous with the purchase of another (cheaper) house. Yet, the dangers to the mortgagee are obvious. Even assuming that the sale price will cover the debt, there is a risk that the mortgagor will make no serious attempt to sell and will use the argument as a ploy to procrastinate and retain possession. Pitching the price too high is effective to discourage potential purchasers. The risk of there being no sale is more obvious where the mortgagor has attempted but failed to sell the house for some time before possession proceedings.

The original approach of the courts was to order possession unless there was evidence of a purchaser, in which case postponement for around three months might be permitted.[259] *National & Provincial BS* v *Lloyd*[260] heralds a more relaxed approach. Postponement for the length of the mortgage was not feasible as the monthly payments could not be afforded. However, the Court of Appeal applied the *Norgan* principle of a 'proper opportunity of making good his default' to capital repayment. They asked whether the mortgage debt would be cleared by the sale of the property. If so, postponement of possession might follow if there is clear evidence that sale would take place within 'six or nine months or even a year'. The facts involved the sale of four barns, and the court held that no such evidence had been presented, bearing in mind that three years had elapsed since initial default.

Bristol & West BS v *Ellis*[261] provides an excellent example of the working of *Lloyd*. The borrower wished to postpone sale for three to five years whilst her children were completing their education. The total debt was £77,000 plus costs; she was willing to pay £5,000 and had valuations of £80,000 and £85,000 for the house. The Court of Appeal was clearly willing to contemplate postponement for more than the year mentioned in *Lloyd*. This flexibility is to be welcomed.

As in *Lloyd*, the court in *Ellis* placed great stress on the safety of the security: if the lender is certain to recover the sum lent, then there is little need for an early sale. However, much more caution is required where the security is weak. In such cases, little or no postponement to allow sale is appropriate. The borrower would not have a problem if able to pay interest on the loan and arrears, but that is not the scenario under discussion. If the security is less than the value of the debt, then possession will be immediate.[262] Further, protracted failure

---

[258] Recognised in *Target Home Loans Ltd* v *Clothier* [1994] 1 All ER 439.

[259] *Royal Trust Co of Canada* v *Markham* [1975] 1 WLR 1416; *Target Home Loans Ltd* v *Clothier* [1994] 1 All ER 439.

[260] [1996] 1 All ER 630.

[261] (1996) 73 P&CR 158.

[262] *Cheltenham & Gloucester plc* v *Krausz* [1997] 1 WLR 1558 stresses that, in cases of negative equity, there is no jurisdiction under the legislation to postpone possession to enable the mortgagor to sell. For the effect of this on applications for sale under LPA, s 91(2), see p 623 below.

to sell may well lead the court to consider that the borrower has had the chance to sell and that possession should be ordered after, at best, a short delay. On the facts, the court concluded, perhaps harshly, that the security was inadequate to justify such a postponement as had been sought. The court was influenced by the possibility of price fluctuation over several years, together with the tendency of agents to produce unduly optimistic valuations.

A rather different question is whether the borrower can retain possession whilst the lender sells the land. In *Cheltenham & Gloucester plc v Booker*,[263] the Court of Appeal thought that this was theoretically possible. However, it would apply only if the mortgagee did not need possession, the mortgagor's presence would not adversely affect the price and the mortgagor would co-operate and give possession on completion. These requirements would virtually never be satisfied: the court stressed that the person with the conduct of the sale normally needs to be in possession.

A variation on the sale analysis is that the mortgagor may receive capital which would enable arrears to be paid off. In *Citibank Trust Ltd v Ayivor*,[264] the mortgagor was suing the mortgagee for failure to communicate a surveyor's finding of dry rot. If successful, the damages would exceed the arrears. Mervyn Davies J was reluctant even to consider the existence of such a counterclaim. It may be questioned whether such reluctance was justified, although it is easier to agree with the judge's doubts as to whether any damages would in fact be used to clear the arrears.[265] Whether a claim against a third party could be considered is not clear.[266] On the other hand, a challenge to the validity of the mortgage will not be prejudged by assuming a liability greater than the sum lent.[267]

Protecting partners

A significant question concerns the position of partners (whether or not spouses) of mortgagors in default, especially where the relationship has broken down and the partner is left in possession of the house. We are here considering cases where the partner is not a party to the mortgage.

Most mortgagees will not be too concerned by the source of payments, so long as they are received. Statute provides that payments by spouses (and those in civil partnerships), or cohabitants with a court order for occupation, are as good as payments by the mortgagor.[268] Further, such persons are normally entitled to be joined as parties[269]; notice of possession proceedings has to be given to those who have registered their statutory rights of occupation.[270] A distinct danger is that, unless spouses and other partners are involved at an early stage of default, arrears may become awkwardly large by the time of court proceedings.

---

[263] [1997] 1 FLR 311. As there was negative equity, this was based upon common law powers to postpone possession.
[264] [1987] 3 All ER 241.
[265] The repairs still needed to be carried out: it was not as if the arrears had arisen because money had been spent on repairs.
[266] A claim not settled after five years was accorded little weight in *Abbey National Mortgages plc v Bernard* (1995) 71 P&CR 257.
[267] *Household Mortgage Corporation v Pringle* (1997) 30 HLR 250.
[268] Family Law Act 1996, ss 30(3) (cf s 35(13) for former spouses), 36(13).
[269] Ibid, s 55.
[270] Ibid, s 56; for this right to occupy, see ss 30–31.

(f) The human rights dimension

Could the present law be challenged on the basis of human rights infringement? This is most likely as regards the Article 8 respect for home.[271] A challenge by the mortgagor may be unlikely to succeed, given both the s 36 discretion and the essentially consensual nature of the power of sale which possession is required for.[272] However, an interesting argument has been mounted that home rights of children, in particular, are nowhere taken into account.[273] This was discussed in Chapter 3 – the argument seems unlikely to succeed after *McDonald* v *McDonald*.[274]

(g) Duties of the mortgagee in possession

The courts have recognised the extraordinary nature of the mortgagee's right to possession by insisting that the mortgagee must account for profits made (or which should have been made).[275] The normal benefit to the mortgagee is the interest on the loan. There is no question of the mortgagee's being able to benefit twice over: by possession and by receipt of interest. This strict duty to account is intended to persuade mortgagees not to take long-term possession save in quite exceptional cases. Where possession is sought for sale, then the duty to account has no substance because possession is for so short a period; leasing the land in the intervening weeks is impracticable. It would be otherwise if the mortgagee were to delay selling for a considerable period.

The mortgagee must obtain the best rent available from the property, although essential expenses such as insurance costs will be allowed. The courts may reject expenses that are not 'absolutely necessary'[276] and will not allow the mortgagee any form of payment for time spent in managing the property.[277] Greater problems arise where the mortgagee continues a business on the land, as illustrated by the leading case of *White* v *City of London Brewery Co*.[278]

The mortgagee in *White* was a brewer, who took possession of a mortgaged public house. Unemployment in the area had resulted in lower sales of beer. Initially, the brewery ran the pub at a loss, employing a manager. Subsequently, it was let to the manager as a tied house (that is, only the mortgagee's beer could be sold), the rent being low on account of the difficulty in making a profit. Although the pub itself was unprofitable, the mortgagee brewer made large profits by the sale of beer to the pub. The major question was whether the mortgagee must account for these profits. The Court of Appeal unanimously held not: the profits came from the business of brewing, not from the pub itself. This represents a limit to the strict accounting rule, although it can be justified because brewing profits would be made by any brewer whose beer was sold. On the other hand, the mortgagee

---

[271] Nield [2013] King's LJ 147. See also *Ropaigealach*, n 243 above.
[272] *Horsham Properties Group Ltd* v *Clark* [2009] 1 WLR 1255 (p 27 above); *McDonald* v *McDonald* [2016] 3 WLR 45.
[273] Nield and Hopkins (2013) 33 LS 431.
[274] [2016] 3 WLR 45; p 25 above.
[275] See *Robertson* v *Norris* (1859) 1 Giff 428 (65 ER 986). Accounting takes place on redemption.
[276] *Trimleston* v *Hamill* (1810) 1 Ball&B 377 at p 385.
[277] *Comyns* v *Comyns* (1871) 5 IR Eq 583.
[278] (1889) 42 Ch D 237. For failure to continue it, cf *AIB Finance Ltd* v *Debtors* [1998] 2 All ER 929.

could not charge an abnormally low rent and compensate for that by higher beer profits. In particular, a tied house invariably has a lower rent, and the mortgagee had to account for the differential between that and the full normal rent.[279]

Where the mortgagee in possession is running a business, normal business expenses are deductible. However, the courts will scrutinise costs of materials supplied by the mortgagee.[280] In addition, if a prudent person would not have used the property in the way the mortgagee has, then the mortgagee will be liable for any reduction in the value of the property caused thereby, whilst having no right to recover any trading losses incurred.[281]

If the mortgagee occupies the property personally, then the value of the property or (in the case of a business) the profits[282] must be accounted for. It appears that other collateral benefits will be ignored. In the Australian case of *Fyfe* v *Smith*,[283] the mortgagee was in possession of a hotel. It was held that he was not required to account for the benefit of living in the hotel, on the basis that the room had no rental value. This purports to follow the *White* analysis, in stressing the rental value of the property. However, it does appear generous when the mortgagee has derived a benefit directly from the property.

(iii) *Sale*

If the mortgagor is unable to repay the loan, then sale is the most likely remedy.[284] The mortgagee can sell the full estate of the mortgagor, despite having merely a long lease or legal charge. Sale has great advantages over foreclosure: it does not require court approval,[285] nor can it be set aside if properly carried out. In addition, the mortgagee can bring a personal action for any balance of the debt over the money raised by sale,[286] though few mortgagors will be able to pay the balance. From the mortgagor's point of view, sale has to be regarded as a disaster simply because the property is lost. However, there is the consolation of being entitled to any money left over after the debt and sale expenses have been satisfied.

(a) When is there a power of sale?
The power of sale originated as an express power, included in virtually every mortgage. Today it is implied by the Law of Property Act 1925, although it is common for mortgage deeds to make explicit provision overriding the statutory power. If there are successive

---

[279] Calculated at £20 pa on a lease negotiated at £60 pa, to be contrasted with £1,990 profits from the sale of beer: an interesting example of the economics of the industry.

[280] *Robertson* v *Norris* (1859) 1 Giff 428 (65 ER 986): higher prices for materials taken on credit not allowed, despite being usual whilst the mortgagor was in possession.

[281] *Marriott* v *The Anchor Reversionary Company* (1861) 3 De GF&J 177 (45 ER 846).

[282] *Robertson* v *Norris* (1859) 1 Giff 428 (65 ER 986); *Chaplin* v *Young (No 1)* (1864) 33 Beav 330 (55 ER 395); *White* v *City of London Brewery Co* (1889) 42 Ch D 237.

[283] [1975] 2 NSWLR 408; Markson (1979) 129 NLJ 334.

[284] For a discussion of sale, unorthodox in part, see Robinson [1989] Conv 336, 412.

[285] *Horsham Properties Group Ltd* v *Clark* [2009] 1 WLR 1255. This would be changed by the proposals discussed earlier (at p 610).

[286] As the claim is under a mortgage, the limitation period for the capital debt is 12 years from the date it is due: *West Bromwich BS* v *Wilkinson* [2005] 1 WLR 2303. In most mortgages, this will be the date of default (or shortly after).

mortgages of the same property, then each has a power of sale. However, any sale has to be subject to prior mortgages[287] and in unregistered land subsequent mortgagees have the severe disadvantage of not holding the title deeds.[288]

There are two principal statutory provisions relating to the power of sale. Section 101(1)(i) (applicable to mortgages by deed, including registered charges[289]) confers the power when the mortgage money has become due. What does this mean? If there is provision for redemption after six months (the old form of mortgage), the mortgage money would be treated as due at that time. The wording is more difficult to apply to a modern instalment or endowment mortgage, in which final payment is postponed for a long period. However, it is normal for the entire loan to be made payable immediately on default in payment of instalments or interest; the mortgage money then becomes due. In order to avoid any uncertainty, it is common to include a provision that, *for the purposes of s 101*, the mortgage money is due after six months.[290]

The second provision, s 103, states that the power cannot be exercised unless one of three conditions is satisfied:

(1) three months' notice requiring repayment has been given. This is most likely to apply to the traditional six-month redemption mortgage,[291] in which the length is initially indeterminate;

(2) interest is in arrear for two months; or

(3) some other breach has occurred.

Protecting purchasers

It is generally said that s 101 governs when the power *arises* and s 103 governs when it is *exercisable*. What is the difference? All the purchaser has to do is to ensure that the power has arisen (s 101). Investigation of the exercisability of the power would involve details as to the mortgagor's conduct that would clog up the sale process. Accordingly, s 104(2) enacts that after conveyance the purchaser is protected against any irregularity and is under no obligation at any stage to investigate whether the sale is authorised.[292] It is the mortgagee's duty to ensure that the power is exercisable. It follows that a sale in breach of s 103 can be prevented prior to conveyance, but that after conveyance the mortgagee (not the purchaser) may be liable in damages for any loss caused.

Despite the purchaser's apparently unlimited protection under s 104(2), the courts have denied protection to those who are aware of a defect: the section cannot be used as an instrument of fraud.[293] Thus in *Waring* v *London & Manchester Assurance Co Ltd*[294]

---

[287] LPA, s 104(1).

[288] The deeds are held by the first mortgagee: ibid, ss 85(1), 86(1).

[289] LRA, s 51; *Swift 1st Ltd* v *Colin* [2012] Ch 206 shows that powers can apply without registration, when the charge can only be equitable.

[290] Wurtzburg and Mills, *Building Society Law* (15th edn), Appendix C.

[291] Notice cannot be served within the six months: *Selwyn* v *Garfit* (1888) 38 Ch D 273.

[292] 'Authorise' must be a reference to s 103 and not to s 101.

[293] *Bailey* v *Barnes* [1894] 1 Ch 25 (Stirling J), citing *Parkinson* v *Hanbury* (1860) 1 Dr&Sm 143 (62 ER 332); *Selwyn* v *Garfit* (1888) 38 Ch D 273 (both cases on express powers of sale). *Meretz Investments NV* v *ACP Ltd* [2007] Ch 197 at [317]–[325] states that 'shut-eye' (but not constructive) knowledge precludes protection, as does knowledge of an agent (noted, but not discussed, on appeal: [2008] Ch 244).

[294] [1935] Ch 311 at p 318.

Crossman J said: 'Of course, if the purchaser becomes aware [before conveyance] of any facts showing that the power of sale is not exercisable, or that there is some impropriety in the sale, then, in my judgment, he gets no good title on taking the conveyance.'

This analysis needs to be reconsidered in the light of LRA, ss 23(2)[295] and 52. The Law Commission explains the latter as intended to provide further protection for purchasers.[296] This further protection is said to apply if the purchaser is aware of the problem (the *Waring* point) or if the power has not arisen at all (most likely because the date of redemption has been postponed). On the *Waring* point, the added protection may prove illusory, given that the Law Commission contemplates that there may be personal liability for inducing breach of contract in this scenario.[297]

As regards the power that has not arisen, we must consider the wording of s 52. It provides that, for the protection of purchasers, 'the proprietor of a registered charge is to be taken to have . . . the powers of disposition conferred by law on the owner of a legal mortgage'. Any limitation on powers is effective only if entered on the register. The problem is that the 'powers of disposition conferred by law' appear to be the powers conferred by s 101[298] and, of course, these powers apply only when the mortgage monies are due. Doubtless s 52 provides protection if the charge provides for the powers not to arise at that stage, but it is difficult to see how it provides comprehensive protection for purchasers.

At what stage is the purchaser protected? Section 104(2) does not apply until conveyance and LRA, s 52 similarly appears to operate on transfer (it protects a 'disponee'). However, the purchaser receives some protection at the contract stage. The contract of sale is treated as a partial exercise of the power of sale, with the result that it overreaches the mortgagor's rights. It follows that there is no right to redeem after the contract of sale.[299] Although it might be argued that the mortgagor should be given every opportunity to redeem, it is essential to give early protection to the purchaser in order that mortgaged property can be sold at its full value. If there were a risk that the sale could fall through at the last minute, fewer people would be prepared to make offers. Speculators certainly would be happy to make derisory offers, but the average purchaser will be selling their existing house at the same time and needs to be certain that the purchase will go through. Anything that reduces the purchase price works to the disadvantage of the mortgagor, who is entitled to any surplus.

Can the mortgagor prevent sale?

We will assume that ss 101 and 103 are complied with. In practice, it is unusual for the decision to sell to be challenged directly. The mortgagor who wishes to prevent a sale will normally rely on fighting possession proceedings. However, a difficult question has arisen

---

[295] *Skelwith (Leisure) Ltd* v *Armstrong* [2016] Ch 345 holds that s 23(2) applies to the exercise of the powers of a mortgagee. This can be significant, as s 24 extends s 23 to persons entitled to be registered. *Skelwith* is doubted by Law Com CP 227, paras 5.41, 19.09.

[296] Law Com No 271, paras 7.7–7.8.

[297] Ibid, para 7.7, note 31.

[298] Supported by *Skelwith (Leisure) Ltd* v *Armstrong* [2016] Ch 345 at [48] in the context of LRA, s 23.

[299] *Waring* v *London & Manchester Assurance Co Ltd* [1935] Ch 311, approved by the Court of Appeal in *Property & Bloodstock Ltd* v *Emerton* [1968] Ch 94 and *National Provincial BS* v *Ahmed* [1995] 2 EGLR 127.

as to whether a mortgagee's sale should be allowed if the mortgagor is on the point of selling the land so as to provide funds for redemption. In *Duke* v *Robson*,[300] the mortgagees had obtained possession and contracted to sell the land. The mortgagor had earlier contracted to sell the land to the claimant, who now sought to restrain the mortgagees' sale. The Court of Appeal held that the power of sale was not affected by the claimant's contract. It was only by tendering the money required for redemption that the mortgagee's sale could be prevented and, as has been seen above, such tender is only effective before the mortgagee contracts to sell. Although the analysis appears harsh, the merits of the case were weak: the claimant had failed to complete the contract over an extended period, and the contract price was too low to satisfy the debt.

The Law Commission recognised the potential unfairness to the mortgagor if the mortgagee insists on ignoring a viable contract and goes ahead with a mortgagee's sale. Such a scenario is unlikely for most houses, simply because the mortgagee will usually be unable to obtain possession and therefore be unable to sell. It was recommended that, following notice of the mortgagor's contract to sell, the mortgagee who acts unreasonably in selling should be liable in damages.[301]

(b) Duties owed by the mortgagee

These concern the manner in which the sale is conducted and constitute the most litigated issue regarding sale. It should be remembered that the mortgagor is vitally affected by the sale price. If it is greater than the mortgage debt and expenses, then the balance goes to the mortgagor. If it is less, then the mortgagor is liable for the balance. A danger demonstrated time and again in the cases is that the mortgagee is concerned to get enough money to clear the mortgage debt and makes no effort to get more.[302]

In the early nineteenth century, the mortgagee was seen as a trustee, owing the normal duties of a trustee when selling land.[303] Although the trust analogy was subsequently rejected (the mortgagee has a substantial interest in the property),[304] it remained clear that the mortgagee could not ride roughshod over the interests of the mortgagor.[305] This meant that the mortgagee had to set out to obtain a proper price and also that there could be no sale to the mortgagee or the mortgagee's agent.[306]

However, the most difficult question was whether the duty was a subjective one not to harm the mortgagor or an objective one to take reasonable care to obtain a proper price. Most of the nineteenth-century cases are expressed in subjective terms. Typical is the

---

[300] [1973] 1 WLR 267. See also *Routestone Ltd* v *Minories Finance Ltd* [1997] 1 EGLR 123 and the discussion on timing of sale at p 621 below.

[301] Law Com No 204, paras 7.16 et seq.

[302] Although it is rare to get auctioneers' evidence that 'I don't think we endeavour to get the best price in a mortgagees' sale': *Pendlebury* v *Colonial Mutual Life Assurance Society Ltd* (1912) 13 CLR 676 at p 686.

[303] *Downes* v *Grazebrook* (1817) 3 Mer 200 (36 ER 77) (Lord Eldon LC); *Robertson* v *Norris* (1858) 1 Giff 421 (65 ER 983). Devonshire argues for a fiduciary duty on mortgagees in *The Reform of Property Law* (eds Jackson and Wilde), Chapter 15.

[304] *Nash* v *Eads* (1880) 25 SJ 95; *Warner* v *Jacob* (1882) 20 Ch D 220; *Farrar* v *Farrars Ltd* (1888) 40 Ch D 395. The process is well described by Waters, *The Constructive Trust*, Chapter 3.

[305] *Farrar* v *Farrars Ltd* (1888) 40 Ch D 395; *Kennedy* v *De Trafford* [1897] AC 180.

[306] *Martinson* v *Clowes* (1882) 21 Ch D 857.

dictum of Kay J in *Warner* v *Jacob*[307] that 'If he exercises it *bona fide* [to realise the debt], without corruption or collusion with the purchaser, the Court will not interfere even though the sale be very disadvantageous, unless indeed the price is so low as in itself to be evidence of fraud.' Other cases, however, refer to a duty to take care, usually without any recognition that this may be a very different test.[308]

Disentangling these cases is a difficult exercise,[309] but fortunately, we have a strong 1970s Court of Appeal decision that a duty of care is owed. In *Cuckmere Brick Co Ltd* v *Mutual Finance Ltd*,[310] the mortgagee failed to mention the existence of planning permission when advertising the land for sale and selling it at auction. Planning permission is often crucial to the value of land. The court stressed that the mortgagee could choose when to sell and that no objection could be taken that it would have been better to wait for some time. Once the decision to sell has been taken, however, care must be taken to obtain what Salmon LJ described as 'the true market value' and Cairns LJ the 'proper price'[311]; a majority held that there had been a breach of duty on the facts. The court recognised the difficulties posed by the earlier cases, but was obviously influenced by the twentieth-century development of liability in tort for negligence. It may be noted that breach of the duty results in liability in damages; without some impropriety or bad faith, the sale itself cannot be challenged.[312]

Subsequent cases have accepted *Cuckmere Brick*, although with some qualifications. In *Standard Chartered Bank Ltd* v *Walker*,[313] the benefit of the duty was extended from mortgagors to guarantors of debts. Lord Denning MR explained the duty in terms of the tort of negligence. However, limits were signalled by the Court of Appeal in *Parker-Tweedale* v *Dunbar Bank plc*.[314] The case was unusual: the mortgagee was sued by a beneficiary of a trustee mortgagor. It was held that liability to mortgagors is based upon an equitable duty and not upon tort. It follows that ideas such as proximity should not be seen as being at the heart of *Cuckmere Brick*.

On the facts of *Parker-Tweedale*, the nature of the beneficiary's rights was not sufficient for equity to allow an action against the mortgagee: the beneficiary was adequately protected by the duty to the trustee mortgagor. Although this probably does not affect the

---

[307] (1882) 20 Ch D 220 at p 224. See also *Kennedy* v *De Trafford* [1897] AC 180.
[308] The leading examples are Lindley LJ in *Farrar* v *Farrars Ltd* (1888) 40 Ch D 395 at p 395 (played down by the same judge in *Kennedy* v *De Trafford* [1896] 1 Ch 762 at p 772) and *McHugh* v *Union Bank of Canada* [1913] AC 299 (Privy Council, but not fully discussed); see also *Wolff* v *Vanderzee* (1869) 20 LT 353 and *Tomlin* v *Luce* (1889) 41 Ch D 573 (Kekewich J).
[309] This is most graphically shown by Australian cases. Most have striven to avoid reaching a conclusion, with the remainder being divided as to the proper approach. See *Forsyth* v *Blundell* (1973) 129 CLR 477; also *Commercial & General Acceptance Ltd* v *Nixon* (1981) 38 ALR 225 and [1988] Conv 4. Although some more recent cases (including *Upton* v *Tasmanian Perpetual Trustees Ltd* (2007) 242 ALR 422) have declined to apply the English approach, that has been adopted in legislation: Butt (2012) 86 ALJ 442.
[310] [1971] Ch 949.
[311] These terms (also 'best price') are regarded as synonymous in *Michael* v *Miller* [2004] 2 EGLR 151 at [131].
[312] *Corbett* v *Halifax BS* [2003] 1 WLR 964; Thompson [2004] Conv 49. A purchaser who is unaware of the undervaluation would in any event be protected by LPA, s 104.
[313] [1982] 1 WLR 1410 (action against receiver appointed by debenture holders); followed in *American Express International Banking Corp* v *Hurley* [1985] 3 All ER 564.
[314] [1991] Ch 12. Note the criticism of the confusion of equity and negligence in Meagher, Gummow and Lehane, *Equity: Doctrines and Remedies* (5th edn), paras 2.215–2.230.

liability to guarantors,[315] it would seem difficult to argue that a duty is owed to creditors of the mortgagor.[316]

Subsequently, the Privy Council in *Downsview Nominees Ltd* v *First City Corporation Ltd*[317] emphatically rejected any general duty of care (i.e. going beyond getting a proper price) owed by the mortgagee: any such duty would be inconsistent with the rights of the mortgagee to choose how to enforce the security.

What must the mortgagee do in order to satisfy the duty to obtain a proper price? It is clear that the sale, which may or may not be by auction,[318] must be advertised properly. This involves advertising in the normal range of places for the type of property[319] with a full description of it[320] and allowing a reasonable time before auction or the acceptance of an offer below a proper valuation.[321] If these requirements are ignored, then arranging a public auction provides no guarantee that the sale cannot be challenged.[322] If they are complied with, then a mortgagee who exercises a reasonable judgment will be protected even if the judge considers that the property is worth more.[323]

It must be borne in mind that valuation is often difficult. For most houses, it is possible to be fairly clear about their value from recent sales of similar houses; any significant deviation looks suspicious. A difficult question may arise if, as in *Horsham Properties Group Ltd* v *Clark*,[324] a house is sold without vacant possession. Especially where this is to avoid the court's discretion to suspend possession, can it be argued that a relatively low price is the proper price for property without vacant possession? The answer is unclear. For commercial property, particularly where linked to a specific business, valuations are less reliable. The reports are full of examples of wild differences between optimistic and pessimistic valuations.[325] The truth is often that the higher valuation could be achieved only if the right sort of purchaser (perhaps just one person or company) were to be interested. The courts are reluctant to say that the mortgagee must wait a long time before concluding a sale of such property.

How far is the mortgagee bound to spend money putting the property in a condition to sell well? Obviously, some expenditure on advertising and such-like is essential. More awkward is the Irish case of *Holohan* v *Friends Provident & Century Life Office*.[326]

---

[315] *China & South Sea Bank Ltd* v *Tan Soon Gin* [1990] 1 AC 536 (PC). *Downsview Nominees Ltd* v *First City Corporation Ltd* [1993] AC 295 reaffirms that a duty is owed to subsequent mortgagees (their security is diminished if the sale is for an unduly low price).

[316] Bentley [1990] Conv 431; *Latchford* v *Beirne* [1981] 3 All ER 705 at p 709 (overruled in *Standard Chartered* as regards guarantors).

[317] [1993] AC 295; Devonshire (1995) 46 NILQ 182.

[318] LPA, s 101(1)(i).

[319] *American Express International Banking Corp* v *Hurley* [1985] 3 All ER 564 (specialist lighting equipment); *Pendlebury* v *Colonial Mutual Life Assurance Society Ltd* (1912) 13 CLR 676.

[320] *Cuckmere Brick Co Ltd* v *Mutual Finance Ltd* [1971] Ch 949 (failure to advertise planning permission).

[321] This does not prevent the acceptance of a high offer within a short period: *Johnson* v *Ribbins* [1975] 2 EGLR 78. A quick sale is more readily defended if the mortgagor has been attempting to sell, showing that a higher offer is unlikely to be received: *Bank of Cyprus (London) Ltd* v *Gill* [1980] 2 Ll Rep 51.

[322] *Tse Kwong Lam* v *Wong Chit Sen* [1983] 1 WLR 1349 (PC).

[323] *Michael* v *Miller* [2004] 2 EGLR 151.

[324] [2009] 1 WLR 1255.

[325] A valuation based on a crash sale is unacceptable: *Predeth* v *Castle Phillips Finance Co Ltd* [1986] 2 EGLR 144 (derelict bungalow).

[326] [1966] IR 1.

A mortgagees' sale was stopped because they refused to consider buying out tenants, when that would have achieved a markedly higher price. The case is awkward because it seems hard on mortgagees to say that they must risk more money before realising their security. A more conventional line was more recently taken in *Silven Properties Ltd* v *Royal Bank of Scotland plc*[327]: a mortgagee can sell immediately without taking any pre-marketing steps. This provides useful clarity, although it would have been reasonable for the law to have required the expenditure of moderate amounts, at least where this is strongly recommended and would not delay sale.

One small but important point should be added. The mortgagee is liable for any carelessness of an agent conducting the sale: it is no defence that a competent estate agent or auctioneer has been employed. This was held in *Tomlin* v *Luce*[328] and, although the point had been conceded, is supported by *Cuckmere Brick*.

Although the sale price has been the crucial issue in most recent cases, the motive for the sale was central to *Meretz Investments NV* v *ACP Ltd*.[329] Despite the conventional wisdom that the motive for exercising powers is irrelevant,[330] Lewison J considered that a motive to recover the sums owing was essential. However, it suffices if there are mixed motives, of which this is one. In practice, this will make it very difficult to challenge decisions to sell.

(c) The timing of sale

The conventional view is that the mortgagee can choose when to sell. There can be no complaint that there should have been an earlier sale,[331] and the courts have constantly said that the mortgagee need not postpone sale in order to obtain a better price.[332] Nor can it be objected that land was sold at a time of recession and low land prices. On the other hand, the conduct of a sale will usually demand that a reasonable time be allowed for advertisements and receipt of offers,[333] although the mortgagee is not bound to wait as long as an owner who is intent on getting the very best price.[334]

One may posit a difficult case between these extremes. If there is a seasonal market in a certain type of property so that prices are much lower at certain times of the year, can the mortgagee sell at the time of low prices or will the law require a delay of several months? In *Standard Chartered Bank Ltd* v *Walker*,[335] Lord Denning MR thought that the mortgagee could not sell 'at the worst possible time'; this was in the context of a sale of

---

[327] [2004] 1 WLR 997 at [16]: no need to seek planning permission or find tenants.

[328] (1889) 41 Ch D 573, approved on appeal: 43 Ch D 191.

[329] [2007] Ch 197 at [288]–[339] (not considered on appeal: [2008] Ch 244). The possible wrongful motive was to prevent commission payments becoming payable to the claimant.

[330] *Nash* v *Eads* (1880) 25 SJ 95, but contrast *Clark* v *National Mutual Life Association of Australasia Ltd* [1966] NZLR 196.

[331] *China & South Sea Bank Ltd* v *Tan Soon Gin* [1990] 1 AC 536; *Downsview Nominees Ltd* v *First City Corporation Ltd* [1993] AC 295.

[332] *Warner* v *Jacob* (1882) 20 Ch D 220; *Farrar* v *Farrars Ltd* (1888) 40 Ch D 395 (Chitty J); *Cuckmere Brick Co Ltd* v *Mutual Finance Ltd* [1971] Ch 949.

[333] *Predeth* v *Castle Phillips Finance Co Ltd* [1986] 2 EGLR 144, in which four weeks was insufficient (Thompson [1986] Conv 442); *Skipton BS* v *Stott* [2001] QB 261. It may be that three months should be allowed, absent an excellent offer.

[334] *Predeth* v *Castle Phillips Finance Co Ltd* [1986] 2 EGLR 144 at p 148 (Ralph Gibson LJ).

[335] [1982] 1 WLR 1410; Fox LJ stressed the right to choose the time of sale.

specialist machinery on a cold February day. However, mortgagees were accorded greater freedom by the Court of Appeal in *Silven Properties Ltd* v *Royal Bank of Scotland plc*[336]: the dicta of Lord Denning were regarded as inconsistent with later cases. Accordingly, the mortgagee can choose to sell at any time.

(d) Sale to the mortgagee and related issues

A sale to oneself is no exercise of the power of sale.[337] The courts have rejected sales to trustees for the mortgagee[338] and to agents connected with the sale.[339] There is an obvious danger that the price will not be negotiated at arm's length. Even at an auction, the fact that an agent is bidding may discourage other bids and so depress the price.[340] There is no requirement of proof of fraud or a low price before the sale will be set aside.[341] The courts have not applied such a strict rule where the purchaser is a relative, friend or employee of the mortgagee[342] or a company in which the mortgagee is interested.[343] On the other hand, the courts are suspicious in these cases and demand proof that no conflict of interest is involved. The sale is likely to be approved if steps have been taken to ensure a proper price has been received.

(e) The destination of the proceeds of sale

It must be remembered that the balance of the purchase price, after deduction of the loan capital, interest and expenses, cannot be retained by the mortgagee. In a straightforward case, the balance will be paid to the mortgagor. Any mortgages with a lower priority to the selling mortgagee are overreached by the sale; the balance is paid to the overreached mortgagee who has the next priority.[344] A mortgagee who pays the balance to the wrong person is liable in damages, at least where there is notice of the subsequent mortgagee to whom payment should have been made.[345] Obviously, the selling mortgagee should take steps to discover subsequent mortgages, principally by checking whether they are registered. Subsequent mortgagees must in turn account in a similar manner for any balance left after deduction of their mortgage debts.

(f) The court's jurisdiction to order sale

The court has jurisdiction to order sale under LPA, s 91(2) if either party seeks sale in an action for foreclosure, redemption or sale. This useful jurisdiction tends to be employed in

---

[336] [2004] 1 WLR 997 at [15]. Nicholls V-C had been more receptive to a duty to delay in *Palk* v *Mortgage Services Funding plc* [1993] Ch 330, discussed below.

[337] *Williams* v *Wellingborough BC* [1975] 1 WLR 1327 (despite the mortgagee's possessing a valid right of pre-emption); reversed on its special facts by Housing Act 1985, Sched 17, para 1.

[338] *National Bank of Australasia* v *United Hand-in-Hand and Band of Hope Company* (1879) 4 App Cas 391 (PC). The courts are suspicious if the mortgagee later buys the property from the purchaser: *Robertson* v *Norris* (1858) 1 Giff 421 (65 ER 983).

[339] *Downes* v *Grazebrook* (1817) 3 Mer 200 (36 ER 77); *Martinson* v *Clowes* (1882) 21 Ch D 857 (secretary of building society bona fide buying at auction).

[340] Lord Hatherley LC in *Tennant* v *Trenchard* (1869) LR 4 Ch App 537 at p 547.

[341] *Farrar* v *Farrars Ltd* (1888) 40 Ch D 395.

[342] *Corbett* v *Halifax BS* [2003] 1 WLR 964 (sale to employee not affected where employee had no role in the sale process).

[343] *Farrar* v *Farrars Ltd* (1888) 40 Ch D 395; *Tse Kwong Lam* v *Wong Chit Sen* [1983] 1 WLR 1349 (PC).

[344] LPA, s 105, using the opaque words 'person entitled to the mortgaged property'.

[345] *West London Commercial Bank* v *Reliance Permanent BS* (1885) 29 Ch D 954.

exceptional cases – for example, where a power of sale has been defectively drafted.[346] Even a valid power of sale may be useless if the mortgagor employs the spoiling tactic of threatening purchasers with a challenge to the validity of the sale. So long as the chances of success of such a challenge are 'utterly remote', the court may order a sale in order to protect the purchaser and ensure that a sale can go ahead.[347]

More unexpected is an application by the mortgagor. Mortgagors generally have no problem in selling if the purchase price exceeds the debt, as the mortgage will be redeemed out of the proceeds of sale. In *Palk* v *Mortgage Services Funding plc*,[348] however, the house was worth less than the debt (negative equity). The mortgagee wanted to lease the house, even though the rent would be no more than a third of the interest. The mortgagee hoped that market conditions would improve so that the house could be sold at a higher value later. The mortgagors realised that the effect of this would be that their debt would be increasing. Their personal liability for the debt meant that the mortgagee could delay a sale at their expense. They wished to sell now, leaving a debt of around £75,000 that they had a reasonable chance of paying off in the future. The Court of Appeal was impressed by these arguments and ordered sale.

Palk shows that even though the mortgagee can normally decide when to sell, this does not affect the court's independent jurisdiction. However, it seems probable that the facts of the case are exceptional. In most cases, any prospect of suing the mortgagors for the balance will be illusory,[349] and the mortgagees will be taking the entire risk upon themselves.

The utility of *Palk* was reduced by a hostile Court of Appeal in *Cheltenham & Gloucester* v *Krausz*,[350] in which the mortgagee itself wished to sell. It was held that the court has no jurisdiction to stop the mortgagee from taking possession in a negative equity scenario, despite the mortgagor's wishing to sell. The practical effect is that the mortgagee will have control over sale. Millett LJ further suggested that *Palk* does not justify an order for sale where the mortgagee is seeking possession in order to sell.[351] Yet there is much to be said for the argument that s 91(2) itself may authorise giving possession to the mortgagor for the purpose of selling,[352] albeit that a mortgagee wishing to sell (as in *Krausz*) would normally be given conduct of the sale.

Where the mortgagee does not seek possession, *Polonski* v *Lloyds Bank Mortgages Ltd*[353] indicates that the court will readily order sale at the mortgagor's request. The mortgagor wished to move to rented accommodation in order to find better social conditions and schools for her children: the court ordered sale to facilitate this. The result in *Polonski* of converting secured liability into unsecured personal liability may be viewed as 'very difficult to justify'.[354]

[346] *Twentieth Century Banking Corporation Ltd* v *Wilkinson* [1977] Ch 99.
[347] *Arab Bank plc* v *Merchantile Holdings Ltd* [1994] Ch 71 at p 90.
[348] [1993] Ch 330. It may be significant that there was no term postponing the date of redemption.
[349] One may question whether it was substantial in *Palk*.
[350] [1997] 1 WLR 1558; Kenny [1998] Conv 223.
[351] Criticising the order in *Barrett* v *Halifax BS* (1995) 28 HLR 634, despite the striking fact that the mortgagor had obtained an offer which the lender thought to be reasonable.
[352] Dixon (1998) 18 LS 279.
[353] [1998] 1 FLR 896 (£12,000 negative equity).
[354] Thompson [1998] Conv 125 at p 132.

(iv) *Receivers*

The power to appoint a receiver arises and becomes exercisable in the same situations as the power of sale.[355] A receiver will normally be appointed where there is rental income from tenants. The receiver will receive that income and usually pay it, less expenses, to the mortgagee to cover interest and (if the mortgagee requests) capital.[356] The receiver is used as a substitute for taking possession, in order to avoid the strict accounting rules. Distinctly artificially,[357] LPA s 109(2) deems the receiver to be the agent of the mortgagor, with the result that the mortgagee is not liable for any breach of duty.[358]

Further reading

Bamforth, N [1996] CLP Pt 2, pp 207–244: Lord Macnaghten's puzzle: the mortgage of real property in English law.

Nield, S and Hopkins, N (2013) 33 LS 431: Human rights and mortgage repossession: beyond property law using Article 8.

Rudden, B (1961) 25 Conv 278: Mortgagee's right to possession.

Thompson, M (2003) 'Mortgages and undue influence' in *Modern Studies in Property Law*, Vol 2 (ed E Cooke), Chapter 7.

Watt, G (2007) 'The lie of the land: mortgage law as legal fiction' in *Modern Studies in Property Law*, Vol 4 (ed E Cooke), Chapter 4.

Whitehouse, L (1997) 'The right to possession: the need for substantive reform' in *The Reform of Property Law* (eds P Jackson and D Wilde), Chapter 9.

---

[355] LPA, ss 101, 109(1).
[356] This is a brief summary of s 109(8). It should be noted that repairs must be authorised by the mortgagee.
[357] *Nijar* v *Mann* (1998) 32 HLR 223 at p 228.
[358] *Medforth* v *Blake* [2000] Ch 86; Omar [2005] Conv 380.

Index